ODHAMS
ENQUIRE WITHIN

First Published 1951

Made and printed in Great Britain by
ODHAMS (WATFORD) LTD., WATFORD
S.951.T.

ODHAMS
ENQUIRE WITHIN

A COMPREHENSIVE BOOK

OF REFERENCE FOR THE HOME

AND THE OFFICE

ODHAMS PRESS LIMITED

LONG ACRE, LONDON

CONTENTS

HOW TO USE THIS BOOK

THERE can be few people who, in their daily lives in home, workshop or office, do not require the answers to countless topical questions, or instructions as to how to perform the increasing number of essential tasks which fall to the lot of the ordinary householder. It is the aim of this volume to provide the answers to most of these everyday problems in an easily accessible and comprehensible form. How wide its net has been cast can be gathered from a glance through the list of contents on the two preceding pages.

Nearly all the sections have been arranged alphabetically. Having turned up the appropriate subject by reference to the contents pages, the reader will then experience no difficulty in finding the required entry. A few sections, such as the Radio and Television Guide and the chapter on Dogs, Cats and Poultry, do not lend themselves to such treatment if their subject matter is to be arranged logically. But these sections, like the rest of the book, are provided with ample headings, and the reader should easily find the information he seeks. The section on Law for Everyman is divided, for ease of reference, under four main headings which are themselves subdivided alphabetically.

It will be found that some sections are far more lavishly illustrated than others. This is inevitable and, it will be agreed, desirable. For example, a great deal of tedious explanation of handyman jobs, or of needlework or knitting methods, can be avoided by including straightforward drawings or diagrams. In many cases an adequate explanation is, in fact, impossible without some visual aid. On the other hand, the Legal section does not require such illustrations.

This volume, then, has been designed to compress as much useful information as handily as possible into the least possible space, and to ensure that the information given shall be readily found when required. At the same time, its pages contain much that will be read out of sheer interest.

PERSONALITIES OF THE TWENTIETH CENTURY

Short biographies of notable people in all walks of life who are living or have been alive since the year 1900.

ABERCORN, Duke of; James Albert Edward Hamilton. Was in the Life Guards, and afterwards Conservative M.P. for the City of Londonderry. In 1913 succeeded to title. Treasurer to King's Household, 1903–5. Governor of Northern Ireland for six successive years from 1922, 1928, 1934. (1869–.)

ABERCROMBIE, Prof. Sir L. Patrick (knight). Architect and town-planner, he devised scheme for re-creation of London after bomb devastation. First obtained architectural and town-planning experience in Manchester; won open competition, 1913, for re-designing Dublin. Has since planned improvements in many English areas. (1879–.)

ACHESON, Dean. Secretary of State, U.S.A., since 1949. Formerly prominent U.S. lawyer. A firm admirer of Britain, he was most active during the Second World War in promoting aid for that country. Assistant Secretary of State, 1941, Under-Secretary, 1945. (1893–.)

ACLAND, Sir Richard T. (baronet). Wealthy landowner who in 1943 gave his 16,000-acre Devonshire estate, estimated worth £250,000, to the nation. Liberal M.P. for Barnstaple, 1935, later became Independent. Founded Common Wealth Party, 1943, but left it two years later. In 1947 became Labour M.P. for Gravesend. (1906–.)

ADDISON, Rt. Hon. Viscount; Christopher Addison. Was Professor and Examiner in Anatomy, Cambridge and London Universities, 1901. First entered Parliament as Liberal, and later as Labour. Minister of Munitions, then Minister of Reconstruction (1917). First Minister of Health, 1919–21. Leader, Labour Party, in House of Lords. (1869–.)

ADRIAN, Edgar Douglas. Professor of Physiology at Cambridge University since 1937. In 1925 was appointed Oliver Sharpey Lecturer, Royal College of Physicians, and from 1929–37 was Foulerton Research Professor, Royal Society. (1889–.)

AGA KHAN, Rt. Hon. Sultan Sir Mahomed Shah. Spiritual leader of Ismaili Mohammedans all over the world. Founded the All-India Moslem League and represented India at the Geneva World Disarmament Conference, 1932. Fabulously wealthy and keen racehorse owner. Derby winner, 1930 (Blenheim), 1935 (Bahram), 1936 (Mahmoud). (1877–.)

AGATE, James Evershed. Began work, when nineteen, in a cotton mill. Left it in 1898 and spent sixteen years in the Manchester cotton trade. Next turned to dramatic criticism, beginning with *Manchester Guardian.* Also wrote several books, including his *Ego* series. (1877–1947.)

AINLEY, Henry Hinchliffe. Once an accountant, he first appeared at the Lyceum Theatre, London, 1900. Toured America in 1903. Served in the First World War; later became joint manager, St. James's Theatre. Played many leading Shakespearean and other rôles. (1879–1945.)

ALANBROOKE, Field-Marshal Viscount; Alan Francis Brooke. Entered the Royal Field Artillery from Woolwich in 1902 and rose to G.O.C. Anti-Aircraft Command, 1939, and same rank Southern Command, 1939–40. Commanded Second Army Corps, B.E.F., 1940, and next year Chief of Imperial General Staff until 1946. (1883–.)

ALCOCK, Capt. Sir John (knight). Aviator. Assisted in the bombardment of Constantinople during the First World War. With Whitten Brown won *Daily Mail* £10,000 prize for Newfoundland-Ireland flight, 1919. Killed near Rouen in crash. (1892–1919.)

ALEKHINE, Alexander. Russian chess player. After taking law degree, entered Russian Foreign Office. Served in Red Cross in First World War. Won world record for blindfold chess and held championship of the world from 1927 to his death except for 1935–7. Author of books on chess. (1892–1946.)

ALEXANDER, Rt. Hon. Viscount; Albert Victor Alexander. Began as office boy in a leather factory, afterwards became a clerk. Took an interest in Socialist politics and particularly the Co-operative movement. Became M.P. in 1922, and was appointed First Lord of the Admiralty in 1929, and again in 1940. Minister of Defence, 1946–50. (1885–.)

ALEXANDER, Field-Marshal Viscount; Harold Rupert Alexander. Governor-General of Canada since 1946. Commanded a battalion when twenty-four. Served in both world wars, and in the second gained distinction first in Burma and afterwards in Middle East as C.-in-C. Allied Forces; then in North Africa as Deputy C.-in-C. to General Eisenhower. Later became Supreme Allied Commander, Mediterranean theatre. Afterwards victor over the Axis forces and Governor of Italy. (1891–.)

ALINGTON, Very Rev. Cyril Argentine. Formerly Headmaster of Shrewsbury, 1908–16, he was appointed headmaster of Eton in 1916. Chaplain to the King, 1921–33. Was Dean of Durham 1933-51. (1872–.)

ALLEN, Sir Hugh Percy (knight). Organist, St. Asaph Cathedral, 1897; Ely, 1898. New College, Oxford, 1901–18. Director of Royal College of Music, 1919–37. Professor of Music, Oxford, from 1918. President, Royal College of Organists. (1869–1946.)

ALLENBY, Field-Marshal Viscount; Edward Henry Hynman Allenby. Enlisted in the Army in 1879, first saw active service in Bechuanaland; went through the South African War, and also the First World War as Corps Commander. Saw more service in Egypt, where he afterwards became High Commissioner in 1919. (1861–1936.)

ALTRINCHAM, Rt. Hon. Lord (baron); **Edward William Grigg.** After serving in the First World War was appointed, 1919, military secretary to the Prince of Wales on Empire tour. Later as Nat. Lib. M.P. held Government secretarial posts in London. Was Governor of Kenya Colony, 1925–31, and made Under-Secretary for War in 1940. (1879–.)

AMERY, Rt. Hon. Leopold Stennett. Early in career, *Times* correspondent in Europe, then war correspondent during Boer War. Afterwards barrister-at-law. Became Conservative M.P., 1911, and at different times held Secretaryships at Colonial Office, Admiralty (there later First Lord), and as Secretary of State for India, 1940. (1873–.)

AMMON, Rt. Hon. Lord (baron); **Charles George Ammon.** When a boy of twelve began at three shillings a week in a fancy-bottle works. Later became a sorter in a post office, then Lab. M.P. for Camberwell. In 1924, and again in 1929, was appointed Parliamentary Secretary to the Admiralty. (1873–.)

AMUNDSEN, Capt. Roald. Norwegian explorer. After studying medicine went to sea, 1894. Joined Arctic expedition in 1901, and about nine years later sailed for the Antarctic. Reached South Pole, 1911. Flew over North Pole, 1925. Death presumed in 1928. (1872–1928.)

ANDRADE, Prof. Edward N. da C. Quain Professor of Physics, London University, 1928–50. Served in France, 1915–7, and afterwards collaborated with the late Lord Rutherford in gamma-ray research. Gave valuable aid in the Second World War at Ministry of Supply and in the field. Also a poet. (1887–.)

ARLISS, George. Was for sixty years on the British and American stage and screen following his first appearance at Elephant and Castle Theatre, London, 1887. Made his American screen début in 1920, his later pictures including *The Green Goddess*, *Disraeli*, and *The Iron Duke*. (1868–1946.)

ARNAUD, Yvonne. Actress. Made her début at the Adelphi Theatre, London, in *The Quaker Girl* (1911). Stage successes in London and New York include *The Girl in the Taxi* (1912), *Kissing Time* (1919), *Henry V* (1934), *Love for Love* (1943), *Traveller's Joy* (1948). Entered films in 1924, appearing in *Tons of Money*, *Canaries Sometimes Sing*, *A Cuckoo in the Nest*, and others. (1895–.)

ASHFIELD, Rt. Hon. Lord (baron); **Albert Stanley Ashfield.** Chairman London Transport Board, 1933–47. Taken to the U.S.A. when a boy, he began with the Detroit City Street Railways. In 1907 returned to London to become General Manager District and Tube Railways. Coalition-Unionist M.P., 1916–20. Appointed President Board of Trade, 1916. (1874–1948.)

ASSHETON, Rt. Hon. Ralph. Landowner in Lancashire and Yorkshire, also a barrister. Was High Sheriff of Lancashire, 1919, and later Deputy Lieutenant. Tory M.P. since 1934 (with brief gap in 1945). Was Chairman of the Conservative and Unionist Party. (1901–.)

ASTOR, Lt.-Col. Hon. John J. A.D.C. to Viceroy of India, 1911-4. Commanded Household Siege Battery in First World War. Unionist M.P., 1922–45. President of Press Club and Newspaper Press Fund. Member of B.B.C. General Advisory Committee 1937–9; chairman *Times* Publishing Company. (1886–.)

ASTOR, Viscount Waldorf. Proprietor of *The Observer*, Conservative M.P. for Plymouth from 1910–9, he became Parliamentary Secretary to the Prime Minister, 1918, Minister of Food, 1918, and then Minister of Health, 1919–21. Chairman Royal Institute of International Affairs, 1935–49, and a keen racehorse owner. (1879–.)

ASTOR, Viscountess (*née* Nancy Langhorne). First woman M.P. to sit in the House of Commons. Settled in Britain from Virginia, U.S.A., and in 1919 successfully contested Plymouth as a Conservative. Retired from active politics in 1945. Was a keen protagonist of temperance and child welfare. Noted for her wit. (1879–.)

ATHLONE, Maj.-Gen. the Earl of; formerly Prince Alexander of Teck. Governor of Windsor Castle since 1931. Served in the South African War and First World War. Was Governor-General of the Union of South Africa, 1923–31, and of Canada, 1940–6. (1874–.)

C. R. Attlee.

ATTLEE, Rt. Hon. Clement Richard. Labour Prime Minister since 1945. Educated at Haileybury and from there went on to University College, Oxford. Began his career by practising law from 1906 to 1909, and after social work in London's East End as Secretary, Toynbee Hall, 1910–3, he lectured and taught at the London School of Economics. Saw active service in the Gallipoli campaign, First World War, and left the army with the rank of major. In 1922, elected to Parliament as Labour. Became in turn Under-Secretary for War, Postmaster-General and, in 1940, Deputy Prime Minister in the National Government. (1883–.)

AUCHINLECK, Field-Marshal Sir Claude John (knight). Joined the army in 1904, and was in First World War. Organized British withdrawal from Narvik in the Second World War and was later C.-in-C. Middle East. Transferred to same position, India; became, in 1946, Supreme Commander, Indo-Pakistan forces, until his retirement in November, 1947. (1884–.)

AUDEN, Wystan Hugh. Poet. Entered teaching profession and was Associate Professor of English Literature, Ann Arbor University, Michigan. Received the King's Gold Medal for poetry, 1937. First volume of poems published 1930. His many books include *The Orators*, *The Dance of Death*. (1907–.)

AURIOL, Vincent. First President of Fourth French Republic, elected 1947. Entered the Chamber of Deputies in 1914 as a Socialist and became a leading financial authority in his party. Held various ministerial appointments, 1936–9, and voted against Pétain on the fall of France in 1940. Was active in the Resistance movement and escaped to England in 1943. Paid a state visit to Britain in 1950. (1884–.)

BACKHAUS, Wilhelm. German pianist. Born in Leipzig, pupil of Reckendorf. Spent much time on tour. Won the Rubinstein prize whilst tutor at Royal College of Music, Manchester, 1905. Taught at Sondershausen Conservatoire, 1907. Sought refuge in Switzerland during the Second World War, after which he resumed foreign engagements. (1884–.)

BADEN-POWELL, Lt.-Gen. Lord (baron). Cavalry officer in Matabele War, 1896–7. Besieged in Mafeking in South African War, holding out for seven months. In 1908 founded Boy Scout Movement in Great Britain, becoming Chief Scout. (1857–1941.)

BAIRD, John Logie. Scots electrical engineer. Subject to constant ill-health, he went to Trinidad and there started a jam factory. Afterwards at Hastings, England, made the first television projector. In 1931 televised pictures in relief and in colour. (1888–1946.)

BALDWIN, Earl; Stanley Baldwin. Beginning his Parliamentary career as Conservative M.P. in 1908, his first important post was President Board of Trade, 1921–2; later Chancellor of the Exchequer. Prime Minister in 1923, 1924, and 1935. Two important events during his time were the General Strike, 1926, and the abdication of King Edward VIII (now Duke of Windsor), December, 1936. Retired May, 1937. (1867–1947.)

BALFOUR, Earl; Arthur J. Balfour. Entered Parliament as Conservative in 1873, and after holding Government secretarial posts became Leader of the House of Commons in 1891, and was head of his party in Opposition, 1892. Was Prime Minister, 1895–1902 and 1902–5, and Lord President of the Council, 1919–22 and 1925–9. (1848–1930.)

BANTING, Sir Frederick Grant (knight). Joint discoverer with C. H. Best of insulin, for which he received part of the Nobel Prize, 1923. Commenced research, University of Toronto, 1921. Awarded Starr Gold Medal for Doctorate, Toronto, 1922. Professor of Medical Research, Toronto, 1923. (1891–1941.)

BANTOCK, Sir Granville (knight). Toured the world with the Gaiety Company, 1894–5, and after conducting at Festivals in Great Britain and Canada became Professor of Music, Birmingham University, 1908–34. Composed a large number of works. (1868–1946.)

BARBIROLLI, Sir John (Giovanni Battista) (knight). Son of an Italian father and a French mother, he first appeared as violoncellist at Queen's Hall, 1911. Founded and conducted Barbirolli Chamber Orchestra, 1925. Permanent Conductor, New York Philharmonic Symphony Orchestra, 1937–42, and of Hallé Orchestra since 1943. (1899–.)

BARING, Hon. Sir Evelyn (knight). Is High Commissioner for the United Kingdom in the Union of South Africa and for Basutoland, Bechuanaland and Swaziland. Also Governor of Southern Rhodesia, 1942–4. In 1929 was appointed Secretary to Agent of the Government of India in South Africa. (1903–.)

BARING, Wing-Commander Hon. Maurice. Diplomatist and author. Entered Diplomatic Service, 1898. Attaché at British Embassy, Paris, 1898, and was in the Foreign Office, 1903–4. Staff Officer, Independent Air Force, 1918. Author of many books. (1874–1945.)

BARKER, Sir Herbert (knight). Specialist in manipulative surgery and now honorary surgeon, Noble's Hospital, Douglas, I.o.M. Before that appointment successfully treated over forty thousand cases. Had at one time to contend with prejudice from medical profession. Representations were made to the Prime Minister by a group of eminent surgeons and he was knighted in 1922. (1869–1950.)

BARNES, Rt. Hon. Alfred J. A designer by trade, he entered Parliament as Labour in 1922, representing the south East Ham Co-operative movement. Was chairman of the Co-operative Party, 1924–45, and in the latter year was appointed Minister of War Transport. Minister of Transport since 1946. (1881–.)

BARNES, Rt. Rev. Ernest William. Anglican Bishop of Birmingham since 1924. A rebel against orthodoxy, he has played a prominent part in more than one controversy concerning Church and Politics. Canon of Westminster, 1918–24. Gifford Lecturer, Aberdeen, 1927–9. (1874–.)

BARRIE, Sir James Matthew (baronet). In 1887 produced his first volume, *Better Dead*, a satire on London life. Other works included: *When a Man's Single*, *A Window in Thrums*, *The Little Minister*. Plays: *The Admirable Crichton*, *Peter Pan*, *A Kiss for Cinderella*. (1860–1937.)

BARRINGTON-WARD, Robert M'Gowan. Editor of *The Times*, 1941–8. After leaving Oxford he became Editorial Secretary to *The Times*, 1913, and during First World War served in the Duke of Cornwall's Light Infantry. Assistant Editor of *The Observer*, 1919–27. (1890–1948.)

BARRY, Rt. Rev. Frank Russell. Bishop of Southwell since 1941. Fellow and Lecturer of Oriel College, Oxford, 1913–9. Made Archdeacon of Egypt, 1923, then Vicar of St. Mary the Virgin, Oxford, and Canon of Westminster, 1933–41. (1890–.)

BARTLETT, Vernon. Independent M.P., 1939–50, and journalist. Formerly special correspondent on the Continent for *The Times*, and has also been connected with other national newspapers. London Director, League of Nations, 1922–32. (1894–.)

BATEMAN, Henry Mayo. Studied drawing and painting at Westminster and New Cross Art schools, and later achieved fame with his humorous drawings in leading weekly and monthly magazines. Author of *Burlesques; A Book of Drawings*. (1887–.)

BATES, Sir Percy E. (baronet). Shipping expert. Formerly a director of *The Morning Post*, he became chairman of Cunard Steamship Co., Ltd., and Cunard White Star Line, 1934–46. (1879–1946.)

BATTEN, Miss Jean Gardner. Granted a private pilot's licence at London Aeroplane Club, 1930; solo flight from England to Australia (women's record), 1936; solo flight from Australia to England, 1935. Other records included a flight across the Atlantic Ocean to South America. (1909–.)

BAX, Sir Arnold E. T. (knight). Master of the King's Musick since 1942. After studying at the Royal Academy of Music in London, he went to Ireland, lived there for several years and, under the pen-name of Dermot O'Byrne, wrote a number of Irish stories. Contributions to music include symphonies, chamber and other compositions. Gold medallist, Royal Philharmonic Society. (1883–.)

BAX, Clifford. Studied art at the Slade School and Heatherley's. Lived in Germany, Belgium and Italy, and afterwards in England took up literary and dramatic work. Wrote several books and also plays, the first, produced in 1912, being *The Poetasters of Ispahan*. (1886–.)

BAYLIS, Lilian Mary. After being a girl violinist became a concert entertainer in England and South Africa. Later was manager of the "Old Vic," London, from 1898, and then of Sadler's Wells Theatre, when it reopened in 1931. (1874–1937.)

BEARSTED, Viscount; Marcus Samuel. Travelled widely in the Far East and Japan. Introduced transport of petroleum in bulk through Suez Canal. Was Lord Mayor of London, 1902–3. Created a Viscount 1925 for "services of the utmost importance to the fighting forces." (1853–1927.)

BEATTY, Admiral Earl; David Beatty. Entered the British Navy, 1884, and served in the Sudan and China campaigns and in the First World War. Commanded the First Battle Cruiser Squadron at Battle of Jutland, 1916. Appointed Admiral of the Fleet, 1919. (1871–1936.)

BEAVERBROOK, Rt. Hon. Lord (baron); **William Maxwell Aitken.** Canadian by birth, he entered English politics as a Conservative and acquired the *Daily Express* and other newspapers. During the Second World War was, in turn, Minister of Information, and of Aircraft Production and of Supply. Was made Lord Privy Seal in September, 1943. (1879–.)

BECKETT, Joseph. First boxing matches won in 1914. Defeated Bombardier Wells, 1919, becoming British heavyweight champion. Beat Frank Goddard, but was defeated by Georges Carpentier in one round, 1919, and again in 1923, when he retired from the ring. (1894–.)

BEECHAM, Sir Thomas (baronet). Displayed a talent for music at an early age, later toured with a travelling opera company and in 1905 made his first London appearance with the Queen's Hall Orchestra. Achieved worldwide reputation as conductor. (1879–.)

BEERBOHM, Sir Max (knight). Essayist, satirist and caricaturist. Succeeded Bernard Shaw as dramatic critic of *The Saturday Review*. Has produced several books of essays and also caricatures. (1872–.)

BELCHER, George Frederick A. Studied at the Gloucester School of Art, then specialized in humorous drawings of London life, especially of charwomen. Contributed to *Punch* and other periodicals. Author of *Taken from Life*, *Characters*, *Odd Fish*. Elected Royal Academician, 1945. (1875–1947.)

BELL, Rt. Rev. G. Kennedy A. Bishop of Chichester since 1929. Lecturer and Tutor, Christ Church, Oxford, 1910–4. Dean of Canterbury, 1924–9. Won the Newdigate Prize in 1904. Editor, *Poems of Life and Death*. (1883–.)

BELL, Miss Gertrude. Traveller and archaeologist. Her close knowledge of Syria, Asia Minor and other parts of the East led to the Government employing her for special work during the First World War (mentioned in dispatches four times). Oriental Secretary to the High Commissioner, Baghdad, 1920–6. (1868–1926.)

BELLENGER, Capt. Rt. Hon. Frederick John. Served in the First World War, 1914–8, in Royal Artillery (twice wounded), and in France, 1940. Entered Parliament as Labour M.P. and, after being Financial Secretary to the War Office, was Secretary of State for War 1946–47. (1894–.)

BELLOC, Hilaire. Son of a French barrister, he served in the French artillery before settling in England. Was Liberal M.P., 1906–10. Author of essays and a long list of books which include *The Crisis of Our Civilization*, *The Question and the Answer*, *The Great Heresies*, *The Last Rally*. (1870–.)

BENES, Dr. Eduard. Born in Bozlany, Bohemia, he studied in Prague, Paris, London and elsewhere. During First World War worked for the liberation of the Czechoslovak people. After being Minister of Foreign Affairs, became Prime Minister, 1921, and President, Czechoslovak Republic, 1935. Resigned, 1938, but resumed office in London, 1940, as President, Czechoslovak National Committee. Re-elected President, June, 1946, for seven years. (1884–1948.)

BENN, Sir Ernest J. P. (baronet). London publisher. Chairman, Benn Brothers, Ltd., 1922–41, and Ernest Benn, Ltd. Founded the Society of Individualists. Author of *The Confessions of a Capitalist*, *If I were a Labour Leader*, *The Case of Benn v. Maxton*. (1875–.)

BENNETT, Enoch Arnold. Gave up law for journalism and eventually achieved fame as a writer of novels portraying life in the six Staffordshire towns known as "the Potteries." His work includes *The Old Wives' Tale*, *Clayhanger*, *Riceyman Steps*. Plays: *Milestones* (with Edward Knoblock), *The Great Adventure*. (1867–1931.)

BENNETT, Rt. Hon. Viscount; Richard Bennett. After being admitted to the Bar, entered the Canadian Parliament. Became successively Minister of Justice, Attorney-General, Prime Minister and Minister of External Affairs (1930–5). As leader of the Conservative Party, represented Canada at the Imperial Conference, London, 1930. (1870–1947.)

BERGMAN, Ingrid. Swedish film actress; star in American films. First appeared on the screen in her own country. Hollywood début, 1939, in *Escape to Happiness*. Other successes include *Dr. Jekyll and Mr. Hyde*, *For Whom the Bell Tolls*, *Bells of St. Mary's*. (1917–.)

BERGNER, Elisabeth (Mrs. Paul Czinner). Born in Vienna, she has played in Shakespearean and other rôles. First notable screen appearance was in *Nju*, and on the stage has acted in *The Boy David*, *Catherine the Great* and other plays. Naturalized British subject. (1900–.)

BERNERS, Lord (baron); **Gerald Tyrwhitt-Wilson.** Was Hon. Attaché in Diplomatic Service, 1909–20. Composed the opera *La Carrosse du Saint Sacrement*, and ballets including *Triumph of Neptune*, *A Wedding Bouquet*, *Cupid and Psyche*. Exhibited his oil paintings in 1931 and 1936. Author of an autobiography and other books. (1883–1950.)

BERNHARDT, Sarah. Made her stage début in Paris at the Comedié Française in Racine's *Iphigénie* in 1862. Served as ambulance worker in Paris in First World War. Acted in London and also toured Europe and Australia. Established her own theatre in Paris in 1899. Leg amputated in 1915. (1845–1923.)

BESSBOROUGH, Earl of; Vere Brabazon Ponsonby. Barrister-at-law, Inner Temple, 1903. First sat in Parliament as Conservative for Cheltenham, 1910, then Dover, 1913–20. Served in the First World War, 1914–8, and was Governor-General of Canada, 1931–5. Deputy Lieutenant of County Kilkenny. (1880–.)

BEVAN, Rt. Hon. Aneurin. Minister of Health 1945–51. Was Minister of Labour for a short time, 1951. Before he was nineteen became elected to the local urban district council. Later prominent in South Wales Miners' Federation. Introduced National Health Act, 1946. (1897–.)

BEVERIDGE, Lord (baron); **William Henry Beveridge.** Studied and taught law. Next turned to sociology and economics. Was Permanent Secretary, Ministry of Food, 1919, and Director, London School of Economics, 1919–37. Devised scheme for national welfare which became known as the "Beveridge Plan." (1879–.)

BEVIN, Rt. Hon. Ernest. Foreign Secretary, 1945–1951. Lord Privy Seal, March–April, 1951. As a boy worked on a farm; in after years became known as "the dockers' K.C." because of his successful presentation of their case in the 1920 dispute. Two years later became General Secretary of the Amalgamated Transport and General Workers' Union, then chairman of the General Council, T.U.C., and in May, 1940, Minister of Labour in the National Government. Was M.P. for Woolwich East. (1881–1951.)

Ernest Bevin.

BINNEY, Admiral Sir T. Hugh (knight). In the First World War was Gunnery Officer, H.M.S. *Elizabeth*. Rear-Admiral, First Battle Squadron, 1936–8. In Second World War commanded Orkneys and Shetlands, 1939–42. Appointed Governor of Tasmania, 1945. (1883–.)

BINYON, Lawrence. Well known as an author, playwright and poet, he won the Newdigate Prize in his early days, when at Trinity College, Oxford, in 1890. In the U.S.A. was Norton Professor of Poetry, Harvard University, 1933–4, and in 1940 was Byron Professor, Athens University. (1869–1943.)

BIRDWOOD, Field-Marshal Lord (baron); **William Riddell Birdwood.** Descended from a family long connected with India, he saw much active service there and later went through the South African War. In 1915 commanded the Australian and New Zealand Corps at Gallipoli. (1865–.)

BIRKENHEAD, Earl of; Frederick Edwin Smith. Famous for his legal handling of Court actions. Was also author of *International Law*. In 1914 helped to organize Ulster's resistance to Home Rule. Served in the First World War, and in Parliament, as Conservative, became Lord Chancellor, 1919; Secretary for India, 1924–8. (1872–1930.)

BIRKETT, Rt. Hon. Sir Norman (Mr. Justice) (knight). Born in humble circumstances, he reached Cambridge University by sheer ability, became barrister-at-law and entered Parliament as Liberal. In 1941 was appointed High Court Judge. (1883–.)

"BIRMINGHAM, George A." (Canon James Owen Hannay.) Vicar of Holy Trinity Church, Kensington Gore, London, 1934–50. In 1916 was appointed Temporary Chaplain to the Forces; in 1924 became Rector of Mells, Somerset. Author of a number of novels under his *nom-de-plume*. (1865–1950.)

BISSET, Capt. Sir James G. Son of a Scottish ironmonger, he began in the British merchant service at age of fifteen. In 1907 was a junior officer, Cunard Line. Commanded a destroyer in First World War, and the *Queen* liners, 1939–47. Commodore, Cunard-White Star Co., 1944–7. (1883–.)

BLANESBURGH, Lord (baron); **Robert Younger.** Queen's Counsel in 1900, he was afterwards appointed Judge, High Court of Justice, 1915, then Lord Justice of Appeal, 1919–23, when he represented Great Britain on the Reparations Commission at Paris. Was made a life peer. (1861–1946.)

BLEDISLOE, Rt. Hon. Viscount; Charles Bathurst. An expert on agriculture, he was elected to Parliament as Conservative for the Wilton Division, South Wilts., and in 1916 became Parliamentary Secretary, Ministry of Food. At the Ministry of Agriculture, 1924–8. Was Governor-General, New Zealand, 1930–35. (1867–.)

BLISS, Sir Arthur (knight). Composer. Director of Music, B.B.C., 1942–4. Served in First World War (wounded; mentioned in dispatches). Professor of Music, University of California, 1940. Assistant Overseas Music Director, B.B.C., 1941–2. (1891–.)

BLOMFIELD, Sir Reginald (baronet). President, Royal Institute of British Architects, 1912–4. A Vice-President, Royal Historical Society. Amongst his works are the Menin Gate, Ypres, and Lambeth Bridge. (1856–1942.)

BLUM, Leon. President of the Socialist Party of France. Became prominent in the Dreyfus case. A Socialist from 1899, he was elected to *Chambre des Députés* in 1919 and was Prime Minister in 1936, 1938 and 1946. (1872–1950.)

BLUMENFELD, Ralph D. Born in Wisconsin, U.S.A., he gained his early journalistic experience as a reporter on the *Chicago Herald.* After being London correspondent for the *New York Herald* became news editor *Daily Mail*, then editor *Daily Express*. Chairman of its Board of Directors. (1864–1948.)

BLUNDEN, Edmund Charles. Fellow and Tutor in English Literature, Merton College, Oxford, 1931–43. Professor of English Literature, Tokio University, 1924–7, he was awarded the Hawthornden Prize, 1922. Author of *Poems*, 1914–30, *Undertones of War*, and other works. (1896–.)

BOHR, Niels Henrik David. Born in Copenhagen, Denmark, he was appointed Professor in Theoretical Physics, University of Copenhagen, 1916. In 1912 came to England, and as a result of his research work on the atom became known as "the founder of modern atomic theory." Author of works on atomic theory, etc. (1885–.)

BONDFIELD, Rt. Hon. Margaret. Began as a shop assistant and eventually became a trade-union official. Entered Parliament as Labour in 1923, made chairman General Council T.U.C., 1923. In 1929 was the first woman to attain Cabinet rank as Minister of Labour. Has held many public offices. (1873–.)

Margaret Bondfield.

BONE, Sir Muirhead (knight). A former art student of Glasgow, his subsequent drawings earned him a reputation which led to his appointment as official artist on the Western Front and later with the Fleet in the First World War. (1876–.)

BONHAM-CARTER, Lady Violet. Has for several years taken an active interest in the Liberal Party and became its President. Was before that President of the Women's Liberal Federation, 1923–5. Was a member of the Executive Council of the League of Nations Union. (1887–.)

BOOTH, "General" William. Salvation Army founder. Born in Nottingham, he set up in London's East End, in 1865, an obscure "Christian Mission" which developed into the famous Salvation Army with depots all over the world. (1829–1912.)

BOROTRA, Jean. French lawn-tennis player. Won singles Lawn-tennis Championship at Wimbledon, 1924 and 1926. Member of French team which won Davis Cup from the U.S.A., 1927. With Brugnon won Men's Doubles at Wimbledon, 1932–3. (1899–.)

BOTTOMLEY, Horatio. Journalist and politician. Founded the *Hackney Hansard*, the *Financial Times* and later *John Bull.* Prosecuted after failure of Hansard publications, but was acquitted. Entered Parliament as a Liberal in 1906, and resigned in 1912. In 1918 was elected Independent M.P., South Hackney, which he had previously represented. Prosecuted 1922 for Victory Bond Club misappropriations and sentenced to seven years' imprisonment. Released 1927. (1860–1933.)

BOUGHTON, Rutland. Founded Glastonbury Festival Players 1914. Has composed a number of operas and musical dramas, the most successful of which was *The Immortal Hour*, and a musical setting to Gilbert Murray's *Alcestis*. (1878–.)

BOULT, Sir Adrian Cedric (knight). Conductor B.B.C. Symphony Orchestra, 1930–50. At sixteen could play many classical compositions on the piano. Afterwards studied at the Leipzig Conservatory, later conducted for the Royal Philharmonic Society, London, and in December, 1944, was awarded the Society's gold medal. (1889–.)

BOURCHIER, Arthur. Made his first stage appearance in Wolverhampton, 1899, having earlier assisted in founding Oxford University Dramatic Society and built theatre. Acted in many famous rôles, including "Old Bill" in Bairnsfather's *The Better 'Ole*, and as "Long John Silver" in *Treasure Island.* (1864–1927.)

BOURNE, His Eminence Cardinal Francis. Ordained Priest, 1884, he became Rector, Southwark Diocesan Seminary, 1889. Later was appointed Domestic Prelate to Leo XIII; Bishop of Epiphania, 1896; of Southwark, 1897, and Archbishop of Westminster, 1903; Cardinal, 1911. Author of *Occasional Sermons*, 1930; *Congress Addresses.* (1861–1935.)

"BOWEN, Marjorie" (Margaret Gabrielle Long). Writer of novels, historical studies, plays and biographies under the pseudonyms Marjorie Bowen, George R. Preedy, and Joseph Shearing. Educated in Paris, Rome and London. Her *Viper of Milan*, published in 1917, won her immediate success. (1888–.)

BOX, Sydney. Film director and producer. During Second World War produced many propaganda and training films for British Government. Managing Director of Gainsborough Pictures since 1946. Productions include *The Man Within, The Brothers, Jassy, Holiday Camp, Good-time Girl.* (1907–.)

BOYER, Charles. First appeared on the stage in Paris, 1920; made his film début in silent pictures in Paris. Went to Hollywood 1932 and 1935 and has also appeared in British films. Among his films are *The Constant Nymph*, *Gaslight*, *Confidential Agent*, and *Cluny Brown*. (1899–.)

BRABAZON, Rt. Hon. Lord (baron); **John Cuthbert Moore-Brabazon.** Was the first air pilot in Great Britain to be granted the Royal Aero Club's certificate for flying. In 1909 won the *Daily Mail* £1,000 prize for flying an all-British machine. Minister of Aircraft Production, 1941–2. (1884–.)

BRACKEN, Rt. Hon. Brendan. Was Conservative M.P. for North Paddington, 1929 to July, 1945, and during that time, 1940–1, was Parliamentary Private Secretary to Winston Churchill as Prime Minister. Was later Minister of Information, 1941–5, and then First Lord of the Admiralty, 1945. (1901–.)

BRADBURY, Lord (baron); **John Swanwick Bradbury.** Joint Permanent Secretary to H.M. Treasury, 1913–9, he was principal delegate Reparations Commission, Paris, 1919–25. Prime Warden of the Goldsmiths Company, 1938–9. Chairman, Bankers' Clearing House Committee. (1872–1950.)

BRADLEY, General Omar Nelson. Born in Randolph County, Missouri, he studied at the West Point Military Academy and later became Lt.-Col. U.S. Army, 1936. Commanded U.S. troops in Northern Tunisia and Sicily, 1943, and in invasion of France, 1944. In 1948 became Chief of Staff, U.S. Army. (1893–.)

BRADMAN, Sir Donald George (knight). Australia's ace batsman, he has scored numerous centuries since he first made 118 runs when he played for New South Wales against South Australia in 1927. His highest Test score in England was 334 runs, at Leeds in 1930. His highest score was 452 runs not out, scored for New South Wales against Queensland in 1929. (1908–.)

Sir Don Bradman.

BRAGG, Sir W. Lawrence (knight). Professor of Experimental Physics at Cambridge since 1938. Was awarded Nobel Prize for Physics for X-ray research work. In First World War was director of submarine research and later in the Army helped to develop in France sound-range detection of enemy guns. Director, National Physical Laboratory, 1937–8. (1890–.)

BRAITHWAITE, Dame Lilian. Played Shakespearean parts in Sir Frank Benson's Company, and in modern plays with Sir George Alexander, Sir Herbert Tree, Cyril Maude and others. Appearances include *A Bill of Divorcement*, *Mr. Wu*, *Full House*, *Arsenic and Old Lace*. (Died 1948.)

BRANGWYN, Sir Frank (knight). Painter and etcher. Born in Bruges of Welsh extraction. Member of a number of foreign academies, he was awarded the Albert Medal of the Royal Society of Arts in 1932. (1867–.)

BRENTFORD, Viscount; William Joynson-Hicks. Popularly known as "Jix" before being raised to the peerage, he was a solicitor, and in Parliament as Conservative became Postmaster-General, 1923, then Minister of Health. Afterwards Home Secretary. Helped to defeat the Prayer Book Measure, 1927. (1865–1932.)

BRESSEY, Sir Charles Herbert (knight). Architect and highways expert. Served in First World War, Lt.-Col. R.E., and in 1919 joined the Ministry of Transport, later becoming Chief Engineer and then Principal Technical Officer. Author of "Bressey Report" on Development Survey of Greater London, 1935–8. (1874–1951.)

BRIDGES, Sir Edward (knight). Son of the late Robert Bridges, Poet Laureate. After leaving Oxford University served in the First World War as Captain and Adjutant. Entered Civil Service, was appointed Secretary to the Cabinet, 1938, and since 1945 Permanent Secretary, H.M. Treasury. (1892–.)

BRIDGES, Robert. Poet Laureate. Studied medicine at Barts and practised until retirement in 1881. Meanwhile had written much unpublished poetry until his first volume of poems was issued in 1873. Following that came many lyrics, odes for music and volumes of verse, including *The Testament of Beauty*. Poet Laureate, 1913. (1844–1930.)

"BRIDIE, James" (O. H. Mavor). Served with R.A.M.C. in Mesopotamia throughout First World War and was later Professor of Medicine, Anderson College, Glasgow. First London play, *The Anatomist*, 1931. Author of many books and plays. (1888–1951.)

BRITTEN, Edward Benjamin. Son of a dentist, he preferred a musical career and before his teens had composed sonatas, quartets and songs. Studied at the Royal College of Music and has since produced, among other works, *Peter Grimes* and the music for *This Way to the Tomb*. (1913–.)

BROOKE, Capt. the Rt. Hon. Sir Basil (baronet). Prime Minister of Northern Ireland since 1943 and Minister of Commerce, 1941–5. He served in the First World War, and in 1929 was elected Unionist M.P. Minister of Agriculture, N.I., 1933–41. (1888–.)

BROOKE, Rupert Chawner. Born in Rugby. His first volume of poems published in 1911. Saw active service as sub-lieutenant with Royal Naval Division in First World War. Best-known poem, *The Soldier*, contains the oft-quoted lines: "Some corner of a foreign field, that is forever England." Died of sunstroke at Syros, Aegean Sea. (1888–1915.)

BROWN, Flt.-Lt. Sir Arthur Whitten (knight). Aviator. Shared the *Daily Mail* prize of £10,000 with the late Sir John Alcock for the first transatlantic flight, from Newfoundland to Ireland, in 1919. (1886–1948.)

BROWN, Rt. Hon. Ernest. Son of coxswain Brown of Torquay's lifeboat, he became a lecturer on politics and in 1927 entered Parliament as Liberal. Has been Minister of Labour, 1935–40, later Secretary for Scotland and Minister of Health, 1941–3. Baptist lay preacher. (1881–.)

BROWN, Ivor, J. C. Left the Civil Service to take up journalism and was dramatic critic at different times for *Manchester Guardian*,

Saturday Review, *Observer*, and other papers. Also author of books. (1891–.)

BRUCE, Rt. Hon. Viscount; Stanley Melbourne Bruce. Australian statesman. Came to England to study and when back in Australia entered Parliament, becoming Commonwealth Treasurer, then Prime Minister, 1923. After filling other Government posts, represented Australia at International Conferences and at League Assemblies. Was High Commissioner for Australia in London. 1933–45. (1883–.)

BRUNSKILL, Muriel. Contralto. Studied abroad and made her English début at the Aeolian Hall, 1920. Sang at Covent Garden and in provinces, 1922–7. Has also toured Canada, U.S.A., Australia, New Zealand and Holland. (1899–.)

BRYANT, Arthur W. M. Barrister-at-law, Inner Temple. Educational Adviser, Bonar Law College, Ashridge, 1929–49. Watson Chair in American History Lectures, London University, 1935. Author and producer of pageants and of historical biographies, etc. (1899–.)

BUCHANAN, Jack. Actor-manager and film producer. Was born in Scotland and made his first appearance on the stage, Glasgow, 1912, then appeared at the Apollo Theatre, London. First film appearance in *The Happy Ending*. Director, Riverside Studios, Hammersmith. (1891–.)

BUCHMAN, Frank. Born in Pennsburg, U.S.A., of Dutch-American parentage, he became Minister of Lutheran Church at Overbrook, Pennsylvania, 1902. Resigned to found Lutheran settlement. Travelled in India and Far East. Founded a First Century Christian Fellowship, 1921, now known as the Oxford Group Movement. (1878–.)

BUDGE, Sir E. A. Wallis (knight). World-famous author and excavator. Conducted excavations at Aswan, in the Sudan, Nineveh and in Mesopotamia. Keeper of Egyptian and Assyrian Antiquities, British Museum, 1893–1924. Author of several authoritative works. (1857–1934.)

BURGHLEY, Lord; David George Burghley (heir to the Marquess of Exeter). A noted hurdler, he won many inter-university events and British championships, and won the Olympic low hurdles in 1928. Elected to Parliament as Conservative in 1931, he was first Parliamentary Secretary, Ministry of Supply. Governor-General, Bermuda, 1943–5. (1905–.)

BURNS, Rt. Hon. John. Labour leader. Was the first working man to attain Cabinet rank in Britain. Had become M.P. (Labour) for Battersea, 1892. In 1887 was imprisoned for six weeks for resisting the police over the right of public meeting in London. President Board of Trade, 1914–8. (1858–1943.)

BURROWS, Sir Frederick (knight). Appointed Governor of Bengal in 1946. Worked on the Great Western Railway, afterwards enlisting in the Grenadier Guards, 1914. Member National Union of Railwaymen's Executive Committee, and President, 1943. (1889–.)

BURT, Rt. Hon. Thomas. Worked for eighteen years as a miner, and was Secretary Northumberland Miners' Association, 1865–1913. Entered Parliament as Labour for Morpeth, 1874, and in 1891 became President Trade Union Congress. Parliamentary Secretary Board of Trade, 1892–5. (1837–1922).

BUSONI, Ferruccio Benvenuto. Italian musician. Professor of Music at Helsinki, 1888–90; Moscow, 1890; Boston, 1891–3. In 1920 was appointed Professor of Composition, Berlin Academy of Arts. Gave many recitals in Great Britain. Works include orchestral, operatic, chamber and piano music. (1866–1924.)

BUTLER, Professor Nicholas Murray. President of the Pilgrims' Society since 1928, and President since 1901 of Columbia University. A world-famous scholar, he has received numerous honorary degrees and gold medals. (1862–1947.)

BUTLER, Rt. Hon. Richard Austen. Attained schoolboy ambition to enter Parliament as Conservative for Saffron Walden in 1929. Has held secretarial posts, India Office, Ministry of Labour, and in the Foreign Office, 1938–41. Minister of Education, 1941–5. Responsible for Education Act, 1944. (1902–.)

BUZZARD, Sir E. Farquhar (baronet). Regius Professor of Medicine, Oxford, 1928–42. Physician-in-Ordinary to the King, 1932–6. Harveian Orator, Royal College of Physicians, 1941. (1871–1945.)

BYNG, Field-Marshal Viscount; Julian Hedworth George. Commanded the South African Horse in the South African War, later C.-in-C. Egypt. In the First World War was in France as head of the Canadian Corps. After retirement from the Army became Governor-General, Canada, 1926. (1862–1935.)

BYRNES, James F. U.S.A. statesman. Began as office-boy in a legal office, became solicitor, then member of Congress, 1911–25. Director of War-Mobilization in Second World War. Was U.S. Secretary of State, 1945. (1879–.)

CADOGAN, Rt. Hon. Sir Alexander George (knight). Began in the Foreign Office as a junior clerk in 1915 and twenty years later was appointed Ambassador at Peking. In August, 1944, as Permanent Under-Secretary of State for Foreign Affairs, he represented Great Britain at the Dumbarton Oaks Conference, which prepared the way for the formation of U.N.O., at which he was later Britain's permanent representative. (1884–.)

CALDECOTE, Rt. Hon. Viscount; Thomas Walter Inskip. A barrister-at-law, became Conservative M.P. in 1931 and later was first Solicitor-General, then Attorney-General. As Sir Thomas Inskip was Minister for the Co-ordination of Defence at the outbreak of Second World War. Lord Chancellor, 1939–40. (1876–1947.)

CAMERON, Basil. One-time conductor of seaside orchestras, he later conducted the Royal Philharmonic Society's concerts in London, Prague, Los Angeles, Budapest and San Francisco. Joint conductor, Promenade Concerts, London. (1885–.)

CAMPBELL, Commander A. B. Author and broadcaster. Joined the Merchant Service and, in 1900, the Royal Naval Reserve. Was a member of the B.B.C. "Brains Trust" and has lectured and written books. (1881–.)

CAMPBELL, Major Sir Malcolm (knight). First man in a racing car to reach 150 miles an hour, on Pendine Sands, Carmarthen, 1925. Set up higher records in America in his famous *Bluebird* cars, and in June, 1947, tried to beat his own speed-boat record of 141·74 miles an hour with a jet-propelled boat, but had to postpone the attempt after achieving 110 miles an hour. (1885–1949.)

Sir Malcolm Campbell.

CAMPBELL, Miss Sybil. Called to the Bar in 1922, she practised on the Midland circuit until 1939. Then became Assistant Divisional Food Officer in London during the war. Since 1945 has presided at Tower Bridge Police Court. (1889–.)

CAMROSE, Viscount; William Berry. Brother of Lord Kemsley, he was fourteen when he began his newspaper career on the *Merthyr Times*. Then came to London at twenty-two and founded the *Advertising World*. Afterwards acquired other newspaper interests, including control of *Daily Telegraph*. In 1939 was appointed Principal Adviser, Ministry of Information. (1879–.)

CAPABLANCA, Jose Raoul. Cuban chess champion. Showed a remarkable talent for chess when only four years of age. Was World Champion, 1921–7, when he was defeated by Alekhine. (1888–1942.)

CARNEGIE, Andrew. Millionaire philanthropist. Born in Dunfermline, Scotland, was taken to U.S.A. when a boy in 1848. Began work in a Pittsburgh cotton-mill, later telegraph boy, then Telegraph Superintendent, Pittsburgh. Next joined Pennsylvania Railroad and made a fortune. Founded Carnegie libraries and the Carnegie Hero Fund. (1835–1919.)

CARRUTHERS, Violet Rosa (Violet Markham). Deputy Director, Women's Section, National Service Department, 1917, and later worked in connexion with the Industrial Court and was elected Mayor of Chesterfield, 1927. Has served on various trade boards and committees. (1872–.)

CARUSO, Enrico. Italian operatic tenor. Born in Naples, he studied singing and scored his first success at Naples in *La Traviata*, 1896. Made his début in America in 1903 and was leading tenor in New York for eighteen years. Appeared at Covent Garden. (1873–1921.)

CASALS, Pau; formerly Pablo, name now converted to the Catalan form. Violoncello virtuoso. Professor at Barcelona Conservatoire, 1897. Founder and conductor of Orquesta Pau Casals, Barcelona, 1919. In addition to concert appearances, formed trio with Cortot and Thibaud. Composed symphonies and chamber music. (1876–.)

CASEMENT, Roger (former Sir). One-time British Consul in Africa, and in Brazil. He was found guilty of treachery during First World War by trying to persuade Irish prisoners-of-war to fight for Germany. Was condemned to death, degraded from knighthood, and hanged at Pentonville, 1916. (1864–1916.)

CASEY, Rt. Hon. Richard G. Australian statesman. In 1914 joined up in Australia as a private and returned home after the war as a major. Became Australian Minister to the U.S.A., and later Minister of State in Middle East, 1942–3. Governor of Bengal, 1943–6. (1890–.)

CATTO, Lord (baron); **Thomas Sivewright Catto.** Born in Peterhead, Aberdeenshire, he began in a local shipping office, then worked abroad and eventually turned to banking. In 1940 was appointed a director of the Bank of England. Governor, 1944–9. (1879–.)

CAVAN, Field-Marshal the Rt. Hon. the Earl of; Horace Edward Lambert. Served in South African War and in First World War, commanded Guards' Division and Tenth Italian Army. Captain, Gentlemen-at-Arms, 1929–31. Commanded troops at Coronation, 1937. (1865–1946.)

CAVELL, Edith Louisa. Nurse. Born at Swardleston, Norfolk. Was matron of an infirmary in Brussels when the First World War broke out in 1914. Arrested by Germans and charged with assisting refugees to escape. Sentenced to death and shot, 1915. Body brought to England and buried in Norwich Cathedral precincts. (1865–1915.)

CECIL, Rt. Hon. Viscount; Edgar Robert Cecil. First entered Parliament as Conservative; then turned Independent. In 1918 was appointed Assistant Secretary of State for Foreign Affairs. Minister of Blockade, 1916–8. Lord Privy Seal, 1923–4. Was actively interested in League of Nations Union, of which he became President. Awarded Nobel Peace Prize, 1937. (1864–.)

CHAMBERLAIN, Rt. Hon. Arthur Neville. Birthplace, Birmingham. Second son of Joseph Chamberlain and half-brother of Sir Austen Chamberlain. Entered Parliament as Conservative, Ladywood Division, Birmingham, 1918. Was three times Minister of Health and twice Chancellor of the Exchequer. As Prime Minister, 1937–40, flew to see Hitler in 1938 in vain effort to prevent war. (1869–1940.)

CHAMBERLAIN, Rt. Hon. Sir J. Austen. As Conservative M.P. became Financial Secretary to the Treasury. Later, Chancellor of the Exchequer. Was Secretary of State for India, 1915–7. In 1924 became Foreign Secretary, and in 1931 First Lord of the Admiralty. (1863–1937.)

CHAMBERLAIN, Rt. Hon. Joseph. Began life as a Birmingham business man. Was later thrice elected Lord Mayor of that city. As its M.P. he became in turn President of Board of Trade, President of the Local Government Board, and Secretary of State for Colonies, 1895–1903. Ardent Tariff Reformer. (1836–1914.)

CHAPLIN, Charles Spencer. Born in Kennington, London. As a boy appeared in variety. In Hollywood became a star comedian in silent films. Besides acting, produces and directs his pictures, writing script and music. (1889–.)

CHARLES, Sir Noel H. H. (baronet). British Ambassador to Italy 1944–7. After serving in First World War was appointed to secretarial posts abroad, then becoming Minister in Rome, 1939–40; Lisbon, 1940–1. British Ambassador to Brazil, 1941–4. (1891–.)

CHATFIELD, Admiral of the Fleet, Rt. Hon. Lord (baron); **Ernle Montacute Chatfield.** Began as a "middy," rose to Flag-Captain under Sir David Beatty and, after seeing active service in First World War, was appointed Fourth Sea Lord at the Admiralty in 1919, becoming First Sea Lord, Chief of Naval Staff, in 1933, and Minister, Co-ordination of Defence, 1939–40. (1873–.)

CHERWELL, Rt. Hon. Lord (baron); **Frederick Alexander Lindemann.** Professor of Experimental Philosophy, Oxford, since 1919. An experimental pilot in First World War, flying new machines before they were released for use. As Professor Lindemann was Personal Assistant to the Prime Minister, Mr. Winston Churchill, 1940–2. (1888–.)

CHESTERTON, Gilbert Keith. Author and journalist. Attended classes at Slade School. Began career reviewing art-books. Contributed to *Illustrated London News*, *New York Times* and other publications. Founded and edited *G.K.'s Weekly*. Works include *The Napoleon of Notting Hill*, *The Innocence of Father Brown*, and poems. (1874–1936.)

CHETWODE, Field-Marshal Rt. Hon. Lord (baron); **Philip Walhouse Chetwode.** Served in South African and First World Wars, and was Commander of the Desert Corps, Egypt, 1916–7. Made Adjutant-General in 1922, Commander-in-Chief, Aldershot, 1926, and Commander-in-Chief, India, 1930. (1869-1950.)

CHEVALIER, Albert. Vaudeville actor. Child actor at age of eight, he made his first professional appearance with the Bancrofts in 1877. Was associated for many years with the Kendals, Sir John Hare and Pinero. Achieved fame on the music-hall stage and toured with his own entertainment in Cockney imitations, notably, *My Old Dutch* and *Mrs. 'Enery 'Awkins*. (1861–1923.)

CHIFLEY, Rt. Hon. Joseph B. Prime Minister of Australia, 1945–9. Once an engine-driver on New South Wales Railways, he became Minister for Defence in the Scullin Government, 1929–32. Commonwealth Treasurer in 1941. Attended Empire Premiers' meeting, London, 1946. (1885–.)

CHIANG KAI-SHEK, Generalissimo. President of China. Met Sun Yat-sen and other revolutionaries in Japan, 1905. Studied at National Military Academy, Paoting, 1906, and at Tokyo. Joined revolutionary army in Chinese Revolution, 1911. Chairman State Council, Generalissimo, 1928; resigned, 1931. President of China, 1943, resigned 1949. Leader of Kuomintang remnant forces on Formosa, 1949, following defeat on mainland by Chinese Communist armies. (1887–.)

CHRISTIAN X, His Majesty King. Succeeded to the throne of Denmark, 14 May, 1912. A democratic monarch, he gained universal respect in April, 1940, when German forces occupied his country. He refused to leave Copenhagen, preferring to share the misfortunes of his people. (1870–1947.)

CHRISTIE, Agatha M. C. (Mrs. Max Mallowan) of American parentage, she achieved fame in Great Britain as a writer of detective stories, many of her thrillers being clever elucidations of involved mysteries by a Belgian detective, Hercule Poirot. Books include *Towards Zero*, *Death Comes as the End*, *Sparkling Cyanide*.

CHURCHILL, Rt. Hon. Winston Leonard Spencer. Has had a career full of military, journalistic and political activities. Beginning as soldier and war correspondent in Cuba, South Africa and elsewhere, he entered Parliament in 1900 as Conservative, but after disagreeing with tariff-reform proposals crossed to Liberals as Free-trader. Became President Board of Trade, and was First Lord of the Admiralty at outbreak of First World War. In 1916, as Lt.-Col., commanded 6th Royal Fusiliers in France. Returned to Parliament in 1917 as Minister of Munitions. Rejoined Conservatives in 1924 and was appointed Chancellor of the Exchequer. In history, however, his highest place of honour will be his courageous leadership of the nation as Prime Minister during the Second World War. Awarded O.M., 1946. (1874–.)

Winston Churchill.

CITRINE, Rt. Hon. Lord (baron); **Walter Citrine.** Chairman Electricity Board since 1947. Apprenticed to be an electrician, he became in time Assistant General Secretary, Electrical Trades Union, and afterwards Assistant Secretary, Trades Union Congress, 1924, and General Secretary, 1926. Director, *Daily Herald*, 1929. Served on Government's Economic Advisory Council, 1930–3. (1887–.)

CLARENDON, Rt. Hon. Earl of; George Herbert Villiers. Became Parliamentary Under-Secretary of State for Dominion Affairs, 1925, and in 1931 became Governor-General of Union of South Africa. Lord Chamberlain since 1938, and Chancellor, Order of St. Michael and St. George, since 1942. (1877–.)

CLARK, Sir Kenneth McKenzie (knight). Worked in Florence for two years, and in 1931 was appointed Keeper, Department of Fine Art, Ashmolean Museum, Oxford. During the Second World War was Controller Home Publicity. Director of the National Gallery from 1934 until his retirement in 1945. (1903–.)

CLARK, General Mark W. United States Army. Served in the First World War and in the Second made a dramatic trip in 1942 with other American officers in a submarine to North Africa on a secret mission concerning invasion plans. Commanded American forces in Italy and captured Rome, 1944. (1896–.)

CLAYTON, Rev. Philip T. B. Toc-H founder. Was a Brigade Chaplain, 6th Division, in First World War. Opened Talbot House, Poperinghe, and refounded it later as Toc-H. Vicar, Allhallows, Barking-by-the-Tower, London, since 1922. (1885–.)

CLYDESMUIR, Rt. Hon. Lord (baron); **John Colville.** Formerly director of various companies, he was afterwards, as Conservative M.P., made Parliamentary Under-Secretary of State for Scotland, 1935. Financial Secretary Treasury, 1936; Secretary of State for Scotland, 1938. Appointed Governor of Bombay, 1943. (1894–.)

CLYNES, Rt. Hon. John Robert. Began his career in a Lancashire cotton-mill and taught himself by wide reading. Joined the trade-union movement and rose to prominence in it. As Labour M.P. was Food Controller, 1918–9, when he introduced the rationing system for the first time in Britain. (1869–1949.)

COATES, Albert. Orchestral conductor. After brief business career in St. Petersburg, studied music at Leipzig, where he conducted at Opera House. Returned to England in 1919 and later conducted London Symphony Orchestra. Has also conducted in New York and elsewhere. Composer of two operas. (1882–.)

COATES, Eric. Composer and conductor. As a violinist won a scholarship at twenty for the Royal Academy of Music. In 1908 joined the Hambourg String Quartet and later Sir Thomas Beecham's Orchestra. Has numerous compositions to his credit, including the well-known *London Suite*. (1886–.)

COBHAM, Sir Alan John (knight). Served three years in France in First World War; R.F.C., 1917, later R.A.F. After demobilization, flew ten thousand civilian passengers, 1919. Joined de Havilland Aircraft Company, 1921. Started Spanish air-line to Morocco, 1922. Won King's Cup Race, 1924; Britannia Trophy, 1925. Flew London–Cape Town and back, 1925. Made many other notable flights. (1894–.)

COCHRAN, Sir Charles Blake (knight). Showman. Once worked in a surveyor's office, then became a music-hall singer. Unsuccessful, went to America, did odd jobs and, after returning to London, entered the show business as producer. Staged the first Rodeo in England, 1924. Many successes followed. (1872–1951.)

COLE, G. Douglas H. Economist and novelist. Made a name for his work on Guild Socialism, and as an expert in economics and the history of social conditions in England. As a sideline has written many crime novels in collaboration with his wife. (1889–.)

COMPTON, Denis Charles Scott. Middlesex and England cricketer, and Arsenal footballer who played for England in war-time internationals. Batsman and slow bowler. In 1947 scored 3,816 runs, the most made in a season in first-class cricket. Made eighteen centuries in same season, beating Hobbs's record by two. (1918–.)

COMPTON, Fay. Actress. Made her first appearance in Pelissier's Follies and in 1914 appeared in American production of *Tonight's the Night*. Acted in London in *Peter Pan*, 1918; *Mary Rose*, 1920, and with John Barrymore in *Hamlet*, 1925. (1894–.)

CONNAUGHT, Field-Marshal H.R.H. the Duke of. Third son of Queen Victoria. Joined the Royal Engineers and in 1874 was made Duke of Connaught and Strathearn. Saw service in Egypt and India and was Governor-General of Canada, 1911–6. Opened Union Parliament in South Africa, 1919. (1850–1942.)

"CONRAD, Joseph" (Theodor Josef Konrad Korzeniowski). Author. Born in Poland. Served for four years in French ships, then became a Master in British Merchant Service and naturalized British subject. Wrote much on seafaring subjects, his novels including *The Nigger of the Narcissus*, *Typhoon*. (1857–1924.)

COOPER, Rt. Hon. Sir Alfred Duff (knight). Entered Foreign Office before First World War, in which he served. Afterwards as Conservative M.P. became in turn Financial Secretary to Treasury, 1934; Secretary of State for War, 1935; First Lord of the Admiralty, 1937, and Ambassador to France, 1944–7. (1890–.)

COOPER, Gladys. First stage appearance in Colchester, 1905. After that acted in several musical comedies: *Our Miss Gibbs*, *Dollar Princess* and others, until she graduated into serious plays in 1911. After ten years in America returned to the London stage in 1948. (1889–.)

CORK AND ORRERY, Admiral of the Fleet the Earl of; William Henry Boyle. Rear-Admiral Commanding 1st Cruiser Squadron, 1926–8, he afterwards commanded the Reserve Fleet and then the Royal Naval War College, 1928–32. First and Principal A.D.C. to the King, 1936–8. (1873–.)

COTTON, Thomas Henry. Golf champion. Became a professional at Langley Park, 1927. Won Kent Professional Championship 1926–30; British Open, 1934, 1937; also Italian, German and Czechoslovak Open. Represented Great Britain *v.* America 1929, 1937. (1907–.)

COURTNEIDGE, Cicely (Mrs. Jack Hulbert). Born in Australia, she made her first stage appearance in Manchester, 1901. Has appeared in musical comedies and in revues. Appeared in several of her husband's films. (1893–.)

COWARD, Noel. Wrote his first play, *The Rat Trap*, when he was eighteen. In 1916 toured the provinces in *Charley's Aunt*. One of his earliest successes was his play, *The Vortex*. Among others are *Bitter Sweet*, *Cavalcade*, *Blithe Spirit*, *Sigh No More*. (1899–.)

CRERAR, General Henry. Canadian Army. Won distinction as a gunnery officer in the First World War. Was appointed Professor of Tactics, Royal Military College, Kingston, 1927, and during the Second World War was an army commander in the field. Chief of General Staff, Canada, 1940–1. (1888–.)

CRIPPS, Rt. Hon. Sir Stafford (knight). Was Chancellor of the Exchequer, 1947–50. Years ago did scientific research work, then began a legal career. Joined Labour Party in 1928, was expelled in 1937 because of his views. In the National Government was British Ambassador to Russia,

Sir Stafford Cripps.

1940–2, and after being accepted into the Labour Party again was President of Board of Trade, 1945–7. (1889–.)

CROMER, Earl of; Evelyn Baring. Administrator. From India, where he was Secretary to the Viceroy, 1872–6, he was sent to Egypt and there became Controller-General in 1879, afterwards being made Agent and Consul-General there in 1883. (1841–1917.)

CRONIN, Archibald Joseph. Formerly a doctor practising in London, he spent a holiday writing a novel. It was *Hatter's Castle*, a best-seller which changed his career. Then came *Three Loves*, *Grand Canary*, *The Stars Look Down*, *The Citadel*, and other books. (1896–.)

CROSBY, "Bing" (Harry L.). Was intended for the law, but got his first variety engagement when a boy. Spent ten years broadcasting and recording and began in films in 1930. Among them are *Going My Way*, *The Bells of St. Mary's*, *Blue Skies*. (1904–.)

CROSS, Rt. Hon. Sir Ronald H. (baronet). United Kingdom High Commissioner in Australia, 1941–5. A merchant banker, he entered Parliament as a Conservative, and after being Government Whip was made Parliamentary Secretary, Board of Trade, 1938, then Minister of Economic Warfare, 1939. Governor of Tasmania, 1951–. (1896–.)

CULBERTSON, Ely. American bridge expert. Years ago learned bridge from his wife, worked out with her a system on the game and became recognized as an expert player; and from his books on bridge and other forms of instruction accumulated a fortune. (1891–.)

CUNNINGHAM, Gen. Sir Alan G. (knight). Served in the First World War. Commanded Royal Artillery, 1st Division, 1937–8, and in 1940 commanded the 9th, 51st and 66th Divisions, and in 1941 was given command of 8th Imperial Army, Middle East. High Commissioner in Palestine, 1945–8. (1887–.)

CUNNINGHAM, Admiral of the Fleet Viscount; Andrew Browne Cunningham. Before he was thirty was in command of the 900-ton *Scorpion* in First World War. In 1932 was made Naval A.D.C. to the King. As C.-in-C. Mediterranean he crippled the Italian fleet at Taranto in November, 1940; Admiral of the Fleet, January, 1943. (1883–.)

CURTIS-BENNETT, Sir Francis Noel (knight). K.C.V.O. Entered the Civil Service, 1905; at the Ministry of Health, 1920; H.M. Treasury, 1930. Chairman of a large number of athletic associations. (1882–.)

CURZON, Marquess (of Kedleston); George Nathaniel Curzon. Conservative M.P. for Southport, he held secretarial posts first for India and then for Foreign Affairs, and when only thirty-nine was appointed Viceroy and Governor-General of India in 1898. Instituted several administrative reforms, one being the partition of Bengal, which aroused bitter criticism. Resigned in 1905 over a difference of opinion with Lord Kitchener on Army control. (1859–1925.)

DALADIER, Edouard. French politician. In 1919 was elected to the French Chamber of Deputies as a Radical-Socialist. Subsequently held important posts under Herriot, Briand and other Prime Ministers. Formed his first government in January, 1933. Minister of Foreign Affairs, 1940. (1884–.)

DALE, Sir Henry Hallett (knight). Secretary of the Royal Society, 1925–35; became President in 1940. Shared Nobel Prize for Medicine, 1936. Is connected with many scientific organizations throughout the world. Director of Laboratories, Royal Institution, and Fullerian Professor, 1942–6. (1875–.)

DALTON, Rt. Hon. Hugh. Labour M.P. Read for the Bar, turned to economics and he became a lecturer at the London School of Economics. Minister for Economic Warfare, 1940–2. President of Board of Trade, 1942–5, then Chancellor of Exchequer, July, 1945 to November, 1947. Later Chancellor of Duchy of Lancaster and Minister of Local Government and Planning. (1887–.)

DARLAN, Amiral De la Flotte Jean François. Entered the French Navy, served in the 1904 Chinese campaign and later in the First World War. In the Second World War he revealed pro-German tendencies as Minister of National Defence in Pétain Government, 1941–2. Was assassinated by Frenchman. (1881–1942.)

DARWIN, Sir Charles Galton (knight). Scientist. Director National Physical Laboratory since 1938. Was attached to Royal Engineers and R.A.F. for scientific work in First World War. When Tait Professor of Natural Philosophy, Edinburgh, was awarded the Royal Society's medal in 1935. Master of Christ's College, Cambridge, 1936–8. (1887–.)

DAVIDSON, Most Rev. and Rt. Hon. Randall T. Anglican Archbishop. Dean of Windsor and Domestic Chaplain to Queen Victoria from 1883 to 1891, when he was made Bishop of Rochester. Then of Winchester, 1895–1903. Archbishop of Canterbury, 1903–28. Created Baron Davidson of Lambeth, 1928. (1848–1930.)

DAVIES, Rt. Hon. Clement. Liberal M.P. and party leader; King's Counsel. At twenty-four was urging reform of the House of Lords. Has been a member of various Royal Commissions and Committees of Enquiry. Entered Parliament in 1929. (1884–.)

DAVIES, Sir Henry Walford (knight). Mus. Doc. Cantab., 1898; from 1898 organist of Temple Church for twenty-five years. Also Professor of Counterpoint, Royal College of Music, 1895. Musical Director of the Royal Air Force during First World War. Director of the National Council of Music in Wales, 1923. Master of the King's Musick, 1934. Composed many works. (1869–1941.)

DAWSON of Penn, Rt. Hon. Viscount; Bertrand Edward Dawson. Physician. At one time assistant physician at the London Hospital, he was the first physician to be raised to the peerage. Was Physician Extraordinary to King Edward VII and Physician in Ordinary to King George V. (1865–1945.)

DEEPING, George Warwick. Novelist. Practised as a doctor for a year, then became an author and won an early success with his romantic historical novels. Later books dealt with modern problems. His works include *Old Pybus*, *Sorrell and Son*, *Reprieve*, *Mr.*

Gurney and Mr. Slade, The Impudence of Youth. (1877–1950.)

de GAULLE, Gen. Charles A. French leader. In the Second World War refused to accept the capitulation of Marshal Pétain to the Germans and rallied under him all "free Frenchmen" willing to continue fighting their country's aggressor. President of the Government and head of the French armies, 1945–6. (1890–.)

de la MARE, Walter. Poet and author. His first published book was *Songs of Childhood* (poems), 1902; followed by *Motley and other Poems*; *The Veil and other Poems*; a play, *Crossings*; *Collected Poems.* Later works include *The Burning Glass* and *The Traveller.* (1873–.)

DELIUS, Frederick (C.H.). Born in Bradford. Went to Florida as a planter, 1883, but preferred music. After studying at Leipzig, settled at Grez-sur-Loing, France, where in later years he suffered from partial blindness. In his music he symbolized the influence of nature on the human emotions. Wrote six operas and a variety of other works. (1862–1934.)

Frederick Delius.

"DEMPSEY, Jack" (William Harrison). Irish-American boxer who defeated Jess Willard, world heavyweight champion, in 1919. Retained championship for seven years, during which he gained a sensational victory over Georges Carpentier, the French champion, in 1921. Was twice defeated by Gene Tunney. Retired 1927. (1895–.)

DEMPSEY, Gen. Sir Miles C. (knight). Of Irish descent. Born in Wallasey, Cheshire, he served in Royal Berkshire Regiment in First World War, and rose to prominence in the Second as a tank expert. Commanded an army corps at the battle of El Alamein, 1942. Commanded British Second Army, 1944–5. (1896–.)

DERBY, Earl of; Edward George Stanley. First entered Parliament in 1892, later became Financial Secretary, War Office, then Secretary of State for War, 1916, again in 1922, and in the interval Ambassador to France. Famous racehorse-owner. Won the Derby, 1924, 1933, and 1942, One Thousand Guineas seven times, and other classic races. (1865–1948.)

DE VALERA, Eamon. Irish statesman. Born in New York of a Spanish father and an Irish mother, he was taken to Ireland when a boy. A leader of the Irish insurrection, 1916. Death sentence commuted to penal servitude for life. In 1919 he escaped from Lincoln Gaol. Prime Minister of Eire, December, 1937, to February, 1948. (1882–.)

DEVONSHIRE, Duke of; Edward William Spencer Cavendish. The title borne by the Cavendish family goes back to 1694. Elected a Member of Parliament in 1923, he was Under-Secretary of State for Dominion Affairs, 1936–40, and for India and Burma, 1940–2, and for the Colonies, 1943–5. (1895–.)

DEWAR, Sir James (knight). Physicist. Born at Kincardine-on-Forth, he was noted for his researches on gases, and was the first to liquefy and afterwards solidify hydrogen. Invented the vacuum flask, and in 1899 with Sir Frederick Abel discovered cordite. President of the British Association, 1902. (1842–1923.)

DEWEY, Thomas E. Governor of New York since 1942. Practised at the Bar, rose to Attorney in 1933, and showed his fearlessness of American gangsters as Special Prosecutor in investigation of organized crime in New York. Republican candidate for Presidency, 1944 and 1948. (1902–.)

DICK, Sir William Reid (knight). Sculptor, born in Glasgow. Designed Kitchener Memorial Chapel for St. Paul's Cathedral; and among his other works are the bronze eagle on R.A.F. Memorial, Embankment, London; lion on Menin Gate; bust of King George V, and London statue of President Roosevelt. (1879–.)

"DIETRICH, Marlene" (Mary von Losch). Film actress. Born in Berlin. First achieved fame in her picture *The Blue Angel.* Had before that appeared on the stage in Berlin and Vienna and in films in Germany. Made her Hollywood screen début in *Morocco.* In 1937 became an American. Later films include *Knight Without Armour* and *Golden Earrings.* (1905–.)

DILL, Field-Marshal Sir John Greer (knight). Born in Northern Ireland, he served in both World Wars and South African War. Director of Military Operations and Intelligence, 1934–36, he was afterwards C.-in-C. in Palestine and Trans-Jordan. Appointed Chief of Imperial General Staff, 1940–1. (1881–1944.)

DIONNE. Monsieur and Madame. Parents of the world-famous quintuplets born at Callandar, Ontario, 1934, making twelve children in family. Quintuplets were attended by Dr. Dafoe and were made wards of King George VI, who received them on his Canadian visit, 1939.

DISNEY, Walter E. Artist-cartoonist. Producer of "Mickey Mouse" and "Silly Symphonies" since 1928. Served in First World War as Red Cross ambulance driver. Went to Hollywood, 1923. First full-length film: *Snow White and the Seven Dwarfs*, 1938. Among his successes are *Pinocchio, Fantasia, Dumbo, The Reluctant Dragon* and *Bambi.* (1901–.)

Walt Disney.

DODD, Francis (R.A.). Artist. Studied at Glasgow School of Art. Was an official artist in First World War. His portraits of generals and admirals on active service were published in 1917. Two of his works are in Tate Gallery, of which he was a Trustee, 1929–35. (1874–1949.)

DONEGALL, Marquess of; Edward Hamilton. Was a special writer for several national newspapers. Was an Honorary Attaché at Brussels Embassy in 1925. (1903–.)

DONOGHUE, Stephen. One of the most famous English jockeys in racing history, he began riding in 1909 and achieved first big success winning the Cambridgeshire Stakes, 1910. Rode 143 winners in 1920 and won the Derby six times, 1915–25, thus establishing a record on the Turf. (1884–1945.)

"*Steve*" *Donoghue.*

DORLING, Capt. Henry Taprell. Better known as "Taffrail," author of novels and short stories. Served with Navy in First World War and during that period received gold medal from Swedish Government for life-saving at sea, 1917. Books include *The Shetland Plan*, *The Navy in Action* and *Chenies*. (1883–.)

DORMAN-SMITH, Rt. Hon. Sir Reginald H. (knight). Governor of Burma, 1941–6. Served with the 15th Sikhs, Indian Army, and in 1935 entered Parliament as Conservative. Was appointed Minister of Agriculture in 1939. Liaison officer between the Home Defence Forces and Government Departments, 1940. (1899–.)

DOWDING, Air Chief-Marshal Lord (baron); **Hugh Caswall Dowding.** Served in the First World War, and in the early days of the Second World War contributed much to Britain's defences. Commanded R.A.F. Fighter Command in Battle of Britain. Retired in 1942. (1882–.)

DOYLE, Sir Arthur Conan (knight). Practised as a doctor for some years until he achieved success as a writer of crime stories with his first book, *A Study in Scarlet*, in which appeared that great detective of fiction, Sherlock Holmes. Other Sherlock Holmes stories include *The Hound of the Baskervilles* and *His Last Bow*. Among his historical novels are *The White Company*, *The Exploits of Brigadier Gerard* and *Uncle Bernac*. His play, *A Story of Waterloo*, was produced by Irving. Ardent spiritualist. (1859–1930.)

DRAPER, Ruth. American diseuse. First appeared at Aeolian Hall, 1920, and displayed unrivalled technique and artistry. Using no scenery and little change of costume, she conveys impression of a crowded stage and possesses remarkable imitative ability. Royal Command performance, Windsor Castle, 1926. (1884–.)

DRINKWATER, John. Poet and dramatist. Spent twelve years in insurance companies. Co-founder of The Pilgrim Players, 1907, now Birmingham Repertory Theatre. First play (in verse), *Cophetua*. His other plays include *Abraham Lincoln*, in which he played the title rôle, *Mary Stuart*, *Oliver Cromwell*. (1882–1937.)

DUGDALE, Major Sir Thomas (baronet). After leaving Sandhurst, served with the Royal Scots Greys in First World War. Elected M.P., 1929; became Secretary of State for Colonies, 1931; for Air, 1935; and Parliamentary Private Secretary to Prime Minister, 1935–7. Was Lord of Treasury, 1937–40, and Chairman of Conservative Party, 1942–4. (1897–.)

du MAURIER, Sir Gerald (knight). Actor. Made stage début at Garrick Theatre, London, 1894. First success in *The Admirable Crichton*. Other hits as Captain Hook in *Peter Pan*, and in *Raffles*. Among his later successes were *Bulldog Drummond*, *The Last of Mrs. Cheyney*, and, on the screen, *Escape*, and *Catherine the Great*. (1873–1934.)

DUNCAN, the Rt. Hon. Sir Andrew Rae (knight). Industrialist. Conservative M.P. for the City of London, 1940–50. Was twice appointed President of Board of Trade, 1940 and 1941, and twice Minister of Supply, later in 1940 and in 1942. Was Coal Controller, 1919–20. Director of Bank of England, 1929–40. (1884–.)

DUNSANY, Lord (baron); **Edward John Moreton Drax Plunkett.** Short-story writer, poet and dramatist. Served in South African and First World Wars and has travelled extensively in the Far East. His books include *Time and the Gods*, *Seven Modern Comedies*, *Fifty Poems*. Plays: *The Glittering Gate*, *The Bureau de Change*. (1878–.)

EARHART, Amelia (Mrs. G. P. Putnam). American aviator. Became a teacher and later was the first woman to fly the Atlantic, 1928. She crossed the Atlantic alone in 1932 and established a record by making the flight in thirteen and a half hours. Disappeared on a world flight in 1937. (1898–1937.)

EBBISHAM, Lord (baron); **George Rowland Blades.** Entered a printing firm and subsequently became its head. Elected to Parliament in 1918, and in 1926–7 was Lord Mayor of London. In his early days was a noted cricketer. Treasurer of the Conservative Party, 1931–3. (1868–.)

EDDINGTON, Sir Arthur Stanley (knight). Astronomer and physicist. Fellow, Trinity College, Cambridge, he was first appointed Chief Assistant, Royal Observatory, Greenwich, in 1906, and soon became known as one of the best mathematical astronomers of his day. Awarded Royal Medal, Royal Society, 1928. President of the Royal Astronomical Society, 1921–3. (1882–1944.)

EDE, Rt. Hon. James Chuter. Labour Secretary of State for Home Affairs, 1945. A scholarship took him from an elementary school to Cambridge. Afterwards took up teaching, becoming president of the Surrey Teachers' Association. Parliamentary Secretary, Board of Education, 1940–5. (1882–.)

EDEN, Rt. Hon. Robert Anthony. Conservative M.P. An expert at Oriental languages, he graduated from Oxford and was elected to Parliament in 1923. Before that served in the First World War. In Parliament rose to prominence as Foreign Secretary, 1935–8, and again under Churchill, 1940–5. (1897–.)

Anthony Eden.

EDISON, Thomas Alva. American inventor. Of mixed Dutch and Scottish descent, he was first a newsboy. Next turned to inventing and in his lifetime produced more than a thousand inventions, including the quadruplex telegraph, phonograph, incandescent lamp and numerous other appliances. Suffered from deafness. (1847–1931.)

EDWARD VII. King of Great Britain and Ireland, Emperor of India. Succeeded to the throne 1901. Possessed a striking personality, was genial and fond of sport, yet a firm ruler. Helped to establish *L'Entente Cordiale* with France, 1904, and the Anglo-Russian agreement was enhanced by his visit to Russia, 1908. Known as the Peacemaker. (1841–1910.)

EGERTON, Sir Alfred (knight). Scientist. Professor of Chemical Technology, Imperial College of Science, 1936–48, and Secretary to the Royal Society since 1938. Formerly member of the Advisory Council of the Department of Scientific and Industrial Research. (1886–.)

EINSTEIN, Prof. Albert. Scientist. Born of Jewish parents in Ulm, Germany, in 1901 became a naturalized Swiss subject until 1909. Was twenty-six when the publication of his special theory on relativity brought him world-wide fame. Exiled from Germany 1933 and came to England. Now a naturalized American, and Professor of Theoretical Physics at Princeton, U.S.A. Nobel Prize for Physics, 1921. Announced a general theory of gravitation, 1949. (1879–.)

Prof. Einstein.

EISENHOWER, Gen. Dwight D. American Army. Born in Tyler, Texas, he studied at West Point Academy and later became Chief of Staff to General MacArthur in the Philippines, 1935–40. Was chosen in the Second World War to command the Allied Forces in North Africa, but became Supreme Commander of all the Allied forces at the invasion of Western Europe. Chief of Staff, U.S.A. Army, 1945–8. President Columbia University. In 1950 he was appointed Supreme Commander of the United Nations Forces in Western Europe. (1890–.)

Gen. Eisenhower.

ELGAR, Sir Edward (baronet). Composer. He first learnt from his father who was a church organist. *The Wand of Youth* and *Salut-d'Amour* were among his early works. Later the *Enigma Variations*, *The Dream of Gerontius*, a choral work, and his "Pomp and Circumstance" marches were great successes. (1857–1934.)

ELIOT, Thomas Stearns (O.M.). Poet. Born in America, he became a naturalized British subject in 1927. Lectured at Trinity College, Cambridge, 1926, and later was appointed Norton Professor of Poetry, Harvard, U.S.A. Among recent works are *Practical Cats, Four Quarters, What is a Classic?* (1888–.)

ELIZABETH, Queen. Formerly Lady Elizabeth Angela Marguerite Bowes-Lyon, the youngest daughter of the Earl and Countess of Strathmore and Kinghorne. In 1923 married the Duke of York (now King George VI) and was crowned Queen Consort in 1937. With the King toured Canada and U.S.A. in 1939, and South Africa in 1947. (1900–.)

ELIZABETH, Princess (Duchess of Edinburgh). Heiress-Presumptive to the British Throne. Elder daughter of King George VI and Queen Elizabeth, she was born in London. Studied Constitutional Law and History under Sir Henry Marten, then Vice-Provost of Eton. Is a Colonel of the Grenadier Guards and in the Second World War was gazetted a Lieutenant in the **A.T.S.** In November, 1947, married H.R.H. Prince Philip, Duke of Edinburgh. See Philip, H.R.H. Prince. Son, Prince Charles, born 1948. (1926–.)

Princess Elizabeth.

ELLERMAN, Sir John Reeves (baronet). Shipping magnate. Entered shipping industry 1892, joining Board of Frederick Leyland and Co.; subsequently elected chairman. Acquired financial interests in other shipping lines, as well as in *The Times*. Left over sixteen million pounds. (1862–1933.)

ELLINGTON, Marshal of the Royal Air Force Sir Edward L. (knight). Saw service in the First World War. Director-General of Military Aeronautics, 1918. Commanded R.A.F. Middle East, 1922–3. Air Officer Commanding-in-Chief, Air Defence of Great Britain, 1929–31. Chief of Air Staff, 1933-7. (1877–.)

ELLIOT, Col. the Rt. Hon. Walter. Conservative M.P. Served as a doctor in First World War. Took his first seat in Parliament as a Unionist, in 1918, and later held important ministerial posts. Appointed Minister of Health in 1938. (1888–.)

ELMAN, Mischa. Russian violinist. Made his début in Berlin when thirteen, and sprang to prominence as a brilliant child prodigy. About a year later played in London. A naturalized American subject. (1891–.)

ELTON, Lord (baron); **Godfrey Elton.** He was expelled from Labour Party in 1931, because of his support of Ramsay MacDonald, Prime Minister, when the latter joined Stanley (afterwards Lord) Baldwin in Government partnership. Secretary Rhodes Trust since 1939. (1892–.)

EPSTEIN, Jacob. Sculptor. Born of Russo-Polish parents, his first important sculpture, in 1908, for the British Medical Association, aroused great controversy. His figure of Christ, and "Rima," the W. H. Hudson Memorial in Hyde Park, were also the subjects of criticism. Portraits in bronze include one of Bernard Shaw. (1880–.)

EVANS, Dame Edith (Mary). Actress. First appearance, King's Hall, Covent Garden, 1912. Toured with Ellen Terry in variety, 1918, and after that acted in Shakespeare's plays. For a year, from 1925, was associated with the Old Vic and then acted in Shaw's plays. (1889–.)

EVATT, Rt. Hon. Herbert Vere. Australian statesman. Born in New South Wales, he was first a teacher of philosophy, then turned to law, becoming King's Counsel. Later in the Australian Parliament succeeded to the post of Attorney-General and Minister for External Affairs in 1941. (1894–.)

EWINS, Dr. Arthur J. Scientist. Took up first appointment in 1899. One of the discoverers of the drug "M. and B. 693," which has been successfully used in treatment of cerebro-spinal fever, pneumonia, and other diseases. (1882–.)

EYSTON, Capt. George Edward Thomas. British racing motorist. Served as Captain in First World War; became the holder of land speed records three times, in America, his last being broken by John Cobb at 394 miles an hour in 1947. Segrave Trophy, 1937; Author of motor-racing books. (1897–.)

FARNOL, Jeffery. Author. Began to write at age of nineteen; went to New York, 1902, became a theatrical scene-painter and in intervals wrote *The Broad Highway*, which after being rejected by several publishers became a best-seller. Returned to England, 1910. Other novels include *The Money Moon*, *The Amateur Gentleman*, *Chronicles of the Imp*, *Murder by Nail*. (1878–.)

FAROUK, King of Egypt. In 1935, when fifteen, came to England to complete his education, part of which was acquired at the Royal Military Academy, Woolwich. Until he attained the age of eighteen was under a Regency Council. Succeeded his father, King Fuad, in 1936. (1920–.)

FIELDS, Gracie (C.B.E.). Variety star. Joined theatrical troupe at age of seven, then went to work in a cotton mill. When seventeen began her variety career in the revue *Yes, I Think So*. Has sung in many countries, and during the Second World War entertained the troops overseas. (1898–.)

FISHER, Most Rev. and Rt. Hon. Geoffrey Francis. Archbishop of Canterbury. Comes from a long line of Midland country parsons. Educated at Marlborough, and after being ordained went back to Marlborough as an assistant master. In 1914 became Headmaster of Repton School and in 1932 Bishop of Chester. Bishop of London, 1939. (1887–.)

FISHER, Admiral of the Fleet, Lord (baron); **John Arbuthnot Fisher.** Born in Ceylon, he entered the Royal Navy at fourteen. Served in Crimean War, 1855, and in the attack on Alexandria, 1882. In 1904 became First Sea Lord. Was criticized in Whitehall for his insistence on reforms. Introduced the Dreadnought type of battleship. (1841–1920.)

FISTOULARI, Anatole. Conducted first concert at age of seven at Kiev. Gave first symphony concert with London Symphony Orchestra, 1942, and since has conducted at Covent Garden and abroad. (1907–.)

FITZROY, Capt. the Rt. Hon. Edward A. Former Speaker. Conservative M.P., he was Deputy Chairman of Committees, House of Commons, 1922–4, 1924–8, and Speaker 1928–43. (1869–1943.)

FLEMING, Sir Alexander (knight). Discoverer of penicillin. Came to London from Ayrshire in the eighteen-nineties, spent some years in a shipping office and then turned to medicine. Isolated penicillin after a chance discovery of the antiseptic properties of a mould. Shared the Nobel Prize for Medicine with Sir Howard Florey, 1946. (1881–.)

Sir Alexander Fleming.

FLEMING, Sir J. Ambrose (knight). Inventor of thermionic valve and many other devices in connexion with electric lighting, wireless telegraphy and telephony. Was for some years adviser to Marconi's Wireless Telegraph Company. (1849–1945.)

FLEMING, Peter. Explorer. Served in Norway, Greece and elsewhere in Second World War. Travelled extensively in Asia, generally as Special Correspondent of *The Times*, and has embodied his observations and experiences in *News from Tartary*, *The Flying Visit*, and other books. (1907–.)

FOCH, Marshal Ferdinand. Generalissimo of the Allied Armies in the First World War. Son of a lawyer, he took up a military career instead, and for a time was a professor of military history and strategy. Dictated the Armistice terms to a defeated Germany in November, 1918. (1851–1929.)

FORBES, Joan Rosita (Mrs. Arthur T. McGrath). Explorer. Seized by an urge for adventure as a girl, she first went to Australia, then crossed to Africa in a small vessel, and has since then travelled alone in Syria, Palestine and elsewhere. Author of many travel books. (1893–.)

FORBES-ROBERTSON, Sir Johnston. Actor. Made stage début in 1874, and later had leading rôles with the Bancrofts, Henry Irving, Barrett and John Hare. Became actor-manager at the Lyceum, 1895. Was the possessor of a magnetic personality and spoke with excellent diction. (1853–1937.)

FORD, Henry. American industrialist. At one time a jeweller's assistant, he conceived the idea of making a petrol motor vehicle. His first motor was finished in 1892. Founded the Ford Motor Co., and eventually became the second richest man in the world. (1863–1947.)

FORMBY, George. British comedian and film star. Was a jockey before going on the stage as George Hoy. Screen appearances include *No Limit*, *Feather Your Nest*, *Keep Fit*, *Trouble Brewing*, *Come on, George*. (1904–.)

FORSDYKE, Sir Edgar John (knight). Has been a director, and Principal Librarian, of the British Museum, 1936–50. Is an authority on Greek and Roman antiquities and is a member of committees of British schools of Archaeology in Athens, Rome and Iraq. (1883–.)

FORSTER, Edward M. Author. Was member of a committee to examine the law relating to defamatory libel and its possible alteration. In 1937 was awarded the Benson Medal by the Royal Society of Literature. Author of many works, including *Passage to India*, *A Room with a View*, *Nordic Twilight*, *Virginia Woolf*. (1882–.)

FRANCO, Gen. (Don Francisco Franco Behamonde). Caudillo of Spain. Saw service in Morocco and helped to form the Spanish Legion. Later Military Governor of Balearic islands. Chief of General Staff, 1934. Generalissimo of Nationalist armies throughout the civil war, 1936–9. (1892–.)

FRANKAU, Gilbert. Author. Travelled round world, and after working in his father's tobacco business wrote his first book, *Peter Jackson, Cigar Merchant*. Later came *Self-Portrait*, *Wine, Women and Waiters*, *Experiment in Crime*, *World Without End*, *Selected Verses*. (1884–.)

FRASER, Admiral of the Fleet Lord (baron); **Bruce Austin Fraser.** One-time Flag Captain, East Indies, he later commanded H.M.S. *Glorious* and from 1939–40 was Chief of Staff, Mediterranean Fleet. Commander-in-Chief, Pacific Fleet, 1944–. First Sea Lord, 1948. (1888–.)

FRASER, Rt. Hon. Peter. New Zealand statesman. Scotsman. Worked in London for a time, made his first political speech in Hyde Park and after going to New Zealand joined the Labour Party. Became in turn Minister of Education, Health, Marine and Police. Prime Minister, 1940–9. (1884–1950.)

FRASER, Lt.-Col. Sir W. Ian (knight). Though blinded in the First World War, he began to take an active interest in politics and welfare, first as Member L.C.C. and then as Conservative M.P., from 1924. Governor British Broadcasting Corporation 1937–41. Chairman, St. Dunstan's, since 1921. Has attended conferences in the Dominions, U.S.A. and European capitals. (1897–.)

FREUD, Prof. Sigmund. Austrian scientist. After qualifying as a doctor, he took up the study of neurology and after that concentrated on the influence of the unconscious mind. His first book, *Studies About Hysteria*, originated science of psycho-analysis. Some of his works have been translated into English. (1856–1939.)

FREYBERG, Lt.-Gen. Sir Bernard C. (knight). Governor-General of New Zealand since 1946. Soldier and Administrator. Swam ashore in Gulf of Xeros, lighting flares to deceive the Turks (D.S.O.). Won Victoria Cross at Beaumont Hamel, 1916. Assistant Quartermaster-General, Southern Command, 1931–3. Retired, 1937. Commander-in-Chief Allied Forces in Crete, 1941. Commanded Second N.Z.E.F., 1939. (1890–.)

FRY, Charles Burgess. Became prominent as an athlete while studying at Oxford. In 1912 captained the English cricket team against Australia. Played for England in association football for some years, and held the world's record long jump. Author of books on sport. (1872–.)

FYFE, Rt. Hon. Sir David P. Maxwell (knight). Lawyer and Conservative M.P. Practised on Northern Circuit before entering Parliament and in 1942 became Solicitor-General. Was Deputy Prosecutor in 1946 at Nuremberg Trials of German major war criminals. (1900–.)

FYFFE, Will. Variety and film actor. Made his early stage appearance in his father's company and later achieved popularity in variety and in films. (1885–1947.)

GALSWORTHY, John. First a lawyer, he found his true bent in writing and issued his early books under the nom-de-plume of John Sinjohn. Later achieved success, notably with his *Forsyte* series of novels. Plays include *The Silver Box*, *Strife*, *The Skin Game*. (1867–1933.)

GANDHI, Mohandas Karamchand. Indian leader. Took an active lead on behalf of the depressed classes among his countrymen. Advocated the withdrawal of British power from India, but won wide respect as a believer in non-violence and a peacemaker. Assassinated in January, 1948, six months after he had seen India achieve Dominion status. (1869–1948.)

Mahatma Gandhi.

GARBETT, Most Rev. and Rt. Hon. Cyril F. Archbishop of York since 1942. One-time Vicar of Portsea, he was afterwards ordained Bishop of Southwark, and later Bishop of Winchester. In 1943 gave up half his income of £9,000 a year. Author of several religious works. (1875–.)

"GARBO, Greta" (Greta Lovisa Gustafsson). First a clerk and then a mannequin in a Stockholm store. Made her screen début in *Atonement of Gosta Berling*. In 1926 went to Hollywood for her first American film, *The Torrent*. (1905–.)

GARVIN, James Louis. First wrote for *Newcastle Chronicle*, and after working on other provincial papers came to London and became in turn editor of *The Outlook*, *Pall Mall Gazette*, and *Observer*. Achieved prominence as a writer on foreign and fiscal topics. (1868–1947.)

GEORGE II, King of the Hellenes. Succeeded Constantine I in 1922, and when Greece became a Republic in March, 1924, he left the country until recalled to the throne in 1935. Was forced to flee again following Italian invasion of his country, and lived in London till his return to Greece, 1946. (1890–1947.)

GEORGE V, King of Great Britain and Northern Ireland, Emperor of India. Second son of Edward VII, he was first created Duke of York and then Prince of Wales. In the interval married Princess May of Teck, now Queen Mary. His tour of the British Dominions and India helped to fit him for the throne, to which he succeeded in 1910. Was greatly loved and respected by his subjects at home and abroad. (1865–1936.)

GEORGE VI, King of Great Britain and Northern Ireland. Sub-Lieutenant at Battle of Jutland, 1916, he was later drafted to the Royal Flying Corps as captain. Showed great interest in industrial welfare and made the industrial life of his country a special study. Married Lady Elizabeth Bowes-Lyon, 1923, and, on abdication of Edward VIII, succeeded to the throne, 1936. Visited South Africa, 1947, with the Queen and his two daughters, Princess Elizabeth and Princess Margaret. (1895–.)

H.M. King George VI.

GIBBS, Sir Philip (knight). Was appointed educational editor in a London publishing house not long after leaving Eton. Later held editorial positions on national newspapers, and was war correspondent during the First World War. Best-known novel, *The Street of Adventure.* (1877–.)

GIBSON, George. In 1913 became General Secretary Mental Hospital and Institutional Workers' Union, and in 1940 Chairman Trades Union Congress. Is also chairman of various committees and a member of the Overseas Settlement Board, 1936–9. Director of the Bank of England, 1946–9. (1885–.)

GIELGUD, A. John. Well known for his fine interpretations of Shakespeare, his acting as Hamlet gained high praise in America in 1937. In addition to acting in or producing other plays has also appeared in films. (1904–.)

GIGLI, Beniamino. Italian tenor. Made his operatic début in 1914 in *La Gioconda* at Rovigo. The tone quality of his voice soon brought him offers from the principal opera-houses of the world. First Covent Garden, London, appearance was in 1930. Has sung in the U.S.A. and elsewhere. (1890–.)

GILBERT, Sir William Schwenck (knight). Was a civil servant until after studying law he became a barrister. But his real gift lay in verse- and play-writing, and in association with Arthur Sullivan he helped to produce the series of famous operas *H.M.S. Pinafore, Pirates of Penzance, The Mikado,* and others. Drowned at Harrow. (1836–1911.)

GILBEY, Sir H. Walter (baronet). Wine merchant, a prominent sportsman and agriculturist, he was a notable figure in social London of the 'nineties, a racehorse owner, and a member of the Jockey Club. Chairman Royal Agricultural Hall Company. (1859–1945.)

GILL, Arthur Eric. Studied at Chichester Art School and later became widely known for his war memorials and other designs. Achieved fame as a typographer, particularly for his Gill Sans type. Author of books and essays. (1882–1940.)

GILLIES, Sir Harold Delf (knight). A New Zealander by birth and during the Second World War became known in London as "the Miracle Man" because of his cures by plastic surgery. In earlier days was a Cambridge rowing blue, an international golfer and painter in oils. (1882–.)

GIRAUD, Gen. Henri. A general in the French Army, strategist and tactician, he achieved fame in both World Wars for his successful escapes from German prisons. After his last escape in 1942, he took his stand on the side of the Allies. Became Commander-in-Chief, French Forces, 1943. (1879–1949.)

GLOUCESTER, Henry William Frederick Albert, Duke of. Third son of George V, he toured East Africa in 1928, visited Japan, 1929. Served in Second World War as a Major-General. Was appointed Governor-General of Australia, 1945–6. (1900–.)

GOEBBELS, Dr. Josef. Nazi German Minister of Propaganda. Broadcast with satire, irony, and frequent inaccuracy, during the Second World War. Became associated with Hitler in 1924. Committed suicide with his family, Berlin, 1945. (1897–1945.)

GOERING, Field-Marshal Hermann. Head of the German Air Force, he had commanded an Air Squadron during the First World War, and before and during the Second World War achieved prominence as a close collaborator of Hitler. Played a leading part in rise of Nazism. Committed suicide while awaiting his execution as a war criminal. (1893–1946.)

GOOSSENS, Eugène. Orchestral conductor, violinist and composer, of Belgian ancestry though born in London, he began his musical education at Bruges. Has conducted Sir Thomas Beecham's Orchestra and others in London and America. His opera, *Judith,* was produced at Covent Garden in 1929. (1893–.)

GORT, Field-Marshal Viscount; John Standish Vereker. Began his army career in 1905 in the Grenadier Guards. Won the Victoria Cross in 1918 and was mentioned in dispatches nine times. Appointed Chief of Imperial General Staff in 1937, he was made C.-in-C. British Field Force, 1939. Later Governor of Gibraltar, then Malta. (1886–1946.)

GOUGH, Gen. Sir Hubert (knight). Served in South African War and in the First World War. Commanded the 5th Army, which was almost annihilated and forced to retreat; this led to his becoming one of the central figures in a great controversy. Established Home Guard School, Hurlingham, 1940. (1870–.)

GOWRIE, Brig.-Gen. Earl of; Alexander Gore Hore-Ruthven. Governor-General of Australia from 1936 to 1945. Served in Soudanese, Egyptian and First World Wars. Commanded Welsh Guards, 1920–4, and was Governor of South Australia, 1928–34. (1872–.)

GRACE, Dr. William Gilbert. Member of a cricketing family, he was educated for medical profession. Cricket, however, soon absorbed all his attention and he became captain of the Gloucestershire county eleven until 1899, as well as an outstanding cricketing personality. His highest score as batsman was 344 runs. Also skilful bowler and fieldsman. (1848-1915.)

GRAHAM, Stephen. Lived with Russian peasants, tramped in the Caucasus and Crimea and accompanied Russian pilgrims to Jerusalem. Served in First World War. Has taken part in much exploration and travelled extensively. His works include *Undiscovered Russia*, *A Life of Alexander II.* (1884–.)

GRAINGER, Percy A. Studied in Australia until age of ten. Came to London, 1900. Has given many concerts in Great Britain and over a hundred on the Continent; has also played at Royal Command Performances. Composer of *Kipling Setting*, *English Dance*, *Hill Songs.* (1882–.)

GRANVILLE, Vice-Admiral Earl; William Spencer Leveson-Gower. Governor of Northern Ireland since 1945. Assisted in suppression of slave trade and piracy in Red Sea, 1902–3, and later made a journey through Yemen. Served in First World War, and in 1929 was appointed Naval A.D.C. to the King. Rear-Admiral Commanding Coast of Scotland, 1931–3. Retired from Navy, 1935. (1880–.)

GRANVILLE-BARKER, Harley Granville. Made his stage début, 1891, toured the provinces, later becoming joint manager, Court and Savoy Theatres, London. Influenced by Bernard Shaw in his dramatic works. Member of Academic Committee, Royal Society of Literature. Adapted French and German plays for English stage. (1877–1946.)

GREENE, Rt. Hon. Lord (baron); **Wilfred Arthur Greene.** Served in First World War; he was made King's Counsel in 1922. Lord Justice of Appeal, 1935–7, he was during that time made principal, Working Men's College. Master of the Rolls, 1937–50. (1883–.)

GREENWOOD, Rt. Hon. Arthur. Formerly Lecturer, University of Leeds, and afterwards Assistant Secretary, Ministry of Reconstruction, he was made Minister of Health in 1929, and Minister without Portfolio, 1940. Deputy Leader, Labour Party, 1935. Lord Privy Seal, 1945–7. Author of *The Labour Outlook*, *Labour's Case.* (1880–.)

GREGG, Most Rev. John A. F. Archbishop of Armagh and Primate of all Ireland since 1939. After leaving Cambridge devoted himself to the Church. Was appointed to ecclesiastical posts, and then became bishop in 1915. In 1920 was made Archbishop of Dublin. (1873–.)

GREGORY, Sir Richard A. (baronet). Editor of *Nature*, 1919–39. Emeritus Professor of Astronomy, Queen's College, London. President of the British Association for the Advancement of Science, 1940–6. Author of *Religion in Science and Civilization*, *Science in Chains*, *British Scientists.* (1864–.)

GRIERSON, Sir Herbert J. C. (knight). Formerly Professor at Aberdeen University and then in 1915–35 Professor of Rhetoric and English Literature, Edinburgh University. Rector of Edinburgh University, 1936–9. Author of *The Background of English Literature* and other *Collected Essays*, *Lyrical Poetry from Blake to Hardy.* (1866–.)

GRIFFIN, His Eminence Cardinal Bernard. Spiritual father to two and a half million Roman Catholics in England and Wales. Studied for five years at the Venerable English College, Rome, and later gained a reputation as a leading canon lawyer. Archbishop of Westminster, 1944. (1899–.)

GRIFFITHS, Rt. Hon. James. Labour Minister of National Insurance, 1945–50. Worked in the mines of West Wales before being made President South Wales Miners' Federation, in 1934. Labour attaché to the British Embassy, Washington, 1941. Toured the U.S.A. explaining British Labour views, 1944. Sponsored Bill for National Security by Insurance, which was passed. Appointed Colonial Secretary, 1950. (1890–.)

GRIGG, Rt. Hon. Sir P. James (knight). Went to Cambridge University by means of scholarships, entered the Civil Service and later worked as principal private secretary to five successive Chancellors of the Exchequer. In India for a time as Finance Minister, returned for a secretarial post at the War Office, afterwards becoming its head. (1890–.)

GROMYKO, Andrei. In 1939 was sent to Washington as a member of the Soviet Embassy and, when his chief, Litvinov, was recalled in 1943, he was appointed Soviet Ambassador at Washington. In the same year was made Minister to Cuba. Soviet delegate to U.N.O. (1908–.)

GROSSMITH, George. Became an entertainer in 1870, and later achieved popularity in leading rôles in Gilbert and Sullivan operas. Resumed the rôle of entertainer in 1889 and made big hits in London, the provinces and in America. Father of two famous theatrical sons, George and Lawrence. (1847–1912.)

GUEDALLA, Philip. A former lawyer and legal adviser to the War Office and Ministry of Munitions, he turned biographer and historian with *The Hundred Days*, *Gladstone and Palmerston*, *The Duke*, *Mr. Churchill—a Portrait*, and other books. (1889–1944.)

GUSTAV V, King of Sweden. Succeeded his father, Oscar II, in 1907, after a thorough preparation for rulership which included wide travel and ability to speak five languages. Was related by family ties to the English nobility. In the Second World War maintained a difficult neutrality. (1858–1950.)

HAAKON VII, King of Norway, second son of King Frederick VIII. As Prince Charles, he married Princess Maud, daughter of King Edward VII. When Norway separated from Sweden in 1905, he was elected King of Norway. After German capture of Norway in 1940, the King took refuge in London until 1945. (1872–.)

HAIG, Field-Marshal Earl; Douglas Haig. In the First World War commanded the 1st Army, and in 1915 was appointed Commander-in-Chief of the British Forces in France. In his later years laboured for the welfare of ex-service men, resulting in the formation of the British Legion. (1861–1928.)

HAIGH, Rt. Rev. Mervyn G. Bishop of Winchester since 1942, was temporary Chaplain to the Forces during the First World War. Mentioned in dispatches. Later became private secretary, first to Archbishop Davidson and then to Archbishop Lang.

Chaplain to the King, 1929–31, and Bishop of Coventry, 1931–42. (1887–.)

HAILE SELASSIE, Emperor of Ethiopia. Proclaimed Heir-Apparent and Regent in 1916, he was crowned King in 1928 and Emperor in 1930. On the invasion of Ethiopia by Italy went into exile, 1936–40. Restored to the throne, 1941. (1891–.)

HAILSHAM, Rt. Hon. Viscount; Douglas McGarel Hogg. Was a noted leading counsel in his day, and in 1922 was elected a Conservative M.P. Attorney-General, 1922–4, and 1924–8, Secretary of State for War, 1931–5, Lord Chancellor, 1935–8, Lord President of the Council, 1938. (1872–1950.)

HALEY, Sir William (knight). Spent some years in journalism in London and the provinces, and in 1943 joined the B.B.C. as Editor-in-Chief. Appointed Director-General in 1944. (1901–.)

HALIFAX, Earl of; Edward Frederick Lindley Wood. After holding various Government posts, was given a peerage in 1925 as Baron Irwin and in the following year was appointed Viceroy of India. After again returning to Government posts in England, was made British Ambassador to U.S.A.,1941–6.(1881–.)

Lord Halifax.

HALL, Admiral Sir W. Reginald. Entering the Navy in 1883, he became a gunnery expert. On the outbreak of the First World War was appointed Director of Intelligence Division, Admiralty. Elected Conservative M.P. in 1919. Principal Agent, Unionist Party, 1923–4. (1870–1943.)

HALL, Rt. Hon. Viscount; George Henry Hall. Worked in colliery at age of twelve, afterwards made checkweigher, and in 1922 was elected Labour M.P. Became Civil Lord of the Admiralty, Parliamentary Under-Secretary, Colonial Office, 1940, and in 1946 was appointed First Lord of the Admiralty. (1881–.)

HALSEY, Admiral Sir Lionel (knight). Began his naval career on board H.M.S. *Britannia* in 1885, served in the South African War, and in H.M.S. *Iron Duke* at Battle of Jutland in the First World War. Commanded Royal Australian Navy, 1918–20, and was Chief of Staff to Prince of Wales, 1919–22, on tour of Australia, New Zealand and Canada. (1872–1949.)

HAMMOND, Walter R. Played for Gloucestershire as an amateur cricketer, 1920, and when he turned professional in 1923 scored over a thousand runs in his first season for that county. Has since played for England against Australia, New Zealand, South Africa and the West Indies. (1903–.)

HANDLEY, Tommy. Was articled clerk in Liverpool, next became commercial traveller; after serving in the First World War got a part in the chorus of an Edinburgh show. Made his first broadcast in 1924, and began his famous *Itma* series in 1939. (1896–1949.)

HANKEY, Rt. Hon. Lord (baron); **Maurice Pascal Alexs Hankey.** In 1895 joined the Royal Marines, retired as colonel, 1929. In 1939 joined the War Cabinet as Minister without Portfolio until 1940, when he was appointed Chancellor, Duchy of Lancaster. Paymaster-General, 1941–2. (1877–.)

HANNEN, Nicholas J. Spent sixteen years in China and Japan. Studied for Foreign Office, was then apprenticed to Sir Edwin Lutyens, architect. Went on stage, 1910, and achieved his first success as Nelson in *The Dynasts*. Was an opponent of Sunday theatres. (1881–.)

HANNON, Sir Patrick (knight). His active interest in Irish agriculture led to his appointment as assistant secretary and subsequently chief organizer of the Irish Agricultural Organization Society. In 1921 was elected to Parliament as Unionist for Birmingham, which he represented until 1950. (1874–.)

HARDIE, James Keir. Worked in the mines and when twenty-three became Secretary of Lanarkshire Miners' Union. Founded *The Miner*, which became *The Labour Leader*. First elected to Parliament as Labour, he afterwards helped to found the Independent Labour Party. (1856–1915.)

HARDWICKE, Sir Cedric (knight). Studied at Royal Academy of Dramatic Art and made his first appearance at the Lyceum, in *The Monk and the Woman.* Served in First World War and later joined the Birmingham Repertory Company. Film rôles in *The Rome Express*, *Jew Suss*. (1893–.)

HARDY, Thomas. Intended being an architect and was a prizeman of the Royal Institute of British Architects and of the Architectural Association. Known chiefly for his novels, which include *Tess of the D'Urbervilles*, *Desperate Remedies*, *Under the Greenwood Tree*. Also poet and dramatist. (1840–1928.)

HAREWOOD, Earl of; Henry George Lascelles. From Sandhurst joined the Grenadier Guards and in 1907 became A.D.C. to Governor-General of Canada. Was wounded in First World War. Married H.R.H. Princess Mary (Princess Royal), 1922. A.D.C. to the King in 1936. (1882–1947.)

HARRIMAN, William Averell. During the Roosevelt administration was Ambassador to Moscow and for a short period under President Truman was Ambassador in London. Has had much to do with American shipping and railroads on boards of directors. U.S.A. Secretary of Commerce, 1946–8. (1891–.)

HARRIS, Marshal of the Royal Air Force Sir Arthur T. (knight). By his planning and direction as Chief of Bomber Command, intensive mass air raids on Germany during Second World War contributed much to destruction of enemy war material. Also served in First World War. Now retired. (1892–.)

HARTY, Sir H. Hamilton. Was organist in several Irish churches. Came to London, 1900, and achieved a reputation as accompanist. Composer of *Comedy Overture*, *The Wild Geese* and other works. International reputation as conductor, and was Chief Conductor, London Symphony Orchestra, 1933. Director Hallé Orchestra, 1920–33. (1880–1941.)

HARVEY, Sir John Martin. Actor. Made his début at Court Theatre, 1881, and acted with Irving until 1896. Became manager of Lyceum, 1899, and won great reputation as Sydney Carton in *The Only Way*. Other notable appearances in *The Lyons Mail*, *The Burgomaster of Stilemonde*. (1863–1944.)

HASTINGS, Sir Patrick (knight). Was first mining engineer and then for a time a journalist. Served in South African War, and by 1904 had qualified as barrister-at-law and became K.C. in 1919. Was Attorney-General in the first Labour Government of 1924. Has also written plays. (1880–.)

HAWTREY, Sir Charles. Made first stage appearance under name of Bankes. In 1884 produced *The Private Secretary*, in which he achieved an immense success. In the following year became manager of Her Majesty's Theatre, London, and later of the Comedy Theatre. Acted also in New York. (1858–1923.)

"HAY, Ian" (Maj.-Gen. J. Hay Beith). A language master until authorship attracted him. His experiences in the First World War provided him with rich material. Novels include *Happy-Go-Lucky*, *A Knight on Wheels*, *The First Hundred Thousand*. *Happy-Go-Lucky* was later dramatized as *Tilly of Bloomsbury*. (1876–.)

"HAY, Will" (W. T. Thomson). Was apprenticed to the engineering trade, but adopted instead a stage career in 1909. In 1923 went on a world tour in his comic rôle of a not-too-knowledgeable schoolmaster. An amateur astronomer. (1888–1949.)

HEADLAM, Rt. Rev. Arthur C. Fellow of All Souls, Oxford, he was ordained rector of Welwyn, Herts, in 1896, and several years later became Canon of Christ Church, Oxford, 1918–23, and then Bishop of Gloucester in 1923. Retired in 1945. Author of *Christian Unity* and other books. (1862–1946.)

HEARST, William Randolph. U.S.A. newspaper proprietor. Son of an American mining magnate, he took over from his father the *San Francisco Examiner* and introduced many improvements. Now owns a number of newspapers in the States. Alleged to be anti-British in his policy. (1863–.)

HEIFETZ, Jascha. Former Russian child prodigy who began learning the violin when three years of age and set out on a musical tour of the Continent when twelve. Has played in England and in the U.S.A., where he became a naturalized American. (1901–.)

HENSON, Leslie Lincoln. As a comedian appeared at seaside concert parties and in the provinces and in 1915 made his London début at the Gaiety. Also appeared in films in *Alf's Button*, *Tons of Money*, and has produced a number of plays. (1891–.)

HERBERT, Sir Alan P. (knight). Writing for *Punch* as a freelance, he joined the staff of the paper in 1924. In 1918 was called to the Bar, following legal studies, but kept to writing humorous prose and verse. As Independent M.P., introduced the Marriage Bill, 1938. (1890–.)

HERRIOT, Edouard. Instead of following family tradition by joining the French Army, he became a professor of rhetoric, then turned to politics. As leader of the Radical Socialist Party achieved premiership for the first time in 1924. Was anti-German in Second World War. (1872–.)

HERTZ, Very Rev. Joseph Herman. Rabbi born in Hungary. Emigrated from Slovakia to New York in childhood. Later in South Africa was expelled by President Kruger for pro-British sympathies. In 1913 became Chief Rabbi, United Hebrew Congregation of the British Empire. Author of several educational books on Jewish and non-Jewish subjects. (1872–1946.)

HERTZOG, Gen. Hon. James B. M. Born in South Africa of Dutch and German parentage, he was a general in the South African War against the British. Remained anti-British. Was Minister of Justice in the first Union Cabinet. Later held other posts and became Prime Minister, 1924–39. (1866–1942.)

HESS, Dame Myra. Born in London, she studied the piano at Royal Academy of Music, passing her first examination when aged seven. Later her fine renderings of some of the earlier classics, Bach, Mozart, and others, brought her world-wide success as a pianist. Gold Medallist, Philharmonic Society, 1941. (1890–.)

HEWETT, Sir F. Stanley (knight). Surgeon Apothecary to George V, Queen Alexandra, the Prince of Wales (now Duke of Windsor) and his household, he continued in the same post to George VI and Queen Mary since 1936. Has held various appointments at St. Thomas's and West London Hospitals. (1880–.)

HILTON, John. Formerly an engineering foreman and manager, he afterwards became assistant secretary, Director of Statistics, Ministry of Labour, and later a popular B.B.C. broadcaster, dealing with everyday problems in a way which showed his wide sympathy and understanding of human nature. (1880–1943.)

HITLER, Adolf. Austrian, naturalized German, and once a building artisan, his anti-Semitism and lust for power plunged the nations into a Second World War. Wounded in the First World War, he became member of National Socialist German Workers' Party, 1919, and after the failure of the first Nazi revolution late in 1923 he was arrested and put in prison, where he wrote *Mein Kampf*, a book which became the "bible" of Nazi ideology. Became head of the German State, 1934, is believed to have committed suicide shortly before the capture of Berlin by the Allies in May, 1945. (1889–1945.)

Jack Hobbs.

HOBBS, John Berry. Starting on the ground staff of the Surrey County Cricket Club, he was eventually made a playing member and excelled as a batsman. By 1935, when he retired, he had made the still unsurpassed record of 197 centuries, including twelve in

Tests against Australia. Played many times for England. (1882–.)

HOGG, Major the Hon. Quintin McGarel, Conservative M.P. President of the Oxford Union, 1929. Wounded in the Second World War. Fellow of All Souls' College, Oxford, since 1931. Barrister-at-law, Lincoln's Inn, 1932. M.P. for City of Oxford 1938–50, when he succeeded to Hailsham peerage. (1907–.)

HOOVER, Herbert. Of Quaker descent, he worked for some years as a mining engineer. In the First World War was made Chairman, American Relief Committee. After that was appointed Food Administrator, U.S.A., in 1917, then Secretary of Commerce, 1921–8. U.S. President, 1929–33. (1874–.)

HOPE, Bob. Film and stage comedian. Born in Eltham, London, S.E., the son of a stone contractor and of a Welsh singer, his family went to live in America when he was four. Began as a boxer, next turned to stage comedy. Film début in *The Sidewalks of New York*. (1903–.)

HOPKINS, Harry L. The late President Roosevelt's closest friend and adviser and acted as his personal representative during the Second World War. He was given the responsibility of administering the Lend-Lease Bill. Visited London and Moscow in 1941. Was formerly U.S.A. Secretary of Commerce. (1890–1946.)

HORDER, Lord (baron); **Thomas Jeeves Horder.** Began his medical career at St. Bartholomew's Hospital as a demonstrator of biology. Has since won an international reputation as a physician. During Second World War inspected air-raid shelters and advised improvements. (1871–.)

Lord Horder.

HORE-BELISHA, Rt. Hon. Leslie. Served in First World War, afterwards barrister, journalist and then Liberal M.P. After holding secretarial posts, was made Minister of Transport. Invented "Belisha beacons" to mark pedestrian crossings. Head of War Office, 1937. Resigned, 1940. Minister, National Insurance, 1945, until General Election in July of same year. (1893–.)

HORNER, Arthur. Worked on the railway first, then in a colliery. Opposed First World War and was court-martialled and served sentence for agitation. Joined Communist Party, 1919, and in 1946 was elected Secretary, National Union of Mineworkers. (1894–.)

HORSBRUGH, Florence. During the First World War did excellent work in canteens and national kitchens, for which she was awarded the M.B.E. Elected to Parliament in 1931 as a Conservative, she was first woman M.P. to move the Address in House of Commons, 1938. Parliamentary Secretary Ministry of Health, 1939–45.

HOWARD, Leslie. At one time a bank clerk, he became a professional actor and, after service in the First World War, toured in *Peg O' My Heart*, *Charley's Aunt* and other plays. Achieved wide popularity through Hollywood films. Shot down in a non-military aeroplane, 1943. (1893–1943.)

HOWES, Bobby. English stage comedian, who began as a boy at the Battersea Palace. Later in a stage dancing team for two years, with Royal Gotham Quartette for three years. Served in First World War. Has appeared in various revues and plays. (1895–.)

HUDSON, Rt. Hon. Robert S. Attaché in Diplomatic Service, 1911, he was elected to Parliament as a Unionist in 1924, and in 1931 was appointed Parliamentary Secretary, Ministry of Labour. Among his other posts were Minister of Health, Minister of Shipping, and in 1940–5 Minister of Agriculture. (1886–.)

HUGHES, Rt. Hon. William Morris. Born in Wales, came to London and took post as school teacher and in 1884 went out to Queensland. Ten years later was an M.P. in the New South Wales Parliament. Became Prime Minister, 1915, Minister for Health, 1934, and again in 1936, and Minister for the Navy, 1940. (1864–.)

HULBERT, Jack. Son of a doctor, he preferred a theatrical career and while an undergraduate at Cambridge produced and took a leading part in revues. Later made his professional stage début in *The Pearl Girl* at the Shaftesbury Theatre. Has also co-starred with his wife, Cicely Courtneidge. (1892–.)

HULL, Cordell. U.S.A. politician. Born in a log cabin among the mountains of northern Tennessee, he worked his way to the Bar and became attorney-at-law. Later became a member of Congress and in 1933 was made Secretary of State. Retired in 1945. (1871–.)

HUMPHREYS, Rt. Hon. Sir Travers (knight). Called to the Bar, 1889. Counsel to Crown at Middlesex Sessions; North London Sessions, 1905; Junior Counsel to Crown, Central Criminal Court, 1908. Recorder successively of Chichester, Cambridge. Judge King's Bench Division since 1928. (1867–.)

HUNTLEY, G. P. Irish actor who began at the age of six in his father's company. Accompanied the Kendals to U.S.A. four times. He acted in *A Runaway Girl*, *Kitty Grey*, *Three Little Maids*, *Miss Hook of Holland*. (1868–1927.)

HURD, Sir Archibald (knight). After editing weekly naval journal, joined *Daily Telegraph*, 1899, and was its naval expert, 1899–1928. Was engaged in propaganda work in First World War. Joint Editor, *Brassey's Naval Annual*, 1922–8. Chairman, Shipping World Ltd. Author of several nautical works. (1869–.)

HUTTON, Leonard. Yorkshire and England batsman. First played for county in 1934, and in 1938 made 364 against Australia, highest ever made in any Test match. Following a fractured arm, imperfectly set during the war, he had to remodel his strokes but has since batted as well as ever. (1916–.)

HUXLEY, Aldous L. Totally blind at sixteen, learned Braille and to type by touch. At nineteen the darkness partly lifted, leaving one eye fairly good. Managed to improve his sight and wrote a book, *The Art of Seeing*. Author of many novels including *Antic Hay*, *Point Counterpoint*. (1894–.)

HUXLEY, Julian Sorell. Brother of Aldous, he has held several academic appointments, including Senior Demonstrator in Zoology, Oxford University, and Professor of Zoology, King's College, London. Was secretary of the Zoological Society, London, 1935–42. Director-General U.N.E.S.C.O., 1946–8. Author of many scientific books (1887–.)

ILIFFE, Lord (baron); **Edward Mauger Iliffe.** Entered his father's publishing business and during the First World War was appointed Controller Machine Tool Department, Ministry of Munitions. In 1923 he became Unionist member for Tamworth. Owns provincial newspapers, in addition to his London publishing house. (1877–.)

Dean Inge.

INGE, Very Rev. William Ralph. Was an Assistant Master at Eton, 1884–8, and after being ordained became Vicar of All Saints, Ennismore Gardens, 1905, and Dean of St. Paul's, 1911–35. Has written a number of books on religion. (1860–.)

INMAN, Lord (baron); **Philip Albert Inman.** Lord Privy Seal during 1947, he is Chairman of Charing Cross Hospital and formerly of the British Broadcasting Corporation. Was President of the National Brotherhood Movement, 1938. (1887–.)

INONU, Gen. Ismet. President, Republic of Turkey, 1938–50. Succeeded Kemal Ataturk, founder of the Turkish Republic. Fought the British in the Dardanelles campaign, but in the Second World War rejected German attempts to turn him against Britain, while Turkey remained neutral. (1884–.)

INVERCHAPEL, Rt. Hon. Lord (baron); **Archibald John Clark-Kerr.** Entered Diplomatic Service, 1906, and during the First World War served in Scots Guards. Was appointed afterwards to diplomatic posts in Tangier, Cairo, Chile and Sweden. In 1935 became Ambassador to Iraq, then Ambassador to China and in 1942 to Russia. Ambassador to U.S.A., 1946–8. (1887–.)

INVERFORTH, Rt. Hon. Lord (baron); **Andrew Weir.** Born at Kirkcaldy, he established the firm of Andrew Weir & Co., shipowners, and accumulated a large fortune. In 1917 was given the post of Minister of Supply and became Minister of Munitions in 1919. (1865–.)

IRELAND, John. In 1912 produced his first composition entitled *The Forgotten Rite*. Later on became examiner to the Associated Board, Royal Schools of Music. Composer of chamber music, trios and ballads, notably *Sea Fever*, *Songs to Hardy's Poems*. (1879–.)

IRONSIDE, Field-Marshal Lord (baron); **William Edmund Ironside.** Began his military career with the Royal Artillery, 1899. Won distinction in the South African War. Served in the First and Second World Wars, becoming Chief of the Imperial General Staff in 1939. Governor, Gibraltar, 1938. (1880–.)

IRVING, Sir Henry (knight) (John Henry Brodribb). Born in Somerset, he was brought to London and started as a clerk. Before he was twenty turned to the stage and achieved fame as Mathias in *The Bells*. Later acted with Ellen Terry at Lyceum, London, which he managed for twenty-four years. (1838–1905.)

ISAACS, Rt. Hon. George Alfred. Labour M.P. Minister of Labour from 1945 to 1951; then appointed Minister of Pensions. Son of a printer, he followed the same trade, became secretary of the National Society of Operative Printers and Assistants and later, in Parliament, was first Parliamentary Private Secretary to the Dominions Secretary, and to the First Lord of the Admiralty, 1942–5. (1883–).

ISAACS, Rt. Hon. Sir Isaac (knight). Born in Melbourne, he became a member of the Victorian Legislative Assembly in 1892 and in the following year was made Solicitor-General, becoming Attorney-General in 1894, and again in 1900 until his retirement. Was Chief Justice, 1930–1, and Governor-General, 1931–6. (1855–1948.)

ISMAY, Lord (baron); **Hastings Ismay.** Has seen active service in Somaliland; spent many years of his Army career in India, and in the Second World War was chief of Prime Minister Churchill's military staff, accompanying him to Washington and elsewhere. (1887–.)

IVEAGH, Earl of; Edward Cecil Lee Guinness. Son of a well-known philanthropist, he became Unionist M.P. in 1908. Has been Chancellor of Dublin University since 1927. Was a keen oarsman and yachtsman. (1874–.)

JACOBS, William Wymark. Was a clerk in the Post Office and during that time was the writer of successful short stories. His novel, *The Skipper's Wooing*, soon brought him fame, and this was followed by many other short stories about seafaring men. His ghost story, *The Monkey's Paw*, was later dramatized. (1863–1943.)

JEANS, Sir James Hopwood. Astronomer and scientist. Beginning as a teacher of applied mathematics, he became one of the foremost figures in the world of astronomical science. President, Royal Astronomical Society, and later of the British Association. Wrote many popular expositions of astronomy, (1877–1946.)

JELLICOE, Admiral of the Fleet Earl. Entering the British Navy in 1872, he first saw active service in Egypt, 1882, and later at the relief of Peking, 1900. At the outbreak of the First World War was in command of the Grand Fleet. In 1916 he defeated the German High Seas Fleet at the battle of Jutland. Chief of Naval Staff, 1917. Governor-General of New Zealand, 1920–4. (1859–1935.)

JINNAH, Mohamed Ali. First Premier and Governor-General of Pakistan (Moslem India). President of the Moslem League claiming to represent some eighty million Moslems in India. A one-time barrister and one of the founders of the Indian National Congress, he afterwards separated himself and his Moslem followers from the Hindus. Author of *Pakistan*. (1876–1948.)

JOAD, Cyril E. M. Was at the Board of Trade, later Ministry of Labour (1914) until his retirement in 1930. Head of the Department of Philosophy and Psychology, Birkbeck College, University of London, since 1930. An original member B.B.C. "Brains Trust." Author of works on philosophy. (1891–.)

C. E. M. Joad.

JOFFRE, Marshal Joseph J. C. (O.M.). Appointed French Generalissimo for over two years of the First World War, his handling of military situations made him the object of much criticism and he resigned in December, 1916. He shared, however, with General Gallieni the success of the battle of the Marne, 1914. (1852–1931.)

JOHN, Augustus E. (R.A.). Artist. Famous as a portrait painter, he was born in Wales and after completing his art studies in London and Paris was an instructor of drawing at University College, Liverpool. Among the many celebrities who have sat for his portraits is Madame Suggia, the violoncellist. (1878–.)

JOHN, Sir W. Goscombe (knight). Well-known portrait sculptor, he was awarded the Royal Academy Gold Medal and Travelling Studentship, 1889, and Gold Medal, Paris Salon, 1901. His principal works include: King Edward VII, King George V and Queen Mary; equestrian statue of King Edward VII, Liverpool, and memorial to Lord Salisbury, Westminster Abbey. (1860–.)

JOHNSON, Amy (Mrs. James A. Mollison). Airwoman. Worked for a time in a London solicitor's office. Then, after qualifying as a pilot, established her first record by solo flight to Australia, 1930. Next year flew to Japan and then with her husband flew to the Cape. Perished in air accident. (1904–41.)

JOHNSTON, Rt. Hon. Thomas. Was a journalist when he first became Labour M.P. for West Stirlingshire in 1922. Was appointed Parliamentary Under-Secretary for Scotland, 1929–31, and in 1931 became Lord Privy Seal. Secretary for Scotland, 1941–5. (1882–.)

JONES, Sir Harold Spencer (knight). Astronomer Royal. Was Assistant Director Inspection of Optical Supplies, Ministry of Munitions, during First World War and in 1923 was appointed Astronomer, Cape of Good Hope. Has been Astronomer Royal since 1933. President Royal Astronomical Society, 1937. (1890–.)

JONES, Robert ("Bobby") Tyre. American golfer. Admitted to Georgian Bar, 1928. National Amateur Golf Champion, 1924, '25, '27, '28, '30. National Open Champion, 1923, '26, '29, '30. Won Open Championship of Great Britain, 1926, '27, '30. Amateur champion, Great Britain, 1930. (1902–.)

JOWITT, Rt. Hon. Viscount; William Allen Jowitt. Lord Chancellor. Started his Parliamentary career as a Liberal and within a week changed to Labour. Had already been practising at the Bar and one of his most famous cases was the Rasputin libel action against an American film company, 1934. Solicitor-General, 1940. (1885–.)

JOYCE, James. Born in Dublin, his early work consisted of chamber music and a volume of verse. His *Portrait of the Artist as a Young Man*, published 1916, showed psychological characterization. Wrote novel, *Ulysses*, in Paris, banned in England, and which aroused great controversy in Britain and in the U.S.A. (1882–1941.)

JULIANA, Louise Emma Maria Wilhelmina. Queen of the Netherlands. Only child of Queen Wilhelmina, who abdicated for reasons of ill-health in 1948. Married Prince Bernhard, 1937. Four daughters: Beatrix (b. 1938), Irene (1939), Margriet (1943), Maria Christina (1947). (1909–.)

KENT, George, Duke of. Fourth son of George V and Queen Mary, and youngest brother of George VI. Entered Royal Naval College, Osborne, 1916; joined H.M.S. *Iron Duke*, 1921, and served on China Station. Retired 1929. Married Marina, daughter of Prince Nicholas of Greece, 1934. Was killed in an aeroplane crash in August, 1942, while flying to Iceland on active service. (1902–42.)

KEYES, Admiral of the Fleet Lord (baron); **Roger John Keyes.** Son of a general, he entered the Navy in 1885. During the First World War distinguished himself at the battle of Heligoland Bight and by the naval raid on Zeebrugge. Became Commander-in-Chief Mediterranean Station, 1925–8. Unionist M.P., 1934–43. (1872–1945.)

KEYNES, Lord (baron); **John Maynard Keynes.** Famous economist. One-time secretary of the Royal Economic Society and a director of the Bank of England, he was sent to the United States in 1941 to confer with the Washington Administration on the operation of the lease-lend proposals. Author of several books on economics. (1883–1946.)

KILLEARN, Rt. Hon. Lord (baron); **Miles Wedderburn Lampson.** Entered the Foreign Office, 1903; became Acting High Commissioner in Siberia, 1920; British Minister to China, 1926–33; High Commissioner for Egypt and Sudan, 1934–6, and British Ambassador to Egypt, 1936–46. (1880–.)

KINDERSLEY, Lord (baron); **Robert Molesworth Kindersley.** At fifteen began as a clerk at ten shillings a week and eventually rose to Governor, Hudson's Bay Company, 1916–25. A Director of the Bank of England, he was High Sheriff, Sussex, 1928, and President, National Savings Committee, 1920–46. (1871–.)

Mackenzie King.

KING, Rt. Hon. W. L. Mackenzie. Prime Minister of Canada, 1935–48. Born in Ontario of Scottish descent, he was a prominent figure in Canadian politics since becoming Deputy Minister of Labour, 1900. Was Prime Minister and Secretary of State for External Affairs, 1935–46. (1874–1950.)

KING-HALL, Commander Stephen. Well known as a broadcaster and writer, he was on Admiralty Naval Staff, 1919–20, 1928–9, and as Intelligence Officer, Mediterranean Fleet, 1925–6. M.P. (Independent National), Ormskirk, 1939–45. Awarded Gold Medal, Royal United Service Institution, 1919. (1893–.)

KIPLING, Rudyard. Born in India, his first book, *Schoolboy Lyrics*, was published in 1881. Ultimately gained fame with his *Barrack Room Ballads*, followed by his tales depicting jungles and life in India. Awarded Nobel Prize for Literature, 1907. (1865–1936.)

Rudyard Kipling.

KITCHENER, Field-Marshal Earl (of Khartoum); **Horatio Herbert Kitchener.** Entered Royal Engineers, 1871. Took part in attempt to rescue General Gordon. Commander-in-Chief against Boers. Will best be remembered, however, as Secretary of State for War after hostilities broke out in 1914. Drowned on his way to Russia, 1916, in H.M.S. *Hampshire* when she struck a mine. (1850–1916.)

KNIGHT, Harold (R.A.). Studied at Nottingham School of Art and in Paris. His work has been awarded gold, silver and bronze medals. His pictures are hung in a number of public collections. (1874–.)

KNIGHT, Dame Laura (R.A.) (wife of the above). Studied art in Nottingham and won Princess of Wales Scholarship. Won Gold Medal, San Francisco, 1905. First exhibited Royal Academy, 1903. She is represented at Tate Gallery, British Museum, and in many public collections in Britain and abroad.

KNOX, Edmund G. V. Joined the staff of *Punch*, 1921, and was its editor 1932–49. Served in France in the First World War and was wounded. Most of his humorous contributions are written under pseudonym "Evoe". (1881–.)

KNOX, Rt. Rev. Monsignor Ronald A. Roman Catholic priest and author, he was Fellow and Lecturer, Trinity College, Oxford, 1910; Roman Catholic Chaplain, Oxford University, 1926–39, and Domestic Prelate to the Pope, 1936. Is the author of witty essays, religious works and ingenious detective novels. (1888–.)

KOO, Vi Kyuin Wellington. English Secretary to former President of China, he has held several other important posts, among them being Prime Minister, Minister of Foreign Affairs, 1926–7. Chinese Minister to France, 1932, and Ambassador to Great Britain, 1941–6, and to U.S.A. since 1946. (1888–.)

KORDA, Sir Alexander (knight). Film producer. Born in Hungary, he was first a teacher, then journalist, but found greater success in the making of films. Began in Budapest, then went to Hollywood and eventually settled in London, where he founded London Film Productions Ltd., 1932. (1898–.)

KREISLER, Fritz. World-famous violinist. Born Vienna. Could read music before he was six and made his concert début as violinist when seven. After three years' study won gold medal. Made London début 1902. Now American. (1875–.)

LATHAM, Lord (baron); **Charles Latham.** Labour leader of London County Council, 1940–7. Joined Labour Party in 1905, and in 1915 was elected President, National Union of Clerks. Is chairman of several trade concerns and was a member of the London Passenger Transport Board. (1888–.)

LAUDER, Sir Harry (knight). Was a mill boy in flax-spinning mill, subsequently becoming a miner. Made his stage début at Arbroath and his first London appearance at Gatti's. Made his name in variety. Knighted in 1919. (1870–1950.)

LAUGHTON, Charles. First a Scarborough hotel manager, he made his stage début, 1926, in *The Inspector-General.* Gold medallist of the Royal Academy of Dramatic Art, he excels in character parts and has appeared in Shakespearean and other rôles. Chief film successes as Henry VIII in 1933, as Captain Bligh in *Mutiny on the Bounty.* (1899–.)

LAVAL, Pierre. Became first Minister of Labour, then three times Prime Minister in 1931, 1935, and in 1942. Collaborated with the Germans during occupation of France in the Second World War and was executed by shooting, 1945. (1883–1945.)

LAW, Rt. Hon. A. Bonar. In 1900 was elected Unionist M.P. and soon gained a reputation as a speaker. From being Colonial Secretary, then Lord Privy Seal, became Prime Minister in 1922. Ill-health led to his resignation early in 1923. (1858–1923.)

LAWRENCE, David Herbert. English author and poet. Best-known works: *The White Peacock* (1911); *Sons and Lovers* (1913); *The Rainbow* (1915, suppressed by the police); *The Plumed Serpent* (1926); *Lady Chatterley's Lover* (1928, banned in England; expurgated edition, 1932); *Collected Poems*, 1928. (1885–1930.)

LAWRENCE, Col. Thomas Edward (later T. E. Shaw). One of the most romantic figures of the First World War, his expert knowledge of Arab affairs led to the Government engaging him on special work. He organized and led an Arab army and held Damascus until relieved by General Allenby. Afterwards, shunning publicity, he became Aircraftman Shaw in the R.A.F. Killed in motor-cycle accident. (1888–1935.)

T. E. Lawrence.

LAWSON, Rt. Hon. Lord (baron); **John James Lawson.** Worked in a mine at age of twelve, and in

1919 was elected Labour M.P. Financial Secretary, War Office, 1924. Parliamentary Secretary, Ministry of Labour, 1929–31. Became Secretary of State for War, 1945. Resigned in 1947 owing to ill-health. (1881–.)

LAYE, Evelyn. Made stage début at Brighton, 1915; first appearance in London, 1918. Has played in *The Merry Widow*, *Madame Pompadour*, *Lilac Time*, *Bitter Sweet* (also in New York). First film rôle in *The Luck of the Navy*, 1928. (1900–.)

LAYTON, Lord (baron); **Walter T. Layton.** Newspaper proprietor and economist, he was Director-General of Programmes, Ministry of Supply, 1940–2. Earlier in his career was a lecturer on economics and member of various Government committees on economy. Leading supporter of European unity. (1884–.)

LEACOCK, Prof. Stephen. Born in Hampshire, he was taken to Canada when a boy. Became the author of biographies and books on economy, but achieved wider popularity as a humorous writer of short stories and parodies. Books include *Nonsense Novels*, *Moonbeams from the Larger Lunacy*. (1869–1944.)

LEATHERS, Rt. Hon. Lord (baron); **Frederic James Leather.** The first man to be given complete charge of all shipping and transport, from railways to highways, during the Second World War. Had been associated with shipping in First World War. Coal Adviser to Ministry of Shipping, 1940. Later Minister of War Transport. (1883–.)

LEE, of Fareham, Rt. Hon. Viscount; Arthur Hamilton Lee. Colonel in First World War, he entered Parliament as Conservative and became Minister of Agriculture in 1919 and First Lord of the Admiralty in 1921. Gave Chequers to the nation, 1921. (1868–1947.)

LEEPER, Sir Reginald W. A. (knight). Ambassador to the Argentine, 1946–8. Entered the Foreign Office in 1918 as a temporary clerk and two years later was Second Secretary. In 1923 and again in 1927 was appointed First Secretary, Warsaw Legation, and, following other appointments, was Ambassador to Greece, 1943–6. (1888–.)

LEESE, Lt.-Gen. Sir Oliver W. H. (baronet). Following service in First World War, held various staff positions, one being instructor at the Staff College, Quetta, India. As tank expert in the Second World War, served under Field-Marshal Montgomery, at Alamein, and later in Italian Campaign, 1943–4. (1894–.)

LEGGETT, Sir Frederick W. (knight). Chairman, London and South-eastern Board for Industry, 1947–8. Began Civil Service career in 1904, later held various secretarial posts. In 1926 became Chief Adviser to Minister on industrial conditions in Canada and United States. Chief Industrial Commissioner, 1940. (1884–.)

LEHAR, Franz. Hungarian composer and conductor of military bands in Budapest, Vienna and other cities. He became famous as the composer of a series of operettas, notably *The Merry Widow*, *The Count of Luxembourg*, *Gypsy Love*, *The Land of Smiles*, *Guiditta*. (1870–1948.)

LEIGH, Vivien (Lady Olivier). Stage and film actress. First stage appearance Queen's Theatre, London. Played Ann Boleyn in *Henry VIII*, Queen Anne in *Richard II*; Ophelia in *Hamlet* in Denmark; in *Romeo and Juliet* in New York City. Film appearances include *Gone with the Wind*, *Caesar and Cleopatra*. (1913–.)

LEITCH, Cecilia ("Cecil"). Won the British Open Ladies' Golf Championship in 1914, 1920–1 and 1926; the French Ladies' Championship five times; the English Close Championship twice. Played as British representative in twelve series of international matches. (1890–.)

LENGLEN, Suzanne. French lawn-tennis player, she first achieved prominence by winning the French championship at St. Cloud, in 1914. Champion of France, 1919–23 and 1925–6. Ladies' Singles Champion, Wimbledon, 1919–23 and 1925. Turned professional, 1926. (1899–1938.)

LENIN (Vladimir Ilyich Ulianov). In 1891 became a lawyer, but the revolutionary spirit in him soon asserted itself, which led to his imprisonment in 1895. Released and again imprisoned, he escaped to Finland. Leader of Russian Revolution, 1917, he became eventually dictator of Russia as President of the Soviet of People's Commissaries. After death his body was embalmed and placed in a mausoleum. (1870–1924.)

Lenin.

"LENO, Dan" (George Galvin). Began career as an acrobat, and was champion clog-dancer of northern England, 1880. Won a leading position in music-halls as comedian and appeared in pantomimes at Drury Lane from 1888. (1860–1904.)

LEOPOLD, III. King of the Belgians. Succeeded Albert in 1934. Married Princess Astrid of Sweden (killed in car accident). The armistice he was forced to seek from the Germans in the Second World War brought him much criticism from some quarters, but his actions were approved by National Committee. The Germans placed him under house arrest and later removed him to Germany. After the war, remained in exile. (1901–.)

LE QUEUX, William T. Possessing a marked aptitude for mystery fiction, he became the successful author of exciting novels about spies and crime. His books include *Guilty Bonds*, *Fatal Fingers*, *Blackmailed*. Forecast war against Germany in *The Great War in England*, *The Invasions*, 1910. (1864–1927.)

LEWIS, Cecil Day. After leaving Oxford University became an assistant master at Summerfields, Oxford, in 1927, and in the same year edited *Oxford Poetry*. Other teaching posts followed later elsewhere. His works include *Collected Poems*, 1929–33, *A Hope for Poetry*, *Child of Misfortune*, *Anatomy of Oxford*. (1904–.)

LEWIS, D. B. Wyndham. Author and journalist, was the original "Beachcomber" of the *Daily Express*; wrote later for the *Daily Mail* and *News Chronicle* (as Timothy Shy). Author of *François Villon*, *King Spider*, *Emperor of the West*, *At the Sign of the Blue Moon*. (1884–.)

LEWIS, John L. U.S.A. labour leader and President of the United Mine Workers of America since 1920. In his early days worked at various jobs, including mining, and on defence of the American miners since; has figured prominently in leading national strikes connected with mining. (1880–.)

LEWIS, Sinclair. First attracted literary attention in America with his book, *Main Street*, which satirized American provincial life. *Babbitt* followed in 1922, enhancing his newly-acquired fame. Later books include *Arrowsmith*, *The Man Who Knew Coolidge*. Has written plays. Awarded Nobel Prize for Literature, 1930. (1885–.)

LIDDELL HART, Capt. B. H. Wounded in First World War. Military correspondent, *Daily Telegraph*, and later of *The Times*. Military editor, *Encyclopaedia Britannica*. Evolved Battle Drill System and Torrent Method of Attack, which were officially adopted. Author of several books. (1895–.)

LIDGETT, Rev. J. Scott. Born in Lewisham, London, he became a Methodist minister and in 1891 helped to found the Bermondsey Settlement. Was editor *Methodist Times*, 1907–18. Joint editor *Contemporary Review* since 1911. First President, United Methodist Churches. Author of many theological works. (1854–.)

Rev. J. Scott Lidgett.

LIE, Trygve. Norwegian statesman and lawyer, his first important job was as secretary of the Norwegian Labour Party. Then became legal adviser to trade unions, 1922–35. Member of Norwegian Cabinet, 1939, he was afterwards appointed as the first Secretary-General United Nations Organization. (1896–.)

LILLIE, Beatrice (Lady Peel). Born in Toronto, she came to London in 1914 and made her début as a comedienne. Her appearances include *Tonight at 8.30*, *Plays and Music*, *Big Top*. Made her film début in 1926. Has often appeared in New York. (1898–.)

LINDBERGH, Col. Charles A. American aviator, he gained worldwide fame in 1927 for his solo flight from New York to Paris. Was in England, 1936–7. Lost much in popularity, even in the States, for alleged pro-German views. (1902–.)

LINDRUM, Walter. Australian billiard-player. Began playing at age of nine and made his first thousand break at age of seventeen. After increasing his reputation in Australia, he came to England, 1931. Made world's record break of 4,137 in 1932. British professional champion in 1933. (1898–.)

LINDSAY, Lord (baron); **Alexander Dunlop Lindsay.** Master of Balliol College, Oxford, since 1924. Served in First World War and in 1922 was appointed Professor of Moral Philosophy, Glasgow University. Vice-Chancellor, Oxford University, 1935–8. Author of *The Essentials of Democracy*. (1879–.)

LINKLATER, Eric. Born at Dounby, Orkney Islands, he first studied medicine, then went out to India as assistant editor, *Times of India*, Bombay. After his return to England became assistant professor of English literature at Aberdeen University. Author of several books. (1899–.)

LINLITHGOW, Marquess of; Victor Alexander John Hope. Following service in the First World War, was appointed Civil Lord of the Admiralty, 1922. Was Viceroy and Governor-General of India, 1936–43 (term of office twice extended). (1887–.)

LIVINGSTONE, Sir Richard (knight). Vice-Chancellor, Oxford University, 1944–7. President, Corpus Christi, Oxford, since 1933. Held a temporary post as Assistant Master, Eton College, 1917–8, and was later Vice-Chancellor, Queen's University, Belfast, 1924–33. President, Hellenic Society, 1938, and Classical Association, 1940–1. (1880–.)

LLEWELLIN, Rt. Hon. Lord (baron); **John Jestyn Llewellin.** Served in First World War, and was called to the Bar in 1921. From 1929 to 1945 was Conservative M.P. Held minor ministerial posts, 1931–42. President, Board of Trade, 1942; Minister of Food, 1943–5. (1893–.)

"LLOYD, Marie" (Marie Wood). The most popular comedienne of her time, she made her début as Bella Delmore in 1885, and later as Marie Lloyd. Her vivacious personality and portrayals in song of the London Cockney won her a very large following among music-hall audiences. (1870–1922.)

LLOYD GEORGE, Earl; David Lloyd George. Liberal statesman, was an outstanding figure in the House of Commons, where his "silver-tongued oratory," enlivened sometimes by caustic wit, was heard, in his position as Cabinet Minister, for seventeen years. His parliamentary career had begun in 1890, and from being first President of the Board of Trade he progressed through various posts to Prime Minister, 1916–22. Became "Father" of the House of Commons in 1929. (1863–1945).

LLOYD GEORGE, Lady Megan. Youngest daughter of the above, she began her political career in 1929 as Liberal M.P. In 1936 was made President, Women's Liberal Federation. Was Member of League of Nations Union Executive Committee. Chairman, Welsh Parliamentary Party, 1944. (1903–.)

LOCKHART, Sir Robert H. Bruce (knight). Entered the Consular Service and was appointed a Vice-Consul in 1911. In 1918 headed a Mission to the Soviet Government, was arrested and imprisoned in the Kremlin, then released and exchanged for Litvinoff. Deputy Under-Secretary Foreign Office, 1941–5. (1887–.)

LÖHR, Marie. Came to England from Sydney, Australia, and made her London début in 1901. Soon established herself as a comedienne, though later she played part of the Empress in *Casanova*. Made film début in *Aren't We All.* Became manager, Globe Theatre, 1918–25. (1890–.)

LONDONDERRY, Marquess of; Charles Stewart Vane-Tempest-Stewart. As Conservative was appointed Under-Secretary for Air in 1920 and in 1931, Lord Privy Seal in 1935. Lord Lieutenant of Durham since 1928. Chief Commissioner, Civil Air Guard, 1938–45. Worked for many years to advance Britain's progress in the air. (1878–1949.)

LONSDALE, Earl of; Hugh Cecil Lowther. Famous as a patron of the boxing ring, the turf and other sports, he was Mayor of Whitehaven in 1894, and later served in the South African War. Chairman, Westmorland Quarter Sessions; J.P., Westmorland and Rutland. Later became Lord Lieutenant of Cumberland. (1857–1944.)

Lord Lonsdale.

LONSDALE, Frederick. Attained popularity as the author of stage comedies of social life, including *Spring Cleaning*, *The Last of Mrs. Cheyney*. Collaborated in musical comedies, *The Balkan Princess*, *The Maid of the Mountains*. Wrote scripts for films, including *The Devil to Pay*. (1881–.)

LOPOKOVA, Lydia (Lady Keynes). Russian ballet dancer. Became famous in Paris and New York before her début in Diaghileff's Russian Ballet, 1918. Created rôles of Columbine in *Carnival* and the can-can dancer in *La Boutique Fantasque*. Appeared at Covent Garden, Coliseum and Alhambra, London. (1892–.)

LOTHIAN, Marquess of; Peter Henry Kerr. Held official positions in Orange River Colony, and back in England became Secretary to Prime Minister in 1916, then Chancellor, Duchy of Lancaster, and later Parliamentary Under-Secretary, India Office, and was British Ambassador to U.S.A., 1939–40. (1882–1940.)

LOUIS, Joe. American heavyweight boxer, born in Alabama, son of a cotton picker. Won world heavyweight title by defeating James J. Braddock in 1937, and successfully defended his title twenty-five times before retiring in 1948. (1914–.)

LOW, David. Cartoonist. Born in Dunedin, New Zealand, he contributed cartoons to several papers in that country and Australia. Came to London in 1919 as cartoonist to the *Star*, in which he also collaborated with F. W. Thomas in *Low and I.* On *Evening Standard* 1927–50, and *Daily Herald* since. (1891–.)

"LUDWIG, Emil" (Emil Cohn). Born in Breslau, he began career as dramatist. First wrote plays only, mainly in verse, later psychological essays and biographies. Books include *Bismarck*, *The Germans*, *Versailles*. (1881–1948.)

LUNT, Alfred. American actor, who with his wife and partner, known professionally as Lynn Fontanne, had for years appeared in American and Canadian cities before achieving fame together. First London appearance, 1924. (1893–.)

LUTYENS, Sir Edwin L. (knight). Co-architect of New Delhi, India, and designer of the Cenotaph, Whitehall, London, his work is widespread, from English country houses to the British Embassy building in Washington, and Government House, New Delhi. President, Royal Academy, 1938–45. (1869–1945.)

LYNN, Ralph. Actor. Made début at Wigan, 1900; acted in provinces and U.S.A. Appeared at the Empire, 1914. Began acting in successful farces, among them being *It Pays to Advertise*, *Is Your Honeymoon Really Necessary?* Film début in 1929. (1882–.)

LYTTLETON, Rt. Hon. Oliver. Politician. Served in First World War, and afterwards specialized in metal industry, and travelled to inspect mines abroad. Later as Conservative M.P. became President Board of Trade, 1940–1. Minister of State in Middle East, then Minister of Production, 1942–5. (1893–.)

LYTTON, Earl of; Victor Alexander Lytton. He was born in Simla, India; educated at Cambridge, and in 1916 was appointed Civil Lord of the Admiralty. Governor of Bengal, 1922–7. Viceroy and Acting Governor-General of India, 1925. Author of biographies and other works. (1876–1947.)

LYTTON, Sir Henry (knight). Was long associated with the leading comic rôles of Gilbert and Sullivan operas. Made his début in Glasgow in 1884 in the chorus of *Princess Ida*, and appeared throughout British Isles, U.S.A., and Canada. (1867–1936.)

MACARTHUR, Gen. Douglas. American Army. Became the youngest general in the U.S. forces. Chief of Staff, U.S. Army, 1930–5, then Field-Marshal, Philippines Army, 1936. In Second World War was given the defence of Australia. Appointed C.-in-C., Allied Forces, South-west Pacific area, 1942. Since the end of the war, U.S. C in-C., Far East. In the Korean war commanded United Nations forces brilliantly until April, 1951, when his dismissal was a major sensation. (1880–.)

Gen. MacArthur.

MACARTHUR, Mary. Social worker, was secretary, Women's Trade Union League. Formed National Federation of Women Workers, organizing especially for chain workers, lace finishers and others in the trade. Member, National Insurance Advisory Committee. (1880–1921.)

MACAULAY, Rose. First success was *Potterism*, 1920, a skit on departmental life. Has done more serious work since, though humour and satire are skilfully blended in her books. These include *Mystery of Geneva*, *Two Books of Verse*, *Going Abroad*, *John Milton*, *Personal Pleasures*, *Life Among the English.*

MACCARTHY, Desmond. First attracted attention by the style of his writing when he was dramatic critic for *The Speaker*, 1904, and *The New Statesman*, 1913. Afterwards editor of *The New Quarterly* and later of *Life and Letters*. Author of *Criticism, Experience*. (1877–.)

McCORMACK, Count John. Famous Irish tenor. Won gold medal at Irish National Festival, 1902. Made début in *Cavalleria Rusticana* at Covent Garden, 1907, and afterwards added to his reputation when singing on the Continent and in the U.S.A. Became naturalized American, 1919. Created a Papal Count by Pius XI. (1884–1945.)

John McCormack.

McCRACKEN, Esther H. Playwright. Spent eight years with Newcastle Repertory Theatre Company and has appeared at Playhouse, Newcastle, since 1929. *Daily Herald* published her short story, *The Willing Spirit*. First three-act play, *Quiet Wedding*. Other work includes *Living Room*, *Quiet Weekend*. Late transport driver, W.R.N.S. (1902–.)

McCULLOCH, Derek. Served in First World War. Later worked on Central Argentine Railway, 1923. In 1926 joined the staff of the B.B.C., later as "Uncle Mac" being appointed Director of the Children's Hour. Was responsible also for several other features and programmes. (1897–.)

MACDONALD, Rt. Hon. James Ramsay. Labour politician. Born at Lossiemouth, Scotland, son of a farm-labourer. Began as a clerk and in 1906 was elected to Parliament as Labour. Became first chairman of the Independent Labour Party, then leader, 1911–4, of the Labour Party. Lost Parliamentary seat in 1918, but returned in 1922. Prime Minister and Foreign Secretary, 1924, he formed first British Labour Government. Was again Premier 1929–35, during which period he formed a National Government. (1866–1937.)

Ramsay MacDonald.

MACDONALD, Rt. Hon. Malcolm. Son of the above. Commissioner-General for the United Kingdom in South-east Asia since 1948. After becoming Labour M.P., filled a succession of posts, including Dominions Secretary, Colonial Secretary and Health Minister. Was High Commissioner in Canada, 1941–6. Governor-General, Malaya and Borneo, 1946–8. (1901–.)

MACFARLANE, Lt.-Gen. Sir Frank Mason (knight). After serving in the First World War, was attached to the Staff College, Quetta, India. Held other staff appointments elsewhere and has also been military attaché at continental capitals. Governor of Gibraltar, 1942–4, and Labour M.P., 1945–6. (1889–.)

McGOVERN, W. Montgomery. Professor of Political Science. Born in Brooklyn, U.S.A., he has stayed during his world travels in monasteries in China, Japan and other eastern countries, while engaged on research work. Once reached Lhasa, Tibet, in disguise without discovery. Also explored the Amazon. (1897–.)

McGOWAN, Lord (baron); **Harry Duncan McGowan.** Joined Nobel's Explosives, Ltd., when fifteen and rose to become chairman, Imperial Chemical Industries, Ltd. Also a director, Midland Bank, and of General Motors Corporation, New York. President, Society of Chemical Industries, 1931. Chairman, Financial Company of Great Britain and America. (1874–.)

MACKENZIE, Compton. One-time stage actor who turned author and achieved success with his novel, *Carnival*, and also with his next, *Sinister Street*. Served with Royal Naval Division in First World War, when he was military control officer in Athens; later Director Aegean Intelligence Service. Also wrote *Gallipoli Memories*, *Four Winds of Love*. (1883–.)

MACMILLAN, Rt. Hon. Harold. Politician and publisher. After service in First World War, was A.D.C. to Governor-General of Canada, 1919–20, and later as Conservative M.P. became Parliamentary Secretary, Ministry of Supply, 1940, and of Colonies, 1942. Minister in North-west Africa, 1942–5. Secretary for Air, 1945. (1894–.)

MACMILLAN, Rt. Hon. Lord (baron); **Hugh Pattison Macmillan.** Lord of Appeal in Ordinary, 1930–9 and 1941–7. In 1918 was appointed Assistant Director of Intelligence, Ministry of Information, and in 1924 Lord Advocate of Scotland. Minister of Information, 1939–40. Chairman of Pilgrim Trust. Lord of Appeal since 1947. (1873–.)

McNEILE, Lt.-Col. Cyril ("Sapper"). Novelist. Son of a naval captain, he enlisted in the Royal Engineers in 1907; later served in First World War. As a writer made a hit with his first book, *Sergeant Michael Cassidy*. Author also of *Bulldog Drummond* and its sequels. (1888–1937.)

MAETERLINCK, Count Maurice. Belgian poet and dramatist. Born at Ghent, he began practising law until success followed his first poetical works, *Serres Chaudes*, 1889. His play, *The Blue Bird*, aroused wide interest. Awarded Nobel Prize for literature, 1911, and in 1914 his works were recorded on the papal index. (1862–1949.)

MAISKY, Ivan M. U.S.S.R. Assistant Commissioner for Foreign Affairs. Formerly a journalist. Chief of press department, Moscow Foreign Office, 1922. Minister to Finland, 1929–32. Negotiated several pacts. Ambassador to Great Britain, 1932–43. President at League of Nations Council, 1939. (1884–.)

MANNERHEIM, Field-Marshal (baron); **Gustavas von Mannerheim.** Born in Abo, Finland, he enlisted in the Russian Army, served in the Russo-Japanese War and later commanded a cavalry corps during the Russian revolution. Afterwards returned to Finland and in 1918 was elected Regent. Later President, Council of National Defence. (1869–1951.)

MANN, Thomas. German author, who began as a clerk in his birthplace, Munich, then took to journalism and joined staff of *Simplicissimus.* His novel, *Buddenbrooks,* made his name. Won Nobel Prize for literature, 1929. Most of his works have been translated into English. (1875–.)

MANNIN, Ethel (Mrs. R. Reynolds). Writer who began her career as a shorthand-typist, afterwards becoming associate editor of *The Pelican,* 1918. Attracted attention by her first novel, *Martha,* and has since written, among others, *Commonsense and the Child, Red Rose, Commonsense and Morality,* and *The Blossoming Bough.* (1900–.)

MAO TSE-TUNG. Founder member and chairman of Chinese Communist Party's central committee. Led Communist opposition to Kuomintang (Chinese Nationalists) with which he had co-operated, 1924-7. Now head of Chinese government. Born in Hunan, son of a small landowner. (1894–.)

MARBLE, Alice. American lawn-tennis player. Women's coach, Queen's Club, London, since 1947. No. 1 player in U.S.A. Won Pacific Coast singles and mixed doubles, 1932; toured Europe, 1934. Singles champion, Wimbledon, 1939. Has played in several Wightman Cup contests. (1913–.)

MARCHANT, Prof. Sir Stanley (knight). Appointed sub-organist, St. Paul's Cathedral, 1916, he later became organist, and in 1930 was elected President, Royal College of Organists. Later on Music Advisory Board, B.B.C. Professor, Royal Academy of Music, 1913–36, and Principal from 1936. (1883–1949.)

MARCONI, Guglielmo, Marchese. Italian inventor, who in 1895–6 established wireless communication over a mile and in 1899 transmitted messages from France across to England. In 1901 successfully flashed wireless signals across the Atlantic from Cornwall to Newfoundland. Received Nobel Prize for physics, 1909, Albert Medal, Royal Society of Arts, and other honours. (1874–1937.)

Marconi.

MARGARET ROSE, Princess. Younger daughter of King George VI and Queen Elizabeth. Studied music with Miss Lander. Her first public engagement was the launching of the *Edinburgh Castle,* October, 1947. Also launched aircraft-carrier *Bulwark,* 1947. Patroness, Princess Margaret Hospital, and various societies. Colonel-in-Chief, Highland Light Infantry. (1930–.)

MARQUAND, Rt. Hon. Hilary A. Minister of Pensions, 1948–51. Descended from a line of Guernsey seafarers and merchants, he was born in Cardiff, and at twenty-nine became one of Britain's youngest professors, his work being connected with industrial relations. Afterwards as Labour M.P. was Parliamentary Secretary, Board of Trade, appointed Minister of Health, January, 1951. (1901–.)

MARSHALL, Gen. George Catlett. U.S. Secretary of State, 1947–9, when he initiated the European Recovery Programme (the famous "Marshall Aid") to provide financial assistance to war-stricken countries of Europe. Was Chief-of-Staff, U.S. Army, 1939–45, when he was largely responsible for direction of U.S. military war effort, and special envoy to China, 1945–7. (1880–.)

Gen. Marshall.

MARTEN, Sir C. Henry (knight). Provost of Eton College and tutor in constitutional law and history to H.R.H. Princess Elizabeth since 1945. Assistant master at Eton, 1896. House Master, 1907–27. Lower Master, 1926–9. Vice-Provost, 1929–44. President, Historical Association, 1929–31. Author of works on history. (1872–.)

MARTIN, B. Kingsley. Editor, *New Statesman,* since 1931. Formerly at London School of Economics, he joined the editorial staff of the *Manchester Guardian* in 1927. Author of *The Triumph of Lord Palmerston, Low's Russian Sketch Book.* (1897–.)

MARY, H.M. The Queen Mother. Born in Kensington, the eldest daughter of the Duke of Teck. In 1891 became betrothed to Duke of Clarence, but after his death married his brother, the Duke of York, later crowned King George V. Previous to that, as Princess of Wales toured the Empire with him, visiting India and Canada. (1867–.)

MARY, Victoria Alexandra Alice. English Princess. Third child and only daughter of King George V and Queen Mary. Created Princess Royal in 1932. Married (1922) Viscount Lascelles, later Sixth Earl of Harewood (1929). Two sons were born to them, George Henry Hubert, the present Earl of Harewood, and Gerald David. (1897–.)

MASEFIELD, John (O.M.). Poet Laureate since 1930, he began as a sailor, left the sea on reaching America and after odd jobs on the land settled down in England to writing. Also prose writer and dramatist. Plays include *Philip the King, Tristan and Isolt.* Has also written numerous prose works. (1875–.)

MASKELYNE, John Nevil. Famous illusionist. At the age of sixteen began practising conjuring, but afterwards became a clock-maker in Cheltenham. Following his exposure of a stage spirit illusion, he took up conjuring as a career and acquired world fame in partnership with Devant. (1839–1917.)

MASON, Alfred Edward Woodley. Novelist. Scored his first success with *The Courtship of Morrice Buckler,* published in 1896. After that wrote many other novels, including *The Four Feathers* (1902), *The Broken Road, No Other Tiger, At the Villa Rose.* Also wrote plays. Elected Liberal M.P., 1906. (1865–1948.)

MASSEY, Rt. Hon. Vincent. Canadian administrator. Chancellor, Toronto University, since 1947. Was Associate Secretary, War Cabinet Committee, Ottawa, 1918, and Canadian Minister to U.S.A., 1926–30. High Commissioner in Britain, 1935–46. Holds several honorary degrees. Author of *Good Neighbourhood* and other addresses. (1887–.)

MAUDE, Cyril. Actor. Born in London and obliged for health reasons to live first in Canada and then in America, he made his first stage appearance at Denver, Colorado. London début in 1888. Has played many successful comedy rôles. (1862–1951.)

MAUGHAM, W. Somerset. Author and dramatist. Qualified as doctor, but became an author. First novel was *Liza of Lambeth.* Was doctor and secret service agent in First World War. Author of many books and cynical plays, including *East of Suez, Our Betters, The Breadwinner, The Moon and Sixpence, Cakes and Ale.* (1874–.)

MAWSON, Sir Douglas. Explorer. Professor in Geology, Adelaide University, since 1920. On scientific staff, Shackleton's Antarctic Expedition, 1907, he became leader of the Australian Antarctic Expedition, 1911–4, and the British and New Zealand Expeditions, 1929–31. Awarded King's Polar Medal (two bars) and others. (1882–.)

MAXTON, James. Politician. An active member of the Independent Labour Party, he was its chairman from 1926 until 1931 and again in 1934–9. Entered Parliament in 1922 as I.L.P. and was frequently prominent in debates. Author of *If I Were Dictator*, 1935, and *Lenin.* (1885–1946.)

MEAD, Frederick. One of London's best-known magistrates, he presided at Marlborough Street Police Court, 1907–33. Became barrister-at-law, Middle Temple, 1869. Counsel to the Treasury, Middlesex Sessions, 1879–86; Central Criminal Court, 1886–9, and Metropolitan magistrate, 1889–1933. (1847–1945.)

MEIGHEN, Rt. Hon. Arthur. Canadian Conservative leader. Called to the bar, 1903, and elected to the Canadian Parliament in 1908, he became Solicitor-General, then Minister of the Interior, and Prime Minister, 1920–1 and 1926. Attended Prime Ministers' Conference, London, 1921. (1874–.)

MELBA, Dame Nellie (Helen P. Mitchell). Australian soprano. After learning to play the organ, she studied in Paris and became an operatic singer in Brussels, 1887. Achieved fame in London, Paris and New York. Her leading rôles were Mimi in *La Bohème* and Juliet in *Romeo and Juliet.* (1861–1931.)

MELCHETT, Lord (baron); **Alfred Moritz Mond.** Barrister-at-law, Inner Temple, 1894, he entered Parliament as Liberal in 1906, was Commissioner of Works, 1916–21, Minister of Health, 1921–2. Joined the Conservative Party in 1926, and was later Founder-President, Institute of Coal. (1868–1930.)

MENUHIN, Yehudi. Famous violinist. Born in New York, he began his violin studies at the age of four and made his début at San Francisco when only eight. While still a boy, played in New York and London (1916–.)

MENZIES, Rt. Hon. Robert G. Australian politician. Practised law; entered Parliament, 1928, and became Attorney-General and Deputy Premier, Victoria, 1932–4. In 1935 was made Commonwealth Attorney-General; Minister for Railways; Prime Minister, 1939–41, and from 1949. (1894–.)

MERRIMAN, Rt. Hon. Lord (baron); **Frank Boyd Merriman.** Judge. Called to the bar 1904. Served in First World War, and in 1920 was appointed Recorder of Wigan. As Conservative M.P., he became Solicitor-General, 1928–9; 1932–3. President, Probate, Divorce and Admiralty Division since 1933. (1880–.)

MIDDLETON, C. H. Horticulturist and broadcaster. Held national diploma in horticulture and associate of honour, Royal Horticultural Society. First broadcast *The Week in the Garden*, 1931, and after that regularly 1931–45. Wrote several books on gardening. (1887–1945.)

MILNE, Alan Alexander. Author and playwright, he began a journalistic career in London, 1903, later becoming assistant editor of *Punch*, 1906. Made his reputation with his book, *When We Were Very Young*, and its sequels. Also wrote plays, including *Mr. Pim Passes By.* (1882–.)

MILNE, Field-Marshal Lord (baron); **George Francis Milne.** Entered Army, 1885, and served in the Sudan campaign and in the South African and First World Wars. Chief Staff Officer, Second Army. G.O.C.-in-C. Eastern Command, 1923–6. Chief of Imperial General Staff, 1926–33. Governor, Tower of London, 1933–8. (1866–1948.)

MITCHELL, Sir P. Chalmers. Biologist. Lecturer on biology at London hospitals, 1892–4. Examiner in biology, Royal College of Physicians, 1892–6 and 1901–3. Secretary, Zoological Society of London, 1903–35. Served in First World War and in the A.R.P. in the Second. Author of *The War in Spain.* (1864–1945.)

MITCHELL, Reginald J. Famous aircraft designer who designed the winning flying-boat for Schneider Trophy contest, 1922, and the seaplane which won contests of 1929 and 1931. Won international fame as designer of the "Spitfire" fighter. (1895–1937.)

MOISEIWITSCH, Benno. Russian pianist, now British subject. Studied at Imperial School of Music, Odessa, winning Rubinstein Prize at age of nine. Made his début at Queen's Hall, London, 1909. Has toured the Dominions, U.S.A., and the Continent. (1890–.)

MOLLISON, James A. British aviator. Made record solo flight Australia to England in eight days, 1931; England-Cape record in just over four days, 1932. Made first U.K. to U.S.A. flight with Amy Johnson (his wife), 1933, and England-India record in twenty-two hours, 1934. (1905–.)

MOLONY, Rt. Hon. Sir Thomas (baronet). Irish lawyer, Vice-Chancellor, Dublin University, since 1931, he began his legal career in 1887. Solicitor-General, 1912–23. Attorney-General, 1913, and Lord Chief Justice, Ireland, 1918–24. Former Lord Justice of Appeal (Ireland). (1865–1949.)

MOLOTOV, Vyacheslav Mikhailovich. Commissar for Foreign Affairs, U.S.S.R., 1939–49, and Member of Supreme Soviet.

Took part in Revolution, 1905; arrested and deported; exiled from Petrograd, 1912. Went to Siberia, 1915; escaped, 1916. Member Revolutionary Committee, 1917. Chairman, Council of People's Commissars, 1939–40. (1890–.)

MONTGOMERY, Field-Marshal Viscount (of Alamein); Bernard Law Montgomery. Chairman Western European Commanders-in-Chief Defence Committee since 1948. Chief, Imperial General Staff, 1946–8. Entered the Army, 1908, served first in India, later in First World War, and afterwards was instructor Staff College, Quetta, India, 1934–7. Appointed to the command of the Eighth Army, 1942, during the Second World War, he won spectacular victories in North Africa, and later commanded the British 21st Army Group in the invasion of Europe. (1887–.)

Viscount Montgomery.

MOORE, Grace (Mrs. Valentin Parera). American opera singer and film actress. Studied under various European masters, and made her début at Metropolitan Opera House, New York, 1928. Film début in *One Night of Love*, 1933. Covent Garden, London, début in *La Bohème*, 1935. Killed in Copenhagen air crash, 1947. (1901–47.)

MORAN, Lord (baron); **Charles McMoran Wilson.** President of Royal College of Physicians. Gold medallist, London University, 1913, and member of senate. Awarded Italian silver medal in First World War. Examiner in medicine, Universities of Cambridge, Liverpool and Wales. Knighted, 1938. Physician, St. Mary's Hospital. (1882–.)

MORGAN, John Pierpont. American banker. Joined Duncan Sherman, bankers, 1857, and Drexel Morgan (later J. P. Morgan and Co.), 1871. Financed enormous railway and shipping schemes and created United States Steel Trust. He was world's greatest art collector and gave huge donations to Yale and Harvard universities. (1837–1913.)

MORGENTHAU, Henry. German-born U.S.A. financier, he went to the United States in 1865 and was Ambassador to Turkey, 1913–6. Was President of Central Realty Bond and Trust Company, 1899–1905, and of Henry Morgenthau Co., 1905–13. Author of *Secrets of the Bosphorus*, 1919. (1856–1946.)

MORRISON, Rt. Hon. Herbert S. Politician. Lord President of the Council, 1945–1951, when he succeeded Ernest Bevin as Foreign Secretary. Entered Parliament as Labour in 1923. Joined the National Government as Minister of Supply, 1940, afterwards becoming Home Secretary. (1888–.)

MOTTISTONE, Maj.-Gen. Rt. Hon. Lord (baron); **Edward Bernard Seely.** Politician. Barrister-at-law, 1897. Served in South African and First World Wars. As Liberal M.P. became Under-Secretary of State for War, 1911; later Under-Secretary of State for Air. Deputy Minister of Munitions, 1918. (1868–1947.)

MOUNTBATTEN, Vice-Admiral Earl (of Burma); Louis Francis Albert Victor Mountbatten. Viceroy and Governor-General of India, 1947–8. Beginning as a naval cadet in 1913, he rose to Lt.-Commander, then Captain, and in the Second World War was Chief of Combined Operations, 1942. Supreme Commander, South-east Asia, 1943–6. K.C.B., 1945. Personal Naval A.D.C. to the King since 1937. (1900–.)

MOUNTEVANS, Admiral Lord (baron); Edward Ratcliffe Evans. Also known as "Evans of the *Broke*." Was second-in-command, British Antarctic Expedition, 1909; returned in command after Scott's death, 1913. Served in First World War. C.-in-C., the Nore, 1935–9. London Regional Commissioner, Civil Defence, 1939–45. (1881–.)

MOYNIHAN, Lord (baron); **Berkeley George Andrew Moynihan.** Surgeon. Was President of the Royal College of Surgeons, 1926–32, and an honorary Maj.-Gen., Army Medical Service. Made a great name when consulting surgeon, Leeds General Infirmary and 2nd Northern General Army Hospital. Linacre Lecturer, Cambridge, 1936. (1865–1936.)

MUNNINGS, Sir Alfred J. (knight). President of the Royal Academy, 1944–9. Born at Mendham, Suffolk, his boyhood drawings of horses and ponies revealed his particular talent. Years later won the gold medal of the Paris Salon and in the First World War was official artist. (1878–.)

MURRAY, David L. Author. Served in Military Intelligence in the First World War. He was dramatic critic of *The Nation and Athenaeum*, 1920–3, afterwards joining the staff of *The Times*, and becoming editor of *The Times Literary Supplement*. Author of *Disraeli*, *Regency*, *Tale of Three Cities*. (1888–.)

MURRAY, George Gilbert. Author and politician. Left Australia at age of eleven. Fellow of New College, Oxford, 1888. Became Professor of Greek, Glasgow University, 1889–99, and later Oxford University, 1908–36. Chairman, League of Nations Union, 1923–8. Prolific author. Translator of Euripides and other Greek playwrights. (1866–.)

MUSSOLINI, Benito. Italian Dictator (styled *Il Duce*). Founded Fascist Party in Italy, 1919, and led the march on Rome, 1922. Became Prime Minister and dictator, 1922. In 1936 joined forces with Hitler. Made war on Abyssinia, 1935–6. Executed by Italian partisans, 1945. (1883–1945.)

NANSEN, Fridtjof. Norwegian Arctic explorer. His crossing of the Greenland ice-field first brought him fame. In 1895 went to the North Pole, reaching the farthest point north then attained. Became Norwegian Minister to Great Britain, 1906–8. Won Nobel Peace Prize, 1922. Was instrumental in separating Norway from Sweden. (1861–1930.)

NARES, Owen R. Actor-manager. Born at Maiden Erleigh, Berks, he was trained for the stage and made his début at the Haymarket Theatre, London, in 1909. Also toured the provinces, but acted mostly in London.

Among his successes were *The Fanatics, Diplomacy, Counsel's Opinion.* (1888–1943.)

NASH, Heddle. Operatic tenor. Saw service in the First World War. Studied in Milan and became leading lyric tenor there. Returned to England, 1925. Appeared with great success in *Rigoletto* and other operas.

NASH, Rt. Hon. Walter. Minister of New Zealand in U.S.A., 1942–4. Born in Kidderminster, where he began as office-boy. Afterwards in New Zealand became secretary, Labour Party, 1922, and National President, 1935–6. In 1929 entered New Zealand Parliament, and was appointed Minister of Finance, 1935. (1882–.)

NATHAN, Rt. Hon. Lord (baron); **Harry Louis Nathan.** Minister of Civil Aviation, 1946–8. A practising solicitor, he served in the First World War and in 1929 entered Parliament as Liberal, changing to Labour in 1934. Author of *Free Trade Today*. (1889–.)

"NEAGLE, Anna" (Mrs. Herbert Wilcox). Actress. Was a dancer in Charlot and Cochrane revues and cabarets, London and New York, 1926–30. Has acted in stage plays and in films: *Nell Gwyn, Victoria the Great, Sixty Glorious Years, The Courtneys of Curzon Street, Spring in Park Lane.* (1908–.)

NEHRU, (Pandit) Jawaharlal. Prime Minister and Minister of Foreign Affairs, India, since 1947. Was educated in England. Took an active part in the Indian National Congress and its aims, which were directed against British rule. Was imprisoned several times. In 1946 became Vice-President of an Interim Government composed of Hindus and Moslems, until his present post. (1889–.)

Pandit Nehru.

NEWALL, Marshal of the R.A.F. Lord (baron); **Cyril Louis** Newall. Served in the Gurkhas, Indian Army, in 1909, and two years later in England learned to fly. Served in the R.A.F. in the First World War. Commanded the R.A.F., Middle East, 1931–4. Chief of Air Staff, 1937–40. Governor-General and C.-in-C., New Zealand, 1941–6. (1886–.)

NEWMAN, Ernest. Music critic and author. Was musical critic, *Manchester Guardian*, 1905, *Birmingham Post*, 1906–19, and then *Sunday Times*. His works include studies on Wagner and Elgar, and biographies of Wolf and Strauss. (1868–.)

NICHOLSON, Sir William N. P. (knight). Born at Newark-on-Trent, he studied art and gained distinction as a stained-glass window designer and woodcut artist. His landscapes include "Málaga Bull Ring" and "La Ropa." Has illustrated Kipling's *Twelve Sports.* Author of *The Pirate Turns.* (1872–1949.)

NICOLSON, Hon. Harold. Politician and writer. Born in Teheran, Iran, and educated in England, he entered the Foreign Office and held diplomatic posts in Madrid and Constantinople. Became National Labour M.P. in 1935. Governor of the B.B.C., 1941–6. Biographer of Lord Curzon. (1886–.)

NIJINSKY, Vaslav. Russian ballet-dancer. Born in Kiev, he was trained at St. Petersburg School of Ballet. Made his début in 1907 and afterwards attracted wide attention by the fine technique of his dancing. First appeared in London in 1911. Choreographer of *L'Après-midi d'un faune*, and other productions. (1890–1950.)

NIKISCH, Arthur. Hungarian musician. A prodigy pianist at the age of eight, he became chief conductor at Leipzig opera house in 1879. Conductor of Boston Symphony Orchestra, 1889–93, he conducted in several European cities also, and in Covent Garden, 1914. (1855–1922.)

NIMITZ, Fleet Admiral Chester W. Chief of Naval Operations, United States, 1945–7. Graduated from the naval academy at Annapolis and began as a midshipman. In 1918 commanded the submarine force, Atlantic Fleet, and was head of the U.S. Bureau of Navigation, 1939–41. C.-in-C., U.S. Pacific Fleet, 1941–5. (1885–.)

NOEL-BAKER, Rt. Hon. Philip J. Secretary of State for Air, 1946–7, and for Commonwealth Relations, 1947–50, and since then Minister of Fuel and Power. At Cambridge won a scholarship in international law. Served in First World War and in the Second was at the Ministry of Transport. Became Labour M.P. in 1929. Author of *Private Manufacture of Armaments* and other books. (1889–.)

NORFOLK, Duke of; Bernard Marmaduke FitzAlan-Howard. Earl Marshal of England. Premier Duke and Earl. Was in charge of King George VI's Coronation, 1937. He was Joint Parliamentary Secretary to the Ministry of Agriculture from 1941 to 1945. (1908–.)

NORMAN, Rt. Hon. Lord (baron); **Montague Collet Norman.** Served in the South African War and afterwards as a banker became the most powerful figure in British finance. Was elected Deputy Governor, Bank of England, 1918; Governor, 1920–44. Re-introduced the gold standard in 1925. It was abandoned 1931. (1871–1950.)

NORWOOD, Sir Cyril. President, St. John's College, Oxford, 1934–46. Was a civil servant, 1899 to 1901, when he became an assistant master, Leeds Grammar School. Afterwards Headmaster in turn of Bristol Grammar School, Marlborough College and Harrow (1926–34). (1875–.)

NOVELLO, Ivor. Playwright, actor-manager. Born in Cardiff, his first song was published when he was fifteen. Made a hit with his later song "Keep the Home Fires Burning." Has appeared in many plays and written several, *Perchance to Dream, We Proudly Present* and others. (1893–1951.)

NOYES, Alfred. Born in Staffordshire, his first book of verse was published in 1902 and was followed by several other poetical works. Was temporarily attached to Foreign Office, 1916. Among his publications are *The Flower of Old Japan, The Last Man.* (1880–.)

NUFFIELD, Viscount, William Richard **Morris.** Motor manufacturer and philanthropist. Started his career as a bicycle repairer, 1894. Won seven county bicycle championships, 1900. Began manufacturing cars, 1912. Now head of largest British car-manufacturing concern. Has given many millions to hospitals and is head of Nuffield Foundation. (1877–.)

NURMI, Paavo. Finnish runner. Broke world records for the mile, 1923; two miles, 1931; five miles, 1924; six miles, 1930; ten miles, 1928. Won many Olympic victories, but was barred from Olympic Games in 1932 owing to his professional status. (1897–.)

OAKSEY, Rt. Hon. Lord (baron); **Geoffrey Lawrence.** Lord Justice of Appeal, 1944–47. Served in First World War. Was Attorney-General to Prince of Wales, 1928–32, and from 1924–32 Recorder of Oxford. Judge of the High Court, 1932–44. Presided at Nuremberg Trials, 1945–6, of German major war criminals. (1880–.)

O'CONNOR, Rt. Hon. Thomas P. Irish politician and journalist. Born in Athlone, Ireland, he began as junior reporter on *Saunders' Newsletter*, Dublin, 1867, and first entered Parliament in 1880. Was the founder and first editor of the *Star*, London. Also founded *The Sun*, *M.A.P.*, and *T.P.'s Weekly*. (1848–1929.)

O'KELLY, Sean Thomas. Irish politician. President of Eire since 1945. M.P. (Republican), 1918–24. Irish Envoy to France and Rome, 1919–22, and to U.S.A., 1924–6. Co-founder of Sinn Fein movement and first Speaker of Dail Eireann. Minister of Finance, Education, 1939–45. (1882–.)

OLIVIER, Sir Laurence (knight). Actor. First appeared at Shakespeare Festival, Stratford-on-Avon, and played with Birmingham Repertory Company, 1925–8. Appeared at Old Vic, 1936, in Shakespearean rôles. Actor-producer in *Romeo and Juliet*. Films include *Wuthering Heights*, *Henry V*, *Hamlet*. (1907–.)

Sir Laurence Olivier.

OPPENHEIM, E. Phillips. Novelist. Won a reputation as a writer of society, popular and mystery novels, many of which dealt with espionage. Lived for several years in the south of France. His many books include *The Million Pound Deposit*, *Murder at Monte Carlo*, *The Spymaster*, *The Inevitable Millionaires*. (1866–1946.)

ORCZY, Baroness (Mrs. Montagu Barstow). Novelist. Born in Hungary, she studied painting at the Heatherley School of Art, London, and exhibited at the Royal Academy. Began writing in 1900 and first won world fame with *The Scarlet Pimpernel*, a novel of the French Revolution. Other works include *A Spy of Napoleon*, *No Greater Love*. (Died 1947.)

ORR, Lord Boyd (baron); **John Boyd Orr.** Director-General, United Nations Food and Agricultural Organization, 1946–7. Professor of Agriculture, Aberdeen University, 1942–5. Was Independent M.P., 1935–6, and for Scottish Universities, 1945–6. Ministry of Food's Adviser at Washington. (1880–.)

OWEN, Frank. Journalist. Editor of the *Daily Mail*, 1947–50. Previous to that was with the *Evening Standard* as editor. During Second World War edited *S.E.A.C.* (South East Asia Command) *News*, a British Army publication. (1905–.)

OXFORD AND ASQUITH, Earl of; Henry Herbert Asquith. A Liberal from his Oxford University days, he studied law and became Queen's Counsel, 1890. Entered Parliament in 1886, was Home Secretary under Gladstone and Chancellor of the Exchequer under Campbell-Bannerman, whom he succeeded as Prime Minister in 1908. In May, 1915, formed a coalition government, remaining Prime Minister until 1916. (1852–1928.)

PADEREWSKI, Ignaz Jan. Polish patriot, politician and pianist. Made his musical début at Vienna, 1887, and in London three years later. His brilliant technique won him world fame. Made tours and raised funds for Polish sufferers in First World War. Premier of Poland, 1919. (1860–1941.)

Paderewski.

PAGE, Rt. Hon. Sir Earle (knight). Australian politician. Was one of Australia's leading surgeons and joined the Australian Imperial Forces to serve in First World War. Afterwards gave up surgery, and as M.P. since 1919 has been Minister of Commerce, Minister of Health and Prime Minister. (1880–.)

PAGE, Sir F. Handley (knight). Aircraft designer and manufacturer. First engaged in aeronautics, 1907, and became an aeronautical engineer and designer in 1909, when he founded Handley Page Ltd. In 1928 patented the slotted wing to provide more stability for aeroplanes in flight. (1885–.)

PAGET, Gen. Sir Bernard (knight). Principal of Ashridge College, 1946–9. Served in the First World War. Was Commandant, Staff College, Camberley, 1938–9; Chief of General Staff, Home Forces, 1940. C.-in-C., South-eastern Command and Home Forces, 1941–3. C.-in-C., Middle East, 1944–6. (1888–.)

PANKHURST, Emmeline. Militant suffragette. Wife of a barrister, with whose help she founded the Women's Franchise League, 1889. Founded Women's Social and Political Union, 1903, led English suffragettes and was imprisoned eight times for disturbances designed to call attention to the "votes for women" campaign. (1858–1928.)

PARK, Air Chief Marshal Sir Keith R. (knight). Allied Air C.-in-C., South-east Asia, 1945–6. A.O.C., Malta, 1942–3, Middle East, 1944. Commanded No. 11 Fighter Group during the Battle of Britain. (1892–.)

PARTRIDGE, Sir Bernard. Artist. Was engaged in stained-glass designing and decorative painting, and the illustrating of books.

In 1891 he joined the staff of *Punch* and regularly contributed cartoons that became widely known. Was once on the stage. (1861–1945.)

PASSFIELD, Lord (baron); **Sidney Webb.** Labour politician. Londoner by birth and expert economist, helped to found the London School of Economics. As Labour M.P. he and his wife, Beatrice Webb, took active interest in unemployment and social conditions. President, Board of Trade, 1924; Secretary for the Colonies, 1929–31. Wrote several books. (1859–1947.)

PAUL-BONCOUR, Joseph. French Senator and barrister. At one time Independent in politics, he became actively interested in the French Radical-Socialist party, becoming Minister of Labour, 1911. Resigned from Socialist Party, 1931. Afterwards was in turn War Minister, Prime Minister, and Foreign Minister, 1932–4; also Foreign Minister, 1938. (1873–.)

PAVLOVA, Anna. Russian ballet-dancer. Born in St. Petersburg, she made her début there at the Imperial Opera House, afterwards foremost ballet-dancer in Europe. London début, 1909. Later toured America. Appeared many times in Diaghileff's Ballet Company, notably in *Le Cygne* (The Swan). (1885–1931.)

PEACH, L. du Garde. Author and dramatist. Served in First World War. Lecturer in English language and literature, Gottingen University. Author of stage and radio plays. (1890–.)

PERRY, Frederick J. Tennis champion. Formerly table-tennis champion of the world, he attained equal success as a lawn-tennis player. Won the Davis Cup for Great Britain in 1933. In the same year, and later, won French, American, and Australian championships in singles and doubles. (1909–.)

PERSHING, Gen. John J. Was C.-in-C., U.S. Army. First saw active service in the Spanish-American War and again in military expeditions in Philippines. C.-in-C., American Expeditionary Forces in Europe, in First World War. Chief-of-Staff, U.S. Army, 1921–4. Freeman, City of London, 1919. (1860–1948.)

PERTH, Earl of; Eric Drummond. Diplomat. Was a Private Secretary to Prime Minister, 1912–5; to Foreign Secretary, 1915–9. Was Secretary-General to the League of Nations, Geneva, 1919–33, and Ambassador to Italy, 1933–9. Chief Adviser on Foreign Publicity, Ministry of Information, 1939–40. (1876–.)

PÉTAIN, Marshal Philippe. Former Chief of French State. Commanded Infantry Division at battle of Marne and operations at defence of Verdun, First World War. Secretary for War, 1934. Ambassador to Spain, 1939–40. Chief of Vichy France, 1940–4, and Prime Minister, 1940–2. Tried for collaboration with Germany and imprisoned since 1945. (1856–.)

PETHICK-LAWRENCE, Rt. Hon. Lord (baron); **Frederick William Pethick-Lawrence.** Politician. Editor *The Echo*, and later of *Labour Record and Review*. Was imprisoned for nine months for activities connected with militant suffragette disturbances. In 1923 was elected Labour M.P. Secretary for India and Burma, 1945–7. Headed Cabinet Delegation to India, 1946. (1871–.)

PHILIP, Prince (Duke of Edinburgh). Formerly Lieut. Philip Mountbatten, R.N., and Prince Philip of Greece. Brought up in England by Earl Mountbatten and educated in Germany and Scotland, he entered the Royal Navy, 1939, and served in Mediterranean, 1940. Was at battle of Matapan, 1941 (dispatches). Naturalized British subject, 1946. Married H.R.H. Princess Elizabeth, November, 1947, after being made Duke of Edinburgh and a Prince of the British royal household. (1921–.)

PHILLPOTTS, Eden. Novelist and dramatist. Worked in an insurance office, studied for the stage, but became an author. Has specialized in scenes of Devonshire life, particularly of Dartmoor, and has written many poems, novels and plays. Works include *The Human Boy, Children of the Mist, Widecombe Fair*. (1862–.)

PICCARD, Auguste. Swiss balloonist and scientist, and first since Coxwell and Glaisher to make a balloon ascent into the stratosphere, 1931. Second ascent, 1932. Zurich Polytechnic and Brussels University. (1884–.)

PICKTHORN, Kenneth W. Historian. After service in First World War became Dean of Corpus Christi College, Cambridge, 1919–27, then Tutor, 1927–35. President, Corpus Christi, 1937–44, and lecturer in History. Conservative M.P. for Cambridge University, 1935–50. Author of *History of the Peace Conference* and other books. (1892–.)

PINERO, Sir Arthur W. (knight). Dramatist. Was an actor from 1874 to 1881, when he became a dramatic author. Produced clever comedies at Court Theatre, London, 1885–93, notably *Sweet Lavender*. Other plays include *The Second Mrs. Tanqueray, The Gay Lord Quex, Trelawney of the Wells*. (1855–1934.)

PIUS XII; Eugene Pacelli. Pope since 1939. Born in Rome, he was ordained priest, 1899. Became Archbishop of Sardes, 1917, and Cardinal in 1929. Secretary of State to the Pope, 1930–9. Succeeded Pius XI. (1876–.)

PONSONBY of Shulbrede, Lord (baron); **Arthur Augustus William Ponsonby.** Politician. Entering the Diplomatic Service, 1894, he became Principal Private Secretary to Prime Minister, 1906–8, and then Liberal M.P., afterwards Labour. Was Parliamentary Secretary, Ministry of Transport, 1929–31, Chancellor, Duchy of Lancaster, 1931, and Leader of Opposition, House of Lords, 1931–5. (1871–1946.)

PORTAL of Hungerford, Marshal of the R.A.F. Viscount; Charles Frederick Portal. Served for a time in the Army in the First World War, and before it ended was a colonel in the Royal Flying Corps. Commanded British Forces, Aden, 1934–5. In April, 1940, became A.O.C.-in-C., Bomber Command, and in October of the same year Chief of Air Staff (until 1945). (1893–.)

"POY" (Percy H. Fearon). Cartoonist. Studied at Chase School of Art, New York, and subsequently under Prof. Herkomer at Bushey. First cartoons appeared in *Judy*. Became cartoonist, *Manchester Evening Chronicle*, 1905, and later on *Sunday Chronicle, Daily Despatch, Evening News, Daily Mail*, 1935–8. (1874–.)

PRIESTLEY, John Boynton. Author and broadcaster. Born in Bradford, he began as journalist at seventeen. Later served in First World War, and then became critic on *Daily News* and a publisher's reader. Won fame with his novel, *The Good Companions*, 1929, and has also written several plays. (1894–.)

J. B. Priestley.

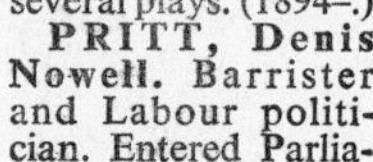

PRITT, Denis Nowell. Barrister and Labour politician. Entered Parliament as Labour but was expelled from the party, 1940. Independent Labour, 1945–50. Late chairman, Howard League for Penal Reform. Chairman, Society for Cultural Relations with U.S.S.R. Author of *Revolt in Europe, A New World Grows*, etc. (1887–.)

PROCTER, Mrs. Dod (R.A.). Artist. Wife of the late Ernest Procter, also artist, she was elected A.R.A. in 1934 and R.A. in 1942. Her picture, "Morning," was hung at the Royal Academy in 1927 and was bought for the nation. Others include "The Tall Girl" and "The Sleeping Girl."

QUEENBOROUGH, Lord (baron); **Almeric Hugh Paget.** Lived for several years in the U.S.A., farming and ranching. After returning to England became Conservative M.P. and was three times President of the National Union of Conservative and Unionist Associations. (1869–1949.)

QUICKSWOOD, Rt. Hon. Lord (baron); **Hugh Richard Cecil.** Served in Royal Flying Corps in First World War. Elected Conservative M.P., 1895–1906, and 1910–37. Provost of Eton, 1936–44. (1869–.)

RAMSAY, Admiral Hon. Sir Alexander (knight). Served in Dardanelles in First World War. Rear-Admiral, Aircraft Carriers, 1933–6, and then C.-in-C., East Indies, until 1938. Fifth Sea Lord and Chief of Naval Air Service, 1938–9. In 1919 married Princess Patricia of Connaught. (1881–.)

RANJITSINHJI, Prince Kumar Shri. Maharaja of Nawanagar. Famous Indian cricketer and leader. Educated at Cambridge, he became renowned as a cricketer, and later played for Sussex, heading the averages. Champion batsman of England, 1896, 1900. Went to Australia, 1897–8. Served in First World War. (1872–1933.)

RANK, Joseph Arthur. Film magnate. Besides being joint managing director of his family's milling firm, he is chairman of Odeon Theatres, Ltd., Gaumont-British Picture Corporation, Ltd., J. Arthur Rank Organization, Ltd., British and Dominions Film Corporation, Ltd. Has also financial interest in American companies. (1888–.)

RATTIGAN, Terence. Dramatist. Left Oxford University to write plays. His first accepted play was *French Without Tears*, at Criterion Theatre, where it ran for two and three-quarter years. Air-gunner, R.A.F., 1940. Wrote R.A.F. play, *Flare Path*, 1942. Won *Daily Mail* Film Award with *The Way to the Stars*. (1911–.)

RAYLEIGH, Lord (baron); **Robert John Strutt.** Physicist. After leaving Cambridge, won the Rumford medal of the Royal Society, of which he afterwards became foreign secretary. President, Physical Society, 1934–6, and then President of the British Association. (1875–1947.)

READING, Marquess of; Rufus Daniel Isaacs. Went to sea when fourteen and afterwards worked in a London city office. Studied law, elected Liberal M.P. and became Solicitor-General, 1910, and Attorney-General, 1910–3. Lord Chief Justice, 1913–21. In 1918 was appointed Special Ambassador to U.S.A. Viceroy of India, 1921–6. Foreign Secretary, 1931. (1860–1935.)

REILLY, Sir Charles. For more than thirty years Emeritus Professor of Architecture, Liverpool University. Director of the Liverpool School of Architecture, 1904–33. In 1943 was awarded the Royal Gold Medal for Architecture. Wrote several books, including *Scaffolding in the Sky, A Semi-architectural Autobiography*. (1874–1948.)

REITH, Rt. Hon. Lord (baron); **John Charles Reith.** Administrator. Served in First World War and in 1919 was at the Ministry of Munitions. Became Director-General, B.B.C., in 1927. In 1940 was first Minister of Information, then Minister of Transport, and later Minister of Works. (1889–.)

RENNELL, Lord (baron); **James Rennell Rodd.** Diplomat. Entered diplomatic service, 1883, and in 1897 was appointed special envoy to Abyssinia. Became Minister to Sweden, 1904–8, and Ambassador to Italy, 1908–19. His Parliamentary career as Conservative extended from 1928 to 1933. Author of *Social and Diplomatic Memoirs*. (1858–1941.)

REYNAUD, Paul. French politician. Served in First World War. Was elected a Deputy, 1919; later was Minister of Colonies and, in 1940, Premier. In Second World War fled to Bordeaux, was interned and handed over to Germans. Repatriated, 1945. (1878–.)

RHONDDA, Viscount; David Alfred Thomas. Colliery director and politician. President, South Wales Liberal Federation, 1893–7, and Liberal M.P. Was President of Local Government Board, 1916–7. As Food Controller, 1917, he instituted compulsory rationing. (1856–1918.)

RICHARDS, Gordon. Jockey. Began as a clerk, then turned to horse-racing as a career. Became apprentice to Martin Hartigan and eclipsed Archer's record by winning the greatest number of races in the history of the Turf. Between 1920 and 1950 he had ridden four thousand winners. (1904–.)

RICHARDSON, Sir Ralph David (knight). Actor. Made stage début at Brighton, 1921, in *The Merchant of Venice*, then toured the provinces and later joined Birmingham Repertory Theatre. London début in July, 1926. Toured South Africa in 1929. First film *The Ghoul*, 1933. Other films include *The Four Feathers, The Silver Fleet*. (1902–.)

ROBERTS, Field-Marshal Earl; Frederick Sleigh Roberts. Born in Cawnpore, India, he was destined to win military distinction in that country. Won the V.C., 1858, and rose to be C.-in-C., India, 1885. His appointment as C.-in-C. in South Africa, 1899, was followed by reversal of British failures against Boers. Relieved Kimberley, 1900. (1832–1914.)

ROBERTSON, Rt. Hon. Sir Malcolm Arnold (knight). Diplomat. Was First Secretary in Washington, 1915–8, and British High Commissioner, Rhineland, 1919. Consul-General at Tangier, 1921. Minister Plenipotentiary to Argentine, 1925–7, and Ambassador, 1927–9. Was Conservative M.P., 1940–5. (1877–.)

ROBESON, Paul Le Roy. Negro singer and actor. Born in Princeton, New Jersey. After a university education, made his first appearance on the concert platform, New York, 1925. Acted in *Emperor Jones*, London, 1925, and in *Show Boat*. Afterwards played the title rôle in London and U.S.A. in *Othello* and other productions. (1898–.)

"ROBEY, George" (George E. Wade). Music-hall comedian. Made professional début at the old Oxford Theatre, London, 1891, after achieving success there as amateur in matinée trial show. Has since appeared in many pantomimes, plays, variety acts and films. (1869–.)

ROBSON, Flora. Actress. Awarded the Bronze Medal, Royal Academy of Art, she made her first appearance on the stage in 1921 at the Shaftesbury Theatre, London. Afterwards acted in repertory for several years, and then with equal success appeared in films. Rôles mostly emotional. (1902–.)

ROCKEFELLER, John D. American oil-magnate. Started as a commission agent, built up oil concerns from the combination of which he accumulated vast sums of wealth, becoming a multi-millionaire. Gave liberally to various objects, among them the Rockefeller Foundation. (1839–1937.)

RODIN, Auguste. French sculptor. Served in National Guard in Franco-Prussian War. His sculptures, "L'Age d'Airain" and "Saint Jean-Baptiste," were purchased by the State in 1884. His famous group, "Les Bourgeois de Calais," is at Calais (a replica is in Victoria Tower Gardens, Westminster). (1840–1917.)

RONALD, Sir Landon. Principal, Guildhall School of Music, 1910–38, and noted conductor. Conducted grand opera at Covent Garden and accompanied Melba to America, 1894. Conducted at concerts at Albert Hall and elsewhere. Composer of many works. (1873–1938.)

Franklin D. Roosevelt.

ROOSEVELT, Franklin Delano. Great American statesman and Britain's staunch supporter in Second World War. Former lawyer, entered politics, 1910. First official position, 1913, as assistant naval Secretary of State. Twice Governor of New York State. Despite physical disability, served three Presidential terms, 1932, 1936, 1940, and began a fourth (elected 1944). Attended war conferences at Yalta and Teheran. (1882–1945.)

ROPER, E. Stanley. Organist, composer and choirmaster to the King, St. James's Palace; formerly Principal, Trinity College of Music. Honorary assistant organist, Westminster Abbey. Professor, Trinity College of Music. (1878–.)

ROSEBERY, Earl of; Archibald Philip Primrose. One of the outstanding figures of early Liberal power, associated with Gladstone. He filled many important posts, including Lord Privy Seal, 1885, Foreign Secretary in the following year and again in 1892–4. Prime Minister, 1894–5. Prominent racehorse owner. (1847–1929.)

ROSS, Sir Edward Denison (knight). Oriental authority. After extensive travels, became Professor of Persian, University College, London, 1896–1901. Keeper of Stein Antiquities, British Museum, 1914–6, and then Director, School of Oriental Studies, until 1937. Gold Medallist, Royal Asiatic Society, 1935. (1871–1940.)

ROSS, Sir Ronald (knight). Expert on tropical medicine. He discovered life-history of malaria parasites in mosquitoes, 1897–8. Served in Indian Medical Service, 1881–99. Was awarded Party's Gold Medal, 1895, and Nobel Prize for medicine, 1902. Director-in-Chief, Ross Institute, Putney Heath. (1857–1932.)

ROTHERMERE, Rt. Hon. Viscount; Harold Harmsworth. Newspaper proprietor. Younger brother of Lord Northcliffe, with whom he became actively associated in newspaper enterprises. Endowed chairs of English literature, American history (Oxford) and Naval history (Cambridge). Director-General, Army Clothing, 1916. Air Minister, 1917–8. (1868–1940.)

ROTHSCHILD, Lord (baron); **Nathaniel Victor Rothschild.** Scientist. Fellow of Trinity College, Cambridge, 1935–9. During the Second World War was engaged in highly confidential anti-sabotage work, for which he was awarded the George Medal and the American Legion of Merit. Joined Labour Party, 1945. (1910–.)

ROYDEN, A. Maude. Nonconformist preacher. Worked in a Liverpool settlement and later was actively interested in women's suffrage movement. Assistant Preacher, City Temple, 1917–20. In 1928 made the first of several preaching tours in U.S.A. Other tours made in Canada, India, and Palestine. Wrote *Problem of Palestine* and other books. (1876–.)

RUGBY, Lord (baron); **John Loader Maffey.** British representative to Eire, 1939–49. Was in the Political Department, India, 1905, and then saw service with the Mohmand Field Force. Governor-General of the Sudan, 1925–33. Permanent Under-Secretary, Colonial Office, 1933–7. (1877–.)

RUSSELL, Earl; Bertrand Arthur William Russell. Philosopher and author. First attracted attention with his *Principles of Mathematics*, 1903, followed, in 1910, by *Principia Mathematica*, written in collaboration with Prof. A. N. Whitehead. Other books include *An*

Outline of Philosophy, *Problems of Philosophy*, *The A, B, C of Relativity*, *Our Knowledge of the External World*, *History of Western Philosophy*. (1872–.)

SALAZAR, Antonio de Oliveira. Prime Minister of Portugal since 1932; Foreign Minister since 1936. Has also been in turn Minister for Finances, of Colonies and of War. Was Professor of Economics, Sciences, Coimbra University. Drafted new Constitution, 1933. (1889–.)

SALISBURY, Frank O. Portrait and figure painter. Studied in Italy, Germany and France. Has exhibited at Royal Academy since 1899. Portraits of King George V, King George VI, Queen Mary, Archbishop of Canterbury, President Roosevelt. Has also depicted many notable events. (1874–.)

SALISBURY, Marquess of; James Edward Hubert Gascoyne-Cecil. Served in South African War. As Conservative M.P. was Lord Privy Seal, 1903–5 and 1924–9, and President, Board of Trade, in 1905. Lord President of Council, 1922–4. Chancellor, Duchy of Lancaster, 1922–3. Leader, House of Lords, 1925–9. (1861–1947.)

SALISBURY, Rt. Hon. the Marquess of; Robert Arthur James Gascoyne-Cecil. Began his career in the City (London) with a firm of bill-brokers. Later as M.P. (1929–41) when styled Viscount Cranbourne, was appointed Parliamentary Under-Secretary of State for Foreign Affairs, 1935, followed by other important Conservative Government positions. Conservative leader, House of Lords, 1942 (until 1947 as Baron Cecil of Essendon). (1893–.)

SALTER, Rt. Hon. Sir J. Arthur (knight). Independent M.P., 1937–50, and Gladstone Professor of Political Theory, Oxford University, 1934–44. Assistant Director of Transport, Admiralty, 1915. As Parliamentary Secretary to Ministry of Shipping, 1939–41, represented Britain at Washington Conference. Parliamentary Secretary War Transport Ministry, 1941–5. Conservative M.P., 1951. (1881–.)

SAMMONS, Albert. Violinist. After being taught for a short while was able to play solos at the age of eight. First important engagement at Harrogate, 1903. Specializes in works by Elgar and Delius and has played with many important orchestras. (1886–.)

SAMUEL, Rt. Hon. Viscount; Herbert Louis Samuel. Politician. On leaving Oxford, lived for a time in London's East End to study the conditions of the poor and specialized in social reform. Afterwards as Liberal M.P. held several important posts, among them Postmaster-General (twice), Home Secretary, 1916, and 1931–2, and High Commissioner, Palestine, 1920–5. Liberal leader, House of Lords, from 1944. (1870–.)

SANDOW, Eugen. German wrestler and physical culture exponent. Won world fame as wrestler and gymnast; world's weight-lifting champion, 1891. Gave other remarkable exhibitions of his strength. Opened a remedial centre in St. James's, London. (1867–1925.)

SANKEY, Rt. Hon. Viscount; John Sankey. Well known as an ecclesiastical lawyer, he afterwards gained prominence in Labour politics. Was Lord Chancellor, 1929–35, also took an active part in the Indian Round-Table Conference. In 1919 investigated mining industry and considered nationalization. (1866–1948.)

SARGENT, Sir Malcolm (knight). Has been called "Britain's Ambassador of Music." Has conducted on the Continent, in the United States and elsewhere. Conductor-in-Chief, Royal Choral Society, since 1928, Hallé Orchestra, 1939–43, Liverpool Philharmonic Orchestra, 1942–8, and Huddersfield Choral Society since 1932. (1895–.)

SASSOON, Siegfried. Poet. Served in First World War and published war poems, *Counter-Attack*, *Satirical Poems*. He gained the Hawthornden Prize with *Memoirs of a Fox-Hunting Man*. This was followed by *Memoirs of an Infantry Officer*, 1930. Other volumes include *The Old Huntsman*, *Rhymed Ruminations*. (1886–.)

SAUNDERS, Hilary St. George. Librarian, House of Commons, since 1946, and author. After being on the staff of the League of Nations, began writing crime novels with the late John Palmer, their pen-name being "Francis Beeding." Has also written his own official histories of the Second World War. (1898–.)

SAYERS, Dorothy L. (Mrs. Atherton Fleming). Novelist. Became well known as a writer of mystery novels, after publishing two volumes of verse. Amongst her thrillers are *Lord Peter Views the Body*, *The Nine Tailors*, *Strong Poison*. Plays include *Busman's Honeymoon*, *The Man Born to be King*. (1893–.)

SCHACHT, Hjalmar. President of the German Reichsbank in the Nazi régime. Opposed adoption of Hague Agreement and resigned his Presidency, 1930; reappointed, 1933. Was Minister of Economics and later Minister without Portfolio. Tried as war criminal at Nuremberg and acquitted, 1946; sentenced by De-Nazification Court, 1947, but acquitted on appeal, 1948. (1877–.)

SCHARRER, Irene (Mrs. S. Gurney Lubbock). Pianist. Made her début in Germany at age of seventeen. Has played at Queen's Hall Symphony Concerts, London Symphony and Royal Philharmonic Concerts and made many concert appearances on the Continent.

SCOTT, Charles Prestwick. Famous as editor, *Manchester Guardian*, which he guided with Liberal views to a position of wide influence during the years of his association with it, 1872–1929. Entered Parliament as Liberal in 1895. Opposed the policies which, he alleged, led to the Boer War and the First World War. (1846–1932.)

SCOTT, Sir Giles Gilbert (knight). Architect. When twenty-three won a competition for a design for the Anglican Cathedral at Liverpool. Also designed the new University Library and new buildings at Clare College, Cambridge, and carried out restoration work at Chester Cathedral and elsewhere. (1880–.)

SCOTT, Sir Harold Richard (knight). Commissioner, Metropolitan Police, London. After leaving Cambridge entered the Civil Service. Was Permanent Secretary to the Ministry of Aircraft Production, 1943. Has held secretarial posts at Ministry of Labour and at the Ministry of Home Security. (1887–.)

SCOTT, Capt. Robert Falcon. Antarctic explorer. Commanded *Discovery*, National Antarctic Expedition, 1901. Discovered and named Ross Island and King Edward VII Land. In 1910 commanded the British Antarctic Expedition and reached the South Pole, but was forestalled by Amundsen. Scott's body found, 1912. (1868–1912.)

SCULLIN, Rt. Hon. James H. Australian politician. A journalist by profession, he became M.P. in 1910. Leader of Federal Labour Party, 1928–35. Prime Minister of Australia, 1929–31. Resigned, 1935. (1876–.)

SEGRAVE, Major Sir Henry (knight). British racing motorist. Served in the First World War until wounded, then took up motor racing, 1918. Broke world record at 231 m.p.h. Was killed on Lake Windermere after breaking world's motor-boat record. (1896–1930.)

SELBORNE, Earl of; Roundell Cecil Palmer. Administrator and politician. Conservative M.P., 1910–40. Held various Government posts (as Viscount Wolmer), including Postmaster-General, 1924–9. After going to the Lords he became Minister of Economic Warfare, 1942–5. (1887–.)

SHACKLETON, Sir Ernest Henry (knight). Explorer. Commanded British Antarctic Expeditions, 1907 and 1914. Director of Equipment and Transport, Mobile Forces, North Russia Winter Campaign, 1918–9. Commander, the *Quest* Antarctic Expedition, 1921. After catching influenza, died of heart failure. Author of *The Heart of the Antarctic*. (1874–1922.)

Sir Ernest Shackleton.

SHANKS, Edward R. B. Author, poet and critic. Served in First World War. First winner, Hawthornden prize for imaginative literature, 1919. Lecturer in poetry, Liverpool University, 1926. Author of *The Dogs of War*, *The Universal War and the Universal State*, and other books. (1892–.)

SHAW, George Bernard. Irish playwright and author. Son of an Irish civil servant, "G.B.S." was born in Dublin, began in a land agent's office and when twenty decided, in his own words, to "plunge into London." Began reviewing books for the *Pall Mall Gazette*, next became art critic for the *World*, and later dramatic critic for the *Saturday Review*. Plays include *Arms and the Man*, *Caesar and Cleopatra*, *Pygmalion*, *Saint Joan*. Awarded Nobel Prize for literature, 1925. Was Socialist, vegetarian, and teetotaller. (1856–1950.)

Bernard Shaw.

SHAWCROSS, Rt. Hon. Sir Hartley (knight). Labour M.P., Attorney-General 1945–51, Appointed President of Board of Trade, 1951. Barrister, 1925, he lectured at Liverpool University. As chief prosecutor for the United Kingdom took a prominent part in the Nuremberg trial of German major war-criminals. (1902–.)

SHEPPARD, Very Rev. H. Richard. Canon Residentiary. Before becoming Precentor, St. Paul's Cathedral, London, he did valuable work as Vicar, St. Martin-in-the-Fields, 1914–27. Dean of Canterbury, 1929–31. Author of *The Impatience of a Parson*, *Sheppard's Pie*. (1880–1937.)

SHINWELL, Rt. Hon. Emanuel. Labour M.P. and Minister of Defence. Began in his father's tailoring shop, then changed to clerk in the Glasgow office of the Sailors' and Firemen's Union, and became interested in trade unionism. As Minister of Fuel and Power introduced the coal industry nationalization bill, made law in May, 1946. Was Secretary for War, 1947–50. (1884–.)

SIBELIUS, Jean Julius. Finnish composer. Comes of a peasant stock, and of a musical family. Was intended for the law but chose a musical career instead. Professor of the Violin, Helsingfors Conservatoire, 1893. Awarded Government pension for his services. Has visited Great Britain and U.S.A. (1865–.)

SIMON, Rt. Hon. Viscount; John Simon. Liberal statesman. Called to the Bar in 1898, he became Solicitor-General in 1910 and later Attorney-General. Among other posts has been Home Secretary, Foreign Secretary and Lord Chancellor, 1940–5. (1873–.)

SINCLAIR, Rt. Hon. Sir Archibald (baronet). Personal Military Secretary to the Secretary of State for War, 1919–21; Liberal M.P., 1922–45; Secretary of State for Scotland, 1931–2; Secretary for Air, 1940–5, and Leader, Parliamentary Liberal Party, 1935–45 (1890–.)

SINCLAIR, Upton. American author. Caused a sensation in 1906 when he exposed in his book, *The Jungle*, the conditions in the U.S. canning industry. Continued to expose other industrial evils in later books, among them being *Oil*, *Mountain City*, *King Midas*, *Bill Porter*. (1878–.)

SITWELL, Edith. Poetess. She made a name with her book *The Mother and other Poems*, 1915, followed by an anthology of poems each year until 1921. She gave poetry recitals to a musical accompaniment. Later works include *Green Song*, *A Song of the Cold*, and *Fanfare for Elizabeth*. (1887–.)

SLIM, Field-Marshal Sir William (knight). Chief of Imperial General Staff since 1948. Commandant, Defence College, 1946–7. Deputy Chairman Railway Executive, 1948. Fought in France, Belgium, Gallipoli and Mesopotamia during the First World War. Subsequent posts include Instructor, Staff College, Camberley. In Second World War was C.-in-C., Allied Land Forces, South-East Asia. (1891–.)

SMITH, Rt. Hon. Sir Ben (knight). Chairman West Midlands Divisional Coal Board since 1946. Organizer of Transport and

General Workers' Union. Labour Whip, 1925. Was Labour M.P., 1923–31 and 1935–46; Parliamentary Secretary, Ministry of Aircraft Production, 1942; British Resident (for supply), Washington, 1943–5, and Minister of Food, 1945–6. (1879–.)

SMUTS, Field-Marshal Rt. Hon. Jan Christiaan. Prime Minister, Minister of External Affairs and Defence, South Africa, 1939–48. Born in South Africa, and of Boer descent, he fought the British in the Boer War, but then became one of Britain's most loyal supporters. In the First World War put down an anti-British rebellion in South Africa in addition to giving other valuable help. Was first Prime Minister, 1919–24. In Second World War was present at conferences in London and in the Middle East. Helped to found the League of Nations. (1870–1950.)

Field-Marshal Smuts.

SMYTH, Dame Ethel M. Composer. Born in London. Studied in Leipzig and later attracted attention in London with her composition *Mass In D.* Her operas include *Fantasio*, *Der Wald*; other works, *The Wreckers*, *The Boatswain's Mate.* Also wrote a "battle hymn" for suffragettes. (1858–1944.)

SNOWDEN, Rt. Hon. Viscount; Philip Snowden. Politician. Entered the civil service, 1886; retired, 1893. Became journalist and lecturer. After entering Parliament as Labour, he was Chancellor of the Exchequer, 1924 and 1929–31. Was a virile personality in the House of Commons. (1864–1937).

SOLOMON. Pianist. His first public appearance at the piano was made at Queen's Hall, London, 1910, when eight years of age. Subsequently studied on the Continent and reappeared at Wigmore Hall, 1921. After that toured the British Isles, U.S.A., France, Germany, Holland, Italy, Australia, and New Zealand. (1902–.)

SOMERVELL, Rt. Hon. Sir Donald (knight). Served in First World War. Made K.C., 1929, and elected Conservative M.P., 1931. Afterwards Solicitor-General, 1933–6, then Attorney-General. Lord Justice of Appeal since 1946. Was Home Secretary for a few months in 1945. (1889–.)

SOMERVILLE, Admiral of the Fleet Sir James Fownes (knight). Began his naval career in 1898. Served in First World War, C.-in-C., East Indies, 1938–9. Was on the retired list, but put on special service the same year. Conducted Madagascar and Andaman Islands campaigns. C.-in-C., Eastern Fleet, 1942–4. (1882–1949.)

SOSKICE, Rt. Hon. Sir Frank (knight). Solicitor-General 1945–51. Attorney-General, 1951. Called to the Bar, 1926; has appeared mainly in commercial cases. M.P. (Labour) since 1945 except for short interval in 1950. (1902–.)

SOULBURY, Rt. Hon. Lord (baron); **Herwald Ramsbotham.** Chairman, Assistance Board, 1941–8. Barrister-at-law, 1911. Served in First World War, and in 1929 became Conservative M.P. After being Parliamentary Secretary, Board of Education, and later Agriculture, he was appointed Minister of Pensions in 1936, and was President Board of Education, 1940–1. (1887–.)

SOUTHWOOD, Viscount; Julius S. Elias. Newspaper proprietor and company director. From being a newspaper boy, became chairman and managing director, Odhams Press Ltd., and associated companies, including *Daily Herald* (1929) Ltd., chairman Illustrated Newspapers Ltd., chairman Hospital for Sick Children and Penny-a-week Red Cross Fund. A generous benefactor to charities. (1881–1946.)

SPAHLINGER, Henry. Director, Bacteria-Therapeutic Institute, Geneva. Introduced bovine anti-tuberculous vaccine. Now devotes his researches to raising vitality and defence against chronic disease. Has written on tuberculosis and tetanus. (1882–.)

SPENDER, John Alfred. Journalist. Joined *Pall Mall Gazette*, 1892, and four years later, as editor, *Westminster Gazette.* Was a member of Lord Milner's Special Mission to Egypt, 1919–20. Visited India in 1926 and wrote his *Reminiscences* and, later, *Life of Sir Henry Campbell-Bannerman.* (1862–1942.)

SPILSBURY, Sir Bernard (knight). British pathologist, crime diagnostician, and authority on forensic medicine. He took his medical degree in 1905 and lectured at St. Bartholomew's and other London hospitals. Pathologist to the Home Office for twenty-five years, he was called in by Scotland Yard in nearly every important case of suspected murder by poisoning. His expert evidence frequently proved a decisive factor. (1878–1947.)

SQUIRE, Sir John C. (knight). Journalist. Was literary editor, *New Statesman*, 1913; acting editor, 1917–8; editor, *London Mercury*, 1919–34. Contested Cambridge University, 1918; Brentford and Chiswick, 1924. Governor Old Vic, 1922–6. Chairman English Association, 1926–9. Author of *Outside Eden*, *Reflections and Memories*, *Water Music* and many other works. (1884–.)

STACPOOLE, H. de Vere. Author. Practised for some time as a doctor. Travelled widely and took part in deep-sea expeditions. First literary success, *Fanny Lambert*. Became famous through his novel, *Blue Lagoon.* Author of *An American at Oxford*, *Men and Mice*, *Story of My Village.* (1865–1951.)

Generalissimo Stalin.

STALIN, Generalissimo Joseph Vissarionovich. President, Soviet Council of Ministers; real Dictator of U.S.S.R.; State Defence Committee; member Supreme Soviet. Arrested for political activity on many occasions. Exiled near

Arctic Circle, 1913–7. Joined Lenin in Revolution, 1917. Secretary Communist Party, 1924–41. Attended International Conferences during Second World War. (1879–.)

STETTINIUS, Edward R. (Jnr.). American Secretary of State, 1944–5. Was Vice-President General Motors Corporation, 1931. Later became a member President's Advisory Committee, Council of National Defence, 1940. Under-Secretary of State, 1943–4. (1900–1949.)

STOKOWSKI, Leopold. Conductor, N.B.C. Orchestra, Radio City, New York. Among other orchestras he has conducted are the Cincinnati, Philadelphia, San Francisco, and Hollywood orchestras. Appeared with Deanna Durbin in film *A Hundred Men and a Girl.* Has made symphonic transcriptions of Bach's works. (1887–.)

STRABOLGI, Lord (baron); **Joseph Montague Kenworthy.** Politician. Holder of an ancient English title which after falling into abeyance was revived in 1916. Began naval career 1902, and in politics has been Liberal, then Labour. Books include *Singapore and After*, *Sea Power in the Second World War*, *Conquest of Italy*. (1886–.)

STRACHEY, Rt. Hon. John. Labour M.P. and Minister for War, 1950; Minister of Food, 1946–50. In 1931 broke away from the Labour Party but returned and became Under-Secretary for Air, 1945–6. Introduced bread rationing in July, 1946. Author of several books on politics. (1901–.)

STRAUSS, Richard. German composer. Was Director Vienna State Opera, 1919–24. Compositions include *Der Rosenkavalier*, *The Woman Without a Shadow*, *Schlagobers Ballet*, *Intermezzo*, *Arabella*, *Friedenstag*, *Die Schweigsame Frau*, *Daphne*. (1864–1949.)

STRAVINSKY, Igor. Russian composer, whose work has done much to develop modern music. Diaghileff commissioned him to compose the ballet music for *The Fire Bird*, 1910. Other works include *Petrouchka*, *Oedipus Rex*, *Persephone*, *Jeu de Cartes*. (1882–.)

SUGGIA, Guilhermina. Portuguese violoncellist. Studied at Leipzig. Made her début at Gewandhaus Concerts, Leipzig. Has toured in principal European countries. Augustus John painted a striking portrait of this musician. (1888–1950.)

SUMMERSKILL, Edith (Mrs. Jeffrey Samuel). Minister of National Insurance since 1950; Parliamentary Secretary to the Ministry of Food, 1945–50. Labour M.P. since 1945. Qualified as a doctor. (1901–.)

SUTCLIFFE, Herbert W. Yorkshire and England cricketer. With J. B. Hobbs, he made eleven century partnerships. With P. Holmes created a new record of 555 for first wicket versus Essex, 1932. He made his hundredth century for Yorkshire, 1937, and his fifty-thousandth run, 1939. (1894–.)

SWAFFER, Hannen. Journalist. Came to Fleet Street from the provinces when the great popular newspapers were coming into being. Began as reporter on *Daily Mail*, later on *Daily Mirror*, *Daily Sketch*, *Daily Express* and, from 1931, *Daily Herald*. Former editor *Weekly Dispatch*. (1879–.)

SWINNERTON, Frank A. Novelist and critic. Notable amongst his novels is *The Merry Heart*, which was followed by books on George Gissing and Robert Louis Stevenson. Later works include *The Fortunate Lady*, *Thankless Child*, *A Woman in Sunshine*, *English Maiden*. (1884–.)

SWINTON, Maj.-Gen. Sir Ernest (knight). Chichele Professor of Military History, Oxford University, 1925–39. Served in South African and first World War. Pioneer in introduction of tanks, 1916, and raised the heavy section, Machine Gun Corps. Later was appointed Controller of Information, Department of Civil Aviation. (1868–.)

SYKES, Maj.-Gen. Rt. Hon. Sir Frederick (knight). Administrator. Served in the South African War and also in the Royal Flying Corps in First World War. His knowledge of such Eastern countries as Persia, Baluchistan, and Turkey, led to his services being used in those countries. In 1922 became Conservative M.P. (1877–.)

SZIGETI, Joseph. Hungarian violinist. Made his début on the Continent at age of thirteen. Stayed in England for seven years, touring with Busoni, McCormack, and Melba. Later toured United States, the Far East, Australia, and New Zealand. Has transcribed many works. (1892–.)

TANNER, Jack. Trade-union leader. Member Economic Planning Board, 1947. At thirteen sailed before the mast to China. Later in engineering trade. Served on committees and in 1939 was elected President Amalgamated Engineering Union. Afterwards President, British Section, International Metal Workers' Federation. (1889–.)

TAUBER, Richard. Tenor and conductor. Born in Austria, he made his début as a singer at Dresden. Later became naturalized British subject. Appeared in many operas on the Continent and in England. Also appeared in the films *Blossom Time*, *Land Without Music*, *Paganini*. (1893–1948.)

TAWNEY, Prof. Richard H. President Workers' Educational Association since 1928. Chancellor, British Embassy, Washington, 1942. Professor of Economic History, London University, 1931–49. Author of works on economics including *Religion and the Rise of Capitalism*, *Equality*, and *Land and Labour in China*. (1880–.)

TEARLE, Godfrey. Actor. Born in New York. Made English début, 1893. He acted in *White Cargo*, *The Acquittal*, *Late Night Final* and Shakespearean rôles. He appeared in the films *The Shadow Between*, *These Charming People*. Was the first President British Actors' Equity Association. (1884–.)

Lord Tedder.

TEDDER, Marshal of the R.A.F. Lord (baron); **Arthur William Tedder.** Chief of Air Staff, 1946–9. During First World War was transferred from the infantry to the Royal Flying Corps. Early in Second World War commanded R.A.F.,

Middle East; in January, 1943, became Deputy Chief, British Air Staff; later Deputy Supreme Commander to Gen. Eisenhower for the invasion of Europe. (1890–.)

TEMPLE, Most Rev. and Rt. Hon. William. Former Archbishop of Canterbury. Was Headmaster of Repton School and afterwards Rector, St. James's, Piccadilly. From Canon of Westminster in 1919, became Bishop of Manchester, 1921, then Archbishop of York. Afterwards transferred to Canterbury. Was editor of *The Challenge*. (1881–1944.)

TEMPLEWOOD, Viscount; Samuel John Hoare. Began his Parliamentary career as Conservative in 1900 and in 1922 became Secretary of State for Air and later for India. As Foreign Secretary came in for criticism over his attitude towards the Abyssinian War started by Italy under Mussolini, 1935. Later Ambassador to Spain, 1940–4. (1880–.)

TERRY, Dame Ellen (Mrs. James Carew). Actress. Was eight years old when she first appeared on the stage in Charles Kean's revival of *The Winter's Tale*. Later, in *The Taming of the Shrew*, began to attract attention by her acting. Joined Bancroft, 1875, and became leading lady at Lyceum Theatre. (1848–1928.)

TERRY, Fred. Actor. Brother of Ellen Terry, his acting career began at the Haymarket in 1880. Visited U.S.A., 1885, then confined his stage appearances to London in Shakespearean and other leading rôles. Two of his successes were *Sweet Nell of Old Drury* and *The Scarlet Pimpernel*. (1863–1933.)

TERTIS, Lionel. Leading viola player. Played in the principal British and U.S.A. orchestras in 1923–4. Has also been viola player in quartettes, is a zealous propagandist for his instrument and has arranged many compositions for the viola. (1876–.)

THOMAS, Sir Miles (knight). Chairman B.O.A.C. Formerly with Morris Motors, Ltd. Served in First World War as aerial fighting instructor at Heliopolis, Egypt. In Second World War concerned with tank development. Author of *Defence of Mobile Columns against Dive-bombing*, 1941. (1897–.)

THOMAS, Sir T. Shenton (knight). Administrator. Was Assistant Chief Secretary, Uganda, 1918; Deputy Chief Secretary, Nigeria, 1921, and Colonial Secretary, Gold Coast Colony, 1927. Afterwards Governor, Nyasaland Protectorate and, later, Gold Coast, Straits Settlements, and High Commissioner, Malay States, 1934–42. (1879–.)

THORNDIKE, Dame Sybil. Actress. A badly sprained wrist, due to too much piano practice, led her to give up her ambition to be a concert pianist and to become an actress. Has acted in Shakespearean plays in Britain and America. Also many other rôles. (1882–.)

Dame Sybil Thorndike.

THORNE, Will. Politician. Worked at a hairdresser's at age of six. A founder of National Union of General and Municipal Workers, 1889, and was its General Secretary, 1889–1934. In the meantime had entered Parliament as Labour M.P. Autobiography, *My Life's Battles*. (1857–1946.)

TILDEN, William T. Lawn-tennis player. Editor *Racquet Magazine*. Was a journalist, later joining film industry. Has been world tennis champion three times, seven times U.S.A. champion and ten years played in Davis Cup matches. Author of *Art of Lawn Tennis* and several other books. (1893–.)

TILLETT, Benjamin. Early in his career went to sea, and later became interested in trade unionism. As Secretary Dock Workers' Union, organized Dock Strike, 1889. Afterwards Secretary Transport and General Workers' Union. Labour M.P. from 1911. Chairman General Council T.U.C., 1928–9. (1860–1943.)

"TILLEY, Vesta" (Lady de Frece). Actress and famous male impersonator. Stage début at age of four at Nottingham. Made a great reputation as impersonator and became, too, a popular vaudeville artist. Retired in 1920. Author of *Recollections of Vesta Tilley*. (1864–.)

TIMOSHENKO, Marshal Semyon Konstantinovich. Member Supreme Soviet, U.S.S.R., and Hero of the Soviet Union, 1940. Served in Tsarist Army, 1915, and took part in the Civil War, 1918–21. Appointed People's Commissar of Defence, 1940–1. Marshal of the Soviet Union, 1940. (1895–.)

TITO, Marshal Josip (Josip Broz). Croatborn Prime Minister, and Minister for Defence, Yugoslavia, since 1945. By trade a locksmith. Served in Austro-Hungarian Army in First World War. Took part in Communist activities. Served four years' imprisonment for conspiracy, 1930. Organized partisan forces in Second World War. (1892–.)

TIZARD, Sir Henry Thomas (knight). Before the First World War was acquiring a reputation as a promising young physicist. Assistant Controller of Experiments and Research, R.A.F., 1918–9. Chairman Aeronautical Research Committee, 1933–43. Chief Scientific Adviser, Ministry of Aircraft Production, 1941–3. President, British Association, 1948. (1885–.)

TOSCANINI, Arturo. Famous conductor. Studied at the Parma Conservatoire, Parma, Italy, where he was born. Has conducted at the Scala Opera House, Milan; Metropolitan Opera House, New York; at the Bayreuth and Salzburg Festivals, and in London. Has rigidly refused to respond to encores. (1867–.)

TOVEY, Admiral of the Fleet Lord (baron); **John C. Tovey.** In First World War was Lt.-Commander of the *Onslow*. In Second World War first commanded destroyers, Mediterranean Fleet. C.-in-C. Home Fleet, 1940–3, and of the Nore, 1943–6, having been promoted to Admiral, 1943. (1885–.)

TRACY, Spencer. American film actor. First stage appearance, 1922. Made film début, 1930, in *Up the River*. Has since been screened in *Dante's Inferno*, *Captains Courageous*, *Stanley and Livingstone*, *Dr. Jekyll and Mr. Hyde*, *Thirty Seconds Over Tokyo*, *Before the Sun Goes Down*, *Cass Timberlaine*. (1900–.)

TRAVERS, Benjamin. Dramatist and novelist. Served in the Royal Air Force in First and Second World Wars. His best-known plays include *A Cuckoo in the Nest, Rookery Nook, Stormy Weather, Foreign Affairs, Banana Ridge, Pot Luck, Dishonour Bright, Spotted Dick.* (1886–.)

TREE, Sir Herbert Beerbohm. Actor-manager. Stage début in 1877, and in 1887 took over the management of the Comedy Theatre, and later acquired the Haymarket and His Majesty's Theatres. Attracted attention in the comedy *The Private Secretary*. Specialized in Shakespeare's and Sheridan's plays. (1853–1917.)

TRENCHARD, Marshal of the R.A.F. Viscount; Hugh Montague Trenchard. Enlisted in Royal Scots Fusiliers, 1893, served in the Boer and First World Wars. Planned the Cadet College, Cranwell, and did much to improve efficiency of the R.A.F. Was Commissioner, Metropolitan Police, 1931–5. (1873–.)

TREVELYAN, George Macaulay (O.M.). English historian. Has written a number of histories of various periods particularly relating to England, and is noted for his entertaining style. First successes, however, dealt with Italy in Garibaldi's time. (1876–.)

TROTSKY, Leon (Leiba D. Bronstein). Russian revolutionary. Banished to Siberia, 1898, he escaped and came to England. Returned to Russia, 1905. Exiled to Tobolsk, but escaped. Went to France and later U.S.A., 1916. Chief organizer, Revolution, 1917. Commissar for Foreign Affairs under Lenin, but was banished by Stalin in 1929. Assassinated in Mexico. (1879–1940.)

TRUMAN, Harry S. President United States of America since 1945 (death of Roosevelt). Studied Law at Kansas City. Was farmer for thirty-three years. Elected Senator, 1934, opposing the New Deal. Defeated Henry Wallace at Democratic Convention, 1944, becoming Vice-President. Conferred with Mr. Churchill and Marshal Stalin, 1945. Defeated Thomas Dewey for President, 1948. (1884–.)

Harry S. Truman.

"TWAIN, Mark" (Samuel L. Clemens). American humorist. After being a printer, became a pilot on the Mississippi River and later reporter in California. Then tried journalism and mining in San Francisco. Visited England on holidays. Best-known books are *The Innocents Abroad, Adventures of Tom Sawyer.* (1835–1910.)

TWEEDSMUIR, Lord (baron); **John Buchan.** Author of many popular novels. Became Governor-General of Canada, 1935–40. Private Secretary to Lord Milner, 1901–3, and Director of Information, 1917–8. Entered Parliament as Conservative, 1927. Books include *The Thirty-nine Steps, The Three Hostages, Greenmantle.* (1875–1940.)

TYRWHITT, Admiral of the Fleet Sir Reginald (baronet). Served in First World War, in which he commanded the destroyer flotillas in the battles of Heligoland Bight and Dogger Bank. C.-in-C., China Station, 1927–9. C.-in-C., Nore, 1930-3. Admiral of the Fleet, 1934. (1870–.)

ULLSWATER, Viscount; James William Lowther. Speaker of House of Commons (as Sir James Lowther), 1905–21. Called to the Bar, 1879, and in 1883 first entered Parliament as Unionist. Under-Secretary for Foreign Affairs, 1891. He presided at several Commissions and Committees and represented Great Britain at a number of International conferences. Author of *A Speaker's Commentaries.* (1855–1949.)

VACHELL, Horace Annesley. Novelist and former President Dickens Fellowship. Enlisted in Army, 1883. A prolific author, he has written many novels, including *The Hill, Quinney's, Gift from God, The Wheel Stood Still, Hilary Trent*, and the plays *The Case of Lady Camber, Fishpingle, Humpty Dumpty.* (1861–.)

VANBRUGH, Dame Irene (Mrs. Dion Boucicault). Actress. President Royal Academy of Dramatic Art, London. Acted with Toole, 1889, Tree, 1892, Alexander, 1893, Bourchier, 1895. Her plays include *Mr. Pim Passes By, Seven Women, Fit for Heroes, King Maker*, and many others. (1872–1949.)

VANBRUGH, Violet (Mrs. Arthur Bourchier). Actress. Made her first success as Ann Boleyn in *Henry VIII*, 1891, subsequently appearing in many notable Shakespearean and other productions. (1867–1942.)

VANSITTART, Lord (baron); **Robert Gilbert Vansittart.** Chief Diplomatic Adviser to the Foreign Secretary, 1938–41. Served under Foreign Office in Paris, Teheran, Cairo, Stockholm. Has held parliamentary secretarial posts in London, and is noted for his trenchant writings on German aggressiveness through the centuries. (1881–.)

VAUGHAN WILLIAMS, Ralph (O.M.). Composer. Travelled collecting folk tunes. Served in First World War and afterwards became Professor of Composition, Royal College of Music; then conductor of Bach Choir. Compositions include *The Poisoned Kiss, Dona Nobis Pacem, Five Variants on Dives and Lazarus*, and several symphonies. (1872–.)

VIAN, Admiral Sir Philip. Appointed Commander-in-Chief, Home Fleet, 1950. Fifth Sea Lord, 1946–9. Became famous by leading the attack on the *Altmark* in Second World War. Took part in the Normandy invasion, 1944. (1894–.)

VOROSHILOV, Marshal Kliment Yefremovich. Marshal of Soviet Union since 1935, and Vice-Chairman of the Council of People's Commissars. Member of State Defence Committee and of Supreme Soviet since 1940. Was engaged in underground political work, 1915–7, and People's Commissar for Home Affairs, Ukraine, 1919. (1881–.)

WAKEFIELD, Viscount; Charles Cheers Wakefield. Governing director of the firm bearing his name. Was Lord Mayor of

London, 1915–6. Took keen interest in aviation, financing Mollison's flight to Cape Town and Segrave's racing activities. Purchased and endowed Talbot House (Toc H). (1859–1941.)

WAKEHURST, Lord (baron); **John de Vere Loder.** Governor, New South Wales, 1937–46. After service in the First World War, entered the Foreign Office, 1919, as a clerk. In 1924 was elected to Parliament as Conservative. Author of *Our Second Choice, Preparation for Peace*, and other books. (1895–.)

WALBROOK, Anton (Adolph W. Wohlbruck). Actor. Son of a famous clown. Made his stage début, 1920, and since then has played over two hundred parts. First film appearance in 1931, his films including *The Student of Prague, Victoria the Great, Sixty Glorious Years.* (1900–.)

WALKDEN, Lord (baron); **Alexander George Walkden.** Began as a railway clerk and in 1906 became General Secretary Railway Clerks' Association. Member General Council, T.U.C., 1921–36, becoming chairman in 1932. Entered Parliament as Labour in 1929 and continued to show his interest in railway matters. (1873–1951.)

WALLACE, Edgar. Novelist, journalist. Though born of unknown parents, and poorly educated, he became the most prolific writer of his day. After free-lancing, he served in South Africa as war correspondent. Following return to London, became reporter, then writer of feature articles, racing tips, short stories, detective novels and plays. Works include *The Four Just Men, Sanders of the River, The Fellowship of the Frog* (novels): *The Squeaker, On the Spot* (plays). (1875–1932.)

Edgar Wallace.

WALLACE, Henry A. Vice-President, U.S.A., 1941–5. Comes from Iowa of Scots-Irish stock. One-time editor of *Wallaces' Farmer* and then Secretary of Agriculture. Believer in plain diet, plain living and is a constant advocate for world peace. Defeated in Presidential election, 1948. (1888–.)

WALLS, Tom. Actor, racehorse-owner and trainer. Made stage début, 1905. Toured U.S.A. and Canada, 1906–7. Joint manager Shaftesbury Theatre, 1922, acting in *Tons of Money* (two years' run). Subsequently appeared in many stage comedies and also films. Won the Derby, 1932, and owned winners of many races. (1883–1949.)

WALPOLE, Sir Hugh (knight). Novelist. Was a schoolmaster. Served with Russian Red Cross in First World War and afterwards turned to writing. His novels include *The Prelude to Adventure, The Secret City* (Tait Black Prize), *The Cathedral* (dramatized, 1932), *The Herries Chronicle.* (1884–1941.)

WAND, Rt. Rev. John William Charles. Bishop of London since 1945, and formerly Bishop of Bath and Wells. During the First World War served as Chaplain to the Forces. Afterwards Chaplain Royal Air Force, and then University Lecturer in Church History. Archbishop of Brisbane, 1934–43. (1885–.)

WARNER, Sir Pelham F. (knight). Cricketer, editor *The Cricketer.* Temporary Deputy Secretary Marylebone Cricket Club, 1939–45. Played cricket all over the world. Visited Australia with English team, 1903, 1911. Played for Middlesex, 1894–1920, when after retiring became joint manager M.C.C. team, 1932–3. (1873–.)

WATSON-WATT, Sir Robert Alexander (knight). Inventor of Radar. Scientific Adviser on Telecommunications, Air Ministry, 1940–9. and in Ministries of Supply, Transport, and Civil Aviation, 1946–9. Was Director of Communications Department, Air Ministry, 1938–40. (1892–.)

WAVELL, Field-Marshal Viscount; Archibald Percival Wavell. Viceroy of India, 1943–7, he was descended from a military family and himself served in the South African and First and Second World Wars. Commanded troops, Palestine, 1937–8, and then became C.-in-C., Southern Command, until 1939. General Officer Commanding Middle East, 1940–1. Wrote autobiography, 1944. A.D.C. General to the King from 1941. (1883–1950.)

F.M. Lord Wavell.

WEATHERHEAD, Rev. Leslie D. Minister, City Temple, since 1936. In First World War was Army Chaplain in Kurdistan and Persia. Minister, Brunswick Methodist Church, Leeds, 1925–36. Lecturer in Psychology, Workers' Educational Association. Is a prolific author. (1893–.)

WEIR, Sir John. Physician-in-Ordinary to the King since 1937 and to Queen Mary since 1936, to the Prince of Wales, 1923–36, to late Queen of Norway, 1929–1938, to Duke and Duchess of York, 1936. Consulting Physician, London Homoeopathic and other hospitals. (1879–.)

WEIR, Rt. Hon. Viscount; William Douglas Weir. Scottish engineer. Served on the Air Board, 1917–8, and became Director-General Aeronautical Production and Minister of the Royal Air Board. Secretary of State and President of Air Council. Director-General of Explosives, Ministry of Supply, 1939, and Chairman of Tank Board, 1942. (1877–.)

WELLES, Sumner. U.S.A. Under-Secretary of State, 1937–43. From Harvard University entered the Foreign Service and from time to time held important posts at Tokyo, Cuba, and Honduras, and in 1940 reported on conditions in Europe. (1892–.)

WELLS, Herbert George. Author. Apprenticed to a chemist at age of thirteen, then became a draper. Attended Normal School of Science and became a demonstrator and lecturer in biology. Entered journalism in 1893. First successful novel was *The Time*

Machine, 1895. Author of *The Outline of History*, *War of the Worlds*, *The Invisible Man*, *Kipps*, *Mr. Britling Sees it Through* and many other works. (1866–1946.)

WEST, Rebecca (Mrs. H. M. Andrews). Author. When seventeen tried a stage career, but admits she was not a success and turned to writing. Has contributed to many British and U.S.A. newspapers. Author of *Henry James*, *D. H. Lawrence*, *The Harsh Voice*, *Ending in Earnest*, *St. Augustine*, *The Rake's Progress* (with Low), *Black Lamb and Grey Falcon*, *The Meaning of Treason*. (1892–.)

WESTMINSTER, Duke of; Hugh Richard Arthur Grosvenor. Major of the Cheshire Yeomanry, landowner. A.D.C. to Viscount Milner, and to Field-Marshal Earl Roberts in South African War. Served in First World War. Formerly Personal Assistant Controller of Mechanical Department, Ministry of Munitions. (1879–.)

WETHERED, Joyce (Lady Heathcoat-Amory). Golfer. Won English Ladies' Championship, 1920, 1921–4, and represented England in a number of international matches. She defeated Cecil Leitch, 1922, and was defeated, 1923, but won again in 1924, 1925. (1902–.)

WIGRAM, Lord (baron); **Clive Wigram.** Permanent Lord-in-Waiting to the King. Was Keeper of His Majesty's Privy Purse during the reign of King George V and also his private secretary. Before that was A.D.C. to the Viceroy of India, 1895, 1899–1904. (1873–.)

WILKINS, Sir G. Hubert. Australian explorer. Photographic correspondent with Turkish troops, 1912–3. Served in First World War, and in 1919 was navigator England–Australia flight. Naturalist with Shackleton's expedition, 1921–2. Commander Arctic submarine expedition, 1931, about which he wrote a book. (1888–.)

WILKINSON, Rt. Hon. Ellen C. As Labour M.P., first elected in 1924, she became a forceful personality in the House of Commons. Held Cabinet rank as Minister of Education, 1945–7, and before that Parliamentary Secretary Ministry of Pensions, and then at Home Office. Twice went to Spain during the Civil War, 1937. (Died 1947.)

Ellen Wilkinson.

WILHELMINA, Queen of the Netherlands 1890–1948. For eight months preceding her accession her mother acted as Regent. Became Queen Regnant in 1898. In 1901 married the Duke of Mecklenburg-Schwerin. Exiled in England during Second World War, when her Government was transferred to London. In 1948, owing to ill-health, abdicated her throne in favour of her daughter, Princess Juliana. (1880–.)

WILLIAMS, Emlyn. Welsh actor and dramatist. Son of a Welsh sailor. Was prominent in the Oxford début of J. B. Fagan's play *And So to Bed*. Has written several plays, including *A Murder Has Been Arranged*, *Glamour*, *Night Must Fall*. (1905–.)

WILLIAMS, Rt. Hon. Tom. Minister of Agriculture since 1945. One of fourteen children of a Derbyshire miner, he too went into the pit, afterwards becoming a checkweigher. Elected Labour M.P., 1922, held secretarial posts, then became Parliamentary Secretary, Minister of Agriculture, 1940–45. (1888–.)

WILLKIE, Wendell. American politician. Was a presidential nominee, 1940, and Leader of the International wing of Republican Party. Wielded tremendous political influence and rallied Roosevelt's opponents in support of administration's foreign policy for the sake of wartime unity. (1892–1944.)

WILLS, Helen (Mrs. Aidan Roark). American lawn-tennis player. Was world's amateur woman tennis champion at the age of twenty-three. American lawn tennis champion, 1923–5, 1928–9, 1931, English champion, 1927–30, 1932–3, 1935–8, and French champion, 1927–30. (1905–.)

WILMOT, Rt. Hon. John. Minister of Supply, 1945-7. Gilbart Prizeman in Banking, King's College, London. Served in First World War. Became Labour M.P. in 1933, and in 1942 was appointed Parliamentary Private Secretary to the President of the Board of Trade; to Minister of Economic Warfare, 1940–2. (1895–.)

WILSON, Field-Marshal Lord (baron); **Henry Maitland Wilson.** A.D.C. to the King since 1941. Served in South African and the First and Second World Wars. In 1939 was C.-in-C., Egypt, afterwards serving in Greece and Palestine, and in 1942 in Persia and Iraq. C.-in-C., Middle East, 1943. In 1944 headed the British Staff Mission to U.S.A. (1881–.)

WILSON, T. Woodrow. American President of Scots-Irish descent, he attracted political attention first as a Congressman and in 1912 won the presidential election as a Democrat. Introduced his famous fourteen points, the basis of the First World War's Armistice terms. A founder of the League of Nations. (1856–1924.)

WINANT, John Gilbert. American Ambassador to Great Britain, 1941–6. Became New Hampshire Senator, 1921, and twice served as Governor, 1925–7 and 1931–5. Chairman, Social Security Board, 1935–7. Director International Labour Office, 1938–41. (1889–1947.)

WINDSOR, H.R.H. The Duke of. (Successively Prince of Wales and King Edward VIII.) Trained for the Navy. Invested Prince of Wales and created K.G., 1911. Served in First World War, then visited the Dominions and South America. Succeeded to throne, January, 1936; abdicated, December, 1936. Married Mrs. Wallis Warfield Simpson, 1937. Governor of Bahamas, 1940–5. (1894–.)

WINGATE, Maj.-Gen. Orde. Commissioned in Royal Artillery, 1923. Served in Sudan and in Palestine until 1939. He became a legendary figure as head of Military Mission, Abyssinia, 1940. Commanded famous Chindit Expedition against Japanese in Burma, 1943. Killed in air crash in Burma. (1903–44.)

WINNINGTON-INGRAM, Rt. Rev. and Rt. Hon. A. Foley. Bishop of London, 1901–39, he became noted for his untiring work in connexion with social welfare. Was first head of Oxford House, and rector, Bethnal Green, 1895, afterwards Canon of St. Paul's, and then Bishop of Stepney. Dean of Chapels Royal, 1901–39. (1858–1946.)

WINSTER, Lord (baron); **Reginald Thomas Fletcher.** Governor and C.-in-C. of Cyprus 1946–9. As M.P. was first Liberal and then in 1929 joined Labour Party. In 1945 became Minister of Civil Aviation. Author of *The Air Defences of Great Britain, The War on our Doorstep.* (1885–.)

WINTERTON, Earl; Edward Turnour. Unionist M.P. for Horsham since 1904. Controlling editor *The World* until 1910. After service in the First World War became Under-Secretary for India, 1922–4: 1924–9. Chancellor, Duchy of Lancaster, 1937–9, and Paymaster-General in the latter year. (1883–.)

WOLFIT, Donald. Actor-manager and producer. Entertained the troops in the First World War as a boy reciter, then at seventeen became a teacher. As an actor has specialized in Shakespearean rôles, appearing in the provinces, London, Canada, and U.S.A. (1902–.)

WOOD, Haydn. Composer and violinist. Studied the violin at the Royal College of Music and afterwards toured with Madame Albani for eight years, during that time visiting the Dominions. Composer of nearly two hundred songs, notably "Roses of Picardy." (1882–.)

WOOD, Sir Henry J. Conductor. Began his career at ten years of age as an organist, but made his professional début as a conductor in 1889. Founded London's Promenade Concerts. Conducted in America, Canada and elsewhere in the Dominions. (1869–1944.)

WOODERSON, Sydney. English athlete. Ran for Blackheath Harriers and held the Amateur Athletic Association 1 mile championship, 1935–9. Holder of British 880 yd., 1 mile (in 4 min. 6·4 sec., in 1938, which was then also a world record) and 3 miles (1946) records. Achieved his fastest mile (4 min. 4·4 sec.) in Sweden, 1945, after several years' war service. (1914–.)

Sydney Wooderson.

WOOLF, Virginia. Writer and critic. Married Leonard Woolf, author and publisher (1912), and with him controlled the Hogarth Press, which he founded in 1917. Works include *The Voyage Out* (1915), *A Room of One's Own* (1929), *The Waves* (1931). (1882–1941).

WOOLTON, Lord (baron); **Frederick James Marquis.** Once lived among the poor in his native Liverpool and helped in social welfare. At outbreak of Second World War was given charge of clothing the conscript army. When Minister of Food, 1940–3, displayed notable administrative ability. Minister of Reconstruction, 1943–5. Chairman, Conservative Party, since 1946. (1883–.)

WOOTTON, Barbara (Mrs. G. P Wright). Professor of Social Studies, London University, since 1948. Member Central Advisory Council for Education, England, 1947. Lecturer in Economics, Girton College, Cambridge, 1920–2, she was appointed Principal, Morley College, 1926. Director of Studies (Tutorial Classes), London University, 1927–44. Governor of B.B.C., 1950. (1897–.)

WRENCH, Sir Evelyn (knight). Founder of Overseas Club. Chairman *The Spectator*, since 1925. In 1904 joined Lord Northcliffe's staff, retiring 1912 to devote himself to imperial work. Founded English-speaking Union. Public Relations Officer with American troops in India, 1942. (1882–.)

WRIGHT, Sir Almroth. Pathologist. Studied at three continental universities. Was the originator of the system of anti-typhoid inoculation: therapeutic inoculation for bacterial infections. Served in First World War. Great authority on hay-fever and its treatment. Prominent opponent of women's suffrage. (1861–1947.)

WRIGHT, Orville. American pioneer aviator. With his brother, the late Wilbur Wright, was the first to fly a heavier-than-air machine, 1903. Invented control system. Awarded gold medal by French Academy of Sciences, 1909. Served in First World War. Director Wright Aeronautical Laboratory, Dayton. (1871–1948.)

WRIGHT, Lord (baron); **Robert Anderson Wright.** Lord of Appeal in Ordinary, 1932–5, and again 1937. His legal career began when called to the Bar in 1900. K.C., 1917, he became afterwards Judge of High Court (King's Bench) 1925–32. Master of the Rolls, 1935–7. (1869–.)

WYNDHAM, Sir Charles. Actor-manager, Criterion Theatre, London, 1876–1919. Intended for medical profession. He fought in the American Civil War. Made his début in U.S.A. with Wilkes Booth. London début, 1865. Acted in English and German. Built Wyndham's and New Theatres, 1899–1903. (1837–1919.)

YPRES, Field-Marshal the Earl of; John French. First entered Navy at fourteen. Served four years, then transferred to the Army. Commanded cavalry in South African War. Chief of Imperial General Staff, 1912–4. As C.-in-C. Expeditionary Forces, First World War, showed courage and ability in the battles of Mons and Ypres. (1852–1925.)

YSAYE, Eugene. Famous Belgian violinist. Won fame as solo violinist and conductor, 1879. Professor of Violin, Brussels Conservatoire, 1886. Three years later made London début. Conductor Covent Garden, 1907, and Cincinnati Orchestra, 1918–22. (1858–1931.)

ZETLAND, Marquess of; Lawrence John Dundas. Became Conservative M.P., 1907, and Governor of Bengal. 1917–22. Secretary of State for India, 1935–40; Burma, 1937 until 1940, and in that year narrowly escaped assassination when hit by bullets fired by an Indian. Has travelled extensively in the East. (1876–.)

GREAT NAMES THROUGH THE AGES

Brief biographical notes on some of the more famous men whose lives have helped to mould or enrich their own and succeeding ages

AESCHYLUS (525–456 B.C.). Father of the Greek tragic drama.

ALCIBIADES (450–404 B.C.). Athenian statesman and general; pupil and friend of Socrates.

ALEXANDER THE GREAT (356–323 B.C.). King of Macedonia. Conquered Persia, Syria, Phoenicia, Egypt. Founded Alexandria.

ALFRED THE GREAT (849–901). King of Wessex. Conquered Danes at Ethandune. Began *Anglo-Saxon Chronicle.*

ARCHIMEDES (287–212 B.C.). Greek mathematician who lived in Sicily. Inventor of Archimedean screw. Discovered laws of specific gravity.

ARISTOPHANES (d. *c.* 384 B.C.). Great comic dramatist of Athens; wrote fifty-four plays, eleven of which exist.

ARISTOTLE (384–322 B.C.). The most famous of Greek philosophers, disciple of Plato, and tutor of Alexander the Great.

AUGUSTINE, St. (d. *c.* 613). Missionary monk sent by Pope Gregory the Great in 597 to convert the English. First Archbishop of Canterbury.

BACH, Johann Sebastian (1685–1750). One of the greatest of German musical composers; master of contrapuntal style.

BACON, Francis (1561–1626). English philosopher and statesman; famous for *Novum Organum* and *Essays.*

BACON, Roger (*c.* 1214–*c.* 1294). English philosopher and scientist. Laid foundations of deductive scientific method.

BEETHOVEN, Ludwig Van (1770–1827). Great German composer. Broke away from earlier musical conventions and laid foundations of romantic movement.

BISMARCK, Otto, Prince Von (1815–98). Unified Germany under Prussia after defeating Austria and France; German Chancellor.

BLAKE, Robert (1599–1657). Great English admiral. Won victories over Spanish and Dutch fleets and Barbary pirates.

BOTTICELLI, Sandro (1444–1510). Italian painter; most famous for his "Spring" and "Birth of Venus."

BRAHMS, Johannes (1833–97). German musician; last of the great classical composers.

BUNYAN, John (1628–88). Author of *The Pilgrim's Progress*, which, owing to religious persecution, he wrote in Bedford Gaol.

BURNS, Robert (1759–96). Scotland's greatest poet. Wrote poems in native dialect.

BYRON, George Gordon, Lord (1788–1824). English poet. Died in Greek War of Independence at Missolonghi. Best works *Don Juan* and *Childe Harold.*

CAESAR, Julius (102–44 B.C.). Roman general and statesman. Campaigned in Gaul and Britain. Refused crown; was assassinated by Brutus and others.

CALVIN, John (1509–64). French religious reformer. Zealous Protestant, leading theologian of the Reformation.

CAXTON, William (*c.* 1422–91). English printer, who set up first English printing press.

CERVANTES, Miguel de (1547–1616). Spanish writer; world-famous as the author of *Don Quixote.*

CEZANNE, Paul (1839–1906). French painter, pioneer of Impressionism, known chiefly for landscapes.

CHARLEMAGNE (742–814). Frankish king who extended rule from Spain to the Elbe. Crowned Emperor at Rome in 800.

CHARLES I (1600–49). King of England whose quarrel with Parliament led to civil war and his own execution.

CHARLES V (1500–58). Holy Roman Emperor and King of Spain. Opponent of the Reformation.

CHAUCER, Geoffrey (*c.* 1340–1400). English poet, famed for his *Canterbury Tales.*

CHOPIN, Frederic (1810–49). Polish composer and pianist; excelled as a composer for the piano.

CICERO, Marcus Tullius (105–43 B.C.). Most famous of all Latin prose writers; also great orator and notable politician.

CLEOPATRA (69–30 B.C.). Famous Egyptian queen whose beauty fascinated Caesar and Antony.

CLIVE, Robert (1725–74). British soldier and administrator; laid foundation of British Empire in India. Victor of Plassey.

COLERIDGE, Samuel Taylor (1772–1834). British poet and literary critic; famous for his *Ancient Mariner.*

COLUMBUS, Christopher (1447–1506). Italian navigator; discovered America, 1492.

CONFUCIUS (*c.* 550–478 B.C.). Great Chinese moralist and philosopher. Spent many years in government service.

CONSTABLE, John (1776–1837). British painter; great interpreter of the English landscape.

CONSTANTINE THE GREAT (288–337). Roman Emperor: set up new capital at Byzantium (renamed Constantinople). Adopted Christianity.

COOK, James (1728–79). British navigator, who explored much of the Pacific. Claimed New Zealand and Australia for Britain.

CROMWELL, Oliver (1599–1658). Parliamentary leader during English Civil War. Later became Lord Protector.

DANTE ALIGHIERI (1265–1321). Greatest of all Italian poets. His masterpiece, *The Divine Comedy*, was inspired by his love for Beatrice.

DARWIN, Charles Robert (1809–82). British biologist. Put forward theory of evolution in *The Origin of Species*.

DAVY, Sir Humphry (1778–1829). British chemist, who invented the miner's safety lamp.

DEBUSSY, Claude Achille (1862–1918). French composer. Led revolt against nineteenth-century style.

DESCARTES, René (1596–1650). French philosopher and mathematician. Founded analytic or algebraic geometry.

DICKENS, Charles (1812–70). Most popular English novelist of the nineteenth century; his first great success was *Pickwick Papers*.

DONATELLO (1386–1466). Greatest of Italian Renaissance sculptors.

DRAKE, Sir Francis (*c.* 1545–96). English sailor, fought Spaniards and was vice-admiral against the Armada; was the first Englishman to sail round the world.

ELIZABETH, Queen (1533–1603). Queen of England whose reign was marked by a great increase in material prosperity, the growth of English sea-power, and the excellence of its literature.

EUCLID (third century B.C.). Greek mathematician of Alexandria. Systematized and developed knowledge of geometry.

EURIPIDES (*c.* 480–406 B.C.). Greek tragic poet; credited with over ninety plays.

FARADAY, Michael (1791–1867). Celebrated chemist and physicist; famed for his discoveries in the field of electricity.

FRANCIS OF ASSISI, St. (1182–1226). Founder of Franciscan order, devoted to life of poverty and self-denial.

FREDERICK THE GREAT (1712–86). King of Prussia. Extended Prussian power in Germany.

GAINSBOROUGH, Thomas (1727–88). English landscape and portrait painter.

GALILEO (1564–1642). Italian physicist and astronomer. Invented first practical telescope, use of pendulum in clocks. Paved way for Newton.

GAMA, Vasco Da (1469–1524). Portuguese navigator; rounded Cape of Good Hope and reached India.

GARIBALDI, Giuseppe (1807–82). Italian soldier and patriot who played leading part in liberation and unification of modern Italy.

GAUTAMA (*c.* 550 B.C.). Founder of Buddhism. Forsook wealth to become a beggar and teacher.

GIBBON, Edward (1737–94). Famous historian; wrote *The Decline and Fall of the Roman Empire*.

GOETHE, Johann Wolfgang Von (1749–1832). Great German poet, novelist and dramatist; famous for epic drama *Faust*.

GUTENBERG, Johannes (1400–68). German inventor of printing with movable type. Set up first printing press.

HALS, Frans (1589–1666). Dutch painter; best-known picture, "The Laughing Cavalier."

HANDEL, George Frederick (1685–1759). German musical composer of operas and oratorios, famous for his *Messiah*.

HANNIBAL (247–183 B.C.). Carthaginian general and military genius, first successful against Romans, finally defeated by Scipio at Zama.

HASTINGS, Warren (1732–1818). British administrator; first governor-general of India.

HAYDN, Joseph (1732–1809). Austrian composer. Played important part in development of the symphony.

HEGEL, Georg Wilhelm Friedrich (1770–1831). German philosopher whose theories influenced Karl Marx and Fascism.

HENRY IV (1553–1610). King of France. Consolidated France after religious wars and granted religious toleration.

HENRY VII (1457–1509). First Tudor King of England. Established order and prosperity after Wars of Roses.

HENRY VIII (1491–1547). King of England whose reign marked the Reformation in England. Became head of English Church.

HOLBEIN, Hans (1497–1543). German painter, worked largely in England under royal patronage.

HOMER (*c.* 850 B.C.). Greek poet, reputed author of the *Iliad* and the *Odyssey*.

HORACE (65–8 B.C.). Roman poet notable for odes, satires, and epistles.

HUGO, Victor (1802–85). French poet and novelist; a leading Romanticist, wrote *Les Misérables*.

IBSEN, Henrik (1828–1906). Norwegian dramatist, biting critic of established institutions; also wrote *Peer Gynt*.

IVAN THE GREAT (1440–1505). First Czar of Russia; he put an end to Tartar rule.

JEFFERSON, Thomas (1743–1826). American statesman and president, probable author of Declaration of Independence.

JENGHIZ KHAN (1162–1227). Mongol ruler who conquered Turkistan and most of China.

JOAN OF ARC (1412–31). French heroine who inspired French resistance to the English; burnt as a heretic at Rouen.

JOHNSON, Dr. Samuel (1709–84). Famous English writer and conversationalist; leader of London's literary circle of his day.

KANT, Immanuel (1724–1804). German philosopher. His work marked new era in philosophical thought.

KEATS, John (1795–1821). English romantic poet; *Hyperion, Endymion* among his best-known work.

KNOX, John (*c.* 1505–72). Scottish ecclesiastic; leader of Reformation in Scotland.

LEONARDO DA VINCI (1452–1519). Italian painter, sculptor and scientist; painted the "Mona Lisa." A genius years in advance of his time.

LINCOLN, Abraham (1809–65). American statesman; President 1861 and 1864; abolished slavery.

LINNAEUS (Karl Von Linnë) (1707–78). Swedish naturalist. Laid foundation of modern systematic botany.

LISTER, Joseph, Lord (1827–1912). English surgeon, founder of antiseptic surgery.

LIVINGSTONE, David (1813–73). Scottish missionary who explored central Africa.

LOUIS XIV (1638–1715). King of France; his reign was marked by the magnificence of the royal court and the greatness of its culture.

LOYOLA, Ignatius de, St. (1491-1556). Founder of the Society of Jesus (Jesuits).

LUTHER, Martin (1483–1546). German leader of the Reformation and founder of Protestant Church; translated the Bible into German.

MACHIAVELLI, Niccolo (1469–1527). Florentine statesman who influenced political thought through his book *The Prince.*

MAGELLAN, Ferdinand (1470–1521). Portuguese explorer; died on expedition which sailed round the world.

MARCUS AURELIUS (121–180). Roman Emperor, a follower of Stoic philosophy. Recorded his principles in *Meditations.*

MARLBOROUGH, John Churchill, Duke of (1650–1722). Brilliant English general renowned for victories of Blenheim, Ramillies, Oudenarde, Malplaquet.

MARX, Karl (1818–83). German philosopher whose teaching forms the basis of Communist theory.

MENDELSSOHN-BARTHOLDY, Felix (1809–47). German composer.

MICHELANGELO BUONARROTI (1475–1564). Italian painter, sculptor, architect and poet. Outstanding Renaissance figure.

MILTON, John (1608–74). Greatest of England's epic poets; sightless, he wrote *Paradise Lost, Paradise Regained.*

MOLIÈRE (1622–1673). French comic dramatist; ridiculed social pretensions.

MOZART, Wolfgang Amadeus (1756–91). Austrian composer famous chiefly for his symphonies and operas.

MUHAMMAD (or Mohammed or Mahomet) (*c.* 570–632). Founder of Mohammedan religion; recorded his teaching in the *Koran.*

NAPOLEON BONAPARTE (1769–1821). Military genius who became French emperor and master of Europe. Finally defeated at Waterloo.

NELSON, Horatio, Viscount (1758–1805). Greatest figure in British naval history. Won battles of the Nile, Copenhagen, and Trafalgar.

NEWTON, Sir Isaac (1642–1727). English mathematician and philosopher; discovered law of gravity; inventor of calculus.

NIGHTINGALE, Florence (1820–1910). Laid foundations of modern military hospital system and general standards of nursing.

NOBEL, Alfred Barnhard (1833–96). Swedish chemist; inventor of dynamite and gelignite. Instituted the Nobel Prizes.

OVID (43 B.C.–A.D. 18). Roman poet who retold classic myths in his *Metamorphoses.*

PALESTRINA (1526–94). Italian composer. Master of polyphonic music whose influence is still felt.

PASCAL, Blaise (1623–62). French Puritan philosopher, mathematician and writer.

PASTEUR, Louis (1822–95). French chemist and bacteriologist; famed for his researches in preventive medicine.

PERICLES (495–429 B.C.). Great Athenian statesman, general and orator.

PETER THE GREAT (1672–1725). Emperor of Russia who expanded, reformed and westernized his dominions.

PHIDIAS (d. 432 B.C.) Greatest sculptor of ancient Greece. Executed Parthenon frieze and supervised its building.

PITT, William (1759–1806). English statesman; Prime Minister for twenty years. Reformed national finances; opposed revolutionary France.

PLATO (427–347 B.C.). Greek philosopher; disciple of Socrates and tutor of Aristotle; renowned for his *Dialogues.*

POE, Edgar Allan (1809–49). American writer, master of the short story; his mystery tales unsurpassed.

POLO, Marco (1254–1324). Venetian traveller and explorer; journeyed to China, Burma, Southern India, and Persia.

PTOLEMY (second century A.D.). Egyptian astronomer and geographer, who held that the earth was fixed and that the heavenly bodies moved round it.

PYTHAGORAS (*c.* 582–500 B.C.). Greek philosopher, astronomer and mathematician.

RACINE, Jean (1639–99). French tragic dramatist; best-known plays include *Andromaque, Iphigénie, Phèdre.*

RAPHAEL, SANZIO (1483–1520). Italian painter and architect, painted frescoes for Vatican and St. Peter's.

REMBRANDT VAN RIJN (1606–69). Great Dutch painter noted for his light and shade effects. Painted mostly portraits.

REYNOLDS, Sir Joshua (1723–92). British portrait-painter; first president of the Royal Academy.

RICHELIEU, Cardinal (1585–1642). French statesman who raised his country to be the foremost in Europe.

ROBESPIERRE, Maximilien (1758–94). French revolutionist; leading figure in Reign of Terror, later guillotined.

RUBENS, Peter Paul (1577–1640). Flemish painter; famous for rich and glowing colour.

SCHUBERT, Franz (1797–1828). German composer, notable for his songs, symphonies.

SCHUMANN, Robert (1810–56). German composer; notable for his works for piano and the voice.

SCOTT, Sir Walter (1771–1832). Scottish poet and novelist. Well known are *The Lady of the Lake, Marmion* and the Waverley novels.

SHAKESPEARE, William (1564–1616). England's greatest poet and playwright. His thirty-seven plays include *Hamlet, Romeo and Juliet, Julius Caesar.*

SHELLEY, Percy Bysshe (1792–1822). English romantic poet; he combined great lyrical and intellectual powers.

SHERIDAN, Richard Brinsley (1751–1816). Author of the comedies *The School for Scandal* and *The Rivals.*

SIDNEY, Sir Philip (1554–86). Elizabethan scholar, poet and soldier; died fighting Spaniards in Holland.

SOCRATES (469–399 B.C.). Greek philosopher and soldier; the tutor of Plato, whose writings contain Socrates' teaching.

SOPHOCLES (495–406 B.C.). Greek tragic dramatist. Wrote about a hundred plays but only seven survive.

SPENSER, Edmund (1552–99). English soldier and poet; wrote *The Faerie Queene.*

STEPHENSON, George (1781–1848). British engineer; built the first successful locomotive and the first passenger railway.

STERNE, Laurence (1713–68). British humorist. Remembered for his witty *Tristram Shandy.*

STEVENSON, Robert Louis (1850–94). Scottish novelist and poet. Wrote *Treasure Island, Dr. Jekyll and Mr. Hyde, Kidnapped.*

STRAUSS, Johann (1825–99). Austrian composer famous for his waltzes and light operas.

SULLIVAN, Sir Arthur Seymour (1842–1900). British composer who collaborated with W. S. Gilbert in the Savoy operas.

TASMAN, Abel Janszoon (1602–59). Dutch navigator who discovered Tasmania and New Zealand.

TCHEKHOV, Anton Pavlovich (1860–1904). Russian writer and playwright; master of the short story.

TENNYSON, Alfred, Lord (1809–92). Great poet of Victorian era; Poet Laureate. Wrote *Idylls of the King.*

THACKERAY, William Makepeace (1811–63). British novelist and humorist; author of *Vanity Fair*, etc.

THUCYDIDES (*c.* 471–*c.* 399 B.C.). Greek historian who recorded events of Peloponnesian War.

TITIAN (1477–1576). Italian painter, greatest of Venetian school; credited with nearly a thousand works.

TOLSTOY, Leo Nikolaievich, Count (1828–1910). Russian novelist; wrote *War and Peace, Anna Karenina.*

TRAJAN (*c.* 53–117). Roman emperor who added Dacia (Rumania) and other eastern provinces to his empire.

TSCHAIKOVSKY, Peter Ilyich (1840–93). Russian composer of operas, ballets, etc.

TURNER, Joseph Mallord William (1775–1851). British painter noted for his imaginative landscapes.

TYNDALE, William (1490–1536). English translator of the Bible; strangled and burnt at the stake near Brussels for heresy.

VAN DYCK, Sir Anthony (1599–1641). Flemish painter who many times painted Charles I of England. Excelled in portraits.

VERMEER, Jan (1632–75). Dutch painter, noted particularly for his interiors.

VICTORIA, Queen (1819–1901). Her reign, which began in 1837, was marked by great expansion of Britain's imperial and industrial power.

VIRGIL (70–19 B.C.). Author of the *Aeneid*; greatest of all Latin epic poets.

VOLTAIRE, François Marie Arouet De (1694–1778). French philosopher and writer, whose writings paved way for the French Revolution.

WAGNER, Richard (1813–83). German operatic composer, whose innovations greatly influenced musical art. Composed several operas based on Nordic mythology.

WALPOLE, Sir Robert (1676–1745). British statesman; regarded as first Prime Minister and founder of cabinet system.

WALTON, Izaak (1593–1683). English angler and writer; wrote *The Compleat Angler.*

WASHINGTON, George (1732–99). American soldier and statesman; led colonists in American War of Independence and became first president.

WATT, James (1736–1819). British engineer; made and developed the first practical steam-engine.

WELLINGTON, Arthur Wellesley, Duke of (1769–1852). British soldier and statesman; fought in India, and in Spain and at Waterloo against Napoleon's armies.

WESLEY, John (1703–91). English divine, who founded the Methodist Movement.

WILLIAM THE CONQUEROR (1027–87). Duke of Normandy who defeated Saxon King Harold at Hastings and became King of England.

WOLSEY, Cardinal Thomas (*c.* 1471–1530). English statesman who fell from power through inability to obtain papal sanction for Henry VIII's divorce from Catherine of Aragon.

WORDSWORTH, William (1770–1850). Foremost of the "Lake Poets"; stressed the beauty of nature.

WREN, Sir Christopher (1632–1723). English architect; built St. Paul's Cathedral and many London churches.

WYCLIFFE, John (*c.* 1324–84). English reformer who translated the Latin Bible into English.

XENOPHON (*c.* 435–354 B.C.). Greek historian and scholar; commander of the Greek forces against Artaxerxes; campaign recorded in his *Anabasis.*

XERXES (*c.* 519–465 B.C.). Persian King; defeated Spartans at Thermopylae; himself defeated at Salamis.

ZOLA, Emile (1840–1902). French writer of realistic novels, e.g., *La Fortune des Rougons.*

ZOROASTER (*c.* fifth century B.C.). Persian religious teacher; was contemporary with Buddha.

DICTIONARY OF DATES

Important and interesting events in the world's history

B.C.

c. 3000 Beginning of written record of events in Egypt and Babylonia.
c. 2500 Old Kingdom in Egypt; pyramid age.
c. 2350 First Babylonian empire won by Sargon.
c. 2000 Middle Kingdom in Egypt.
c. 1750 Hammurabi, king of Babylon; his code of laws.
c. 1650 Cretan civilization at its height; palace at Knossos.
c. 1500 New Kingdom in Egypt.
c. 1190 Trojan War.
c. 1100 Tiglath-pileser I extended the power of Assyria.
Chow dynasty founded in China.
c. 1050 David, king of Israel.
933 Death of Solomon.
c. 800 Building of Carthage.
776 First Olympiad.
770 Invasion of Palestine by Assyrians.
753 Traditional date of foundation of Rome.
745 Assyrians conquered Babylonia.
721 Assyrians deported Israelites.
657 Byzantium founded by Greeks.
625 Fall of Nineveh to Medes and Chaldeans.
608 Battle of Megiddo; Jews defeated by Egyptians.
c. 600 Marseilles founded by Greek settlers.
c. 625 Birth of Gautama, founder of Buddhism.
586 Jerusalem taken by Nebuchadnezzar.
569 Nebuchadnezzar conquered Egypt.
c. 550 Birth of Confucius, Chinese philosopher.
538 Persians conquer Babylon.
510 Roman Republic established.
c. 496 Battle of Lake Regilius.
492 Darius of Persia invaded Greece.
490 Battle of Marathon; Greeks defeated Persians.
481 Xerxes of Persia invaded Greece.
480 Battles of Thermopylae and Salamis; Persians defeated by Greeks.
469 Pericles entered public life in Athens.
457 Return of Jews to Palestine.
440 The Parthenon at Athens begun.
431–404 Peloponnesian War between Athens and Sparta.
427 Plato born.
399 Persecution and death of Socrates.
390 Rome burnt by the Gauls.
384 Birth of Aristotle.
356 Birth of Alexander the Great.
336 Accession of Alexander the Great to throne of Macedonia.
333 Battle of Issus.
332 Alexander conquered Tyre and Egypt; foundation of Alexandria.

B.C.

331 Alexander defeated Persians at Arbela.
327–325 Alexander's India campaigns.
323 Death of Alexander at Babylon.
312 The Appian Way constructed.
264–241 First Punic War between Rome and Carthage.
260 First Roman fleet launched.
218–201 Second Punic War.
218 Hannibal crossed Alps, invaded Italy.
216 Romans defeated by Hannibal at Cannae.
214 Great Wall of China begun.
212 Death of Archimedes at siege of Syracuse.
207 First gold coinage at Rome.
202 Scipio the Elder defeated Hannibal at Zama.
149–146 Third Punic War.
146 Carthage destroyed by Scipio the Younger.
106 Births of Pompey and Cicero.
102 Birth of Julius Caesar.
58 Gallic wars began.
55 Caesar invaded Britain.
48 Pompey defeated at Pharsalia. Murder of Pompey in Egypt.
47 Caesar occupied Alexandria.
46 Caesar reformed calendar.
44 Caesar assassinated.
42 Battle of Philippi.
32 War between Octavian and Mark Antony.
31 Battle of Actium; Antony defeated by Octavian.
27 Roman Empire established; Octavian (Augustus) first emperor.
30 Deaths of Antony and Cleopatra.
c. 4 Birth of Christ.

A.D.

26–36 Pontius Pilate, governor of Judea.
29 The Crucifixion.
43 Invasion of Britain by Aulus Plautius.
47 London founded by Romans.
51 Caractacus captured and taken to Rome.
61 Boadicea led revolt against Romans.
68 Martyrdom of St. Peter and St. Paul. Death of Nero.
70 Fall of Jerusalem to Emperor Titus.
78 Agricola commanded in Britain.
79 Destruction of Pompeii.
84 Agricola defeated Picts and Scots.
c. 95 St. John the Evangelist banished to Patmos.

A.D.

c. 122 Hadrian's Wall begun.
208 Severus visited Britain.
Roman invasion of Caledonia.
Severus rebuilt Hadrian's Wall.
262 Temple of Ephesus destroyed by Goths.
305 St. Anthony established first monastery.
324 Christianity became official Roman religion.
330 Constantinople founded.
370 Saxons landed on coasts of Gaul.
378 Romans defeated by Goths near Constantinople.
385–404 St. Jerome translated Bible into Latin (the Vulgate).
395 St. Augustine made bishop of Hippo.
406 Vandals invaded Gaul.
410 Sack of Rome by Visigoths.
411–418 Roman legions withdrawn from Britain.
420 Death of St. Jerome.
439 Vandals took Carthage.
449 Hengist and Horsa (Saxons) landed in Britain.
455 Sack of Rome by Vandals.
457 Hengist established kingdom of Kent.
476 End of Western Roman Empire.
477 South Saxons landed in Britain.
495 West Saxons landed in Britain.
527 Justinian Code established.
539 Destruction of Milan by Goths.
540 St. Benedict issued his "rule."
551 Silkworms introduced into Europe.
553 Goths expelled from Italy by Justinian.
565 Ethelbert, king of Kent.
568–571 Lombards conquered Italy.
c. 570 Birth of Muhammad.
590 Gregory the Great, bishop of Rome.
593 Ethelfrith founds kingdom of Northumbria.
597 Christianity introduced to Britain by Augustine.
602 Augustine became first archbishop of Canterbury.
609 Muhammad preached at Mecca.
619 Tang Dynasty founded in China.
622 Muhammad's flight to Medina (the Hegira).
629 Muhammad re-entered Mecca.
632 Death of Muhammad at Medina.
The *Koran* compiled.
634 Moslems conquered Syria. Arab conquests began.
711 Moslems invaded Spain.
732 Charles Martel defeated Moslems at Poitiers.
774 Lombards overthrown by Charlemagne.
785 Haroun Al Raschid, caliph of Baghdad.
c. 787 Danes landed in England.
800 Charlemagne crowned Emperor in the West.
814 Death of Charlemagne.
828 Egbert became first king of England.
849 Alfred the Great born.
871 Alfred king of Wessex.
875 *Anglo-Saxon Chronicle* begun.

A.D.

878 Alfred defeated Danes at Ethandune.
1002 Massacre of the Danes in England.
1013 Sweyn (Denmark) became king of all England.
1017 Canute, king of England.
1027 Birth of William of Normandy (William the Conqueror).
1054 Great Schism between Roman and Greek Churches.
1066 Harold, king of England.
Harold's defeat at Hastings.
1073 Hildebrand became Pope.
1076 Jerusalem taken by the Turks.
1079 William the Conqueror planted New Forest.
1084 Normans sacked Rome.
1086 Domesday Book begun.
1087 William II, king of England.
1093 Anselm, archbishop of Canterbury.
1096–1099 First Crusade.
1099 Jerusalem captured by Crusaders.
1100 William Rufus killed in New Forest.
1118 Order of the Knights Templars founded.
1124 David I, king of Scotland.
1137 Birth of Saladin.
1138 Battle of the Standard; Scots defeated.
1141 Stephen taken prisoner at battle of Lincoln.
1147–1149 Second Crusade.
1162 Thomas Becket, Archbishop of Canterbury.
Jenghiz Khan, first Mongol emperor, born.
1165 William I, king of Scotland.
c. 1167 Oxford University founded.
1169 Invasion of Ireland by Strongbow.
1170 Murder of Becket.
1173 Saladin, Sultan of Egypt.
1174 Damascus taken by Saladin.
1182 Birth of St. Francis.
1187 Jerusalem captured by Saladin.
1189–1192 Third Crusade (Richard I).
1191 Acre captured by Crusaders.
1192 Richard imprisoned by Duke of Austria.
1193 Death of Saladin.
1194 Richard liberated; his return to England.
1199 John, king of England.
1202–1218 Fourth and fifth Crusades.
1203 Murder of Prince Arthur by King John.
1204 Crusaders captured Constantinople.
c. 1208 Cambridge University founded.
1210 Invasion of China by Jenghiz Khan.
c. 1214 Birth of Roger Bacon.
1215 Sealing of Magna Carta.
Jenghiz Khan captured Peking.
1221 Jenghiz Khan invaded Persia.
1227 Jenghiz Khan died.
1231 Inquisition established in Italy.
1241 Mongol invasion of Europe.
1249–1254 Sixth Crusade.
1254 Birth of Marco Polo.

A.D.
1261 Greeks recaptured Constantinople from Latins.
1264 Battle of Lewes; Henry III taken prisoner.
1265 First parliament of Simon de Montfort.
Gunpowder invented by Roger Bacon.
Dante born.
1269–1272 Seventh Crusade.
1280 Conquest of China by Mongols completed.
1282 Conquest of Wales by Edward I.
1284 Birth of first Prince of Wales at Caernarvon.
1291 Swiss Confederation founded.
1296 Invasion of Scotland by Edward I.
1297 Wallace's victory at Stirling.
1298 Wallace defeated at Falkirk by English.
1302 Battle of "the Spurs."
1306 Robert Bruce, king of Scotland.
1314 Battle of Bannockburn.
1329 Ottoman empire established.
1338–1452 Hundred Years War.
c. 1340 Chaucer born.
1345 Discovery of Canary Isles by Spain.
1346 Battle of Crécy; French defeated by English.
1347 Capture of Calais by Edward III.
1348–1349 The Black Death in England.
1356 Battle of Poitiers; French defeated by English.
1367 The Kremlin founded.
1368 Ming Dynasty founded in China.
1369–1380 Wycliffe's translation of the New Testament.
1381 The Peasant Revolt under Wat Tyler.
1388 Battle of Otterburn between Percies and Douglases.
1397 Denmark, Norway, and Sweden united.
1399 Order of Knights of the Bath instituted.
1402 Hotspur defeats Scots at Homildon Hill.
1403 Battle of Shrewsbury; Hotspur killed.
1411 St. Andrews University founded.
1414 John Huss burned at Prague for heresy.
1415 Capture of Harfleur and victory at Agincourt by Henry V.
1418 Henry the Navigator began explorations.
1428 Siege of Orleans by the English.
1429 Orleans captured by Joan of Arc.
1431 Joan of Arc burnt at Rouen.
1440 Eton College founded by Henry VI.
1447 Vatican library founded.
1450 Jack Cade's insurrection.
Printing with movable type invented by Gutenberg.
1452 Birth of Leonardo da Vinci.
1453 Capture of Constantinople by Turks.
1455–1485 Wars of the Roses.
1460 Battle of Northampton.
1466 Henry VI imprisoned in Tower.
1467 Birth of Erasmus.

A.D.
1469 Machiavelli born.
1471 Battles of Barnet and Tewkesbury.
Deaths of Warwick the Kingmaker and Henry VI.
1475 Birth of Michelangelo.
1476 Caxton set up printing press at Westminster.
1477 Birth of Titian.
1480 Russians threw off Mongol allegiance.
1483 Edward V murdered; Richard III succeeded.
Luther, Raphael born.
1485 Battle of Bosworth; end of Wars of Roses.
1488 Diaz rounded Cape of Good Hope.
1492 Columbus discovered the New World.
1497 Birth of Holbein.
Newfoundland discovered by Cabot.
1498 Vasco da Gama sailed round Cape to India.
1499 Turks captured Lepanto in Greece.
1500 Emperor Charles V born.
Brazil discovered.
1502 University of Wittenberg founded.
c. 1505 Birth of John Knox.
1506 Madagascar discovered.
1509 Henry VIII married Catherine of Aragon.
1512 Trinity House founded.
1513 War with Scotland; battle of Flodden.
Balboa first saw Pacific Ocean.
1516 More's *Utopia* published.
1517 Luther's *Theses* published.
1519–1521 Mexico conquered by Cortez.
1520 Martin Luther burned the Papal Bull.
Magellan entered Pacific.
1521 Magellan discovered the Philippines.
Henry VIII designated Defender of the Faith.
1525 Baber founded Mogul Empire in India.
1526 Tyndale's New Testament.
1529 Fall of Wolsey.
Suliman the Magnificent besieged Vienna.
1533 Cranmer, Archbishop of Canterbury.
1534 Luther's Bible completed.
Canada discovered.
Church of England established.
Society of Jesus (Jesuits) founded.
1535 Coverdale's English Bible.
1539 The Great Bible published.
Dissolution of monasteries in England.
1541 Mississippi discovered by De Soto.
1546 Death of Luther.
1547 Cervantes born.
1549 Book of Common Prayer first used.
1550 Beginning of Protestantism in England.
1552 Edmund Spenser born.
1554 Lady Jane Grey executed in the Tower.
Sir Philip Sidney born.
1556 Cranmer, Ridley, Latimer burnt.
Emperor Charles V abdicated.
1558 Loss of Calais by England.
Elizabeth, Queen of England.
1562 Hawkins began slave trade (Africa).
1563 Potato introduced into England from South America.

A.D.

1564 Shakespeare and Marlowe born.
1565 Marriage of Mary Stuart and Lord Darnley.
Drake's first voyage to West Indies.
1566 Suliman the Magnificent died.
Rizzio murdered.
1567 Revolt of Netherlands against Spain.
Murder of Darnley.
Mary Stuart married Bothwell.
Mary Stuart imprisoned.
1571 Lepanto; Don John of Austria defeated Turks.
1572 St. Bartholomew's Day massacre in France.
1573 Donne and Inigo Jones born.
1574 Ben Jonson born.
1576 Frobisher's first attempt to discover N.W. Passage.
1577 Rubens born.
1577–1580 Drake sails round the world.
1582 University of Edinburgh founded.
1584 Virginia discovered.
1585 Expedition of Drake against Spanish West Indies.
1586 Death of Sir Philip Sidney.
Trial of Mary Queen of Scots.
1587 Mary Queen of Scots beheaded.
Drake attacked shipping at Cadiz.
1588 The Spanish Armada destroyed.
1590 Battle of Ivry. Spenser's *Faerie Queen* and Sidney's *Arcadia* published.
1593 Izaak Walton born.
1597 Galileo invented thermometer.
Bacon's Essays published.
1598 Edict of Nantes granting religious toleration in France.
1599 Van Dyck, Oliver Cromwell and Blake born.
1600 East India Company chartered.
1602 *Hamlet* published.
1603 Elizabeth died; Union of England and Scotland; James VI of Scotland and I of England.
1604–1611 Authorized version of the Bible.
1605 Gunpowder Plot.
1606 *Don Quixote* published. Rembrandt born.
1607 First permanent English Settlement in America.
1608 Telescope invented.
Milton born.
1610 Henry IV of France assassinated.
Hudson Bay discovered.
1612 English factories established in India.
1614 Logarithms invented.
1616 Shakespeare and Cervantes died.
Manchus invaded China.
Circulation of blood discovered.
1618 Thirty Years War began.
1620 Pilgrim Fathers sailed to America.
1622 Birth of Molière.
1623 First folio Shakespeare's works published.
1624 Richelieu became chief minister of France.
1625 Charles I king.
1626 Death of Francis Bacon.
1628 Petition of Right.

A.D.

1632 Taj Mahal begun.
Gustavus Adolphus of Sweden killed at battle of Lützen.
1633 Galileo condemned by Inquisition.
Samuel Pepys born.
1635 French Academy founded.
1636 Hampden resists imposition of ship-money.
Harvard College, U.S., founded.
1637 Trial of John Hampden.
1640 The Short Parliament; the Long Parliament begun.
1641 Strafford tried and beheaded.
1642 Battle of Edgehill.
Tasmania discovered.
Newton born.
1643 Barometer invented.
1644 Battle of Marston Moor.
William Penn born.
End of Ming dynasty in China.
1645 Battle of Naseby.
George Fox began his ministry.
1648 Battle of Preston.
The "Rump" Parliament.
Pascal's experiment with atmospheric pressure.
Treaty of Westphalia, end of Thirty Years War.
1649 Charles I tried and executed.
England declared a Commonwealth.
Cromwell stamped out Irish rebellion.
1650 Battle of Dunbar.
Marlborough born.
1651 Battle of Worcester; Prince Charles escaped to Continent.
1653 Cromwell, Lord Protector.
Blake destroyed Dutch fleet.
Walton's *Compleat Angler* published.
1657 Cromwell refused crown.
1658 Cromwell died; Richard Cromwell succeeded as Protector.
1659 Richard Cromwell retired.
1660 Restoration of Charles II.
Royal Society founded.
1665 The Great Plague of London.
1666 The Great Fire of London.
1667 *Paradise Lost* published.
Swift born.
1668 Bombay granted to East India Company.
1670 Hudson's Bay Company formed.
1671 *Paradise Regained* and *Samson Agonistes* published.
1672 Addison born.
1674 Nieuw Amsterdam became British by treaty and was renamed New York.
1675 Building of new St. Paul's Cathedral begun.
Greenwich Observatory founded.
1676 Robert Walpole born.
1678 Popish plot invented by Titus Oates.
The Pilgrim's Progress published.
1679 Habeas Corpus Act.
1680 Penny Post established in London.
1681 William Penn founded Pennsylvania.
1683 The Great Frost.
Last Turkish attack on Vienna defeated.
1685 Revocation of Edict of Nantes.
Bach and Handel born.

A.D.
1688 William of Orange became king of England.
Alexander Pope born.
1689 Bill of Rights.
Peter the Great became Czar of Russia.
1690 Battle of the Boyne.
1692 Massacre of Glencoe.
1694 Voltaire born.
Bank of England founded.
1695 Censorship of the Press abolished in England.
1701 War of the Spanish Succession began.
Frederick I became king of Prussia.
1702 Queen Anne on British throne.
1703 John Wesley born.
1704 Battle of Blenheim; Gibraltar captured by British.
1706 Battle of Ramillies.
1707 Union of English and Scottish Parliaments.
1708 Battle of Oudenarde.
1709 Battle of Malplaquet.
Dr. Johnson born.
Piano invented.
1710 St. Paul's Cathedral completed.
1711 South Sea Company formed.
Marlborough deprived of all his offices.
1712 Rousseau born.
Frederick the Great of Prussia born.
1715 Jacobite rebellion; battles of Sheriffmuir and Preston.
1717 Horace Walpole born.
1719 *Robinson Crusoe* published.
1720 South Sea Bubble burst.
1724 Kant, German philosopher, born.
1725 Robert Clive born.
1727 Gainsborough born; *Beggar's Opera* first produced.
1728 Behring Strait discovered.
Oliver Goldsmith born.
1730 Burke and Cowper born.
1732 Washington, Warren Hastings and Haydn born.
1733 Pope's *Essay on Man* published.
1736 James Watt, pioneer of the steam engine, born.
1739 Methodist revival under Wesley and Whitfield began.
1740 James Boswell born.
1740–1748 War of Austrian Succession.
1742 Handel's *Messiah* produced.
Fall of Walpole.
1745 Jacobite Rebellion in Scotland.
Battles of Prestonpans and Falkirk.
1746 Battle of Culloden.
1749 Goethe born.
1750 Westminster Bridge opened.
Fielding's *Tom Jones*, Johnson's *Rambler* published.
1751 Arcot taken by Clive.
1753 British Museum founded.
Marie Antoinette born.
1755 Lisbon destroyed by earthquake.
1756 Calcutta captured by Suraja Dowlah; the Black Hole of Calcutta.
Mozart born.
1756–1763 Seven Years War.

A.D.
1757 Clive's victory at Plassey.
Calcutta re-taken by the English.
Admiral Byng shot.
1758 Nelson born.
1759 Wolfe's victory and death at Quebec.
Wilberforce, Pitt and Danton born.
Eddystone lighthouse completed.
1761 Clive's victory at Pondicherry.
1762 Catherine the Great became Empress of Russia.
1763 Peace of Paris; Canada became British.
1764 Spinning jenny invented.
1768 Cook's first voyage round the world.
Royal Academy of Arts founded.
1769 Watt's first steam-engine.
Napoleon Bonaparte and Wellington born.
1770 Beethoven and Wordsworth born.
1772 First partition of Poland.
Cook's second voyage round the world.
Coleridge born.
1773 The Boston Tea Party.
1774 Warren Hastings, first Governor-General of India.
1775 American War of Independence began; Boston invested by Washington; battle of Bunker Hill.
Lamb, Turner and Jane Austen born.
1776 American Declaration of Independence.
Adam Smith's *Wealth of Nations* published.
1777 The Stars and Stripes adopted.
1778 Cook discovers Sandwich Islands and Hawaii.
Gibbon's *Decline and Fall* published.
1779 Cook killed at Hawaii.
1780 The Gordon Riots in London.
1781 George Stephenson, railway engineer, born.
1783 Peace treaty between Britain and United States of America.
1784 Dr. Johnson died.
1786 Impeachment of Warren Hastings.
Burns's *Poems* published.
1788 First U.S. Congress at New York.
British penal settlement established at Botany Bay (New South Wales).
1789 Fall of the Bastille.
George Washington became first President of U.S.A.
1791 Flight to Varennes.
Michael Faraday born.
1792 French Republic proclaimed.
Gas first used in England for lighting.
1793 Louis XVI and Marie Antoinette executed.
Second partition of Poland.
1794 Danton executed; fall of Robespierre.
Battle of Glorious First of June.
1795 The Directory; Bonaparte became prominent.
Third partition of Poland.
English take Cape of Good Hope.
1797 Pound notes issued in England.
1798 Battle of the Nile.
1799 Bonaparte became First Consul.
1800 Malta captured by British.
Union of England and Ireland.

A.D.

1801 Battle of Copenhagen.
1802 Peace of Amiens between Great Britain and France.
First steamship plied on the Clyde.
1804 Bonaparte, Emperor of France.
1805 Trafalgar; death of Nelson.
Battle of Austerlitz.
1806 Napoleon defeated Prussia at Jena.
Title of Holy Roman Emperor abolished.
Death of William Pitt.
1807 Britain abolished slave trade.
1808–1814 The Peninsular War.
1809 Darwin, Mendelssohn born.
Battle of Corunna; death of Sir John Moore.
Battle of Talavera.
1811 Battle of Albuera.
1812 Napoleon's retreat from Russia; Moscow burnt.
Dickens born.
1813 Battle of Vittoria.
1814 Napoleon abdicated.
Scott's *Waverley* published.
1815 Battle of Waterloo; Napoleon exiled.
Invention of safety lamp by Humphry Davy.
1816 Telegraph invented.
1819 First steamship crossed Atlantic.
Queen Victoria born.
Singapore founded.
1820 Florence Nightingale born.
1821 Napoleon died at St. Helena.
1822 Caledonian Canal opened.
Negro republic of Liberia founded.
1824 Byron died in Greece.
Lord Kelvin born.
1825 Stockton-Darlington railway opened.
1826 London Zoological Society founded.
1827 Beethoven died.
Battle of Navarino.
1828 The New Corn Laws.
Meredith, Tolstoy, Ibsen and Jules Verne born.
1829 George Stephenson's *Rocket*.
Metropolitan police force formed.
Catholic Emancipation Act in Britain.
1830 Liverpool-Manchester Railway opened.
Belgium broke away from Holland.
1831 Discovery of electro-magnetic induction by Faraday.
Poland annexed by Russia.
1832 Death of Scott and Goethe.
Reform Bill passed.
Greek independence recognized.
1833 Abolition of slavery in British colonies.
Alfred Nobel, Swedish scientist, born.
1834 Poor Law system revised.
1835 Froebel established first school.
1836 Adelaide founded.
London University founded.
1837 Victoria came to the throne.
Electric telegraph invented by Samuel Morse.
Dickens's *Pickwick Papers*.
John Constable died.
1838 National Gallery, London, opened.

A.D.

1839 First English colony in New Zealand.
Discovery of gold in Australia.
1840 Penny Post established in Great Britain.
Marriage of Queen Victoria and Prince Albert.
Thomas Hardy born.
1841 Self-government granted to Canada.
1842 First Coal Mine Act.
Hongkong ceded to Great Britain.
First International Peace Congress, at London.
1843 Opening of Thames tunnel.
1844 First message sent by electric telegraph.
1845 Franklin's last voyage.
Potato famine in Ireland.
1846 Repeal of the Corn Laws.
Planet Neptune discovered.
1847 Salt Lake City founded by Mormons.
Chloroform discovered.
1848 Revolutionary movements in Europe.
Gold discovered in California.
1850 First submarine telegraph between England and France.
Wordsworth died.
1851 Great Exhibition in London.
1852 Napoleon III, emperor of the French.
Duke of Wellington died.
1854–1856 Crimean War; Alma, Balaclava, Inkerman, Siege of Sebastopol.
1855 Livingstone discovered Victoria Falls.
1857 The Indian Mutiny.
1858 Siege of Lucknow.
Atlantic cable laid.
Livingstone explored Lake Nyassa.
1859 Darwin's *Origin of Species* published.
1860 First ironclad battleship launched.
Oil found in Pennsylvania.
Barrie born.
1861 Victor Emanuel, first king of Italy.
Prince Albert died.
1861–1865 American Civil War.
1862 Source of the Nile discovered.
Bismarck became minister of Prussia.
Slavery abolished in the U.S.
1863 David Lloyd George born.
1864 Nobel invented dynamite.
International Red Cross founded.
1865 Lincoln assassinated.
Kipling born.
1866 Battle of Sadowa; Prussian victory over Austria.
1869 Suez Canal opened.
1870–1871 Franco-Prussian War.
1871 Meeting of Livingstone and Stanley.
1873 Death of Livingstone.
Typewriter invented.
1874 Winston Churchill born.
1875 Suez Canal shares bought by Britain.
Capt. Webb first man to swim English Channel.
1877 Queen Victoria proclaimed Empress of India.
1877–1878 Russo-Turkish War.
1878 Congress of Berlin.
1881 Revised version of the New Testament published.

A.D.

1883 Egypt occupied by Britain.
Karl Marx died.
1885 Khartoum captured; Gordon murdered.
1887 First motor-car built.
1890 Cecil Rhodes became Prime Minister of Cape Colony.
Opening of the Forth Bridge.
Heligoland ceded by Britain to Germany in exchange for Zanzibar.
1894 Manchester Ship Canal opened.
War between China and Japan.
1895 Jameson raid.
Kiel Canal opened.
Bell invented telephone.
X-rays discovered.
1896 Matabele War.
Marconi discovered wireless.
Olympic Games revived.
1898 Battle of Omdurman.
1899–1902 Boer War.
1900 Boxer rising in China.
1901 President W. McKinley of U.S. assassinated.
Death of Queen Victoria.
1902 Death of Cecil Rhodes.
1903 Wilbur and Orville Wright flew first aeroplane.
1904–1905 Russo-Japanese War; Japanese victorious.
1907 Boy Scout movement founded by Baden-Powell.
1909 North Pole reached by Commander Peary.
Blériot first man to fly English Channel.
1911 South Pole reached by Amundsen.
1912 Scott died on way back from South Pole.
Titanic lost on maiden voyage to America.
1913 Balkan War.
1914–1918 First World War.
1914 England declared war on Germany; battles of Mons, Tannenberg, Marne (first), Ypres (first).
1915 Battles of Dardanelles, Mesopotamia, Loos, Ypres (second), Neuve Chapelle.
Poison gas first used by Germans.
1916 Battles of Jutland, Verdun (first), Somme (first); Kitchener drowned.
Lloyd George, Prime Minister.
1917 Baghdad taken. Battles of Arras, Cambrai, Paschendaele, Verdun (second), Ypres (third); Jerusalem taken.
1918 Battles of Somme (second), Marne (second); armistice (11 November).
1919 Interned German fleet scuttled at Scapa Flow.
Treaty of Versailles.
Alcock and Brown flew the Atlantic.
1920 League of Nations established.
Joan of Arc canonized.
1922 Fascist march on Rome; Mussolini came to power.
1924 Lenin died.
First Labour Government in Britain.

A.D.

1925 Locarno Conference.
1927 Beam radio service to Australia begun.
Canberra, new capital of Australia.
Lindbergh flew Atlantic alone.
1929 Byrd flew over the South Pole.
1930 Amy Johnson flew alone from England to Australia.
1931 Alfonso XIII of Spain abdicated.
1932 Franklin Delano Roosevelt elected President of the United States.
1933 Hitler came to power.
German Reichstag destroyed by fire.
1934 Scott and Black made record flight to Australia.
1935 Mussolini invaded Abyssinia.
1936 Germany and Italy concluded anti-Comintern pact.
Edward VIII abdicated.
Hitler marched into Rhineland.
1938 Munich Agreement between Chamberlain, Daladier, Hitler and Mussolini.
1939 Hitler conquered Poland.
1939–1945 The Second World War.
1940 Norway, Denmark, Netherlands, Belgium, and France (in part) occupied by Germany; Mussolini declared war on Allies; Battle of Britain.
First campaign in the Western Desert.
1941 Hitler invaded Russia. Japanese attacked Pearl Harbour; Hongkong, Singapore fell to Japanese; Malaya overrun.
Atlantic Conference.
1942 Japanese occupied Burma. Battle of El Alamein; Allied landings in North Africa. Battle of Stalingrad. Naval battles of Coral Sea and Midway Island.
1943 Campaigns in Sicily and Italy. Mussolini forced to resign; Italy surrendered.
Death of Mussolini (28 April).
British offensive in Burma.
1944 Rome captured. Allies landed in France (D-Day, 6 June); France, Belgium liberated.
Flying bombs on London.
Civil war in Greece.
1945 Death of Roosevelt, four times President of U.S. (12 April).
Death of Hitler (30 April).
Unconditional surrender of Germany (7 May).
Atom bombs on Hiroshima (6 August) and Nagasaki (9 August).
Unconditional surrender of Japan (14 August).
Labour Government in Britain.
Potsdam Conference.
1946 First meeting of United Nations General Assembly.
1947 Coal mines in Britain nationalized.
1948 Assassination of Mahatma Gandhi.
United Europe movement launched at The Hague.
Harry S. Truman elected President of U.S.
1949 State of Israel set up.

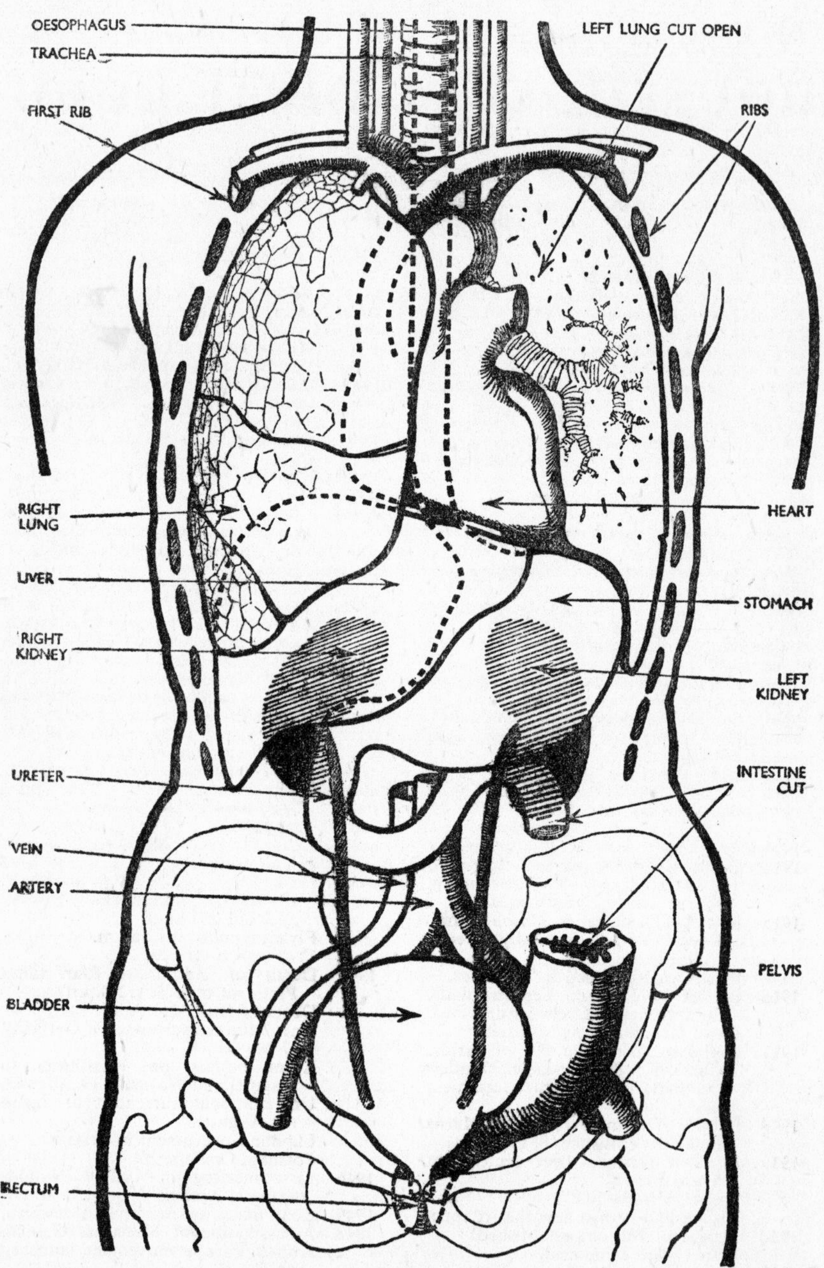

The general arrangement of the human body, showing the main organs. More detailed illustrations of many of these organs appear on later pages.

HOUSEHOLD MEDICAL GUIDE

Concise information on the structure of the human body and its chief ailments, and authoritative advice on their treatment. The section is arranged alphabetically.

ABDOMEN. The part of the trunk of the body lying below the diaphragm, which is the partition that separates it from the chest above. It contains the principal organs of digestion: the stomach, intestines, liver, pancreas; and also the spleen and the kidneys. Its lower part is called the pelvis and contains the rectum, the urinary bladder and, in the female, the reproductive organs. The lining of the abdominal cavity, called the peritoneum, serves as an attachment for keeping the various organs in place; but their chief support lies in the strength of the abdominal muscles.

ABORTION. This is also known as miscarriage. It is the expulsion of a child from the womb earlier than the twenty-eighth week of pregnancy, after which it is known as premature labour. Criminal abortion is abortion deliberately contrived by either drugs or instruments. It is illegal from the moment of conception. Abortion may be legally produced by doctors if the life or health of the mother is in danger, but not for social considerations.

The majority of abortions are not intentional, and are due to several different causes. They tend to occur most frequently at about the twelfth week of pregnancy. The onset is signalled by pains and by bleeding. About 20 per cent of all pregnancies end in abortion from one cause or another. The fact of having one does not signify that the next pregnancy will not be perfectly normal; but any woman who has a succession of abortions should be competently examined with a view to discovering the cause. When an abortion occurs, a doctor or midwife should be called in, and any material which is discharged should be kept for their inspection.

ABRASIONS. Grazes of the skin. In the absence of infection these heal quickly; but as a fairly large area is exposed to infection inflammation is likely if no care is taken. Washing with soap and water, followed by the application of an antiseptic and a clean dressing, is all that is needed.

ABSCESS. A localized collection of pus, or matter, shut off from surrounding tissues by an inflammatory reaction. It produces the usual signs of inflammation: redness, swelling, heat and pain. The presence of fluid gives rise to a phenomenon called fluctuation; that is to say, if two fingers are placed over an abscess, pressure with one will displace the fluid and cause the other finger to rise. It is an invariable rule that any abscess should be opened, as soon as it is discovered; though, in some cases, it may be possible to withdraw the pus through a hollow needle. See GUMBOIL.

ACIDITY. By gastric acidity a tendency to bring back, or regurgitate, sour fluid from the stomach into the mouth is usually meant. The contents of the stomach are normally acid, so that what is really wrong is not the sourness, but the fact of regurgitating it. This is usually due to irritation of the stomach as a result of taking overhot fluids, alcoholic drinks, too many condiments, or very greasy food. See HYPERCHLORHYDRIA and HYPOCHLORHYDRIA.

ACIDOSIS. A condition in which the blood is slightly more acid than usual. This normally happens after severe exertion and is soon cured by rapid breathing, which gets rid of carbonic acid gas by the lungs. The term acidosis is also wrongly applied to a condition called ketosis, which occurs in children who do not digest fats well. The full digestion of fat is impossible unless a sufficiency of starch or sugar is also present. When partly digested, fat gives rise to toxic substances (ketones), which cause "biliousness." Such children are easily cured by cutting down fats and increasing sugars. Glucose is very popular for this purpose, but any sweet food will do as well. Ketosis can be definitely diagnosed from an examination of the urine, in which ketones are excreted.

ACNE. The well-known pimply face of youth is due to acne. At puberty, the grease glands of the skin often enlarge and become overactive. Such enlarged glands harbour bacteria, and the first result is the blackhead. Neglected blackheads become infected by other germs, and red pimples result.

Young people with greasy skins should wash well with plenty of hot, soapy water to get rid of the extra grease, and then should sponge with cold water to close the pores up. Witch-hazel and alibour water are useful astringents. Blackheads should be squeezed out with a comedo extractor, which can be bought from most chemists. It is better not to use the finger-nails, which damage the skin. A little skin spirit may be rubbed in after removing blackheads. Acne which has progressed to the pimply stage is not easy to cure, and is better left to a doctor or a skin specialist. Vaccines and ray treatments are often used, and ointments containing sulphathiazole or penicillin are very helpful.

ADDISON'S DISEASE. A disease of the supra-renal ductless glands (situated above the kidneys), producing wasting, weakness and darkening of the skin, It is now treated by a hormone called desoxycorticosterone which is implanted under the skin in small pellets.

ADENOIDS. An enlargement of the lymphatic tissue normally present in the throat at the back of the nose and due to infection by colds and catarrhal organisms. The enlargement causes obstruction to breathing, and blocks the eustachian tubes leading to the ears, causing deafness. Neglected adenoids cause an ill-shaped palate, chronic catarrh, breathing through the mouth, "nasal" speech, and deafness. Treatment consists of surgical

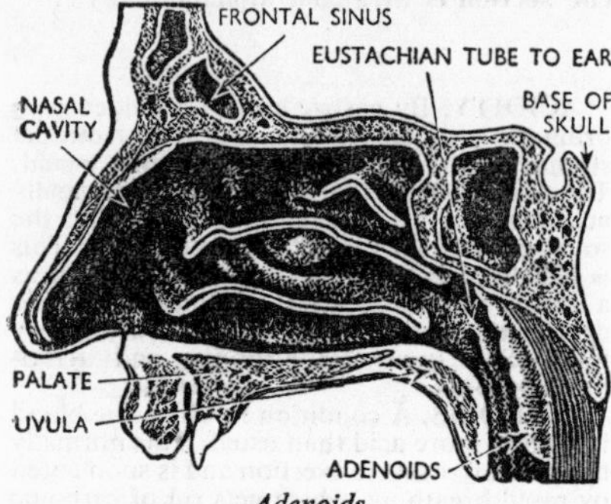

Adenoids.

removal—a very slight operation—followed by breathing exercises to keep the nasal passages clear.

ADHESIONS. Fibrous bands formed after inflammation. In a joint, they limit its movement, and may be cured by manipulation. Adhesions occur in the chest after pleurisy, and in the abdomen after peritonitis. When abdominal they may cause kinks in, and obstruction to, the intestines.

ADRENALIN. The hormone formed by the supra-renal glands. It is poured out into the blood during such emotions as fear and anger, causing more rapid heart-beat, dry mouth, pale skin, and a cessation of digestive processes. As adrenalin dilates the bronchial tubes, it is used to stop asthmatic attacks. It is sometimes used in collapse and shock, and is also combined with local anaesthetics in order to constrict small blood vessels and keep the anaesthetic localized for a longer period.

AGUE. An old term for malaria. As the onset of a malarial attack is characterized by a fit of shivering (a rigor), the word ague is sometimes used for any feeling of chill and shivering.

AIR EMBOLISM. A rare cause of sudden death, occurring after accidental injuries or, possibly, operations, in which a volume of air has entered a large blood vessel, and formed a kind of "air lock" in some vital organ, obstructing the circulation.

AIR SWALLOWING. This is the most common cause of gastric flatulence (see FLATULENCE) and of belching. It occurs more especially in anxious or worried people. A sense of fullness in the stomach impels them to make efforts to belch. These efforts are accompanied by gulping down quantities of air. Finally, the swallowed air returns, with a sense of relief, confirming the original false idea; so the process is repeated.

ALBUMINURIA. The presence of albumen in the urine. This is detected by boiling acidified urine in a test tube, when the albumen coagulates, as white of egg does, and forms an opaque cloud. It can occur harmlessly in adolescents, when it is found after exercise but never in the morning after resting. Apart from this, it usually indicates disease of the kidneys, though the severity and type of such disease have to be judged by other signs, such as breathlessness, swollen feet, raised blood pressure, etc., and by blood tests. During pregnancy, albuminuria is a warning of possible toxaemia. See ANTENATAL CARE.

ALCOHOL, EFFECTS OF. See INTOXICATION.

ALIMENTARY SYSTEM. The digestive system, consisting of the alimentary canal—mouth, throat, gullet, stomach, small and large intestines, and rectum—and of the associated organs, such as the pancreas and the liver. Its function is to break down food into simple substances which can be absorbed and utilized by the body in providing energy and repairing waste.

ALLERGY. A condition in which the body has become sensitized to one or more substances, so that absorption of, or even contact with, such substances produces disease symptoms. Typical allergic disorders are nettlerash (see URTICARIA), hay fever, asthma and, in some cases, migraine and eczema. The harmful substance may be some foods, such as shellfish, fruit, milk or eggs; it may be a dust or pollen which is inhaled, or a plant which comes into contact with the skin. Such substances are quite harmless to normal people, and only affect those who have become sensitized to them. It is sometimes possible to identify the substance by suitable skin-tests, and to create an immunity by a series of graduated injections. When this cannot be done, injections of peptone or of blood are sometimes successful. Adrenalin and ephedrine are used as drugs to counteract allergic symptoms. It is now thought that allergic symptoms are due to the release into the tissues of a substance called histamine, to which the drug benadryl acts as an antidote.

ALOPECIA. Baldness. Alopecia areata—commonly spoken of as alopecia—consists of circular patches of baldness, varying in size from that of a sixpence to a patch of two inches or more in diameter, unaccompanied by any evidence of skin disease. This complaint is sometimes associated with sepsis elsewhere in the body, such as with septic tonsils or infected tooth roots; but is often a sequel to general ill-health or anxiety. Ultra-violet rays and stimulating lotions are often prescribed, but this disease tends to clear up spontaneously in nine to twelve months, without treatment. The general health more than the scalp should receive attention.

AMENORRHOEA. Absence of menstruation. This may be primary, as when menstruation has never occurred; or secondary, when it has been normal, but has ceased. Primary amenorrhoea may be due to structural abnormalities in the female reproductive organs, to defects in the supply of hormones from the ductless glands, or to general disease, such as

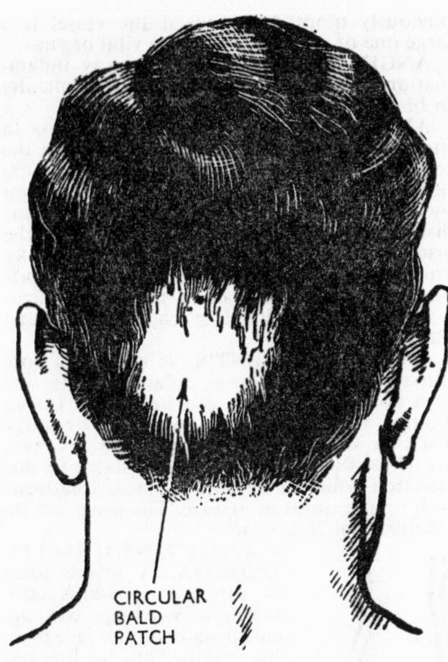

Alopecia.

diabetes, tuberculosis, anaemia, etc. Secondary amenorrhoea may be due to pregnancy, to general ill-health, to operative removal of the womb (hysterectomy), to X-ray or radium treatment, or to the change of life (see MENOPAUSE). Amenorrhoea in itself is quite harmless, contrary to the popular idea that it retains poisons in the system. It is of importance only in that its cause should be discovered.

AMNESIA. Loss of memory. This may be due to head injury, to various diseases of the nervous system, to toxins, including alcohol, or to psychological causes, such as hysteria. Old people tend to lose their memory for recent events, while retaining it for things long past.

ANAEMIA. Literally, a deficiency of blood, the term anaemia being applied to a number of blood disorders. Chlorosis, or microcytic anaemia, or simple anaemia, is due to lack of iron, sunshine, fresh air, etc., and can be rapidly cured by adequate doses of iron, preferably as ferrous sulphate. Secondary anaemia is caused by loss of blood, and is treated by blood transfusions, fluids, iron and liver. Pernicious anaemia, also known as Addison's anaemia or macrocytic anaemia, is a disease in which the bone-marrow does not form new red blood cells to replace wastage. Injections of liver are a specific treatment, in that they stimulate the marrow to form these cells; but the injections usually have to be continued every few weeks for an indefinite period. Dried hog's stomach, taken in capsules by way of the mouth is also effective. Aplastic anaemia is a rarer form, in which the marrow will not respond to such stimulation.

Leukaemia is a form of anaemia in which the white blood cells multiply enormously. It is sometimes treated by X-ray (see RADIOTHERAPY). Symptoms of anaemia are pallor, breathlessness, coldness and general weakness; but as all these can exist with normal blood, a definite diagnosis can be made only by a blood examination. See BLOOD.

ANAESTHESIA. The production of unconsciousness, usually for the purpose of surgical operations. Anaesthesia may be produced by inhaling drugs, by having them injected into the blood stream, by having them absorbed from the intestine, or by injecting them into the fluid around the spinal cord. Inhalation was the original method and is still largely used.

To the early nitrous oxide (dental gas), ether and chloroform, have been added trichlorethylene, cyclopropane, and other volatile substances. Basal anaesthetics, chiefly barbiturates, such as evipan and pentothal, can be injected into a vein and produce unconsciousness in a few seconds. Solutions of percaine and other drugs injected into the spinal canal cause paralysis and loss of sensation from the waist down and are used for operations on the lower abdomen and legs. Spinal anaesthesia greatly reduces shock because nerve impulses to the brain are cut off. Paraldehyde and avertin are injected into the lower bowel to produce unconsciousness after they have been absorbed. Accessory drugs, such as nembutal, morphine, omnopon, etc., are used before operations, to produce a sleepy condition. The latest addition is curare, which is used to produce complete relaxation of the muscles so that very little additional anaesthetic is required.

The modern anaesthetist is often a whole-time specialist who has the choice of many methods at his disposal to suit widely differing cases. In consequence, anaesthesia has become very much safer and very much less unpleasant than it once was.

ANAL FISSURE. A crack in the skin, rather like a split lip, in the margin of the anus, usually at the back. This leads to intense pain when the bowels are moved, which continues for about an hour afterwards. It can usually be relieved very quickly by injecting a slow-acting local analgesic, such as proctocaine, which not only takes away the pain but abolishes the spasm and permits healing. Some severe cases, however, require a minor operation.

ANALGESIA. Abolition of the sensation of pain without the loss of consciousness. Local anaesthetics are more properly referred to as local analgesics. They are substances such as procaine, which can be injected under the skin to deaden nerve endings, can be injected into the trunk of a nerve to deaden all the tissues supplied by that nerve, or can be applied to a surface, such as the lining of the nose or throat, or the surface of the eye. Thus, cocaine drops may be placed in the eye before extracting a bit of grit; or the nerves at the sides of a finger may be injected before removing a finger-nail.

Analgesia is also the term applied to a slight degree of anaesthesia, sufficient to abolish pain without completely rendering the patient unconscious. This may be done when painful dressings have to be changed; and it is the usual method employed during childbirth (see BIRTH and CONFINEMENT). In this case it may be carried out by injecting drugs such as scopolamine (twilight sleep) or pethidine; by inhaling nitrous oxide and air (the official method allowed to midwives), or trilene and air; by small doses of chloroform; or by injecting nerve roots in the method known as caudal analgesia which, although largely employed in the United States, is not so popular in Britain. A good deal of research is still being carried out into methods of analgesia.

ANASTOMOSIS. Surgically joining one hollow organ to another, such as when a short-circuit is made between the stomach and small intestine as in cases of duodenal ulcer.

ANEURIN. Vitamin B_1—the anti-neuritic vitamin whose absence from the diet leads to beri-beri. See VITAMINS.

ANEURISM. A dilatation in the wall of a blood vessel. It may be congenital; it may be due to injury or to disease. As the vessel wall becomes thinned, there is danger of its bursting with consequent haemorrhage. It is obviously more dangerous if the vessel is a large one or is situated in some vital organ.

ANGINA, LUDWIG'S. A brawny inflammation of the neck tissues, causing difficulty in breathing and swallowing.

ANGINA PECTORIS. Literally, a pain in the chest. The term is applied to pain in the region of the heart, often spreading to the neck and insides of the arms, and brought on by exertion. It is usually associated with some disease of the muscle of the heart or of the arteries supplying that muscle (see CORONARY THROMBOSIS). The pain of angina pectoris may be relieved by taking tablets of nitroglycerine, or by inhaling capsules of amyl nitrite.

ANGINA, VINCENT'S. A variety of sore throat, sometimes also of inflamed gums, due to a specific microbe; also known as trench mouth. It is frequently conveyed by dirty drinking vessels. Absence of vitamin C (see VITAMINS) makes the gums more liable to this infection which is curable by local treatment with preparations of arsenic. The germ can be identified microscopically.

ANGIO-NEUROTIC OEDEMA. A severe form of urticaria in which considerable swellings can occur, usually on the face or in the mouth. Thus the lips and eyelids may be swollen out of all recognition. This is an allergic disease. See ALLERGY.

ANKLE, SPRAINED. See JOINTS, DISLOCATIONS AND SPRAINS OF.

ANKYLOSIS. Union of the bones which form a joint, so that the joint becomes fixed. Ankylosis may be due to inflammation, arthritis or injury.

ANOREXIA. Loss of appetite. The cause must usually be sought in the general health.

ANOSMIA. Loss of the sense of smell. It may follow injury or diseases of the nose and nasal sinuses. See SINUS.

ANTENATAL CARE. The care of an expectant mother from the time of conception until the confinement (see BIRTH). By the introduction of clinics for this purpose, antenatal care has in some ways been divided off from the total care of the expectant mother; but this is to be deplored, and it should be realized that the process of having a baby begins at conception and continues until about six weeks after the birth, by which time a normal mother should be fully in control of a normal baby. The actual birth, though dramatic, is only one incident in a process which

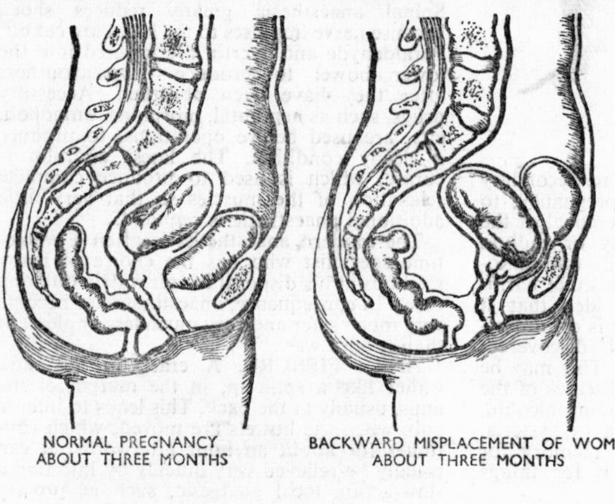

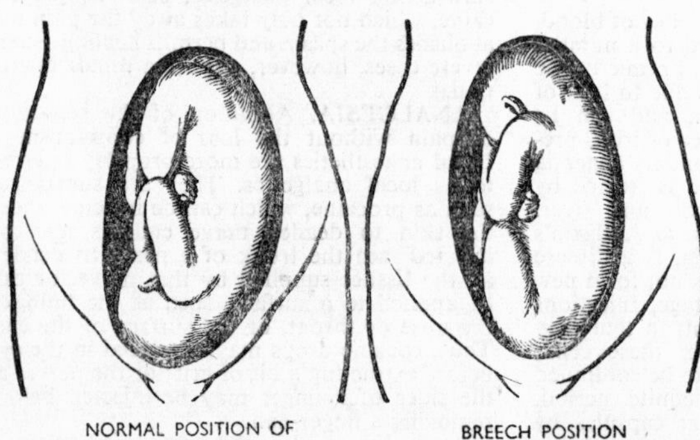

Antenatal care. The correction of abnormal positions (shown here compared with the normal) of the womb in early pregnancy and of the baby before birth is a purpose of antenatal care.

takes many months, and the whole process should be supervised by the same doctor and/or midwife throughout. Before antenatal care became general many babies were lost, and so were some mothers, simply because acute emergencies occurred which could have been foreseen and, to some extent, prevented. By suitable supervision it is possible to forestall a great many of the more dangerous complications of pregnancy and childbirth.

Antenatal care should include three things: first, general care of the physical health of the expectant mother, including suitable rest, diet, exercise and attention to any minor ailments such as defective teeth, etc. Second, special attention to the pregnancy itself, including watching for difficulties if the mother is small in relation to her baby, correcting any early malpositions of the womb and any late malpositions of the baby; having pre-natal radiograms (that is, X-ray photographs) if necessary; regular testing of the urine to anticipate any toxic troubles, and care of the breasts and nipples. Instruction should also be given in proper preparations for the confinement if this is to take place at home; alternatively, arrangements should be made for admission to a nursing home or hospital. Third, the mother should be told about herself, reassured that she is normal, that she will have analgesics if necessary, that she is to disregard old wives' tales and realize that having a baby is a normal human function and not a thing to be dreaded; in general, her psychological outlook should be adjusted so that she is happy and not miserable about the whole thing.

Many mothers think that antenatal care is rather fussy and can be left until the last months, but it is wise to begin it immediately after pregnancy is established. If this were a regular rule, many early abortions (see ABORTION) could be prevented. It is important that such things as urine tests and blood-pressure examinations should be done regularly, and it is very important to have regular supervision in the last few weeks, when the actual position of the child in the womb can be discovered. With all this, it is equally important to avoid any suggestion of invalidism, and to lead as normal a life as possible.

ANTHRACOSIS. A chronic disease of the lungs as a result of inhaling coal-dust.

ANTHRAX. A disease of the skin or the internal organs, usually acquired by infection from furs, skins and hides. It is due to a specific germ, the anthrax bacillus.

ANTIBIOTIC. An animal or vegetable preparation which has the power of killing harmful organisms, as distinct from the chemical disinfectants.

ANTISEPTIC. A chemical substance used to prevent infection, either by killing microbes or by sufficiently reducing their vitality that they cannot multiply. There are plenty of substances, such as pure carbolic, which will kill germs almost instantly; but when those germs are on or in a human being the problem is complicated by the necessity of not injuring the tissues while killing the germs. It is almost impossible to render human skin germ-free, but the majority of harmful germs can be removed from unbroken skin by *thorough* washing, followed by rubbing on surgical spirit (70 per cent alcohol).

On open wounds or cuts, a 1-in-1,000 solution of acriflavine or proflavine may be used; or, where there has been much infection, powders of flavine, of the sulpha drugs or mixtures of these with penicillin may be applied. While penicillin is by far the most effective agent against some of the common infecting organisms, there are others against which it is quite ineffective. When germs are actually in the blood stream, the sulpha drugs and penicillin, and possibly newer antibiotics, such as streptomycin and bacitracin, are, with the exception of the use of quinine in killing the malaria parasite and of arsenical preparations in killing the germ of syphilis, the only valuable antiseptics. The ordinary chemical antiseptics either cause more harm to the tissues than to the germs, or are themselves inactivated in the presence of blood and other bodily fluids.

Disinfection of the air of a room can be accomplished either by air-conditioning apparatus, or by spraying with aerosols, such as propylene glycol. Disinfection of water is accomplished by chlorination. Bedding, surgical instruments and many other things are best disinfected by superheated steam, though this requires special apparatus.

ANTITOXIN. An antidote formed by the body against the poisons of bacteria. Such antitoxins are formed in infectious disease and account for the natural process of recovery. They can be produced artificially by injecting dead bacteria (see VACCINE); if this is done to an animal, its serum, containing much antitoxin, can be used by injection to hasten the recovery of a human being. See SERUM, DIPHTHERIA, and LOCKJAW.

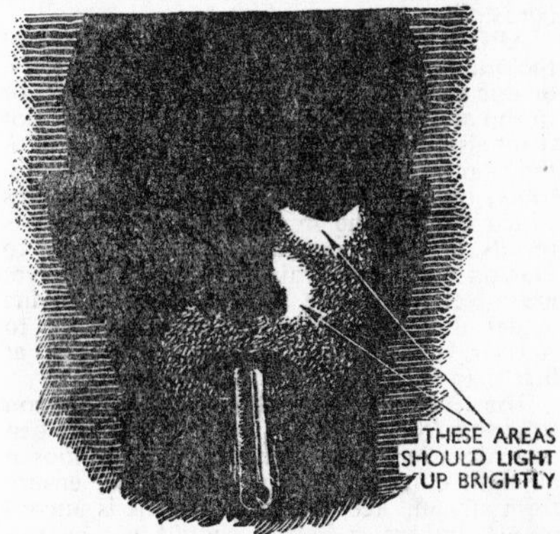

Antrum. An infected antrum is revealed in the dark by placing a bright light in the mouth. In this figure the right side is infected.

ANTRUM. A hollow in the cheek-bone communicating with the inside of the nose. It is liable to become infected in catarrhal diseases, leading to pain in the face. See SINUSES.

ANXIETY NEUROSIS. Roughly speaking, a state of emotional tension, brought about by mental stress, characterized by undue fears, sleeplessness, headaches and many subjective symptoms, such as palpitations, sweatings, fainting attacks, and loss of appetite. The treatment is by psychotherapy.

AORTA. The main artery leaving the heart by the left ventricle; it divides and subdivides inumerable times to form all the arteries of the body. It is the "mother" of all the arteries, which supply oxygenated blood to the body.

APERIENTS. Substances which produce an action of the bowels. Different types of aperients have different actions. Salines, such as Epsom salts, function by retaining water in the intestine, and this water acts as a flush. Vegetable laxatives, such as senna, aloes, and cascara, act chiefly on the lower bowel and have purely an irritant action, persuading the bowel to contract and so urge on its contents. Castor oil is inactive until it reaches the small intestine and mixes with bile. After acting once, it constipates, as does rhubarb. Calomel and phenolphthalein are both irritants of the whole of the intestines. The more violent aperients are known as purgatives. See also LAXATIVES.

APHASIA. Loss of the power of speech. May be due to injury to the brain, to hysteria or to organic disease. The most frequent cause is a "stroke"—a haemorrhage into the brain. In right-handed people, the speech centre is on the left of the brain. Haemorrhage on the left side causes right-sided paralysis (see APOPLEXY) with loss of speech. Left-handed individuals suffer loss of speech when the haemorrhage is on the right side of the brain. As a rule, there is a good deal of recovery, usually preceding recovery of the paralysis.

APHONIA. Loss of voice, which is usually because of some disease of the larynx or vocal cords. See LARYNGITIS.

APOPLEXY. A stroke. Damage to part of the brain by haemorrhage from a burst artery, or due either to clotting in a blood vessel, or to the arrival in a small brain artery of a clot from elsewhere in the body. In some parts of the brain, this may lead to only slight symptoms; but when it affects those nerve-centres which control the muscles, sudden paralysis results of the opposite side of the body to that on which the brain is injured. As nerves are affected at some little distance from the actual damage, and as these are likely to recover, there is usually more paralysis at first than there is after a few weeks.

The immediate treatment of a person suffering from a stroke is to put him to bed in a room in which the light is shaded, loosen all tight clothing, remove false teeth, ensure fresh air, and keep him warm. If he is unconscious, hot-water bottles should *not* be put next the skin or they may cause severe burns. Alcohol, in any form, must *not* be given, as it raises the blood pressure and may increase the haemorrhage. Note that the paralysed limbs will be more stiff and rigid than the unaffected ones. This is easily tested by gently bending the knees and elbows.

APPENDICITIS. Inflammation of the appendix, a small finger-shaped organ attached

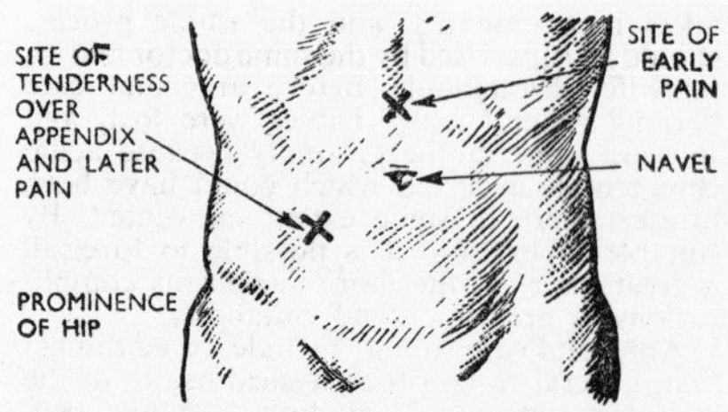

Appendicitis. Some of the symptoms.

to the beginning of the large intestine. The position is roughly half-way between the navel and the right hip-bone. The onset of appendicitis usually causes pain, not at this point, but in the mid-line just below the junction of the ribs. There may be vomiting and a rise of temperature, but this is not invariable. After an hour or two, the pain shifts, and becomes localized to the appendix area, which is then tender when pressed. While many cases of appendicitis have been known to recover without an operation, there is always danger of peritonitis and the only safe course is to have the appendix removed as soon as appendicitis is diagnosed.

ARTERIO-SCLEROSIS. Hardening of the arteries. Is a normal accompaniment of old age, but occurs earlier in some people than in others. The reason is unknown. If the arteries become completely obstructed, the circulation fails, and gangrene may result. If a high blood pressure breaks a hard and brittle artery in the brain, apoplexy may result. There is no known cure for arterio-sclerosis.

ARTERY. One of the blood vessels by which fresh blood containing oxygen leaves the heart on its way to the different parts of the body. See AORTA and HAEMORRHAGE.

ARTHRITIS. Inflammation of a joint. The two common varieties are rheumatoid and osteo-arthritis. Rheumatoid arthritis usually attacks the smaller joints, such as those of the fingers and wrists. It is usually associated with infection elsewhere in the body, especially in tonsils, sinuses and tooth roots. Osteo-arthritis attacks larger joints such as hips and knees, but may affect any joint. It is not thought to be due to infection, but to a degeneration of the bone and cartilage of the joints. Treatment of these conditions is very difficult; and is often carried out in special clinics or spas. In the case of rheumatoid arthritis, it may involve search for the source of the infection, splinting of affected joints during the acute stages, treatment by gold injections and a well-balanced diet, wax baths, electrical treatment, such as diathermy and short-wave therapy, with remedial exercises and occupational therapy as the condition improves.

Osteo-arthritis may need the co-operation of the orthopaedic surgeon in resting or exercising joints and in the devising of suitable splints for support and rest. Manipulative surgery may be needed in breaking down adhesions. Some success has been achieved by injecting solutions of lactic acid into arthritic joints to increase their mobility and allay the pain, and also by the administration of thyroid gland in combination with iodine and aspirin. The help of the masseuse is invaluable, and electrical stimulation of flabby muscles may be needed. Arthritis can also be an acute infectious condition, in which the joint has to be operated on and drained, or a tuberculous one, needing prolonged immobilization, and the usual treatment of tuberculosis. The new drug, cortisone, promises a revolution in the treatment of arthritis.

ARTIFICIAL LIMBS. The success of an artificial limb in making the wearer independent partly depends on the degree of amputation and partly on the confidence and determination of the wearer. High amputations provide more difficulties than those near the extremities, and the more natural joints which are preserved the better. It is almost impossible to fit a satisfactory limb when the amputation has been through the shoulder or the hip-joint. An artificial foot is a much more useful thing than an artificial hand; but hands are now so well made that many crafts can be performed with them.

ASCITES. A collection of fluid in the peritoneal cavity. See DROPSY.

ASCORBIC ACID. Synthetic vitamin C, the fruit vitamin, which provides protection against scurvy. See SCURVY and VITAMINS.

ASEPSIS. The *absence* of disease-producing bacteria as distinguished from disinfection, which consists of *killing* germs and their spores already present. When Lister first proved that wound infection was due to germs, he regarded their presence as inevitable, thinking they were always in the air and so got into operation wounds. He therefore adopted disinfectant methods—spraying the air with carbolic, and using this in dressings. While he thus reduced mortality very remarkably, the disinfectants were found to be injurious in themselves.

Later, it was found possible entirely to exclude bacteria from a normal operation by strict attention to cleanliness, by boiling instruments, and by sterilizing gowns, towels, gloves—in fact everything used. The modern operation ritual, developed on these lines, is known as asepsis. It involves a great deal of training and attention to detail and cannot, usually, be applied in the home.

ASTHMA. A disease in which there is spasm of the smaller bronchial tubes, leading to great difficulty in breathing—more especially in breathing out. It is apt to recur in attacks of varying duration, often during the night. Bronchitis is not only a predisposing factor, but also results from many asthmatic attacks, so that a vicious circle of asthma—bronchitis—asthma is set up. There is usually an underlying tendency to this disease, which may be inherited; and also an allergic condition (see ALLERGY), by which taking certain foods, or coming into contact with certain substances or animals, will precipitate an attack. Spasms are often cut short by an injection of adrenalin or by taking ephedrine tablets. Breathing exercises are helpful, and a book giving such exercises may be obtained from the Asthma Research Council, at King's College, Strand, London, W.C.2. It is better to have the exercises demonstrated by a physiotherapist.

It is important for asthmatics to live in a dust-free atmosphere as far as possible. They should have plastic curtains, and rubber or linoleum floor-coverings. The dusting of their rooms should be done with a damp cloth or a vacuum-cleaner, and special attention should be paid to the tops of doors and picture-rails. Residence at the seaside is often helpful in some cases, but different patients vary widely in the kind of district which suits them.

ATHEROMA. Hardening of the arteries, with deposition of lime salts.

ATROPHY. Wasting; the term is usually applied to muscular wasting, or to the thinning of bones in old age.

ATROPINE. A drug obtained from the deadly nightshade (*Atropa belladonna*) and used to relieve asthma to abolish spasmodic pains, and to dry up secretions as a preliminary to anaesthesia.

AURICULAR FIBRILLATION. A form of heart disease in which the rhythm is disordered, resulting in a completely irregular pulse and considerable breathlessness. It is usually controlled by taking digitalis and can sometimes be cured by the drug quinidine. Some cases are due to rheumatic heart disease, others to exophthalmic goitre. Curing the goitre often results in a cure of the fibrillation.

AUSCULTATION. Listening to sounds inside the body, usually with a stethoscope. Most useful as an aid to the diagnosis of heart and lung diseases. It is an art, rather than a science, and requires considerable experience.

AUTOHAEMOTHERAPY. The injection into a muscle of the patient's own blood obtained from a vein. It is used successfully in the treatment of allergic diseases. See ALLERGY.

AXILLA. Medical term for the armpit.

BABY, CARE OF. This is too large a subject for brief reference, and mothers should learn all they can from the many reliable books on this subject, from their doctors and midwives, and from infant-welfare clinics. A few points may be made, however. Babies are usually tougher as regards exposure than many people think; they will stand cold water, firm handling, fresh air, and many varieties of supposedly unsuitable foods. They do not do well if exposed to germs in crowded stuffy rooms, if disturbed when they want to sleep, or if deprived of vitamins. Although it helps the mother to feed a baby at regular intervals, it is a mistake to be "clockbound." An obviously hungry baby should be fed, even if its feed is not due. Babies get thirsty, especially in the summer, and need a lot of water as well as their feeds. They do not like being wrapped in many layers of clothes on a hot day when their mothers wear little but a frock. The result is a peevish baby with a sweat rash. Nappy rashes are mostly due to urine decomposing and forming ammonia. If nappies smell of ammonia, they should be boiled daily; washing is not enough.

Babies should gain at least a pound a month, but will sometimes gain a pound in a week. It is much more common to underfeed babies than overfeed them. If in doubt, multiply baby's weight in pounds by 2½—it should get that number of ounces of breast milk in twenty-four hours. To find the amount taken by a breast-fed baby, weigh it before and after a feed. Babies do better in charge of their own mothers than with grannies, nannies or in crèches. They like being cuddled and they like sucking their thumbs. Both are good for them! They do not like being dropped; nor do they like sudden noises, but they don't mind a continuous noise at all.

BACILLARY DYSENTERY. See DYSENTERY.

BACILLURIA. Infection of the urinary apparatus by bacteria, generally indicated by turbid urine which smells of fish. It is usually curable by sulpha drugs, but may indicate disease of the kidneys. See KIDNEY DISEASES.

BACKACHE. This can be due to so many disorders that it is ridiculous to attempt to cure it with a backache pill. It may be due to rheumatic disorders in the muscles or the spine; to disease of the vertebrae, kidney disorders, neuritis, constipation, womb troubles, pleurisy or bronchitis. In fact, only a very complete examination will arrive at the cause. Until the cause is discovered, treatment can be only empirical, such as taking a couple of aspirin tablets.

BACTERIA. Germs, or microbes—tiny living organisms, which are visible through a microscope. They have an amazing power of reproducing themselves, forming millions of descendants in twenty-four hours by simply splitting in two. They are of different sizes and shapes: round ones are called cocci, rod-shaped ones bacilli, and corkscrew-shaped ones spirilla. Some bacteria prefer to live at our expense, and in doing so form poisons which make us ill. Much medical work is concerned with means of killing them and frustrating their activities. Others are harmless, and quite a number are beneficial; for example, those which inhabit our intestines not only help us to digest our food, but

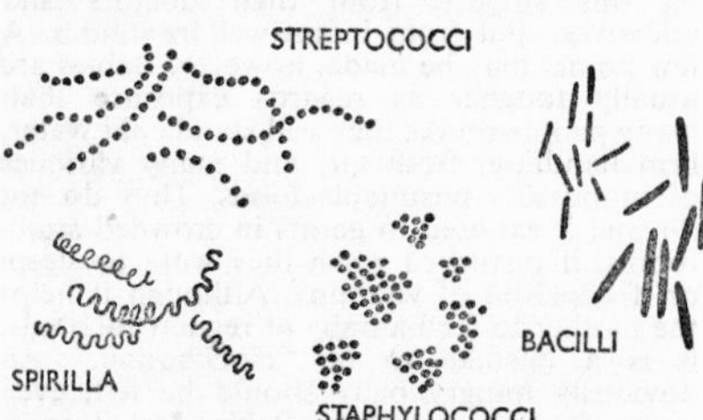

Bacteria. Some varieties (greatly enlarged).

actually synthesize vitamins for us. If we could be quite rid of bacteria, we should die from want of these beneficial ones.

BAKER'S ITCH. Dermatitis due to contact of the skin with flour and sugar.

BANDAGES. The two points to remember in bandaging are: (1) not to apply a bandage without a dressing underneath it and (2) to fix it so that it will not come off. Both these ends are best served by using a generous supply of cotton-wool under the bandage. This prevents constriction and keeps the bandage from slipping. A neat bandage not only looks better, but is more comfortable.

Fancy bandages for the top of the head are very difficult to apply, and the triangular first-aid bandage, arranged as a cap, is more useful. Crêpe bandages are used to support varicose veins, and should be applied spirally without twists. When using crêpe bandages no dressing is put underneath, as their own elasticity is sufficient; they should be discarded when they lose their stretch. See BANDAGES, etc., in First-aid chapter.

BARBER'S RASH. This is also known as sycosis and is an infection of the hair roots of the beard, resulting in a collection of pimples on the chin and cheeks. It is difficult to cure, but usually succumbs to penicillin injections. If resistant, it may need X-ray treatment.

Barber's rash.

BARBITURATES. A class of drugs used to promote sleep, to sooth emotional people, or as an aid to anaesthesia. They include luminal, medinal, pentothal, nembutal, etc. All barbiturates may be habit-forming and should be taken only on medical advice.

BARIUM MEAL. Opaque meal used in radiology.

BAYER 205. A drug used to cure African sleeping sickness.

B.C.G. VACCINE. A vaccine for the prevention of tuberculosis, favourably reported on in Scandinavia, and under trial in England.

BED-PANS. There are two kinds: the circular type of bed-pan is for a patient able to sit up; while the wedge-shaped sort, or slipper, is for the patient who can only lie down.

BEDSORES. Sores on the back of the trunk and limbs in bedridden patients, due to constant friction or prolonged weight on unhealthy skin. Prevention involves careful nursing: daily washing and drying, rubbing-in alcohol to

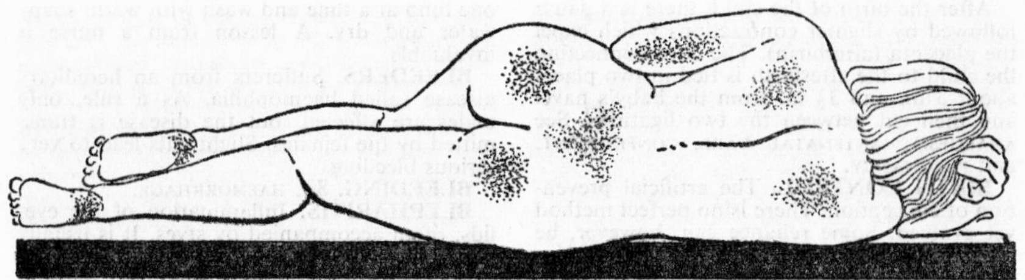

Bedsores. These may occur on pressure-bearing areas, including backs of the elbows and heels.

harden the skin, and powdering with talcum. If bedsores are starting, the use of an air ring, or, better, a water bed or an air bed, to relieve pressure, is indicated. Air rings should be two-thirds empty; full ones are uncomfortable.

BEDWETTING. See ENURESIS.

BEE STING. Extract the sting if still there. Apply a compress soaked in 20 per cent Glauber salts or Epsom salts. Some people are allergic to bee stings (see ALLERGY), and develop considerable and painful swellings, with feelings of faintness and exhaustion. This can usually be quickly relieved by an injection of adrenalin or a tablet of ephedrine every half an hour. Benadryl, also, may be tried. Treatment is the same for wasp stings and mosquito bites. A sting in the mouth may be dangerous from swelling of the tongue.

BELL'S PALSY. Facial paralysis. One side of the face loses its expression, wrinkles disappear, smiling is lop-sided and the patient cannot whistle. Food is apt to collect inside the cheek on the paralysed side. Bell's palsy is often due to exposure to draught, such as may be encountered on a long railway journey through sitting by the open window, but it may be due to ear troubles. This condition may also result from too sudden immersion in cold water while the skin is perspiring, particularly after strenuous exercise. Treatment is

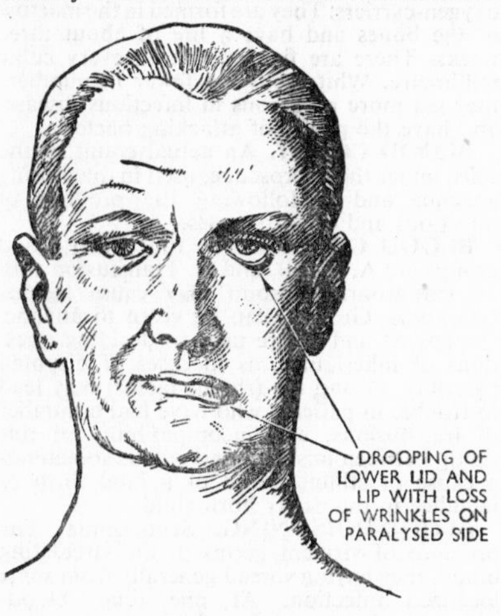

Bell's palsy.

by electrical stimulation, often aided by strapping the cheek with sticking plaster. It is best done by a qualified physiotherapist.

BENEDICT'S SOLUTION. An alkaline solution of copper salts, used in testing urine for sugar (see DIABETES). To one inch of the solution in a test tube, add eight drops of urine and boil it; a yellow colour resulting indicates sugar.

BERI-BERI. A combination of neuritis and dropsy, due to absence of the anti-neuritic factor, vitamin B_1, from the diet. See ANEURIN and VITAMINS.

BICARBONATE OF SODA. A household remedy for indigestion. It occurs in the composition of most stomach powders. In small doses after meals, it eases pain and discomfort, and taken before meals sometimes helps the appetite and promotes digestion. Bicarbonate of soda may be applied externally, as a paste for itching and irritation, such as that due to nettlerash or to the stings of plants and insects. See URTICARIA and INDIGESTION.

BILE. Fluid secreted by the liver, and poured into the intestine after meals. It is essential in the digestion of fats, and is bright green in colour. The bitter yellowish fluid sometimes vomited, and somewhat erroneously called bile, is gastric juice. Obstruction of the flow of bile leads to its absorption into the system and a staining of the skin yellow or greenish yellow. See JAUNDICE.

BILIOUS ATTACK. This term usually implies an attack of vomiting, giddiness, and headache. The term is not a medical one and is inaccurate, as bile is seldom concerned. The trouble is also called a chill on the liver, though the liver is not usually involved. Most such attacks are attacks of gastritis but some are due to constipation and others to migraine. A mild aperient and twelve hours on water or a glucose drink usually effects a cure.

BIRTH. The onset of birth is sometimes heralded by a slight bleeding, called a show. The true indication is the beginning of regular contractions of the womb, usually accompanied by momentary pain, beginning in the small of the back and working round to the thighs. It is the regular repetition of such pains which indicates that labour has started. These "first-stage pains" continue for a varying period, averaging twelve to sixteen hours, while the cervix (the neck of the womb) enlarges sufficiently to admit the baby's head. Then there is generally a loss of clear fluid (the forewaters), followed by stronger contractions as the child is expelled.

After the birth of the child, there is a pause followed by slighter contractions which expel the placenta (afterbirth). The cord connecting the child to the afterbirth is tied in two places about 3 in. and 3½ in. from the baby's navel and then cut between the two ligatures. See ANALGESIA, ANTENATAL CARE, CONFINEMENT, and PREGNANCY.

BIRTH CONTROL. The artificial prevention of conception. There is no perfect method yet evolved. Some reliance can, however, be placed on the so-called "safe times." The principle of this is that a woman normally produces an egg-cell only once a month, about the fourteenth day before the onset of menstruation. As this only lives about forty-eight hours unless fertilized, and as male sperms live only three days, pregnancy is possible only from the seventeenth day before menstruation to the twelfth day before menstruation. In practice, this is more reliable with women who are perfectly regular than with those who are not; but it cannot be *completely* relied on in any case.

Apart from this, most methods resolve themselves into those which prevent access of the sperms to the womb, and those which aim at killing the sperms. Access is prevented by the rubber sheath (condom) worn by the male, or by using some form of rubber occlusive pessary by the woman. Such a pessary should be individually fitted, and should be left in place at least six hours after intercourse.

Killing the sperms is attempted with various chemical pessaries, tablets and injections, none of which is wholly reliable, but the best are probably the various jellies. The combination of an occlusive pessary with a sperm-killing paste is as near 100 per cent security as can be obtained. Metal pessaries should not be used, as there is great danger of injury and infection.

BIRTHMARK. See NAEVUS.

BISMUTH. Bismuth carbonate is used for indigestion and for diarrhoea.

BITES AND STINGS. See BEE STING.

BLACKHEADS. See ACNE.

BLACKWATER FEVER. A severe complication of malaria. See MALARIA.

BLANKET BATH. A useful way of washing a feverish person or helpless invalid. Take off the sheets and cover with a blanket. Expose one limb at a time and wash with warm soapy water and dry. A lesson from a nurse is invaluable.

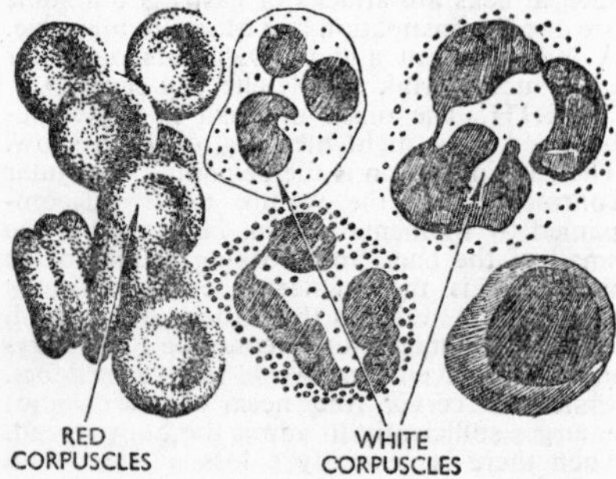

Blood cells or corpuscles (greatly enlarged).

BLEEDERS. Sufferers from an hereditary disease called haemophilia. As a rule, only males are affected, but the disease is transmitted by the females. Slight cuts lead to very serious bleeding.

BLEEDING. See HAEMORRHAGE.

BLEPHARITIS. Inflammation of the eyelids, often accompanied by styes. It is usually curable by sulphathiazole ointment, for which a doctor's prescription is required. In mild cases, "golden ointment" may cure this condition.

BLINDNESS. Blindness may be due to many sorts of injury or disease of the eye. In some cases it is curable, for example, by the surgical treatment of a separated retina; or by transplanting a cornea to replace a damaged one. When blindness is incurable, much can be done by such training as is given at St. Dunstan's to make blind people independent and able to earn their own living. The blind can learn to read by braille, or can have books spoken by long-lasting gramophone records which play for about twenty minutes each side.

BLISTER. A bleb on the skin full of clear fluid; it may be due to injury, to burns or to infection by germs. The skin over and around a blister should be gently wiped with cotton-wool dipped in flavine, peroxide or some other bland antiseptic, before the blister skin is cut away with sterile scissors and an aseptic dressing applied. See ANTISEPTIC and ASEPSIS.

BLOOD. An extremely complicated fluid, consisting of red and white corpuscles (cells) floating in colourless plasma. It conveys oxygen and nourishment to the tissues, takes away carbon dioxide and waste matter, and is able to attack bacteria and neutralize their poisons. It has the power of clotting when shed, thereby stopping haemorrhage.

BLOOD CELLS. The red cells are the oxygen-carriers. They are formed in the marrow of the bones and have a life of about three weeks. There are five million to every cubic millimetre. White cells are fewer in number; they get more numerous in infectious disease. and have the power of attacking bacteria.

BLOOD COUNT. An actual count of the cells, under the microscope, used in diagnosing anaemia and in following the progress of infections and other diseases.

BLOOD GROUPS. The four main blood groups are A, B, AB, and O. Transfusion with an inappropriate group may cause serious symptoms. Group O can be given to anyone. Groups M and N are used in deciding questions of inheritance, as in cases of disputed paternity. Group Rh (rhesus factor) may lead to trouble in patients who have had a number of transfusions, and incompatibility of this group between husband and wife is sometimes a cause of stillbirth and of a fatal form of jaundice in the newly born child.

BLOOD-POISONING. Septicaemia. The presence of virulent germs in the circulating blood, they having spread generally from some localized infection. At one time, blood-poisoning was very often fatal, but now it is usually curable with sulpha drugs or penicillin.

BLOOD PRESSURE. Arterial blood pressure varies with the pulse wave. The pressure at the height of the beat is called the systolic pressure, and varies from 100 to 150 mm. of mercury. Anything above this, when at rest, is abnormal, but, in healthy people, the pressure rises considerably with exercise, during emotion or even after smoking. The seriousness of a high blood pressure depends entirely on what disease is causing it. It is a symptom, not a disease in itself any more than is a temperature.

BLOOD TESTS. These are of many kinds; in anaemia, the cells may be counted. The amount of sugar may be analysed in diabetes, and the amount of nitrogenous urea ascertained in kidney disease. The presence of antibodies (see ANTITOXIN) to various diseases may indicate the presence of those diseases or the patient's immunity to them; such serum tests are performed in cases of suspected typhoid and of syphilis.

BLOOD TRANSFUSION. This has now been standardized and made a relatively simple performance, much aided by the "blood banks" which were set up in wartime and are able to supply blood at short notice, without the necessity of the donor actually being present. Blood transfusion is a life-saving procedure in many emergencies apart from war, and the good offices of donors are needed and appreciated at all times.

BOIL. An infection of the root of a hair, resulting in a raised red lump with pus forming at the centre. It may quickly be cured by injections of penicillin. For small boils application of a compress of 20 per cent Epsom or Glauber salts, changed every three hours, is effective. Do not use hot fomentations, which encourage the infection to enter other hair roots and create more boils and pimples. See also CARBUNCLE.

BORACIC POWDER. Boric acid. A very weak antiseptic, useful as an eye lotion, and to apply in solution to sore nipples in nursing mothers. The dry powder is not antiseptic, and there is no point in using *dry* boric lint for any purpose.

BOW LEGS. Resulting from rickets in infancy (see RICKETS). If very severe, bow legs can be straightened by an operation.

BRADYCARDIA. A slow pulse. It is normal in many people, especially athletes; but if below about fifty per minute it may indicate disease.

BRAIN. A collection of billions of nerve-cells. The organ of the mind, receiving information through the senses, capable of memory and judgment, and of originating action. Vital centres are at the base of the brain; motor areas are on the surface above the ear, and the centre for sight is at the back. But many areas are ill-defined in use, and damage to them may be followed by very little incapacity; this is especially so with the frontal lobes. See APOPLEXY, CEREBRAL HAEMORRHAGE, CEREBRO-SPINAL FLUID, CEREBRO-SPINAL FEVER, and CEREBRAL TUMOUR.

BREAST, DISEASES OF. Abscess of the breast is due to germs entering through the

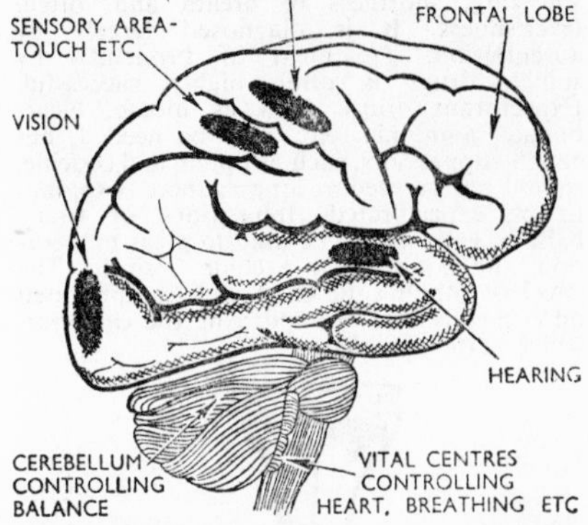

Brain, showing principal sensory areas, etc.

nipple and can usually be prevented by swabbing the nipple with boracic lotion, before and after feeding, with a soap-and-water wash twice a day. Cancer is *not* painful in its early stages. It first appears as a small hard lump, quite easily felt, and is at this stage curable in the great majority of cases. Many innocent lumps can appear in breasts, but any lump should be medically examined to be on the safe side. Chronic mastitis is a painful disorder in which a sort of ropy thickening is felt, which is tender; it can be accompanied by cysts. In most cases it does not need operation, and can be treated medically.

BREAST FEEDING. A new-born baby should be put to the breast almost at once, though milk does not appear for the first three days. There is a thin fluid, called colostrum, which helps the child's bowels to act, and the suction brings the milk in. For babies over 7½ lb. four-hourly feeding is generally most convenient, but a hungry baby may need to be fed more often. Babies that "won't take the nipple" need cuddling, not smacking. They should be allowed to play with the breast for a short time and not have it thrust at them. See BABY, CARE OF.

BREATHLESSNESS. Although normal after hard exercise, if it occurs after slight exertion it may be due to anaemia, to heart, lung or kidney disease, etc., and needs a thorough investigation.

BRIGHT'S DISEASE. Nephritis. Inflammation of the kidneys, resulting in their inability properly to get rid of the waste products of the body. The condition may be either acute or chronic. Symptoms are puffiness, especially of eyelids, hands and ankles; breathlessness; headaches; defective vision, and loss of appetite. The treatment is by rest, dieting, etc. The chronic form of this disease usually tends to get worse as time goes on, but can be controlled to some extent by careful supervision. See also KIDNEY DISEASES.

BRONCHIECTASIS. A disease of the bronchial tubes, with dilatation of their cavities.

BRONCHITIS. Catarrhal inflammation of the bronchial tubes, resulting in coughing, wheezing, shortness of breath and, often, feverishness. It is diagnosed largely by auscultation. Treatment of bronchitis by sulpha drugs is often highly successful. Expectorant drugs, such as ipecac, bicarbonate, ammonia, etc., may be needed, but cough-suppressors, such as opium and codeine, should not be used as long as there is sputum to be expectorated. Inhalations of friar's balsam, etc., should be used in great moderation, and not so as to exclude fresh air. The effect of rubbing the chest with camphorated oil is merely that of vaporizing the camphor, which is then inhaled.

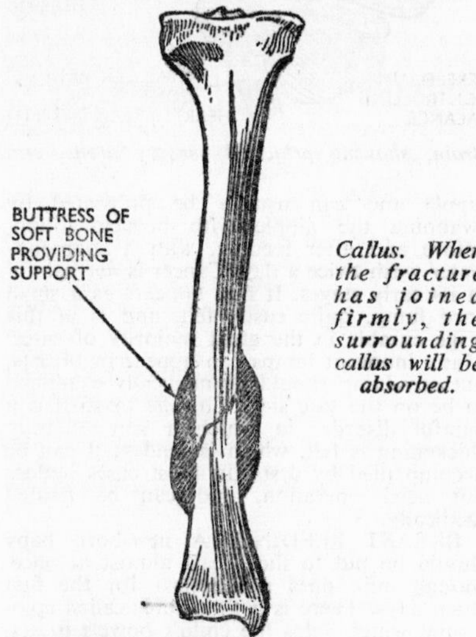

Callus. When the fracture has joined firmly, the surrounding callus will be absorbed.

BRONCHO-PNEUMONIA. A patchy pneumonia, affecting usually both lungs, developing often insidiously from an attack of bronchitis and tending to clear up gradually in about fourteen days if no specific treatment is used. Nowadays it is usually cleared up quickly with sulpha drugs or penicillin. The patient should have complete rest, easily digested food at frequent intervals and plenty of fresh air. Warmth is needed but should not be obtained by stuffiness.

BRONCHOSCOPY. Inspection of the inside of the windpipe and bronchial tubes through an instrument inserted through the mouth and down the windpipe.

BRUISE. Bleeding below the skin or in muscles, etc. Immediate application of cold compresses limits the extent of the bruise. Subsequent vigorous use and massage helps the blood clot to absorb and disappear.

BURNS. These are fully dealt with in the chapter on First-aid (page 140). Blisters should be treated (see BLISTER). The application of flavine, sulphonamide or penicillin prevents sepsis. The patient should be treated for shock. Where the burn is extensive call a doctor.

BURSITIS. Swelling in a bursa—a pocket containing a little fluid situated where friction may arise, such as over the kneecap and on the point of the elbow. Bursitis is due to injury in most cases. The fluid may be withdrawn through a hollow needle and a tight bandage applied. Housemaid's knee is a bursitis.

CALCIFEROL. Synthetic vitamin D which prevents rickets. See VITAMINS.

CALCULI. Stones, as in the kidney, bladder, and gall bladder. Small ones may pass, with considerable pain. Larger ones need to be removed by operation. There is no drug which dissolves or disperses stones.

CALLOSITY. Thickening of the skin where it is subject to hard pressure or friction, such as on the soles of the feet and on the hands of manual workers. It acts as a protection to the soft tissues.

CALLUS. The ring of soft bone which forms round the site of a fracture, holding the ends together while firm union takes place. After the fracture has united, the callus usually becomes absorbed.

CALORIE. The unit of heat. It is used as a measure of the energy value of foods. The average adult requires 2,800 to 3,000 calories a day, largely supplied by starch, sugar, and fat.

CANCER. There are several diseases under the general heading of cancer, but the common feature of them is that, in some organ, certain cells abandon their usual duties and concentrate on reproducing themselves, thus creating a growing mass or tumour. When this remains localized, it is described as benign or innocent. The feature of a cancerous tumour is that cells break off from it, spread through the lymphatic vessels or the blood stream and start new tumours, called secondaries, in other parts of the body. If the original tumour is removed before any secondaries have begun, a cure is generally obtained; but the existence of secondaries makes treatment much more difficult. See also RADIOTHERAPY.

CARBOHYDRATES. Sugary and starchy foods.

CARBUNCLE. A large boil which has penetrated below the skin. It often has more than one head. See BOIL.

CARCINOMA. A variety of cancer. See CANCER.

CARIES, DENTAL. Decay of the teeth. It is primarily due to a defective enamel coating, resulting from a shortage of vitamin D (see VITAMINS) in the diet, or in the mother's diet in the case of milk teeth, when the teeth are forming. A contributory cause is crowded teeth, causing food particles to collect between them and ferment.

CARMINATIVE. A drug which soothes flatulence and dispels wind; peppermint, ginger and sal volatile are examples.

CAROTID ARTERY. The main artery taking blood to the head and neck. It runs from the inner end of the collar-bone to the top of the Adam's apple, where it forms the external carotid, which supplies the face, and the internal carotid, which supplies the brain.

CARRIER. A person who carries disease germs without himself suffering from the disease, so spreading infection to other people. Typhoid and diphtheria are examples of diseases which may be spread in this way by people who are themselves immune.

CATARACT. A disease in which the lens of the eye loses its transparency, thus causing

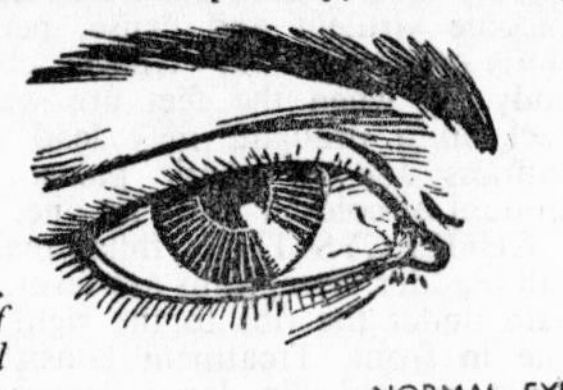

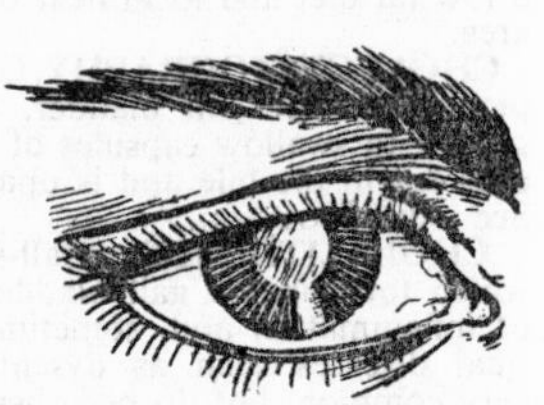

Cataract. The pupil of the normal eye is transparent and does not reflect light. In cataract it becomes opaque and dull, making the eye blind.

blindness. By operation, the opaque lens is removed, and spectacles are worn to compensate, giving fairly good vision.

CATARRH. A moist exudation from mucous surfaces, due to infection with various germs. It is common in the nose and its associated passages. In chronic cases there may be some nasal obstruction, or some disease of the sinuses (see SINUS). A starchy diet, anaemia, lack of fresh air, too much smoking and repeated exposure to colds, all tend to cause catarrh.

CELLULITIS. Inflammation of connective tissues, such as those below the skin, resulting in a thickened, brawny, painful swelling.

CELLULOSE. The stringy material of plants. It forms most of the roughage in our diets and helps the bowels to act. We cannot digest it, though herbivorous animals can do so; it is for this reason that grass is not a suitable diet for us.

CEREBRAL HAEMORRHAGE. Bleeding into the brain. See APOPLEXY, and BRAIN.

CEREBRAL TUMOUR. A growth in the brain. See BRAIN and CANCER.

CEREBRO-SPINAL FEVER. Spotted fever; meningococcal meningitis. An inflammation of the membranes covering the brain, due to a germ called the meningococcus. It may be spread by carriers (see CARRIER) and used to be fatal, but is now usually cured by penicillin. See MENINGITIS.

CEREBRO-SPINAL FLUID. A straw-coloured fluid bathing the brain and spinal cord. Among other functions, the fluid acts as a cushion to the brain in case of injury to the head. See LUMBAR PUNCTURE.

CHANCRE. A venereal sore. Soft chancre is a local disease, but hard chancre is the primary evidence of syphilis. See SYPHILIS and VENEREAL DISEASE.

CHEIROPOMPHOLYX. A skin disease characterized by a crop of blisters on the palms of the hands or soles of the feet.

CHEST. The upper part of the trunk, separated by the diaphragm from the abdomen below (see ABDOMEN). It is enclosed by the ribs, so that movement of these and the diaphragm enables the chest's volume to vary and breathing to take place. It contains the lungs and heart, with large blood-vessels and important nerves.

CHICKEN-POX. The rash of chicken-pox appears in the first twenty-four hours and consists of small oval blisters surrounded by a red margin. Generally, the rash is more profuse on the trunk than on the limbs; it may be very slight or may cover the whole body. There are no serious complications. The incubation period is ten to twenty-one days and the rash lasts about fourteen days. There may be fever at first, but if there is none, bed is unnecessary, though the patient should be isolated. Chicken-pox is due to the same virus as is the cause of shingles (see HERPES); herpes may be caught from chicken-pox and vice versa. There is no specific treatment.

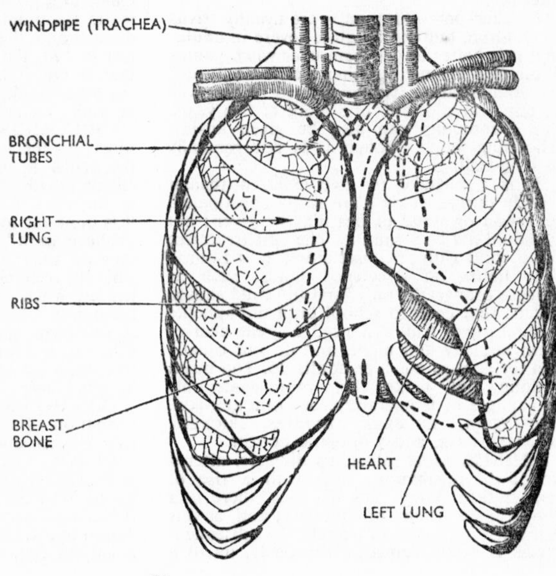

Chest showing position of the principal organs.

CHILBLAIN. Itching purple swellings on the extremities, due to spasm of the tiny veins from cold. Prevention consists of eating more fats, taking exercise and keeping the extremities warm. Treatment of chilblains is by ultra-violet and infra-red rays (see RAYS), by rubbing them with liniments, by bathing them in alternate hot and cold water, and by tight bandaging just above the chilblains for ten minutes at a time to increase congestion. Broken chilblains may be healed with a mixture of bleaching powder and petroleum jelly.

CHILDBIRTH. See BIRTH.

CHILDREN'S AILMENTS. Children need more food than do adults in proportion to their size, and adolescents eat a good deal more than adults. They need more proteins, because they are growing, and more fats and carbohydrates to supply energy. As their energy output is high, they require much more rest and it is important to get them to bed early. Temperature in children is more unstable than in adults and a temperature of 105 is not necessarily a cause for alarm; it depends entirely on the ailment causing it.

One unsolved problem is that school age coincides with the age at which a child's immunity from most infectious diseases is at its lowest. Children of five, who have met little infection and have no immunity, are plunged into crowded classrooms where colds, influenza, measles and whooping-cough are almost certain to appear. It is best to recognize the fact that a child has to have some infections in order to acquire immunity, and to be prepared for about a half of the first year of schooling to be spent at home. Provided that such ailments are taken in time, and the child put to bed, little harm is done and immunity is gradually built up. Sheltering a child from infections means only more severe attacks in later life.

Chicken-pox and mumps are usually trivial in children, but can be quite severe in adults, and it is better to get them over when young. Protection against diphtheria can be afforded by immunization, two injections being given at one year old, and one more at five years. Some immunity can also be given against whooping-cough, though it is not generally as long-lasting.

It is a mistake to give children regular weekly purges. If they are really constipated, magnesia or syrup of figs may be given; but it should *not* be a routine. The best treatment for a child with an upset stomach is twenty-four hours on sweetened fluids, such as glucose orangeade, only, and the child should not be sent back to school until the appetite has returned. Children need a great deal of fresh air, day and night, and do not usually feel the cold as much as adults do. Too much coddling only makes them more susceptible to changes of temperature. See CHICKEN-POX, DIPHTHERIA, ENURESIS, MEASLES, RICKETS, SCARLET FEVER, and WHOOPING-COUGH.

CHILLS. Most infectious diseases, after a period of incubation, start with a rise of temperature. When this happens, there is a shiver and a feeling of chilliness; and, as this is the first indication of trouble, the subsequent illness is often blamed, erroneously, on to a "chill." Chilling *can* cause illness, but it usually has to be fairly severe. Sitting about in wet clothes, or spending a night in the open, may reduce the bodily temperature so that resistance is lowered and germs in the throat, which would ordinarily be innocuous, become virulent and cause, perhaps, bronchitis or pneumonia. Uneven chilling of the body, as when the feet are warm but the neck in a draught, may lead to muscular stiffness and rheumatic pains. But a mild amount of cold air hurts no one.

CHOLECYSTITIS. Inflammation of the gall bladder. Symptoms are fever, nausea, and pain under the ribs to the right of the mid-line in front. Treatment consists of sulpha drugs or penicillin, large quantities of fluids, a low fat diet and local heat over the painful area.

CHOLECYSTOGRAPHY. Obtaining X-ray pictures of the gall bladder, by getting the patient to swallow capsules of a dye which is excreted in the bile and is opaque to X-rays. See RADIOLOGY.

CHOLELITHIASIS. Gall-stones; stones which form in the gall bladder after attacks of inflammation and, sometimes, after intestinal diseases such as dysentery. They are very common, but do not always give rise to symptoms. Small gall-stones may try to pass into the intestine and, in doing so, give rise to great pain until they are passed. Repeated attacks of this "gall-stone colic" necessitate operation to remove the gall bladder.

CHOLERA. A tropical disease, characterized by intense diarrhoea and collapse. Contracted by drinking infected water.

CHOREA. It is also known as St. Vitus's dance and is a form of rheumatic fever in children, affecting the nervous system. The child performs continuous purposeless movements and grimaces. It may have other rheumatic symptoms; there is a danger of heart disease and the child should have complete rest in bed. Patients often do better at home than in hospital, as they have a habit of copying other similar cases; they should, however, be under medical care.

CIRCUMCISION. Removal of the male foreskin—the loose skin covering the end of the penis. A very ancient traditional rite or custom, with religious sanctions, originating in the East. From a medical point of view, it is done far too frequently, as many parents "believe in it" without any clear idea why they do so. It is unnecessary when it is possible to retract the foreskin, but may be needed when the foreskin is very long and redundant, or when the opening is very small. A new-born male baby naturally has a foreskin which adheres to the penis underneath; this needs no treatment and corrects itself as he gets older.

CIRRHOSIS. Hardening, owing to the formation of fibrous tissue. Cirrhosis of the liver is often due to chronic alcoholism.

CLINIC. Literally, the term "clinic" means *at the bedside* and is, therefore, a misnomer for the modern clinic, which usually has no beds. It has come to mean a building where examination and treatment of some particular kind is carried out, such as antenatal clinics (see

ANTENATAL CARE), infant-welfare clinics, tuberculosis clinics, fracture clinics and so on. The idea is to concentrate people requiring a certain kind of medical service at a place where facilities for that service are available. It is rather a mass-production method of dealing with individual problems, but where individual methods are impracticable for reasons of cost, or lack of facilities, it has great advantages.

COCCYDYNIA. Pain in the coccyx—the tailbone at the lower end of the spinal column. It often follows a fall, the instrumental delivery of a child, other difficulties in labour, or other injury, and may be difficult to cure. Electrical treatment may be successful.

COD-LIVER OIL. A useful addition to diet, not only for the calorific value of the fat in it, but for its content of vitamins A and D (see VITAMINS). If it proves difficult to digest, it may be given as an emulsion, or with malt; but many of the malt preparations contain too small a proportion of the oil.

COLDS. There are probably a number of different diseases called colds. A person with chronic catarrh may have periodic flare-ups, which he calls colds, as may one with sinus trouble (see SINUS). The running nose of hay fever, however, is due to allergy. The true cold is due to an ultra-microscopic virus (see VIRUS) and is intensely infectious.

Infection is spread not only by coughing and sneezing, but by the unhygienic practice of shaking hands. The air of a room where people are sneezing is highly infectious, and is difficult to sterilize, though experiments are being made in this direction (see ANTISEPTIC). Treatment of a severe cold is not very satisfactory. Drugs such as benzedrine dry up the secretions, aspirin removes headache, and inhaling or gargling with preparations of iodine and chlorine help to keep the infection under. A few days in bed is far the best remedy, but is not always practicable.

COLIC. Spasmodic pain in the intestines or in some other hollow internal organ. Intestinal colic is characterized by severe spasms of pain with relief between. It can be eased by pressure and heat and by taking warm drinks. Belladonna is used to counteract it. It may be due to constipation, diarrhoea, unsuitable food, etc. Gall-stone colic and renal colic are due to the passage of gall-stones and kidney-stones respectively.

COLITIS. Inflammation of the colon, or large intestine. There are a number of diseases under this heading, such as ulcerative colitis, dysentery and mucous colitis. The characteristic is diarrhoea and colicky pains, sometimes with bleeding from the bowel.

COLLAPSE. There are many causes of collapse, such as injury, loss of blood, heart disease, emotional strain and prolonged exposure. It is usually fairly sudden in onset. Muscular weakness leads to inability to stand or sit; the pulse is rapid and feeble, breathing shallow and sighing and the skin pale and cold. The lips may be bluish, as also may the finger-nails. Treatment is that of the condition causing collapse, plus moderate warmth (not great heat), plenty of fluids, sugar or glucose, complete rest by lying flat on the back, and possibly blood transfusion. See SHOCK.

COLON. The large intestine; it starts in the lower right-hand side of the abdomen, proceeds upwards to the liver, across to the spleen on the left side, then down to the pelvis, where it leads into the rectum.

COLOSTOMY. An artificial opening made into the colon. It is usually made to provide

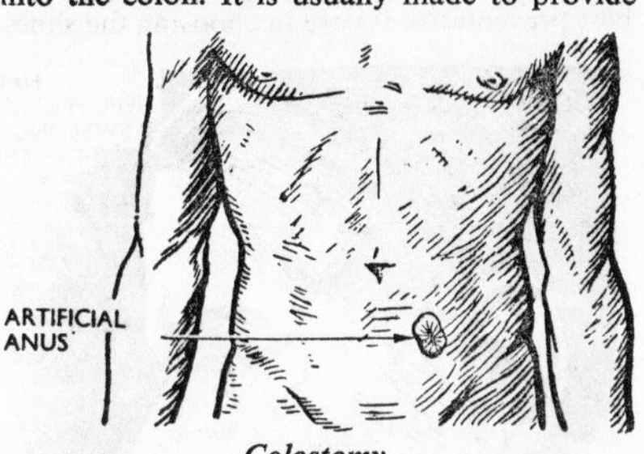

Colostomy.

an artificial outlet for the bowel in diseases of the rectum.

COMA. Unconsciousness, deeper than sleep, so that the patient cannot be roused.

CONFINEMENT. It may take place at a hospital or nursing home. If, however, the birth of a child is to take place at home, arrange for a quiet room, with a single bed, preferably with linoleum on the floor and a minimum of bric-à-brac and unnecessary furniture. If there is no running hot and cold water, there must be a washstand with at least two large bowls, and arrangements made for plenty of hot water. Mackintosh sheet and drawsheets, cotton-wool, an antiseptic, methylated spirit, Gamgee tissue, boracic lotion, clean towels, soap, and a *clean* nail-brush are the chief things to provide. See ANTENATAL CARE and BIRTH.

CONJUNCTIVITIS. Pink-eye; a bloodshot eye, rather painful, which may discharge or weep. The lids may be stuck together in the morning. Bathe the eye with a one-per-cent solution of boracic, using an eyebath. See a doctor if it does not improve in twenty-four hours. Steaming sometimes gives relief to the pain.

CONSTIPATION. Difficulty in evacuating the bowel. It is not as serious as is often supposed, and many people would remain quite well with an evacuation twice a week. It may be due to sedentary habits, to drinking insufficient fluids, or to not taking enough roughage in the diet. Constipation is often much easier to relieve with a suppository or a small enema than by taking aperients, which merely upset the stomach. See APERIENTS.

CONTAGION. Acquiring disease by actual contact, as opposed to infection. Some diseases, for example, the common cold, are both infectious and contagious. Chicken-pox is chiefly contagious and impetigo is contagious. Germs cannot fly about of their own volition. See INFECTION.

CONTRACEPTION. See BIRTH CONTROL.

CONVULSIONS. See FITS.

CORN. A hard painful lump, usually on a toe. It is due, in the first place, to pressure and is painless until germs are rubbed into it and it becomes inflamed. An inflamed corn may need poulticing or surgical treatment. Pressure may be relieved by corn rings, and the hard skin may be removed by cutting, or by corn paints. But corns will always recur if a joint rubs against an ill-fitting shoe, and the best preventative is care in choosing the shoes.

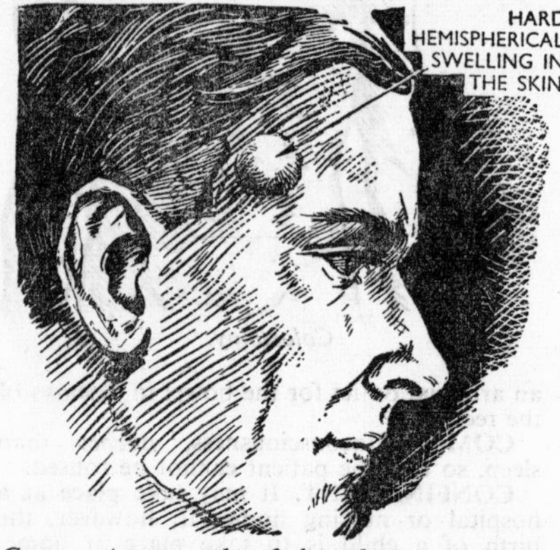

Cysts. An example of the sebaceous variety.

CORNEA. The clear substance in front of the coloured part of the eye. If injured, it may lead to blindness. See EYE.

CORONARY THROMBOSIS. Clotting in the coronary artery, the main artery supplying the heart. It causes sudden pain in the chest (see ANGINA PECTORIS) and collapse. Sometimes it is fatal, but many cases recover, with some scarring left in the heart muscle, but with comparatively good health. See HEART and ELECTROCARDIOGRAM.

COUGH. A spasmodic contraction of the throat muscles designed to remove sputum. It is produced by sputum reaching the throat from above or below, and also by anything irritating the throat, such as local dryness. When there is sputum, the cough is useful and should be encouraged; when there is none, it is useless and needs to be repressed. Therefore, one sort of cough mixture is unsuitable for all coughs and may be actually harmful. See BRONCHITIS, COLDS, and PNEUMONIA.

CRAMP. A painful muscular spasm produced by the over-tiring of a group of muscles, especially when they are cold. It also occurs when there has been a loss of salt from the body, as in excessive sweating. Cramp can be due to interference with the blood supply of the muscles (see ARTERIO-SCLEROSIS), or to various nervous diseases. Severe cramp occurs in strychnine poisoning and in lockjaw.

CROUP. Laryngeal spasm. The term "croup" is often applied, incorrectly, to any husky, crowing cough; but while true croup is dangerous, this type of cough is not especially so. Babies can get a form of crowing breathing, due to spasm of the vocal cords, which is relieved by a warm sponge on the neck, and cured by giving cod-liver oil.

CYANOSIS. Blueness of the lips, face and extremities, due to defective circulation. This may be merely local, or may be due to heart disease, etc.

CYSTITIS. Inflammation of the urinary bladder (see BACILLURIA). It causes frequent and painful micturition, often with thick cloudy urine which sometimes contains blood. The doctor may be able to make a diagnosis from a specimen of urine, but a fuller investigation is often needed. Modern treatment with sulpha drugs is usually successful.

CYSTS. Hollow swellings, filled with various fluids. They may be trivial as in small sebaceous cysts of the skin, or serious as with large ovarian cysts. Dermoid cysts contain hair, teeth and other extraneous objects, and may turn cancerous if not removed.

DEAFNESS. Deafness may be due to trouble in the external, the middle, or the internal ear. In the external ear, it may be due to plugging with wax or a foreign body, or to some inflammatory condition such as boils or eczema. Middle-ear deafness may be due to catarrh or to abscess formation, caused by infection from the back of the nose via the eustachian tube; or it may be due to a hardening of the small bones which conduct vibrations from the eardrum. Most external-ear troubles are curable and the deafness quickly subsides.

In acute inflammations of the middle ear, hearing usually recovers in a few weeks after the inflammation has settled down, but perforation of the drum does not always heal, and may lead to deafness. Otosclerosis is now being treated by an operation called fenestration, in some cases with dramatic success, but it is too early to say if all cases can be cured. All such conditions need expert attention. Internal-ear deafness usually involves the auditory nerve and is therefore incurable. In external, or in middle-ear deafness, sounds may be heard by conduction through the bones of the skull; but not in internal-ear deafness. The degree of deafness may be tested by an audiometer and, from this, suitable hearing aids prescribed.

DEFICIENCY DISEASES. Diseases due to a lack of vitamins. See VITAMINS.

DEFORMITIES. These may be congenital or due to acquired disease. Such things as hare-lip and cleft palate are due to failure of the child to complete its development in the early weeks of pregnancy. They *may* be due to illness in the mother at that time, and German measles is thought to be one such cause. Pigeon chests, bow legs and knock knees are due to rickets and hunchbacks are due to tuberculosis of the spine. Other curvatures of the spine may be due to faulty posture, to stooping over school desks, or to internal disorders; for instance, chronic disease of one lung will cause a lateral curvature of the spine. The treatment of deformities is the function of the orthopaedic surgeon, aided by physiotherapists.

DELIRIUM. Wandering speech, due through fevers or other causes to toxins reaching the brain. It requires no special treatment unless the patient becomes restive and violent.

Deformities. Both knock knees and bow legs are due to rickets.

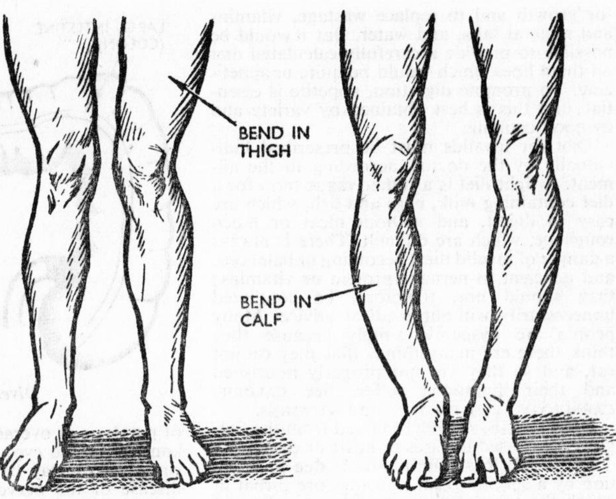

when he should be gently restrained so as not to hurt himself. Delirium is very common in small children when they are feverish, and is not an indication of danger.

DEMENTIA. Loss of mental power and judgment. See MENTAL DISEASES.

DENGUE. A tropical disease, due to a virus transmitted by the mosquito bite. "Measley" rashes and pains in the limbs occur.

DEPRESSION. People of mercurial temperaments are subject to fits of depression alternating with periods of happiness. Prolonged depression is likely to be due to the effects of some disease, such as influenza. Really severe depression, termed melancholia, occurs in mental diseases.

DERMATITIS. Inflammation of the skin. It includes some forms of eczema and, strictly speaking, includes impetigo, pimples, boils and any other inflammatory condition. Industrial dermatitis has a special importance, both because of its interference with production and because of claims under the National Insurance Act. It may be due to contact of the skin with oils, powders or industrial solvents, to exposure to radiation, or to handling foodstuffs (see BAKER'S ITCH). It may take an eczematous form, or that of a mass of small boils.

Prevention lies in strict cleanliness, the use of barrier creams and the elimination from unsuitable jobs of people with sensitive skins. Diagnosis may be difficult in distinguishing it from non-industrial dermatitis. Treatment, in the main, consists of the use of soothing applications containing zinc, ichthyol and various oils. See ECZEMA and IMPETIGO.

DERMOID CYST. Dermoids are congenital, being malformations during development of the child. See CYSTS.

DIABETES. Chief symptoms are thirst, frequent passing of large quantities of urine, and loss of weight. But some cases remain fat and have no thirst; these may be first discovered as diabetics by circulatory troubles or even dimness of vision. Diabetics pass sugar in the urine (see BENEDICT'S SOLUTION), but so do some people who have not got diabetes, and a blood test (see BLOOD TESTS) may be needed to distinguish them. Diabetes is due to the failure of the islets of Langerhans in the pancreas to form insulin. Insulin is needed before the body can utilize sugar as a source of energy.

The symptoms of diabetes can be prevented by administering insulin hypodermically before meals containing starch or sugar (see CARBOHYDRATE), but this usually has to be continued indefinitely, and there is so far no cure which will make the body form its own insulin again. Untreated diabetics are unable to digest fat (see ACIDOSIS), and the undigested fat forms poisons which may cause unconsciousness known as diabetic coma; the treatment for this is insulin. An overdose of insulin can also cause coma (see COMA) the treatment for which is to administer sugar. It is thus vital for a diabetic and his friends to distinguish between diabetic coma and insulin coma, as the treatments are exactly opposite.

DIAPHRAGM. The midriff; a muscular partition between the chest and the abdomen. It is the most important muscle in respiration because it descends on breathing in; also a very important muscle in any straining effort in which the breath is held.

DIARRHOEA. Loose and frequent motions of the bowel. It may be due to too much aperient or to injudicious diet, especially onions, plums, rhubarb or blackcurrants, in susceptible people. Diarrhoea is frequently due to infections, such as colds and influenza, and is very severe in dysentery, cholera and sometimes in typhoid. Mild attacks may be cured by a dose of castor oil, which clears out the offending substance and then constipates. Bismuth is useful, in twenty-grain doses every three hours. Infective cases are often medically treated by sulphaguanidine, which kills the responsible bacteria; but this should not be taken without medical advice as beneficial bacteria also may be killed. Normally, the diet should be milky, but in acute cases twenty-four hours' starvation with water only is well worth while.

DIATHERMY. See ELECTRICAL TREATMENT.

DICK TEST. A skin test to determine susceptibility to scarlet fever.

DIET. A balanced diet should contain fats and carbohydrates to provide energy, protein for growth and to replace wastage, vitamins and mineral salts, and water. But it would be possible to provide a carefully calculated diet on these lines which would be quite unappetizing. To promote digestion, appetite is essential, and this is best obtained by variety and by good cooking.

Diet for invalids must be prescribed individually by the doctor, according to the ailment. A light diet is a rather vague term for a diet containing milk, eggs and fish, which are easy to digest, and without meat or much roughage, which are difficult. There is always a danger of invalid diets becoming unbalanced, and deficient in perhaps protein or vitamins; they should not, therefore, be continued unnecessarily without medical advice. Many people are dyspeptic simply because they think there are many things that they cannot eat, and so they are not properly nourished and their digestions suffer. See CALORIE, CARBOHYDRATES, PROTEIN and VITAMINS.

DIGITALIS. A drug obtained from the foxglove; it is used in cases of heart disease.

DIPHTHERIA. Diphtheria is due to infection by a specific germ, causing sore throat in which the tonsils are covered by an adherent grey-white membrane which may spread on to the palate and uvula, or down to the larynx and windpipe. Powerful toxins are formed in the throat and, being absorbed into the bloodstream, cause great prostration, damage to the heart and to the nervous system. Death may be caused by heart failure or by obstruction to breathing.

Diphtheria may be largely prevented by immunization, usually done at one year of age and repeated at five. It is treated by serum obtained from horses which have been rendered immune. When serum is given early, the results are dramatic, quick recovery taking place; it is important to give it before too much general damage has been done. Obstruction to breathing is treated by tracheotomy. See CROUP and IMMUNIZATION.

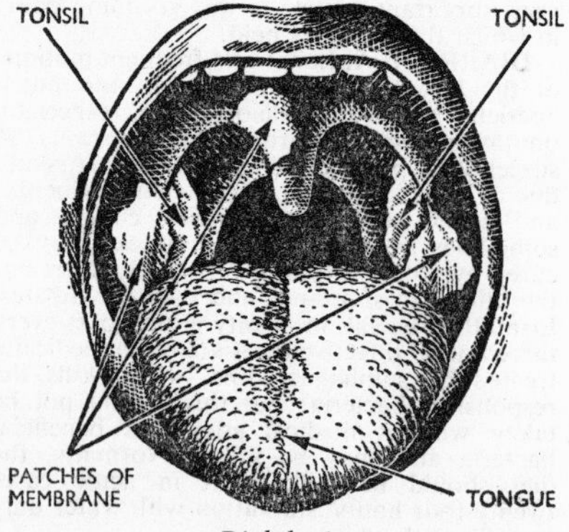

Diphtheria.

DIPLOPIA. Double vision. If it occurs when only one eye is used, it may be due to disease in the eyeball. When double vision occurs only on using both eyes, it is the result of paralysis or overaction of the small muscles controlling the eye, producing a tendency to squint. This may be due to local trouble, to disease of the nervous system or to certain toxins, as in food poisoning and alcoholism. See INTOXICATION, NERVOUS DISEASE, and PARALYSIS.

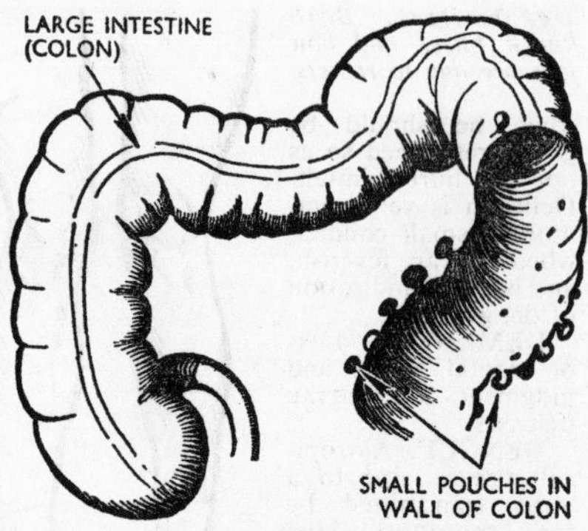

Diverticulosis.

DIPSOMANIA. Drunkenness. See INTOXICATION.

DISLOCATED JOINT. See JOINTS, DISLOCATIONS AND SPRAINS OF.

DISSEMINATED SCLEROSIS. A disease, the cause of which is unknown, in which patches of scarring take place in the spinal cord and brain leading to paralysis of various groups of muscles. The symptoms vary widely and, while the disease is chronic, spontaneous improvement often occurs. See NERVOUS DISEASES.

DIVERTICULOSIS. A disease of the colon. Tiny pouches form in the wall of the intestine, due to weakness in the muscular coat. These fill with food residues, which ferment from time to time and cause attacks of diverticulitis—abdominal pain and tenderness, sometimes with vomiting. Diagnosis is made by radiology, and treatment consists of a diet without much roughage, and taking paraffin and powdered kaolin.

DRAWSHEET. A sheet folded three times from side to side and placed lengthways across a bed so that it may be gradually drawn across as it becomes soiled.

DROP FOOT. A foot which cannot be raised at the ankle joint, so that the toe drags in walking. It is due to paralysis of the muscles in the front of the shin and may be treated by electrical means (see ELECTRICAL TREATMENT), and by shortening the tendons.

DROPSY. An accumulation of fluid in the tissues due to disease of the heart or kidneys, or to obstruction to the circulation, as in liver disease. The treatment is that of the disease causing it, including measures, such as purgatives and sweating, to get rid of fluid. Fluid may also be removed by tapping.

DRUGS. Medicines; substances which alter the bodily reactions or attack bacteria, etc.; they are taken by the mouth or administered by injection. Dangerous drugs, legally

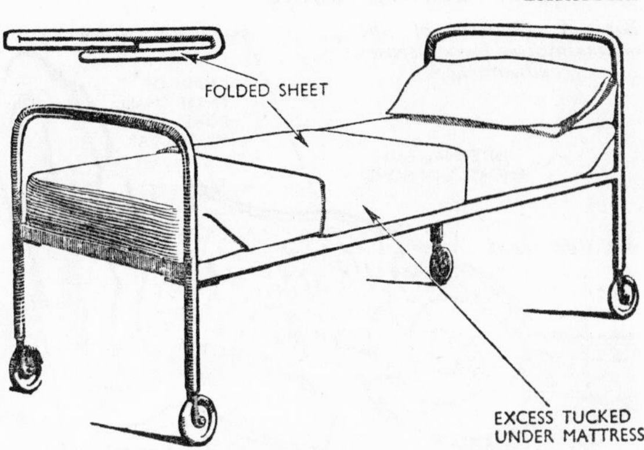

Drawsheet. A useful idea in home nursing. (*See page* 82.)

such drugs as morphia, cocaine and heroin, which may cause addiction, may be supplied only on a medical prescription.

DUODENAL ULCER. Ulceration in the duodenum —the first three inches of the intestine after leaving the stomach. It is largely due to psychological causes, such as strain and anxiety. The symptom is pain just below the ribs on the right side of the mid-line, often boring through to the shoulder-blade behind, and coming on about two hours after a meal. The pain is apt to come on in the night and is sometimes accompanied by vomiting. It is usually relieved by the taking of food. Diagnosis is usually confirmed by radiology. Treatment is medical in the first instance, and comprises two-hourly bland feeding, alkalis, rest, etc. Mental rest is as essential as physical rest, because worry retards recovery. Bleeding from the ulcer may need surgery, as also may obstruction due to scarring near the stomach outlet. Sometimes ulcers perforate the wall of the intestine, causing collapse and severe abdominal pain; urgent operation is then necessary. See GASTRIC ULCER.

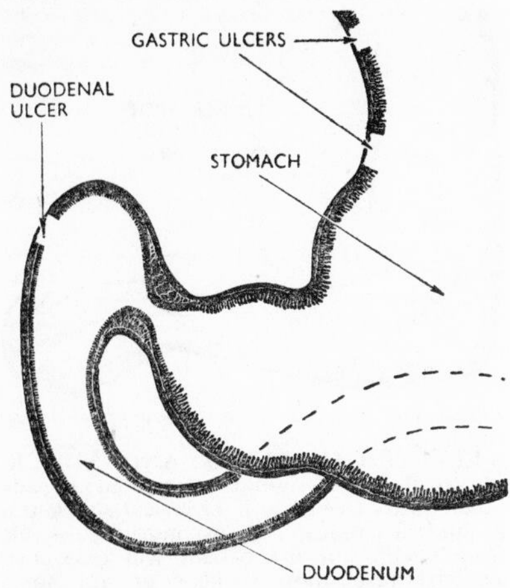

Duodenal and gastric ulcers.

DUST DISEASES. Chronic diseases of the lungs due to inhaling certain dusts, such as coal-dust and quartz. See ANTHRACOSIS.

DWARFS. They may be perfectly proportioned or deformed, highly intelligent or mentally deficient. Cretins are mentally deficient, are caused by thyroid deficiency and are curable if treated early. Achondroplasia is an hereditary disease in which the trunk is normal but the limbs are short and bowed; intelligence is normal. Most circus dwarfs are achondroplasic. Stunted growth can be caused by disease, especially kidney disease, in childhood.

DYSENTERY. Severe diarrhoea, often with bleeding from the bowel and great prostration. Tropical dysentery is of two main kinds—bacillary and amoebic, distinguished by bacteriological examination of the motions. Amoebic dysentery is treated by emetine, obtained from ipecacuanha; bacillary dysentery by sulphaguanidine and other sulpha drugs. A mild form of dysentery, called Sonne dysentery, has been very prevalent in England in recent years. See DIARRHOEA.

DYSMENORRHOEA. Painful menstruation. This is of several types and may have many different causes. Pain may be due to trouble in the womb itself or in the ovaries, it may have psychological causes, or it may be a result of congestion through constipation or sedentary habits. Mild dysmenorrhoea can usually be controlled by adequate exercise and attention to the bowels. If severe enough to interfere with work, a gynaecologist should be consulted.

DYSPEPSIA. Impaired digestion. See INDIGESTION.

EAR DISEASES. While there are many diseases of the ear, by far the commonest serious disease is acute otitis media—inflammation of the middle ear. This usually follows catarrhal diseases, such as colds, measles or whooping-cough, or those with sepsis in the throat, such as scarlet fever and tonsillitis. The infection reaches the ear from the throat by way of the eustachian tube. It may subside rapidly, or pus may form and an abscess result. If this is unrelieved, it will burst through the eardrum and cause an ear discharge. Or infection may go backwards into the hollow of the mastoid bone and cause mastoid disease. The first sign of most of these troubles is earache, which should always be taken seriously. Also see DEAFNESS and EARACHE.

EARACHE. In the majority of cases, earache is due to inflammation in the ear, and of the eardrum. It may be due to only a mild catarrh and may quickly subside on the application of heat to the outside with a hot-water

Ear. A diagram of the organs involved in ear diseases and earache.

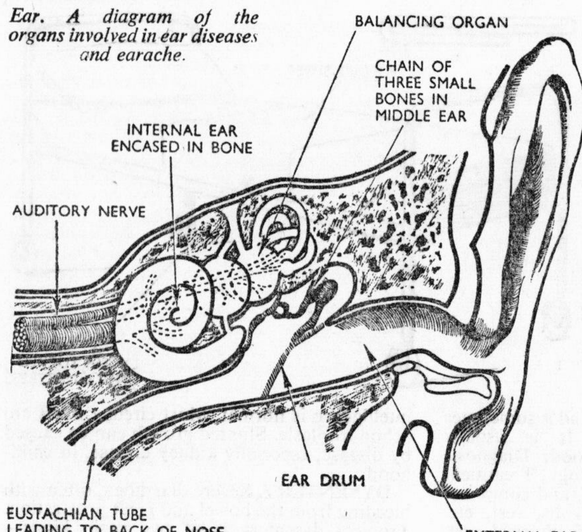

bottle; but if the ache is at all severe and persistent, a doctor should always be consulted, because it is necessary to inspect the eardrum before any idea of the seriousness can be obtained. *Never pour anything* into the ear, unless instructed to do so by the doctor, or considerable damage may be done. See First-aid Chapter (page 144).

ECTOPIC PREGNANCY. Pregnancy outside the womb. The egg-cell has to travel from the ovary to the womb, and after fertilization it may develop in the tube instead of moving into the womb. In such a case, it has not room for full growth and usually ruptures the tube. Sudden pain in the side, with slight bleeding from the vagina, occurring in early pregnancy, calls for medical advice in case this complication has occurred. It is not, however, very common. See ANTENATAL CARE and PREGNANCY.

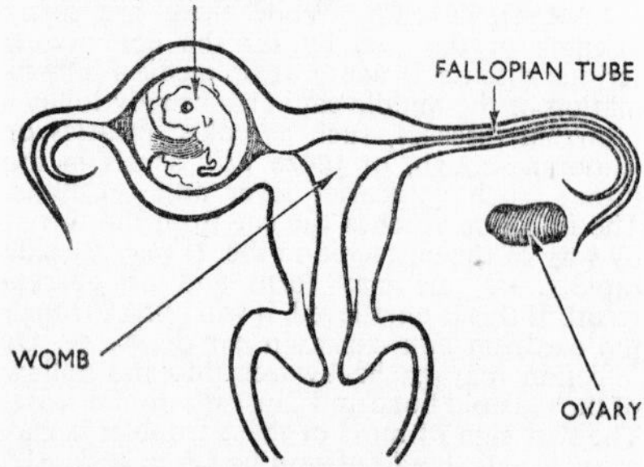

Ectopic pregnancy.

ECTOPIC TESTIS. A testicle which has not descended into the scrotum (the pouch holding the testes); fairly common in young boys and may right itself before puberty. It can often be hastened by injections of hormones (see ENDOCRINES). In a few cases, an operation may be necessary. A testicle which remains in the groin is easily injured and is always sterile.

ECZEMA. An attack of eczema begins with an eruption of tiny pimples, which soon grow together into a red, irritable rash which often oozes and weeps. Eczema may be a result of dietary troubles or of local irritation: it often follows scratching due, for example, to scabies or to urticaria. Treatment is by local applications as for dermatitis. Extensive eczema is very prostrating and may need complete rest in bed for several weeks. It is apt to take many months before complete recovery. See DERMATITIS and SKIN.

ELBOW, TENNIS. A pain at the outer side of the elbow, caused by jerking movements of the forearm, as in the backhand drive at tennis, or in hammering, carpet beating, etc. Acute cases should be strapped and bandaged. Chronic ones may need manipulation. See JOINTS, SPRAINS OF.

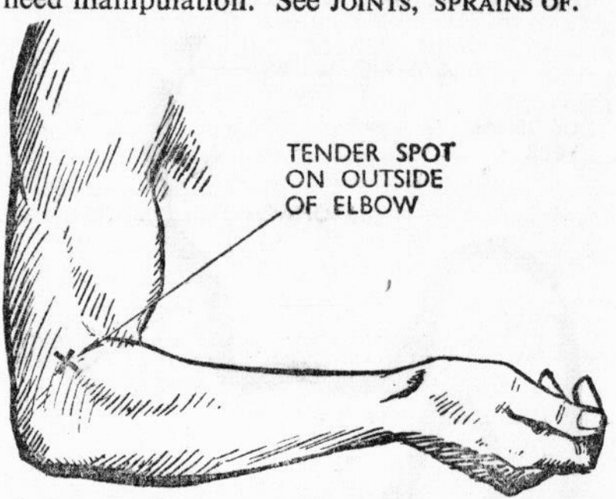

Elbow showing where tennis elbow pains occur.

ELECTRICAL BURNS AND SHOCK. Electrical burns should be treated as any other burns (see BURN). Electrical shock can produce a condition almost indistinguishable from death, but the patient will recover if artificial respiration is kept up for some hours.

ELECTRICAL TREATMENT. Electric currents may be used in medicine in various ways. The body consists largely of salt water, and a current passed through this dissociates it into sodium and chlorine, which combine with water to form caustic soda and hydrochloric acid, both caustic. Therefore a needle, carrying a constant current, passed into a hair root will form caustic and destroy the root of the hair. Both constant and interrupted currents are used to stimulate paralysed muscles.

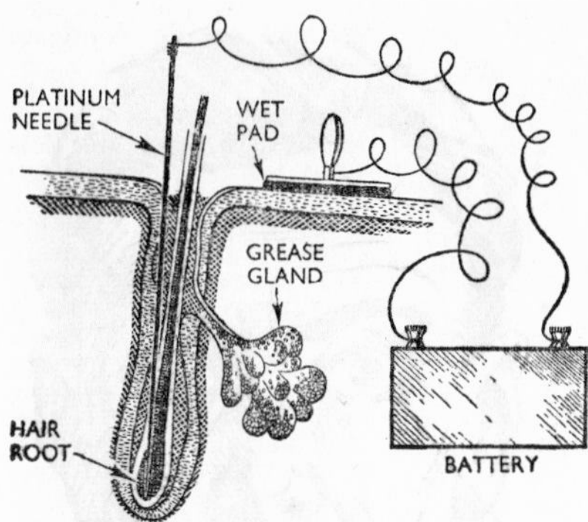

Electrical treatment. A diagram of the apparatus and method used to destroy unwanted hair.

External heating can be produced by electric blankets, radiant-heat cradles, etc., and slightly more penetrating heat by infra-red rays; while heat can be produced inside the tissues by diathermy and short-wave therapy. All these are employed to relieve rheumatic troubles (see RHEUMATISM). Ultra-violet rays are used for their general tonic effect, also to produce vitamin D in the skin and cure rickets —though cod-liver oil is equally effective (see RICKETS and VITAMINS); and these rays are used locally to heal up ulcers. Ionization is a means of driving some drug into the body by passing a constant current through the appropriate tissues, and is useful in some skin diseases.

ELECTROCARDIOGRAM. A record of the small electrical currents given off by the heart as it contracts. Used in diagnosing heart diseases. See CORONARY THROMBOSIS and HEART.

EMBOLISM. A clot of blood detached from one part of the circulatory system, as after phlebitis, and arriving in some other organ where it suddenly obstructs the blood supply. If in a vital organ, such as the brain, the heart or a lung, an embolism can be very serious. See APOPLEXY.

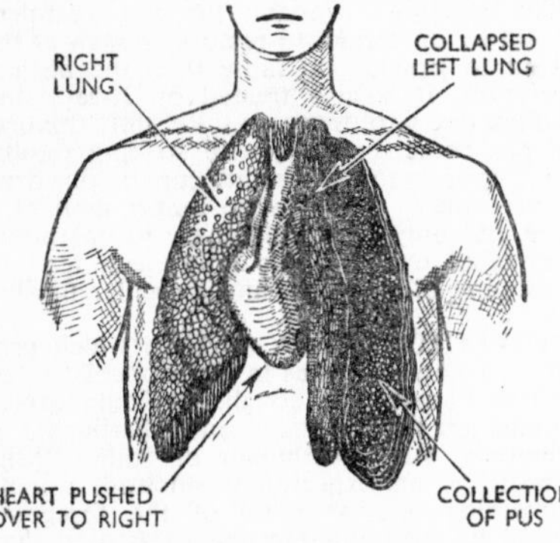

Empyema.

EMETICS. Drugs which cause vomiting, such as weak mustard water and salt and water (normal saline solution).

EMPHYSEMA. The over-stretching of the air spaces of the lungs, so that they join up with each other and provide larger spaces with less surface area, and consequently cause difficulty in breathing. Emphysema is often a sequel of chronic bronchitis and of asthma.

EMPYEMA. A large abscess or collection of pus, lying between the lung and the inner wall of the chest. It is often a consequence of pneumonia, or it may follow chest wounds. An acute empyema is accompanied by high temperature, pain in the shoulder and difficulty in breathing. Treatment involves withdrawing the pus, either by operation or through a hollow needle. The subsequent injection of penicillin into the cavity often hastens recovery.

ENCEPHALITIS. Inflammation of the brain. Encephalitis lethargica, known as sleepy sickness, is an infectious disease, in which paralysis of various muscles may occur, together with fever and prostration. It may leave serious after-effects, especially a form of shaking palsy (see PARKINSONISM).

ENDOCARDITIS. Inflammation of the lining of the heart, more especially attacking the valves (see HEART); it is due in most cases

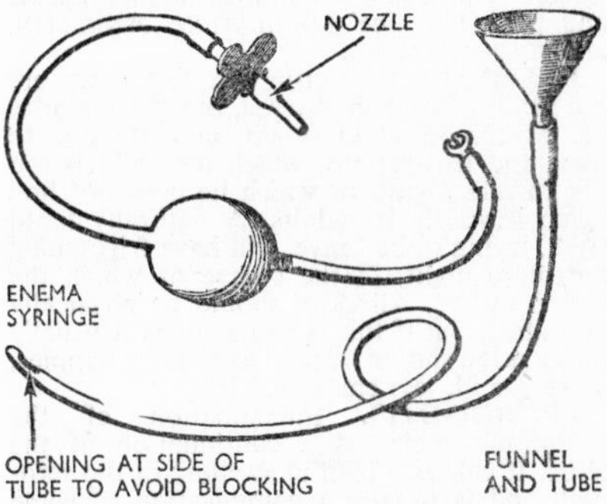

Enema. Two types of apparatus for giving an enema: a syringe and tube and funnel.

to rheumatic fever. Malignant endocarditis is a septic infection in a heart already damaged by rheumatic endocarditis; it was almost invariably fatal, but, in recent years, recoveries have followed very large doses of penicillin. Even then, it leaves a severely damaged heart.

ENDOCRINES. The hormones are substances formed by the ductless glands. The principal glands concerned are the pituitary, in the skull, which forms at least eight hormones and controls all the others, the thyroid, the supra-renals (see ADRENALIN), and the sex glands (see OVARY and TESTIS). Insulin is a hormone formed by the pancreas (see INSULIN and DIABETES). The effects are varied, and taking mixed hormones in a pill is senseless.

ENEMA. An enema is sometimes ordered by a doctor when it is inadvisable to give an aperient. It may be given either with an enema syringe or with a rubber tube and funnel. Make a quart of soapsuds, at about 105 deg. F.

—about the heat of a hot bath. If the syringe is employed, use the shorter nozzle supplied, put the butt end in the soapy water, squeeze the bulb until the solution comes through in order to avoid introducing air into the lower bowel and so producing distressing flatulence. Then gently insert the nozzle well lubricated with petroleum jelly into the rectum, and squeeze the bulb slowly and gently. Alternatively, hold the funnel about a foot above the patient and pour in from a jug. The patient should lie on the left side, and the enema should be given quite slowly.

ENTERIC. Typhoid fever, conveyed by food or water, is essentially an infection of the intestine, with general effects due to absorption of toxins. It starts with a gradual rise of temperature, colicky pains in the abdomen, and with headache and prostration. There may be a slight rash, of "rose spots," chiefly round the ribs. Diagnosis is made from the blood or from the motions.

Prevention is obtained by inoculation, which should be repeated every year. The infection can be conveyed by carriers. Treatment comprises rest in bed and good nursing and keeping up nourishment. A watch must be kept for complications, such as perforation or haemorrhage. Recently typhoid has been successfully treated with a combination of sulphathiazole and penicillin. See INOCULATION, PENICILLIN, and SULPHONAMIDES.

ENURESIS. Bedwetting. A few cases are the result of organic disease, but the majority are psychological in origin, and are due to fears and frustrations, which the child is too shy to talk about, or which he does not find taken seriously by adults. A naturally timid child, trying to be brave, will have frightening dreams at night, in the course of which the bed is wetted. All cases should be physically examined, but if this is negative, as it usually is, attention should be paid to giving a happier, more placid, less emotional life.

EPIDIDIMITIS. Inflammation of the epididimis, which is a continuation of the testis. It causes a painful swelling in the scrotum, and is usually a complication of some disease of the bladder or urinary passages—sometimes due to gonorrhoea (see VENEREAL DISEASE), or to cystitis—or it may follow operations on the bladder or the prostate. Epididimitis tends to recover with complete rest; some form of support should be worn.

EPILEPSY. See FITS.

EPISTAXIS. See NOSE BLEEDING.

ERYSIPELAS. An acute skin infection, due to streptococcus (see BACTERIA). Infection enters by some crack or scratch, and the whole surface becomes hot, red and slightly raised, advancing with a clear line demarcating it from normal skin. The temperature may be raised, and there may be shivering attacks. Penicillin or sulphonamides usually produce a rapid cure.

ERYTHEMA. A red rash. The rashes of measles and scarlet fever both come into this class; so do the red blotches of food poisoning, and the redness of sunburn.

EXOPHTHALMIC GOITRE. A disease of the thyroid gland. The thyroid produces a hormone (see ENDOCRINES) which controls the

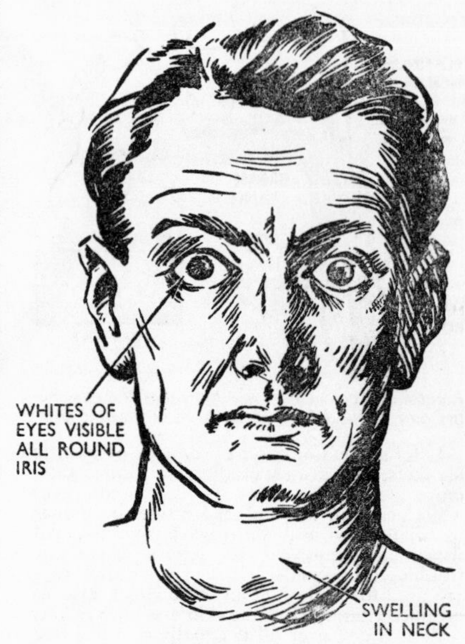

Exopthalmic goitre.

rate at which food is used up and energy produced. An overacting thyroid accelerates this process and produces the symptoms classed as exophthalmic goitre: a swelling in front of the neck below the Adam's apple, loss of weight, great excitability, fine trembling of the hands, a rapid pulse with palpitations and, frequently, prominent, staring eyes, from which the disease takes its name. These symptoms may not *all* be present in a given case.

The activity of the thyroid can be estimated by taking the basal metabolic rate—the rate at which oxygen is breathed in and carbon dioxide breathed out. The cause of this disease is uncertain, but it is definitely related to emotional disturbances, and perhaps to tonsillar infections. Probably the best treatment is still by operation, to remove enough of the gland to provide no more than the normal secretion. It is also treated by X-rays and radium (see RADIOTHERAPY). Recently thiouracil has come into use, with striking results, but it is early to say whether cure by this drug is permanent. Iodine is no longer used as a cure, but only as a preliminary to operation. Untreated exophthalmic goitre can lead to poisoning of the heart and auricular fibrillation.

EXPECTORANT. A medicine which promotes a flow of mucus in the bronchial tubes and so "loosens" a cough. Common expectorants are squills, ipecacuanha, carbonate of ammonia and bicarbonate of soda. "Mist expect" is an expectorant mixture, usually containing one or more of the foregoing drugs. Expectorants are much less used than formerly in acute disease, because sulpha

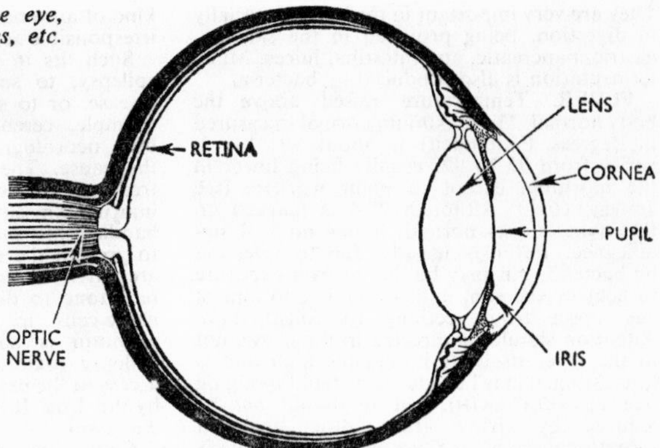

Eye. Principal features of the eye, referred to under Eye Diseases, etc.

drugs have now made it possible to cure the bronchitis, etc., and thus stop the cough at its source, but they are sometimes useful in chronic bronchitis. Expectorants should not be used for dry irritating coughs, which need, instead, a suppressor, such as codeine.

EYE DISEASES. This is an enormous subject, and it must be said at once that all eye diseases should be under the care of an oculist if the sight is to be preserved. Foreign bodies in the eye can sometimes be washed out by blinking, by bathing with weak salt water (one teaspoon of salt to the pint of water), or a drop of castor oil may be instilled. Any firmly wedged foreign body should be seen by a doctor as soon as possible.

Pink, bloodshot eyes may be due to conjunctivitis, and improve by bathing; but the inflammation may be more deep-seated. Cloudiness of the coloured part of the eye indicates iritis; violent pain in the eye may be due to glaucoma. Dimness of vision may be due to an opacity, such as cataract, or to the fact that the eye is not focusing properly, in which case glasses are indicated. Short sight is caused by an overlong eyeball, so that only near objects can be focused on the retina. Long sight is due to an overshort eyeball, with which near objects cannot be focused at all.

Astigmatism means that the eye focuses differently in different diameters; for example, a vertical object may be clear, but a horizontal one out of focus. For this, cylindrical glasses are worn. Squint may be due to muscular paralysis (see DIPLOPIA) or to long sight. After the age of forty, the eye has difficulty in focusing on near objects, and most people begin to need reading glasses.

Even people with perfect vision may need glasses if they do constant fine work near the eyes, otherwise eyestrain will result. Eyestrain headaches are usually absent in the morning but gradually come on during the day, and are intensified by reading or close work. There is a pain in the forehead and temples, and a feeling as though the eyes are being pressed on in their sockets. See CATARACT, CONJUNCTIVITIS, IRITIS, OPHTHALMOSCOPE, and RETINA.

FAECES. Motions; stools; matter passed from the lower bowel. The shape of the faeces is imparted as they leave the body and has no relation to any disease higher up. The colour and consistency vary with diet; meat makes them dark and milk makes them pale. Black motions may be due to bleeding, for example, from a duodenal ulcer, or may be due to taking bismuth or iron. In obstruction of bile duct the motions are pale. Senna may give them a yellow colour and calomel a green hue. See CONSTIPATION and DIARRHOEA.

FAINTING. Contrary to popular opinion, this does not often indicate heart disease. Attacks of indigestion and flatulence are the commonest cause. Fainting may also be due to overtiredness, to undernourishment, to too much heat or too much cold. Adolescents have a tendency to faint, especially when growing rapidly. They usually need more rest and more food—especially more proteins (see PROTEIN and DIET).

When a person faints, the patient should be left lying flat, and *not* propped up. Smelling salts, sal volatile (30 drops in plenty of water), or a glass of cold water, may be used to revive the patient. It is important to provide plenty of fresh air and get the patient away from crowds. Fainting is often emotional, due to the sight of blood or of an accident, or to the receipt of bad news. In this way, it provides a form of protection, providing unconsciousness instead of distressing experiences.

FALLOPIAN TUBES. The tubes, leading from the ovary to the womb, through which the egg-cell passes, and in which it is fertilized. See BIRTH, ECTOPIC PREGNANCY, SEX, and STERILITY.

FAMILY-PLANNING CLINICS. Some people seek information on birth control, others on wider aspects of marriage. The Marriage Guidance Council, 78 Duke Street, Grosvenor Square, London, W.1, has been established to give help on marriage in all its aspects.

FATS. Oily and greasy substances which are edible (butter, margarine, olive oil, meat fat, etc.), and which provide the body with heat and energy. See DIET.

FATTY DEGENERATION. Changes in the bodily organs, in which the normal cells are replaced by fat that is detrimental to the efficiency of the organ. It usually follows some chronic inflammation.

FAUCES. The folds of membrane, at the back of the throat, between which the tonsils lie. See TONSILS.

FEEBLE-MINDEDNESS. See MENTAL DEFICIENCY.

FERMENTS. Chemical substances which, if present in small quantities, initiate very large chemical changes in other substances.

They are very important in the body, especially in digestion, being provided in the salivary, gastric, pancreatic, and intestinal juices. Much fermentation is also produced by bacteria.

FEVER. Temperature raised above the body normal. The maximum normal (measured in degrees Fahrenheit) is about 99; but it varies from 95 to 99, usually being lower in the morning, except in night workers (see TEMPERATURE). Although 98·4 is marked on thermometers as normal, it has no real significance. Fever is usually due to infection by bacteria, but may be due to over-exposure to heat or the sun, and, in babies, to almost any upset from teething to constipation. Attention should be directed to the cause, not to the fever itself. If it remains high and is exhausting, it may be reduced by tepid sponging (see BLANKET BATH), but it should *not* be reduced by giving drugs, other than in exceptional cases, as fever is one of Nature's natural reactions to infection and helps to defeat the germs.

FIBROMA AND FIBROADENOMA. Fibroids; a class of non-malignant tumours, consisting largely of fibrous tissue, the cause of which is unknown. They may occur in any part of the body and need surgical removal. Fibroids occur in the womb, and may cause excessive menstrual loss, constipation, pain in the pelvis and interference with pregnancy.

FIBROSIS. Internal scarring resulting from injury or disease.

FIBROSITIS. A name given to a class of disorders characterized by muscular pains and aches, such as lumbago. Often there are definite spots which are tender to pressure, known, technically, as "nodules." In such cases, immediate relief may sometimes be given by having local anaesthetics (see ANALGESIA) injected into these spots. Otherwise, treatment consists of warmth, massage and various forms of electrical treatment. The pain may be relieved by aspirin. Many people have faith in the rubbing in of preparations of wintergreen, though taking aspirin is probably more effective. See RHEUMATISM.

FINGER-NAIL. See NAILS.

FINGER, SEPTIC. See WHITLOW.

FIRST-AID. See pages 129–161.

FISTULA. An abnormal canal, leading from one part of the body to another, often discharging pus or mucus. Rectal fistula may cause a permanent weeping discharge near the anus. It may be due to injury by a fishbone, or to tuberculosis. It needs thorough surgical attention, in which the whole of the false passage must be removed in order to provide a cure.

FITS. Convulsions; the sudden loss of consciousness, accompanied by violent spasmodic movements of the limbs. The tongue may be bitten, and urine may be passed. After the convulsive movements stop, usually in a few minutes, unconsciousness or partial unconsciousness may continue for a while. If the limb movements are violent they must *not* be forcibly restrained. The limbs are *guided* so as to avoid danger to the patient or bystanders. When the patient recovers consciousness, he is generally unaware of what has happened. In a few cases, he may pass into a kind of automatic state, when he may perform irresponsible actions and have to be restrained.

Such fits in an adult may be due to true epilepsy, to some toxic state as in kidney disease, or to some disease of the brain, for example, cerebral tumour. An examination by a neurologist may be needed to establish the cause. The actual fit does not call for treatment except to prevent the victim injuring himself—a piece of wood or a knotted handkerchief may be placed between the teeth to prevent the tongue being bitten. Epileptics are often treated by small doses of phenobarbitone to diminish the excitability of the nerve-cells in the brain. Treatment with epanutin is based on the theory that, in epilepsy, toxic substances from the blood gain access to the brain, and this access is prevented by the drug. It has the advantage of being less depressing.

Convulsions in babies, while the symptoms are similar, are hardly ever epileptic. They may be due to rickets, to constipation, to teething, or to the onset of some feverish illness, such as measles. Where an adult will have a shivering attack at the onset of infectious disease, a baby will have a convulsion. The baby should be kept warm, and it often helps to place it in a warm bath till the fit is over, with the addition of cold compresses to the back of the head. It should then be allowed to sleep. If constipated, an enema should be given (see ENEMA), or a glycerine or soap suppository may be used.

After sleeping, the baby's temperature should be taken. If feverish, a watch should be kept for other signs of illness; for example, a rash, a cough or vomiting; and medical attention should be sought. If the child has not been having cod-liver or halibut oil, this should be commenced in full doses.

Fits due to kidney or brain disease need treatment for the basic disease, which is usually a specialized matter.

FLATULENCE. Gas in the stomach or intestines. In the stomach the gas is usually air which has been swallowed. The effort to bring it up causes gulping, which results in swallowing more air, and so the discomfort is intensified. A carminative, such as peppermint, is an effective remedy. Gas in the intestines results from the fermentation of cellulose from roughage, or of undigested starch due to imperfect mastication (chewing). Taking aperients, and thus hurrying starch on before it has had time to digest, increases such flatulence. Peas and beans should be cut down, as should woody vegetables and skins and stalks. A few doses of powdered kaolin (a teaspoon in water, after meals) are helpful.

FLAVINE. See ANTISEPTIC.

FOCAL INFECTION. Localized infection, as in a tonsil or at the root of a tooth, which causes absorption of toxic substances, with effects in remote parts of the body. It is thought to play a part in rheumatic disorders. See RHEUMATISM.

FOOD POISONING. The old idea of ptomaine poisoning is obsolete; it was thought that decomposing food formed poisonous substances, called ptomaines, and that these caused the symptoms, such as diarrhoea and sickness, fever, headache, etc., of food poisoning. Actually, decomposing food, in itself, is harmless—witness the eating of high game and decomposing cheeses, which are appreciated for their flavours.

All food poisonings (except those due to definitely poisonous substances such as deadly-nightshade berries) are due to the contamination of food by harmful bacteria. This contamination arises in the handling of the food: for example, a typhoid carrier employed as a cook can easily cause an epidemic of typhoid. A person with a septic finger, or a boil on the hand, who is allowed to handle food can cause an epidemic of gastro-enteritis.

Prevention of food poisoning lies in a much better standard of cleanliness in the trades which handle food. In the home, foods which have been cooked well are usually safe because the heat destroys bacteria. Foods eaten raw, such as fruit and salads, should always be well washed. The crust of bread is a possible source, and loaves ought always to be delivered wrapped. If they are placed in the oven for a few minutes, however, any infection is much reduced. See GASTRO-ENTERITIS.

FOOT. The two great principles in avoiding foot troubles are to choose really well-fitting shoes, and to keep the feet scrupulously clean. Ill-fitting shoes result in bunions, hammer toes, dropped arches and corns. Lack of cleanliness leads to skin infections, especially the so-called "athlete's foot"—a soggy, itching rash between the toes, due to germs picked up while going barefoot. This can usually be cleared up by frequent washing and dusting boracic into the socks. Early bunions can be treated by wearing wider shoes and having the anterior arch of the foot strapped up. Severe bunions need operation to straighten the toe. Shoes that are too short cause pain in the joint of the big toe, and this may be relieved by wearing a metatarsal bar—a bar of leather—across the back of the sole, behind the toe-joint. See also BRUISE, CHILBLAIN, CORN, and JOINTS, SPRAINS OF.

FOREIGN BODY. See EYE DISEASES, EARACHE and First-aid chapter, page 147.

Foreign bodies *in the windpipe or bronchial tubes* sometimes occur through children placing metal objects in their mouths and inhaling them, and they sometimes result from a tooth being inhaled after extraction. The effect is a severe cough, which continues and leads to a localized bronchitis. This becomes chronic, until the cause is discovered, usually by X-ray (see RADIOLOGY). The offending body has to be removed by a chest specialist, through a bronchoscope (see BRONCHOSCOPY). A foreign body *in the throat* is usually removed by passing the finger down as far as possible and then hooking out the offender. If this fails, the patient's feet should be raised above the head and the back should be slapped between the shoulder-blades.

FRACTURES. Broken bones. These may be due to direct or to indirect violence. Impact with a motor-car or a bullet will cause a direct fracture of a bone. The majority of fractures are, however, due to indirect violence. For example, falling on the outstretched hand may fracture the forearm bone above the wrist, or falling upon the point of the shoulder (the common hunting accident) may fracture the collar-bone, according to where the thrust of the body's weight is taken. In a simple fracture, the skin is intact; in a compound fracture, there is a wound leading down to the break, or the broken bone may be protruding. Simple fractures remain aseptic, but compound fractures become infected by bacteria and are much more difficult to heal.

The principle of treatment of a fracture is to bring the broken ends into line and to keep them there until the bone unites; this may take from three to ten weeks. Within the first week, a ring of soft bone forms round the break (see CALLUS), and this acts as a natural splint till union is complete, after which it is absorbed. When a fracture takes place, there is nearly always damage to soft structures in the neighbourhood—muscles, tendons, blood-vessels and nerves—and attention must be paid to this damage as well as to the fracture. Splinting of a fracture should include the joints on both sides of the fracture (for example, a broken forearm bone needs wrist and elbow fixed) so as to prevent movement of the broken parts. Too rigid adherence to this rule may result in stiffness of these joints, and modern fracture treatment includes preliminary splinting, followed by early movement of joints to preserve their mobility.

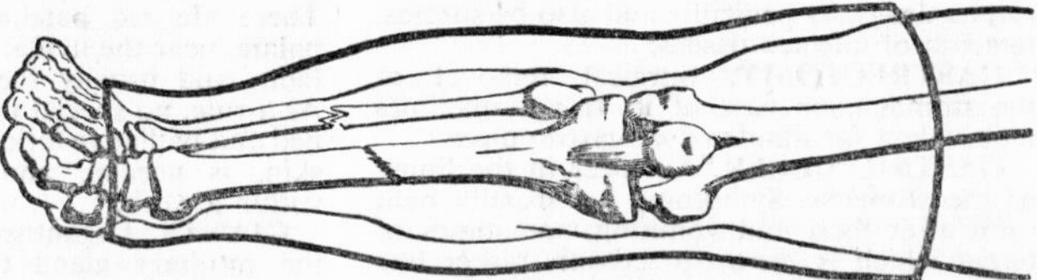

Fractures. An example showing fractures of both shin-bones encased in plaster enclosing knee and ankle joints and ensuring immobility of the broken bones.

In elderly people, broken bones do not always unite well and may need to be fixed by pins or screws. This applies especially to fractures of the neck of the femur inside the capsule (the hip) in old people, who may be bedridden unless the fracture can be successfully pinned.

FURUNCULOSIS. Boils. See BOIL.

GALL BLADDER. An appendage to the liver which acts as a reservoir for bile, discharging it into the intestine. See BILE.

GALL STONES. See CHOLELITHIASIS.

GANGRENE. Local death of a part of the body, due either to a cutting-off of the circulation or to poisoning of some kind. It may occur in arterio-sclerosis, in diabetes,

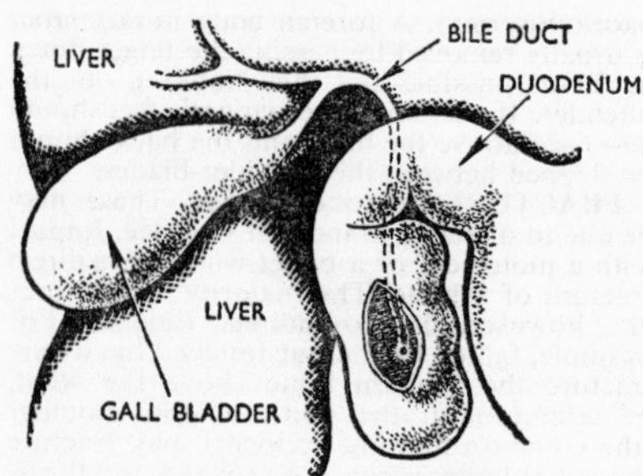

Gall bladder (see page 89).

after frostbite, or in gas-gangrene. It may be necessary to amputate the affected part.

GAS-GANGRENE. A very severe infection of wounds by specific microbes, causing gangrene and the formation of bubbles of offensive gas. It was the cause of much mortality in the First World War, but considerably less in the Second. It is treated by serum, by sulpha drugs, by penicillin and also by surgical removal of infected tissues.

GASTRECTOMY. Surgical removal of the stomach, or part of it. It is sometimes undertaken for duodenal or gastric ulcer.

GASTRIC ULCER. An ulcer in the lining of the stomach. Symptoms are usually pain soon after food and vomiting, sometimes of blood which is brown in colour, rather like coffee grounds, from the action of the gastric juice. If the blood is red, it has not come from the stomach (see HAEMATEMESIS). Causes of gastric ulcer are emotional strain, as in duodenal ulcer, but also infections of the mouth, particularly septic teeth and tonsils. Diagnosis is usually confirmed by radiology, the treatment being similar to that for duodenal ulcer. See also DUODENAL ULCER.

GASTRITIS. Inflammation of the stomach. The term is usually applied to a catarrhal infection, resulting in gastric pain and vomiting and often occurring in epidemics. Gastritis may be due to food poisoning, or to swallowing deleterious substances. Chronic gastritis may result from the over use of alcohol, too much smoking, chronic nasal catarrh or gall-bladder disease. The acute attacks are best treated by twenty-four hours of starvation, taking nothing but a sweetened fruit drink until all tendency to vomit has ceased. Treatment of chronic gastritis involves a search for the cause.

GASTRO-ENTERITIS. Inflammation of stomach and intestines, usually producing both vomiting and diarrhoea. Its causes and treatment are similar to gastritis. In some forms it may be cured by certain of the sulpha drugs, especially sulphaguanidine. Gastro-enteritis can also be the result of food poisoning or a complication of influenza and other infectious diseases.

GASTRO-ENTEROSTOMY. An operation to short-circuit the stomach to the small intestine, thus preventing food from going the normal way through the duodenum. It is sometimes used as treatment for duodenal ulcer, especially when scarring has caused obstruction to the duodenum. See ANASTOMOSIS and DUODENAL ULCER.

GENERAL PARALYSIS. General paralysis of the insane, or G.P.I., due to syphilitic disease of the brain (see SYPHILIS). The symptoms often include delusions of grandeur, a tendency to spend money recklessly, an exaggerated sense of well-being, and an aggressive manner with a loud bellowing voice. There may be difficulty in walking and clumsiness in other movements. Treatment should be undertaken by a mental specialist (psychiatrist). See MENTAL DISEASE and PSYCHOTHERAPY.

GERMAN MEASLES. This ailment, also known as rubella, has nothing to do with measles, and an attack of one does not protect against the other. It is usually a mild disorder without complications. There is no premonitory cold and cough, as in measles. The rash appears in the first twenty-four hours and may vary from a general red flush to separate red patches on the face and trunk. Pain in the neck is often complained of, and enlarged glands may be felt in the back of the neck. There are red patches on the back of the palate, near the uvula. There is no aversion to light, and usually the temperature is slight. As a rule, no special treatment, beyond rest in bed and palliative lotions applied to the itching skin, is needed, and recovery takes place within a week.

GIANTS. Gigantism is due to disease of the pituitary gland (see ENDOCRINES). This gland, situated inside the skull, forms a hormone which controls growth. Disease can make it over-active, producing too much growth hormone, and excessive bodily growth then takes place. X-ray of the skull shows an enlarged hollow where this gland rests.

GIDDINESS. The medical term for this is vertigo. The balance of our bodies is co-ordinated by the cerebellum (see fig. on page 75). Information as to our position in space reaches the brain from the eyes, from a special

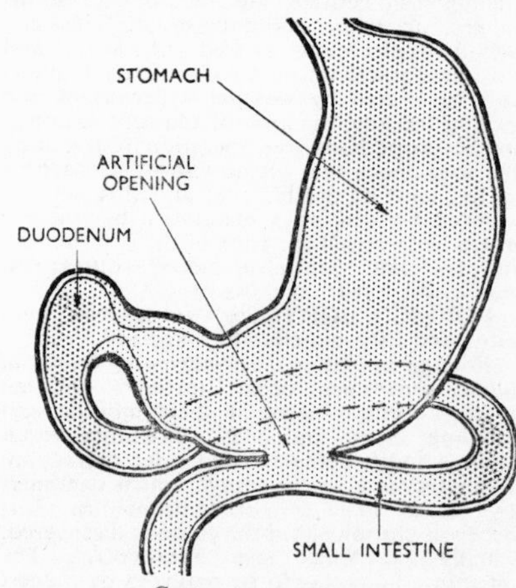

Gastro-enterostomy.

balancing organ in the ear, from the sense of touch (particularly in the soles of the feet), and from the sensation of tension and pressure in joints and muscles. Giddiness may result from trouble in any of these places.

Cerebellar diseases cause constant giddiness; but it is usually possible to maintain balance if only one of the "informative" organs is out of use. Thus we are not giddy in the dark; but a person with numbed feet, or with ear trouble, having now his feet or his ears, as well as his eyes, out of action, is giddy. Ear trouble is probably the commonest cause of giddiness. It may be owing to nothing more than wax in the ears, or may be due to disease of the balancing organ itself (Menière's disease). Temporary giddiness is often due to some toxin, as from a cold or from food upsets, reaching the brain.

GINGIVITIS. Inflammation of the gums (see ANGINA, VINCENT'S). It may be due to septic tooth roots, or to infection from dirty crockery, etc. It is often associated with a deficiency of vitamin C (see VITAMIN).

GLAND. A secreting organ. The lymphatic glands, situated in the neck, armpit, groin and other places, form white blood corpuscles (see BLOOD) and help to check any spread of infection into the blood. In doing this they enlarge and become tender, acting as filters to the lymph circulation. In chronic infections, such as tuberculosis, they may become so diseased that they have to be removed. They also become enlarged in Hodgkin's disease and in some forms of anaemia, as well as in some severe infectious diseases, such as plague.

Other glands, such as the liver, the pancreas and the sex glands, form secretions which are discharged through ducts: bile from the liver into the intestine, sperms from the testis into the seminal vesicles, and so on. Ductless glands (see ENDOCRINES) are those which discharge their secretion straight into the blood stream; for example, the thyroid, the suprarenal and the pituitary.

GLANDULAR FEVER. A feverish illness in which the lymphatic glands are enlarged and painful.

GLOSSITIS. Inflammation of the tongue, which feels sore and has a shiny, pink appearance. It may be due to infection from teeth or tonsils, from antrum or sinus trouble (see SINUS), or to infection from drinking utensils, etc. Chronic glossitis is sometimes due to syphilis, but more frequently to a deficiency of nicotinic acid. See VITAMINS.

GLUCOSE. A form of sugar manufactured from starch. All starchy and sugary food is converted to glucose in the processes of digestion, and is absorbed into the body as glucose. The advantage of taking glucose is solely that it needs no further digestion. It is, therefore, suitable for administration to very exhausted people; and it can be given as a form of nourishment by injection in cases where no food can be taken by mouth at all. But people with normal digestions can get all the nourishment which glucose can give by taking any other form of starch or sugar.

GLYCOSURIA. Passing sugar in the urine. It is a sign of diabetes, but it can also occur harmlessly and is then known as renal glycosuria. This condition is distinguished from diabetes by blood tests and needs no treatment. See DIABETES.

GOITRE. A swelling in the front of the neck, below the Adam's apple, due to enlargement of the thyroid gland. There are a number of different kinds of goitre, besides exophthalmic goitre (see EXOPHTHALMIC GOITRE). In contrast to this disease, simple goitre, or Derbyshire neck, is a result of a deficiency of iodine in the food and water supply. The gland starved of iodine, enlarges to try to do its best with what iodine it can get. This type of goitre can be prevented and cured by giving either iodine or thyroid extract.

Nodular goitres are not uniform enlargements; they are, rather, round lumps in the gland, either on one side or on both, but seldom symmetrical. This type of goitre is usually curable only by operation. Cancer of the thyroid gland forms a type of goitre which is hard, sometimes painful, and grows quickly. It is not at all common, compared with the other kinds. See CANCER.

GOLD TREATMENT. Certain gold salts are used by injection in the treatment of tuberculosis and of arthritis. Selection of suitable cases and the supervision of treatment must be left to an expert, or more harm than good may result.

GONORRHOEA. See VENEREAL DISEASE.

GOUT. A disease in which acute, painful swellings occur in the joints, often the big-toe joint. At one time it was very common, but is now a comparative rarity. It is associated with excess in eating and drinking, particularly red meats and fermented liquors. The tendency to gout seems to be hereditary. Certain foods are not completely burned up in the body, and an excess of uric acid is formed. A gouty person is unable to rid himself of this excess, and it combines with sodium salts to form crystals of sodium biurate which are deposited in the joints.

An attack of gout comes suddenly, with a red, glazed, swelling of the joint, which may last for several days. It is often preceded by an attack of bad temper and irritability. Chronic gout leads to the formation of "chalk stones" in the joints, which may penetrate the skin. Hard gouty nodules are also found in the edges of the lobes of the ears. The drug colchicum is specific in curing an attack of gout, while atophan is used as a preventative because it helps in the elimination of uric acid. Gout has no connexion with other rheumatic complaints, which are unassociated with uric acid.

GRAFTING. This consists of taking tissues from one part of the body, or even from someone else's body, and making them grow in some other part. It is extensively used in plastic surgery, for the repair of disfigurements and of useless limbs. As a rule, grafts cannot be made from one species to another, and they do not take as successfully from one person to another, as when transplanted in the same individual. Blood transfusion is, in a sense, grafting, and great care has to be taken in selecting suitable blood (see BLOOD TRANSFUSION). Normally bone grafts well, and pieces of rib or shin bone can be used to make new noses and jaw bones.

Skin grafts are of various kinds. Where a raw surface has to be covered, wafer-thin pieces of skin may be razored from the thigh and applied to the raw area. Where a whole thickness is wanted, as in making a new nose, a pedicle graft—skin undercut and rolled rather like a sausage roll—is detached almost

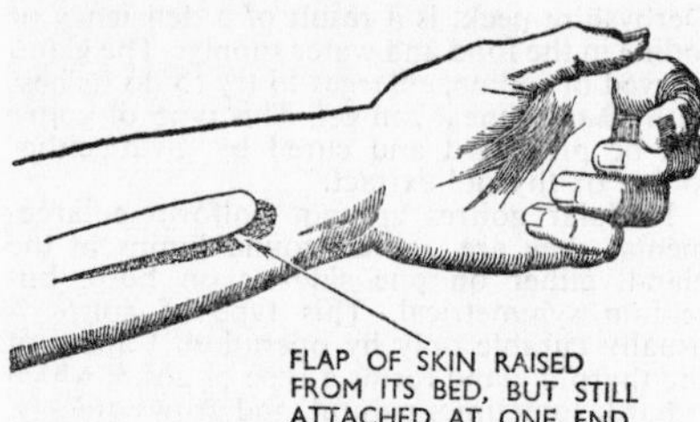

Grafting. This flap of skin is ready for grafting to some other part of the body. When it has "taken" it will be cut free from the arm.

completely, say from the arm or forehead; but is left with a blood supply until it has acquired a new one from the place to which it is now attached, after which it is freed from its original site. Corneal grafts consist of the transparent cornea taken from one person's eye and transplanted to another's (see BLINDNESS).

GRAVES' DISEASE. See EXOPHTHALMIC GOITRE.

GREENSTICK FRACTURE. A bone which is broken half through, the other half being bent as when a green stick is broken. This occurs in children, whose bones are still partly cartilage. A greenstick fracture causes deformity of the limb, but usually little pain as there are no moving fragments. See FRACTURE.

GREY HAIR. See HAIR, GREY.

GROWING PAINS. Transient pains in the limbs of children, formerly thought to be due to growth but now known to be due to a form of rheumatic fever. It is very important that such children should receive medical care, as there is great danger of valvular disease of the heart in neglected cases. It is characteristic of "growing pains" that they move from one part of the body to another. A child who complains of pains always in the same limb is more likely to be suffering either from a joint disease or from muscular strain.

GUMBOIL. An abscess at the root of a tooth, which spreads to produce a very painful swelling below the gum. This can be relieved by lancing, but the proper treatment is extraction of the offending tooth, which should be done as soon as possible, thereby allowing the contents of the abscess to drain away. It is not advisable to wait until the swelling has subsided. As local anaesthetics cannot be used in such cases, the extraction is usually done under gas.

GUMS, BLEEDING. This may be due to gingivitis, to pyorrhoea, to scurvy, to injury, or to the extraction of teeth. Bleeding after tooth extraction may be due to a general tendency to bleed easily, but is more often due to the tearing of small blood-vessels during the extraction, followed by too much use of a mouth wash. The clot, which should stop the bleeding, is continually washed away. Such bleeding can nearly always be controlled by biting on a tightly rolled piece of cotton wool. If very severe, the dentist should be revisited, as he may think it advisable to stitch the gum. The common practice of going to a doctor about it is ill-advised; it is a job for the dentist.

HAEMATEMESIS. Vomiting of blood. Blood which has actually been in the stomach becomes changed to a brown fluid. Bright blood may be vomited from varicose veins in the gullet, or from other diseases of this region. Brown blood may be due to bleeding in the stomach from a gastric ulcer, or may be due to swallowing blood, for example, from a bleeding nose (see NOSE BLEEDING) or after tooth extractions (see GUMS, BLEEDING).

HAEMATOMA. A collection of blood under the skin or inside the body (see BRUISE). A large clot may need to be emptied surgically.

HAEMATURIA. Bleeding when passing urine. It may be due to injury or to disease of the bladder, the kidneys or the urinary passages. It should always be invesitgated by a doctor or urologist.

HAEMOGLOBIN. The red colouring matter of blood. This exists in two forms: haemoglobin, purple in the veins; and oxy-haemoglobin, a bright vivid red, in the arteries. Its function is to carry oxygen from the lungs to the tissues.

HAEMOPTYSIS. Coughing-up blood. This may come from the throat, when it is usually a dullish red and may clot, or from the lungs, when it is usually frothy and bright red, being charged with oxygen. Haemoptysis occurs in tuberculosis, but also in heart disease, in bronchiectasis, in some forms of anaemia, in scurvy, and other diseases. It always calls for a complete examination to determine its cause. In tuberculosis, coughing of blood does

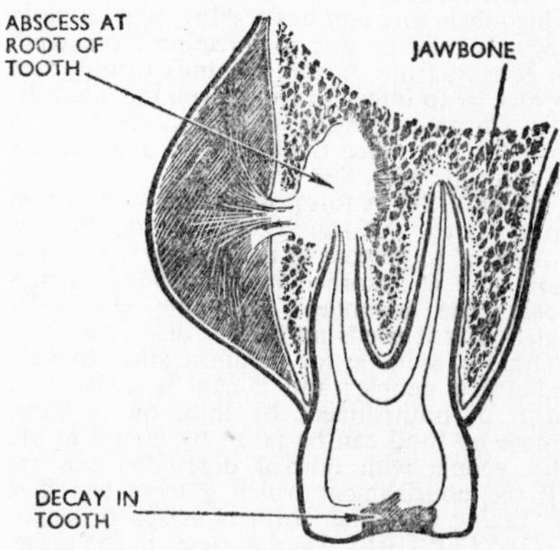

Gumboil caused by abscess at root of tooth.

not necessarily indicate severity of the disease, but can be a very useful warning.

HAEMORRHAGE. Loss of blood, either externally or internally. It can occur when a blood-vessel is cut or torn, or when it is

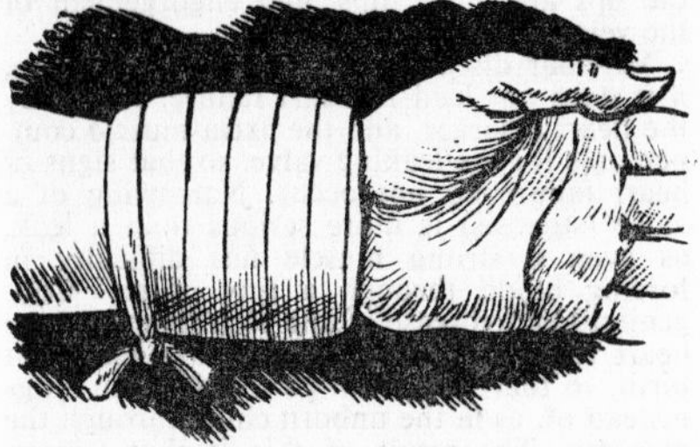

Haemorrhage. Bleeding from the wrist may be stopped by a pad and firm bandage (above), *and from the palm of the hand by gripping a rolled bandage* (below).

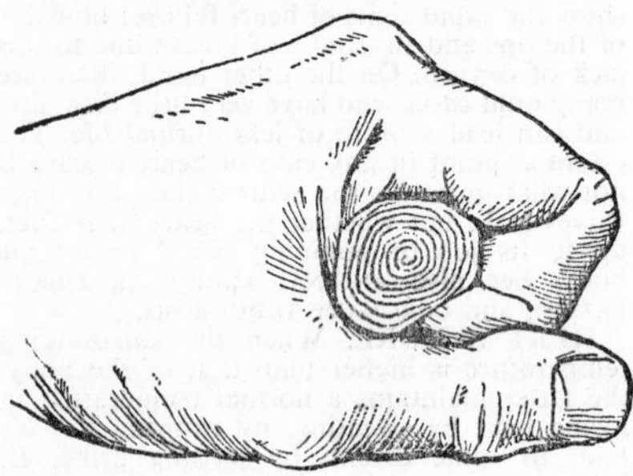

eroded by disease or ruptured by high blood pressure (see APOPLEXY and BLOOD PRESSURE). Blood from an artery is a vivid red, being charged with oxygen, pumps out in spurts with the beats of the heart, and is very likely to lead to severe loss of blood. Blood from a vein is a dull red in colour, wells out slowly and is easily stopped by pressure. Blood from capillaries is the ordinary bleeding one sees from cuts and grazes, and which stops spontaneously after a few minutes, when a clot forms.

Arterial bleeding is the only kind difficult to stop. If the artery above the wound can be pressed back against a bone, it will stop at once. Otherwise pressure may be applied higher up the limb (see First-aid chapter), or a tourniquet may have to be applied. Arterial bleeding during operations is controlled by applying special forceps and then ligaturing the vessel.

Internal haemorrhage is far more dangerous than external, as it is apt to be overlooked. Collapse of a patient after injury or after operation, accompanied by pallor, sighing respiration, rapid, weak pulse and impending unconsciousness, should raise suspicion of internal haemorrhage. The only satisfactory treatment is immediate surgery, and the patient should be kept flat and got to hospital as soon as possible. Fluids may be given to replace the blood lost. It is important to form, if possible, an idea of whether the bleeding has stopped or is continuing, in deciding how urgent the case is. See ARTERY, BLEEDERS, BLOOD, HAEMATEMESIS, HAEMATURIA, HAEMOPTYSIS, GUMS BLEEDING, NOSE BLEEDING, and VARICOSE VEINS.

HAEMORRHOIDS. See PILES.

HAIR DISEASES. The hair roots are involved in boils, in barber's rash, in ringworm and in other skin diseases. The hair may break off short if affected by ringworm at the root, but is not greatly subject to infection in itself. It is chosen as a site for egg-laying by lice, and it may lose its lustre when the general health is poor. Straight hair is circular in section, curly hair oval. The object of permanent waving is to flatten the hair so that it can be curled.

HAIR, GREY. Grey hair is a normal accompaniment of advancing years. In some people there is an hereditary tendency to go grey when young. There is no known treatment to prevent or to cure this. While certain vitamins will prevent rats from going grey, they do not have this effect on humans.

HAIR, LOSS OF. Baldness is more common among men than among women and was once attributed to wearing hard hats, thought to interfere with the circulation of the scalp. It has also been attributed to cutting the hair and thus preventing the weight of the hair from stimulating the roots. Nowadays both sexes cut the hair and neither wears hard hats, but men still go bald. Endeavours to cure baldness are usually profitless. See also ALOPECIA.

HALLUCINATIONS. Seeing and hearing things which do not, to other observers, exist. Often a sign of mental disease.

HAY FEVER. Continual sneezing, redness of the eyes and congestion of the nose, due to inhaling grass pollens or other dusts. Prevention can sometimes be obtained by injections of the offending substance; but these have to be done very often and may be needed to be repeated annually. Benadryl, taken in capsules four times a day, gives great relief. Some people are relieved by ephedrine or by benzedrine. Hay fever is also treated by ionization (see ELECTRICAL TREATMENT) and by autohaemotherapy. It is a form of allergy.

HEADACHE. A universal experience which may be trivial, or may be due to serious disease. It is often very difficult to diagnose the cause, and the diagnosis may involve examining every organ of the body. Dyspeptic headaches are often throbbing. Eyestrain headaches are like a tight band round the forehead. Worry headaches suggest a nail being driven into the top of the head. Neuralgic, shooting headaches may be due to bad teeth or to ear trouble. But liver and kidney troubles, lung disease, fevers—almost any ailment—can cause headache. Some headaches can be relieved by aspirin, others by a dose of salts. If neither of these works, then a doctor should be consulted. Headaches which do not disturb sleep are seldom due to organic disease. See MIGRAINE.

HEAD INJURIES. As the brain is protected by a solid bony skull, many injuries involve only the scalp and have the same effect as cuts or bruises elsewhere. More severe injury may lead to concussion of the brain with unconsciousness, followed by vomiting, and a varying period of loss of memory. Very severe injuries lead to fracture of the skull. If the vault of the skull is fractured, bits of bone may be sticking out of the wound, or a crackling "broken egg-shell" feeling may be obtained with the finger-tips.

Fractures of the base of the skull lead to unconsciousness, and, possibly, to bleeding and discharge of cerebro-spinal fluid from the ears and the nose. Such fractures are especially dangerous in that the vital centres lie at the base of the brain (see BRAIN). Head injury which seems slight at first, but is followed by unconsciousness twenty minutes later, is due to bleeding inside the skull and needs immediate treatment. All head injuries should be taken seriously, and the patient must be kept under medical observation until it is certain that no complications are likely to arise. Damage to the brain may lead to persistent headaches or to fits, apart from the more obvious results of paralysis, unconsciousness or even death.

HEARTBURN. A burning sensation below and to the left of the breastbone, occurring in certain types of indigestion. It is sometimes associated with a copious flow of saliva, and is usually relieved by a dose of bicarbonate of soda or magnesia. See INDIGESTION.

HEART DISEASES. There are many diseases of the heart which may roughly be classified into diseases of the valves and heart lining (endocarditis), and diseases of the

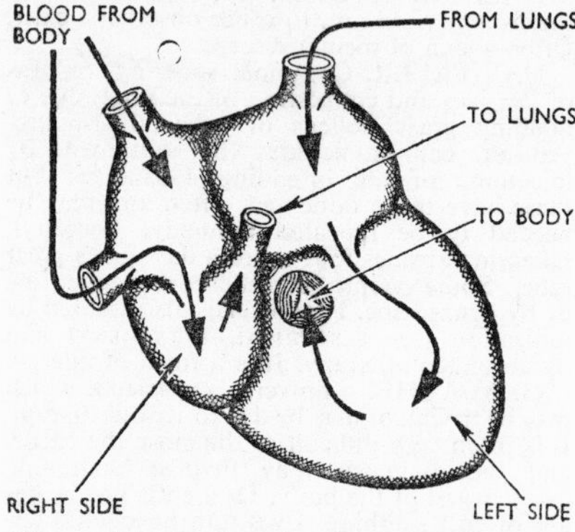

Heart (diagrammatic). Heavy arrows show the course of the blood stream through the heart.

muscle of the heart (myocarditis). Rheumatic fever is one of the principal causes of heart disease and accounts for most cases of valvular disease, which may also be due to syphilis. The heart muscle can be weakened by any severe infection of the body, and is affected directly by disease of the artery supplying it (the coronary artery). One of the main causes of heart disease in old people is hardening of this artery (see ARTERIO-SCLEROSIS).

The chief disturbing features in heart cases are heart pain (see ANGINA PECTORIS) and heart failure. Failure occurs when the heart can no longer find the strength to accept the blood coming to it and pump it on effectively. The signs of this are increasing breathlessness, especially, at first, on exertion; blueness of the lips and finger-tips, and engorgement of the veins on the neck and face.

Valvular disease is not necessarily serious, if it does not lead to heart failure. Normally the heart enlarges, and the extra muscle compensates for the leaking valve, so that signs of heart failure do not occur. Narrowing of a valve (stenosis) is more serious than a leak, as even a strong muscle has difficulty in forcing blood through a tiny orifice. Congenital heart disease is due to a failure of the heart to make certain anatomical changes at birth, so that blood can go through the lungs instead of, as in the unborn child, through the placenta. The result of this is that venous blood, instead of going to the lungs for a fresh supply of oxygen, is apt to be returned direct to the general circulation.

Severe cases of congenital heart disease show the usual signs of heart failure: blueness of the lips and shortness of breath due to this lack of oxygen. On the other hand, there are many mild cases who have very little disability and can lead a more or less normal life. The essential point in any case of heart disease is not what murmurs the heart makes, nor what valves leak, but whether the heart is, in fact, up to its job of pumping blood round the body. See also ANGINA, AURICULAR FIBRILLATION, and CORONARY THROMBOSIS.

HEAT STROKE. When the surrounding temperature is higher than that of the body, the latter maintains a normal temperature in losing heat by sweating, by expiring hot air and, to some extent, by passing urine. If, however, external heat is excessive, and if the supply of fluids is insufficient, the body may not be able to lose enough heat, and its temperature then rises, perhaps to 110 deg. F., producing a state of collapse and the condition known as heat stroke. Treatment is by immersion in cold water. See FEVER and TEMPERATURE.

HEMIANOPIA. Partial loss of vision, so that only half of the usual picture is seen. It is due to diseases of, or pressure on, the optic nerves, or to migraine.

HEMIPLEGIA. Paralysis of one side of the body, generally due to a stroke. See APOPLEXY.

HEPATITIS. Inflammation of the liver. Infective hepatitis, supposed to be due to a virus, causes epidemics of jaundice.

HEREDITARY DISEASE. Very few diseases are strictly hereditary. Epilepsy and gout often are; and there are some rare diseases such as haemophilia, and a form of blindness with mental defect; also a mild type of jaundice, due to an inherited fragility of the red blood cells. There is, however, an hereditary tendency to a lack of resistance to some diseases, possibly tuberculosis; and to a weakness in some tissues, such as in families which tend to break their bones, to get varicose veins, or to have hernia.

Hereditary disease should be distinguished from congenital disease which includes infections acquired at birth, such as syphilis and gonorrhoea, and defects of structure (see

DEFORMITIES) due to a failure of the unborn child to develop properly. Mental disorders are possibly more frequently inherited than physical ones. Insanity runs in families sometimes, and so does a tendency to psychoneuroses (see NEUROSIS). Allergic diseases (see ALLERGY) also have an hereditary tendency.

The modern conception of the hereditary transmission of disease tends more towards the more or less proved theory of predisposition at birth.

HERNIA. Rupture; the protrusion of part of the abdominal contents, generally a loop of the intestine, forming a bulge beneath the skin. It is most common in the groin, especially in males, who have the remains of a canal through which the testis descended into the scrotum before birth. This canal, which should become sealed-off after the testis has descended, frequently remains open, and a subsequent strain at any time in later life will cause a loop of intestine to enter it, forcing it wide open; after this, coughing, straining and the lifting of heavy weights tends further to increase the bulge. The canal is called the inguinal canal, and a hernia here is known as an inguinal hernia.

Just below the groin there is another potential weak spot, where the large blood vessels enter the thigh. A hernia here is called a femoral hernia, and is proportionately more common in females. Other herniae can occur at the navel (umbilical hernia) and in weak scars after operations (post-operative hernia).

It is characteristic of a hernia that the bulge appears on standing, straining or coughing, and disappears on lying down. The danger is that the loop of intestine may be nipped, be unable to return whence it came, and thus have its circulation interfered with. This disaster is called a strangulated hernia and calls for immediate operation to relieve the obstruction.

Treatment of hernia is by truss or by operation. A truss does not cure a hernia, except sometimes in babies where the canal may seal itself off if the intestine is kept from protruding for some months. It does, however, prevent danger of strangulation and relieve discomfort, and, as long as it is well fitting, ordinary activities may be indulged in safely. The object of operation is to close the canal through which the hernia occurred and to prevent any recurrence.

HERPES. Herpes febrilis, or herpes simplex, is the name for the "cold spot" or group of little blisters round the lips which frequently accompany the common cold. They may often be prevented or cured by taking extra vitamins, especially nicotinic acid. What is usually meant by herpes, however, is herpes zoster, or shingles. This is a form of neuritis resulting from the infection of a nerve root at the spine, which may occur at any age of life. The inflamed nerve causes considerable pain of a "toothachey" character, and groups of small blisters form on the skin over the area supplied by the nerve.

It may occur anywhere in the body, but always follows the anatomical distribution of the particular inflamed nerve. When it affects the forehead, blisters can occur on the eyeball, which is supplied by the same nerve, and this may result in loss of sight, so that every care should be taken in shingles in this situation. When it affects the upper part of the chest it will also go down the inner side of the arm because this is supplied by the same nerve. Similarly, herpes on the buttock is accompanied by groups of blisters down the back of the leg, following the course of the sciatic nerve.

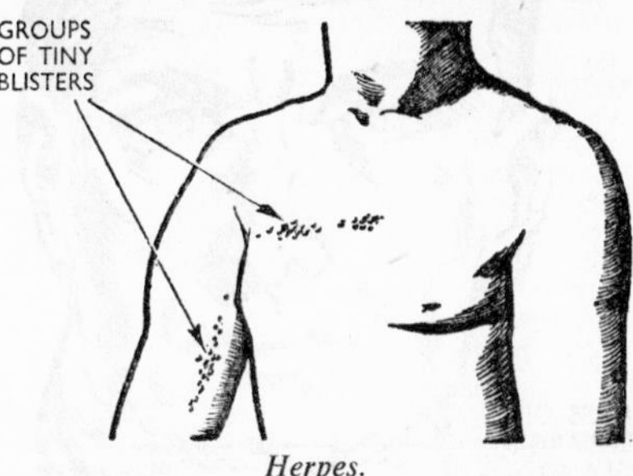

Herpes.

The blisters dry into scabs which peel off, often leaving scars and taking two to three weeks, as in chicken-pox. That is the end of the rash but, unhappily, the pain often persists much longer. The actual rash needs only a soothing ointment, such as calamine. Aspirin or other pain-relieving drugs may be desirable. Much relief is generally obtained from radiant heat or infra-red rays (see RAYS). Injections of liver extract in the first days of the attack often materially diminish the pain and shorten the course of the complaint. Attention should be paid to general nourishment, and extra vitamins should be given. If pain is severe, plenty of rest should be taken, and a holiday during convalescence is desirable.

HICCOUGH. This distressing symptom is due to spasms of the diaphragm. It may be a result of irritation of the gullet or stomach by strong condiments or over-hot food; it is a symptom of stomach disorders, such as gastritis, as well as of general abdominal disorders, such as peritonitis and obstruction. It frequently results from nervous disorders—hysteria, neurosis—and from serious disease of the nervous system (for example, meningitis), as well as from diseases which directly affect the diaphragm, such as pleurisy, peritonitis and pericarditis.

The usual case is due to some dietary indiscretion, and can be relieved by holding the breath, by pressing hard on the chest, or by inhaling smelling salts. There is also a form of epidemic hiccough; this can be very persistent and distressing and may have to be relieved by hypnotic drugs, or even by anaesthetics.

HODGKIN'S DISEASE. Lymphadenoma; a disease of the lymphatic glands (see GLAND), which swell enormously. It is accompanied by a progressive anaemia. The cause is unknown and treatment unsatisfactory, though some relief can be given by nitrogen mustard.

HORMONES. See ENDOCRINES.

Hodgkin's disease (see page 95).

HOUSEMAID'S KNEE. A swelling in front of the kneecap. See BURSITIS.

HYDROCELE. A fluid swelling round the testis, usually following some injury. It can become very large and hold a pint or more of fluid. Immediate relief can be given by tapping this fluid off, but it nearly always accumulates again and permanent cure can be obtained only by an operation in which the membrane which secretes the fluid is removed.

HYDROCEPHALUS. Water on the brain. The brain is surrounded by cerebro-spinal fluid. This has its own circulation and, if it is obstructed, the fluid accumulates. Such obstruction can be due to a congenital defect, resulting in the birth of a hydrocephalic baby, or may be the result of meningitis. The pressure, in a baby whose skull has not united, results in an enormous head, and the interference with the nerve cells of the brain causes various paralyses and mental defects. Treatment is unsatisfactory; such children require continual nursing care and seldom survive as adults.

HYPERCHLORHYDRIA. An excess of acid in the gastric juice. Wide variations occur in perfectly normal people, but excess acid is often present in cases of dyspepsia and of gastric and duodenal ulcer, and part of the treatment may consist of attempts to neutralize this acid. This is commonly done by alkaline mixtures or powders of various proportions of chalk, bicarbonate of soda, magnesia, and bismuth.

As chalk and bismuth are constipating, while magnesia is a laxative, the effect of these powders on constipation may be varied by altering the composition. They are not entirely harmless, partly because an excess may result in too much alkali in the blood (alkalosis), resulting in mental confusion and muscular weakness, and partly because they are often taken, mistakenly, in cases of dyspepsia resulting from too little hydrochloric acid (see HYPOCHLORHYDRIA), thereby aggravating the condition. People with hyperchlorhydria seldom get cancer of the stomach, so there is something to be said for not interfering too much with this condition.

HYPERPIESIA. A condition of raised blood pressure. See BLOOD PRESSURE.

HYPERTROPHY OF THE HEART. Enlargement of the heart; it is often a compensation for a valvular leak, thereby ensuring a good circulation by increasing the heart's pumping power. See HEART DISEASES.

HYPOCHLORHYDRIA. A condition in which hydrochloric acid is deficient in the gastric juice. This results in the pepsin in the stomach being unable fully to digest the food. Such people have poor appetites and tend to prefer savoury and spicy foods which stimulate the stomach to form some acid. They suffer from flatulence, generally have poor muscular development and tire easily.

While the condition can be treated by taking the acid as a medicine, this is nasty stuff to take, and equally good results can be obtained by taking alkalis, such as bicarbonate of soda, *before* meals. Although alkalis taken after meals neutralize acid and make the condition worse, when taken before meals they stimulate the stomach to produce acid. This is the better method because, in practice, it is impossible to drink sufficient acid to replace the deficiency.

HYPOGLYCAEMIA. A deficiency of sugar in the blood. This can occur in starvation, as a result of pancreatic disease, or can be due to an overdose of insulin in treating diabetes. Slight hypoglycaemia leads to fainting fits and to attacks in which the patient does unusual things without being aware of it; he may even attack people. Severe hypoglycaemia causes coma. See COMA and DIABETES.

HYSTERIA. A condition in which the symptoms of some illness appear in a patient without his actually having that illness, and in which there is some advantage to be gained by being ill. But it differs from malingering in that it is not deliberate, and the patient is not conscious of any wish to deceive. The actual symptoms may vary enormously with the circumstances, with the patient's acquaintance with some particular ailment, and with the powers of his body to reproduce the symptoms for him. There may be different sorts of paralysis, fits, loss of speech or appetite, skin rashes, tumours, or even, in women, a simulated pregnancy.

In diagnosis, genuine organic disease has to be excluded, and the patient's subconscious motive has to be discovered. There is often an hereditary tendency; but the onset is frequently due to some calamity or to some unendurable position, coupled with a longing for sympathy, love, position in life, or with some other strong emotion. Hysterical subjects have often been spoilt as children, and so have not learnt to face up to the difficulties of life. Later on they find themselves unable to acquire a "thick skin." Treatment is difficult and a matter for both the medical man and the psychologist. Relations should realize that the fundamental trouble is the patient's inadequate way of dealing with difficult situations, and that he has to be re-educated to meet difficulties as other people do.

When symptoms are endangering health—as does, for example, refusal to eat—then drastic treatment, such as hypnosis or auto-suggestion, may be needed; but it has to be understood that curing the symptoms does not cure the complaint, and results merely in some other symptom being developed which may, of course, be a less harmful one.

Quackery of all kinds has a great field among hysterical people, because they are all very suggestible and can be apparently cured by any sort of strong suggestion. It is a mistake to tell hysterical people that they should get married, or have a child; it does not cure them and is merely unfair on the partner or the child. A suitable occupation, a hobby, and a more healthy attitude to life's troubles and anxieties are more likely to give good results.

IDIOCY. A degree of mental defect so severe as to make the patient unable to look after himself or to guard himself against ordinary dangers. See MENTAL DEFICIENCY.

ILIUS. Dilatation of the intestine with obstruction.

IMBECILITY. Incapacity to be educated or to manage affairs. A state of mental deficiency less severe than idiocy.

IMMUNITY. The natural power of the body to resist disease, especially disease caused bv bacteria. Partly this resistance is accompanied by a healthy state of the skin and lining membranes, so that bacteria cannot penetrate, and this depends on an adequate supply of vitamins. Partly it is due to the power of the white blood cells to attack bacteria circulating in the blood. Partly it depends on the power of the body to form chemical substances, called antibodies, which neutralize bacterial poisons.

The bodily immunity can be raised by general healthy living and a good diet, keeping bacteria at bay; more specifically by either stimulating the production of antibodies or by supplying them artificially. Stimulation is achieved by injecting vaccines or toxoids, made from the particular germ against which immunity is desired. Artificial immunity can be provided by injecting the serum of an animal which has been itself immunized with vaccines or toxoids. See SERUM, TOXIN, and VACCINE.

IMMUNIZATION. The production of immunity, especially, of late years, against diphtheria. Babies less than one year old are not susceptible to this disease, but their immunity rapidly disappears and is very little at five years old. About 80 per cent of adults are immune. It is therefore customary to immunize at one year old, and to reinforce this with an additional injection at five. The reaction, if any, is very slight, but a hard nodule is left for some time at the site of the injection. See IMMUNITY.

IMPETIGO. A contagious skin disease, very common among school children (scrum rash). Blisters appear, which very soon change to scabs, and spread very quickly ove the skin. Impetigo may arise as a secondary infection on an already existing scabies, making the latter difficult to diagnose It is due to a streptococcus (see BACTERIA) and can be cured with ointments of sulphathiazole (see SULPHONAMIDES) or of penicillin.

Sufferers should use their own linen and towels and be excluded from school It is best to cover the sores with dressings to prevent scratching and the spread of infection. If the rash is on the face, a mask (with holes for the eyes, nose and mouth) may be made and ointment applied to this.

IMPOTENCE. The inability to perform the sexual act (see SEX), the term being usually applied to the male. Impotence may be due to old age, to disease, such as diabetes, to lack of hormones (see ENDOCRINES), or to psychological causes. Investigation should include examination for constitutional diseases—anaemia, diabetes, tuberculosis, etc. Lack of hormones will usually be indicated by a general trend to femininity: shrill voice, underdeveloped sexual organs, lack of hair on the face, etc.

In the majority of the cases, impotence is due to psychological causes. It is, for example, common among returned soldiers, not, as their wives suspect, because they have been unfaithful, but because, on the contrary, they have got into the habit of repressing their sexual desires and cannot quickly lose the habit. It also occurs in people who have had a faulty upbringing in sexual matters and have been taught to consider sex disgusting. Such an attitude, coupled with a strong religious nature and a feeling of guilt or sin, often leads to impotence. The cure lies in a more sane and sensible approach to the subject.

INCONTINENCE. Inability to control the passage of urine or stools (see ENURESIS). It may be due to emotional causes, especially fright, to local disease in the parts affected, to any severe illness, or to old age. In bedridden patients, very careful nursing is required in such cases, or bedsores will develop (see BEDSORES). Unbleached cotton-wool and sphagnum moss are useful absorbents; mackintoshes and drawsheets are necessary (see DRAWSHEET). Patients with urinary incontinence may be able to wear a rubber urinal, which can be purchased from any surgical instrument firm.

INDIGESTION. Any kind of upset due to imperfect digestion or to disease of the digestive organs. Regurgitation of sour food may be a result of eating too quickly, of taking food which is too hot, alcohol, strong tea or other irritants. Pain immediately after food may be due to gastric ulcer, or to gastritis. Pain two hours after food may be due to duodenal ulcer or to spasm of the bowel. When pain in the abdomen is unrelated to mealtimes, it is probably owing to flatulence and colic in the bowel, to constipation or to diarrhoea. In short, indigestion is not a disease, but is a vague term for all sorts of symptoms which may be caused by one of many disorders. These have to be sorted out by medical examination, and possibly by radiology. See CONSTIPATION, DIARRHOEA, DUODENAL ULCER,

FLATULENCE, GASTRIC ULCER, GASTRITIS, HEARTBURN, HYPERCHLORHYDRIA, and HYPOCHLORHYDRIA.

INFANTILE PARALYSIS. More correctly termed poliomyelitis, this is a disease due to inflammation of the spinal cord by a virus.

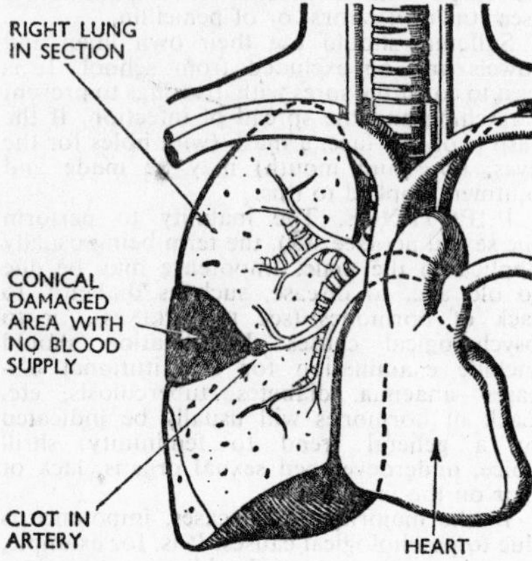

Infarct. An example in the right lung.

It is more common among children and young adults, and is spread by carriers. Infection is usually by droplets of nasal secretion, but may also be carried by milk and, possibly, by insects. The results of recent research in U.S.A. would appear to show that the virus is more frequently conveyed by excreta (faeces). Paralysis does not occur in the early days of the infection. The child is flushed, miserable and drowsy, restless, frightened, and usually irritable, giving the impression of being tense and preoccupied. There may be some jerky movements of the limbs. The child resents being touched, and may vomit and complain of headache. So far it is rather like a severe attack of influenza, though influenzal patients do not generally resent being made comfortable. The temperature may be 103 or 104.

Within a few days, pains in the back and limbs and increasing weakness in one or more limbs appear. The temperature may have fallen, but the child's movements are unsteady and noticeably weaker in one limb than in the others. At this stage paralysis may quickly become widespread, and the child become quite helpless, but, as time goes on, recovery from a great deal of this usually occurs.

The legs are most commonly involved. Paralysis of the chest muscles may lead to inability to breathe, and it is in cases of this kind that the so-called "iron-lung" is used as a mechanical method of artificial respiration. After the stage of rapid improvement some paralysis may or may not remain, but if it does it is often permanent, the nerve cells affecting that part having been destroyed by the infection.

Treatment involves prolonged rest, sometimes with splinting of the affected limbs, followed by massage and electrical treatment. Good results have been claimed for doses of potassium chlorate during the early stages. The serum of a person who is convalescent from the disease contains antibodies (see IMMUNITY) and is given with beneficial results. But it has to be given early in the disease, and some authorities are sceptical of its use. It is important, during convalescence, to re-educate the muscles by mechanical devices and by occupational therapy.

INFARCT. Damage in some organ due to a clot of blood stopping up a blood-vessel.

INFECTION. The invasion of the body by bacteria. Often this term is used when the bacteria arrive from a distance, through the air or in water or food, as opposed to contagion, when they are acquired by actual contact with a sick person. Germs may enter through cracks, pricks or cuts in the skin, or through any of the apertures of the body. The healthy intact skin is nearly germ-proof if kept clean.

Typhoid, cholera, dysentery and food poisoning are examples of disease carried by food and water; measles, influenza, colds are diseases in which the germs are conveyed on droplets of saliva coughed or sneezed through the air; impetigo and chicken-pox are conveyed by contact with the patient; while other diseases require an insect or animal to carry the germ, e.g., malaria is conveyed by the bite of a mosquito, plague by that of a rat flea, and typhus by the bite of a louse.

A knowledge of the method, in any particular disease, by which the germs are spread, is essential to the proper control of infection. See CONTAGION.

INFLUENZA. An acute infectious disease, due to a virus. It occurs in epidemics, often in the winter months. These epidemics tend to recur in cycles, but the reason for this is not understood. Some immunity can be obtained by injecting a vaccine made from inactivated mixed viruses; the protection lasts for three months, and the injection should then be repeated.

Influenza has a sudden onset, with aching pains, weakness, and high temperature, and the patient must promptly go to bed. Influenza may be complicated by catarrhs, by pneumonia, or by digestive disturbances. Victims should realize that true influenza can be an exhausting illness from which it takes some time to recuperate. The practices of trying to fight against it or to ward it off, and that of hurrying back to work before strength has returned, not only spread infection but lay the patient open to attacks of depression, palpitations, and muscular weakness.

A feverish cold is *not* influenza. The latter is not necessarily accompanied by catarrh at all. Its great characteristic is its sudden onset, with prostration and generalized aches and pains. Influenzal pneumonia results from secondary infection by catarrhal germs; it can often be controlled by sulpha drugs and penicillin, although these are without effect on the virus itself. In nursing influenza, do not make the patient over-hot through fear of a chill. He will be more comfortable if kept cool, and must have windows wide open. Sweats indicate the need for a blanket bath.

Large quantities of fluids, such as tea or lemonade, should be drunk—up to eight pints a day. Aspirin can be given for the aches and pains. It may be necessary to give a saline laxative, such as Epsom salts or magnesia. It is important that the patient should not get up until the evening temperature has remained normal for two nights. Some days should be allowed after that for a gradual return of strength. Extra supplies of vitamin C (see VITAMINS) are to be given both during the illness and during convalescence.

INFRA-RED RAYS. Invisible rays used as a local application in the treatment of some diseases and injuries where deep penetration is called for.

INOCULATION. The injection of vaccines to provide protection against disease. See IMMUNITY.

INSOMNIA. Some people need far less sleep than others, and are able to keep fit on a few hours of sleep every night, It is a mistake for them to regard themselves as victims of insomnia, and better to adjust their routine to fit in. True insomnia may be due to mental or to bodily causes. Pain of any sort needs relief according to its cause. Discomfort from excessive heat or cold, from itching, from stuffiness or from draughts, should be attended to.

Insomnia is a common feature of feverish illnesses and may need the use of drugs for its relief, because a refreshing sleep hastens recovery. A habit of insomnia can be formed, just as can a habit of sleeping; so that to go to bed feeling quite certain that sleep will not come generally guarantees that it will not. Much insomnia is due to mental anxiety and worry, especially to the habit of going over the day's affairs. All worries are magnified at night. Letting the mind chase from one thing to another banishes sleep most effectively. It is almost impossible to make the mind a blank, but it is fairly easy to insist on keeping the mind on one subject only, refusing to let it stray to anything else. This is the most effective cure, as one subject, if not a worrying one, quickly becomes boring and sleep follows.

There are, of course, many hypnotic drugs, but it is a great mistake to get into the habit of using them. While they are of the greatest help in illness, they should be restricted to temporary use. Otherwise they lose their effectiveness, the dose has to be increased, and a bad habit is established. A warm drink, perhaps an aspirin and deliberate relaxation will usually produce sleep.

INSULIN. See DIABETES and ENDOCRINES.

INTERTRIGO. A red, itching rash in places where sweat and friction occur, especially under heavy breasts. It should be treated by frequent washing and powdering.

INTESTINAL OBSTRUCTION. This may occur from severe constipation, from tumours (see CANCER), from strangulated hernia (see HERNIA), or from adhesions, twists or inflammations of the intestine. Symptoms are complete constipation, without passing even gas, vomiting (later bringing up foul matter from the lower intestine), and severe abdominal pain with collapse. Relief is given by the operation of colostomy in cases where the cause cannot be dealt with immediately. See COLOSTOMY.

INTESTINES. The alimentary canal from the stomach as far as the rectum. Its length varies, but may be 24 ft. See ABDOMEN.

INTOXICATION. Strictly speaking, poisoning by any toxin, but usually refers to acute alcoholic poisoning. A person is drunk if he is unable to carry out his intentions with safety to himself and other people. People vary enormously, however, in the amount of alcohol they can take without getting drunk. Alcohol is not a stimulant. Its action is to depress the nervous centres in the brain. It acts first on the higher centres, controlling action, before it affects the emotional centres, leaving, therefore, the intoxicated person under the impression that he is a fine fellow who is doing everything very well indeed.

Actually he is less perceptive and less able to perform intricate actions. The normal repressions of civilized life are dulled, so that a drunk person behaves more like an animal and shows his real nature. After reason has returned there is a "hangover," which can be countered to some extent by taking vitamins B and C (see VITAMINS). It is a mistake to take more alcoholic drink as a cure for the aftereffects; if there is no appetite, a saline and sweet drinks should be given.

INTUSSUSCEPTION. A tucking of one part of the bowel into the adjacent length, as when turning the finger of a glove inside out. It is most common in young children and causes intestinal obstruction. See INTESTINAL OBSTRUCTION.

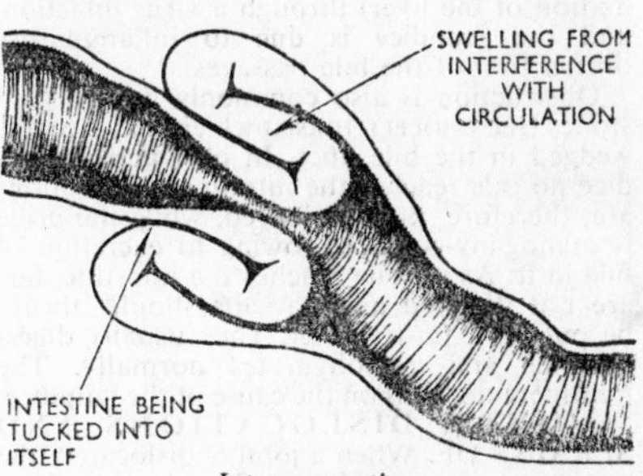

Intussusception.

IONIZATION. See ELECTRICAL TREATMENT.

IRITIS. Inflammation of the iris—the coloured part of the eye, round the pupil. See EYE DISEASES.

IRON. Haemoglobin, the pigment of the blood, contains iron, and a small daily intake of iron in the food is necessary for its replenishment. Iron also occurs in many other organs of the body. Simple anaemia can be cured quickly by adequate doses of iron. It is not cured by taking haemoglobin itself, for that substance is broken down in the stomach and the small amount of iron it contains is insufficient to do good. Ferrous salts of iron, such as ferrous sulphate, in doses of about twenty grains a day, are most effective.

ITCHING. Itching is a symptom in many skin diseases, especially scabies, eczema, and urticaria. It can also occur without any sign of a rash, especially in old people with dry skins. Scratching makes itching worse; the best treatment is, if possible, to cure the disease quickly. Sweating always makes itching worse; hot sunshine, violent exercise and hot fires should be avoided.

Calamine, coal-tar preparations and ointments containing local anaesthetics are all used to allay itching. Small doses of infra-red (see RAYS) are sometimes used. In persistent cases a dose of X-rays (see RADIOTHERAPY) will usually give relief. In cases of itching round the back passage (pruritus ani), toilet paper should be discarded and cotton-wool used; great cleanliness should be observed and a search should be made for threadworms. Prompt relief can be given by injecting into the skin a slow-acting local anaesthetic (see ANALGESIC). See THREADWORMS.

JAUNDICE. Yellowing of the skin. This is not a disease, but may be the symptom of various disorders. It can be classified roughly into two kinds. One is obstructive jaundice, in which bile is unable to leave the liver and is re-absorbed into the system, staining the skin and other organs; the other is "haemolytic" jaundice, which occurs in certain blood disorders, when red blood cells break down and release their pigments. The common epidemics of jaundice are produced by hepatitis (inflammation of the liver) through a virus infection, and the jaundice is due to inflammatory obstruction of the bile passages.

Obstruction is also commonly due to gallstones (see CHOLELITHIASIS) which may become wedged in the bile duct. In obstructive jaundice no bile reaches the intestine, the motions are, therefore, putty-coloured, while the urine is mahogany-coloured, owing to excretion of bile in it. As no bile reaches the intestine, fats are not digested and patients should always be put on a fat-free diet. They usually digest proteins and carbohydrates normally. The treatment depends on the cause of the jaundice.

JOINTS, DISLOCATIONS AND SPRAINS OF. When a joint is dislocated, the two bones forming it are forced away from their normal relationship and the usual movement at that joint becomes impossible. Dislocation is always accompanied by a certain amount of tearing of the ligaments surrounding the joint. If this tearing does not completely heal, afterwards the joint loses its former support, and subsequent dislocations may occur very easily.

When the ligaments are torn, but the force is not sufficient to move the bones out of alignment, then the joint is said to be sprained. Both sprains and dislocations follow some sudden movement which goes beyond the normal range of that particular joint. Common injuries are to the ankle, when the toe is caught and the weight of the body forces the joint apart; to the shoulder, when there is a fall on the elbow or the outstretched hand; to the knee, when the body goes over sideways with the foot held; or to the elbow, following a fall on the hand.

It will be noted that, in the majority of cases, the weight of the body causes all the damage. Consequently, many such injuries can be avoided by learning to fall on the soft parts of the body with all muscles relaxed. Putting out a hand to save oneself is probably the most common cause of injury. Dislocations and sprains of the wrist, elbow and shoulder, and fractures of the arm or collar-bone, are all due to this automatic action; whereas a fall on the buttock would, at most, result in a bruise.

In distinguishing a fracture from a dislocation, it should be remembered that a broken limb usually has more movement than it ought, whereas a dislocated one has less. In a sprain there is pain and tenderness at and about a joint, but if the limb is compared with the sound one there is no deformity, apart from bruising and soft swelling. The commonest sprain is of the ankle, and the diagnostic point is a tender spot just below the outer ankle bone, where the ligament has been wrenched. The bone itself is not painful to touch, whereas in a fracture it is. Often exact diagnosis of these injuries cannot be made without X-ray (see RADIOGRAPHY), and this should be used if there is any doubt.

The essential point in treating a sprain is to prevent further swelling, by cold water bandaging or by tight binding over cotton-wool. When the swelling has subsided, the joint should be strapped or bandaged so as to support the weakened ligament. With such

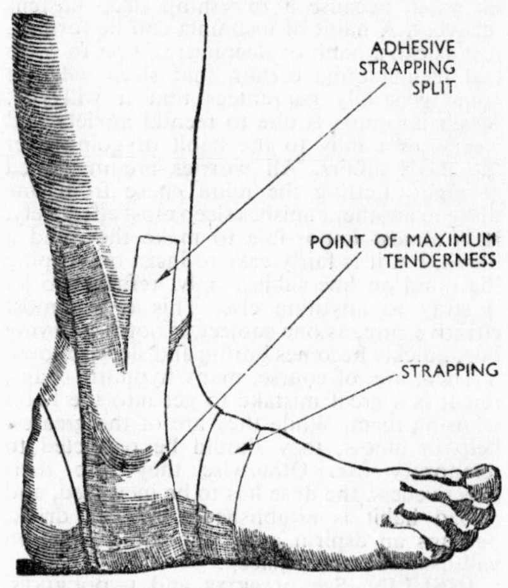

Joints. Strapping for a sprained ankle.

support, active exercise is all to the good. A dislocation or a fracture should receive medical attention.

A dislocated shoulder, if seen before stiffening has set in, may be put in place as follows: Assuming it is the patient's left arm, seize his elbow in your left hand and pull gently down towards his feet. Take his wrist in your right hand, and rotate his forearm outwards so that it points, at first, to you and then away from his body. During this manoeuvre, a click will be felt and the joint will go into place.

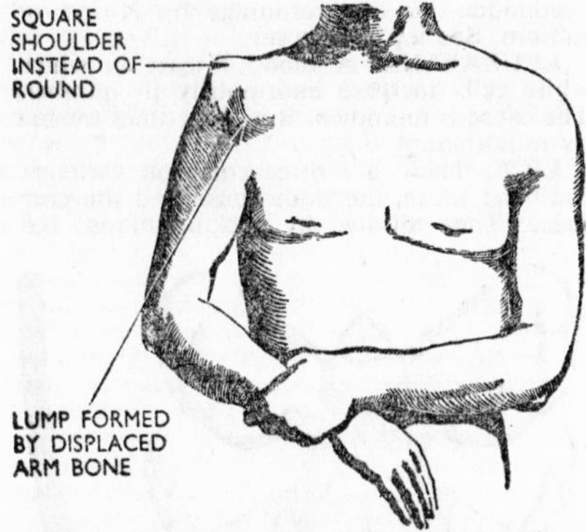

Joints. Symptoms of a dislocated shoulder.

Great force is *not* required and should not be used. The downward pull on the elbow *must* be maintained all the time the forearm is rotated. Afterwards, the arm should be put in a sling.

JUGULAR VEIN. The main vein of the neck; it takes blood from the face and the brain to the heart.

KIDNEY DISEASES. There are many diseases of the kidneys. Bright's disease has now been subdivided into six or seven varieties of inflammation, some being due to bacterial infection, some to degeneration and some to arterial diseases (see BRIGHT'S DISEASE). The kidneys suffer to a greater or lesser extent in all acute infections. In Great Britain scarlet fever is the commonest cause of nephritis (inflammation of the kidneys), and the first sign may be the passage of blood in the urine (see HAEMATURIA).

Such an attack needs prolonged rest in bed, with a diet low in proteins. Milk is not a good diet, but other fats and carbohydrates (even barley sugar and toffee) are excellent. Fluids should be kept within three pints a day (one and a half pints for a child), the bowels should be kept well open, with salts or cascara (salts should not be given if the patient is having sulpha drugs). Convalescence may be slow, and chills should be carefully guarded against.

In chronic nephritis the diet need not be so much restricted and more variety than is generally allowed is quite safe. Common salt should be avoided, and alcohol is unwise. Dropsy and other complications may need special measures. Stone in the kidney may cause aching in the back, or blood in the urine, but often causes no symptoms until the stone tries to move out towards the bladder. This produces agonizing pain in the lumbar region and the groin which may need morphia for its relief. The pain travels downwards and ceases when the stone enters the bladder. Stones may have to be removed by operation. They can usually, but not always, be seen by X-rays (see RADIOLOGY).

Modern methods of examining the kidneys are so accurate that exact information can be obtained in almost every case, by urine and blood examinations, by X-rays, and by examination of the inside of the bladder with a cystoscope. Most old-wives' tales about kidney diseases are inaccurate and misleading. Gin and methylene blue pills are *not* good for the kidneys, nor is barley water any better than plain water. It does not, as a rule, help to "flush them out"—in fact, in many kidney diseases fluids should be restricted. In all cases it is best to have medical advice.

KNEEJERKS. With the knees crossed, if the tendon below the knee is tapped, the muscles should jerk the leg up. This reflex is abolished in some diseases, notably locomotor ataxy, and is increased in others, such as certain psycho-neuroses, disseminated sclerosis and other forms of paralysis (for example, apoplexy). It does not by itself provide diagnosis of any disease, but is an adjunct to other methods of examination.

KYPHOSIS. Hunchback. See SPINE.

LACTATION. Milk normally enters the breasts about the third day after childbirth (see BREAST FEEDING), and further production is encouraged by the child's suction. It should disappear after weaning. If it does not, and the breasts become engorged and painful, the flow of milk can be stopped by administering oestrogens (see OESTRIN and ENDOCRINES). There is no need for the old-fashioned binding and purging.

LARYNGISMUS STRIDULUS. Sudden alarming attacks of breathlessness in children, due to a spasm of the vocal cords; it is associated with rickets and adenoids. The child wakes, gasping for breath, stops breathing altogether, becomes red and blue in the face and then takes a large crowing breath. After the attack the child is perfectly normal and can speak (with laryngitis the voice is lost).

Repeated attacks can lead to great exhaustion. Warm and cold sponges to the front of the neck relieve attacks, or a finger may be placed in the mouth and the tongue pressed forward. Removal of adenoids and administration of cod-liver oil prevent further attacks.

LARYNGITIS. Inflammation of the larynx, which contains the vocal cords, causing loss of voice, and sometimes causing pain in breathing and coughing. Patients should not try to speak, but may whisper. Inhalations of steam, with creosote, friar's balsam, eucalyptus or menthol give relief. Kaolin poultices or hot compresses may be applied to the Adam's

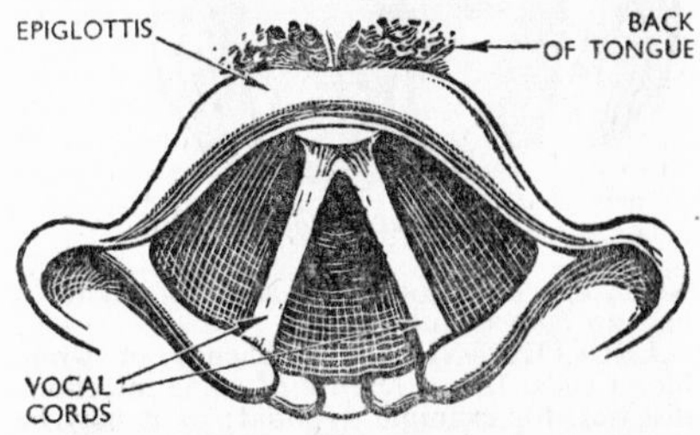

Laryngitis. The larynx seen from above.

apple. A soothing cough linctus usually gives relief. Penicillin lozenges may help, depending on the particular germ causing the inflammation. Cold air should be avoided.

LARYNX. That part of the air passage which contains the vocal cords and the "Adam's apple," which is the largest of the cartilages comprising the voice-box. See LARYNGITIS.

LAXATIVES. Substances causing the bowels to move. Laxatives have a gentle action, as opposed to purgatives. Salines, cascara, senna, medicinal paraffin, agar and magnesia are all laxatives. See APERIENTS.

LEAD POISONING. It can occur in some industries handling lead, and is characterized by griping abdominal pain with constipation, by paralysis of the limbs due to muscular wasting, to fits and anaemia. There is sometimes a blue line along the gums.

LEPROSY. A disease, widespread throughout the world, due to infection by the lepra bacillus. Close contact in the home is usually necessary for infection. Incubation may take many years, so that the chief danger is to a child brought up in a household with a leper. Leprosy takes two forms: one affects the skin and soft tissues, and the other affects the nervous system. Early cases are often curable by modern methods.

LEUCOCYTES. The white blood cells. See BLOOD CELLS.

LEUCODERMA. A skin disease in which the power of forming pigment is lost. Sunshine, therefore, causes patches of brown and white

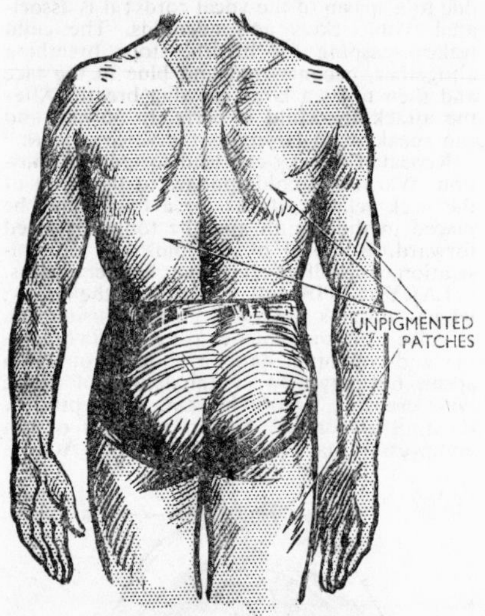

Leucoderma.

which are unsightly. The cause is unknown and no cure is known.

LEUCOPAENIA. A deficiency of white blood cells. It is a feature of some infectious diseases, for example, typhoid; or it may be the result of poisons or of some drugs, such as acetanilide, or of overdosage by X-rays or radium. See RADIOTHERAPY.

LEUKAEMIA. A blood disease in which white cells increase enormously in number. The cause is unknown. It is sometimes treated by radiotherapy.

LICE. There are three common varieties, the head louse, the body louse and the crab louse. They all live by sucking blood, but

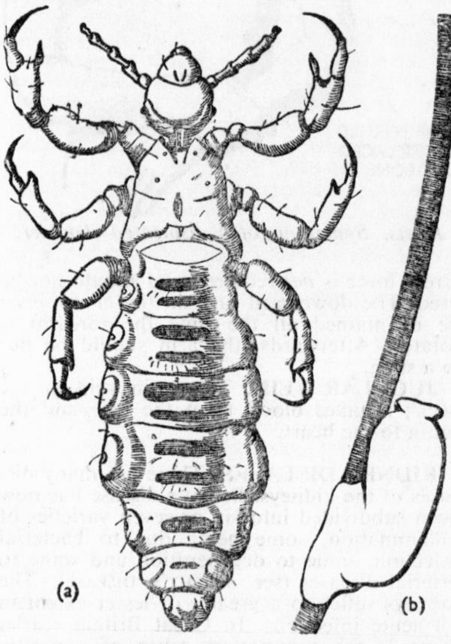

Lice. (a) *Fully developed head louse;* (b) *nit stuck on a hair.*

whereas the body louse lays its eggs in the seams of the undergarments, the others lay theirs on hairs, where they are called nits. The head louse lays one egg on a hair, but the crab louse infests the hairs on the abdomen and beneath the arms and lays many eggs on one hair. Lice and nits are killed by one application of lethane hair oil; lice can also be killed by D.D.T. powder, and by steaming garments. Lice spread diseases, including typhus and trench fever.

LICHENIFICATION. A smooth scaly state of the skin resulting from friction.

LICHEN PLANUS. An itchy skin rash, in pinkish patches, made up of small angular scales. The cause is unknown, but it may be due to worry and the need of a holiday. In severe cases, rest in bed and quite prolonged treatment may be required. See ITCHING.

LIGAMENTS. Fibrous bands binding joints together. See JOINTS, DISLOCATIONS AND SPRAINS OF.

LIGATURES. Strands of catgut, silk and other materials used in operations for tying blood-vessels. Catgut has the advantage of becoming ultimately absorbed, but it is more difficult to sterilize than other materials.

LIPIODOL. A substance which is opaque to X-rays: it is used to inject into various cavities of the body before taking photographs. See RADIOGRAPHY.

LIPOMA. A tumour or lump composed of fat. It is very common, as a soft rounded lump, sometimes tender, under the skin. The only cure is surgical removal. Such a tumour is not cancerous.

LIVER. A large organ which lies under the right ribs and below the diaphragm. It acts as a warehouse and a chemical laboratory, storing many foodstuffs in simple form until they are required, and then releasing them into the blood. It also forms various chemical substances of which one is the bile, another is heparin, which helps to prevent blood clotting too quickly, and a third is a substance which prevents pernicious anaemia and is used in this disease by injection.

The liver can become inflamed in hepatitis, producing jaundice, can become the seat of tropical abscesses in dysentery, and can become scarred and fibrous in cirrhosis. It is seldom the seat of primary cancer, but often contains secondary growths when the primary growth is in the bowel. "Liverishness" is a vague term with no specific meaning (see BILIOUS ATTACK). "Liver salts" are usually aperients and have no direct action on the liver. The liver becomes enlarged in some heart diseases owing to its congestion with blood.

LOCKJAW. A disease of the nervous system, also known as tetanus, with violent painful spasms of the muscles, sometimes ending in death. It is due to toxins formed by the tetanus bacillus, which gets into wounds, especially deep wounds contaminated by garden dirt or manure. It can be prevented by injections of tetanus toxoid, and treated by antitoxin. See SERUM.

LOCOMOTOR ATAXY. See TABES.

LORDOSIS. A curvature of the spine with exaggerated incurving of the small of the back. See SPINE.

LUMBAGO. Pain in the muscles of the back. It often comes on very suddenly, and is disabling. The pain is especially apt to occur after jerking movements in cold weather. An acute attack may be treated by hot baths, electric pads or other forms of heat with aspirin in full doses (three every two hours). When easier, it often helps to strap the back across with 2-in. strapping plaster in four or five strips, one above the other.

Chronic cases may need electrical treatment and should be examined for septic troubles, such as tooth abscesses or infected tonsils. Lesser degrees of backache without a sudden onset may not be muscular, but may be due to flatulence or other abdominal disorders. Prolonged standing, especially in people with flat feet, leads to a lumbago type of backache.

LUMBAR PUNCTURE. The withdrawal of cerebro-spinal fluid by inserting a hollow needle into the lower part of the spine. It is used for the diagnosis and treatment of many nervous diseases.

LUNGS, DISEASES OF. See ASTHMA, BRONCHIECTASIS, BRONCHITIS, BRONCHO-PNEUMONIA, EMPYEMA, PNEUMONIA, TUBERCULOSIS.

LYMPHANGITIS. Inflammation of the lymphatic vessels, commonly seen as red streaks up the arm or leg when there is a septic place on the hand or foot. The treatment consists of dealing with the septic place which is causing it.

LYMPHATICS. Small vessels conveying lymph over the body and passing through the lymphatic glands. See GLANDS.

M. & B. The initials of the drug firm which first developed sulphapyridine as a cure for pneumonia, calling it M. & B. 693. Popularly, the term M. & B. is frequently used for all drugs of this nature, often known as sulpha drugs, but confusion may arise because many drugs supplied by this firm are stamped M. & B., but are not sulpha drugs. Without any desire to detract from their pioneer work, it is better to speak of the sulpha drugs as sulphonamides.

MALARIA. A disease caused by a minute parasite, conveyed to human beings by the bite of the female anopheles mosquito. The parasite attacks and destroys the red blood cells, causing attacks of fever and progressive anaemia. In chronic cases this leads to jaundice and to enlargement of the spleen. There are at least four different types of malarial parasite, causing different forms of malaria. Benign or simple tertian malaria causes fever every other day; quartan malaria causes fever every third day. Malignant tertian, or subtertian, malaria has fever either daily or every other day. In addition, there is a mild type which occurs only in equatorial Africa.

The malignant tertian is the most severe and dangerous. The typical malarial attack begins with severe shivering, followed by feverishness, and then profuse sweating. The patient may feel vaguely unwell for several days before an attack occurs. There are a great many variations from the typical attack: there may be vomiting and diarrhoea, jaundice, delirium, muscular cramps, abdominal pains, and cerebral forms, with coma or fits.

Another type may produce symptoms resembling a heart attack. Chronic cases may develop blackwater fever, in which blood is passed in the urine. Relapses are very common; but malignant tertian seldom relapses after one year's freedom, and benign tertian seldom after three years. Quartan may persist longer.

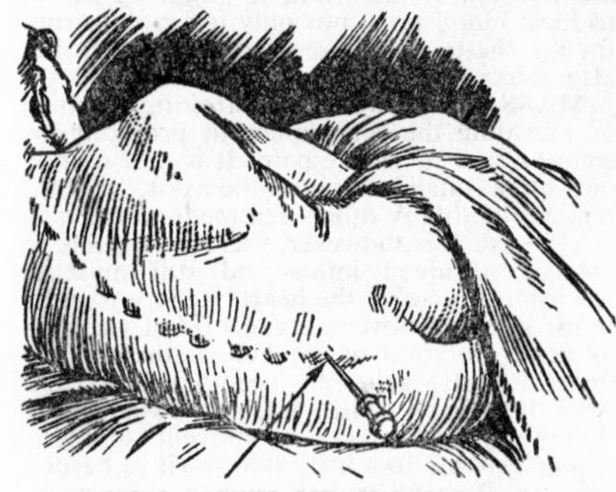

NEEDLE INSERTED BETWEEN VERTEBRAE

Lumbar puncture.

Prevention consists of eliminating mosquitoes and taking precautions against their bites. The classical treatment was by quinine; but new drugs have now been evolved, such as mepacrine and paludrine, which are not only curative, but largely preventative.

MALIGNANT DISEASE. See CANCER.

MALTA FEVER. An infectious disease characterized by very prolonged bouts of fever, with many relapses. It is due to drinking infected milk—usually goat's milk. A similar disease called undulant, or abortus, fever is acquired from infected cow's milk. The usual case lasts for three or four months, may occasionally recover in a few weeks, but sometimes takes several years. There are often rheumatic pains, and bronchitis or pneumonia may occur as a complication. It is unaffected by penicillin or by sulphonamides. The complications need careful attention.

MANIA. Mental disease characterized by great excitement and sometimes by violence. There is sometimes an hereditary tendency. See MENTAL DISEASES.

MANTOUX TEST. A skin test for tuberculosis. While a negative test implies freedom from the disease, a positive test does not mean that the disease is active.

MARASMUS. Chronic wasting in small children. It may be due to various diseases, and a diagnosis of the cause is essential.

MARRIAGE. The question sometimes arises of the desirability of marriage in people who are cousins, or who have some hereditary disease. The question of cousin marriage depends on whether the family is perfectly healthy for several generations. If it is, there can be no objection; but if there is any hereditary disorder, the chances of transmitting it are greatly increased, and it is better to marry outside the family. Tuberculosis should be a bar to marriage if it is active, but healed cases may marry. Each individual should take medical advice on this point.

Epilepsy is definitely hereditary, and couples marrying where this disease is in the family should avoid having children (see BIRTH CONTROL). It would be wise for all couples to have a medical examination before marriage, both to see that general health is good and to see that the reproductive organs are normal. In addition, it might be useful to have blood tests, not only for syphilis, but for the rhesus factor (see BLOOD GROUPS). See also ANTENATAL CARE, BIRTH, and SEX.

MASSAGE. A system of stroking, rubbing or kneading the soft tissues to promote circulation and to relieve pain. It is best carried out by a qualified physiotherapist, in conjunction with any other treatment which may be ordered. It is, however, useful to be able to massage sprained joints and stiff muscles. Always rub *towards* the heart. Relieve pain by gentle stroking movements; get rid of swellings by gentle rotation of the ball of the thumb; treat muscular aches by deep kneading and pounding. Apply a little talcum powder to the skin before massaging to prevent soreness. Afterwards rub in a little skin spirit to harden the skin. Remember that active movement by the patient is more useful than any amount of massage, which is merely a substitute when the patient is unable to move the limb himself. As soon as possible he should be encouraged to change over to his own efforts.

MASTITIS. Inflammation of the breast. See BREAST, DISEASES OF.

MASTOID. The bone behind the ear. It may become inflamed, followed by abscess formation, and necessitate an emergency operation. There is danger of inflammation spreading into the skull and causing meningitis. See EAR DISEASES and MENINGITIS.

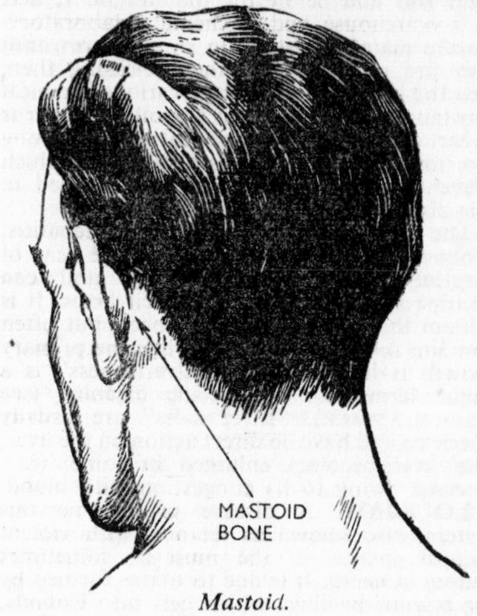

Mastoid.

MASTURBATION. In its widest sense the procurement by any solitary means of sexual excitement and satisfaction. The term is often misunderstood and there are many widespread and false beliefs about the practice. While there are social and individual reasons for avoiding the practice, it is now fully accepted that medically speaking it results in no physical harm to the individual. The stories that the practice results in the development of terrible diseases are quite untrue and should never be repeated, particularly to children. The psychological harm done by the fear which these stories induce is generally the worst aspect of masturbation, and there is no doubt that the currency they have been given has been extremely injurious to many generations. Masturbation normally results from an urge to satisfy an overwhelming desire. If indulged in to excess, it becomes a habit and occupies the mind when thoughts and energy should be better employed. It does, moreover, mitigate the urge to adventure into the world and find a mate and is socially undesirable in that sense. Generally speaking, the habit is not prolonged beyond childhood. If it is, there is probably some deep-seated discontent or neurosis troubling the patient. The cure in such cases is psychological rather than physical. In dealing with children who indulge in the practice it is most important not to frighten them in any way, or indeed to arouse in them any sense of sin. Their basic trouble should rather be discovered and they should be given plenty of interesting and stimulating things to do. These should normally be sufficient to divert them from the practice or break them of the habit.

MEASLES. An infectious disease of children and, sometimes, of adults. Usually, one attack confers immunity, but second attacks do occur rarely After about ten days' incubation the disease begins with a rise of temperature and all the signs of a severe cold—sneezing, running at the eyes, coughing and headache. There is a dislike of bright light, and the eyes may be bloodshot. During this stage, Koplick's Spots may be found inside the cheeks and the lower lip. They are pinpoint bluish-white spots on a scarlet background, occurring in little groups of half a dozen and, if seen, are diagnostic of measles. They do not always occur, however.

There may also be, at this stage, vague blush-red rashes on different parts of the body. The true measles rash does not appear until the fourth day, and may be delayed as much as ten days. It starts on the forehead and behind the ears, and soon spreads downwards over the whole body. The spots at first are separate, rather the size and appearance of pink confetti, but later run together.

After the rash is well out, the temperature often becomes lower, and the patient feels better and coughs less. In an uncomplicated case the rash lasts about four days, but often leaves some staining of the skin which may take a week or two to clear up. The eyes should clear about the third day after the rash appears, after which the room need no longer be darkened. The cough persists about a fortnight.

Nursing care for the ordinary case includes either darkening the room or, if the day is

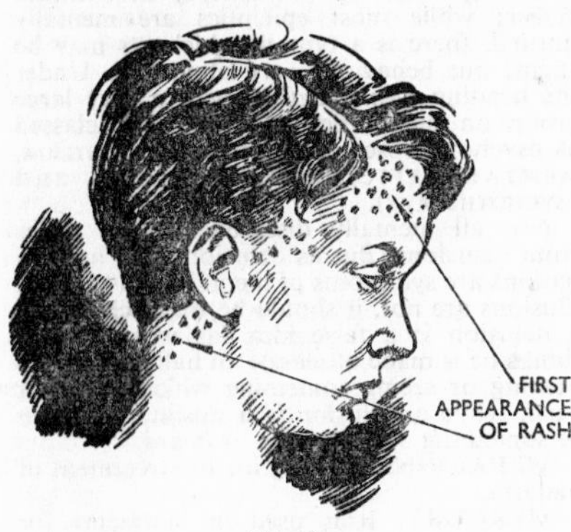

Measles.

dull, arranging the bed with the patient's back to the light; bathing the eyes with boracic two or three times a day; using a mouthwash of boracic or thymol; tepid sponging if there is fever (see BLANKET BATH) and giving some simple linctus for the cough.

Earache is the commonest complication and can lead to serious trouble, with middle-ear disease (see EAR DISEASES) and mastoid trouble. *Never* pour anything into the ear without medical instructions. It is safe to put a hot-water bottle outside it and to give aspirin, but the ear should be examined by a doctor as soon as possible. The other important complication is chest trouble—bronchitis and broncho-pneumonia. The advent of penicillin and sulphonamides has made such complications much easier to clear up than formerly. The patient should not read while the eyes are sore, or the sight may be affected.

Measles is a disease which must always be taken seriously, and for which medical advice should always be sought. It is especially serious in babies under the age of two years. It is possible to protect children of this age, if they have been in contact with a case, by injections of the serum of someone who has had the disease. The protection lasts only a few months, but confers protection for the time being and postpones the disease until the child is older. It is also possible to give partial protection, resulting in a modified attack, which itself confers immunity against further attacks. Such injections should be given within a few days of contact with a case. See IMMUNITY.

MEDIASTINUM. The partition, containing the heart and great blood-vessels, which separates the two lungs.

MELAENA. Passing blood with the motions. When this blood comes from some spot near the anus, the blood may be bright (as when the trouble is piles). When the bleeding occurs higher up, as in cases of duodenal ulcer, the blood becomes changed and causes a tarry black motion. Taking iron and bismuth in medicines may also cause black motions; and a chemical test may be necessary to decide that blood is present.

MEMORY, LOSS OF. See AMNESIA.

MENINGITIS. Inflammation of the meninges—the membranes covering the brain and the spinal cord (see BRAIN, CEREBRO SPINAL FEVER, CEREBRO-SPINAL FLUID). This disease can be due to several different bacteria and the symptoms and treatment differ. The epidemic form results from spreading by carriers and occurs in crowded and damp surroundings, for example, military camps.

Septic organisms arising from mastoid disease or sepsis elsewhere in the body can cause septic meningitis. There is also an influenzal form and one due to a virus. The majority of these infections yield to treatment by penicillin and by sulphonamides, and the mortality has dropped from about 70 per cent to about 5 per cent. The tubercular form, however, is still resistant to treatment, though great hopes have been raised by the use of streptomycin.

Meningitis is ushered in with fever and headache, often with dislike of light. Stiffness of the neck may be an early sign, and there may be a squint or other form of paralysis. Diagnosis, however, is not always straightforward, though it can usually be made by an examination of the cerebro-spinal fluid (see LUMBAR PUNCTURE). Many cases clear up entirely, but in others weakness of limbs or eye muscles and headache may persist. As a rule, cases should be treated in hospital, or nursed by professional nurses; meningitis is not a disease in which home nursing is adequate.

MENOPAUSE. Change of life. The end of the reproductive period in a woman's life, when menstruation ceases and pregnancy is no longer possible. The age at which it occurs varies between 38 and 58, average 45. Menstruation may cease suddenly and finally, but more often the periods become gradually scantier and occur at longer intervals. Excessive bleeding may happen, but is abnormal, and medical advice should always be sought.

There is too great a tendency to regard any abnormality which occurs at this time as due to age, so that no advice is sought for it. It has to be remembered that this is also the age when fibroid tumours and cancer can start, and that excessive loss may be due to such serious things—which can be cured if taken in time, but which may have a tragic sequel if neglected.

Owing to the cessation of ovarian activity, the female endocrines are deficient for a time, and this leads to hot flushes. In some women these are slight and can be disregarded, but others suffer acutely. It is quite possible to control these flushes by suitable glandular treatment, and medical advice should always be taken. This is the only ailment which is strictly due to the menopause. Sufferers from "middle-age spread," from high blood pressure, from rheumatism, or from other complaints, should have the treatment appropriate to their complaint and not be satisfied to endure it and blame their age.

MENORRHAGIA. Excessive loss during menstruation. There are many causes, and medical advice should always be sought.

MENSTRUATION. The flow of blood from the womb, occurring roughly once a month, which takes place in women during the child-bearing period of life—approximately between the ages of 15 and 45. The lining of the womb goes through a cycle of changes every month, to prepare it to receive a fertilized egg-cell. This culminates in a state of great activity and congestion. If no pregnancy occurs, the lining membrane breaks down and bleeds for four or five days, after which it begins to build up again. If a pregnancy does occur, the fertilized egg-cell embeds itself in the spongy tissues, break-down does not take place, and there is no bleeding. Menstruation may, from one point of view, be regarded as the miscarriage of an unfertilized egg-cell. See ABORTION, AMENORRHOEA, DYSMENORRHOEA, MENOPAUSE, MENORRHAGIA, OVARY, PUBERTY, and SEX.

MENTAL DEFICIENCY. In childhood, mental deficiency may be congenital or acquired. When children are born mental defectives the commonest types are mongolism (see MONGOL), hydrocephalus, malformation of the brain, injury to the brain at birth, or "congenital amentia" when the child is backward and the brain does not develop, though the head appears normal.

Mental defect may be acquired by children subsequent to brain injuries resulting from encephalitis, meningitis, syphilis, hereditary epilepsy (see FITS), or from cretinism which is a defect of the thyroid gland, and is remediable by taking thyroid extract. The Mental Deficiency Act (1913) provides for care of these children, and in many districts there are special schools in which they can be trained as far as their intelligence will allow. They should not be at school with ordinary children, both for their own sakes and that of the others.

MENTAL DISEASES. These are as complex in their own way as physical diseases, and there are almost as many beds in mental hospitals as in hospitals for physical disorders. The care of mentally diseased people is the sphere of the psychiatrist, and is a highly specialized matter.

As suitable treatment often involves interference with the patient's liberty of action, various legal forms have to be observed before admission to mental hospitals; and these legal forms sometimes deter people from obtaining the treatment they should have. It must be realized that these formalities are only for the patient's protection and have no bearing on the treatment he will receive. Modern treatment of mental disorders is highly successful, and a majority of patients are discharged in a few months and are able to return to their normal occupations.

Mental disorders can be roughly classified as follows: *schizophrenia*, a disorder in which the emotions are separated from the reason, and the patient, while retaining his intelligence, performs illogical actions—in some cases, a sort of apathy or stupor alternates with periods of excitement; *paranoid states*, in which there are hallucinations or delusions that the patient is being persecuted or used for experimental purposes; *manic-depressive psychoses*, in which periods of excitement and talkativeness alternate with periods of depression and suicidal tendencies; and the *organic psychoses*, in which some bodily disease affects the brain. There is also *epilepsy with mental defect*; while most epileptics are mentally normal, there is a type in which fits may be slight, but behaviour very abnormal. Under the heading *mental deficiency* is a very large group on the borderline of normal, classed as psychoneuroses or neuroses (see HYSTERIA, MENTAL DEFICIENCY, NEUROSIS, and PSYCHOTHERAPY).

Not all mentally diseased persons suffer from delusions. But as delusions and hallucinations are symptoms of mental disease, while illusions are not, it should be made clear that a delusion is a false idea (as when a man thinks he is made of glass); an hallucination is hearing or seeing something which does not exist, while an illusion is a misinterpretation of something actually seen or heard.

MEPACRINE. A drug for the treatment of malaria.

MERCURY. It is used in ointments for various skin diseases. At one time it was the chief treatment for syphilis and is still used to some extent, though supplanted by arsenic and by penicillin. Calomel is subchloride of mercury. Corrosive sublimate, very poisonous, used as an antiseptic is perchloride of mercury.

MESENTERY. The tissues by which the intestines are attached to the abdomen.

METABOLISM. The whole process by which food is absorbed, used in providing energy and waste products eliminated. The rate at which this is done can be measured by estimating the oxygen breathed in and the carbon dioxide breathed out in a given time. This is called the basal metabolic rate, and is often used to indicate the activity of the thyroid gland. See GOITRE.

MICTURITION, DISORDERS OF. The most common urinary complaint in children is bedwetting (see ENURESIS). The too frequent passing of water may be due to nervous strain, or to disease of the bladder or urinary passages. Pain on passing water may be due to inflammation of the bladder (see CYSTITIS). It is not usually possible to diagnose such disorders from the appearance of the urine, but all sufferers should let the doctor have a specimen for test because a great deal of information can be obtained from microscopical and chemical examination.

All these disorders are capable of exact diagnosis by modern methods, including X-rays (see RADIOLOGY), and examination by cystoscope, through which the inside of the bladder can be inspected. Urine which is clear on being passed but which deposits a sediment on cooling does not, as a rule, indicate anything other than the need to drink more fluids. Highly coloured urine is the rule in fevers. Urine smelling of fish indicates infection. Baby's nappies smelling of ammonia need boiling—the trouble lies in the nappy, not the baby.

MIGRAINE. Severe attacks of headache, usually one-sided and incapacitating. The cause varies; it may be a result of eyestrain, or may be due to sinus infection (see SINUS), or to idiosyncrasy to certain food (see ALLERGY). Any of these may produce congestion of the blood-vessels in the membranes covering the brain, and so a headache. If the cause can be discovered it should be treated.

The congestion, and the headache, can often be relieved by preparations of ergot or other drugs. Severe cases have been cured by operations on the nerves in the neck which control the blood flow to the brain. Some cases are entirely due to psychological causes and can be cured by psychological treatment. There is a great variation between individuals and every sufferer from migraine should be separately examined and advised.

MILK. A very valuable food, especially for the young, but also a great source of infection because it is easily contaminated by bacteria which thrive and multiply in it. All milk should be heat-treated before use unless its freedom from germs can be guaranteed in some other way. The appearance of freshness or richness is no guide as to its safety. Tuberculosis is among the serious dangers of infected milk.

MISCARRIAGE. See ABORTION.

MITRAL DISEASE. Disease of the mitral valve of the heart; the valve either may not close properly (mitral regurgitation), or may be partially closed by scarring so that it cannot fully open (mitral stenosis). See HEART DISEASES.

MOLE. A pigmented nodule on the skin, which may carry a few hairs. There is a very dark variety which occasionally becomes cancerous (see CANCER). Black moles should, therefore, be thoroughly removed by a competent surgeon. Other moles will often disappear if the hairs are removed by electrolysis, or the moles themselves may be treated by freezing, cauterization, or removal.

MONGOL. A backward child with a rather "Chinese" type of face. The eyes appear to slant, the child sucks its tongue and lolls it out of its mouth, and there may be a slight squint. The child has small hands, with tapering fingers, and the little finger curves inwards. Many mongols have some congenital abnormality, such as heart disease.

The cause of mongolism is unknown, though they sometimes are born to parents at the end of a long family, or to a comparatively old mother. Possibly illness of the mother, especially german measles in the early months of pregnancy, may be connected. Mongols are backward in development and backward mentally, but they are usually musical and very affectionate. Their expectation of life is not good, and many die in their teens.

MORPHINE. The active principle of opium; it is used to relieve pain.

MOSQUITOES. These insects are responsible for the spread of malaria, yellow fever, dengue, and filariasis. Prevention of these diseases is largely a matter of controlling the breeding of these insects. For the treatment of mosquito bites, see BEE STING.

MOUTH BREATHING. This is primarily due to nasal obstruction which, in children, is usually caused by adenoids. In older people obstruction may be due to a bending of the septum, or partition, in the nose, to the presence of polypus or other growth. After a clear nose has been established, mouth breathing may persist as a habit which should be broken by regular breathing exercises.

MOUTH, CARE OF. See GINGIVITIS, GLOSSITIS, SCURVY, STOMATITIS, TEETH, TONGUE, and TONSILLITIS.

MUCOUS COLITIS. A form of looseness of the bowel associated with the passage of large quantities of mucus, often in the form of complete casts of the bowel itself. This complaint is not thought to be due to infection or organic change in the bowel, but to an increased tendency to secrete mucus, which is associated with emotion and nervous tension. The treatment is psychological, rather than physical, and it is quickly cured by a happy, contented mind. See COLITIS.

MUCOUS MEMBRANE. Just as the skin covers the outside of the body, so mucous membrane lines its apertures; the mouth, the throat, the nose, the rectum and bowel, the urinary and sexual passages, and so on. It is of a different construction from skin, and is much moister. When irritated, it secretes more mucus for its own protection; hence the stream of mucus from the nose in a cold or in hay fever, and the passing of mucus from the lower bowel both in constipation and in diarrhoea.

MUCUS. A clear, rather viscous fluid secreted by mucous membranes.

MUMPS. An infectious disease, also termed epidemic parotitis, which is due to a virus usually affecting the salivary glands of the mouth. The chief of these is the parotid gland, lying below and in front of the ear, hence the most evident swelling is in this neighbourhood. But the glands below the chin can be swollen as well, and the disease can affect other glands, such as the pancreas, the breasts, the ovaries and the testes.

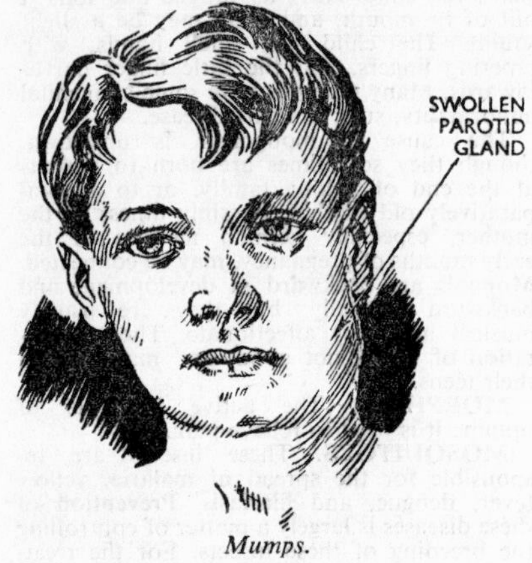

Mumps.

The commonest of these complications is inflammation of the testes (orchitis). This does not occur in boys under the age of puberty, but over that age it is very serious, as it may cause sterility. Complications in girls are much less common. The incubation is from fourteen to twenty-one days, and infection is present four days before any swelling appears. The infection lies in the saliva. The patient remains infectious until a week after all swelling has gone.

Most cases of mumps are mild and need little beside rest, warmth and a light diet. Chewing is very painful, but swallowing is not, so that the patient can take any soft food. Mild cases in boys and men over the age of fifteen should be taken seriously and kept in bed, owing to the danger of orchitis. There is no point in wrapping up the face unless the patient finds it more comfortable; most of them dislike it. A mild mouthwash should be used, and tasty foods, which stimulate the salivary glands, should be avoided.

MURMUR. An abnormal sound produced in the heart and heard with a stethoscope. Some sounds indicate disease, but others are of no importance at all. The differentiation is a matter for a doctor. See HEART DISEASES.

MUSCLE. A tissue with powers of contracting and expanding, joining two or more bones together so as to produce movement at joints. Muscle is developed by exercise and becomes flabby if unused. Besides this "voluntary" muscle there is involuntary muscle which is present in the wall of the intestines, in the womb and other organs which have to make automatic movements. There is also heart muscle, which is a special variety with unusual recuperative powers, so that it does not need—for it cannot have—prolonged rest. Heart muscle benefits by exercise in the same way as any other muscle, and it is unlikely to be strained by any effort of which ordinary muscles are capable.

MYALGIA. Pain in muscle, commonly experienced as muscular stiffness after exercise, and as lumbago and other pains after chilling or wetting. It may be treated by heat, massage, and exercises.

MYASTHENIA GRAVIS. A chronic disease in which the muscles become paralysed. The paralysis is worse on exercise and improves after resting. The drug prostigmin gives considerable temporary relief.

MYCOSIS. Disease due to fungi; actinomycosis, often acquired from cattle, is the commonest variety. There are also several skin diseases caused by fungi, the commonest being athlete's foot, the result of fungi being picked up when going barefoot, which can be treated with Whitfield's ointment.

MYELITIS. Inflammation of the spinal cord. When localized to one area of the cord it may lead to paralysis of both legs. See POLIOMYELITIS.

MYOCARDITIS. Inflammation of the heart muscle. See HEART DISEASES.

MYOSITIS. Inflammation of muscles. It may be due to septic organisms and result in abscesses. It can occur, apart from sepsis, in the course of several diseases; in scurvy, in which there is haemorrhage into the muscles; and in a form of tapeworm that can be caught by humans from underdone pork, in which the larvae are found in the muscles. There is also myositis ossificans, in which bone forms in the muscles and causes stiffness and disuse.

MYXOEDEMA. The opposite condition to exophthalmic goitre; underactivity of the thyroid gland, leading to increase in weight, sluggishness (both physical and mental), slow pulse, dry skin, loss of hair and swelling round the ankles and above the collar bones. It is curable by taking thyroid extract in adequate dosage. The dose may be considerable and should be under medical supervision.

NAEVUS. A birth-mark. In the majority of cases, naevi consist of a collection of dilated blood-vessels in, or just under, the skin. Small spider-web naevi are very common in new-born babies and usually disappear without treatment. Capillary naevi are scarlet and slightly raised above the skin level. They can usually be cured by freezing with carbon-dioxide snow. When larger blood-vessels are involved, very thick purple naevi occur, which may need treatment by radium, or even surgical removal with subsequent skin grafting.

The disfiguring "port-wine" stain is a variety of naevus which is very difficult to eradicate with good result as far as appearance is concerned. Naevi are definitely *not* caused by any fright suffered by the mother before the birth of the child, and are congenital defects due to an error in development of blood-vessels of the skin. Some naevi take the form of pigmented patches, and these can often be eradicated by freezing.

NAILS. Outgrowths of the skin, similar in construction to hair The bed from which the nail grows is exposed to injury and inflammation, the result of which is often the permanent growth of deformed and thickened nails. A blow on the nail results in an accumulation of blood beneath; this is very painful, but can be relieved at once by drilling a tiny hole in the nail, with the point of a penknife, to release the clot. Splinters beneath the nail should be removed at once, or sepsis will probably follow. If necessary, cut away a V-shaped piece of nail so that the splinter can be properly grasped with forceps. Yellow pus beneath the nail can be treated only by removing the nail under an anaesthetic or a local analgesic.

Concave nails are usually due to anaemia; transversely ridged nails to general illness, and white spots to injury. Pitted nails are caused by infection by fungus, and may need removal or radiotherapy. Spongy, red quicks are usually brought about by immersion in dirty water used for scrubbing and washing up; rubber gloves should be worn until they are cured. "Ingrowing toenail" is a false name; the trouble is due to the toe itself enlarging, from tight shoes or too much walking, so that it overlaps the nail. The most satisfactory cure is to have a portion of the enlarged soft tissues removed. It does not, as a rule, help to remove part of the nail.

NAUSEA. A feeling of sickness, without actual vomiting.

NECK. This contains many vital structures: the gullet and windpipe, the large blood-vessels supplying the head, and the main nerves to the heart, lungs and stomach; also the larynx, with which we speak, and the thyroid and parathyroid glands.

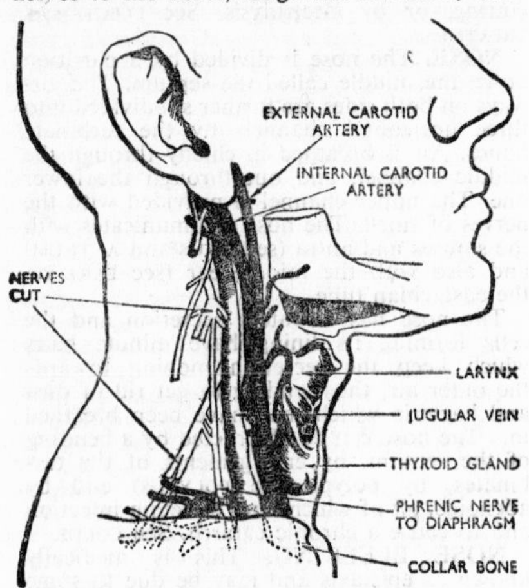

Neck, showing the principal organs.

NEPHRITIS. See BRIGHT'S DISEASE and KIDNEY DISEASES.

NERVES. Specialized cells, each consisting of a body with a tail, sometimes of considerable length. These tails, in bundles, run from the brain and spinal cord all over the body. They transmit sensory impressions to the brain, and impulses for movement from the brain to the muscles. Vast numbers of them are collected in the brain itself (see BRAIN). The term nerve is also applied to the bundles of individual nerve fibres.

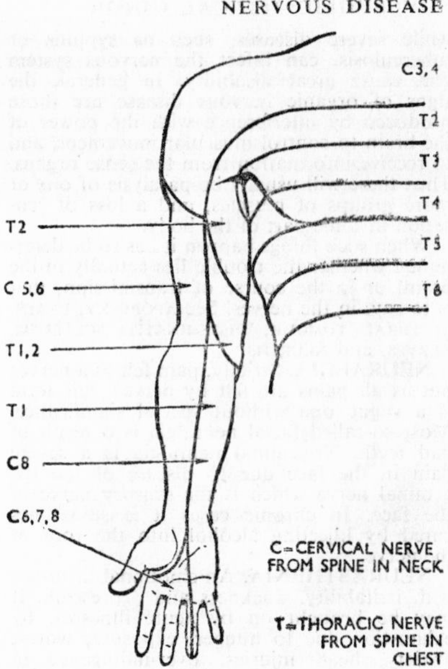

Nerves. Distribution of sensory nerves to the arm, showing areas affected by neuritis or herpes or any one nerve.

There are twelve pairs of nerves leaving the skull: the cerebral nerves, including the optic nerve (sight); the olfactory nerve (smell); the auditory nerve (hearing); the nerves controlling movements of eyes, facial muscles, tongue, etc.; and sensory nerves from the face and scalp. Pairs of nerves also leave the spine between each pair of vertebrae (see SPINE), and these nerves are partly sensory and partly motor.

In addition to all these there are the nerves of the "autonomic" system, working from large ganglia, such as the solar plexus, and controlling heart rate, digestive movements, blood flow, sweating and other involuntary activities of the body. These last are to a great extent under the control of the ductless glands (see ENDOCRINES) and are also influenced by the emotions.

NERVOUS DISEASE. By this is meant actual organic disease of the brain and nerves, but not mental or emotional disorders (see MENTAL DISEASES and NEUROSIS). The study of nervous diseases is known as neurology. The nervous system suffers in many general bodily disorders and cannot be considered by itself. For instance, neuritis may be due to alcohol, beri-beri, diabetes, diphtheria, dysentery, scarlet fever and other disorders.

Tumour of the brain cannot be considered apart from cancer elsewhere (see CANCER).

while severe diseases, such as syphilis or tuberculosis, can infect the nervous system and cause great disability. In general, the signs of organic nervous disease are those produced by interference with the power of the brain to control muscular movement, and to receive information from the sense organs. Thus there will usually be paralysis of one or more groups of muscles, and a loss of sensation in some part of the body.

When such things happen it has to be determined whether the trouble lies actually in the brain, or in the course of transmission, that is to say, in the nerves. See APOPLEXY, BRAIN, CEREBRAL TUMOUR, DISSEMINATED SCLEROSIS, NERVES, and NEURITIS.

NEURALGIA. Strictly, pain felt in a nerve; but as all pains are felt by nerves, this term is a vague one without special significance. Most so-called facial neuralgia is a result of bad teeth. Trigeminal neuralgia is a severe pain in the face due to disease of the trigeminal nerve which is the sensory nerve of the face. In chronic cases it is sometimes cured by injecting alcohol into the root of the nerve.

NEURASTHENIA. An emotional disorder, with irritability, weakness and depression. It may be brought on by acute illnesses, by exhaustion due to hunger, exposure, worry, anxiety, head injuries, over-indulgence in alcohol or strong coffee. The patient complains of headaches and general pains, giddiness, flushings, lack of interest and inability to concentrate; he may also have mild obsessions, such as a compulsion to go round the house twice at night to make sure it is locked up. Treatment depends largely on the removal of the cause.

NEURITIS. Inflammation of a nerve (see NERVOUS DISEASE). It is usually accompanied by pain and weakness in the affected part of the body. Treatment consists in removal of the cause, the administration of vitamin B in those cases due to vitamin deficiency (see VITAMINS), rest and splinting of affected limbs, and, subsequently, massage and electrical treatment. See BELL'S PALSY and HERPES.

NEUROSIS. A general term for emotional disorders, more properly called psychoneurosis; including the hysterias, neurasthenia and various other states caused by psychological disturbances. See OBSESSION and PSYCHOTHERAPY.

NIGHT SWEATS. These occur in pulmonary tuberculosis (see TUBERCULOSIS), but also in any condition which produces fever at night. They are also common in people who are run down from any cause, and may be due to nothing more than a surplus of bedclothes. Troubled sleep and nightmares can also cause a person to awake in a sweat.

NIPPLE. Nursing mothers easily suffer from cracked and infected nipples (see BREAST FEEDING). It is a mistake to apply hardening agents, such as friar's balsam, alcohol or witch-hazel, as these increase the liability to cracking. The ideal is to aim at a soft, prominent nipple, free from any infection. Before a baby is born, the nipples may be drawn out, using a little lanolin on the fingers. When feeding, they should be washed with warm, soapy water before and after every feed. Usually this is sufficient; but they may also be swabbed gently with boracic lotion. If they are inflamed, a doctor should be consulted.

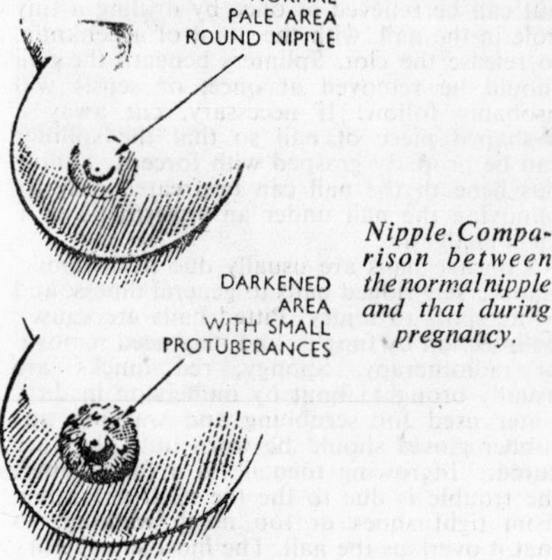

Nipple. Comparison between the normal nipple and that during pregnancy.

Bleeding from the nipple may be a sign of serious disease, and should receive attention as soon as noticed. During pregnancy the area round the nipple becomes pigmented and small nodules stand out on it. Hairs round the nipple are common in brunettes and, if disfiguring, may be removed by shaving, by cutting, or by electrolysis. See ELECTRICAL TREATMENT.

NOSE. The nose is divided by a partition down the middle called the septum. The airways on both sides are further subdivided into three horizontal channels by the turbinate bones. Air is breathed in chiefly through the middle channel, and out through the lower one. The upper channel is provided with the nerves of smell. The nose communicates with the sinuses and antra (see SINUS and ANTRUM) and also with the middle ear (see EAR) via the eustachian tube.

The nose has a watery secretion and the cells forming its lining have minute hairs which keep the secretion moving towards the outer air, thus tending to get rid of dust and bacteria which may have been breathed in. The nose can be obstructed by a bending of the septum, by enlargements of the turbinates, by polypi (see POLYPUS) and by adenoids, all of which tend to retain infection and to cause a chronic catarrh. See COLDS.

NOSE BLEEDING. This is medically known as epistaxis and may be due to some disease of the nose itself, to congestion of the lining, as in colds, hay fever and high blood pressure; to blood diseases, such as anaemia and scurvy; to congestion during menstruation or when menstruation is suppressed for any reason. It is very common among children and may arise from the most trivial causes, such as blowing the nose, going into cold air or getting excited.

The patient should be made to lie down with the head on one side, and cold compresses

Nose bleeding. Treating it with a gauze plug.

should be applied to the nose and mouth. It is a mistake to lean forward over a bowl. If bleeding continues, the nose may be plugged : cotton-wool or gauze should be tightly rolled to the shape and length of a cigarette, and this should be gently introduced and plugged well back. Bleeding generally arises from a point about ¾ in. inside the nose and on the septum (see NOSE), so that small plugs, inserted merely in the nostril, are useless. Keeping the mouth open with a cork often stops nose bleeding.

NUMBNESS. This may occur in various nervous diseases, also in disorders of the circulation, such as chilblains, "dead" fingers, Raynaud's disease, and in a limb which has been subjected to prolonged pressure.

NURSING. The general art and craft of caring for the sick and injured, under medical direction. It includes, necessarily, a good knowledge of the structure and functioning of the body, a knowledge, too, of disease processes, methods of treatment, the use of drugs, etc. But it is essentially a practical rather than a theoretical business, and can be learnt only by actual training in hospitals. A knowledge sufficient for nursing simple cases at home can be acquired by attending lectures and practical classes and by reading books on home nursing.

Every mother should, for instance, be capable of taking a temperature, giving a blanket bath, using a bed-pan and a drawsheet; she should understand the necessity for fresh air as well as warmth in the sick-room, and should be able to bandage a cut and use an antiseptic. The directions for nursing ordinary ailments are given under the respective diseases. See ANTISEPTIC, BANDAGE, BED-PANS, BLANKET BATH, DRAWSHEET, and TEMPERATURE.

OBESITY. Fatness; it is more common in some races, such as the Dutch, Germans, and Jews, than in others. It tends to run in families. Obesity is most common in babies, in children at puberty, in men after forty, and in women during pregnancy or after the menopause. It is commoner among women than men. It always indicates that the calorie value of the food taken is greater than the body needs for exercise. This may be due to eating too much, or to a small output of energy; people who give up vigorous exertion, for example, often continue to eat as much as they did before, and so put on weight.

The energy output is controlled to a great extent by the ductless glands, especially the thyroid, but also the pituitary and the sex glands (see ENDOCRINES); and an inability to put out enough energy to get rid of the food consumed may be due to glandular disorders. In mild cases, reducing calorie intake, by cutting down carbohydrates and fats, may be sufficient, but severe cases need more drastic dieting.

A simple method is to have a weekly fast day, on which only fruit, green vegetables and water are taken. Fats should be reduced as much as possible and carbohydrates modified, but protein foods should be maintained. Extra exercise helps. Gland treatment should be adopted only after careful medical examination. The indiscriminate use of thyroid is apt to upset the heart. See EXOPHTHALMIC GOITRE.

OBSESSION. An obsession may be a persistent idea, an impulse or urge to do something, an unreasoning fear, or an endless search. Obsessions are characteristic of mental diseases and of neuroses.

OBSTETRICS. The science and art of midwifery. See BIRTH.

OBSTRUCTION. See INTESTINAL OBSTRUCTION.

OCCUPATIONAL DISEASES. Diseases arising in the course of industry, for which compensation is payable. The schedule varies in different industries, but includes anthrax, poisoning by lead, mercury, phosphorus, benzene, dope, carbon disulphide, manganese, etc., hookworm disease, cancer due to tar, cataract in glass-workers, nystagmus in miners, beat elbow, beat hand and beat knee. Also included are glanders in those who look after horses, telegraphists' and writers' cramp, dermatitis and ulceration due to dusts and liquids (see DERMATITIS). Any worker claiming compensation must be seen by the Examining Surgeon of the factory.

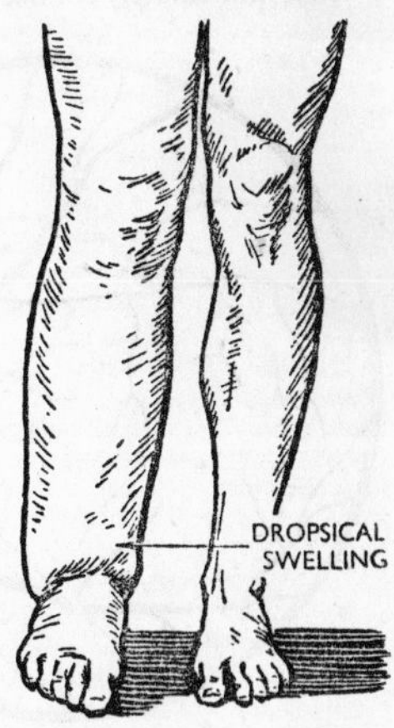

Oedema. Swollen leg due to an obstruction in the blood circulation.

OEDEMA. Fluid dropsical swellings, which pit when they are pressed. Such swellings may be due to heart or kidney disease, or to varicose veins or other causes of obstruction to the circulation.

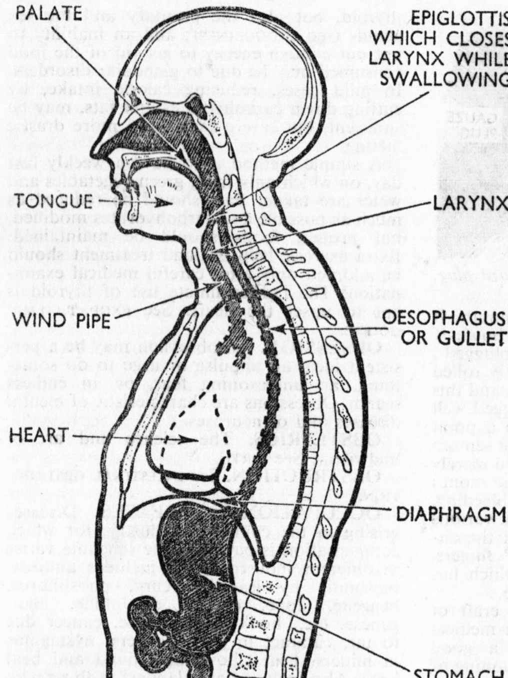

Oesophagus, or gullet. Diagram of the chief organs.

OESOPHAGUS. The gullet; the tube leading from the mouth to the stomach. It separates from the windpipe at the larynx and finishes by passing through the diaphragm, when it immediately connects with the stomach.

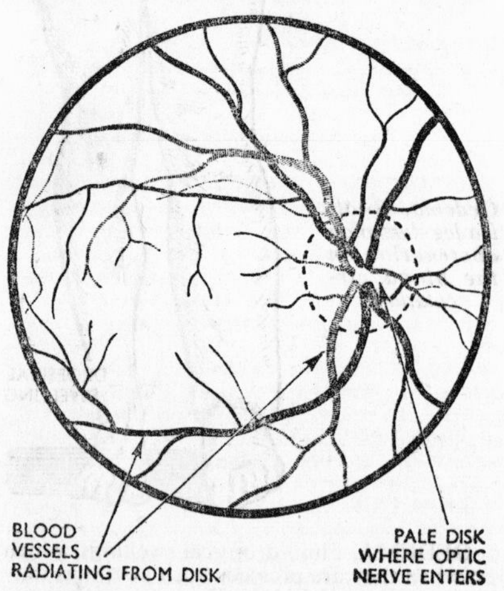

Ophthalmoscope. Retina of the eye as seen through an ophthalmoscope.

The gullet is subject to damage from swallowing scalding fluid, which causes obstruction, and can be the site of cancer.

OESTRIN. A chemical hormone formed by the ovary (see ENDOCRINES). It plays a part in regulating menstruation and is also responsible for the formation of the general sexual characteristics of women. Synthetic substitutes have been developed which can be taken by mouth, are largely used in treatment, but should never be taken without medical advice.

ONYCHIA. Inflammation of the nails. See NAILS.

OPHTHALMOSCOPE. An instrument for examining the interior of the eye. It is essentially a means for looking along a beam of light.

ORCHITIS. Inflammation of the testis. It may be due to mumps, to gonorrhoea, or to infections from the bladder reaching the testis. See also EPIDIDIMITIS.

ORTHOPNOEA. Ability to breathe only when sitting upright; it occurs in some forms of heart disease.

OSTEITIS. Inflammation of bones.

OSTEO-ARTHRITIS. See ARTHRITIS.

OSTEOMYELITIS. Inflammation of the bone marrow; a very serious disease which may follow general infection by the same type of bacteria that cause boils and carbuncles. There are severe pain and signs of inflammation over the affected bone. The patient has a high temperature and may have violent shivering attacks. Osteomyelitis is a complication of wounds and injuries of bones, and of open fractures. Operation is frequently needed to drain away pus. The use of penicillin, combined with surgery, has greatly

Osteomyelitis. Inflammation of the bone marrow.

altered the outlook, and rapid cures are often obtained in cases which formerly relapsed frequently and needed many operations.

OTITIS. Inflammation of the ear. See EAR DISEASES.

OVARIAN TUMOUR. Cysts are common in the ovary; they may be quite small, or may reach the size of a football and have to be removed. Cancerous growths can occur (see

CANCER), and also dermoid cysts. Ovarian disorders always cause disorders of menstruation. If abnormal bleeding or pain is always investigated there is no fear of overlooking these diseases. Large ovarian tumours are sometimes confused with pregnancy.

OVARY. The female sex gland. There are two—one on either side of the womb, low down in the pelvis. At birth the ovaries contain a definite number of immature egg-cells.

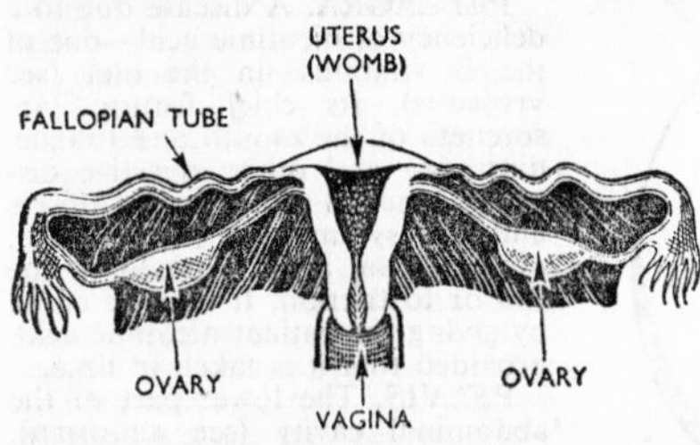

Ovary. Lay-out of the female reproductive organs.

and this number is never increased. At the age of puberty the egg-cells begin to mature in turn, so that, on the average, one ripens each month from the age of fifteen to that of forty-five, approximately. When no more egg-cells are available, menstruation ceases, and pregnancy is no longer possible (see MENOPAUSE). The ovary also secretes two chemical substances, called oestrin and progestin, which control menstruation and pregnancy.

PAIN. The purpose of pain is to draw our attention to injury and to disease. If there were no pain we should be continually burning or injuring ourselves, and disregarding the symptoms of illness. For this purpose it is imperfect because some dangerous conditions, for example, early cancer, are not painful, and because the severity of the pain is unrelated to the severity of the disease. For instance, a tiny abscess at the root of a tooth is excruciatingly painful, whereas quite a large one internally may be far less so.

When the illness or injury is cared for, the purpose of pain has been served, and pain should then be relieved. This may be done by anaesthesia or by the use of pain-relieving drugs, such as morphine or aspirin. It is always

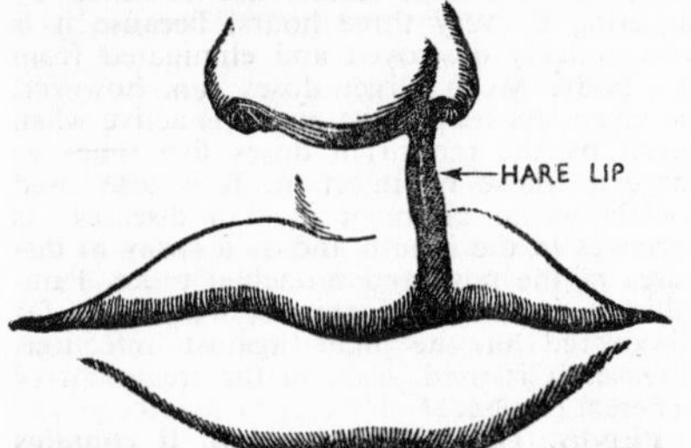

Palate. *Hare lip is often a sign of cleft palate.*

difficult to gauge the severity of another person's pain. A rough, but useful, classification is (*a*) a pain which you can forget; (*b*) a pain you cannot forget, and (*c*) a pain which makes you forget everything else. Morphine is usually necessary only for class (*c*).

PALATE. The roof of the mouth. The hard palate, in front, is bony; the soft palate, at the back, contains cartilage (gristle). Cleft palate, often associated with hare lip, is a congenital defect, resulting from interference with development at an early stage of antenatal life. It can be repaired by plastic surgery.

PALLOR. Pallor does not necessarily indicate anaemia. The colour of the skin depends on its translucence, and thick skins are usually sallow. The gums and finger-nails are a better indication, and should be a good red colour. Temporary pallor is produced by shock and by fainting attacks. See FAINTING and SHOCK.

PANCREAS. An organ lying behind the stomach; it is also known as the sweetbread. The pancreas has two functions: one is to secrete digestive juices, which it discharges into the intestine, and the other is to form an internal secretion essential for the use of sugar by the body. See INSULIN and DIABETES.

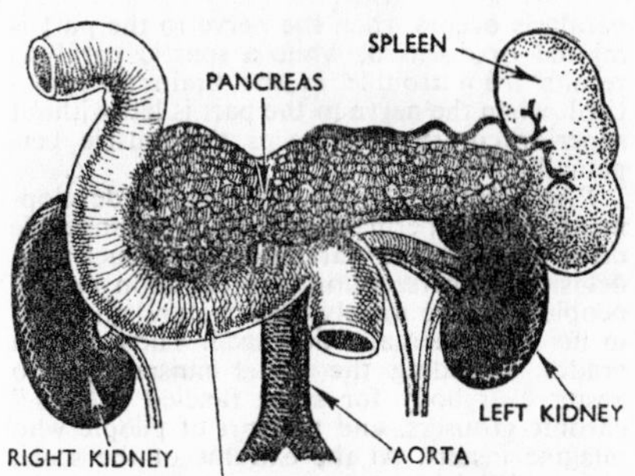

Pancreas and neighbouring organs.

PAPILLOMA. A warty growth, a simple non-malignant tumour, which has a tendency in some situations to spread and to recur after removal. Papilloma of the bladder may cause haematuria. It is cured by cauterization and by radiotherapy. See HAEMATURIA.

PAPULE. A small, raised swelling of any sort.

PARAESTHESIA. Abnormal sensations, such as the burning feeling in a limb during neuritis, or the creeping feeling of "insects on the skin" which occurs after taking some drugs. Paraesthesia occurs in the course of many nervous diseases.

PARALYSIS. Inability to move a limb or a group of muscles. It may be a result of the muscles having degenerated, but more usually it is due to some disease of the nerve supplying the muscle (see APOPLEXY and NERVOUS DISEASE). Paralyses are divided into two types, flaccid or flabby, and spastic or rigid. A flaccid

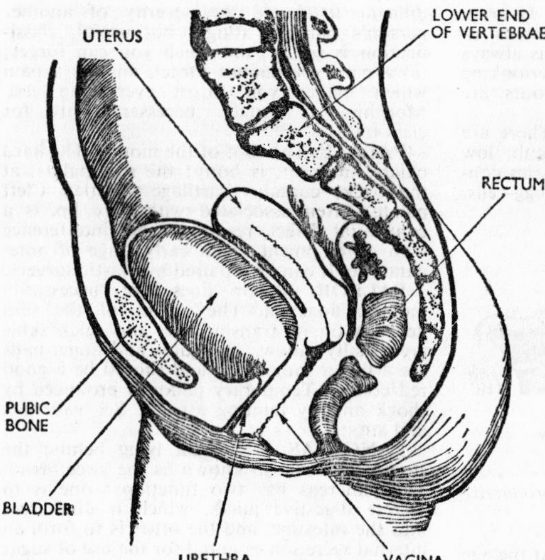

Pelvis (female), a ring of bones which contains the rectum, bladder and sexual organs.

paralysis occurs when the nerve to the part is injured or diseased, while a spastic paralysis results from trouble in the brain or spinal cord, when the nerve to the part is left without superior control and keeps the muscle perpetually in a rigid state.

PARANOIA. Strictly speaking, the development of a permanent and unchangeable delusion. But mild paranoid states, such as a delusion of persecution, are common among people who are merely sensitive and shy, and in no sense mentally deranged. There are all grades, including the social nuisances who pester everybody for some fancied "rights," chronic grousers, and the sort of people who imagine insults. At the extreme of the scale, paranoid delusions become dangerous to the patient, or to others, and constitute insanity. See MENTAL DISEASES.

PARASITES. Many diseases are caused by animal parasites. The scabies mite causes skin disease; the louse causes dermatitis, also typhus and trench fever. Another form of typhus is due to a tick. Intestinal worms are common parasites, especially in the tropics. See THREADWORMS.

PARATHYROID. One of four small glands in the neck, behind the thyroid gland. Their secretion is necessary for the utilization of calcium by the body in the formation of bones, teeth, etc. Removal of the parathyroid leads to convulsive spasms and death.

PARKINSONISM. Symptoms arising after encephalitis, resembling the symptoms of Parkinson's disease (paralysis agitans). These include progressive weakness with muscular rigidity, trembling of the limbs, lack of facial expression and a very peculiar walk in which the trunk is bent forward, the arms held away from the body, and a series of short stumbling steps taken, with difficulty in raising the feet. It is a chronic progressive condition, which may be partly relieved by treatment but cannot be cured.

PAROTID GLAND. One of the salivary glands of the mouth, situated just below and in front of the ear; it swells in mumps.

PELLAGRA. A disease due to a deficiency of nicotinic acid—one of the B vitamins—in the diet (see VITAMINS). Its chief features are soreness of the mouth and tongue, diarrhoea and other digestive disorders, mental and nervous upsets and a symmetrical skin rash, especially on areas exposed to the sun or to friction. It may be cured by giving the patient nicotinic acid, provided that it is taken in time.

PELVIS. The lower part of the abdominal cavity (see ABDOMEN). It is contained in a bony basin, formed by the hip-bones and the lower end of the spine (the sacrum). In men the pelvis contains the rectum, the urinary bladder, the prostate gland and the seminal vesicles, with some loops of the small intestine. In women it contains the rectum, bladder, vagina, uterus, and ovaries (see OVARY).

PEMPHIGUS. A skin disease characterized by large inflammatory blisters. Acute pemphigus is generally due to infection, and can be cleared up by penicillin or by sulphonamides. Chronic pemphigus is a very exhausting condition which may be very difficult indeed to cure. There is also a syphilitic variety.

PENICILLIN. This drug is produced by a mould, *Penicillium notatum*, and is extracted and purified from the broth in which the mould is grown. It has the almost unique power of destroying certain bacteria by preventing their growth and reproduction, while being entirely harmless to human beings and animals. Moreover, it is effective in the presence of blood and of pus. It is limited to certain germs, and does not affect others—tuberculosis and influenza are not cured by penicillin. But it destroys the germs of sepsis and those of pneumonia and most forms of meningitis.

Penicillin is usually administered by injection, and the best results are obtained by injecting it every three hours, because it is very quickly destroyed and eliminated from the body. Much larger doses can, however, be given less frequently, and it is active when given by the mouth in doses five times as large as those by injection. It is also used locally as an ointment in skin diseases, as lozenges in the mouth and as a spray in diseases of the nose and bronchial tubes. Penicillin is probably the greatest weapon so far discovered in the fight against infectious disease. It is used, also, in the treatment of venereal disease.

PENIS. The male sex organ. It contains the urethra, the pipe by which urine is discharged from the bladder. The seminal fluid from the testes (see TESTIS) reaches the urethra about an inch below the bladder, and is discharged from the same orifice. The organ consists chiefly of erectile tissue, enabling it to become large, rigid and erect, for the purpose of insertion into the vagina.

The end is supplied with very sensitive nerves, stimulation of which causes the reflex muscular action which expels the seminal fluid. This sensitive end, the glans, is covered with the foreskin, for protection, but this is sometimes surgically removed (in the operation of circumcision).

PERICARDITIS. Inflammation of the pericardium, the membranous bag enclosing the heart. It is a dangerous disease, as it not only embarrasses the action of the heart, but directly poisons the heart muscle. Treatment is according to the kind of infection, but it may include penicillin. An operation is sometimes needed to drain off fluid.

PERIOSTITIS. Inflammation of the periosteum, the membrane which covers bones. It may follow injury or local infection and can lead to osteomyelitis.

PERISTALSIS. The automatic movements of the intestine during the process of digestion.

PERITONEUM. The smooth membrane lining the abdomen.

PERITONITIS. Inflammation of the peritoneum. It is usually secondary to some inflammatory condition, such as appendicitis, or to a perforated ulcer (see DUODENAL ULCER and GASTRIC ULCER). It may lead to a localized abscess which has to be drained surgically, or may spread over the entire abdomen (generalized peritonitis), which is a very toxic condition and may cause death. Treatment may be by surgery, by penicillin or by sulphonamides. The tuberculous variety may need long treatment by rest, fresh air, etc.

PHARYNGITIS. Catarrhal inflammation of the pharynx, the space at the back of the nose and mouth. It is a common complication of colds and sore throats and leads to coughing and to pain on swallowing.

PHARYNX. The upper part of the throat, from the nose to the larynx.

PHLEBITIS. Inflammation of a vein. This or thrombophlebitis, which means phlebitis

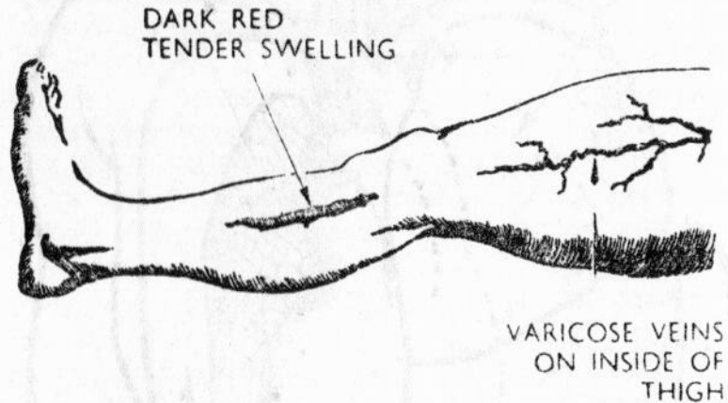

Phlebitis, or inflammation of a vein.

complicated by clotting in the vein, is a common complication of varicose veins. The whole vein swells, becomes red and very tender. It usually subsides under treatment by sulphonamides, but should be rested for at least two weeks because there is a danger of the clot separating, getting into the circulation, and causing infarct. Cooling lotions, such as evaporating lead lotion, may be applied as compresses. See VARICOSE VEINS.

PHOBIA. An unreasoning fear; a form of obsession. See OBSESSION.

PHYSIOTHERAPY. The science of physical medicine, a generic term covering a wide field of treatment, embracing light therapy (infra-red, ultra-violet and chromotherapy), electrotherapy (galvanism, faradism, diathermy and other forms of applied electricity), remedial exercises, massage, and rehabilitation.

PILES. These are really varicose veins inside the anus. They are produced by anything causing congestion in this neighbourhood, such as straining during constipation

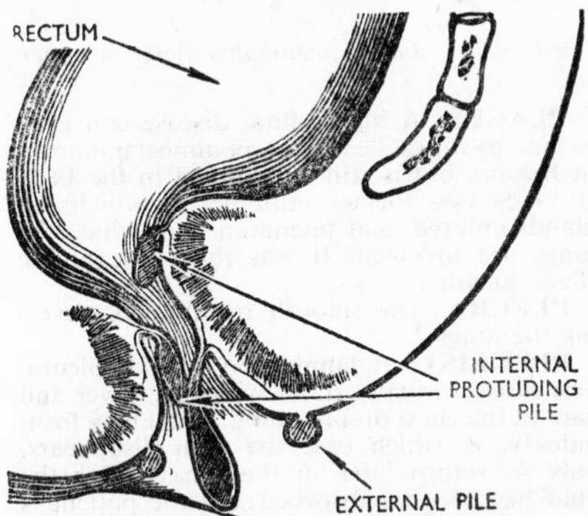

Piles, a form of varicose veins.

or diarrhoea, or by prolonged standing, liver diseases, pelvic obstruction from pregnancy or growths. They usually protrude from the back passage, but may be pushed back. They sometimes bleed quite profusely.

If the blood in a pile clots, it becomes tense and painful (thrombosed pile). This condition can be relieved at once by a small incision under a local analgesic to let the clot out. Immediate relief can be given by hot-water compresses or by sitting in a hot bath. If untreated, the clot gradually becomes absorbed over a period of about three weeks. Piles may be cured by operation, or by injection; but it is necessary to discover the cause and put it right, or they will recur. Slight cases can be relieved by various forms of suppository, or simply by introducing petroleum jelly on the finger.

It helps to adopt a crouching attitude during the passage of motions. Lower lavatory seats would prevent many cases, but the use of a footstool has the same effect. When piles have been bleeding and are sore, cotton-wool should be used instead of toilet paper. Violent pain on passing a motion is not usually due to piles, it is more often because of anal fissure (see ANAL FISSURE).

PITUITARY. See ENDOCRINES.

PITYRIASIS. A widespread skin rash, with a branny scaling. It may be accompanied by fever. The cause is unknown. Pityriasis may be confused with seborrhoea.

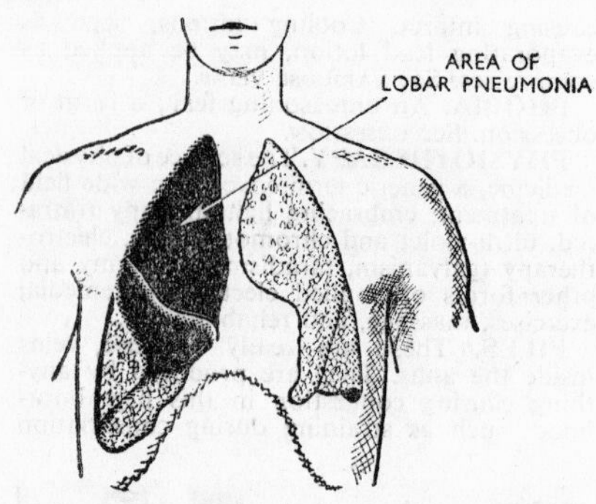

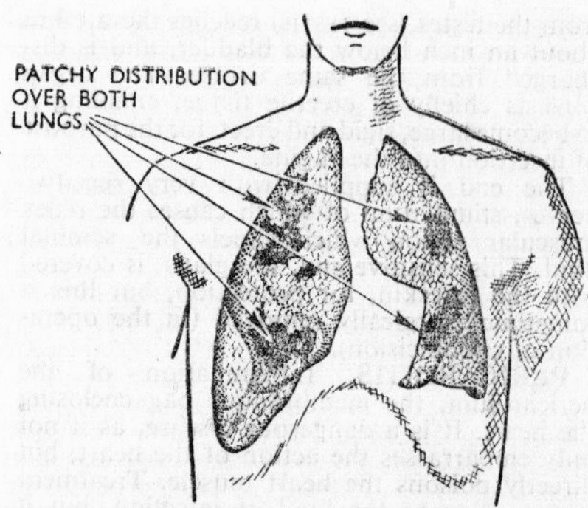

Pneumonia. Lobar pneumonia (left) *in upper part of right lung, and broncho-pneumonia* (right).

PLAGUE. A highly fatal disease conveyed to man by the rat flea. It is now almost unknown in Britain, but is still widespread in the East, It takes two forms: bubonic, in which the glands enlarge, and pneumonic, in which the lungs are involved. It was the cause of the Black Death.

PLEURA. The smooth membranes covering the lungs.

PLEURISY. Inflammation of the pleura. The disease usually starts with high fever and pain in the chest on breathing. Fluid may form quickly, in which case the pain disappears, only to return later in the illness after the fluid has become absorbed and the patient is recovering. "Dry" pleurisy, without fluid, may follow a chill, or accompany pneumonia. When fluid forms it may be clear, or may contain pus. The former variety is sometimes tuberculous, and anyone who has had pleurisy should be kept under observation, have the lungs X-rayed at intervals, etc., until reassurance is obtained about this. When pus is present we have an empyema.

Patients with pleurisy usually lie on the affected side, both to relieve pain and to make breathing easier. The pain may be relieved by poulticing with kaolin poultice, changed every three or four hours. Only a doctor can decide if fluid is present and, if it is, whether it should be removed. Nursing care is required, as the patient must not be allowed to do things for himself. This necessitates bed-pans, draw-sheets and blanket baths. Cooling drinks may be given. The patient must be kept warm, but at the same time must have fresh air.

PNEUMONIA. There are two chief varieties: lobar pneumonia and broncho-pneumonia. The first affects one or more lobes of the lung, leaving the rest alone. It is usually of sudden onset, often following a chill, but may be caught from another patient. Before modern treatment with sulphonamides and penicillin it ran a course of about ten days, and ended with a crisis, at which the temperature suddenly fell to normal with an attack of sweating.

Broncho-pneumonia is of patchy distribution over both lungs; it is the commoner variety, often being secondary to bronchitis or to influenza. If untreated, it does not end in a crisis, but clears up gradually over about three weeks (see BRONCHO-PNEUMONIA). Nowadays, both varieties have lost most of their terrors because of the use of modern drugs which cut the infection short, as soon as diagnosed, and lead to rapid recovery.

It is important to realize, however, that, although the patient may feel well and have a normal temperature, the lung may not have altogether cleared up. X-ray (see RADIOLOGY) will often show that congestion is still present, and adequate convalescence should always be given. Pneumonia patients should be nursed as for pleurisy. Bedclothes should not be heavy and fresh air must be plentiful. Diet should be very light, but fluids, preferably with glucose, should be given in quantity.

PNEUMOTHORAX. Air in the pleural cavity, that is, between the lung and the chest. This may be brought about spontaneously, for example, in the course of tuberculosis due to a cavity extending through the surface of the lung and allowing air to escape. Or it may

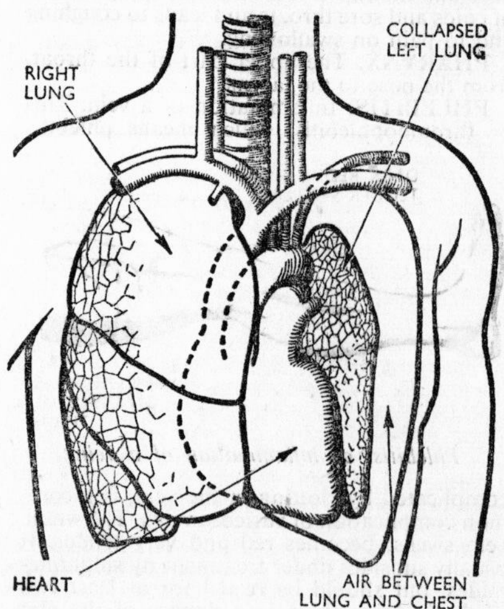

Pneumothorax causing collapse of left lung.

be done deliberately, by puncturing the chest with a needle and admitting air or other gas under pressure in order to collapse, and so rest, a diseased lung; in this case, it is known as artificial pneumothorax.

Spontaneous pneumothorax can also happen through a penetrating wound of the chest. It is accompanied by considerable shock and difficulty in breathing. When there is a wound of the chest, through which air is entering, this should be sealed as soon as possible.

POISONS AND THEIR ANTIDOTES. Poisons may be taken accidentally or suicidally. Depressed or insane people sometimes take poison—usually the one most readily available, for example, in the home, coal-gas or disinfectants. A chemist may take morphia; a photographer, cyanide. In cases of suspected poisoning, send for a doctor and keep, not only any remains of the poison, but any material which may have been vomited and clothes, etc., which may be stained. Unless corrosive poisoning is suspected because of burns around the mouth, give an emetic at once. Mustard and water, salt and water, or washing-up water may be used. Do not, however, give an emetic if the patient is unconscious, or he may choke. In case of corrosive poisoning a neutralizer should be given. Types of poisons and their treatment are described in detail in the entry POISONING in the First-aid chapter.

POLIOMYELITIS. See INFANTILE PARALYSIS.

POLYPUS. A soft lump growing from a mucous membrane, usually as the result of some inflammatory process. It is common in the nose and in the ear, where it causes obstruction and deafness. Polypi are usually fairly easily removed, generally under a local anaesthetic, but a search should always be made for the cause, which may be more difficult to cure. In the nose they are often secondary to disease of the antra and sinuses.

POULTICE. A method of applying moist heat. It is useful to relieve pain, for example, in pleurisy or rheumatism. Sometimes it is employed on inflammatory swellings, whitlows, etc., but it should be used with great caution if there is any pus present, because the tendency to sogginess of the skin may cause inflammation to spread. Linseed and bread poultices have been replaced by kaolin poultices, made chiefly from china clay and glycerine; they may be bought ready for use in tins with full instructions. Remember to take the lid off the tin before heating, or there may be a slight explosion.

PREGNANCY. Human pregnancy lasts approximately 280 days. The usual calculation is to take the first day of the last menstrual period, and add nine calendar months and one week. If those months do not include February, then add five days instead of one week. For example, if the first day of the last period was 12 August, the confinement can be expected about 19 May.

Conception actually occurs about fourteen days after the start of a period, but, as this is always uncertain, it is simpler to reckon from a date which is usually known accurately. The date thus found is only approximate, and

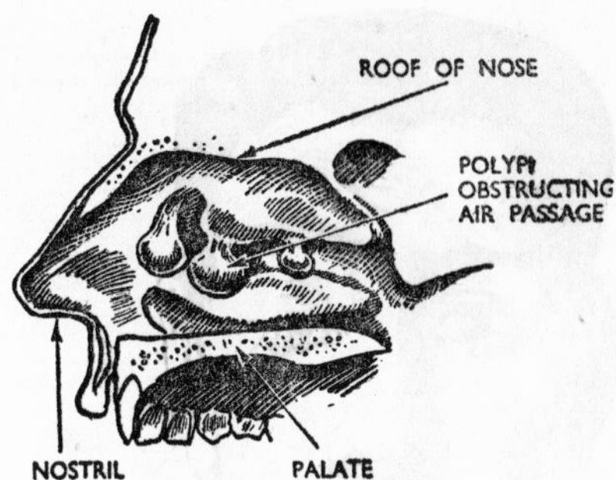

Polypus. These are common in nose and ear.

the baby may be born up to ten days before or after. In exceptional cases, pregnancy has been known to last several weeks longer. See ANTENATAL CARE, BIRTH, and SEX.

PRENATAL CARE. See ANTENATAL CARE.

PROCTITIS. Inflammation of the rectum. It may be secondary to piles or other disease of the rectum, and can be due to threadworms or to gonorrhoea. It causes pain and bleeding on passing motions, with irritation and aching over the lower spine. The condition needs medical treatment, and may yield to sulphonamides or penicillin.

PROGNOSIS. The outlook in any case of illness; an estimate of how long it will last, and whether recovery will take place or any complications ensue. It is one of the most difficult tasks of a doctor, depending to a great extent on experience and judgment.

PROSTATE. A gland, found only in the male, which is situated at the base of the

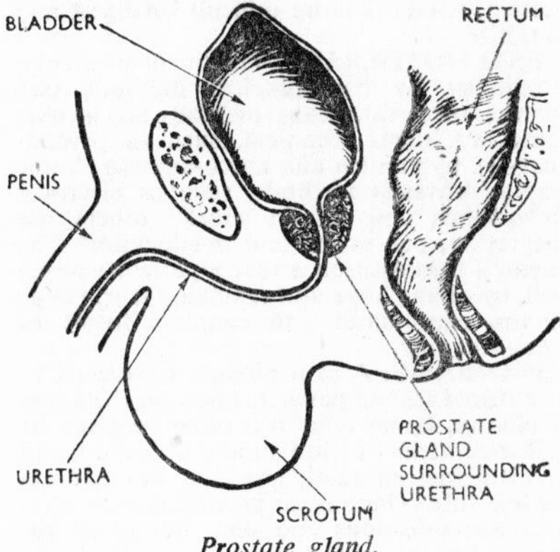

Prostate gland.

urinary bladder. It is about the size of a chestnut, and develops secretions which are added to the male semen. In elderly men the gland sometimes enlarges and can cause obstruction to the flow of urine. Early symptoms are frequency of, and difficulty in, passing water, with some dribbling at the end of the

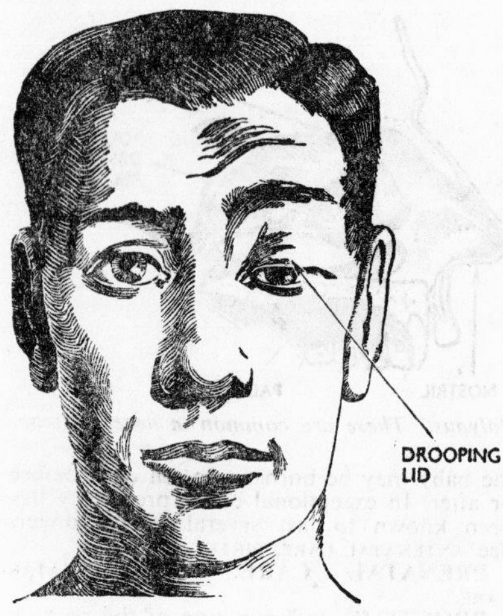

Ptosis.

act. An enlarged prostate can be removed surgically or, sometimes, a canal can be cut through it with a cautery. Cancer of the prostate gland is the first form of cancer to be controlled by a drug (see CANCER).

PROTEIN. Complicated chemical substances containing nitrogen, and necessary in the diet for growth and for repair. Proteins can be used to supply energy, in the absence of carbohydrates and fats, and constitute a large part of the cells of the body. In diet, we speak of first-class proteins, for example, meat protein, which is easily assimilable; and of second-class proteins, such as vegetable protein, which is more difficult to digest and to utilize.

PSYCHOTHERAPY. Treatment of mental conditions by psychological methods (see MENTAL DISEASES). Many methods are in use; some are highly technical, such as psychoanalysis, hypnotism and narco-analysis. Some employ physical methods, such as electrical convulsions and insulin shock; others use suggestion, persuasion and re-education. The doctor's firm assurance that a patient will get well, by giving hope and removing fear, is one of the commonest and simplest forms of psychotherapy.

PSORIASIS. A skin disease, characterized by chronic scaling patches, often on the knees or elbows. Great relief can often be given by such ointments as ichthyol and dithranol, and by medicines containing arsenic, but relapses are the rule. There is an hereditary tendency. It is not infectious and does not affect the general health.

PTOSIS. Dropping of the eyelids; it may be due to a paralysed muscle or it may be congenital. Ptosis is sometimes cured by a plastic operation.

PUBERTY. The age, in both sexes, at which the power of reproduction commences. In boys it is usually between thirteen and sixteen years and in girls generally between eleven and fifteen years, though it may occur outside these limits. In both sexes, puberty is accompanied by development of the sex organs, and by growth of hair on the abdomen and in the armpits.

In boys the penis develops and becomes erectile, the testes enlarge, the hair on the face grows and the voice breaks. In girls the breasts develop and the figure takes on the feminine shape. Girls begin to menstruate (see MENSTRUATION). Boys may have a discharge of semen from the penis, usually during sleep, perhaps every week or so. This is a natural happening, and not in any way harmful.

Puberty, in both sexes, is apt to be accompanied by some mental stress, by physical tiredness, sometimes by irritability, and by a change of attitude to parents, brothers and sisters. Unfortunately, it usually coincides with working for examinations or taking up industrial employment, which adds to the strain. The majority of adolescents pass through it without difficulty, but signs of strain should call for extra rest and, if necessary, for medical advice.

PUERPERAL FEVER. Fever occurring during the puerperium. This may be caused by infection at the confinement, either by germs already present in the birth passages, or by germs introduced at the time. In either case, fever develops about the third or fourth day. It may be due to phlebitis, in which case fever may develop about the tenth or twelfth day; or it may be a result of inflammation of the breasts, when it may occur at any time during lactation (see NIPPLE).

Prevention consists of treating any discharge or inflammatory condition beforehand, of the usual antiseptic precautions by those in attendance, and of attention to cleanliness and to the general health. Modern treatment by sulphonamides or penicillin has robbed puerperal fever of most of its former terrors.

PUERPERIUM. The lying-in period after childbirth.

PULMONARY DISEASE. See BRONCHITIS; EMPYEMA; LUNGS, DISEASES OF; PLEURISY; PNEUMONIA; and TUBERCULOSIS.

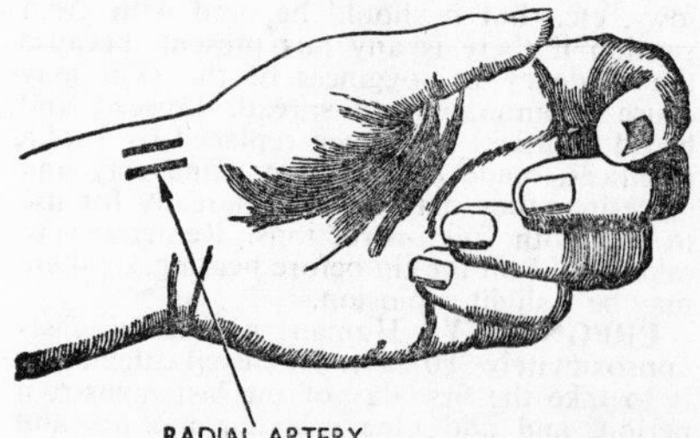

Pulse. It is best felt in the radial artery.

PULSE. This is most easily felt at the wrist on the same side as the thumb. Its average rate is 72 to the minute, but wide variations, from 40 to 90, occur in perfect health. The pulse gets more rapid in feverish conditions, and with exercise. After exercise it should return to its normal rate within two minutes.

The pulse may be irregular in heart disease, but there is a form of irregularity in which it varies with respiration, quickening and slowing rhythmically, which is quite normal, especially in the young. "Missed" beats are actually due, in most cases, to an extra beat occurring too soon after the preceding one and being too weak to reach the wrist. They cause an unpleasant sensation, but are usually not dangerous. They may be due to dyspepsia or to fatigue.

PURGATIVES. See APERIENTS.

PURPURA. A rash consisting of small "blood spots" which do not fade on pressure. Severe measles sometimes causes a purpuric rash; it may also occur in many forms of poisoning, and in some blood diseases.

PUS. The creamy, golden or greenish material, sometimes referred to as "matter," which exudes from infected wounds. It consists of a mixture of dead bacteria with numerous white blood-cells (see BLOOD-CELLS) which have been poured out to attack the infection.

PYAEMIA. Pus in the bloodstream; a very grave form of septicaemia (see BLOOD-POISONING).

PYELITIS. Inflammation of the passages leading from the kidneys to the bladder. It is accompanied by pyuria and by frequent passing of water. There may be fever and pain in the back and loins. It is a complication of pregnancy (see ANTENATAL CARE) and also a complication of cystitis. Frequently it is treated successfully with sulphonamides and copious fluids.

PYLORUS. The outlet of the stomach into the duodenum. It is a muscular valve which remains closed during the digestion of food in the stomach. Between two and three hours after food is swallowed, it opens and allows food to pass into the intestine. This accounts for the pain of duodenal ulcer occurring two to three hours after meals.

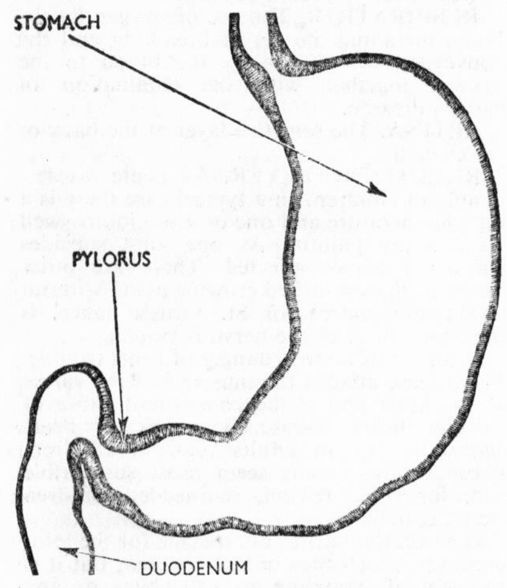

Pylorus, the outlet valve from the stomach.

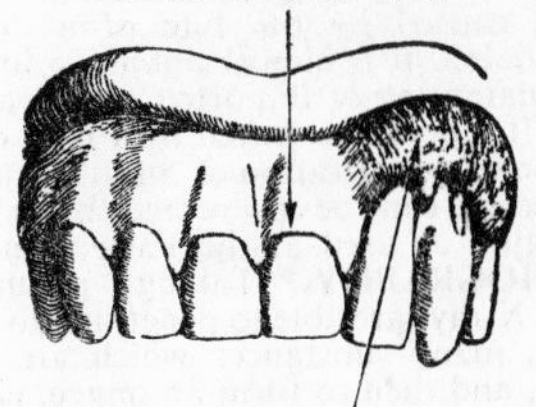

Pyorrhoea.

PYORRHOEA. Literally, a running of pus. Pyorrhoea alveolaris is a septic condition of the tooth sockets, accompanied by a discharge of pus and shrinking of the gums. In the early stages much can be done by expert dental treatment, and by taking vitamin A (see VITAMINS); but when the disease has been allowed to progress extraction of the teeth is often the only cure.

PYREXIA. Medical term for fever.

PYURIA. Pus in the urine. This is always due to infection, which may be in the passage from the bladder (see URETHRITIS), in the bladder (see CYSTITIS), in the passages from the kidneys (see PYELITIS) or in the kidneys.

QUININE. A drug obtained from cinchona bark and used in the treatment of malaria. It is occasionally used as a tonic, but has no special virtues apart from its bitterness, which increases appetite. It is sometimes used in other fevers, but is not specific except in malaria. Another use for quinine is in soluble pessaries for birth control.

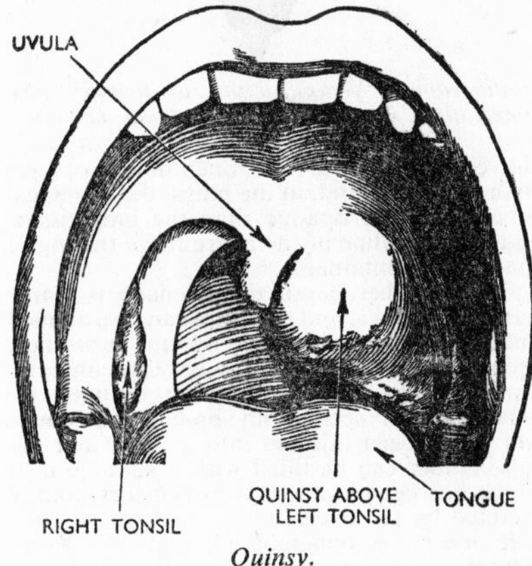

Quinsy.

QUINSY. An abscess behind the tonsil; usually a complication of chronic infection of the tonsils. Immediate relief is usually given by lancing the quinsy. It may be necessary to have the tonsils removed in order to prevent a recurrence of the complaint.

RABIES. An acute disease of the nervous system, caused by the bite of a dog with hydrophobia. It is almost unknown in Britain since quarantine of imported dogs was introduced. If a person is bitten by a mad dog, the traditional cauterization is of little use, but the disease can be prevented by a special inoculation as used at the Pasteur institutes.

RADIOGRAPHY. Taking pictures by X-rays. X-rays are able to penetrate, to varying degrees, many substances which are opaque to light, and then to form an image, either on a photographic plate or on a fluorescent screen. As bones are relatively opaque to X-rays, a shadow picture of a broken or diseased bone is readily obtained. In X-raying

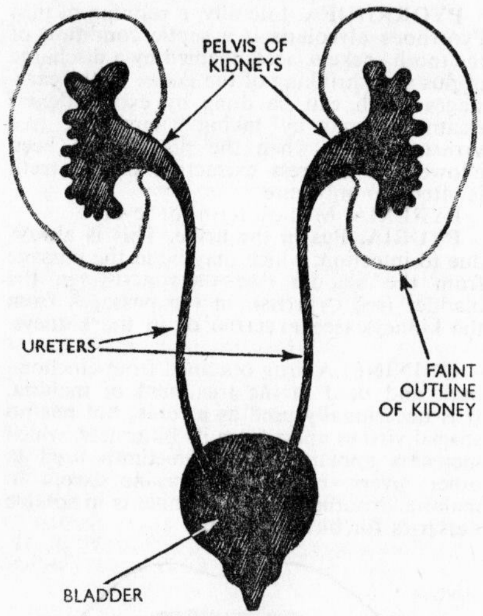

Radiography. X-ray picture of urinary passages after injection of an opaque substance.

the chest, the heart is much more opaque than the lungs; and, in the lungs, the bronchial tubes are more opaque than the lung tissue, so that an outline of the heart and a tracing of the lungs is obtainable.

On the other hand, the stomach is transparent to X-rays, and a picture can be obtained only by filling it with some opaque substance, such as a meal mixed with barium sulphate. Similarly, the kidneys may be outlined by making them secrete an opaque substance which has been injected into a vein; and the gall-bladder can be filled with a suitable dye, which has been swallowed in capsules, and is excreted by the liver.

It must be remembered that all X-ray pictures are shadowgraphs only, and not pictures in the sense of ordinary photographs. Their interpretation, therefore, calls for considerable training and experience, and is subject to error. An X-ray is *not*, as is often thought, the final and irrevocable word in diagnosis, though it is extremely valuable when taken in conjunction with other evidence.

RADIOLOGY. The art of interpreting X-ray pictures obtained by radiography.

RADIOTHERAPY. The treatment of disease by X-rays, and by radium or other sources of radiation. All such rays are destructive to living cells; but they exercise what is called a selective action, being, as a rule, more destructive to rapidly growing cells than to others. As cancer cells, in particular, are rapidly growing, they can be destroyed by a dose which normal cells will survive. The actual technique of administering such rays so as to do good and not harm is, of course, very complicated.

RASHES. Eruptions on the skin. They are of many kinds: those occurring in infectious diseases, such as measles, scarlet fever and chicken-pox; those which may occur as the result of some internal or external irritant, as in urticaria or dermatitis; those due to bacterial infection, such as impetigo, or to the attacks of parasites, as in scabies; and others whose cause is unknown, such as psoriasis. Apart from those occurring in infectious disease, rashes come within the province of the skin specialist.

RAYS. Various forms of radiation are used in medicine. See RADIOTHERAPY, INFRA-RED RAYS and ULTRA-VIOLET.

RECTUM. The lowest part of the bowel, in which residues accumulate for disposal. Inflammation leads to proctitis. See PILES and PROCTITIS.

REFLEX. Automatic action which occurs in response to some simple stimulus. Examples are blinking the eye at the approach of a fly, and the jerking of the knee when struck just below the kneecap (see KNEEJERK). The presence of certain reflexes is very important in the diagnosis of nervous diseases.

REHABILITATION. A branch of physical medicine involving the re-training of a patient in respect of his or her disability for the resumption of his or her normal occupation.

REPRODUCTION. See SEX.

RESPIRATION. The use of oxygen by the body, including the act of breathing and the conveyance of oxygen by the blood to the tissues, together with the elimination of carbon dioxide.

RETINA. The sensitive layer at the back of the eyeball.

RHEUMATIC FEVER. An acute disease, mainly of children. In a typical case there is a high temperature and one or more joints swell up and are painful. As one joint subsides another becomes affected. There are other forms, such as so-called growing pains, without fever; and chorea, or St. Vitus's dance, is rheumatic fever of the nervous system.

In all forms there is danger of heart trouble. The disease attacks the muscle and the valves of the heart and is the commonest cause of valvular heart disease. The risk of heart disease is less in adults than in children. Those in their teens seem most susceptible and, for some reason, red-headed children are most liable.

The salicylate drugs are specific for the joint swellings, which they quickly reduce; but it is doubtful if treatment by salicylates or any other drug helps rheumatic heart disease.

Hence the importance of complete rest in bed, for at least six weeks, in every case. This is essential even in cases which seem trivial, because these are the ones in which heart disease may occur before it has been suspected.

RHEUMATISM. A term rather vaguely used to include a great variety of painful afflictions of the joints, the muscles, the nerves and the fibrous connective tissues of the body. These diseases are dissimilar and the treatment varies considerably. Acute rheumatism is another name for rheumatic fever. Rheumatism of the joints is called arthritis; of the nerves, neuritis; of the muscles, myalgia; and of the fibrous tissues, fibrositis.

Many forms of rheumatism seem to have some connexion with climatic conditions and are especially prevalent in damp changeable climates, such as that of the British Isles. The relationship of clay, sand, or chalk subsoils with rheumatism is obscure, but probably is important only if it leads to dampness of the house. With proper building and drainage it should not matter greatly what the subsoil is.

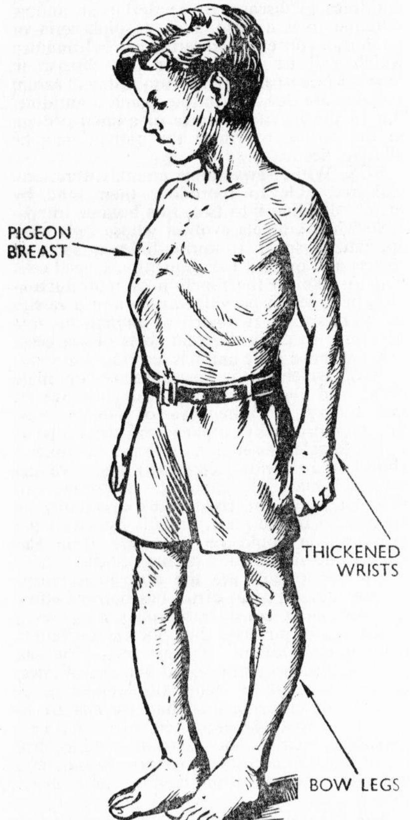

Rickets. Some visible symptoms.

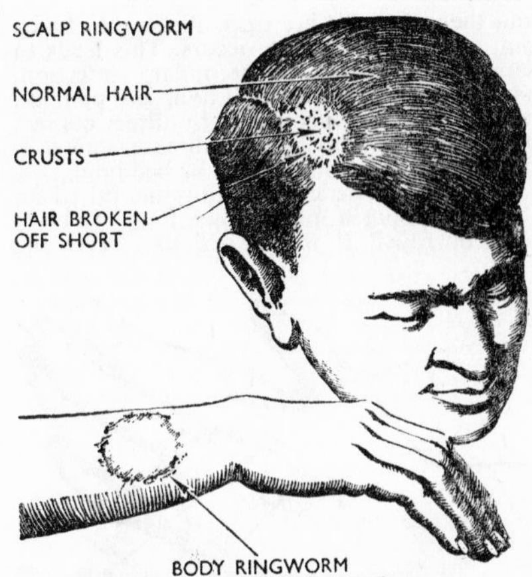

Ringworm. Scalp and body varieties.

RHEUMATOID ARTHRITIS. See ARTHRITIS.

RHINITIS. Inflammation of the nose. Catarrhal rhinitis is the common cold (see COLDS). Vasomotor rhinitis is a continual running nose due to allergy. See ALLERGY and HAY FEVER.

RICKETS. A disease of children in which the bones are soft and the teeth do not develop properly. There may also be fits, sweating of the head, bulging of the forehead, tender wrists and ankles, bow-legs, pigeon-chest, and knock-knees. The disease is readily diagnosed by X-rays (see RADIOGRAPHY). It is due to imperfect absorption of calcium from the diet, due to a lack of vitamin D (see VITAMINS), and is preventable by taking cod-liver oil.

RINGWORM. A group of skin diseases caused by infection by fungi. Ringworm of the scalp infects the hair roots and is difficult to cure, except by X-ray treatment (see RADIOTHERAPY) which makes the hair fall out, bringing the fungus with it. Ringworm of the body is often acquired from animals, and is often easily cured by Whitfield's ointment or sundry mercurial preparations. Athlete's foot, scaling between the toes, is another variety.

RUBELLA. See GERMAN MEASLES.

RUPTURE. See HERNIA.

SAL VOLATILE. A preparation of ammonia, used to relieve fainting and to treat flatulence. The dose is ten to thirty drops in half a teacup of water.

SANATORIUM. A hospital for the long-term treatment of tuberculosis, where proper nursing, rest, fresh air and good food can be obtained, in addition to special forms of modern treatment.

SARCOMA. A rapidly growing variety of cancer, affecting chiefly bones and connective tissues. It usually occurs at a younger age than other forms of cancer.

SCABIES. A skin disease due to a mite, the female of which burrows under the skin and there deposits her eggs. When they hatch out, very severe itching occurs. This leads to scratching and so to secondary infection, which may take the form of boils and pimples, or of impetigo. Infection is by direct contact with someone who has the disease, and it is rarely acquired from clothes or bedding.

The characteristic is the tiny line raised on the skin, about a quarter-inch long, which is the "burrow." It is possible to extract the

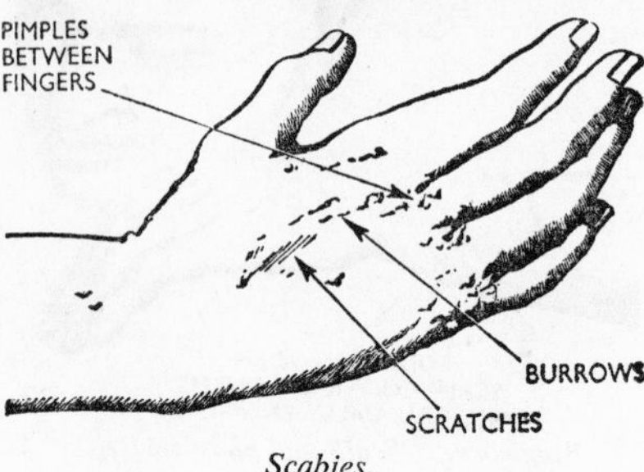

Scabies.

mite from the burrow on a needle, and examine it under a microscope, to confirm the diagnosis. The modern treatment is by rubbing in an emulsion of benzyl benzoate.

It is important that everyone in a house who may be infected should be treated simultaneously; and it is also important *not* to continue treatment more than two days, through excess of zeal, as this drug is itself irritating if used too much.

SCALDS. Burns caused by steam and hot liquids. Treatment is the same as for burns.

SCARLET FEVER. A form of acute tonsillitis, accompanied by a pin-point rash all over the trunk, by a scarlet tongue and by subsequent peeling of the skin. The sore throat may occur with no rash, or the rash with but slight sore throat, so that it is sometimes difficult or impossible to distinguish this disease from other forms of tonsillitis. There is some danger of inflammation of the kidneys (see NEPHRITIS) about three weeks after the onset, so that all cases should be kept in bed at least a month.

Scarlet fever of late years has tended to be very mild, and it is less to be feared than either measles or whooping-cough. It is sometimes confused with German measles, but in scarlet fever the rash never occurs on the face, although the cheeks may be flushed with a contrasting pallor around the mouth.

Scarlet fever is as infectious as other kinds of tonsillitis. The infection lies in the throat and any discharge there may be from the nose or ears; but the peeling is not infectious. The incubation period is four days; quarantine is eight days.

SCIATICA. Pain down the back of the buttock, thigh and leg as far as the ankle and along the course of the sciatic nerve. It may be due to neuritis, or to pressure on the nerve, perhaps in the pelvis from constipation, tumours, etc., or even in the spine from displacement of one of the disks of cartilage between the vertebrae. It seldom clears up completely under six weeks, and may recur. Rest of the affected leg in a partly flexed position is important.

SCURVY. A disease, due to lack of vitamin C (see VITAMINS), in which haemorrhage occurs from almost any part of the body. The gums bleed, the teeth are loosened and painful bruises appear after the slightest knock.

SEBORRHOEA. A scurfy skin disease, particularly of the scalp. It may be treated by frequent shampooing.

SEMEN. The fluid ejaculated by the male in sexual intercourse. It contains millions of spermatozoa, which are the male cells. If one of these spermatozoa fertilizes a female egg-cell, conception results. Blood in the semen may result from sexual excitement without intercourse resulting, or from disease of the prostate or the testis.

SEPTICAEMIA. See BLOOD-POISONING.

SERUM. When blood is allowed to clot, a clear fluid, called serum, separates from it. This contains a great variety of substances, including those chemical bodies which act as antidotes to disease. By rendering an animal immune to a disease, such as diphtheria or tetanus, a concentrated serum can be obtained which will be curative for this disease in humans (see IMMUNITY). Serum rash and serum sickness are due, not to the chemical antidote, but to the inevitable trace of animal protein in the serum, to which the patient may be allergic. See ALLERGY.

SEX. While very simple animals were, and still are, able to reproduce their kind by merely dividing into two, this became impossible when animals evolved whose cells were specialized so as to form different sorts of tissues and organs. Consequently, special cells had to take on the function of reproduction and, in order to provide variety and diversity in the offspring, two sorts of animals became necessary to carry different sorts of sex cells.

So we have male animals, carring testes (see TESTIS), which form spermatozoa, or male cells; and female animals, carrying ovaries (see OVARY), forming ova or female cells. Special reproductive organs were also evolved: in the female, the uterus or womb in which a child could develop (see BIRTH), and a vagina by which male cells could be introduced, and through which the child could eventually be born; and in the male, a penis by which the spermatozoa could be introduced into the vagina and fertilization accomplished.

The sex organs are the only ones which are not developed at birth, but become effective only after considerable physical growth, at the age of puberty, thus preventing infants from having infants of their own. The sex act is subject to many social and moral laws, chiefly designed to secure the well-being of children by ensuring that their parents are in a position to look after them properly. This necessary restraint of a strong instinct has led to much unnecessary mystery; fortunately, however, sex education is now more usual than it was.

SEX HYGIENE. This is chiefly a matter of the mental attitude to sex. Unlicensed sexual indulgence leads to venereal disease and to the birth of illegitimate children, who are seldom wanted or properly cared for. On the other hand, mere repression of a strong instinct is apt to lead to neurosis. The way out is, on the one hand, in the sublimation of this instinct by various forms of creative work; and, on the other hand, in facilities for early marriage.

Physically, sex hygiene amounts to no more than simple cleanliness of the sex organs; they easily become inflamed if they are allowed to accumulate dirt and bacteria.

SHINGLES. See HERPES.

SHOCK. A state of collapse occurring after injury or in the course of surgical operations. The patient is pale, with a rapid, almost imperceptible pulse and very shallow breathing. Treatment is fully described in the First-aid chapter on page 158.

SINUS. In the skull there are hollow spaces (sinuses) communicating with the nose; these may become infected in catarrhal diseases, causing chronic pain, headache, slight fever and other disabilities. Radiography will often demonstrate fluid in these spaces, and this can be washed out with suitable instruments. In severe cases, operation for proper drainage may be necessary. See ANTRUM.

SKIN. The largest organ in the body; it is not only a protective covering, but is concerned in the regulation of heat by sweating and flushing, and also in the elimination of fluids, etc. It may suffer in general diseases or from complaints of its own (see RASHES).

SLEEPING SICKNESS. Trypanosomiasis; a disease of Central Africa, conveyed by the bite of the tsetse fly.

SLEEPY SICKNESS. See ENCEPHALITIS.

SMALLPOX. An epidemic disease due to a virus. There is great weakness, fever, general aching and sickness. After a vague red rash on the first day, the typical rash comes on the third day, starting on wrists and forehead. This rash, although similar to a chicken-pox rash, becomes filled with pus, which a chicken-pox rash does not. The fever rises after the rash comes out. Complications are septicaemia, pneumonia, and ear infections. Protection may be obtained by vaccination.

SORE THROAT. In cases of mild sore throat, gargling with aspirin crushed in water relieves the pain. See ANGINA, VINCENT'S; PHARYNGITIS, QUINSY, SCARLET FEVER, and TONSILLITIS.

SPINE. The spine is formed of a series of bones: seven in the neck, twelve in the back (thoracic region), five in the small of the back (lumbar region), with a fused mass, called the sacrum, below that and a few rudimentary tail bones, called the coccyx. The bones enclose a canal, through which runs the spinal cord as low as the first lumbar vertebra. Nerves are given off from the cord between each pair of vertebrae.

Spinal disease may affect the bones, or the cord, or both. Spondylitis, or arthritis of the spine, is a painful form of osteo-arthritis (see ARTHRITIS). Tuberculosis of the bones leads to the collapse of vertebrae, resulting in hunch-back. Diseases of the cord, such as infantile paralysis and myelitis, lead to paralysis of the body below the level of the disease.

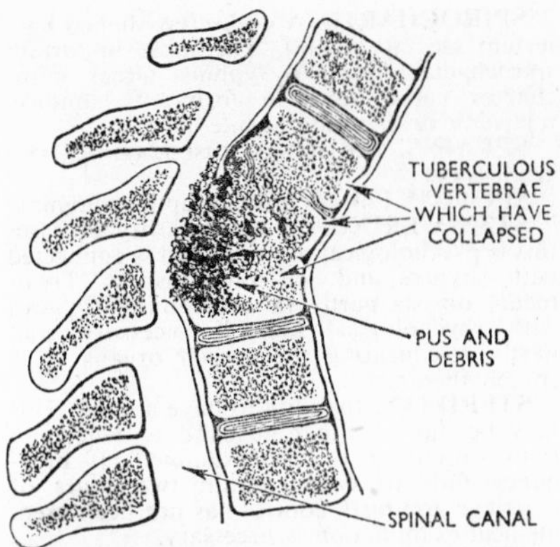

Spine, showing effect of tuberculosis.

Tumours or other obstructions in the canal cause pressure, and pain or paralysis below that level. Scoliosis is a lateral curvature, or a bending of the spine to one side; kyphosis is a convex bend in the spine, and lordosis is a hollow back.

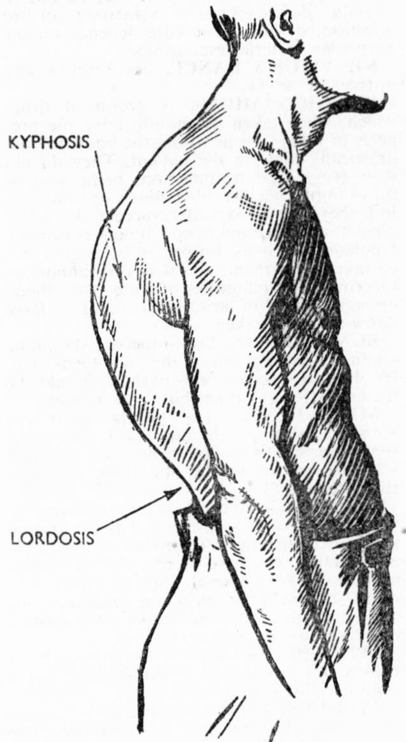

Spine. Two kinds of bending of the spine.

SPIROCHAETE. A corkscrew-shaped bacterium (see BACTERIA). The most important spirochaetal disease is syphilis. Other spirochaetes cause yaws, a form of jaundice, relapsing fever, and rat-bite fever.

SPRAINS. See JOINTS, DISLOCATIONS AND SPRAINS OF.

SPUTUM. Phlegm brought up by coughing.

STAMMERING. In the majority of cases this is psychological in origin and is connected with shyness and self-consciousness. Treatment consists partly in overcoming shyness, with psychological help if necessary, and partly re-educating the speech organs by a speech therapist.

STERILITY. Inability to have a child. This may be due to either husband or wife, and both should always be examined. If pregnancy fails to occur within two years of marriage and birth control has not been used, medical examination is necessary.

STILL-BIRTH. The birth of a dead child. The child may die from various causes before labour begins or from injury during it.

STOMACH DISORDERS. See DYSPEPSIA, FLATULENCE, GASTRIC ULCER, GASTRITIS, HEARTBURN, HYPERCHLORHYDRIA, HYPOCHLORHYDRIA, INDIGESTION, NAUSEA, and VOMITING.

STOMATITIS. Inflammation of the mouth, sometimes with ulceration. It may be due to vitamin deficiency (see VITAMINS) or to infection, or both. The cure depends on the particular bacteria responsible.

ST. VITUS'S DANCE. See CHOREA and RHEUMATIC FEVER.

SULPHONAMIDES. A group of drugs which, when taken by mouth, have the property of killing germs within the body without drastically injuring the patient. They do not stop every kind of infection, being useless, for example, against tuberculosis or influenza. But they are remarkably successful against pneumonia, meningitis and blood poisoning. Sulphates, such as Epsom salts, should not be taken with them, and it is very important to drink large quantities of water with them, or suppression of urine may occur if large doses are being taken.

SUNBURN. Exposure to the sun should be gradual, ceasing when the skin gets red. If blistering occurs the blisters should be treated as for any other burn. See BURNS.

SUPRA-RENAL. The glands above the kidneys, forming adrenalin, are called the supra-renals. Disease of them leads to Addison's disease or to the alteration of sexual characteristics.

SWEATING. General sweating is due to hot weather or to exercise and tends to cool the body. Sweating in the palms of the hands is emotional; excessive sweating in the armpits may also be emotional. Smelly sweat is a result of bacterial infection and can be treated with formalin baths or boracic powder, plus scrupulous cleanliness.

SYNCOPE. Failure of the circulation. Such failure may be caused by heart disease, but is commonly due to fainting.

SYPHILIS. Usually contracted by sexual intercourse. The first sign is the primary sore—a hard ulcer the size of a sixpence, or larger—on the penis. In females it may be inside the vagina and may be overlooked. It heals by itself, but six to eight weeks later the secondary stage sets in with vague ill-health, slight wasting and fever, and a coppery rash on the trunk, which may take many forms or be absent altogether. There are also sore throat, often with ulcers on the tonsils or tongue, anaemia, iritis, some enlargement of the glands, especially in the neck and at the elbows, and various other signs.

When this stage, which may last many months, is over, nothing more may happen for years, until the tertiary stage begins. This may take the form of disease in any part of the body, the heart, the nervous system, the joints, the lungs or the liver. It may imitate any disease. Finally, there is the quaternary stage, chiefly characterized by locomotor ataxy, and by general paralysis of the insane.

Syphilis, if untreated, is by far the most serious disease common to man, with endless possibilities of disaster. Fortunately, because of propaganda and free clinics, it is being brought under control, and the later stages are now seldom seen. Diagnosis is helped by various blood tests, of which the Wassermann test is the best known. Treatment is by long courses of injections of arsenical preparations, mercury, bismuth and penicillin. True prevention consists in avoiding irregular intercourse; but the use of calomel cream after intercourse affords some protection.

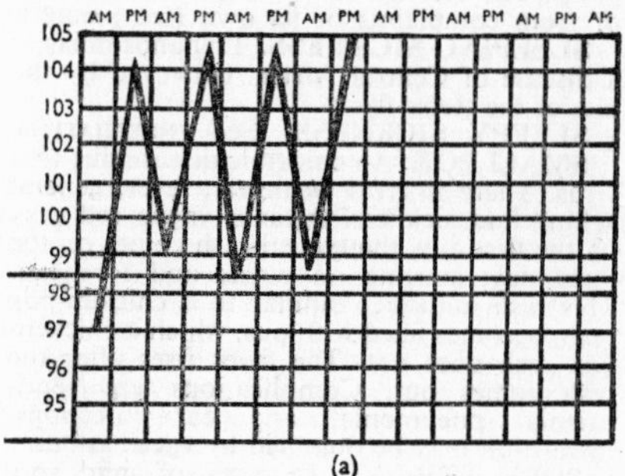

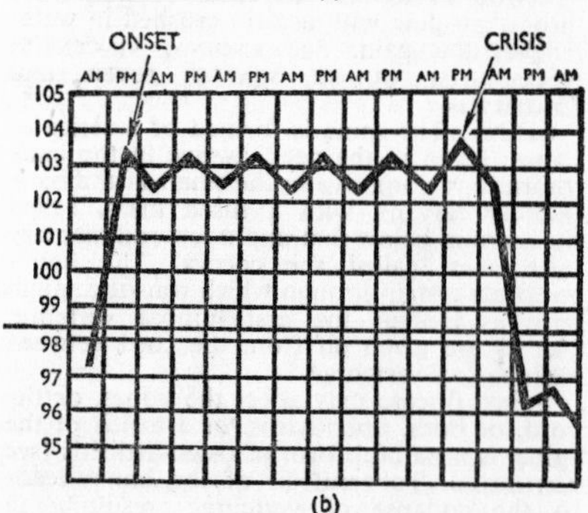

Temperature. Charts showing typical temperature variations in (a) *a septic complaint, for example, empyema, and* (b) *lobar pneumonia.*

TABES. Locomotor ataxy, late syphilis of the spinal cord, which produces difficulty in walking, causing a staggering, widespread gait and loss of sensation in the feet; there are also various bodily pains and other symptoms.

TEETH. There are twenty milk teeth, the first being the lower front teeth, cut at six months, and the last the four back teeth at the age of two and a half years. There are thirty-two permanent teeth, the first being the first molars, behind all the milk teeth, at six years; the last to be cut are the last molars, or wisdom teeth, at about twenty-one. See GINGIVITIS, PYORRHOEA, RICKETS, and SCURVY.

TEMPERATURE. To take a patient's temperature, a clinical thermometer is used. It retains its reading until shaken down; do this with a flick, as in cracking a whip, until the mercury reads 95 or less. Put the thermometer *under* the tongue (not immediately after a hot drink) and leave it there for two minutes if a "half-minute" thermometer, and four minutes if a "one-minute" thermometer. Then read off the height of the mercury and, afterwards, wash the thermometer in cold water.

TESTIS. The male sex organ, of which there are two, contained in the scrotum. The testis forms spermatozoa (male cells) and also a chemical secretion which causes the usual male characteristics—beard, low voice, etc. See EPIDIDIMITIS, HYDROCELE, and ORCHITIS.

TETANUS. See LOCKJAW.

THREADWORMS. Can be recognized in the motions as pieces of dirty cotton, about half an inch long, which move. The adult worm lives for thirty days. Eggs are not laid inside the body, but the worm comes out of the anus at night and lays them on the skin, causing irritation and leading to scratching. Eggs which get under the finger-nails may, in a child, be transferred to the mouth, thus starting new worms.

The only reliable cure is to break this vicious circle by binding up the anus at night with a pad covered with white precipitate ointment, and by putting on two pairs of shorts over the top. Keep nails very short, and always wash the hands before meals. Infection will then die out naturally in thirty days. Worm pills are unreliable for this variety.

THROMBOSIS. Clotting of blood, for example, in phlebitis, from which separation of a clot may lead to infarct, or in the coronary artery, leading to coronary thrombosis. Thrombosis is usually due to inflammatory conditions damaging the walls of blood-vessels, but it may occur as a complication of operations, through slowing of the circulation and lack of movement of the patient.

THRUSH. A fungus disease, usually of babies, starting in the mouth as white spots on the tongue (not to be confused with milk curds). If neglected, thrush leads to considerable gastric upset. The spots should be scrubbed away with a rag dipped in boracic. Bottle teats should be boiled. Mother's nipple should be wiped with boracic before and after feeds, and washed frequently.

THYROID. The gland in the neck governing the rate of metabolism. See EXOPHTHALMIC GOITRE, GOITRE, METABOLISM, and OBESITY.

TONGUE. A furred tongue is caused by the growth of bacteria on it. It may be cleaned with toothpaste on a rag. The tongue is dry in fevers, and in thirst from any cause; brown in intestinal upsets, and scarlet in scarlet fever. It is always furred in smokers.

TONSILLITIS. Inflammation of the tonsils which, when infected, swell and become red and painful; the glands at the angles of the

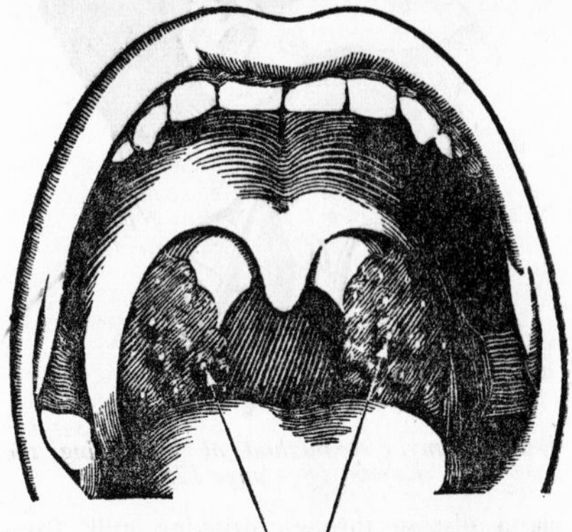

Tonsillitis.

jaw swell, too. When the tonsils are septic, they exude yellow pockets of pus. As long as they return to normal after attacks they serve a useful purpose and should be retained.

When, however, the tonsils remain large, red and discharging, especially when the glands remain large, too, they are better removed, because they are sources of chronic infection for the rest of the body. In small children, tonsils are normally large, and should not be removed for this reason alone. See ADENOIDS; ANGINA, VINCENT'S; and DIPHTHERIA.

TONSILS. Two masses of lymphatic tissue situated one on each side at the back of the mouth. They act as filters, preventing bacteria from gaining access to the bronchial tubes and lungs. See TONSILLITIS.

TOXIN. Literally, any poisonous substance. The term is usually applied to the poisons formed by bacteria. See ANTITOXIN.

TRACHEOTOMY. The operation of making an incision in the windpipe and inserting a tube. It is a life-saving measure in any obstruction of the larynx, whether owing to diphtheria, to a growth, or to a foreign body which has been swallowed.

TREMOR. Shaking of the body, especially of the hands. It occurs in many nervous disorders, in alcoholism, and in old age.

TUBERCULOSIS. Disease due to infection by tubercle bacilli. It may affect the bones and joints, the kidneys and sex organs, the lungs, the lymphatic glands, the nervous system, or the skin; or it may be a generalized infection of the whole body (miliary tuberculosis). Roughly, lung and skin disease is acquired from human beings, and bone and

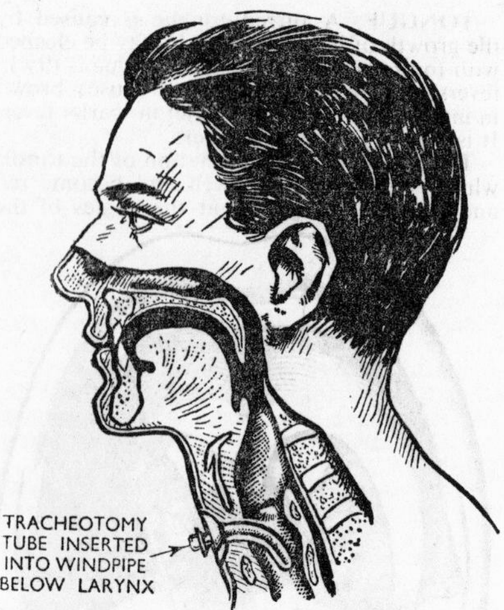

Tracheotomy. A method of by-passing the larynx. (See page 125.)

gland disease through drinking milk from infected cows, but there are exceptions to both. Tuberculosis of birds is not very infectious to humans.

Bone tuberculosis is characterized by early pain in bones or joints, with restriction of movement. Usually it is diagnosable by radiography, but if neglected it leads to deformities from collapse of the diseased bone. Treatment includes splinting, rest, fresh air, good food and vitamins.

Gland tuberculosis results in chronic swellings of the glands in the neck, under the arms, etc., which may break down and form abscesses.

Pulmonary tuberculosis begins with debility and slight cough. Usually, the temperature is slightly raised at night. There may be night sweats, then loss of weight. Any undiagnosed cough which lasts over three weeks should be suspect. Early cases are nowadays detected by mass-radiography. If neglected, the tuberculosis goes on to form cavities in the lung. Many people are naturally immune. General treatment: rest and fresh air. Special treatment, designed to rest the lung: artificial pneumothorax (see PNEUMOTHORAX); paralysis of the diaphragm by cutting the phrenic nerve; surgical removal of ribs to collapse the lung. It is sometimes successfully treated by gold. Pleurisy may be a sign of tuberculosis and should be taken seriously.

Skin tuberculosis (*lupus vulgaris*) is treated by Finsen light, and recently by enormous doses of vitamin D, with great success.

Kidney tuberculosis may start with increased frequency of passing water, loss of weight and general ill-health. It may be necessary to remove the diseased kidney.

Prevention of tuberculosis involves avoiding infected milk, in better social conditions with no overcrowding, and in good diets.

TUMOUR. A lump. It may be cancerous (see CANCER) or it may be composed of fibrous tissue (fibroma), of fibrous and glandular tissue (fibroadenoma), of fat (lipoma) or of blood clot (haematoma). Or it may be hollow, and is then known as a cyst. The seriousness depends partly on its nature and partly on whether, by its size, it presses on any vital organ. Some tumours, while not cancerous, bleed and may lead to anaemia; examples are fibroid tumours of the womb.

TWILIGHT SLEEP. See ANALGESIA.

TYPHOID FEVER. See ENTERIC.

TYPHUS. An exhausting disease, prevalent in eastern Europe, caused by a virus and conveyed by the bite of the louse. A vaccine is now available for protection against the disease.

ULCER. An actual loss of tissue, appearing as a shallow hole with a sharply defined edge. It may occur on the legs from either varicose veins or syphilis. See DUODENAL ULCER and GASTRIC ULCER.

ULTRA-VIOLET. Radiation of somewhat shorter wavelength than visible light. It is produced by mercury-vapour lamps or carbon arcs. Ultra-violet rays produce sunburn on the skin, give a feeling of well-being and cause the skin to form its own vitamin D (see VITAMINS). They are, therefore, curative in rickets—but not more so than cod-liver oil, which is much cheaper.

URAEMIA. Blood poisoning, due to kidney disease, leading to the retention of waste products which cannot be eliminated. It may be diagnosed by blood tests, is a dangerous condition and is liable to end in coma and death. Uraemia may be a cause of fits, headaches and dimness of vision.

URETHRITIS. Inflammation of the urethra, the passage from the bladder. Although commonly caused by gonorrhoea, it is often due to other germs. It causes pain on passing water, and pyuria. The treatment depends upon the cause. See PYURIA.

URIC ACID. A waste product of the body, normally excreted by the kidneys. In gout there is an excess of uric acid; but uric acid is *not* a cause of other forms of rheumatism.

URINE. This contains, besides water, salts, urea and other waste matter. It should be clear and straw-coloured; but on a vegetarian diet it may be cloudy with phosphates. If concentrated, it will deposit a red cloud of urates on standing. This is not a sign of disease. See DIABETES, KIDNEY DISEASES, and PYURIA.

URTICARIA. Nettlerash; an itching rash in the form of large weals, usually a result of allergy. It may follow gastric upsets, the bites of insects, or contact with plants and some kinds of wood and other substances. The cause should be discovered, if possible, and eliminated; or it may be possible to be desensitized by a series of injections. The drug benadryl is used successfully to alleviate the symptoms, but does not remove the cause. Applications such as calamine and coal-tar may be used to relieve the itching. When urticaria follows stomach upsets, a dose of magnesia is often helpful or, if diarrhoea is present, a dose of bismuth.

UTERUS. The womb; a muscular organ measuring about three inches by one and a half inches, but capable of enormous expansion during pregnancy. It is situated in the pelvis, communicating with the vagina below, and by the fallopian tubes with the ovaries on each side. See OVARY.

VACCINATION. Inoculation which gives immunity against small-pox, by causing a local attack of cow-pox, which is the same disease, modified and rendered comparatively harmless by having passed through cattle. The lymph is obtained from clean and healthy calves and is sterilized by glycerine before use.

Complications are rare, and are much less common in babies than in older people who are vaccinated for the first time. Consequently, if there is any likelihood of vaccination being needed throughout life, it is much better to have a primary vaccination as a baby. Normally, vaccination produces a blister after three or four days; this comes to a height in a week, and then scabs and disappears in about another week.

VACCINE. A vaccine is not used for vaccination, so the word is rather misleading. A vaccine is made by growing, in an incubator, the germs against which immunity is desired. The germs are then killed, counted and mixed with saline. The result, being dead germs, cannot give the disease, but as it contains the toxin of the disease it can stimulate the patient's resistance. The most successful use of vaccines is against typhoid fever. See IMMUNITY.

VAGINA. The passage, in females, leading from the vulva to the uterus.

VALVULAR DISEASE. Distortion of the valves of the heart, leading to leakage and to obstruction of blood flow. See HEART DISEASES and RHEUMATIC FEVER.

VARICOSE VEINS. A vein is said to be varicose, not when it is merely large and prominent, but when it is twisted and tortuous.

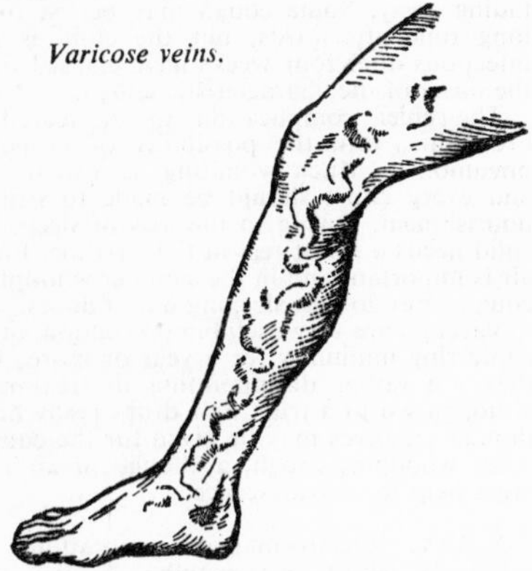

Varicose veins.

The most common site is on the inner side of the leg and thigh, but varicose veins are also found on the abdomen, the chest, and in other parts of the body. A pile is a form of varicose vein in the lower bowel.

The circulation in veins is largely due to muscular action, and hardly at all to the heart impulse, which is expended in the capillaries. Veins have flap valves every few inches, so that the muscles can propel blood only in one direction. There may be hereditary weakness of the valves, or there may be obstruction to the vein; and in the case of the leg, much standing may provide little muscular action to keep the blood moving. Consequently the valves give way entirely, and the weight of the stagnant column of blood distorts the vein.

Complications are mainly due to circulatory congestion; they are swelling of the ankles, eczema and ulceration. Treatment of these is unlikely to be successful unless the veins are also treated. Treatment of the veins includes discovery and cure of the cause; for example, if pregnancy is the cause, it is little use treating the veins until the pregnancy is over, though they can be supported with bandages.

Treatment may be by operation, by injection, by ligature or by a combination of methods, varying with the severity of the veins. In most cases, it helps to sleep at night with the foot of the bed raised, thus helping the blood to flow in the right direction.

VASOMOTOR SYSTEM. A system of nerves controlling the size of the very small veins and arteries, and thus controlling the circulation. Disorders of this system are responsible for chilblains, "dead" fingers, blushing, fainting and many other symptoms.

VEIN. One of the blood vessels by which used, impure blood returns to the heart in order to be pumped to the lungs for restoration of its oxygen. See HAEMORRHAGE, VARICOSE VEINS.

VENEREAL DISEASE. Disease caught by sexual intercourse. The two principal kinds are syphilis and gonorrhoea; both can, however, be acquired in other ways, but this is far more unusual than is commonly believed. Babies can get infected eyes from their mothers during birth (gonorrhoea), or can have syphilis transmitted to them (congenital syphilis). Nurses and doctors occasionally receive syphilitic infection on the finger while attending to patients. Syphilis of the lip can be caught by kissing. Free, confidential advice and treatment can be obtained at most large towns. See GONORRHOEA and SYPHILIS.

VERRUCA. A wart. See WARTS.

VERTIGO. See GIDDINESS.

VINCENT'S ANGINA. See ANGINA, VINCENT'S.

VIRUS. The name given to organisms too small to be seen under an ordinary microscope. Viruses are also so small that they pass through a porcelain filter which keeps back ordinary bacteria.

Viruses probably contain only one very large molecule of matter, but are able to absorb nourishment and to reproduce themselves. They are responsible for many diseases, including influenza, the common cold, measles, chicken-pox, and mumps. They are also the cause of canine distemper.

VITAMINS. Tiny quantities of chemical substances, present in a normal diet and necessary for health.

Vitamin A is found in animal fats, eggs, cod-liver oil and halibut oil; it can also be produced in the body from carotene, present in green vegetables and carrots. Deficiency of vitamin A leads to dry eyes, catarrh, intestinal infections, and night blindness.

Vitamin B_1 is obtained from the germ of cereals, yeast, etc. It is essential for the nervous system, and its deficiency leads to neuritis and beri-beri.

Vitamin B_2 has at least two components, riboflavin and nicotinic acid. Its sources are the same as for B_1. Deficiency of riboflavin causes stunting of growth, unhealthy skin, sores at the angles of mouth and eyes, and loss of hair. Deficiency of nicotinic acid causes pellagra.

Vitamin C, ascorbic acid, is found in fresh fruits and vegetables. It is destroyed by boiling, but is retained in some canned fruits. Deficiency of vitamin C leads to scurvy.

Vitamin D is found in animal fats, cod-liver oil and halibut oil. It can also be formed by the skin when exposed to ultra-violet. Deficiency of it in children leads to rickets.

Vitamin K is important in the clotting of blood.

VOCAL CORDS. See LARYNX.

VOMITING. The return of food from the stomach. This may have emotional causes, it may be a result of disturbance of the equilibrium, as in sea-sickness and air-sickness, or it may be due to gastritis, to gastric or duodenal ulcer, to poisoning, to intestinal obstruction, or to inflammatory diseases, such as appendicitis. It can also occur in disease of the brain, such as cerebral tumour. The treatment depends on the cause.

WARTS. Verrucae; they may be flat, hard lumps on the skin, slightly raised above the surface and rather irregular in outline, or they may grow on stalks. When they occur on the sole of the foot they get trodden level with the skin, and are often mistaken for corns. Warts are infective, due to a virus, and may, therefore, be acquired in shaking hands, or in walking barefoot at swimming baths.

They may be treated by caustics, by ionization, or by X-rays (see RADIOTHERAPY); or they may be removed surgically.

WASSERMANN REACTION. A serum test for syphilis.

WATER-BORNE DISEASES. Diseases in which the infection may be conveyed by contaminated drinking water. They include typhoid, paratyphoid, dysentery, cholera and many minor forms of gastro-enteritis.

WATERBRASH. A rush of saliva to the mouth as the result of an attack of indigestion. It can usually be relieved by taking a dose of bicarbonate of soda.

WHITLOW. A septic finger. It is usually caused by infection entering through a prick or small cut, and can be a very serious matter, leading to stiffness, or even loss, of the finger. When the prick is slight, only penetrating the surface layer, the usual result is a blister full of pus. If this is disinfected and emptied, by removing the blister skin with sterile scissors, prompt healing follows.

Deeper penetration leads to infection, first of the soft pulp of the finger and, if deeper still, of the tendons (or leaders) and their sheaths. Through these sheaths infection may spread quickly down to the palm of the hand. It should be emphasized that much harm can be done by going on too long with home treatment, such as poultices, when a finger should be properly opened, under an anaesthetic, and the infection dealt with.

After the finger has been opened, but not before, such modern aids as penicillin may prevent the further spread of infection and lead to rapid healing.

WHOOPING-COUGH. Pertussis; a disease which usually attacks children, though adults can have it. The incubation period is two to three weeks, after which the disease begins very insidiously as a slight cold and cough, often not being suspected for the first week. The characteristic feature is the long succession of staccato coughs, all on one outgoing breath, until the child is red in the face and can cough no more. It then takes a long crowing inspiration, which is the whoop. But this noise is not always present, whereas the characteristic cough always is.

The child also looks puffy round the eyes, and may have a small whitish ulcer under the tongue, where it shoots forward over the lower front teeth in coughing. Sometimes the eyes become bloodshot, or a little blood may be coughed up. It is about the only sort of cough in which a child will cough out phlegm —they usually swallow it.

The violence of the attacks, which may recur every half-hour, or less often, and are more severe at night than in the daytime, may cause vomiting. The child's food should not be stopped on this account; but an effort should be made to give food immediately after an attack, so as to give it an opportunity to digest before the next attack comes on.

Whooping-cough takes about a fortnight in coming on, is really severe for the next fortnight, and then takes another fortnight in fading away. Some cough may persist for a long time afterwards, but the child is not infectious after four weeks have elapsed from the onset of the characteristic cough.

The chief complication to be feared is bronchitis, with the possibility of bronchopneumonia. Much vomiting is exhausting, and every effort should be made to sustain nourishment. Owing to the loss of sleep, the child needs a lot of rest in the daytime. Fresh air is important and in the summer whooping-cough cases do best sleeping out of doors.

Vaccines are very useful in prevention, often conferring immunity for a year or more; but they are rather disappointing in treatment, although worth a trial. Few drugs really help, though sedatives may be given for the cough. After whooping-cough, a change of air is a great help to convalescence.

X-RAY. Electro-magnetic vibrations of extremely short wavelength. X-rays will penetrate many substances which are opaque to light. They have a destructive effect on living tissues. See RADIOGRAPHY and RADIOTHERAPY.

ZINC. Zinc oxide is used in soothing ointments and, combined with castor oil, is a favourite application for rashes in babies.

FIRST-AID

A rapid-reference guide to emergency treatment

INTRODUCTION

THE science of first-aid occupies a very definite department in the province of medicine and surgery. It is concerned with that period which elapses between the occurrence or discovery of an injury and the arrival of medical aid. The lack of skilled assistance during this critical period has been the cause of much loss of human life. The Second World War proved beyond doubt the necessity for everyone to possess at least a rudimentary knowledge of first-aid.

It must be clearly understood that the person who administers first-aid does not take the place of a doctor, and on no account must he attempt to assume the duties and responsibilities of a medical man. Such responsibilities as the re-dressing of wounds and other *after*-treatment is outside the scope of first-aid. The responsibilities of the practitioner of first-aid cease as soon as medical aid is available, but, having made his report to the doctor, he should stand by in case his further assistance may be required.

Diagnosis means finding out what is wrong. This is attained by summing up the history of the case with the symptoms and signs. Symptoms are the complaints made by the patient. Signs are those features found out by examining the patient, such as a rapid pulse, flushed face, laboured breathing, inflamed areas, etc.

There are certain rules in first-aid which should never be broken. First and foremost is the cardinal rule that, in all cases, arrangements for obtaining medical aid must be made immediately. In the case of a street accident or similar incident, where the patient cannot be left alone, an intelligent person should be sent to the nearest telephone booth to obtain medical assistance. Ensure that the doctor is supplied with the correct name of the street and locality where his services are required. Much valuable time may be saved by also giving the doctor his quickest route.

A rapid survey of the patient's immediate surroundings may prove invaluable. Take stock of such items as fencing, gates and onlookers' coats and scarves which could be improvised, respectively, for emergency splints, stretchers, rugs and slings. Every injury case must be treated for *shock* in addition to the particular treatment called for by the patient's injuries. Shock, in varying degree, accompanies all injuries, no matter how slight. The more serious the injury, the greater is the degree of shock.

The recognition and treatment of shock are fully dealt with in the ensuing pages, but it may be stated here that this condition is always accompanied by a lowering of the body temperature. It follows, therefore, that in order to lessen shock all cases of injury must be kept warm. This can be done by wrapping the patient in blankets, rugs or coats, and by applying hot-water bottles or bags. These last should always be wrapped in flannel or similar material and the heat tested on the first-aider's own elbow or forearm before applying to the patient's body.

The injured person should be supported with pillows or cushions in that position which affords him the greatest relief from pain. Support of the injured part helps to prevent aggravation of the injury.

Death must never be assumed because signs of life are absent. There are certain cases where even a medical man cannot, with certainty, state whether the patient is alive or dead. In any case, it is preferable not to risk allowing a living person to die from want of treatment. No matter what injuries are present, severe bleeding must always be treated immediately, as haemorrhage increases shock.

Always remember that shock kills. Many fatally injured persons die from shock before they have lived long enough to succumb from the actual injuries received. Always remove the cause of injury if possible, or remove the patient from the cause. Every injured person requires air. If attending a street accident, make any crowd that has gathered stand well back from the patient. If breathing has ceased, immediate measures must be taken to restore it. See ARTIFICIAL RESPIRATION.

Each wound, no matter how slight, must immediately be covered with a clean piece of dressing. A wound should never be handled except by hands that have previously been thoroughly scrubbed in hot water containing disinfectant solution. This is termed *sterilization* of the hands. When this procedure is impossible, a piece of clean dressing should be placed between the wound and the fingers.

Millions of germs live on the hair and surface skin of the normal, healthy body. Amongst them are germs which produce sepsis (suppuration), but they can do so only if and when they gain entrance to the body through a scratch or abrasion of the skin surface; hence the necessity for the careful cleansing of wounds and the avoidance of contaminating a wound with unsterilized hands.

When a bone is broken, the patient must not be moved until the broken bone has been made immovable, always provided, of course, that the patient's life is not endangered by his position, as, for example, when he is touching a live electric rail or in a collapsing building.

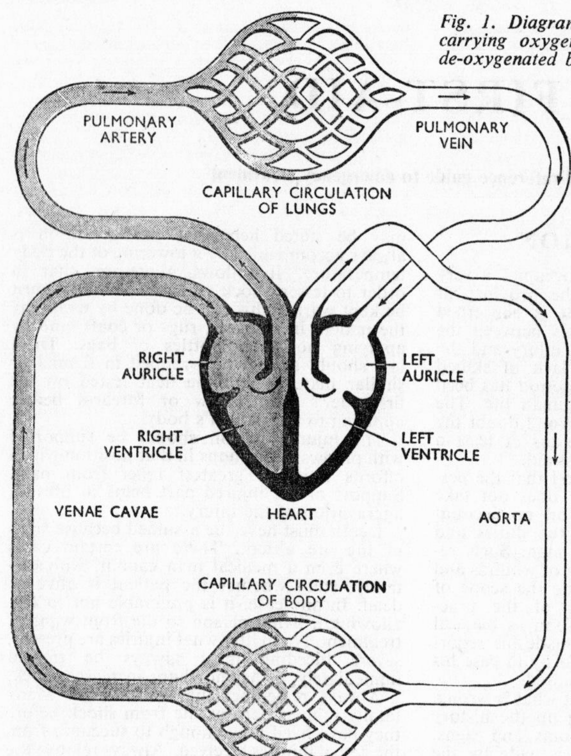

Fig. 1. Diagram of the blood system. Vessels carrying oxygenated blood are shown clear; de-oxygenated blood-vessels are shown shaded.

The body of an injured person should be uncovered as little as possible consistent with making an adequate examination, as exposure increases shock. If clothing has to be removed, avoid cutting material unnecessarily. In removing a jacket, remove the arm from the sleeve on the sound side first. If this is not possible, slit up the *seam* on the injured side. If necessary, shirts and vests should be slit down the front and removed as in the case of the jacket. In the case of other garments, when necessary slit up the seams.

It is important to learn to adopt a confident, reassuring manner when dealing with a patient, and every endeavour must be made to allay the patient's mental anxiety, for mental anxiety increases shock. In no circumstances must the patient's condition be discussed within his hearing. No matter how serious the injuries inflicted and no matter how unlikely are the possibilities of recovery, it is a bounden duty to be optimistic and reassuring towards the patient.

Respiration, or breathing, consists of two acts—breathing in (inspiration) and breathing out (expiration). In the normal, healthy adult the rate of breathing varies from fifteen to twenty breaths per minute. In inspiration, the chest capacity is enlarged partly by the action of the muscles between the ribs and partly by the movement of the *diaphragm*, which is a large muscular sheet dividing the chest from the abdomen or belly. Inspiration is a muscular act. In expiration, which is performed without muscular effort, the chest cavity is diminished in size. This is brought about by the rising upwards of the diaphragm and the falling of the ribs.

At each inspiration air is drawn into the lungs, where the oxygen is extracted and conveyed by the blood to all the tissues of the body. Oxygen is necessary for the production of heat and energy and is, in fact, one of the essentials to human life and functioning. The blood, having given off its oxygen to the tissues, takes on the used products—waste matter, for the most part gases—and returns to the lungs, where on expiration the waste gases are breathed out of the body.

The heart is a muscular organ which acts as a pump for the circulation of the blood. It is situated in the chest behind the breastbone, or *sternum*, between the lungs and immediately above the diaphragm. It has four cavities, two on either side of a central partition. The two upper cavities are called the right and left *auricles*, the two lower the right and left *ventricles*. As the left ventricle, full of fresh oxygenated blood from the lungs, contracts, blood is forced into the arteries. The walls of the arteries are extremely elastic, which causes them to dilate, thus producing the regular expansion known as the *pulse*. The pulse corresponds with each heart-beat and may be felt wherever the finger can be placed on an artery, which is usually where it lies over a bone. The large artery leaving the left ventricle (the aorta) divides and subdivides and forms all the arteries throughout the body. The minute hair-like arteries underneath the skin surface are known as *capillaries*. When the oxygen has been given off to the tissues, the blood enters the veins and begins to take up the waste products. The minute veins join up and get larger and larger until they have all united to form two large veins (the *venae cavae*) which discharge their used blood into the right auricle of the heart, whence it is conveyed to the lungs to be re-oxygenated. Fig. 1 is a diagrammatic representation of the circulation. A grasp of the general principles involved is of the greatest use in the practice of first-aid.

ABDOMEN, WOUNDS IN WALL OF. **With an internal organ protruding.** Keep the patient on his or her back with the knees well drawn up, no matter whether the wound is vertical (in the direction from head to toes) or transverse (across abdomen from side to side). Raise the head and shoulders.

On no account attempt to replace any internal organ (usually the bowel) protruding through the wound. Cover such organs with a piece of gauze, lint or soft towel, wrung out of sterilized warm water at body temperature (98·4 deg. F. or 39 deg. C.). If readily available, one teaspoonful of common salt may be added to each pint of water used. This is normal saline solution. Change the application as it cools (approximately every fifteen minutes). Cover this dressing with cotton-wool or similar clean, soft material. Give nothing by the mouth in case the stomach or gut is torn.

The patient is usually in severe shock. Apply hot-water bottles (wrapped in flannel or similar soft material) to both sides of the body. Keep the patient warm, avoiding undue pressure on the abdomen. Allay mental anxiety. Remove the patient to hospital as speedily as possible.

With no protrusion of organs. If the wound is *vertical*, keep the patient flat on his or her back, with the legs straight to close the wound.

If the wound is *transverse*, keep the patient on his or her back, with the knees drawn well up and the head and shoulders raised. This position keeps the transverse wound closed. Apply an antiseptic and a dry dressing to the wound, fixing the dressing in position with a broad bandage tightly applied. Treat shock by keeping the patient warm and allaying any anxiety, but give nothing by the mouth. See also HAEMORRHAGE and SHOCK.

ACIDS, BURNS BY CORROSIVE. For immediate relief, if readily available, bathe the part with an alkaline (antacid) lotion, such as a dessertspoonful of baking soda (bicarbonate of soda) or washing soda (carbonate of soda) in one pint of warm water. Failing this, thoroughly flood the burnt part with water, preferably but not essentially warm water. If a water-tap is at hand, and none of the abovementioned alkaline lotions is immediately available, place the burnt part under the tap and thoroughly flush with water. Then treat as a burn. See BURNS and POISONING.

AIR HUNGER. This is usually due to bleeding from an internal organ. The patient, who is in a collapsed condition, throws his or her arms about, tugs at the clothing around the neck and calls out for air.

Immediate arrangements should be made to have the patient moved as speedily as possible to hospital, special care being taken to lessen the effects of shock.

Give nothing by mouth, except in haemorrhage from the lungs, when ice, if available, may be given to suck. If the seat of the haemorrhage is known, apply a cold compress over the area. See HAEMORRHAGE.

ALCOHOL, FIRST-AID USE OF. The administration of alcohol should, generally speaking, be withheld until ordered by the doctor. There are, of course, exceptions to this rule, as in the case of ordinary fainting fits. After rendering the local treatment for a bite from a rabid animal, alcohol, such as brandy or whisky, may be administered. For an adult give two tablespoonfuls, or in the case of a child two teaspoonfuls, in a wineglassful of water.

Again, in treating poisoning by prussic acid and cyanide of potassium, after artificial respiration has been performed and breathing restored, brandy, whisky or sal volatile, diluted with an equal quantity of water, may be given freely, if the patient can swallow.

Poisoning by. See POISONING.

ALKALIS, BURNS BY CORROSIVE. If the burn is caused by quicklime, brush off any that remains on the part. If readily available, bathe the affected part with an acid lotion, such as vinegar, lime-juice, or lemon-juice, diluted in an equal quantity of warm water. If the above are not at hand, flush the part with warm water as for a corrosive acid burn. Then treat as a burn. See BURNS and POISONING.

AMMONIA BURNS. Strong ammonia is a corrosive alkali. See ALKALIS, BURNS BY CORROSIVE.

ANKLE, FRACTURE OF. See LEG, FRACTURE OF. **Sprain of.** See SPRAIN.

ANTISEPTICS. The term antiseptic and disinfectant have come to be regarded as meaning the same thing, but, strictly speaking, an antiseptic is a substance used to *prevent* sepsis (contamination by disease germs), whereas a disinfectant is a substance used to *combat* sepsis which has already occurred. The antiseptics and disinfectants in common general use are carbolic acid, acraflavine and numerous proprietary substances sold with full directions for use.

Carbolic acid, which is the standard, classical disinfectant, has the great disadvantage of being a corrosive poison which, in concentration, is able to inflict serious burns. Some proprietary antiseptics are stated to be non-corrosive and non-poisonous and can, therefore, be recommended as safe and reliable for the home first-aid outfit. The directions for dilution should always be carefully followed.

APOPLEXY. This condition, commonly referred to as a "stroke," usually occurs in elderly people and is due to the rupture of a minute blood-vessel in the brain, with bleeding into the brain tissue. It is usually associated with a high blood-pressure in a patient with hardened arteries. The patient, suffering from an apoplectic seizure, is usually unconscious, with a flushed face and full, slow pulse. There is stertorous (snoring) breathing and loss of power on one side of the body, or loss of speech if the patient remains conscious.

Having noticed these signs, raise the eyelids. One pupil will be larger than the other and will not react to light. (Normally, a light shone upon the eyes causes the pupils to contract.)

Treatment: Undo all clothing about the neck, chest and waist. Ensure an abundance of fresh air. Promote warmth to the lower part of the body by applying protected hot-water bottles to the legs and feet. Apply cold water continuously to the head. Keep the patient absolutely quiet in a darkened room. Give nothing by mouth, until advised by the doctor, who should, of course, be sent for immediately.

ARM BONES, FRACTURE OF. The bone may be broken (1) in the upper part; (2) in the middle of the shaft; (3) at or actually in the elbow joint; (4) in the forearm.

Treatment: The purpose of first-aid treatment is to fasten the broken part so that it cannot be moved or jogged. Usually this is best done as follows:

Near the shoulder. Apply a broad bandage with the upper edge level with the top of the shoulder. Pass it round the limb and body and tie it on the opposite side under the armpit. Then apply a small arm-sling. (See Fig. 2.)

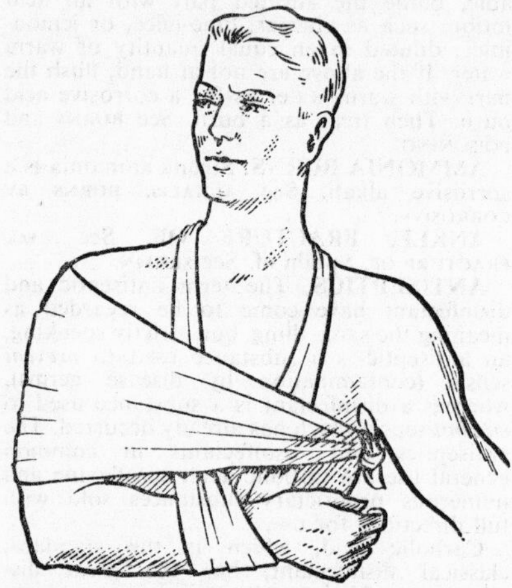

Fig. 2. Fracture of arm close to shoulder.

Middle of the shaft. Place the forearm, at right-angles to the upper arm, across the chest. Having applied a small arm-sling, apply splints reaching from the shoulder to the elbow to the front, back and outer side of the arm. To secure the splints, apply bandages above and below the fracture. (See Fig. 3.) When no splints are available, secure the arm to the side by two broad bandages.

Elbow joint. In these fractures it is difficult to ascertain the exact extent of the injury, owing to the large amount of swelling usually present. The patient usually holds the damaged arm in a right-angle position. Two splints are taken, one reaching from the armpit to below the elbow, the other reaching from beyond the elbow to the finger-tips. Tie them together to form a right-angle. Apply this right-angled splint to the side of the arm that is least swollen, securing it in position by bandages round the upper arm and forearm. A third bandage is applied as a figure of eight round the hand and wrist. A small arm-sling is then applied. (See ELBOW JOINT.)

If there is much swelling at the site of the injury, apply a cold compress.

Forearm. Either or both of the bones in the forearm may be fractured. A fall on the outstretched hand commonly results in an impacted fracture of the lower end of the radius. This fracture is called a Colles' fracture. The general signs and symptoms of fracture are usually present.

Fig. 3. Treatment of fractured upper arm bone.

The first-aid treatment of these fractures is the same whether one bone or both are fractured. The forearm is placed across the chest at right-angles to the arm, with the thumb uppermost and the palm turned to the body. Splints, reaching from the elbow to the fingers, are applied to the forearm, one on the front and the other on the back. These are held in position by two bandages, one applied round the forearm above the fracture and the other

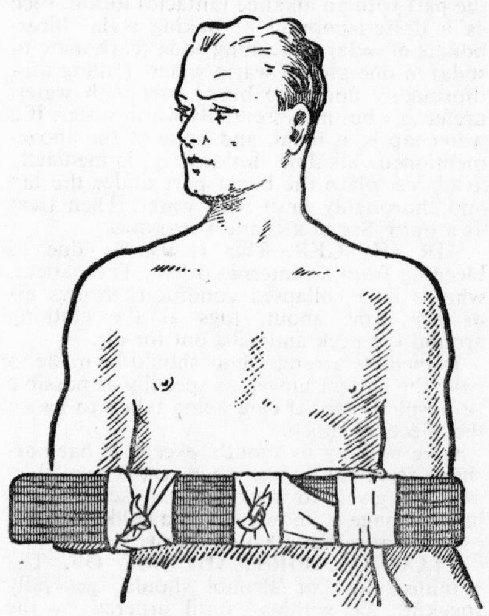

Fig. 4. Splinting for fractured forearm.

applied as a figure of eight round the hand and wrist. (See Fig. 4.) A large arm-sling is then applied to support the arm.

Sprains of. See SPRAIN.

ARM-SLINGS. Large arm-sling. This supports the hand and forearm. Spread out a triangular bandage as in Fig. 5. Put one end over the sound shoulder, passing it round the neck so that it just appears on the shoulder of the injured side. Bring the point behind the elbow of the injured limb with the forearm occupying the middle of the bandage. Bring the other end up to the first end and tie them. Curl the point round the elbow and secure to the front of the bandage with a safety-pin.

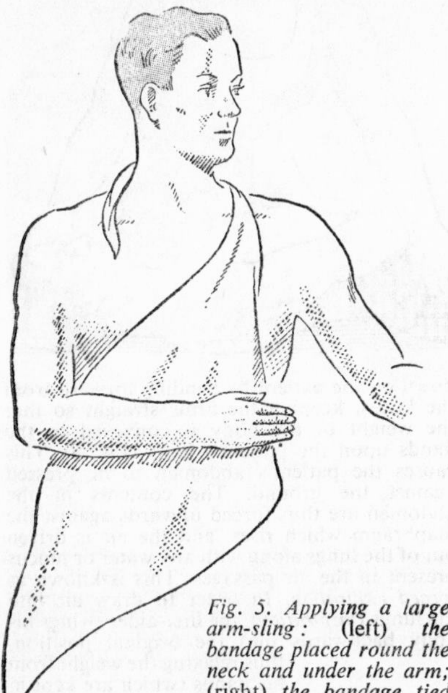

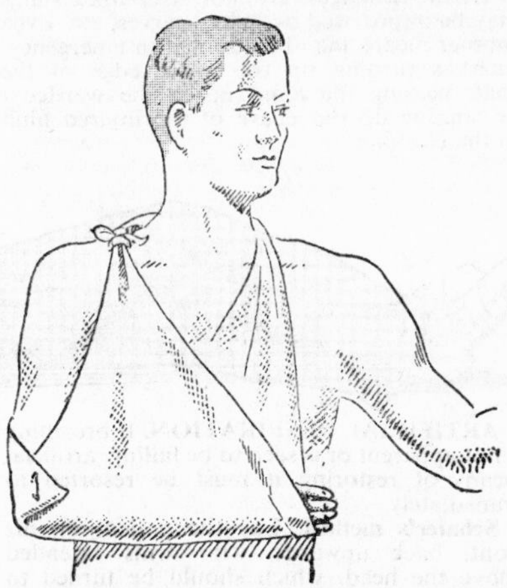

Fig. 5. Applying a large arm-sling : (left) *the bandage placed round the neck and under the arm;* (right) *the bandage tied and the point pinned.*

Small arm-sling. This allows the elbow to hang free while giving support to the hand and wrist. Make a broad bandage from a triangular sling. Pass one end over the shoulder of the sound side and round the neck so that the end lies on the shoulder of the injured side. Place the wrist and hand in the centre of the bandage, then bring the second end up to the first and tie them together.

The St. John sling. Place the left forearm across the chest with the palm resting on the breast-bone and the fingers pointing towards the right shoulder. Take a triangular bandage and hold it with its point in the right hand and one end in the left hand. Place the bandage on the left forearm with the point well beyond the elbow and the end on the right shoulder. Support the left elbow and tuck the base of the bandage under the left hand and forearm. Carry the lower end across the back to the right shoulder. Tie the ends in the hollow above the right collar-bone. With the left hand hold open the side of the bandage lying on the left forearm and with the right hand

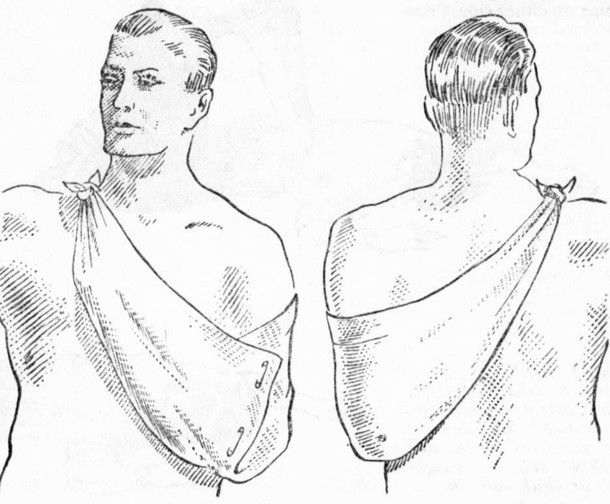

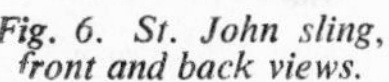

Fig. 6. St. John sling, front and back views.

tuck the point well in between the left forearm and the side of the bandage being held open. Pass the resulting fold over the back of the arm and pin it to part of the bandage on the back. (See Fig. 6.)

When the injury is on the right side, substitute "left" for "right" and vice versa.

When bandages are not available, slings may be improvised by belts, scarves, etc. Even simpler means may be adopted in emergency, such as turning up the lower edge of the coat, passing the hand inside the waistcoat or pinning up the sleeve of the injured limb to the clothing.

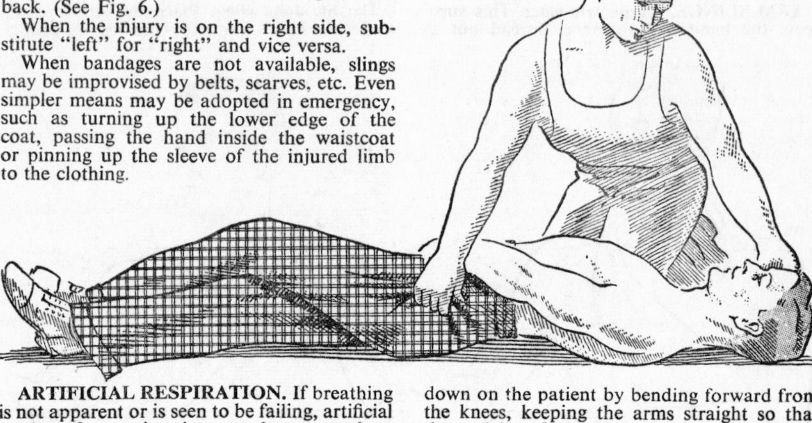

Fig. 7. Artificial respiration: turning a patient over.

ARTIFICIAL RESPIRATION. If breathing is not apparent or is seen to be failing, artificial means of restoring it must be resorted to immediately.

Schafer's method. Lay the patient on his front, back upwards, with arms extended above the head, which should be turned to one side, to keep the mouth and nose off the ground. To turn the patient on to his front, kneel at his side, place his arms close to his body, cross his far leg over the near leg, protect his face with one hand, grasp the clothing at his hip with the other and pull him quickly over. (See Fig. 7.)

Kneel alongside of the patient, facing his head. Place both hands on the small of the patient's back with the wrists close to one another, and the fingers passing over the loins on either side. Press down on the patient by bending forward from the knees, keeping the arms straight so that the weight of the body is conveyed to the hands upon the patient's loins (Fig. 8). This causes the patient's abdomen to be pressed against the ground. The contents of the abdomen are thus forced upwards against the diaphragm which rises, and the air is driven out of the lungs along with any water or mucus present in the air passages. This is known as *forced expiration.* In order to draw air into the lungs (*inspiration*), the first-aider swings his body backwards into the original position, thus relaxing the weight from his hands (which are kept in the same position), and so the pressure on the patient's abdomen being also relaxed the internal organs assume their former position, the chest cavity is enlarged and air is drawn into the lungs.

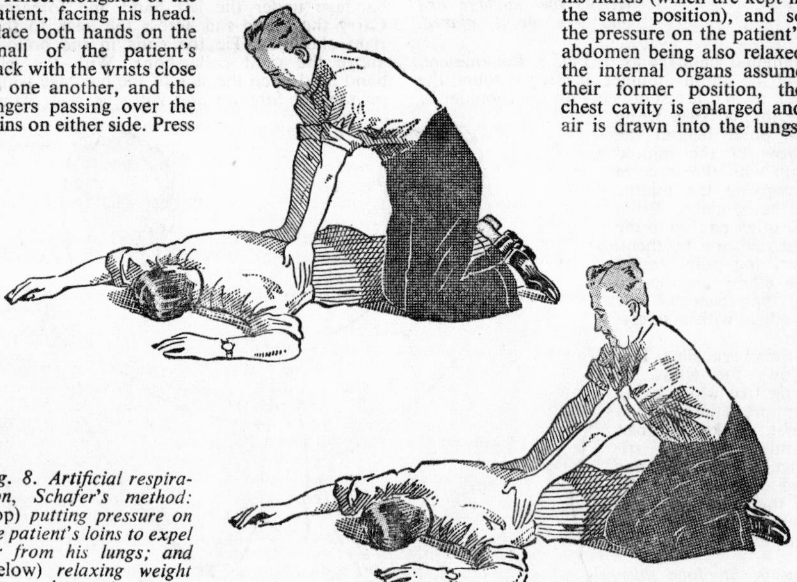

Fig. 8. Artificial respiration, Schafer's method: (top) *putting pressure on the patient's loins to expel air from his lungs; and* (below) *relaxing weight to draw air in.*

These two movements are alternated by swaying backwards and forwards from the knee-joints at the rate of twelve times a minute. The pressure stage is retained for approximately two seconds and stage of relaxation for three seconds. The movements must be steady and regular in rhythm.

When natural breathing returns, regulate the movements to correspond with it. The circulation should be assisted by rubbing the limbs vigorously towards the heart and by the application of warmth to the body.

After the restoration of natural breathing the patient should be carefully watched in case breathing fails again. If this should occur, immediately resort again to artificial respiration.

In all cases artificial respiration must be persevered with either until respiration is restored or until a doctor pronounces life to be extinct.

Sylvester's method. This method is performed with the patient on his back and is only used when it is inadvisable to turn the patient upon his face, e.g., in the case of fractured ribs or long bones, etc. Whereas Schafer's method is performed by one person, Sylvester's method requires an assistant to hold out the tongue. If this is not done there is risk of the patient choking through the tongue falling back over the windpipe.

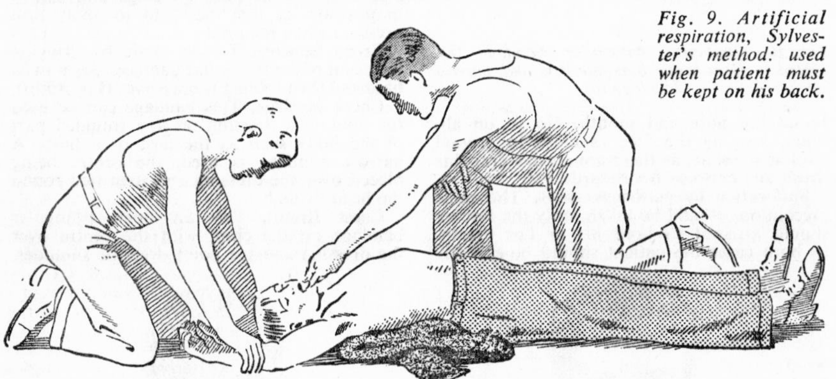

Fig. 9. Artificial respiration, Sylvester's method: used when patient must be kept on his back.

Kneel behind the patient's head. Grasp his arms below the elbows and draw the arms outwards and upwards towards you (Fig. 9). This movement increases the cavity of the chest and air is drawn into the lungs. Then press the patient's arms and elbows slowly downwards and inwards against the chest on each side of the breast bone. This causes the air to be expelled from the lungs. These two movements are repeated alternately and regularly at the rate of about twelve times a minute, pressing down for two seconds and relaxing for about three seconds. The remainder of the treatment is the same as in the case of Schafer's method.

ASPHYXIA. Continuous lack of air results first in struggling attempts to take breaths, and finally in a state of unconsciousness associated with absence of breathing and this is known as *asphyxia*. This condition may be brought about in several ways:

By drowning.
By outside pressure, e.g., strangulation, hanging, smothering, etc.
By a foreign body stuck in the throat.
By swelling of the throat tissues through, e.g., insect stings, scalds, corrosive fluids, and ordinary inflammation.
By the inhalation (breathing) of poisonous gases.
By inhaled vomit in an unconscious person.
By pressure on the chest, for example, by being buried under debris, or by pressure from a crowd.
By "swallowing the tongue" when unconscious.
By certain nervous affections.

The treatment consists in first removing the cause of the asphyxia or else removing the patient from the cause, whichever is the more expedient. Quickly undo all clothing about the neck, chest and waist. Ensure an abundance of fresh air. Never give anything by the mouth while the patient is unconscious. If breathing is absent, immediately commence artificial respiration and keep it up until medical aid takes over. On return to consciousness, when breathing has been restored, treat for shock.

Additional treatment in special cases:

Strangulation. Remove the constriction from the throat immediately.

Hanging. Do not wait to raise the alarm, but grasp the legs and raise the body up to take the strain off the rope round the neck, or cut the rope and free the neck.

Choking. Bend the patient forwards and slap the back between the shoulder-blades. If this does not dislodge the foreign body from the throat, encourage vomiting by passing a finger down the throat.

Swelling of the throat. Sit the patient, if possible, before a fire or stove. Apply repeated hot compresses to the throat. Provided the patient is breathing, give ice to suck. If no ice is available, give sips of cold water. Butter and olive oil tend to ease the pain.

Suffocation by smoke. Before entering the room to rescue the patient, tie a wet cloth

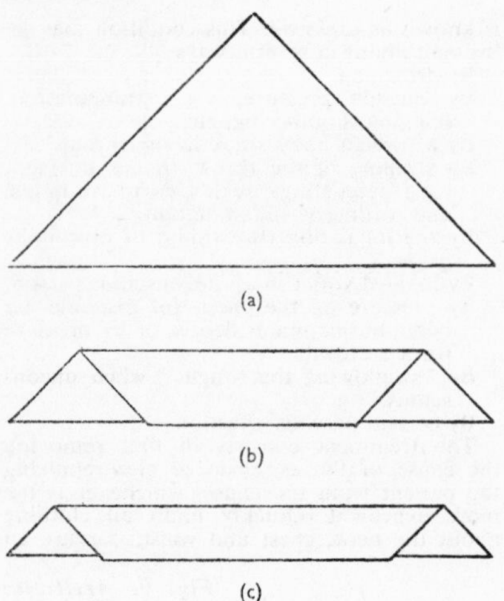

Fig. 10. Bandages: triangular bandage (a), *folded to form broad bandage* (b), *and narrow bandage* (c).

round the nose and mouth. Go in on all-fours, keeping the face as close to ground level as possible, as there are always draughts (fresh air) between floorboards.

Suffocation by poisonous gases. The same precautions should be taken, only the rescuer should attempt to hold his or her breath. In both cases the patient should be speedily dragged out of the dangerous atmosphere before treatment is attempted.

If the gas is known to be of a deadly nature the rescuer must wear a suitable gas-mask.

Inhalation of vomit in the unconscious is avoided by keeping the subject on his side or face, with the head low, so vomit will tend to run out of the mouth, not down the windpipe.

Swallowing the tongue. When an unconscious person is found to be struggling for breath it is always wise to put a finger into the throat and see that the tongue has not fallen back, or that dentures are not displaced (these must always be removed).

See also ELECTRIC SHOCK.

BANDAGES. The triangular bandage is more commonly used in first-aid than the roller bandage, as it can be put to a variety of uses. It is made by cutting diagonally across a 40-in. square of cotton, linen or similar firm material. (See Fig. 10(a).)

The triangular bandage may be used as an arm-sling, for keeping dressings and splints in position on the body and to apply firm pressure when required.

Broad bandage. This is made by bringing the point of the triangular bandage down to its base and then folding it once over (Fig. 10(b)).

Cheek bandage. This bandage can be used for holding a dressing on any rounded part of the body such as the face or a limb. A narrow bandage is used, the centre being placed over the dressing and then tied round the head or limb.

Chest (front). Lay an open triangular bandage on the chest with the centre over the dressing and the point over the shoulder.

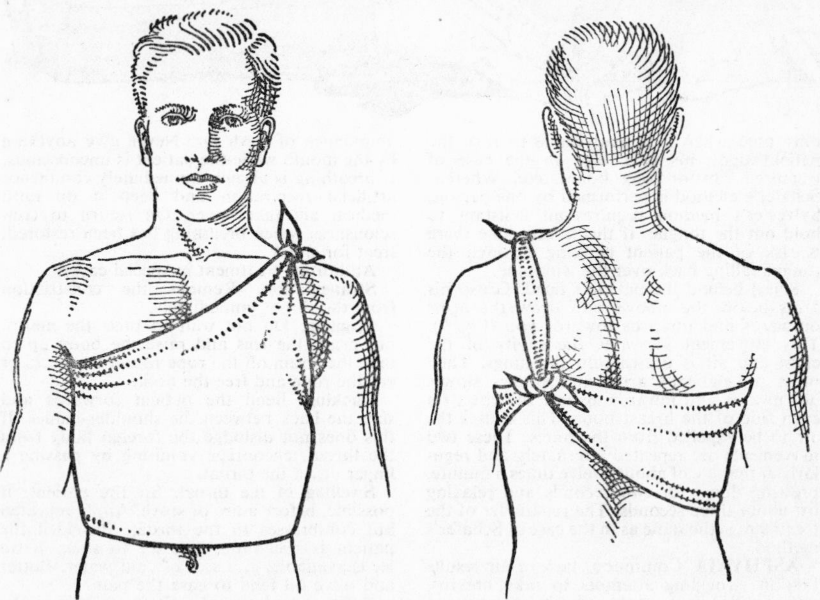

Fig. 11. Triangular bandage applied to the front of the chest.

Turn the lower border inwards for about three inches and carry the ends round the body and tie at the back, leaving one end longer than the other. Draw the point over the shoulder and tie to the longer end. (See Fig. 11.)

Chest (back). Apply as for the front, only begin at the back.

Elbow. Fold about three inches of the base of the bandage inwards and lay the bandage over the back of the elbow with the point up the back of the arm. Cross the ends over the

Fig. 12. Bandage for elbow. The flap is pinned down over the knot in position shown by the dotted line.

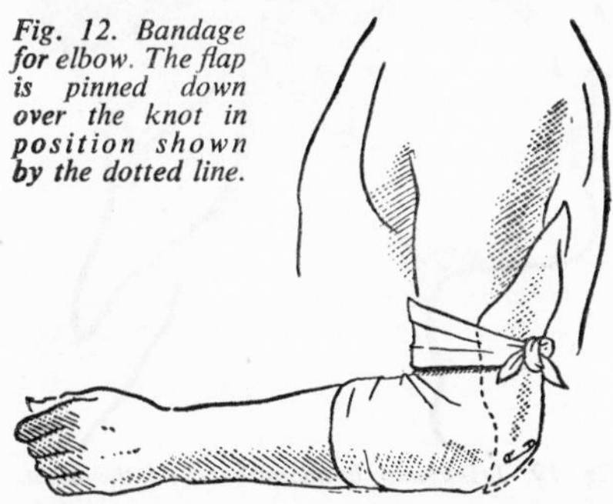

front, then bring them round to the back of the limb and tie them above the elbow. Bring the point down over the knot and fix to the bandage with a safety-pin. (See Fig. 12.)

Finger. A narrow roller bandage tied round the wrist should be used. (See Fig. 13.)

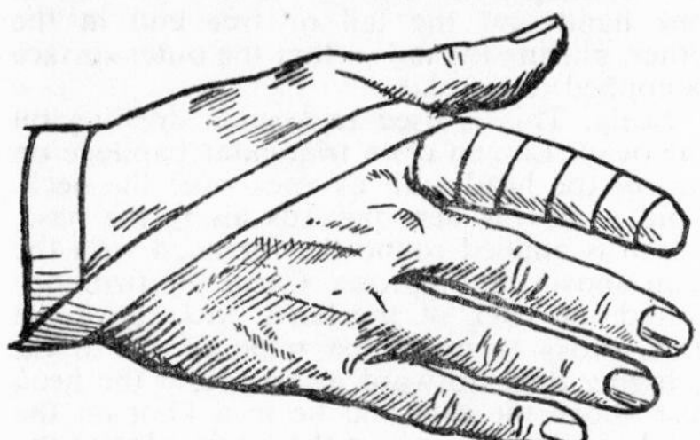

Fig. 13. Bandaging a finger.

Foot. Place the sole of the foot on the centre of a triangular bandage with the toes pointing towards the point. Bring the point over the instep and the ends forward and cross them. Bring the ends round the ankle and tie them. Draw the point forward and pin to the bandage over the instep. (See Fig. 14.)

Forehead. Bandage as for cheek.

Hand. Fold a narrow hem along the base of the bandage. Place the hand palm downwards on the open bandage with the wrist on the folded base and the fingers towards the point. Bring the point back over the wrist, then pass the ends round the wrist and tie them. Draw the point over the knot and pin to the bandage over the hand. (See Fig. 15.) Apply a large arm-sling.

Head, side of. Bandage as for the cheek.

Hip or groin. Tie a narrow bandage round the body above the haunch bones, with the

Fig. 14 (right). *In bandaging the foot the point is pinned down over the knot as for the elbow. The hand bandage, Fig. 15* (below). *is similar.*

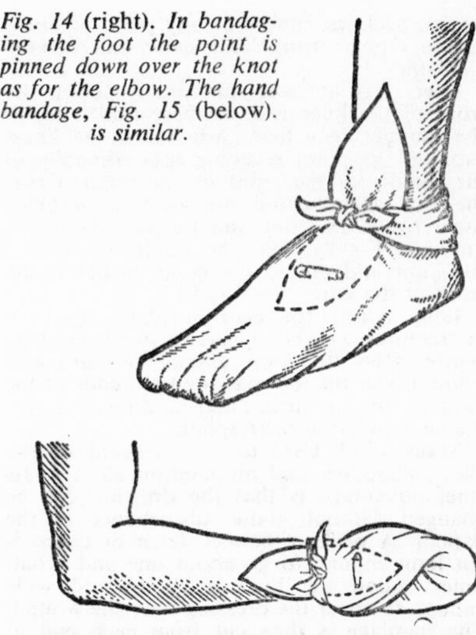

knot on the side to be bandaged. Put the point of another bandage under the first and turn it down over the knot. Fold a hem inwards along the base of this second bandage and bring the ends round the thigh, tying them on the outside so as to secure the base of the bandage to the limb. Draw the point over the knot of the first bandage and pin it to the

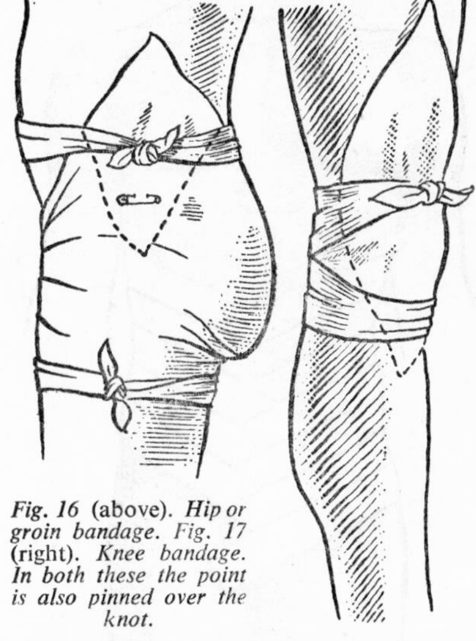

Fig. 16 (above). *Hip or groin bandage. Fig. 17* (right). *Knee bandage. In both these the point is also pinned over the knot.*

outside of the second bandage. (See Fig. 16.)

Improvised bandages. When a triangular bandage is not available, bandages may be improvised from belts, handkerchiefs, scarves, straps, neckties, braces or any piece of linen, cotton, tape or string that is easily and speedily available.

Knee. Lay a triangular bandage upon the front of the knee with its base folded in, in the manner of a hem, just below the knee-cap, and its point reaching approximately to the middle of the front of the thigh. Cross the free ends behind the knee, then bring them round in front and tie just above the kneecap. Finally, fold the point down over the knot and pin to the bandage below the front of the knee. (See Fig 17.)

Loop. Is used for securing splints to a limb in fractures. Double a narrow bandage at its centre. Pass the loop under the limb and bring it over the top, passing both ends of the bandage through it in opposite directions. Tie the ends over the *outer* splint.

Many-tailed. Used to fix a dressing on the chest, abdomen and amputation stumps. Its chief advantage is that the dressing can be changed without undue disturbance of the patient A piece of flannel, linen or calico is cut long enough to go about one and a half times round the limb or body and wide enough to cover the dressing over the wound. The bandage is then cut from each end in equal, parallel strips, the width varying from two to four inches, according to the part to be bandaged. In applying the bandage the tails are crossed over each other so that each subsequent tail secures the preceding one. (See Fig. 18.)

Narrow. This is made by folding the *broad* bandage along its long axis. **(See Fig. 10(c).)**

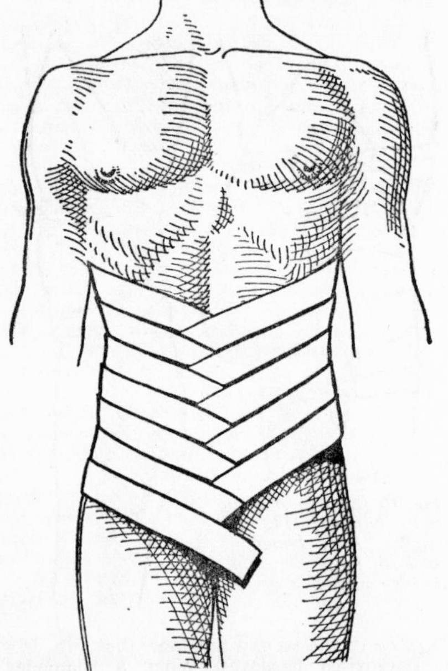

Fig. 18. Many-tailed bandage applied to abdomen.

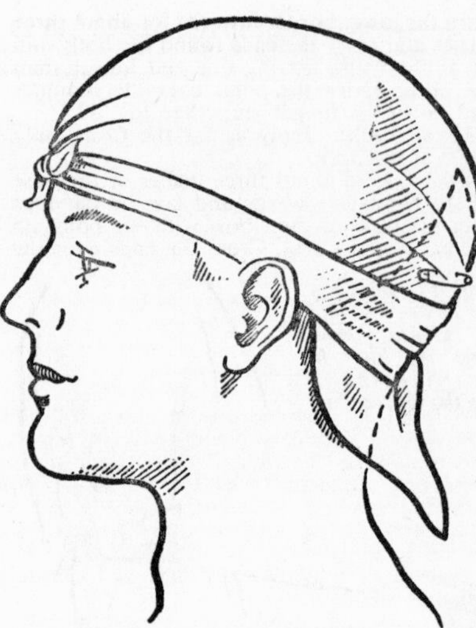

Fig. 19. Triangular bandage used on the head.

Roller. This is made of cotton, unbleached calico, flannel or domette, and is used for retaining dressings and fixing splints to limbs. When the bandage is opened for use, the roll is referred to as the *head* of the bandage and the free end is termed the *tail.* In applying this bandage, the head or roll is grasped in one hand and the tail or free end in the other, placing the tail so that the outer surface is applied to the skin.

Scalp. This is used to keep a dressing on the head. Lay an open triangular bandage on top of the head with its apex over the neck. Fold a narrow hem inwards along the base, which is applied round the forehead with the hem above the eyebrows. Carry the two ends round the back of the head, just above the ears, cross them at the nape of the neck, bringing them forward again round the head just above the ears and tie in a knot on the forehead so as to secure the lower edge of the bandage. Draw the point downwards, then turn it up and pin it to the bandage on top of the head. (See Fig. 19.)

Shoulder. Place the centre of a triangular bandage on the shoulder with the point up the side of the neck. Fold a hem inwards along the base, carrying the ends round the arm and tying them to secure the lower border of the bandage. Apply a small arm-sling. Turn down the point of the bandage over the knot in the sling, draw it tight and pin it in position.

See also ARM-SLINGS.

BITES. Animal. Hydrophobia is a disease resulting from the bite of an animal such as a dog, fox or wolf suffering from rabies. The poison travels from the bite along the nerves to the central nervous system, i.e., the brain and spinal cord. If a person has been bitten by a rabid animal or one suspected of rabies, means must be taken to promote bleeding in order to wash the poison out of the wound.

Immediately tie a bandage between the bite and the trunk of the body. The constriction should be tight enough to congest the limb and ensure bleeding, but not so tight as to stop the arterial circulation, in which case bleeding will entirely cease. It should always be possible to feel the pulse while constricting the limb.

Keep the bitten limb hanging low. Bathe the wound with warm water in which sufficient crystals of permanganate of potash have been dissolved to make the solution a pale pink colour. Give two tablespoonfuls of brandy or whisky in a wineglassful of water or hot black coffee. In the case of a child, reduce the dose of alcohol to two teaspoonfuls.

If a doctor cannot be obtained within a few minutes after the bite has been inflicted, the wound should be cauterized. This is done by removing the constricting bandage and applying a caustic to the wound, such as a pointed pledget of cotton-wool dipped in carbolic acid or a silver nitrate pencil. In order to destroy the poison effectively, every tooth mark must be separately and carefully probed and cauterized.

It is usually advised that if more than half an hour has elapsed since the person has been bitten, the above treatment is proceeded with but the wound is not cauterized. The reason for this is that after half an hour the poison will have entered the system and cauterizing will merely seal the wound and shut the poison into the body.

Frost. This is due to exposure to extreme cold of parts of the body which are at the extremities of the circulation, such as the ears, nose, fingers and toes.

Sensation is lost in the part, which becomes first a waxy white colour and later assumes a purplish appearance. Owing to the loss of sensation, the patient is frequently unaware of his condition.

Immediately apply mild friction (gentle rubbing) to the part and apply gentle warmth. Do not bring the patient into a warm atmosphere until the sensation and circulation have been restored, otherwise the affected tissue may die. Avoid the application of moisture in any form.

Insect. Always extract the sting, if it is present. Swab the wound freely with spirit or a solution of baking soda (bicarbonate of soda), washing soda (carbonate of soda) or a wet blue-bag. This relieves the pain. A dry dressing is finally applied.

Snake. These are dangerous to life and immediate action must be taken to prevent the poison spreading throughout the body.

If the bite is on a limb, immediately tie a bandage round the upper arm or thigh (according to the limb bitten) between the wound and the heart, and tie it tight enough to stop the circulation. It is useless to place this constriction round the forearm and leg, as the blood-vessels lie between the bones in these regions. Keep the bandage in position for about twenty minutes. This prevents the poison from travelling into the circulation. Then relax the bandage for one minute until the skin becomes pink again. This assists the blood to "bleed out" the poison from the wound. Then tighten up the bandage again. Repeat this manoeuvre regularly until the arrival of the doctor.

Keep the bitten person completely at rest. If able to swallow, give hot drinks, such as strong coffee or tea. *On no account give alcohol.* It is of the utmost importance to reassure the patient, as fear will seriously aggravate the condition.

Wash the wound, preferably with a pale-pink solution of potassium permanganate, to remove any dried poison. Should breathing fail, immediately apply artificial respiration.

BLADDER, BLEEDING FROM. If not due to disease, this condition is commonly caused by fracture of the pelvis. There is either inability to pass water or only very little is passed and that is tinged with blood. Where the pelvis or crutch is injured the patient must on no account try to pass water, as if the bladder is torn it will leak into the tissues. The patient should be removed to hospital as soon as possible, special care being taken to lessen shock. Apply a cold compress over the affected area. Give nothing by mouth.

BLEEDING. See HAEMORRHAGE.

BLISTERS. See BURNS AND SCALDS.

BOWEL, BLEEDING FROM. See HAEMORRHAGE FROM AN INTERNAL ORGAN.

BRAIN, COMPRESSION OF. This is a disturbance of the functions of the brain caused by a blow or fall on the head or the lower part of the spine or by a fall from a height on to the feet. The condition is the result of pressure on the brain by a blood clot or by other pressure such as a fragment of bone in a fracture of the skull.

The face is flushed. The pulse is full and slow and the breathing is noisy, like snoring. There is loss of power and sensation in the limbs on one or other side of the body. If the base of the skull has been fractured, there may be bleeding from the nose and ear. The pupil of one eye may be larger than the other. The eyes do not react to light and the patient cannot be roused. The signs of compression may not appear at once. Compression is frequently preceded by concussion.

The general rules for insensibility (see INSENSIBILITY) are adopted as far as possible. Hot-water bottles (wrapped in flannel or similar material) are applied to the lower limbs and the sides of the abdomen. Cold-water compresses are applied continuously to the head, the patient being kept at complete rest in a darkened room.

Concussion of. Concussion or stunning is produced in the same manner as compression, but is of a temporary nature. There is no pressure exerted upon the brain.

The patient is in a stupor, which may clear up rapidly or else deepen into coma. The face is pale, the skin is cold, the breathing shallow and the pulse weak and rapid. Unlike compression, concussion develops at once.

The treatment is the same as for compression.

All cases of head injury, no matter how slight, should be instructed to consult a doctor before resuming work.

Haemorrhage within. See APOPLEXY.

Injuries to. See SKULL, FRACTURE OF.

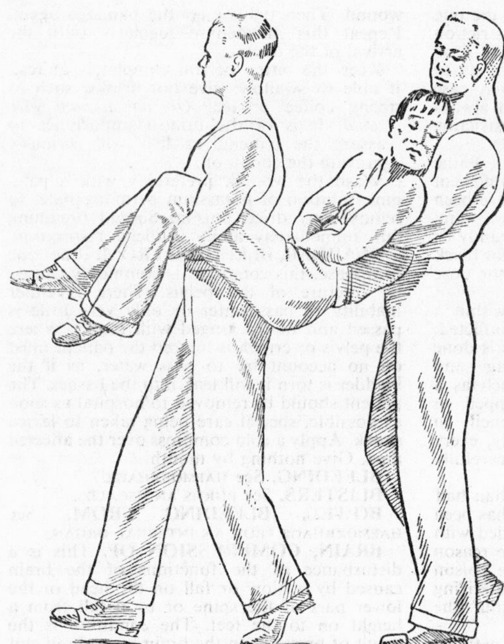

Fig. 20. Carrying an injured person: fore-and-aft method.

BREAST BONE, FRACTURE OF. When the fracture can be felt or is suspected, all clothing about the chest should be loosened. The patient is then placed upon the back and removed to shelter. Cold-water compresses may be applied for the relief of pain.

BREATHING. See RESPIRATION.

BRUISES (CONTUSIONS). A blow on the skin surface of any part of the body causes haemorrhage from the minute vessels beneath the skin (the capillaries). The blood seeps to the surface and produces the characteristic discoloration. Apply a cold compress to the affected part.

"BRUSH BURNS." See FRICTION BURNS.

BURNS AND SCALDS. Burns are caused by (1) dry heat, such as fire or a piece of hot metal; (2) a rail, wire or other material charged with a strong electric current or by lightning; (3) corrosive acids, such as oil of vitriol, and corrosive alkalis (antacids), such as caustic soda, quicklime or strong ammonia; (4) Friction (see FRICTION BURNS). A **Scald** is a burn produced by damp heat, such as steam, boiling water, hot oil or tar.

The effects of a burn or scald may be merely a reddening of the skin or blisters may be formed. In more severe burns or scalds the deeper tissues of the body may be injured. The chief danger of a burn or scald is *shock*, which comes on at once. The shock sustained is proportionate to the area of skin surface affected. A small deep burn is not necessarily dangerous to life, but an extensive skin burn over the chest and abdomen is likely to prove fatal from shock, more especially in the case of young children. The general principles of treatment are fundamentally the same as for other wounds and consist of the exclusion of air from the burn, relief of pain and the prevention and treatment of shock. (See also SHOCK.)

The first-aider should wash his hands if possible before handling the case. Do *not* remove clothing unless absolutely necessary, and do *not* break blisters. Cover the whole of the affected area with sterile gauze or other clean material which has been wrung out of a solution of baking soda (one dessertspoonful to a pint of warm water) or warm saline solution (one teaspoonful of common salt to a pint of warm water). If a first-aid box is available and contains a 1 per cent solution of picric acid, the dressing may be wrung out of this solution instead of the above. If none of the above solutions are available, the burn should be immediately covered with a piece of clean gauze or linen. Contrary to common belief, burns, other than the very smallest, must *never* be covered with grease (butter, oil, etc.). The patient is kept at rest, covered with warm blankets or coats, and is given quantities of warm, weak, sweetened tea.

A young child, severely burnt or scalded, may be placed in a warm bath (body temperature) in which has been dissolved baking soda (one dessertspoonful to one pint), without removing the clothes, and kept in the bath until medical aid arrives.

By corrosive acids. See ACIDS, BURNS BY CORROSIVE.

By alkalis. See ALKALIS, BURNS BY CORROSIVE.

CARBOLIC ACID BURN. See ACIDS, BURNS BY CORROSIVE.

Poisoning. See POISONING.

CARRYING INJURED PERSON. It is always best to leave an injured person where he lies until the doctor has seen him. This is especially true after falls, etc., when the backbone may be broken. If he is flexed (curled up) at all in the process of moving, the broken bones may pinch the spinal cord, causing a permanent paralysis which might have been avoided. If urgent moving is imperative (falling masonry, etc.) he should be carried face down by legs and shoulders so the back is extended (arched backwards), or laid face up on a stretcher. If a patient has to be moved, the method selected must always depend upon the nature and extent of the injuries, the number of helpers available, the amount of room space and the route to be traversed.

Fore-and-aft method. (See Fig. 20.) This method should only be used when space does not permit of the hand-seat method, and if the legs are not fractured.

Four-handed seat. This method is used when the patient can assist the bearers by using one or both arms. The bearers stand behind the patient, facing one another. Each grasps his own left wrist with his right hand and then each bearer grasps the other's right wrist with his left hand (Fig. 21). The bearers then stoop down and the patient is told to place one arm round the neck of each bearer

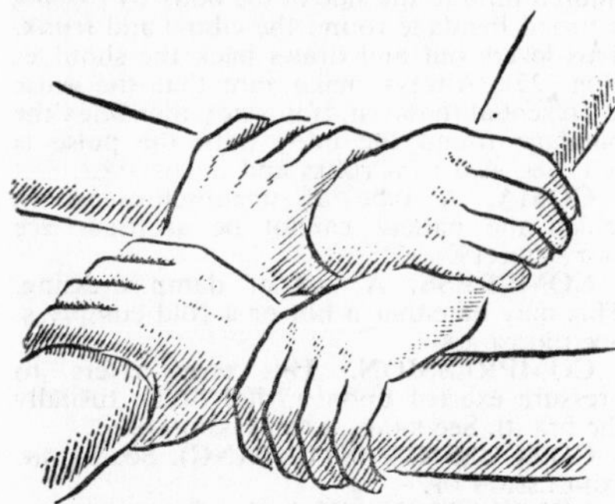

Fig. 21. Four-handed seat.

in order to raise himself up to sit on their hands. The bearers then rise together and step, the right-hand man with his right foot and the other man with his left foot.

Three-handed seat. This seat is used for carrying a patient who can use his arms but requires either of his lower limbs supported. Two bearers stand behind the patient facing one another.

To support the left leg, the bearer standing on the patient's right grasps his own left

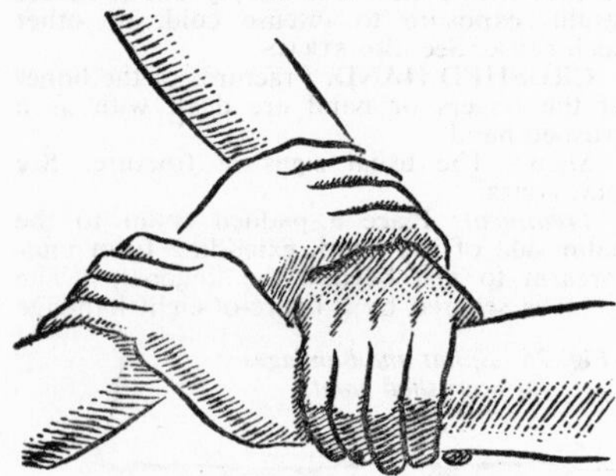

Fig. 22. Three-handed seat.

wrist with his right hand, holding the other bearer's right wrist with his left hand. The other bearer then grasps his companion's right wrist with his own right hand. This leaves his left hand free to support the patient's left leg.

To support the right leg proceed as above, substituting right for left and vice-versa.

The patient then places an arm round each bearer and sits on their hands. The bearers

Fig. 23. Two-handed seat or "hook-grip."

step off as previously described. (See Fig. 22.)

Two-handed seat or "hook-grip." Used in carrying a patient who is unable to steady himself by using his arms.

The bearers stand as before, each passing an arm under the patient's back, grasping his clothing with their hands. Their other arms are passed under the middle of his thighs with their hands clasped together, the left bearer with his palm upwards and the right with his palm downwards. (See Fig 23.)

"Human crutch." The bearer stands at his patient's injured side with his arm round his waist, grasping the clothing at his hip. Placing the patient's arm round his neck, the bearer then grasps his wrist with his own free hand. (See Fig. 24.)

"Pick-a-back." Provided the patient is conscious and able to hold on, he may be carried by the ordinary "pick-a-back" method.

Stretcher. Where the above methods are not practical, as in the case of unconscious

Fig. 24. "Human crutch."

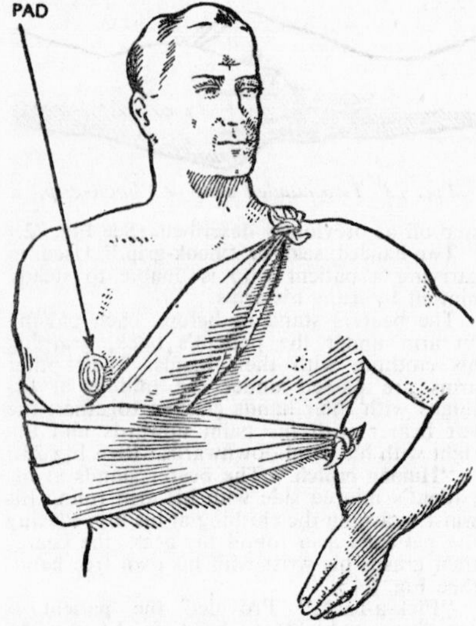

Fig. 25. Treatment for fractured collar-bone.

and seriously injured cases, the ordinary stretcher is used for transporting the patient. Where a stretcher is not available, it may be improvised by stretching and securing a blanket or other strong material between two stout poles. An alternative method consists in turning one or two coats inside out, passing two poles through the sleeves and then buttoning up the coats. A hurdle, shutter or other broad piece of wood, well padded with clothes or other soft material, may be utilized as a stretcher in emergency.

All such improvised stretchers should be carefully tested before being used.

CARTILAGE. See JOINTS.

CHEEK. Bandaging of. See BANDAGES.

Control of bleeding from. A small piece of ice or a little cold water may be held in the mouth, but if the bleeding is excessive and is from the front part of the cheek, compress the part by a piece of sterilized gauze or other clean material held between the finger and thumb.

CHEST OR THORAX. Asphyxia resulting from pressure on. See ASPHYXIA.

Bandaging of. See BANDAGES.

Bleeding within. See RIBS, FRACTURE OF.

CHLOROFORM POISONING. See POISONING.

CHOKING. See ASPHYXIA.

CLOTHING ON FIRE. When a person's clothing catches fire, approach him holding a coat or rug in front for self-protection. Wrap it round the patient, lay him quickly on the floor, and roll him over and over to extinguish the flames.

COAL-GAS POISONING. See POISONING.

COLLAPSE. See SHOCK.

COLLAR-BONE (OR CLAVICLE), FRACTURE OF. Usually caused by a fall on the point of the shoulder.

Signs: The patient usually supports the elbow on the injured side with his hand, inclining his head towards the injured side. The fractured ends can usually be felt through the skin and the general signs and symptoms of fracture are present.

Treatment: Remove the coat from the sound side first. In the case of a male, unfasten the brace on the injured side. Place a firm pad in the armpit, which acts as a fulcrum. Apply a St. John sling, then firmly secure the injured limb to the side of the body by passing a broad bandage round the elbow and trunk. This levers out and draws back the shoulder (Fig. 25). Always make sure that the pulse is present at the wrist. If it is not, then relax the bandage round the body until the pulse is felt. See also FRACTURES and ARM-SLINGS.

COMA. A type of unconsciousness in which the patient cannot be aroused. See INSENSIBILITY.

COMPRESS. A wet or damp dressing. This may be either a hot or a cold compress. See DRESSINGS.

COMPRESSION. This term refers to pressure exerted upon a vital organ (usually the brain). See BRAIN, COMPRESSION OF.

CONCUSSION (STUNNING). See BRAIN, CONCUSSION OF.

CONGESTION. Of brain. See APOPLEXY and SUNSTROKE.

Of limb in bite from rabid animal or snake (see BITES); due to prolonged pressure (see HAEMORRHAGE).

CONTAMINATION OF WOUNDS. See SEPSIS and ANTISEPTICS.

CONTUSION. See BRUISES.

CONVULSIONS OR FITS. See INSENSIBILITY.

CRADLE. See CARRYING INJURED PERSON.

CRAMP. An acute pain felt in a muscle or group of muscles and caused by any interference with their blood supply due to severe strain, exposure to intense cold, or other such cause. See also STRAIN.

CRUSHED HAND. Fractures of the bones of the fingers or hand are dealt with as a crushed hand.

Signs: The usual signs of fracture. See FRACTURES.

Treatment: Place a padded splint to the palm side of the hand, extending from mid-forearm to just beyond the finger-tips. The splint is secured by a figure-of-eight bandage

Fig. 26. Splint and bandages for a crushed hand.

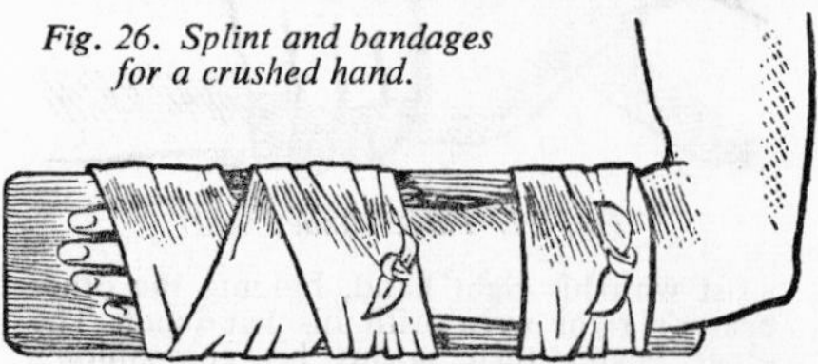

round the hand and wrist and a narrow bandage round the forearm. (See Fig. 26.) The arm is then put up in a large arm-sling.

CRUSHED FOOT. This is dealt with in a similar manner to a crushed hand. Having carefully removed the shoe and stocking, a padded splint is applied to the sole of the foot and fixed in position by a narrow bandage applied as a figure of eight over the instep and ankle (Fig. 27). The bandage is tied on the

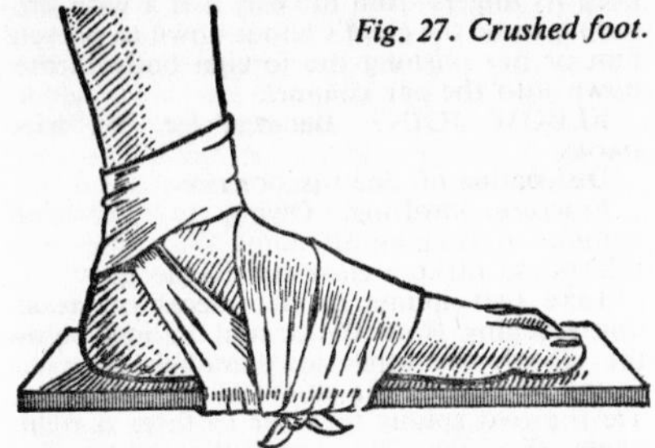

Fig. 27. Crushed foot.

outside of the splint, and the foot is supported in a slightly raised position with a pillow or cushion.

CRUTCH. See CARRYING INJURED PERSON.

CYANIDE POISONING. See POISONING.

DELIRIUM. A confused mental state liable to occur in high fevers. It is also found in certain cases of poisoning (deliriant poisons). See also POISONING.

Signs: The patient rambles incoherently. The pupils are dilated and the pulse is rapid.

Treatment: High temperatures may be reduced by rapidly and carefully sponging the body with tepid water. See also POISON.

DIAGNOSIS. This term is applied to the recognition of the condition or injury from which the patient is suffering. To form a diagnosis, three factors are desirable.

(1) *History:* This is obtained from the patient or from witnesses and gives a clue to the cause of the injury.

(2) *Symptoms:* These are the patient's own feelings as described by himself, e.g., pain, inability to perform certain functions, etc.

(3) *Signs:* These are facts discovered by the examiner for himself, e.g., colour of face, pulse rate, breathing, deformity of a limb, etc.

A diagnosis cannot be made with safety on history and symptoms alone, as they are dependable upon the reliability of the patient and the witnesses. Their value is largely as corroboration of what the examiner finds out by his own examination of the patient, i.e., *signs.*

DIGITAL PRESSURE is a means of controlling bleeding and consists in the application of the thumb or thumbs to the bleeding point. If the bleeding point is not immediately seen, grasp the whole wound and squeeze it tightly for a few seconds. On slowly relaxing the fingers the bleeding point will be seen and can then be controlled by direct digital pressure. See also HAEMORRHAGE.

DISINFECTANTS. See ANTISEPTICS.

DISLOCATION. Of a cartilage. Usually occurs in the knee joint following a sudden wrench which causes one or more of the cartilages to be displaced or torn. The resulting condition is known as "footballer's knee."

The *symptoms, signs and treatment* are similar to those in the case of a dislocation of a joint. (See below.)

Of a joint. This consists in the displacement of one or more bones forming a joint. The joints most frequently dislocated are those of the shoulders (Fig 28), elbow, thumb fingers, and lower jaw.

Symptoms and *signs:* Pain, swelling, loss of power, deformity and fixity of the joint. The fixity enables a dislocation to be distinguished from a fracture.

Treatment: Never attempt to put a dislocated joint back into position yourself. Instead, support the injured joint with pillows or folded rugs in the position which gives

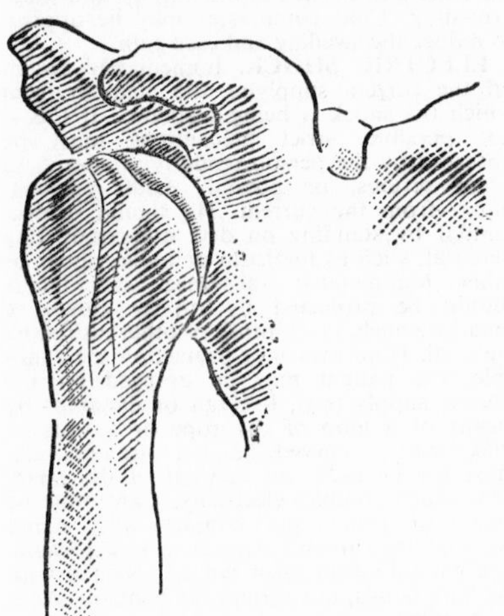

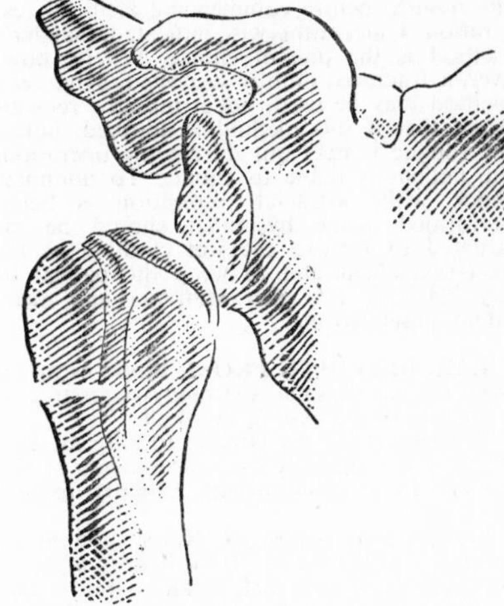

Fig. 28. Dislocation of the shoulder: (left) *the normal joint, and* (right) *when dislocated.*

greatest comfort to the patient. If the pain is severe, carefully expose the part and apply a cold compress. If this fails to give relief, apply a hot compress. Move the patient into shelter as soon as possible and treat for shock until medical aid arrives.

DISPLACED CARTILAGE. See DISLOCATION OF A CARTILAGE.

DRESSINGS. A dressing is any covering applied to a wound or other injury.

Dry. This is used to prevent dirt and disease germs entering a wound. The dressing of choice is a piece of sterilized gauze. If using lint, apply the hard side next to the wound. Any scrupulously clean piece of soft, uncoloured material may be improvised for a dressing.

Wet. (1) *A cold compress* consists of a piece of gauze or other material which is applied to the affected part after it has been well wrung out of cold water. It must be frequently renewed to keep it cold and moist. A cold wet dressing or compress is used to ease pain, reduce swelling and to control internal haemorrhage.

(2) *A hot compress* is a hot, wet dressing prepared by soaking a piece of lint or flannel in very hot water and then wringing it well out. It is applied for the relief of pain. It is usual to cover this dressing with a piece of oiled silk or other waterproof material in order that the damp heat may be retained as long as possible.

All dressings are covered with cotton-wool before being bandaged in position.

DROWNING. This condition results in obstruction of the air passages as a result of the water inhaled into the lungs. The lack of fresh air produces the condition of *asphyxia* with subsequent unconsciousness.

Treatment consists in the immediate application of artificial respiration. It is important to remember in all cases of drowning accidents to remove any weeds, dentures, stones or other foreign bodies which may have got into the mouth, before commencing artificial respiration. Unless otherwise indicated, Schafer's method is the one of choice. Where, however, a fractured limb is suspected, Sylvester's method may be used, but it must be remembered that if this method is adopted, unless the tongue is held out during the operation, the patient is liable to choke. To minimize shock while artificial respiration is being performed, some bystander should be instructed to remove the wet clothing as far as is expedient and to wrap the patient in dry blankets. See also ASPHYXIA and ARTIFICIAL RESPIRATION.

EAR, BLEEDING FROM. Blood escaping from the ear passage is strongly suggestive of a fracture of the base of the skull.

Treatment: Do *not* attempt to plug the ear. Apply a dry dressing over the outside of the ear and fix in position with a lightly applied bandage.

Foreign body lodged in. Never attempt to syringe or probe the ear. If the history suggests the presence of an insect, it can be floated out by filling the ear with warm olive or almond oil. If this fails to remove the foreign body, make no direct attempt to dislodge it, as serious consequences may result. Take the patient to a doctor as soon as possible. In the case of a child who cannot be induced to keep its fingers from the ear, it is a wise procedure to tie the child's hands down to prevent him or her pushing the foreign body farther down into the ear channel.

ELBOW JOINT. Bandage for. See BANDAGES.

Dislocation of. See DISLOCATION.

Fracture involving. Owing to the great amount of swelling attending this injury it is difficult to make a clear-cut diagnosis.

Take two splints or flat pieces of wood, one reaching from the armpit to just below the elbow, the other long enough to reach from just beyond the elbow to the finger-tips. Tie the two splints together to form a right-angle. (See Fig. 29.) Apply the right-angled

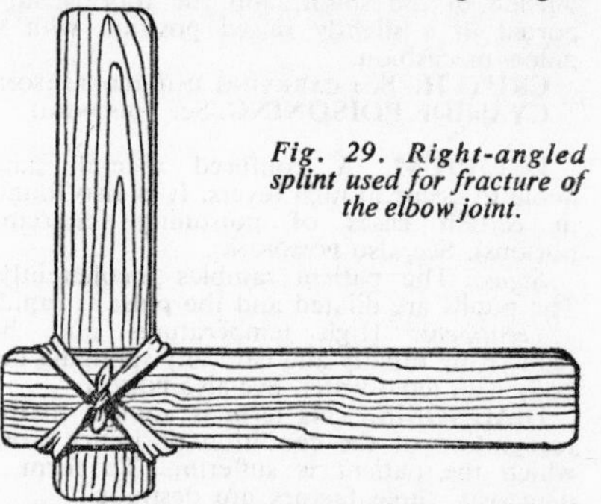

Fig. 29. Right-angled splint used for fracture of the elbow joint.

splint, well padded, on the side that is least injured of the bent limb. Secure the splint in position by three bandages: round the arm, round the forearm and a figure of eight round the hand and wrist. Put the arm up in a small arm-sling. Cold compresses may be applied to reduce the swelling and ease pain.

ELECTRIC SHOCK. Immediately switch off the current supplying the medium from which the shock is being sustained. If this is not possible, strict precautions must be observed by the person rendering first-aid, to avoid serious, or possibly fatal, personal injury from the current. He should protect himself by standing on dry, non-conducting material, such as linoleum or india-rubber or other non-metallic substance. His hands should be protected by rubber gloves, a tobacco pouch, mackintosh or other insulating material. If no means of protection are available, the patient may be dragged off the electric supply (e.g., live rail or dynamo) by means of a loop of dry rope or a walking stick with a curved handle. An umbrella must *not* be used, on account of the metal ribs, which conduct electricity. Care must be taken to avoid any contact with damp material, the patient's armpits, or wet clothing. The patient's skin must not be touched with the bare hands, nor should his boots or shoes be handled.

In electric shock breathing is suspended and artificial respiration must be started at once and kept up until natural breathing is restored. This restoration of breathing may take a long time, and it is usual for the artificial respiration to be undertaken in relays by several persons. No relaxation is permissible if breathing is to be restored. Shock is severe and burns are frequently present. See also SHOCK and BURNS.

EMETIC. This is any substance which, when taken internally, tends to induce vomiting. The usual emetics used domestically are: (1) mustard powder, one tablespoonful in a tumblerful ($\frac{1}{2}$ pint) of lukewarm water; (2) salt, two tablespoonfuls in a tumblerful of lukewarm water.

An emetic is administered in cases of non-corrosive poisoning in order to make the patient vomit and so try to get rid of the poison he has swallowed. An emetic must *not* be given if the poison is of a corrosive nature, that is, when the patient's mouth and lips are burned. See also POISONING.

EPILEPSY. This disease occurs in persons of any age, but is most frequent in young adults. It is associated with fits.

Signs: The patient falls to the ground, sometimes with a scream. The face is flushed at first and then becomes livid. There is frequently frothing at the mouth and, almost invariably, biting of the tongue. Convulsions occur, affecting the whole of the body and limbs, as a result of which the patient may injure himself or others, through his violent movements. He frequently wets or dirties himself.

Treatment: Pull the patient away from any source of danger, such as a fireplace or an electric conductor and move all light furniture out of the way. Wrap a pencil, cork, or similar hard object in a clean handkerchief and introduce it between his teeth to prevent him biting his tongue. No matter how violent the patient may become, do not forcibly restrain his threshing legs and arms, but guide them in such manner that he does not damage himself or any bystanders.

Adopt the general rules for treatment of insensibility as far as they are applicable. See also INSENSIBILITY.

EXAMINATION OF A PATIENT. The following rules are intended to guide the beginner in acquiring a regular and orderly method of approaching and examining a patient so that speed and efficiency may be combined in diagnosis and treatment.

The approach: Go up to the patient speedily, noting the surroundings for possible sources of danger and clues to diagnosis, always taking first-aid material with you, if it is available. Speak encouragingly to the patient as you approach, warning him to lie still. Detain anyone who may afford information or be of assistance to you. Control any crowd present, if the case is out-of-doors, and see that the patient is allowed plenty of fresh air. Obtain the history of the accident from the patient and bystanders, the position of the pain and any other symptoms.

The examination: If you consider the information given you by your patient or bystanders to be unreliable, then depend entirely upon your own powers of observation. The following routine examination should be performed:

(1) Note if severe haemorrhage is present.

(2) Note if breathing is present and, if so, the character of the breathing—slow or quick, deep or shallow or stertorous (snoring). Smell the breath, but do not assume drunkenness merely because the breath smells of alcohol. The patient may have been given an alcoholic stimulant. In any case, acute alcoholic poisoning is a serious condition.

(3) Feel the patient's pulse by placing the first three fingers on the wrist about one inch above the ball of the thumb and half an inch from the outer (thumb) side of the wrist. Note whether the pulse is slow, quick, feeble, strong or absent altogether. If absent, place the hand over the left breast to find out if the heart is beating. The *apex* beat can be felt in the normal subject about three-quarters of an inch below and internal to the left nipple.

(4) Examine the head, noting the colour of the face and if there is any bleeding from the nose, ears, eyes or mouth. Note if the lips are burnt (corrosive poisoning). Note the presence of any foreign bodies. Examine the eyes and note if the pupils are equal, dilated or minutely contracted. Note if they react to light.

(5) Examine the body and limbs for fractures, dislocations or wounds. Compare the two sides of the body (arms and legs) for limpness. Note if the skin is hot or cold, dry or moist.

If, however, the patient is conscious and his information appears to be reliable, the above examination may be considerably abridged. While examining a patient, uncover him as little as possible, as exposure increases shock.

EXTENSION OF A BROKEN LIMB. See FRACTURES.

EYE. Removal of foreign body. Instruct the patient not to rub the eye. In the case of a child, tie its hands down. First pull down the lower eyelid (Fig. 30), when the foreign body, if seen, can be removed with a camel-hair

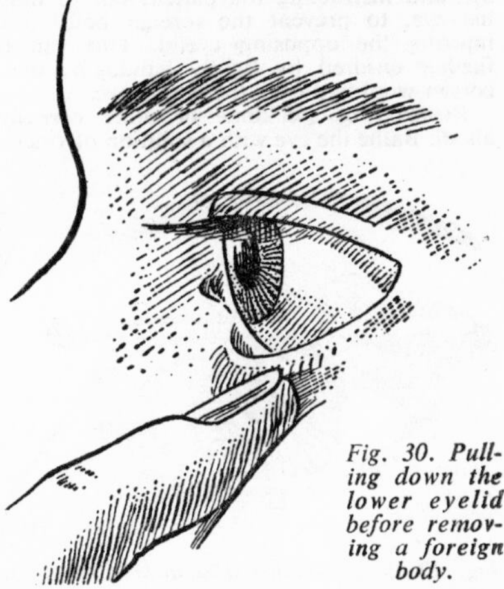

*Fig. 30. **Pulling down the lower eyelid before removing a foreign body.***

brush or the moistened corner of a clean handkerchief.

If the foreign body is beneath the upper eyelid, with the finger and thumb lift the lid forward and push up the lower lid beneath it (Fig. 31). Then instruct the patient to open his eye. The lashes of the lower lid sweep

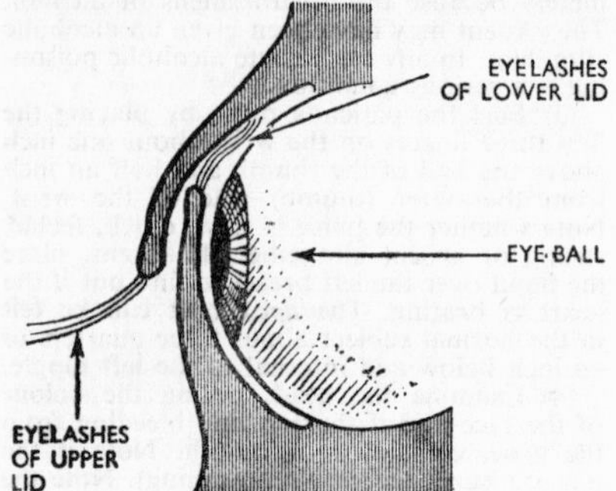

Fig. 31. ***One method of removing a foreign body from beneath the upper eyelid.***

down the inner surface of the upper and so dislodge the foreign body. If the first attempt is unsuccessful, repeat the manoeuvre several times if necessary. If still unsuccessful and no doctor is available, seat the patient facing the light and stand behind him with his head leaning back on your chest. Place a match-stick on the upper lid just above the edge, pressing it backwards. Evert the eyelid by pulling the lashes over the stick (Fig. 32). Then, having located the foreign body, remove it as described above.

When a foreign body is embedded and fixed in the eyeball, as in the case of a "steel," it can be safely removed only by a doctor. The first-aid treatment, pending the arrival of the doctor, consists in dropping a few drops of castor oil or medicinal paraffin into the eye and instructing the patient not to move his eye, to prevent the foreign body from injuring the opposing eyelid. This can be further ensured by lightly bandaging on a cotton-wool pad over the whole eye.

Removal of quicklime or other corrosive alkali. Bathe the eye with a solution of vinegar and water (one part in four) and treat as for foreign body embedded in the eyeball.

Removal of vitriol or other corrosive acid. Bathe the eye with a solution of baking soda (one dessertspoonful to the pint of water) and proceed as above.

In the case of *any* corrosive substance in the eye, when the neutralizing agents suggested are not immediately available, the eye should be freely washed out with cold water.

FAINTING (SYNCOPE). This is due to the sudden slackening in the blood supply to the brain. It may be caused by a variety of conditions, such as haemorrhage, hunger, extreme fatigue, enclosure in a stuffy atmosphere, fear or sudden shock.

Signs: The patient feels giddy and tends to fall to the ground. The breathing is quick and irregular, pulse rapid and weak, face is pale and the skin cold and clammy.

Treatment: Sprinkle the face with hot and cold water alternately. Apply friction to the limbs in a direction towards the heart and apply warmth over the pit of the stomach and the heart. Smelling salts may be used with care, having first smelt their strength before applying them to the patient's nostrils. Treat the cause of the faint, if known, e.g., external or internal haemorrhage, and adopt the general rules for the treatment of insensibility as far as they are applicable. See also HAEMORRHAGE and INSENSIBILITY. If hunger has induced the faint, feed sparingly to begin with. Leave the patient lying flat, as the blood supply to the brain is best that way. Attempting to make him sit up may only cause him to faint again.

FEMUR. See THIGH-BONE.

FIBULA. The outermost of the two leg bones. See LEG, FRACTURE OF.

FINGERS. Bleeding from. See HAEMORRHAGE.
Dislocation of. See DISLOCATION.
Fractures of. See CRUSHED HAND.

FIRST-AID. The practice of first-aid is strictly limited to the assistance required at the time of the emergency with such material as is available. At no time should the first-aider take the place of the doctor, who should be sent for immediately. See also INTRODUCTION (page 129).

FITS. These may be genuine or assumed (as in the case of hysteria). Genuine fits are associated with a period of unconsciousness

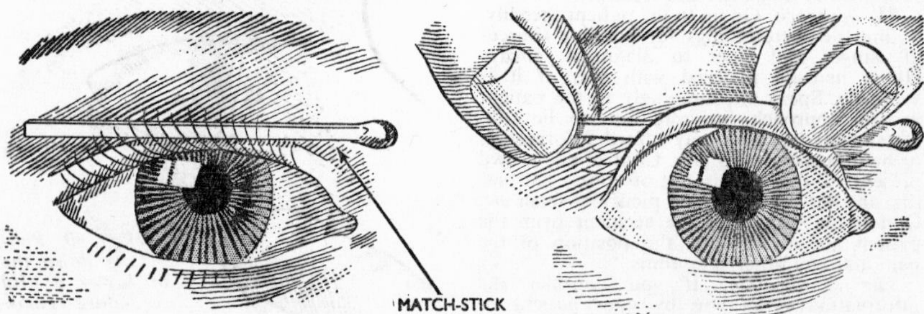

Fig. 32 Using a match-stick to raise the upper eyelid when the method shown in Fig. 31 has failed.

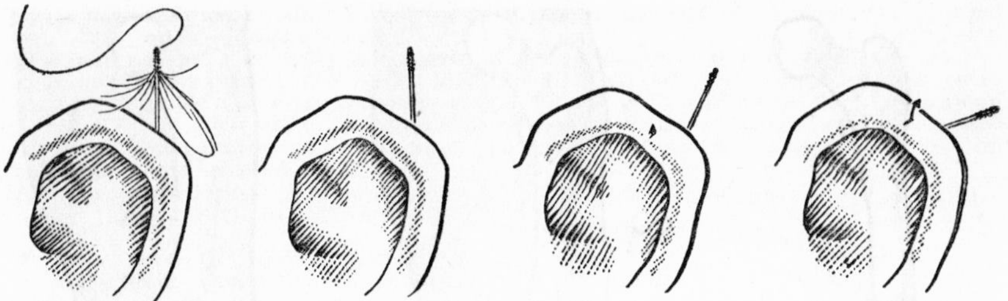

Fig. 33. Removing a fish-hook from the ear: (left to right) *the hook embedded; line and feathers removed and hook sterilized: point pressed through forming new opening; barb completely through.*

and are caused by a disordered functioning of the heart (fainting fits) or nervous system (apoplexy, epilepsy, etc.). See also APOPLEXY, EPILEPSY and FAINTING.

FISH-HOOK EMBEDDED IN THE SKIN. If the hook is a large one, immobilize the limb in a sling or splints and take the patient to a doctor at once.

If the hook is small, do not attempt to withdraw it, as the barb will catch in the tissues and produce a lacerated wound. Instead, paint the hook and the surrounding skin with an antiseptic solution and then force the point outwards *through* the skin until the barb is clear, when it should be cut off with a pair of pliers, and the remainder of the hook withdrawn from the other side (Fig. 33). Apply a dressing to the wound.

FOOD POISONING. See POISONING.

FOOT. Bandage for. See BANDAGES.

Bleeding from. See HAEMORRHAGE.

Crushed. See CRUSHED FOOT.

FOREARM. Bleeding from. See HAEMORRHAGE

Fractures of. See ARM BONES, FRACTURE OF.

FOREHEAD. Bandage for. See BANDAGES.

Bleeding from. See HAEMORRHAGE.

FOREIGN BODIES. In ear, eye and nose. See EAR, EYE and NOSE.

In stomach. In the case of objects accidentally swallowed, give nothing by the mouth but take the patient to a doctor immediately. Use transport if possible, particularly in the case of swallowed pins, needles, or other sharp objects. Smooth and rounded objects need not necessarily cause alarm.

In throat. To dislodge the obstruction, bend the patient's head and shoulders forward and smack him hard on the back between the shoulder-blades. If this is unsuccessful, pass two fingers down to the back of the patient's throat and induce vomiting. In the case of an infant or small child, hold the patient upside down by the feet and smack the back between the shoulder-blades. If unsuccessful, induce vomiting as above.

In a wound these should be removed only if they are clearly seen and easily got at; otherwise they should be left alone. See also HAEMORRHAGE.

FOUR-HANDED SEAT. See CARRYING INJURED PERSON.

FRACTURES. A fracture is the term applied when a bone is broken. It is not in the province of first-aid to "set" a fracture, but to keep the broken ends immobilized so that they cannot produce further injury to the surrounding tissues. This is done, in the case of the limbs, by the application of well-padded splints. See also SPLINTS. Where splints are not obtainable, the uninjured limb may sometimes be used as a splint against which to fix the broken limb. In examining a suspected fracture, no more clothing is removed than is absolutely necessary on account of the fact that exposure increases shock. The correct method of removing clothing has been described in the INTRODUCTION.

Extension. Before applying a splint, it is necessary to place the fractured limb very carefully in as natural a position as possible. No force must be used. In the case of the leg and thigh, if there is shortening of the limb, kneel down behind the sole of the foot. Cup the heel in the palm of one hand and place the other over the instep and, with a gentle and even movement, pull upon the foot until the limb regains a more normal length (Fig. 34). This procedure is known as *extension.* Having done this, the limb must

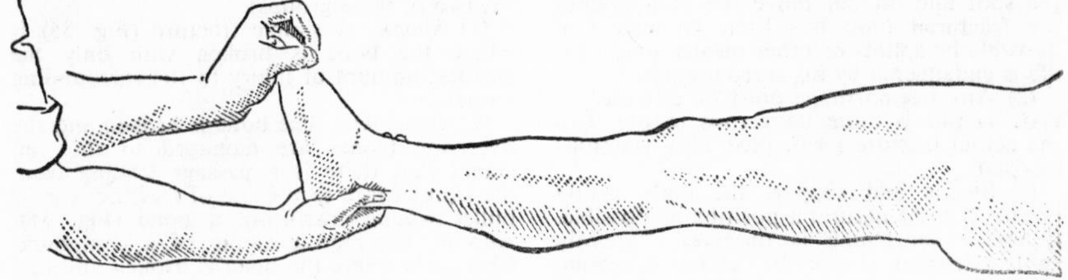

Fig. 34. Method of applying extension to a fractured thigh-bone before splinting.

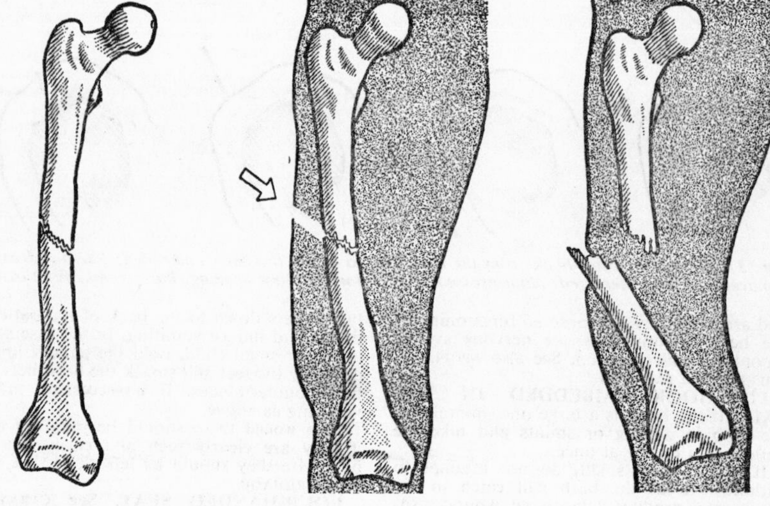

Fig. 35. (Left) *a simple fracture;* (centre and right) *compound fractures. In the centre there is a wound, indicated by the arrow, leading to the fracture; on the right the fractured bone protrudes.*

not be let go until it is secured by splints. It is usual to ask a bystander to slip his or her hands over those of the first-aider and to retain the extension, while the first-aider applies the splint or splints.

Signs and *symptoms* (seven in number):

(1) Pain at or near to the site of the fracture.

(2) Loss of power in the fractured limb.

(3) Swelling round about the fracture.

(4) Deformity of the fractured limb. Frequently the contraction of the muscles causes the broken ends of the bone to override one another, producing a shortening of the limb.

(5) Irregularity of the outline of the bone.

(6) Unnatural movement. This movement can be felt at the seat of fracture, if the patient moves or flinches.

(7) Crepitus. This is the name given to the bony grating felt or heard when the broken ends move against each other.

It is specially to be emphasized that in no circumstances should the first-aider *attempt to elicit* the last two signs (unnatural movement and crepitus), but it may be stated that, almost invariably, the patient produces them by his own restlessness.

Treatment: (1) Attend to the fracture on the spot and do not move the patient until the fractured limb has been rendered immovable by splints or other means, unless his life is endangered by his surroundings.

(2) Any haemorrhage must be attended to first, as this is more dangerous to life than the actual fracture itself. (See also HAEMORRHAGE.)

(3) Steady and support the limb, gently placing it in as natural a position as possible. If undue shortening is observed, carefully apply extension, as described above. *Extension must never be attempted in the case of a compound fracture when the bone is protruding, nor when a complicated or comminuted fracture (see below) is suspected.*

(4) The proper application of splints, bandages and slings where they are indicated.

Bandages must be applied firmly for security, but not so tightly as to arrest the circulating blood in the limb. In securing a limb to a splint or splints the narrow bandage is used, passing it twice round the limb and securing it with a reef-knot on the outer splint. On the trunk of the body the broad bandage is used, passing it once round the body and securing it on the uninjured side either by a reef-knot or by several safety-pins. For securing splints adhesive plaster may be used, if bandages are not available. Of the bandages applied near a fracture the upper one should be secured first. If an improvised round splint, such as a broom-handle or a policeman's truncheon, is being used, an extra turn of the bandage round the splint is required to secure it in position.

Where there is an element of doubt (for instance, where excessive swelling masks the other signs), always treat as a fracture.

Varieties of. Fractures are classified into six types. All fractures fall into one or, it may be, two of these groups:

(1) *Simple.* A simple fracture (Fig. 35) is where the bone is broken with only the smallest amount of injury to the surrounding tissues.

(2) *Compound.* The bone is broken and the overlying tissues are damaged to such an extent that there is a passage leading from the skin surface to the site of fracture, e.g., a bullet wound fracturing a bone (Fig. 35). Another common example of a compound fracture is where the bone is broken and one or both of the fractured ends protrude through the skin surface (Fig. 35). The chief danger

of this fracture is the complication of sepsis (suppuration) through germs obtaining access to the seat of fracture.

(3) *Complicated.* The bone is broken and there is also some injury to an internal organ

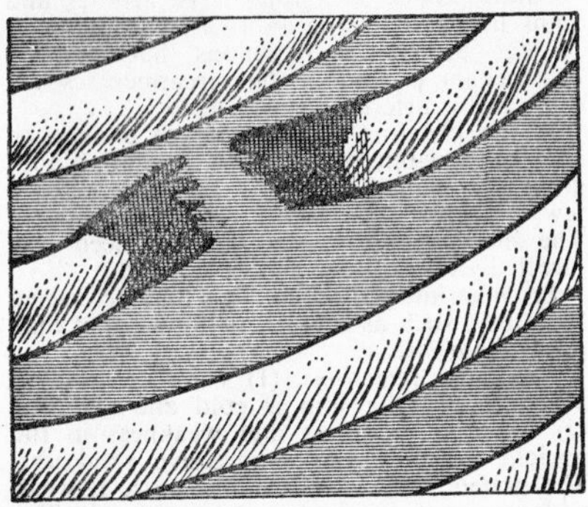

Fig. 36. Complicated fracture; a broken rib has been bent, injuring the lung beneath.

or structure, e.g., the brain, lung (Fig. 36), or some important blood-vessel or nerve.

(4) *Comminuted.* The bone is broken into more than two fragments (Fig. 37).

(5) *Greenstick.* Strictly speaking, this is not a fracture but a bending of the bone. It occurs in children before the bones are fully ossified, that is to say, while the bony tissue is still unformed from the cartilage or gristle of early life. What bone is present may split and the remainder—the cartilage—bends (Fig. 37).

(6) *Impacted.* Here the bone is broken and the broken ends (fragments) are driven into one another (Fig. 37). In the case of greenstick and impacted fractures, no crepitus (bony grating) is heard, as there are no loose fragments.

FRICTION BURNS. These constitute the so-called "brush-burns" produced by friction, e.g., scraping of the skin against a brick wall, contact with a revolving wheel, sliding down a rope, etc. Treat as a burn. See BURNS.

FROST BITE. See BITES.

FUNGI, POISONING BY. See POISONING.

GAS, POISONING BY. See POISONING.

GERMS. See ANTISEPTICS.

GREENSTICK FRACTURE. See FRACTURES.

GRISTLE. See JOINTS.

GUMS, BLEEDING FROM. When this accompanies brushing of the teeth or "sucking" the teeth, it is usually due to a germ infection of the gums and a dentist should be consulted. Where, however, the bleeding follows upon a direct injury, the bleeding can usually be controlled by direct digital pressure. See HAEMORRHAGE.

HAEMORRHAGE (BLEEDING). This may be *arterial*, *venous*, *capillary*, or a combination of any of these three types.

Arterial. The blood from an artery is bright red, as it is taking oxygen to the tissues. It spurts from the side of the wound nearest the heart and fountains out in jets corresponding to the heart-beats.

Treatment: The objects of first-aid treatment are to stop the bleeding, lessen shock and prevent contamination or sepsis.

(1) Place the patient in the most suitable position commensurate with the fact that the bleeding will be less in a sitting position and still less in the supine position, corresponding to the slowing down of the heart's action in these positions.

(2) Except in the case of a fractured limb, raise the bleeding part.

(3) Expose the wound sufficiently to deal with it, bearing in mind that exposure increases shock. Apply pressure with the thumb or fingers directly on the bleeding point, having a piece of sterile gauze or other clean material between the fingers and the wound to prevent contamination by the fingers.

If a fracture or an immovable foreign body (see FOREIGN BODIES) is suspected below the bleeding point, avoid the direct pressure described above and apply *indirect pressure*, that is, pressure as near the wound as possible on the heart side, where the artery can be pressed against underlying bone. This is known as a *pressure point* (see HAEMORRHAGE FROM SPECIAL REGIONS).

(4) As soon as practicable, substitute for digital pressure a pad of sterile gauze or other clean material and bandage it firmly in position. If blood soaks through the pad, do not remove it but apply other pads on top, securing them firmly in position.

(5) Where a broken bone or foreign body is suspected directly beneath the bleeding point, apply

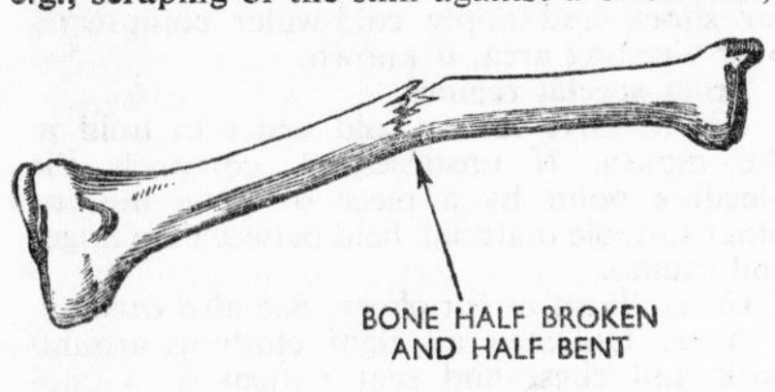

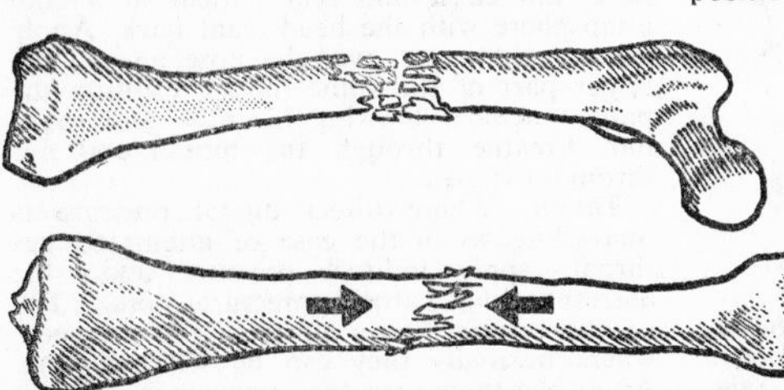

Fig. 37. Three further types of fracture: greenstick (top); *comminuted* (centre); *impacted* (bottom). *The arrows indicate the impact driving the fractured ends of the bone together.*

pads all round the point of haemorrhage to such a height as will allow complete covering of the wound. Secure in position with a firm bandage.

(6) If the above methods fail to control the bleeding, then apply a tight bandage round the limb as near to the wound as possible and on the heart side. It is preferable to use a piece of rubber tubing (see TOURNIQUET). At the end of every fifteen to twenty minutes the bandage or tubing should be relaxed and then re-tightened if the bleeding has not ceased, for there is a great risk of causing gangrene by cutting off the blood for too long. This method is used in the case of an amputated limb.

(7) Keep the affected part at rest, using a sling for the upper limb and, if necessary, splints for the lower limb.

(8) When the bleeding has stopped, keep the patient warm, allay mental anxiety and, except in the case of internal haemorrhages, give plenty of fluids, preferably warm, sweetened tea.

Where it is impossible to apply direct pressure to stop bleeding successfully, as in the case of wounds of the throat and in the uppermost parts of the arm and leg, special pressure points are indicated for the application of indirect pressure.

Capillary. This bleeding, which is from the very minute blood-vessels, is such as occurs when the outer skin is grazed. The blood is red in colour and usually oozes out from all parts of the wound.

Capillary haemorrhage is usually easily controlled by firm pressure with a small gauze pad and bandage.

Venous. Blood from a vein is dark red. It flows from the side of the wound farthest from the heart and issues in a steady continuous stream.

Venous haemorrhage is controlled by direct digital pressure, which is substituted, as soon as practicable, by a pad and bandage as in the treatment of arterial haemorrhage. If necessary, a bandage may be applied close to the wound *on the opposite side to the heart.* Indirect pressure is not employed in the arrest of venous haemorrhage.

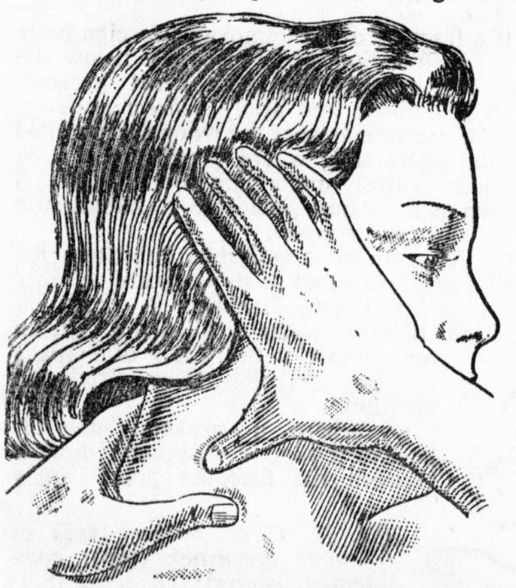

Fig. 38. Both hands are required to stop bleeding from a cut throat. The lower thumb blocks the carotid artery, the other the jugular vein.

Mixed. Since as a rule, large arteries and veins lie close to one another, it is common to get arterial and venous haemorrhage together in a wound. The treatment is the same as for arterial haemorrhage.

If the bleeding point (arterial) cannot be seen on account of the brisk flow of blood, grasp the wound tightly in the fingers for a few moments, then slowly relax the pressure. The bleeding point will then be seen and direct digital pressure can be applied.

From an internal organ. This may be caused by injury, such as a crush or blow, or it may result from disease.

Signs and *symptoms:* (1) The face and lips are pale and the skin is cold and clammy. (2) There is giddiness and weakness in the upright position and progressive weakness. The patient may faint. (3) The pulse is weak and may not be felt at the wrist. (4) The breathing is quick and laboured and accompanied by yawning. The patient exhibits air hunger, i.e., he tosses about, tugging at his collar and calls for air. (5) Finally the patient sinks into unconsciousness.

Internal haemorrhage may occur from the:

Bladder. This is commonly a complication of fracture of the pelvis. There is inability to make water, or if it is passed it is tinged with blood.

Kidneys. Blood escapes with the urine and commonly there is pain and swelling over the injured kidney.

Liver, pancreas (sweetbread), spleen or intestines. There is pain in the abdomen, which is held rigid and may be distended.

Lungs. This is a common complication of fracture of the ribs. The blood is coughed up and is bright red and frothing, due to the presence of oxygen.

Stomach. The blood is vomited up and frequently has a coffee-grounds appearance.

Treatment: Give nothing by mouth. Treat for shock and apply cold-water compresses over bleeding area, if known.

From special regions.

Cheek. Give ice or cold water to hold in the mouth. If unsuccessful, compress the bleeding point by a piece of clean lint, or other suitable material, held between the finger and thumb.

Gums. Treat as for cheek. See also GUMS.

Nose. Unfasten all tight clothing around neck and chest and seat patient in a cool atmosphere with the head leant back. Apply ice or cold water over the nose and to the upper part of the spine (neck). Caution the patient against blowing his nose and make him breathe through the mouth and not through the nose.

Throat. Where direct digital pressure is unavailing, as in the case of attempted cut throat, apply indirect pressure upon the corresponding carotid pressure point. The carotid arteries lie on either side of the neck, where normally they can be felt pulsating. Apply the thumb on the artery as in Fig. 38.

Fig. 39. Pressure applied to the subclavian artery to stop bleeding in the upper arm.

pressing the artery against the spinal column behind it, taking care to avoid the windpipe. It is invariably necessary to apply pressure with the other thumb directly above the wound to arrest the bleeding from (1) the large vein (jugular vein) which runs alongside the artery and which is usually wounded at the same time, and also from (2), the upper end of the carotid artery, from which the back-flow of blood is usually very considerable. The digital pressure must be kept up, by relays of assistants if necessary, until the arrival of the doctor.

Tongue. Treat as for cheek.

Tooth socket. Give ice or cold water to hold in the mouth. If this does not stop the haemorrhage, sit the patient in a good light with the head back and the mouth wide open. Plug the tooth socket firmly with a piece of cotton-wool, leaving a good-sized piece protruding from the socket. Over this place a cork or small roller bandage and instruct the patient to bite down hard on it.

Upper arm. In arterial bleeding high up in the upper limb in the neighbourhood of the armpit, direct pressure may be found impossible. In such cases resort must be made to indirect pressure. Bare the neck and upper chest. Place the patient's arm against his body and incline his head towards the injured side. It will be found that a hollow appears behind the collar-bone (the so-called "salt-cellar"). Standing slightly behind the patient, place the thumb in the centre of this hollow and press downwards (Fig. 39). The pulsation of the subclavian artery will be felt as it lies on top of the first rib. Press the thumb down so as to compress the artery against the rib and so shut it off. This pressure must be maintained by relays of assistants if necessary, until the arrival of medical aid.

Lower arm. Digital pressure may be applied to the brachial artery, pressing it against the humerus. Alternatively, a pad and bandage beneath the armpit may be used on the axillary pressure point.

To find the brachial artery pressure point, grasp the arm from behind at about its centre, and press the fingers in deeply until the pulsation of the artery is felt; then compress it against the bone (humerus) as in Fig. **40**. If

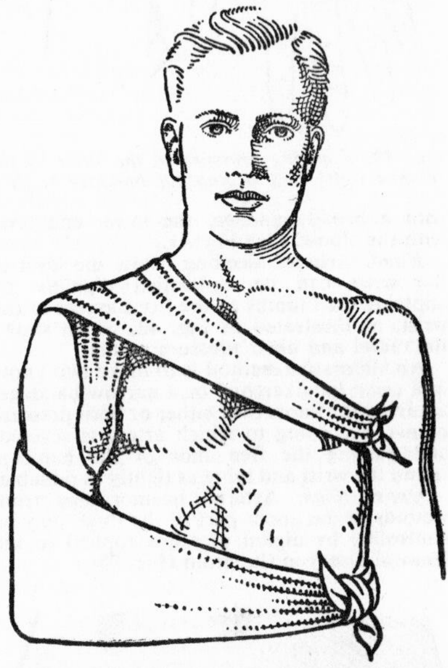

Fig. 41. A pad and two bandages can be used to put pressure on the artery in the armpit.

this fails, a firm pad may be put into the hollow of the elbow-joint and the elbow kept tightly flexed.

To apply pressure to the axillary artery fill the armpit with a firm pad, such as a folded narrow bandage, then place the middle of a narrow bandage over the pad. Cross the ends firmly over the shoulder of the affected side and tie under the armpit on the sound side. Bend the forearm and secure it to the body

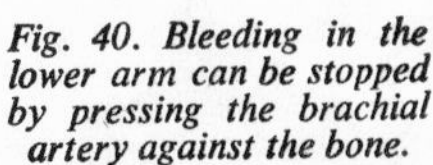

Fig. 40. Bleeding in the lower arm can be stopped by pressing the brachial artery against the bone.

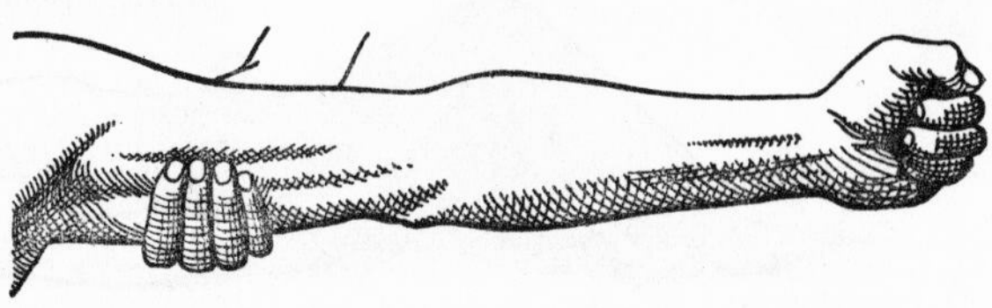

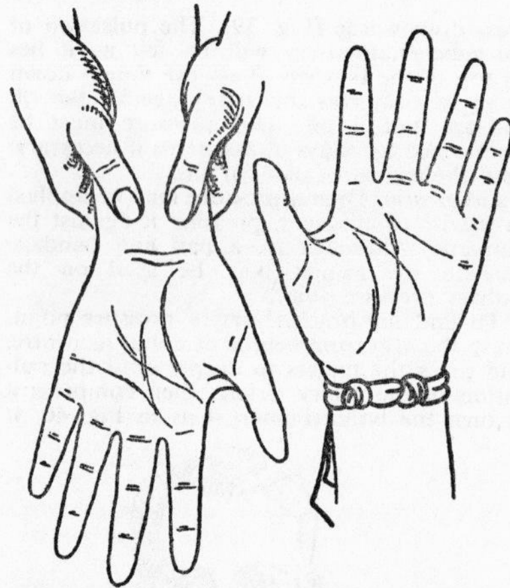

Fig. 42. Applying pressure to the wrist by the thumbs (left) *and a knotted bandage* (right).

with a broad bandage, the lower end level with the elbow. (See Fig. 41.)

Hand. Arterial bleeding below the level of the wrist can be controlled digitally by applying the thumbs to the front aspect of the wrist, as illustrated in Fig. 42, which shows the radial and ulnar pressure points.

An alternative method is to make two knots in a clean handkerchief or a narrow bandage, applying the knots over either or both pressure points, according to which artery is severed, and passing the free ends of the bandage round the wrist and tying as tightly as possible.

Upper thigh. Arterial haemorrhage from wounds in the upper part of the thigh may be controlled by digital pressure applied to the femoral artery in the groin (Fig. 43).

Lay the patient on his back and kneel down beside him facing his head. Bend back the knee and hip on the injured side. This produces a fold in the clothing at the groin (Fig. 43). Place the thumbs one on top of the other at the centre of this fold and press down firmly, compressing the femoral artery against the edge of the pelvis. This pressure must be maintained by relays of assistants until the arrival of medical aid.

Leg. Apply a tourniquet to the femoral artery in the thigh, by placing a large firm pad over the inner side of the thigh, just below the groin. Place the centre of a narrow bandage, preferably of rubber or rubber tubing, over the pad and tie a half reef-knot on the outer side of the thigh. On this lay a stout piece of stick or a metal rod and secure it to the bandage with a full reef-knot. Twist the rod round and so tighten the bandage until the artery is compressed against the bone (femur). Do not neglect to loosen, without removing, the tourniquet every fifteen minutes and, if bleeding recurs, re-tighten, or gangrene of the limb may result. (See Fig. 52.)

HAND. Bandage. See BANDAGES.

Fractures of. See CRUSHED HAND.

Seats. See CARRYING INJURED PERSON.

HEAT CRAMPS arise from lack of salt. When a person has been sweating profusely, as by great exercise in hot weather, they lose much salt in the sweat, and may then suffer from cramp. This is quickly relieved by giving slightly salted water (a teaspoonful to a pint) to drink.

HEATSTROKE AND SUNSTROKE. These produce more or less the same symptoms and the treatment is the same for both conditions. Sunstroke may result from the continued exposure to the sun's rays in very hot weather. Heatstroke is the result of confinement in an abnormally hot atmosphere. The condition produced is the result of a congestion of the brain and spinal cord.

Signs and symptoms: A flushed face, difficult breathing, a rapid, bounding pulse with sickness, giddiness and thirst. The skin is dry and burning and a high temperature with stertorous (snoring) breathing and unconsciousness may ensue.

Treatment: The patient is removed into a cool atmosphere and stripped to the waist. The body is then sponged continuously with cold water, and ice-bags or cold compresses are applied to the head and spine until the acute symptoms abate. At the same time, the patient should be fanned vigorously. When consciousness has returned, give one table-

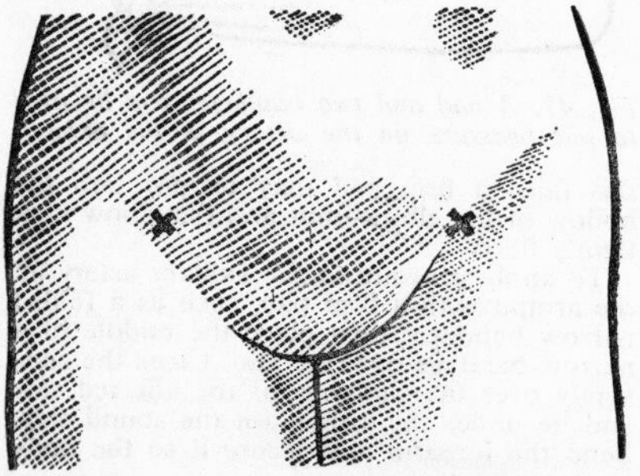

Fig. 43. Bleeding in the thigh is controlled by pressure in the groin (marked X, left*). The point may be found in the fold of the clothing (arrowed* below*) when the knee is raised.*

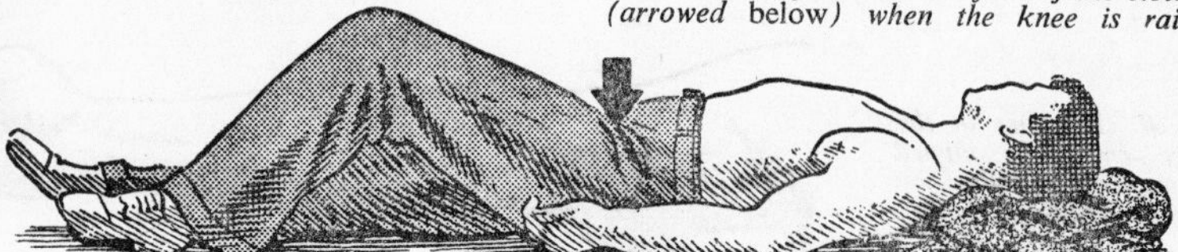

spoonful of Epsom or Glauber salts in a tumblerful of water. Cold drinks may be freely given.

HERNIA OR RUPTURE. This consists of a protrusion of a portion of bowel through the tissues of the abdomen under the skin. It is more common in the male sex, where it occurs in the groin.

Hernia results from lifting or pushing a heavy weight.

Signs and symptoms: Sudden pain and the appearance of a small, circumscribed swelling in the groin. There is a varying degree of shock and sometimes vomiting.

Treatment: Place the patient in a reclining position on his back with the head and shoulders raised and supported by pillows. Bend the knees back and place a pillow underneath them. (See Fig. 44.) Apply a cold compress over the swelling.

HIP. Bandage. See BANDAGES.

Dislocation of. See DISLOCATIONS.

"HOOK-GRIP." See CARRYING INJURED PERSON.

HUMAN CRUTCH. See CARRYING INJURED PERSON.

HUMERUS. The bone of the upper arm.

Fracture of. See ARM BONES.

HYDROPHOBIA. The disease produced in the human being who has been bitten by an animal suffering from rabies. See BITES, ANIMAL.

HYSTERIA (HYSTERICAL FITS). The patient, usually a young woman, suddenly loses control of her emotions as a result of some strong mental excitement. She throws herself on to a couch or chair or adopts some other comfortable position and simulates a fit, clutching at anyone or anything, crying and laughing alternately. Some patients may be violent, kicking and biting, others turn up their eyeballs, grimace and froth at the mouth. Unconsciousness may be assumed, but is never genuine.

Treatment: Avoid any suggestion of sympathy with the patient. Speak firmly and coldly to her and, if advisable, leave her to herself.

INFANTILE CONVULSIONS. These are the common fits of infancy.

Signs: These may vary, but there is usually twitching of the limbs and body. The face is at first pale but later may become livid. There may be squinting, holding of the breath and frothing at the mouth.

Treatment: Usually they pass over before there is time to do much. If, however, they are prolonged, quickly prepare a hot bath. Strip the child naked and, having first tested the heat of the water with the elbow, support the child in the bath so that the child is immersed in the water up to the neck. Apply a cold compress or a sponge lightly wrung out of cold water to the head. Keep the child in the hot bath until the convulsions have ceased or the doctor has arrived.

On removal from the bath, dry the child and wrap it in warm blankets, continuing to keep the head cool. If the convulsions

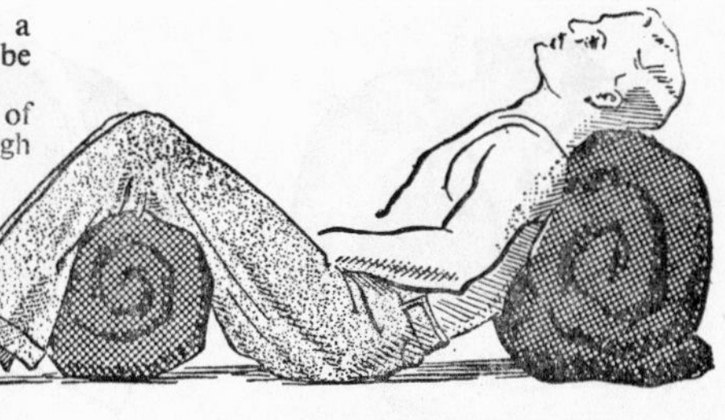

Fig. 44. Position in which to place a patient suffering from hernia or rupture. All strain must be taken off the abdomen.

recur, repeat the treatment described above.

INSECT STINGS. See BITES.

INSENSIBILITY. When caused by interference with the breathing this is called *asphyxia* (see ASPHYXIA).

Insensibility may also occur with the breathing present, either with convulsions as in epilepsy, hysteria and infantile convulsions, or without convulsions as in concussion and compression of the brain, shock, fainting, apoplexy and sunstroke, all of which are dealt with under their appropriate headings.

Loss of consciousness is due to interruption of the action of the brain. Apart from natural sleep, the insensibility may be partial (*stupor*) or complete (*coma*). In stupor it is possible to arouse the patient, but in coma it is impossible. If the upper eyelid is lifted up, the pupil (the central black part) will contract in the light in stupor, but not in coma. In stupor the patient objects to having his eye touched, but not in coma.

General rules for treatment: If breathing is absent or not apparent, perform artificial respiration. If breathing is present, lay the patient on his back with the head turned to one side, and, if his face is pale, keep the head and shoulders low and raise the feet. If the face is flushed undo all tight clothing about the throat, chest and waist, have an abundance of fresh air and, in addition, apply the special treatment advocated for the condition which produced the insensibility. Give nothing whatsoever by mouth to an unconscious patient.

Remove the case to shelter as soon as is expedient, and do not leave the case until he can be placed in responsible hands. On return to consciousness water may be given in sips, and if the pulse is feeble or other signs of shock evident give hot, strong, sweetened tea or coffee, provided there is no suspicion of external or internal haemorrhage. The patient may then be allowed to sleep if he shows the desire except in cases of hypnotic poisoning, a condition generally recognizable by the minutely contracted pupils of the eyes. See POISONING.

INTERNAL ORGAN, HAEMORRHAGE FROM. See HAEMORRHAGE.

INTESTINES (BOWELS). Haemorrhage from. See HAEMORRHAGE, INTERNAL.

Injury to. See ABDOMEN.

IODINE POISONING. See POISONING

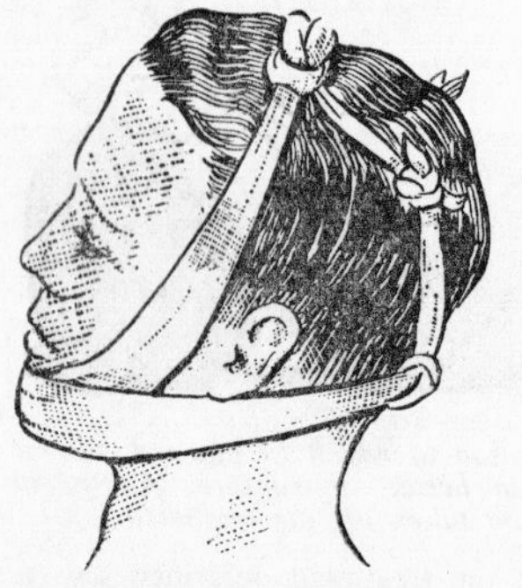

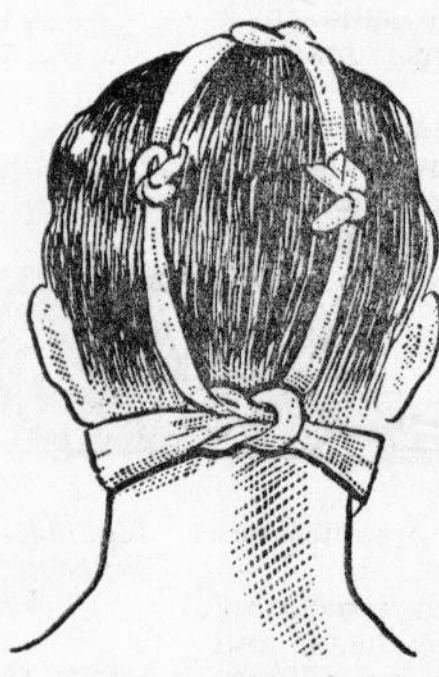

Fig. 45. Supporting bandages for a broken jaw. Two narrow bandages are used with the ends tied at the back of the head to prevent slipping.

JAW, FRACTURE OF LOWER. *Signs and symptoms:* Pain, inability to speak or to move the jaw without pain, irregularity of the teeth, grating of the fragments (crepitus) and bleeding from the gums.

Treatment: With the palm of the hand press the lower jaw gently up against the upper jaw, which can be utilized as a splint. Apply the centre of a narrow bandage under the chin, tying the ends above the forehead. Apply a second narrow bandage with its centre in front of the chin, its upper edge just clearing the lower lip, and tie the ends behind the neck. Tie the corresponding ends of both bandages together (see Fig. 45). If the patient, who has probably swallowed blood, shows an inclination to vomit, remove the bandages from the chin, support the jaw and turn the head to the sound side. Re-apply the bandages when the vomiting has ceased.

JOINTS. Dislocations of. See DISLOCATION.

Displacement of cartilages of. See DISLOCATIONS.

JUGULAR VEIN. This large vein, which lies alongside the carotid artery on either side of the neck, conveys the used blood (venous blood) from the brain back to the right side of the heart and thence to the lungs, where the waste products are got rid of in expiration (breathing out). It is commonly involved in injuries of the carotid artery alongside of it. See also HAEMORRHAGE.

KIDNEYS, HAEMORRHAGE FROM. See HAEMORRHAGE.

KNEE. Bandage. See BANDAGES.

Cap (Patella). A flat oval-shaped bone lying immediately beneath the skin in front of the knee joint which it is designed to protect.

Fracture of. Fractures of the kneecap may be by direct violence, e.g., a kick or blow, in which case they are of a *comminuted* type, or it may be caused by indirect violence, such as in stepping off a bus or kerb, when the fracture is of a simple transverse type. The usual signs of fracture are present.

Treatment: Keep the patient on his back with head and shoulders raised and straighten and support the injured leg. Apply a well-padded splint along the back of the leg, reaching from the lower fold of the buttock to just beyond the heel. Secure the splint to the limb by bandages round the thigh and leg. Apply a double figure-of-eight bandage round ankle, foot and splint, tying it on top of the splint below the foot. Raise the foot on a pillow and apply a narrow bandage with its centre just above the kneecap, cross the ends round the splint and tie in front just below the kneecap. Apply cold compresses over the kneecap to reduce the pain and swelling. (See Fig. 46.)

KNOTS. The ends of a triangular bandage are secured by *reef*-knots. The first "tie" of the knot is made in the ordinary manner, but the second is reversed. (See Fig. 47.) It is customary, having tied the ends, to tuck in any of the bandage left over.

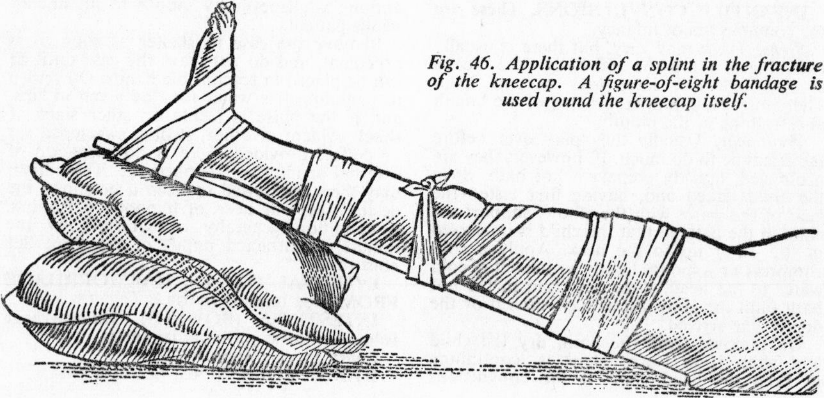

Fig. 46. Application of a splint in the fracture of the kneecap. A figure-of-eight bandage is used round the kneecap itself.

Fig. 47. Reef-knot used in tying the ends of bandages. It will not come undone by pulling.

LACERATED WOUNDS. See WOUNDS.

LEG, FRACTURE OF. Either one or both bones may be broken.

Signs: When both bones (*tibia* and *fibula*) are broken the usual signs of fracture are present. When only one bone is broken, the other acts as a splint and the deformity may not be noticeable. When the *fibula* (the outer bone) is broken just above the ankle it is frequently mistaken for a simple strain.

Treatment: Steady the limb, holding it by the foot and ankle, and draw the foot into its natural position. The foot must be held in this position until the splints are applied. Two splints are required, each extending from just above the knee to just beyond the foot. If only one splint is obtainable, it should be placed on the outer side of the leg. The splints must be well padded. Secure the splints to the limb by five bandages as follows: above and below the fracture, just above the knee, around ankles and feet (as a figure of eight), and a broad bandage round *both* knees as in Fig. 48. If no splint is available, tie the two limbs together by bandages round feet, ankles, knees and thighs. See also FRACTURES and BANDAGES.

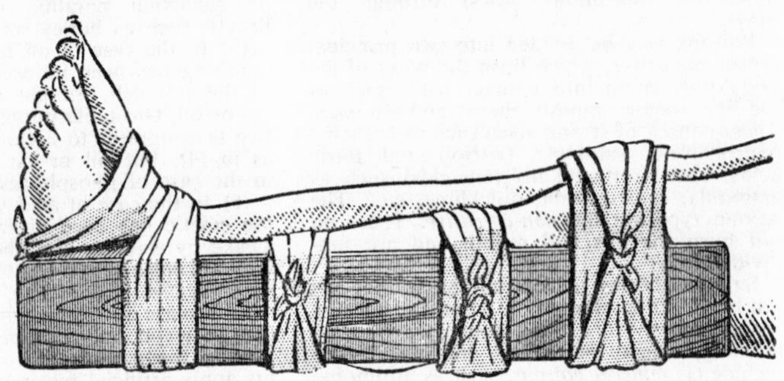

Fig. 48 Splint and bandages for a fractured leg. Both legs are tied to the splint at feet and knees, but not intermediately.

LIGAMENT. A ligament is that part of a muscle which is attached to bone. A rupture of one or more fibres in a ligament constitutes a sprain. See SPRAINS.

LIGHTNING, STROKE BY. See ELECTRIC SHOCK.

LIPS, BLEEDING FROM. Bleeding due to actual injury of the lip or lips must be distinguished from blood issuing from the mouth or from other parts, such as the throat or lungs. See HAEMORRHAGE.

LIVER, HAEMORRHAGE FROM. See HAEMORRHAGE and RIBS, FRACTURE OF.

LOOP BANDAGE. See BANDAGES.

LUNGS, HAEMORRHAGE FROM. See RIBS, FRACTURES OF, and HAEMORRHAGE FROM INTERNAL ORGANS.

MANY-TAILED BANDAGE. See BANDAGES.

METALLIC POISONING. See POISONING.

MUSCLES, INJURIES TO. See SPRAINS and STRAINS.

NERVOUS SYSTEM, AFFECTIONS OF AND INJURIES TO. See INSENSIBILITY.

NOSE. Bleeding from. See HAEMORRHAGE.

Foreign body in. Instruct the patient to breathe through the mouth and not to inhale. If the end of the foreign body is not protruding, do not interfere with it. Take the case to a doctor at once. In the case of a child, tie its hands down if necessary.

OPIUM POISONING. See POISONING.

PANCREAS ("SWEETBREAD"), HAEMORRHAGE FROM. See HAEMORRHAGE.

PARALYSIS. Inability of a part or parts of the body to function as a result of some interference cutting off the nervous supply between the brain or spinal cord and the part affected. See also SPINE, FRACTURES OF, and INSENSIBILITY.

PELVIS. This is the name given to the lower abdomen and the bony girdle formed by the hip bones and the lower spine. The bones are shaped like a basin and form a natural protection for the organs in the lower abdomen (belly).

Fracture of. This fracture is usually the result of a crushing injury and is particularly serious in view of the risk of damage to important organs such as the bladder and lower bowel.

Signs: The patient is unable to stand, nor can he move his legs without difficulty and great pain. Always examine the lower limbs. If the thighs and legs are uninjured it is safe to assume that there is a fracture of the pelvis. The commonest injury to the bladder consists of penetration by a fragment of splintered bone. Where injury to the pelvis has occurred the patient must not be allowed to pass water; if his bladder has been torn urine would then be forced into his tissues.

Treatment: Lay the patient in the position of greatest ease and relief from pain, bending or straightening the lower limbs as he desires.

Apply a broad bandage round the pelvis at hip level, making it sufficiently secure to support the injured parts but not so tight as to press any broken bones inwards. A figure-of-eight bandage is applied round the feet and ankles and a broad bandage round the knees, securing them together.

The patient should only be removed into shelter on a stretcher, if doctor or ambulance are not immediately available.

PERCHLORIDE OF MERCURY POISONING. See POISONING.

PHOSPHORUS POISONING. See POISONING.

PICK-A-BACK TRANSPORT. See CARRYING INJURED PERSON.

PLANT STINGS. Treat as for Insect Bites.

POISONING. A poison is any substance which, if taken into the body in sufficient quantity, is able to destroy life. It may be taken accidentally or intentionally either by the mouth, by injection under the skin or by inhalation (poisonous gases) through the lungs.

Poisons may be divided into two principal types: *corrosives*, which burn the parts of the body they come into contact with, such as the lips, tongue, mouth, throat and stomach. These consist of strong acids such as carbolic, hydrochloric, sulphuric (vitriol) and nitric acids, and strong alkalis (antacids) such as ammonia, caustic soda, quicklime, etc. The second type are the *non-corrosive.* These do not burn the lips and mouth and are subdivided into:

Irritant poisons, which, although they do not burn, cause an intensely irritating, burning sensation in the throat and stomach, producing retching, colicky pains and diarrhoea. They include (1) *mineral poisons,* such as antimony, arsenic, copper, iodine, lead, mercury (quicksilver), phosphorus, etc.; (2) *food poisoning,* due to decomposing food; (3) *poisonous plants,* including some berries and fungi.

Hypnotic poisons, which induce a tendency to sleep, developing sooner or later into coma. These include all preparations of opium, such as morphia, heroin, and also all medicines used for inducing sleep.

Deliriant poisons, which produce delirium and finally coma, such as alcohol, belladonna, chloroform and stramonium.

Convulsant poisons, which produce convulsions (fits), such as prussic acid, cyanide of potassium and strychnine. These are very rapid in their action. The patient's features become livid and the fits may follow one another in quick sequence. Between the convulsions the patient is in a state of profound collapse.

General Rules for Treatment:

(1) Send immediately for a doctor, stating briefly such information as you possess, mentioning whether the lips are burned and naming the poison if known.

(2) If breathing is failing, commence artificial respiration at once.

(3) If the lips and mouth are burned *do not give an emetic.* Give an *antidote,* that is, something that will neutralize the corrosive poison. (*a*) If the poison is known to be an *acid,* immediately give one of the following alkalis (antacids): lime-water in large quantities, or a tablespoonful of magnesia or chalk in about half a pint of water. Repeat frequently. (*b*) If the poison is known to be an *alkali,* immediately give one of the following acids: vinegar, lemon or lime-juice, in either case diluted with an equal quantity of water. Repeat frequently. (*c*) If these remedies are not available, or if it is not known whether the corrosive poison is an acid or an alkali, give copious draughts of cold water or milk.

If the lips and mouth are *not* burned, *promptly give an emetic.* (See EMETIC.) Repeat the emetic every few minutes until vomiting occurs. If an emetic is not readily available, induce vomiting by putting two fingers down to the back of the throat.

(4) In the case of a *corrosive* poison, after the antidote has been given, apply a hot compress over the front of the neck to reduce swelling of the throat tissues. To relieve the pain, give milk, butter, margarine, olive oil or medicinal paraffin, or else demulcent drinks, such as barley water or thin gruel.

(5) In the case of an *irritant* poison, after vomiting has been induced and the contents of the stomach brought up, give a dose of castor oil, two tablespoonfuls to an adult and two teaspoonfuls to a child. Relieve the pain as in (4), but oil or fat must not be given in the case of phosphorus poisoning.

(6) In the case of an *hypnotic* poison, after the emetic has been given, keep the patient awake by walking him about or slapping his face and chest with a wet towel. *On no account let him sleep.* Give strong, black coffee freely.

In the case of a *convulsant* poison, the emetic can be given only between the convulsions. During the periods of collapse between the fits apply artificial respiration.

(7) In *all* cases of poisoning give, if available, milk, flour and milk beaten up together, or strong tea.

(8) All vomited matter must be carefully preserved, and also any foodstuffs or other substance suspected of being the source of the poison. The vessels which may have contained the poison must not be washed, but carefully set on one side and handed over to the medical authority on his arrival.

Treatment in Special Cases:

(1) Carbolic acid (phenol). The ordinary signs and symptoms of a corrosive poison are present. There is also the characteristic odour of the breath.

Treatment: In addition to adopting the general rules insofar as they are applicable, give, if possible, half a pint of medicinal paraffin or, failing this, one tablespoonful of Epsom or Glauber salts in a tumblerful of milk or water.

(2) Corrosive sublimate (perchloride of mercury). This is *not,* as the name might imply, a corrosive poison. The signs and symptoms are those of an irritant (non-corrosive) poison and there are, of course, no signs of burns on the lips, tongue or throat.

Treatment: Before administering the emetic, give (if available) unlimited quantities of white of eggs mixed with milk or water. The general rules are also applied where appropriate.

(3) Iodine. The signs and symptoms are those of an irritant poison. There is also intense thirst and the vomited matter is either yellow or blue.

Treatment: Before the emetic, give starch and water freely. This helps to "fix" the iodine and so minimize absorption of the poison into the system. Failing starch, give thin cornflour or arrowroot.

(4) Phosphorus. This is an irritant poison with the usual signs and symptoms. In addition, there may be the pungent odour of phosphorus about the breath and the lips show a phosphorescence in the dark.

Treatment: Having adopted the general rules which apply, give one tablespoonful of Epsom or Glauber salts in a tumblerful of water. *On no account give oil or fat in any form,* as these only hasten the absorption of the phosphorus into the system.

(5) Opium and all its preparations. Having adopted the general rules which are applicable, after the emetic has acted give as many *permanganate of potash* crystals as will lie on a sixpenny piece. Repeat the dose in half an hour. Failing this, give warm water to drink.

(6) Alcohol. The stage of drunkenness is followed by collapse and finally coma.

Treatment: Promote warmth of the body and ensure rest and shelter. Give hot, strong coffee and also apply the general rules which are appropriate.

(7) Strychnine. This poison is contained in many vermin-killers. It is a convulsant poison. The patient struggles for breath, the face turns a livid hue and violent convulsions ensue, in which the patient arches his body until he rests upon his head and feet.

Treatment: Between the convulsions give an emetic and perform artificial respiration. Adopt those general rules which apply.

(8) Prussic acid and cyanide of potassium. The usual signs and symptoms of a convulsant poison are present with, in addition, a smell of bitter almonds. As the action of these poisons is extremely rapid, treatment must be applied instantly.

Treatment: Whether breathing has ceased or not, apply artificial respiration. In addition to the general rules which apply, if the patient can swallow give freely brandy, whisky, or sal volatile, diluted with an equal quantity of water.

PRESSURE POINTS. See HAEMORRHAGE.

PRONE POSITION. Lying flat on the abdomen (belly).

PRUSSIC-ACID POISONING. See POISONING.

PULSE. This is the regular and rhythmic expansion of an artery corresponding to the heart beat. The pulse of the radial artery in the wrist is the one commonly taken. It corresponds to a pressure point and may be felt by placing the tips of the index, middle and ring fingers on the anterior (palm) surface of the lower forearm, about one inch above the wrist and half an inch from the outer side. The average normal pulse rate is about seventy-one beats to the minute, but anything between seventy and eighty may be regarded as normal.

PUNCTURED WOUNDS. See WOUNDS.

QUICKLIME BURNS. See ALKALIS, BURNS BY CORROSIVE.

RABIES. A disease common (in certain countries) in dogs, foxes and wolves. A human being bitten by such a *rabid* animal is liable to develop HYDROPHOBIA. See also BITES, ANIMAL.

RESPIRATION. See INTRODUCTION.

Artificial. See ARTIFICIAL RESPIRATION.

RIBS. Fracture of. Fractures of the ribs may be *simple* or *complicated.* In the latter case there is, in addition to the fracture, injury to some internal organ, usually the lungs.

Simple fracture. That is, where the fracture is not complicated by injury to an internal organ.

Signs: The usual signs and symptoms of fracture are present.

Treatment: Apply two broad bandages round the chest firmly enough to afford adequate support. The centre of the first bandage is placed immediately above, and that of the second bandage immediately below, the seat of fracture. The lower bandage must overlap the upper to half its extent. In this way a double thickness of bandage is over the fracture. The bandages are tied on the opposite side of the body. The arm on the injured side is placed in a large arm-sling. (See Fig. 5.)

Complicated fracture. That is, where an internal organ is injured. As already stated, the internal organ usually injured is the lung beneath, which is penetrated by one of the fragments. In fractures of the lower ribs, on the right side, however, the liver may be injured, and if the injury is on the left side the spleen may be involved. (See HAEMORRHAGE FROM AN INTERNAL ORGAN.) If the lungs are injured, bright red, frothy blood is coughed up. (See also Fig. 36.)

Treatment: Do not apply any bandages round the chest. Lay the patient down with the body inclined towards the injured side. Loosen any tight clothing and apply a cold compress to the seat of injury. If the lungs have been punctured by a fragment of bone, as evidenced by bright red, frothy sputum, give small pieces of ice to suck or sips of cold water. Place the arm on the injured side in a large sling and apply the general treatment for haemorrhage from an internal organ as far as is applicable.

RING PAD. This is used to arrest haemorrhage when a fracture or foreign body is suspected beneath the bleeding point and direct pressure is, therefore, inadvisable.

To make a ring pad, pass one end of a narrow bandage round the fingers. Pass the other end through the ring thus made and continue passing it through and through until the whole of the bandage is used up. (See Fig. 49.)

RUPTURE. See HERNIA.

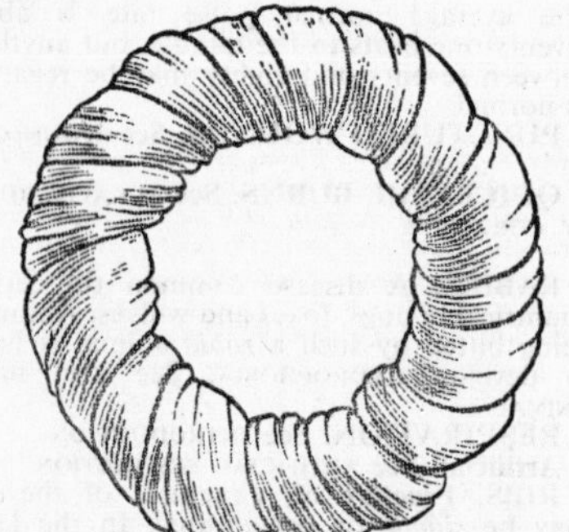

Fig. 49. Ring pad. This is used to stop bleeding when direct pressure is impracticable.

SALINE SOLUTION. This is made by adding one teaspoonful of common salt to a pint of sterile (boiled) water and is known as normal saline. This solution may be used for any purpose in which a sterile solution is required, e.g., washing wounds and applying (at body heat) to an exposed internal organ, as in wounds of the abdomen. See also ABDOMEN, WOUNDS IN WALL OF.

SCALD. An injury produced by damp heat, the appearance and treatment of which are identical with those of a burn. See BURNS.

SCALP. Bandaging of. See BANDAGES.

Bleeding from. This is treated, as in other haemorrhages, by digital pressure, followed by the application of pads and bandage. When the presence of a foreign body or a fractured skull is suspected, apply a ring pad. See also HAEMORRHAGE and RING PAD.

SEPSIS AND ANTISEPSIS. Sepsis is contamination of a wound by pus-producing germs. As these pus-producing organisms are found upon the hands and other exposed parts of the normal healthy individual, it is of the utmost importance that wounds should be handled as little as possible. See also ANTISEPTICS and WOUNDS.

SHIN BONE OR ANKLE BONE. Fracture of. See LEG, FRACTURE OF.

Sprain of. See SPRAIN.

SHOCK is the result of a sudden depression of the nervous system and occurs after all accidents. The severity of shock is dependent upon the severity of the injury inflicted. It may also result as a reaction to sudden horror, fear or relief. In cases of very severe injuries the patient may die from shock alone. There are two types of shock, *primary* and *secondary*.

Primary shock occurs at the moment of injury. Its severity varies from the slight faintness following a simple extraction of a tooth to the possibly fatal degree following upon a severe crush or wound of the abdomen, involving internal organs.

Signs: The face and lips are pale, the skin cold and clammy with beads of *cold* perspiration. The pulse is feeble and rapid and may not be felt at the wrist. The patient may become unconscious.

The condition may pass off after a few seconds or minutes, according to the severity of the case, or it may be so severe that the patient dies if immediate steps are not taken to combat the shock.

Treatment: Immediately arrest any severe haemorrhage. Loosen all clothing about the throat, chest and abdomen. Lay the patient on his back in a comfortable position with his head turned to one side. Allow him plenty of fresh air. Allay the patient's mental anxiety, treat pain and prevent any further aggravation of his injuries. Raise the lower limbs, placing the head low and apply warmth in the form of overcoats, blankets, etc., and the application of hot-water bags or bottles (carefully wrapped up to prevent burning) to the sides of the body, between the legs and to the feet. In applying warmth, avoid sweating.

Provided that there is no suspicion of internal haemorrhage or injuries to an internal organ, the patient may be stimulated by such methods as are immediately available. See also STIMULATION AND STIMULANTS.

Secondary (or surgical) shock. This results from very severe haemorrhage, severe crushing injuries and follows upon serious surgical operations. The condition may appear anything from one to twelve or more hours after the injury has been sustained.

Signs: As in primary shock, in addition to which the pupils are dilated and, in serious cases, the facial pallor may give place to lividity (blueness), first appearing in the lips and ear lobes. The more rapid the pulse, the more serious is the condition. Stupor may develop into coma.

Treatment: As for primary shock.

From electricity and lightning stroke. See ELECTRIC SHOCK.

SHOULDER. Bandage. See BANDAGES.

Blade (scapula), fracture of. This fracture is caused by direct violence, e.g., a fall or blow upon the shoulder-blade.

Signs: The usual signs of fracture.

Treatment: Apply the centre of a **broad bandage** in the armpit of the **injured side,**

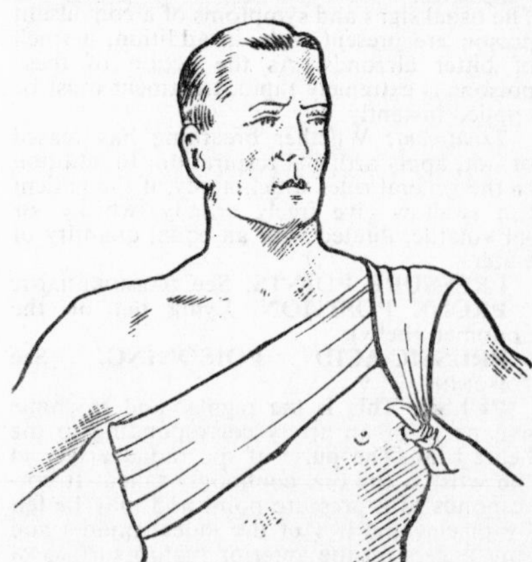

Fig. 50. Bandage for a fractured shoulder-blade.

crossing the ends over the uninjured shoulder and tying them in the sound armpit. The limb is best supported in a St. John sling. (See Fig. 50.)

Joint, dislocation of. See DISLOCATION OF A JOINT.

SKIN. Fish-hook imbedded in. See FISH-HOOK EMBEDDED IN THE SKIN.

Foreign body imbedded beneath. See FOREIGN BODIES, HAEMORRHAGE, and WOUNDS.

Needle imbedded in. If a needle, which has penetrated the skin, disappears below the skin surface, on no account attempt to probe for it. Leave it alone. Take the patient at once to a doctor or hospital, immobilizing the limb by the application of a sling in the case of the upper limb or splints in the case of the thigh, leg or foot.

SKULL. Fracture of. This may be a fracture of the *vault* (upper part of skull) or a fracture of the *base* (lower part).

Fracture of the vault. This usually results from direct violence, such as a fall or blow upon the upper part of the head.

Signs: Swelling, irregularity of outline and unconsciousness. If signs of compression are evident, this indicates pressure upon the brain by a fragment of bone.

Treatment: See COMPRESSION OF BRAIN and also INSENSIBILITY.

Fracture of the base. This is caused by indirect violence, such as a fall from a height on to the feet or lower part of the spine. Unconsciousness may come on at once and blood may be seen trickling from the ears or nose. Injury to the brain is common in this fracture.

Treatment: See BRAIN, COMPRESSION OF, and also INSENSIBILITY.

SLINGS. See ARM SLINGS.

SMOTHERING consists of pressure from outside the body obstructing the air passages. This will result in asphyxia and loss of consciousness.

Treatment: Remove the cause of the asphyxia or the patient from the cause, whichever is easier. Adopt the general rules for asphyxia as far as they are applicable to the case. See also ASPHYXIA.

SNAKE BITE. See BITES.

SPINE (BACKBONE), SPINAL CANAL AND SPINAL CORD. The spine is composed of a series of thirty-three bones called *vertebrae.* These bones are arranged one on top of each other, seven in the neck (*cervical vertebrae*), twelve in the back (*dorsal vertebrae*), five in the loin or lumbar region (*lumbar vertebrae*), beneath which are five fused together to form a bony mass called the *sacrum.* The remaining four vertebrae are joined together to form the end of the spine or *coccyx*, which is considered to be the vestigial tail in man.

Each of these vertebrae consists of a bony mass called the *body*, from the sides of which bony processes extend backwards and unite to form a ring. Thus a bony tube, the spinal canal, is formed by a series of these rings, one on top of the other. The spinal cord is lodged in this canal. Between the bodies of the vertebrae are thick wedges of gristle (cartilage) which allow of movement of the spine as a whole. These cartilaginous wedges also act as buffers and help to break the shock of a fall upon the feet.

Fracture of. The spinal column may be fractured either by direct violence, such as a blow or a fall upon the back, or by indirect violence, such as a blow or fall upon the top of the head. Injury to the spinal cord, as a result of such fractures, is a very serious complication, resulting in either complete or partial loss of power and sensation (i.e., paralysis) in all parts of the body below the site of the injury. It is wiser always to suspect fracture in all cases of injury to the spine associated with pain and shock, even though there are no signs of paralysis.

Treatment: At once warn the patient to lie still. Treat immediately for shock (see SHOCK) and do not leave the patient alone until the doctor or ambulance arrives.

If medical aid is not readily available, place pads between the ankles, knees and thighs. Apply a bandage in the form of a figure of eight round the ankles and feet, tying the knot under the soles of the feet. Secure the knees and thighs by means of broad bandages and empty the patient's pockets of any hard or bulky articles.

With the greatest possible care the patient is carried into shelter *on his back*, that is, face upwards, on a stretcher, stiffened by boards padded by a folded blanket. He must not be allowed to curl up even for a moment, as the broken bone can then squeeze the spinal cord and cause paralysis. In the absence of a stretcher, a shutter, door or board may be used, provided it is at least as long and as wide as the patient's body. Small pillows or other padding are used to support the neck and small of the back in their normal curves.

SPLEEN, INJURIES TO. See HAEMORRHAGE and RIBS, FRACTURE OF.

SPLINTS are used to immobilize injured limbs and joints. To render a fractured limb immovable, splints must be firm and long enough to immobilize the joints immediately above and below the fractured bone. They must be well padded to prevent the occurrence of pressure sores on the skin. See also ARM BONES, FRACTURE OF; ELBOW JOINT, etc.

Improvised splints. Where regulation splints are not available use may be made of pieces of smooth planking of suitable length and width, broom-handles, policemen's truncheons, etc. When round objects such as the latter are being used it is necessary to put an extra turn of bandage round the splint to secure it to the limb.

SPRAIN. The sudden twisting or wrenching of a joint is liable to cause a tearing of the fibres of a ligament (see LIGAMENTS), resulting in pain and swelling and possibly also in discoloration.

Treatment: Rest the limb in a comfortable position and apply cold compresses continuously. Finally apply a firm bandage, wrung out of cold water. Treat as a fracture in all doubtful cases.

STRAIN. This is caused by the over-stretching of the belly or fleshy part of a muscle, resulting in the tearing of the muscular fibres. A sudden sharp pain is felt at the point of injury and there may or may not be swelling of the muscle.

Treatment: Support the injured limb or part and apply a hot compress.

STERILIZATION AND STERILITY. Sterility is the term used to describe complete freedom from contamination, that is, germ life. Sterilization is the method used to obtain that state. Boiling in water for three minutes will sterilize instruments. For thorough sterilization, before handling a wound, the hands and arms should be scrubbed from finger-nails to elbows with soap and hot water, using a hard nail-brush. The hands and forearms are then bathed in a dilute solution of disinfectant. See also ANTISEPTICS and SEPSIS AND ANTISEPSIS.

STERNUM (BREAST BONE). This is situated in the middle line of the chest. The upper ten ribs on either side join up to the breast bone in front and to the spinal column behind, thus forming a bony casing which affords protection to the heart, lungs and other structures within.

Fracture of. See BREAST BONE.

STIMULATION AND STIMULANTS. The stimulants used in first-aid are commonly hot sweetened tea or strong coffee with plenty of sugar. Hot fluid meat extracts may also be used for purposes of stimulation. If smelling salts are used they should be tested first to ascertain their strength, before their application to the patient.

The administration of alcohol should be withheld pending the arrival of the doctor, except in the case of a bite from a rabid animal and in the after-treatment of poisoning by prussic acid and cyanide of potassium.

STINGS. See BITES.

STOMACH. Foreign bodies in. If pins or other sharp objects have been swallowed, give nothing by mouth and take the patient to a doctor, by transport, at once. Smooth and rounded objects such as buttons and coins need not necessarily cause alarm once they have reached the stomach, as these are usually passed, in due course, in the normal way.

Haemorrhage (bleeding) from. See HAEMORRHAGE.

STRAMONIUM POISONING. See POISONING.

STRANGULATION. See ASPHYXIA.

STRETCHER. See CARRYING INJURED PERSON.

STROKE, APOPLECTIC. See APOPLEXY.

STRYCHNINE POISONING. See POISONING.

STUNNING (CONCUSSION). See BRAIN, CONCUSSION OF.

STUPOR. See INSENSIBILITY.

SUFFOCATION. See ASPHYXIA.

SUNSTROKE. See HEATSTROKE.

SUPINE. This is the position of lying on the back, as used in the transport of spinal injuries and fractures of the lower limbs.

SYMPTOMS. See DIAGNOSIS.

TENDONS OR LIGAMENTS, SPRAINS OF. See SPRAINS.

THIGH BONE. Fracture of. The thigh bone, or *femur*, may be broken at the hip joint, knee joint, or in its shaft.

Signs: The usual signs of fracture are present (see FRACTURES). In addition there is considerable deformity about the foot, which lies over on its outer side. There is also considerable shortening of the injured limb, as the leg is drawn up by spasmodic contraction of the powerful thigh muscles, causing overriding of the fractured ends.

Treatment: Very carefully apply extension. (See EXTENSION under entry FRACTURES.) Apply a narrow bandage as a figure of eight round the ankles and feet. Then pass seven bandages underneath the patient's body in th following manner and order: (1) under the back below the armpits; (2) under both hips; (3) under both ankles; (4) under both thighs, above the fracture; (5) under both thighs, below the fracture; (6) under both legs, and (7) under both knees, using a broad bandage. Place a well-padded splint along the outside of the fractured limb, extending from the armpit to just beyond the foot. Secure the splint to the body and limb by tying the bandages in the same order as above. The bandages are knotted on the outside of the splint with the exception of the one round the ankles, which is applied as a figure of eight and tied under the soles of the feet. (See Fig. 51.)

Since in this fracture the danger of shock is very great, anti-shock measures must be adopted at once. See SHOCK.

Bleeding from. See HAEMORRHAGE.

THREE-HANDED SEAT. See CARRYING INJURED PERSON.

THROAT. Cut. See HAEMORRHAGE FROM THE THROAT.

Foreign body in. See ASPHYXIA.

Scald of. See BURNS.

Swelling of tissues of. See ASPHYXIA.

THUMB, DISLOCATION OF. The general rules for the treatment of dislocation are applied as far as possible. See DISLOCATION OF A JOINT.

TIBIA OR SHIN BONE, FRACTURE OF. See LEG.

TONGUE, BLEEDING FROM. Treat as for bleeding from cheek. See HAEMORRHAGE.

Fig. 51. The long splint is used in the treatment of a fracture (marked here by an arrow) of the thigh bone.

TOOTH SOCKET, BLEEDING FROM. See HAEMORRHAGE.

TOURNIQUET. A method of controlling arterial haemorrhage, named after Dr. Tourniquet, a French army surgeon, who first applied this method. Apply a firm pad over the *pressure point*, that is, the nearest point above the bleeding site, where the artery lies over a bone. Place a narrow

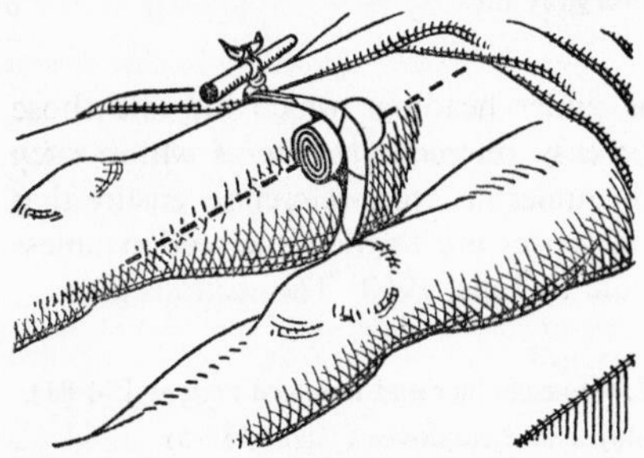

Fig. 52. Tourniquet applied to the femoral artery (indicated by dotted line) in the thigh.

bandage round the limb at this point and tie its ends in a half-knot on the opposite side to the pad. Lay a short, strong stick or similar object on the half-knot and tie a reef-knot on top of the stick. Turn the stick round to tighten the bandage and so press the pad down upon the artery against the bone and thus arrest the flow of blood beyond that point. The stick can be fixed in position by the ends of the bandage. An example of the application of a tourniquet to the thigh is shown in Fig. 52.

The tourniquet should only be drawn tight enough to control the bleeding and should be slowly relaxed every fifteen to twenty minutes, until the bleeding has stopped. Tourniquets are dangerous things, as they often cause gangrene of the limb by cutting off the blood supply. Direct pressure should always be used where possible.

TRANSPORT. See CARRYING INJURED PERSON.

TRIANGULAR BANDAGE. See BANDAGES and SLINGS.

TRUNK. The main part of the human body, excluding the limbs.

Bandage for. See BANDAGES.

TWO-HANDED SEAT. See CARRYING INJURED PERSON.

ULNA. The innermost bone of the forearm.

Fracture of. See ARM BONES.

UNCONSCIOUSNESS. See INSENSIBILITY.

VARICOSE VEINS. A permanently over-stretched and tortuous vein, the wall of which has lost its natural elasticity. In health a vein has a series of small valves in the internal walls which prevent the blood accumulating to excess in any one portion of its course. A vein becomes *varicose* when these valves are damaged. The veins of the leg are those usually affected. The condition results from several causes, such as prolonged standing, tight garters or suspenders, pregnancy, or any other cause of pressure on the large veins.

Bleeding from. *Treatment:* Lay the patient on the back and, provided there is no fractured bone, raise up and support the affected leg. Having exposed the bleeding point, apply direct digital pressure. Then apply a firm bandage on the side of the wound farthest from the heart and a second bandage on the side of the wound nearest the heart. Apply a dry dressing to the wound. Place a wad of cotton-wool on top of the dressing and secure in position with a bandage. Keep the leg elevated.

VEIN, BLEEDING FROM. Treat as for bleeding from varicose veins. See also HAEMORRHAGE.

VERTEBRAE. The bones forming the spine.

VERTEBRAL COLUMN. The spine.

Fracture of. See SPINE, FRACTURE OF.

VITRIOL. Burn. See BURNS BY CORROSIVE ACIDS.

Poisoning. See POISONING.

WIND-PIPE OR TRACHEA. See ASPHYXIA.

WOUNDS. Abdominal (belly). See ABDOMEN.

Associated with severe bleeding. See HAEMORRHAGE.

Types of. (1) *Contused* wounds are accompanied by much bruising of the tissues and result from a blow with a blunt instrument. In this type the chief danger is sepsis (contamination by pus-producing germs), as healing is delayed by reason of the damage sustained by the tissues.

(2) *Incised* wounds are caused by a sharp instrument, such as a razor-blade or a surgeon's knife. The tissues and blood-vessels are "clean-cut" and when the healthy edges are brought together the wound heals rapidly. The chief danger is haemorrhage.

(3) *Lacerated* wounds, such as shell wounds, have torn, irregular edges. As they usually involve considerable loss of tissue, healing is delayed. Sepsis is the chief danger.

(4) *Punctured* wounds, which may be very deep, have comparatively small openings. They are caused by a stab from a sharp-pointed instrument such as a needle, stiletto, knife or bayonet. Severe haemorrhage may result if a large blood-vessel is pierced, and sepsis is an ever-present danger on account of the likelihood of fragments of clothing being driven into the tissues.

General treatment of: Immediately arrest any severe bleeding (see HAEMORRHAGE, TREATMENT OF) and, with a pair of sterilized scissors, cut a piece of sterile gauze, lint or other suitable material, large enough to cover the entire wound, taking care not to touch with the fingers that part of the dressing which is to be applied to the wound. Place a piece of cotton-wool on top of the dressing and fix the whole in place with a bandage.

If a foreign body is in the wound or a fracture is suspected pads should be placed round the wound to prevent direct pressure on the wound by the bandage.

WRIST OR CARPUS. Fracture of. See ARM BONES, FRACTURE OF FOREARM.

Sprain of. See SPRAIN.

LAW FOR EVERYMAN

A simple explanation of legal problems as they affect everyday life

This chapter is divided into nine sections under headings which indicate those aspects of the law described in them. For easy reference the items within each section are arranged alphabetically, though numerous cross-references ensure that each subject can be fully covered. Cross-references are to the same section unless otherwise stated. The chapter is up to date to June, 1950. The sections are:

1. HUSBAND, WIFE AND CHILD

ADOPTION. Adoption in the full sense of the word was not recognized by English Law prior to the Adoption of Children Act, 1926, which came into operation on 1 January, 1927. Until then, parents always had a legal right to reclaim their children from the custody of anyone to whom they had entrusted the children, and that, too, in spite of any solemn agreement by the parents to surrender the children for ever.

But now, under the Act (as amended in certain particulars by later Acts of 1939 and 1949), a person desiring to adopt an infant (only infants, that is, under twenty-one years of age, may be adopted) may apply to the Chancery Division of the High Court, or the County Court, or the Magistrates' Court for an adoption order. Such an order will not be made, however, without the consent of the infant's parents or guardian or of those who are liable to contribute to its support, except in exceptional circumstances such as where the child has been deserted or ill-treated.

Who may adopt. There are certain restrictions as to who may obtain an adoption order. Thus, the applicant must be either at least twenty-five years of age and at least twenty-one years older than the infant, or must be twenty-one and a relative of the infant, or must be the mother or father of the infant (that is, where the infant is illegitimate).

Only one person may apply, except that a husband and wife may apply jointly. A sole applicant who is a male will not be granted the adoption of a female except in special circumstances. Moreover, when the applicant is a husband alone or a wife alone the consent of the other spouse is necessary, except where the other spouse is incapable of giving consent or where the spouses are living apart.

Adoption orders may be obtained also by registered adoption societies and by local authorities.

Effect of adoption. An adoption order has the effect of extinguishing all the rights, duties, obligations and liabilities of the parents or guardians of the infant as regards the infant's future custody, maintenance and education, as well as regards the right to consent to the infant's marriage, and transferring all such rights, etc., to the adopter. The adopter then stands to the infant in these matters as if the infant were the lawful child of the adopter's own marriage.

It is important to note, too, that the order deprives the adopted infant of any rights in property to which it would have been entitled under any intestacy or provision had there been no adoption. Therefore, if either of the infant's natural parents should die without leaving a will, the infant would not be entitled to share in the parent's estate; so also the adopted child would take no share under any provision of its natural parent's will in favour of "my children," for example.

On the other hand, for purposes of succession to property on death the adopted child is treated as the natural child of the adopter and is entitled to the full rights of a natural child under his will or intestacy. In the case of provisions for children under wills or other instruments, however, it is only where these are made after the date of the adoption order that the adopted child ceases for such purposes to be the child of its natural parents and becomes the child of the adopter.

Register of adoptions. There is kept at the General Register Office in Somerset House, London, a special Register of Adopted Children. Whenever an adoption order is made, the court, as a matter of course, sends particulars of the adoption to Somerset House to be entered in this special Register. A certified copy of the entry in the Register is proof of the adoption. Thereafter all copies of the usual birth certificate of that child are endorsed with the word "adopted" and the date of the adoption; but a short form of birth certificate is now also obtainable which says nothing about adoption. See CHILDREN.

AFFILIATION. See ILLEGITIMATE CHILDREN.

BREACH OF PROMISE. An engagement to marry is, in the eyes of the law, a contract between the man and the woman. Such a contract involves mutual promises to marry each other, though a promise need not be expressed but may be inferred from conduct.

Breach of promise is, therefore, breach of contract, and that is why damages may be sued for. That, too, is why the man is entitled to sue the woman, just as the woman may sue the man, though a man generally would have far more difficulty in proving such loss as would entitle him to damages. An infant, that is, a person under twenty-one years of age, cannot be sued for breach of promise, but he or she may sue the other party.

It would be a defence for a man in a breach-of-promise action that, when he became engaged to the woman, he was unaware that she had been unchaste, or that, since the engagement, she had been unchaste with a third party. Likewise a woman is entitled to break off an engagement on the man's bad character coming to light. A promise of marriage given in consideration of the other party permitting sexual intercourse is void and no action can lie for breach of it.

When a promise is made by a person already married at the time, the other party can sue for breach if he or she was unaware of the existing marriage when the promise was made. When a woman breaks off an engagement without justification, the man is entitled to the return of the engagement ring and of any other gifts made by him in contemplation of marriage (though not of presents given merely to win the woman's favour); such articles are also returnable, in the absence of any other agreement, when the engagement is broken off by mutual consent.

CHANGE OF NAME. The law regarding change of personal name is still a little uncertain on some points. It appears, however, that in strict law a christian name (baptismal name) may be legally changed at confirmation, but at no other time and in no other way (unless by Royal Licence or Special Act of Parliament). This, however, is of no practical importance, and no untoward consequences can follow from the use of an assumed name so long as it can be proved that the person was in fact known by that name.

Surnames are in a different position. The law regards them merely as identifying labels and there is no legal obstacle to anyone changing his surname at will; an assumed surname is as good in law as the original one. The really important thing in this connexion is that, where the surname has been changed, evidence of identity should be preserved; that is to say, for example, that the person now known as Tom Jones should be able to prove that he is the same person as was formerly known as Tom Smith.

For this purpose of preserving evidence, it is a common practice for the person either to insert an advertisement in a local and/or national newspaper, or else to execute a deed poll. A deed poll is simply a deed to which there is only one party, as contrasted with an indenture, which is a deed having two or more parties.

The terms of a deed poll may be preserved for all time by enrolling the deed in the Central Office of the Supreme Court, London (fee £2), and it is usual to enrol in this way a deed poll relating to change of name.

A child's surname is, of course, bestowed upon it by its parents in the first instance, and is generally the surname of the father. An illegitimate child, however, is usually given its mother's surname, though, so far as the law is concerned, it could be given the surname of its father, or indeed of anyone else.

From what has been stated in the foregoing, it will be evident that a child may change its name, or have its name changed for it by its parents, without formality; and, in the case of very young children, there is not usually any need to take steps, such as advertisement or execution of deed, to preserve evidence.

CHILDREN. At the outset, it is advisable to bear in mind that, in relation to its parents, a child is always a child in the eyes of the law, no matter how old it may be, whereas a child under twenty-one years of age is legally an infant; in other words, there are children and there are infant children.

This distinction is of importance because, as will be seen, some rules of the law regarding children apply to children even after they have reached their majority, e.g. their rights of succession to property on death, whereas there are other rules, particularly in connexion with contracts, that apply only to infant children. The position of illegitimate children, again, is governed by a number of special rules of law and such children are, therefore, considered under a separate heading (ILLEGITIMATE CHILDREN).

Registration of birth. The birth of a child, whether born alive or still-born, must be registered in the district Register of Births and Deaths. The duty of registering the birth lies in the first instance on the father or mother, but failing them, the duty lies on the occupier of the house where the birth occurred, or anyone present at the birth, or the person having charge of the child. In the case of foundlings, the finder or anyone taking charge of the child must register the birth within seven days.

Registration may, and normally should, be made within forty-two days after the birth, by appearing personally at the registration office, giving the required particulars and signing the register. After the expiry of the forty-two days, but before the lapse of three months from the date of birth, it is still permissible to register; in this case, however, the procedure is to make and sign a written declaration before the registrar.

If the birth is not registered within the forty-two days, moreover, the registrar can, at any time up to twelve months from the date of birth, require the person whose duty it is to register to attend his office and do so. Once the twelve months have expired, registration can be made only with the consent of the Registrar-General.

The particulars required by the registrar are: (1) date and place of birth; (2) name (if any) and sex of child; (3) name and surname and rank or profession of father; (4) name and maiden surname of mother; and (5) signature, address and description of informant. There are penalties for giving false particulars.

In the case of an illegitimate child, the father is not under any duty to register the birth and his name must not be entered on the register except at the joint request of himself and the mother. But where an illegitimate child has become legitimate by the subsequent marriage of its parents (see ILLEGITIMATE CHILDREN), application may be made by the parents to the Registrar-General within three months of the marriage to have the birth of the child re-registered.

Within twelve months of registering the birth, it is permissible to have the child's name altered on the register, or, where no name was originally entered, to have one entered. After the twelve months, no alteration in name can be made on the register.

There is kept at Somerset House, Strand, London, a complete public record of all births registered in England and Wales since 1 July, 1837. Anyone is entitled to search these records, either *generally*, that is, without specifying the particular entry for which he is searching (fee £1 for six consecutive hours' search), or *specially*, that is, where the object of search is specified (fee 1s. for search covering records over a period up to five years). Officials will search on behalf of anyone who does not attend personally (fee 2s. 6d. per five years). Similar searches may be made in the records of the local Superintendents of births and deaths (fee 5s. and 1s. respectively). In both cases a certified copy of any entry may be obtained for a fee of 2s. 7d.; such a certified copy is what is commonly known as a birth certificate. A short form of birth certificate is now also obtainable (fee 6d.) on which the only particulars are name, sex, place and date of birth. Since no particulars of parentage or adoption may be given on this short form it is of convenience especially to persons who are illegitimate or adopted.

It is important to bear in mind that, in addition to the duty of registering the birth, there is also laid on the father, and on anyone else who attends the mother at the birth, the duty of notifying the birth to the local Medical Officer of Health. Such notice must be sent in writing within thirty-six hours of the birth; the fine for failure to do so is £1. See also GUARDIANSHIP.

CIVIL WRONGS (TORTS). Civil wrongs, or torts as the lawyers call them, cover such diverse wrongs as trespass, negligence, libel and slander, nuisance, deceit, and others. A husband cannot sue his wife for torts committed by her against him, and it is only where it is for the protection and security of her own property that a wife may sue her husband. The position remains the same when the spouses are living apart; and, even if they are divorced, one cannot sue the other for a tort committed during the marriage.

The most important aspect of the matter, however, is the question of the husband's liability for his wife's torts. Prior to 1935, a husband was liable for torts committed by his wife during the marriage; so that if, for example, a wife slandered her neighbour the neighbour could sue the husband for damages. Not only so, but the husband was liable to the extent of any property he acquired through his wife on marriage for torts committed by his wife before marriage. Since 1935, however, a husband is no longer liable for his wife's torts, whether committed before or after marriage, unless, of course, he has actually joined with her in committing the tort; the wife alone is liable for her own torts.

CRIMES. As regards liability under the criminal law, husband and wife are in some respects in a special position. The only crimes for which one spouse may prosecute the other are assault, battery, personal injuries and theft (but theft only if they are living apart, and even then only if it was committed by the spouse when leaving or deserting the other or about to do so or after the separation).

Again, a wife cannot be convicted as an accessory after the fact to a felony committed by her husband, which means that if, knowing he has committed a felony, she helps him to escape apprehension, trial or punishment, for example by hiding him or by destroying incriminating evidence, she would not be guilty of an offence. But a husband may be guilty as an accessory after the fact to a felony committed by his wife (though he would not be criminally liable if the wife's offence were merely a misdemeanour). Nor can husband and wife be guilty of criminal conspiracy, which is a mere agreement between two or more persons to do an unlawful act, whether they actually do it or not.

Apart from these exceptions, husband and wife are subject to the criminal law like anyone else. A husband is not, as such, liable for his wife's crimes in which he has not taken any part. The former rule that misdemeanours and felonies (other than treason and murder) committed by a wife in the presence of her husband were presumed to have been committed under his coercion, so that she could not be considered guilty, was abolished in 1925. Now a wife would have to prove that her husband actually did subject her to physical coercion, and such proof is a defence except in cases of treason and murder.

DIVORCE. See MATRIMONIAL PROCEEDINGS.

GUARDIANSHIP. The law regards an infant child (one under twenty-one years of age) as in need of certain protection and guidance, and a guardian is a person recognized by the law as entitled to exercise such protection and guidance. In relation to its guardian, an infant is known as a ward. A female infant ceases to be a ward should she marry before reaching twenty-one, that is to say, the guardianship ceases.

The word "guardian" can be used in other senses, such as guardian *ad litem* (a person appointed to act for a child in an action against the child) but it is employed here only in the sense indicated—its most usual sense.

Who may be guardian. The father is, in the first place, the child's natural guardian. On the father's death, the mother automatically becomes guardian. Either parent may, however, by deed or will, appoint a third party to act as joint guardian with the surviving spouse.

Even if the terms of the deed or will purports to make the third party sole guardian, nevertheless the appointment will be regarded by the law as joint, since the surviving spouse is in the eyes of the law a guardian in any event and cannot be deprived of the office merely because the other spouse has appointed someone else. Moreover, such a third party may act as joint guardian only if the surviving spouse consents.

In the event of a dispute between the surviving spouse and the third party, application may be made to the court—the Chancery Division of the High Court, or the County Court or the Magistrates' Court—for settlement of the question.

The father may forfeit his rights to guardianship by reason of misconduct, cruelty or criminal acts towards his ward, and, in that event, the court would probably appoint the mother to be guardian, especially if the child were very young. (The mother has no legal claim to the office as of right so long as the father is alive.)

But, in these or any other circumstances, once the question has come before the court as to who is entitled to be guardian, the court, while giving proper consideration to the claims of parents and other relatives, is bound to regard the welfare of the infant as the chief consideration overriding all others. It is, therefore, possible for the court to appoint a stranger in blood to be guardian, even while the father and mother are alive.

Where the infant is sixteen years of age or over, the court is bound to have regard to the infant's wishes in the matter and will not make an appointment contrary to those wishes.

Only the High Court can remove and appoint guardians. But, in other questions, such as disputes between joint guardians or questions of custody, both the County Court and the Magistrates' Court have jurisdiction. The Magistrates' Court, however, has no jurisdiction regarding custody where the child has reached sixteen years of age, nor can it award a sum of more than £1 per week for the child's maintenance.

Guardianship of person and of property. Guardianship is of two kinds, that is, guardianship of the infant's person and guardianship of the infant's property. A surviving parent is guardian in both senses, and so is a guardian appointed by the will or deed of a deceased parent. A father, however, so long as the mother is alive, is guardian only of the infant's person.

So, if the infant possessed property, it would be necessary to have a guardian appointed by the court to administer the property. In the absence of special circumstances, the court would probably appoint the father to that office too, but, here again, the chief consideration is what is best for the welfare of the infant.

Guardianship of the infant's person means not merely custody of the infant, but a general right of control and upbringing. The right of custody includes the right to put the child into the custody of another, but, where any such agreement is made by a father as guardian, he may change his mind and refuse to carry it out; even when he has transferred the child, he can get it back unless it would be injurious to the child to allow him to do so.

But an undertaking by the husband in a deed of separation to give custody to the wife is binding. The court may take away the right of custody from the father (while still allowing him to retain the other rights of guardianship), and give it to someone else, for example, the mother, and may at the same time order the father to make periodical payments for the child's upkeep.

A guardian of the child's person is responsible also for the ward's education and religious upbringing. In the matter of education, where the guardian is not a parent, the wishes of the parents, so far as known, should be followed; while as regards religion the guardian is obliged, in the absence of special circumstances, to bring up the child in the father's religion.

A guardian of the ward's property is under a duty to receive the income of the property and apply it towards the ward's maintenance. He is not obliged to be out of pocket himself. A parent, however, must maintain his child at his own expense, and even, generally, when the child has property of its own, but that is a liability arising from parenthood and not from guardianship.

Wards of court. Formerly an infant automatically became a ward of court if any proceedings concerning the infant were taken in the Chancery Division of the High Court, but since 1949 an infant can become a ward of court only under an order of the court made on an application for that purpose. Both the person and property of a ward of court come under the control of the court. The ward, therefore, cannot be taken beyond the jurisdiction of the court, and his education and religious upbringing are subject to the general direction of the court.

The ward may not marry without the consent of the court, any marriage without such consent being treated as contempt of court and severely punished. Before consenting to a proposed marriage, the court will see that proper financial provision is made in favour of the ward by the person proposing to marry the ward, and will also protect a female ward's own property from the control of her proposed husband.

ILLEGITIMATE CHILDREN. In general, the policy of the law with regard to the illegitimate child and its parents is to recognize the mother and ignore the father. Thus the father's name may not be entered in the Register of Births except at the joint request of the mother and himself. But a short form of birth certificate is now also obtainable by anyone in which no particulars at all are given about parentage. See CHILDREN. The father, as such, is not liable for the child's maintenance. It is the mother alone who is liable, and her liability remains until the child is sixteen years of age, though, if the mother should die before then, her estate does not continue liable.

While the father is not, in the first instance, liable for the child's maintenance, nevertheless he may come under liability in various ways. Thus he may be made liable for certain payments under an affiliation order made by the court; he is liable to repay to the Assistance Board or the local authority any sums spent on the child by way of assistance; or he may himself adopt the child and so become liable as adopter; or he may bind himself by contract with the mother to maintain the child, though, in this case, the mother continues to be primarily liable in law, so that if the father failed to fulfil his contract the law would require the mother to support the child.

Anyone legally adopting the child (see ADOPTION) becomes liable for its maintenance instead of the mother; and, if the mother should marry a man who is not the father of the child, that man would become primarily liable until the child reached the age of sixteen years or the mother died, whichever event first happened.

Rights of succession. The rights of an illegitimate child to share in the estate of its parents in the event of their dying intestate (without leaving a will) are very different from the rights of a legitimate child. The illegitimate child has no claim whatever to share in the father's estate. Where it is the mother's estate that is concerned, however, the illegitimate child has a right to share only if the mother has left no legitimate descendants (children or remoter issue) surviving her, and takes, in that event, the same share as it would have taken had it been legitimate. Where an illegitimate child has pre-deceased its mother, but has itself left issue, then the issue are entitled between them to the same share in the mother's estate as the child itself would have taken.

Where the illegitimate child dies intestate, the father has no claim to any share in the child's estate. The child's mother, however, is entitled to the same share in the child's estate as she would have taken had she been the sole surviving legitimate parent. As the law now stands, the child's spouse and his or her own children would have certain claims in priority to the child's mother.

Affiliation proceedings. The object of affiliation proceedings is to have the father of the child declared by the court to be the father, and to make him liable, by an order of the court, to contribute to the child's maintenance. The proceedings are taken by the mother, and must be commenced within twelve months of the child's birth; they may be commenced even before the birth.

If the mother was unmarried, she loses her right to take proceedings if she marries, but, once she obtains an order, it continues in force in spite of her subsequent marriage. A woman already married who gives birth to an illegitimate child is not, however, barred from taking proceedings on account of her being married. Proceedings are begun by the mother applying to the local magistrates for a summons against the alleged father.

After considering all the evidence at the hearing—and whatever other evidence is given, the mother's own evidence is essential—the magistrates may find the defendant to be the father of the child and may order him to pay the mother a weekly sum of up to £1 for the maintenance and education of the child, plus an additional sum to cover confinement expenses.

In the absence of any stipulation to the contrary, the order remains in force until the child is thirteen years of age or dies before that. But the magistrates may lay down that the order shall terminate at an earlier age than thirteen, or that it shall continue until any age up to sixteen. The order may also be subsequently revoked, restored or varied by the court in the light of fresh evidence.

How an illegitimate child may become legitimate. Until 1927, the only way by which an illegitimate child could ever become legitimate was by special Act of Parliament declaring the child to be legitimate. But, by the Legitimacy Act, 1926, it is now provided that, if the parents of an illegitimate child shall subsequently marry each other, the child shall automatically become legitimate, provided that, at the time of the marriage, the father is domiciled in England or Wales, and provided also that, when the child was born, neither parent was married to a third person.

(It should be noted that the Act does not require the father to be resident in England or Wales when the marriage takes place, but only that he shall be domiciled there. To be domiciled in a particular country means to have an intention to make that country one's permanent home, so that, for example, an Englishman who goes abroad even for many years is considered to be still domiciled in England if it is proved that he had a firm intention to return and settle in England.)

Legitimation takes place only as from the date of the marriage or, in the case of marriages entered into prior to 1 January, 1927, only from that latter date.

The somewhat curious result therefore follows that a person made legitimate under the Act may be illegitimate up to a certain time. This may have important consequences, especially in rights of succession under a will or in intestacy, for a person would not, in such cases, be able to take any provisions in favour of legitimate children that came into effect during the period of that person's illegitimacy.

But, once a person becomes legitimate, then not only he but his wife and his descendants also are entitled to claim as legitimate in the estate of anyone dying after that date. And the Act generously provides that where the parents do not marry until after the child has died, then, for purposes of succession by and to the child's own spouse and issue, the child is to be treated as legitimated from the date of the marriage. The marriage of the parents is enough of itself to make the child legitimate, without any other procedure, but, where it is desired to have authoritative evidence of legitimacy, application may be made to the court for a Declaration of Legitimacy.

INCIDENTAL CONSEQUENCES OF MATRIMONIAL PROCEEDINGS.

Financial provisions for spouses. *Alimony.* This is money which the court orders one spouse to pay for the support of the other. The order is usually made against the husband for the support of the wife, but, as is stated in the following, there is one case where the wife may be ordered to support her husband. There are two kinds of alimony:

(1) "Alimony pending suit" (that is, to be paid until the proceedings are over) may be awarded in proceedings for divorce, nullity, judicial separation and restitution of conjugal rights, where the wife is not able to maintain herself adequately. An award may be made to the wife even when she is the respondent. The amount awarded is usually such amount as will bring up the wife's income to one-fifth of the joint income of husband and wife, but it may be less or more than that, according to circumstances. The court may subsequently vary the amount.

(2) Permanent alimony may be awarded to a wife who has obtained a decree of judicial separation, even when the decree has been obtained by the husband against the wife. It may even be awarded to the husband where the wife petitions on the ground of his insanity. The amount is usually one-third of the husband's income or, where the wife has some income of her own, such sum as will make her income up to one-third of the joint income.

But it is in the discretion of the court to award what it thinks fit in all the circumstances; and the court may subsequently vary the amount in the light of changed circumstances. If the husband fails to make the alimony payments he is liable for any necessaries supplied to her. The obligation to pay permanent alimony lasts only during the joint lives of husband and wife, so that the death of one of them brings it to an end.

Maintenance. This is financial provision which the court may award to a wife on a decree of divorce or of nullity being made. An award may even be made to a husband when the wife obtains decree of divorce against him on ground of his insanity, this being the only case where a husband may be awarded maintenance.

The amount is fixed in relation to the financial position of both husband and wife, their conduct in the matters giving rise to proceedings, and the station in life of the party to whom the award is made. The award may be in the form of a weekly or monthly allowance payable only so long as both parties are alive; or it may take the form of a capital sum or annual allowance secured to the wife for life (or some shorter period); or it may be in both forms. The amount of the allowance may be subsequently varied by the court.

Even where the husband obtains decree of divorce against his wife on the ground of her adultery, he may be ordered by the court to make her a small compassionate allowance; such allowances to a guilty wife are not, however, very often awarded.

Settlements. When a husband obtains a decree of judicial separation or of divorce on the ground of his wife's adultery, desertion, or cruelty, the court may order a settlement of her property to be made for the benefit of the husband and/or the children of the marriage. A similar order may be made where a wife refuses to obey a decree for restitution of conjugal rights.

Settlements are made in favour of husbands, not of wives: wives, as stated in the foregoing, have other rights in the form of maintenance. Not only may the court order a settlement to be made but, where there was a marriage settlement already in existence under which either husband or wife is a beneficiary, and there has been a decree of divorce or nullity (but not judicial separation), the court has power to make variations in the settlement so as to ensure that the innocent spouse and the children are not financially prejudiced in consequence of the dissolution of the marriage.

Maintenance and custody of children. In proceedings for divorce, nullity, judicial separation or restitution of conjugal rights, the court has power to make provision for the custody, maintenance and education of the children of the marriage. In questions of custody, the vital consideration is the welfare of the child. Therefore, in certain circumstances, custody may be given even to the guilty spouse, though that is not usual. In any event, where custody has been given to one parent, the court may allow the other parent to have access to the child at certain times.

Damages and costs against co-respondent. In proceedings for divorce or judicial separation, the husband may claim damages against the co-respondent with whom the wife has committed adultery; but a wife petitioner cannot claim damages against the other woman. Damages are intended to compensate the husband for the loss of his wife and the injury to his feelings and honour. The amount awarded will depend on all the circumstances, but is usually very moderate, and nowadays the inclination of the courts is towards the view that to be deprived of an adulterous wife can be no great loss.

But, apart from damages of this kind claimed incidentally to matrimonial proceedings, there is also a separate common law action available to either husband or wife against a third party who has enticed away the other spouse. This action for enticement is based merely on loss of the other spouse's society and adultery is not necessary to the action at all). Costs may also be awarded to a petitioner against a co-respondent, whether a man or a woman.

INFANT'S CONTRACTS. In the matter of contracts, the law regards an infant (a child under twenty-one) as specially in need of protection and is, therefore, very indulgent towards the infant, making it easy for him to escape from his contractual obligations. But there are certain kinds of contracts that are binding on an infant, and these are dealt with first.

Binding contracts. There are two classes of contracts that are binding on an infant.

(1) First, there are *contracts under which necessaries have been supplied.* An infant is bound to pay for necessaries actually supplied. It is, therefore, important to understand what the law regards as necessaries. Food, clothing and shelter are necessaries, and so are medical attention and education.

These items do not, however, complete the list, for the law takes the view that whatever is reasonably required to maintain an infant in the particular standard of life in which he happens to be is to be regarded as a necessary. Thus, while clothes are necessaries in all cases, expensive clothes would not be regarded as necessary for a poor infant, though they probably would be for an infant in affluent circumstances. And, while a piano or a motor-car for personal use might well be regarded as a necessary for the well-to-do infant, they would not ordinarily be so regarded in the case of a poor infant.

There are, therefore, really two questions involved in deciding in any particular case whether an article is a necessary: first of all, whether the article or service is, in the circumstances, of a *kind* that is to be regarded as a necessary, and secondly whether the quality of such article or service is reasonably suitable. So the motor-car that is a necessary for the affluent infant and not for the poor one would probably be held not to be a necessary even for the affluent infant if it were an unreasonably luxurious car of high price.

There is a further and most important consideration in determining whether a thing is a necessary, and it is that the thing must be suitable to the infant's actual requirements at the time it is supplied. Therefore, if the infant already has an adequate supply of a particular thing, any further supplies of that thing cannot be regarded as necessaries, and the supplier cannot compel the infant to pay for them, even if he was unaware of the fact that the infant was already well supplied.

It will be apparent from the foregoing that anyone supplying goods or services to an infant incurs a definite risk because of the difficulty of determining beforehand whether, in the eyes of the law, the goods will be considered as necessaries in the particular case. But, if it is established that the goods supplied or the services rendered are necessaries, then the infant is liable and must pay for them.

Here, however, there are two points to be observed. Firstly, it is only where necessaries have actually been supplied and accepted that the infant is liable to pay. He cannot be compelled to carry out a contract not yet fulfilled, so that although, for example, he has ordered necessaries, yet if he refuses to accept delivery of them he cannot be held liable.

Secondly, even where the infant is liable on the contract, he is liable to pay only a reasonable price and not necessarily the contract price. Therefore, if he were supplied with necessaries for which he had agreed to pay £5, and if it were established that £5 was an excessive price but that £3 10s. was the reasonable price, his liability then is to pay only the £3 10s.

Finally, it is an overriding condition of an infant's liability for necessaries supplied that the contract must be for the infant's benefit. If it is not, then it is void. At first sight, it may be difficult to see how necessaries can ever be considered not for the infant's benefit. Such a situation, however, does arise, for example, where unreasonably harsh conditions are attached to the supply of the goods, as where it was made a condition of the hire of a motor-car to an infant that he should be absolutely liable for injuries to the car whether or not they resulted from his own negligence.

(2) The second kind of contract that is binding on an infant is a *beneficial contract of service.* A contract of apprenticeship is a common instance of this kind of contract. The governing consideration with such a contract is whether it is for the benefit and advantage of the infant. The mere fact that some of the terms of the contract were unduly burdensome and prejudicial to the infant would not of itself be enough to make the contract void. What must be looked at is the effect of the contract as a whole, and if, when so regarded, it can be said that the contract is for the infant's benefit, then it is binding.

Void contracts. The contracts now to be dealt with are those that are void in the sense that, unlike the voidable contracts discussed immediately following, they can never at any time be enforced against the infant. This class of contracts consists of the following:

(1) Contracts for the repayment of money already lent or to be lent.

(2) Contracts for goods supplied or to be supplied (other than necessaries).

(3) All accounts stated with infants. An "account stated" is a statement of account made up by the creditor, showing a sum due to him on trading or a balance due on cross-trading, which sum or balance the debtor has acknowledged to be due. Ordinarily, the creditor can sue for the sum or balance alone, without specifying the individual items comprised in it. Where the debtor is an infant, however, the law says, in effect, that this cannot be done, but that all items must be detailed. The result is that the infant is given an opportunity of challenging any item open to objection on grounds of infancy.

The law declares that all the contracts in this group are "absolutely void," but it is not clear just what that means. The contracts, of course, as has already been stated, can never be enforced against the infant. It would appear, too, that they cannot be enforced by the infant against the other party, but this point has not yet been decided and the contrary view is held in some quarters.

It is, however, settled that, if goods have actually been supplied to an infant under a contract in this group, the supplier cannot sue the infant for their recovery, in spite of the fact that he is also barred by the law from suing the infant for payment. On the other hand, by way of levelling up matters it would seem, the law also lays down that, if the infant on his part has paid money or delivered goods to the other party, he cannot recover the money or the goods if he has received any benefit whatever under the contract.

Voidable contracts. This class of contract comprises all contracts entered into by an infant other than those contracts that are binding or void (as explained in the foregoing). And of voidable contracts themselves there are two kinds.

In the first place, there are contracts that are voidable in the sense that they are only binding if the infant does not repudiate them, as he may, either before reaching full age or within a reasonable time thereafter.

This particular kind of voidable contract is confined to contracts under which an infant acquires an interest in something of a permanent nature with continuing obligations, for example, land or shares in a company or an interest in a partnership.

What length of time after full age will be considered reasonable for purposes of repudiation depends on the particular circumstances of each case and no general rule can be laid down other than that, if a party desires to repudiate and has not done so by the time he reaches twenty-one, then the sooner he does so the better. It is conceivable that a delay of a year or even less might make repudiation impossible.

If the infant repudiates in time, then he ceases to be liable for any obligations that have already arisen under the contract but which he has not yet carried out. Moreover, the contract, having been lawfully repudiated, is at an end, so he is not liable for any future obligations either. On the other hand, any payments that may have been made by the infant cannot be recovered by him if he has had any benefit out of the contract.

So where an infant repudiates an agreement he has made to enter into partnership, and the repudiation is made before the partnership actually commences or at any rate before he has had any benefit out of it, he is able to recover any money he has paid in advance towards the prospective partnership. But if the partnership has, in fact, commenced before the repudiation and the infant has had benefits, for example, use of his partner's premises, then he cannot recover the advance payment.

In the second place, there is the much more common kind of voidable contract that is voidable in the sense that it can never be enforced against the infant, though the infant may enforce it against the other party. A promise to marry made by an infant is an example of such a voidable contract.

Ratification of infant's contract. The question may arise whether an infant after reaching full age may ratify a contract entered into by him during infancy, so as to make the contract enforceable against him when otherwise it would not be. The answer is that the law, in its desire to protect infants, does not allow such ratification, not even if the infant should have received fresh consideration for his ratification.

Of course, after the infant came of age he could enter into an entirely fresh contract to the same effect as the unenforceable one and, provided there is fresh consideration, such a fresh contract would be binding on him. As may be imagined, however, it is sometimes a matter of great difficulty to say whether a particular transaction is a ratification or an entirely fresh contract. There is one special case, however, where the law will not give effect to even a fresh contract (as distinct from a ratification) and that is the case of a fresh promise to pay a debt contracted during infancy.

JOINT CONTRACTS BETWEEN ADULT AND INFANT. Where an adult and an infant have together jointly undertaken contractual obligations, the question arises whether the other party to the contract can sue both the adult and the infant, or either of them. Here, the rule is that if the nature of the contract is such that it can be carried out only by the two of them together (for example, a music-hall special "double act") and also of a kind that does not bind the infant, then the adult is released; but, if it can be performed by the adult alone, then he must perform it.

JUDICIAL SEPARATION. See MATRIMONIAL PROCEEDINGS.

MAINTENANCE. See RIGHTS AND DUTIES OF HUSBAND AND WIFE and INCIDENTAL CONSEQUENCES OF MATRIMONIAL PROCEEDINGS.

MARRIAGE OF INFANTS. An infant (a person under twenty-one years of age) intending to marry requires the consent of his or her parents or guardian, except when the infant is already a widower or widow. When both parents are living together the consent of both is required, but if only one parent is alive and there is no other guardian then the consent of the one parent is sufficient. When the parents or guardian refuse consent, application may be made to the court (usually the Magistrates' Court) for its consent, which, if given, is sufficient. When consent cannot be obtained because of the absence or inaccessibility or disability of the person whose consent is required, the Superintendent Registrar of Marriages may dispense with it.

The marriage of an infant without the requisite consent is not invalid. But, if either party to the marriage, for the purpose of procuring banns or registrar's certificate, falsely declares that consent has been obtained, he or she may be liable to a criminal prosecution; moreover, the parent or guardian of the innocent party may take proceedings through the Attorney-General to prevent the guilty party acquiring any property through the marriage.

MATRIMONIAL PROCEEDINGS. This section deals with the different kinds of relief which the courts may grant to husbands and wives where one spouse has committed some matrimonial offence, or where in other circumstances relief ought to be given. First of all, the different reliefs are each dealt with separately, the grounds on which the relief may be granted being stated and the effect of the relief on the marriage relationship.

Under the heading INCIDENTAL CONSEQUENCES OF MATRIMONIAL PROCEEDINGS there are described certain incidental rights, such as the right to financial support or the right to custody of children, that emerge in favour of one spouse or the other in consequence of matrimonial proceedings having been begun or successfully terminated.

Apart from proceedings to obtain magistrates' orders, all matrimonial proceedings are heard by the Divorce Division of the High Court or at Assizes.

Magistrates' orders for separation and maintenance. Magistrates' Courts may make separation orders, the effect of such an order being that the husband and wife are no longer bound to cohabit, though they remain legally husband and wife. The order, indeed, has the same effect in all respects as a decree of judicial separation granted on the ground of cruelty.

The wife may apply for a separation order on various grounds, including the conviction of the husband for assault upon her, or his desertion, persistent cruelty, adultery, habitual drunkenness, or wilful neglect to maintain her or her infant children. The only grounds on which a husband can obtain an order are his wife's adultery, or persistent cruelty to his children, or habitual drunkenness. A separation order ceases to have effect if the parties resume cohabitation, or if the wife commits adultery.

Where a husband wilfully neglects to maintain his wife, she may apply to the magistrates for a maintenance order. Such an order may be granted also by way of addition to a separation order. The maximum amount that may be granted is £5 per week plus 30s. each per week for the children of the marriage until they reach the age of sixteen (or if necessary for education or training up to twenty-one).

High Court orders for maintenance. Since December, 1949, the High Court, too, can award a wife maintenance for herself and children and it is not restricted to any amount.

Judicial separation. A decree of judicial separation may be granted on any of the grounds that would entitle the petitioner to petition for divorce, or on the ground of failure to comply with a decree for restitution of conjugal rights. A decree of judicial separation entitles the petitioning spouse to live apart from the other; such living apart, therefore, does not constitute the matrimonial offence of desertion.

The decree does not alter the marriage relationship; the parties are still married, are still lawful husband and wife, the only difference being that the party obtaining the decree is excused from the obligation of cohabiting with the other party. There is, however, one result affecting the rights of a spouse to share in the estate of the other spouse who has died intestate (without leaving a will) and it is that a husband is excluded from any such share in any property that has been acquired by or has devolved upon the wife during actual separation under the decree; and this is so even where it was the husband who obtained the decree. There is no similar exclusion of a wife from property acquired by the husband during the separation.

Restitution of conjugal rights. Where one spouse has, without lawful excuse, broken off cohabitation with the other, in other words, deserted the other, then the other may petition the court for a decree of restitution of conjugal rights, that is to say, a decree ordering the offending spouse to resume cohabitation. The breaking off of cohabitation, it should be emphasized, must be without lawful excuse. Where the respondent has good reason for deserting, the petitioner's decree will not be granted. What amounts to desertion and good reason is explained below and, in particular, reference is made to desertion as a ground for divorce. Decree may also be granted on the ground that there never was any cohabitation at all.

Failure of the respondent to obey the decree of restitution is itself a ground for judicial separation, as has been already stated. Refusal to obey also entitles the petitioner to an order against the respondent for periodical payments for the support of the petitioner and any children of the marriage. Such payments may be ordered to be paid even by a wife respondent to a husband petitioner if the wife has property or income of her own.

Dissolution of marriage. In the case of each of the three forms of relief described in the foregoing, it is important to observe that, notwithstanding the order or decree granted by the court, the marriage itself remains valid and subsisting, and the parties remain legal husband and wife. The forms of relief about to be described, however, have this in common, that the relief consists essentially in dissolving the marriage altogether so that, after final decree has been granted, the parties are no longer husband and wife and are free to marry again. Dissolution of marriage in this way results from either a decree of divorce or a decree of nullity.

Divorce. The following are the grounds on which either husband or wife may petition for divorce:

(1) Adultery of the other spouse;
(2) Desertion by the other spouse, without lawful cause, for at least three years prior to presenting the petition;
(3) Cruelty;
(4) Incurable insanity.

Desertion. This means intentionally bringing to an end the normal cohabitation of married life. Cohabitation means simply the sharing of their society or company by each spouse with the other; in law, it does not necessarily imply sexual intercourse, so that the refusal of sexual intercourse by a spouse does not of itself constitute desertion (though it is a lawful cause that would entitle the other spouse to desert).

Again, although desertion usually involves, in fact, living apart, yet living apart is not necessary to constitute desertion. There have been cases of desertion where the parties remained under the same roof, but the respondent shut himself off from the petitioner.

If the respondent has lawful cause for deserting, then, of course, the desertion is not a ground for divorce; but the lawful cause must be some strong and substantial reason, such as the adultery or other serious misconduct of the petitioner, or, as mentioned above, his or her refusal of sexual intercourse.

A spouse living apart under a voluntary agreement for separation is not in desertion.

In all cases of desertion, the petitioning spouse must be able to show that he or she has not repulsed any genuine efforts at reconciliation that may have been made by the deserting spouse; any such repulsion would have the legal effect that the desertion was thereby ended. But the deserted spouse is not under any obligation to attempt to induce the deserting spouse to return.

Cruelty. The cruelty must amount to injury or apprehended injury to body or mind. Thus the constant nagging of a scolding wife, for instance, does not of itself constitute cruelty but, if it caused the husband to have a nervous breakdown or threatened to do so, it would be cruelty.

Incurable insanity. The respondent must be incurably of unsound mind and must have been continuously under care and treatment in a mental institution for at least five years immediately preceding the petition.

As has been stated, the foregoing grounds entitle either a husband or a wife to petition for divorce. But, in addition, there are three grounds open only to a wife; they are rape, sodomy and bestiality committed by the husband since the marriage.

A spouse who has obtained a magistrates' separation order (see opposite, Magistrates' orders for separation and maintenance) or a decree of judicial separation, may subsequently petition for divorce on the same grounds; the court may then treat the earlier order or decree as sufficient proof of the cruelty or desertion, etc., thus saving the expense of calling witnesses again. But the petitioner himself must, nevertheless, give evidence.

A petition for divorce cannot be presented until the expiry of three years from the date of marriage except by leave of a judge of the High Court, which may be granted on grounds of exceptional hardship to the petitioner or exceptional depravity on the part of the respondent.

When petition may be refused. Even if the petitioner is able to prove the facts on which the petition is based, it does not follow that decree of divorce will necessarily be granted. In the first place, the court must, on the evidence, be satisfied as to the following:

(1) That, where the ground of the petition is adultery, the other spouse has not connived at or condoned the adultery. (Connivance means either actively aiding or passively permitting the respondent's conduct. Condonation means pardon granted by the petitioner on condition that the respondent "goes straight" in future; but if, after obtaining pardon, the respondent should subsequently commit a matrimonial offence, the original offence is revived and the petitioner can then found a petition for divorce on the original offence, even if the subsequent offence is not itself a ground for divorce; therefore, subsequent desertion for less than three years, which is not itself a ground for divorce, would let in a petition on the ground of a prior condoned adultery.)

(2) Where the ground is cruelty, that the respondent has not condoned the cruelty.

(3) That there is no collusion between petitioner and respondent, that is to say, that the proceedings are not taken by agreement between them.

If the court is not satisfied as to these three matters, it must refuse to grant divorce.

In the second place, there are certain circumstances where the court has a discretion to grant or refuse decree; they are: (*a*) where, whatever the ground of the petition, there has been adultery, unreasonable delay in petitioning, or cruelty on the part of the petitioner; (*b*) where, when the petition is grounded on adultery or cruelty, there has been desertion or wilful separation by the petitioner prior to the adultery or cruelty; (*c*) where, when the petition is grounded on adultery or insanity or desertion, it is proved that the wilful neglect or misconduct of the petitioner has conduced to the adultery, insanity or desertion.

Adultery on the part of the petitioner is, therefore, always a ground on which the court may in its discretion refuse to grant the petition, and a petitioner who has himself or herself committed adultery must, in the petition, ask the court to exercise its discretion in his or her favour, and must lodge with the court a separate document, called a discretion statement giving particulars of the adultery and any other relevant facts to enable the court to exercise its discretion.

Nullity of marriage. A decree of nullity is the second form of relief that results in the complete dissolution of the marriage. Here, however, an important distinction must be drawn between a so-called "marriage" which is void from the very beginning and which, indeed, never was a marriage at all in law, and, on the other hand, a voidable marriage which is a valid legal marriage that may be made void by a decree of court.

(1) A "marriage" of the first kind may be void because some essential required for a valid legal marriage was wanting at the time it took place. Thus, a marriage will be invalid if one of the parties already has a living lawful spouse, or if the parties are within the prohibited degrees of blood-relationship or affinity, or if either of them is under sixteen years of age, or if, for some reason (for example, insanity or intoxication or intimidation), one of the parties was unable to give a real consent to marriage, or if there was some defect in the formalities of the marriage of which both parties were aware.

Since there never was a valid marriage at all in this case, it is not necessary to go to the court for relief. The court, however, has authority to grant a declaration that such a "marriage" is void, and interested parties usually obtain a declaration so as to have official proof of the fact. Any children of such a "marriage" are, of course, illegitimate.

(2) In the case of a voidable marriage, however, relief can be obtained only by recourse to the court. Here the marriage is quite valid from the beginning, and the parties are legally husband and wife, but it is open to one of the parties on certain grounds to petition the court for a decree of nullity. The grounds on which such a decree may be granted are:

(*a*) Physical incapacity of the respondent to consummate the marriage, that is, to have sexual union; such incapacity must have existed at the time of the marriage. Mere sterility does not amount to incapacity.

(*b*) Wilful refusal of the respondent to consummate the marriage.

(*c*) That either party was, at the time of the marriage, mentally defective within the meaning of the Mental Deficiency Acts or subject to recurrent fits of insanity or epilepsy. Insanity, if incurable, is also a ground for divorce, as has been shown; but as a ground for nullity proceedings the insanity need not be incurable, though it must have existed at the time the marriage took place. Either party may petition on this ground—even the insane party.

(*d*) That the respondent was, at the time of the marriage, suffering from venereal disease in a communicable form (whether acquired innocently or not).

(*e*) That the respondent wife was at the time of the marriage pregnant by some person other than the petitioner.

Where nullity is sought on any of grounds (*c*), (*d*) or (*e*), proceedings must be taken within a year of the date of marriage. Moreover, the court must be satisfied in these cases that the petitioner was at the time of the marriage ignorant of the facts alleged, and that, since discovering the facts, the petitioner has not voluntarily had intercourse with the other party.

The effect of a decree of nullity, as has been shown, is retrospective so that the parties are considered in the eyes of the law never to have been husband and wife at all. Nevertheless, in the interest of any children that may have been born of such a voidable marriage it is provided by Act of Parliament that such children are legitimate. But children born of a marriage which is void from the beginning (see above) are illegitimate.

Decree nisi and decree absolute. In proceedings for divorce and for nullity—and only in these two cases—the decree granted by the court in the first instance is called a decree nisi. This means that the decree is provisional or conditional (*nisi* being a Latin word meaning "unless"), but that it may be made absolute after the expiry of six weeks, on application to the court. The purpose of the six-week period is to allow an opportunity for anyone to inform the court of any circumstances, such as collusion or suppression of material facts, that would prevent a decree absolute being granted.

Any private person at all may so inform the court, but private intervention is rare, such action normally being taken by the King's Proctor, who is an official specially appointed for this and similar purposes in connexion with divorce and nullity proceedings. It is important to note that the marriage is not dissolved by a decree nisi, but only by a decree absolute. Between the dates of the two decrees, therefore, the parties are still husband and wife and neither is free to marry.

Presumption of death as ground for dissolution. Where there is no certain evidence that a spouse has died, but there are reasonable grounds for presuming that death has occurred (as, for example, if he or she has disappeared in a disaster), the other spouse may apply to the court for a declaration of presumption of death and dissolution of marriage. The circumstances from which a presumption of death may be inferred are, of course, most various, and it is for the court to decide in any particular case whether the presumption should be made.

There is one case, however, where the court is obliged to presume death, and that is where the absent spouse has been continuously absent for a period of at least seven years and the petitioner has no reason to believe that he or she has been living during that time, and there is no evidence that he or she was actually alive within the seven years. It should be noted that a marriage is not dissolved on grounds of presumed death unless and until a declaration to that effect is obtained from the court.

NULLITY OF MARRIAGE. See MATRIMONIAL PROCEEDINGS.

RESTITUTION OF CONJUGAL RIGHTS. See MATRIMONIAL PROCEEDINGS.

RIGHTS AND DUTIES OF HUSBAND AND WIFE.

Maintenance. A husband must maintain his wife according to his means. If he does not, she has implied authority to pledge his credit for necessaries suitable to *his* station in life; this authority exists also when the husband has deserted his wife or, by his misconduct, has caused her to leave him.

A husband whose wife becomes chargeable to the Assistance Board or the local authority, in consequence of his wilful failure to support her when he is able to do so, may be prosecuted under the criminal law. The Assistance Board or the local authority, moreover, may obtain an order against the husband for repayment of the cost of the wife's support as well as for her future support. If a wife deserts her husband, he is not liable for her support so long as she is in desertion; and if a wife commits adultery, his obligation to support her terminates altogether.

A wife is liable to support her husband (when he is unable to support himself) only if she has separate property of her own; but she is not under a legal duty to work in order to support him.

For enforcement of rights to maintenance see MATRIMONIAL PROCEEDINGS.

Right to each other's society. Husband and wife have each a right to the society of the other, so that each is bound to reside and cohabit with the other. But a husband is not entitled to use force either to prevent his wife leaving him or to bring her back; the law gives him other remedies in such an event. See MATRIMONIAL PROCEEDINGS.

Rights of property. Until the reforms, which began with an Act of 1857, most of the rights in and control over a woman's own property passed to her husband on marriage, except property given to a woman specifically for her separate use. Today, a married woman has full and unfettered rights in her own property just as if she were unmarried.

Until recently, when property was given to a woman by an instrument which imposed what is called a restraint on anticipation, such a woman, while she was married, could not dispose of the capital or assign the income of the property—in other words, she could not do anything that would prevent her being entitled to each full instalment of income as it fell due, though, of course, once the income did come into her hands, she could do what she liked with it.

But all such restraints, even if already in force, were abolished by Parliament in an Act of December, 1949.

Husband and wife may transfer property to each other, either for consideration or by way of gift, though if a husband has exercised undue influence on his wife to make the transfer it can be set aside by the court. When the transaction is by way of gift, the intention to make a gift must be capable of being clearly shown.

But the law presumes certain transactions to be by way of gift. Thus, where a husband purchases property or investments in his wife's name or transfers his own property from his name to hers, it is presumed, in the absence of any indication to the contrary, that he has made a gift to her; so, too, where the husband puts the property or investments into their joint names, the wife is presumed to be joint owner and, therefore, will take the whole by survivorship if the husband dies without leaving a will. But this rule does not apply where money is kept at a bank in joint names on current account (as distinct from deposit account).

The law is not so ready to presume a gift from a wife to her husband, and, where a wife puts her property into her husband's name alone or into their joint names, the law presumes rather that the husband is a trustee for his wife. A husband claiming a gift in such circumstances must provide clear proof.

Wife's debts and contracts. Where a woman has contracted debts before marriage, she remains liable for them after marriage to the extent of any property she may have of her own. Her husband is not liable for such debts, except to the extent of any property he may have acquired through the wife by the marriage; for example, under a marriage settlement.

With regard to contracts made by a wife during marriage, the position is that, if she makes them on her own behalf, she herself is liable, but if she makes them as agent for someone else she is not liable. The most usual case of a wife contracting as agent is, of course, where she contracts on behalf of her husband. Even then it is frequently only by implication that she is considered her husband's agent.

Thus, unless the contrary is proved, a wife is considered to be her husband's agent for the purpose of obtaining necessaries, and, therefore, to have his authority to pledge his credit for that purpose, so making her husband and not herself liable on the contract with the supplier; and this is so even if, as is usually the case, the wife says nothing to the supplier about her being her husband's agent.

What constitutes necessaries is to be determined by considering first the husband's actual style of living (whatever his means may be), and second whether they are the sort of things that it is usual for a wife to buy. If the purchases are of articles of luxury, or even excessive quantities of articles that would otherwise be necessaries, the husband will not be presumed liable.

The presumption will be rebutted and the husband will escape liability if it is proved that he, in fact, prohibited his wife from pledging his credit; and that is so whether the supplying tradesman was aware of the prohibition or not. Nor will the husband be liable if the wife is already adequately supplied with necessaries or has an adequate allowance for obtaining them, or even if she has a fixed allowance, agreed between her and her husband, for running the household.

It is apparent, therefore, that a tradesman supplying a wife with what, on the face of it, are necessaries cannot be sure that he can rely on the husband's credit; there are several possible risks and, if he wishes to be on the safe side, he should refer to the husband before supplying.

This question as to the husband's liability frequently arises where the husband and wife are living apart, and the answer then depends on the particular circumstances. If the separation is voluntary and the agreement makes provision for the wife's support, or if she undertakes to support herself, then the husband is not liable. But, if he fails to pay her what he agreed to pay, she would be entitled to pledge his credit so as to make him liable. If the separation is a judicial one (under decree of the court) the wife cannot pledge the husband's credit unless he fails to pay her any alimony that may have been awarded by the court. The third case is where the husband deserts his wife or puts her out of the house, or so misconducts himself or ill-treats her as to justify her in leaving him; if, in any such event, he fails to provide for her support she is entitled to pledge his credit. It is worth noting that, wherever a wife is entitled to pledge her husband's credit in such circumstances of separation, she is regarded by the law as her husband's agent by necessity, and her right remains valid notwithstanding that the husband may have expressly forbidden the tradesmen to give her credit.

The wife's right to pledge her husband's credit comes to an end on his death; she cannot thereafter make his estate liable. Adultery by the wife also terminates the right, and it is immaterial whether the supplying tradesman is aware of the fact or not.

Wife's savings. Any savings made by a wife from the income of her own property are, of course, her own. Where, however, the savings are out of an allowance provided by the husband for housekeeping or for dress and similar purposes, the position depends on whether the husband and wife are living together or apart. If together, the savings belong to the husband unless it can be proved he meant the wife to have them; if apart, the question is to be settled by reference to the terms of the separation agreement, if any, and all the circumstances of the case.

RIGHTS AND DUTIES OF PARENTS. The rights and duties of parents as guardians are dealt with under GUARDIANSHIP. Parenthood as such gives rise to other rights and duties, however, and it is these that are here considered.

With regard to maintenance of a child unable to support itself, the legal liability actually arises under the National Assistance Act of 1948 (which repealed and took the place of the former Poor Law). Both the father and mother are liable, insofar as they are able to meet it, to make repayment to the Assistance Board or the local authority of any sums expended by way of assistance on a child under sixteen years of age, even if illegitimate. There is no corresponding liability on a child to pay for assistance granted to its parents. Apart from that, a parent who wilfully neglects or deserts a child may be liable to criminal prosecution.

There is a legal duty laid on parents and guardians to cause a child between five and fifteen to receive an efficient elementary education, but the mode and place of education and its duration beyond the legal minimum are in the discretion of the guardian who, as has been stated, is usually (but not necessarily) the father or the mother.

The father has the right to determine in what religion the child shall be brought up, and the child must usually continue to be reared in that religion until he is twenty-one, even if the father should die or lose his right to custody or guardianship. A father cannot divest himself of this right even by agreement with the mother before marriage.

A parent is entitled to the earnings of an infant child residing with him, and also to the services of such a child. A parent has a claim on his own behalf against a third party who has wrongfully caused the death of his child, provided the parent has suffered actual or probable financial loss in consequence of the child's death; and a child has a corresponding right of action in respect of the death of its parents.

But, when the child is merely injured, the parent has no similar right on his own behalf; in such a case, his right of action can be only in the form of a claim for damages for loss of the infant child's services. So when an infant is seduced, the law does not look upon the mere seduction as an injury to the parent; but if, as a result of the seduction, the parent loses the child's services, for example, during confinement, then the parent has a course of action.

If, however, the parent has not, in fact, been in receipt of services from the child, for example, where the child is living away from home, then the parent has no cause of action.

SEPARATION. See MATRIMONIAL PROCEEDINGS.

2. HOUSEHOLDER AND LANDLORD

ANIMALS. The law classifies animals as domestic and wild. The former class includes horses, cattle, sheep, pigs, poultry, dogs and cats, and all these may be the subject of a charge of larceny. Only a qualified ownership is recognized in wild animals such as deer, hares, rabbits, pigeons and wild fowl.

A domestic animal is presumed to be harmless, and therefore its owner is not liable for any damage which it may commit contrary to its nature, but, if it be shown that the owner was aware of its vicious tendencies, he may be liable in negligence. Strict proof of negligence is required before the award of damages. A customer in a restaurant, who sued the proprietor for injuries caused by a cat, failed because he could not prove that the cat was known to be vicious towards human beings.

It is a general rule of law that the owner of horses, cattle, sheep, or pigs is bound to take care that the animals do not stray on to the land of his neighbour; and he is responsible for the consequences of trespass whether or not the escape was due to his negligence. But he may escape liability if he can show that the person who has suffered damage is under a duty to him (e.g., as tenant) to keep his land or garden fenced and has not done so.

Trespass may be committed when any part of the animal is over the boundary, as, for example, when a horse kicks another animal through a broken fence.

Obviously, such animals as horses and cattle must cause damage if they trespass in a garden or vegetable plot, and the natural propensity of an animal to stray is recognized by the law. Dogs and cats, by their nature, stray, but in ordinary circumstances they do not cause damage; therefore, no action can be brought in respect of trespass by them.

There is liability, however, if the owner deliberately sends his dog in search of game or rabbits on another man's land. It is an offence to poison a trespassing dog without reasonable excuse and without the owner's consent. If a dog is actually causing damage, attacking sheep or poultry, it may be killed. Any trespassing dog or other animal may be impounded, and held to secure payment of compensation for the damage.

A claim for damages against the owner of a cat, which had trespassed on a neighbour's land and killed his chickens, was unsuccessful, but a farmer who claimed because domestic pigeons kept in his neighbour's dovecot flew over his land and ate his corn succeeded in his action. No claim can arise for loss caused by a wild animal, although, as already stated, the owner of land has a qualified ownership in wild animals on his land.

The court dismissed a claim by a householder whose garden vegetables had been destroyed by wild rabbits, though, if it had been shown that the neighbouring landowner had overstocked his land with rabbits, the claim would have been allowed. Where a savage animal is kept as a pet and, through negligence of its owner, escapes and causes damage, the owner is liable. See also Section 7.

ELECTRICITY. See WATER, GAS AND ELECTRICITY.

FENCES. See HOUSEHOLDER'S RESPONSIBILITIES.

FREEHOLD. See INTEREST IN LAND.

FURNISHED HOUSES. See LANDLORD AND TENANT.

GAS. See WATER, GAS AND ELECTRICITY.

HOUSEHOLDER'S RESPONSIBILITIES. Fences. There is no obligation on a person (apart from any agreement) to fence his land, but, if fencing is erected, it must not be dangerous to other persons. Barbed-wire fences adjoining a highway, if a nuisance, may be removed on an order of the magistrates at the owner's expense. If, through lack of a fence or hedge, cattle and sheep trespass and cause damage on a neighbour's land, the owner is responsible.

In some districts there is a restriction imposed by local acts or bye-laws in the height of fences adjoining a highway, but, generally speaking, there is no limit to the height of a fence between adjoining houses, though if it interferes with a neighbour's rights of light an action may follow.

Party walls. Party walls separating adjoining houses are deemed to be severed vertically between the respective owners, and each owner has a right of support and use over the half which belongs to his neighbour. In the case of a flat or one room let as a dwelling, all the walls and the floor and ceiling may, in effect, be party walls.

Right to support. A man must exercise his rights over his own property without causing damage or nuisance to the property of his neighbour. Obviously, the removal of support afforded to neighbouring land by one's own soil is an interference with the natural rights of property, and is actionable. There is no right to any particular kind of support, but only to the ordinary employment of the land. Excavation close to a neighbour's land may damage the foundations of his house and lead to a claim for damages.

Being a right *ex jure naturae* (springing from the natural law), the right to support does not depend on statute but is incidental to the ownership of the land. An adjacent building (as distinct from the soil on which it stands) has no natural right to support, but a right to support may be acquired by express grant (for example, it may be implied where semi-detached houses are built in a row). Accordingly, great care is required before undertaking structural alterations which interfere with the right to support. This applies particularly in the case of blocks of flats.

Dilapidations. A householder is under no obligation to his neighbour (again, apart from agreement) to keep his home in repair or paint it so as to preserve the standard of the district. Nevertheless the local authority has wide powers if the state of dilapidation renders the house dangerous. In such cases the owner may be called upon to execute the necessary repairs and, if he does not do so, the work may be carried out by the authority at his expense.

Overhanging trees. Overhanging trees or the roots of trees from a neighbour's land may be cut without notice being given to the neighbour, who has no redress in law, even if the cutting causes the loss of his trees. Similarly, an owner can remove water-spouts or eaves which project over his land.

When trees obstruct a highway, the local authority may order the occupier of the land to prune them. On default, a summons may be issued, and the magistrates have power to order the necessary work to be done within ten days (penalty £2 fine). If fences obstruct the view of road users at corners and render the highway dangerous, they may be removed, suitable compensation being payable to the owner of the land.

In a case where a householder was sued because a branch of an elm tree fell and damaged the plaintiff's cart on the highway, the court held that there was no liability on the householder as he had not been negligent because he did not know the tree was diseased and likely to cast the branch.

But in another case, damages against a landowner were awarded to a pedestrian who, when on the highway, was injured by a tree branch falling on him. The evidence showed that the tree was so old that it had become dangerous and that the danger was so apparent that an ordinary person could have seen it.

INJURIES. See LIABILITY IN TORT.

INTEREST IN LAND—FREEHOLD AND LEASEHOLD. English law recognizes two kinds of interest in land, *freehold* (sometimes called an estate in fee simple), which is really absolute ownership, and *leasehold*, which means that the land is held for a fixed term of years and then returns to the owner.

Freehold. Obviously, in buying a house, it is advisable to obtain a freehold, though even a freehold may be subject to restrictions. These may arise in several ways. The original owner may have sold the land subject to certain covenants running with the land, that is to say, there are obligations which bind all subsequent purchasers. Such covenants may concern the use of land; for example, that it may be used only for the erection of residential property of a certain character; or the covenants may confer a right-of-way over the land on the public or on adjoining owners.

Apart from these restrictions, the area may have been included in a town planning scheme by the local authority with the result that the use of the property must conform to the requirements of the scheme.

Care is needed, therefore, in buying a house or land and, although it is possible to acquire a freehold without taking professional advice, the ordinary person, unaccustomed to property deals, should always consult a solicitor and also ask for a surveyor's report in the case of a house which is not new. Otherwise he may find himself faced with heavy bills for new drains or repairs to the building.

Although a freeholder enjoys absolute ownership, that does not mean that he can do as he likes with his own. If he wishes to make considerable alterations, for instance, to add another bedroom or to erect a garage, he can do so only after submitting plans to the local authority, and all work done must comply with the building bye-laws; in recent years it has also been necessary to obtain a building licence.

In 1925, Lord Birkenhead, then Lord Chancellor, succeeded in getting through Parliament six statutes (known generally as the Law of Property Acts) with the design of codifying the complicated body of law relating to land which contained many ancient rules and principles unsuited to modern days. The intention was that all land should eventually be registered in the Land Registry, and that the owner should hold, as proof of his title, one document, a land certificate, instead of the usual conveyance or title deeds written in legal language.

The register itself contains all the covenants and charges over the land, and the land certificate is a simple document giving a description of the land and the owner's name. This can be passed from the owner to any fresh owner without formality, and all the new owner has to do is to go to the registry and produce the certificate so that it can be cancelled, the register corrected, and a new land certificate issued to him.

In practice, of course, the transaction of buying land with a registered title is not quite so simple. It is always necessary, for instance, to search the register just before the purchase money is paid over, to make sure that no charge has been registered against the land and that there has been no misrepresentation in regard to what is being actually sold; and various other precautions must be taken in respect of unpaid taxes, rates and insurance.

So far this system of registered title is in operation only in the counties of London and Middlesex and in the boroughs of Eastbourne, Hastings and Croydon.

Leasehold. The term leasehold is usually applied to the grant of a lease of land for a long period, 99 years or 999 years. In the latter case, it is a freehold in all but name, and it is often held on a nominal rent (sometimes called a peppercorn rent). Leases for 99 years are granted mostly for building, on payment of a lump sum, at a yearly ground rent. A lease for a longer period than three years must be made by deed. The lease is assignable and the person to whom it is assigned holds it on the same terms as did the original lessee, and is under the same obligations.

Unless there is agreement to the contrary, the Law of Property Act, 1925, implies, in every contract for the sale of freehold or leasehold land, the following covenants: (1) that the vendor is in a position to convey the land; (2) that the purchaser shall have quiet enjoyment; (3) that the land is free from encumbrances; and (4) that the vendor will do what is necessary to assure (that is, convey) the land to the purchaser. In addition, on the sale of a leasehold, there is an implied covenant that the lease is valid, that the rent due has been paid, and that all the covenants have been duly fulfilled.

Once a contract for the sale of land has been made, either party to it who fails to carry out his contract can be compelled to do so by an action claiming specific performance or, if the innocent party prefers it, the payment of damages. If the purchaser or vendor dies after making the contract, but before the conveyance is completed, the contract must be carried out by the executor.

In all deals in land, the buyer must keep a sharp watch over his own interest. It is not the duty of the vendor, for instance, to disclose that at certain seasons the land is likely to become flooded, or that a noisy factory interferes with the quietness of the house.

After purchasing a home and meadow adjoining, a buyer found that there was a public right-of-way across the meadow, and brought an action on the ground that he had been misled by the vendor. But the court refused relief, maintaining that a buyer must look after himself, and that, if he had done so, the fact that there was right-of-way detracting from the value of the meadow would have been discovered.

LANDLORD AND TENANT. A tenant is a person granted exclusive possession of land or of a house or flat or other building for a limited time at a rent payable to the owner (the landlord), weekly, monthly, or yearly as the case may be. There are four kinds of such tenancies:

(1) **Tenancy on sufferance;** this means remaining in possession of the premises, after the right to possession has expired, without the landlord's assent or dissent. Such a tenancy can be terminated without notice by the landlord.

(2) **Tenancy at will;** this arises when a person enters into possession of a house with the landlord's consent but without an agreement. It may be ended at any time without notice.

(3) **Periodic tenancy;** this may be yearly, half-yearly, quarterly, monthly, or weekly, and arises by agreement and continues until determined by notice to quit given by either side. Apart from agreement to the contrary, the length of the notice must correspond with the period of the letting—a week for a weekly tenancy, and so on—and the notice must expire at the end of the period. In the case of yearly tenancies, six months' notice must be given to expire within the tenancy year.

(4) **Tenancy for a fixed term;** this arises when a landlord lets a house for a specified number of years, usually seven or fourteen, with an option for renewal on a break clause at stated periods. Such leases should be in writing but there is no legal requirement that this should be done except in regard to leases of over three years which must be made by deed under seal. They sometimes bear hardly on a tenant because of special repairing clauses, and it is wise to submit such documents to a solicitor before completion.

The advantage of a written tenancy agreement is that it sets out the rights and liabilities of the parties, the rent payable and the time of payment, responsibility for rates and insurance, the duration of the tenancy, and so on. If there is no agreement, the tenant is bound to use and keep the premises in a tenant-like manner, and, whether there is a written agreement or not, there is imported into all tenancies an implied covenant of quiet enjoyment.

Repairs. What is, perhaps, not generally known is that a landlord, by the act of letting, does not guarantee that the premises are fit for habitation or that they will be kept in a state of repair throughout the tenancy. To this principle of the common law there is a statutory exception in the case of houses let at a rent not exceeding £40 in London and

£26 elsewhere. In such cases, the landlord is also permitted by statute to enter the premises at all reasonable times in order to see the state of repair on giving twenty-four hours' notice in writing.

Where a tenant expressly agrees to execute repairs, he must do so without a formal demand by the landlord. But where the landlord has undertaken repairs, he must be requested by the tenant because (apart from any statutory or contractual permission) the landlord has no right to enter the leased premises in order to see their condition for himself.

Fixtures. A fixture firmly attached to the land or building, for example, a tool shed, is generally known as a landlord's fixture and cannot be removed by the tenant. But where a tenant affixes a cupboard or other removable fixture for his own convenience during his tenancy, he is entitled to remove it, though he must not damage the premises in doing so. Tenant's fixtures, as they are called, must be removed before the end of the tenancy or they become the landlord's property.

Rent. Rent is payable throughout the tenancy, and this obligation remains even though the premises are destroyed by fire or rendered uninhabitable by flood or storm, unless there is a clause in the agreement to the contrary. Rates are payable by the occupier of premises but, where small houses are concerned, they are usually paid by the landlord. A tenant who pays rates due from the landlord can deduct the amount from the next payment of rent.

Upon failure by the tenant to pay the rent, the landlord may adopt one of the following courses: (1) sue for the arrears in an ordinary action; (2) distrain on the furniture and effects of the tenants in the house; (3) where there is a clause in the lease or tenancy agreement providing for re-entry on forfeiture, re-enter and resume possession of his property.

It is now the law that no action can be brought, nor can a distress be levied, to recover rent arrears after six years, whether the lease is made by deed or not.

A landlord can levy a distress personally, though usually he acts through a certificated bailiff, which is the wiser course. There is power to seize all movable goods belonging to the tenant, except the following which are privileged from distress: fixtures, perishable goods, loose cash but not money in a bag, goods delivered to a person in the way of his trade, for example, shoes sent to a cobbler for repair, articles in actual use, wearing apparel, the bedding of the tenant or his family, tools of the tenant's trade, goods belonging to a lodger or stranger having no interest in the property. (These must be set out in a formal written declaration to the distrainor.)

When distrained, the goods may be sold within five days (extended to fifteen in some cases) at auction, and any money obtained above the debt due and costs must be given to the tenant. Illegal distress renders a landlord liable to civil proceedings.

The right of re-entry may be exercised with or without an order of the court, and, in either event, a tenant may ask for relief against forfeiture. As a rule, this is granted on terms, for the judges have no liking for this remedy and are specially reluctant to make orders against tenants who have failed to comply, say, with a covenant to repair or to maintain the house or land. The landlord who is asking for forfeiture must first serve a notice on the tenant specifying the breach of the covenant, demanding compensation in money for the breach if he so desires, and calling on the tenant to remedy the breach if possible. Although the forfeiture of a lease puts an end to any sub-lease granted under it, a subtenant also may be given relief on terms.

LEASEHOLD. See INTEREST IN LAND.

LIABILITY IN TORT. The occupier of a house or land is under a duty not to cause injury or damage to those who enter his premises or land, and this duty is greater in the case of invitees and licensees, that is those who so enter by his express or implied invitation or permission, than it is where trespassers, who enter without leave, are concerned.

An invitee is, strictly speaking, someone who enters on business, for example, a plumber who comes to execute repairs. The occupier must take care to protect such an invitee against an unexpected or unusual danger as, for example, a flight of steps in a dark passage or anything in the nature of a concealed trap. It was said in one leading case that the duty towards a licensee is less than this, for he must protect himself from obvious dangers; but if there is a hidden danger, the occupier must warn him against it.

The trespasser, the person who comes on land without any right, is regarded differently in law. He must take care of himself. There is no duty on the householder to warn him of the state of the premises—he is supposed to take those as he finds them. Any special measure designed to injure a trespasser is, however, unlawful.

These rules apply also to children except that account must be taken of the irresponsibility of children in deciding what is a danger and what is adequate warning.

An action for negligence against her host was brought by a visitor to a house because she sustained serious injuries by falling over highly polished linoleum, but it failed. The judge held that a polished floor was not a hidden danger.

In most cases the claims arise out of some alleged structural defect of which the householder was aware or ought to have been aware. If he could not possibly have been aware of the danger, as in the case of the diseased tree which fell on a highway and injured a passer-by, and the evidence showed that the owner did not know the tree was dangerous, the claim against him must fail. He would be liable if he had known of the defect and failed to remedy it, or if he had actually caused the danger.

Injury or damage caused by an escape of gas or water is actionable if it is shown that the escape is due to the defendant's negligence. In a case where a man, in burning garden refuse, had made a bonfire close to the boundary of his land and destroyed his neighbour's fence, he was ordered to pay damages. Damage caused by something which is designed to benefit the tenants in a house, or the tenants of semi-detached houses, is not actionable without proof of negligence.

The householder or landowner has himself a civil right of action against trespassers for any damage caused. There is no possibility of succeeding in a criminal prosecution unless some damage is proved. In one of the leading cases it was held that the fact that the owner of a field had proved that sixpennyworth of damage had been caused to his grass was sufficient to justify the infliction of a fine by the justices. Trespassers, however, can certainly be removed with the use of no more force than is necessary, though where a violent trespasser is concerned the best course is to send for the police.

Damages can be recovered, in the Metropolitan Area, for trespass against a person who sticks bills or advertisements on another's property without his consent, and, in other districts, there are local bye-laws which make bill-sticking a summary offence.

LODGERS. See LANDLORD AND TENANT and SUB-TENANTS AND LODGERS.

MORTGAGES. It is not always convenient for a buyer of a house or other property to put down the full purchase price in cash, and if so he pays a proportion and borrows the remainder on mortgage. This simply means that he pledges his house as security for borrowed money. A deed is drawn up which differs in form according to whether the owner (the mortgagor) has a freehold or leasehold title.

In a mortgage of freehold, the owner grants the mortgagee (the lender) a lease for three thousand years, subject to the condition that the lease shall cease when the mortgage is redeemed by the payment back of the full sum borrowed with all interest due. A leasehold mortgage is made by a sub-lease for a term one day shorter than that held by the borrower, subject to a provision for termination on redemption.

There is also another form of mortgage, known as an equitable mortgage, which arises when an owner borrows money by depositing his deeds of title with the lender; but this is usually adopted only as a temporary expedient for a short loan, as the protection afforded to the mortgagee is not so effective as it is when a proper mortgage deed is executed.

A building-society mortgage differs in some respects from an ordinary mortgage, though the same law applies with regard to the remedies of the mortgagor and mortgagee, and it is not right to say that a special law applies to building-society mortgages. Each society consists of borrowing and advancing members and, when a borrowing member is granted a mortgage, he is subject to the particular rules of the society regarding the payment of principal and interest, often by monthly instalments. Some societies impose fines or forfeiture in the event of failure to pay the amount owing at the stated time.

So long as the mortgagor keeps to the terms of his contract he cannot be troubled by the mortgagee, but should he default in paying any principal sum or interest due, the mortgagee has several courses open to him. These are as follows:

(1) He can take possession of the land and take the profits from it to meet the debt due; or (2) he can put in a receiver to administer the land; or (3) he can, if the mortgagor does not comply with a notice to pay the sum due in three months, or where there is two months' interest due, or where the mortgagor has broken some covenant in the deed apart from the covenant to pay, sell the land; or (4) he can obtain a foreclosure order from the court under which the land vests in him without giving the mortgagor the right to redeem.

The last remedy is carefully dispensed by the court, and it is now more usual to order the sale of the land. If it should bring in more than is due to him, the mortgagee must hand over the balance to the mortgagor.

While in possession, a mortgagee has wide powers over the land. He may, for example, grant leases or cut and sell ripe timber trees. The cost of the mortgage deed and the release on redemption fall on the mortgagor. Unless otherwise declared in the will, a bequest of mortgaged property means that the beneficiary takes the estate subject to the mortgage.

NUISANCE. An action for nuisance may be maintained against a householder who causes fumes or smells which interfere with the ordinary standard of comfort of human existence. Many different kinds of annoyances have been held to amount to nuisances in law under this head, and have been restrained by injunction. Among them are the burning of bricks or offensive refuse, fumes from chemical works, the deposit of offensive refuse, and the smells from a fried-fish shop.

Apart altogether from the private remedies open to persons aggrieved by such nuisances as noxious smells or fumes or the carrying on of dangerous trades, there are remedies provided by the Public Health Acts under which heavy penalties may be inflicted by the magistrates. In consequence, it is advisable, in such cases, to refer the matter to the local sanitary inspector; he will take action if the nuisance affects the general public as well as persons in the immediate vicinity.

Another common form of nuisance arises from noise and vibration. Loudspeakers and piano-playing late at night can be prevented by injunction, and so can vibration caused by machinery. In one case, the court awarded compensation to the owner of some ancient property which had been damaged by vibration set up by a deep excavation at the other side of the street. See also NUISANCE in Section 8.

PETROL. See STORAGE OF PETROL.

RENT RESTRICTION ACTS. Passed as emergency legislation in the First World War, the Rent Restriction Acts have been renewed from year to year and now constitute a formidable body of statutory law with hundreds of judicial decisions on the true legal meaning of the Acts. The object of the Acts is to control rents in order to prevent landlords letting to the highest bidder and turning out tenants unable to meet ever-increasing rents.

The premises protected by the Acts are houses or parts of houses let as separate dwellings; but they must be let unfurnished and without board or attendance. Since the house must be a separate dwelling a tenant is not protected if he shares any "living accommodation" (and this includes a kitchen, but not a bathroom) with his landlord. But sharing with another tenant does not destroy his protection. A letting for business purposes is not protected (but if only partly for business and partly for dwelling it is protected) nor is a letting at a rent that is not more than two-thirds of the rateable value. If a house is let with more than two acres of land (agricultural land or allotments or poultry farm) it is outside the Act. A special provision excludes council houses.

Even if a dwelling does not fall within the above exceptions, it may be outside the Acts by reason of the rent. The statutory limit has varied from time to time, but now (under the 1939 Act) dwelling houses with rateable values of not more than £100 a year in the Metropolitan Police area on 6 April, 1939, and not more than £75 elsewhere on 1 April, 1939, are protected.

The figure shown in the Current Valuation List is accepted as the rateable value. New property built since the dates named is assessed at the first assessment. It does not follow that a suite of rooms in a large house valued for rates above the statutory figure is excluded. In such cases, an application can be made by the sub-tenants of rooms for an apportionment of the rent of the whole house.

Once a house is within the Acts, it is spoken of as a controlled house and has a standard rent. This means the rent at which the accommodation was let on 1 September, 1939, or, if not then let, the rent at which it was first let. The standard rent of houses which were controlled before the 1939 Act came into operation (2 September, 1939) is the amount at which they were let on that day or if not then let the rent at which they were last let before that date.

In regard to houses which were first brought under control by the 1939 Act, the only increases allowed above the standard rent are a sum for any increase in rates payable by the landlord and an allowance (8 per cent) in respect of structural alterations and improvements made since 2 September, 1939. Any excess payment above the standard rent is recoverable by action in the County Court subject to a limit of two years in all. Disputes regarding the standard rent or apportionment where a house is subdivided are decided by the County Court.

In the case of houses and flats let for the first time after 1 September, 1939, the Rent Acts did not prevent a landlord from demanding any rent he could get and that rent became the standard rent. Now, as a result of the Landlord and Tenant (Rent Control) Act, 1949, that position has been changed. The landlord or the tenant can apply to the rent tribunal (see below) to determine the reasonable rent, and if that figure is less than the standard rent it becomes the standard rent from the day on which the tribunal gave its decision. In determining what rent is a reasonable rent the tribunal must not pay regard to the fact that a premium has been paid in respect of the grant, renewal, or continuance of the tenancy.

It is an offence (punishable summarily by a fine of £100 with repayment of premium at the discretion of the court) to require the payment of any "key money" or other premium in addition to the rent as a condition of the grant, renewal, or continuance of a controlled tenancy. Premiums as a condition of the assignment of a tenancy are likewise prohibited. Agreements for the payment of premiums made since 25 March, 1949, and before 2 June, 1949, which would be unlawful under the Act can be set aside at the option of the parties thereto.

Where the purchase of any furniture, fittings or other articles has been required as a condition of the grant, renewal, continuance or assignment of a tenancy, and the price exceeds the reasonable price of such articles, the excess shall be treated as if it were a premium required to be paid as a condition of the grant, renewal, continuance or assignment of a tenancy and the above provisions apply.

A rent book must be used for weekly tenancies. It must contain full particulars of the standard rent.

Any provision in a lease that the Rent Acts are not to apply is invalid. A tenant who remains on after his lease has expired is known as a statutory tenant, because he holds only under the protection of the Acts (though on the same terms as under his contractual lease), and can be turned out only by a County Court order. To obtain such an order, the landlord must, in all cases, satisfy the court that it is reasonable to do so and prove *one* of the following eight grounds:

(1) That suitable alternative accommodation (that is, a house affording the tenant equivalent accommodation at a similar rent, close to his place of work and giving a like security of tenure) is or will be available on the day on which the possession order becomes effective.

(2) That the rent is in arrears, or the tenant has committed some breach of covenant, for example, a covenant not to use the house for business purposes.

(3) That the tenant or some person residing has committed a nuisance or annoyance to adjoining occupiers, or has committed waste, that is, destroyed the house or fixtures or the garden and so has caused the value of the house to deteriorate.

(4) That the tenant has given notice to quit and that the landlord would be seriously prejudiced if he did not obtain possession.

(5) That the tenant has, without the landlord's consent, sublet the whole of the house or, when part was already sublet, the remainder.

(6) That the home is overcrowded and the court is satisfied that the tenant could have abated the overcrowding if he had taken reasonable steps.

(7) That the landlord reasonably requires the home for some person in his whole-time employment, providing the tenant was given the tenancy because he was in the landlord's employment and that such employment has ceased, or the County Agricultural Committee

certifies that the home is required for a workman whose work is necessary to the proper working of a farm or holding.

(8) That the home is reasonably required by the landlord (not being a landlord who has become landlord by purchase since September, 1939) for himself, or his son or daughter over eighteen years, or his father or mother; but, in such a case, no order may be made if in all the circumstances (including the question of accommodation for both parties) greater hardship would be caused by granting than by refusing the order.

No distress can be made in respect of a controlled tenancy without the leave of the County Court. In practice, an immediate order is rare and, where the claim for possession rests on non-payment of rent, it is usual to make a suspended order, conditional to the payment of arrears.

The widow of a statutory tenant is entitled to continue the statutory tenancy providing she was living with her husband when he died. Where the tenant leaves no widow or is a woman, any member of his or her family who has lived with the tenant for six months can succeed.

Furnished houses. Until recently, furnished houses were not controlled, but now, under the Furnished Houses Rent Control Act, 1946, special rent tribunals have been established which have power, on the application of either landlord or tenant, or on the matter being referred to them by the local authority, to fix rent. The landlord, on a written demand by the tribunal, is bound to supply certain particulars regarding the letting, and the tribunal may inspect the premises. A day is fixed for the hearing and landlord and tenant may appear either in person or by legal representatives.

Rent may be fixed at a higher or lower figure than which is actually being paid. It is registered with the local authority, and it is then illegal to charge a higher rent (penalty, £100 fine or six months' imprisonment or both). Notice to quit given within three months after the tribunal's decision or during the period when the matter is pending decision is ineffective. By the Landlord and Tenant (Rent Control) Act, 1949, the tribunal now has power to give a longer period of security of tenure. When a period of three months security has been granted, the tenant, on receiving notice to quit, may apply to the tribunal for an extension and may be granted successive extensions of three months. He must apply before the notice to quit becomes effective.

The 1946 Act applies to furnished lettings with or without services, such as heating, lighting or hot water, but not to a letting with board. Hence it does not apply to a hostel or a suite of rooms in an hotel.

A landlord who lets premises furnished implies, by so doing, that the premises are fit for habitation at the beginning of the tenancy, but this is not a continuing warranty that the premises will so remain throughout the tenancy.

RENT. See LANDLORD AND TENANT and RENT RESTRICTION ACTS.

REPAIRS. See LANDLORD AND TENANT.

SOLICITORS' CHARGES IN PURCHASE OF PROPERTY.

Vendor's solicitor. For negotiating a sale by private contract, one per cent up to £3,000; one half per cent over £3,000 and up to £10,000; one quarter per cent over £10,000. For deducing title to freehold or leasehold, preparing contract and completing conveyance, one and a half per cent up to £1,000; one per cent on second and third £1,000; one-half per cent over £3,000 and up to £10,000; one-quarter per cent thereafter.

Purchaser's solicitor. As for vendor's solicitor.

Mortgagee's solicitor. For negotiating loan, one per cent up to £3,000; one-quarter per cent over £3,000 and up to £10,000; one-eighth per cent after.

Mortgagee's solicitor. For investigating title, preparing and completing mortgage, one and a half per cent on first £1,000; one per cent on second and third £1,000; one-half per cent over £3,000 and up to £10,000; one-quarter per cent after that.

Mortgagor's solicitor. As for mortgagee's solicitor.

Lessor's solicitor. For preparing and completing lease, seven and a half per cent on rent up to £100; £2 10s. on every complete £100 thereafter up to £500 rent; £1 on each £100 rent thereafter. Minimum charge £5.

Lessee's solicitor. For perusing draft and completing, one half the amount payable to the lessor's solicitor.

All charges are now increased by fifty per cent. A solicitor who acts for both sides usually reduces his charges and, by the agreement of sale, or the agreement to grant a lease, the legal costs may fall to be paid by the buyer or the lessee as the case may be. Interest of four per cent may be charged after one month from demand.

STORAGE OF PETROL. Petrol must be kept in metal vessels so constructed and maintained as to be secure against breakage and the leakage of the liquid or vapour. The storage place should be properly ventilated with an entrance to the open air, and must be equipped with a fire extinguisher or other means of fire prevention.

The storage place must not form part of, or be attached to, any building used as a dwelling house unless it is separated therefrom by a substantial floor or partition made of non-inflammable material. It must not be situated under a staircase or other means of exit. Not more than sixty gallons of petrol, including that in the tank of a vehicle, must be kept in any storage place. Heavy fines may be imposed for breach of the petroleum regulations.

SUB-TENANTS AND LODGERS. A subtenancy is created when the tenant lets the whole or part of the premises which he holds from his landlord, and it may arise with or without the landlord's consent. If the tenant agrees to surrender his tenancy, the subtenant becomes the direct tenant of the landlord, and even when the tenant becomes a bankrupt, and his tenancy is disclaimed by the receiver of the bankrupt's estate, a sub-tenant may ask the court to give him an order for a new tenancy.

Where the tenant has forfeited the lease, through failure to pay the rent or to observe other covenants, application may be made by the sub-tenant for an order vesting the tenancy in him. Sub-tenants of a controlled house are protected under the Rent Restrictions Acts in the same way as tenants.

A lodger is not a tenant or sub-tenant; he merely has a right to occupy a room or part of a room in a house, paying for such accommodation with or without board, the householder retaining general control over the house, including the lodger's room. A lodger is often referred to in law as a licensee to distinguish him from a trespasser or person who has no right to come and go in the house.

The goods of a lodger are protected from any distress levied on his immediate landlord, but to gain this exemption the lodger must set out, in a written declaration in statutory form, an inventory of his goods, particulars of his rent and undertake to pay his rent in future to the bailiff until the distress is satisfied. If, in spite of his declaration, his goods are taken, the lodger can apply to the Justices for a restoration order or bring a civil action for damages.

A lodger or sub-tenant may also be called upon by the local authority to pay rates in arrears from the immediate landlord. The authority is empowered by statute, in such cases, to give, on receipt of the sum due, a discharge from payment of such rent; though the lodger or sub-tenant has a clear right of set-off against his rent.

A lodger is entitled to a reasonable notice to quit unless, by his conduct, he has made himself objectionable to his landlord. Malicious damage by a lodger to fixtures is an offence, and the theft by him of any article from his lodgings is a felony. A landlord is bound to take reasonable care of his lodger's property and may be liable for loss if it is stolen or destroyed through his negligence.

WATER, GAS AND ELECTRICITY. By statute, a duty is imposed on local authorities to ensure that every occupied house has an adequate and efficient supply of water. In most cases, the water is supplied by the authority, or by a company of statutory undertakers, at a charge based on the rateable value of the house. Where the owner and not the occupier is responsible for the payment of rates, the suppliers must not cut off the water on non-payment, but may recover the sum due from the occupier. In other cases, the supply may be cut off for non-payment. Water rates are recoverable summarily before the magistrates, and a commitment order may be made for non-payment. Water stored in pipes or reservoirs may be the subject of larceny. It is an offence to pollute water in a reservoir used in a public water-works.

Gas and electricity are supplied under a statutory obligation contained in special Acts, and the undertakers are not liable, in ordinary circumstances, for default arising out of the supply as they would be in the case of an ordinary private contract to maintain supply. They are under an obligation to provide a supply to any person whose premises are within twenty-five yards of a main supply.

It is an offence to steal gas or electricity, that is to say, to tap the supply pipes or to interfere with the recording of the amount consumed. The meter is the property of the suppliers—though they usually charge the consumer for the hire of it—and cannot be taken under a distress warrant. The undertakers are responsible for maintenance and defects up to the point where the gas pipe or cable from the supply main enters the meter, and the consumer is liable from the point where pipes or wires leave the meter.

If the consumer has decided to quit the premises, he should give the notice stated in the contract; otherwise, he will be liable until the undertakers are notified. The undertakers by their servants have a right to enter premises at all reasonable times to inspect and read meters, and it is an offence to hinder or prevent them from so doing. Payment of sums due for gas or electricity supplied can be enforced before the magistrate as a civil debt by the issue of a distress warrant or commitment order.

3. INSURANCE

ACCIDENT INSURANCE. Insurance against personal injuries or death from accident is not a contract of indemnity (see INSURANCE, DEFINITION OF), so the insurance company cannot deduct from the sum named in the policy any money recovered by the injured person from the person who caused the accident.

In order to claim, it must be shown that the injury is due to an injury within the meaning of the policy, a question to be decided on the facts of each case. It has been held that pneumonia or septicaemia following an accident is an accidental injury, but where an insured person by his own reckless conduct causes injury to himself he cannot recover. Thus, where a trespasser on a railway line was injured by a train, the court held there was no liability under an accident policy.

BURGLARY INSURANCE. This form of insurance is a contract of indemnity, and what is said below about fire insurance applies also to burglary insurance. If the assured is robbed, he can recover only the amount of his loss. Sometimes there is disagreement as to the value of articles, particularly jewellery. Insurance companies do not insist on an exact inventory of the insured goods, but they often limit the amount payable for certain valuables, precious stones, fur coats, wearing apparel and the like, and, therefore, agreement beforehand as to the goods covered in the policy is advisable.

Under certain types of policy, the assured is protected whether the goods are in his own house or not, and so a claim can be made for loss by theft while travelling or staying away from home. The best kind of policy is the "all-in" type which affords protection against fire, theft and the act of God, that is, any event not due to human agency, such as storms and floods.

FATAL ACCIDENTS. Under the Fatal Accidents Act of 1846, sometimes called Lord Campbell's Act, the widow, widower, son, daughter or parents of a person killed through the negligence of another can sue for damages if they were dependent on the deceased for their subsistence. The action must be brought within twelve months after the fatal accident, and in assessing damages the court does not take into account any policy of insurance payable in respect of the death.

In 1934 the Law Reform (Miscellaneous Provisions) Act changed the law by affording further relief in death claims. Before that date, any right of action which a person himself may have had after being injured died with him. It is provided by the 1934 Act that such rights survive for the benefit of his estate, and an action, therefore, can now be brought for the benefit of his estate by his executor or administrator.

Thus the number of persons who may be afforded relief from the death is no longer restricted to near dependant relatives as under the 1846 Act, but extends to others who are entitled to benefit from a share in his estate under a will or on intestacy. Damages can be awarded for pain and suffering endured by the deceased and for loss of the expectation of life.

FIRE INSURANCE. A contract of fire insurance is an agreement to indemnify against loss, and the amount recoverable under it is limited, therefore, to the actual loss, payable either in money or by replacement of goods. Such a policy cannot be assigned without the insurance company's consent.

If a person makes an agreement to purchase a house, he should make arrangements at once with regard to fire insurance either by the assignment of the policy existing on the house or by a new policy, because if the home should be destroyed before completion he will not have a claim to the insurance money or to replacement.

On receipt of a proposal form for fire insurance and payment of the whole or part of the premium, the company issues a cover note which guards the assured against risk until the company accepts or refuses his proposal. In fire insurance an insurable interest is essential; mortgagors, mortgagees, lessors and lessees all have such an interest.

Conditions. Strict compliance with the conditions attached to a fire insurance policy is essential. It is a serious mis-statement, for instance, to omit to declare that petrol is stored on the premises or wrongly to describe the premises. If the risk changes by reason of building alterations, the company must be informed at once. When insuring household goods, especially valuable paintings and jewellery, it is well to put a value on them and so give the company the opportunity to accept the valuation.

The phrase "loss by fire" usually stated in policies means loss by actual ignition, damage by water used in extinguishing the fire, damage caused by the firemen, and loss caused if goods are thrown out of the building. After a fire, the insurers are entitled to enter the premises to assess the damage.

Where a house is totally destroyed, the insurers may be required to lay out the insurance money in rebuilding at the request of the person interested. But a tenant cannot force his landlord to rebuild, though the tenant (unless there is a clause to the contrary in the lease) remains responsible for the rent.

INSURANCE, DEFINITION OF. Insurance is a contract by which one party (the insurer), usually a company or Lloyd's underwriters, undertakes, in consideration of a sum paid in annual premiums by the other party (the assured), to indemnify against a stated risk by promising that, should the event happen which is provided against, the insurer will pay the assured, or his executors or administrators, the actual amount of his loss up to some stated figure. But accident and life insurance is an exception to this; for these the contract usually is to pay a named sum or benefit irrespective of the actual loss.

LIFE INSURANCE. Policies may be issued for payment at death, or at a stated time or death, whichever first happens. They may be taken out on one's own life or on the life of another in whom one has what is called an insurable interest. Thus a creditor may insure his debtor's life; a wife may insure her own life or that of her husband for her own separate use.

If a wife so expresses it, a policy taken out by her for her husband and children creates a trust for them. Similarly, when a husband takes out a policy on his own life for the benefit of his wife and children, a trust is created and, if the husband should become bankrupt, the policy cannot be sold to satisfy his debts.

Children. A parent, as such, has no insurable interest in the life of his child, nor a child in his parent; but if there is some pecuniary interest apart from the relationship, for instance, where an adult child is maintained by a parent, an insurable interest is created. It is lawful to insure in a burial society to meet the expense of burying a parent, grandparent, child, grandchild, brother or sister. The amount payable, under the Friendly Societies Act, in respect of the death of a child is limited as follows: under three years of age, £6; under six years, £10; and under ten years, £15.

Proposals. In contracts of insurance good faith is essential. If there is concealment, misrepresentation or non-disclosure of material facts, the insurer may be in a position to avoid the policy. For this reason, it is necessary to fill up the proposal form carefully, and to give full and truthful answers to the questions asked. The insurer can insist on proof of age. In a case where a person insured his life and failed to disclose the fact that he suffered from a disease which materially altered the risk, the court held that the insurance company was not bound by the contract.

The contract is binding as soon as it is concluded, and cover against the risk begins at that time unless there is a stipulation in the contract that it shall not commence until the first premium is paid. Non-payment of a premium within the stated time—often a little extra time (days of grace) is allowed—ends the contract, which can then be revived only by further agreement. In the case of life insurance the company generally require fresh evidence of continued good health and the payment of an extra sum.

Death by suicide or in flying accidents or at sea or on military service is excluded from most life policies. A policy of life or endowment insurance may be assigned, but, to protect himself, the person to whom it is assigned should give notice to the company. Otherwise, on the bankruptcy of the assured, the policy will probably pass to the trustee.

MOTOR-CAR INSURANCE. Any person using a motor vehicle on a highway without having in force an insurance policy against injury to other persons, either in his own name or in the name of the owner of the vehicle, is liable to a fine or imprisonment or both. A cover note is sufficient to protect against prosecution. The insurance policy must be issued by an authorized insurance company or underwriter, and it must cover liability against claims for death or injury arising out of the use of the vehicle.

Where the car is insured for social or domestic purposes only, it is a breach of the policy to take passengers for reward.

In a relevant case, the Court of Appeal decided that an insured person who habitually drove three of his fellow workers each day to their place of employment, receiving from them an amount equivalent to their railway fares, could not be indemnified, under a policy giving cover while the car was being used for domestic and social purposes, against damages awarded to a passenger who was injured in the car.

NATIONAL INSURANCE. See under Section 4.

WORKMEN'S COMPENSATION. See under Section 4.

4. EMPLOYER AND EMPLOYEE

COMPENSATION FOR INJURIES TO WORKMEN. At common law a workman who can prove that he has suffered physical injury through the negligence of his employer is entitled to damages at large. Three duties rest on an employer: (1) he must provide a safe place to work; (2) he must provide safe appliances and machinery; and (3) he must provide a safe system of work. It has been held these obligations extend to operations incidental to a worker's employment and, for example, cover such accidents as a fall on a slippery floor. In a recent case the injured worker was about to clean a teacup when she fell, sustaining injury, and her claim for damages was allowed. "It would be an extravagant result," said the Court of Appeal, "if the common law obligation of the employer suddenly came to an end the moment the workman ceased to perform the precise acts he was employed to perform and did something that was ordinarily and reasonably incidental to his day's work."

In factories and workshops to which statutory regulations apply a workman injured through breach of safety regulations by the employer can sue for damages on that ground.

But there is in practice considerable difficulty in establishing negligence at common law, and it was for that reason that the first Workmen's Compensation Act was passed in 1897 giving a limited class of workman the right to compensation from his employer for accidents arising "out of and in the course of" his employment. "Accident" under the Act did not mean only a broken limb or cut, but included a long list of diseases, known as industrial diseases, attributable to a man's work, such as silicosis, dermatitis, writer's cramp, and so on. Widows and dependants could claim in the event of fatal accident. During the half-century in which the Compensations Acts operated many changes were made from time to time in the amount of benefits and the scope of the Acts was enlarged. They ceased to have effect in 1947, but matters arising out of claims before that date can still be litigated in the county courts. See NATIONAL INSURANCE (INDUSTRIAL INJURIES) ACT, 1946.

MASTER AND SERVANT. So far as the home is concerned, the law of master and servant means that branch of it which deals with domestic servants, that is to say, housekeepers, cooks, maidservants, grooms, gardeners and chauffeurs. The contract of service in such cases is usually made verbally, and in case of dispute the court must decide its exact terms after hearing evidence on both sides and reading any relevant correspondence.

Where no time is specified, the contract is held by custom to be subject to one month's notice on either side or to the payment by the master of one month's wages without board or lodgings in lieu of notice. At the end of the first month the contract may be determined provided notice is given by either side at or before the end of the first fortnight of the service. This is based on custom and has been held to be lawful by the King's Bench Division.

Although a servant breaks the contract by leaving without giving the proper notice, the master is liable for the wages due to the servant, unless the agreement between them provides otherwise. If he can prove that he has incurred expenses which he would not have incurred if the servant had not left without notice, the master may claim damages, but such actions are rare.

Contracts with servants are usually made by a wife, and in such cases she, being presumed to act as agent for her husband when they are living together, can make an agreement which binds him in law. A married woman living separate from her husband is herself liable. Strictly speaking, persons under twenty-one, being legally infants, cannot enter into binding contracts and so cannot sue, but exception is made in regard to contracts of employment for the infant's benefit. Under such agreements, an action may be brought in the County Court for wages as though the infant were of full age.

Where a domestic servant, for instance, a gardener or chauffeur, is permitted to occupy a home or flat belonging to the master while in employment, such occupation gives him no rights under the Rent Restrictions Acts to a statutory tenancy. If he does not vacate the premises when he ceases to be employed, the master is entitled to an order for possession.

A servant who is incompetent or dishonest or immoral or drunken or wilfully disobedient may be dismissed without notice; but this is a drastic step to take and, unless the misconduct of the servant is gross and can be conclusively proved, it is safer for the master to offer the wages due in lieu of notice.

There is no legal obligation upon a master to give a reference, or character as it is often called. If a reference is given, either orally or in writing, it should be truthful and should reveal information which can be proved if need be. Where it is suspected that a servant has been dishonest, the matter should be reported to the police for such action as they decide. A master who, on his responsibility, searches the boxes of his servant may involve himself in an action for trespass.

NATIONAL INSURANCE. The National Insurance Act, 1946, establishes an extended system of national insurance providing pecuniary payments by way of unemployment benefit, sickness benefit, maternity benefit, retirement pension, widow's benefit, guardian's allowance and death grant. The existing Acts relating to unemployment and national health insurance were repealed by the new Act, which also makes payments compulsory to the National Health Service since 1947.

Formerly national insurance was confined to employed persons in receipt of an income below a fixed limit, but, under the 1946 Act, insured persons include: (1) all persons gainfully employed under a contract of service in Great Britain; (2) self-employed persons gainfully occupied who are not employed persons; and (3) non-employed persons who do not fall into either of classes (1) and (2). Contributions are payable weekly, and are as follows, the amounts shown in italics referring to the contributions payable from October, 1951.

Employed persons. Men between eighteen and seventy (excluding those over sixty-five who have retired from regular employment) earning more than 30s. a week, 4s. 7d. (*4s. 9d.*); earning less than 30s., 2s. 8d. (*2s. 9d.*). Women between eighteen and sixty-five (excluding those over sixty who have retired from regular employment) earning more than 30s. a week, 3s. 7d. (*3s. 9d.*); earning less than 30s., 2s. 2d. (*2s. 3d.*). Boys under eighteen, 2s. 8d. (*2s. 9d.*). Girls under eighteen, 2s. 2d. (*2s. 3d.*).

Employers' contributions in respect of employed persons. Men over eighteen earning more than 30s. a week, 3s. 10d. (*4s.*); earning 30s. a week or less, 5s. 9d. (*6s.*). Women over eighteen earning more than 30s., 3s. (*3s. 2d.*); earning 30s. a week or less, 4s. 5d. (*4s. 8d.*). Boys under eighteen, 2s. 3d. (*2s. 4d.*). Girls under eighteen, 1s. 9d. (*1s. 10d.*).

Self-employed persons. Men between eighteen and seventy (excluding those over sixty-five who have retired from regular employment), 6s. 2d. (*6s. 6d.*). Women between eighteen and sixty-five (excluding those over sixty who have retired from regular employment), 5s. 1d. (*5s. 5d.*). Boys under eighteen, 3s. 7d. (*3s. 9d.*). Girls under eighteen, 3s. 1d. (*3s. 3d.*).

Non-employed persons. Men between eighteen and sixty-five, 4s. 8d. (*5s.*). Women between eighteen and sixty-five, 3s. 8d. (*4s.*). Boys under eighteen, 2s. 9d. (*2s. 11d.*). Girls under eighteen, 2s. 3d. (*2s. 5d.*).

Regulations require an employer to pay contributions for a pensioner who earns over a certain amount.

NATIONAL INSURANCE (INDUSTRIAL INJURIES) ACT, 1946. This Act repeals the Workmen's Compensation Acts, and under it the Minister of National Insurance now controls the whole system of compensation for industrial injuries. It introduces entirely new law by removing all liability from the employer and setting up a State service administered by the Government. Instead of a defined class being within the scheme, as under former Acts, all persons employed under a contract of service are brought in, which means that, with the exception of professional men and employers, everyone will be protected and everyone must contribute. There is power to exempt certain classes of employees under the Act by regulation.

The employer and employee each pay half the contribution per week: 4d. each for a man over eighteen years of age, and 2½d. below eighteen, for a woman over eighteen 3d. per week and below eighteen 2d. The employer is made responsible for payment of the contributions, but may deduct the worker's share from wages, unless a worker is, say, an apprentice not working for a money payment, when the employer must pay the full contribution himself.

As under the former scheme, the worker can claim in respect of injury due to accident arising out of, and in the course of, his employment, and also for disease caused by the nature of his work; but the benefits differ. Where an insured worker is incapable of working owing to an accident, he can claim injury benefit, 45s. a week or 7s. 6d. for any day of incapacity, with increases, if necessary, for children or adult dependants.

This benefit is limited to a maximum period of 156 days (excluding Sundays), but it may be brought to an end earlier if the workman himself applies for disablement benefit. This latter benefit can be claimed (1) for permanent injury, (2) for substantial loss (over twenty per cent) of physical or mental faculty, or (3) if on the end of the 156 days in receipt of injury benefit the worker's physical or mental powers are permanently affected.

If the disablement is over twenty per cent, a weekly disablement pension can be granted according to the following rates: 100 per cent, 45s.; ninety per cent, 40s. 6d.; eighty per cent, 36s.; seventy per cent, 31s. 6d.; sixty per cent, 27s.; fifty per cent, 22s. 6d.; forty per cent, 18s.; thirty per cent, 13s. 6d.; twenty per cent, 9s. (three-quarters only allowable under eighteen years of age). For disablement below twenty per cent, a gratuity not exceeding £150 is payable. There are provisions under the act for increases to be granted to disablement pensioners because of unemployability, special hardship, the need of constant attendance, hospital treatment, children and adult dependants.

Death benefit is a pension of 30s. for widows with an allowance for children, and in certain cases a parent or adult dependant may be granted a pension of 20s.

Where benefit is claimed, the worker has to apply in the first place to the local insurance officer, a civil servant, who has power to allow the claim or reject it in whole or in part. Appeal lies to the local appeal tribunal, a body composed of a chairman appointed by the Minister and representatives of the employers and the employees, and from that tribunal within three months to the Industrial Injuries Commissioner, who is a barrister. Questions of law may be referred to a tribunal of three commissioners.

In addition, the Minister has power to decide certain special questions, for example, whether the worker was in insurable employment, the liability for contributions and the assessment of the amount and duration of disability; and, on certain of these matters, there is a right of appeal from his decision to the High Court. There is also provision for medical boards, and a special medical tribunal for appeal against their decisions.

Proceedings before the local appeal tribunals and the Commissioner are to be in public, except where the Commission or the Tribunal otherwise decides.

SERVANT. See MASTER AND SERVANT.

WORKMEN'S COMPENSATION. See COMPENSATION FOR INJURIES TO WORKMEN and NATIONAL INSURANCE (INDUSTRIAL INJURIES) ACT, 1946.

REFERENCES. See MASTER AND SERVANT.

5. BUSINESS AFFAIRS

AGENCY. An agent is one who is authorized by another to do acts for him and, usually, in his name, the person who gives the authority being known as the principal. No special form of written or verbal appointment is necessary unless the agent is to have power to execute a deed on behalf of the principal, and in this case the agent must be appointed by a special form of writing known as a "Power of Attorney."

In some cases, indeed, the relationship of principal and agent arises automatically as where a wife orders something necessary for the household, in doing which she is her husband's agent and, to that extent, entitled to pledge his credit.

Liabilities of principal and agent. A principal is responsible under contracts made by his agent in so far only as the agent has authority to contract, but a principal is liable for wrongful acts done by his agent if they are committed within the scope of the agent's ostensible authority. On the other hand, a principal is not liable for wrongful acts of the agent if such acts are done outside the scope of the agent's authority or solely for the agent's private purposes.

Normally an agent is not liable personally on contracts made by him on behalf of a principal, but he will be so liable if the other party to the contract is not aware that he is acting as an agent. If, however, the other party afterwards discovers the name of the principal, on whose behalf the contract was made, he can sue either the principal or the agent, but not both.

Ratification. Where an agent holds himself out as such without authority, the principal on whose behalf he assumed that authority may afterwards accept responsibility for the agent's acts, and in this case the principal is said to "ratify." A principal who ratifies becomes fully liable on the contract.

Illegal commissions. When acting as an agent, a person may not make any profit without the consent or knowledge of the principal. If he does so, for example, receives a secret commission from someone with whom he is dealing on his principal's behalf, both he and the person paying the secret commission are liable to punishment under the Prevention of Corruption Act, 1906, by fine or imprisonment or both. The principal can also claim repayment to himself of the illegal profit, and sue a guilty third party for damages.

The authority of an agent ends if expressly withdrawn by the principal, and on the death or bankruptcy of either or the lunacy of the principal.

ARTICLES OF ASSOCIATION. See LIMITED LIABILITY COMPANIES.

BANKING. The relationship between a bank and its customers is that of debtor and creditor. A banker is not accountable to a customer for the use he makes of the customer's money while it is "in the bank," and if a bank became insolvent its customers would have no greater rights than other creditors.

Secrecy as to the state of a customer's account is an obligation of a bank, and disclosure may be made only with the customer's prior consent, for example, in giving a banker's reference, except under legal compulsion.

Cheques. A cheque is an unconditional order in writing by a customer to a banker requiring the banker to pay a definite sum of money on demand to, or to the order of, a named individual, or to the bearer of the cheque.

Unless marked "not negotiable," cheques are almost as good as money to the extent that whoever takes them in good faith, after giving value, is entitled to be paid the sum named on them. If, however, the words "not negotiable" appear on the front, the cheque can still be transferred from one person to another, but no one after the person named on the cheque as payee will get or be able to give a better title (or right to possession) to the cheque than that possessed by the person from whom he obtained it.

Cheques drawn in favour of "Bearer" can be cashed on demand by whoever presents them to the bank on which they are drawn, but cheques drawn in favour of a named individual must be "endorsed," that is, the payee named must sign his name on the back of the cheque. If a cheque is crossed, that is to say, if two parallel lines are drawn across the front, it cannot be cashed over the counter, but can only be paid into a bank, which will then collect the amount from the bank upon which it is drawn. The words "account payee" added to the crossing mean that the money can be paid only into a banking account in the name of the person in whose favour the cheque is drawn.

A cheque need not be made out on a form supplied by a bank, but must bear a two-penny stamp. It can be made out for any amount from a penny upwards, and may be dated on a Sunday.

A bank is bound to honour a customer's cheques provided there are sufficient funds to the customer's credit or the deficiency is less than the amount which the bank has previously agreed to allow that customer to overdraw. If a cheque is wrongly dishonoured, the bank will be liable to pay damages to the drawer for the injury to his credit and reputation.

Authority to pay cheques drawn by a customer ceases on receipt by the bank of an explicit order from the customer, and on the customer's death, insanity, or bankruptcy, or on receiving notice of an act of bankruptcy.

Forged cheques. The signature of a customer is supposed to be known to his bank and, if payment is made on a forged signature, the bank is liable. In other cases of forgery, however, for example, where the amount on a cheque has been altered, the bank will not be responsible unless it has failed to use reasonable care. See also MONEY.

BANK-NOTES. See MONEY.

BANKRUPTCY. The law of bankruptcy is a comparatively modern method of dealing with the age-old problem of a person who, possibly through no fault of his own, cannot pay his debts. The position which has now been reasonably achieved by a succession of Acts of Parliament is that an insolvent debtor can surrender all his remaining property for division amongst his creditors and then start life afresh free from his previous debts and obligations.

Bankruptcy proceedings can be commenced either by the debtor or his creditors, but by creditors only where a debtor has either been served with a special form of notice, known as a bankruptcy notice, or has committed what is called an "act of bankruptcy."

Acts of bankruptcy. An act of bankruptcy is committed whenever one of the following steps is taken:

(1) The debtor hands over his property to a trustee for the benefit of creditors generally;

(2) the debtor hands part of his property over to someone else with the intention of defeating creditors' claims;

(3) the debtor creates what is known as a "fraudulent preference," that is to say, he pays one creditor generously without being able to pay other creditors on an equivalent scale;

(4) the debtor obviously and deliberately avoids his creditors;

(5) the debtor's goods have been seized in execution by the sheriff without redemption of the debt for which they were seized; or

(6) the debtor himself has filed in court either a declaration of his inability to meet his debts, or a petition in bankruptcy, or the debtor has specifically given notice to any of his creditors of his inability to pay his debts.

Receiving order. On the filing of a petition, except in cases where the debtor successfully opposes a creditor's petition, a receiving order will be made which places all the debtor's property in the charge of the Official Receiver. The Receiver then convenes a meeting of the creditors at which the debtor may make a proposal, for acceptance by his creditors, to pay his debts by instalments or to pay a sum of not less than five shillings in the £; and, in default of any such acceptable proposal, the creditors can resolve that the debtor be adjudicated bankrupt.

In the latter event, a trustee will be appointed to take over the bankrupt's property, sell it, and distribute the proceeds among the creditors. The bankrupt will also have to face a public examination to ensure that all property available for creditors has been handed over.

Disqualifications attaching to bankrupt. An undischarged bankrupt is disqualified from holding certain public offices or from acting as director of a company, and may not obtain credit over £10 without disclosing his bankruptcy. He may, however, apply for his discharge from bankruptcy at any time after his public examination has been concluded.

The court will consider such an application and may grant, refuse or suspend the discharge, or grant it on condition that some portion of the bankrupt's future earnings is set aside for his creditors. In some cases, however, the court has no power to grant an immediate discharge, for example, where the assets realize less than ten shillings in the £ of the debts, or where the bankrupt has not kept proper account books. See also DEEDS OF ARRANGEMENT.

CAPITAL. There are several applications of the term capital to the affairs of a limited company, of which the following are in general use:

Nominal (authorized or registered) capital. The total face value of all shares the company has power to issue.

Issued capital. The total face value of the shares which the company has actually issued.

Paid-up capital. The total amount which has been paid by shareholders on the issued capital.

Reserved capital. Any portion of the nominal capital which the company may, by special resolution, declare shall not be called up except in the event of the company being wound up.

Fixed capital. The property owned by a company and essential to the carrying on of business, for example, factories and plant.

Floating (circulating) capital. Money, raw materials and property which the company has bought for re-sale.

The nominal capital of a company may be increased by a resolution carried at a general meeting, subject to any special provisions in the company's Articles of Association (see LIMITED LIABILITY COMPANIES). A reduction of capital, however, requires a special resolution, which must be confirmed by the courts.

CHEQUES. See BANKING.

CLOSING TIMES. See SHOPS.

CONTRACTS. A contract may be shortly defined as an agreement, between two or more persons, which is enforceable at law. The parties must be agreed upon the terms, and there must also be present in every contract both an offer or proposal and the acceptance of that offer or proposal.

Contracts are divisible into two classes; they are *specialty* contracts (contracts under seal) and *simple* contracts. The former require to be embodied in a properly executed deed; contracts made by corporations (except certain routine matters), promises made without consideration, transfers of a British ship, and leases for more than three years are enforceable only if made by deed.

Consideration. Simple contracts, on the other hand, include every contract, written, verbal, or even implied from the conduct of the parties, which is not a specialty contract. As distinct from a deed, a simple contract is not enforceable unless there is present something known as consideration, that is to say, unless a party to a simple contract who makes a promise receives some benefit in return for that promise.

The law of consideration is rather technical and involved, but it may be briefly stated that consideration is some right, interest, profit, or benefit accruing to one party, or some forbearance, detriment, loss, or responsibility given, suffered or undertaken by the other.

Although a simple contract can, normally, be in any form, certain contracts are enforceable only if made in writing. These include: (1) bills of exchange; (2) assignments of shares; (3) contracts of marine insurance; (4) promises by executors or administrators to pay damages out of their own funds; (5) promises to be guarantor or surety for another; (6) agreements in consideration of marriage; (7) contracts for sale of land or interest in land; (8) contracts not to be performed within one year; and (9) certain contracts for the sale of goods.

Illegal and voidable contracts. Some contracts are illegal, that is, neither party can sue the other for breach of them. Illegal contracts include agreements against public policy, for example, to commit a crime, agreements to impede the course of justice, agreements in general restraint of marriage, agreements in restraint of trade (where the restraint is wholly unreasonable), wagering and gaming contracts, and contracts to lend money for betting or to pay betting debts.

Voidable contracts are such that the person not at fault can refuse to carry them out, or carry out his part of the contract and insist upon performance by the other party. An example of such a contract is where one party enters into the contract owing to misrepresentations made by the other party. See also INTERFERENCE WITH BUSINESS.

COPYRIGHT. Copyright is the sole right to produce or reproduce published or unpublished original literary, dramatic, musical and artistic works. Copyright also applies to performing a play or delivering a lecture.

No form of registration is necessary. The copyright belongs to the author or originator as soon as the work is written, painted, or performed. The writer of every letter, for example, owns the copyright in it; this means that no one else has any right to publish it, or communicate its contents to another person, without the writer's permission.

Authors and composers usually assign their copyright to a publisher by a contract, the publisher paying them royalties in return. Sometimes an author sells his copyright outright to a publisher, but it is more usual to grant a licence to the publisher to print and publish for a period subject to the payment of royalties.

Normally, copyright in a work lasts for the life of the author and for fifty years afterwards, so that he can leave the copyright to anyone in his will; or his executors can make use of it for the benefit of his creditors or next-of-kin.

Anyone infringing a copyright, that is, publishing another's work or substantial parts of it without permission, can be sued for damages, or for an injunction (an order of the court forbidding him to continue infringing the copyright), and any copies he has made may be confiscated.

There is no copyright in a mere idea. Copyright exists in the form in which ideas are expressed in writing or in art. A work to be copyright must be original in its expression or form. The words in a dictionary, for example, are not copyright, but a dictionary itself may be copyright, and so may anthologies, directories, or maps, because of the skill and labour involved in compiling them.

The work, to be copyright, must be original in the sense that it is not copied from another work, though it may be a translation of a foreign work. The translator has copyright *in the translation*, though not in the original work, because he has employed his labour and skill in choosing and arranging the words in his own language to interpret the original work.

In the same way a report of a speech or a photograph of a picture may be copyright. The owner of the copyright has no monopoly of the subject-matter, as he has in a patent, but only in the originality in the expression of thought. Copyright is not infringed by making short extracts or quotations from a copyright work. A plagiarism, as such infringement is called, must be a substantial extract.

There is no copyright in works that are grossly immoral, blasphemous, or seditious, nor in a work which contains false statements calculated and intended to deceive the public. A work which infringes another copyright is not itself copyright, even though it may contain much original matter. A most interesting example is the copyright in Basic English which the British Government bought from the inventor for the public. The words are merely words of the English language, but to constitute "basic" English they were selected and compiled so as to create an original work.

A copyright work first published in any part of the British Dominions is protected in Britain. By international arrangement, British copyright is protected in most countries except the United States of America, and foreign works are protected in Britain.

DEBENTURES. A debenture is, strictly speaking, a document issued by a company by which the company undertakes to repay money that it has borrowed; and the total of the face value of the debentures issued by a company is known as its loan capital. In practice, however, debentures usually give some security for repayment in the form of a charge over the whole or a part of the company's assets, as well as guaranteeing payment of a fixed rate of interest on the loan.

Failure by the company to honour the obligations contained in debentures entitles the holders of those debentures to take and sell the property charged and pay themselves from the proceeds in preference to any other creditors of the company.

Debentures must be registered with the Registrar of Companies within twenty-one days of their creation, otherwise they become void.

Classes of debentures. There are two classes of debenture in common use, namely, *registered debentures* and *debentures to bearer*. The former can be transferred only by a document registered with the company, but the latter are negotiable instruments and pass their rights from one person to another by mere delivery.

Unlike shares, which may not normally be issued for less than their nominal value, debentures may and frequently have been issued by companies for less than the amount for which they are to be redeemed and in respect of which interest is payable. See SHARES.

DEBTS. A debt is a sum of money owed by one person to another, either of a fixed amount or to be ascertained by future valuation. There are three kinds of debt, known respectively as debts of record, specialty debts, and simple contract debts.

A *debt of record* is a court judgment enforceable against the debtor; a *specialty debt* is one arising from a document under seal; all others are *simple contract debts*.

If a simple contract debtor does not pay anything for six years or in writing acknowledge the debt, the creditor loses his right to sue for the money owing. In the case of specialty debts, the time limit is twenty years, and, in cases where land has been mortgaged as a security for the debt, the time limit is twelve years.

Although imprisonment for debt is, generally speaking, abolished, payment of a debt of record can be enforced by committal to prison if it can be proved that the debtor has had the means to meet the judgment but has failed to do so.

Accord and satisfaction. In the settlement of a debt, otherwise than by payment of the exact amount due, there must be what is called "accord and satisfaction." An agreement whereby the creditor takes less than the sum due is ineffective unless there is some consideration for abandoning the balance of the debt; for example, if a creditor accepts £50 in payment of a debt of £100, he does not lose his right to sue for the other £50, since there is no consideration for his abandoning that right. If, however, he agrees to accept £50 *and something else*, however trivial (even a pin), there is accord and satisfaction, and the debt is extinguished.

DEEDS OF ARRANGEMENT. When a person is in financial difficulties, he may sometimes avoid the stigma of bankruptcy by entering into a private settlement with his creditors, known as a deed of arrangement. From the creditors' point of view, such an arrangement is usually profitable, as it avoids the legal expenses of bankruptcy and thereby leaves more of the debtor's property available for division among his creditors.

Deeds of arrangement are of various kinds, the principal being:

Deed of assignment, whereby the debtor transfers all his property to a trustee for proportionate division among the creditors.

Deed of composition, whereby the debtor agrees to pay a certain amount in the £, either in a lump sum or by instalments, in full settlement of his debts.

Deed of inspectorship, whereby the debtor carries on his business under the control of inspectors appointed by the creditors.

Any such deed must be stamped and registered within seven days of its execution; it becomes void unless, within twenty-one days thereafter, consent to it is obtained from a majority in number and value of the creditors. See also BANKRUPTCY.

GOODWILL. See SHOPS.

INNS AND INNKEEPERS. An inn is a place for passengers, travellers and wayfarers, and it is a legal offence for an innkeeper to refuse accommodation and food at any hour of the day or night to a traveller who is ready to pay for them. Such refusal can be justified only when all accommodation is already occupied; or the traveller is an objectionable person by reason of his condition, behaviour or reputation; or if the innkeeper has some other reasonable excuse, it having been ruled that "he is not obliged to serve the last crumb in his house to any traveller who might arrive at any moment."

The duty to receive a traveller includes a duty to receive his luggage as well as his horse and carriage (the latter term probably including a motor-car).

Liability for lost property. The innkeeper was, at one time, fully liable for loss or damage to a guest's property, except where it could be shown that the loss was due to the guest's own default. But since 1863, by the Innkeepers' Liability Act passed in that year, an innkeeper is not liable to pay more than £30 in respect of any loss, unless the loss was due to the wilful act, default, or neglect either of the innkeeper or his servants, or the property was expressly deposited with the innkeeper for safe custody. The innkeeper can obtain the statutory benefit only if a notice containing the relevant section of the Act is conspicuously exhibited in the entrance hall of the inn.

It is the duty of an innkeeper to take reasonable care to ensure the safety of his guests and, in particular, to provide them with food and drink that is harmless and reasonably fit for human consumption. He must also keep a register showing the name, address and nationality of every guest who sleeps on the premises, with certain additional particulars in the case of guests of other than British nationality.

Innkeeper's lien. If a guest fails to pay his bill, the innkeeper, apart from his ordinary right to sue for this, has a special remedy by lien, that is, a right to detain all the property brought to the hotel by the guest until the bill is paid. If the bill is not paid within six weeks, the innkeeper has the right to sell the property by public auction after advertising his intention to do so in a London and local newspaper and, from the proceeds, pay himself the amount of the bill and the costs of the sale. Any balance remaining must be held and paid on request to the defaulting guest.

INTERFERENCE WITH BUSINESS. It is wrong to interfere, without justification, in another's business affairs. That includes interfering with any contract or agreement existing between other parties. For example, there is a contract of service between a master and his employee or servant, and anyone wrongly enticing a servant to break that contract may be liable to pay damages to the master. The same applies to contracts between professional artists, singers, actors and the like and theatre managements or producers, or film companies.

But a person is not liable to pay damages if he did not know that a contract or business arrangement existed.

In some cases, interference with a contract does not make the interferer liable—as when the film censor bans a film in the interests of public morality, although that may interfere with a contract to show the film. Similarly a father who persuades his daughter to break off her engagement (which is a contract) with a drunkard, cannot be made to compensate her fiancé.

A doctor who advises a man to give up work on a contract because it is injuring his health would also escape liability. These forms of interference are justifiable.

Passing off. Any false statement about a man's business or goods, or passing off goods as those of another, although they may be equally good or better, may render the offender liable to pay damages to the injured party.

If a person's name is the same as a well-known maker of advertised goods, he should make it clear in some way that he is not the same as the well-known established trader with whose products he would be competing.

I O U. See MONEY.

LEGAL TENDER. See MONEY.

LIEN. See INNS AND INNKEEPERS and SHOPS.

LIMITED LIABILITY COMPANIES. A limited liability company is a corporation whose property is owned by persons, known as shareholders, in proportion to the number of shares of the company that each holds, but where a shareholder is not liable for the debts of the company once he has paid the full face value of the shares he holds. The rights and duties of companies have been strictly defined by a succession of Acts of Parliament since 1862, the most recent being the Companies Act, 1948.

There are two classes of limited liability company, public and private companies. A *private* company is one with not more than fifty shareholders (apart from profit-sharing employees), which may not make a public issue of shares or debentures, and the rules of which restrict the right to transfer shares. Any other company is a *public* company, even if it does not actually offer shares to the public.

Formation of company. In order to form a company it is necessary for certain documents to be prepared, signed by at least seven persons (two in the case of a private company), and submitted for registration to the Registrar of Companies together with the appropriate fees. The documents which have to be registered are the Memorandum of Association and the Articles of Association, together with a list of directors in the case of public companies, and, in the case of all companies, a statement of the capital, the address of the registered office, and a sworn declaration by a solicitor or an official of the company that all legal requirements have been complied with.

The Memorandum of Association is a vital document, to the extent that it must contain what are known as the objects of the company, that is, the things which the company is entitled to do; and throughout its existence the company will be debarred from any form of enterprise for which authority cannot be found in its Memorandum.

The Articles of Association are usually longer and more detailed than the Memorandum, and they form a binding contract between the shareholders and the company, dealing with such matters as internal management, voting rights of shareholders, and the qualifications and powers of directors. It is not absolutely essential for a company to provide its own Articles of Association, but where this is not done the affairs of the company will automatically be governed by a set of model Articles, which are set out in the First Schedule to the Companies Act, 1948.

Assuming that the documents submitted to the Registrar are approved, a certificate of incorporation will be issued; this is the commencement of the legal existence of the company, and, in the case of a private company, permits it to commence business. A public company, however, before carrying on business, must obtain from the Registrar a further certificate entitling it to do so.

Winding up. Whilst the registrar has power to remove from the Register of Companies any company which has ceased to carry on business, a company, which has in law an artificial and distinct personality, can cease to exist only if it is wound up.

Winding up may be either compulsory (by order of the court, usually on the petition of an unpaid creditor) or voluntary (by the company itself, most usually when the objects for which the company was formed have been fulfilled) or, in rarer cases, under the supervision of the court, which resembles a combination of the two other methods.

In any event, the essential to a winding up is the appointment of some person as liquidator, whose duty is to get together the company's property, sell it to the best advantage, and distribute the proceeds among the creditors and shareholders.

MONEY. Bank-notes. These are promissory notes payable to bearer, and whoever takes them in good faith and gives value for them is bound to be paid their face value on presenting them to the bank by which they were issued. The holder is under no obligation to endorse them by writing his name on the back, as is sometimes demanded. If a bank improperly refused to cash its own notes, it would have to cease business. For practical purposes, the Bank of England is today the only bank which issues bank-notes in England, though there are a number of banks which still retain the right to do so. See also BANKING.

Legal tender. This is such coinage and notes as, when they are offered in payment of a debt, the creditor is bound to accept. Any other form of payment may be refused. The following are good legal tender: gold coins and Bank of England notes up to any amount, silver coins up to £2, and bronze coins up to 1s. A person to whom money is paid is not bound to give change.

Receipts. Strictly speaking, a receipt cannot be lawfully demanded by the person making payment, but where the amount paid is £2 or over, the recipient is liable to a fine of £10 if he refuses to give a receipt bearing a 2d. stamp or gives an unstamped receipt. Where a receipt is given without the money being actually received, for example, if payment is made by a cheque which is dishonoured, the receipt is not conclusive evidence against the person signing it; he can still sue the debtor.

IOUs. An IOU requires no stamp, and is of no legal importance other than as evidence of a debt. The transaction which gave rise to the debt must be proved. A court will not give judgment on the strength of an IOU signed by a defendant and nothing else. If the transaction is one that the courts do not recognize, for example, a bet, the plaintiff will not obtain judgment in his favour.

Promissory notes. A promissory note, or note of hand, is an unconditional promise in writing, signed by the maker, engaging to pay, on demand or at a fixed future date, a certain sum of money to, or to the order of, a specified person or to the bearer. A bank-note is an example of a promissory note payable to bearer on demand.

Mistake. Money paid under a mistake of fact, for example, money paid to the wrong person, may be recovered; but money paid under a mistake of law, that is, money paid under the mistaken impression that a legal liability to make the payment existed, is not recoverable. A person can also recover money obtained from him by deceit, extortion, or actual or threatened violence.

PARTNERSHIP. Partnership is the relationship between persons carrying on in common, with a view to profit, any trade, occupation or profession; but whilst the profit motive is the basis of partnership, it is obvious that, if losses instead of profits result, they will likewise be shared by the partners.

In determining whether or not a person is a partner in a business, the *prima facie* (at first sight) test is the right of such person to receive a share of any profits. Neither the joint ownership of property, however, nor the sharing of gross returns is, in itself, sufficient to constitute a partnership; nor will a presumption of partnership arise from (1) the receipt by an employee of a share of profits by way of remuneration; (2) the receipt by a widow or the children of a deceased partner of a portion of the profits by way of annuity; (3) the receipt of a portion of the profits as part of the purchase price on the sale of a business; or (4) the payment of a debt out of accruing profits.

Forming a partnership. No written agreement is essential to the formation of a partnership and, in fact, partnership often arises by implication from a course of dealing. Writing is, however, required in the case of a partnership which is intended to last for more than a year or, more rarely, is to commence only at a future date exceeding a year ahead.

In practice, it is always advisable, when entering into partnership, to provide clearly, by written agreement (known as the "Articles"), for at least the following matters: (1) the scope of the business; (2) the duration and method of ending the partnership; (3) the name of the firm; (4) the capital of the firm and how this is provided; (5) how moneys shall be banked and who shall sign cheques; (6) who shall manage the business; (7) how profits and losses shall be shared, and (8) what shall happen if a partner dies or the partnership is dissolved for any other reason.

In the absence of any contrary provision in the Articles, partners share equally in profits and contribute equally to the firm's losses.

Persons dealing with a firm are in no way concerned with the Articles of Partnership. Each partner is, in normal partnership, personally liable for the debts of the firm, and his property may be taken to satisfy creditors.

Since 1907, however, it has been possible to form *limited partnerships*, in which the liability of a limited partner does not exceed the amount of capital which he puts into the firm. In a partnership of this kind there must be at least one general partner whose liability is unlimited; but a limited partner may not interfere with the conduct of the firm's business. A limited partnership must be registered with the Registrar of Joint Stock Companies, and any person may inspect the register on payment of a shilling fee.

A partnership may not consist of more than twenty (or, in the case of banking, ten) partners and where a partnership has an unlawful object the partners lose all legal rights against one another.

Liability of partners. All partners are liable under contracts made by one of them in the scope of the firm's business, and even if a partner is forbidden to contract on the firm's behalf the firm will be responsible to persons who contract with that partner in ignorance of the prohibition. The firm is likewise liable for wrongful acts done by a partner within the scope of the partnership business.

Sale and dissolution. Sale of a partner's interest, if permitted by the Articles, does not necessarily make the purchaser a partner, but entitles him only to the seller's share of the profits and capital. If a partner dies or becomes bankrupt, the partnership, in the absence of any agreement to the contrary, ceases to exist. And if a partner becomes a lunatic, or incapable of performing his duties to the other partners, or by his conduct adversely affects the business, or if the business can only continue at a loss, the partnership may be dissolved by court order.

PATENTS. A patent is a grant from the Crown, through the Patent Office, of a monopoly in respect of an invention. It takes the form of what are known as Letters Patent, which declare that the holder has the sole right to make, use, and sell the invention in the United Kingdom, Northern Ireland and the Isle of Man.

Ordinary Letters Patent run for sixteen years from the date of application, provided payments of the necessary fees are kept up. The first payment of £5 lasts for four years and after that there is an increasing annual payment. At the end of the sixteen years, extensions may be obtained on application.

Any person, married woman, infant or alien may apply for a patent, but the applicant must be the true and first inventor of the thing or process to be patented. It must not have been in use by any other person and it must be the applicant's own property.

The Patent Office supplies forms of application, and a description with complete drawings (or samples, if it is a chemical product) is usually required. The Comptroller of Patents, who has a staff of Examiners, decides whether the invention is sufficiently original and different from others in the Register of Patents to be patented.

A *provisional* patent can be obtained for one year for a fee of £1. This prevents anyone else from obtaining a patent for the same or very similar invention during that time, and gives the inventor time to test and improve his invention before the final registration. If, however, improvements are made after the grant of full patent, they can be protected by obtaining a *patent of addition.*

Once Letters Patent have been granted, and the invention is entered in the Register as patented, they protect the rights of the inventor and they are his property, like any other property. He can sell them or leave them in a will, or he can assign the rights in them or grant a licence to a manufacturer, for example, in return for payment known as royalties. Anyone who makes or sells the patented invention without a licence from the person who has the Letters Patent (known as the patentee) is said to infringe the patent and can be sued for damages.

Before an invention can be patented, it must be "a manner of new manufacture," and that may apply to the process of manufacture or the thing manufactured. New in this sense means different in some substantial way from previous things of the same kind.

The granting of patents is governed by the Patents and Designs Act, 1907, and many subsequent amending acts. The law of patents is very technical and it is usual to employ firms of experts known as patent agents to deal with all the necessary forms, specifications, drawings, etc., although it is possible, in the case of a simple invention, for the inventor to obtain Letters Patent himself.

The fact that a person has secured a patent for an invention does not protect him against actions by other persons who may claim that he has no right to it, or that his invention infringes some patent they hold. The matter may then have to be settled in the courts.

PROMISSORY NOTES. See MONEY.

RAILWAY TRAVEL. Railway authorities, being of comparatively modern development, derive most of their privileges and responsibilities from Acts of Parliament. In particular the maximum fares which they are entitled to charge passengers are regulated by the Transport Tribunal, and they are bound to accept as an intending passenger any person who tenders the fare unless that person's condition, for example, by reason of drunkenness or disease, would be unduly offensive to other passengers.

The railway authority is bound to carry a passenger between the places mentioned on his ticket, but not necessarily by any particular train, or at or within any particular time. The authority must allow him to take a certain amount of luggage free of charge, and is responsible for making its premises safe and preventing any harm coming to him during the journey. The latter liability may be reduced and usually is in the case of workmen's and excursion tickets, but any such limitation must be brought to the passenger's notice.

A passenger must, on proper demand, produce a ticket, pay the fare, or give his correct name and address. If he fails to do one or other of these things, he may be arrested.

RECEIPTS. See MONEY.

RECEIVING ORDER. See BANKRUPTCY.

SALE OF GOODS. The law relating to the sale of goods was consolidated by the Sale of Goods Act, 1893. This defines a contract of sale as one whereby the seller transfers, or agrees to transfer, the ownership in goods to the buyer for a money consideration. The difference between a sale and an agreement for sale is that the latter becomes a sale only when the conditions subject to which the property is to be transferred are fulfilled.

As a rule, the owner alone can give a good title, that is to say, a right of possession which cannot be disputed, to goods sold, the principal exceptions to this rule being: (1) sale by an authorized agent of the owner; (2) sale of a negotiable instrument by the holder; (3) sale of a pledge by a pawnbroker after the time for redemption has elapsed, and (4) sale in "market overt," that is, sale in any public market on a market day, or, in a shop in the City of London, of goods of a class normally sold by that shop.

Form of contract. A contract of sale may be in any form, but where the value of the goods is £10 or more it must be in writing and signed by the person against whom it is to be enforced, as otherwise, although the contract may be perfectly lawful, it cannot be enforced in court. Writing is not, however, required if the buyer receives the goods or pays part of the price or gives something in "earnest" to bind the bargain, or does or says something which implies a recognition of the contract, as, for example, offering to resell the goods to someone else.

If the goods have, unknown to the parties, perished at the time of sale, the contract is said to be "frustrated," that is, there is no contract and neither party can sue the other.

Where no price is fixed, a reasonable price must be paid, but, if the price is to be fixed by a third party and that party does not make a valuation, the agreement to sell becomes void. If, however, the valuation is prevented by the buyer or seller, the one in fault will be liable to pay damages.

Delivery of goods. Unless the parties have so agreed in their contract, the seller is not bound to send or convey the goods to the buyer. He need only give the buyer reasonable facilities for obtaining the goods.

Where the goods are sent through a carrier, the seller should contract with the carrier on behalf of the buyer, otherwise the buyer can refuse to regard delivery to the carrier as delivery to himself and, if the goods are lost or damaged in transit, he can sue the seller. Where goods are sent by sea, notice must be given to the buyer to enable him to insure; otherwise the goods travel at the seller's risk.

A buyer is not bound to take more or less than he has contracted for, but he must pay for what he takes. If other goods are mixed with the goods ordered, the buyer may accept what he ordered and reject the others, or he may reject the whole consignment. A buyer is not bound to return rejected goods, but must inform the seller of the rejection, and, in the absence of agreement, a buyer is under no obligation to accept delivery by instalments.

If the buyer wrongfully refuses goods which he has ordered, he is liable to pay damages to the seller to compensate him for any loss he may thereby sustain.

Conditions and warranties. On a sale of goods, a very important distinction exists between two kinds of undertakings which are found in contracts, namely conditions and warranties. A condition is a matter said to go to the root of the contract and, if a condition is not fulfilled, the buyer is entitled to cancel the contract. A breach of a warranty, on the other hand, normally only gives the buyer a right to damages.

The old rule of law was that "the buyer should beware" and that conditions and warranties could not be implied into a contract, but, by the Sale of Goods Act, the following conditions may now be implied: (1) that the seller has a right to sell; (2) that, where goods are sold by description or sample, they must correspond with the description or the sample, as the case may be; (3) that, where the buyer relies on the seller's skill or knowledge, the goods must be fit for the purpose for which they are required; and (4) that, where a seller deals in a particular class of goods which are sold by description, the goods shall be of merchantable quality.

The only implied warranties are: (1) that the buyer shall have quiet possession, and (2) that the goods are free from any charge or incumbrance in favour of any third party.

SHARES. The capital of a company usually consists of shares which entitle their holders to receive a proportionate share of the company's trading profits or, in the event of a winding up, of the company's available assets. A company may not normally issue shares at less than their face value, though they may afterwards fetch much less than this in the open market if the company's affairs are not prospering. Shares may carry special rights of participation in the profits, and the most usual kinds are preference shares, ordinary shares and deferred shares.

Preference shares are usually entitled to a fixed percentage of the profits before anything is paid on ordinary shares. Cumulative preference shares are, in addition, entitled to any arrears of their fixed percentage which have not been paid in preceding years.

Ordinary shares usually take a larger share of the profits when a company is prospering, but take nothing until the preference shareholders have received their full entitlement.

Deferred shares, which are usually taken by promoters, or issued as a bonus to ordinary shareholders, take all profits, if any, which have not been distributed to preference and ordinary shareholders.

Transfer of shares. Shares may be bought, sold, and transferred as provided by the company's articles, usually by deed and registration of the transfer with the company, but until the transfer is registered (which may take up to two months) the seller will be regarded as still the shareholder.

Every shareholder is entitled to receive from a company a share certificate; this certifies the number of shares he holds. When the shares of a company are fully paid, the company may issue share warrants in place of shares. A share warrant differs from a share, as the rights under it pass by mere delivery from one person to another, and no registration of the transfer is required.

Stock. When shares have been fully paid, they may be converted into stock. The only advantage of stock over shares is that, whereas it is possible to deal only in units of a certain number of shares, stock may be held in amounts of any value, e.g., £23 2s. 10d. Stock may be either registered in the books of the company like ordinary shares, or may be payable to bearer, in which case it resembles share warrants.

SHOPS. A shop, for the purposes of the Shop Acts (from which, and regulations made thereunder, the law relating to the management of shops is mainly derived), includes all premises where any retail business is carried on, including hairdressing, the sale of intoxicating liquors and refreshments, and retail sales by auction.

Every shop assistant must leave work not later than 1.30 p.m. on at least one weekday, and specified times are to be allowed for meals. A person under eighteen may not be employed in a shop for more than forty-eight hours including meal-times in any one week, and seats must be provided for female assistants in the proportion of one seat to three assistants in every room.

Closing times. Unless it belongs to an exempted class, a shop must close on one weekday not later than 1 p.m. The classes exempted from early closing are shops retailing intoxicating liquors, refreshments, motor, cycle and aircraft supplies and accessories, newspapers and periodicals, meat, fish, vegetables and other perishable articles, tobacco and smokers' requisites, medicines and medical and surgical appliances, and stalls at exhibitions and fairs.

All shops, with certain specified exceptions broadly corresponding to the exemptions from early closing, must be closed for the serving of customers not later than 8 p.m., except on one day of the week known as the "late day" when they may remain open until 9 p.m.

During the period November to February closing hours of 6 p.m. and 7.30 p.m. respectively are substituted, subject to powers of local authorities to extend these times, under certain conditions, to 7 p.m. and 8 p.m. respectively.

Compensation for goodwill. Until 1927 the tenant of business premises had no security of tenure at the end of his lease or tenancy agreement, and it was often the case that a shopkeeper who had built up a substantial goodwill from nothing was at the mercy of his landlord when his tenancy came to an end.

The Landlord and Tenant Act of 1927 entitles certain tenants of business premises at the end of a tenancy of a number of years, to claim compensation for improvements, including goodwill, which add to the letting value of the property, and even, in cases where compensation in money would not be an equitable adjustment, to claim to be given a further lease.

Liability to customers. The responsibility of a shopkeeper for the safety of persons entering his premises is a heavy one, as a customer is what the law calls an invitee, that is to say, he comes into the shop upon business in which there is a mutual interest between him and the shopkeeper. The duty of the shopkeeper to a customer is to have the premises reasonably safe for him, to take precautions to prevent injury to him, and to warn him of any unusual dangers of which the shopkeeper is, or should be, aware.

Similarly, there is a duty to keep the premises in a safe condition externally. For example, if a passer-by were injured through a defect in a hanging sign or awning, the shopkeeper would be liable for damages.

Bailment and lien. In cases where a shopkeeper receives goods from a customer for repairs, there is said to be a "bailment." The shopkeeper, while the goods are in his possession, is the bailee, and the customer the bailor. In such cases the bailee is under a duty (unless he expressly contracts out) to look after the goods with reasonable care, but will not be liable if the goods are damaged or stolen without any fault of his.

The shopkeeper will also have what is called a lien on any goods on which he has expended work or money; that is to say, he will have the right to retain possession of the goods until he has been paid his proper charges.

TRADE-MARKS. A trade-mark is a distinctive mark, stamp, or similar device attached to goods, indicating that the goods are manufactured or supplied by the person or persons who have affixed it. In particular, a trade-mark tends to identify the producer or supplier of a thing and not the thing produced; in that respect it differs from a trade name, the object of which is an advertisement of the character of the goods themselves and may be attained by describing either the producer or the article or both.

Subject to a trade-mark being distinctive, the sole right to its use belongs to the first person who applies it to his goods, and a rival trader can be restrained by injunction from applying it to goods of his own.

Registration. Since 1875 it has been possible to strengthen the true owner's rights to a trade-mark by registration, but, having regard to the technical complications which surround an application to register a trade-mark, it is always advisable to use the advice and services of a patent agent for this purpose.

To qualify for registration, a trade-mark must contain at least one of the following essential particulars: (1) the name of a real person or firm represented in some special way; (2) a signature; (3) an invented word or words; (4) an ordinary word which has no direct reference to the goods; (5) any other distinctive mark.

Application to register a trade-mark may be made in one or more of thirty-four classes, amongst which will be found almost every possible kind of article. Any one registration lasts for seven years from the date of application, and may be renewed indefinitely for further periods of fourteen years on payment of renewal fees.

TRUSTEES. Where one person holds property not for his own benefit but for the benefit of another, a trust is said to exist. The person holding the property is called a trustee, and the person for whose benefit it is held is known as the beneficiary or, in legal language, a *cestui que trust.*

Any person who is legally qualified to hold property can be a trustee, and there may be many trustees or many beneficiaries of the same trust. In no event, however, can one person be both the sole trustee and the sole beneficiary of the same trust, and where the trust property is land not more than four trustees can now be appointed.

Appointment. Trustees may be appointed expressly by: (1) the document creating the trust; or (2) the person or persons having power to appoint, either under the terms of the trust, or under the Trustee Act, 1925; or (3) the beneficiaries, if they are all of age and between them fully entitled to the benefit of the trust property; or (4) by the High Court.

What is called an "implied" trust will arise when a person acquires or holds property in circumstances where the law presumes that a trust was intended; for example, if a person buys property in the name of another, there will be a presumption that the other holds the property as trustee for the purchaser.

Duties. The duties of a trustee are laid down primarily by the document (if any) creating the trust, and are further stringently prescribed by the Trustee Act, 1925. When it is considered that a trustee is normally unpaid for his services, and that, in his administration of the trust, he is generally as liable for a mistake as for a wilful breach of trust, it will be seen that the position of trustee is not one to be lightly undertaken.

A trustee can, however, and, in any case of difficulty, should, apply to the Chancery Division of the High Court for directions. In all proper cases, the costs of such an application will be ordered to be paid out of the trust estate, and the trustee's responsibility limited to following the court's directions.

6. DEATH

BURIAL. Registration of death. When a death occurs, notice must be given personally to the local Registrar of Births and Deaths. The doctor in attendance must send a certificate to the Registrar stating the cause of death and also hand to the person whose duty it is to register the death a notice that he has issued such a certificate. In the case of sudden, violent, or unnatural death, it is the duty of the householder where it takes place to notify the police so as to permit of a coroner's inquest being held.

Responsibility for burial. When there are no near relatives or executor (see WILLS) to bury a dead person, it is the duty of the householder where the death took place to provide a decent burial. In the case of bodies washed up by the sea and unclaimed, the duty falls upon the parish where they are found. In all cases the reasonable expenses of the funeral are a first charge upon any property the dead person may have left.

Every person dying within a parish has a right to burial in the parish churchyard or burial ground. The burial must be done in a decent and orderly manner, but no form of religious service is legally necessary.

INTESTACY. Where a person dies without leaving a valid will he is said to be intestate and, in that event, all the property which he possessed at the time of his death will pass according to a table of succession laid down in the Administration of Estates Act, 1925.

Letters of administration. Before, however, the property can be distributed, it is necessary for someone (usually a near relative, but possibly a creditor) to take out Letters of Administration. Application is made at the Principal or a District Probate Registry and must include an affidavit setting out the whole estate of the intestate, a further affidavit setting out the applicant's right to act, and a bond for double the value of the estate as security for its proper administration.

In due course, if the application is in order, a document called Letters of Administration will be issued; this authorizes the person or persons named therein to wind up the estate, pay the funeral expenses and debts of the intestate, and hand over the residue of the property to the persons entitled under the Administration of Estates Act, 1925.

WILLS. A will must be in writing, signed at the end by the testator, that is, the person making it. It must be signed in the presence of two witnesses, who in the presence of the testator and each other should sign their names also. If the will leaves anything to a witness, or to the wife or husband of the witness, the gift is void. To make a valid will a person must be twenty-one years old or more, and of sound mind.

The law has attached special meanings to words and phrases commonly found in wills and, unless a will consists of a few simple bequests which can be clearly identified and stated, it is advisable to employ a solicitor.

A will is revoked by the testator marrying after it is made. It may also be revoked by a new will, or by destroying it with the intention of revoking it, or by a statement of intention to revoke made in writing and signed and witnessed with the same formalities as a will.

It can be varied without entire revocation by means of a codicil, which is a document setting out the desired variations in the will, signed by the testator in the presence of two witnesses.

Executors. It is important to appoint in a will one or more persons as executors, whose duty is to see that the provisions are carried out. On the death of the testator, the executors will then obtain a grant of probate, that is, authority to carry out the provisions in the will. If an executor is not named in the will, some person will have to apply for and obtain Letters of Administration before the testator's wishes can take effect. See INTESTACY.

7. LIABILITY FOR DANGEROUS THINGS, ETC.

DANGEROUS LAND AND STRUCTURES. Owners or occupiers of dangerous land or of buildings, bridges, gangways, scaffolding, trains, and omnibuses are under a very strict liability to see that they are reasonably safe for any persons who may enter upon them. It is the *occupier* who is liable, though he may sometimes be the owner as well. Presumably, it is because he is in a position to know more about the land or structure or vehicle and its defects than anyone else and, therefore, has a duty to take care to see that no one is taken unawares by any defect in the structure.

The occupier is most strictly liable to anyone who comes on to his premises under a contract, e.g., after paying for admission. The occupier or owner gives an implied guarantee that the structure is reasonably fit for the purpose for which it is made, and is therefore safe. He is not, however, liable for unknown defects that could not be discovered by reasonable means.

But the person who goes, for example, on to a dangerous place like a motor-racing track takes the risk of such accidents as may happen in motor racing, and he cannot get damages if he is injured, provided, of course, that such protective devices as were provided were not faulty.

A person who comes on to a structure to do something in which both he and the occupier have a common interest—for example, one who enters a shop to make a purchase —provided he uses reasonable care, is entitled to expect the occupier shall also use reasonable care to make the premises safe and protect him from injury by warning him of any defects. If the occupier is negligent in this, he may be liable to pay damages.

A person who has express or implied permission to go on to a structure for his own purposes, but not with any advantage to the occupier, is entitled only to be warned of any concealed danger of which the occupier knows. A trespasser, who has no right on the land or structure at all, must take things as he finds them. He is not entitled to be warned of dangers or traps, but the occupier has nevertheless a duty to refrain from doing anything deliberately to harm the trespasser, or from showing a reckless disregard for his safety. If he fails in this duty, even a trespasser may get damages from him.

Warning to children. If an occupier knows, or ought to know or to anticipate, that children are likely to be attracted by his premises or structure, such as a pond or sandpit, and are too young to appreciate the danger they may run, he is bound to protect them from injury so far as he can by warnings which they can understand or by other means, such as fencing or locking up. What is reasonably safe for an adult may not be safe for a child, and what may be a warning to an adult may not necessarily be understood by a child.

DANGEROUS THINGS. A person who has a dangerous thing, such as a loaded gun, a bottle of poison, a machine saw and so on, has a duty to take a very high degree of care to see that such a thing does not injure anyone who might possibly come into contact with it, or to whom it might be sold or sent. The nature of the thing calls for a corresponding degree of care, and a wider range of persons may be affected by some dangerous things than by others. So the liability of the owner or user becomes very strict indeed.

Some things which cannot normally be classed as dangerous may become dangerous owing to their condition; examples are a bicycle with a cracked front fork, a car with defective brakes, and a chair with a rotten leg. The question whether a thing is a dangerous thing at the time it causes an injury is a matter for a judge to decide. If he decides that it was dangerous, then, whether the owner knew it or not, the owner will find it hard to escape liability. If he can prove that he took every possible care to see that the thing was safe he may do so.

If a dangerous thing is transferred to another person in pursuance of a contract, the liability of the person who transferred it will be regulated by the terms of the contract, which may say that the seller is not liable for defects afterwards discovered. In the case of giving or lending a dangerous thing, the giver or lender is liable for damage it may do only if he knew of its danger and wilfully or carelessly omitted to warn the recipient.

But whether a thing is sold or given, the person who hands it over has a duty to warn the recipient if he knows or expects that, in certain circumstances, it may become dangerous. If a thing is dangerous because of a defect, and that defect should or could have been discovered on reasonable inspection by the injured party, then that party cannot claim damages for injury caused. But in such a case it is important that the person who handed the thing over should reasonably have expected that it would be examined.

If a thing is not dangerous when it is handed over, but becomes so by the act of the user, the latter, if injured, has no remedy.

In some cases, such as dangerous machinery and dangerous manufacturing processes, there may be a duty to take care imposed by statute which orders the owner to fence the machinery or take other appropriate precautions. Omission to take such precautions is negligence, and this entitles an injured person to damages.

A person who, for his own purposes, brings on to his property and collects and keeps there anything likely to do mischief if it escapes, must keep it at his peril. If he does not do so he is responsible for all the damage which is the natural consequence of its escape. An example of this is building a reservoir on his land, or starting a musk-rat farm. The dangerous thing must be something not normally kept on the property.

Liability is excused only if the escape was due to the fault of the person claiming damages, or if he consented to the act or derived some benefit from it. Escape due to interference by a stranger is also a good defence if proper precautions were taken. "Act of God," which means some cause not brought about by human agency, as, for example, a gale or an earthquake, also excuses liability.

DANGEROUS WORKS OR OPERATIONS. If a person does work or starts some operation near another's property, and it involves danger to that property, he must take proper care to see that no injury is caused. He is not only liable himself, but he is also liable if his employee or a contractor whom he engages to do the work neglects to take proper care.

Thus if he digs a hole in his garden near his neighbour's wall he must make sure that it does not weaken the ground supporting the wall and cause a collapse. If he lights a bonfire he must see, not only that the smoke does not cause a nuisance to his neighbour, but that the fire cannot spread into neighbouring property by sparks. A man who, for example, employs a photographer to take a flashlight of his friends at a dance is liable to pay for all the damage done if the flashlight sets fire to a lady's dress or to the dance hall.

8. SUNDRY OFFENCES

CONSPIRACY. When two or more persons combine for the purpose of injuring another person unlawfully, and cause him damage, they can be sued and made to compensate him for the damage. Anyone can boo or hiss at a theatre if he does not like the act. But if several people get together to hiss an actor off the stage to ruin him, they can be made to pay damages.

Again a trade association, consisting of traders formed into a body to protect their own interests, may lawfully induce a wholesaler to stop supplies to a particular trader, and, that trader will have no redress provided the association's motive was merely to protect its own interests and not to injure the trader.

Anyone complaining of conspiracy in the civil courts must prove that he has actually suffered damage. Conspiracy which renders the offenders liable to pay damage will usually also make them liable to criminal prosecution.

DEFAMATION. Defamation is the publishing of a false and damaging statement about a person. Generally speaking, a defamatory statement which is spoken is slander and one which is written or printed is libel. Conduct, such as gestures accompanying a harmless statement, may also amount to defamation if it injures a person's reputation. Putting a waxwork figure of a man in the "Chamber of Horrors" may be libellous.

Once the words, or writing, or conduct has been published, that is, made known to others, the person defamed can bring an action for damages. The burden is then on the person who published the defamatory statement to prove that the words were true, or are fair comment on a matter of public interest, or that he had a justifiable reason for publishing them (in which case the statement or the occasion on which it is made is said to be privileged), if he is to escape paying damages. In all libels and some slanders the person defamed is assumed to have suffered damage, and does not need to prove it.

Before a defamatory statement can be actionable it must be regarded as injuring the reputation of the person defamed in the minds of ordinary reasonable people by holding him up to hatred, ridicule or contempt; so that, when such an action is tried, it is for the jury to say whether the words are defamatory or not, once the judge has decided that they are capable of having a defamatory meaning.

Words, though apparently harmless enough in themselves, may be defamatory because of the circumstances in which they are uttered, or the person to whom they are published. They are then said to be defamatory "by innuendo." Any early apology and withdrawal as soon as one is accused of libel will do much to reduce damages and often make an action unnecessary or not worth pursuing. Defamation is further explained under the separate headings of LIBEL and SLANDER.

LIBEL. This is a written or recorded defamatory statement. It is generally regarded as more serious than slander because it is in a more permanent form and usually more deliberate. On this account, a person who is libelled can claim damages whether he can prove actual cash damage or not.

To be actionable the defamatory words must be published. Merely writing them is not libel. But if anyone other than the person referred to reads the writing (or printing), then the libel is said to be published. If a postman reads a libellous postcard the libel is published and, indeed, the law presumes that a postcard or a telegram has been read by someone besides the addressee unless the contrary is proved. A person may be libelled although not mentioned by name, even if the maker of the statement had no idea he existed. It is not the intention of the writer that matters, but the fact of damage to the person libelled.

Testimonials or "characters," however damaging, if given honestly and without malice to persons entitled to receive them, are safe, being protected by privilege. The burden is on the employee who says he is libelled to prove dishonesty or malice if he seeks damages. And, generally, a statement in which the writer and the reader have a common interest is protected by privilege.

Fair and accurate reports, though not complete, of judicial or parliamentary proceedings, are protected by privilege, even though they are only condensed summaries.

It is a good defence to an action for libel or slander that the words complained of are fair comment or criticism on a matter of public interest. But the facts, on which the comment or criticism is based, must be true for the comment to be fair.

Libel may be the subject of criminal proceedings if it is such that it may cause a breach of the peace. In this case it need not be published to a third person, but writing it to the person libelled is enough to lead to criminal prosecution. A libel about a dead man with the intention of injuring his living descendants may be criminal, though it cannot be grounds for an action for damages, because only the person libelled can take a civil action for damages.

A person may be libelled not only by a written or printed statement, but by a talking film, a waxwork, a photograph or cartoon. It is a libel on a famous author to publish an inferior article or story over his name if he did not write it.

NEGLIGENCE. Everyone has a duty to take care not to injure his "neighbour," that is, any other inoffensive person whom he might reasonably expect to be affected by his actions. If he neglects that duty and, by carelessness, injures and causes damage to his neighbour, he is guilty of negligence and can be sued and made to pay damages to the injured party.

Before an action can be brought for negligence, the negligent party must have a legal duty, not merely a moral duty, to take care. The plaintiff must show that it was a duty recognized by law, and there is a very wide range of cases where the law has said that a duty to take care existed. The law says a man must take reasonable care to avoid acts or omissions which he can reasonably foresee will be likely to cause injury. If he omits to do what an ordinary reasonable man would do in the same circumstances, he is negligent.

When a ginger-beer manufacturer sold a stone bottle of ginger beer with a snail in it, and later a woman who drank the ginger beer, which she bought from a retail shop, became ill, she successfully sued the manufacturer for negligence.

Persons professing particular skill, such as surgeons or solicitors, are expected to exercise such skill as is usually shown by such persons, and anything short of that may be held to show negligence.

In some cases it is said that the thing speaks for itself—as when a barrel fell out of an upper-storey window and injured a passer-by. Barrels do not move of themselves; somebody must have handled it negligently to let it fall out of the window, and people who handle barrels near open windows have a legal duty to take care not to let them fall on passers-by. They are responsible for all the damage which is a direct consequence of their negligence, and the plaintiff in such a case is not required to prove how the accident was caused—it speaks for itself.

Similarly, objects must not be left lying about in the dark where people are likely to pass and trip over them, nor cars left on a slope with brakes off or inefficiently adjusted. If, as a result, anyone is hurt, the injured party has an action for damages. If anyone interfered with such a car, however, causing it to run downhill, the man who left it would not be responsible for the resulting injury.

But in the case of things which are dangerous in themselves, such as explosives or poisons, or animals such as wild animals in a zoo, a much greater standard of care is demanded; and, if they are allowed to cause damage, the owner is almost always responsible. His liability is said to be strict liability. (See DANGEROUS THINGS in Section 7.)

If the person who is injured was partly responsible for his own injury, as by stepping off a pavement without looking both ways, although the driver of a vehicle which strikes him may have been driving much too fast or not looking ahead, the injured party is said to be guilty of contributory negligence. Formerly, in such a case, he could not recover any damages in compensation at all. Since the Law Reform (Contributory Negligence) Act, 1945, the total damage is estimated (both parties may be injured) and apportioned between the two according to their respective degrees of negligence so far as these can be estimated.

A master is usually liable for the negligence of his servant or employee acting in the course of his duties.

NUISANCE. A nuisance is anything obnoxious or injurious to the public (public nuisance) or to a private person (private nuisance) which interferes with their enjoyment of land (including buildings). In the case of a public nuisance, such as obstructing the public highway, a private individual cannot bring a civil action against the obstructor unless he suffers in some way in which the rest of the public does not suffer. The remedy for a public nuisance is usually prosecution under the Public Health Acts or under a local bye-law.

Mere annoyance is not nuisance that gives a right of action. Before an action can be brought to make the offender abate (stop) nuisance (and possibly pay damages as well), the nuisance must involve an interference with the use or enjoyment of land or some right over it, causing damage to the plaintiff. Nuisances such as a bad smell, persistent loud noise, and large quantities of black smoke all come within this definition.

Because of this rule, only the owner or occupier of property can sue for nuisance, but he may sometimes sue the owner or occupier of the property from which the nuisance comes as well as the person creating the nuisance. Thus a lodger or visitor to any premises cannot sue for nuisance, but someone who has a right to own or occupy the property in future can sue if the nuisance threatens to damage it permanently.

A person is liable for a nuisance originating on his property even if it was there before he took over the property. He is also liable for any nuisance his family, guests, or servant may create on his property. Although in theory a person must suffer some actual damage before he can sue anyone for nuisance, it will usually be presumed that he has suffered damage if such damage was a likely consequence of the nuisance, and it would then be unnecessary to prove actual damage.

In a sense, all noises and smells are a nuisance to somebody in some small degree, so before they can be stopped by a legal action they must amount to more than this and cause substantial annoyance. If a neighbour is creating a nuisance and will not stop it by polite request, the remedy is to apply to the court for an injunction or court order to him to abate it, and the plaintiff can sue for damages as well if damage has been or is likely to be caused.

It is generally no defence to say that the complainant came to the district knowing the nuisance was there, if the nuisance is greater than it ought to be in such a district. But if a person goes to live, say, in a coal-mining district, he must expect the discomforts which the usual residents normally endure. It is no defence that a business, such as a tannery or fried-fish shop, is a man's living or useful to the public generally. He must conduct it in such a manner and in such a place that it is not a nuisance. Thus what would be a nuisance in one district may not be considered a nuisance in another.

If a person allows a nuisance to continue a long time without objecting to it, he may lose the right to object. For example, if a man puts up a wall or hoarding which blocks the light from his neighbour's windows, which is a nuisance, and no objection is made for twenty years, the neighbour loses the right to object. Similarly, if anyone blocks a footpath which some persons are entitled to use, they lose the right after twenty years.

The right to sue for a nuisance may also be lost if the person affected stands by without objecting and allows someone to do something which will obviously create a nuisance.

If it can be shown that a man took every precaution to avoid a nuisance arising on his property, or that it arose against his orders, or by the act of a trespasser on his property, he may, in some cases, escape liability; but in most cases he is liable for any nuisance arising from his premises, however and by whomsoever it is caused.

SLANDER. Slander is a defamatory statement which is spoken. In most cases, anyone who claims that his reputation is injured by slander must prove that he has suffered some substantial damage, that can be estimated in cash, directly due to the slander, before he can bring an action against the slanderer.

But if the slander says that a person is guilty of any crime punishable by imprisonment, or that he is suffering from a grave contagious or infectious disease, or that he is guilty of misconduct or incompetence in his trade, profession or calling, or where a woman is concerned, that she is unchaste or immoral, then, in any of these cases, damage is presumed as a matter of course and need not be specially proved in court.

A damaging statement about a person's goods or his right to property, if false and made with intent to injure that person, can also be actionable if it results, or is almost certain to result, in damage that can be specified. This is sometimes called slander of goods, slander of title, or trade libel.

A slander to be actionable must be spoken to a third person, that is, someone other than the person slandered. The slanderer's husband or wife is not regarded as a third person if they are living together. Husband and wife cannot sue one another for slander or libel.

In judicial proceedings a judge or magistrate, a barrister, a solicitor, and witnesses are privileged and can make defamatory statements, even maliciously, without being liable to pay damages. So can Members of Parliament in the course of Parliamentary debates.

Some slanderous statements, if made honestly by someone having a duty or an interest to do so to another person who has a right to know or ought to be told, are also covered by privilege. They include giving a "character" about a servant and similar communications. But if the speaker is proved to have acted at all through ill-will or malice, the protection of privilege is destroyed and he or she may be liable to pay damages.

TRESPASS. The common meaning of trespass is "going without right or permission on to another person's land." It applies to any unjustifiable interference with possession of land. Trespass is not a crime, so one cannot be prosecuted for it (the notice-board which says "trespassers will be prosecuted" has been called a "wooden lie"), except where a special bye-law applies, as on railway property. A civil action can, however, be brought against a trespasser.

When there is trespass, inadvertently or otherwise, on another's land, the occupier (or his servant) can order the trespasser off by the same way as he came on, and, on refusal, the occupier can use such force as is necessary, but no more, to remove him. The trespasser should give his name and address and offer a small sum to cover any possible damage.

Even touching a neighbour's property may be trespass, such as leaning a ladder against his wall, letting your animals stray on to another's land, or planting a tree on another's land. Flying very low over another's land, shooting over it, or on to it, or letting a notice-board or horse's head project over the fence, also may be a trespass.

A trespass by, for example, putting something on another's land may make the trespasser liable for continuing damages until the thing is removed. Tunnelling under another man's land is as much trespass as walking on it or building on it.

Trespass may sometimes be justified, and, in such a case, the occupier of the land has no remedy against the trespasser. For example, a policeman chasing a criminal on another's land or into a private house is not a trespasser. Nor is a man who goes there to escape an attacker or who pulls down another's building to prevent a fire burning his house. A landlord does not commit trespass when he goes into a house to distrain for rent.

No one is allowed to set traps to injure trespassers, except in a dwelling house during hours of darkness. At other times, if a trespasser were injured by a trap, he could get damages for the injury. Trespassing animals may be seized and detained until damage is paid for, but if this is done the owner of the animals cannot be sued for damages in addition. A railway engine has been seized for trespass.

There are also special kinds of trespass; these are known as trespass to the person, which includes assault, etc., and trespass to goods, which is any wrongful interference with another's goods, such as chasing his cattle, chalking on his wall or beating his dogs.

9. COURTS AND PROCEDURE

APPEAL. See COURT OF APPEAL and COURT OF CRIMINAL APPEAL.

ASSIZES. These are held in the principal towns (Assize towns) by a High Court Judge "on circuit." Sometimes a K.C. or County Court Judge is specially appointed a Commissioner of Assize. As such he has the same judicial powers as a judge. Assizes are really the High Court being taken round the country, to avoid bringing all criminals, litigants and witnesses to London. All crimes punishable by death or imprisonment for life must be tried at Assizes, as well as many other crimes made triable there by statute. Divorce and some civil cases are also dealt with at Assizes. All criminal cases at Assizes are tried by jury.

No appeals are heard at Assizes. Appeals against conviction or sentence at Assizes go to the Court of Criminal Appeal, and other appeals to the Court of Appeal.

Only barristers may represent the parties at Assizes, as in the High Court, though any litigant may if so minded conduct his case in person. He is then allowed to call witnesses, to cross-examine the other side's witnesses and to make submissions in law to the Court and address the jury. The judge's title is "Mr. Justice ——" and he is addressed as "My Lord." He wears red when on criminal cases.

Accused persons are tried at the Assizes for the district in which they are alleged to have committed the crime, unless the judge orders, for some special reason, such as excessive delay or local public feeling, that they be tried at some adjoining Assizes.

BREWSTER SESSIONS. Justices of the peace appointed as Licensing Justices must hold an annual general licensing meeting within the first fourteen days in February of each year (known as the Brewster Sessions) for the purpose of granting Justices' Licences to deal in or sell intoxicating liquor. The Licensing Justices can grant new "on" and "off" licences, renewals, transfers, removals, provisional grants of on-licences, and provisional ordinary removals.

A Court of Petty Sessions can grant an occasional licence. No justice who has any beneficial interest in brewing or selling liquor in the district or in adjoining districts may act for any licensing purpose.

CENTRAL CRIMINAL COURT ("Old Bailey"). This is the equivalent of Assizes for the County of London, Middlesex and parts of Surrey, Kent, and Essex, though offences committed elsewhere may be tried there if thought advisable. It is a branch of the High Court of Justice and has jurisdiction in criminal cases only.

Usually, several courts are sitting at the same time at the Old Bailey. The judges are High Court judges of the King's Bench Division (who try the more serious cases), the Recorder of London, the Common Serjeant, and the Judge of the Mayor's Court. The Lord Mayor and Aldermen of the City of London and the Lord Chancellor are nominally judges of the Central Criminal Court, but never sit as such. Every judge at the Old Bailey is addressed as "My Lord," and the Recorder and High Court Judges wear red.

Offences committed on the high seas must, and very grave offences committed under martial law may, be tried at the Central Criminal Court.

CHANCERY DIVISION. See HIGH COURT.

CORONERS' COURTS. A coroner is a "royal officer" whose duty is to inquire into the cause of death of any person who is killed or dies in unusual or suspicious circumstances, or who dies in prison. He has also the duty of inquiring into "treasure trove" and deciding who shall be the owner.

He should sit with a jury, and usually does so when a crime is suspected; but he has power to dispense with a jury. Evidence in a coroner's court is taken on oath; any interested parties may be represented by counsel or solicitors, who may cross-examine witnesses.

A coroner may commit for trial any person who he believes, as a result of his inquiry, or inquest, may possibly be guilty of murder or manslaughter, and he may issue a warrant for the arrest of such a person. In practice, however, it is more usual in cases of that kind to adjourn the proceedings in the Coroner's Court, so as to give the police an opportunity to investigate the case independently.

COUNTY COURTS. These were founded as the poor man's courts, and they remain the court of the humbler litigant, because it is there that matters involving claims of not more than £200 for debt or damage are dealt with. Even if the amount in dispute is over £200, the parties can have their case tried in the County Court if both agree. Any defendant who wishes to do so can have the action transferred to the High Court if the claim is more than £100 and, in some cases, even when it is less; but it is very rarely desirable to do so, because the costs in a County Court action are very much less than in a High Court action.

Actions for recovery of land and for possession of houses are tried in the County Court only if the rent or value of the land or house does not exceed £100 a year or the house is "controlled" under the Rent and Mortgage Interest Restriction Acts. A house is controlled if its rateable value does not exceed £75 a year in the provinces, or £100 a year in London.

The County Court can also deal with certain matters of equity (concerning the administration of estates, trusts, mortgages, deeds, and partnerships) where the value or money involved does not exceed £500, and, by agreement between the parties, even where it does exceed that sum. Certain bankruptcy matters and applications under the Adoption of Children Acts are also dealt with.

A County Court judge must be a barrister of at least seven years' standing. He is known as "His Honour, Judge ——," and he is addressed in court as "Your Honour." He wears a judge's wig and a black and purple gown. The registrar of a County Court must be a solicitor of at least seven years' standing. He wears a wig and black gown and may try minor matters where the claim does not exceed £10, or where the defendant does not appear or admits the claim.

County Courts deal only with civil, not criminal, matters; but the judges can commit a defendant to prison for non-payment, disobedience of court orders, or contempt in the face of court.

Parties can appear and argue their cases in person in a County Court or they may be represented by a solicitor or a barrister. But if the amount awarded is small, a barrister's fee will not be allowed in the costs unless the judge gives a certificate to say that the case required a barrister. Proceedings and rules of evidence are the same as in the High Court, but rather more latitude is allowed to litigants and witnesses, particularly where they are not legally represented.

Appeals from decisions of the registrar go to the judge. Appeals from the judge's decisions go to the Court of Appeal.

COURT OF APPEAL. This consists of the Lord Chancellor, ex-Lord Chancellors, Lords of Appeal in Ordinary (Judges of the House of Lords), the Master of the Rolls, the President of the Probate, Divorce, and Admiralty Division, and eight Lords Justices of Appeal. These last have the title "Lord Justice ——." They are usually appointed from the judges of the High Court, but sometimes members of the Bar are made Lords Justices. The Lord Chancellor may also request the attendance of a High Court judge or ex-judge.

Three judges of the Court of Appeal constitute a court for hearing appeals from the decisions in the various divisions of the High Court, and from County Courts, Mayor's Court and other "Courts of Record" on civil matters. The Court of Appeal does not hear evidence (though it has power to do so in its discretion), but reviews the evidence given in the lower court and hears arguments from counsel. It can allow or dismiss the appeal, or order a new trial.

COURT OF CRIMINAL APPEAL. This is part of the High Court of Justice and hears appeals from Assizes, the Central Criminal Court (often referred to as the Old Bailey), and Quarter Sessions. In some cases the leave of the court has to be obtained before it will hear an appeal, and it may refuse leave. The court has wide powers to quash convictions, dismiss appeals or quash sentences and substitute a lesser or greater sentence as it thinks proper. It may also order an unsuccessful appellant to pay costs or award costs against the Crown.

Although convicted persons may appeal against conviction, the prosecution cannot appeal against an acquittal. The court can hear fresh evidence, but sentence must not be increased simply as the result of the fresh evidence. An appellant against conviction attends his appeal in person, even when he has to be brought from prison. Usually appeals against sentence are heard in the absence of the appellant.

The judges are the Lord Chief Justice and the judges of the King's Bench Division, not less than three and always an odd number sitting, and their decision is by a majority. All judges are addressed as "My Lord."

DOMESTIC PROCEEDINGS COURTS. Magistrates hear domestic proceedings (that is, proceedings between husband and wife for separation, maintenance and custody of children) separately from other business. In such cases the court consists of not more than three justices of the peace, one of whom is a woman, and they normally sit in private, only court officials, the parties and their counsel and solicitors, and the Press being present. But a stipendiary magistrate or a London metropolitan police magistrate may sit alone as a court. Newspaper reports of the proceedings are much restricted.

Probation Officers who have been asked to attempt a reconciliation, but have failed, may furnish reports, but these are not evidence. After the magistrates have made their decision, but not before, the Probation Officer may be asked to report as to how much maintenance ought to be paid.

The Domestic Proceedings Courts may also, on application, give consent to the marriage of a minor whose parent or guardian unreasonably refuses consent.

EVIDENCE. Witnesses must always give evidence on oath. If they give false evidence they may be prosecuted for perjury. Witnesses can give evidence only of what they *know*, not what they have been told or what they think, or their opinion (unless they are being called as expert witnesses on technical matters about which they are qualified to speak). If a witness cannot remember or is uncertain as to a fact, he should say so.

Witnesses are not allowed to read their evidence. But they may refresh their memory from notes if the notes were made at the time of the incident referred to, or very soon after. Husband and wife cannot give evidence against one another except in certain cases such as neglect, desertion, assault, rape and incest. An accomplice cannot be called by the prosecution to give evidence against a fellow accused charged in the same indictment. He may be called, however, if they are not being tried together, though his evidence requires to be corroborated.

Witnesses being examined may not be asked leading questions, that is to say, questions which suggest the answer desired. In cross-examination, they can be asked leading questions and questions otherwise apparently irrelevant to test their reliability.

Certain documents may be put in evidence without the writer being present, but the rules on this are complicated and legal advice is necessary.

HIGH COURT. This consists of three Divisions: King's Bench, Chancery, and Probate, Divorce and Admiralty. Every judge of the High Court is knighted on appointment, and receives a salary of £5,000 a year with a pension of £3,750 after fifteen years; he is known as "Mr. Justice ——" and addressed as "My Lord."

King's Bench Division has a minimum of seventeen judges, presided over by the Lord Chief Justice of England. In this Division are tried actions on contracts, and civil wrongs such as libel, negligence (claims for damages after accidents, etc.); and the judges of this Division go on circuit to try criminal cases at Assizes. They also hear appeals from Magistrates' Courts on points of law and, for this purpose, three or more judges sit as a "Divisional Court." A judge may try a case with or without a jury.

Chancery Division has six judges. In this Division are brought all actions about patents, partnerships, most company matters, trusts, mortgages, administration of estates, deeds, guardianship of infants and other matters assigned to it by statute.

The Probate, Divorce and Admiralty Division has a President and several other judges. Probate covers all matters affecting wills and intestacies, and Divorce covers nullity proceedings as well as divorce. Admiralty is concerned with ownership of ships, collisions and salvage.

Judges of the High Court are appointed for life. They may resign, or be promoted to the

Court of Appeal. They cannot be removed from office except by a petition to the King by both Houses of Parliament.

HOUSE OF LORDS. This is the highest Court of Appeal in the country, and its decisions are final and binding in all other courts. The House, sitting as a Court of Appeal, usually consists of five judges who have been made Law Lords. They are peers and are known as Lords of Appeal in Ordinary. They do not wear robes, but they meet as members in the House of Lords and hear arguments from counsel at the Bar of the House. The hearings are public.

The Law Lords do not, strictly speaking, deliver judgment, but make speeches in which they give their opinion on the case and the reasons for it. The Lord Chancellor, or some ex-Lord Chancellor or very senior Law Lord, presides and moves, as a resolution of the House, that the appeal be allowed or dismissed. The other Law Lords then make their speeches and the decision is by majority.

Before the House of Lords can hear an appeal from the Court of Criminal Appeal, the Attorney-General has to certify that the case contains some point of law of sufficient public importance. The poorest prisoner can have his case taken to the House of Lords if necessary, without cost. Appeals in civil cases may be made from the Court of Appeal with the leave of that court; this will be granted in cases of great importance, though not usually if the judges have been unanimous in their decision. But the House of Lords itself may give leave.

The full House of Lords also sits as a court on rare occasions to try other matters, such as contempt or breach of privileges of the House, and, by means of a committee, it decides claims to peerages.

INQUESTS. See CORONERS' COURTS.

JUDICIAL COMMITTEE OF THE PRIVY COUNCIL. This is the highest Court of Appeal in the British Empire for matters outside the jurisdiction of the English Courts and the House of Lords. It is, in effect, the King in Council to whom the appeal is made, the King deputing the work of actually hearing the case to certain legally qualified members of his Privy Council. The members of the Judicial Committee—usually five sit at a hearing—are Law Lords and judges who have held high judicial office in the dominions, British possessions or India.

Appeals are heard from the decisions of the Appeal Courts all over the Empire (though not now from South Africa, Canada, or India), and the poorest man sentenced to death or imprisonment in any part of the Colonial Empire can, when the circumstances justify it, have his case brought up to the Privy Council. The judges do not deliver a judgment or dismiss or allow appeals, but make a report of their opinion to the King, humbly advising His Majesty, who acts accordingly.

The Judicial Committee is not confined to appeals from the Empire, but hears also appeals in Admiralty Prize cases and appeals from certain Ecclesiastical Courts. It has also jurisdiction under the Endowed Schools Act, and, in the matter of copyright, it can license the re-publication of books after the death of the author.

Leave to appeal to the Privy Council is granted only when the case raises a question of great legal or public importance.

JUVENILE COURTS. These are special sittings of the magistrates' courts for the trial of offenders under the age of seventeen years (they may also be tried in the criminal courts). They are presided over by justices specially selected as a Juvenile Court panel, and the courts are held quite apart from the ordinary Magistrates' Courts. They are conducted *in camera*—that is, the public is excluded—and the names of children brought before a Juvenile Court may not be disclosed or given publicity in any way.

A Juvenile Court can fine an offender, put him or her under the care of a probation officer or other suitable person, or send him or her away to a remand home or approved school. At Juvenile Courts children are never "convicted" or "sentenced." There may, however, be a "finding of guilt" against them and an "order made" on such finding.

Juvenile Courts have power to deal with children who are not charged with any offence at all if their parents or guardians report that they are out of control, or if they need care and protection because they have no parents or guardians. These courts may also hear applications under the Adoption of Children Act, 1926, and make adoption orders which may be either permanent or for a probationary period not exceeding two years.

KING'S BENCH DIVISION. See HIGH COURT.

MAGISTRATES' COURTS. Otherwise known as Police Courts or Courts of Summary Jurisdiction, these are the local courts of Petty Sessions. The court consists of two or more justices of the peace, that is, local magistrates or in London a metropolitan magistrate and in certain cities and towns a stipendiary (paid) magistrate sitting alone, who must be a barrister.

The court must be held always in the usual petty sessional court house. In some minor matters, a lay justice of the peace may sit alone, but he cannot impose a sentence of over fourteen days or a fine of over 20s. Justices of the peace, being local citizens unpaid and without legal qualifications, are advised on points of law by the clerk, who is a solicitor.

Magistrates' Courts may deal with certain civil (non-criminal) matters, such as bastardy, dogs, husband and wife, master and servant, poor law, rates, etc. But their main business is dealing with petty crime, which includes breaches of local bye-laws, motoring offences, drunkenness, breaches of the peace, and so on. Ninety per cent of the crime of the country is dealt with at petty sessions, which are known also as courts of summary jurisdiction because they dispose of the matter there and then.

In some more serious indictable offences with which magistrates may deal summarily, they must give the accused the choice of being tried by jury if he so wishes. Certain offences, however, are too serious to be tried summarily and must be committed to Quarter

Sessions, or, in very grave matters such as murder, to Assizes. Magistrates may grant or refuse bail in these cases at their discretion, but, if they refuse, the accused may apply for bail to a High Court judge. They should grant bail unless good cause is shown for not doing so.

In cases where the accused is committed to Quarter Sessions or Assizes (or the Central Criminal Court) the statements of witnesses and accused are taken down and read over and signed by the persons making them; these statements are known as depositions. The accused need not make any statement unless he wishes, but may wait until his trial.

An accused person may be represented by a solicitor or a barrister before the magistrates, and, if he is too poor to pay fees, he may ask for a certificate for free legal aid. If this is granted, a solicitor and barrister (if necessary) will be provided. The magistrate, whether a justice of the peace or stipendiary, is addressed as "Your Worship" by everybody except a barrister, who addresses him as "Sir."

The rules of evidence are the same as in any other court (see EVIDENCE) and the prosecution must prove the case beyond reasonable doubt to the satisfaction of the magistrates. If they do not do so, the charge or summons is dismissed.

Proceedings in Magistrates' Courts may be started by a private person or by the police "applying" for a summons, and the police are in no better position than is anyone else in this respect. A summons may be issued on what is known as oral information, that is, a statement which, if true, supports the charge or complaint. A summons must always be answered, preferably in person, but, if that is impossible, a letter explaining why it is impossible should be written at once. A summons should never be ignored, however innocent the recipient of it may be.

Proceedings sometimes start by the police arresting the accused without a warrant, as may be done on reasonable suspicion of felony and in some other cases, for example, when someone attempts to drive a car on the road but is too drunk to do so. Where a felony, such as burglary, has been committed or attempted, and in some other cases, a private citizen may arrest the offender and have him brought before the magistrates. In other cases, magistrates may issue a warrant for arrest to a citizen or police constable who gives information on oath. For procedure in a Magistrates' Court see PROCEDURE.

A convicted person may appeal against the magistrates' decision. On giving notice of appeal, the magistrates may require a surety, usually of £20, as a guarantee that the appellant will go on with the appeal and is not merely wasting time. He does not have to find the money unless he fails to go on.

Appeal is usually heard at Quarter Sessions and, if it is against conviction, the case is re-heard entirely. If it is against sentence, the court hears arguments why the sentence should be reduced. Quarter Sessions may allow the appeal, dismiss the appeal or, if it thinks fit, can increase the sentence. Appeals from either the magistrates or from Quarter Sessions on a point of law usually take the form of what is known as "case stated" before a Divisional Court, consisting of two judges of the High Court. They can allow the appeal, dismiss it, or send the case back to the magistrates with instructions, as they think fit.

MAYOR'S AND CITY OF LONDON COURT. The jurisdiction in this Court is much the same as in a County Court. The judge ranks and wears robes as a County Court judge, but is addressed as "My Lord."

OLD BAILEY. See CENTRAL CRIMINAL COURT.

POLICE COURT. See MAGISTRATES' COURTS.

PRIVY COUNCIL. See JUDICIAL COMMITTEE OF THE PRIVY COUNCIL.

PROBATE, DIVORCE AND ADMIRALTY DIVISION. See HIGH COURT.

PROCEDURE. Civil cases. In the *High Court* and the *County Court*, when the names of the parties are called, the advocate for the plaintiff gives a summary of his case and the facts upon which he relies. He then calls and examines his witnesses. They are then cross-examined by the other side. When all the witnesses have been heard, the defendant's advocate may submit that there is no case, or outline his defence and then call witnesses, and they in turn are examined and cross-examined. At the end, the defendant's advocate summarizes his case, and then the plaintiff's advocate may reply. If the defendant does not call any evidence, his advocate has the last word.

In the County Court, if the plaintiff is not represented, he goes straight into the witness-box, takes the oath and gives his evidence; the procedure is then as already described.

When the parties and their advocates have finished, the judge sums up and, if there is a jury, they give their verdict, and the judge gives judgment accordingly. In the County Court, if it is intended to appeal the fact should be mentioned, because in some cases, for example, where the amount in dispute is under £20, this requires leave of the judge.

In a *Magistrates' Court*, when the case is called, the complainant goes into the witness-box and gives evidence. When he or she has done so, the defendant may ask questions to challenge what has been said or test the truthfulness of the witness. But he is not allowed to make statements or speeches; he must ask questions, or his solicitor or counsel (barrister) must ask them for him.

Then witnesses for the complainant are called, sworn, make their statements and may be questioned (cross-examined). When they have all been heard, the defendant goes into the box and is sworn, the same procedure being followed. In maintenance proceedings, the defendant may be questioned as to his means. Solicitors or counsel for each side may address the magistrate, who then gives his decision.

Criminal cases. In the *Magistrates' Court*, proceedings are started by an information laid before the justices followed by a summons to the defendant to attend the court. A summons should never be ignored. If the person summoned cannot attend, he should write to the court giving reasons and asking for an adjournment. The reasons must be strong ones —serious illness, too far away to return in time or without great expense. The defendant may appear in person or have a solicitor or barrister to represent him. If it has not been possible to get witnesses to the court in time, an adjournment should be asked for.

If the offence is one that can be dealt with summarily, the case is called on and the defendant goes into the dock or stands before the court. The charge is read out to him and he is asked whether he pleads "guilty" or "not guilty," and he *must* answer one or the other.

If he pleads "guilty," it is not necessary to call witnesses. The prosecution gives a brief outline of the facts, the defendant or his advocate then says what is possible in his favour, as to good character or mitigation, and the Bench then gives judgment.

If the defendant pleads "not guilty," the prosecution outlines the case and puts witnesses into the witness-box, one after another. Each is sworn, questioned and cross-questioned. Then the defendant puts his witnesses up to be questioned and cross-questioned, and at the end the defendant or his advocate may address the Bench but the prosecution may not reply. If the defence chooses to address the court before calling witnesses it may not thereafter again address the court except by permission and in that case the prosecution may reply. The Bench then gives judgment.

For some offences the accused may choose either to be tried summarily by the magistrate or to be tried on indictment before a jury. In these cases he is told so and asked to choose. If he decides to be dealt with then and there, procedure is as already described. But if he decides to be tried by jury, or the offence is one which must go to a jury at Sessions or Assizes, he is asked to plead "guilty" or "not guilty." Witnesses for the prosecution are called and their statements taken down in writing, read over to them and signed. (They may be cross-examined by the defence, but this can be reserved until the trial.)

When they have finished, the magistrate reads over the charge and explains it. The accused may then give evidence and call witnesses but, generally, he does not do so and "reserves his defence." Whatever he says is taken down, read over to him, and signed by the justices. They then, if they think there is sufficient evidence, commit him for trial. He may be kept in custody or let out on bail. If he asks for bail and it is refused, he can apply for it to a High Court judge.

At *Sessions* or *Assizes*, the accused is called, the indictment, or charge, read over to him and he pleads "guilty" or "not guilty." If "guilty," procedure is as in a Magistrates' Court.

If he pleads "not guilty," a jury is sworn and the accused is given the chance to object to any juror.

Then prosecuting counsel outlines the case, calls his witnesses, who give their evidence and are cross-examined, after which the accused or his counsel may open the case for the defence and call his witnesses. If the accused does not call any evidence other than his own, he or his counsel has the last word. Then the judge sums up and the jury give their verdict, which must be unanimous.

If the verdict is "not guilty," the accused is discharged. If "guilty," the police officer who handled the case is called and states what he knows about the accused, his past record, etc. He may be questioned about this if the accused challenges its correctness. Then the accused is asked if he has anything further to say and he or his counsel may speak in mitigation of sentence. The judge then passes sentence.

An accused person who thinks he has a good defence and cannot afford counsel can ask for free legal aid at the Magistrates' Court or before he is tried at Sessions or Assizes. If it is a serious case, or it appears there is a genuine defence, and the accused has little means, free legal aid is usually granted.

At the *Court of Criminal Appeal* the accused is present but not heard. Only counsel may address the court and no witnesses are called.

QUARTER SESSIONS. These are courts held by two or more justices of the peace for the borough or county. They try criminal cases (indictable offences) sent to them from the Magistrates' Courts (popularly called Police Courts) except those cases of more serious crimes which are sent for trial at Assizes. Quarter Sessions also hear appeals from decisions of magistrates in Petty Sessions and deal with certain administrative business.

A person convicted at a Magistrates' Court (Petty Sessions) can appeal to Quarter Sessions against conviction and sentence, or against sentence alone if it is considered too severe. Even when he has pleaded guilty in the lower court he can still appeal against sentence, though the court of Quarter Sessions has power to increase the sentence if it is thought too lenient. Here the appeal against conviction amounts to a complete re-hearing, and additional evidence may be brought if notice is given to the other side.

The administrative and civil business dealt with by Quarter Sessions includes licensing, orders for closing or diverting highways, appointing visiting Committees of Justices for prisons, and lunacy matters and mental homes. Appeals are also heard against bastardy (affiliation) orders, rating, highways, and the refusal or transfer of licences.

Borough Quarter Sessions are presided over by a Recorder alone. He must be a barrister of at least five years' standing.

County Quarter Sessions have a permanent chairman, who is usually legally qualified, a barrister or solicitor, and may be paid.

In Quarter Sessions all criminal cases are tried by jury. Recorders, Chairman and Justices at Quarter Sessions are addressed as "Sir," except at the North London and South London and Middlesex Sessions where the Chairman is addressed as "My Lord."

Appeals from Quarter Sessions sitting as an original court of trial and not as a court of appeal from the Magistrates' Court go to the Court of Criminal Appeal.

ENCYCLOPAEDIA OF GARDENING

A guide to the cultivation of flowers, fruit and vegetables, and to the care and making of gardens.

The main part of this Encyclopaedia of Gardening is arranged in alphabetical order under the headings of the various flowers, fruits, vegetables, garden pests, fertilizers, garden equipment, and other items of interest to the gardener. Following this on pages 266–75 are charts (to which there are many cross-references in the alphabetical section) dealing with fertilizers, plant diseases, garden pests and vegetable growing. Finally, on pages 276–8, under the title of "Your Garden Month by Month" there is a calendar of the gardener's activities for the year.

ABELIA. (Caprifoliaceae.) 2 ft.–10 ft. Evergreen and deciduous flowering shrubs. Hardy varieties used on warm sheltered walls outdoors. *Soil:* equal parts loam, peat, sand. *Prune:* lightly after flowering. *Propagation:* layers in March or cuttings in July. **Best to grow:** *A. floribunda*, crimson, semi-evergreen, June. *A. grandiflora*, hardiest, pink, July–October. *A. triflora*, creamy-pink, June, 10 ft. *A. Schumanni*, rose, June–September, 5 ft.

ABUTILON. Indian Mallow. (Malvaceae.) 2 ft.–6 ft. Most are greenhouse plants, though one or two will grow in sheltered positions outdoors. *Soil:* ordinary. *Prune:* youngest shoots in March. *Propagation:* cuttings or seed in March. **Best to grow:** *A. vitifolium*, 15 ft., mauve or white, May. *A. megapotamicum*, red and yellow, June to September, 6 ft. on wall.

ACACIA. (Leguminosae.) Evergreen flowering shrubs or small trees. Suitable for cool greenhouses. *Soil:* turfy loam, leaf-mould, coarse sand with charcoal added. *Prune:* after flowering. *Propagation:* seeds in March, cuttings of half-ripened shoots in sandy peat in June. **Best to grow:** *A. armata*, 6 ft.–10 ft., yellow, January. *A. Baileyana*, 15 ft.–20 ft., yellow. *A. dealbata*, the mimosa sold in markets, may be planted outside in southern gardens, 30 ft., pale yellow, February.

ACACIA, False. *Robinia*. (Leguminosae.) Hardy deciduous trees and shrubs with white or pink flowers (Fig. 1). Plant October–February in sunny position. *Propagation:* seed, grafting. **Best to grow:** *R. hispida*, 8 ft., deep rose. *R. viscosa*, small tree, pale rose.

ACAENA. New Zealand Burr. (Rosaceae.) Hardy, trailing perennials. Evergreen. Suitable for rockeries. *Plant:* October–March. *Soil:* moist sandy loam. *Propagation:* seeds in March, root division in April, cuttings in August. **Best to grow:** *A. Buchananii*, 1 in.–2 in., carpet of blue-green leaves, red burrs. *A. Novae Zealandiae*, 2 in., trailing bronze foliage, purple burrs.

ACANTHUS. Bear's Breech. (Acanthaceae.) Hardy herbaceous perennials with ornamental foliage. *Plant:* October–April, in beds, borders, or cool greenhouse. *Soil:* light. *Propagation:* seed, root division in October or March. **Best to grow:** *A. mollis*, 3 ft.–4 ft., white, rose-lilac. *A. spinosus*, 3 ft.–4 ft., purplish.

ACHILLEA. Milfoil, Yarrow. (Compositae.) Hardy herbaceous perennials. *Plant:* October–April; dwarf species in rockeries, tall ones in borders. Lift seldom. *Soil:* ordinary. *Propagation:* seeds in spring, root division in autumn. **Best to grow:** *A. millefolium roseum*, 2 ft.–3 ft.,

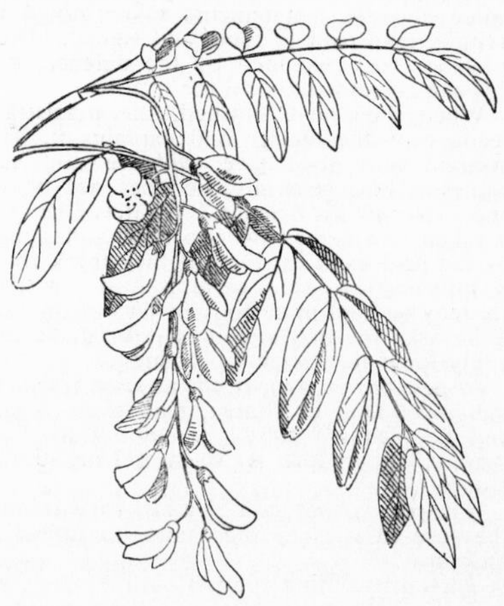

Fig. 1. False Acacia, a native of America.

rose. *A. Ptarmica flore pleno*, 2 ft., good varieties being The Pearl, Boule de Neige, Perry's White. *A. rupestris*, 8 in., tufted, white. *A. Eupatorium*, 5 ft., golden-yellow.

ACONITE. Winter Aconite, Eranthis. (Ranunculaceae.) Hardy, tuberous-rooted, early-flowering perennials (Fig. 2). *Plant:* October–December, 3 in. apart in wild garden, shrubberies or rockeries. *Soil:* ordinary.

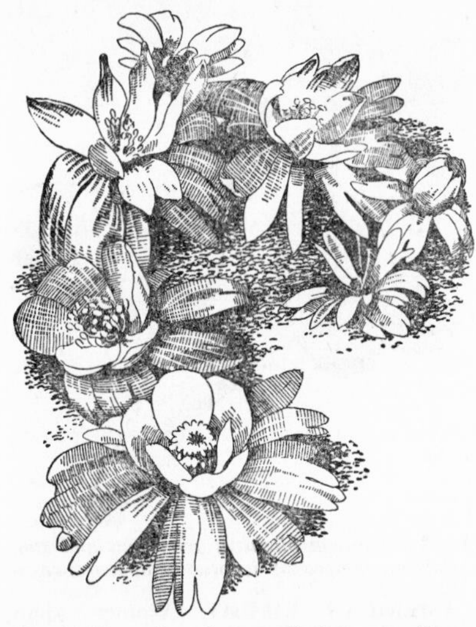

Fig. 2. The yellow flowers of winter aconite are surrounded by whorls of leaflets.

Propagation: seed or division. **Best to grow:** *E. hyemalis*, 3 in., yellow, January. *E. Tubergenii*, 6 in., yellow, February.

ACONITUM. See MONKSHOOD.

ACORUS. (Aroideae.) Hardy perennial aquatic. *Soil:* sunny marshy spots or shallow water. *Propagation:* division in March. **Best to grow:** *A. Calamus*, 3 ft., yellow. *A. gramineus*, and variegated forms, 2 ft.

ACTINIDIA. (Ternstroemiaceae.) Deciduous hardy climbing shrubs. Fleshy berries are edible. *Plant:* October–March against walls, tree-stumps or pergolas. *Soil:* ordinary. *Prune:* thin out and shorten branches in February. *Propagation:* seeds, cuttings or layers. **Best to grow:** *A. arguta*, one of the hardiest; white, fragrant; June. *A. Henryi*, semi-evergreen, white, needs protection. *A. Kolomikta*, leaves blotched with white and red.

ADIANTUM. Maidenhair. (See FERNS.)

ADONIS. (Ranunculaceae.) Hardy annuals for mixed borders and hardy perennials for rockeries. *Plant:* October. *Soil:* moist and sandy. *Propagation:* March-sown seeds for annuals and perennials; root division for perennials in October. **Best to grow:** *A. aestivalis*, Pheasant's Eye, 1 ft., crimson, June (annual). *A. amurensis*, 1 ft., yellow, spring (perennial).

AFRICAN LILY. *Agapanthus.* (Liliaceae.) Cool greenhouse herbaceous plant often grown in tubs for loggias and terraces, but will winter outdoors if protected. Grow in full sunlight, watering freely during March–September, moderately afterwards. Feed liquid manure during growth. Re-pot every 4–5 years. *Soil:* two parts loam, one leaf-mould, half sand. *Propagation:* division in spring. **Best to grow:** *A. umbellatus*, 3 ft., blue or white, April. *A. Mooreanus*, 2 ft., hardy, blue, late flowering, and its white variety.

AGAPANTHUS. See AFRICAN LILY.

AGARICUS. See MUSHROOMS.

AGAVE. American Aloe. (Amaryllidaceae.) Tender perennials with ornamental foliage. Many species often take years to flower. Culture as for Agapanthus. *Propagation:* offsets. **Best to grow:** *A. americana variegata*, dark green and yellow leaves.

AGERATUM. (Compositae.) Half-hardy annuals for sunny beds or borders. *Plant:* 6 in.–8 in. apart in June. *Soil:* ordinary. *Propagation:* sow under glass in March, cuttings from stock plants kept in pots. **Best to grow:** varieties of *A. mexicanum*, 18 in.–2 ft., Imperial Dwarf White, Imperial Dwarf Blue, Blue Ball, Covent Garden, Swanley Blue.

AGROSTEMMA. (Caryophyllaceae.) Hardy perennials allied to Lychnis. *Soil:* ordinary. *Propagation:* seeds. **Best to grow:** *A. coronaria*, 2 ft.–3 ft., crimson, August.

AILANTHUS. Tree of Heaven. (Simarubaceae.) Handsome hardy deciduous tree from China. Large divided leaves turn yellow in autumn. *Plant:* sheltered position in November. *Soil:* ordinary. *Propagation:* root suckers in frames in August. **Best to grow:** *A. glandulosa*, 30 ft.–60 ft., whitish-green flowers. *A. pendulifolia*, a weeping variety.

AJUGA. Bugle. (Labiatae.) Hardy perennials, forming spreading mats of broad leaves and blue spikes. *Soil:* moist. *Propagation:* cuttings. **Best to grow:** *A. reptans atropurpurea*, dark purple foliage. *A. reptans variegata* (Rainbow), variegated foliage. *A. genevensis*, 6 in., blue and white.

ALCHEMILLA. Lady's Mantle. (Rosaceae.) Hardy herbaceous perennials for rockeries and wild garden. *Soil:* ordinary. *Propagation:* seed or root division. **Best to grow:** *A. alpina*, 6 in., green flowers, silver foliage. *A. mollis*, 1 ft., greenish-yellow.

ALDER. *Alnus.* (Betulaceae.) Hardy deciduous trees and shrubs allied to birches. *Soil:* ordinary, or moist places. *Propagation:* seeds or cuttings of firm wood after leaf fall. **Best to grow:** *A. cordata*, 50 ft. for chalk or damp positions. *A. glutinosa*, 50 ft.–60 ft. (common alder). *A. incana*, 12 ft., catkins 5 in. long.

ALISMA. Water plantain. (Alismaceae.) See WATER PLANTS.

ALLIUM. See CHIVE, LEEK, ONION, SHALLOT.

ALLOTMENTS. Where land is available an allotment can be obtained by any local resident on demand through the Local Authority. Allotment Holders' Charter or Act compels local councils to establish allotment committees where required in every borough or urban district with a population of ten thousand upwards, unless exempted by the Ministry of Agriculture, after consultation with the Ministry of Health. The Act provides for compensation to allotment holders in certain cases on termination of their tenancies. It provides for six months' or longer notice to quit in the case of land let by private landlords, except under certain conditions.

Copies of Allotments Act are obtainable from the Ministry of Agriculture and Fisheries. Allotment cultivation, see VEGETABLE GARDEN.

ALLOTMENTS SOCIETY, THE NATIONAL. The headquarters of allotment movement in England and Wales. *Objects:* circulation of all matters appertaining to the allotment movement, and the securing of improved legislation and better conditions for allotment holders. Society's journal published at 3d. quarterly. *Subscription:* individual members, 5s. per annum; associates, 4d. per annum after purchase of 2s. 6d. share by the association on joining. Details from the Secretary, Drayton House, Gordon Street, London, W.C.1.

ALMOND. *Prunus Amygdalus.* (Rosaceae.) 20 ft.–30 ft. Deciduous tree flowering in March; suitable for towns. *Soil:* well-drained warm loam. *Propagation:* budding on seedling plums; plants from seed are seldom hardy. **Best to grow:** *P. Amygdalus Pollardii,* large pink flowers.

ALNUS. See ALDER.

ALPINES. Plants named thus come from high altitudes such as the Alps. Usually perennials of squat growth requiring light, open soils and cool root-run. Grown in rock gardens and cold greenhouses in Britain. See ROCK PLANTS.

ALSTROEMERIA. Peruvian Lily. (Amaryllidaceae.) Tuberous-rooted perennials. *Plant:* October in sunny sheltered borders. *Soil:* well-drained and sandy. *Propagation:* division in autumn, March-sown seeds in warm greenhouse. **Best to grow:** *A. aurantiaca,* 2 ft.–3 ft., orange with red streaks, July. *A. Ligtu* hybrids, 2 ft.–4 ft., cream, salmon and rose, July.

ALYSSUM. (Cruciferae.) Dwarf annuals and perennials for sunny borders, edging and rockeries. Perennials flower from May–June, annuals throughout the summer. *Soil:* preferably sandy. *Propagation:* March-sown seeds under glass. **Best to grow:** *A. saxatile,* 1 ft., yellow, and its varieties *compactum, variegatum, sulphureum. A. maritimum,* 6 in.–10 in., white, fragrant.

AMARANTHUS. Love-lies-bleeding. (Amarantaceae.) Half-hardy annuals with brilliant tail-like flowers, used for bedding out in June, or pot-plants for greenhouses. *Soil:* ordinary. *Propagation:* March-sown seeds under glass. **Best to grow:** *A. caudatus,* 2 ft.–3 ft., crimson-purple. *A. hypochondriacus* (Princes Feather), 4 ft.–5 ft., crimson.

AMARYLLIS. Belladonna Lily. (Amaryllidaceae.) Deciduous, bulbous plant grown in well-drained borders at the foot of a south wall. *Plant:* 9 in. deep and 12 in. apart in September. *Soil:* sandy loam with leaf-mould. *Propagation:* offsets. **Best to grow:** *A. Belladonna,* 18 in., rose, and varieties *purpurea maxima* and *kewensis.*

AMELANCHIER. Snowy Mespilus. (Rosaceae.) Deciduous, hardy, spring flowering trees and shrubs. *Plant:* November in open shrubberies. *Soil:* ordinary. *Propagation:* seeds or layers in spring, cuttings in autumn. No pruning required. **Best to grow:** *A. alnifolia,* 10 ft.–20 ft., white, April. *A. canadensis,* 20 ft.–30 ft., white, April, rich autumnal colouring.

Fig. 3. American blight attacks fruit and elm. It is recognized by its woolly appearance.

AMERICAN BLIGHT. Woolly Aphis (Fig. 3). See PEST CHART.

AMPELOPSIS. See VITIS.

ANAGALLIS. Pimpernel. (Primulaceae.) Trailing hardy annuals, and perennials best treated as annuals. Suitable for rockeries or sunny borders. *Soil:* ordinary. *Propagation:* annuals, sow seeds in March under glass, transplant in June; perennials, March root division, or seeds sown outside in April. **Best to grow:** *A. grandiflora* (syn. *A. linifolia*), blue, May to September.

ANCHUSA. (Boraginaceae.) Hardy annuals and perennials for borders and rockeries. *Plant:* October or March. *Soil:* ordinary. *Propagation:* seeds and root cuttings (for perennials). **Best to grow:** perennials, *A. italica,* 4 ft.–5 ft., varieties Dropmore (deep blue), Opal (light blue). *A. myosotidiflora,* 2 ft., pale blue. Annual, Blue Bird, 2 ft.

ANDROMEDA. (Ericaceae.) Hardy dwarf evergreen shrub with pink clustered waxy flowers. *Soil:* boggy peat in sheltered borders. *Propagation:* layers in September or cuttings. *A. polifolia,* 2 ft., June.

ANDROSACE. Rock Jasmine. (Primulaceae.) Hardy perennial alpine plants. *Plant:* March or April in sunny rockery or pots in Alpine house. *Soil:* sandy peat or loam with grit. *Propagation:* seeds or cuttings in September; division of roots in October. **Best to grow:** *A. carnea,* green mats of leaves with pink flowers. *A. Chamaejasme,* 2 in., blush-pink, May–June. *A. sarmentosa,* 6 in., bright rose, May and June.

ANEMONE. Wind Flower. (Ranunculaceae.) Hardy herbaceous and tuberous-rooted perennials. *Plant:* tubers 3 in. deep and 6 in. apart, autumn or spring, in sun or shade. *Soil:* deep, rich, with decayed manure added. *Propagation:* seeds of tuberous varieties sown outside in January or July, or offsets removed annually after flowering. **Best to grow:** Herbaceous varieties, *A. alpina*, 2 ft., white, May. *A. Pulsatilla*, 1 ft., purple, April. *A. japonica*, 4 ft., white or rose, September, good for mixed borders. Tuberous varieties, *A. blanda*, 6 in., blue, January–March. *A. coronaria* (poppy anemone), various colours. *A. hortensis*, 1 ft., crimson, May. St. Brigid, Empress, Aldeborough are selections of these two varieties. *A. nemorosa* (wood anemone), 6 in., white, rose or lavender, April.

ANGELICA. (Umbelliferae.) Perennial herb used for confectionery. See HERB GARDEN.

ANNUAL. Plant raised from seed that flowers, seeds and dies in one season. R.H.S. definition of exhibition annuals is "plants, which in this country naturally and ordinarily begin and end their growth, ripen seed and die (irrespective of frost), within twelve months."

ANTHEMIS. Rock Chamomile. (Compositae.) Hardy perennials for sunny borders or rockery. *Plant:* October or March. *Soil:* ordinary. *Propagation:* seed sown outdoors in April, division in March. **Best to grow:** *A. tinctoria*, 2 ft., yellow, June. *A. Sancti-Johannis*, 2 ft., orange, June.

ANTIRRHINUM. Snapdragon. (Scrophulariaceae.) Hardy perennials, but used mostly as annuals and biennials, either outdoors or as pot plants. *Plant* out in warm, dry beds or borders in May. For massed effects plant dwarf (Tom Thumb), 6 in. apart, intermediate, 1 ft., and tall varieties 1½ ft. *Soil:* ordinary with lime added 2 oz. per square yard when preparing beds. *Propagation:* pot plants, seed sown in cold frame or in house in July or August. Outdoors, sow in March under glass or outside in April. Cuttings of young shoots in cold frames in August. **Best to grow:** pot plants, varieties Majestic, Orange Glow, Victory, Royal Rose, Red Emperor.

ANTS. See PEST CHART.

APHIDES OR APHIS. See PEST CHART.

APPLE. See FRUIT AND ITS CULTURE.

APPLE BLOSSOM WEEVIL. See PEST CHART.

AQUILEGIA. See COLUMBINE.

ARABIS. (Cruciferae.) Hardy perennials, trailing plants for walls, rockeries, edging, and carpeting for spring-flowering bulbs. *Plant:* October–November. *Soil:* ordinary. *Propagation:* seeds, cuttings, division. **Best to grow:** *A. albida flore pleno*, 8 in., white, double, February to May. *A. albida variegata*, white-edged leaves.

ARBUTUS. Strawberry tree. (Ericaceae.) Hardy evergreen trees and shrubs with scarlet globular fruit. *Soil:* loam, with peat or leaf-mould. *Propagation:* seeds; keep plants in pots until planted outdoors as they transplant badly. **Best to grow:** *A. Unedo*, 10 ft., white flowers, September.

ARCTOTIS. (Compositae.) Half-hardy annuals and perennials used best as annuals for beds and borders, preferably in full sun. *Soil:* loamy, enriched with leaf-mould, sand and charcoal for pot plants. *Propagation:* seeds. **Best to grow:** *A. grandis*, 2 ft., white, summer.

ARENARIA. Sandwort. (Caryophyllaceae.) Low-growing, hardy herbaceous perennials or rock plants. *Soil:* ordinary, sun or shade. *Propagation:* seeds or division. **Best to grow:** *A. balearica*, 2 in., white, June, good for edges of stone walks. *A. montana*, 3 in., large white flowers, April.

ARNICA. (Compositae.) Hardy, herbaceous perennials for sunny borders. *Soil:* ordinary. *Propagation:* seeds or division. **Best to grow:** *A. montana*, 1 ft., yellow, May–July. *A. Chamissonis*, 2 ft., yellow, July–September.

ARTEMISIA. (Compositae.) Wormwood, Tarragon, etc. Evergreen and deciduous hardy shrubs and perennials. *Soil:* well drained, not rich, sunny position. *Propagation:* cuttings, division in October. **Best to grow:** *A. Abrotanum* (Old Man), 2 ft.–4 ft., fragrant, yellow, August. *A. lactiflora*, 5 ft., cream, August–October.

ARTICHOKE, Chinese. *Stachys tuberifera.* (Labiatae.) Perennial tuberous-rooted plant doing best in sunny position. *Plant:* tubers March–April, water freely in dry weather. Plant 9 in. apart and 4 in. deep in rows 18 in. apart. *Soil:* well drained and deeply dug.

ARTICHOKE, Globe. *Cynara Scolymus.* (Compositae.) Large perennials of which the immature flower heads are edible. Water freely during summer. *Plant* in rich, deeply dug soil as they are gross feeders. *Propagation:* seed or offshoots of older plants. *Cultivation:* see VEGETABLE CHART.

ARTICHOKE, Jerusalem. *Helianthus tuberosus.* (Compositae.) Edible tubers that do best in an open soil in a sunny position. Useful as a summer screen for odd corners of the garden. Prepare ground in February, digging deeply and adding manure. Cut stalks down in early winter. Lift tubers as required for use. *Cultivation:* see VEGETABLE CHART.

ARUM LILY. *Richardia.* (Aroideae.) Herbaceous perennials for greenhouse or living-room. After flowering (October–May) stand plants outside until autumn. Water freely March–May, moderately September–March, applying stimulants during flowering period. Re-pot annually in autumn. *Soil:* two parts fibrous loam, one of leaf-mould and sand. *Propagation:* seeds, suckers, or division. **Best to grow:** *R. africana*, 3 ft.–4 ft., white, winter and spring.

ASPARAGUS. (Liliaceae.) Includes the edible species grown in the vegetable garden and the decorative-foliage pot plants.

Edible Asparagus requires deep digging with manure added in October–November when preparing the 3 ft.–4 ft. wide beds, which can be of any convenient length. Make pathways between the beds 1 ft. wide. *Plant* 2–3-year-old crowns in April, setting them 15 in. apart each way and 3 in.–5 in. below the surface. Start cutting shoots after the second or third year and never cut after June. Mulch each autumn with decayed manure. *Soil:* rich sandy loam is best. *Propagation:* seed.

Greenhouse species are grown in pots or tubs or as climbers against walls. *Plant* or pot in March, watering freely during the summer. Apply liquid manure occasionally. *Soil:* loam, leaf-mould, and sharp sand. *Propagation:* seed, root division. **Best to grow:** *A. plumosus, A. Sprengeri.*

ASPERULA. Woodruff. (Rubiaceae.) Hardy dwarf annuals and perennials suitable for shady rockeries or under trees. *Soil:* light. *Propagation;* seed, division of perennials. **Best to grow:** *A. odorata*, Sweet Woodruff, 6 in., white, May. *A. orientalis*, annual, 1 ft., sky-blue, August.

ASPIDISTRA. (Liliaceae.) See ROOM PLANTS.

ASPLENIUM. Greenhouse and hardy ferns. See FERNS.

ASTER, China. *Callistephus.* (Compositae.) Half-hardy annual transplanted out end of May. Treat carefully and grow without a check. *Soil:* dig in well-decayed manure. Apply 6 oz. lime per square yard in March. *Propagation:* sow seeds in cold frame in March. Singles, sow outdoors in flowering positions in April. **Best to grow:** dwarf types (9 in.–12 in.), Chrysanthemum-flowered, Liliput, Dwarf Bouquet. Tall ($2\frac{1}{2}$ ft.–3 ft.), Californian Giant, Comet, Ostrich Plume. All available in separate colours and named varieties.

ASTRANTIA. (Umbelliferae.) Hardy herbaceous perennials for wild garden, shady borders, woodland walks. Plant October–March. *Soil:* ordinary, preferably cool and moist. *Propagation:* division in winter or spring. **Best to grow:** *A. major*, 2 ft., white, June. *A. maxima*, 2 ft., rose-pink, June.

AUBERGINE. Egg Plant. *Solanum melongena.* (Solanaceae.) For greenhouse cultivation, grown mostly for decoration but the fruits can be eaten. *Soil:* two parts loam, one part each of leaf-mould and decayed manure with sand. *Propagation:* seed in temperature of 75 deg. F. Sow January–March, transplanting gradually to 6-in. pots. Syringe foliage daily, water freely, giving liquid manure occasionally.

AUBRIETIA. (Cruciferae.) Hardy trailing perennials. Carpet growth suitable for walls, edging to borders, spring bedding and rockeries. Trim straggling plants after flowering. *Soil:* light sandy or ordinary. *Propagation:* cuttings, seeds. **Best to grow:** modern hybrids are best, e.g., Church Knowle (lavender), Prichards A.1 (blue), Vindictive (red), Gloriosa (pink), Carnival (purple).

AUCUBA. Spotted or Variegated Laurel. (Cornaceae.) Evergreen shrub suitable for hedges, either in the open or shade. *Soil:* ordinary. *Propagation:* seeds or cuttings in September–October. **Best to grow:** *A. japonica*, 6 ft.–10 ft., and its varieties. See also SHRUBS AND TREES.

AURICULA. *Primula Auricula.* (Primulaceae.) Alpine types have yellow blooms with white or yellow eye, smooth stems and no powder. Florists' types are covered with mealy powder. Will thrive in dry soils. Seed germination is erratic and may not take place for two years if seed is old. *Propagation:* seeds or division. **Best to grow:** *P. Auricula alpina*, yellow. *P. Auricula*, Blue Velvet, purple-blue. *P. Auricula*, Old Red Dusty Miller, red.

AZALEA. Brilliant-flowered evergreen or deciduous shrubs, now included with the rhododendrons. Those used for pot culture include the Indian azalea which is evergreen. The most commonly grown Ghent azalea is deciduous. After flowering, these plants can be put in sheltered positions outdoors and left in their pots if preferred. Bring them into the home or greenhouse for the winter and re-pot firmly. Remove all seed-pods.

Outdoor azaleas thrive in the same soil as rhododendrons and the latter's dark evergreen foliage forms an excellent background to the brilliant flowers and autumn colouring of the azaleas. *Plant:* in autumn, and mulch annually with decayed manure or leaf-mould. *Prune:* do not prune, except straggly growth of pot plants. *Soil:* pot plants, three parts peat, one loam, and half of leaf-mould and silver sand. Outdoors, sandy peat and leaf-mould.

BALSAM. *Impatiens Balsamina.* (Geraniaceae.) Quick-growing white, rose or scarlet, half-hardy annuals. Grown as pot plants or planted outdoors in June in sun or shade. *Soil:* ordinary; for pot culture fibrous loam, leaf mould and sand. *Propagation:* seeds in greenhouse, March–April.

BAMBOO. *Bambusa, Arundinaria.* (Gramineae.) Hardy and half-hardy evergreen plants with decorative leaves. Quick-growing and suitable for warm sheltered woodland walks or dells. Also on moist banks of streams or ponds. Grass-like growth from 18 in.–15 ft. *Propagation:* division, or seed when obtainable.

BARBERRY. See BERBERIS.

BARTONIA. (Loasaceae.) Quick-growing hardy annual, excellent for filling gaps in sunny borders. *Soil:* ordinary. *Propagation:* March sowing where it is to flower, with subsequent thinning to 1 ft. apart. **Best to grow:** *B. aurea* (syn. *Mentzelia*), 18 in., yellow, summer.

BASIL. See HERB GARDEN.

BASS, BAST or RAFFIA. Used for tying plants. Derived from dried vegetable fibre.

BAY. *Laurus nobilis.* (Lauraceae.) 20 ft.–40 ft. Evergreen hardy trees with dark green aromatic leaves used for flavouring. *Soil:* ordinary. Will grow in open sunny positions, sheltered shrubberies or borders. *Prune:* in April to keep the plants shapely.

BEANS, Broad. *Vicia Faba.* (Leguminosae.) Thrive in any soil though best in deep moist positions. Best to sow on ground manured for previous crop, giving dressings of lime, superphosphate and sulphate of potash to the ground in early autumn or winter.

First sowings in October or November need to be thicker than for successional sowings from January to May. Intercrops of early lettuce can be taken between the bean rows. Set seeds in flat-bottomed drills taken out with a hoe. As blossoms set, the bean tops can be pinched out to check black-fly. **Best to grow:** for November sowing use Mazagan; January–February, use long-pod varieties like Eclipse, Bunyards Exhibition; March, sow Windsor varieties. See also VEGETABLE CHART.

BEANS, Climbing French. Grow these climbing French varieties like scarlet runners.

BEANS, Dwarf, French or Kidney. *Phaseolus vulgaris.* (Leguminosae.) These hardy annuals can be raised in frames, under cloches, or in temperatures of about 55 deg., and may be either hardened off and planted out or cropped as they stand in the boxes or frames. Protect from frost and water well.

Sow outdoors, 3 in. deep, from mid-April in sunny positions. Thin out to 1 ft. apart, watering freely in dry weather. Protect from slugs. See also VEGETABLE CHART.

BEANS, Haricot. Grow like dwarf beans, leaving plants to mature in the ground. Sow as early as possible to let seeds ripen. When pods are brown, hang bunched plants to dry. Store in very dry conditions, shell beans for use. **Best to grow:** Comtesse de Chambord, Brown Dutch.

BEANS, Scarlet Runner. *Phaseolus multiflorus.* (Leguminosae.) Require manure and deep digging. Prepare a trench a foot deep with compost or manure added. Thin plants to 9 in.–12 in. apart. Spraying the plants with soft water on fine evenings encourages the pods to set. Growing points must be pinched out if beans are grown without stakes. Mulch plants and water in dry weather. Pick regularly. See also VEGETABLE CHART.

BEECH. *Fagus.* (Cupuliferae.) Hardy deciduous trees growing well on chalky soils or at the seaside. *Propagation:* seeds or grafting of named varieties. **Best to grow:** *F. sylvatica* (common beech), 70 ft.–80 ft. For hedging, plant 9 in. apart. *F. sylvatica cuprea* (copper beech), *F. sylvatica pendula* (weeping beech), *F. sylvatica purpurea* (purple beech).

BEETROOT. *Beta vulgaris.* (Chenopodiaceae.) Sow beet on ground manured for previous crop, never on freshly manured land. Early crops are raised in frames from February to March. Lift for storage in October, twist off tops and select best roots for storing in dry sand, peat or soil, in damp, frost-proof shed. See Fig. 4. See also VEGETABLE CHART.

BEGONIA. (Begoniaceae.) Warm greenhouse fibrous- and tuberous-rooted perennials. Ornamental leaves and showy flowers suitable for bedding out, hanging baskets or decorative pot plants.

Outdoor culture: start tubers in boxes of loam, leaf-mould and sand, in gentle heat in March. After hardening off, plant outside in June. Lift tubers in September, and after drying them off, place in frost-proof store. *Pot culture:* start in February–March in equal parts loam and leaf-mould with half-part dry cow manure and half-part sand. Feed with liquid manure during full growth and shade from sun. After flowering gradually withhold water, keeping fibrous-rooted plants rather dry till March. Keep tubers quite dry and store pots on their side until February. *Propagation:* fibrous- and tuberous-rooted, by seeds sown in 60 deg. F. in January, also by cuttings; ornamental-leaved kinds by leaf cuttings in spring or summer, in heat.

BELLADONNA LILY. See AMARYLLIS.

BELLIS. Daisy. (Compositae.) Double-flowered varieties of this dwarf hardy perennial are used for edges or spring flower-beds. Plant in October–March in sun or shade. *Soil:* ordinary. *Propagation:* divide in June after flowering; seed sown outside in June. **Best to grow:** *B. perennis flore pleno* and its varieties, Alice (pink), Rob Roy (red), Dresden White (white), Dresden China (pink).

BENEFICIAL INSECTS. Quite a number of garden insects are not harmful and can be helpful to the gardener. Never destroy the following: *Devil's Coach-horse* or Cocktail Beetle, a long black beetle which cocks up its tail. *Centipede,* distinguished by yellow-brown, flat body, with one pair of legs to each segment. (*Millipedes* are harmful.) *Ground Beetle,*

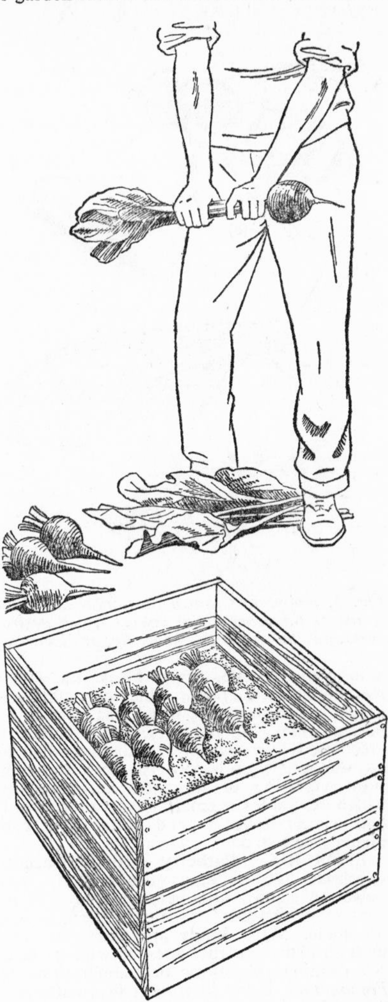

Fig. 4. To store beetroot, twist off the tops and store in dry sand in a cool place.

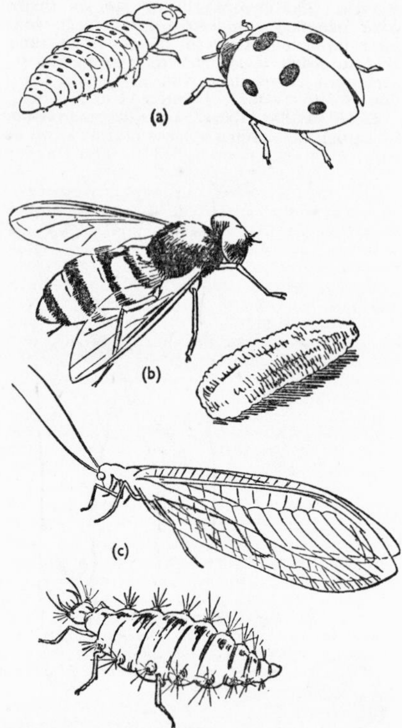

Fig. 5. Above are shown the larval and adult forms of three beneficial insects which destroy pests: (a) *ladybird;* (b) *hover fly;* (c) *lacewing.*

a long oval beetle, nearly black but with a metallic lustre. *Ladybird*, which eats aphis and greenfly. *Lacewing Fly*, which has large transparent wings, big red eyes, and a thin pale green body. *Ichneumon Fly*, distinguished by its slender, wasp-like waist, and the constant vibration of its antennae. *Hover-fly*, which resembles a small wasp but has only two wings; it hovers and darts about over plants. See Fig. 5.

BERBERIS. Barberry. (Berberidaceae.) Evergreen and deciduous shrubs, hardy, both flowering and ornamental-leaved. *Plant:* September–October or March–April, in sun or shade. Many kinds are useful to form undergrowth in shrubberies or wild gardens. No pruning except for occasional thinning. *Propagation:* layers in spring; firm cuttings in September, inserted in cold frames. Seed sown in sheltered borders October–November. **Best to grow:** *B. Aquifolium* (syn. *Mahonia Aquifolium*), 4 ft.–6 ft., yellow, April. *B. Darwinii*, 6 ft.–12 ft., orange-yellow, April–May. *B. japonica*, *B. Bealei*, 6 ft., scented, yellow flowers in winter. *B. stenophylla*, 6 ft.–10 ft., golden yellow, April–May, excellent for hedges, sloping banks, or specimens. Above mentioned are evergreen.

Deciduous varieties: *B. Thunbergii.* 3 ft.–8 ft., orange-scarlet autumn foliage. *B. vulgaris purpurea*, 6 ft.–10 ft., yellow with purple foliage. *B. rubrostilla*, 6 ft., vivid red berries.

BIENNIALS. Those plants which normally mature from seed in two years. The first season's growth of leaf and shoots stores energy for flower and seed production the following season, when the plant subsequently dies. Many perennials are grown as biennials as the flowers are of better quality and more suitable for bedding. Sweet williams and wallflowers, though perennials, are usually grown as biennials, whilst the Canterbury bells are true biennials. Carrots and parsnips are biennial vegetables.

BIG BUD. See PEST CHART.

BIRCH. *Betula.* (Betulaceae.) Deciduous hardy trees and shrubs, with ornamental bark. Suitable for any position, especially seaside or town. *Propagation:* seeds, layers. **Best to grow:** *B. alba* (silver birch), 50 ft. *B. alba Youngii*, weeping variety.

BIRD CHERRY. *Prunus Padus.* See PRUNUS.

BLACKBERRY. See FRUIT AND ITS CULTURE.

BLACK SPOT. See DISEASE CHART.

BLANCHING. Some vegetables at certain stages of growth are covered to exclude the light in order to make them more palatable. Exclusion of light prevents formation of green colouring matter and promotes tenderness and mild flavour.

BLANKET FLOWER. See GAILLARDIA.

BLIGHT. See DISEASE CHART.

BLUEBELL. See SCILLA.

BONEFLOUR. Bonemeal, steamed boneflour. See FERTILIZER CHART.

BORAGE. *Borago.* (Boraginaceae.) Hardy annuals and perennials, useful for sunny rockeries and dry banks. *Soil:* ordinary. *Propagation:* sow seeds yearly or root division for perennials. **Best to grow:** *B. laxiflora*, blue, creeping, perennial, August. *B. officinalis* (common borage), 1 ft.–2 ft., blue, annual.

BORDEAUX MIXTURE. A fungicide of copper sulphate (blue-stone) used against potato blight, apple and pear scab, celery leaf spot, and sold in proprietary forms or mixed at home in wood or enamel vessels (not galvanized iron). Prepare as follows for:

Potatoes:		9 oz. copper sulphate 6 oz. quick-lime 5 gal. water
Fruit trees:		4 lb. copper sulphate 6 lb. slaked lime 100 gal. water
Celery:		4 lb. copper sulphate 5 lb. slaked lime 40 gal. water.
General use:	(*a*)	4 lb. copper sulphate 5 lb. slaked lime 40 gal. water
	(*b*)	4 oz. copper sulphate 5 oz. slaked lime 2½ gal. water

Dilute lime with bulk of water, stir in blue-stone dissolved in a little water, and use within twenty-four to thirty-six hours.

BORECOLE or KALE. *Brassica oleracea acephala.* (Cruciferae.) Biennials, grown as annuals for winter greens. Very hardy and easy to grow on ordinary deep soil. See also VEGETABLE CHART.

BOX. *Buxus.* (Euphorbiaceae.) Hardy evergreen shrubs. For topiary work, or suitable for hedges or bushes in any position, sun or shade; grows well on poor chalky soil. Trim annually, April or October, but not in frosty weather. *Plant:* April or September. *Propagation:* cuttings 3 in. long in August or September, division or layers September–October. **Best to grow:** *B. sempervirens* and its varieties e.g., *var. suffruticosa*) used for edgings.

BRACHYCOME. Swan River Daisy. (Compositae.) Half-hardy annual suitable for sunny bed or border. *Soil:* ordinary. *Propagation:* seed sown in temperature of 55 deg. in March. March-sown seed under glass, transplanted out in May. Sown outside in April and thinned to 6 in. apart. **Best to grow:** *B. iberidiolia*, 1 ft., white or blue.

BRASSICA. See members of cabbage family, especially BORECOLE, BROCCOLI, BRUSSELS SPROUTS, CABBAGE, CAULIFLOWER.

BREASTWOOD. Young shoots that grow directly outwards at right-angles from the

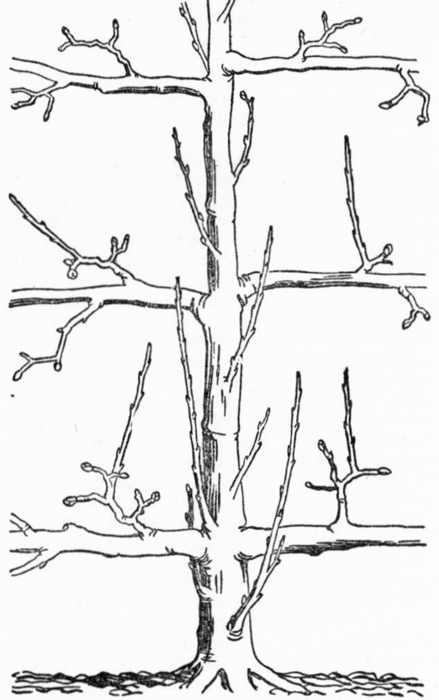

Fig. 6. Breastwood is the unwanted growth coming from the central stem and fruiting spurs of a trained tree and must be cut out during pruning.

wall or support of wall-trained trees. This growth is cut out to keep plants in orderly shape. See Fig. 6.

BROCCOLI. *Brassica oleracea botrytis asparagoides.* Broccoli is similar to cauliflower but coarser and more hardy, and matures during winter and spring. Select good and successional varieties. Protect curds by bending over leaves in severe weather. **Best to grow:** autumn use, Early Roscoff; winter use, Roscoff No. 1; spring use, Snow White.

BROCCOLI, Purple Sprouting and White Sprouting. Flowering sprouts are gathered immature in spring as required. Culture as for broccoli. See also VEGETABLE CHART.

BRUSSELS SPROUTS, *Brassica oleracea bullata gemmifera.* (Cruciferae.) Crop from November to April; thrive best on fertile, manured soils, but avoid newly dug-in fresh manure. Apply as top-dressing a mixture of ½ oz. sulphate of potash, 2 oz. superphosphate, and 8 oz. soot, using this quantity per square yard. Never apply fertilizers after August. Do not cut off tops until all the sprouts are gathered. **Best to grow:** dwarf, Little Gem; medium, Fillbasket; tall, Exhibition. See also VEGETABLE CHART.

BUDDING. See PROPAGATION OF PLANTS.

BUDDLEIA. (Loganiaceae.) Deciduous flowering shrubs, which do well in open sunny positions, sheltered shrubberies or against walls. *Plant:* April or October. *Prune: B. variabilis* group hard back in March. Thin out and shape *B. globosa* and *B. alternifolia* after flowering. *Soil:* light. *Propagation:* 4 in. long cuttings in September or seeds outdoors in spring. **Best to grow:** *B. Colvilei*, 10 ft.–12 ft., crimson, summer. *B. globosa*, 10 ft.–15 ft., orange, May–June. *B. variabilis* and its varieties, 6 ft.–10 ft., rosy-lilac, summer. *B. alternifolia*, 10 ft., long mauve sprays, June.

BULB FLIES AND MITES. See PEST CHART (Narcissus fly).

BULBOCODIUM. Spring Meadow Saffron. (Liliaceae.) Hardy bulbous plant flowering before the leaves appear in February–March. Crocus-like flowers are rosy-purple, and are suitable for sun or shade. *Plant:* bulbs 3 in. deep and 3 in. apart in September, replanting them every two years. *Propagation:* offsets.

BULBS are built up of fleshy leaf-bases which store the plant food, thus enabling the plant after its resting period to grow and flower in a comparatively short space of time. In early spring, bulbs are thus enabled to flower in woods before overhead foliage causes dense shade. It is essential that after flowering the leaves should be allowed to complete their full development in order to provide for the next season's growth. *Soil:* open, well-drained soil in general; bulbs should never be in contact with fresh manure. *Propagation:* remove offsets or young bulbs which are formed at the base of the old ones. They require to be planted in separate beds as it may be several years before these small bulbs bloom. Bulbils in the axils of certain lily leaves are treated in the same way. Seed is sown in frames or sheltered positions outside in March. Scales from most lilies, when planted in sand, leaf-mould or peat in July–September, will form bulbils at the base of the scales. Hyacinths and *Scilla sibirica* can be propagated by specialists by scooping and cross-cutting the base of the bulb.

Planting: give dressings of lime and bonemeal to ground that is in good heart, prior to planting. Plant bulbs with their own depth of soil above them; always have the base of the bulb in contact with the soil. Sand under each bulb will aid drainage on very heavy soils. Space out bulbs on bed before planting, never allow them to be baked through by the sun. Put all bulbs in the bed at the same depth, as those deeper will flower later. Plant spring-flowering bulbs in October, or earlier if possible.

Planting in grass (naturalizing). Bulbs must be planted in natural drifts; handfuls of bulbs can be tossed over the ground and planted where they fall. Special bulb planters will make a hole for each bulb and replace the plug of turf above the bulb; otherwise, square pieces of turf can be removed with a spade, then one or more bulbs placed beneath.

Storage and drying: certain bulbs, such as tulips and the summer-flowering gladioli, are lifted annually. After growth has died down, lift and dry off bulbs, remove dead foliage and sort out. Store in cool dry place (not in full sunshine). Crocuses, *Muscari* (grape hyacinth), bulbous iris, and narcissus, can be left until they need thinning. Lift tulips and hyacinths in June–July, gladioli in October. Bedding bulbs can be lifted earlier and heeled in till they die back (watering occasionally), if the space is required for other plants.

Indoor culture: choose good bulbs. Specially prepared bulbs can be obtained for Christmas flowering. Plant in pots or boxes in autumn, with nose of bulb above soil level, using plenty of crocks and a compost of fibrous loam and sand; bulbs can be almost touching each other. It is better to plant one type of bulb to each pot, to ensure their flowering together. Stand pots outside in frames or yard, cover with 4 in. of ashes, for seven or eight weeks, bringing into heat and light gradually. *Bulbs in bowls:* most bulbs can be grown in bowls when fibre is used, since the latter requires no drainage. This method is cleaner in the house. Keep bowls in darkness in an airy, frost-proof place, never put in a hot cupboard, as roots dry out; if a cupboard is used, leave the door open for ventilation; covering bowls with blanket or thick material will suffice. Bring bulbs gradually into the light when ready. Soak fibre in water before use, squeezing out the moisture so that fibre holds together when squeezed. Choose deep bowls for narcissus and half-fill with fibre before pressing in the bulbs; pack in fibre round the sides to within ½ in. of the rim. *Water* regularly every ten days or so with tepid water; keep fibre just moist. Never let it dry out completely, but be careful also not to overwater. *Bulbs in water:* certain bulbs, especially hyacinths, will grow in water in special glasses. Keep water-level just below the base of the bulb. Put a lump of charcoal in the bottom of the glass to keep the water sweet. *Bulbs in stones:* pebbles or small stones can be used as a growing medium with the base of the bulb just above water-level. Crocuses grown in bowls containing pebbles need cool conditions till flowers open.

BULRUSH. *Scirpus lacustris.* (Cyperacea.) Hardy perennial marsh or water plant suitable for bog-gardens, margin of ponds. *Plant:* October–April. *Propagation:* division in March; seeds.

BURGUNDY MIXTURE. This resembles Bordeaux mixture and is made with washing soda (sodium carbonate) and blue-stone (copper sulphate). Not used for fruit owing to injury to plants.

BUTCHERS' BROOM. *Ruscus aculeatus.* (Liliaceae.) Hardy evergreen shrub, ornamental green leaves, with red berries in winter. Suitable in shade or sun. *Plant:* October or April. *Soil:* ordinary. *Propagation:* by division in October.

CABBAGE. *Brassica oleracea.* (Cruciferae.) Successional sowings of different varieties will maintain a supply of cabbage through the whole year. Deeply worked soil with manure and compost added is essential; give regular dressings of lime to ground used for cabbage crops. *Spring cabbage:* always plant firmly and refirm if frosts lift them during the winter. Planting can be closer than required and alternate plants cut as greens to allow others to heart. Dress with nitrate of soda round each plant (avoiding foliage) in early spring. *Summer and autumn cabbage:* if greens are short the stumps can be cut across the top to allow further buds to sprout. See also VEGETABLE CHART.

CABBAGE BUTTERFLY. Parent of cabbage caterpillar. See PEST CHART.

CABBAGE CATERPILLAR. See PEST CHART.

CACTUS. (Cactaceae.) This is a vast family with over three thousand distinct varieties, many of which live in hot, waterless deserts. Cactus cultivation was much in vogue in Victorian times, when miniature greenhouses were found in many drawing-rooms. Full-sized greenhouses and sunny windows may be used so long as excess moisture and frost are avoided. *Cultivation:* plant in clean disinfected pots, giving good drainage by one-quarter filling each pot with crocks. Use two parts garden soil (free from manure and humus) and one part clean sand; lumpy soils are best, and as cacti are lime-lovers, add builders' rubble. Prickly plants can be held with wooden tweezers when potting. Do this by trickling in the soil round the plant and pressing gently. Give spring stimulants of bonemeal, salt or complete fertilizers. *Watering:* though not requiring water as often as most plants, cacti require water regularly, especially in hot weather; often once a day is necessary. From September–October watering once a week is sufficient, then once a fortnight till February, after which the watering can be increased. *Cereus* and *Opuntia* require rather more water than the others. *Propagation:* cuttings of portions which should be left to dry twenty-four hours before inserting in sandy soil; handle carefully and do not water for fourteen days. When growth starts, pot in usual soil. Any cactus, when cut in pieces with a sharp knife, will root in from two to three weeks.

CALCEOLARIA. (Scrophulariaceae.) Half-hardy or greenhouse shrubs and herbaceous perennials (Fig. 7). Keep shrubby varieties in pots in greenhouses or windows, or outdoors

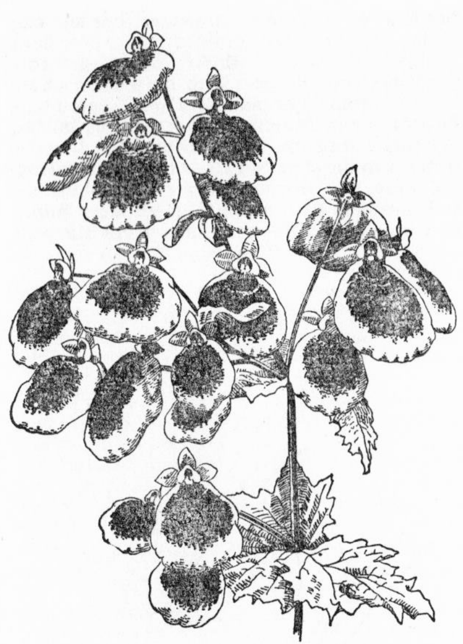

Fig. 7. Calceolarias make a good display for bedding or growing under glass.

in summer in sunny or shady borders. Pot in March, avoiding any check, and when established give liquid manure. Plant out in May. *Propagation:* cuttings in autumn. The herbaceous plants should be sown in July under glass; pot up and water moderately till April, after which water freely. Discard plants after flowering. Hardy types may be planted in moist shaded positions in rock garden; water well in hot weather. Sow annuals in March. *Soil:* ordinary, with leaf-mould; for potting, two parts sandy loam, one leaf-mould. Always pot lightly.

CALENDULA. See MARIGOLD.

CALLIOPSIS. *Coreopsis.* (Compositae.) Hardy annuals and perennials suitable for sunny, well-drained beds or borders. *Soil:* moist and ordinary for perennials; annuals do well in ordinary town soils. *Propagation:* annual by seed sown where plants will flower in April, perennials by seed sown outdoors in April; division in October or March. **Best to grow:** perennials, modern hybrids of *C. lanceolata* (such as Perry's variety), 3 ft., yellow, June–September.

CALLUNA. Ling. Scotch Heather. (Ericaceae.) Hardy evergreen shrubs for bog or peat soils, or open beds, borders or shrubbery edges. Excellent flowers for bees, differ from true heaths by large coloured calyx and four tiny bracts at base. *Propagation:* division in October or April. **Best to grow:** *C. vulgaris*, 1 ft., purple, and such varieties of this as *Alportii*, crimson; *alba*, white; *H. E. Beale*, long sprays of double pink flowers.

CALYCANTHUS. Allspice. (Calycanthaceae.) Hardy deciduous flowering shrubs suitable for south or west walls, or sheltered shrubberies in southern England. *Propagation:* seeds or layers, July–August.

CALYSTEGIA. (Convolvulaceae.) Trailing and climbing hardy perennials for sunny positions. Deciduous. *Soil:* ordinary; best to restrict root area to prevent spreading. *Propagation:* seeds outside in April; division in October or March.

CAMPANULA. Harebell. Canterbury Bell. Bell Flower. (Campanulaceae.) Large family of hardy annuals, biennials and perennials. Shorter types suitable for sunny border edgings, rockeries, hanging baskets; taller kinds for herbaceous borders and greenhouses. *Soil:* ordinary; pot plants require equal parts leaf-mould, loam, sand. Re-pot in March. *Propagation:* seeds sown in spring, biennials sown May–June, perennials by division or cuttings. **Best to grow:** Biennials, *C. Medium*, Canterbury Bell, 3 ft., also variety *calycanthema* (Cup-and-Saucer). Perennials, *C. carpatica*, 1 ft., blue, with varieties *alba*, white; Ditton Blue, blue; Isobel, violet; *C. pusilla*, 3 in., quickly spreading carpet for rockeries and edgings; *C. persicifolia* and such varieties of this as Telham Beauty, 3 ft., china blue; *Moerheimi*, 2 ft., double white; *Backhousei*, 3 ft., single white.

CANARY CREEPER. *Tropaeolum peregrinum.* (Tropaeolaceae.) Half-hardy, yellow-flowered climber (Fig. 8), grows rapidly as an annual for trellis or low fences, and does well on north aspect. Sow where it is to flower,

Fig. 8. Canary creepers can be grown as climbers or trailing from window-boxes or hanging baskets.

in April. *Soil:* light ordinary; water freely in dry weather. Perennials include *T. polyphyllum*, golden yellow, suitable for sunny bank, rockery walls (*plant* August–November); *T. speciosum*, brilliant flame flowers covering shaded walls, hedges, fencing (*plant* October or March in moist soil, water in dry weather, and mulch in October). *Propagation:* root division.

CANDYTUFT. *Iberis.* (Cruciferae.) Hardy annuals and evergreen perennials for sunny beds, borders or rockeries. *Soil:* light ordinary. *Propagation:* seeds; also cuttings for perennials. **Best to grow:** Perennials: *I. corifolia*, 1 ft., white, May–June; *I. sempervirens*, 9 in., white. Annuals: *I. coronaria* (Rocket candytuft), 1 ft., white; *I. umbellata* (common candytuft), 1 ft., purple.

CANKER. See DISEASE CHART (Apples).

CANNA. (Scitaminaceae.) Tropical herbaceous plants, used for pot culture or as pot plants for bedding outside from June–September. Lift and place in boxes for winter, keep nearly dry in a frost-proof shed. Pot in March in minimum temperature of 40 deg. *Propagation:* seeds or division. (Soak seeds for twenty-four hours in tepid water and notch before sowing.)

CAPE GOOSEBERRY. *Physalis.* (Solanaceae.) Hardy and greenhouse perennials. The fruit within the large calyx of the greenhouse variety is edible. Outdoors, sunny, well-drained borders are suitable. Gather stems with calyx-like Chinese lanterns in September and hang upside down in a dry place for winter decorations. *Propagation:* seeds or division. Lift and replant every three years. **Best to grow:** *P. Alkekengi*, 1 ft.–2 ft., white flowers; *P. Francheti* (hardiest), 1½ ft.–2½ ft., white flowers.

CARAWAY. *Carum Carvi.* (Umbelliferae.) Hardy biennials, seeds used for confectionery purposes. Sow in ordinary soil in spring.

CARDAMINE. (Cruciferae.) Hardy perennial herbs, flourishing in damp shady places, preferably front of shady borders. *Propagation:* seeds or division. **Best to grow:** *C. pratensis* (Cuckoo Flower, Lady's Smock), 18 in., pale purple, May, and its double variety, *C. pratensis flore pleno.*

CARDOON. *Cynara cardunculus.* (Compositae.) Grown for its edible leaf-stalks and closely related to the globe artichoke. Sow seeds in April over manured trenches, 18 in. wide, 1 ft. deep and 4 ft. apart. Dibble three or four seeds every 18 in. and cover with cloche or inverted flower-pot. Remove all but the strongest plant from each group, and protect from late frosts and hot sun. Keep moist and blanch with hayband round the drawn-up leaves and mound with soil. Plants are then ready in eight weeks.

CARLINA. Carline Thistle. (Compositae.) Hardy perennial stemless thistles for open dryish borders and rockeries. Useful for poor soils. *Propagation:* seed where it is to grow in April. **Best to grow:** *C. acanthifolia*, white, June; *C. acaulis*, white and silver thistles, July.

CARNATIONS. Pink. Picotee. Sweet William. Malmaison. Marguerite Carnations. Dianthus. (Caryophyllaceae.) Hardy perennials and biennials for greenhouse or sunny borders or rockeries. *Culture:* border carnations prefer well-drained soil, especially chalky, in towns, window-boxes or roof gardens. Deep digging with only small quantities of compost or manure. *Plant:* September–October or in March, and increase in July by layering young non-flowering growths. Incision is made in the stem at two or three inches from the base and opened, then pressed into the soil and held with a pin (Fig. 9). Keep moist, and shade exhibition blooms from the sun.

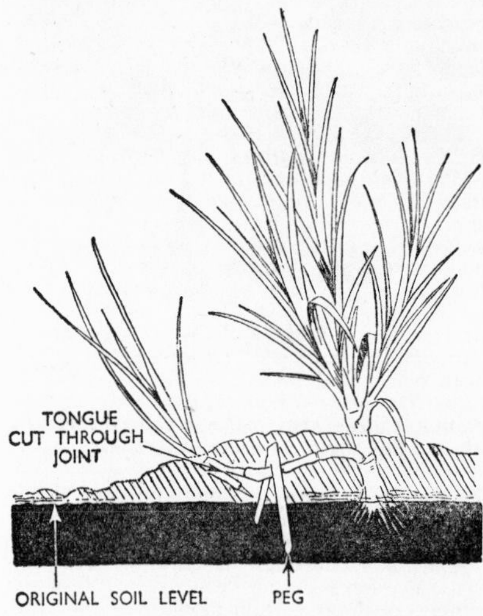

Fig. 9. Layering a carnation.

Carnations *under glass* require three parts turfy loam, one part of equal portions decayed cow manure, and wood ashes and sand with bonemeal added. Pot rooted cuttings singly into 3-in. pots and stand in temperature of 45–50 deg. Stop at third or fourth joint, and at intervals when shoots are a few inches long, till September. Pot on, and stand outside from May to September, then house, giving ample ventilation; syringe daily in spring and summer. Feed when well rooted, remove all but terminal bud, and support growths. *Propagation:* cuttings in sand, November–March. *Malmaison carnations:* large self-coloured flowers grown under glass, and treated as above. Plant rooted layers in August–September. Water moderately in winter, and feed with liquid manure when buds form; ventilate freely, and shade from sun. *Propagation:* layers in July.

Pinks: useful for borders, requiring ordinary soil and sunny borders. Plant in autumn or spring 9 in. apart. *Propagation:* heel cuttings in July; division; seeds.

Sweet williams: raise outdoors as biennials in ordinary soil for sunny beds or borders. Plant 12 in. apart in autumn. *Propagation:* seed sown in summer.

Marguerite carnations: perennials that are always used as annuals. Suitable for open borders or pot plants for conservatory; wide range of colour, and growing 2 ft. high; fragrant flowers. *Propagation:* seed sown under glass in January.

Best to grow: *Indoor:* Perpetual Robert Allwood (red), Pink Spectrum (pink), Doris Allwood (mauve), Allwood's Purity (white), Tangerine. *Border Carnations:* Montrose (geranium), Lavender Clove (mauve), Talisman (pink).

CARNATION RUST. See DISEASE CHART.

CARPINUS. Hornbeam. (Corylaceae.) Hardy deciduous trees good for open exposed positions; rapid growth; valuable for hedges, which should be planted as three-year-old seedlings 3 ft. apart. *Prune:* hedges every autumn. *Propagation:* seed. **Best to grow:** *C. Betulus* and its varieties (for hedges).

CARROT. *Daucus Carota.* (Umbelliferae.) Hardy biennials, grown for their roots of which there are various types: long-rooted (tapering roots), intermediate, stump-rooted, short-horn (conical short roots). *Soil:* deep, well-drained sandy loam is best; use ground manured for previous crop; never grow where fresh manure is near the surface of the soil, or the roots will fang. Choose south borders or frames for early crops, using short-horn varieties. Hotbed and frames require short-horn types. Seed broadcast thinly or sown in drills 6 in. apart. Water moderately. Before planting, dress with mixture of 1 oz. sulphate of potash, 2 oz. superphosphate and ½ oz. sulphate of ammonia, applying this quantity per square yard. For the main crop thin rows to 4 in.–6 in. apart, do so on dull days after sunset and water rows after thinning to avoid carrot fly. Lift for storage in October, twist off tops and select best roots for storage in clamps, or boxes covered with dry sand or soil in a frost-proof shed. On heavy soils or for exhibition, sow seed in dibber holes filled with fine soil, use stump-rooted varieties for heavy soils. **Best to grow:** frames and early sowings: Early Nantes, Early Horn. Main crop: James' Intermediate, Early Chantenay.

CARUM. See CARAWAY.

CASTANEA. Sweet chestnut. (Cupuliferae.) Hardy deciduous trees bearing edible nuts. Dry nuts in autumn, and store in air-tight jars, or cool dry place. *Plant:* November, in sandy, lime-free soil.

CASTOR-OIL PLANT. *Ricinus* (Euphorbiaceae.) Half-hardy annuals with ornamental foliage (Fig. 10). Requiring rich soil, plenty of water, and shade from the sun. *Propagation:* March-sown seeds which have been soaked in tepid water for a few hours. Sow in pots. Castor oil is obtained from *Ricinus communis.*

CATALPA. Indian Bean Tree. (Bignoniaceae.) Flowering and ornamental-leaved trees that are hardy and deciduous. *Soil:* well-drained. Suitable for sunny, sheltered lawns. *Propagation:* seeds, cuttings. **Best to grow:** *C. bignonioides.*

CATKIN. Stemless flower-like spike of certain trees. Tiny flowers are crowded together on the downward hanging "tail." Certain species of trees have male and female catkins on different plants.

CATMINT. *Nepeta Mussinii.* (Labiatae.) Excellent for large masses of colour in borders or edgings or as backgrounds to pink flowers. Lavender-blue flowers last well from May–October; the foliage is fragrant. *Propagation:* seeds; division. Similar to *N. Mussinii* is the brighter blue *N. ucranica.*

CAULIFLOWER. *Brassica oleracea botrytis cauliflora.* (Cruciferae.) Has a shorter season than broccoli and requires deeply dug and manured ground, whereas broccoli is grown on land manured for previous crop. Winter plants in frames or under glass that have been sown in September. Transplant with care, as cauliflowers transplanted too deeply are often "blind." Apply 1 oz.–2 oz. superphosphate per square yard before planting; if growth is slow give dressing of nitrate of soda or sulphate of ammonia in spring at 1 oz. per yard run. Break leaves over curds to keep them clean. Hoe regularly. See also VEGETABLE CHART.

CEANOTHUS. (Rhamnaceae.) Hardy and half-hardy evergreen and deciduous flowering shrubs. Require shelter of south or west walls or fences in full sunshine. *Plant:* October or March when soil is not wet or cold. *Prune:* late-flowering types on walls, like Gloire de Versailles, cut back to 2 in. of old wood; specimen bushes require trimming in March. Spring-flowering species, prune lightly after flowering. *Propagation:* seeds, cuttings, layers. **Best to grow:** deciduous: *C. azureus*, 8 ft.–10 ft., blue, May; the hybrids, Gloire de Versailles, lavender blue; and Marie Simon, rose, flowering from July onwards. Evergreen: *C. dentatus*, 10 ft., blue, May; *C. Veitchianus*, 10 ft., blue, June.

CEDAR. *Cedrus.* See CONIFERS.

CELERIAC. *Apium graveolens rapaceum.* (Umbelliferae.) Close relation of celery with the same flavour, and easier to grow. The turnip-like root (Fig. 11) is cooked or eaten raw in salads. No trenches are necessary;

Fig. 10. Castor-oil plant, grown for its foliage.

Fig. 11. Celeriac, an easily grown vegetable.

sow seed under glass, and trim plants of side-shoots before setting out. Water after planting, and remove side-shoots as they grow. Grows on poorer and drier soils than celery, though celeriac needs a longer season of growth. See VEGETABLE CHART.

CELERY. *Apium graveolens.* (Umbelliferae.) Plants grown in trenches 15 in.–18 in. wide, and 3½ ft.–4 ft. apart. Dig in manure or compost generously at bottom of 1 ft. deep trenches (Fig. 12). Soil between trenches, when mounded neatly and firmly, will carry a crop of lettuce, radish or even peas if the trenches are made early enough. Celery plants are raised under glass, pricked out, and later hardened off before being planted in trenches, either in two staggered rows or one single row. Water after planting. Water through season if weather is dry. Remove suckers and tie stalks together with raffia before earthing up when plants are nearly full grown. Gradually earth up until stems are covered, taking care to prevent soil from falling into the celery hearts (Fig. 13). Brown paper can be wrapped round stems before earthing. Slope soil neatly away from the exposed leaves and cover the latter with bracken or some protection against frost. (See also VEGETABLE CHART.) Doré, or self-blanching celery, requires no earthing up.

Fig. 12. Digging a celery trench, using two lines.

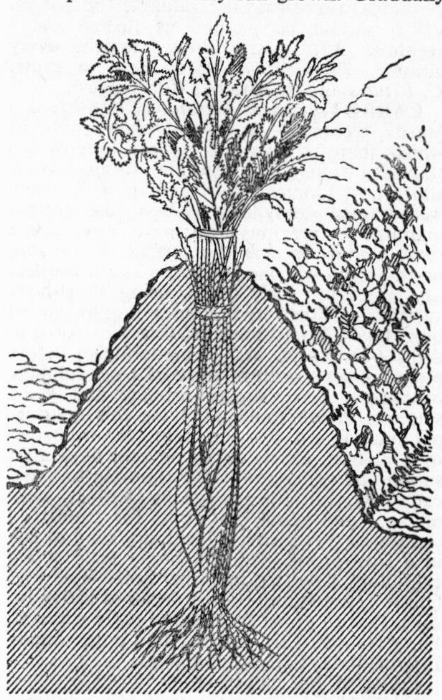

Fig. 13. Celery after the final earthing-up.

CELERY FLY. See PEST CHART.

CELOSIA. Cockscomb. (Amarantaceae.) Greenhouse annuals, of which the *Celosia plumosa* can be used for summer bedding. The red and yellow cockscomb, *Celosia cristata*, must be grown in heat from seed sown in March; prick out and water carefully, keeping plants near the glass. Raise plants for bedding by sowing outdoors in April, or by usual method of sowing under glass in February.

CELSIA. (Scrophulariaceae.) Biennials for flower-beds or borders resembling yellow *Verbascum. Soil:* ordinary. *Propagation:* seed sown under glass in autumn or spring, outdoors in April or August. Sown in heat, they will flower as annuals.

CENTAUREA. Cornflower. Sweet Sultan. (Compositae.) Annuals and perennials excellent for mixed sunny borders, and cut flowers. *Soil:* ordinary. *Propagation:* annuals: sow outdoors in April in flowering positions, and thin out 4 in.–6 in. apart. Perennials: seed outside or under glass in April. Division of roots. Replant perennials every three or four years. **Best to grow:** annuals: *C. Cyanus* (cornflower), 3 ft., blue, rose, white; summer, *C. moschata* (Purple Sweet Sultan), 2 ft., *C. moschata alba* (white), *C. moschata flava* (yellow). Perennials: *C. macrocephala*, 3 ft., golden yellow. *C. montana*, 15 in., blue, and its varieties *alba* (white) and *rosea* (deep rose).

CENTRANTHUS. Valerian. (Valerianaceae.) Hardy annuals and perennials familiar in wild places. Very effective in a mass; excellent for walls, rockeries and borders on poor chalky soils. *Propagation:* seeds, division. **Best to grow:** *C. ruber*, 2 ft., red, and its white variety, *alba.*

CERASTIUM. (Caryophyllaceae.) Hardy evergreen and deciduous perennials. Make a white carpet of bloom. Useful for old walls, rockeries, rock edgings, or carpeting for summer bedding. Rampant in any soil, requiring plenty of room to spread. *Propagation:* seeds; division. **Best to grow:** *C. tomentosum*, 9 in., *C. Biebersteinii*, 9 in.

CERATOSTIGMA. (Plumbaginaceae.) Hardy deciduous shrubs for ordinary soils and sunny positions. *Propagation:* cuttings; division. **Best to grow:** *C. plumbaginoides*, 1 ft., blue, autumn. *C. Willmottianum*, 2 ft., deep blue, July–October.

CERCIS. Judas-tree. (Leguminosae.) Hardy, deciduous flowering trees. Flowers pea-shaped and rosy-purple. Bladder-like pods. *Soil:* rich, deep, well-drained. *Prune:* prune old branches in February. *Propagation:* seed sown ¼ in. deep in sandy soil at 55–65 deg. in March; transplant outdoors in June; layers in autumn or spring. **Best to grow:** *Cercis siliquastrum*, 40 ft., rose, May.

CHEIRANTHUS. Wallflower. (Cruciferae.) Hardy fragrant perennials, used chiefly as biennials for sunny beds, borders, old walls, rockeries. Popular spring bedder flowering from April–May. *Soil:* ordinary, add dressing of lime or old mortar rubble before planting out firmly in September–October at 1 ft. apart. *Propagation:* sow seeds outdoors in May, transplanting seedlings 6 in. apart to a firm nursery bed when three or four leaves have formed. To sow on old walls, place seed in crevices with a little soil and cow manure. **Best to grow:** varieties of *C. Cheiri* as follows: Vulcan (crimson-brown), Fire King (orange-red), Cloth of Gold (yellow), Phoenix (blood-red). *C. Allioni* (Siberian wallflower), bright yellow, early summer.

CHELONE. (Scrophulariaceae.) Hardy herbaceous perennials resembling pentstemon. Suitable for borders of deep rich soil. *Propagation:* seeds, cuttings, division. **Best to grow:** *C. barbata*, 2 ft., scarlet. *C. Lyoni*, 1 ft., purple.

CHERVIL. See HERB GARDEN.

CHESTNUT, Horse. *Aesculus.* (Sapindaceae.) Hardy deciduous flowering trees for shrubberies, lawns, woods, and parks. *Soil:* deep and well drained. *Propagation:* seeds. **Best to grow:** *Ae. carnea*, 40 ft., pink, June. *Ae. Hippocastanum*, 80 ft., white, May.

CHESTNUT, Sweet. Spanish Chestnut. See CASTANEA.

CHICORY. *Cichorium Intybus.* (Compositae.) The blanched leaves of forced roots are used for autumn and winter salad. *Soil:* ordinary, well manured and moist. In November when leaves have died down, the roots (preferably 2 in. across at the top) are lifted and stored in ash, sand, or a trench where the temperature is cool but frostproof. *Blanching plant:* store roots 5 in. apart both ways in boxes of moist soil, with root tops 1 in. above the surface. Place in a dark, airy shed at 45 deg.; syringe regularly. *Propagation:* seeds sown May–June and thinned 9 in. apart. **Best to grow:** Witloof variety.

CHIMONANTHUS. Winter Sweet. (Calycanthaceae.) Fragrant, deciduous winter-flowering shrub, suitable for sunny south or west wall. Plant in October or March in moist sandy loam. *Prune:* February, removing flowered shoot to 1 in. of base, leaving main branches untouched. *Propagation:* seeds; layers in September–October; suckers. **Best to grow:** *C. fragrans*, 6 ft.–9 ft., yellow and red flowers appearing without leaves in December and January.

CHINA ASTER. See ASTER, CHINA.

CHIONODOXA. Glory of the Snow. (Liliaceae.) Hardy deciduous bulbs for sunny rockeries or borders. Replant every three years 1 in. apart and 1 in. deep. *Propagation:* seeds, offsets. **Best to grow:** *C. Luciliae*, 6 in., blue and white, March, and its variety, *gigantea. C. sardensis*, gentian blue.

CHIVE. *Allium Schoenoprasum.* (Liliaceae.) Bulbous-rooted perennial used as onion flavouring in salads. Plant in March 6 in. apart in rows 8 in.–9 in. apart on ordinary soil. Replant every three years. Cut closely to surface when required.

Fig. 14. Choisya makes a good flowering hedge.

CHOISYA. (Rutaceae.) Hardy evergreen shrubs with shiny foliage and white flowers in summer (Fig. 14). Plant in sheltered shrubberies and hedges in April or September.

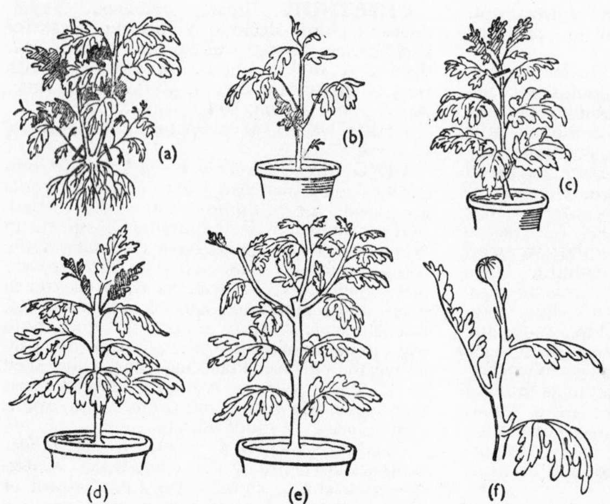

Fig. 15. Stages in raising and disbudding chrysanthemums: (a) *cuttings taken from base of plant in autumn;* (b) *rooted cutting;* (c) *first stopping when plant is 6 in.–7 in. high;* (d) *same plant a short time later with side shoots visible;* (e) *plant ready for second stopping when the three new shoots are pinched out evenly;* (f) *flowering bud with all other side shoots and buds removed from its stem.*

Propagation: cuttings March–June. **Best to grow:** *C. ternata*, 6 ft.

CHRYSANTHEMUM. Ox-Eye Daisy. Marguerite. Pyrethrum. Corn Marigold. Shasta Daisy. (Compositae.) A large genus including annual, herbaceous perennial and shrubby plants.

Annuals: require ordinary rich soil in sunny borders. Sow seed under glass in March and plant out in May, or sow outdoors in April, thinning to 9 in. in June. Species include *C. carinatum*, 2 ft., white, yellow and purple, summer. *C. segetum* (Corn Marigold), 18 in., yellow.

Perennials: suitable for sunny borders. Require dividing and replanting every three years in autumn or spring. *Soil:* ordinary. *Propagation:* seed. Cuttings under glass January–March, or in cold frames in December. Division in March. Raise growth for cuttings from plants placed in cold frames after the dead flower stems have been cut down. See also Fig. 15. These old plants can be discarded or replanted outdoors afterwards. The hardy perennials include: *C. coccineum* (Pyrethrum), excellent for cutting in early summer. Require fairly rich, well-drained soil. Autumn planting is best. They have a long flowering period and when cut back often produce a second crop. Single varieties: Kelway's Glorious, scarlet; Eileen May Robinson, shell-pink; Snowflake, white. Double varieties: Queen Mary, salmon-pink; Carl Vogt, white; Lord Rosebery, crimson. *C. leucanthemum* (Marguerite, Ox-Eye Daisy), 2 ft., white, summer. *C. maximum* (Shasta Daisy), 1½ ft.–2 ft., white, summer; and its varieties, Beauté Nivelloise and Mayfield Giant.

Tender perennials: Marguerites require equal parts loamy soil, leaf mould and silver sand. Pot rooted cuttings into 3-in. to 5-in. pots, stand in full sun from July–September and in cold frame till November. Bring into heat and give liquid manure. Raise stock yearly from cuttings.

Treatment of greenhouse varieties. Culture: Pot rooted cuttings into 3-in. pots, continue potting in easy stages (as roots fill the pots) to 9-in.–10-in. pots, using increasing firmness to encourage short joints. Use three parts fibrous loam (never sieve), one part peat (or leaf mould), and manure, sand, wood ash or charcoal. Add lime and complete fertilizer, or soot and bonemeal (3-in. pot to each bushel of soil). Place plants in final pots on ash standing ground or on slates, gravel or boards, in sheltered, sunny positions. To stop, pinch growing tip when 4 in.–6 in. high to form a bushy plant. Most decorative types are stopped again after a further 6 in. of growth. Necessity for one or two stoppings varies with different varieties. Never stop directly after potting.

Disbud down each stem, leaving terminal flowering bud for decorative and exhibition types. Singles are grown as sprays or disbudded. Bring plants into greenhouses before frosts in October. Water freely outdoors, keeping plants sprayed in hot weather. Water moderately inside. Stake plants and tie-in continuously. Commence feeding liquid manure when flower buds form and top-dress with compost and complete fertilizer from mid-July.

Decorative varieties can be planted 18 in.–2½ ft. apart in borders for the summer; lift with a good ball of soil in September and plant in beds or boxes indoors. After flowering all plants are cut to within 4 in. of soil level.

Propagation: from January onwards, choose firm, healthy, short-jointed growth for cuttings. Make cuttings 2 in.–3 in. long; cut cleanly beneath a leaf node and insert very firmly into well-drained pots or boxes of sandy soil. Water in cuttings and keep sprayed with warm water in temperature of 50 deg. Give air as they strike, and pot up carefully when well rooted.

Cascade Chrysanthemums. Stop when rooted cuttings are 6 in. high to fifth pair of leaves. Grow on one central stem unchecked and stake this at a slope of 45 deg. pointing north. Pinch all side shoots at third pair of leaves and tie plant tip to a string fixed to the ground. Result is a cascade of blooms. Bring indoors in September. Varieties for the open border include Millersdale, white; Imperial Yellow, yellow; Sweetheart, pink; Barbara, salmon;

Gladiator, crimson; Royal Bronze, bronze. Indoor varieties: Market Gold, golden-yellow; May Wallace, pink; Birmingham, red; Christmas Beauty, yellow; Gladys Paine, salmon; Molly Nicolson, pinkish-bronze.

Korean Chrysanthemums, usually hardened off in 3-in. pots and planted outdoors 1 ft.–2 ft. apart in May. Varieties include The Moor, double, wine-red; Venus, single, rose-pink; Ceres, single, deep gold-copper; Bubble, double, yellow-bronze; Vulcan, red.

CINERARIA. *Senecio.* (Compositae.) Annuals and perennials for greenhouse, used occasionally for summer bedding. Seeds sown under glass from April to August will bloom from Christmas to May. *Soil:* fibrous loam, leaf-mould, charcoal. Sow thinly and prick out, pot into 3-in. pots and grow in cold frames; keep shaded and water very carefully. Give liquid manure twice weekly from September, and house in October. **Best to grow:** *C. stellata* and *C. stellata cactus*, tall, star-like blooms. *C. grandiflora*, dwarf, large flowers. *C. intermediate*, medium in height and size of flowers. Many shades of blue, crimson, magenta, rose and white.

CISTUS. Rock Rose. (Cistaceae.) Hardy and half-hardy evergreen shrubs for dry, sunny positions, against walls or on rockeries, for temperate climates only. *Propagation:* seed in April, cuttings in August. **Best to grow:** *C. laurifolius*, 6 ft., white, June. *C. ladaniferus*, white. Silver Pink, 2 ft., suitable for rockery.

CLARKIA. (Onagraceae.) Hardy annuals, excellent for sunny mixed borders or as pot plants. *Soil:* light ordinary. *Propagation:* sow outdoors in April or September, or in pots in autumn for April–May flowers. Winter plants in cold frames. **Best to grow:** Varieties of *C. elegans*, 3 ft., white, rose, salmon, and other pinkish colours.

CLEMATIS. (Ranunculaceae.) Showy hardy climbers and herbaceous perennials. Evergreen and deciduous plants for light, well-drained soils containing lime. Grow well on arches, old tree-stumps, arbours, trellises, and also on north walls. *Prune:* climbers usually fall into two groups, those that flower late on new wood and those that flower early on older wood. Prune first group hard back to a few inches of the base of new growth, or of old stems before growth commences in February, Second group, thin out and remove weak growth in dormant season. Varieties: *Viticella*, *Jackmanii*, treat as first group. *Florida*, *lanuginosa*, thin in February. *Montana*, *alpina*, *flammula*, *Armandi*, *paniculata*, *tangutica*, remove old growth to keep in bounds. **Best to grow:** named hybrids of *C. Jackmanii*, Crimson King, Comtesse de Bouchard, pink. *C. lanuginosa*, Nellie Moser, pink; Lady Northcliffe, lavender; *C. florida*, Duchess of Edinburgh, white; Belle of Woking, mauve. *C. patens*, The President, violet. *C. Armandi*, 20 ft.–30 ft., evergreen, white to rose, April.

CLERODENDRON. (Verbenaceae.) Stove climbing and hardy flowering shrubs. *Soil:* ordinary, in sheltered warm positions outdoors. *Propagation:* seeds, cuttings, division, root suckers. **Best to grow:** *C. Fargesii*, 8 ft., white flowers, blue berries, hardy.

CLIANTHUS. (Leguminosae.) Semi-evergreen, climbing shrubs for warm sheltered east or west walls or greenhouses. *Soil:* well-manured loam. *Propagation:* seeds, cuttings. **Best to grow:** *C. puniceus* (Parrot's Beak), 3 ft., crimson, May.

CLICK BEETLE. See PEST CHART (Wireworm).

CLIMBING PLANTS. Natural climbers fix themselves to supports by means of aerial roots (ivy), adhesive pads (Virginia creeper), twining tendrils, leaf-stalks, prickles, thorns or twining stems (nasturtiums, sweet peas, rambler roses). Besides the natural climbers, certain plants (such as winter jasmine) can be tied in and trained against walls, trellis and fences. *Plant:* remember chiefly that once climbers are established it is usually impossible to move them and consequently the ground must be dug deeply and enriched with manure and bonemeal before planting. It is usually essential to dig in moisture-holding humus, like leaves, spent hops, compost or decayed manure, in order to counteract the dryness beneath walls, especially where rain is kept off by the eaves of a house. Plant firmly and tie climber to a support. **Best to grow:** annual climbers for new gardens: *Humulus japonicus* (hops), Canary creeper, nasturtium, sweet peas, *Ipomaea*, *Cucurbita* (gourds). Climbers for north walls: *Cotoneaster horizontalis*, *Jasminum nudiflorum*, *Kerria japonica plena*. Climbers for sunless walls: *Polygonum baldschuanicum*, *Ampelopsis Veitchii*, Mermaid (rose). Climbers for porches: for very dense growth, *Clematis montana*, jasmines, honeysuckles, *Humulus* (hops), *Alberic Barbier* (rose), ivy. Climbers for pergolas and verandas: roses, wistaria, clematis, vines, *Passiflora*, *Forsythia*, jasmines. Self-clinging climbers for walls: *Ampelopsis Veitchii*, ivy, *Vitis Henryana*, *Hydrangea petiolaris*. Climbers and shrubs for walls: *Ceanothus Veitchianus*, *Chimonanthus fragrans*, clematis, honeysuckles, *Pyracantha coccinea*, climbing roses, wistaria.

CLIVIA. (Amaryllidaceae.) Bulbous-rooted greenhouse evergreen. *Soil:* two-thirds loam, one-third decayed manure and sand. Pot in February. Water freely March–September and moderately at other times. *Propagation:* seeds; division of suckers. Minimum temperature 40 deg. **Best to grow:** *C. miniata* and its varieties, 2 ft., bright orange-red.

CLOCHE. Glass covering to set over low-growing plants to protect from excessive rain, frost and cold. Old pattern are bell-shaped heavy glasses, modern continuous cloches are designed as tent-shaped or barn-shaped structures. Consist of sheets of glass held together by metal frames or clips.

CLUMP. Term applied to growths of some herbaceous plants, such as Michaelmas daisies. Large clumps produce smaller and poorer flowers than smaller ones. Divide regularly, keeping young outside growth. To divide, lift plants, inset two forks back to back and lever apart.

COAL-ASH. Sifted finely, the ash is used for paths. Unburnt coal is not recommended.

COBAEA. (Polemoniaceae.) Half-hardy, evergreen, climbing perennial, used often as an annual for quick growth outside in summer.

Soil: light, moderately rich. Very rich soil encourages too much leaf-growth. Plant in full sun. **Best to grow:** *C. scandens*, purple, summer.

COLCHICUM. Autumn Crocus. Meadow Saffron. (Liliaceae.) Hardy bulbous plants (Fig. 16), flowering without leaves in autumn. Excellent for naturalizing in shrubberies, under shade of trees. *Plant:* 6 in. apart and 6 in. deep in July–August, in ordinary soil. *Propagation:* seed sown outdoors or cold

Fig. 16. The leaves of the autumn crocus appear after the delicate blooms have finished.

frame in August–September, transplant when two years old; division of bulbs in August. Seedlings do not flower for four or five years. **Best to grow:** *C. speciosus*, 9 in., rosy-purple, September; also white variety.

COLEUS. (Labiatae.) Ornamental-leaved greenhouse perennial. *Soil:* two parts turfy loam, one part well-decayed manure, leaf-mould and sand. *Propagation:* sow in heat in March, cuttings usually taken at any time. Pinch out growth points to obtain dwarf, well-shaped plants. Minimum temperature 50 deg.

COLLINSIA. (Scrophulariaceae.) Hardy annuals raised easily from seed sown outdoors in spring. Flowers resemble snapdragons and appear from May to August. **Best to grow:** *C. bicolor*, 1 ft., purple and white.

COLUMBINE. *Aquilegia.* (Ranunculaceae.) Long-flowering herbaceous perennials (Fig. 17) for sun or shade, in light ordinary soils. *Propagation:* seeds, division in April or September. **Best to grow:** *A. alpina*, 12 in.–18 in. for rockeries, blue and white; long-spurred hybrids of *A. vulgaris*, 2 ft., for borders, colours various, May–July.

COLUTEA. Bladder Senna. (Leguminosae.) Hardy, deciduous flowering shrub for open or shady shrubberies. Suitable for town gardens and ordinary soil. *Prune:* trim weak shoots in November. *Propagation:* seeds, cuttings. **Best to grow:** *C. arborescens*, 10 ft., yellow, August.

COMPOST. Term for a mixture of soil for sowing seeds or potting. Usually includes loam, leaf-mould or peat, always sand, occasionally decayed manure, charcoal, fertilizer. The John Innes Horticultural Institution recommends two basic composts, as follows:

1. *For potting:*
   - 7 parts loam
   - 3 parts peat
   - 2 parts sand

   To every bushel add ¾ oz. chalk and ¼ lb. base fertilizer, consisting of:
   - 2 parts hoof and horn
   - 2 parts superphosphate of lime
   - 1 part sulphate of potash
2. *Seed compost:*
   - 2 parts loam
   - 1 part peat
   - 1 part sand

   To every bushel add 1½ oz. superphosphate and ¾ oz. chalk.

COMPOST HEAP. This consists of all garden refuse that will rot down, such as leaves, annual weeds, lawn mowings, green refuse, and even peelings and scraps from the house. Object is to return vegetable matter to the soil. Choose a site out of view and heap in a neat pile, building corners first, or sink in a pit. At regular intervals, turn sides to middle, compress well; water if very dry,

Fig. 17. Long-spurred columbines make fine displays for borders or for cutting.

(a)

(b)

Fig. 18. Making a compost heap: (a) *apply a dressing of sulphate of ammonia to the garden refuse;* (b) *add a layer of soil, and water well.*

adding lime and sulphate of ammonia, as these hasten the decomposition of the vegetable matter. There are also proprietary fertilizers sold for this purpose. It is beneficial to add layers of poultry, rabbit, or other animal manure. Never include weed tap-roots or diseased material. Covering with soil when the heap is completed is advantageous. Best not to build heaps higher than four feet. (See Fig. 18.)

CONE FLOWER. *Rudbeckia.* (Compositae.) Hardy annuals and perennials, excellent for cutting. Suitable for ordinary soil in sunny, well-drained borders. Replant and divide perennials every three years. *Propagation:* seeds, division for perennials.

CONIFERS are the cone-bearing trees which belong to the natural order Coniferae. Almost all are evergreen. Narrow foliage is adapted to prevent too rapid evaporation, making trees suitable for cold climates where roots cannot easily absorb the cold soil water. Commonly grown conifers are pines (*Pinus*), larches (*Larix*), spruce (*Picea*), junipers (*Juniperus*), *Arbor Vitae* (*Thuya*) and cedars (*Cedrus*). All are very decorative, as well as their timber being of value. *Soil:* most soils are suitable if not waterlogged or very barren peat. Poor chalk soils are not suitable, unless there is two feet of soil above the chalk. *Plant:* best to plant when trees are small, weather showery, and the soil warm, in April or September. Prepare site by deep digging. *Pruning:* this is not necessary except to remove dead wood or broken branches. Some conifers need shelter from frosts. Use hardier conifers for protection from the north and east.

Conifers for screens and hedges: Cupressus Lawsoniana, Taxus baccata (yew), *Thuya Lobbii. Conifers for lawns and specimen trees: Cedrus atlantica, Cedrus Deodara* (Deodar), *Cedrus Libani* (Lebanon), *Sequoia gigantea* (*Wellingtonia*). *Conifers for shelter belts: Pinus austriaca, Larix europaea* (larch). *Conifers for rockeries: Thuya occidentalis*, varieties *Ellwangeriana* and *compacta*, *Cupressus* (syn. *Chamaecyparis*) *obtusa*, variety *nana*, *C. Lawsoniana*, varieties *Fletcheri* and *Elwoodii*, *C. obtusa minima*, only 6 in. high, for trough or scree garden, *Juniperus procumbens* for creeping growth, and *J. communis compressa* for conical spike.

CONVALLARIA. See LILY OF THE VALLEY.

CONVOLVULUS. (Convolvulaceae.) Hardy annuals, perennials and shrubs, mostly trailing or climbing. Climbers more commonly grown. *Soil:* ordinary, warm positions. *Propagation:* seed. **Best to grow:** *C. mauritanicus* and *C. Cneorum* for rockeries; *C. tricolor*, 1 ft., annual, blue and white.

CORDON. A method of growing fruit trees, apple, pear, gooseberry, red and white currants as a single stem covered with short, fruiting spurs (Fig. 19.) Cordons are trained in vertical, oblique or horizontal positions, and can also be double vertical or triple vertical (grid-iron) shaped. Plant single oblique

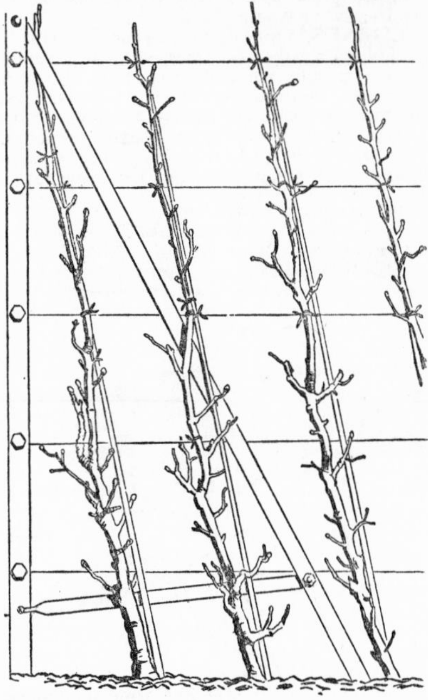

Fig. 19. Cordon apples after winter pruning.

cordons 2 ft.–3 ft. apart in rows 6 ft.–8 ft. apart. Horizontal cordons 5 ft.–15 ft. apart, but vertical gooseberries can be spaced 1 ft. apart. Double vertical cordons (simple U-form), 5 ft.–6 ft. apart.

Training: single cordons: summer prune laterals 5 in.–6 in. from the base when 12 in. long. Plant in oblique position and train by tying stem to a cane against supporting wires, and as growth reaches the top lower the stem and cane and re-tie. Repeat as the growth reaches the limit. *Double vertical* (simple U-form): head back maiden shoot (one year old) to 12 in.–15 in. of ground. During the summer, train top two shoots horizontally each side on canes 6 in.–8 in. long. Bend these shoots round to grow vertically. Prune leaders back one-third of growth in winter, choosing an upward bud. Spur back all laterals. *Triple cordon:* treat as for double cordon, making first cut above a bud pointing upwards. Use this shoot to train vertically. Use dwarfing stocks for apples and pears.

COREOPSIS. See CALLIOPSIS.

CORM. This is a swollen and fleshy underground stem bearing a terminal bud, resembling a bulb in appearance, but the construction is more solid. Examples: crocus, gladiolus.

CORNFLOWER. See CENTAUREA.

CORN SALAD. Lamb's Lettuce. *Valerianella olitoria.* (Valerianaceae.) Hardy annual, the leaves of which are used for winter and spring salads. *Soil:* ordinary; sunny dry border. *Propagation:* sow outdoors in August to September; thin to 6 in. apart. Can be intercropped with winter onions. Gather leaves separately, or whole plant.

CORNUS. Dogwood. (Cornaceae.) Hardy deciduous shrubs and trees, with ornamental foliage, usually white flowers (Fig. 20). *Soil:* ordinary. *Propagation:* layers, suckers. **Best to grow:** *C. mas* (Cornelian Cherry), 15 ft., yellow, and its variegated-leaved varieties. *C. Nuttallii*, 30 ft.–40 ft., white, May. *C. sanguinea*, 8 ft., green, attractive red branches.

Fig. 20. Cornus sanguinea, *a variety of cornus.*

CORTADERIA. See PAMPAS GRASS.

CORYDALIS. Fumitory. (Fumariaceae.) Hardy annuals and perennials for sunny and shady borders, rockeries, old walls. Foliage is attractive, resembling ferns. *Propagation:* seeds, division.

CORYLUS. Hazelnut or filbert. See NUTS.

COSMOS. (Compositae.) Half-hardy, graceful, feathery-leaved annuals. Excellent for cutting. *Soil:* ordinary; warm dryish borders. *Propagation:* sow seed under glass in spring. Transplant 2 ft.–3 ft. apart in May. **Best to grow:** *C. bipinnatus*, 3 ft., rose, purple, white, July to September.

COTONEASTER. (Rosaceae.) Favourite hardy evergreen and deciduous flowering shrubs, bearing red berries in autumn. For any position in sun or shade against walls, over rocks, shrubberies. *Propagation:* cuttings. **Best to grow:** *Evergreen: C. microphylla*, 2 ft.–3 ft. *C. salicifolia*, 12 ft.–20 ft. *Deciduous: C. horizontalis*, 18 in., flat growing. *C. conspicua*, 4 ft., *C. Wardii*, 6 ft.

COTYLEDON. (Crassulaceae.) Greenhouse and hardy evergreen succulent plants. Hardy types suitable for rockeries. *Soil:* ordinary. *Propagation:* cuttings. Echeveria is synonym for some species. **Best to grow:** *C. simplicifolia*, 6 in., bright yellow.

CRABS. Crab Apple, *Malus pumila* and other species. (Rosaceae.) Grown as ornamental trees for shrubberies or specimen trees on ordinary soil. **Best to grow:** for flowering: *Sargenti*, 10 ft., bushy, white; *theifera*, 20 ft., late, white; *purpurea*, 20 ft., purplish-rose, and its varieties *Eleyi* and *Lemoinei*. For fruiting: John Downie, orange; Transcendant, yellow; Cheal's Crimson.

CRASSULA. (Crassulaceae.) Perennials for the greenhouse. *Propagation:* seed sown in April or by cuttings 2 in.–3 in. long. Stop in spring and remove top leaves to encourage shoot growth. **Best to grow:** *C. coccinea*, 1 ft.–3 ft., scarlet, June to August.

CRATAEGUS. Thorns. (Rosaceae.) Decorative berried trees and shrubs for woods and shrubberies, lawns, hedges. *Soil:* ordinary, limed. *Propagation:* seeds; budding and grafting choice varieties on common hawthorn. *Plant:* hedges November–March, in trenches dug two feet deep. Trim July and August. **Best to grow:** *C. Oxyacantha* (common hawthorn), 15 ft., white, and its varieties, *alba plena* (double white), *coccinea plena* (double scarlet). *C. prunifolia*, small tree, crimson berries, red autumn leaves.

CRAZY PAVING. See PATHWAYS.

CREEPING JENNY. *Lysimachia nummularia.* (Primulaceae.) Evergreen creeping, yellow-flowered plant for ordinary moist shady rockeries, margins of beds, ponds or streams. Useful for planting in hanging baskets, bowls and tubs, in two parts loam, one part leaf-mould and some sand. *Propagation:* division. Golden-leaved variety is *L. nummularia aurea.*

CRESS, garden. *Lepidium sativum.* (Cruciferae.) Grown with mustard as a salad crop. *Propagation:* sow thickly and evenly on soil, flannel, or hessian. Do not cover seeds with soil, but cover with brown paper. Water well when sowing and this should suffice to keep seed moist enough during growth. Sow cress three days before the mustard.

CRESS, Land. *Barbarea praecox.* (Cruciferae.) Coarse-leaved plant useful for salad. *Soil:* ordinary; moist borders.

CRESS, Water. *Nasturtium officinale.* (Cruciferae.) Aquatic salad-plant rich in vitamins, easily raised without running water. Sow seed or plant cuttings in April and again in August in a trench 1 ft. deep and 2 ft. wide. Put six inches of rotted manure in trench bottom covered with three inches of soil. Flood frequently with water.

CROCUS. (Iridaceae.) Hardy flowering bulbs for all positions. *Plant:* spring-flowering varieties October–December, autumn varieties August–September; bulbs two or three inches deep and apart; leave undisturbed four or five years. Always allow the foliage to die right down. Excellent for naturalizing in grass. Will not force, but will grow indoors if kept cool. *Propagation:* offsets; corms from seed take from two to four years to flower. (Further culture, see BULBS.) **Best to grow:** *C. vernus*, numerous Dutch forms in cultivation; Purpurea grandiflora, large purple; Yellow Mammoth, large golden yellow; King of the Whites, King of the Striped, white and blue. Autumn-flowering: *C. nudiflorus*, *C. speciosus*, *C. pulchellus.* Spring-flowering: *C. chrysanthus*, *C. Sieberi*, *C. Tomasinianus.*

CROCUS, Autumn. See COLCHICUM.

CROWN IMPERIAL. *Fritillaria Imperialis.* (Liliaceae.) Tall hardy bulbous plants with graceful yellow or red bell-flowers, April–May. Suitable for sunny borders. Plant 6 in.–8 in. deep in October and leave undisturbed. *Propagation:* division, when two flower stems produced. From seed they take from four to six years to flower.

CUCUMBER. *Cucumis sativus.* (Cucurbitaceae.) Half-hardy trailing plants for greenhouse or frames. Ridge cucumbers grow outdoors. *Greenhouse:* sow end February in heat,

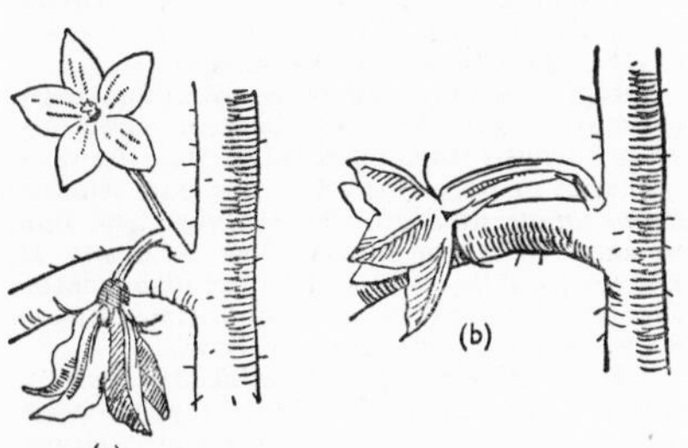

Fig. 21. Cucumber flowers; (a) *male;* (b) *female.*

mid-April without, singly in pots. Plant when two rough leaves form, singly on prepared mounds or beds 3 ft. apart, or one or two plants per frame. *Soil:* equal parts roughly broken turfy loam, well-rotted strawy manure, with potful old soot and bonemeal. Prepare beds on slating or corrugated iron, spread ash or straw for drainage, then 6-in. layer of compost. Mound half a barrow-load of the compost for each plant. Train plants up to the roof of house, then pinch growth. Tie in laterals 15 in. apart. *Frames:* pinch growth at third leaf, stop laterals at six leaves. The secondary laterals produce fruit. Water freely, syringe, shade and feed with liquid manure. Pinch out male flowers (Fig. 21). **Best to grow:** Improved Telegraph. See also VEGETABLE CHART. *Ridge cucumbers:* mound soil in full sun outdoors and stop at first six leaves, peg down laterals, water freely and feed liquid manure.

CUCUMBER CANKER OR COLLAR ROT. See DISEASE CHART.

CUPRESSUS. See CONIFERS.

CURRANT. See FRUIT AND ITS CULTURE.

CUT FLOWERS ALL THE YEAR. By choosing carefully, a succession of material for indoor decoration throughout the year is possible, even from a small garden. Here is a short list of flowers and shrubs for each month.

January: *Chimonanthus fragrans*, *Hamamelis mollis*, ivy, winter heliotrope, sea buckthorn, *Iris stylosa.*

February: *Cyclamen Coum*, *Erica carnea*, *Daphne Mezereum*, *Garrya elliptica*, *Cornus mas.*

March: *Allium*, *Crocus*, *Forsythia*, snowdrop, almond blossom.

April: bird-cherry, broom, anemone, Siberian wallflower, daffodil, primrose, flowering currant, wallflower, primrose, tulip, hyacinth.

May: columbine, double *Arabis*, *Deutzia*, *Dielytra*, peony, pink, honesty, pyrethrum, *Gypsophila*, lupin, lilac, iris.

June: asparagus, *Campanula*, cornflower, *Delphinium*, *Erigeron*, guelder rose, *Heuchera*, Iceland poppy, stock, oriental poppy, lily.

July: *Antirrhinum*, aster, campanula, catmint, *Calliopsis*, *Chrysanthemum maximum*, grasses, lily, marigold, sweet pea, carnation, rose.

August: *Ceanothus*, cornflower, *Dahlia*, *Escallonia*, larkspur, *Leycesteria*, *Nigella*, *Phlox*, poppy, *Montbretia*, *Solidago*, sea holly, carnation, *Gladiolus.*

September: *Chrysanthemum*, *Gladiolus*, *Godetia*, red-hot poker, sunflower, rose, *Nasturtium.* scabious, *Rudbeckia*, *Physalis*, mountain ash, sweet sultan, *Cosmos.*

October: aster, *Chrysanthemum*, cornflower, *Dahlia*, everlasting flower, heather, *Helenium*, marigold, Michaelmas daisy, beech leaves.

November: autumn crocus, *Chrysanthemum*, heather, marigold, all kinds of berries, rose-hips.

December: winter jasmine, *Chimonanthus fragrans*, iris, *Cotoneaster frigida* (berries), sea buckthorn (berries), holly, ivy, and (in the house) bulbs in bowls and pots.

CYCLAMEN. (Primulaceae.) Hardy and greenhouse flowering tubers. *Outdoor cultivation:* Excellent for grass under deciduous trees, shady nooks in rockeries. Plant 12 in. apart, $1\frac{1}{2}$ in. deep, top-dress annually with rich soil and old cow manure when plants have died down. *Greenhouse culture:* Re-pot corms at soil level, July–August, using two parts loam, one leaf-mould. Grow in gentle heat during winter. Increase water supply when growth begins. Keep roots dry and cool after flowering. Year-old plants are best; discard after two years. *Propagation:* hardy types, sow in cold frame October–November. Tender types in August–November or January–March in heat. **Best to grow:** hardy varieties: *C. Coum*, pink, crimson base, January–March. *C. europaeum*, scented, crimson, July. *C. neapolitanum*, pink and white varieties, September. Tender species: *C. persicum*, and its varieties.

CYDONIA. Quince. (Rosaceae.) Early flowering trees and shrubs, of which the fruit can be used for preserves. Suitable for sunny shrubberies or sheltered walls. Grown as fans on walls, as bushes or standards. *Prune* out unwanted wood, spur back in June. *Propagation:* seeds, layers, suckers, cuttings. **Best to grow:** *C. japonica* (syn. *Chaenomeles lagenaria*), 8 ft.–10 ft., scarlet. *C. Maulei*, 2 ft.–4 ft., orange-red.

CYNOGLOSSUM. Hound's Tongue. (Boraginaceae.) Hardy perennials requiring ordinary soil or loam with leaf-mould and sand. For sunny rockeries and borders. *Propagation:* seeds, division. **Best to grow:** *C. amabile*, 18 in., bright blue, annual. *C. nervosum*, 1 ft., deep blue.

CYPRESS. See CONIFERS (*Cupressus*).

CYPRESS, Summer. See KOCHIA.

CYTISUS. Broom. (Leguminosae.) Evergreen and deciduous shrubs. Bright pea-shaped flowers of wide colour range. Plant October–December. **Best to grow:** *C. albus*, *C. praecox*, *C. scoparius*, *C. purpureus*, for shrub borders. *C. Ardoinii*, *C. kewensis* on sunny rockeries.

DAFFODIL. See NARCISSUS.

DAHLIA. (Compositae.) Tuberous-rooted perennials extensively used for summer bedding and borders. Prepare soil deeply with manure for show flowers, preferably during previous autumn. Tall varieties plant in full sun 3 ft.–5 ft. apart and bedding varieties 1 ft.–2 ft. apart, during June. Drive in stakes before planting tall varieties. Water during dry weather and feed with liquid manure; remove dead flowers and disbud for exhibition blooms. When growth is blackened by frost, lift tubers and store in a dry, frost-proof shed. *Propagation:* division; cuttings from tubers started into growth under glass in heat during February–April. **Best to grow:** The following outline of the modern classification of garden dahlias gives a named example of each class. *Single:* Perplex, orange-red. *Star:* White Star, white. *Collarette:* Kingsbrook Scarlet, intense red. *Paeony-flowered:* Bishop of Llandaff, scarlet. *Formal decorative:* Jersey Beauty, pink. *Informal decorative:* Dorothy Tattam, salmon. *Double show:* Grandee, red. *Pompon:* Snow Girl, white. *Cactus:* Dolly Varden, white. *Semi-cactus:* Boldness, red. *Dwarf bedding:* Maureen Creighton, crimson.

DAISY. See BELLIS and CHRYSANTHEMUM.

DAISY, Michaelmas. See MICHAELMAS DAISY.

DAPHNE. (Thymelaeaceae.) Fragrant winter- and spring-flowering deciduous and evergreen shrubs. Trailing species for rockeries, erect species for open borders. *Soil:* sandy peat and leaf-mould for outdoor types; two parts loam, one part peat and sand, for greenhouse species which are housed from September–June and summered outdoors. *Propagation:* cuttings in autumn; layer trailing species. **Best to grow:** *Evergreen: D. Blagayana*, trailing, white, March–April. *D. Cneorum major*, trailing, pink. Garden hybrid, *D. Somerset*, 30 in., pale pink, May–June. *Deciduous: D. Mezereum* (also variety *alba*), 3 ft.–5 ft., rosy purple or white, February–March. This will propagate by seed. *Greenhouse: D. odora*, 4 ft., evergreen, purple, March.

DELPHINIUM. Larkspur. (Ranunculaceae.) Showy annuals and perennials for borders. Sow annual larkspur outside in April or September or under glass in March. Perennial species require deeply-dug rich soil. Add manure, bonemeal and lime. Strawy manure on heavy soils aids drainage. Mulch with decayed manure in spring, giving liquid manure when flower-spikes form. Never allow the plants to dry out completely. Replant and divide every three or four years in spring. Plant 2 ft.–3 ft. apart. Remove flower-spikes after flowering to prolong season. *Propagation:* division, cuttings, seed. **Best to grow:** Perennial hybrids divided into two classes, *Belladonna* or sprayed loose-flowered types, and the close-flowered spikes derived from *D. elatum hybridum*. *Belladonna:* Moerheimi, white; Wendy, blue, white eye. *D. elatum hybridum:* Mrs. Townley-Parker, 5½ ft., sky blue, white eye; Innocence, white; Duchess of Portland, gentian, white eye; Blue Gown, ultramarine, black eye; Cynthia Bishop, deep purple-violet.

DEUTZIA. (Saxifragaceae.) Deciduous, hardy flowering shrubs, with clusters of small blooms. For sunny, well-drained borders of ordinary soil. *Prune:* shorten flowered shoots in July. *Propagation:* soft and hard wood cuttings in sandy soil. **Best to grow:** *D. gracilis*, 2 ft., white, April. *D. scabra* (syn. *D. crenata*), 8 ft., June, and its varieties, *plena*, double, and *Watereri*, rosy.

DIANTHUS. See CARNATIONS.

DICENTRA (syn. **Dielytra**). Bleeding Heart. (Fumariaceae.) Hardy herbaceous tuberous- and fibrous-rooted perennials for borders, rockeries or pots. Protect during cold winters. *Propagation:* division, root cuttings 2 in. long in sand in warm house. **Best to grow:** *D. spectabilis*, 2 ft., pink and white, also suitable for pot culture. *D. cucullaria* (Dutchman's Breeches), 6 in., white and yellow.

DICTAMNUS (syn. **Fraxinella**). Burning Bush. (Rutaceae.) Fragrant-foliaged, herbaceous perennial. Sunny or shaded dryish borders. Foliage exudes oil, which burns when lit, but does not harm the foliage. *Propagation:* seeds; root division in March–April. Crimson and white varieties, 2 ft.

DIERVILLA (syn. **Weigela**). (Caprifoliaceae.) Hardy, free-flowering deciduous shrubs for any soil. Clusters of pink or red flowers. *Prune:* shorten flowered stems after blossoms die, thin out and remove dead wood in winter. *Propagation:* cuttings, hard wood in autumn, soft wood in June. **Best to grow:** *D. grandiflora*, *D. rosea* and named varieties.

DIGITALIS. See FOXGLOVE.

DIMORPHOTHECA. Star of the Veldt. (Compositae.) Quick-growing tender annuals, and perennials usually grown as annuals in sunny warm borders. *Propagation:* seeds sown in open ground in April. **Best to grow:** *D. aurantiaca*, 1 ft., orange, annual.

DORONICUM. Leopard's Bane. (Compositae.) One of the first flowers in the herbaceous border. Yellow, daisy-like perennials for sun or shade, and excellent for cutting. *Propagation:* root division. **Best to grow:** *D. plantagineum*, 2 ft., yellow, April–May.

DRABA. (Cruciferae.) Alpine perennials forming rosettes of lance-shaped leaves. *Soil:* ordinary, for crevices in rockeries and old walls. *Propagation:* easily from seeds, division.

ECHINOPS. Globe Thistle. (Compositae.) Effective biennials and perennials for sunny, well-drained borders. Very hardy and easy to grow. *Propagation:* seed, division. **Best to grow:** perennials, *E. bannaticus* (syn. *E. ruthenicus*), 2 ft.–3 ft., metallic blue; *E. sphaerocephalus*, 5 ft., pale blue.

ECHIUM. Viper's Bugloss. (Boraginaceae.) Annuals, biennials and perennials for dry places and wild gardens. A good plant for bees. *Propagation:* seeds, cuttings, division. **Best to grow:** *E. creticum*, Blue Bedder, 1 ft., annual; *E. vulgare*, 3 ft., blue, biennial.

ELAEAGNUS. Oleaster. (Elaeagnaceae.) Deciduous and evergreen flowering shrubs with ornamental foliage. *Soil:* ordinary. Plant deciduous species October–December, and evergreens April–September. *Propagation:* seeds under glass; cuttings in September; layers in spring. **Best to grow:** Deciduous: *E. angustifolia*, 15 ft.–20 ft., silvery-white and yellow, June. Evergreens: *E. pungens*, 6 ft., and its varieties *E. pungens aureomaculata*, golden-leaved, and *E. pungens variegata*, silver-leaved.

ELM. Ulmus. (Ulmaceae.) Hardy deciduous trees. Any soil for common species, rich loam with gravel subsoil for wych elm (*U. montana*). Suitable for parks and woodlands up to 1,500 ft. *Propagation:* ripe seed; grafting named varieties. **Best to grow:** *U. campestris* (common elm), 70 ft.–120 ft.; *U. montana* (wych elm), 100 ft.–125 ft., and its weeping variety, *Camperdowni*.

ENDIVE. *Cichorium Endivia.* (Compositae.) The leaves of this hardy vegetable are blanched and used for winter salads. To obtain tender leaves grow quickly on rich soil on open or sheltered south or west borders. Cover with pot or boxes to blanch, three weeks before required. See also VEGETABLE CHART.

ERANTHIS. See ACONITE.

EREMURUS. (Liliaceae.) Herbaceous perennials with tall graceful spikes of flowers, which rise from a rosette of rush-like leaves. Require well-drained rich soil, or warm borders sheltered from winds. Protect crown during winter, and mulch in autumn. Water freely in hot weather. *Propagation:* division in September, seeds sown under glass and planted out when a year old. Plants bloom after two years. **Best to grow:** *E. robustus*, 8 ft., pink, July.

ERICA. Heath. (Ericaceae.) A large genus of tender and hardy evergreen flowering shrubs. Most require peaty soil, but varieties of *E. carnea*, *E. mediterranea* and *E. darleyensis* are tolerant of lime. Soil for pot plants: two parts fibrous peat, one part sand. *Propagation:* division, layers, seeds, cuttings of soft tips in August. **Best to grow:** for greenhouse, *E. hyemalis*, pink; *E. gracilis*, rose; *E. canaliculata*, white. For open ground, *E. carnea*, 9 in., pink, January–March, and many white or coloured forms; *E. mediterranea*, 5 ft., rose-pink, April; *E. arborea alpina*, 8 ft., white, May; *E. vagans*, 18 in., pink, several varieties, August to October.

ERIGERON. Fleabane. (Compositae.) Hardy herbaceous perennials resembling Michaelmas daisies, flowering June–July. *Soil:* ordinary moist borders or rockeries. *Propagation:* seeds, division. **Best to grow:** *E. alpinus*, 12 in., for rockeries; varieties of *E. hybridus* like Beauty of Hal, lavender; Elsie, rose; Mrs. H. Beale, violet; also varieties of *E. speciosus*.

ESCALLONIA. (Saxifragaceae.) Delightful flowering shrubs for sheltered walls or hedges in mild districts, does well by the sea as a shrub or hedge. *Soil:* well drained. *Propagation:* seeds, cuttings, layers in October· suckers replanted in April. **Best to grow:** evergreen, *E. langleyensis*, 8 ft., crimson, June; *E. macrantha*, 3 ft.–6 ft., rose-red, June. Deciduous, *E. Philippiana*, varieties Donard Brilliance, red-crimson; Donard Gem, pale pink; Apple Blossom, pale pink.

ESCHSCHOLTZIA. Californian Poppy. (Papaveraceae.) Thrives in dry, sunny places and produces bright poppy-like blooms, which last well in water. Hardy annuals easily grown from seed sown outside in autumn or spring. **Best to grow:** *E. californica*, orange-yellow, and numerous varieties.

EUCALYPTUS. Australian Gum. Blue Gum. (Myrtaceae.) Mostly half-hardy evergreen trees that grow to very great heights in favourable gardens. Curved lance-shaped grey leaves are fragrant. Often grown in pots for conservatories or living-rooms. *Soil:* light, poor. *Propagation:* seed. Sow annually for pot culture. Pruning unnecessary. **Best to grow:** *E. Gunnii* is the hardiest for growing outdoors. *E. citriodora* and *E. globulus* are good pot-plants for the warm greenhouse.

EUPATORIUM. Hemp Agrimony. (Compositae.) Tender and herbaceous perennials. Outdoor species; plant in open borders or shrubberies in ordinary soil. Greenhouse plants; use equal portions loam, manure with a little sand. Prune after flowering and keep dryish whilst plants are resting. *Propagation:* hardy species, divide; cuttings of tender species. **Best to grow:** hardy species, *E. purpureum*, 6 ft., purple, August. Greenhouses, *E. riparium*, *E. micranthum*, 4 ft., white.

EUPHORBIA. Spurge. Poinsettia (Euphorbiaceae.) Include greenhouse shrubs and hardy flowering perennials. Hardy species are very suitable for wild garden. Greenhouse, *E. pulcherrima.* Use fibrous loam, decayed manure and sand. Slightly root-prune plants when young shoots develop, then re-pot and prune to leave two or three buds in April. Pot and keep in a sunny frame during the summer. Return to greenhouse for winter and keep dryish. *Propagation:* form young plants from shoots removed in May; insert shoots singly in pots of sandy loam and peat in a propagating case. Pot on and harden off and put in summer position in cold frame. Water freely, shade from sun, feed liquid manure. *Hardy species: E. epithymoides,* 1 ft., vivid greenish-yellow, May; *E. palustris,* 2 ft., similar to preceding; *E. myrsinites,* prostrate, yellow, April, fleshy grey foliage.

EVENING PRIMROSE. *Oenothera.* (Onagraceae.) Annual, biennial and perennial plants for light ordinary soil. *Propagation:* seed, division, cuttings. **Best to grow:** *Oe. biennis,* 5 ft., pale yellow; *Oe. Youngii,* 2 ft., golden-yellow; *Oe. linearis,* 1 ft., golden-yellow. *Oe. taraxacifolia,* white, trailing. All summer-flowering.

EVERLASTING FLOWERS. Flowers of *Helichrysum, Rhodanthe, Xeranthemum* and *Acroclinium,* that can be dried and preserved. The colour of the crisp, scaly bracts will keep for some months. Gather blooms in autumn, bunch, and hang upside-down to dry off.

FAGUS. See BEECH.

FERNS. Include hardy and half-hardy plants for fernhouse, garden, home. Most ferns require shade and moisture, though certain species, like the male fern (*Nephrodium Filix-mas*), will grow in sunny borders. *Soil:* add decayed leaves and sand to ordinary garden soil, and equal parts loam, peat, leaf-mould and sand, and good crock drainage for pot-plants. *Propagation:* root division for most types, spores from lower sides of fronds (leaves) in summer. Brush lower frond surface on sandstone or fine soil, or lay a piece of frond on sand. Cover with bell-jar, pot up tiny plants. Re-pot ferns every year, dividing with a sharp knife, keeping young outside growth. Indoors, over-watering and cold draughts cause many failures. Ferns for tropical houses include Adiantum (maidenhair), Platycerium (stag's horn), Gymnogramme (gold fern, silver fern).

Greenhouse ferns: Asplenium (lady fern), *A. caudatum, A. bulbiferum. Adiantum* (maidenhair), *A. gracillimum, A. Williamsii, Polypodium* (polypody, oak fern, beech fern). *Pteris* (bracken, spider fern).

Hardy ferns: Osmunda regalis (royal fern), 5 ft.–6 ft. Suitable for waterside. *Phyllitis Scolopendrium* (hart's-tongue), 2 ft. *Nephrodium Filix-mas* (male fern), 2 ft. *Blechnum Spicant* (hard fern), 2 ft. *Onoclea sensibilis* (sensitive fern), 2 ft., suitable for a moist, shady place.

FERTILIZERS. All plants have certain food requirements. The elements in the soil essential for their well-being may not be present, either because the soil in some districts is naturally deficient of vital elements, or because the ground has been continually cultivated and the natural stores have been used by previous crops.

The main nutrient substances are *nitrogen, phosphates* and *potash.* These are added either in organic forms, such as farmyard manure, fish manure, green crops or compost heap, or as inorganic chemical fertilizers. Some chemical fertilizers supply plant food in a more soluble and available form than the natural manures which take time to break down in the soil. Each fertilizer has its own reaction as a plant food. *Nitrogen* encourages leaf and shoot growth. *Potash* encourages sturdy growth, increases resistance to disease, and increases the sugar in roots and fruits. *Phosphates* encourage root growth and early ripening. Certain manures can be mixed together to make a complete fertilizer or bought already mixed. Lime is also essential to the garden, since it corrects soil acidity and makes plant foods more available (see LIME). Liquid manure is used during the growing period,

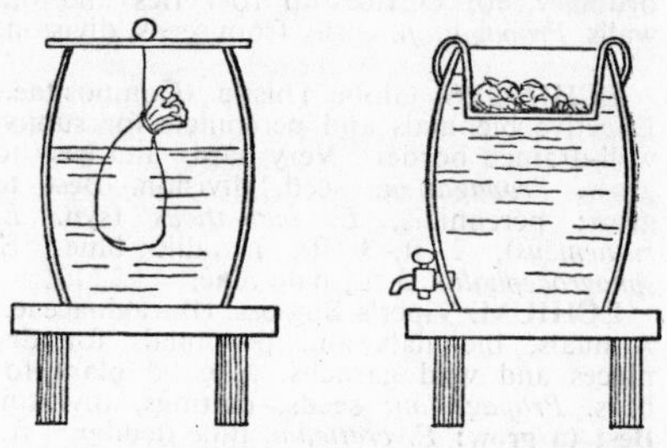

Fig. 22. Two ways of obtaining liquid manure from a solid base. Either method prevents small particles clogging up the tap.

and given in a dilute form alternately with ordinary watering (see Fig. 22). Certain quick-acting fertilizers are given as top dressings to crops; these highly concentrated materials are given in small quantities and cultivated into the soil. Prevent these fertilizers coming in contact with the plant foliage or scorching will result. Some crops are greedy feeders, while others, for example the legumes (peas and beans), have the quality of adding to, instead of taking from, the amount of nitrogen in the soil, and thus following crops may require no further addition of nitrogenous fertilizer. A general estimate of the quantities of artificial fertilizers required for a half-acre garden, for lawns, flower beds, etc., is: 4 cwt. basic slag, 2 cwt. superphosphate, ½ cwt. Kainit, ½ cwt. sulphate of ammonia, ¼ cwt. nitrate of soda. Under the Fertilizers and Feeding Stuffs Act the percentage of the constituents in a fertilizer must be declared, unless the vendor is selling a specially requested mixture. See also FERTILIZER CHART.

FIG. *Ficus Carica.* (Urticaceae.) Will grow on a poor soil by a sheltered south wall or protected under glass. Exposure to the sun through the day is essential. Root restriction is necessary, the roots being confined in pots or specially built holes, concreted or bricked in to keep the plant within bounds. Put a layer of broken bricks or gravel on the hole bottom, then a foot layer of turves, grass side down, above which a foot layer of mixed fibrous loam and broken rubble is placed. *Plant:* in autumn, fan-train trees against wall. *Prune:* remove dead wood, and thin in winter. Disbud unwanted shoots in summer and pinch young growth to five or six leaves. If excessive growth root-prune in October.

Fruit is borne on one-year-old or two-year-old wood, and young wood should be trained from the base to replace the old branches. Water freely every ten days in dry summers. Protect roots in severe weather with litter, and the stems with mats, straw or hay. *Propagation:* cuttings of half-ripe one-year-old wood, 4 in.–6 in. long, outdoors in autumn. **Best to grow:** Brown Turkey.

FILBERT. See NUTS.

FLAX. *Linum.* (Linaceae.) Hardy annuals and perennials for ordinary soil and sunny positions. Annuals often grown broadcast in masses, and thinned when large enough to handle. *Propagation:* seed, division. **Best to grow:** Annual: *L. grandiflorum*, 1 ft., and its varieties, *coccineum*, scarlet; *splendens*, rose; *rubrum*, red. Perennial*: L. narbonense*, 2 ft., pale blue, June; *L. flavum*, 1 ft., yellow, July.

FORGET-ME-NOT. *Myosotis.* (Boraginaceae.) Early-flowering hardy perennials, used for carpet bedding for bulbs, edges to borders, rockeries in moist shady positions. *Soil:* ordinary. *Propagation:* seeds sown in April; division. Most species, especially for carpet bedding, are treated as biennials. **Best to grow:** *M. alpestris*, 6 in., and its variety, Ruth Fischer, for rockeries or bedding; *M. palustris*, 6 in.–12 in., blue, and its pink and white varieties.

FORSYTHIA. (Oleaceae.) Favourite early-flowering deciduous shrubs that are hardy and bear sprays of golden bloom on leafless branches. For south or west walls, shrubberies, specimen shrubs. *Soil:* ordinary. (Fig 23.)

Fig. 23. Forsythia produces a brilliant yellow bloom in early spring.

Prune: hard back after flowering. *Propagation:* softwood cuttings in July; layers. **Best to grow:** *F. intermedia*, 8 ft., March, and its variety, *spectabilis; F. suspensa*, 8 ft., March, and its varieties, *Fortunei* and *Sieboldii; F. Giraldiana*, 10 ft., February; *F. ovata*, 4 ft., compact, March.

FOXGLOVE. *Digitalis.* (Scrophulariaceae.) Hardy biennials and perennials for wild gardens, shaded borders and woodlands. *Soil:* ordinary, most shaded positions. *Propagation:* seed sown outdoors in April, transplant in autumn. **Best to grow:** *D. purpurea* (common foxglove); raise as a biennial. *D. ambigua*, 3 ft., soft yellow, June, perennial.

FREESIA. (Iridaceae.) Attractive greenhouse pot-plants. Fragrant yellow, cream, mauve and rose flowers appear after Christmas. Re-pot annually in equal parts decayed manure, loam, leaf-mould and sand. Plant 1 in.–2 in. deep and 2 in. apart in August to flower in January. October for February, November for March, and in December for April. Keep in cold frame until growth starts, then near glass in cool greenhouse. Feed liquid manure when flowering, water freely, and dry plants off gradually after flowering, keeping bulbs quite dry until July–August. *Propagation:* soak seed for a day before sowing in August, sow thinly and leave undisturbed for a year; offsets.

FRENCH GARDENING. A system of intensive crop production under frames. Requires a quantity of horse manure and deeply dug rich black soil. Succession of five or more vegetables (mostly salad crops) are produced during a single season, by careful planning and intercropping. Soil is specially mounded during winter, and built up on hot-beds of manure covered with frames during mid-January. Alternative methods of cropping under cloche or cold frames are also used. Main essentials are good supplies of water, manure and labour. See also HOT-BED.

FRUIT AND ITS CULTURE. With a little careful planning and provided the soil is reasonably suitable, most kinds of fruit trees and bushes can be grown in any garden. To grow fruit it is essential to start with a good clean reliable stock suited to the local soil and conditions, and to maintain it in normal balanced growth, free from pests and diseases.

Walled-in and open kitchen gardens. Shelter of walls affords excellent opportunity to grow wall-trained trees. Peaches, apples, pears, apricots, plums, red and white currants and gooseberries can be trained on walls or as espaliers and cordons to line pathways through the garden. For several different methods of training trees see Fig. 24.

Orchard or plantation. Often under grass where less cultivation is required. The usual large standard or bush trees take longer to bear fruit and the essential pruning, spraying, fruit thinning and picking are more difficult and expensive. For dessert apples planting of dwarf bushes is now recommended and these have the advantages of earlier cropping, and are easier to manage.

Planning. Essential factors of soil, site, varieties for succession, and method of growing trees must be decided. Land on a south

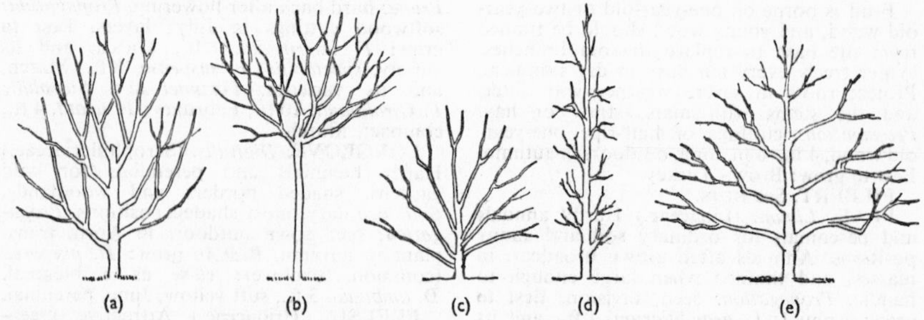

Fig. 24. Methods of training trees: (a) *bush;* (b) *half-standard;* (c) *fan;* (d) *cordon;* (e) *pyramid.*

slope, with shelter on north and east sides and exposed to full sun is ideal. Certain fruits have preferences but generally speaking good, deep, well-drained soil will grow most fruits. Soft fruits, like gooseberries, raspberries, loganberries and black-currants, are best in moist, heavy soils. Apples, pears, plums and cherries are usually grafted on named stocks whose performances are known.

Certain stocks are dwarfing, others make large vigorous trees, and the nurseryman should be consulted over the amateur's requirements. Always ensure that self-sterile varieties of fruit trees (of which there are many) have pollinators planted in close proximity, preferably one or more pollinators to every nine trees of the same variety. For large-scale work, under-cropping of soft fruit amongst apples and pears is not recommended, as the difficulties of spraying, manuring and cultivation are great. Gooseberries and strawberries are perhaps the most suitable if interplanting is done.

Planting. Prepare ground well, dig a wide deep hole, loosening the bottom soil, and spread out roots on a slightly mounded base, tread soil down in layers to make absolutely firm. Union of stock and variety (usually a slight swelling at stem base) must be above soil level. Stake while planting (Fig. 25). Plant in autumn or in spring, not later than March.

Manure. Dessert apples, red currants, gooseberries: chief requirement is potassium, with small amounts of nitrogen. Cooking apples, pears, raspberries, loganberries, blackberries and strawberries require plentiful potassium supplies with heavier applications of nitrogen than for the above. Plums, damsons, peaches, nectarines, cherries, black-currants, cobnuts, filberts need the most nitrogen, with potassium in moderate quantities. Fresh manure is injurious, it produces excessive leaf and wood growth, whereas chemical fertilizers act more quickly and do not produce a rank growth. But well-decayed manure, given annually as a mulch before flowering, is beneficial. Lime is also necessary in certain cases; add one ounce to a square yard in spring.

Winter pruning. Always make clean cuts, slightly above and slanting upward to a bud. Never leave snags, remove all dead and diseased wood and burn the latter. To remove branches, cut flush with the main stem; and cover large wounds with white-lead paint to keep out the wet and disease. On the general principle that hard cutting back encourages strong woody shoots, the pruning of trees and bushes in early years is more severe than the general pruning at a later stage.

Forming young trees and bushes of pear, apple, plum, cherry. A single-stemmed young tree is pruned back in winter to a bud at required distance from the ground to form the main stem, which should measure for bushes 30 in., for half-standards 4½ ft., and for standards 7 ft. Subsequent shoots form the main branches. These are cut hard to 3 in.–4 in. of their base. Leaders selected for main branches are evenly spaced and tree centre is kept open and clear to allow maximum light

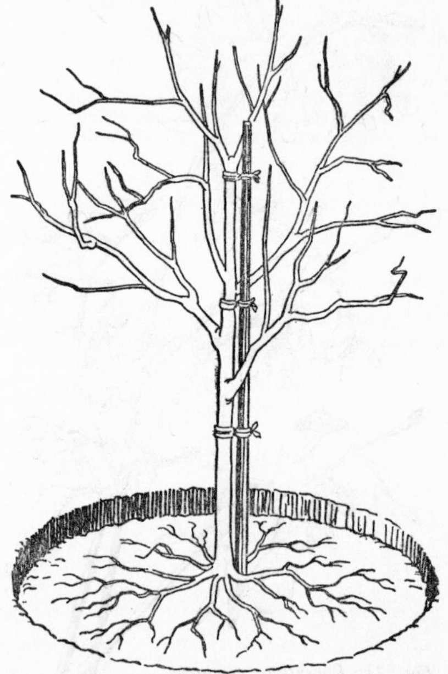

Fig. 25. A tree should be staked at the time of planting to avoid damaging the roots.

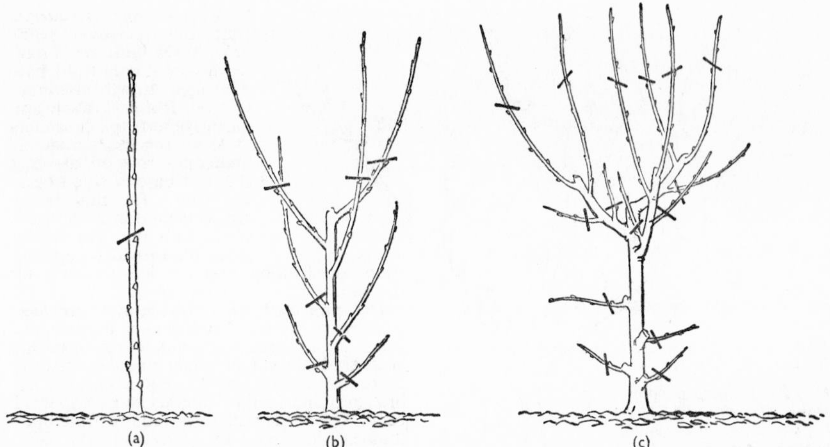

Fig. 26. Pruning from maiden apple tree to bush: (a) *maiden;* (b) *second year;* (c) *third year.*

and air to ripen fruit. Prune second-year leaders to 6 in.–8 in., always selecting outward-growing bud. (See Fig. 26.)

To form gooseberry and red-currant bushes. In their second winter the main stem is cut hard back, and laterals to an outward bud at 2 in.–3 in. from their base. Choose eight or nine leading shoots in following winter to form open-shaped bush. Remove suckers. (See Fig. 27.)

To form black-currant bushes. Cut all shoots of one- to two-year-old bushes to within two inches of their base. Keep centre open.

General winter pruning of established fruit. Apple and pear: fruit is borne on spurs of two- (or more) year-old plump, rounded fruit-buds. Certain varieties of "tip-bearers" develop fruit-buds on short laterals; for example, Worcester Pearmain, Grenadier, Bismarck, Irish Peach, Gladstone. For cordons, espaliers and dwarf bushes, cut leaders (main shoot growth of branches) to an outward bud, leaving two-thirds of the current season's growth, and laterals (side shoots from leaders) to three or four buds. For standards, remove overcrowded branches, leave short laterals for tip-bearers in early years and shorten back laterals to encourage spur-bearing in later years. (See Fig. 28.) For natural spur-bearers like James Grieve, Cox's Orange Pippin, Lord Derby, Edward VII, Miller's Seedling, Ribstone Pippin, Egremont Russet, shorten back laterals. Leaders are pruned lightly on trees coming into bearing, and later cut away one-half to a third according to the habit of the tree. (See Fig. 29.) Each variety has its own characteristics which need to be studied, bearing in mind that to bring young trees early into cropping after frameworks are made requires light pruning, provided the good shape of the tree is retained, and that weaker growers need harder pruning than strong growers. Prune Blenheim Orange, Bramley's Seedling and Belle de Boskoop lightly.

Summer pruning. Only laterals on espaliers and cordons are shortened to five or six leaves when growth is as thick as a lead pencil, in July. Apples are usually a fortnight later than pears.

Pears, damsons and cherries fruit on one- to two-year-old wood. Remove broken and diseased wood and thin out growth in late spring. Protect big cuts with lead paint directly the wounds are made, to avoid entry of disease.

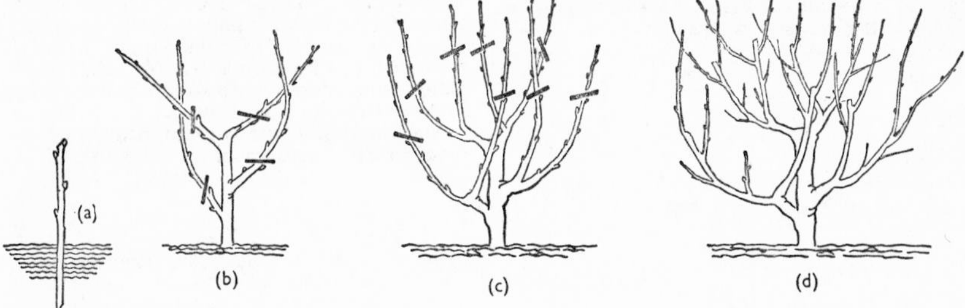

Fig. 27. Pruning red-currants from cutting to three-year-old bush: (a) *cutting;* (b) *one-year bush;* (c) *two-year bush;* (d) *three-year bush.*

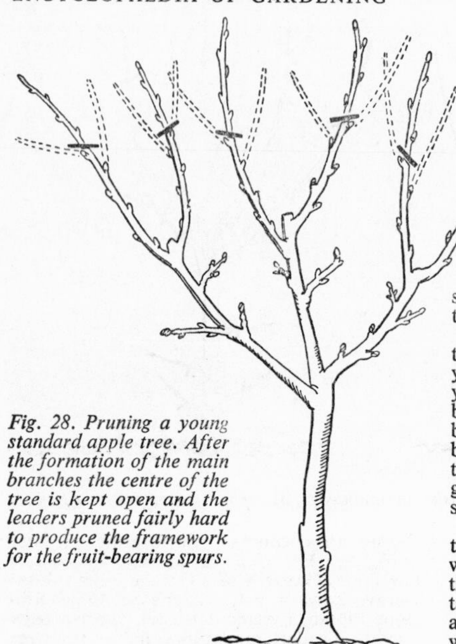

Fig. 28. Pruning a young standard apple tree. After the formation of the main branches the centre of the tree is kept open and the leaders pruned fairly hard to produce the framework for the fruit-bearing spurs.

Blackberries, loganberries and related berries fruit on one-year-old growth. During summer tie in young canes. After cropping, remove all fruited, diseased and weak canes. Tie in from five to eight strong canes per plant. Raspberries fruit on young wood. Cut fruited canes to ground level in autumn. Remove weak and remote canes. Tie in five or six canes per plant about five or six inches apart (Fig. 30).

Black-currants bear better fruit on younger growth than old. After gathering the fruit cut old fruited growths to ground level, or down to newest shoots on the stem. Keep well thinned out.

Red-currants fruit on older wood. Cut leaders to 6 in. in winter to outside buds, laterals to three or four buds.

Gooseberries fruit on one-year-old wood. For quality, prune like red-currants, but cut leaders to inward-growing bud in all cases. For quantity thin out and cut leaders back half to two-thirds. Prune in winter or in spring where birds peck the buds.

Peaches and nectarines fruit on previous year's growth. On fan-trained trees tie in new shoots from base of fruited growth in winter. Cut out fruited growth and during summer pinch leaders at 18 in. (or less if space is limited). Grow on the best shoot at base of wood bearing fruit. Tie this in as replacement for next year's crop. Rub out shoots not required, provided terminal shoot on fruiting wood is left to draw up the sap.

Old neglected trees. Overgrown crowded trees need careful thinning over a period of years. Never remove too much growth in one year, gradually cut out badly placed or crossing branches to open up tree centre. Shorten tall branches and in time laterals can be spurred back. Weak, starved trees require fruit buds thinned if they are overcrowded. Give generous nitrogen dressings to trees in this state.

Spraying. Pests and diseases must be checked to give clean fruit from healthy trees. Trap winter moths on grease-bands placed round tree trunks in autumn. Spraying with winter tar-oil washes destroys eggs of certain pests and burns up moss and lichen. Apply winter washes as drenching sprays with good pressure. Cover-washes, which lay a protective film on leaves against leaf-eating insects, must be applied as a fine misty spray over the foliage. Contact-washes for leaf-piercing and sucking pests kill by contacting the bodies; drenching high-pressure sprays are necessary. Dusts are easily applied, but are soon washed off by rain. Stirrup pumps are serviceable for spraying small areas of low trees.

General cultivation. *Apples:* Cox's Orange Pippin needs a pollinator such as Worcester Pearmain or James Grieve. *Pears:* Glou Morceau pollinates the self-sterile Doyenne du Comice. *Plums:* Oullin's Golden Gage pollinates the self-sterile Coe's Golden Drop. *Cherries:* self-sterile Early Rivers requires Governor Wood or Bigarreau as a pollinator.

Selected varieties for gardens. Cherries: Early Rivers, black; Governor Wood, white; Morello, sour red, self-fruitful; Bigarreau, black. *Pears:* Williams' Bon Chrétien; Conference; Doyenne du Comice; Winter Nelis. *Dessert Plums:* Victoria; Coe's Golden Drop; Green Gage. *Cooking plums:* Czar; Monarch. *Dessert apples:* Cox's Orange Pippin; Laxton's Fortune; Laxton's Superb; Worcester Pearmain; James Grieve. *Cooking apples:* Arthur Turner; Bramley's Seedling.

Strawberries. Choose clean healthy stock. Plant in early autumn or spring 12 in.–18 in.

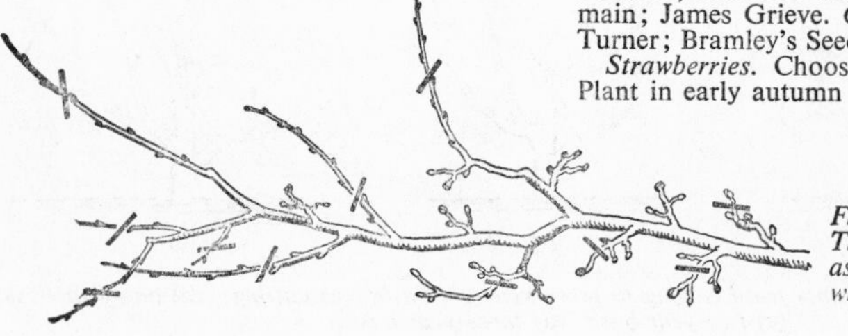

Fig. 29. Pruning apple. The leader is not cut back as hard as the laterals which are spurred back to encourage buds.

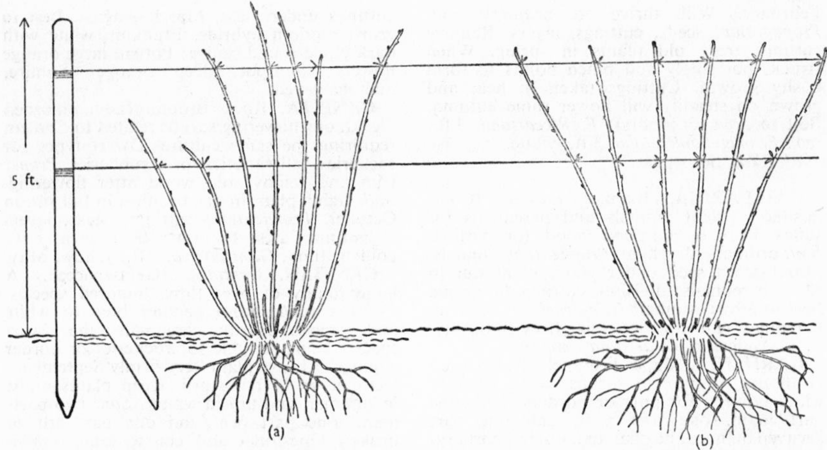

Fig. 30. Training raspberries on horizontal wires; (a) *badly pruned, and* (b) *well pruned.*

apart in rows 2½ ft.–3 ft. apart on well-manured ground. Disbud spring-planted strawberries during first season. Prick in sulphate of potash and bonemeal every winter. Straw down in mid-May and remove runners from fruiting plants. *Propagation:* Layers (Fig. 31). Renew beds every three to five years.

Fig. 31. To propagate strawberries, peg down runners into pots of mixed compost. When these have rooted, sever from the parent plant.

Fruit Storage. To keep fruit in sound condition, keep it in a cool, dry place, and where air can circulate freely (Fig. 32).

FUCHSIA. (Onagraceae.) Graceful hardy and tender shrubs for pot-plants or sheltered shrubberies, south or west walls, or for summer bedding. *Greenhouse pot-plants* require two parts fibrous loam, one part manure and leaf-mould with sand. Pot February–March, watering moderately until May and afterwards freely until October, then very slightly. Pot-plants for summer can be planted out in June and stored for winter in the greenhouse. *Outdoor Fuchsias:* Prune shoots to base in

Fig. 32. Slatted wood trays fitted into a wooden framework are ideal for fruit storage.

February. Will thrive in ordinary soil. *Propagation:* seeds, cuttings, layers. Remove cuttings from old plants in spring. When struck, pot singly and pinch points to form bushy growth. Cuttings taken in heat and grown on steadily will flower same autumn. **Best to grow** (outdoors): *F. Riccartonii*, 3 ft., red; *F. magellanica alba*, 3 ft., white.

FURZE. See GORSE.

GAILLARDIA. Blanket Flower. (Compositae.) Bright annuals and perennials for sunny beds or borders; good for cutting. *Soil:* ordinary, dry, light. *Propagation:* annuals. March-sown seed under glass, plant out in May. Perennials: division, cuttings in spring. **Best to grow:** Annual: *G. pulchella*, var. *picta*. Perennial: named varieties like Ipswich Beauty, E. T. Anderson, *G. aristata* Dazzler.

GARDENIA. Cape Jasmine. (Rubiaceae.) Hothouse evergreen shrubs with fragrant white flowers, for pots or borders. *Soil:* one part loam, one part peat, and one part decayed manure and charcoal. Pot in February-March. Syringe during summer except when in flower, when liquid manure is beneficial. *Propagation:* cuttings of young shoots inserted in sandy peat during early spring. Require 75 deg. F.

GARRYA. (Cornaceae.) Hardy evergreen shrubs with catkin-like flowers. *Soil:* ordinary. Requires wall shelter in northern districts. Plant in May. *Propagation:* hardwood cuttings under frames or bell-glass in September. Layers in September. *Prune:* trim shoots and remove dead wood in May. The staminate (male) plant is the more ornamental of the two available forms. **Best to grow:** *G. elliptica*, 5 ft.–10 ft., greenish-white, March (Fig. 33).

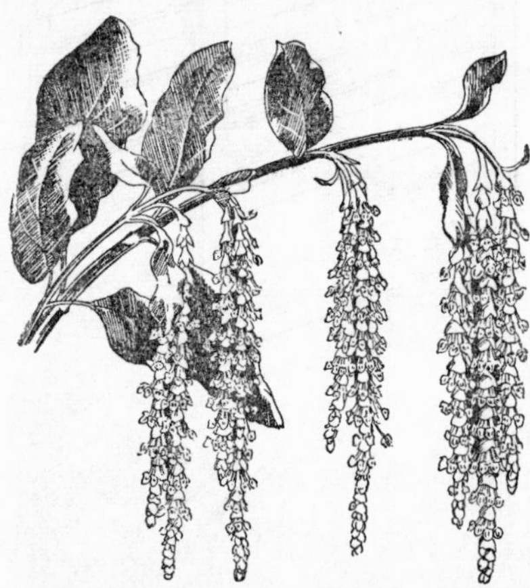

Fig. 33. Garrya, a spring-flowering shrub

GAZANIA. Treasure Flower. (Compositae.) Brilliant, half-hardy perennials, with orange or yellow daisy-like flowers that will bloom from cuttings during first year. Grown outdoors are suitable for sunny border edgings or rockeries, also grown as pot-plants. *Soil:* ordinary; also seaside chalk soil. *Propagation:* cuttings under glass, March–August. **Best to grow:** modern hybrids, Franklin, white with dark circle round centre; Pottsii, large orange flowers; Sunspot, deep orange; Sunfire, mahogany red.

GENISTA. Rock Broom. (Leguminosae.) Deciduous flowering shrubs related to *Cytisus*, requiring the same culture. Dwarf types for rockeries, tall varieties for shrubberies. *Prune:* trim and remove old wood after flowering. *Soil:* light; plant in dry position in full sun in October. *Propagation:* cuttings, seeds, layers in autumn. **Best to grow:** *G. cinerea*, 8 ft., golden, June; *G. hispanica*, 2 ft., yellow, May.

GENTIAN. *Gentiana.* (Gentianaceae.) A large family of over three hundred species. Colours range from gentian blue to white and yellow. Hardy perennials, the dwarf species being suitable for rockeries or border edgings. Always plant very firmly September–October or March–April. Keep plants moist in summer, and dry in winter. *Soil:* two parts loam, one part peat and one part grit or broken limestone, and coarse sand. *Propagation:* seeds sown in well-drained pots of sandy soil, root division in March. **Best to grow:** *G. acaulis*, 3 in., tubular deep blue flower, March–June; *G. Farreri*, 6 in., Cambridge blue, requires lime-free soil; *G. sino-ornate*, 6 in., royal blue, and easy to grow; also its cross, *G. Macaulayi*, 6 in., turquoise blue, for any soil; *G. lutea*, 36 in., yellow, requires lime-free soil; *G. verna*, 4 in., azure blue, peaty loam, do not disturb; *G. saxosa*, 3 in., white, good garden soil.

GERANIUM. Crane's Bill. (Geraniaceae.) Hardy herbaceous perennials with seed-pods resembling the beak of a crane. Dwarf types for rockeries, tall species for sunny borders. *Propagation:* seed sown in open in April; division. **Best to grow:** *G. Wallichianum*, 2 ft., blue, June; *G. sanguineum*, 1 ft., crimson, June; *G. Endressii*, 1 ft., pink, June. See also PELARGONIUM and Fig. 34.

GLADIOLUS. Sword Lily. (Iridaceae.) Half-hardy deciduous flowering corms. Modern hybrids are divided into three types: the most popular, the large-flowered class, 2 ft.–4 ft.; *Primulinus*, 1½ ft.–3 ft., which have hooded flowers smaller than the first type and are free-flowering but less vigorous; and *Colvillei*, early, small, wide-open flowers, usually forced under glass. *Soil:* light, well-drained and enriched with moisture-holding humus or decayed manure. Choose sheltered place that has good drainage. Plant out after frosts in March–April, at fortnightly intervals for succession. Place corms 4 in. deep and 6 in. apart, either in clumps in the border or farther apart in rows for cutting or bedding. If soil is heavy, place a little sand in the hole to ensure good drainage. Stake heavy spikes and feed liquid manure when flowers open. Lift in November, dry off and store corms in a cool frost-proof place. Plant smallest corms separately, as flowers do not appear for two or three years. *Greenhouse varieties:* use one part loam, one part decayed manure and sand. Pot October–November and plant 1 in. deep and allow five corms per 6-in. pot. *Propagation:* seeds, bulbils. **Best to grow:** modern hybrids of large flowered types, Bit of

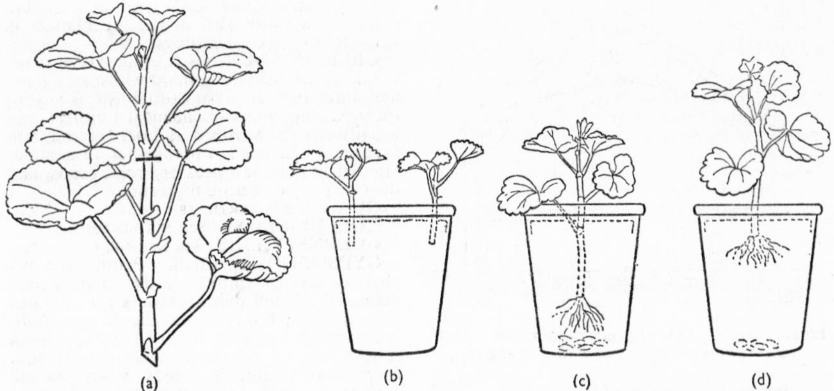

Fig. 34. Propagating pelargoniums (geraniums). (a) *make a cut below a joint (shown by line), trim off lower leaves;* (b) *insert cuttings, which should be about 3 in. long, round edge of pot of sandy compost; when cuttings have developed, re-pot;* (c) *shows the wrong way;* (d) *the correct.*

Heaven, orange yellow; Van Tienhoven, flaming red; Gold Dust, yellow; Rosa Van Lime, pink; Mrs. Mark's Memory, magenta; Snow Princess, white; New Europe, geranium-red with cream patches; Picardy, salmon-pink.

GLAUCIUM. Horned Poppy. (Papaveraceae.) Seed-pods of this hardy perennial are long and horn-like. Flowers resemble single poppies. It will flower the first year from seed. *Soil:* ordinary; sunny warm positions. *Propagation:* seeds sown outdoors in May, transplanted July–August.

GOAT'S BEARD. *Spiraea Aruncus.* See SPIRAEA.

GODETIA. (Onagraceae.) Gay flowering annuals for summer bedding, spring pot-plants or borders. Easily grown and excellent for cut flowers. *Propagation:* seeds sown outdoors in March or under glass and transplanted in May for earlier flowering. Pot-plants require leaf-mould, loam and sand. **Best to grow:** modern hybrids like Double Sybil Sherwood, Lady Albermarle, Duke of York, Bridesmaid.

GOLDEN ROD. *Solidago.* (Compositae.) Hardy herbaceous perennials, which grow in sunny or shady positions or near water. *Plant:* October to April. *Soil:* ordinary. *Propagation:* divide every three or four years, or propagate by seed in April.

GOOSEBERRY. See FRUIT AND ITS CULTURE.

GORSE. (Furze.) *Ulex.* (Leguminosae.) Hardy, spiny, evergreen shrubs, which thrive if left undisturbed on sunny banks, rockeries and in woodlands. *Soil:* poor sandy, or ordinary ground. Plant shrubs from September to April. For hedges, place in single row 18 in. apart. *Propagation:* sow seed outdoors in April; cuttings. **Best to grow:** *U. europaeus flore pleno*, 4 ft., double yellow.

GRAFTING. See PROPAGATION OF PLANTS.

GRAPE. See VITIS.

GRAPE HYACINTH. *Muscari.* (Liliaceae.) Attractive early flowering hardy bulbs for most garden soils, under trees or rockeries, border edges, or for pot culture. Plant 2 in. deep, and 2 in.–4 in. apart in lines or masses, from August to November. Lift and replant, dividing bulbs every third year. **Best to grow:** *M. conicum*, variety Heavenly Blue, 8 in., April; *M. botryoides album*, 6 in., white, March.

GRASSES. Ornamental. Can be most attractive amongst border flowers to fill gaps, to provide background and colour contrasts, or even to prevent colour clashing. Fresh or dry grasses make useful indoor decoration. To dry the grass, harvest before the seed ripens, and hang bunches upside down in a cool place for a few weeks. Ordinary garden soil will grow grasses. Most are hardy annuals which can be sown outdoors in spring. Hardy annuals: *Agrostis* (cloud grass), 1½ ft.; *Avena* (animated oat), 2 ft.; *Briza* (Quaking Grass), 1 ft.; *Eragrostis* (feather or love grass), 1 ft.–3 ft.; *Hordeum* (squirrel-tail grass), 2 ft., for dry position; *Lagurus* (hare's-tail grass), 1 ft. Half-hardy annuals: *Coix* (Job's tears), Indian grass, 2 ft. high; *Zea* (Indian maize or corn), 3 ft.–5 ft.; sow in heat and transplant. Perennials: *Aira* (hair grass), 12 in.–18 in.; *Dactylis* (gardener's garters, cock's foot), 6 in.–8 in.; *Eulalia* (zebra-striped grass), 6 ft.–10 ft.; *Stipa* (feather grass), 2 ft.–3 ft.

GREENHOUSE. A great deal of enjoyment can be had from the smallest greenhouse. Both hot and cold houses will produce flowers and fruit out of season for comparatively small expense. Greenhouses vary slightly in construction, according to the space available and the type of plant.

Construction can be full span standing independently (Fig. 35), a three-quarter or half span (lean-to) against a wall. Inside, plants are bedded out in borders, or grown in pots on single or tiered stages.

Heating is usually done by boilers outside and below the level of the house. Use rain or soft water in the pipes, since hard water will fur them up. Oil-radiators or hurricane lamps can be used, but lamps must be kept clean as

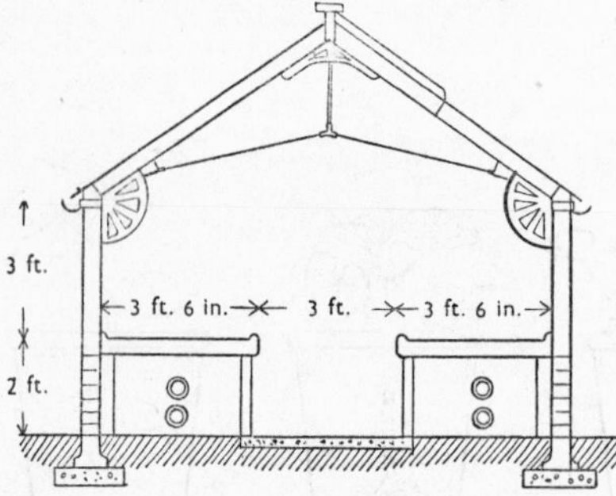

Fig. 35. A good type of greenhouse has a central pathway and pipes under the staging.

the fumes are detrimental to plants. *Cool house:* requires small heating apparatus to keep up the minimum night temperature of 45 deg. Probably most useful of all heated houses, as a wide range of decorative plants can be grown, besides providing sufficient heat to raise young stock in early spring. *Warm house* (intermediate): minimum night temperature of 50 deg. gives wider range for sub-tropical foliage and flowering plants. *Stove house:* with minimum night temperature of 60 deg. for tropical plants.

Ventilation. It is necessary to study the weather in relation to crops within the house, and the time of year. Avoid cold draughts, but keep house well aired by opening ventilators gradually in the morning and shutting them before sunset and before the house has got cold. Object is to trap last of sun's heat in the house to keep atmosphere warmer during the night. Guiding principle is to keep temperature continually even according to the day's weather. Open top ventilators first, then side ventilators, choosing the sheltered side on a windy day. In frosty weather plants can be protected with paper coverings. Shading from intense summer sun may be necessary by means of blind or spray outside on the glass, using a thin coating of distemper, starch and whitening.

Watering needs great care. Never over-water or let the plants dry right out; give generous waterings regularly, preferably with rainwater. Water-tanks inside the house provide water with the chill off. Very cold water in winter or in hothouses at any time is detrimental. Syringing in summer promotes growth, cleans foliage, keeps temperature down and controls red spider mite and thrips. Keep paths and gravel or ash on staging damp. Never leave houses wet during winter months or cold summer nights.

Cleanliness is of prime importance in greenhouse work; an annual clean-out is essential for all staging, corners, glass, woodwork, water-tanks and gutters. If plant diseases have been observed, fumigate house and disinfect water for cleaning. Never use creosote, as fumes are detrimental to plants. Always keep houses clean of rubbish, remove dead and diseased growth. A propagating case, with good drainage and sandy loam and a glass lid, placed in a warm part of the greenhouse, is suitable for striking cuttings.

GREEN MANURING. Certain green crops are dug back into the ground whilst still green and immature as a substitute for farmyard manure. Subsequently chemical fertilizers are usually dug in. Mustard at 2 oz. per rod, and rape at ½ oz., are sown together in summer after early potatoes, peas or broad beans, and then dug in just before flowering.

GUANO. See FERTILIZER CHART.

GUELDER ROSE. See VIBURNUM.

GUERNSEY LILY. See NERINE.

GYPSOPHILA. Chalk Plant. (Caryophyllaceae.) Delightful hardy annuals and perennials. Small dainty flowers are valuable for rockeries, borders and cut flowers. *Soil:* ordinary and chalky. Old mortar or brick rubble can be mixed in with garden soil. *Propagation:* annuals, seeds sown on soil surface in April and thinned to 3 in.–6 in. apart. Perennials, seed sown outdoors in April and transplanted to permanent position in summer; also cuttings and division. **Best to grow:** annual, *G. elegans*, 2 ft., white. Perennial, *G. paniculata*, 2 ft.–3 ft., white, and its varieties *flore pleno* (double), Bristol Fairy; *G. repens*, creeping, 6 in., white.

HALF-HARDY ANNUALS. These plants are too tender to stand the cold of winter or early spring outdoors. Sow in cold frame or greenhouse February–March, and transplant outdoors May–June.

HALF-HARDY BIENNIALS AND PERENNIALS. These may be grown in the open air only in the most favoured parts of the British Isles.

HAMAMELIS. Witch-Hazel. (Hamamelidaceae.) Hardy shrubs with delightful flowers appearing without foliage in mid-winter. *Soil:* deep rich loam in a damp position by lake margin, shrubbery or border. *Propagation:* layers in October–November; grafting. **Best to grow:** *H. mollis*, 10 ft., deep yellow; *H. japonica*, 12 ft., lemon yellow, December–February.

HEATH, HEATHER. See CALLUNA and ERICA.

HEDGES are used as boundaries and add more interest and beauty to a garden than walls or fences. Informal hedges of attractive plants take up more room than clipped hedges which must be trimmed regularly throughout the summer. To plant, prepare ground well and plant as for individual shrubs.

Evergreen hedges form attractive backgrounds for deciduous shrubs and herbaceous plants. Evergreen-hedge plants include: holly, *Ilex aquifolium*, slow-growing impenetrable barrier, 12 ft. high, requiring one trim a year. Yew, *Taxus baccata*, good windscreen, 10 ft.–12 ft. high, but does not do so well near towns; one clip per year; poisonous to animals, so not recommended for outside boundary. Box, *Buxus sempervirens*, grows to 6 ft.; good for shady places, but slow growing. *Buxus sempervirens suffruticosa* is suitable for dwarf edgings. Privet, *Ligustrum*, quick-growing semi-evergreen; requires several clippings. *Lonicera nitida*, quick growing, easily rooted from cuttings; good for low and narrow hedges. *Cupressus macrocarpa*, quick growing, not very hardy, and transplants badly. *Cupressus Lawsoniana*, very quick growing, 12 ft.–20 ft. high.

Deciduous hedges can be made from beech, *Fagus sylvatica*, for chalk soils; hornbeam, *Carpinus Betulus;* hawthorn, *Crataegus oxyacantha.*

Informal hedges: *Berberis stenophylla, Ceanothus, Escallonia, Fuchsia, Hydrangea, Rhododendron*, lavender, lilac.

Seaside hedges: *Olearia Haastii, Veronica*, holly, blackthorn, tamarisk, buckthorn.

HELENIUM. (Compositae.) Useful hardy herbaceous perennials for borders and cut flowers. *Soil:* ordinary. *Propagation:* division. Stake tall varieties, and cut stems down in November. **Best to grow:** Moerheim Beauty, The Bishop, Madame Canivet; *H. autumnale* and its varieties, Riverton Beauty, Rubrum, Chipperfield Orange.

HELIANTHEMUM. Sun Rose. (Cistaceae.) Evergreen hardy flowering shrubs. *Soil:* light sandy soil on rockeries or border. *Prune* into shape in March. *Propagation:* cuttings or division. **Best to grow:** modern hybrids of *H. nummularium* (syn. *vulgare*), 6 in., apricot; Ben Flada, 9 in., yellow; Ben Lin, 9 in., crimson magenta; Miss Mould, 9 in., salmon; The Bride, 9 in., white.

HELIANTHUS. Sunflower. (Compositae.) Tall hardy annuals and perennials grown in sunny borders of ordinary soil. *Propagation:* division. Seeds sown outdoors in flowering positions. Divide and replant every few years as the roots spread rapidly. **Best to grow:** perennials, *H. rigidus;* varieties, Miss Mellish, Monarch; *H. multiflorus*, and its double form Loddon Gold. Annual, *H. annuus* (common sunflower); large-flowered varieties, Sutton's Giant Yellow and Bronze King; small flowers, Sutton's Miniature.

HELIOTROPIUM. Cherry-pie, Heliotrope. (Boraginaceae.) Fragrant flowered greenhouse shrub, used in window-boxes and beds during summer months. *Soil:* equal parts loam, leaf-mould, sand. Light and rich outdoors. Trim old plants in February. *Propagation:* seeds, cuttings, February–August.

HELLEBORUS. Christmas Rose, Lenten Rose. (Ranunculaceae.) Hardy perennials which flower in winter and early spring. Require rich loamy soil in shade or sun. Do not disturb, and protect with hand lights or cloches in winter. Feed liquid manure during summer, and water in dry weather. Prepare ground with manure before planting. Excellent for cut flowers, lasting well if stems are split. Plants are poisonous. Will grow well in pots indoors. *Propagation:* seeds, division. **Best to grow:** *H. niger* (Christmas Rose), *H. orientalis* (Lenten Rose), and its varieties, Snowdrift (white) and Larissa (pink).

HELXINE. Hundreds and Thousands, Mind Your Own Business. (Urticaceae.) Creeping perennial for carpeting on walls, greenhouse staging, pots in windows. Will ramp if unchecked. *Soil:* ordinary. Water moderately in pots. *Propagation:* division.

HERBACEOUS BORDERS are planted with perennials and can be left undisturbed from three to five years. Annuals are used to fill in gaps; shrubs behind large borders give green colour during winter months. A suggested arrangement is shown in Fig. 36.

To prepare ground, double dig and manure, lime if necessary, consolidate ground and make level. Prepare a plan of bold groups of plants from list of those available and those to be purchased. Take into account season of flowering, colour and height of plants, ranging the tallest at the back and avoiding straight lines. *Plant* in autumn or early spring. Wide borders backed with evergreen hedges (preferably not gross feeders like privet) display

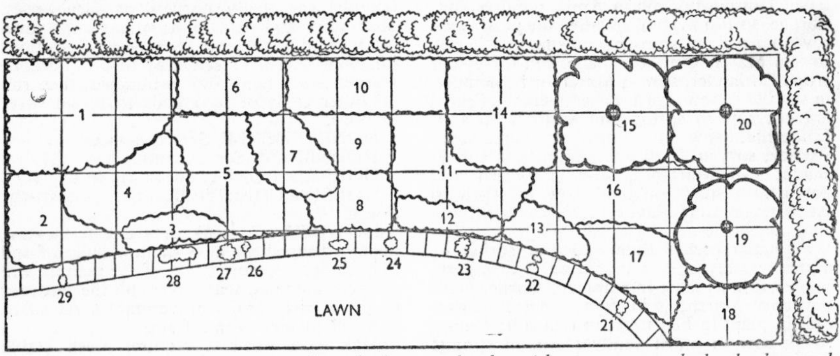

Fig. 36. A suggested arrangement for a herbaceous border with an evergreen hedge background: (1) delphiniums; (2) veronica, "Shirley Blue"; (3) pinks; (4) phlox, "Elstead Pink"; (5) iris (tall varieties at the back, dwarf in front); (6) aster; (7) gypsophila, "Bristol Fairy"; (8) aster, dwarf, "Audrey"; (9) Papaver orientale, *"Lord Lambourne"; (10)* Anchusa italica, *"Morning Glory"; (11)* Coreopsis grandiflora; *(12) geum, "Fire Opal"; (13)* Artemisia pontica; *(14) Russell lupin; (15) lilac; (16) helenium, "Moorheim Beauty"; (17) anthemis, "Perry's variety"; (18)* Lychnis chalcedonica; *(19)* Hamamelis mollis; *(20) Golden cupressus. Rock plants in the paving: (21)* Thymus serpyllum coccineum; *(22)* Sedum spathulifolium rubrum; *(23)* Veronica prostrata; *(24)* Phlox subulata; *(25)* Dianthus deltoides; *(26)* Achillea rupestris; *(27)* Gypsophila repens; *(28)* Armeria maritima alba; *(29) frankenia.*

the flowers best; protection from north side is beneficial. Borders viewed sideways on, from a house, are more attractive.

HERB GARDEN. One of the oldest forms of gardening, which nowadays may be a small patch for culinary purposes or designed on old-world lines, linking, say, the flower garden with the vegetable garden (Fig. 37).

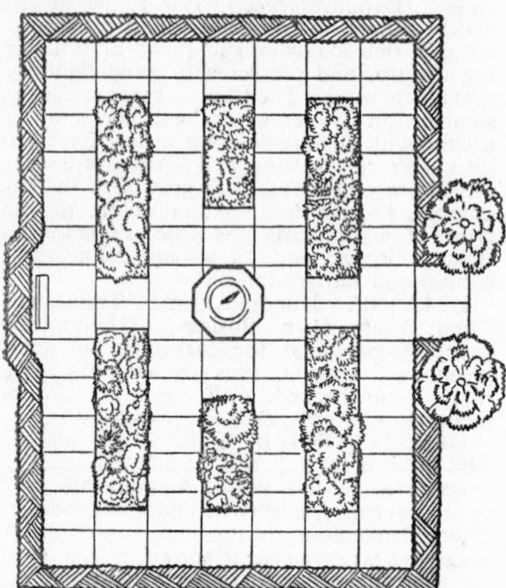

Fig. 37. Plan of a herb garden. The beds can be surrounded either with grass paths or paving. The garden is bounded with a lavender hedge; in the centre is a sundial in line with a seat.

Herbs, grown annually from seed: *Angelica*, sow in March in shady position; Anise (*Pimpinella anisum*), sow in April, requires sun; Basil, half-hardy, sow in April, requires sun; Borage, sow in March, requires sun; Caraway, sow in April, in sun or semi-shade; Chervil, sow in March–October, shade, sun for winter crop; Coriander, sow in March or September, in sun; Dill, sow April, in semi-shade; Fennel (sweet), sow in spring and autumn, in sun; Finocchia, sow in April or September; Parsley, sow in April and summer, in sun or shade; Pot Marigold, sow in March and August, in sun; Purslane, sow in April to August, in sun; Savory, sow in April or summer, in sun.

Perennial herbs: Balm, sow in spring or autumn; Chives, sow in March, 6 in. apart; Fennel (bitter), sow in summer; Garlic, plant February–March, 6 in.–9 in. apart; Horse-radish, plant in February, in rich soil; Penny-royal, sow in moist sandy loam, in spring; Savory (winter), sow in April; Tarragon, plant in April; Marjoram, sow in April.

HESPERIS. Sweet Rocket. (Cruciferae.) Fragrant-flowered hardy perennials for sunny borders or rockeries. *Soil:* ordinary, rich. *Propagation:* seeds, division. **Best to grow:** *H. matronalis*, 2½ ft., white, lilac or pale purple flowers, and its double forms.

HEUCHERA. (Saxifragaceae.) Admirable hardy perennials for front of herbaceous borders in full sunlight. *Soil:* light or peaty. *Propagation:* seed, division. Freshly divided plants should be kept in a sandy nursery bed for a year. **Best to grow:** *H. sanguinea*, 2 ft., red, June–August, and its varieties, Oxfordil (scarlet), Honey Bell (rose), Bloom's Variety (coral red).

HIBISCUS. (Malvaceae.) Mallow-like flowers of tender and hardy annuals and perennials. Stove species need fibrous loam, charcoal and sand. Pot or plant, February–March. *Propagation:* annuals and stove species from seed, division and seed for perennials; shrubs by cuttings and grafts. **Best to grow:** perennial, *H. rosea*, 4 ft.–6 ft., rose. Hardy shrubby species, *H. syriacus*, 6 ft.–8 ft.

HIPPOPHAE. Sea Buckthorn. (Elaeagnaceae.) Deciduous shrubs for seaside or inland borders. Orange berries all winter. *Soil:* ordinary. *Propagation:* seeds, division. **Best to grow:** *Hippophae rhamnoides*, 8 ft.–12 ft. Both male and female plants must be grown if berries are wanted.

HOLLY. *Ilex.* (Aquifoliaceae.) Hardy shrubs bearing berries. Good for hedges, and planting near sea, or on exposed banks in sun or shade. *Soil:* ordinary. *Prune* with secateurs, September–April. *Propagation:* seeds, cuttings. See also HEDGES.

HOLLYHOCK. *Althaea rosea.* (Malvaceae.) Favourite hardy perennial, often grown as biennial or annual in ordinary soil. Requires deeply worked and manured ground, with application of liquid manure from May until blooms open, and copious waterings in dry weather. Stake in summer and cut flower stems to 6 in. from the ground in autumn. *Propagation:* seed sown outdoors in June. Thin to 6 in. and transplant in September. Cuttings of shoots from base of flower stems, for the best double varieties. Hollyhocks may suffer from rust, for which no cure is known.

HONESTY. *Lunaria biennis.* (Cruciferae.) Biennial for shady borders or shrubberies. *Soil:* moist and rich. *Propagation:* seeds sown in May and transplanted to flowering positions following April, or scattered in odd corners. Harvest seed-stems, dry in bunches, then rub off outer cases of seed pods to reveal silver "moons."

HONEYSUCKLE. See LONICERA.

HORNBEAM. See CARPINUS.

HORNED POPPY. See GLAUCIUM.

HORSE CHESTNUT. See CHESTNUT, HORSE.

HOT-BED. Consists of fresh fermenting manure heaped under a shallow layer of soil in a frame. Decomposition of the manure will raise considerable heat and enable the gardener to grow early crops of vegetables on sifted rich soil covered with a frame.

Making a hot-bed requires fresh stable manure containing a certain amount of straw for the hottest beds, whilst dry grass and leaves can be mixed with manure for slower-heating hot-beds. After turning the fresh manure several times (outside to middle), build up the manure evenly and firmly, wider and longer than the frame, as a foundation. Two loads of manure are enough for a single frame. Settle frame on to manure heap, and sift in a 4 in.–8 in. layer of rich garden soil, compress and rake the surface level. Cover soil with a light and allow hot-bed to settle and heat to a steady temperature. Mid-January is the most suitable time to sow seeds in a new hot-bed. Lime the soil.

Cropping table: mid-January, sow short-horn carrot, and inter-plant lettuce seedlings. After lettuces are cut, cauliflower plants can be put in among the carrots. Harvest carrots. During summer the lights are removed, cauliflowers are cut and frame planted up with lettuce and Dore (self-blanching) celery. Regular overhead spraying is essential after lettuces are cut to bring carrots and cauliflowers to maturity.

HUMEA. *H. elegans.* Incense Plant. (Compositae.) Biennial with aromatic foliage for greenhouses, graceful rose-purple flowers appearing in June. *Soil:* loam, decayed manure, leaf-mould and sand, bonemeal. *Propagation:* seed sown in July.

HUMUS is formed from decaying vegetable and animal material, and is the dark organic matter in the soil. It contains potential plant-foods and retains moisture in the ground.

HYACINTHUS. Hyacinth. (Liliaceae.) Delightful spring-flowering hardy bulbs that will force indoors or grow outside in nearly any position. The trade offers special "prepared" bulbs for forcing that are larger and more expensive but the best for indoor work, since their blooms are earlier and bigger than those sold for garden cultivation. Hyacinth bulbs deteriorate more quickly than daffodils and tulips, but forced bulbs when planted outdoors will continue to produce rather smaller flowers in after years. *Outdoors. Soil:* ordinary, though preferably light, must be well drained. Plant 4 in.–12 in. apart and 4 in.–6 in. deep in October. Handle bulbs carefully and place sand in the hole under the bulb to aid drainage. Lift when foliage has died away.

Indoor cultivation. See also BULBS (*in bowls.*) Plant bulbs in September for early flowering. If growth is slow and stunted, a dunce's cap of paper over each bulb will draw the growth up. **Best to grow:** hyacinths suitable for forcing, L'Innocence (white), Lady Derby (pale pink), Bismarck (blue, purple markings), Mauve Queen (reddish-lilac), Queen of the Blues (Cambridge blue), City of Haarlem (deep yellow), Yellow Hammer (canary yellow), Lord Balfour (purple), Electra (red). *Hyacinths for bedding*, City of Haarlem (yellow), Gertrude (rose), Grand Maître (blue), Queen of the Whites (white), Queen of the Pinks (pink).

HYDRANGEA. (Saxifragaceae.) Flowering shrubs, both tender and hardy. **Outdoor culture:** ordinary rich soil in sunny, well-drained borders. Admirable for seaside districts in south and west of England. Apply liquid manure during flowering period, and top-dress with decayed cow manure. Prune out dead wood and straggling shoots.

Indoor culture: the common species with flat flower-heads used for forcing in pots requires compost of two parts loam, one well-decayed manure, and sand. Water freely from March to October, and moderately during winter. Feed with liquid manure and soot when flower-buds appear. ***Prune*** flowered shoots and weak growths in August. Pot plants can be used for bedding, either planted out or with the pots sunk in the ground for the summer months. Lift and bring into a frost-proof room or greenhouse. *H. macrophylla* blooms on growth made during the previous year. *H. paniculata,* pointed heads of flowers bloom on growth made during the same year. Prune hard to two buds from base of each growth during spring.

Propagation: cuttings of thick shoots from plant-base in heat during spring or frame during August. Keep in frost-proof place. Colours of *H. macrophylla* (*hortensis*) vary according to the soil. Changing the pink flowers to blue requires special "blueing powders" that are sold by nurserymen for the purpose. Weekly waterings of alum are equally effective. **Best to grow:** Generale Vicomtesse de Vibraye, Parsifal, Blue Wave.

HYPERICUM. St. John's Wort. (Hypericaceae.) Shrubbery and herbaceous perennials, both hardy and half-hardy. Shrubs will thrive in sun or shade in ordinary soil. Herbaceous species are suitable for sunny borders or rockeries on sandy soil. *Propagation:* seeds, cuttings, division. **Best to grow:** *H. patulum var Forrestii*, 4 ft., shrubby, yellow; *H. olympicum*, 9 in., yellow; *H. reptans*, yellow, creeping.

IBERIS. See CANDYTUFT.

INSECTIVOROUS PLANTS. Insects are trapped by certain plants for food. Flies and other small insects are held captive when they alight on leaves or inside the flowers, by sticky substances on the leaves, the closing of flowers, or by downward-pointing hairs. Digestive juices decompose the body so that the plant can absorb it. Most plants of this type flourish in moist boggy sites. They include sundews (*Drosera*) and butterwort (*Pinguicula*), both native to Britain.

INULA. Flea-bane. (Compositae.) Herbaceous perennials for ordinary soil in moist sunny positions. Suitable for wild garden, borders and rockeries. *Propagation:* division in spring.

IRIS. (Iridaceae.) A large and varied genus of bulbous and rhizomatous perennial flowering plants, many of which are hardy and easily grown in rock garden or border. All like sunny positions. *I. sibirica*, *I. Kaempferi* and *I. ochroleuca* thrive in very moist places. Plant bulbous species in October, 3 in. deep. Others may be lifted and divided (Fig. 38) after flowering or in September. **Best to grow:** Bulbous, *I. reticulata*, 6 in., violet, February, and its blue form, Cantab. *I. histrioides*, 6 in., rich blue, February. *I. Xiphium* (Dutch and Spanish irises), 18 in., June, white, yellow, blue or bronze. *I. xiphioides* (English iris), 2 ft., July, white, lilac, blue or purple. Rhizomatous, *I. unguicularis* (Algerian iris), 1 ft., lavender, December–March; plant near south wall in dry spot. *I. sibirica*, 3 ft., June, deep blue-purple or white. *I. Kaempferi* (Japanese iris), 3 ft., June, white, purple, lavender or red-purple. *I. ochroleuca*, 5 ft., July, creamy-white. The "bearded" or ordinary border varieties, 3 ft. to 4 ft., May–June, cover a very wide range of colours. The following is a

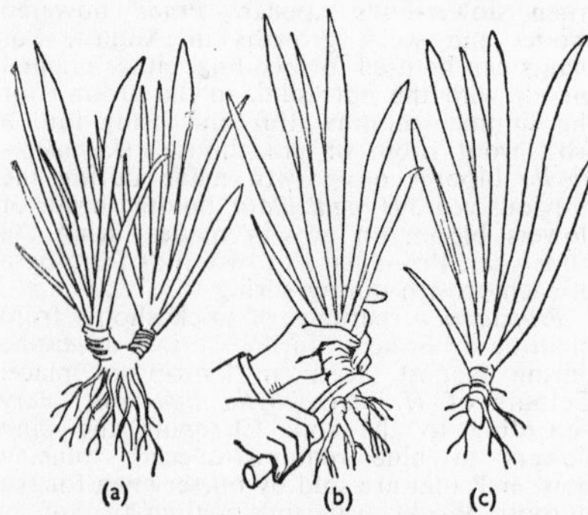

Fig. 38. Divide an iris: (a) *with a central cut; trim off old rhizomes* (b); *ready for planting* (c).

selection from a reliable modern list: White City, white; Aline, pale blue; Mrs. J. L. Gibson, deep violet-blue; Amigo, white and purple; Depute Nomblot, reddish-brown; Sweet Lavender, soft rosy-lavender; Shot Silk, rosy-pink; Golden Hind, golden yellow; Iris King, yellow and brown.

IVY. *Hedera helix.* (Araliaceae.) Hardy climbing evergreen that will make dense covers over old tree stumps, house walls or railings. *Soil:* will grow anywhere, especially on poor ground. Colour of variegated varieties better on poor soil. Plant in spring. *Propagation:* root-cuttings in summer. Cut weak cuttings to ground in first year.

IXIA. African Corn Lily. (Iridaceae.) Half-hardy bulbs. *Soil:* light, sandy. *Plant* annually in September, in sunny, well-drained borders, 4 in. deep and 2 in. apart. Pot plants can be kept in cold pits until roots have formed, and then brought into the greenhouse. *Propagation:* seeds, offsets. There are many named varieties in red, pink, cream or white, and one green (*I. viridiflora*).

JACOBINIA. (Acanthaceae.) Flowering stove plants from Mexico and Brazil. *Soil:* equal parts peat, loam, leaf-mould and sand. *Propagation:* cuttings. **Best to grow :** *J. carnea*, 4 ft., flesh-pink, August.

JAPONICA. See CYDONIA.

JASMINE. *Jasminum.* (Oleaceae.) Tender and hardy climbers and shrubs. Hardy species need ordinary rich loam, and are easily cultivated. Plant from October–March against south or west walls, or in well-drained borders. After flowering prune moderately, removing flowered shoots. *Propagation:* cuttings, layers. **Best to grow:** *J. nudiflorum*, yellow, winter-flowering, excellent in towns against walls or in the open. *J. officinale*, the common, fragrant white jasmine. *J. Stephanense*, a climber with pale pink flowers and glossy black fruits. All hardy and need support.

JUDAS-TREE. See CERCIS.

JUGLANS. See WALNUT.

JUNIPER. See CONIFERS.

KAINIT. See FERTILIZER CHART.

KALE. See BORECOLE.

KELP. Seaweed used as a manure, especially for early potatoes.

KENTISH COBS. Cobnuts. See NUTS.

KERRIA. (Rosaceae.) Deciduous hardy shrub bearing deep yellow blossoms in spring and early summer on arching branches. *Soil:* ordinary. Plant against south or west fences or in shrubberies. *Prune* in May or June by removing old or weak shoots. *Propagation:* cuttings, division. **Best to grow:** *K. japonica*, 6 ft.–10 ft., and its varieties *flore pleno* (double), *variegata* (silver variegated), *variegata aurea* (golden variegated).

KNIPHOFIA. Red-hot Poker. (Liliaceae.) Tall, handsome, herbaceous perennials, making an outstanding show in summer. *Soil:* ordinary rich. *Plant* in November or April, in well-drained sunny positions. Water freely in summer and mulch in April. Protect crown in winter by tying leaves together or covering with straw. *Propagation:* seeds, division, suckers. **Best to grow:** garden hybrids such as The Rocket, 6 ft., terra cotta-scarlet; June Glory, 4 ft., scarlet; Express, 4 ft., salmon-orange; C. K. Butler, 5 ft., yellow and light red.

KOCHIA. *Scoparia.* Summer Cypress. (Chenopodiaceae.) Pretty-foliaged half-hardy annual; pale green, bushy, column of finely cut leaves, turning brilliant crimson in autumn. Used for summer bedding. *Propagation:* sow seeds in cold frame in April; transplant 2 ft. apart in June.

Fig. 39. Kohl-rabi, an uncommon vegetable.

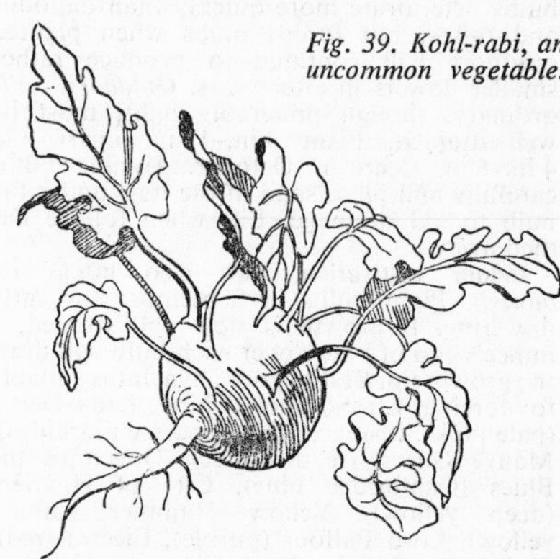

KOHL-RABI. *Brassica.* (Cruciferae.) Turnip-like vegetable with leaves growing from the side (Fig. 39). When sliced and fried make pleasant variation as a winter vegetable. Grow as turnips in drills 18 in. apart. Thin to 1 ft. apart.

LABELS. These can be made of metal or wood. For permanent work the aluminium kind is durable if marked with a lead pencil and then varnished. Wooden labels are best painted to preserve the wood, and make a clean foundation for writing. Smear white paint on with a rag, and rub well in. Mark labels clearly, giving date of sowing, potting, etc. Always keep to one method of labelling pots and boxes.

LABURNUM. (Leguminosae.) Favourite spring-flowering deciduous trees. The branches, laden with golden blossoms, can be trained over pergolas and arches. Specimen trees are useful in shrubberies. *Soil:* ordinary. Plant in October or March, and prune out dead or weak wood directly after flowering. *Propagation:* seed sown outdoors in spring; grafting; suckers. **Best to grow:** *L. vulgare* (common laburnum), 20 ft.–30 ft., and its varieties *pendulum* (weeping), *aureum* (golden-leaved) and its fine long-flowered hybrids *Vossi* and *Watereri. C. alpinum* is a late-flowering species.

LACHENALIA. Cape Cowslip. (Liliaceae.) Deciduous greenhouse bulbous plant with attractive spike of yellow and orange flowers. Plant from five to seven bulbs in a 5-in. pot of three parts loam, leaf-mould and sand in August. Keep pots in cold frame till November, bring into greenhouse and place in a sunny spot. Give liquid manure when buds appear. After flowering dry off bulbs and re-pot annually. *Propagation:* offsets. There are many named varieties.

LANTANA. (Verbenaceae.) Evergreen tender and half-hardy flowering shrub. *Soil:* two parts loam, one part peat, leaf-mould or decayed manure, sand and charcoal. Keep pots in light airy places in greenhouse. Outdoors choose sunny dry position, plant in June and return to greenhouse for winter. *Prune* to shape in February. *Propagation:* cuttings in autumn in sandy peat; seeds sown in 80 deg. in spring.

LARCH. See CONIFERS.

LARKSPUR. (Ranunculaceae.) These annual *Delphiniums* grow to about 3 ft. and are easily raised from seed sown outdoors in spring, or in well-drained soil in September. Can be transplanted from boxes sown under glass in March. Larkspurs make admirable indoor winter decoration if sown in boxes or cold frame in autumn and potted into a compost of loam, leaf-mould and sand. Water moderately and carefully. Colours various. See also DELPHINIUM.

LAUREL. See PRUNUS.

LAURUS. See BAY.

LAVANDULA. Lavender. (Labiatae.) Favourite hardy evergreen shrub. Fragrant flowers are much favoured for drying and distilling for perfume. Plant 1 ft. apart in light soil during March or September. Warm dry, sunny positions are best. *Prune* into shape in March. Harvest blooms when just out, dry slowly and store in a dry place. *Propagation:* seeds sown outdoors in April; soft wood cuttings with or without a heel in September in a frame or under a cloche. **Best to grow:** *L. Spica nana* and *L. Spica nana alba* are dwarf varieties, whilst Grappenhall is giant.

LAVATERA. Mallow. (Malvaceae.) Showy hardy annuals and shrubs. Sow annuals in borders in September or April. Plant shrubs in June in warm border. *Propagation:* seeds, cuttings. *L. trimestris* is a good annual.

LAWNS. Lawns are an old and great attraction of English gardens. To make a lawn, turves can be laid brick-fashion, which though giving a quick result is expensive and rarely free from weeds; otherwise grass seed is sown. Preparations for either method are similar and require much care. The ground must be deeply dug in autumn and left to winter weathering. If soil is too heavy, drain site by laying pipes or coke breeze. Well-rotted manure must always be dug in. The area must be levelled, and undulations smoothed, whilst the actual soil surface must be finely raked. Choose a reliable seed, and broadcast on a calm day in April or late August. Rake seed in, and protect against birds; water in if soil is very dry. Roll lightly two or three times when seedlings are 2 in.–3 in. high. Mow lawn with knives set fairly high. Remove all weeds as they appear. Never roll in worm-casts, but scatter first. Occasional applications of lawn sand from April to June will help growth of grass. Moss grows on acid lawns; dressings of sulphate of iron at $\frac{1}{4}$–$\frac{1}{2}$ oz. to the square yard, mixed with a carrier, or light dressings of lime will check growth, but encourage worms and weeds.

LEEK. *Allium Porrum.* (Liliaceae.) Useful winter vegetable. It is very hardy, and is comparatively free from pests and diseases. Prepare ground well, dig deeply and add plenty of manure. (See Fig. 40.) Earth up to

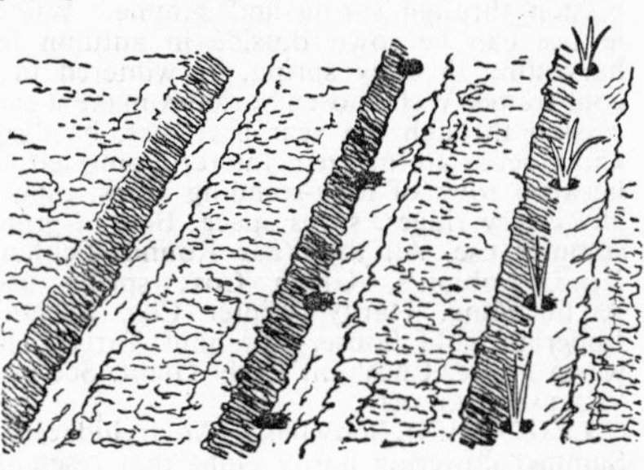

Fig. 40. Planting leeks. Draw a line with a hoe and make holes with a dibber 9 in. apart. Drop a leek into each hole, water well, but do not fill in with soil; let rain gradually wash it in.

blanch leaves. Leave in ground until required for use. Liquid manure should be given weekly. See also VEGETABLE CHART.

LEONTOPODIUM. Edelweiss. (Compositae.) Hardy, silvery-haired perennial that grows in exposed sunny rockeries (Fig. 41.) Protect plants with a sheet of glass during autumn and winter. *Soil:* well-drained, sandy. Cut flowers in August for drying. *Propagation:* seed, division. **Best to grow:** *L. alpinum*, 3 in.–6 in., yellow, May–July.

LEPTOSPERMUM. (Myrtaceae.) Small-leaved evergreen shrub. Half-hardy and early flowering. Needs protection of south wall, except in very warm sheltered gardens. *Soil:* gravelly loam and peat; dislikes chalk soils. *Propagation:* seeds, cuttings. **Best to grow:** *L. scoparium*, 4 ft.–6 ft., white; and its carmine-red variety, Nichollii.

LEPTOSYNE. (Compositae.) Yellow-flowering annuals and perennials. The annuals are useful for cut flowers, are one of the quickest plants to come into bloom, taking only five weeks from seed sown outside in spring. Divide perennials to increase them.

Fig. 41. Leontopodium or edelweiss.

LETTUCE. Valuable salad crop that can be grown outdoors throughout the year. Any soil will grow lettuce, though rich, well-prepared ground is preferable. Sow for succession through spring and summer. Winter lettuce can be sown outside in autumn for harvesting in early spring, or wintered in a cold frame. Well-chosen varieties make a succession through the year if frames, hot-beds and cloches are utilized. Intercropping lettuce between rows of long-standing crops, especially celery ridges, saves space. **Best to grow:** summer use, All the Year Round, Feltham King, Lobjoit's, Green Cos; spring use, Arctic King, Hardy Winter Cos, Sutton's Imperial; cold house, Cheshunt Early Ball; warm house, Cheshunt Early Giant. See also VEGETABLE CHART.

LEUCOJUM. Snowflake. (Amaryllidaceae.) Summer-flowering hardy bulbs that resemble snowdrops. Suitable for borders or naturalizing in grass. Plant bulbs 4 in. deep and 4 in. apart from August to November. Usually flower second year and need only be replanted every five to eight years. *Propagation:* offsets. **Best to grow:** *L. aestivum*, 1 ft., white, May, in sun or shade in borders or woodlands; *L. vernum*, 9 in. white, February, in shady borders or rockeries.

LIGUSTRUM. Privet. (Oleaceae.) Evergreen and deciduous hardy shrubs for hedges, shrubberies or under trees. White flowers and yellow or black berries, and in some varieties variegated leaves. *Prune* evergreens in April and others in autumn. *Propagation:* seed sown in November; cuttings planted outdoors in October and November. For hedges plant 6 in.–9 in. apart from October to April. Trim in June and July. See also HEDGES.

LILAC. *Syringa.* (Oleaceae.) Glorious spring-flowering hardy shrubs that are great favourites for sunny positions. They will grow in any garden soil. Give water or liquid manure in summer to plants on poor soil. *Prune* moderately and remove flowered shoots in June. *Propagation:* cuttings of ripe shoots in August; seed sown outdoors in autumn. Specimen trees are trained as a single stem by removing flower buds and lower buds at early stages. There are many fine varieties.

LILIES. *Lilium.* (Liliaceae.) A vast family of beautiful hardy and half-hardy bulbous plants. These plants are classified according to their habit as lime-lovers or haters, and the flower-shape, whether cupped, trumpet or reflexed. Lilies are best planted in autumn, in soil that has been well prepared and has had leaf-mould dug in. Good drainage is essential. For most types choose partially shaded sites sheltered from wind and sun. Plant bulbs 4 in. deep except for stem-rooting species like *L. auratum*, *L. Henryi* and *L. sulphureum*, which need at least 6 in. of soil over the bulb. Sand placed under each bulb will help drainage, though lilies love moisture. Swamp-lilies are usually planted on an inverted flower pot and surrounded with sand, since only the roots penetrate the mud. Mulch in April with leaf-mould, avoiding fresh manure; apply liquid manure when plants are in flower, and water in very dry weather. Transplant only when they are overcrowded or unhealthy. *Under glass* bulbs are planted singly from September to March in pots of good loam, leaf-mould and sand. Add compost as growth progresses. May be wintered in cold-frame or in the greenhouse. *Propagation:* offsets, spring-sown seed. Cover compost with sand to prevent moss growing. Transplant to boxes or frames. Bulb-scales produce bulbils in their axils when inserted in sandy loam. **Best to grow:** lilies for shade, *Henryi*, *Hansoni*, *Willmottiae*, *Wardii*; lilies for sun, *auratum*, *bulbiferum*, *candidum*, *chalcedonicum*; swamp lilies, *canadense*, *Grayi*, *Parryi*, *paradalinum* (the first three are difficult to grow); for wild garden, *Martagon*, *regale*, *giganteum*, *rubellum*; for rock garden, *dauricum*, *pomponium*, *concolor*. *L. candidum* and *L. Martagon* will grow on most soils. Lilies tolerant of lime, *candidum*, *Henryi*, *Martagon*, *concolor*.

LILY OF THE VALLEY. *Convallaria.* (Liliaceae.) Favourite sweet-smelling hardy perennial. Grows best in shady beds, borders, beneath walls or fences where plants have plenty of root-run. *Soil:* outdoors, use loam, leaf-mould and sand. Plant crowns 2 in.–3 in. apart just below the surface, September–October. Mulch annually in February, apply liquid manure from May to September, and replant beds every four years. A section of the bed can be redone every year. For pots, use equal parts loam, leaf-mould and sand. Plant from eight to twelve crowns per 4½-in. pot and keep in a cold frame until they are brought into the greenhouse in January. **Best to grow:** *C. majalis*, 6 in.; *C. majalis rosea* (tinged with pink); Fortin's Giant (large flowers).

LILIUM. See LILIES.

LIME. Applications of lime to the soil at regular intervals have many beneficial effects. The texture of heavy soils is improved and a finer tilth and better drainage result, and the soil is easier to work. Organic matter undergoes more rapid decomposition on alkaline soils, as the activity of the soil-microbes is increased. This means that more plant food is available. Acid soils are detrimental, and, though they often contain sufficient plant-foods, half of these are insoluble and cannot be assimilated by the plant under acid conditions. Most garden soils need regular applications of lime, about 2 oz.–4 oz. per square yard before digging.

LINDEN. *Tilia platyphyllos.* Lime tree. (Tiliaceae.) Hardy deciduous trees with fragrant flowers good for bees. Suitable for sunny avenues or parks, or adapted for training over arches or lining a shady walk. *Soil:* moist and rich. *Propagation:* seeds. *Prune:* thin out branches.

LINARIA. Toadflax. (Scrophulariaceae.) Hardy annuals and perennials for moist rich soils in borders and rockeries. *Propagation:* seeds, division for perennials in spring. **Best to grow:** *L. dalmatica*, 3 ft., yellow, perennial. Varieties of *L. maroccana*, 1 ft., colour various, annual.

LIPPIA. *L. citriodora.* (Verbenaceae.) Greenhouse deciduous shrub grown for its lemon-scented leaves. *Soil:* loam, leaf-mould and sand. *Prune* shoots in February to within an inch of the base. Re-pot in March or plant near a sheltered south wall. *Propagation:* cuttings of young shoots in warm frame.

LIRIODENDRON. Tulip tree. (Magnoliaceae.) A handsome, hardy, deciduous tree bearing fragrant, greenish, tulip-like flowers (Fig. 42). *Soil:* Well-drained deep loam. *Plant:* from November to May in a sheltered sunny position. Makes fine specimen tree.

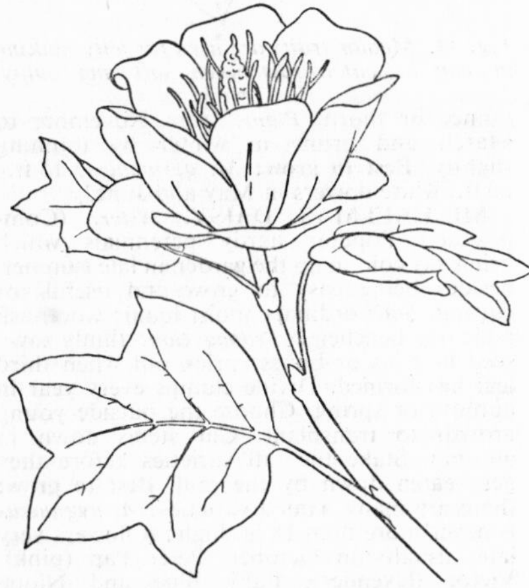

Fig. 42. Flower of the tulip tree.

Propagation: Seed sown outdoors in moist sandy loam. Layering in September. **Best to grow:** *L. tulipifera*, 70 ft.–150 ft., flowers June–July.

LOBELIA. (Campanulaceae.) Bright-flowered hardy and half-hardy perennials. Used for edging, summer bedding, rockeries or borders. *Soil:* moist, rich loam. Those wintered outdoors need protection, though most species are best lifted and placed in a cold frame for winter. *Propagation:* cuttings from shoots taken from plants brought into heat over winter; seeds sown in March in a sandy loam. **Best to grow:** *L. Erinus* and varieties, blue, for bedding. *L. cardinalis*, *L. fulgens* and varieties, 2 ft., scarlet or pink, for borders.

LONDON PRIDE. See SAXIFRAGE.

LONICERA. Honeysuckle. (Caprifoliaceae.) Evergreen or deciduous, hardy and half-hardy shrubs. Fragrant twining species are favourite plants for fences, walls and arbours. Evergreens need protection of south or west walls; deciduous species will grow anywhere. *Plant* in winter, and mulch in March or April. Water during dry weather. *Prune* shoots of previous year's growth during February. *Propagation:* seeds, cuttings, layers. **Best to grow:** *L. Tellmanniana*, 10 ft., deep yellow; *L. japonica Halliana*, 10 ft., cream; *L. sempervirens*, 10 ft., scarlet, evergreen.

LUPIN. *Lupinus.* (Leguminosae.) Both annuals and perennials are grown, the latter being popular in most herbaceous borders. Most soils are suitable, in sun or shade, and cultivation is quite easy. Perennials need mulching in April; they are comparatively short-lived but give glorious colour displays in early summer. *Propagation:* seeds, division of strong clumps. **Best to grow:** modern named hybrids of *L. polyphyllus;* Russell lupins are exceptionally brilliant. *L. arboreus* (tree lupin) has yellow or white flowers.

LYCHNIS. Campion. (Caryophyllaceae.) Hardy annuals and perennials for sunny beds and borders. *Soil:* ordinary. *Propagation:* seeds sown in April outdoors, division for perennials. **Best to grow:** *L. chalcedonica*, 3 ft., scarlet; *L. Flos-jovis*, 18 in., magenta.

LYTHRUM. Purple Loose-strife. (Lythraceae.) Hardy herbaceous and shrubby perennials, suitable for borders or waterside. *Soil:* moist. Water freely in dry weather. *Propagation:* division.

MAGNOLIA. (Magnoliaceae.) Handsome spring-flowering trees. Hardy deciduous and evergreen plants that produce magnificent waxy blooms (Fig. 43). Plant in a sheltered position on lawns and in borders. Evergreens need the protection of a south or west wall. *Soil:* ordinary, preferably a deep sandy loam. Plant in spring, choosing a site sheltered from

Fig. 43. Magnolia, spring-flowering shrub.

the early morning sun. *Prune* straggling shoots of evergreens in spring, deciduous species after flowering. *Propagation:* seeds sown singly under glass directly they are gathered, though they may not germinate for a year or longer after sowing; layers in autumn for common species; grafting for choicer forms. Protect evergreens during severe winters, and never move these plants in the dormant state, but when the buds are moving in spring. **Best to grow:** Deciduous, *M. Soulangeana*, 7 ft.–15 ft., white and purple; *M. stellata*, 10 ft.–15 ft., white, semi-double-flowered; *M. conspicua*, 30 ft.–45 ft., white; *M. parviflora*, 7 ft.–15 ft., white, rosy-crimson centre. Evergreen, *M. grandiflora*, 15 ft.–20 ft., white.

MALCOLMIA. Virginia Stock. (Cruciferae.) Hardy annual for sowing outdoors in September or spring, where plants are to flower. Suitable for rockeries, banks or broadcast for a massed border. *Soil:* ordinary. *Propagation:* seed sown evenly and thinly, thinned out to 3 in. apart.

MALVA. Mallow. (Malvaceae.) Hardy border annuals and perennials, with scented flowers in summer. *Soil:* ordinary. *Propagation:* seeds, division of perennials. **Best to grow:** *M. Alcea*, 4 ft., rose (perennial); *M. moschata*, 2 ft., rose (perennial).

MAPLE. *Acer.* (Aceraceae.) Attractive trees and shrubs with ornamental, simple or delicately feathered leaves. *Soil:* well-drained loams except for the scarlet maple, which thrives on damp soils.

MARGUERITE. See CHRYSANTHEMUM.

MARIGOLD. *Calendula.* (Compositae.) Hardy annuals, known as Scotch pot marigolds, flourish anywhere and give orange blooms throughout the summer. Sow outdoors in flowering positions. The half-hardy French and African marigolds (*Tagetes*) must be sown under glass in March or April, and transplanted out in May in ordinary soil.

MARROW, vegetable. See PUMPKIN.

MECONOPSIS. Himalayan Poppy. (Papaveraceae.) Lovely hardy biennials and perennials for half-shaded positions that are not too dry. *Soil:* light, rich soil that is preferably gritty. Plant in spring and give liquid manure during the flowering season. *Propagation:* divide perennials in March or sow seeds then in a cold frame. **Best to grow:** *M. cambrica*, 2 ft., orange, May (perennial); *M. betonicifolia*, 3 ft., blue, June (perennial); *M. nepalensis*, 6 ft., blue or purple, June (biennial).

MEDLAR. See MESPILUS.

MESEMBRYANTHEMUM. Ice Plant. (Ficoideae.) Numerous annuals and perennials with bright flowers. Many are evergreen and trailing fleshy plants. *Soil:* sandy loam, with leaf-mould and lime. Winter tender species under glass, and plant out in June. *Propagation:* heel cuttings dried in the sun, from March to September; seeds sown in spring under glass for tender species, and outdoors in April for hardy types. **Best to grow:** *M. criniflorum*, 6 in., colours various (annual); *M. tricolorum*, 3 in., red and yellow (annual); *M. edule*, prostrate, yellow (perennial).

MESPILUS. Medlar. (Rosaceae.) Hardy deciduous tree cultivated for its brown fruits (Fig. 44). Fruits are harvested in late autumn for jelly-making. *Soil:* deep ordinary loam. Prefers a sunny position and does well in shrubberies or as specimen tree. *Propagation:* seeds sown in March, or grafted on to pear, quince or thorn. *Plant:* from November to March and prune in winter by thinning slightly. **Best to grow:** *M. germanica*, 15 ft.–20 ft., white flowers in May and June.

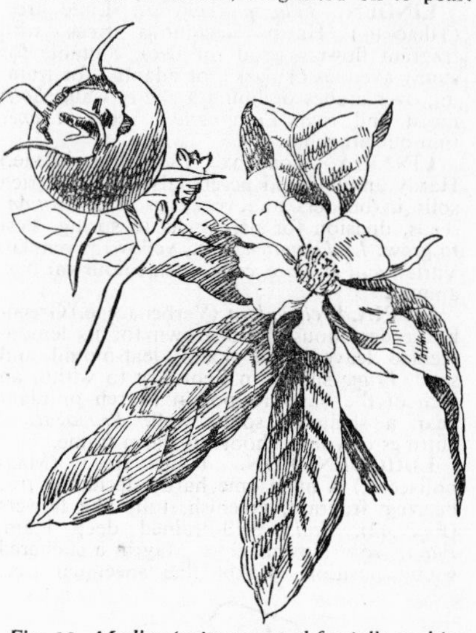

Fig. 44. Medlar fruits are used for jelly-making or can be eaten raw when soft and pulpy.

MICHAELMAS DAISY. *Aster.* (Compositae.) Popular hardy perennials which bring gay colours to the garden in late summer, besides being easy to grow and useful for cutting. *Soil:* ordinary moist loam; wood-ash added is beneficial. *Propagation:* thinly sown seed in pans or boxes; prick out when third leaf has formed. Divide clumps every year in autumn or spring. Choose the outside young growth to transplant. Cut stems down in autumn. Stake the tall varieties before they get beaten down by the rain. **Best to grow:** there are many named varieties: *A. pygmaeus* is never more than 18 in. high; it flowers very late, usually in October. Peter Pan (pink), Victor (lavender), Baby Blue and Niobe (white) are named varieties. *A. Novae Angliae* is tall with thin petals, and flowers from August to September. Good varieties are Barr's Violet, Barr's Pink and S. T. Wright (purple). *A. Novi-Belgii*, the parent of the best known type, grows 3 ft., and flowers August–September. Varieties include Little Blue Boy, Mrs. George Munro (white), and Red Rover (crimson), Blue Jacket, Climax (lavender).

MIGNONETTE. *Reseda odorata.* (Resedaceae.) Deliciously perfumed hardy perennial, often grown as an annual. *Soil:* ordinary, with lime rubble. It grows well on chalk soils. Under glass use two parts loam, one part manure and a little sand. *Propagation:* seeds sown outdoors in spring; thin to 12 in. apart. There are several named varieties.

MIMOSA. See ACACIA.

MINT. *Mentha viridis.* (Labiatae.) Hardy perennial with aromatic foliage. Thrives best in damp, cool ordinary soil. Roots can be laid thinly in 3-in.-wide drills 12 in. apart, or cuttings planted 3 in. apart in rows 12 in. apart to make a new bed. Water in dry weather. Renew beds regularly.

MISTLETOE. *Viscum album.* (Loranthaceae.) An evergreen semi-parasite found on apple, hawthorn, poplar, lime, maple, mountain ash, cedar and oak. To grow, cut a notch in the bark on the underside of a branch. Press in a ripe berry in March or late winter. Choose apple or hawthorn for preference; on oak it spreads very slowly.

MONKSHOOD. *Aconitum.* (Ranunculaceae.) Poisonous-rooted hardy perennials. They grow in cool, shady borders in ordinary soil 2 ft.–6 ft. high; flowers hooded, and usually blue-purple. *Propagation:* divide roots carefully owing to their poisonous nature; seeds sown outdoors in April. **Best to grow:** *A. Napellus,* 4 ft.–5 ft., June; *A. Wilsonii,* 4 ft., July; *A. Fischeri,* 5 ft., July.

MORUS. Mulberry. (Urticaceae.) Hardy deciduous trees bearing white, red or black berries that have long been cultivated. *Plant* November-March in light, deep, moist soil. Select a sunny position, sheltered from the north. On heavy soils, fruit often does not ripen. Gather fruit from August onwards, when it is ready to drop. *Propagation:* seed sown in light sandy soils in May; layers in spring. The common mulberry is *Morus nigra.*

MULBERRY. See MORUS.

MULLEIN. *Verbascum.* (Scrophulariaceae.) Easily grown hardy biennials and perennials for sunny spots. Imposing plants varying from 2 ft.–6 ft., requiring ordinary garden soil. *Propagation:* seeds, division.

MUSCARI. See GRAPE HYACINTH.

MUSHROOMS. *Psalliota* (*Agaricus*) *campestris.* This edible fungus is best grown on prepared beds (Fig. 45) in cellars, sheds, outhouses or frames, which can be kept quite dark and the temperature controlled. Cool, damp and even temperatures are essential, and outdoor beds are only satisfactory in late summer or early autumn.

Fresh horse manure free from shavings is the ideal material for preparing the beds. Stack this outside, and turn after a week; continue to turn daily for a further week, allowing the first violent heat to subside. The manure must decay evenly; water dry parts if necessary. When ready it should smell sweet, and be a dark brown colour. To prepare the bed, build the manure into a ridge-shaped heap outdoors, and a flat heap indoors, treading it down layer by layer. For boxes, make 9 in.–12 in. deep, for indoor beds 8 in.–12 in. deep and 2 ft.–3 ft. wide; outdoor beds 2½ ft. high and 3 ft. wide. Plunge a soil thermometer into the beds, and when the temperature falls to 70 deg. insert sterilized mushroom spawn in small pieces at intervals of 10 in. all over the bed. Cover the beds with 6 in. of straw (12 in. outdoors). After two or three weeks scrape away a little of the manure to see if the spawn is "running" (there should be white filament-like growths penetrating the bed); if so, the bed is ready for casing. This is done by removing straw and covering the manure evenly with a 1-in. layer of loam, beaten smooth with the back of a spade. Replace clean dry straw to keep the bed at an even temperature. Bearing commences from six to eight weeks after spawning. Gather mushrooms by pulling, never by cutting. Spawn can be pressed into loosened soil under grass turf during June.

Fig. 45. Pulling mushrooms from a bed of manure and straw. Mushrooms should never be cut.

MUSK. *Mimulus.* (Scrophulariaceae.) Brightly-coloured hardy annuals and perennials. Plant in moist shady borders in March–May on ordinary soil. *Propagation:* seeds, cuttings, division for perennials.

MUSTARD. *Sinapis alba.* (Cruciferae.) Often dug in as green manure; also used with cress in salads. Treat as cress, sowing seed three days after the cress. See also GREEN MANURING, and CRESS, LAND.

MYRICA. Bog Myrtle. (Myricaceae.) Hardy fragrant-leaved shrubs, deciduous and evergreen. *Soil:* moist, sandy peat. *Propagation:* autumn-sown seeds outdoors, layers or suckers in autumn. **Best to grow:** *M. Gale,* 4 ft., brown catkins in February.

MYRTUS. Myrtle. (Myrtaceae.) Beautiful fragrant-flowered evergreens with aromatic leaves, greenhouse and half-hardy shrubs, of which the latter will grow in sheltered, well-drained sunny borders protected by south or south-west walls. These need added protection of mats or straw in severe weather. Will also grow in tubs. *Soil:* ordinary. *Propagation:* softwood cuttings in heat during the summer. **Best to grow:** *M. communis*, 6 ft., white, July; *M. Luma*, 3 ft., for very sheltered places; *M. Ugni*, 4 ft., white, May, dark red, edible berries. Hardy in Britain only in the south and west.

NAPHTHALENE. It is used as a soil-fumigant scattered and dug into the ground at from 3 oz.–6 oz. per square yard, in autumn and winter. As an evaporating fumigant in glasshouses against thrips and red spider on carnation, use 4 oz.–6 oz. of grade 16 to every 1,000 cu. ft. of glasshouse space. As deterrent against carrot, cabbage and onion fly, sprinkle 1 oz.–2 oz. per square yard from April to July.

NARCISSUS. Daffodil. Jonquil. (Amaryllidaceae.) A large and lovely genus including tiny rock-garden species 3 in.–4 in. high and the trumpet daffodils, pheasant-eye and jonquils. They will grow on most soils, but shelter from the wind is the main requirement; good drainage and early planting in August and September are also essential, and whether planted in shrubberies, borders or naturalized in grass (for which this genus is especially suitable) the bulbs can remain undisturbed until they become overcrowded. Always let foliage die down before lifting. See also general information under BULBS. **Best to grow:** long yellow trumpets, King Alfred; Emperor. Medium cupped, Helios; Croesus; Lady Diana Manners. Short-cupped varieties, Firetail; Horace. Polyanthus type, Paper White; Soleil d'Or. For rockeries, *N. Bulbocodium* (hoop-petticoat); *N. cyclamineus* (like a cyclamen); *N. juncifolius.*

NASTURTIUM. *Tropaeolum majus.* (Geraniaceae.) The hardy annuals that we know as nasturtiums are useful climbing favourites, that will clothe arches, fences, window-boxes and waste patches of ground. They flourish on any soil, and will grow quickly from seed sown outdoors in spring. Modern hybrids have a fine range of colour. The Golden Gleam hybrids are especially showy.

NEMOPHILA. (Hydrophyllaceae.) Hardy annuals which make showy edging plants for borders and beds. *Soil:* ordinary. *Propagation:* seeds sown outside March–April, or August–September for spring flowering. Thin to 6 in. apart. **Best to grow:** *N. insignis*, 6 in., blue.

NERINE. Guernsey Lily. (Amaryllidaceae.) Mostly South African greenhouse bulbs. One species will grow in well-drained, sunny borders, protected by a south wall. Plant 2 in.–3 in. deep in August; top-dress annually during August. Lift and replant every three to five years. Protect with dry litter in winter. Pot culture requires two parts sandy loam, one part decayed cow manure or leaf-mould and one part sand. Pot August–November and keep in a cool house September–May. During summer keep in a cold frame. In summer keep dry. *Propagation:* offsets. **Best to grow:** many beautiful named varieties are suitable for pot-culture; *N. Bowdenii* for the border, 18 in., bright pink, September–October.

NERIUM. Oleander. (Apocynaceae.) Fragrant-flowered, greenhouse evergreen shrub. In spring pot in compost as for nerine. *Prune* after flowering. Requires minimum temperature of 45 deg. from September to March. *Propagation:* cuttings. There are many varieties in red, pink, or white.

NICOTIANA. Tobacco Plant. (Solanaceae.) Delightfully scented half-hardy annuals. Grows best in warm sheltered position from seed sown under glass in February and transplanted outdoors. Soot round the plants deters slugs. Water in dry weather. Grown also as pot-plants. **Best to grow:** varieties of *N. affinis*, 3 ft., purple, rose or white.

NIGELLA. Love-in-a-mist. (Ranunculaceae.) Favourite hardy annual with pretty blue flowers. *Soil:* ordinary. *Propagation:* sow outdoors March–April or autumn in lines or masses; thin to 6 in. apart. Excellent flowers, of which Miss Jekyll is a popular variety of *N. damascena.*

NIGHT-SCENTED STOCK. *Matthiola bicornis.* (Cruciferae.) Hardy annual for ordinary soil. Sow in borders, beds or any odd corners in April. Flowers open at night, giving out a delightful perfume.

NUTS. Certain nuts are comparatively easy to grow, especially the hazel and filbert, which thrive on a poor soil where fruit-cultivation is difficult. Cobnuts and filberts are varieties of the common English hazelnut and are grown as bush-trees planted 15 ft. apart. Walnuts, chestnuts and almonds will fruit in most seasons. *Soil:* dig soil deeply, 2 ft.–3 ft., adding manure and lime. Give dressings of lime occasionally in later years. Plant during dormant season and stake trees immediately.

NYMPHAEA. Water Lilies. See WATER PLANTS.

OAK. *Quercus.* (Cupuliferae.) Deciduous and evergreen trees and shrubs, of which there are many species. They make handsome trees, with good foliage, and are valuable for their timber. *Soil:* deep, rich loam, preferably moist in woodlands, deep soil over chalk. Plant evergreens in September or April, deciduous species from October to February. *Propagation:* seed, grafting. Sow acorns when they ripen in autumn or store in sand until March. Sow 2 in. deep and transplant when a year old. Plant in permanent site when three or four years old. Gradual removal of lower branches during growth will produce shapely trees.

OENOTHERA. See EVENING PRIMROSE.

OLEANDER. See NERIUM.

OLEARIA. Daisy Bush. (Compositae.) Hardy and half-hardy evergreen shrubs, bearing countless daisy-like flowers in summer. *Soil:* sandy, lime-free loam. Plant in sunny sheltered borders, preferably against walls for protection. Cover plants during a severe winter. *Propagation:* cuttings.

ONION. *Allium cepa.* (Liliaceae.) A most valuable vegetable to store for winter use, or to use green in salads. Prepare ground deeply in early autumn; work in manure, wood-ashes and lime. Dress ground when sowing with sulphate of potash at 1 oz. per square yard. Before sowing or transplanting tread ground

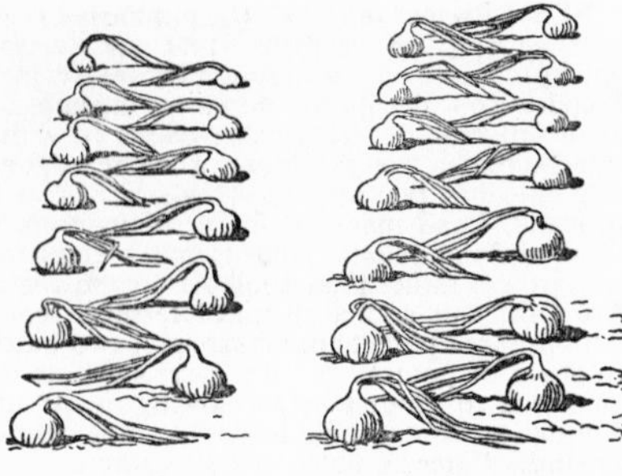

Fig. 46. To hasten the ripening of onions, bend over the tops in late summer.

firmly, and work up a fine tilth, 2 in.–3 in. deep. In mid-August, bend onion tops down to speed ripening (Fig. 46) a fortnight before harvesting, which must be done in fine weather. Dry off bulbs carefully before storing in ropes or bunches (Fig. 47), or on trays of

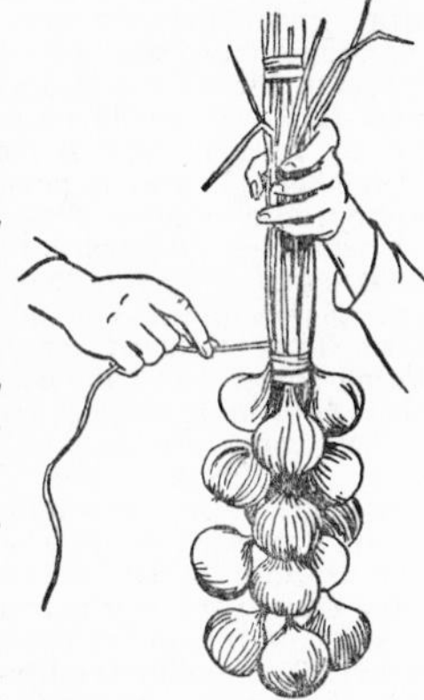

Fig. 47. Stringing onions for storage. Starting at the bottom, bind the neck of each onion on to a rope or stick. If possible arrange the onions in a spiral fashion, as they pack closer together in this way. Hang in a dry shed or room.

slatting or netting. Keep in a frost-proof place. See also VEGETABLE CHART.

ONION FLY. See PEST CHART.

ONION SETS can be used if onion fly is bad or seeds difficult to raise. Press the bulbs into the soil half their own depth, at 9 in. apart in March, and treat as onion seedlings.

ORANGE, Mock. See PHILADELPHUS.

ORCHIDS. An enormous family of plants, many of which have very handsome flowers. Some are suitable for growing in the open garden, but it would not be possible to give an account here of the cultivation of all the varieties available. We give a brief outline of conditions suitable for some of the popular types grown. The novice should start with one or two of the easier cool-house species, such as *Cypripedium insigne* and *Odontoglossum crispum.*

Warm-house orchids: these require a minimum night temperature of 65 deg. to 70 deg., with day temperatures of 70 deg. and over. Well-chopped fibre and sphagnum moss should be packed round the roots. *Orchids for intermediate house:* minimum night temperature in winter is 60 deg., while 65 deg. to 70 deg. is the usual summer night temperature. Osmunda fibre and sphagnum moss are used for potting. *Cool-house orchids:* night temperatures are never less than 45 deg. in winter and 60 deg. in summer; daytime 60 deg. to 70 deg. in summer; pot in fibre and moss. *Hardy terrestrial orchids:* a few species, such as *Orchis maculata*, are easily cultivated in ordinary garden soil. Suitable mainly for rockeries and water gardens, or in sunny well-drained borders. *Resting-period:* after flowering, most orchids require a resting-period. Their flowering seasons vary, but generally speaking most greenhouse orchids are allowed to rest during the winter and are re-potted in February.

ORIGANUM. Marjoram. See HERB GARDEN.

ORNITHOGALUM. Star of Bethlehem. (Liliaceae.) Tender and hardy bulbs. Plant outdoors in August or November, small bulbs 3 in. deep and larger ones 4 in.–6 in. deep and 3 in. apart, in sandy soil. Pot-plants require two parts sandy loam to one part leaf-mould, peat and sand. *Propagation:* offsets; seeds. **Best to grow:** *O. umbellatum*, 6 in., white, April; *O. nutans*, 1 ft., green and white, May.

OSMUNDA. *O. regalis.* The hardy Royal Fern. (Filices.) Suitable for moist positions on pond margins. Water copiously unless growing on the water's edge. The fibre is used for potting orchids and other greenhouse plants. See also FERNS.

OXALIS. Wood Sorrel. (Geraniaceae.) Tender annuals, greenhouse and half-hardy perennials. *Soil:* sandy loam for hardy species in warm borders or rockeries; loam, peat and leaf-mould under glass. *Propagation:* seeds, division. **Best to grow:** *O. floribunda*, 9 in., rose-pink, May; *O. enneaphylla*, 4 in., white or pale rose, for cold greenhouse.

PAEONY. *Paeonia.* (Ranunculaceae.) Majestic-flowered hardy perennials and shrubs. Avoid a dry and eastern aspect or a frosty corner, and plant in sun or shade during October or March in rich, deeply dug soil. Cover crowns with 2 in.–3 in. of soil and allow 3 ft.–4 ft. between each clump. Mulch annually in spring and protect with litter in winter. Paeonies dislike disturbance and only flower freely after three years. For pot-plants use two parts loam, one part manure and one part sand. Pot in October or November, keeping in cool greenhouse until spring. Stand outdoors in warm weather. *Propagation:* seed, root division. There are numerous beautiful named varieties to choose from.

PAMPAS GRASS. *Cortaderia argentea.* (Gramineae.) Graceful plant with feathery plumes rising 7 ft.–10 ft. high. Grows well on light, rich, sandy loams in sheltered shrubberies or lawns. It needs water in dry weather. *Propagation:* seeds sown under glass in spring. The male and female flowers grow on different plants. The female plumes are more attractive and last longer for winter decoration.

PANSY. See VIOLA.

PARSLEY. See VEGETABLE CHART.

PARSNIP. See VEGETABLE CHART.

PASSIFLORA. *P. caerulea.* Passion Flower. (Passifloraceae.) Beautiful flowering greenhouse or half-hardy climber. Outside south or west wall; protection is necessary, and plant base should be covered in severe winters. Prune short growths to 3 in.–6 in. and strong ones to 2 ft.–3 ft. during February. Water and feed with liquid manure in summer. Indoors, these lovely climbers may be grown in pots, tubs or beds, and their shoots trained against walls and rafters. Use equal parts of fibrous loam, peat and a little sand, for compost. Water freely in summer, and treat as hardier species. *Propagation:* cuttings, seeds sown in heat.

PATHWAYS. Prepare ground for paths thoroughly by removing weeds, especially deep-rooting perennials, either by hand or weed-killer. Along the chosen site, take a

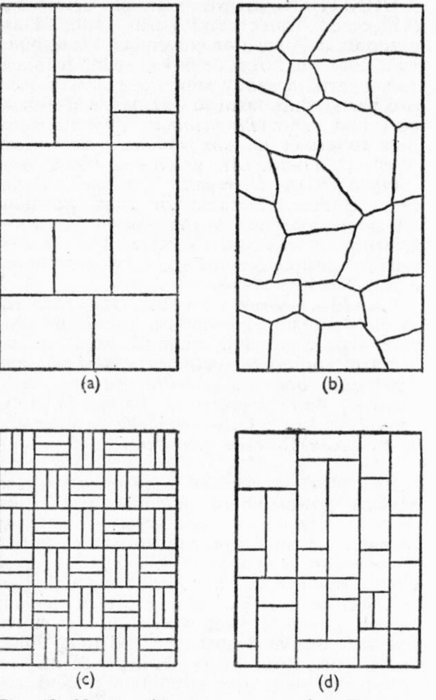

Fig. 48. Neat paths improve a garden. Types of paving shown here are: (a) *random rectangular;* (b) *crazy;* (c) *brick;* (d) *coursed random.*

trench out 6 in.–12 in. deep, lay drains down the centre for 4-ft. paths and down each side for 9-ft. widths. Pack in clinker and broken brick for drainage into half the depth of the trench, then cover with a fine layer of clinkers, coarse gravel, etc. Make this all firm and even, rolling the foundations. Cover with surface material 2 in.–3 in. deep, curving the edges slightly downward to form a camber for better drainage. A binding bituminous material on the surface will prevent weeds growing. Weed-killers are the simplest and quickest method of keeping paths clean. (See Fig. 48 and WEED-KILLERS.) See also "Uses for Bricks and Concrete" (page 500).

PEA. *Pisum sativum.* (Leguminosae.) A popular summer vegetable that appreciates good preparation of the ground before sowing. Prepare soil deeply in autumn, digging in plenty of manure. This helps plants to withstand summer drought. Manure can be worked into trenches two spits deep where peas are to stand. Land manured for previous crop is ideal, as fresh manure tends to make excessive leaf-growth rather than pods. Always sow in a flat drill, and add a chemical fertilizer containing three parts superphosphate, two parts sulphate of potash, and one part sulphate of ammonia to ground before sowing in spring. Autumn sowings should be thicker than spring sowings. Water or mulch in dry weather.

PEACH. See FRUIT AND ITS CULTURE.

PEAR. See FRUIT AND ITS CULTURE.

PELARGONIUM, zonal. Zonal Geranium. (Geraniaceae.) Favourite bright-flowered half-hardy shrubs and herbaceous perennials, usually called geranium. Used a great deal for summer bedding, window-boxes, hanging baskets or pot-plants. *For bedding* cuttings are taken in August or September and wintered in greenhouse or frame, then potted up in loam, leaf-mould and sand, with bone-meal and superphosphate added. Nip terminal shoots in March and also side-shoots to 3 in. long. Remove to cold frame before planting out in June in well-drained beds. Lift in September and store in pots or boxes in cool-house, room or cellar. *Ivy-leaved Pelargonium (P. peltatum):* cuttings as for above. Nip out main shoot points in February or March, train plants to sticks or allow them to hang down from baskets. Apply liquid manure during spring and summer and plant out in June. *Pot-plants:* cuttings are taken in August or September for summer flowering. Pinch points in February and after final potting keep in greenhouse or window during summer. Re-pot following spring. For winter flowers, take cuttings in February or March under glass. During summer plunge in ash outdoors or in a cold frame; bring inside in September. Keep all Pelargoniums fairly dry in winter and give stimulants in summer. They will do well in dryish beds under walls outside in very favourable localities. See also Fig. 34.

PENTSTEMON. (Scrophulariaceae.) Popular hardy and half-hardy herbaceous and semi-shrubby perennials for summer bedding and borders. Their colourful blooms commence in early summer and continue until autumn. Give full sun outdoors and plant in March or April in good soil. *Propagation:* seeds sown in heat in spring or cuttings in cold frame in autumn. **Best to grow:** modern named varieties like King George V (crimson), Day Dream (white and pink), White Bedder (white), Majestic (purple or violet), Alice Hindley (pale bluish rose).

PERIWINKLE. *Vinca.* (Apocynaceae.) Useful evergreen trailing hardy and stove shrubs. Hardy species will cover awkward and ugly corners, banks and bare rockery spaces. Cut shoots right back in January. *Propagation:* cuttings, seeds, division.

PERNETTYA. *P. mucronata.* Prickly Heath. (Ericaceae.) Evergreen hardy flowering shrub, bearing berries, for peaty, lime-free soils.

Plant in moist shady places. *Propagation:* seeds, division, cuttings.

PESTS AND DISEASES. Certain pests and diseases of horticultural crops must be reported to the Ministry of Agriculture; thus, *wart* disease of potato, *Colorado beetle* of potato, and *onion smut*, are notifiable. The sale of plants infected with certain pests and diseases is prohibited. This concerns *big bud mite* of black-currants, apple and pear *canker*, American gooseberry *mildew*, rhododendron *bug*, *woolly aphis* of fruit, *mussel*

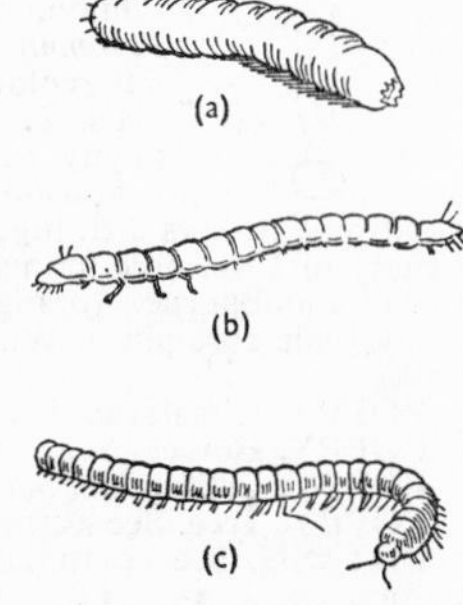

Fig. 49. Some soil pests. Browny-red leather-jackets (a) *are the chrysalis stage of many insects which are pests. The yellow wire-worm* (b) *and the black millipede* (c) *must always be destroyed when found.*

scale infected plants. Dead wood of plum infected with *silver leaf* must be burnt before 15 July. Strawberry plants for sale must come from stock that is disease-free. The guiding rule in connexion with plant pests and diseases is that prevention is better than cure, especially in the case of disease, for often there is no satisfactory control and stocks have to be burnt. See Fig. 49 and also PEST CHART and DISEASE CHART.

PETUNIA. (Solanaceae.) Vivid flowering half-hardy perennials which make showy summer bedding, for which they are frequently grown as annuals. Also grown as basket or pot plants, when two parts loam to one each of decayed manure, leaf-mould and sand are used. For bushy plants, pinch young shoots in February; old plants can be pruned at the same time. Plant outside for bedding in June, and lift again in September to winter under glass. Apply plenty of water in summer and give fertilizers when coming into flower. *Propagation:* cuttings and seeds under glass in April.

PHASEOLUS. See BEANS, FRENCH and BEANS, SCARLET RUNNER.

PHILADELPHUS. Mock Orange. (Saxifragaceae.) Sweet-scented, hardy deciduous flowering shrubs. Countless lovely white blossoms are borne in late spring. *Soil:* ordinary. Plant in sunny position from October to February, and prune directly after flowering, removing flowered shoots only. Water occasionally in summer. *Propagation:* suckers; layers in spring; soft-wood cuttings in heat in April, or cold frame in May. **Best to grow:** *P. purpureo-maculatus*, 4 ft., white, purple spots; *P. Virginale*, 8 ft., double; *P. Belle Etoile*, 8 ft., white, purple eye.

PHLOX. (Polemoniaceae.) Gay-coloured herbaceous perennials, for midsummer display, 3 ft.–4 ft., and alpine species, which bear cheerful blooms 6 in. from the ground. *Soil:* border-plants need deep moist loam; ground that dries out in the summer is not suitable, so choose a shady spot on light land. Mulch in April, and give liquid manure and water in dry weather. Do not disturb too often, but lift and divide when overcrowded. Alpine species: plant in a deep rich loam, enriched with leaf-mould. Used as edgings to borders or massed on rockeries and ledges. Disturb only when overgrown. Annuals: sow under glass in March. Pinch main shoots to make bushy plants. Plant out in June in a rich sunny position. Water in dry weather. *Propagation:* perennials, ripe seed sown under glass; cuttings; division; annuals, seed. **Best to grow:** alpine species, *P. subulata*, 6 in. pink, and many varieties. Tall species, modern hybrids of *P. decussata*, such as Border Beacon (salmon scarlet), Mia Ruys (white), Daily Sketch (rose), Graf Zeppelin (white, crimson eye), Newbird (crimson), Aviator (violet). Annuals, *P. Drummondii* and its varieties.

PIERIS. (Ericaceae.) Hardy evergreen flowering shrubs for sheltered borders and woodland. *Soil:* moist peaty loam. Give water in dry weather. *Prune* straggling growth after blossoms fade. *Propagation:* seeds, division. **Best to grow:** *P. japonica*, *P. floribunda*, 3 ft.–8 ft., white, February.

PIMPERNEL. See ANAGALLIS.

PINE. *Pinus.* See CONIFERS.

PINKS. See CARNATIONS.

PLANE. *Platanus.* (Platanaceae.) This deciduous tree sheds its bark, thrives in towns, flourishing in heavy smoky atmospheres, besides withstanding severe pollarding. Deep soils with plenty of moisture and sunny positions are best. *Prune* and *plant* from October to February. *Propagation:* seeds; heel cuttings taken in autumn.

PLUM. See FRUIT AND ITS CULTURE.

PLUMBAGO. (Plumbaginaceae.) Greenhouse evergreen shrub. *Soil:* three parts loam, one of leaf-mould and sand. *Propagation:* cuttings, division. **Best to grow:** *P. capensis*, 6 ft., pale blue, August.

POINSETTIA. See EUPHORBIA.

POLEMONIUM. *P. caeruleum.* Jacob's Ladder. (Polemoniaceae.) Hardy perennial suitable for open sunny borders and rock gardens. Neat pinnate foliage and blue or white flowers. *Soil:* sandy. *Propagation:* division.

POLYGONATUM. Solomon's Seal. (Liliaceae.) Admirable hardy perennial for deep shade. *Soil:* ordinary moist. *Propagation:* root division. Creeping roots spread very rapidly once established. **Best to grow:** *P. multiflorum*, 2 ft.–3 ft., white, June.

POLYGONUM. Knot Weed. (Polygonaceae.) Includes annuals and perennials, evergreen shrubs and deciduous climbers, all of which have knotted stems. Perennials make excellent waterside plants; annuals thrive on sunny borders. All need water in dry weather. *Propagation:* soft-wood cuttings with a heel; division; seeds; climbers by layering. **Best to grow:** border perennials, *P. amplexicaule*, 3 ft., rose-red flowers, and its dark red variety *atrosanguineum;* rock-garden perennials, *P. affine*, pink, autumn-tinted; annual, *P.*

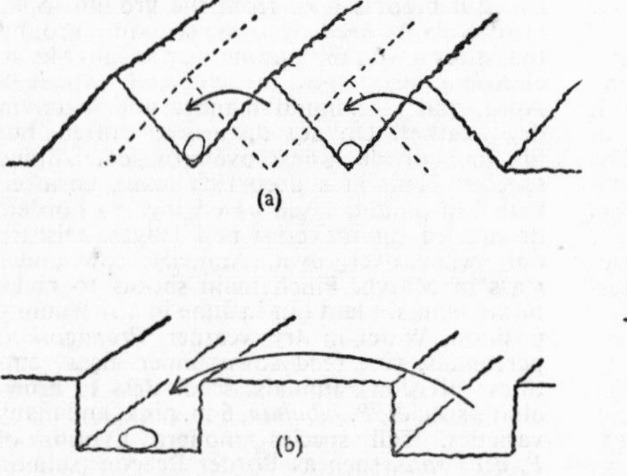

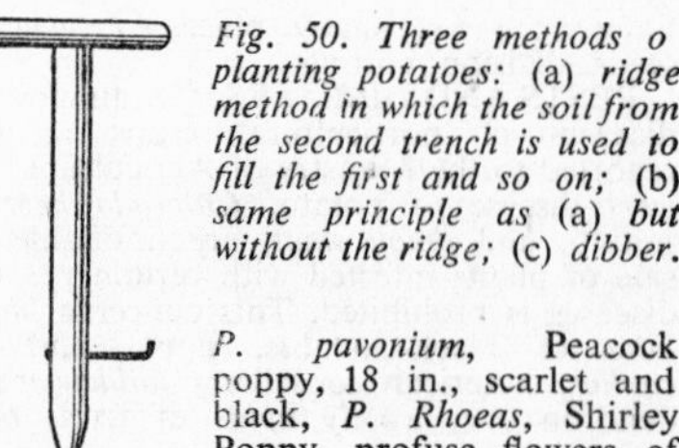

Fig. 50. Three methods o planting potatoes: (a) *ridge method in which the soil from the second trench is used to fill the first and so on;* (b) *same principle as* (a) *but without the ridge;* (c) *dibber.*

orientale, 4 ft., rosy-purple; wild garden, *P. cuspidatum*, 6 ft.–8 ft., creamy flowers; climbers, *P. baldschuanicum*, white.

POPLAR. *Populus.* (Salicaceae.) Quick-growing deciduous trees for moist soils. Will make a good screen in a few years, and are especially suitable for towns. *Soil:* any moist soils; avoid chalk or dry soils. Plant 4 ft.–6 ft. apart for screens. *Propagation:* seeds, cuttings, grafting. **Best to grow:** wind-breaks and screens: *P. nigra betulifolia*, *P. nigra italica* (Lombardy poplar); seaside: *P. alba*, white poplar; chalk soils: *P. canescena*, grey poplar; other species: *P. balsamifera*, balsam poplar, balsam scent when leaves open, *P. nigra*, black poplar.

POPPY. Papaver. (Papaveraceae.) Favourite annuals and perennials that give a wide range of brilliant colour to summer beds and borders. *Soil:* ordinary, deep sandy loam preferable for perennials. *Propagation:* annuals, sow in flowering positions in April for summer blooms, and in September for spring flowering; thin to 1 ft. apart. Perennials, seed, division, root-cuttings taken in autumn. Border species resent disturbance, and should be left from year to year. **Best to grow:** annuals, *P. pavonium*, Peacock poppy, 18 in., scarlet and black, *P. Rhoeas*, Shirley Poppy, profuse flowers of salmon, white, orange, etc., *P. somniferum*, opium poppy, 3 ft., colours various; perennials, *P. nudicaule*, Iceland poppy, 1 ft., various colours, *P. orientale*, oriental poppy, handsome flowers 3 ft. high. Varieties include Beauty of Livermere (crimson), Barr's White, Lord Lambourne (orange scarlet), Mrs. Perry (pale rose-pink), Wunderkind (salmon-pink).

POPPY, Himalayan. See MECONOPSIS.

POPPY, Horned. See GLAUCIUM.

POPPY, Californian. See ESCHSCHOLTZIA.

POPPY, Tree. See ROMNEYA.

POTASH. See FERTILIZERS and FERTILIZER CHART.

POTATO. *Solanum tuberosum.* (Solanaceae.) It is an admirable cleaning crop for weedy ground or newly broken pasture. Dig ground deeply, adding plenty of manure. Dress land at planting time (Figs. 50 and 51) with a mixed fertilizer. Avoid lime, unless soil is sour, to prevent scab.

Seed potatoes the size of an egg are ideal. To sprout (Fig. 52), set the tubers rose end up (round end possessing the most eyes) in a shallow box or tray. Keep in a light airy place protected from frost. If tubers are large they can be cut.

Earth up as the plants grow. Early potatoes are protected from frost by earthing up and covering with straw, bracken, etc.; save seed potatoes only from healthy crops. Best to import new disease-free stock every two years.

When lifting tubers, leave on soil surface to dry for a little, but not long enough for them to go green. Store in clamps or frost-proof sheds; store only sound, healthy tubers. See also VEGETABLE CHART.

POTTING. When mixing composts be sure all ingredients are fresh and disease-free, and the pots properly clean. Wash and scrub off dirt, leaving pots to dry before using them. New pots need to be soaked for some hours

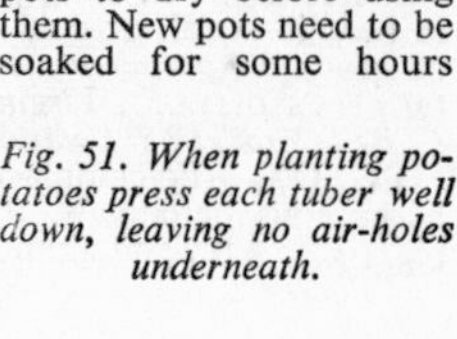

Fig. 51. When planting potatoes press each tuber well down, leaving no air-holes underneath.

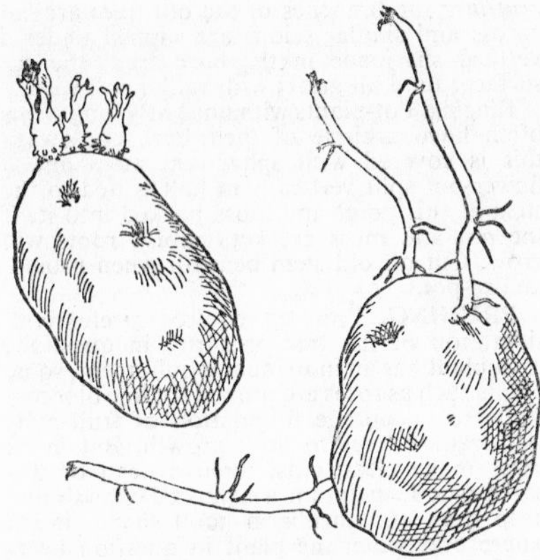

Fig. 52. A well-sprouted seed potato (left) *compared with a badly sprouted example.*

before they are used. Principle for all potting is the same, good drainage of broken crocks laid with hump or curved surface uppermost in the bottom of the pot. Roughage of dried grass or leaves is next laid in and soil firmly and evenly laid on top, sufficiently high to allow ball of soil round plant to rest within the pot at the same soil level. Pack soil round firmly and evenly, leaving a watering space between soil and pot rim. Keep plant exactly in the centre of the pot. Generally speaking, plants with woody stems are potted up more firmly than others.

Keep plants to moderate-sized pots, moving them up to bigger pots as the roots develop.

PRIMROSE. See PRIMULA.

PRIMULA. Auricula. Polyanthus. Primrose. (Primulaceae.) A large family of lovely perennials, greenhouse and hardy plants, with a wide range of colour, that grow on rockeries, in woodlands, bogs, beds and borders, or in greenhouses. *Pot culture:* raise by sowing seed in March, or in June for spring flowering. Pot singly into 3-in. pots, then into 5 in.–6 in. pots in compost of three parts loam, one part leaf-mould, dry cow-manure and sand. *P. obconica*, *P. sinensis* and *P. malacoides* will thrive in cool houses or frames. Keep moist and give liquid manure feeds. *Rock-garden:* well-drained open positions, or in rock crevices or shady banks and wet corners. *P. denticulata* (lavender) and *P. capitata* (purple) for moist and cool spots, *P. marginata* (violet-blue) and *P. spectabilis* (rosy-purple) for drier places. *Bog plants:* plant in sun or shade on peaty soil. *P. Beesiana* (crimson-purple), *P. japonica* (crimson), *P. sikkimensis* (yellow), *P. Florindae* (yellow). *Border: P. vulgaris* (primrose) has double and single varieties, the former preferring lime-free soils. Lift and divide primrose, auricula, cowslip and polyanthus each year after flowering. *Soil:* ordinary, moist. Raise from spring-sown seed. See also AURICULA.

PROPAGATION OF PLANTS. There are various methods of increasing plant stocks, some by natural means and others by methods adapted from man's experimental discoveries.

Seed. A method of propagation used by gardeners and by nature for most plants. Named hybrids bred by man from crossing one species or variety with another often fail to come true to type and colour from seed; in this case other methods are used. Always buy reliable seed annually. The germination power of all seeds fails with age; for example, parsnips are good only in the first year. Certain trees and shrubs are raised from seed sown in a cold frame. Fern spores are grown like ordinary seeds on fine soil in shallow pans set in moist moss. When saving seed select good healthy plants in their prime, and mark them. Allow to ripen, and harvest when dry. Spread out on paper to dry thoroughly before labelling and storing in a frost-proof and dry place. See SEEDS.

Cuttings. Used to obtain plants true to type. It is essential to select good, healthy, typical growth. Use a very sharp knife, and always make a clean cut, and insert the prepared cuttings at once before they have time to dry. The most important point in planting cuttings is to make them absolutely firm. The cutting base must be in contact with the gritty loam. Keep moist until they are rooted; shade from the sun. *Soft-wood cuttings:* choose terminal shoots without flower-buds. The shorter the length the better. Nodal cuttings are cut just below the leaf joint. *Hard-wood cuttings:* ripe wood of 6 in.–8 in. in length is cut below a bud

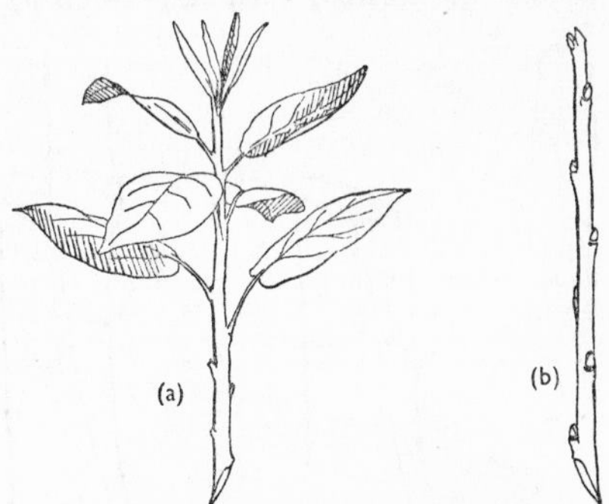

Fig. 53. Hard-wood cuttings (a) *are made of ripened young growth; soft-wood cuttings* (b) *of healthy young growth in spring and summer.*

usually in late summer or autumn. (See Fig. 53.) Unripe tips are cut above a node (leaf joint). *Heel cuttings:* cuttings with part of the main stem adhering. *Root cuttings:* fleshy roots of certain plants are made into 3 in.–4 in. cuttings. Make straight cuts at the top, and slanting ones at the base, to indicate right way up. *Leaf cuttings:* fleshy leaves, like those of certain *Begonias*, are pegged down on sandy soil after the veins have been notched. Divide up the rooted leaf into separate plants.

Division of roots. Herbaceous perennials are divided in autumn or spring with a sharp clean knife, spade, or two forks back to back and then levered apart. Replant young outside growths of the clump.

Layering. Climbers, rock plants, shrubs and border carnations can be increased this way, whilst strawberries do it naturally with their runners. Make a slanting cut on the underside of a stem and peg it down into sandy soil beside the parent plant. Sever when well rooted and later lift and replant.

Budding. Employed to put delicate or new varieties on to old or hardier stocks for roses, fruit trees, shrubs, trees, etc., during June and July. Cut a T-shaped slit 1 in. long in the bark of the stock, gently lever up corners of bark and slip in the bud. Prepare the bud by cutting a shield-shape carrying a leaf and bud out of the stem of the selected variety, approximately 1 in. long. Remove the leaf-blade (leave the stalk) and the wood behind the bud. Slip the bud into the bark of the stock. Bind the bud-shield to the stem with raffia (leaving the leaf-stalk and the bud protruding). Loosen the raffia when the stem swells. Remove other shoots below the bud. Tie in the bud as it grows to the upper stem, and when well established cut out the latter above the union.

Grafting. This is carried out in April. The hardened shoot of the selected variety (scion) is grafted either on to a young root-stock, before the tree framework has been developed, when whip and tongue or saddle grafting is employed; or on to older stocks that have wide branches or stems that require more than one scion to form a branched tree. This last method includes rind or crown grafting, oblique-cleft grafting and frame-working,

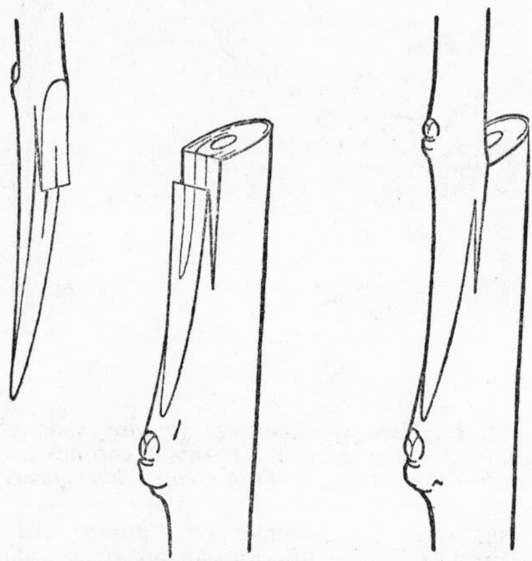

Fig. 54. Whip and tongue grafting before binding.

which involves stub and bark grafting. Grafts (scions) of one-year-old wood are cut 6 in. long, the top above a bud and the base a long slanting cut according to the type of graft required. *Whip grafting:* make a long slanting cut behind a bud on the scion base and on the stock so that they fit exactly together, with the cambium layers (a soft layer directly beneath the bark) touching; a tongue on each cut can be made to interlock (Fig. 54). Grafts are tied well together and waxed. *Rind or crown grafting:* the branches of the old trees are cut across and similar scions are slipped under a vertical slit made in the bark from the cut surface. Bind all grafts with raffia, and wax.

Ringing. Pot-plants with unsightly long stems often have a circle of their bark cut away; this is covered with sphagnum moss and a flower-pot split vertically in half is tied to the stem at this point and moss packed into it. If the pot and moss are kept moist, roots will grow. Cut off old stem beneath when rooted, and re-pot.

PRUNING. Pruning requires careful consideration of the tree or shrub in question; each plant has an individual requirement, some plants such as roses are pruned for fine blooms; fruits to encourage foundation of fruit-bud; wall-trained trees to limit growth. But in all cases make clean cuts, remove dead or diseased wood, maintain a balanced growth and keep trees and shrubs in good shape. Learn where and when the plant in question bears its flowers or fruit, for the success of the pruning depends on this understanding. *Standard and bush roses* are pruned at the end of March to early April. *Ramblers:* remove old flowered growth after blooming. *Shrubs* vary from one genus or species to another. *Fruit:* See FRUIT AND ITS CULTURE.

PRUNUS. (Rosaceae.) There are many lovely flowering varieties of this family, which include almonds, apricots, cherries, plums, peaches and laurels. Most require deep rich soil, rather more sandy for cherries. *Prune* straggling growth and remove dead wood only. *Propagation:* seeds, budding, grafting. **Best to grow:** *P. Amygdalus* (almond), 20 ft.–30 ft.; pink, March. *P. Pissardi*, 20 ft.–30 ft., purple foliage, white flowers. *P. Padus* (bird cherry), 30 ft.–50 ft., white, and its double variety. *P. subhirtella*, 20 ft.–30 ft., shell-pink, and its weeping variety, *pendula*. *P. triloba flore pleno*, 12 ft.–15 ft., rose. Also many beautiful pink or white varieties of the Japanese *P. serrulata.*

PUMPKIN, VEGETABLE MARROW. Cucurbita. (Cucurbitaceae.) Trailing, half-hardy annuals that are easy to grow. Grow on manure or refuse heaps, banks, beds, frames, or in the garden in a hole 15 in. deep, filled with manure and covered with 6 in. of soil. Plant out in May–June, and pinch leading shoots when too long. Water copiously during dry weather, and give frequent feeds of liquid manure. *Propagation:* sow seeds singly in small pots in spring under glass, or outside on growing site May–June.

QUINCE. See CYDONIA.

RADISH. *Raphanus sativus.* (Cruciferae.) Annual used as salad vegetable. Quick-growing crop raised on ordinary light soils, enriched with manure or compost. Sow for succession and water plentifully. For early crops sow in frames, hot-beds or under cloches. See VEGETABLE CHART.

RANUNCULUS. (Ranunculaceae.) Attractive hardy perennials. The buttercup is a member of this large genus. Garden varieties need deep rich loam, alpine species need sand and leaf-mould. *Propagation:* seeds, division. Leave undisturbed for several years. Plant tuberous-rooted species in February, or October–November in warm districts. Place tubers with claw downwards, 2 in. deep and 3 in. apart. Lift after flowering and dry before storing in sand. **Best to grow:** *R. aconitifolius flore pleno*, 18 in., white, May. *R. asiaticus*, 1 ft., May and June; many brightly-coloured varieties.

RASPBERRY. *Rubus Idaeus.* (Rosaceae.) Plant 2 ft. apart in rows 5 ft. apart and train on wires, trellis or between two wires spaced 1 ft. apart. Mulch with decayed manure in April and water with liquid manure during fruiting period. *Propagation:* suckers. See also FRUIT AND ITS CULTURE.

RED-HOT POKER. See KNIPHOFIA.

RHODODENDRON. (Ericaceae.) Magnificent flowered tender and hardy shrubs which include the azaleas. Plant only in lime-free soils. If fresh peaty soil is imported on to chalk soils, the plants survive only for a short time, since the roots penetrate into the chalk subsoil, and the surrounding area drains chalky soil water among the roots. Choose sunny positions, and prepare ground by digging in leaf-mould and well-rotted manure. Plant in September and keep roots balled in soil when moving them, since they are easily damaged. No pruning is necessary, except to remove dead heads. Cutting out weak growths may mean removal of some of next season's flowers, but ensures a finer display in the second year. *Propagation:* seeds sown in peat moss and sand. Cover seed pans with glass and shade until germination takes place after a month. Cuttings and grafts are used in nurseries, but usually require special conditions. There are numerous species and garden hybrids suitable for woodland, borders and rock garden, varying greatly in size and price. The advice of a reputable nurseryman should be sought in the selection of varieties. See also AZALEA.

RHUBARB. *Rheum rhaponticum.* (Polygonaceae.) Grow this vegetable in fairly rich ground that has had manure or compost dug in, though it will grow anywhere if well fed. Plant crowns firmly in February or March, 3 ft. apart, and 2 in. below the soil surface. Leave the stalks the first year. Avoid pulling too many stalks from the same plant and cease to do so after July. To force, place boxes, drainpipes, barrels or special pots over the crowns in January and keep manure or straw over the coverings. Exclude all light. Roots can be lifted in autumn, dried in the air for several days and packed into boxes or beds in the greenhouse. Pack soil between the roots, and water moderately at first and then freely. *Propagation:* seeds, which take two years to form good plants; root-division, with fibres and buds on each new piece. These can be taken from the parent plant without moving it.

RHUS. Smoke Tree. Sumach. (Anacardiaceae.) Deciduous shrubs grown for their brilliant autumn foliage. *Soil:* ordinary, without manure. Poor soils produce more vivid colours. *Propagation:* seeds, cuttings, root-cuttings. **Best to grow:** *R. Cotinus*, 8 ft. (Smoke Tree); *R. typhina laciniata*, small tree.

RICINUS. See CASTOR-OIL PLANT.

ROBINIA. See ACACIA, FALSE.

ROCK CRESS. See AUBRIETIA.

ROCK JASMINE. See ANDROSACE.

ROCK PLANTS. Grow naturally in high altitudes among limestone or other rocks, and when grown in domestic rock gardens the nearest approach to their natural habitat must be provided. Supply lime in the form of mortar rubble or builders' lime and add sharp grit to the soil to ensure the good drainage they naturally require to prevent them "damping off" in wet British climate. During very wet and foggy weather the more delicate plants need the shelter of a piece of glass at an angle against the rock, or supported overhead by four sticks or wires. This is easily done, since most alpine plants are compact, low growers. Their roots penetrate deeply into the soil in rock-crevices and their flower-buds develop under the snow, appearing directly the first warm weather comes, as the summer season is short in mountain areas. For individual plant requirements see under the generic name of each. See also ALPINES.

ROMNEYA. *R. Coulteri.* Californian Tree Poppy. (Papaveraceae.) Though rather a difficult half-hardy evergreen to grow, it produces large, fragrant, white flowers which are very showy in late summer and autumn. Plant in sheltered borders or against a south wall in moist sandy loam during April or May. Always protect carefully in severe weather. *Propagation:* seeds, root cuttings.

ROOM PLANTS. To those who possess "green fingers" the cultivation of plants in the house presents little difficulty. Most room plants need plenty of sunlight; if the room is dark, give the plant a change by placing it in the window or on the greenhouse shelves. Always avoid cold draughts and fluctuating temperatures. If plants are kept in windows, move the pot round to obtain even upright growth, for they will always grow towards the light. Most plants are pale and leggy in dark corners, except the shade-loving types like aspidistras, *Aralia* (*Fatsia*), and hart's-tongue ferns. These shiny-leaved plants will benefit if their leaves are sponged or placed in warm rain to remove dust. Give regular waterings, filling the pot to the brim. If plants are very dry, soak them in a tub or bucket. Rain-water is soft and has more goodness; avoid very cold water during winter; never over-water. A hollow sound when the pot is tapped is a sure indication that the plant is dry. More light, air and water is needed by plants in full growth (for ferns this is the winter) than during the resting season, when water should be gradually withheld. See also BULBS (*Indoor Culture*).

ROSES. *Rosa.* (Rosaceae.) This lovely flowering genus has been cultivated for centuries and is found today in many countries. Roses thrive best in good heavy loam, though a well-drained retentive soil that is deep and rich will give almost as good results. To prepare ground for all types, deep digging is essential. Sticky clays can be lightened with ash, leaf-mould or strawy manure; to light soils add compost, leaf-mould, good heavy loam and cow manure. Only very dry, rotted manure may be dug into the top layers. To all soils give dressings of lime, 2 oz.–8 oz. per sq. yd.; also bonemeal and potash.

Plant in October or November while the soil is still warm enough to allow the roses time to establish themselves before the growing season. Fewer losses occur with autumn planting, which necessitates, however, good soil preparation a month before planting. If there is no time for early preparation, delay planting until February or March. When planting, trim broken roots and spread them carefully out before covering. Cover union of stock and graft with 1 in.–2 in. of soil. Choose sunny open positions away from trees and sheltered from wind. Do not feed in the first year, but subsequently mulch in spring, using well-rotted manure or lawn mowings. A good, balanced fertilizer is two parts sulphate of potash, one part sulphate of ammonia, and three parts superphosphate. Apply in spring at 2 oz. per sq. yd. During the season remove suckers, and keep watered on light soils.

Pruning: March is the chief month, but Noisettes, Pernetianas and Tea Roses can be left until April. Always remove dead and diseased wood. *Climbing roses:* prune according to type. *Ramblers and American Pillar*, that flower on long shoots from the base, cut out those that have blossomed and tie in the new shoots after the flowering season. Other climbers that grow new shoots from existing main stems, remove old wood as far as possible, leaving sufficient stems to cover supports. Shorten laterals to 6 in. and lay in strong shoots to replace older wood removed. Encourage new growth from the base to take the place of the worn-out stems. Climbing varieties of hybrid Teas are best pruned in the spring. *Dwarf polyanthas:* remove or shorten old flowering wood and thin out. *Bush roses:* prune in the first week of April or the last week in March, leaving the most tender varieties until last. Too early pruning encourages young shoots which may be killed by the frost, but prune when top shoots are 1 in.–3 in. long. Hard cutting results in greater growth, so strong bushes require less pruning. Aim to keep the bushes open and well shaped, remove dead wood and thin, weak growths. Prune above a dormant bud, cutting branches to one-third or two-thirds of their length according to the strength of the growth. Choose outward-growing buds. *Standard roses:* prune as bush roses, never cutting below the union where the bush is budded on the stock. Suckers arising from the base (which are usually common briars) must be removed, also the growth below the union on the main stem. Prune slightly harder than ordinary bushes, as fewer shoots are usually produced.

ROSMARINUS. *R. officinalis.* Rosemary. (Labiatae.) Fragrant evergreen shrub suitable for the herb garden, mixed borders or old-world gardens. *Soil:* ordinary, dryish loam mixed with old mortar rubble. Plant in April in a sunny place. Water in summer. *Propagation:* seeds, layers, cuttings.

ROTATION. The fertility of the soil is maintained if a wise and careful cropping plan is carried out. As a result of crop rotation any one group of vegetables rarely comes on the same land except after a two- or three-year interval. This prevents certain crop pests and diseases being carried over from year to year, which is disastrous in many cases (for example, Carrot Fly). Also ground tillage and manuring is properly utilized, since some crops (such as roots) must not be planted over fresh manure (Fig. 55). By rotation and crop planning no

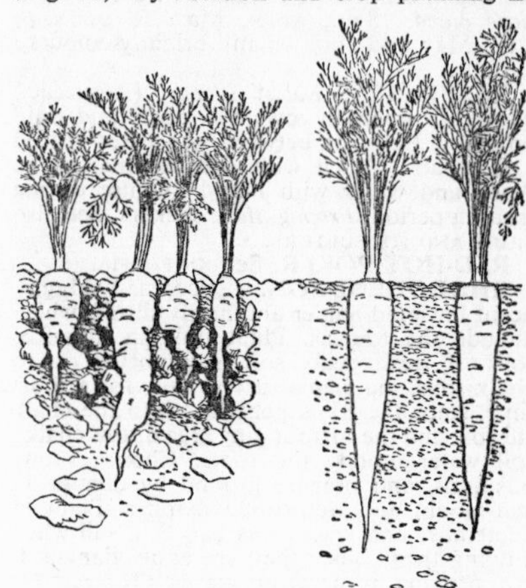

Fig. 55. Root crops planted in stony ground or over fresh manure tend to form fanged roots. Careful thinning helps to produce good shapes.

ground is wasted, and complete sections of the garden, each in their turn, are cleared altogether to allow deep digging and manuring during winter and spring. Certain crops stand outside a rotation scheme; those include permanent crops such as rhubarb, asparagus and onions.

Generally speaking, three-year crop rotations are best, but fundamentally in any scheme green crops and potatoes should be followed by roots. Manure is applied to ground which is to grow onions, leeks, peas, beans, potatoes, spinach, celery and tomatoes. Potatoes and tomatoes should be planted as widely apart as possible, since the same diseases attack them. Runner beans are usually planted where they do not overshadow crops, except the shade lovers.

Catch-crops that can be grown and harvested quickly on vacant ground include lettuce, radish, spring onions, carrots, beet. Intercropping of widely spaced crops such as tall peas is an economy; use lettuce or shade-loving plants. Winter greens can also go out earlier if planted between rows soon to be harvested.

ROWANBERRY. Crab apple. See CRABS.

RUMEX. *R. acetosa.* Sorrel. (Polygonaceae.) Hardy perennial for any soil that is moist. It will grow quickly and spreads like a weed once it is established. *Propagation:* seeds, division.

SAGE. See SALVIA.

SALADS. The skilful gardener will produce this immensely valuable crop most of the year round. Though easy to grow in summer months, careful planning and the use of hot-beds, frames, greenhouse and cloches in colder weather will enable a garden to grow certain salad crops out of season. Most salad crops are surface-rooting and need plenty of moisture. To ensure success the ground needs deep digging and the crop watered regularly. Sow seeds continuously in small amounts to obtain a succession. See also HOT-BED, GREENHOUSE and VEGETABLE CHART.

SALSIFY. *Tragopogon porrifolium.* (Compositae.) Tender roots, resemble a parsnip, are cooked in the same way. Leaves are useful in salads. Sow as parsnips in rows 1 ft. apart on deep light soil. Thin seedlings to 6 in.–8 in. apart and lift in November. Store in dry sand.

SALVIA. (Labiatae.) Hardy and tender annuals, perennials and evergreen shrubs. *Salvia splendens* (vivid scarlet) is often used as a bedding plant; plants raised in heat and planted out in June. *S. patens* (a beautiful blue) is used for mixed borders, its tuberous roots are lifted in October and stored in sand in a frostproof place. Start growth under glass in March and plant out in May. *Soil:* light for outdoors; pot-plants require two parts loam, one part sand, with manure and leaf-mould added. *S. turkestanica*, 5 ft., mauve; *S. haematodes*, 2 ft., lilac; *S. superba*, 3 ft., dark blue, are valuable border perennials.

SAMBUCUS. Elder. (Caprifoliaceae.) Deciduous, white-flowered shrub, bearing black berries in autumn. Plant in dry shrubberies, banks or hedgerows, in sun or shade. *Soil:* ordinary. *Propagation:* soft-wood cuttings.

SAND. Can be used to lighten heavy and badly drained soils, though very sandy soils are considered poor since only a few plants thrive well on them. Sand is an essential ingredient in most potting composts; it not only lightens the compost, but affords better drainage and aeration of the mixture. For seed composts a larger proportion of sand is used, drainage being extremely important. In all composts silver sands are used, preferably coarse-grained. Builders' sand has a binding effect on the soil mixture, making it "set" too much. Dry sand is used to store root vegetables during the winter.

SANTOLINA. Lavender Cotton. (Compositae.) Hardy sub-shrubs with yellow flowers and grey, aromatic foliage. *S. Chamaecyparissus* is usually grown. *Soil:* sandy. *Propagation:* seeds, cuttings. **Best to grow:** *S. Vaccaria*, 1 ft., pink, annual; *S. ocymoides*, red or pink, perennial, for rock garden.

SAVOY. See CABBAGE and VEGETABLE CHART.

SAVORY. See HERB GARDEN.

SAWFLY. See PEST CHART.

SAXIFRAGE. *Saxifraga.* (Saxifragaceae.) This is an enormous family of which the most commonly grown are the charming flowered rock-plants. There are various groups, the four most usual being the *Kabschia* section of cushion plants whose foliage is in tidy tufts of spiny leaves, the mossy saxifrages with hummocks of moss-like foliage, the *Megasea* section with large leathery leaves, and the encrusted group with silver-edged leaves in rosettes. London Pride belongs to a fleshy-leaved section which needs ordinary loam and a position on border edges or rock gardens. Plant them in spring. *Soil:* most of the saxifrages require gritty soil with lime and leaf-mould covered with limestone chips. *Propagation:* seeds, division.

SCABIOUS. *Scabiosa.* (Dipsaceae.) Useful and colourful annuals and perennials for cut flowers and border plants. *Soil:* ordinary; plant in sun or shade in well-drained borders. Give plentiful water supplies in dry weather. *Propagation:* seeds, division. Perennials need lifting and dividing every three or four years. **Best to grow:** perennial, *S. caucasica* and its varieties, Diamond (dark blue), *perfecta* (pale blue), Clive Greaves (mauve), *alba* (white). Annual, many varieties of *S. atropurpurea;* colours and heights various.

SCARBOROUGH LILY. See VALLOTA.

SCHIZANTHUS. Butterfly Flower. Poor Man's Orchid. (Solanaceae.) Showy, half-hardy annuals in various colours. They make fine pot-plants and are also suitable for planting outdoors in May. *Soil:* loam, leaf-mould and sand. *Propagation:* sow seeds under glass in March for transplanting outdoors. For pot-plants, sow in greenhouse or frame in August. Grow on in pots and stake plants with canes.

SCILLA. Squill. Bluebell. (Liliaceae.) Tender and hardy bulbs with attractive blue, white or pink flowers. Like the bluebell, which is a native of British woodlands, many species thrive in sunny borders, rockeries, grass or lawns. *Plant:* August–November, large bulbs 4 in. deep and apart, and the small sizes 2 in. each way, either in lines as edgings or in masses, or naturalized in the turf of an alpine garden. For growing in pots, see BULBS. *Propagation:* offsets; seeds produce flowering bulbs in three or four years. **Best to grow:** *S. hispanica* is a finer and more imposing improvement of the British wild bluebell (*S. nutans*). *S. sibirica* (common squill), 6 in., blue; also *alba*, its white variety, April. *S. bifolia*, 4 in., deep blue, February.

SEAKALE. *Crambe maritima.* (Cruciferae.) The shoots are blanched under glass or outdoors to provide a choice winter vegetable. Raise plants by sowing seed in open ground in good light soil during March. Rows are 1 ft. apart and seedlings thinned 6 in. apart and replanted when one year old, 2½ ft. apart, to grow on until the roots are strong enough to force. Quick results are obtained by purchasing roots, or maintain a stock from 6-in. root cuttings. Plants are put in a permanent bed, 2½ ft. apart, in rows 2 ft. apart, to be lifted as required or forced as they stand outdoors by excluding the light with pots, cloches and straw. Boxes covered with a 1-ft. layer of stable manure are excellent. The main object is to exclude light and frost. Permanent beds must be deeply prepared in winter ready for planting in March. *To force indoors:* lift roots November–December, trim off leaves and side shoots, and store in sand until required. Force by placing five or six crowns in an 8-in. flower-pot and pack with fine soil. Water and put in a temperature of 60 deg.–65 deg. Invert a second flower-pot of the same size over the top and block up the drainage hole. Shoots will be fit to cut in two or three weeks.

SEASIDE GARDENS. Seaside conditions in the British Isles normally provide less extreme temperatures than do inland regions, but at the same time the winds are more violent and the air is salt-laden. The first thing

Fig. 56. Seaside gardens can be protected by a coarse hedge on a high bank.

to do in making a seaside garden is to consider the question of shelter (Fig. 56), and this having been provided, the garden will grow practically any type of plant according to the natural soil of the district.

Before planting any trees or shrubs the condition of the soil should be taken into account. The ordinary rules for soil preparation will apply; that is, heavy soils should be lightened and light soils should be made more retentive of moisture by the addition of strawy manure, leaf-mould, etc. The worst problem will be where the soil is practically pure, sea-washed sand. Here the sand must be prevented from blowing about by the establishment of grasses, the erection of fences, and by pegging down tree branches over the surface. Scotch roses, willows, common privet, broom and tamarisk, with violas and sea pinks (thrift), will constitute the first planting, whilst trees that can be planted almost at once include Corsican vines, maritime pines and Sitka spruce. *Other trees and shrubs for coastal regions:* dogwood, alder, blackthorn, sycamore, hollies, sea buckthorn, whitebeam, certain *Veronicas*, hawthorn, *Lycium barbarum*, *Rosa rugosa*.

SEAWEED. See KELP.

SEDUM. Stonecrop. (Crassulaceae.) The hardy perennials of this large genus are suitable for rockeries and dry borders. *Soil:* ordinary, or sandy with some lime. Plant November or April, in sun. *Propagation:* seeds, division. **Best to grow:** *S. spectabile*, 1 ft., rose-pink, September. *S. populifolium*, 9 in., pink, August. *S. acre*, 3 in., yellow, July. *S. album*, 6 in., white, July.

SEEDS. Seeds vary greatly in shape, size, and thickness of skin (testa), and the chief concern of the gardener is the length of time they retain their power of germination. This may vary from months to many years.

As a result of cross-pollination plants grown from seed may vary considerably, since they inherit the characteristics of both parents. Because of the variations the best seedsmen test samples of all seed sent out, first for germination and secondly for purity of strain. Amateurs who save their own seed will frequently find that though germination may be good, some of the resulting seedlings are worthless, but against this there is the chance of securing a novelty of first-class quality. Home-saved seed must be gathered fully ripe and allowed to dry in the sun for a time before storing. Label all containers and store in a cool, dry place.

To raise seed indoors, use good soil, preferably sterilized; sift the compost, using a fine mesh for smaller seed. Compost must be gritty and open, for seeds frequently fail to germinate on a caked soil. Peat is often substituted for leaf-mould in indoor work, since it is a clean and disease-free material. Peat must be soaked in water and squeezed free of liquid before being added to a compost. Outdoor seed-beds must be finely raked down and well firmed. In all cases, thin, even sowing always repays the extra skill and trouble it takes; if seeds are fine, then a dry carrier of sand or soil can be mixed to assist the gardener to sow more evenly and thinly. Transplant seedlings or thin them in early stages and do not leave them to become overcrowded and leggy. Shade boxes of seedlings and water regularly.

Hardy annuals are usually sown outdoors in spring or autumn; half-hardy annuals in boxes under glass or cold frames (Fig. 57) in early spring, or outdoors from April to May. Biennials and perennials are sown towards midsummer, either under glass or outside according to their hardiness (Fig. 58). See also PROPAGATION and VEGETABLE GARDEN.

SHALLOT. *Allium ascalonicum.* (Liliaceae.) A useful vegetable that is easy to grow, and gives little trouble if grown in open sunny positions and lightish soil that has been well prepared. Land that has been deeply dug and manured for the previous crop is ideal. Cultivation is the same as for onions, though

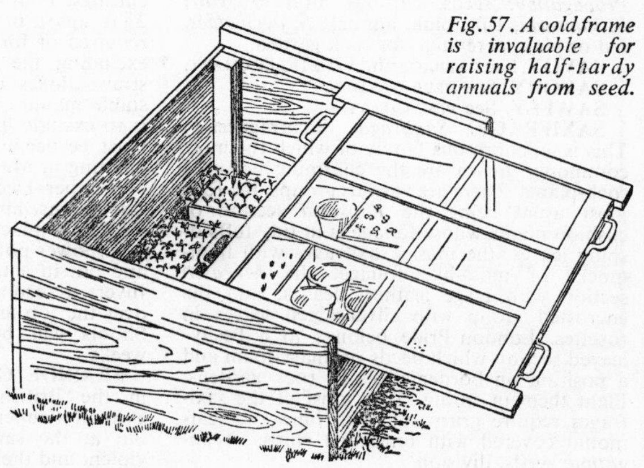

Fig. 57. A cold frame is invaluable for raising half-hardy annuals from seed.

Fig. 58. Sowing seeds outdoors: (a) *make a drill with a hoe;* (b) *sow seeds sparingly in a line in the drill;* (c) *cover the seeds—shuffling along the drill is a convenient method.*

rather less rich. Lift at the end of June, and dry the bulbs off before stringing them in the same way as onions. See VEGETABLE CHART.

SHRUBS AND TREES. These form the architectural outline of a garden and are used to make wind-breaks, boundaries, dividing screens, shelter, and to provide a background for brightly-coloured plants. A shrub border plan is shown in Fig. 59. Undoubtedly there is a reduction of labour in the garden where trees and shrubs are planted in quantity. Before actually planting, visualize them when mature and allow plenty of room.

Deciduous plants must be transplanted when the leaves are absent and evergreens during April or September. Evergreens suffer more from moving than the deciduous trees and shrubs, as the latter have no leaves from which to lose moisture and can adjust themselves more quickly to the change. If evergreens are moved in dry weather, give them regular sprays with tepid water for some days afterwards, as this helps to restore the balance of moisture. If evergreens lose their leaves after being transplanted it is not an unhealthy sign, but f the leaves remain on the plant and shrivel up, this may be a sign of failure.

Planting: for all trees and shrubs prepare the ground well and make up deficiencies, since this cannot be done in later years. Dig ground 2 ft. deep on light soils and deeper still on heavy clays, to improve the texture of the soil. See SOIL. Bonemeal and hoof-and-horn meal are good fertilizers for new sites; spread at 3 oz.–4 oz. per sq. yd. and work well into the soil. Make the hole wider and deeper than required and spread out the roots on a slightly mounded base, holding tree or shrub straight; fill in gently but firmly, with the soil-mark on the stem at ground level; never bury deeply. Fill in the hole gradually, treading down the layers separately as they go in. Stakes can be driven in at planting time to avoid damaging the roots, and this enables a single-handed planter to tie the stem upright before filling in the soil. When transplanting within the garden especially rather tender evergreens, keep a good compact ball of soil round the roots, and a piece of canvas pulled underneath the ball will facilitate movement. Avoid planting in frosty weather, as the roots are chilled when they come in contact with the frozen soil.

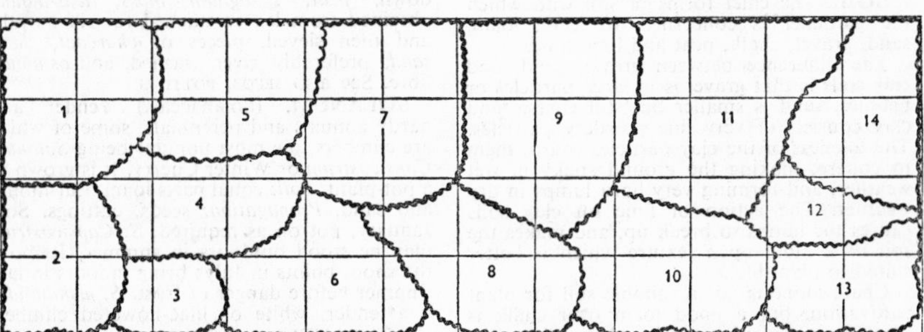

Fig. 59. Suggested plan of a shrub border: (1) Cotoneaster Francheti; *(2)* Cytisus purgans; *(3)* Potentilla fruticosa; *(4)* Kerria japonica; *(5)* Buddleia variabilis; *(6)* Deutzia gracilis; *(7) Escallonia, C.F. Ball; (8)* Philadelphus hybridus, *Manteau d'Hermine; (9)* Forsythia intermedia spectabilis; *(10)* Berberis Wilsonae; *(11)* Ceanothus hybridus, *Gloire de Versailles; (12)* Hypericum patulum Forrestii; *(13)* Lavandula nana compacta; *(14)* Chamaecyparis.

Pruning trees: never allow young trees to grow two leaders, as storms in later years may split the fork. With dry woods such as oaks, beeches and hornbeams, the branches can be pruned at any time, but with sappy woods such as birch, horse-chestnut, conifers and maple the branches can be pruned only in November. To make large cuts, saw beneath the branch a short way before commencing the downward cut. Cover all wounds with white lead paint or tar.

Shrubs: though presenting amateurs with some difficulty, there are a few guiding rules to follow which will help him provided that the general habit of the shrub is first studied. Its method of producing flowers, whether on new or old wood, the time of flowering, and whether the shrub is to provide a hedge, wind-break, or fruit, must all be ascertained. Thinning is often necessary, but the main principle is to maintain a well-shaped plant and encourage new growth from the base to replace the old. Remove all dead wood, weak, thin growth and branches which cross. *Evergreens* need little pruning and, if necessary, do so after flowering. Straggly growth can be removed after frosts are over in spring. *Deciduous shrubs* are divided into two groups: those flowering on old or previous year's wood, and those flowering on new wood. The first group is pruned back directly after flowering, the other generally in autumn or early spring.

SIBERIAN WALLFLOWER. See CHEIRANTHUS.

SLUGS AND SNAILS. See PEST CHART.

SNAPDRAGON. See ANTIRRHINUM.

SNOWDROP. *Galanthus.* (Amaryllidaceae.) One of the earliest flowering hardy bulbs, often commencing to show its white and green blooms in midwinter. Easily cultivated, it is best planted 4 in. deep and 2 in. apart in September, in banks, shady borders, rockeries or in turf. *Soil:* ordinary. Pot plants require two parts loam, one part leaf-mould, and some sand. *Propagation:* seed, though this takes three years to produce flowering bulbs; offsets. Bulbs need lifting only when too overcrowded. **Best to grow:** *G. nivalis* (wild snowdrop), *G. byzantinus*, *G. latifolius.*

SOIL. The chief forms of soil with which the gardener is concerned are clay, loam, sand, gravel, chalk, peat and limestone.

The difference between gravel, sand, and clay soils is that gravel is in large particles or pebbles, sand is smaller but still coarse, and clay consists of very fine powdery particles. The fineness of the clay particles causes them to cohere, making the ground sticky in wet weather, and forming very hard lumps in dry weather. The action of lime on clay soils causes the lumps to break up, and makes the soil of a more open texture which is better suited to plant-life.

Chalk alone is not a suitable soil for plant cultivation, but a good loam over chalk is ideal for many subjects. The chalk allows the water to pass away very rapidly, with the result that soil over chalk is inclined to dry out in summer. Though chalk and lime are practically the same thing, gardens over a chalk subsoil may need regular dressings of lime, the reason being that the lime in the soil is washed down into the subsoil, leaving the surface-layer lime-free. Chalk does not break up stiff soil as does builders' lime, but it is an excellent though slower-working substitute for lime on light soils.

Peaty soils are acid, that is, they are lime-free and contain plenty of decayed vegetable matter and fibre.

Methods of improving soils. For all soils deep digging with the addition of different substances is the keynote to good cultivation of vegetables, fruit and flowers. *Heavy soils:* are usually dug in autumn to allow the big clods to be broken down by winter frosts; other helpful additions are strawy stable manure, leaves, compost, bonfire-ash, grit and lime. This will make the sticky soil more open and porous. *Light soils:* the main requirement of these soils are cow and pig manure, compost, leaves, potash and lime given in regular applications. *Chalk soils:* give dressings of organic manure, and if ground is very light make it compact by rolling. Unless the subsoil is brought up as the digging is done, or lime-hating plants are being grown, give a dressing of lime after the digging is finished.

Methods of digging. Double-digging or mock-trenching is the most usual method of deep digging. The soil is turned over two spits deep (a spit is the depth of a spade, usually less than 1 ft.). But in doing so, as in all digging (except in special cases), the subsoil remains below the top soil in the normal way and is not brought to the surface.

Rockeries. Limestone and other rocks not yet broken down to the condition we call soil are often used by the gardener to made rock gardens. These limestone rocks are ideal for most rockeries, as they retain moisture, but their lime content should be kept in mind. Plants that naturally haunt the limestone valleys and hills will grow well amongst the imported limestone and will generally appreciate additional lime in the soil used for the rock garden.

Pot culture. Certain materials are necessary for pot culture. These include loam, obtainable from surface turf from good pasture or roadsides, stacked for six months and then chopped down, *peat*, *sphagnum moss*, *leaf-mould*, obtained from leaves stacked for six months and then sieved, pieces of *charcoal*, *sharp sand*, preferably river washed, and *osmunda* fibre. See also SEEDS, POTTING.

SOLANUM. (Solanaceae.) Tender and hardy annuals and perennials, some of which are climbers, the most popular being *Solanum Capsicastrum* or Winter Cherry. It is grown as a pot-plant. *Soil:* equal parts loam, leaf-mould and sand. *Propagation:* seeds, cuttings. Sow January, pot on as required. *S. Capsicastrum* may be stood outdoors in summer. Remove the shoot-points in July; bring indoors in late summer before danger of frost. *S. jasminoides* is a tender, white or lilac-flowered climber.

SOLDANELLA. (Primulaceae.) A charming spring-flowering hardy perennial for sheltered moist positions on the rockery. Plant in March or April in sandy loam, peat and leaf-mould. Top-dress with leaf soil and sand in autumn. *Propagation:* seeds, division after flowering. **Best to grow:** *S. alpina*, 3 in., blue; *S. montana*, 6 in., lavender flowers.

SOLOMON'S SEAL. See POLYGONATUM.

SORREL. See RUMEX.

SPARTIUM. Spanish Broom. (Leguminosea.) Bright yellow fragrant-flowered shrub. Hardy deciduous plant resembling a broom with pea-shaped blossom. *Plant:* October–March in open sunny banks or borders in ordinary soil. *Propagation:* seeds. **Best to grow:** *S. junceum*, 6 ft.–10 ft., June–September, and its double form, *flore pleno*.

SPHAGNUM MOSS. Grows in swampy places and retains moisture like a sponge. For this reason it is used for packing flowers and roots, and is also chopped up for use in composts for certain greenhouse plants.

SPINACH. *Spinacia oleracea.* (Chenopodiaceae.) A health-giving vegetable requiring a rich moist soil, since it must be well grown to produce large succulent leaves. Summer crops can be grown in shady places or sown as catch-crops to stand a month. Winter spinach is prickly-seeded and must be sown in sheltered sunny positions outdoors in August. Thin plants 6 in. apart and give dressing of sulphate of ammonia or nitrate of soda in March. See also VEGETABLE CHART.

SPINACH BEET. *Beta.* (Chenopodiaceae.) A form of beetroot grown for its leaves. Plants are hardy and crop for months in any position. Sow once in March and again in August for all-year-round supply. Sow seed in pairs 9 in. apart in rows 18 in. apart and single them later.

SPIRAEA. Meadowsweet. (Rosaceae.) A large genus of many lovely flowering shrubs and herbs of which the herbaceous species are often forced in pots. *Soil:* moist loam. *Propagation:* seeds, cuttings. **Best to grow:** Herbaceous, moist positions on margins of streams; *S. astilboides* (syn. *Astilbe*) and its many named varieties; *S. Aruncus*, 4 ft.–6 ft., cream plumes; *S. venusta*, 5 ft., pale pink; *S. Ulmaria flore pleno*, a fine form of our native meadowsweet. Deciduous shrubs, *S. arguta*, 6 ft.–8 ft., white, April; *S. discolor*, 8 ft.–12 ft., cream-white, July; *S. bumalda*, Anthony Waterer, 2 ft.–3 ft., crimson, July–October.

SPRUCE. See CONIFERS.

STATICE. Sea Lavender. (Plumbaginaceae.) Hardy and half-hardy annuals and perennials for sunny rockeries or borders. Plant March or April in sandy loam. The dried flowers will retain their colour for many months. *Propagation:* seed. **Best to grow:** *S. latifolia*, 2 ft., purple, perennial. *S. Sinuata*, purple or yellow, 1 ft., annual.

STOCK. *Matthiola.* (Cruciferae.) A glorious family providing sweet-scented blooms of many colours for the greater part of the year. Pot-plants for winter decoration require loam, leaf-mould and sand, and should be sown in July in a cold frame. For summer flowers sow in spring under glass, or outside later. Biennials are sown any time during the summer to flower the following year. **Best to grow:** Brompton stocks, biennials, 2 ft., branching growth, bears blooms May–July; best used for bedding. East Lothian stocks, 1 ft., half-hardy annuals resembling Bromptons, flowering June–September; sow in cold frame in August and plant out in following April. Beauty of Nice stock, 2 ft., very showy in early summer. For summer sow under glass in February. For spring sow in cold frame in August.

STOCK, Virginia. See MALCOLMIA.

STONECROP. See SEDUM.

STRAWBERRY. See FRUIT AND ITS CULTURE.

STRAWBERRY TREE. See ARBUTUS.

SUGAR PEA. *Pisum sativum.* (Leguminosae.) Cultivated for its edible pod, instead of the actual peas. For cultivation see PEA.

SUNFLOWER. See HELIANTHUS.

SWEDE. See VEGETABLE CHART.

SWEET PEA. *Lathyrus odoratus.* (Leguminosae.) One of the world's most popular flowers, this hardy annual is easily cultivated in the open garden or under glass.

Outdoor cultivation. Sow seed where it is to grow in March or April, 2 in. deep and 3 in.–6 in. apart, preferably over a trench that has been deeply dug and manured if they are to be grown in a line. Otherwise sow in clumps in the herbaceous border. Sowing in autumn, either in a cold frame or outside, is often practised. All plants must be staked with branches or bamboo canes (Fig. 60) if they are not grown against fences. Water copiously in dry weather and give frequent application of liquid manure to plants in flower.

Cultivation under glass. Sow peas in boxes or pots in September, and keep in a cold frame or greenhouse, potting them on as required in a compost of two parts loam, one part leaf-mould and sand. Transfer to trenches prepared with manure and bonemeal or to pots where they are to flower. Support shoots and water liberally, and feed with liquid manure. Sweet peas under glass may need shading in bright sun as they are apt to scorch and fade and therefore are unfit for exhibition.

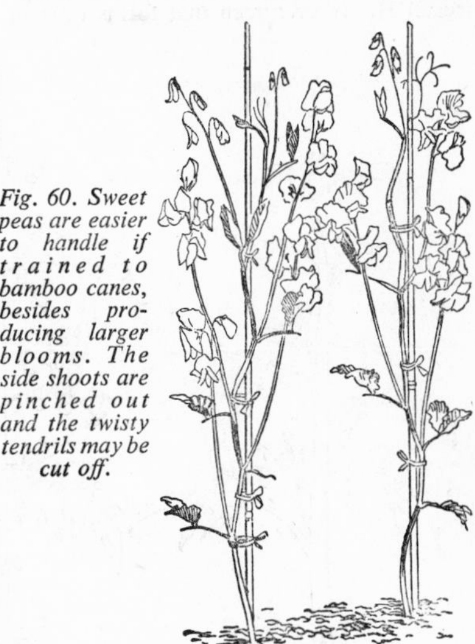

Fig. 60. Sweet peas are easier to handle if trained to bamboo canes, besides producing larger blooms. The side shoots are pinched out and the twisty tendrils may be cut off.

Keen growers for exhibition are recommended to consult the literature of the National Sweet Pea Society, which has done useful work in listing varieties that are too much alike to be exhibited in the same class as separate varieties. **Best to grow:** there are many beautiful varieties of which the following are recommended. Duchess of Gloucester (cherry red), Mount Everest (white, frilled edge), Gigantic (white), Youth (white ground, picotee edge), Powerscourt (lavender), Ambition (deep lavender), Startler (scarlet), Mrs. A. Searles (salmon-cerise), Flamingo (orange-scarlet), Copper Mahogany (mahogany), Lady Lilford (light blue), Purple Monarch (deep purple), Mabel Gower (blue).

SWEET SULTAN. See CENTAUREA.

SWEET WILLIAM. See CARNATION.

SYCAMORE. *Acer pseudo-platanus.* (Sapindaceae.) A hardy tree suitable for exposed and wind-swept positions. It will grow 1,500 ft. above sea-level. Is a good timber tree. *Propagation:* easily raised from seed in any soil.

SYRINGA. See LILAC.

TAMARIX. Tamarisk. (Tamaricaceae.) Hardy deciduous and evergreen shrubs with feathery leaves and attractive pink and white plumes. Plant in winter or early spring in shrubberies or hedges. They are especially suitable for seaside gardens. *Prune* to a good shape, October–March. *Propagation:* hardwood cuttings in autumn.

THALICTRUM. Meadow Rue. (Ranunculaceae.) Herbaceous perennials with divided foliage resembling a maidenhair fern. Easily grown in ordinary moist soil on sunny borders or rockeries. *Propagation:* division in spring. **Best to grow:** *T. dipterocarpum*, 6 ft., lilac and its good variety Hewitt's Double. *T. minus* var. *adiantifolium*, 2 ft., a useful foliage plant.

THRIFT. Sea Pink. Armeria. (Plumbaginaceae.) Hardy evergreen that forms tufts or cushions bearing bright pink globular flower-heads. Easily grown as edging-plants, or on rockeries. *Soil:* ordinary, or sandy loam. *Propagation:* seeds, division. **Best to grow:** *A. cephalotes*, variety Bees Glory, 1½ ft., rose. *A. maritima*, native sea pink, and its varieties *alba* (white), Vindictive (deep pink), 8 in. high. *A. alpina*, 6-in., grass-like foliage, for rockeries.

THYMUS. Thyme. (Labiatae.) Compact trailing plants, excellent for covering bare patches in the rock garden. Herbaceous perennials requiring light ordinary or sandy loam. Replant culinary plants every three or four years, and gather for drying before blossoms appear. *Propagation:* seed sown in April; cuttings; division. **Best to grow:** *T. vulgaris*, culinary thyme. *T. Serpyllum*, varieties red, pink or white, for rock garden.

TIGRIDIA. Tiger Flower. (Iridaceae.) Half-hardy bulbs bearing handsome flowers which, though short-lived, are freely produced over a long period. *Soil:* equal parts loam, leaf-mould and plenty of sand. Plant in a sunny, well-dug position, 3 in. deep and 6 in. apart, in April. Mulch when plants are a few inches high, and water freely in dry weather. Lift bulbs for storing in October. The bulbs are often used as pot-plants. *Propagation:* seeds, offsets. In mild localities plant in south border and leave undisturbed.

TOBACCO FLOWER. See NICOTIANA.

TOMATO. *Lycopersicum esculentum.* (Solanaceae.) The edible fruit of this tender annual is very wholesome. Modern hardier strains can be raised fairly easily if given a little care and attention.

Outdoor cultivation. Plant outside at the end of May or June as soon as the frosts are over. Choose a warm sheltered place, preferably a south border open to the sun, beside a fence or wall. Always plant well away from potatoes, since they are affected by the same diseases. Dig the ground thoroughly and apply artificial manure containing potash; avoid land recently manured with stable manure.

Plant tomatoes running north to south if possible, 18 in. apart, either in double or single rows at least 2 ft.–2½ ft. apart. Plants in double rows are placed alternately 18 in. apart with 9 in. between the double rows. Give each plant a firm stake or string it to an overhead wire supported by stakes. Pinch out all side-shoots and tie in main stem to the stake or twist it round the string (Fig. 61). Plants can be tapped regularly to shake the pollen from flower to flower. Apply stimulants; liquid manure being good when fruit has set. Collect green fruits in late September to colour indoors. Alternatively, the stakes

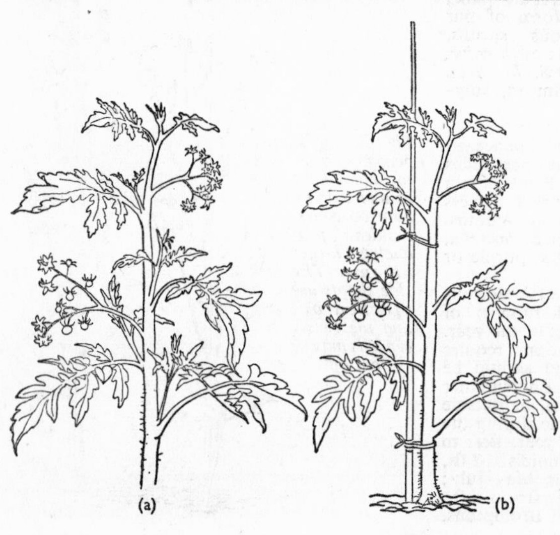

Fig. 61. Tomato plant: (a) *before disbudding;* (b) *after disbudding and staking.*

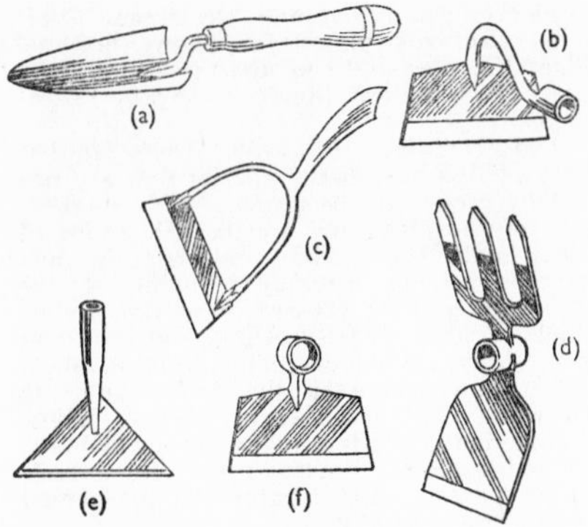

Fig. 62. Useful tools: (a) *hand trowel for planting;* (b) *broad potato hoe;* (c) *Dutch hoe;* (d) *double-purpose hoe, useful on lumpy soils;* (e) *triangle hoe;* (f) *draw hoe.*

can be removed and plants laid along the ground on small supporting forked sticks and covered with cloches.

Propagation: plants are raised from seed sown under glass in March or early April; prick seedlings out later and pot up. Harden off before planting.

Indoor culture. Sow in heat in January or February, or in a cold-house in mid-April. Sow evenly and in a good seed compost (see PROPAGATION). Cover with glass and paper until they germinate. Prick out carefully and grow on in pots, being careful to give them maximum light and no checks. Grow in large pots or plant in borders in the house, 12 in. apart. Train on strings or stakes, removing all side shoots, taking care not to damage terminal shoot. Spray in hot weather; spraying and shaking the plants will assist pollination. Give full ventilation and plenty of water once fruits have set. Avoid too much dampness on cold nights and watch out for disease. Top-dress with well-rotted cow or horse manure or a good compost when the roots appear on the surface.

Apply stimulants when the fruit has set; for example, 1 part nitrate of soda, 1 part dried blood, and 2 parts superphosphate applied at 1 oz. per sq. yd., or ½ oz. per gallon of water and watered on. Green tomatoes can be ripened if wrapped in soft paper and put in a dry cupboard or kept on shelves between straw. Best temperature is 45 deg. to 50 deg. **Best to grow:** outdoors, Harbinger, Sunrise, Essex Wonder, Kondine Red, Market King, Ailsa Craig, Stoner's M.P.; indoors, Potentate, Market King, Sutton's Earliest of All, Sunrise.

TOOLS. The gardener should buy the best tools that he can afford, and see that they are always cleaned and stored away after use.

The following tools are those in common use (some are shown in Fig. 62). *Bulb-planter* removes circular plugs of soil by means of iron circle fixed to the handle. Useful for planting bulbs in grass. *Cloches:* sheets of glass pegged together to form shelters for early or late crops. *Cultivator:* three to five steel prongs fixed to a wooden handle. *Daisy-grubber:* a short-handled, two- or three-pronged tool for inserting beneath lawn weeds. *Dibber:* a pointed piece of wood, sometimes metal-capped, used for planting-out seedlings. Dibbers made from broken spade handles are very effective. The point should be slightly rounded. *Edging-iron:* used with garden line to straighten lawn edgings, or cut turf sods. Consists of half-moon-shaped metal cutter attached to a wooden handle. *Edging-trimmer:* a small tool on the lawn-mower system, which can be run along the lawn edges. *Edging-shears:* shears at right-angles to their long handles.

Forks: border-forks have either four or five square prongs and are small and light. For women, the prongs are sometimes oval, which decreases the weight. Digging forks are heavier than border-forks, and slightly larger, but with the same number of prongs. Potato forks are broader than digging forks and the prongs are usually flattened. Hand forks are useful for working between rock plants, seedlings, etc. A forged fork is always worth the extra money. *Garden line:* a length of rope fixed to a metal pin. It can easily be made at home (Fig. 63). *Hoe:* two main types, draw- or

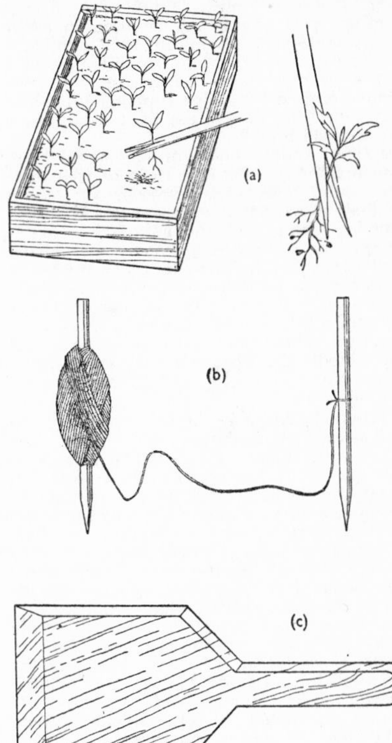

Fig. 63. Some home-made tools: (a) *forked stick for lifting seedlings;* (b) *garden line;* (c) *scraper to remove mud from spade.*

drag-hoe, pulled towards the worker who moves forward over the ground he has actually worked over, and Dutch or flat hoe, pushed away from the user, who walks backward over the ground he has not yet worked. *Hose:* the black corrugated-rubber type does not kink, but is not so lasting as the canvas-wrapped type. For lengths up to 100 ft. a bore ½ in. in diameter is sufficient, and ⅝ in. is adequate for 200-ft. lengths. *Incinerator:* a galvanized-iron bin-like structure with a central flue. The ashes can be used as a fertilizer. *Labels:* white-painted wooden labels are suitable for temporary use. Metal tabs with stamped names are everlasting.

Lawn-mowers should be bought from reliable makers, so that separate parts can be replaced. The machine should be fitted with ball-bearings, the blade adjustments should be easy to manipulate by hand, handle and grass-box should be easily adjustable, gears should be enclosed, and only good-quality oil used. A 14-in. mower is advised for a one-acre lawn. *Rake:* used to give a fine tilth on seed beds before sowing. Usually 6 in.–16 in. wide. *Roller:* double-cylinder type is useful for most gardens. *Secateurs or pruners, shears:* three main types, guillotine, useful for general pruning; parrot-beak can be used in either hand; single-cut type, skilfully used with blade uppermost, is less likely to bruise the growing plant than other types. Shears used with two hands are used for hedge clipping. Long-arm shears on long handle are used for pruning out-of-reach branches.

Spade: straight blade of hammered steel, with preferably a flat iron tread or transverse bar is the best type. *Sprayers:* vary from hand-syringe and bottle-sprayer to a knapsack spraying outfit, and the admirable stirrup-pump. The syringe used chiefly for smaller gardens should have interchangeable nozzles of various sizes. *Trowels* vary from 5 in.–8 in. in length. *Wheelbarrow:* ash or elm wood is recommended, as it does not warp. Detachable tops are obtainable. Pneumatic tyres are undoubtedly the best. *Watering cans:* greenhouse cans need to be lighter than those for outdoor work.

TRADESCANTIA. Spider wort. (Commelinaceae.) Greenhouse and hardy herbaceous perennials. Plant hardy species in shady or sunny borders of ordinary soil. Lift plants and divide every three to five years, in spring or autumn. Flowers last only for a day, but there is a constant succession from June to September. An excellent plant for town gardens. The greenhouse species needs equal parts loam, leaf-mould and sand. It can be grown along the staging edge or underneath, besides as a pot plant. *Propagation:* divide hardy perennials; cuttings in heat. **Best to grow:** *T. virginiana*, 1 ft.–2 ft., blue, and its varieties Merlin (lavender pink), *alba* (white), *delicata* (pale blue). Tender species: *T. zebrina*, variegated foliage, purplish flowers.

TREES. See SHRUBS and TREES.

TRIFOLIUM. Clover. (Leguminosae.) Hardy perennial. *Soil:* ordinary. *Propagation:* seed, division. **Best to grow:** *T. alpinum*, 4 in., pale pink, for rockeries. *T. repens purpureum*, creeping, purple-blotched leaves.

TRITONIA. *Montbretia*. (Iridaceae.) Deciduous bulbous plants for sunny borders. Plant 3 in. deep and 2 in. apart in well-drained good loam during March or April. *Propagation:* offsets.

TULIP. *Tulipa*. (Liliaceae.) These familiar hardy bulbs have many species that are not usually grown in the garden; many of them are very beautiful and are the wild tulips of other lands. The bedding tulips used in most gardens belong, generally speaking, to the following groups: (1) early-flowering tulips, single, double, dwarf-growing, and flowering April–May; (2) Mendel tulips, Triumph tulips, which flower between the earlies and the Darwins; (3) Darwin tulips, breeder tulips, double and single late tulips, flower in May; (4) old-fashioned English tulips, Rembrandt tulips, parrot tulips, bizarre and bybloemen tulips, flower in May.

Culture outdoors. Tulips will grow on most types of soil, a well-drained loam that has been manured for the previous crop is ideal; they do not do well on water-logged, newly-manured land or naturalized in grass. *Plant:* October–November, 4 in. deep, according to the size of the bulb. Plant 7 in.–9 in. apart, but if carpet bedding is used they can be farther apart. Make sure all the bulbs are the same depth down to ensure even flowering. Remove all seed pods and, when the leaves have died right down, lift the bulbs, dry them and store until autumn. If ground is wanted for further bedding, bulbs can be heeled in temporarily elsewhere until they have died down. **Best to grow:** early single, General de Wet (gold), Keizerskroon (scarlet, edged yellow), Prince of Austria (orange-scarlet), Couleur de Cardinal (crimson). Double early, Peach Blossom (pink), Mr. Van de Hoeff (yellow), Orange Nassau (orange-scarlet), Schoonoord (white). Mendel, Van de Erden (scarlet), Mozart (pink and white). Triumph, Rynland (crimson, yellow edge), Bandoeng (mahogany red). Darwin, Clara Butt (pink), Inglescombe Yellow (canary yellow), Farncombe Sanders (brick red), La Tulipe Noire (black), William Copeland (lavender-blue), Carrara (white). Parrot, Fantasy (salmon-pink), Red Champion (red), Blue Parrot (bluish heliotrope).

TULIP TREE. See LIRIODENDRON.

TURNIP. See VEGETABLE CHART.

URSINIA. (Compositae.) Half-hardy annuals bearing brilliant orange-yellow blooms. *Propagation:* sow under glass in February or March, or outdoors in May. *Soil:* ordinary.

VACCINIUM. (Vacciniaceae.) Evergreen and deciduous shrubs bearing berries known as bilberry, whortleberry, huckleberry. Grow in boggy peat or sandy loam, or lime-free soil that has plenty of moisture, in rock garden or shrubbery. *Propagation:* layers in autumn, seeds, cuttings. **Best to grow:** deciduous, *V. Canadense*, 1 ft., white; *V. Myrtillus*, 2 ft., pale pink. Evergreen, *V. Vitis-Idaea*, 6 in.–10 in., pink.

VALERIAN. See CENTRANTHUS.

VALLOTA. Scarborough Lily. (Amaryllidaceae.) Tender evergreen bulb with lily-like blooms that will grow in very sheltered outdoor positions in warm districts. Pot-plants require equal parts loam, leaf-mould and sand. Re-pot in June only when necessary. Outdoors, light sandy loam; give protection in winter. *Propagation:* offsets.

VEGETABLE GARDEN. When choosing a vegetable plot, select land that is open to the sun, that is, not overshadowed by trees or buildings, but where the winds are not too strong and biting. Open situations can be screened on the north and east sides by erecting fences, planting hedges, or even putting in rows of Jerusalem artichokes.

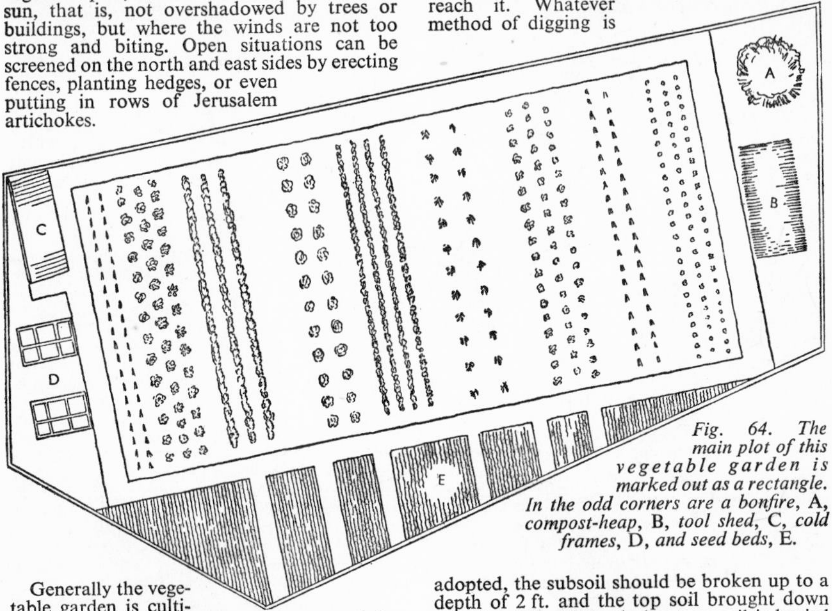

Fig. 64. The main plot of this vegetable garden is marked out as a rectangle. In the odd corners are a bonfire, A, *compost-heap,* B, *tool shed,* C, *cold frames,* D, *and seed beds,* E.

Generally the vegetable garden is cultivated on conventional lines, the crops being grown in rows parallel with each other and running north to south, or as nearly as possible in this direction (Fig. 64).

Make careful plans before laying out, as some crops will be permanent while others change from season to season. Asparagus beds, for instance, are a permanent feature which when once planted will remain for many years. When planning a garden the first thing is to allot a position for the permanent crops, then mark out the area to be used for other crops, and make good serviceable paths.

After this prepare the soil by deep digging (see Figs. 65, 66 and 67). The darker-coloured true soil above the paler subsoil is the most fertile, and should always be kept on the surface where the young plants and seed can reach it. Whatever method of digging is adopted, the subsoil should be broken up to a depth of 2 ft. and the top soil brought down to a fine tilth. If the darker true soil is buried beneath clay or house excavations, bring it to the surface. Incorporate as much decayed manure as possible, stable manure, decayed leaves, compost, household refuse are all suitable. After digging, dust soil with lime, which can be left to be washed in by the rain. If the ground is prepared in winter, leave the surface rough and lumpy, so that the frost can break it down to a fine tilth for seed sowing.

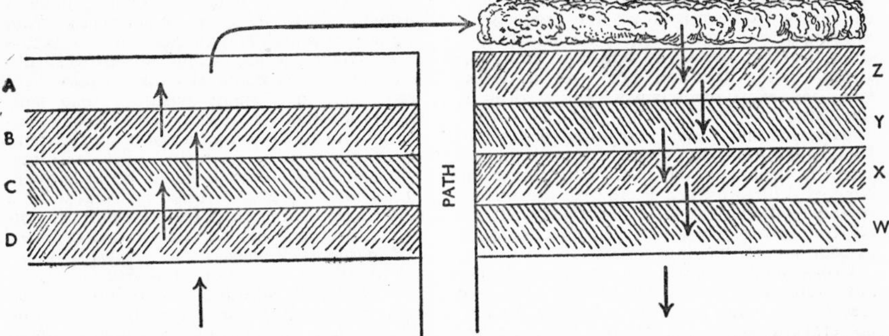

Fig. 65. When double digging begin by piling soil from A *near* Z. *Fill trench* A *with soil from* B *and trench* B *with soil from* C, *and so on to* Z, *which is filled from the original pile. (See also Fig. 67.)*

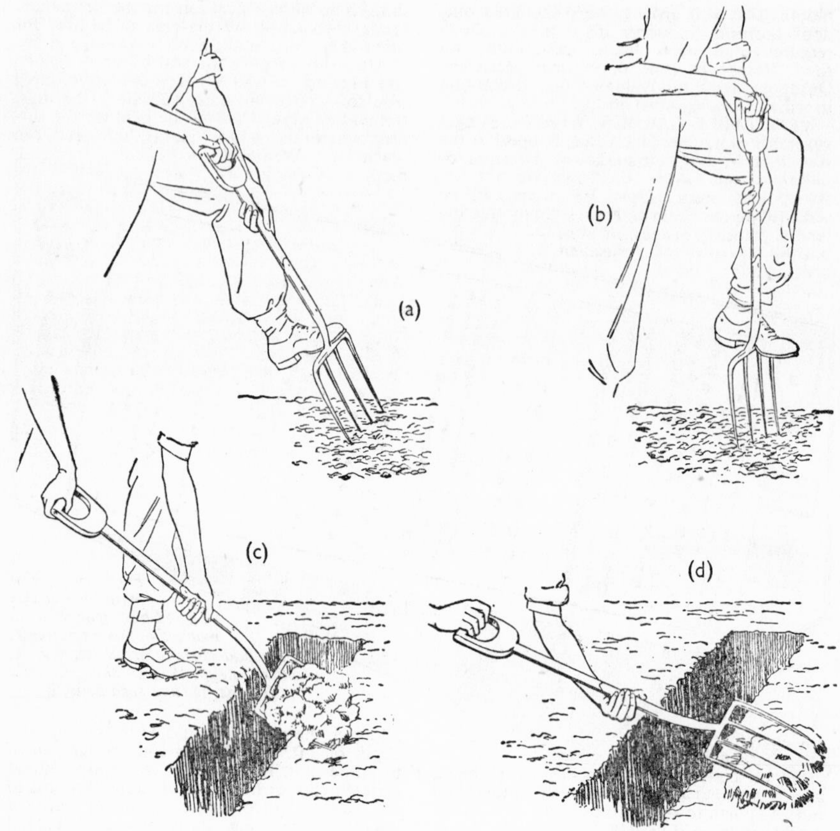

Fig. 66. How to dig. The fork should not be inserted on the slant (a), *but vertically* (b). *Lift out a whole forkful of soil* (c) *and turn it over completely* (d). *Note position of the hands.*

For sowing, use a rake to prepare the surface, then take out drills (long shallow trenches, 2 in.–3 in. deep) with the corner of a draw hoe, guided by a taut garden line. The gardener can move backwards down the line, always keeping a foot firmly planted on it to keep it from moving. Draw the hoe-edge along the string, taking the soil out with a corner (Fig. 58). Most seeds can be scattered along the drill.

Remove line before covering the seeds. Either rake soil over the seeds or push the soil into the drill with the feet. Walk down the covered drill to firm it. Rake over the surface to tidy and to remove the footmarks. Label all rows with name, variety and date, and hoe as soon as the seedlings appear.

Crops hoed regularly are healthier, cleaner and more attractive than neglected ones. The seed-bed or nursery plot for seedlings of cauliflower, cabbage, etc., is set aside to raise crops for transplanting. These are planted as the space becomes available. See ROTATION.

VEGETABLE MARROW. See PUMPKIN.

VERBASCUM. See MULLEIN.

VERBENA. (Verbenaceae.) The half-hardy biennials used as bedding plants make a brilliant show if sown under glass from January to March and planted out in May and June. Other species include flowering shrubs and herbaceous perennials that require light fertile soil in a sunny position. Also half-hardy pot-plants requiring sandy loam, leaf-mould and a little manure. Pot up in February or March and water freely whilst flowering. Nip out shoot points to ensure bushy growth. *Propagation:* seeds, cuttings in August in a cold frame; in February from greenhouse pot-plants. **Best to grow:** varieties of *V. teucrioides*, *V. bonariensis*, *V. venosa*.

VERBENA. Lemon-scented. See LIPPIA.

VERONICA. Speedwell. (Scrophulariaceae.) A large genus of hardy evergreen flowering shrubs and herbaceous perennials. *Shrub culture:* especially valuable for seaside gardens. Plant in September or April in ordinary or peaty soil in a sunny position. Protect in severe weather. Prune to shape in April. *Herbaceous plants:* for sunny borders or rockeries of ordinary soil. Replant and divide every three years. Water well in dry weather.

VIBURNUM. Guelder Rose. Laurustinus. (Caprifoliaceae.) A hardy family including many lovely flowering evergreens and deciduous shrubs. *Soil:* moist sandy loam in warm sheltered shrubberies. Plant deciduous species in October or March and evergreens in September or May. *Prune* to shape and thin out in winter. *Propagation:* layers in October, cuttings. **Best to grow:** evergreens, *V. cylindricum*, 10 ft., white, July–September; *V. Tinus* (laurustinus), 8 ft.–10 ft., white and pink, winter-flowering. Deciduous, *V. Carlesii*, 3 ft.–4 ft., sweet scented, pinkish-white flowers in April, suitable for seaside; *V. fragrans*, 10 ft., fragrant winter flowers of pinkish-white; *V. Opulus* (guelder rose), 10 ft.–15 ft., white, red autumn berries and foliage; *V. tomentosum* var. *plicatum* (the best "snowball" tree).

VINE. See VITIS.

VIOLA. Pansy. (Violaceae.) Favourite free-flowering and free-growing herbs for borders, rockeries or bedding. Show pansies have round blooms with thick velvety petals with a dark centre containing an orange eye. The tufted pansies known usually as violas have smaller blooms and dwarf habit. Fancy pansies have wavy or crinkled edges and a solid orange eye. *Soil:* rich moist loam. Exhibition plants need old manure and bonemeal added when ground is prepared in autumn. Plant in March or April, 10 in. apart, restricting the growth of exhibition plants to 2 in.–3 in. Water freely in dry weather, and stir surface-soil frequently. Feed with liquid manure every week or ten days. The dwarf bedding violas with the stiff erect stem of numerous blooms will grow in most soils. *Propagation:* all species can be raised from seeds. For flowers true to type take cuttings of exhibition and named plants in July and August. Plants can be cut back in late summer and cuttings of vigorous basal

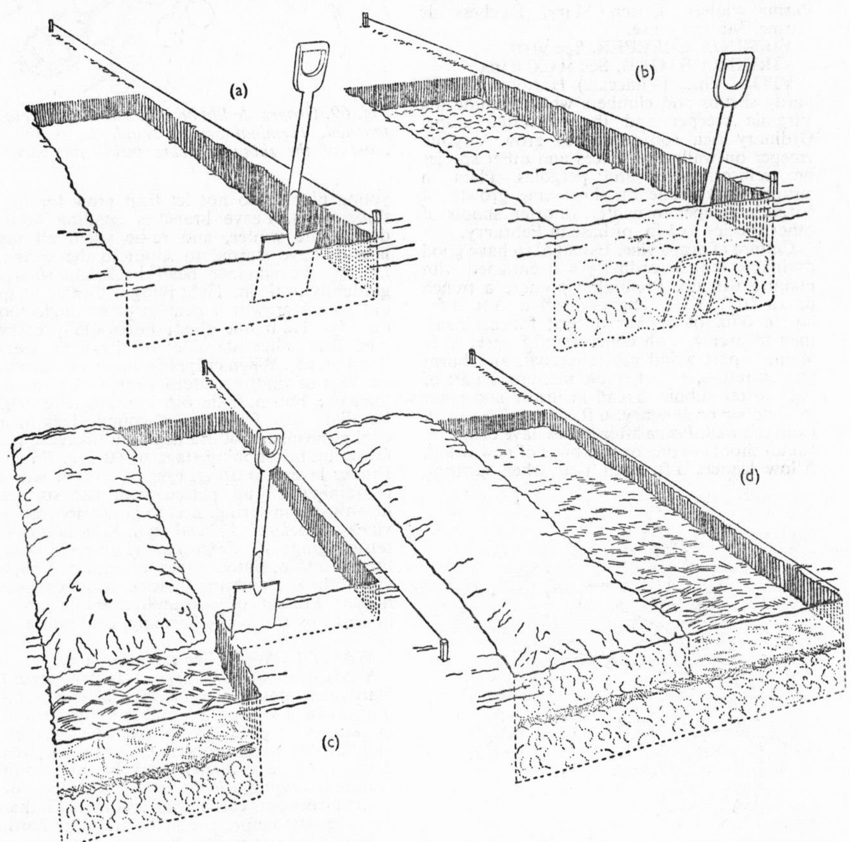

Fig. 67. Double digging: (a) *dig trench, removing soil as in Fig. 66;* (b) *fork bottom of trench, mixing in manure or compost;* (c) *dig next trench, filling first trench;* (d) *second trench forked.*

shoots are struck in frames. **Best to grow:** bedding violas, Blue Stone, Cambridge Blue, Jackanapes (mahogany, red and gold), Haslemere (lavender-pink). Modern show violas are many and varied, and include some glorious colours. *Violettas* have dwarf bushy growth and oval, scented flowers. Rock garden violas, *V. gracilis*, and its varieties, Black Knight (purple and black), Moonlight (creamy-yellow), Cornelia (blue-mauve).

VIOLET. *Viola odorata.* (Violaceae.) Grow these hardy perennials on ordinary soil enriched with old manure in partly shaded positions, preferably facing west. Plant 9 in. apart in rows 12 in. apart in April, water in fine weather, and feed with liquid manure. Remove runners. For winter flowering lift in September and plant in a cold frame close to the glass. Protect from frost but give plenty of air. Break up plants and re-make bed annually. *Propagation:* divide after flowering, cuttings in spring. **Best to grow:** singles, Princess of Wales, La France (both violet), White Czar (white), Admiral Avellan (rose). Double Parma violets, Queen Mary, Duchess de Parme, Marie Louise.

VIRGINIA CREEPER. See VITIS.

VIRGINIA STOCK. See MALCOLMIA.

VITIS. Vine. (Vitaceae.) Hardy and half-hardy shrubs and climbers which include the Virginia creeper and the cultivated grape. Ordinary rich soil outdoors; grow Virginia creeper on walls and fences and other species on trellises, poles and pergolas. Plant in autumn and prune by shortening growth of Virginia creeper in winter. Shorten shoots of other species to 1 in. of base in February.

Culture of grape vine. Essential to have good drainage, though ordinary soil enriched with manure will do. Preferably prepare a trench up to 10 ft. wide. Dig out soil to 3 ft.–4 ft., lay in 6 in. of clinker or grit for drainage, then fill trench with compost of 5 parts turfy loam, 1 part wood ash, charcoal, and burnt garden refuse, 1 part stable manure, 1 part of old mortar rubble. Tread in firmly and plant in October or January, 6 ft. apart, 1 ft.–1½ ft. from the wall. *Prune* after leaves have dropped, cut all shoots to one or two buds of new wood. Allow leaders 3 ft. each year when growing young plants; do not let fruit grow for first three years. Leave branches bending down during the winter, and re-tie when all the laterals have started to shoot in the spring. During the summer bend back the shoots gradually to tie in. Tight tying will often snap out young growth if bent in at an angle too quickly. Train one shoot horizontally every 9 in. from alternate sides of the main stem (see Fig. 68). When cropping, allow one bunch per foot of vine; no lateral should carry more than one bunch. Thin out bunches (Fig. 69). Ventilate very freely, start young vines in a cool atmosphere, 40–45 deg., and increase for flowering in cropping stage to 60 deg. *Propagation:* layers, grafting, eyes of 2 in. of wood containing a bud placed with cut surface downwards in spring. **Best to grow:** decorative vines, *Ampelopsis Veitchii* (syn. *V. inconstans*), self-clinging; *V. Coignetiae* (Japanese vine), huge crimson, tinted leaves in autumn. Grape vine, Black Hamburg (black), cool- or hot-house; Muscat of Alexandria (white), hot-house; Foster's White Seedling, cool house.

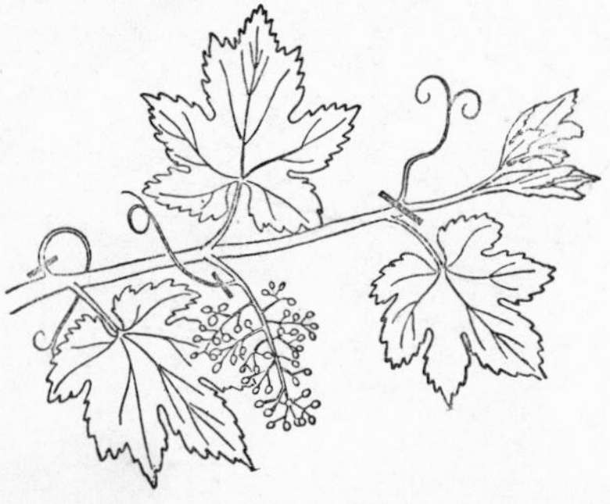

Fig. 68. Remove tendrils from vines and stop shoots at third leaf, just above the joint.

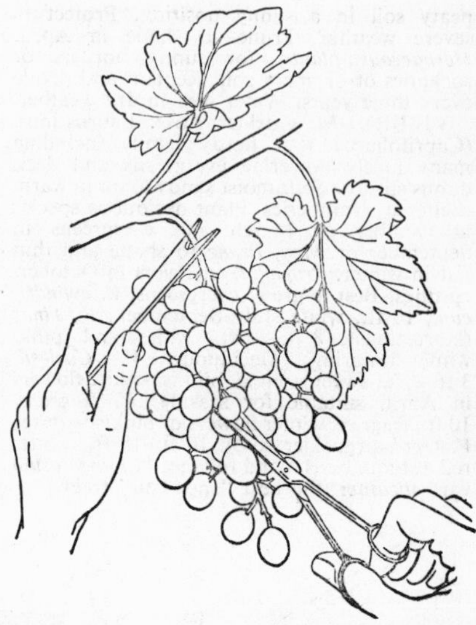

Fig. 69. Grapes should be thinned without being touched. Terminal berries should be retained, most of the thinning being inside the bunch.

WALLFLOWER. See CHEIRANTHUS.

WALNUT. *Juglans regia.* (Juglandaceae.) Hardy deciduous tree valued for its timber and nuts. *Plant:* October–November in open south or south-west positions not overshadowed by buildings or other trees. *Soil:* ordinary, well drained. Store ordinary nuts in sand until required. *Propagation:* seeds; budded or grafted trees bear earlier than seedlings. Gather pickling nuts before the shells are quite hard.

WATERCRESS. See CRESS, WATER.

WATER PLANTS. The three general groups of water plants consist of marginal plants, decorative plants, aerating or oxygenating plants. The last group must be grown in ponds where fish are kept. Fish take oxygen from the water and return carbon dioxide. This will, if absorbed into the water, cause it to become grey and smell unpleasant. Plants in the presence of sunlight absorb the carbon dioxide and thus restore the balance. Plants for cultivation in fish ponds: shallow ponds, *Callitriche obtusangula*, *Ranunculus*, *Myriophullum*; medium ponds, *Elodea canadensis*, *E. crispa*, *E. densa*, *Potomageton*, *Ceratophyllum*.

Among the decorative plants the best known are the *Nymphaeas* or water-lilies. These need 2 ft. depth of water, except for pygmy species which grow in 12 in.–18 in. *Nelumbium*, *Nuphar*, *Brasenia*, and *Sagittaria* are also suitable for growing in ponds for decoration. *Water-lily culture:* plant in the mud of a natural pond or stream by enclosing the roots with a little soil in a loosely-woven basket and dropping it into the bottom of the water. Roots can also be tied between two turves and lowered in the same way. In artificial ponds, put on a 6-in. layer of soil over the bottom. Large water-lilies need 6 ft. between each plant, pygmy species can be as close as 2 ft. Heavy loam enriched with cow manure or bonemeal is best for water-lilies. Plant in May or before the last week in June.

Plant other water plants in the same way if a new pond is being made (Fig. 70). It is generally best to plant before the pond is filled, covering the newly-set roots with a few inches of water only, and gradually adding more as growth continues.

Aquatic plants for warm greenhouse tanks need similar treatment. It will pay the amateur to obtain full details from the firm that supplies the plants. **Best to grow:** water-lilies are obtainable in many modern colours. For tubs, *Nymphaea alba* (white), *N. Moorei* (canary yellow), *N. Marliaca rosea* (flesh, fragrant), *N. pygmaea alba* (dwarf white). For greenhouse tanks, *N. Escarboucle* (bright crimson), *N. coerulea* (blue).

Nuphars are easily cultivated water-lilies, and can be grown by throwing seed into the water. *Nuphar luteum*, the yellow British water-lily, is a commercial variety. *Nelumbiums* are suitable for greenhouse tanks, and are pink and white; usually called water-beans. Floating plants can be classed with decorative aquatics. These include *Azolla caroliniana*, *Hydrocharis morsus-ranae*, *Lemna*, *Stratiotes*.

Some of the best marginal plants are *Acorus*, *Alisma*, *Butomus*, *Caltha*, *Iris*, *Juncus*, *Mimulus* and *Myosotis palustris*.

WEED-KILLERS. These must be carefully mixed and watered on to paths, etc., from a can that is not used for ordinary waterings unless it is scrupulously cleaned out. Do not use weed-killers on ground in which garden plants are growing. Sodium chlorate is one of the best and can be used from ¼ lb. to 1 lb. per gallon according to the resistance of the weeds to be killed. Use a 5 per cent solution of sodium chlorate for paths and drives; it kills bindweed on tennis courts and is excellent for nettles, chickweed, etc. For dandelion and plantain, use 5 parts by weight sulphate of ammonia, 2 parts sulphate of iron mixed with dry soil. Ivy on walls and trees, drill holes in the wood and fill with sodium arsenate.

On lime acid soils, where cornflower, horsetail, heath, sprug, ox-eye daisy, moss and pearlwort grow, kainit applications reduce charlock, chickweed, thistles and speedwell.

Lawn sands and proprietary weed-killers are excellent if the instructions are carefully followed. Beware of concentrated fluids, for they may have a caustic effect on the skin.

WEEDS. Gardeners are required by law to clear their ground of weeds, not for their own benefit, but for their neighbours. In clearing out weeds the soil is aerated by using the hoe, and annual weeds may be turned over to make green manure. Bracken, bindweed, deadly nightshade, charlock, coltsfoot, dock,

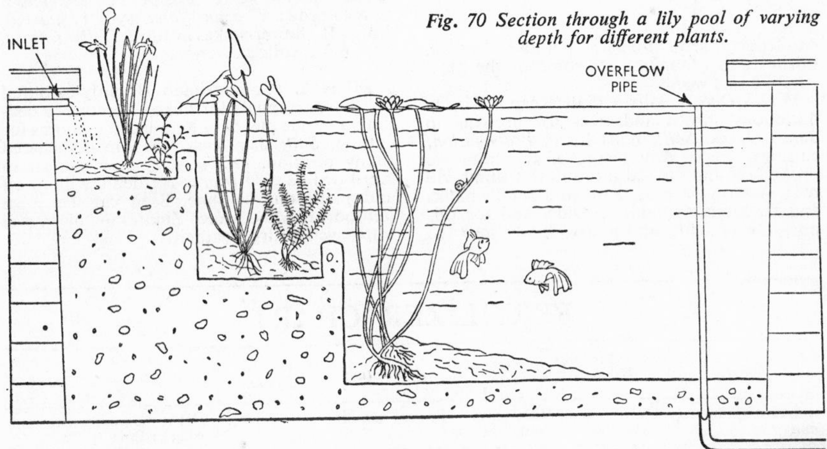

Fig. 70 Section through a lily pool of varying depth for different plants.

Fig. 71. Yucca has pointed leaves and creamy-white drooping flowers on handsome spikes. With one exception yuccas do not flower when young.

dandelion, ground-elder, plantain, nettle, thistles and groundsel are some of the most troublesome weeds.

WILLOW. Salix. (Salicaceae.) Hardy deciduous shrubs and trees for growing in damp places. *Soil:* moist loam. *Propagation:* cuttings, seeds. Any pieces of the branches broken off and pushed into moist ground will root. Willows are used to bind sandy banks and land that is liable to slide, and for this purpose 6 ft.–8 ft. stakes are driven into the ground at right angles to the slope of the bank. Roots quickly grow to bind the soil together.

WISTARIA. (Leguminosae.) Perhaps one of our most beautiful hardy deciduous climbers. Plant against south or south-west walls, sunny archways or porches, or grow as standards in sheltered shrubberies or lawns. *Plant* March or April. *Prune,* in January or February, shoots not required for extension, to 1 in. of their base. *Soil:* deep rich sandy loam. *Propagation:* layer young shoots in spring and summer. **Best to grow:** *W. sinensis,* the commonest species, has white and double varieties.

YEW. See CONIFERS.

YUCCA. Adam's Needle. (Liliaceae.) Evergreen perennial with enormous, handsome spike of white bloom (Fig. 71) which makes appearance at intervals of two or three years. The foliage is sharply pointed and leathery. *Plant* in ordinary soils on dry banks, borders or lawns. Protect in severe weather. *Propagation:* division, cuttings, suckers. Young plants do not flower except *Y. filamentosa.* **Best to grow:** *Y. angustifolia* (syn. *Y. glauca*), 3 ft.–4 ft., flower-spikes in July; *Y. filamentosa,* 3 ft.–6 ft., white flower-spikes.

ZINNIA. (Compositae.) Brightly-coloured half-hardy annuals for mixed borders or bedding. Provide plenty of long-lasting blooms for cutting. *Soil:* deep rich loam, in a sheltered sunny position. *Propagation:* sow in heat in April or in a cold frame. Harden seedlings off and plant out in June. Seed can be sown outdoors in May. Mulch Zinnias in flower, and water well in dry weather.

FERTILIZER CHART

Name	*Action*	*Appropriate soil*	*Application*	*Oz. per sq. yd.*	*Notes*
Sulphate of ammonia	Quick	Wet, heavy; not acid	Spring, summer	½–¾	Not to be mixed with basic slag or lime
Nitrate of soda	Quick	Light, drier	Spring; top dressing	½–1	Not to be mixed with superphosphate or kainit
Nitrate of lime	Quick	Dry	After light rain	1	Do not use in mixtures
Nitro-chalk	Very quick	Heavy	Spring, summer; fork in	1	Lasting effect
Calcium cyanamide	Medium	Most	Winter spring	½–1	Apply 48 hours before sowing; caustic effect on plants; do not mix with ammonium fertilizers
Nitrate of potash (saltpetre)	Quick	Most, deficient in potash	Top dressing or in liquid form	½ in gallon water	Expensive; do not confuse with Chilean potash nitrate
Chilean potash nitrate	Quick	Most	Spring, early summer	½–1	Top dressings
Rape dust	1 year	Most	Spring	4	Base for compound fertilizers
Castor-seed meal	Similar in composition and action to above				
Soot	Medium	Light and medium	Summer; top dressing, spring	½–6	Not to be mixed with lime

Name	*Action*	*Appropriate soil*	*Application*	*Oz. per sq. yd.*	*Notes*
Shoddy or wool refuse	Slow	Most	Winter	7	1 ton good shoddy said to equal 10 tons manure
Poultry manure	Medium	Most	Winter	1 cwt. to 24–40 sq. yd.	Variable composition
Superphosphate of lime	Quick	Chalk loam not acid	Spring, autumn	1½–2½	Good for all crops
Basic slag	Slow	Heavy, wet, peaty	Autumn; fork in	2–4	Do not mix with sulphate of ammonia
Mineral or rock phosphate	Slow	Limey, moist	Autumn, winter	3–4	
Bonemeal	Slow	Light	Autumn	2–3	
Boneflour	Medium	Chalk, light	Spring	2	Top dressing
Dissolved bones	Medium	Chalk	Spring	1½–3	
Sulphate of potash	Quick	Heavy	Spring, autumn	½–1	Top dressing
Kainit	Medium	Medium Light	Autumn; fork in	1–3	Not to be mixed with sulphate of ammonia; very variable in composition
Hoof and horn	Slow	Any	Autumn; fork in after digging	2–6	Best when finely ground
Peruvian guano	Quick	Most	Growing season	2–3	Powerful stimulant
Fish guano	Medium	Most	Few weeks before sowing or planting	2–3	Apply as soon as received
Meat guano	Medium	Most	As soon as received	1–3	
Dried blood	Quick	Any	Growing season	1–4	Also 1 oz. per gallon of water
Town refuse	Slow	Most	Autumn, winter	Barrow-load to 15–45 sq. yd.	Quality depends on origin
Farmyard manure	Medium	Most	Autumn, winter	Good forkful	
Green manuring	Medium	Light and heavy	According to maturity	—	Good substitute for the above
Compost heap	Medium	Any	Autumn, winter	Good forkful	Turn at intervals; sprinkle with sulphate of ammonia or calcium cyanamide
Liquid manure	Medium	Any	Growing season	—	Never use when roots are in a dry state; dilute with water
Free lime: (1) Lump lime or burnt lime; (2) Ground lime; (3) Small lime	—	Most	In autumn during a dry period	According to soil	(1) Cheapest; (2) Rake in after digging
Slaked lime: (1) Hydrated; (2) Carbide waste	—	Most			The purest and quickest
Carbonate of lime: (1) Ground limestone; (2) Chalk; (3) Ground chalk; (4) Dried carbonate of lime; (5) Limestone dust	—	Most			Recommended for compost heaps

Plant attacked	*Disease*	*Part of plant attacked and appearance of disease*	*Control*
Apple	Scab	Scabs on fruits, distorted by early attack; dark green patches on the leaves	Spray with lime-sulphur at following stages: (1) green bud; (2) pink bud; (3) petal fall. Use Bordeaux mixture on sulphur-shy varieties
Apple (and pear)	Canker	Ringed depressed areas round branches and twigs	Apply white-lead paint to large surface wounds made during pruning; remove and burn infected parts
Apple	Mildew	Leaves and shoots white and mealy; flowers small and distorted, may fail to open	Spray with lime-sulphur or Bordeaux mixture (as for scab)
Apple	Brown rot	Flowers wither, turn brown and die; afterwards spurs covered with grey pustules; fruits brown, soft rot, later mummify	Remove and burn all infected wood and mummified fruits
Black-currant	Reversion	In May and June reverted leaves appear in midst of new growth. These are deficient in main veins and serrations (long and narrow); blossoms abnormal and set no fruit	Destroy badly infected bushes; do not propagate from reverted shoots
Brassicas (cabbage, sprouts, etc.)	Club root (finger and toe)	Cause lumps or swellings on the roots; do not confuse with turnip gall weevil	Lime regularly
Beet	Violet root rot	Roots covered with a felt-like mass of violet or purple mycelium; roots often bring up a mass of attached soil	Burn diseased roots: do not use the same piece of ground for this crop for several years
Celery	Leaf spot	Leaves and blanched stems become discoloured and turn brown in patches; small black specks appear on the brown markings	Always purchase guaranteed healthy seed, or soak seed in solution of formaldehyde for 24 hours (1 part formalin to 300 parts water); spray with Bordeaux when disease is seen
Carnation	Rust	Small reddy-brown spots on the underside of leaves; these gradually spread until leaves turn brown and die	Spray under and upper sides of leaves with an equal mixture of proprietary colloidal copper and colloidal sulphur
Chrysanthemum	Rust	Small brown spots on the leaves	Spray with colloidal copper
Cucumber	Canker or collar rot	A soft rot appears on the stem either just above or just below soil level; causes complete collapse of plant	Keep base of plant as dry as possible; dust base of plant with 10 parts dry slaked lime, 2 parts copper sulphate, 3 parts flowers of sulphur
Gooseberry	American gooseberry mildew	Tips of young shoots and fruits coated with thick felt of mycelium; white, turning brown	Spray (washing soda ½ lb., soft soap 2 oz., in 2½ gallons water) at first sign and repeat as necessary
Gooseberry	Die back	Main stem and branches wilt and die	Cut out and burn all infected parts; take care not to make wounds on the branches, where the disease can enter
Grape	Powdery mildew	White mealy mould on young shoots, buds, foliage, blossoms, and fruits	Dust with flowers of sulphur
Lettuce	Grey mould	Old and decaying leaves readily attacked; disease works its way into stem; grey mould appears on decaying parts	Well-drained soil essential; choose good hardy varieties; remove dead and decaying leaves regularly
Lettuce	Downy mildew	Light green or yellow patches on the leaves; white or greyish "down" copiously produced	Good drainage and ventilation essential; remove diseased leaves

CHART

Plant attacked	*Disease*	*Part of plant attacked and appearance of disease*	*Control*
Mint	Rust	Yellowish-orange cushions appear on stems and leaves; plants become distorted in bad cases	Mint tops can be burnt off in late September, using dry straw as a rapid fire is necessary to burn stems and kill the spores but not to damage the roots
Marrow	Grey mould	Attacks flowers and rot spreads to the fruits	Remove rotting flowers and fruits, also any leaves that keep sun and air from the fruits
Marrow	Mildew	Attacks leaves and stems in the autumn, turning them white	Dust plants with ground sulphur when disease appears and at regular intervals
Onion	Smut (notifiable)	Dark opaque spots or streaks within the leaves and scales; soon after the skin splits, exposing black powdery mass	Soil may remain contaminated for at least 5 years, so do not use same plot for onions till this time has elapsed
Onion	Downy mildew	White or grey mildew appears on the leaves, which turn yellow and die	Well drained soil essential; spray repeatedly with Bordeaux mixture
Pea	Mildew	Pods and leaves covered with white powdery patches	Apply sulphur dust when plants are still wet with dew
Pear	Scab	As for apple scab	Green bud stage, lime-sulphur 2½ per cent sprays; white bud stage, lime-sulphur 2½ per cent sprays; petal fall stage, Bordeaux mixture
Peach, Nectarine, Apricot	Leaf curl	Leaves crinkled and swollen when young; yellowish with tinges of red	Spray with Bordeaux mixture dormant branches before buds burst
Plum	Silver leaf	Leaves turn silvery on infected branches	All infected wood must be removed and burnt early in the summer
Potato (and tomato)	Blight	Brown and white mould found on underside of leaves, which go brown and die back from edges; leaves become black and eventually the whole haulm dies	Spray with Bordeaux mixture in June–July (end of July for tomatoes)
Potato	Wart disease (notifiable)	Black cauliflower-looking growths appear on the potatoes: report immediately to the police	Grow immune varieties of potato only
Rhubarb	Crown rot	Bases of the stems become swollen and distorted; leaves turn a puce colour; crown of plant finally rots	Always buy clean stock; burn all infected stock
Rose	Mildew	White powder found over young stems and leaves	Spray with colloidal sulphur and cut out diseased shoots in spring
Rose	Black spot	Purple irregular spots on leaves and stems; later turn black	Spray with colloidal copper in June and repeat
Raspberry	Cane spot	Purplish spots on young canes early in summer getting larger; have grey centres	Spray as soon as the buds begin to move with 7 per cent lime-sulphur; cut back canes in autumn
Raspberry	Mosaic	Yellow mottling of the leaves	Dig up and burn badly infected plants with their young canes
Tomato	Leaf mould	Pale greyish mould appears on the underside of leaves in large spots; leaves eventually die	Use a colloidal copper spray with a good spreader
Tomato	Damping off foot rot	Attacks young plants and seedlings; fungi grow into the tissue either at soil level or in the roots; stems turn brown and collapse	Sterilize pots and boxes and soil with 1 gallon formaldehyde (40 per cent) to 49 gallons water

Pest	Plant attacked	Position, appearance, etc., of attack	Control
American blight or woolly aphis	Apple	Insect occurs in colonies on roots and trees under white woolly material	Paint affected parts with methylated spirit, using stiff brush
Ants	General	Troublesome in greenhouse and garden	Pyrethrum powder applied at intervals until destroyed
Apple-blossom weevil	Apple	Blossom buds; grub eats interior of buds causing "capped blossom"	Spray in winter with tar-distillate wash, remove loose bark, rubbish, etc., put sacking bands round trunks in June; D.D.T. in spring
Apple aphis or green fly	Apple	Leaves and shoots curled and distorted; misshapen fruits	Spray with tar-distillate wash in winter to destroy eggs; nicotine wash in young fruit stage
Apple sawfly	Apple	Young apples attacked by the grub; ribbon-like scars on the surface. Grubs also eat their way into the fruit, causing them to fall	Spray with nicotine wash at petal fall
Apple capsid	Apple	Leaves and fruits, growing points; all active stages of this insect are harmful	Mineral oil washes in winter to destroy eggs; nicotine washes in spring and summer
Apple moths (several types)	Apple	Considerable damage done when numerous caterpillars feed on the foliage	Tar-distillate wash in winter to kill the eggs; lead arsenate spray in spring; grease band in September
Apple sucker	Apple	Blossom trusses and young shoots attacked	Spray with tar-distillate wash in winter to destroy eggs; or a nicotine spray when the leaf buds have burst
Asparagus beetle	Asparagus	Grub attacks shoots and seed heads	Dust beds with derris dust to kill the larvae of the beetle, when damage is seen; burn all dead foliage; after cutting use lead arsenate
Bean aphis or black fly	Broad beans	Attacks mainly the tops of the shoots	Spray with nicotine or pyrethrum at the first sign of attack; pinch tops of plants out
Black-currant mite or big bud	Black-currants	Mites cause the unopened buds to swell, dry up and die or produce distorted foliage	Spray with lime-sulphur when foliage is the size of a shilling piece; burn badly infected bushes
Carrot fly	Carrot	Grubs bore into and feed on roots	Apply at singling time and at regular intervals after, flaked or powdered naphthalene, 2 oz. per sq. yd.
Cabbage-root fly	Cabbage	Grubs destroy inner tissues of stems; eat off young roots	½ oz. naphthalene sprinkled round each plant at intervals; or solu tion of corrosive sublimate poured round each plant at time of planting
Cabbage caterpillars	Cabbage	Caterpillars eat foliage; late summer and autumn attacks most serious	Hand picking the best method; spray with an insecticide containing derris or pyrethrum or D.D.T.
Celery fly	Celery	Brown blisters made by maggot burrowing into the leaves	Remove and destroy blistered leaves; spray with nicotine, 3 per cent
Chafer beetle	General	Grubs are harmful to roots of most plants; the adult beetles attack the foliage	Control grubs by naphthalene applied at the rate of 3–4 oz. per sq. yd. before rain
Cut worm	General	Feed mostly on stems round soil level, "cutting" them off	Poison bait (1 lb. Paris green, 25 lb. bran); keeping ground clean

CHART

Pest	*Plant attacked*	*Position, appearance, etc., of attack*	*Control*
Fruit-tree capsid	Fruit trees	Leaves, fruit, and growing points attacked by all active stages of this insect	Winter, spray with mineral-oil washes to control eggs; spring and summer treatment, spray with nicotine washes
Flea beetle	Turnips and swedes suffer most	Adult beetles eat seedling plants	(1) Aim at rapid growth in early stages; (2) use derris and nicotine dust
Fruit-tree red spider	Apples, plums, damsons, pears	Mites lower vitality of the tree by feeding on the sap which they suck from leaves	Lime-sulphur sprays: (1) pre-blossom, 1 gallon lime to 29 gallons water; (2) post-blossom, 1 gallon lime-sulphur to 99 gallons water
Fruit-tree caterpillar	Apples, plums	Caterpillars feed on foliage	Grease bands in September; lead arsenate in spring, used as a spray
Gooseberry sawfly		Grub attacks fruit and leaves: in bad attacks all parts of the plant are eaten	Hand picking or with spray containing lead arsenate or derris
Millipede	General	Roots of most plants attacked; also bulbs and tubers	Apply naphthalene at 4 oz. per sq. yd. on light soils, 6–8 oz. per sq. yd. on heavy soils
Narcissus fly	Daffodil, snowdrop, etc.	White maggot feeds on interior of the bulb	Soft bulbs should not be planted; cover up when lifted
Onion fly	Onion	Maggots eat into the bulbs	Burn affected plants; early planting; naphthalene applied as a repellent at the rate of 2 oz. per sq. yd.; use sets instead of seedlings
Pea and bean weevils	Peas, beans	Adults attack young plants by eating regular notches round the edges of the leaves	Dressings of soot, lime, basic slag, as deterrent
Pea and bean thrips	Peas, beans	Thrips feed on the flowers, haulms and the pods, causing stunted growth and a mottled silvery appearance	Spray with nicotine when pest first discovered
Pea and bean beetles	Peas, beans	Grubs eat into and damage the seed	Do not sow seed containing living beetles
Raspberry beetle	Raspberry	Grubs eat into and deform berries; adults injure buds and opening flowers	Spray or dust in June with insecticides containing derris
Raspberry moth	Raspberry	Caterpillars burrow into and feed on the interior of the cane tips causing them to die back	Remove and burn all rubbish and cracked canes, also withered shoots containing larvae when seen in spring
Slugs and snails	General	Eat the leaves and stems of plants, also roots and tubers below ground; injury varies according to species	Poison baits (bran and Paris green); quicklime and salt applied at night when the slugs are on the surface
Turnip gallweevil	Turnips, cabbages, savoys, brussels sprouts, etc.	Grub feeds on roots and burrows into the stems causing gall-like growths; grub lives and feeds inside the galls	Use clean stock; if possible remove attacked crop before the larvae leave the galls; burn old cabbage stumps, etc.
White fly	Common pest in garden and greenhouse	Found on underside of the leaves, sucking juices, making the plant weak and dirty	Fumigate with tetrachlorethane, or use a white-fly parasite indoors such as *Encarsia formosa*
Wireworm	General	Attack roots, tubers, etc., by burrowing in and feeding on them	Soil fumigation with naphthalene; thorough cultivation, exposing pest to the birds
Woodlice	—	As for ants	—
Woolly aphis	—	See American blight	—

VEGETABLE

Name	Variety	Season available	Sowing time: Under glass	Sowing time: Outside	Depth (inches)
Beet	Crimson Globe Cheltenham Green Top	All year	—	May	1½
Carrot (maincrop)	James Intermediate	All year	—	March–April	¾–1
Parsnip	Offenham Tender and True	November–March	—	February	¾–1
Turnip (main)	Golden Ball	Autumn	—	May–June	½–¾
,, (winter)	Green Top Stone	—	—	July	½–¾
Swede	Purple and Green Top	—	—	July	½–¾
Leeks	Musselburgh The Lyon	September–May	Last week January	March	½
Onions (pickling)	Paris Silver Skinned Pickling	All year	—	March	¾–1
,, (maincrop)	Best of All	September onwards	January–February	September or March	¾–1
, (salad)	White Lisbon	April–June May–September	—	August March–May	½–1
Shallots	—	August–March	—	—	Half-covered
Potatoes (early)	Arran Pilot	June–July	—	—	4–6
,, (mid-season)	Majestic	August onwards	—	—	4–6
,, (maincrop)	Gladstone	All year	—	—	4–6
Artichoke (Jerusalem)	Purple or white skinned	October–March	—	—	5
Broccoli	Snows Winter White	October–May	February	March–Mid-May	¾–1
Cauliflower (maincrop)	All The Year Round	May–July	September–October	August	½
	Majestic	June–October	January–February	March–April	½
Brussels Sprouts	Wroxton	October–March	February	March–April	½
Cabbage (spring sown)	Golden Acre	July–November	February	April	½
Cabbage (autumn sown)	Offenham	April–July	—	July–August	½
Cabbage (summer grown)	Christmas Drumhead	November–April	—	May	½
Cabbage (savoy)	Best Of All	November–March	—	March–May	½
Cabbage (pickling)	Red Cabbage	September–December	—	March	¾
Kale	Cottagers	November–March	—	Early March–May	½–¾
Celery	Covent Garden Red Sandringham White	October–February	January–February	April	¼

CHART

Germination (days)	Maturity reached in (weeks)	Time to plant or transplant	Distance: Rows (inches)	Distance: Plants (inches)	Average No. of seeds per ounce	Quantity of seed required: 50-ft. row (ounces)	1,000 plants (ounces)	1 acre (pounds)
14–21	18–20	—	18	9	1,700	⅛	—	8–12
10–21	22–26	—	12	4–6	18,500	⅓	—	8
28–50	24–26	—	15	9–12	5,000	¼	—	8
4–10	7–10	—	15	6–8	10,000	¼	—	2–3
4–10	7–10	—	15	6–8	10,000	¼	—	2–3
4–10	7–10	—	15	6	10,000	¼	—	2–3
10–25	32–36	May–June	18–24	6–9	8,000	¼	⅛	2
14–40	—	—	8–12			½		16–30
14–40	20–26	April–May	12–15	4–8	7,000	¾	¼	8–10
14–21	—	—	12	—	—	—	—	40–50
—	22–26	March	12	9		2–3 lb.	—	6–8 seed 10–12 bushels bulbs
20–35	12–24	March	18–24	12	1 peck equals 14 lb. or about 100 tubers	7–10 lb.	—	1 ton
25–35	12–24	March–April	24–30	12		8 lb.	—	1 ton
25–35	12–24	April	24–36	18		6–7 lb.	—	1 ton
—	39–42	February–March	36	12–15	—	7 lb.	—	—
5–14	18–24	May–July	24–30	24–30	14,000	¼	½–1	4 oz.
6–15	22–24	February–March	24	18	14,000	¼	½–1	4 oz.
6–15	18–22	May–June	30	18–24	14,000	¼	½–1	4 oz.
7–14	24–30	May–June	24	24	9,000	¼	1	4–6
7–14	18–22	June–July	18–24	12–15	8,000	¼	1	4–6
7–14	35–40	October	24	18	8,000	¼	1	4–6
7–14	35–40	July–August	24	24	8,000	¼	1	4–6
6–12	18–22	May–July	24–30	18–24	8,000	¼	1	—
6–12	18–23	May–June	24	24	8,000	¼	1	—
7–14	18–20	June–July	24–30	18	8,000	¼	1	—
8–15	22–24	May–June	30	6–9	50,000	Pinch	Pinch	—

Name	*Variety*	*Season available*	*Sowing Time*		*Depth (inches)*
			Under glass	*Outside*	
Lettuce	Summer: All the Year Round. Spring: Arctic King	March–November	January–March	March–June August	½
Chicory	—	October–May	—	May–June	½
Endive	Summer: Green curled Autumn–winter: Batavian Broad-leafed	Autumn–Winter	—	July–August	½
Lambs Lettuce or Corn Salad	—	December–Spring	—	July–September	½
Radish	French Breakfast	April–October	October–February	March–September	½
Garlic	—	—	February–March	—	—
Tomato	Stonor's M.P. Market King	August–November	February–March	—	½
Mustard and Cress	White Mustard Curled Cress	April–September	October–March	April–September	On top soil
Artichoke (globe)	Purple Globe Green	June–October	—	March–April	—
Asparagus	Mary Washington	April–June		March–April	1–2
Rhubarb	Champagne Victoria	Spring–Summer	—	—	—
Sea-kale	—	February–June	—	—	—
Beans (broad)	Broad Windsor Seville Long Pod	June–August	—	November–January March–May	4
„ (dwarf or kidney or French)	Masterpiece	July–September	March–April	May–July	3
„ (runner)	Prizewinner	July–October	April	May–June	3
Peas (early)	Kelvedon Wonder	June–July	—	January–February	2–3
„ (maincrop)	Onward	July–August	—	March–May	2–3
Celeriac	—	October–February	February–March	—	¼
Cucumber (ridge)	Perfection Ridge	August–September	April–May	May	½
Parsley	Dwarf Double Curled	All Year	February	August March–April	½
Spinach	Giant Prickly	June–April	—	March–August	1
Vegetable Marrow	Bush Green	August–October	February–April	May	1

Many of the items mentioned in the above charts, and particularly the vegetables, have individual entries in the alphabetical list given in the preceeding pages. In connexion with vegetables, useful

CHART *(continued)*

Germination (days)	*Maturity reached in (weeks)*	*Time to plant or transplant*	*Distance*		*Average No. of seeds per ounce*	*Quantity of seed required*		
			Rows (inches)	*Plants (inches)*		*50-ft. row (ounces)*	*1,000 plants (ounces)*	*1 acre (pounds)*
6–10	11–26	April–July	12	9–12	26,000	⅛ or less	⅛ or less	—
5–10	—	—	12	9	—	¼	—	—
7–14	11–14	—	12	12	18,000	⅛	¼	—
—	—	—	6–9	6	—	—	—	—
6–12	6–10	—	9	—	4,000	½	—	10
—	—	—	12	6	—	100 cloves	—	—
14–21	18–22	May	24–36	12–15	—	—	½	—
5–10	1–2	—	—	—	—	—	2 of each	—
—	—	April	36	24	—	1 or 16 roots	—	—
30–40	—	March–April	48	12–18	1,000	½–3	1	—
—	—	February–March	30–36	30–36	—	16 plants	—	—
—	—	March–April	18	12–16	—	—	—	—
26–36	20–28	—	24–36	6	12	1–1¼ lb.	—	125–150
10–20	13–15	—	18–24	6–12	50	⅓ or ⅔ lb.	—	56–80
12–20	15–18	—	96	6–9	30	½ lb.	—	56–60
28–36	12–16	—	36	2–3	50–150	¾ lb.	—	3–5 bushels
12–18	12–16	—	36–48	2–3	50–150	¾ lb.	—	3–5 bushels
—	—	May–June	18	18	50,000	—	¼	—
10–20	13–16	May–June	—	30	—	1 packet	—	—
30	12–14	—	12–16	6–9	17,500	¼	—	5–6
6–12	7–14	—	12	6–12	3,000 to 17,500	½–1	—	8
8–14	16–20	May–June	Bush 36	Bush 36	200–300	—	—	2–4

additional information may be found under the headings FRENCH GARDENING, HOTBED, ROTATION, SALADS, SEEDS, and VEGETABLE GARDEN, and on the next three pages in YOUR GARDEN MONTH BY MONTH.

YOUR GARDEN MONTH BY MONTH

JANUARY

Vegetable garden

(1) Make cropping plan.
(2) Order seed and seed potatoes.
(3) For early crop, sow onions, tomatoes, lettuces, cauliflowers, in gentle heat.
(4) Force rhubarb and seakale.
(5) Dig all available ground.
(6) Plant potatoes in frames and pots.
(7) Sow leeks and French beans for succession.
(8) Mulch asparagus beds.
(9) Sow small salads under glass.

As required lift artichokes, celery, leeks, parsnips.

Cut winter cabbages and savoys.

Use from store beet, carrots, haricot beans, potatoes, onions, shallots, swedes, turnips.

Gather spinach-beet, brussels sprouts.

Fruit

(1) Prune late vines.
(2) Start early vines, peaches, nectarines, apricots.
(3) Spray apples, pears, plums with winter wash.
(4) Finish pruning fruit trees.
(5) Clean strawberry bed.

Flower garden and plant houses

(1) Plant deciduous trees and shrubs.
(2) Take chrysanthemum and carnation cuttings.
(3) Prick over bulb beds.
(4) Bring bulbs into greenhouse.
(5) Pot and plant lilies.
(6) Pot rooted carnation and chrysanthemum cuttings.

FEBRUARY

Vegetable garden

(1) Sow beans, round-seeded spinach; (end of the month) onions; (in a cold frame) parsnips, turnips, parsley; early peas.
(2) In gentle heat sow brassicas, early celery, leeks, maincrop tomatoes.
(3) Lift parsnips to check growth; store.
(4) Sprout seed potatoes.
(5) Protect early crops with bracken or litter.
(6) Complete digging, and break down soil.
(7) Prepare trench for runner beans.
(8) Plant Jerusalem artichokes, shallots.
(9) Pot tomato seedlings.

As required lift as for January.

Cut savoys.

Use from store and gather as for January.

Fruit

(1) Prune gooseberries, red-currants, and autumn-fruiting raspberries.
(2) Cut newly planted raspberries down to 6 in. of soil level.
(3) Pollinate and disbud early peaches.
(4) Start second-early vines.

Flower garden and plant houses

(1) In cool house sow sweet peas, half-hardy annuals.
(2) Pot annuals for greenhouse.
(3) Finish planting trees and shrubs.
(4) Complete planting of lilies.
(5) Plant anemones.

MARCH

Vegetable garden

(1) Sow succession of carrots, lettuces, peas, spinach, broad beans.
(2) Sow leeks, onions, main-crop celery, brussels sprouts, cabbage lettuces.
(3) Plant August-sown onions, onion sets, pickling cabbages.
(4) Replant crops that have failed.
(5) Plant rhubarb, horse-radish, seakale.
(6) Prepare new mint bed and sow seeds of herbs.
(7) Pot early tomatoes and make further sowings in heat.
(8) Plant early potatoes.
(9) Melons in a warm greenhouse.
(10) Lift remains of leek crop, to check growth, and "heel in."

Use from store as for February.

Cut brussels sprouts, savoys, turnip tops.

Gather spinach beet, spring greens.

Fruit

(1) Spray black-currants with lime-sulphur wash against "big-bud."
(2) Plant strawberries.
(3) Start vines in unheated greenhouses.
(4) Start grafting.

Flower garden and plant houses

(1) Sow annuals and sweet peas for the greenhouse.
(2) Start pruning roses.
(3) Sow herbaceous perennials and alpines.
(4) Stop chrysanthemums.
(5) Sow cacti, fuchsias, geraniums.
(6) Plant autumn-sown sweet peas, gladioli, montbretias.
(7) Sow annuals and half-hardy annuals in frames.
(8) Start gloxinias, cannas, begonias, dahlias, hippeastrums.
(9) Take dahlia cuttings.
(10) Plant carnation layers.
(11) Clip ivy on walls.

APRIL

Vegetable garden

(1) Sow beet, cabbages, carrots, cauliflowers, onions for pickling, onions for salad, turnips, salsify, kohl-rabi, parsley, endives.
(2) Stake peas.
(3) Prepare celery trenches.
(4) Successional sowings of lettuces, peas, spinach, radishes.
(5) Plant second-early and late potatoes, also globe artichokes and asparagus.

Gather sprouting broccoli, kales, spring greens, turnip tops.

Fruit

(1) Spray gooseberries and black-currants.
(2) Finish grafting fruit trees.
(3) Thin outdoor peaches and nectarines.
(4) Remove grease bands from trees.

Flower garden and plant houses

(1) Complete rose pruning.
(2) Sow zinnias, grass seed.
(3) Pot cyclamen seedlings.
(4) Sow hardy annuals, and greenhouse primulas.
(5) Plant violas, pansies, and antirrhinums.

MAY

Vegetable garden

(1) Plant out autumn and winter greens, late potatoes, celeriac, and summer cabbages.
(2) Sow haricot, French and runner beans, kale, savoys, autumn cabbages, marrows, ridge cucumbers, beetroot, chicory.
(3) Thin beetroot, carrots, lettuces, onions, parsnips, turnips.
(4) Stake runner beans.
(5) Earth early potatoes.
(6) Mulch, if possible, such crops as peas, beans, etc.
(7) Hoe between all crops.
(8) Dig ground recently cleared of late green crops, and prepare for leeks.
(9) Start cutting asparagus.
(10) Prick off and plant celery; prick out winter greens.
(11) Plant tomatoes in unheated greenhouses.
(12) Plant melons and cucumbers in frames.

Gather spinach, sprouting broccoli.
Cut cabbages, lettuces.
Lift leeks as required.
Pull radishes and onions for salads.
Use from store haricot beans and onions.

Fruit

(1) Straw strawberry beds.
(2) Spray apple trees against scab, codling moth, etc.

Flower garden and plant houses

(1) Plant dahlia tubers outdoors.
(2) Stop exhibition chrysanthemums.
(3) Plant early-flowering chrysanthemums.
(4) Plant seedlings of hardy perennials.
(5) Clear beds for summer bedding.
(6) Remove side-shoots from sweet peas.
(7) Sow hardy and half-hardy annuals and cinerarias.
(8) Pot late-flowering chrysanthemums.
(9) Pot begonias, gloxinias, etc.
(10) Plant out bedding plants and half-hardy annuals.
(11) Prick off primulas.
(12) Plant window-boxes, hanging baskets, etc.

JUNE

Vegetable garden

(1) Sow garden swedes.
(2) Successional sowings, beet, carrots, lettuces, runner beans, turnips.
(3) Plant brussels sprouts, early cabbages, cauliflowers, celery, marrows, tomatoes.
(4) Thin beet, carrots, lettuces, turnips.
(5) Stake runner beans, stake and tie tomatoes.
(6) Stop cutting asparagus.

Gather broad beans, peas, spinach.
Cut cabbages, cauliflowers, lettuces.
Pull radishes and onions for salads.

Fruit

(1) Start to thin apples and pears.
(2) Start to summer-prune gooseberries and currants.

Flower garden and plant houses

(1) Sow perennials and biennials, and St. Brigid anemones.
(2) Plunge pot shrubs and roses outdoors.
(3) Prick off cinerarias.
(4) Put chrysanthemums in summer quarters.
(5) Cut back aubrietias, etc.
(6) Start budding roses.
(7) Divide mossy saxifrages.
(8) Sow Brompton stocks and myosotis (forget-me-nots).
(9) Pot cyclamen and cinerarias into flowering pots.
(10) Sow cinerarias, primulas for succession.

JULY

Vegetable garden

(1) Sow cabbages for spring cutting, spinach beet, kale, parsley.
(2) Successional sowings, beet, carrots, lettuces; sow turnips for storing.
(3) Plant late cauliflowers, autumn cabbages, leeks, sprouting broccoli, kale, savoys.
(4) Thin beet, carrots, lettuces, swedes.
(5) Tie tomatoes, and remove side growths as they develop.
(6) Harvest shallots.
(7) Protect cauliflower curds with leaves broken from the plant.
(8) Make an outdoor mushroom bed.
(9) Gather herbs for winter use.
(10) Start to earth up celery.
(11) Lift and store autumn-sown onions.

Gather dwarf and runner beans.
Cut cabbages, cauliflowers, lettuces.
Pull early beet, carrots, onions, early turnips, as required for use.
Lift early potatoes as required for use.

Fruit

(1) Start to prune wall-trained cherries and plums.
(2) Complete thinning of apples and pears.
(3) Peg down strawberry runners.
(4) Remove any tree attacked by silver leaf.
(5) Start to summer-prune apples and pears.
(6) Start to pick apples and pears.
(7) Start to bud fruit stocks.

Flower garden and plant houses

(1) Lift tulips, hyacinths, etc.
(2) Complete stopping of carnations.
(3) Stand out regal and show pelargoniums.
(4) Prick out perennials and biennials.
(5) Layer border carnations.
(6) Summer-prune wistarias, roses.
(7) Plant colchicums and autumn crocuses.
(8) Start to feed chrysanthemums.
(9) Bud roses.

AUGUST

Vegetable garden

(1) Sow cabbages for spring use, onions for spring planting, winter spinach.
(2) Thin beet, carrots, July-sown kales.
(3) Gather herbs for drying.
(4) Earth broccoli and kales.
(5) Stop tomato plants when four trusses of fruit have set.
(6) Start to blanch endives.
(7) Ripen off onions.
(8) Hoe between all crops.

Gather dwarf and runner beans, tomatoes.
Cut cauliflowers, lettuces, marrows, ridge cucumbers.
Pull beet, carrots, onions, turnips as required.
Lift early potatoes as required.

Flower garden and plant houses

(1) Take geranium and shrub cuttings.
(2) Complete trimming of hedges.
(3) Re-pot and start arum lilies.
(4) Pot winter-flowering begonias, lachenalias, freesias for early flowering, greenhouse calceolarias, and cinerarias.
(5) Cut back violas and pansies for propagation.
(6) Sow schizanthus for spring flowering, cyclamen, stocks and mignonette for the greenhouse.
(7) Prune hydrangeas.
(8) Start nerines.

Fruit

(1) Continue to bud fruit stocks.
(2) Pick and summer-prune apples and pears.
(3) Prune summer-fruiting raspberries.
(4) Make new strawberry beds.

SEPTEMBER

Vegetable garden

(1) Sow winter lettuces, turnips for turnip tops.
(2) Plant cabbages for spring cutting.
(3) Thin winter spinach, and turnips for storing.
(4) Bend down tops of spring-sown onions on maturing, lift two weeks later, and dry off on the surface.
(5) Cut off and burn potato tops if badly infected with disease.
(6) If wireworm is troublesome, lift potatoes early in the month.
(7) Continue to earth celery and leeks.

Gather runner beans and tomatoes.
Cut cabbages, cauliflowers, lettuces, marrows, ridge cucumbers.
Pull beet, carrots, turnips, as required for use.
Lift potatoes for immediate use, and for storing when ready.

Fruit

(1) Complete planting of strawberries.
(2) Continue to pick apples and pears.
(3) Fix grease bands.
(4) Prune loganberries.

Flower garden and plant houses

(1) Plant narcissus, lilies, bulbous irises, etc.
(2) Sow grass seed.
(3) Take cuttings of evergreen shrubs, bedding plants, etc.
(4) Plant bulbs in ornamental bowls.
(5) Pot lilies for the greenhouse, primulas, calceolarias, freesias.
(6) Plant anemones.
(7) Prune rambler roses.
(8) Plant rooted carnation layers.
(9) House late-flowering chrysanthemums.
(10) Pot cyclamen seedlings.

OCTOBER

Vegetable garden

(1) Plant cabbages for spring cutting, and winter lettuces.
(2) Earth celery for second time, and leeks.
(3) Protect late cauliflowers from frost.
(4) Tie onions in ropes and hang in a suitable store as soon as the bulbs are thoroughly ripened.
(5) Cut back asparagus, globe artichokes.

Gather brussels sprouts, runner beans, spinach.
Cut cabbages, cauliflowers, lettuce.
Lift potatoes, turnips for storing.

Fruit

(1) Insert hard-wood cuttings.
(2) Gather all remaining apples and pears.

Flower garden and plant houses

(1) Turf and repair lawns.
(2) Lift begonias, dahlias, etc.
(3) Plant spring bedding and herbaceous perennials.
(4) Insert hard-wood cuttings.
(5) Pot hardy plants for the greenhouse.
(6) Rest begonias, gloxinias, etc.
(7) Protect outdoor chrysanthemums.
(8) Bring early arums, freesias, lachenalias into the greenhouse.
(9) Pot cinerarias, stocks, and a last batch of freesias.
(10) Lift gladioli, montbretias.
(11) Sow sweet peas.
(12) Plant tulips and hyacinths.
(13) Make lily of the valley beds.

NOVEMBER

Vegetable garden

(1) Give celery final earthing.
(2) Clear all runner-bean haulms for the compost heap; take up and store bean stakes and those used for tomatoes.
(3) Bastard-trench the ground as it becomes available.
(4) Sow broad beans and hardy culinary peas.
(5) Lift seakale for forcing.
(6) Start to force rhubarb.

Lift and store Jerusalem artichokes, parsnips, horse-radish, salsify.
Gather brussels sprouts, spinach beet.
Lift celery, leeks and parsnips as required.
Use from store beet, carrots, marrows, onions, shallots, potatoes, turnips.

Fruit

(1) Cut and store grapes.
(2) Prune early and maincrop vines.

Flower garden and plant houses

(1) Bring early bulbs into the greenhouse.
(2) Complete planting of tulips and hyacinths.
(3) Put glass over alpines.
(4) Cut back chrysanthemums.
(5) Prune deciduous hedges.

DECEMBER

Vegetable garden

(1) Lift and store July-sown carrots.
(2) Protect celery trenches with straw.
(3) Dig all ground as it becomes available.
(4) Examine regularly vegetables in store.
(5) Continue to force seakale and rhubarb.

Gather brussels sprouts, spinach beet.
Cut winter cabbages and savoys.
Use from store as for November.

Fruit

(1) Continue to prune fruit trees.

Flower garden and plant houses

(1) Start taking chrysanthemums and carnation cuttings.
(2) Bring more bulbs into the greenhouse.
(3) Stop sweet peas.
(4) Continue to cut back chrysanthemums.

EVERYWOMAN'S COOKERY BOOK

A guide to the principles of cooking—with practical recipes and instructions for dishes of all kinds

This Cookery Book has been arranged for the user's convenience in two sections. The first section, "The A.B.C. of Cookery," describes simply but accurately those basic principles of cookery without a knowledge of which no one can confidently face the preparation of food. Here will be found general information on the various processes of cooking, boiling, baking, roasting and so on, as well as essential information on the choice and preparation of meat and fish, dishing and garnishing and other useful items. The second section gives recipes which shortly and simply describe the quantities of ingredients required and the method of preparing and cooking an enormous range of dishes. For ease of reference all recipes have been arranged in alphabetical order, but the liberal use of cross-references makes it easy for the cook to find in a matter of moments exactly what she needs to know.

THE A.B.C. OF COOKERY

COOKING PROCESSES

BAKING is a process of cooking in dry heat, in a closed oven heated by gas, electricity or solid fuel. This method has superseded the old-fashioned method of roasting meat before a clear fire, which is not convenient for modern space and fuel economy. The old term "roast meat" is still widely used, but meat cooked in the oven should correctly be described as "oven-roasted" or "baked."

Baking is a convenient method of cooking, but success largely depends upon familiarity with the oven used and intelligent noting of its reactions, this being the case especially with solid-fuel ovens. The makers of any kind of cooking stove issue directions for its use and these should be followed carefully. It will be found that experience and intelligence together will bring perfection. In addition, most modern stoves are fitted with thermostatic control which simplifies baking.

Points about baking. See that sufficient time is allowed to heat the oven to the required temperature. The average time to heat a gas oven is fifteen minutes, but an electric oven will probably take rather longer. In using gas and electric ovens, plan to fill the oven to capacity, in the interests of fuel economy. This matters less where a solid-fuel stove is kept constantly heated. As a general rule, the top of the oven is the hottest, so bake the dish requiring greatest heat on the top shelf, and set thermostatic control to this temperature. Use the middle shelf for food requiring more moderate heat and the bottom shelf or even the bottom plate for slow baking. Avoid opening the oven door more than is essential, and, when this is necessary, stand at the handle side of the oven door and take a quick look inside, closing the door gently and never slamming it. A volume of cold air entering the oven will cool it considerably, and is most likely to check rising or cause uneven baking.

If relays of baking are necessary in a small oven, begin with those items needing greatest heat. Make full use of residual heat in the oven, that is, the heat which is stored in it. Gas-heated ovens cool more rapidly than electric ones, but even in the former gas may be turned off when a dish is barely cooked. Electric ovens will maintain a steady temperature for some fifteen minutes after the current has been switched off, and can be used for cooking some biscuits or a sandwich cake. Make sure that no food is placed directly over gas jets or in contact with electric elements, or it will burn. A few inches of space must be allowed, so that heat can rise and pass over the top of food while baking. If neither thermostatic control nor an oven thermometer is available, the following home-made test may prove useful until one is sufficiently experienced to test an oven by holding the hand inside it. Put a piece of white kitchen paper on the oven shelf. At the end of three minutes:

(1) If it has turned black the oven is too hot for use. (2) If it has turned brown, the oven is a very hot one, and is correct for such things as bread and puff-pastry. (3) If it has turned russet brown, the oven is a hot one, and is ready for small cakes, short pastry, or the first stage of oven-roasting meat. (4) If it has turned dark yellow, the oven is moderately hot, and is ready for large cakes, and

many casserole dishes and baked puddings. (5) If it has turned light yellow, the oven is very moderate and is ready for such dishes as bread and butter pudding and shortbread.

Baking by systematized temperature

Thermostatic control	*Thermometer reading*	*Description of oven temperature*
Mark 0	200 deg. F.	Drying temperature
Mark ¼	240 deg. F.	
Mark ½	275 deg. F.	Cool
Mark 1	300 deg. F.	
Mark 2	325 deg. F.	Very moderate
Mark 3	350 deg. F.	Moderate
Mark 4	375 deg. F.	
Mark 5	400 deg. F.	
Mark 6	425 deg. F.	Hot
Mark 7	440 deg. F.	
Mark 8	465 deg. F.	Very hot
Mark 9	490 deg. F.	
Mark 10	520 deg. F.	Rarely used as a cooking temperature, but suitable for browning *au gratin* dishes, etc.
Mark 11	550 deg. F.	
Mark 12	575 deg. F.	

Oven-roasting meat. Weigh the meat, wipe and trim it as necessary. Replace wooden skewers with metal ones, and tie the joint into shape. Place on a grid in a deep baking tin (Fig. 1), cover with pieces of dripping and put some pieces also in the tin. Have the oven very hot, and set at Mark 7 or 440 deg. F. for fifteen minutes, to harden the surface albumen. Baste the joint and reduce the heat to a very moderate temperature. Allow twenty minutes to each pound and twenty minutes over for beef and mutton, and twenty-five minutes to the pound and twenty-five minutes over for pork and veal. Stuffed joints take longer, and an extra five minutes should be added for each pound. Allow one and a quarter to one and a half hours if the joint is under three pounds: the former time if the joint has much bone. Baste the meat each fifteen minutes, to help to cook it and to prevent it from becoming dry on the outside; colour and flavour are also improved by basting. Serve on a hot dish with the correct accompaniments served separately, but a little gravy may be poured round the meat if liked.

Fig. 1. Baking or oven-roasting.

BOILING is the process of cooking food by the application of moist heat, the food coming into direct contact with boiling water. It is an economical and easy method of cooking, though watchfulness is necessary to secure perfection. Boiling also renders food easy to digest. The rate of boiling is determined by the ebullition or bubbling caused, which denotes whether the liquid is vaporizing quickly or slowly. Water alone cannot exceed a temperature of 212 deg. F. and an increase of heat beyond this stage merely means more rapid evaporation into steam.

Boiling is sometimes a misleading term, as, with the exception of vegetables, puddings and galantines, the water is not kept boiling the whole time; for example: **Meat** is put into boiling water and kept at that temperature for five minutes, after which it is kept just below boiling point, with the surface stirring very gently. Salt meat is put into cold water and brought slowly to boiling point. **Fish,** though called "boiled," is put into water at simmering point (180 deg. F.), except for salmon, which is put into boiling water to preserve colour and then the temperature is reduced. **Custard,** though called "boiled," must be cooked at a temperature well below boiling point or the eggs will curdle.

There are two distinct aims when boiling: (1) To extract the flavour and juices of the material cooked, as in making stocks, soups, broths. (2) To retain all flavour and food constituents, as in cooking joints, vegetables, puddings. There will, however, be a slight loss of these even though reduced to a minimum, and water used for boiling meat or vegetables should be used for soup-making and sauces, and that of fish should be used as part of the liquid for making the accompanying sauce.

BRAISING is a compound process of cooking, involving steaming and baking. It is especially suitable for small joints, for those which are lacking in flavour or not sufficiently fine-grained for oven-roasting and for older fowls. Hence its popularity on the Continent, where the quality and flavour of meat is frequently less good than in Britain. Food to be braised is placed on a *mirepoix*, which is a bed of vegetables, covered with stock and brought to boiling point. The prepared meat is laid on this and a close-fitting lid covers it (Fig. 2). For two-thirds of the cooking time the meat cooks in the steam rising from the stock and vegetables, after which the lid is removed and the pan placed in a moderately heated oven to brown and crisp the surface of the meat. The meat is then removed and

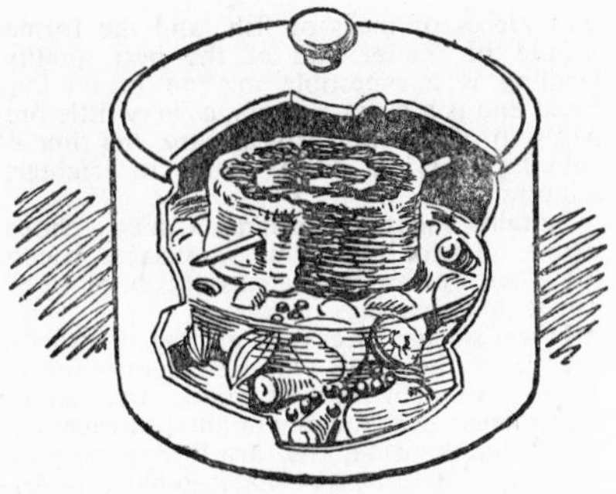

Fig. 2. Braising on a mirepoix *of vegetables.*

placed on a hot dish and the vegetables strained from the stock, which is used to make a sauce to pour round the meat. The vegetables may be chopped and put in little heaps round the meat, although if these can be utilized in soup some freshly cooked vegetables, such as green peas, sliced runner-beans, button mushrooms or spinach, both look and taste better.

The purpose of braising is to save trouble and fuel by cooking both meat and vegetables in one utensil (in which you serve them) and lose none of the goodness of either.

FRYING is the process of cooking food in smoking hot fat, the temperature of which varies according to the kind of food to be fried. Temperature may be judged by the amount of smoke rising from the pan, the denser the vapour rising, the greater the heat. There are two methods of frying:

Shallow fat or dry frying. Little fat is required, merely sufficient to wash over the bottom of the frying-pan. The process is carried out in an ordinary frying-pan, and it is better to use a thick, heavy frying-pan made from wrought-iron or heavy-gauge aluminium. A thin aluminium or enamelled tin pan soon buckles and food burns easily. When the food is browned on one side, it requires turning and

Fig. 3. Shallow fat or dry frying.

the second side is cooked to the correct colour and time allowed for the whole to cook through. Shallow fat frying is suitable for such foods as small thin pieces of meat, liver, kidneys, sliced cooked potatoes, sliced onions, mushrooms, sausages, bacon, pancakes and omelettes (Fig. 3). Fats suitable for shallow fat frying are dripping, clarified fat, or lard. A mixture of margarine and lard or olive oil is satisfactory, though expensive for frying cutlets or fillets of beef.

Deep fat frying is also known as French frying, and for this process a strong, deeper stewpan is required. Any strong saucepan will suffice, but it is convenient to use a special deep fat pan, either round or oval, fitted with a wire frying basket (Fig. 4). Sufficient fat must be used to cover the food fried, or to float it in the case of fritters. A fair amount of fat is needed to start deep fat frying, but it is economical in use once the outlay has been made. Any kind of food can be fried in the same deep fat. There is no transference of flavour, because the food is completely immersed in the fat and juices are sealed inside instantaneously by the great heat. From time to time the store of fat needs a small addition. After use, allow the fat to cool a little, then

Fig. 4. Deep fat frying using a frying basket.

strain it through a fine strainer, or a piece of muslin put into a coarser one, to remove any particles which may have fallen from the food.

Coatings. All foods cooked in this way need a protective coating against the intense heat of the fat, except raw potatoes, or farinaceous mixtures like doughnuts or cheese aigrettes. Coatings used are: egg (or substitute) and breadcrumbs; batter; thin pastry coated with egg and breadcrumbs or crushed vermicelli.

Fats suitable for deep fat frying. Clarified fat or clarified dripping (see page 304); lard; oil. Oil can be raised to a higher temperature than fat. Olive oil is the best for use, but expensive, and the cheaper vegetable oils can be substituted, but are apt to smell strongly.

Special points. The deep fat pan should not be more than three-parts full of melted fat.

Lower the food to be fried gently into the fat, as its moisture will cause the fat to bubble. Keep the hand on the handle of the frying basket, and if it is noted that the fat is bubbling dangerously near the top of the pan, slightly raise the basket and the level of the fat will fall. Place foods coated with batter straight into the fat, or the batter will stick to the wire of the basket and the appearance will be spoiled.

Temperature of fat for deep fat frying. See that the fat is quite still; bubbles rising show that water is present. Average temperatures vary from 320 deg. F., when a slight blue vapour can be seen rising from the centre of the pan, to 400 deg. F., when it will be rising from the whole surface and slightly darker in colour. A fryometer can be obtained to register the temperature of the fat exactly, but provided that the stove is placed in a good light it is not difficult to judge temperature by the amount of smoke rising from the fat. Foods coated with batter do not require the fat quite so hot as those egged and crumbed, but longer time should be allowed to ensure crispness. Thick pieces, such as cutlets of fish, require rather longer time to ensure thorough cooking. Both of these kinds of food should be put into fat which is only just beginning to smoke.

Essentials for success in both methods of frying. Use perfectly clean fat and strain each time after use, also during the frying of the various batches if it is necessary. Use the fat at the correct temperature and fry only a few pieces at one time, as many cold pieces of food put into the fat at one time reduce the temperature too much. Reheat the fat before frying a second batch. Drain fried foods thoroughly on crumpled paper. Fry the food until golden brown and crisp. Serve very hot, but if it is necessary to keep fried food hot before serving, do not cover it or steam will make it sodden. Dish on a paper doily, garnishing savoury food with fried parsley.

GRILLING is a process of rapid cooking beneath a red-hot gas or electric griller, or over or in front of a clear glowing fire (Fig. 5). It is suitable only for small and comparatively thin pieces of meat or fish, and the former should be tender and of the best quality. Grilling is a digestible method of cooking food, and is a quick process, as very little preparation of the food is necessary, the time of cooking varying from eight to eighteen minutes.

Fig. 5. Grilling beneath an electric griller.

Suitable foods for grilling. Cutlets, chops, steaks, fillets of beef, kidneys, sausages, bacon, tomatoes, mushrooms, steaks of fish, or whole fish such as herrings or sole.

Essentials for success in grilling. Brush the outside of the food with melted dripping or oil, to prevent it from becoming dry. Expose it to intense heat for one minute on each side to seal juices inside, and turn it frequently for the remaining time, exposing it to more moderate heat. Avoid piercing the food when turning it so that juices do not escape: use two blunt surfaces (the blade of a knife and a spoon) or special tongs procurable for the purpose.

Time required for grilling meat. This is regulated by the thickness of the meat, and not by weight. Exact time for grilling may vary according to the power of the heat in the griller, but the following are approximate times required:

Steak $1\frac{1}{2}$ in. thick	Well done	18 min.
Steak $1\frac{1}{2}$ in. thick	Underdone	15 min.
Chop 1 in. thick	Well done	12 min.
Chop 1 in. thick	Just cooked	10 min.
Cutlet $\frac{1}{2}$ in. thick	Well done	8–9 min.
Cutlet $\frac{1}{2}$ in. thick	Just cooked	7 min.

Steak for grilling is much improved if it is beaten lightly with a damp rolling-pin, brushed thickly with melted dripping on both sides and left for an hour before cooking. To test when meat is sufficiently cooked: if the meat is still raw in the centre when pressed with the flat blade of a knife, it will rebound slowly; when underdone it will yield readily, but rebound at once; when well done, the surface will yield very little. Meat should appear puffy, and have an even, rich brown coloration on both sides.

Accompaniments for grilled meat. Sprigs of watercress, maître d'hôtel butter, sauté or French fried potatoes. (For recipes, see alphabetical section.) No gravy is served with grilled meat.

HAY-BOX COOKERY involves the principle of the conservation of heat. Food brought to boiling point, and in some cases given a short cooking time, will finish cooking without additional heat except for bringing to boiling point before serving. It is a useful method of cooking for those who are out working all day, as there is no risk of fire or of food becoming over-cooked, even if left for a longer time than stated. It is economical in fuel and a hay-box can be used anywhere, provided that a boiling ring is available. The disadvantages of using a hay-box are that there is loss of vitamin C, because of the length of time of exposure to heat. If a hay-box is used frequently some fresh-cooked vegetables should also be served. Also the type of cooking is rather limited and suitable short-handled utensils must be used.

To make the hay-box. Procure a large wooden box with a strong lid, which should be fastened to the box by hinges (Fig. 6). Cover the outside

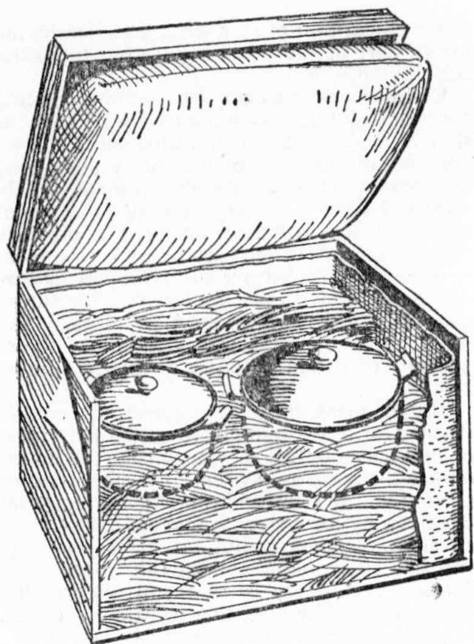

Fig. 6. Hay-box and two casseroles.

with oil-baize or Lancaster cloth, tin-tacked into place. Line the inside in the same way with felt or a clean old blanket. Fill the box with hay, or balls of crumpled newspaper, to within two inches of the top. Make a cushion, stuffed with hay or paper balls, to fit inside the top of the box. This will prevent heat escaping from beneath the lid. Scoop out the required number of nests for the pans in the hay or paper.

Using the hay-box. Use short-handled utensils, preferably earthenware or enamelled iron casseroles. Bring the food to boiling point, and wrap the pan at once in double newspaper or a piece of old blanket. Put it immediately into the prepared box, cover with the cushion and shut the lid firmly. If the food requires a certain amount of cooking before putting into the hay-box, allow the required time and see that it is boiling when put into the box. On removal from the hay-box, bring the food to boiling point and serve. Scrupulously remove any splashed hay or paper, and replenish before using the box again.

Average times. *Meat stews.* Allow half the usual time for cooking and five to six hours in the hay-box. *Pulse* (peas, beans and lentils). Soak in the usual way overnight. Boil for an hour over heat. Allow four hours in the hay-box. *Dried fruit.* Soak overnight. Boil for five minutes over heat. Allow five hours in the hay-box. Or it may be put into the box overnight and left until the morning. (*Note:* it is better to cook fresh fruit in the usual way, to avoid loss of vitamin C.) *Oatmeal.* Boil for ten minutes and leave in the box all night. This method gives particularly well-cooked, creamy porridge.

STEAMING is the process of cooking food in the vapour from boiling water, and it is a most economical method of cooking food, both in regard to the amount of fuel used and also the small amount of loss of weight in the food cooked. It is the most digestible method of cooking and for this reason is an especially suitable process of cooking for children, convalescents and those of delicate digestion. Steaming may be carried out in two ways.

(1) By **direct contact** with steam from boiling water, using either (*a*) a simple round steamer, perforated at the bottom, to fit on to a saucepan already available, or (*b*) a steamer consisting of three or four tiers in which a complete meal may be cooked (Fig. 7). In (*b*) each compartment is identical and, instead of being perforated at the bottom, the steam passes up a tube at the side, reaching all compartments. Each is fitted with a valve, so that if the food in one compartment is cooked the valve may be closed and the food kept hot while the food in the remaining compartments finishes cooking. Naturally, no flavour passes from one compartment to another, and all kinds of food can be cooked in the different compartments without fear of a mingling of flavours. If no steamer is available, the food may be placed in a basin stood in a saucepan with sufficient boiling water to come halfway up the basin, and raised from the bottom by an inverted old saucer or a pastry cutter. The lid is put on and the food cooked by the steam rising from the boiling water. A little boiling water from a kettle must be added from time to time to prevent the pan from boiling dry.

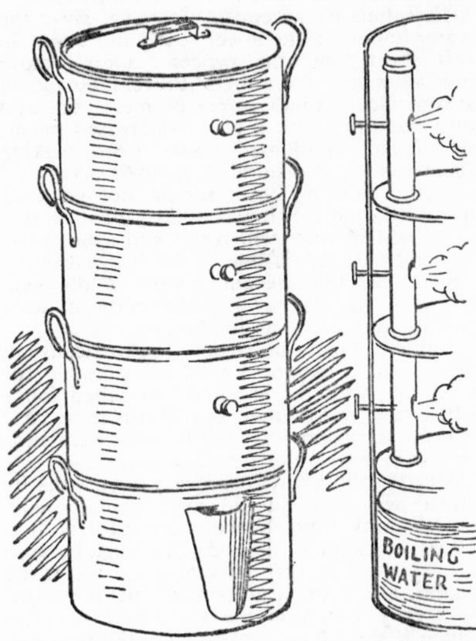

Fig. 7. Three-tiered steamer. Amount of steam entering each compartment is controllable.

(2) By **indirect contact** with steam from boiling water. The food is placed between two plates, stood over a saucepan half-filled with boiling water, and the food is cooked in the steam of its own juices, produced by the

Fig. 8. Stewing in a stewpan on top of a stove and in a casserole in an oven.

heating of the lower plate. This method is suitable only for small pieces of food, such as chops, but the food absorbs no water and its full flavour and food value are conserved.

Essentials for successful steaming. Have the water boiling in the lower vessel and maintain this throughout the process, adding more boiling water if required. Prevent escape of steam. Cover small pieces of meat, fish and also puddings with a piece of greased paper, to prevent condensed steam from making them sodden. No pudding cloth is necessary, and the pudding basin should not be filled quite full when making a pudding for steaming, as a light mixture will result and space must be allowed for rising. Time for steaming depends on the size and texture of the food steamed. As a general guide, allow at least half as long again as for boiling.

Suitable foods for steaming. Practically all foods which can be boiled are suitable for steaming, with the exception of salted foods which tend to lose their salt. If it is more convenient to steam such foods, soak salt meat or fish in cold water for an hour or two.

STEWING is a slow process of cooking by moist heat, and should not be undertaken unless ample time can be allowed for it. It is a most economical method of cooking, because the cheaper, coarser cuts of meat are made tender, and a small amount of fuel is needed to keep the stew at the simmering point at which it should be cooked (160–180 deg. F.). Another advantage is that meat can be cooked with plenty of vegetables, which will save space on the stove and minimize washing up. Any meat juices and flavour which escape from the ingredients are not lost, but are served in the liquid, which forms a sauce.

Stewing can be carried out in a stewpan or saucepan on top of a stove, or may be done in the cooler part of an oven in a casserole, the upper part of the oven being used for other cooking (Fig. 8).

Essentials of success. Success in cooking coarse, tough and gelatinous meat, such as shin of beef, scrag of mutton, sheep's head and ox-tail, depends mainly on not allowing the stew to cook at a high temperature. By means of gentle and long cooking the fibres of the meat are softened and the connective tissue is converted into gelatine. Cut the meat into moderate-sized pieces, removing superfluous fat, which must be clarified for future use. Use the correct proportion of meat and water, the average amount being three-quarters of a pint of liquid to one pound of meat.

Tough meat may be steeped in a little vinegar for a few minutes to soften the fibres, or two teaspoonfuls of vinegar may be added during the cooking process for each pound of meat used. If finer-grained and more tender meat is used for a stew, it may be browned on all sides in smoking-hot fat before stewing, and this adds colour and flavour to the stew. Season, flavour and skim the stew carefully. Cover with a closely-fitting lid while cooking, to avoid loss by evaporation.

Time for stewing meat. The time allowed varies only with the quality and not with the quantity. Allow one and a half hours for veal if fine-grained; two hours for mutton; two and a half hours for beef; three hours for shin of beef or ox-tail.

Flavourings for stews. There is ample scope for varying the flavour of stews. When in season, either celery, mushrooms, leeks, Jerusalem artichokes or tomatoes may be added. Or piquancy may be given by the addition of Worcester sauce, mushroom ketchup, celery salt, chutney, red-currant or crab-apple jelly. For white stews, lemon juice or mixed mustard is a welcome addition.

Casserole cookery consists of stewing in a casserole, which can be made from glazed earthenware, from glass ovenware, or from cast-iron with a porcelain enamel finish (Fig. 9). Glass casseroles are ovenware only, but earthenware and enamelled-iron varieties can be used on the top of a stove (earthenware over moderate heat only, or with an asbestos mat placed underneath). Casseroles have the power of retaining heat and use very little

Fig. 9. Casseroles can be made of earthen- or enamelware or heat-resisting glass.

fuel. They are very durable if handled carefully and food can be sent to table in the casserole, which ensures that it will be piping hot, and also minimizes washing up. Heat casseroles very gradually, avoid lifting with a damp cloth while hot, and do not fill a hot casserole with cold water.

Foods suitable for cooking *en casserole* are: braised food, reheated food, soups of the broth variety, vegetables, stewed fruit. In fact, any food requiring slow, gentle heat can be suitably cooked in casseroles, in addition to meat stews.

MEAT COOKERY

CUTS OF MEAT AND METHODS OF COOKING.

Boiling. *Beef:* brisket; silverside; flank (thick or thin); aitchbone; tongue. *Mutton or lamb:* leg; whole neck or middle neck; breast (boned and rolled). *Veal:* head; fore-knuckle; leg; loin (boned and rolled); hind-knuckle (for stock or soup). *Pork:* hand; spring or belly; leg; head and cheek (brawn).

Braising. *Beef:* as for boiling. *Mutton or lamb:* cutlets; chops; sweetbreads; loin; best end of neck; leg. *Veal:* fillet; shoulder; sweetbreads; loin. *Pork:* not usually braised.

Grilling and frying. *Beef:* rump steak; fillet; kidney. *Mutton or lamb:* chops (loin or chump); cutlets; sweetbreads; kidneys. *Veal:* loin chops; cutlet or fillet; sweetbreads. *Pork:* chops; for frying only, liver and "fry."

Oven roasting. *Beef:* sirloin; wing rib; top rump; back rib; top rib; topside; silverside (fresh); thick flank; aitchbone; heart. *Mutton or lamb:* saddle; loin; best end of neck; leg; shoulder; breast (boned and stuffed); heart. *Veal:* loin; fillet; bladebone or oyster; heart; breast (boned and stuffed). *Pork:* loin (hind and fore); leg.

Pies and puddings. *Beef:* aitchbone; buttock; chuck; thick flank; kidney. *Mutton or lamb:* scrag or middle neck (boned); leg; shoulder. *Veal:* shoulder; fillet; "pie pieces." *Pork:* hand; leg; spare rib.

Stewing. *Beef:* buttock; beefsteak; kidney; thick flank; blade or chuck; gravy beef; ox-tail; shin; cheek; brisket; neck or sticking; clod. *Mutton or lamb:* knuckle (fore or hind); head; breast; scrag; middle neck; trotters; sweetbreads. *Veal:* fillet; breast; shoulder; knuckle; feet (calves); head; sweetbreads. *Pork:* feet; chops (for a casserole stew).

GENERAL POINTS ON CHOICE OF MEAT. Meat should be firm and elastic to the touch and rebound when touched with a finger. Choose small meat, as that from an overgrown animal is likely to be coarse and to have large bones. There should be no offensive smell. *Beef* is in season all the year round, but is more tender in winter, as it can be hung longer. The lean should be bright red and slightly marbled with threads of fat, and the fat should be of cream colour. *Mutton* is out of season only in early summer. Note that the lean is of dark-red colour and the fat white. *Veal* is in season in spring and summer and should be eaten fresh. Joints should be pinkish white in colour; the flesh of an older animal is redder and darker. When veal is young and fresh, the connective tissue is puffy and looks blistered. *Pork* is most seasonable in cold weather, and is seasonable from September to April. It is not easily digested and must be well cooked, being put into a very hot oven at first. Joints should be small, the flesh firm and the lean pinkish-white, the fat smooth and white. *Bacon* should have thin rind, pinkish-white fat, free from black specks, and smooth pink lean. To test a ham, stick the point of a knife into it near the bone, and note that it does not smell unpleasant when withdrawn.

FISH COOKERY

KINDS OF FISH. To the cook there are three groups:

Oily fish in which the oil is distributed throughout the flesh. This class includes salmon, mackerel, herrings and pilchards. The food value of these fish is very good, as they are a source of protein, fat, vitamins and mineral matter including iodine. Oily fish is more satisfying than white fish because of the fat it contains, but it is not so digestible and is suitable for those doing manual work or taking plenty of exercise.

White fish in which the oil is confined to the liver which is removed in cleaning the fish. This variety includes round fish, such as cod, haddock, halibut, whiting, and flat fish, such as plaice, soles, turbot. White fish is more easily digested than oily fish and is suitable for children, convalescents and those of delicate digestion. As white fish lacks fat, the deficiency should be made good in cooking it, or by serving with it sauce containing fat.

Shellfish, such as lobster, crab and oysters. In this variety of fish the fibres are coarse, somewhat tough, and thus are indigestible with the exception of oysters.

Choice of fish. Fish is at its best and cheapest when in season. During the spawning time it is poor in flavour and apt to be watery. Some fish, such as cod, whiting, halibut and haddock, are in season all the year round, but for most there is a close season. Fish should be very fresh and cooked as soon as possible when purchased. Make sure that there is no unpleasant, stale smell; the flesh is firm and the body stiff; the gills are red, the eyes bright and not sunken, and that there are plentiful scales on the body; the skin is fresh and unwrinkled, and, with the exception of turbot, adheres closely to the flesh; in choosing plaice, see that its spots are of bright red-orange colour.

PREPARATION OF FISH. *To clean flat fish,* make a cut just under the gills on the dark side of the fish and scrape out the entrails. *To clean round fish,* cut open the fish on its underside from its head to nearly halfway to the tail. Scrape out the entrails. Next remove the fins and scrape off the scales, working from tail to head. Use a sharp knife lightly to avoid cutting the flesh. Wash thoroughly and dry.

TO FILLET FLAT FISH. In the case of soles, skin the fish before filleting, as the flesh is very delicate. Other fish are skinned after filleting. Four fillets are obtained.

Place the fish on a board (Fig. 10), with its tail towards you and the dark side uppermost.

Make a short cut just above the tail, raise the skin and loosen it round the edge of the fish, using the thumb. Hold the fish firmly and flat with the left hand, dip the fingers and thumb of the right hand in salt and draw back the loosened skin smartly from tail to head. The white skin may be removed from the other side of the fish in the same way, but it is frequently left on the fillets. To remove the fillets, use a sharp-pointed knife, and cut on to the bony framework of the fish from head to tail and round the edge of the fins. Starting at the left-hand side, lift the flesh gently with the point of the knife, for its entire length. Then, with long sweeping strokes and pressing the knife on to the bone, remove the fillet in one piece. Turn the fish round with its head towards you and repeat the process for the second fillet. Turn the fish over and remove the third and fourth fillets in the same way.

TO FILLET ROUND FISH. Place the fish on its side with the tail towards you and cut through the skin and flesh lengthways on either side of the backbone (Fig. 11). Cut the flesh cleanly from each side of the bone in turn, and lay the left hand flat upon it to hold it steady while doing this. Small fish, like herrings, need to be cut along the underside only. Spread out the fish, and turn half over so that the back is uppermost, and loosen the backbone by pressing with the thumbs. Turn the fish over completely and lift out the entire bone. Two fillets are obtained.

TO SKIN A FILLET. Place it skin downwards on a board, narrow end towards you. Hold the end with the thumb and fingers of the left hand dipped in salt and, holding the knife upright in the right hand, push the flesh off the skin using a sawing movement and draw the skin backwards with the left hand.

MISCELLANEOUS

DISHING AND GARNISHING. These are very important branches of the cook's art and efforts should be made in preparing food to appeal to the eye first and so create a desire

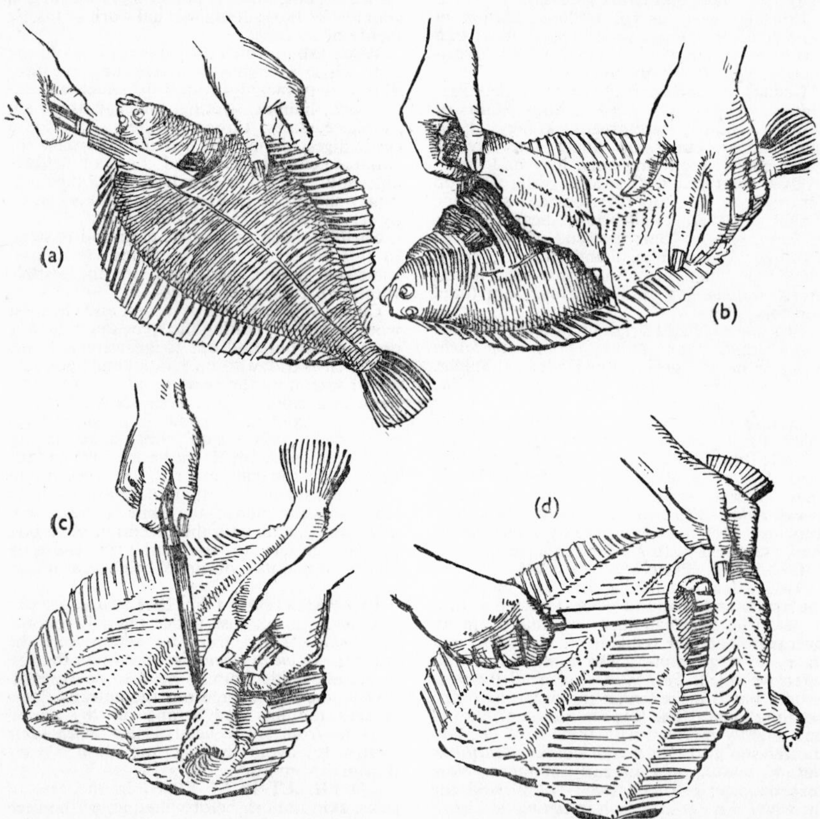

Fig. 10. Skinning and filleting a flat fish: (a) *make a cut under the gills and remove entrails;* (b) *make a cut above the tail and pull off the skin;* (c) *lift the fillet from the bone with the point of the knife;* (d) *remove fillet in one piece with long sweeping strokes.*

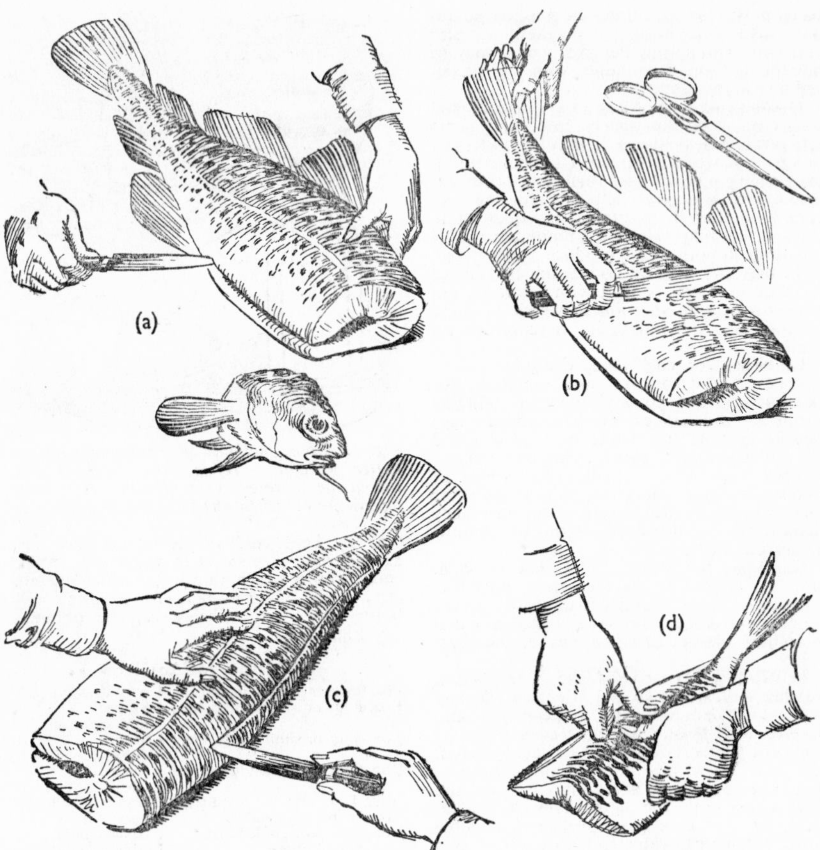

Fig. 11. Filleting a round fish: (a) *cut open fish halfway to tail and remove entrails;* (b) *cut off fins and scrape off scales;* (c) *cut along both sides of backbone and remove fillets;* (d) *with a small fish the backbone may be removed whole by pressing with the thumbs.*

to eat which will help in the digestion of the food served. Do not make the mistake of thinking that it does not matter about trying to make simple food look interesting.

Dishing hot food. Both the food itself and any accompaniments to it should be hot and in readiness for sending to table at the right moment. It is not easy to heat dishes and plates and to keep cooked food really hot, especially if the oven is in use for finishing some other dish. In this case, when the cooker has a rack at the back, the food may be covered and placed on it. (Fried food must not be covered.) If heat is not supplied from the hot-plate by cooking in progress, light one or two burners and turn them down to a glimmer. Heat will rise and keep the dishes hot.

Electric cookers, as a rule, have no rack, but usually have a comparatively large grilling compartment which can be closed. Switch the grill to "low" and store the food in this, being careful not to place any dish immediately below the grill. Saucepans of soups and sauces may be kept hot by standing them in a baking tin with about two inches of simmering water in it. See that dishes of suitable size are in readiness for dishing, and avoid draughts while the dishing is in progress. Dish hot food quickly, and food like grills, soufflés, omelettes and batters should be so timed in their preparation that they may be sent straight to table without delay. Test soups and sauces for correct consistency before serving, as they sometimes thicken on standing. Wipe the rims of dishes with the corner of a teacloth dipped in hot water, to remove any greasiness or splashes of gravy.

Garnishes for hot food. These may consist of vegetables, either cut into neat shapes and cooked separately, or such vegetables as green peas (tinned or fresh), baked tomato slices, small mushrooms, rolls of bacon, forcemeat balls, pastry leaves, border of mashed potato or cooked macaroni or spaghetti, parsley chopped or in sprigs. Paprika pepper may be bought in a small container with a sprinkler top and is economical.

Dishing cold food. All food and accompaniments must be completely cold, and if no refrigerator is available it may be necessary in very hot weather to resort to the methods for keeping milk cold (see IMPROVISED COOLERS, below). Ice is a great help in preparing very cold food, but if unobtainable, equal quantities of washing soda and ammonium nitrate dissolved in cold water produce intense cold. Note that this must on no account be allowed to come in actual contact with the food, but it makes a good solution in which to stand moulds of food which are required to set firmly.

Garnishes for cold food. Consider colour schemes. Sliced beetroot and tomatoes, for example, do not go well together. Suitable garnishes are: slices of hard-boiled egg; sieved egg yolk (the white may be chopped for use separately); capers; chopped pickles; scraped horseradish; small cress; sprigs of watercress; sliced cucumber; sliced radishes; sliced tomatoes; sliced beetroot cut into fancy shapes; and for fish dishes, strips of anchovy or herring fillets, and slices of lemon.

Garnishes for sweet dishes, hot or cold. Shredded almonds; glacé cherries; angelica; crystallized fruits; dates cut in strips; grated chocolate or cocoa and sugar mixed in equal quantities; chopped nuts or crushed breakfast flakes.

IMPROVISED COOLERS. In warm weather milk needs special attention. It may be scalded, poured into a clean jug and covered with muslin. Or proceed as follows: bring the bottle indoors as soon as delivered, run cold water into the washing-up bowl, stand the bottle in it, and continue to run the cold water until the bottle is well chilled. Next, stand it in a large piedish or shallow bowl, containing water to the depth of two to three inches. Cover with a piece of muslin with the ends dipping into the water, and stand the whole thing in the coolest part of the larder in a draught, which will cause evaporation. Butter or other fat may be put into a basin and treated similarly, or a pudding

Fig. 12. Some methods of preserving milk and butter without a refrigerator. Scalded milk should be covered with muslin. The lower figures show earthenware jars for milk and butter.

may be kept cold or its setting hastened. Earthenware jars stood in water will remain cool through sucking up water which evaporates. Types of jar suitable for covering milk bottles and butter dishes can be obtained (see Fig. 12).

HOMELY MEASURES

¼ lb. flour or similar ingredient	1 level teacupful
1 oz. flour or similar ingredient	1 heaped tablespoonful
½ oz. flour or similar ingredient	1 heaped dessertspoonful
¼ oz. flour or similar ingredient	1 heaped teaspoonful
Scant 1 oz. sugar or dried fruit	1 level tablespoonful
2 oz. fresh breadcrumbs	1 teacupful
2 oz. treacle or golden syrup	1 tablespoonful
½ oz. grated cheese	1 tablespoonful
1 oz. lump sugar	6 lumps
½ oz. fat	piece the size of a walnut
½ pint liquid	1 breakfastcupful, or a tumblerful
¼ pint liquid	1 teacupful, or 7 tablespoonfuls

RECIPES

FLOUR. *All the following recipes are arranged for use with plain flour. The required amount and kind of raising agent is given in each case. The disadvantage of using self-raising flour is that the amount of raising agent is fixed and cannot be reduced. Add a pinch of salt when sieving flour for cakes, pastries, scones, etc.*

DRIED EGG. *Dried egg can take the place of shell eggs in any recipe except the very few in which yolks and whites are separated. When possible, sieve the dry powdered egg with the flour and add two tablespoonfuls extra of water or milk when mixing. For creamed mixtures, custards, omelettes, etc., the powdered egg must be reconstituted.*

NUMBER OF PEOPLE SERVED. *Recipes for main-course dishes will provide four portions.*

* * *

ALMONDS, to blanch. Put the almonds into a small enamelled saucepan, covered with cold water. Bring to boil, strain off immediately and run plenty of cold water over them from the tap. Pinch off the skins.

ANCHOVY ROLLS. *Small piece of puff, rough puff, or flaky pastry, or trimmings* (see PASTRY); 6–8 *anchovy fillets; cayenne and*

lemon juice; 2 *teaspoonfuls grated cheese.*
Roll out the pastry to wafer thickness, and cut in pieces large enough to enclose a fillet, as for sausage rolls. Dip the fillets into warm water to remove oil, pat them dry, and lay a fillet on each piece of pastry. Sprinkle with cayenne, cheese and lemon juice. Damp the edges and fold in two lengthwise. Finish and mark the rolls as for tiny sausage rolls (see SAUSAGE ROLLS). Brush the tops with beaten egg or reconstituted dried egg and bake in a hot oven about fifteen minutes, at Mark 7 or 440 deg. F., until golden brown. Serve hot or cold, garnished with sprigs of watercress.

ANCHOVY SAUCE. ½ *pint white sauce* (see WHITE SAUCE, FOUNDATION); *few drops lemon juice;* 2–3 *teaspoonfuls anchovy essence.*
Make the white sauce, using half milk and half fish stock or fish liquor as the liquid. When made, add the lemon juice and sufficient anchovy essence to make the sauce of good flavour and of brownish-pink colour. Re-heat and serve.

APPLE AMBER. *Short pastry, made with* 3 *oz. flour, etc.* (see PASTRY, SHORT); 1 *lb. apples;* 2 *tablespoonfuls water;* 2–3 *oz. sugar; a nut of margarine; yolks of* 2 *eggs; grated rind and juice of* ½ *lemon, or* 1 *level teaspoonful powdered cinnamon.* Meringue: *whites of* 2 *eggs;* 2 *tablespoonfuls caster sugar.*
Line and decorate the sides of a piedish with the pastry. Stew the apples with the water, sugar and margarine until pulped. Rub through a sieve, and add the lemon and beaten yolks. Pour into a piedish and bake at Mark 6 or 425 deg. F. for ten minutes, then reduce the heat to Mark 4 and continue cooking for about a further thirty minutes until set. For the meringue, whisk the whites until stiff, and fold in the sugar lightly. Pile on top of the pudding when it is baked, dredge lightly with sugar, and place in a cool oven until biscuit-coloured and crisp.

APPLE CHARLOTTE. 1–1½ *lb. apples;* 6 *oz. breadcrumbs; grated rind of a lemon, or* 1 *level teaspoonful powdered cinnamon;* 3 *oz. finely shredded suet, or* 2 *oz. margarine in tiny pieces;* 4 *oz. sugar.*
Wipe, peel and core the apples, cut them into small chunks. Mix together the breadcrumbs, lemon rind, chopped suet and sugar. Grease a piedish, and cover the bottom and sides with the crumb mixture. Put in a layer of prepared apple, then of crumb mixture until the dish is full, finishing with a layer of the crumb mixture. Bake in a moderate oven at Mark 4 or 375 deg. F. for one to one-and-a-quarter hours. Serve hot in the piedish, or loosen with a knife and turn out on to a hot dish. Custard may be poured round.

APPLE DUMPLINGS. *To each medium-sized apple allow* 1 *teaspoonful sugar,* 1 *clove or* 1 *teaspoonful marmalade, mincemeat, or other filling; short pastry made with* 2 *oz. flour.*
Make the pastry, and divide into the required number of portions. Mould each to a smooth ball and roll out slightly with a floured rolling-pin. Peel and core the apples and place an apple on each piece of pastry. Work the pastry round the apple, nearly to the top, and put in the sugar and clove. Join and seal the edges of the pastry with a little water. Place the dumplings on a greased baking tin and brush with milk or slightly beaten egg-white. Bake for thirty to thirty-five minutes at Mark 6 or 425 deg. F., slackening the heat towards the end of cooking. Serve on a hot dish, dredged with caster sugar. The centre may be filled with mincemeat, marmalade or chopped dates, or grated lemon rind may be put with the sugar instead of cloves.

APPLE FRITTERS. *Fritter batter* (see FRITTER BATTER); 3–4 *medium-sized apples; caster sugar to dredge.*
Make the batter and set aside in a cool place. Wipe the apples, peel them and cut across in slices of ¼ in. thickness; stamp out the core, using an apple corer or a small round cutter. Have ready a saucepan containing fat, or a saucepan with sufficient dripping and/or lard to float the fritters. When the fat is just beginning to smoke, dip each ring of fruit into the batter and, using a fork through the hole in the centre, lower it gently into the fat. Turn the fritters from time to time, and when golden brown, at the end of about ten minutes, remove from fat and drain on crumpled paper. Serve very hot, sprinkled with caster sugar. *Note:* other fruit may be treated in the same way, such as well-drained tinned apricots or pineapple, bananas peeled, halved and quartered, or pieces of peeled oranges.

APPLE AND NUT SALAD. 4 *red apples;* 2 *oz. shelled nuts;* 2 *tablespoonfuls mayonnaise, or thick salad dressing* (see MAYONNAISE and SALAD DRESSING); 2 *sticks celery* (*optional*); *salt and pepper; a few lettuce leaves, or a handful of small cress.*
Polish the apples, and cut a slice off the stalk end of each. Core the apples, being careful not to take the corer right through. Scoop out some of the pulp of each apple and chop with the nuts and celery, if it is used. Season carefully and moisten with the mayonnaise or salad dressing. Pile the mixture in the apple cases, decorate the tops with shreds of nuts, and serve on individual plates, on lettuce leaves or small cress.

APPLE SAUCE. 1 *lb. apples;* 1–2 *tablespoonfuls water;* ½–1 *tablespoonful sugar; a nut of margarine; few drops of lemon juice.*
Wipe, peel, quarter and core the apples and cut them into small chunks. Put into a saucepan with the water and sugar, and simmer until the apples are pulped. Beat smooth, add the margarine and lemon juice. Re-heat if necessary and serve with roast pork, duck or goose.

APPLE SNOW. 1 *lb. apples;* 2 *oz. granulated or caster sugar; few strips of lemon rind;* 2 *tablespoonfuls water;* 4 *sponge cakes; whites of* 2 *eggs;* ½ *pint boiled custard, made with* 2 *yolks, etc.* (see CUSTARD, BOILED); *glacé cherries; a few pieces of angelica.*

Stew the apples to a pulp with the lemon rind and water; add sugar. Rub through a sieve. Prepare the custard and, while it is still hot, pour it over the sponge cakes which have been sliced and arranged in a fancy dish. Whisk the whites until stiff, and add the cold apple pulp by degrees, continuing the whisking. When stiff and white, pile the apple purée on the sponge cakes and custard and decorate with cherries and angelica.

APPLE SNOW for invalids. 2 *baked apples* (see APPLES, BAKED); *caster sugar; lemon juice or vanilla essence to flavour; white of* 1 *egg.*

Pass the baked apples through a fine sieve, and sweeten and flavour to taste. Whisk the white of egg stiffly, and add the apple pulp by degrees, still whisking. When white and stiff, pile into coupé glasses and serve with a thin slice of sponge cake.

APPLE WATER. 2 *apples, or cores and peelings from* 4 *apples; sugar to taste (about* 3 *lumps); strips of orange or lemon rind;* 1 *pint boiling water; lemon or orange juice to taste.*

Wipe the apples, remove "eye" and stalk, but do not peel or core them. Cut them in slices and put into a jug, or use clean apple peelings and cores. Add the sugar and rind and pour the boiling water over. Stir well and leave covered until cold. Strain off the liquor and add the fruit juice. This forms a healthful and cooling drink.

APPLES, baked. 4 *large cooking apples;* 2 *tablespoonfuls granulated or Demerara sugar;* 4 *cloves;* ½ *oz. margarine or butter;* 3 *tablespoonfuls water;* ½ *pint custard sauce* (see CUSTARD SAUCE).

Wipe the apples and core them without taking the corer right through at the farther end. Cut through the skin of the apples round the centre transversely, and place them on a tin or fireproof dish with the water. Put some sugar, a clove and tiny shavings of margarine in each. Bake in a moderate oven, Mark 4 or 375 deg. F. The length of time required will vary, according to the kind and size of apple, but the average would be one hour. Dish neatly and hand custard and sugar separately.

ARROWROOT. 1 *heaped teaspoonful powdered arrowroot;* ½ *pint milk; flavouring;* 1 *teaspoonful caster sugar.*

Mix the arrowroot smoothly with a little of the cold milk. Boil the remainder of the milk and pour it over the arrowroot, stirring meanwhile. Stir and simmer the arrowroot for five minutes. Add the sugar and flavouring, such as a little grated nutmeg or a teaspoonful of sherry or brandy. Before pouring it into a breakfast cup, note that the consistency is that of thin cream, so that the arrowroot may be sipped from the cup.

ARTICHOKES, boiled. 1 *lb. Jerusalem artichokes;* ½ *pint white coating sauce* (see WHITE SAUCE); *chopped parsley or paprika pepper.*

Scrub and peel the artichokes thinly, using a teaspoonful of white vinegar or lemon juice in the water to keep the vegetable white. Put them into a pan of boiling water, lightly salted and containing a teaspoonful of white vinegar or lemon juice. Simmer gently until tender, the exact time being determined by size and age of the vegetable, but an average time would be forty-five minutes to one hour. Drain very well, then transfer to a hot vegetable dish, and coat promptly with the sauce, or air may discolour the vegetable. Scatter a little chopped parsley or paprika pepper over.

ASPARAGUS. 1 *bundle asparagus;* 1 *piece of toast;* 1–2 *oz. butter; salt and pepper; lemon juice (optional).*

Trim the asparagus from the hard white ends to even and suitable length for serving. Scrape the white parts of the stalks lightly and put the asparagus in water. Tie the stalks into small bundles according to thickness. Have a flat stewpan ready, containing sufficient boiling water to cover the bundles, and cook gently until the green part of the stem can be easily pierced with a fork; the bundles containing the thicker stems must either be put into the pan first, or given rather longer cooking at the end. Time will depend on the thickness of the stems, and may vary from twenty to thirty-five minutes. Drain on a hot dish or plate, then arrange the asparagus neatly on a piece of toast placed at the bottom of a hot vegetable dish. Heat the butter, skim and season it, adding a few drops of lemon juice. Hand separately in a small sauceboat.

AUSTRALIAN PUDDING. ½ *lb. flour;* 1 *level teaspoonful bicarbonate soda;* ¼ *lb. granulated sugar;* 3 *oz. chopped suet;* 2 *oz. currants;* 2 *oz. sultanas;* 1 *tablespoonful marmalade;* 1½ *gills milk.*

Prepare and mix all dry ingredients. Blend the marmalade and milk and mix all together. Put the mixture into a well-greased pudding basin, tie a pudding cloth over and boil for two hours, or alternatively twist a greased paper over and steam for two-and-a-half hours. Turn out on to a hot dish, sprinkle with sugar, and, if liked, serve sweet white sauce separately.

BACHELOR'S PUDDING. 4 *oz. flour; pinch of salt;* 1 *teaspoonful baking powder;* 2 *oz. stale bread;* 1 *gill milk and water;* 2 *oz. chopped suet;* 1½ *oz. sugar;* 2 *oz. mixed currants and sultanas or raisins;* ¼ *teaspoonful mixed spice; extra milk and water for mixing if required.*

Break the crumb of bread into pieces, pour on the boiling milk and water, and leave covered until cold. Then beat until smooth. Pass the flour through a sieve with the salt and baking powder, add suet, sugar, prepared dried fruit and spice. Mix well and add the bread mixture which has been beaten smooth. Mix all well, adding a little more liquid if necessary to make a mixture which will just drop from the spoon. Put into a well-greased pudding basin, tie a pudding-cloth over and boil for two hours, or, alternatively, steam with a greased paper twisted on top for two-and-a-half hours. Unmould on to a hot dish, and pour custard or sweet white sauce round (see CUSTARD and WHITE SAUCE, SWEET).

BACON ROLLS. Remove rind and rust from rashers of streaky bacon, and flatten out each rasher thinly with a knife. Cut across into two or three pieces according to size required, roll each piece up tightly and thread on a metal skewer. Grill or bake gently until cooked. Use as garnish for stewed veal or rabbit, in a mixed grill or as an accompaniment to roast chicken.

BAKEWELL TART. *Rich short pastry, made with 4–5 oz. flour, etc.* (see PASTRY, RICH SHORT); 1 *large tablespoonful red jam;* 1 *large tablespoonful lemon curd;* 1 *oz. margarine;* 1½ *oz. sugar;* 1 *large egg;* 1½ *oz. cake crumbs;* 1½ *oz. ground almonds; rind and juice* ½ *lemon.*

Prepare the pastry and line a shallow tart tin with it (such as an oval tart tin of about eight-and-a-half inches in length, or a sandwich tin of seven inches in diameter). Put a narrow rim of pastry on top of the pastry lining, damping the latter to hold the rim in place. Cut up the edges and draw them up in flutes. Put a layer of jam in the bottom and spread the lemon curd over. For the almond mixture, cream the margarine, add the sugar and cream again. Add the beaten egg by degrees, then mix in the lemon rind and juice, cake crumbs and ground almonds lightly. Bake in a moderate oven until the mixture is set and brown, at Mark 5 or 400 deg. F. for about forty-five minutes. *Note:* instead of ground almonds, fine semolina and one teaspoonful ratafia or half a teaspoonful of almond essence may be substituted.

BAKING POWDER, home-made. 4 *oz. cream of tartar;* 2 *oz. bicarbonate of soda;* 4 *oz. ground rice or cornflour.*

Mix all ingredients together, then pass through a fine sieve several times, until a perfectly smooth powder is obtained. Store in an airtight tin, keeping the lid on the tin firmly, except when in use. Keep in a dry place. *Note:* if preferred, tartaric acid can take the place of cream of tartar. As this is stronger than cream of tartar, two ounces only of tartaric acid are necessary.

BAKING-POWDER ROLLS. 1 *lb. flour;* 4 *heaped teaspoonfuls baking powder;* 1 *small teaspoonful salt;* 2 *oz. lard or margarine; about* ½ *pint milk and water to mix.*

Pass the flour, baking powder and salt through a sieve. Rub in the fat and mix to a dough, which is soft and pliable but not sticky. Knead lightly and cut into six or eight pieces. Mould into balls, flatten with a floured rolling pin, prick the tops, brush with milk and put the rolls on a greased and floured baking tin. Put quickly into a hot oven at Mark 7 or 440 deg. F. Reduce the heat after ten minutes and continue cooking for about twenty minutes in all. The rolls are best eaten new.

BANBURY CAKES. *Puff or rough puff pastry, made with 8 oz. flour, etc.* (see PASTRY, PUFF and ROUGH PUFF); 2 *oz. cleaned currants;* 2 *oz. stoned raisins;* 1 *oz. candied peel;* 2 *oz. sugar;* 1 *oz. butter or margarine;* 1 *tablespoonful cake crumbs; grated nutmeg; mixed spice;* 1 *tablespoonful lemon juice, rum or brandy.*

Make the pastry and set it aside in a cool place. For the filling: pass the currants, raisins and candied peel through a mincer. Add all the remaining ingredients, oiling the butter so that it will combine evenly. To shape and bake the cakes, roll out the pastry a quarter-inch thick, and cut in rounds of about three inches diameter. Place a spoonful of the filling in the middle of each, damp the edges and draw them together to form a ball. Turn each completely over, so that the smooth side is uppermost. Roll a little with a floured rolling-pin, and shape with the sides of the hands into an oval shape. Put the cakes on floured baking tins, and bake for about twenty minutes in a hot oven, set at Mark 7 or 440 deg. F. Brush with a little milk, water or slightly-beaten egg-white, sprinkle with sugar and put back into the oven for a minute or two to dry the glaze.

BARLEY WATER. 2 *oz. pearl barley;* 1 *quart water;* 2–3 *thin strips lemon rind; uice* ½–1 *lemon; sugar to taste.*

Method for clear barley water to serve as a beverage: blanch the barley (see BLANCHING), strain and put it with the water and lemon rind in a saucepan. Simmer gently for one hour, cover and leave until cold. Stir well, add the sugar and lemon juice, strain and serve. The barley water may also be served hot, as soon as it is made, if preferred.

Method for barley water for the dilution of milk: omit the lemon rind and juice; proceed as above, but simmer very gently for rather longer time.

BATTER for Coating. 4 *oz. flour; pinch of salt;* 1 *egg;* 1 *gill milk, or a trifle more* (see below).

Make as for batter for Yorkshire pudding (see below) and leave to stand in a cool place for an hour. The batter must be thick, or it will not adhere to the material to be fried.

BATTER for Yorkshire pudding or pancakes. 4 *oz. flour; pinch of salt;* 1½ *gills milk;* ½ *gill water;* 1 *egg.*

Pass the flour through a sieve and make a well in the centre. Put in the unbeaten egg and some of the liquid. Mix from the middle with a wooden spoon and very smoothly, gradually adding more liquid as required and drawing in the flour from the sides. Add about half of the liquid, and when all the flour has been drawn in beat the batter thoroughly, using a lifting motion to allow air to enter. Continue beating until the surface is covered with small air bubbles, and this will probably take about eight to ten minutes. Stir in the remainder of the liquid. Leave to stand for at least an hour in a cool place. *Notes:* the batter will be lighter if the above proportion of water is used with the milk. The batter is easier to beat, before all the liquid is added. If dried egg is used, sieve it with the flour, and add two tablespoonfuls extra of milk or water.

BEANS, broad. 1½ *pints broad beans after shelling;* ½ *pint parsley sauce.*

Have the beans young and very fresh and do not shell them until required for cooking. Cook in boiling salted water until tender, about fifteen minutes when the beans are young, twenty to thirty minutes when old. Drain the beans and add them to the sauce, which must on no account be too thick. Broad beans are a very suitable vegetable to serve with a piece of boiled ham or bacon.

BEANS, French or runner. *Preparation.* Trim off a rim from the outside of each, slice thinly and wash well. Soak for fifteen minutes in water as cold as possible, then drain very well.
Cooking. Plunge the prepared beans into rapidly boiling water. Boil for twelve to eighteen minutes, very rapidly. Drain and toss in a little margarine or butter, with pepper and salt. *Note:* if the beans are small and very young, slicing is unnecessary, but they will take a little longer to cook.

BEANS, haricot or butter. *Preparation.* Wash them well. Cover with boiling water, adding one teaspoonful bicarbonate of soda to each two quarts of water used. Soak in this for twelve hours, then drain and again wash well.
Cooking. Cook in boiling water with a small nut of bacon fat or dripping. Keep the water just boiling all the time, but not rapidly. Do not add salt until the beans are almost cooked or the skins are toughened. Average time to cook: one-and-a-half hours. Drain, and the liquid may be added to household stock (see STOCK, HOUSEHOLD).
Serving. (1) Toss in a little margarine to moisten, and add chopped parsley. Serve as a vegetable with fish or meat. Or lay slices of fried, grilled or boiled bacon on top and garnish with croûtons of fried bread or toast. (2) Serve in a good sauce, allowing half a pint sauce to each four ounces of beans before cooking. Tomato, curry, brown or onion sauce is suitable. (3) Use as a component of such dishes as vegetable hot-pot or pie.

BÉCHAMEL SAUCE. 1 *pint milk;* 1 *shallot or* ½ *small onion; piece of carrot; stick of celery;* 1 *small bayleaf;* 10 *white peppercorns;* 2 *oz. margarine;* 2 *oz. flour;* ½ *gill evaporated milk or "top" milk; salt.*
Put the milk, sliced vegetables, bayleaf and peppercorns in a saucepan and bring just to boiling point. Cover and leave to stand for ten minutes. Strain off the milk, and make a white sauce with the margarine, flour, and flavoured milk. Simmer for ten minutes, add the evaporated milk, re-warm and use as required.

BEEF, boiled salt. 3–4 *lb. salted silverside or brisket; cold water to cover;* 2 *large carrots;* 2 *large onions;* 2 *large turnips; dumplings* (see DUMPLINGS); ½ *pint mustard sauce* (*optional*) (see MUSTARD SAUCE); *chopped parsley.*
Weigh the meat and allow time for cooking at the rate of twenty-five minutes for each pound and twenty-five minutes over. Wash meat in cold water to remove brine, tie and skewer it into shape. Put the meat into a saucepan with sufficient cold water to cover, and bring slowly to boiling point. Skim and add the prepared root vegetables, cut into halves or quarters according to size. Simmer gently for the required length of time. Prepare and add the dumplings, or cook them separately. Serve the meat on a hot dish, with blocks of vegetables sprinkled with chopped parsley and dumplings arranged round it. Serve the sauce separately in a sauceboat, and some of the beef broth also.

BEEF, fillets of. *About* 1 *lb. fillet steak, in one small thick piece; fried round croûtes of bread for dishing* (see CROÛTONS); *slices of baked tomato* (see TOMATOES, BAKED); ½ *oz. maître d'hôtel butter* (see MAÎTRE D'HÔTEL BUTTER); ½ *pint tomato or brown sauce.*
Cut the meat in slices one-inch thick, beat slightly with a damp rolling pin, and trim if necessary. Prepare the sauce, tomato slices, and maître d'hôtel butter. Melt a little dripping in a frying-pan and, when just smoking, fry the croûtes of bread. Re-heat the fat, and fry the fillets on both sides. Arrange a fillet on each croûte, on a hot dish, putting a slice of tomato and neat piece of maître d'hôtel butter on each. Pour the sauce round. A tablespoonful of cooked vegetable (as for BEEF OLIVES) may be placed at each side if liked.

BEEF OLIVES. 1 *lb. buttock steak;* 2 *tablespoonfuls veal stuffing* (see STUFFING, VEAL); 1 *oz. dripping;* 1 *oz. flour;* ¾ *pint household stock or vegetable water;* 1 *onion; glaze* (see GLAZE, MOCK); *cooked vegetable to garnish;* ½ *lb. mashed potatoes.*
Cut the meat into thin slices across the grain, making them about three inches wide and four inches long. Spread a little of the stuffing down the centre of each slice, roll up and secure with fine string. Fry the meat in smoking hot dripping until lightly browned. Remove the meat and keep it warm while making a brown sauce with the dripping, onion, flour and stock (see STOCK, HOUSEHOLD). When boiling, add the meat and simmer gently for two hours. Remove meat to a hot plate and remove the string. Brush the rolls with glaze, and arrange them on a bed of hot mashed potato which has been piped or forked into place. Boil, skim and season the sauce, strain it round the potato. Have ready a small quantity of suitable cooked vegetable to place at each side, such as dice of carrot and turnip, cauliflower sprigs, green peas (fresh or tinned) or sliced runner beans.

BEEF, roast. For roasting beef follow the general directions given on pages 280 and 285 of "The A.B.C. of Cookery." Fig. 13 shows how to carve two cuts of beef.

BEEF, spiced. 5–7 *lb. round of beef, or aitchbone or brisket;* ½ *oz. baysalt;* ½ *oz. saltpetre;* ¼ *oz. black pepper;* ¼ *oz. powdered allspice;* 1 *level teaspoonful ground ginger;* ½ *level teaspoonful ground cloves;* ½ *level teaspoonful ground mace;* 3 *oz. common salt;* 3 *oz. brown sugar.*
Remove bones, skin and gristle from the meat. Pound and crush the baysalt and saltpetre with a rolling pin, and rub these well into meat, which has been wiped with a damp cloth.

Fig. 13. Carving roast beef. Ribs of beef (left) *should be carved downwards, giving both fat and lean; a round of beef* (right) *is carved horizontally as thinly and evenly as possible. Mutton and pork are carved thicker.*

Put the meat into a bowl, and next day mix the pepper and spices and rub thoroughly into meat. Return the meat to the bowl and sprinkle over the mixed salt and sugar. Turn the meat daily and baste it with the liquid which forms. Allow one day for each pound of meat spiced. Wash the meat in cold water, bind it securely with string and skewers, and boil as for salt beef (see BEEF, BOILED SALT), adding a *bouquet garni* (see BOUQUET GARNI) and a dozen peppercorns. Drain the meat, and press it between two dishes with weights on top. When cold, trim the meat and brush with glaze (see GLAZE, MOCK). Garnish with parsley sprigs or salad plants.

BEEF TEA. 1 *lb. lean beef, as freshly killed as possible;* 1 *pint cold water;* ½ *teaspoonful salt.*

Measure the water and put it into a stone jar or casserole. Remove skin and fat from the meat and shred the lean finely, putting it at once into the water. Add the salt, cover and allow to stand for thirty minutes. Stand the jar in a saucepan containing cold water to come halfway up its sides. Cover the jar closely, bring the water to boil slowly and allow it to simmer for three hours. Stir the contents of the jar occasionally and see that it does not boil. Strain, cool and skim. Re-heat, without boiling, in small quantities as required. Keep the beef tea in a cold place and, as it must not boil in preparation, do not make more than twenty-four hours' supply at one time.

Quick method. Put the shredded meat, water and salt into a small saucepan and allow to stand for fifteen minutes. Stir and press with a small wooden spoon, over gentle heat, until the liquid becomes brownish-red colour and the meat white. Strain and serve.

Raw method. Shred two to three ounces lean beef finely and put it at once into quarter pint of water with a pinch of salt. Leave to stand for thirty minutes, and press through a strainer. Serve at once, in a coloured glass to conceal its unpleasant colour. *Note:* the meat residue from making beef tea may be added to the household stockpot (see STOCK, HOUSEHOLD).

BEETROOT. *Preparation.* Cut off the leaves, leaving about two inches of stem. Shake off the soil, and the beetroot may be washed very gently, but must not be scrubbed, for fear of breaking the skin.

Cooking. Plunge into boiling water, and cook gently until tender. A medium-sized beetroot will take about one-and-a-half hours, but a small globe-beetroot takes about an hour. Drain and, if it is required to skin the beetroot while hot, put it into a bowl and cover it with water, to cool it sufficiently to handle. Otherwise skin it when cold.

Serving. Cut into slices or dice if the beetroot is to be served hot, and coat with white sauce, slightly acidulated with lemon juice or vinegar. For serving cold, slice thinly when cold and sprinkle with vinegar.

Note: if preferred, the beetroot may be placed on a well-greased tin and baked in a moderately hot oven, for the same length of time, Mark 3 or 350 deg. F.

BEETROOT SALAD. 1 *cooked peeled beetroot;* 1 *tablespoonful chopped onion; chopped parsley; French salad dressing* (see SALAD DRESSING, FRENCH); *watercress sprigs.*

Slice the beetroot, and cut out some fancy-shaped pieces and set them aside. Slice the remainder coarsely and mix with the chopped onion and sufficient dressing to moisten. Make into a mound in a salad dish, and arrange the prepared shapes of beetroot over. Sprinkle with chopped parsley, and arrange the watercress round the base of the mound.

BISCUITS, almond. 6 *oz. flour;* 2 *oz. ground almonds* (*or use* 7 *oz. flour,* 1 *oz. semolina and* ½ *small teaspoonful almond or* 1 *teaspoonful ratafia essence*)*;* 4 *oz. margarine;* 4 *oz. caster sugar;* 1 *egg; a few drops water or milk, if necessary.*

Make by creaming method (see CAKE MIXTURES, CREAMED). Knead lightly to a smooth ball. Roll out thinly, prick all over and cut in rounds, preferably with a fluted cutter. Bake in a moderate oven, Mark 5 or 400 deg. F. for about fifteen minutes, until pale golden-brown colour.

BISCUITS, cheese. Make cheese pastry (see PASTRY, CHEESE) and roll out one-eighth inch thick. Cut in small rounds, squares or oblongs. Bake golden brown in a moderate oven set at Mark 5 or 400 deg. F. for ten to twelve minutes, being very careful not to over-brown them. These biscuits may be used as canapes for savouries or hors d'oeuvres.

BISCUITS, Easter. 8 *oz. flour; pinch of salt;* ¾ *teaspoonful mixed spice;* 2 *oz. currants;* 4 *oz. margarine;* 4 *oz. caster sugar;* 1 *egg; a little water or milk if necessary.*

Pass flour, salt, spice through a sieve and add the currants. Shape and bake as for almond biscuits (see BISCUITS, ALMOND).

BISCUITS, ginger. 4 *oz. flour; salt;* 1 *level teaspoonful ground ginger;* ½ *level teaspoonful bicarbonate soda;* 1½ *oz. lard and margarine together;* 1 *oz. sugar;* 1 *tablespoonful golden syrup.*

Sieve the flour, ground ginger, salt and bicarbonate of soda together. Rub in fats and add sugar. Blend with the syrup and knead. The mixture should be firm and dry, but if necessary add a few drops of water to bind it together. Roll out thinly and cut in rounds. Place on a greased tin and bake in a moderate oven set at Mark 4 or 375 deg. F. for fifteen to twenty minutes, reducing heat after ten minutes.

BISCUITS, milk. ¼ *lb. flour;* 1 *level teaspoonful baking powder;* 1 *oz. margarine;* ½ *gill milk; large pinch of salt or* 1 *teaspoonful sugar.*

Pass the flour, baking powder and salt or sugar through a sieve. Put the margarine and milk in a saucepan, warm gently to melt the margarine and pour into the flour. Turn the dough on to a floured board, knead lightly, roll out thinly and prick well. Cut in rounds and place them on a greased tin. Bake in a moderate oven, set at Mark 4 or 375 deg. F., for fifteen minutes until golden brown.

BISCUITS, oaten. 3 *oz. flour; pinch of salt;* ½ *teaspoonful baking powder;* 5 *oz. medium or rolled oats;* 3 *oz. lard and margarine together;* 1 *egg;* 2 *oz. sugar.*

Pass flour, salt and baking powder through a sieve. Add oats and rub in fat. Add sugar. Mix to a firm dough with the beaten egg, adding a little water if necessary. Roll out to one-eighth-inch thickness and cut in rounds, squares or fingers. Bake on greased tins in a moderate oven set at Mark 5 or 400 deg. F. for twelve to fifteen minutes.

BISCUITS, shortbread. 6 *oz. flour;* 2 *oz. ground rice or fine semolina;* 4 *oz. margarine or butter;* 4 *oz. sugar;* ½ *a beaten egg;* 2 *tablespoonfuls "top" milk or cream.*

Mix to a firm dough by rubbing-in method (see CAKE MIXTURES, RUBBED-IN). Roll out to scant quarter-inch thickness, using a little caster sugar mixed with the flour on the board. Cut in fancy shapes and place on a greased tin. Bake in a moderate oven set at Mark 4 or 375 deg. F. for fifteen to twenty minutes.

BISCUITS, Shrewsbury. As for Easter biscuits (see above), but omit currants and spice, and add one teaspoonful grated lemon rind at the beginning of creaming.

BLANCHING. To blanch any ingredient, cover it with cold water in a suitable-sized saucepan, bring briskly to boiling point and strain off the water. This process is used in cookery for various reasons, and the following are examples: to enable the skins of nuts to be removed easily; to remove strong flavour, as in the case of onions; to remove loose starch, as in pearl barley; to cleanse, as in sweetbreads; to whiten, as in the case of potatoes to be browned in fat.

BOTTLED FRUIT. Choice of fruit. Fruit selected for bottling should be as fresh as possible and, with the exception of gooseberries, which are best for bottling when green, should be just firmly ripe. If the fruit is too ripe, it breaks during the sterilizing process. Reject all blemished fruit.

Vacuum bottles. Two types are obtainable from ironmongers and large stores, sizes ranging from half to four pounds. Clip bottles have usually round rubber rings, lacquered tin lids and metal spring clips to keep the lids in place during sterilization and cooling. Screw-band bottles have glass lids, flat rubber bands and screw bands made from lacquered tin or aluminium, to keep the lid in place during sterilization and cooling (see Fig. 14).

Fig. 14. Vacuum bottles for preserving fruit.

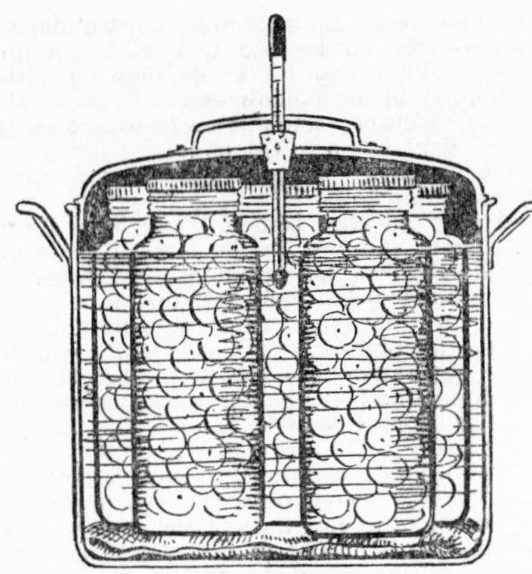

Fig. 15. A thermometer set in a cork inserted in the lid is useful when sterilizing in water.

Preparation for bottling. Rubber rings should be examined carefully before use. It is not advisable to use them more than once, as use tends to stretch them. If unused, they may usually be kept from one season to the next in a tin stored in a cool, dark place. Soak the rings in warm water for quarter of an hour before use. Examine each bottle carefully before use. If a bottle or lid is chipped, or has even a very small crack, it must be discarded, or it will not be possible to obtain an air-sealed bottle when the process is finished. Bottles should be tightly packed with fruit without bruising. If small fruit is used, add water or syrup to cover when the bottle is half-filled, continuing alternately until full, to obtain the correct proportion of liquid to fruit. Hard fruit should be closely filled into the bottles to the top before any liquid is added. Fruit may be preserved successfully in water or syrup as preferred, but if syrup is used the fruit will have a better colour and flavour after storing. One disadvantage of using syrup is that the fruit tends to rise in the bottles during sterilization, which gives a less good appearance for storage. Average proportions: half pound granulated or loaf sugar to one pint water. Dissolve the sugar completely in some of the water, boil up and boil for one minute. Add the remainder of the water, cold, if it is desired to hasten cooling.

Filling the bottles. Fit on the rubber ring. Fill the bottles *slowly* with water or syrup. Tap or jerk the bottles occasionally while filling to remove air-bubbles. Put on the lid and spring clip or screw band, giving this latter about a quarter turn back to loosen it, to allow steam and hot air to escape during sterilization, or the bottle will burst. Spring clips can be fitted quite firmly, as they are so shaped as to rise slightly during sterilization.

Sterilization. *Using a thermometer.* A deep fish-kettle, saucepan or water-boiler may be used for bottling small quantities of fruit, or the washing copper may be adapted. If large quantities of fruit are to be sterilized, it is worth while to obtain a special sterilizing outfit. This will be provided with a fitted false bottom; an ordinary pan must have either a wire frame with short legs, strips of wood nailed together in a trellis, straw, a coarse cloth, or even many folds of newspaper, put at the bottom, to prevent the bottles touching the bottom of the pan. Put in sufficient cold water to cover the bottles, or at least to cover the shoulders, and there must be a lid to prevent the escape of steam.

A thermometer is of great assistance for exact bottling, and during the process the bulb of the thermometer must be immersed in the water surrounding the bottles. It is convenient to have a hole in the lid through which the thermometer can be passed and left in position, so that the lid need not be removed. It is generally possible to get a tinsmith to make a sufficiently large hole in the lid of an ordinary pan (Fig. 15).

The cold water put into the pan should take one-and-a-half hours to reach the required temperature, so that the contents of each bottle will be heated to the centre. Allow times and temperatures as shown below.

Kind of fruit	*Temperature to reach in 1½ hours*	*Time to maintain temperature*
Apples Apricots Blackberries Damsons Gooseberries Greengages Loganberries Mulberries Plums (whole, ripe) Raspberries Rhubarb Strawberries	165 deg. F.	10 min.
Plums (halved and stoned, or unripe)	165 deg. F.	20 min.
Currants (red, black or white)	180 deg. F.	15 min.
Cherries	190 deg. F.	10 min.
Pears	190 deg. F.	20 min.
Tomatoes	190 deg. F.	30 min.

Without a thermometer. Prepare and place bottles in pan as foregoing, cover with cold water and bring to simmering point in one hour. Keep most fruits at simmering point for five minutes, but allow ten to fifteen minutes for cherries and currants, twenty minutes for pears, and thirty minutes for tomatoes.

Cooling the bottles. When sterilization is completed, remove sufficient of the water from the pan so that the necks of the bottles are well above its surface, and use a dry cloth to remove the bottles one at a time. If screw-band bottles have been used, tighten each screw immediately. Stand the hot bottles on a wooden surface to prevent cracking and leave undisturbed until cold, and thereafter for forty-eight hours, before testing.

Oven method of sterilization. After the fruit has been packed into the bottles, but before any liquid has been poured over, stand the bottles on asbestos mats or thick cardboard

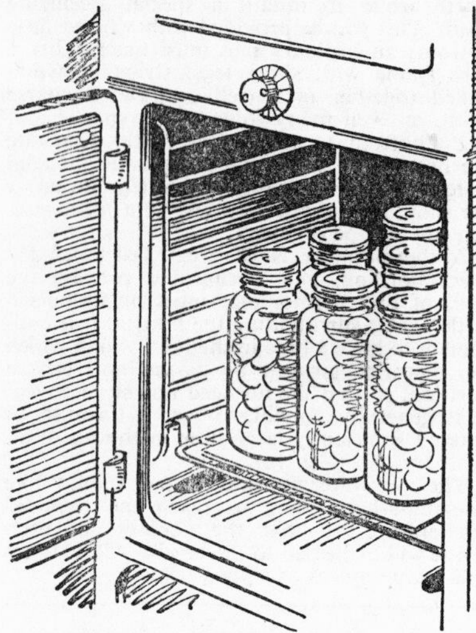

Fig. 16. Sterilizing fruit in the oven.

in a cool oven (Fig. 16), set at Mark $\frac{1}{4}$ or 240 deg. F. for an average of three-quarters to one hour. Have the bottles filled rather fuller with fruit than for the water-bath method, to allow for shrinkage. Put the lids on only, without rubber bands or screw bands or spring clips, or cover the tops of the bottles with a flat tin. This prevents the fruit from burning. When ready the fruit will have changed colour slightly and shrunk somewhat. If the fruit has shrunk much, fill up the bottles from one of

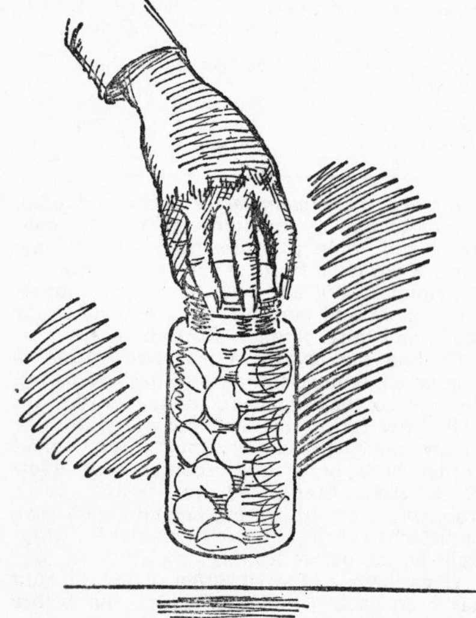

Fig. 17. Testing for vacuum.

them and return to the oven for a few minutes. Remove the bottles one at a time, put on rubber rings, and fill to overflowing with boiling syrup or boiling water. Replace lid, put on spring clip, and if screw bands are used, screw tight at once. On removal from oven these processes must be carried out very quickly, one bottle at a time.

Testing all filled bottles. When bottles are quite cold, test that the lid is firmly held in position by the small vacuum formed. Remove screw band or clip, and test that it may be lifted for a few inches from the table holding by the lid only (Fig. 17). Any bottle which does not respond to this test must be re-sterilized, or a better plan is to use it as stewed fruit as soon as possible. Screw bands can be used again for further bottling, or they may be rubbed with a little petroleum jelly or oil and lightly replaced on the bottles or stored in a box. Clips lose their resilience if left on bottles and should be rubbed with petroleum jelly or oil and stored in a box.

Storage of bottled fruit. Put away in a cool, dry place, airy but protected from light.

Homely methods of bottling. Special covers may be obtained for covering fruit bottled

Fig. 18. Vacuum tops for use with jam-jars.

in jam-jars (Fig. 18), and are generally satisfactory if the makers' directions are followed implicitly. Firm, acid fruit may be oven-sterilized, and mutton fat may be poured on or a mixture of three parts paraffin wax and one part of liquid medicinal paraffin. For success in carrying out this method, note the following points: see that in either case the fat is thoroughly hot, but not smoking hot. Fruit must be completely covered with liquid and well within the neck of the jar. Wipe neck with a clean cloth to remove moisture before pouring in fat to the level of the top of the jar. Do not move the jar until the fat is set, then, if a slight depression is formed in the fat, fill up level with more melted fat. When quite set and hard, tie a preserve cover over to protect from dust. Store carefully as above.

BOTTLED VEGETABLES. The only safe way in which vegetables may be bottled at home is by sterilizing them in a pressure cooker, and this should be done exactly according to the directions given in the book of instructions supplied with each cooker. The use of this piece of equipment by an experienced person will ensure that the vegetables are quite good for use, but in no case must the bottling of vegetables be attempted by any of the methods recommended for the bottling of fruit. All vegetables are likely to be contaminated with organisms from the soil, which are often resistant to moderate heat, and, even if the vegetables appear to be quite good, serious food poisoning may result. Also the composition of vegetables is completely different from that of fruit, and they contain no acid, which is so helpful in the preservation of fruit.

BOUQUET GARNI. 1 *clove; pinch of mixed herbs or a few sprigs fresh herbs; tiny piece bayleaf; tiny piece mace; 2–3 pieces parsley stalk, ½ in. length; 4 peppercorns.*

Place these ingredients on a small square of muslin and tie up with fine string or thread. Use for flavouring soups and sauces. If a flavour of celery is required and no fresh celery is available, one teaspoonful celery seeds may be added.

BRAINS WITH PARSLEY SAUCE. 4 *sheeps' brains; ½ pint white stock or vegetable water; ½ small onion; ½ small carrot; 1 oz. margarine; ¾ oz. flour; 2–3 tablespoonfuls milk; 1 teaspoonful lemon juice; salt and pepper.*

Soak the brains in salted water for two hours. Remove skin and fibres, wash and cleanse very well, cook in boiling water for three minutes, drain and leave in fresh cold water until quite cold. Heat the stock, add the onion and carrot, salt and pepper, and simmer gently for twenty minutes. Make a white sauce with the margarine, flour, flavoured stock and milk. Re-heat the brains in this for ten minutes and add lemon juice and chopped parsley. The brains may be served on slices of buttered toast or mashed potato, as a light luncheon or supper dish.

BRAISED CELERY. 4 *hearts of celery; chopped parsley; mirepoix* (see MIREPOIX).

Cleanse the celery well, leaving the hearts whole, tie each securely with fine string and blanch (see BLANCHING). Prepare the mirepoix and, when boiling, lay the celery hearts on top. Baste well with the liquid, cover with a greased paper and close-fitting lid. Cook until tender, about one hour, basting occasionally. Place the celery in a hot vegetable dish, and keep hot. Strain the stock from the mirepoix and boil it briskly until syrupy and of glazing consistency. Pour this over the celery and sprinkle with chopped parsley. *Note:* Cauliflower or Jerusalem artichokes may be treated similarly. The outer sticks of the celery can be stewed, or used for soup.

BRAISED SWEETBREADS. ¾ *lb. lambs' sweetbreads; mirepoix* (see BRAISING); ½ *lb. cooked mashed potatoes; ½ pint white or béchamel sauce* (see WHITE and BÉCHAMEL SAUCES); *cooked vegetable to garnish.*

Soak the sweetbreads in cold salted water for one hour. Blanch briskly (see BLANCHING) and put at once into cold water to check cooking. Skin, and press the sweetbreads between two plates until cold. Remove any gristle and fat. Prepare the mirepoix, and when boiling lay the sweetbreads on top. Braise gently for one hour. Prepare the sauce, and arrange the hot mashed potato in a neat roll on a hot dish. Lay the sweetbreads on this, and garnish with the cooked vegetable chosen. *Note:* a large heart sweetbread may be used instead if preferred. In this case cut it in slices before arranging on the mashed potato.

BRAISED VEAL. 1½ *lb. slice of fillet of veal; 3 tablespoonfuls veal stuffing; fat bacon; mirepoix* (see MIREPOIX); *cooked green peas or other suitable vegetable to garnish; ½ pint tomato or brown sauce* (see TOMATO and BROWN SAUCES).

Wipe and trim the meat, spread it with the veal stuffing, roll up and secure with short metal skewers and string. Prepare the mirepoix and, when boiling, place the meat on it, covered with slices of bacon fat. Cook over heat until tender, about one-and-a-half hours. Remove meat and place it on a greased tin, in a moderately hot oven, for twenty minutes, to crisp the outside and the bacon. Meanwhile strain the stock from the mirepoix, and boil it briskly until of syrupy consistency. Brush this "half-glaze" over the meat on a hot dish. Pour the sauce round, and arrange the cooked vegetable at each side. If preferred, the vegetables from the mirepoix may be cut up and used instead of freshly cooked vegetable (see BRAISING). *Note:* braised beef can be made by substituting a slice of buttock steak. Allow rather longer time for cooking.

BRANDY SAUCE. 1 *teaspoonful cornflour; ½ pint milk; 1 teaspoonful sugar; yolk of 1 egg; 1–2 tablespoonfuls brandy.*

Mix the cornflour smoothly with the milk. Put these in a small saucepan and stir until boiling. Add the sugar and boil and stir for five minutes. Allow to cool while beating the egg yolk and brandy together. Add and cook over very slow heat until the egg yolk thickens. See that sauce does not curdle by overheating.

BRANDY SNAPS. 4 *oz. golden syrup; 3½ oz. caster or Demerara sugar; 4 oz. margarine; 3½ oz. flour; 1 teaspoonful ground ginger; 1 teaspoonful grated lemon rind; 1–2 teaspoonfuls brandy (optional).*

Melt the syrup, sugar and margarine together gently in a small saucepan. Stir in the flour sieved with the ground ginger, the grated lemon rind and the brandy, if it is used. Drop the mixture in small teaspoonfuls on a greased tin, about three inches apart. Bake in a very moderate oven, set at Mark 3 or 350 deg. F., for seven to ten minutes. When baked and just set, roll up at once round the handle of a wooden spoon which has been greased. If at all overbaked, or if allowed to become too cool, the snaps are too brittle to roll.

BREAD, brown. 1 *lb. wholemeal flour; 1 lb. white flour; 2 oz. lard; 2 teaspoonfuls salt; 1 oz.*

yeast; 1 *teaspoonful caster sugar; rather more than* 1 *pint tepid milk and water.*

Mix together the two kinds of flour, and warm them with the salt. Rub in the lard, and proceed as for BREAD, HOUSEHOLD.

BREAD, currant. For each one pound of flour to be made into dough, allow two ounces currants and one ounce sugar. Warm these and knead into the dough after it has risen and before putting it into the tin to prove. Proceed as for BREAD, HOUSEHOLD.

BREAD, household. 3½ *lb. flour;* 3½ *teaspoonfuls salt;* 1½–2 *pints tepid water;* 1 *oz. yeast;* 1 *teaspoonful caster sugar.*

Warm the flour and salt and pass it through a sieve into a warm mixing bowl. Stir the yeast with the sugar in a cup until liquid and add one-and-a-half pints of the water and pour it into a well made in the centre of the flour. Sprinkle a little of the flour from the sides over the surface. Cover the bowl with a cloth, and set it aside in a warm place for about twenty minutes until the surface of the liquid is covered with bubbles. This part of bread-making is called "setting the sponge." Plunge the hand into the middle, and work in all the flour, adding more tepid water as necessary to make a firm elastic dough. Knead thoroughly for about ten minutes. Return the dough to the floured bowl, stretch a well-rinsed swab over, and set aside in a warm place for one-and-a-half to two hours until the dough has doubled its bulk. Have ready three or four bread tins which are warm and have been greased, knead the dough again lightly for a few minutes, and press the dough into the tins. Put the tins into a warm place for about fifteen minutes to "prove" the dough, when it should begin to rise in the tins. Bake in a hot oven, Mark 8, or 465 deg. F., until the bread has risen and is beginning to brown, then slacken the heat by degrees. Time for baking will be from half to one hour, according to the size of the loaves. When ready, the bread should have a nicely browned crust, and sound hollow when rapped underneath.

BREAD, quickly-made. 1 *lb. flour;* 1 *teaspoonful salt;* ½ *oz. yeast; small teaspoonful caster sugar; about* ½ *pint tepid water.*

Pass the warmed flour and salt into a warm mixing bowl, and make a well in the centre. Cream the yeast and sugar in a warm basin, add the water and pour all into the middle of the flour. Mix thoroughly, adding a little more water as necessary to make a firm elastic dough. Knead for ten minutes. Press the dough into a warm greased tin, to fill it half-full, and set aside in a warm place until the dough reaches the top of the tin. Brush the surface with a little warm milk and bake in a hot oven at Mark 8 or 465 deg. F., for fifteen minutes. Reduce the heat by degrees, and leave the loaf to cook through for forty-five to fifty minutes in all. To test when the loaf is ready, see BREAD, HOUSEHOLD.

BREAD, rolls. 1 *lb. flour;* 1 *teaspoonful salt;* 1 *oz. margarine;* ½ *oz. yeast;* 1 *teaspoonful caster sugar;* 1 *egg; about* ½ *pint milk.*

Sieve the warmed flour and salt into a warm bowl and rub in the margarine. Cream the yeast and sugar, warm the milk until tepid and pour it on to the beaten egg. Pour both on to the yeast, and add all to a well in the centre of the flour. Beat to a smooth dough with the hand, cover with a damp cloth and set aside in a warm place until the dough doubles its bulk, in about an hour. Turn the dough on to a floured board, cut into about sixteen even-sized pieces, and shape into rolls, plaits, twists, etc. Place these on a greased baking tin and set in a warm place to "prove" for about fifteen minutes. Brush with beaten egg or milk, and bake in a hot oven at Mark 7 or 440 deg. F. until the rolls are nicely browned and feel firm, about fifteen to twenty minutes.

BREAD, soda. 1 *lb. flour;* 1 *teaspoonful salt;* 1 *level teaspoonful bicarbonate of soda; about* ½ *pint solid sour milk or buttermilk.*

Sift together the flour, salt and bicarbonate of soda. Mix with the milk to a soft dough. Knead slightly, then flatten with the hands to a round cake. Cut into wedge-shaped pieces, prick each with a floured fork and brush with milk. Put the pieces on a greased baking tin and bake in a hot oven at Mark 7 for about thirty minutes. *Note:* if neither sour milk nor buttermilk is available, add one well-rounded teaspoonful of cream of tartar to the flour when sieving it, and rub an ounce or two of lard or margarine into it before mixing with fresh milk.

BREADCRUMBS, dried. Collect together pieces of stale crust and crumbs of bread, but reject any pieces of crust which are dark in colour. Break up the pieces and put them on a baking tin to dry gradually, without colouring further. They can stand on the rack at the back of the stove, or may be put into the oven, after cooking has been completed. Put the pieces through a rotary grater, or pound, and sieve them. The coarser crumbs may be stored separately as raspings, for coating the outside of a piece of boiled bacon or ham. These crumbs keep for weeks if looked after carefully, and give a more satisfactory surface for egged and crumbed foods than do fresh ones. After use, spread the remaining crumbs to dry thoroughly, sieve and store when cold.

BREAD PUDDING, baked. 4 *oz. stale bread;* 2 *oz. dried fruit;* 2 *oz. sugar;* 2 *oz. chopped suet;* ½ *teaspoonful spice;* 2 *oz. flour;* 1 *level teaspoonful baking powder;* 1 *gill milk;* 1 *egg (optional).*

Break up the bread, pour over the heated milk, cover and soak until soft. Mash with a fork, and add the fruit which has been washed and picked over, sugar, suet, and flour sieved with the spice and baking powder. Beat and add the egg if it is used. Mix all to a soft consistency, pour into a greased piedish and bake in a moderate oven at Mark 4 or 375 deg. F. for fifty minutes to one hour. Custard sauce may be served separately.

BREAD-AND-BUTTER PUDDING. 3–4 *rounds of thinly cut bread and butter (or margarine);* 2 *tablespoonfuls sugar;* 2 *tablespoon-*

nuts, currants or sultanas; 2 *eggs;* 1 *pint milk; vanilla essence.*

Cut the bread and butter into fingers. Place them in a greased piedish in alternate layers with the fruit. Beat the eggs, add the sugar, milk and vanilla essence. Pour these into the piedish, first removing the top layer of bread and butter if a crisp top is liked. Allow to soak for thirty minutes. Sprinkle the top with a little sugar, and grate nutmeg over, if desired. Bake in a moderate oven at Mark 4 or 375 deg. F. until set. Serve hot or cold.

BREAD SAUCE. ½ *pint milk;* 1 *small onion;* 3–4 *cloves;* 1 *blade mace;* 2 *oz. fresh breadcrumbs; salt and pepper;* ½ *oz. margarine.*

Put the milk into a small saucepan, with the onion stuck with the cloves and the mace. Boil up and simmer for fifteen minutes. Strain and return to the saucepan with the breadcrumbs. Stand at the side of the stove and, when required for use, re-heat, adding the seasoning and margarine. Test the consistency of the sauce, which should be that of a soft pulp and, if too thin, boil it for a few minutes, or, if too thick, add a few drops of milk.

BROWN SAUCE. 1 *small onion;* 1 *small carrot;* 1 *oz. dripping;* 1 *oz. flour; salt and pepper;* 1 *pint household stock or vegetable water;* 1–2 *teaspoonfuls Worcester sauce (optional).*

Slice the onion and carrot and fry in the dripping until shrivelled but not browned. Withdraw saucepan from heat and stir in the flour. Cook slowly, stirring from time to time, until the whole (called a brown roux) is a rich brown colour, taking about twenty minutes. Withdraw the saucepan again from the heat, and stir in the liquid. Add pepper and salt and stir until boiling, skim and simmer for thirty minutes. Skim and add Worcester sauce if used, then strain for use. This recipe makes a sauce of flowing consistency, but if needed for coating, reduce the amount of liquid used to half.

BUNS, Bath. ½ *oz. yeast;* 1 *oz. sugar; about* ½ *gill milk or water;* ½ *lb. flour; pinch of salt;* 1 *oz. margarine;* 1 *egg. Additions:* 1½ *oz. sultanas;* 1 *oz. chopped candied peel;* 1 *oz. caster sugar; grated rind* ½ *lemon; crushed loaf sugar for tops.*

Make the dough as for BUNS, CURRANT (see below). Mix together the fruit, caster sugar and lemon rind and knead them very lightly into the mixture. Divide into eight portions and put them on a greased baking tin, leaving the mixture unshaped. Sprinkle with a little of the crushed loaf sugar on the top of each. Set aside in a warm place for about twenty minutes, until about twice their original size. Bake as for currant buns.

BUNS, Chelsea. ½ *oz. yeast;* 1 *oz. sugar; about* ¾ *gill milk or water;* ½ *lb. flour; pinch of salt;* 1 *oz. margarine;* 1 *egg. Additions:* 1 *oz. caster sugar;* 1 *oz. currants;* ½ *teaspoonful mixed spice;* 1 *oz. chopped candied peel; scant oz. oiled margarine.*

Make the dough as for BUNS, CURRANT (see below). Turn it out on to a floured board and roll out into a large square. Brush over with the oiled margarine, and scatter over the sugar, currants, peel and spice mixed together. Roll up firmly, like a Swiss roll, and cut across the roll into slices of about one-and-a-half inch thickness. Place them on a greased baking tin, cut sides to the tin and to the top, and set in a warm place for ten to fifteen minutes. Sprinkle with a little sugar, and bake in a hot oven, set at Mark 8 or 465 deg. F., for five to seven minutes, then reduce heat to moderate, and finish cooking for twelve to fifteen minutes in all.

BUNS, currant. ½ *lb. flour;* ½ *oz. yeast; about* ½ *gill water or milk;* 1 *egg;* 1–1½ *oz. margarine;* 1 *oz. sugar; pinch of salt;* 1–2 *oz. currants. Glaze for buns:* 1 *tablespoonful of granulated sugar;* 2 *tablespoonfuls milk.*

Cream the yeast with one teaspoonful of the sugar, and add the warmed liquid. Warm the flour with the salt and sugar, pass it through a sieve and rub in the margarine roughly. Beat the egg, add the creamed yeast and liquid, and pour all into a well made in the centre of the flour. Knead well and put to rise until the dough has doubled its bulk, about one to one-and-a-half hours. Turn the dough out on to a floured board, and knead in the currants lightly. Divide the mixture into eight portions, and mould each to a ball. Put the buns on a greased baking tin in a warm place for about ten minutes. Bake in a hot oven, set at Mark 8 or 465 deg. F., for seven minutes, then reduce heat to moderate for a further six to seven minutes. Brush over with a glaze made by melting the sugar in the milk and put the buns back into the oven for one minute to dry. *Note:* a baking tin containing a little boiling water and put on the bottom shelf of the oven while the buns are baking will help to keep them soft and thin-skinned.

BUNS, hot cross. ½ *oz. yeast;* 1 *oz. sugar; about* ½ *gill milk or water;* ½ *lb. flour; pinch of salt;* 1–1½ *oz. margarine;* 1 *egg;* 1–2 *oz. currants or sultanas;* 1 *teaspoonful mixed spice.*

Make the dough as for currant buns (see above), passing the spice through a sieve with the salt, sugar and flour. Divide the dough into six pieces and, when shaped to balls, press each with a floured rolling pin and mark deeply with a cross, using the back of a knife. Bake and finish as for currant buns.

CABBAGE, boiled. Remove any coarse and decayed leaves, and cut into quarters. Cut out centre stem, then shred across the quarters fairly finely. Wash the shreds in salted water, and leave them lying in fresh plain cold water for a few minutes to crisp them. Have ready a saucepan containing about one inch of boiling water, salted, and put in the well-drained cabbage. Put on a close-fitting lid, and boil very rapidly for about ten minutes, shaking the pan occasionally. Drain immediately the cabbage is cooked, press it well in a colander and serve as quickly as possible and very hot. Any liquor left over can be used for making gravy. In order to avoid loss of vitamin C, cook the cabbage rapidly in a small quantity of water, and do not overcook.

CABINET PUDDING (plain). 2 *eggs;* ½ *pint milk;* 1 *dessertspoonful sugar;* ½ *teaspoonful vanilla essence;* ¼ *lb. stale bread, cut in dice;* 2 *oz. large raisins, stoned; a strip of candied peel, chopped;* ½ *pint jam sauce* (see JAM SAUCE).

Grease a pudding basin, and decorate it by pressing some of the raisins to the bottom and sides, stoned side downwards. Put the bread into a mixing basin with the remainder of the raisins sliced and the chopped candied peel. Beat the eggs with the sugar, add the essence and milk, pour all over the bread and fruit in the basin, and leave to soak for thirty minutes. Pour all carefully into the prepared basin and twist a greased paper over the top. Steam for about one hour, as for steamed custard (see CUSTARD, STEAMED). Turn out on to a hot dish and pour the jam sauce round.

CAKE MIXTURES, creamed. Cut up the fat if it is firm and cream it in a warm basin until smooth. Add grated lemon or orange rind, if it appears in the list of ingredients. Add sugar and cream again, using an easy, circular, swinging movement, until the mixture is quite soft, white and somewhat resembling whipped cream. Add well-whisked eggs by degrees, beating very thoroughly between each addition. Fold in about a third of the flour which has been sieved with the baking powder if it has been listed. Fold in remaining flour, any fruit or similar addition, and any liquid indicated in the list of ingredients. Have the mixture a little softer than for a rubbed-in mixture, but not soft enough to pour. Cream very thoroughly until the eggs are added, but when the solid ingredients are added simply fold them over lightly, using the side of a metal spoon, and avoiding beating.

CAKE MIXTURES, rubbed-in. Pass the flour through a sieve, with the raising agent used, and a pinch of salt. Cut the fat into the flour, using a round-bladed knife, then rub it in lightly with the finger tips until crumbly and no lumps of fat appear. Add remaining dry ingredients. Mix with a wooden spoon, adding eggs and other liquid, according to the list of ingredients. Make a softish mixture, which would be impossible to handle. For small cakes the mixture should be slightly stiffer. See also method of mixing ROCK CAKES.

CAKE, almond. 4 *oz. margarine and lard together;* 4 *oz. sugar;* 2 *eggs;* 3 *oz. flour and* 2 *oz. ground almonds or* 4½ *oz. flour;* ½ *oz. semolina and* ¾ *teaspoonful almond essence;* 1 *level teaspoonful baking powder; glacé icing* (see ICING, GLACÉ) *or* 1 *tablespoonful jam; chopped browned almonds or grated chocolate.*

Make the mixture by creaming method, adding the ground almonds to the flour after it has been sieved with the baking powder. Spread the mixture in a shallow baking tin, lined with greased paper. Bake in a moderate oven, Mark 5 or 400 deg. F. for twenty-five minutes. When cold, pour the icing on top, or spread with jam, and scatter nuts over. Cut in fingers when cold and set.

CAKE, chocolate. 4 *oz. margarine;* 4 *oz. caster sugar;* 2 *eggs;* 2 *oz. plain chocolate;* 6 *oz. flour;* ¾ *teaspoonful baking powder; few drops vanilla essence;* ½ *gill water.*

Scrape the chocolate with a knife and dissolve it in the water over gentle heat. Boil while stirring, until creamy, and allow to cool. Make by creaming method (see CAKE MIXTURES, CREAMED), beating in the prepared chocolate and vanilla essence, after the eggs have been beaten in. Put the mixture into a six-inch cake tin lined with greased paper. Bake in an oven set at Mark 4 or 375 deg. F. for one-and-a-quarter hours, slackening the heat towards the end of baking.

CAKE, chocolate sandwich. 4 *oz. margarine and lard together;* 4 *oz. caster sugar;* 2 *eggs;* 4 *oz. flour; scant level teaspoonful baking powder;* 2 *teaspoonfuls cocoa; a little milk if required; mock cream or jam.*

Sieve together the flour, baking powder and cocoa. Make by creaming method. Divide mixture into two six-inch greased sandwich tins, and bake in a moderate oven set at Mark 5 or 400 deg. F. for twenty minutes. When cold, sandwich with jam or mock cream (see MOCK CREAM).

CAKE, Christmas. ½ *lb. butter or margarine;* ½ *lb. caster sugar;* 4 *eggs;* ½ *lb. flour; grated rind of a lemon;* ¼ *lb. currants;* ¼ *lb. sultanas;* ¼ *lb. sliced raisins;* ¼ *lb. chopped candied peel;* ¼ *gill brandy, rum or milk; pinch of salt; pinch of baking powder.*

Make by creaming method (see CAKE MIXTURES, CREAMED). Transfer the mixture to a seven-inch cake tin lined with double greased paper, and put the cake on a shelf in the middle of an oven set at Mark 3 or 350 deg. F. Bake for three hours, reducing the heat to Mark 2 at about half-time. *Note:* 2 oz. glacé cherries or shredded almonds may be added to the above fruit if liked. The cake may be made three or four weeks before it is required for use. Put on almond icing if required (see ICING, ALMOND), set aside for three or four days and add white icing.

CAKE, dripping. ½ *lb. flour;* 1 *teaspoonful baking powder;* 1 *level teaspoonful bicarbonate of soda;* 1 *egg or* 1 *level tablespoonful dried egg;* 3 *oz. clarified dripping* (see CLARIFIED DRIPPING); 4 *oz. sugar;* 4 *oz. currants, sultanas or raisins;* 1 *level teaspoonful grated nutmeg;* 1 *level teaspoonful ground ginger or cinnamon;* 1 *tablespoonful brown treacle;* ¼ *pint milk and water.*

Sieve the flour, baking powder, bicarbonate of soda and spices. Add also the dried egg, if it is used, and allow two extra tablespoonfuls of milk and water for mixing. Rub in the dripping, and add the sugar and prepared fruit. Beat the shell egg if used, and add it to the treacle mixed with the milk and water. Make a well in the dry ingredients and pour in the mixed liquids. Mix all thoroughly and spread in a Yorkshire pudding tin (ten inches by eight inches, top measurement) lined with greased paper. Bake in a moderate oven set at Mark 5 or 400 deg. F., and cook for one hour, slackening the heat towards the end of cooking. Cut in squares when cold.

CAKE, eggless. 4 *oz. margarine, lard, or dripping, or some of each;* 4 *oz. sugar;* 3 *oz. currants;* 3 *oz. raisins or sultanas;* 8 *oz. flour;* 1 *level teaspoonful bicarbonate of soda;* 1 *level teaspoonful ground ginger;* 1 *level teaspoonful grated nutmeg;* ½–¾ *gill milk;* 1 *tablespoonful vinegar.*

Cream the fat and sugar thoroughly. Prepare the fruit and mix it with the flour which has been sieved with the bicarbonate of soda and spices. Add the dry ingredients, mixing well, then the milk. Lastly stir in the vinegar quickly, and put the mixture into a greased six-inch cake tin. Put the cake in a moderate oven, set at Mark 5 or 400 deg. F. Cook for one-and-a-quarter hours, gradually slackening the heat after the first half-hour.

CAKE, Genoa. 6 *oz. margarine or butter;* 6 *oz. soft brown sugar; grated rind* ½ *lemon;* 3 *eggs;* ½ *lb. flour; pinch of baking powder;* 6 *oz. currants;* 6 *oz. sultanas;* 2 *oz. candied peel;* 2 *oz. glacé cherries, quartered;* 1½–2 *oz. almonds, split through;* 1–2 *tablespoonfuls milk, water or sherry.*

Make mixture by creaming method (see CAKE MIXTURES, CREAMED). Put it into a seven-inch cake tin, lined with greased paper. Lay the almonds on top, to appear like whole almonds. Bake in a very moderate oven set at Mark 3 or 350 deg. F. for two to two-and-a-quarter hours. *Note:* if it is not possible to obtain soft brown sugar, the cake may be darkened by the addition of a few drops of browning after the eggs have been beaten in.

CAKE, Madeira. 4 *oz. margarine or butter;* 4 *oz. caster sugar; grated rind* ½ *lemon;* 3 *eggs;* 6 *oz. flour; 1 level teaspoonful baking powder; a little milk if necessary, according to size of eggs;* 2 *thin slices of citron peel.*

Make by creaming method (see CAKE MIXTURES, CREAMED). Put mixture into a six-inch cake tin lined with greased paper. Dredge lightly with caster sugar before placing the cake on a tin in the middle of the oven. Set oven at Mark 4 or 375 deg. F. and bake for one to one-and-a-quarter hours. Lay thin slices of citron on top at the end of half an hour.

CAKE, plum. 4 *oz. margarine;* 4 *oz. sugar, preferably caster;* 2 *eggs;* 6 *oz. plain flour;* ¾ *teaspoonful baking powder;* 2 *oz. currants;* 2 *oz. sultanas;* 1 *oz. raisins;* 1 *oz. chopped candied peel; about* ½ *gill milk.*

Make by creaming method (see CAKE MIXTURES, CREAMED). Transfer mixture to a six-inch cake tin lined with greased paper. Put into a moderate oven set at Mark 4 or 375 deg. F. for one-and-a-half hours, slackening the heat towards the end of baking.

CAKE, wedding. 1 *lb. fresh butter;* 1 *lb. brown sugar;* 3 *teaspoonfuls coffee essence; the grated rind of* 1 *lemon;* 8 *eggs* (1 *lb. in shells*); 2 *lb. currants;* 1 *lb. sultanas;* ½ *lb. chopped candied peel;* ½ *lb. sliced raisins;* 2 *oz. ground almonds;* 1¼ *lb. flour;* 2 *heaped teaspoonfuls cocoa;* ½ *teaspoonful powdered cinnamon;* ½ *teaspoonful ground ginger;* ½ *teaspoonful mixed spice;* ½ *gill brandy;* ½ *gill sherry; a large pinch salt.*

Prepare an eleven-inch cake tin as follows: line the tin with two thicknesses of ungreased white kitchen paper. Make as for CAKE, CHRISTMAS.

Bake the cake in a very moderate oven, set at Mark 3 or 350 deg. F., and turning down to Mark 2 at the end of the first hour. Bake for five hours further. Make the cake about three months before it is required, wrapping it in several thicknesses of greaseproof paper, and storing in an airtight tin. *Note:* the cocoa and coffee essence are added to darken the cake and enrich flavour; they do not taste as such when the mixture is baked.

CANAPES. This word applies to the small "platform" on which many hors d'oeuvres and savouries are served. They are cut in small rounds, squares, fingers and fancy shapes, and may consist of:

Toast cut thinly and buttered while hot, to ensure that it will not be hard.

Bread cut into the required shapes and fried.

Cheese pastry cut in shapes and baked.

Small plain biscuits bought at a shop.

Brown bread, cut scant quarter-inch thick and spread with savoury butter.

CANARY PUDDING. 4 *oz. lard and margarine together;* 4 *oz. caster sugar;* 2 *eggs;* 4 *oz. flour;* ¼ *teaspoonful baking powder; flavouring essence; a little milk if necessary, according to size of egg;* 1 *gill jam sauce* (see JAM SAUCE).

Make the mixture by creaming method (see CAKE MIXTURES, CREAMED). Put it into a greased pudding tin or basin, twist a greased paper over and steam for one-and-a-quarter to one-and-a-half hours. Alternatively, divide into six to eight small tins and steam for thirty to forty minutes. Unmould on to a hot dish and pour jam sauce round.

CAPER SAUCE. ½ *pint white sauce* (see WHITE SAUCE, FOUNDATION); 1 *dessertspoonful capers cut in halves;* 1 *dessertspoonful caper vinegar.*

Make the white sauce. Add the prepared capers and the vinegar, and re-heat. *Note:* if the sauce is to be served with boiled mutton, use half meat-boilings and half milk as liquid in making the sauce. The sauce is, however, very good when served with other foods, notably with boiled cod.

CARROTS, Continental method. 1 *lb. carrots;* ½ *oz. margarine or bacon fat;* 1 *gill water or stock;* 1 *heaped teaspoonful chopped parsley.*

Prepare the carrots and slice them finely. Young carrots should be lightly scraped and left whole. Old carrots may be peeled. Heat the fat in a saucepan, put in the carrots, cover and cook for ten minutes, shaking the pan occasionally. Add the water, with some salt and pepper. Cover and simmer from thirty to forty-five minutes, until the slices are tender. Dish up the carrots and keep them hot. Reduce the liquid in the pan a little by boiling with the lid off for a few minutes. Add the chopped parsley and pour over the carrots.

CASSEROLE OF CHICKEN OR RABBIT. 1 *chicken or* 1 *young rabbit;* 1 *tablespoonful* *seasoned flour* (see SEASONED FLOUR); 1½ *oz. fat for frying;* ½ *lb. mushrooms or tomatoes;* 1 *pint stock; fleurons of pastry.*

Cut the chicken or rabbit into joints and dip them in seasoned flour. Fry the joints brown in fat which is heated to smoking point in a frying pan. Remove and drain them, then fry the mushrooms (see MUSHROOMS, FRIED). If tomatoes are used in place of the mushrooms, skin and slice them, but they do not require frying. Pour off the fat, leaving one tablespoonful in the frying pan. Stir in the remaining seasoned flour, cook three to four minutes, then stir in the stock. Stir until boiling, season and boil for three minutes. Pour over the prepared joints and vegetable in a casserole and cover with the lid. Have the oven set at Mark 3 or 350 deg. F., and cook for one-and-a-half hours. Arrange neatly in the casserole, and garnish with fleurons (cut to flower-shape) of pastry.

CASTLE PUDDINGS. 4 *oz. lard and margarine together; grated rind* ½ *lemon;* 4 *oz. caster sugar;* 2 *eggs;* 4 *oz. flour;* ¼ *teaspoonful baking powder; a little milk if necessary;* 1 *gill jam sauce* (see JAM SAUCE).

Make the mixture by creaming method (see CAKE MIXTURES, CREAMED). Put it into six to eight small tins, filling them two-thirds full with the mixture. Bake in a fairly hot oven, set at Mark 5 or 400 deg. F., for twenty minutes. Turn out on to a hot dish and pour the jam sauce round.

CAULIFLOWER, boiled. 1 *cauliflower;* ½ *pint white coating sauce* (see WHITE SAUCE, FOUNDATION).

Remove the coarse outer leaves, and trim off the end of the stump. Make a cross-cut at the end of the stalk. Cleanse well by holding the cauliflower upside down under a running cold-water tap, then soak for fifteen minutes well covered with water. Cook in boiling salted water with the flower downmost, and do not cook too rapidly. Cook for twenty to twenty-five minutes and the cauliflower is ready when the stalk of the flower can be pierced easily with a fork. Drain carefully, put into a hot vegetable dish, and coat completely with well-seasoned white sauce. A little chopped parsley or paprika pepper may be scattered on top.

CAULIFLOWER AU GRATIN. 1 *cauliflower;* 2 *oz. grated cheese;* ½ *pint white coating sauce* (see WHITE SAUCE, FOUNDATION).

Boil the vegetable as in CAULIFLOWER, BOILED. Transfer it carefully to a fireproof dish, and add one ounce of the grated cheese to the white sauce. Coat the cauliflower completely with this, and sprinkle the remainder of the cheese on top. Place under a griller or in a very hot oven until lightly browned. *Note:* Celery, vegetable marrow and Jerusalem artichokes may be treated in the same way.

CHEESE AIGRETTES. 2 *oz. flour;* ½ *oz. margarine;* 1 *gill water;* 1 *egg and* 1 *yolk;* 1½ *oz. finely grated Parmesan or Cheddar cheese; salt and cayenne pepper.*

Warm the flour and pass it through a fine sieve. Bring the margarine and water to boiling point, withdraw from heat and at once shake in the flour and stir very rapidly. Cool slightly, then beat in the yolk, followed by the beaten egg by degrees, beating well. Add the cheese and seasonings and allow the mixture to cool. Have ready a pan containing sufficient fat to float the aigrettes and just beginning to smoke. Drop the mixture into it in small teaspoonfuls. Fry to golden-brown colour, taking about ten minutes. Drain on crumpled paper and serve very hot, sprinkled with a little grated cheese.

CHEESECAKES, chocolate. *Flaky or short pastry, made with* 4–5 *oz. flour, etc.* (see PASTRY, FLAKY and SHORT); 2 *oz. margarine;* 2 *oz. caster sugar;* 1 *large egg;* 1 *oz. flour;* 1 *oz. ground rice or semolina;* 2 *teaspoonfuls cocoa;* ½ *teaspoonful vanilla essence; a few glacé cherries; chocolate icing* (*optional*) (see ICING, CHOCOLATE BUTTER).

Make the pastry, roll it out thinly, cut in rounds and line twelve to fourteen patty tins with it. If liked, a little jam may be put at the bottom of each. Cream the margarine, add sugar and cream again, then beat in the egg by degrees. Mix together the flour, ground rice or semolina and cocoa, and fold in lightly, with the vanilla essence and a very little milk or water if it should be needed. Fill the prepared patty tins three parts full with the mixture and bake in a hot oven set at Mark 6 or 425 deg. F. for twenty minutes. Put half of a glacé cherry on top of each, or, when cold the filled part of each may be coated with icing before putting on the cherry halves.

CHEESECAKES, sponge. *Short pastry, made with* 4–5 *oz. flour, etc.* (see PASTRY, SHORT); 1 *tablespoonful hot milk;* 2 *oz. crumbled stale sponge cake; grated rind* ½ *lemon or grated rind* 1 *orange or* ¼ *teaspoonful mixed spice;* 1 *tablespoonful currants;* 2 *oz. margarine;* 2 *oz. caster sugar;* 1 *egg.*

Make the pastry, roll it out very thinly, cut in rounds and line twelve to fourteen patty tins with it. Pour the hot milk on to the sponge cake, add grated rind or spice and leave to soak until soft. Cream the margarine, add the sugar and cream again. Beat in the whisked egg by degrees, and lastly mix in the soaked sponge cake by spoonfuls until quite smooth. Fill the prepared tins three parts full with the mixture. Bake until set and brown in a hot oven set at Mark 6 or 425 deg. F., for twenty minutes. Serve hot or cold, sprinkled with sugar. *Note:* if the grated rind of an orange is chosen for flavouring, the currants may be omitted if preferred.

CHEESECAKES, Welsh. *Short pastry made with* 3–4 *oz. flour, etc.* (see PASTRY, SHORT); 1 *tablespoonful jam; creamed mixture;* 1 *egg;* 2 *oz. margarine;* 2 *oz. caster sugar;* 2 *oz. flour; pinch of baking powder; a little milk if necessary, according to size of egg; few drops vanilla essence.*

Make the pastry, roll it out thinly and line about a dozen patty tins with it. Put a little jam in the bottom of each. Make a creamed mixture (see CAKE MIXTURES, CREAMED), and put a teaspoonful on top of the jam in each patty tin. Bake for about twenty minutes in an oven set at Mark 6 or 425 deg. F. Dish and sprinkle with sugar.

CHEESE-AND-POTATO PIE. *½ lb. freshly boiled potatoes; ½ gill hot milk; salt and pepper; ½ teaspoonful mixed mustard; 1 teaspoonful finely chopped onion; 1 teaspoonful chopped parsley; 1 egg; 1 teaspoonful baking powder; 2 oz. grated cheese.*

Mash the potatoes very thoroughly while still hot, press them to one side of the pan and heat the milk in the space left clear at the bottom. Beat the milk into the potatoes, using a fork. Transfer the mixture to a warm mixing basin, and whisk in the seasonings and flavourings, then the beaten egg. Shake the baking powder over, and the cheese, and fold all together lightly. Put mixture at once into a greased piedish and bake in a hot oven set at Mark 6 or 425 deg. F. until puffed up and browned. Serve immediately. Served with a green vegetable or baked tomatoes the pie makes an excellent lunch or supper dish.

CHEESE PUDDING. *2 oz. fresh breadcrumbs; ½ pint milk; 1½ oz. grated cheese; scant 1 oz. margarine; 1 egg; salt and pepper.*

Heat the milk and add the breadcrumbs, margarine and seasoning. Leave to soak for thirty minutes. Add the cheese and the well-whisked egg. Pour into a greased piedish and bake in a moderate oven set at Mark 5 or 400 deg. F. Serve at once very hot. *Note:* if preferred, the yolk and white of egg may be separated; the yolk beaten into the mixture and the white stiffly whisked and folded in.

CHEESE SAUCE. *½ pint white sauce* (see WHITE SAUCE, FOUNDATION); *1½–2 oz. dry grated cheese.*

Make the white sauce and, when cooked, stir in the cheese. Re-heat the sauce to melt the cheese, but do not reboil it. This sauce may be used to coat cooked food such as fish or vegetables. A little more cheese may be sprinkled over, and some dried crumbs, and the surface browned under a hot griller. In this case the food must be dished on a fireproof dish or piedish.

CHEESE SOUFFLÉS. *½ oz. margarine; 1 teaspoonful flour; ½ gill milk; yolks and whites of 2 eggs; 1½ oz. grated cheese (Parmesan or Cheddar); salt; a few grains of cayenne.*

For cooking the soufflé, grease a half-pint piedish, a five-inch fireproof china soufflé case, or five or six smallest size paper soufflé cases. If a soufflé case is chosen, tie a band of greased paper round it. Make a sauce (see WHITE SAUCE, FOUNDATION) with the margarine, flour and milk. Cool slightly and beat in the yolks, cheese and seasoning. Whisk the whites of eggs stiffly and fold lightly into the mixture. Pour mixture into the container chosen to fill it three-quarters full, and bake in a moderate oven set at Mark 5 or 400 deg. F. until firm to the touch, well risen and golden brown; about twelve to fifteen minutes for small soufflés, or twenty to twenty-five minutes for the larger sizes. Serve at once, sprinkled with grated cheese.

CHEESE STRAWS. *1 oz. margarine; 1 oz. flour; 1–1½ oz. finely grated cheese; cayenne and salt; a little yolk of egg and water.*

Chop the margarine into the flour which has been sieved on to a board with the seasoning. Add the cheese and again chop all together very finely. Remove the ingredients to a small bowl and mix to a stiff dough with egg-yolk and water. Roll out thinly and cut in straws and rings. Place on a greased tin and bake for a few minutes only, until golden-coloured, in a hot oven set at Mark 6 or 425 deg. F. Place the straws through the rings and serve hot or cold. *Note:* plainer cheese straws may be made by using cheese pastry in the same way (see PASTRY, CHEESE).

CHEESE TARTLETS. *Short pastry, made with 3 oz. flour, etc.* (see PASTRY, SHORT); *1 egg; 3 oz. finely-grated cheese; 1 gill white sauce (coating)* (see WHITE SAUCE, FOUNDATION)*; salt and cayenne pepper.*

Line about a dozen small patty tins with the short pastry, rolled out very thinly. Add the well-whisked egg to the sauce, then the cheese and seasonings. Half fill the prepared tins with this mixture, and bake in a hot oven set at Mark 6 or 425 deg. F., for fifteen to twenty minutes, until golden brown, puffed and set. Sprinkle with grated cheese and serve hot at once. *Note:* if preferred, the yolk of egg may be beaten into the cheese mixture, and the white stiffly whisked and added last.

CHEESE, toasted. *A slice of bread; thin slices new Cheddar cheese; mixed mustard.*

Toast the bread on one side only. Cover the untoasted side with the slices of cheese. Grill lightly until the cheese is softened and faintly brown. Avoid over-cooking the cheese, which will make it tough, or burning it in any part, which will make it most indigestible. Serve at once, flecked with mustard.

CHEESE TURNOVERS. *Short or flaky pastry, made with 4 oz. flour, etc.* (see PASTRY, SHORT and FLAKY); *1 oz. margarine; 2 oz. grated cheese; 1 egg or 1 tablespoonful mashed potato; salt and pepper; a little beaten egg or milk.*

Melt the margarine in a saucepan, add the grated cheese, beaten egg or mashed potato and seasoning. Heat gently until thickened, then set aside to cool. Roll out the pastry thinly, and cut it in rounds or squares. Turn the pieces over so that the smoother side of the pastry will be on the outside, and put a teaspoonful of the cheese mixture on each. Damp the edges and fold over in half, pressing well. Place on a greased baking tin, brush with beaten egg or milk, and bake in a hot oven set at Mark 7 or 440 deg. F. for fifteen minutes. These turnovers are excellent to include in a packed lunch.

CHESTNUTS, baked. *1½ lb. sweet chestnuts; 1½ oz. margarine or butter.*

Prepare the chestnuts by making a small cut in each end of each nut. Drop the nuts into boiling water for ten minutes. Strain and remove outer and inner skins. Place them in a baking tin and pour the melted margarine over them; stir well. Cook in an oven set at Mark 6 or 425 deg. F. for twenty minutes. Drain and use as a garnish for savoury dishes, sprinkled with salt and pepper and chopped parsley.

CHESTNUT STUFFING. ½ *lb. sweet chestnuts;* ¼ *lb. breadcrumbs; salt and pepper;* 2 *tablespoonfuls bacon fat;* 1 *level teaspoonful grated lemon rind;* 1 *egg and a little milk.*

Prepare the chestnuts as described above. Stew the chestnuts in water or stock until tender, drain and pass through a wire sieve or mincing machine. Add all other ingredients, using the beaten egg and a little milk to hold all together. *Note:* the stuffing may be put into the crop of a turkey to be roasted, and veal stuffing in the body of the bird, fried or grilled sausages being cooked separately, or sausage meat can take the place of either of the stuffings.

CHOCOLATE SAUCE, mock. 2 *heaped teaspoonfuls cocoa;* 2 *heaped teaspoonfuls sugar;* 1 *gill boiling water;* 1 *gill milk;* 1 *heaped teaspoonful cornflour.*

Put the cocoa and sugar in a small basin and mix smoothly with the boiling water. Mix cornflour smoothly with a little of the milk. Put both these mixtures into a small saucepan, with the remaining milk and the sugar. Stir until boiling and stir and simmer for five minutes.

CHRISTMAS PUDDING (plain). 6 *oz. breadcrumbs;* 6 *oz. flour;* 6 *oz. suet or lard;* 4 *oz. raisins;* 4 *oz. sultanas;* 4 *oz. currants;* 2 *oz. chopped candied peel;* 4 *oz. sugar;* 1 *level teaspoonful mixed spice;* ½ *level teaspoonful grated nutmeg;* 2 *teaspoonfuls baking powder;* 2–3 *eggs; about* 1 *gill milk or ale to mix.*

Pass the flour through a sieve with a pinch of salt, the spices and baking powder. Add the suet finely chopped, or lard may be rubbed into the flour before other ingredients are added. Mix in the prepared dried fruit and sugar. Beat the eggs and add the milk or ale. Mix all well together and put into a thickly-greased basin. Lay a round of greased paper on top and tie on a pudding cloth. Steam the pudding steadily for five to six hours. If preferred it may be boiled, in which case it is necessary that the pudding basin is filled quite full. When cooked cover with fresh paper and a dry cloth and steam for a further two hours when required for use, and do not make the pudding more than a fortnight beforehand. Turn out carefully on to a hot dish, sprinkle sugar on top and serve with custard or sweet white sauce. *Note:* one tablespoonful brown treacle may be added to the mixture if liked.

CHRISTMAS PUDDING (richer). 4 *oz. breadcrumbs;* 4 *oz. flour;* 5 *oz. chopped suet;* 5 *oz. raisins;* 5 *oz. currants;* 5 *oz. sultanas;* 4 *oz. chopped candied peel; grated rind* 1 *orange;* 6 *oz. brown sugar;* 2 *oz. shredded blanched almonds or ground almonds;* 1 *level teaspoonful mixed spice;* ½ *level teaspoonful grated nutmeg;* 3–4 *eggs;* ½ *gill ale or milk;* 1 *tablespoonful rum or brandy.*

Method as for plain Christmas pudding. If stored in a dry cool place this pudding will keep for two to three months. A richer sauce, such as hard sauce or brandy sauce (see HARD SAUCE and BRANDY SAUCE), may be served with the pudding.

CHUTNEY. ¾ *lb. green cooking apples;* ¾ *lb. raisins or sultanas;* ½ *lb. shallots or onions;* ¾ *lb. tomatoes;* ½ *lb. Demerara sugar;* ¾ *teaspoonful cayenne pepper;* 1 *teaspoonful salt;* 6 *cloves;* 1 *teaspoonful ground ginger;* 1 *pint vinegar.*

Peel and slice the apples and shallots, and stone the raisins. Pass all these through the mincer, or chop them finely. Sultanas may be left whole. Skin and slice the tomatoes. Put all ingredients except the vinegar into a saucepan and cook for half an hour, stirring frequently. Add the vinegar, boil up and simmer gently until a soft brown pulp is obtained, about two-and-a-half hours. While cooking, keep the pan covered with a lid, but the lid may be removed for the last thirty minutes if the chutney appears to be rather thin. Pour into warm, dry jars and cover down when cold. Use bladder or corks to prevent evaporation, or glass-lidded preserving jars are excellent for the purpose.

CLARIFIED DRIPPING. Pour off the dripping from the meat tin into a basin, and pour into it about an equal quantity of boiling water. Stir well and set aside in a cool place. Next day remove the cake of fat, and scrape the bottom free from moisture. Heat the dripping until just beginning to smoke, then pour it into a clean dry basin. Use for frying, sauces or, with some lard or margarine, for plain pastry and cakes.

CLARIFIED FAT. Cut out any flesh, glands or discoloured parts from the fat and remove skin. Cut the fat into pieces of about the size of a walnut. Put it in a saucepan with just sufficient water to cover and add one level tablespoonful of salt to each two pounds of fat. Bring slowly to boiling point, skim and simmer until the water has evaporated, leaving a clear yellow liquid. Allow the fat to cool slightly, then strain into an enamelled bowl. Clarified fat may be chopped when set and used in place of suet in a boiled or steamed pudding, or, if it should be rather soft, it may be rubbed in and so used. Other uses as for clarified dripping. *Note:* if it is required to clarify a small quantity only of fat, cut the fat in pieces, put them in a Yorkshire pudding tin, and then in the bottom of the oven when some other cooking is in progress. When the fat has melted, leaving only shrivelled pieces of skin, strain off the liquid fat and proceed as for clarified dripping (see above).

COATING WITH EGG AND BREADCRUMBS. 1 *egg or egg substitute; dried crumbs.*

Beat up the egg on a plate (a soup plate is convenient) or prepare the substitute. Put a sufficiency of crumbs on a half-sheet of kitchen paper in readiness. If fish is being coated, it must be thoroughly dried and lightly floured.

Put each piece of food to be coated into the egg in turn and brush over with a pastry brush. Lift out the piece on a knife, draining off superfluous egg. Put the piece straight on to the crumbs, and lift both sides of the paper to shake the crumbs over. Pass the coated piece of food from hand to hand lightly to remove loose crumbs, then press in the crumb coating firmly.

COCOA MOULD. 1½ *oz. cornflour;* ½ *oz. cocoa;* 1 *pint milk;* 1½ *oz. sugar;* ½ *teaspoonful vanilla essence; custard sauce* (see CUSTARD SAUCE).

Put the cornflour and cocoa together in a basin and mix them smoothly with some of the milk. Heat the remainder of the milk with the sugar and pour it on to the mixed cornflour and cocoa. Return all to the rinsed saucepan and stir until boiling; continue boiling and stirring for ten minutes. Add vanilla essence, and mould and allow to set.

COD STEAKS, baked stuffed. 2 *cod steaks of about* ½ *lb. each;* 1 *tablespoonful veal stuffing* (see STUFFING, VEAL); 1 *tablespoonful seasoned flour* (see SEASONED FLOUR); 1 *egg or egg substitute for coating*; *dried crumbs* (see page 298); 2–3 *oz. dripping;* ½ *pint anchovy or parsley sauce* (see ANCHOVY SAUCE and PARSLEY SAUCE); *lemon and parsley to garnish.*

Wash the fish and dry it thoroughly. Remove centre bone and fill the cavity with stuffing mixed firmly; secure with string and a skewer. Dip each steak in seasoned flour, then in beaten egg or egg substitute, and roll in dried crumbs. Have the dripping smoking hot in a baking tin, put in the steaks and baste. Bake in a moderate oven at Mark 5 or 400 deg. F. for twenty-five to thirty minutes. Baste occasionally. Drain on crumpled paper, remove string and skewer, and serve on a hot dish. Pour the sauce round and garnish with lemon and parsley.

COFFEE. *For each* ½ *pint freshly boiled water allow* 1 *large tablespoonful freshly roasted and ground coffee.*

Various types of percolator can be procured for making coffee, and it is necessary to follow their makers' directions exactly. Excellent coffee can be made, however, in an earthenware jug as follows: put the coffee in a warm, dry earthenware jug, with a tiny pinch of salt, and stand it in a warm place. Pour on the fast-boiling water and stir well with a spoon. Cover closely and leave to stand in a warm place for ten minutes. Pour off some coffee into a cup and splash it back into the jug again, and repeat this two or three times. Cover again, leave for a minute or two to settle, then strain into a well-heated coffee pot for table. Serve with milk brought just to boiling point.

CORNISH PASTIES. *Short pastry made with* 8 *oz. flour, etc.* (see PASTRY, SHORT); ¼ *lb. raw rump or buttock steak;* 1 *medium-sized potato;* ½ *small onion; salt and pepper; a little water; egg or milk to brush over.*

Cut the meat in very small dice, the potato rather larger, and chop the onion. Mix these on a plate with salt and pepper and sprinkle with water to moisten. Divide into four portions. Make the pastry, cut it into four pieces, and roll each to a round. Damp the edges, put a mound of filling on each, join the edges over the top and crimp them. Place on a greased baking tin and brush over. Put into a hot oven until the pastry is set and beginning to brown, set at Mark 6 or 425 deg. F. Slacken the heat and cook for forty-five minutes in all. Serve hot or cold. Cornish pasties are very useful for a packed lunch.

CRAB, dressed. 1 *cooked crab of medium size;* 1–2 *tablespoonfuls mayonnaise or thick salad dressing; salt and pepper;* 1 *tablespoonful breadcrumbs;* 1 *teaspoonful chopped parsley; paprika pepper; shredded lettuce leaves.*

Twist off the large claws and smaller feelers of the crab (Fig. 19). Separate the upper from the lower shell by pulling and keep the latter intact for dishing. Remove and discard the spongy gills known as "dead men's fingers"; the stomach, a little sac near the head; the intestine, which is of greenish matter. Crack the body-shell and pick out all the meat with a skewer. Crack the claws and remove the meat. Chop all this firm flesh and mix with the mayonnaise and seasoning. Mix the dark meat from the body with the breadcrumbs, and season it. Scrub the shell and chip to the natural line by tapping gently with a skewer and small hammer. Refill with the mixture, put dark meat in a straight band down the centre and the white meat at each side. Sprinkle paprika pepper on the white meat and chopped parsley down the centre. Serve on shredded lettuce, garnished with the small feelers.

CRAB, mock. 1 *oz. margarine;* 3 *oz. grated cheese;* 2 *teaspoonfuls vinegar;* 1 *tablespoonful fresh breadcrumbs; salt and pepper;* 1–2 *teaspoonfuls anchovy essence.*

Cream the margarine and mix in the remaining ingredients. Use as a sandwich filling, or roll into balls with butter-hands and serve on salad. Mock crab is also very successful when piled on small croûtons of cheese pastry (see PASTRY, CHEESE) decorated with chopped parsley or paprika pepper, and served as a cold savoury.

CROÛTONS, to garnish. *Toasted.* Make a slice of toast, cut it into squares of one to one-and-a-quarter inches, then cut diagonally to make triangles; or cut into crescents, using a round cutter. To do this, take out a small piece with the cutter, then move it upwards to cover the toast about a third of its surface, cut through, and a well-shaped crescent will result. Or a crescent-shaped cutter may be obtained.

Fried. Cut shapes as above from a slice of bread. Fry golden brown in deep or shallow fat. Drain well.

CROÛTONS, to serve with soup. *Toasted.* Make a slice of toast a quarter of an inch thick, and cut it into strips a quarter-inch wide. Turn the strips round and cut them across, making the cuts a quarter-inch apart, and dice will result.

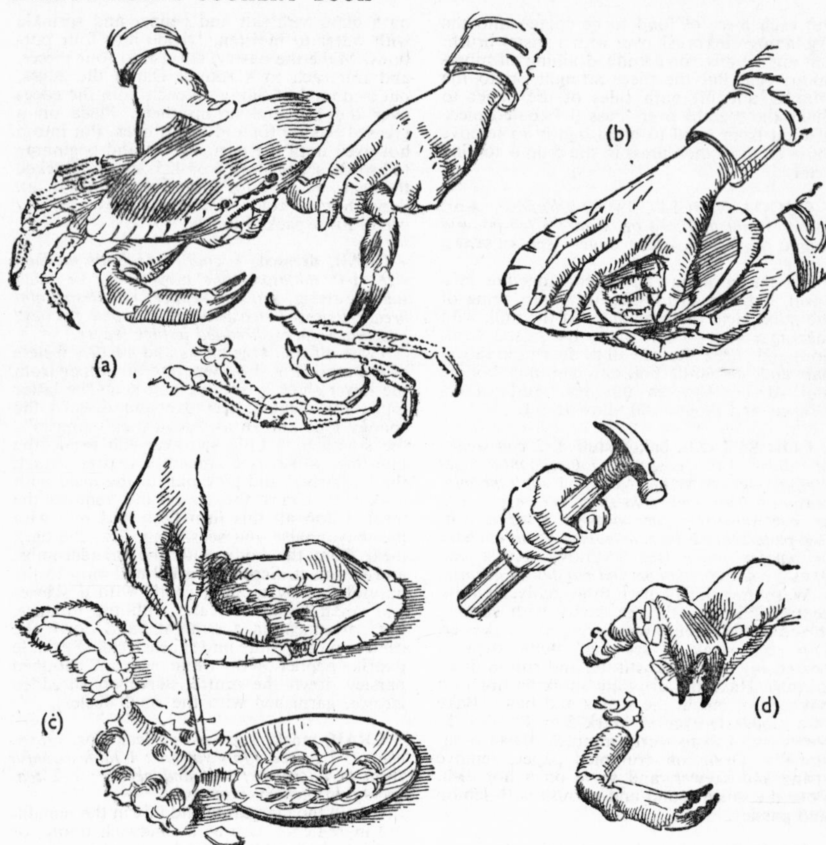

Fig. 19. Dressing a crab: (a) *twist off large claws and smaller feelers;* (b) *separate upper and lower shells and remove gills, stomach and intestines;* (c) *crack body shell and pick out meat with a skewer;* (d) *crack claws and remove meat. (See page 305.)*

Fried. Cut dice as foregoing from a slice of bread cut a quarter-inch thick. Fry in deep or shallow fat, and drain well.

CURRIED COLD MEAT. ½ *pint curry sauce* (see CURRY SAUCE); 1 *lb. cold meat; 4 oz. Patna rice; slices of lemon and gherkin; chutney.*

Prepare the curry sauce and simmer gently for thirty minutes. Cut the meat into dice and add to the sauce, after it has cooled somewhat, or the meat may be toughened. Add the meat and re-heat it without actually cooking it again in a very slow oven for one hour. This may be done on top of the stove, or it may be done in a casserole in the oven. Serve in the casserole, handing boiled rice (see RICE, BOILED) and chutney separately.

CURRIED EGGS. 4 *hard-boiled eggs;* 2–3 *oz. Patna rice;* ½ *pint curry sauce* (see CURRY SAUCE); *slices of lemon and gherkin.*

Make the curry sauce. Cut the eggs in quarters. Place in the sauce and simmer gently for fifteen minutes. Prepare the rice (see RICE, BOILED) and arrange it in a border round a hot dish. Pour the curry into it and garnish with lemon and gherkin.

CURRIED FISH. *About* ¾ *lb. cooked fish;* ½ *pint curry sauce* (see CURRY SAUCE); 3 *oz. Patna rice; slices of lemon and gherkin.*

Make the sauce. Remove skin and bones from the fish, and flake into large pieces. Mix with the sauce and simmer gently for twenty minutes. Alternatively, place in a casserole and re-heat in a moderate oven set at Mark 4 or 375 deg. F. for twenty-five to thirty minutes. Boil the rice (see RICE, BOILED) and arrange it in a border round a hot dish. Pour the curry into it and garnish with lemon and gherkin.

CURRIED FRESH MEAT. 1 *lb. lean veal, pork or mutton;* ½ *pint curry sauce* (see CURRY

SAUCE); 4 *oz. Patna rice; slices of lemon; strips of gherkin.*

Cut the meat into pieces of about one-inch cube. Roll them in the curry powder before making the sauce. Fry the meat lightly in a little fat in a frying pan, remove and drain the meat from fat. Prepare the curry sauce, add the meat, and simmer gently for two hours. Cook the rice (see RICE, BOILED) and arrange it in a border on a hot dish. Place the curry carefully in the middle and garnish with slices of lemon and pieces or slices of gherkin.

CURRIED VEGETABLES. ¾ *lb. cold cooked vegetables;* ½ *pint curry sauce* (see below); *fried or toasted croûtons of bread* (see CROÛTONS); 3 *oz. Patna rice;* 1 *oz. sultanas or a few stewed prunes.*

Cut the vegetables into neat pieces, and any vegetables other than greens can be used in this way. Cooked potatoes, cut into quarter-inch slices, make a good curry. Heat the vegetables in the curry sauce, either by simmering gently on the top of the stove for twenty minutes or by placing the curry in a casserole, in the bottom of an oven in use for other cooking. To steep the vegetables in the curry sauce before re-heating will improve flavour. Boil the rice (see RICE, BOILED) and arrange it in a border with the curry in the middle, or, if cooked in a casserole, serve the curry in it and the rice in a separate dish. Garnish with small heaps of scalded sultanas, or strips of stewed prunes.

CURRY SAUCE. ¾ *pint light-coloured stock or vegetable water;* 1 *tablespoonful fresh or desiccated coconut;* 1 *small apple;* 1 *small onion;* 1 *oz. margarine;* 5 *teaspoonfuls curry powder;* ¾ *oz. flour or ground rice;* 1 *teaspoonful chutney; salt; lemon juice.*

Infuse the coconut in the liquid for ten minutes (see INFUSION). Peel and chop the apple and onion separately. Melt the margarine and fry the onion in it until soft but not coloured. Add the curry powder and flour or ground rice mixed together and cook for a few minutes. Add the stock, the remaining ingredients, and stir until boiling. Put on the lid and simmer gently for thirty minutes. Strain and use as required.

CUSTARD, baked. 2 *eggs;* 1 *oz. sugar;* 1 *pint milk;* ½ *teaspoonful vanilla essence; grated nutmeg; few tiny shavings margarine* (*optional*).

Beat the eggs with the sugar and add the essence and milk. Pour into a greased piedish, grate nutmeg on top and float a few shavings of margarine on the surface. Bake in a slow oven set at Mark 2 or 325 deg. F. until on touching the centre lightly with a finger the custard is found to be set. This will take about an hour. As an extra precaution against curdling, stand piedish in a little water.

CUSTARD, boiled. *Yolks of* 2 *eggs;* ½ *oz. sugar;* ½ *pint milk; few drops vanilla essence; for a rich custard, add* 1–2 *extra egg yolks.*

Beat the eggs (and extra yolks if used), add the sugar and a little of the milk; beat again. Heat remaining milk until steaming, and whisk it on to the egg mixture. Return all to a jug or jar stood in a saucepan of boiling water, and stir continually until the custard thickens and coats the back of the spoon. Turn it at once into a cold basin, add the vanilla essence and stir frequently while cooling. Avoid boiling or even overheating, which will curdle the eggs, and if there should be any sign of curdling, stand the jug or jar at once in a bowl of cold water and whisk.

CUSTARD, caramel. 3 *eggs, or* 2 *whites and* 3 *yolks;* 1 *oz. sugar;* ½ *pint milk;* ½ *teaspoonful vanilla essence. For the caramel:* 3 *oz. granulated or loaf sugar;* ¾ *gill water.*

Dissolve the sugar completely in the water, in a small saucepan. Boil up and boil rapidly without stirring, until the caramel becomes a deep golden-brown colour. Pour at once into a heated small cake tin, or about five dariole moulds, and turn the tin or tins round until the bottom and sides are coated. Pour in the custard, prepared as for CUSTARD, STEAMED. Cook as for steamed custard, unmould carefully and serve hot or cold.

CUSTARD, steamed. 1 *egg and* 1 *extra yolk;* 1 *dessertspoonful sugar;* ¼ *pint milk; few drops vanilla essence.*

Beat the egg and yolk with the sugar, add the essence and milk. Pour into a greased mould or basin and twist a greased paper over. Stand the mould on a folded dishcloth or a wire grid, in a saucepan containing sufficient water to come halfway up the mould. Cook by simmering only and arrange that the mould does not stand directly over the heat. Test by piercing the centre of the custard with a fine skewer, which will be clean when withdrawn if the custard is set. Time for cooking averages about thirty-five minutes, or if divided into small dariole tins about fifteen to twenty minutes. Allow the custard to stand for a minute or two before turning out.

CUSTARD SAUCE. ½ *oz. cornflour;* ½ *pint milk;* 1 *egg* (*or* 2 *yolks*); ½ *oz. sugar;* ½ *teaspoonful vanilla essence or other flavouring.*

Mix the cornflour smoothly with some of the milk and heat the remainder of the milk. Pour the heated milk on to the mixed cornflour. Return all to the rinsed saucepan, add the sugar, stir and boil for eight minutes. Cool slightly, add beaten egg or yolks and cook carefully for a few minutes until the egg thickens. Serve hot or cold and, if the latter, stir often while cooling. Add the essence last.

CUSTARD TART. *Short pastry made with* 4–5 *oz. flour, etc.* (see PASTRY, SHORT); *custard filling:* 2 *eggs;* 2 *teaspoonfuls sugar;* ½ *pint milk;* ½ *teaspoonful vanilla essence; grated nutmeg; few tiny shavings margarine.*

Make the pastry and line a sandwich tin or flan ring with it. Bake for fifteen minutes before adding the custard. Prepare the custard as for baked custard (see CUSTARD, BAKED) and pour it into the pastry case. Reduce heat of oven to Mark 2 or 325 deg. F. and continue cooking until it has set, about forty-five minutes. A custard tart is usually served cold.

DOUGH CAKE. 1 *lb. flour made into bread dough* (see BREAD, HOUSEHOLD); 2–3 *oz. currants;* 2–3 *oz. sultanas;* 1 *oz. chopped candied peel; a little grated nutmeg and mixed spice;* 2 *oz. caster sugar;* 1 *egg;* 1 *oz. margarine.*

Have the dough in a warm basin, add the warmed fruit mixed with the spice, the sugar, beaten egg, and margarine softened but not oiled. Knead all thoroughly with the hand for ten minutes. See that the resulting dough is soft and pliable, if stiff add a little warm milk, or tighten by adding a little more flour. Put the dough in a warmed, greased, seven-inch cake tin, or a bread tin. Set aside in a warm place for twenty to thirty minutes, until risen and puffy. Bake in a hot oven set at Mark 6 or 425 deg. F. for twenty-five minutes, then slacken to Mark 3, cooking for forty minutes in all. Dissolve half a tablespoonful sugar in a small tablespoonful milk, and brush over the top of the cake with this. Return it to the oven for a minute or two to dry.

DOUGHNUTS. ½ *lb. flour;* 2 *oz. margarine;* 1 *oz. caster sugar;* ½ *oz. yeast;* ½ *gill milk;* 1 *egg; jam; lard or deep fat for frying.*

Warm the flour and sieve it, rub in the margarine and add the sugar except for one teaspoonful, which cream with the yeast. Warm the milk, pour it on to the beaten egg and pour both on to the creamed yeast. Mix all well and beat or knead lightly. Cover with a damp cloth and put to rise in a warm place. When the dough has increased to twice its size, cut it in twelve pieces and form into balls. Put them aside in a warm place for a few minutes. Flatten each ball with the floured fingers, put half a teaspoonful of jam in the middle, damp the edges and close up into a ball again. Put in a warm place again for ten minutes. Fry in deep fat or lard which is just beginning to smoke. Turn the doughnuts from time to time and cook for about eight minutes in all. Drain on crumpled paper, then roll in caster sugar. Put the doughnuts on a wire tray to soften.

DUCK, roast. 1 *duck; sage and onion stuffing* (see STUFFING, SAGE AND ONION); *apple sauce* (see APPLE SAUCE); ½ *pint thickened gravy* (see GRAVY, THICKENED).

Singe the duck and cut off the head. Slit the skin at the back of the neck to the backbone. Loosen the skin all round, cut off the neck close to the body, and remove the crop and windpipe. Cut out the vent and remove everything inside the bird. Wipe inside and outside with a wet cloth, scald and scrape the feet. Cut off the toes and the ends of the wings. Place the stuffing in the lower part of the bird. Truss the duck with the feet placed across the back and the ends of the wings caught in under the legs (Fig. 20). Bake in a hot oven, set at Mark 6 or 425 deg. F., for an average of one-and-a-half hours, according to size, slackening the heat towards the end of cooking. Serve with thickened gravy and apple sauce.

DUMPLINGS. ¼ *lb. flour;* 1½ *oz. chopped suet;* 1 *level teaspoonful baking powder; large pinch salt; water to mix to a stiff dough.*

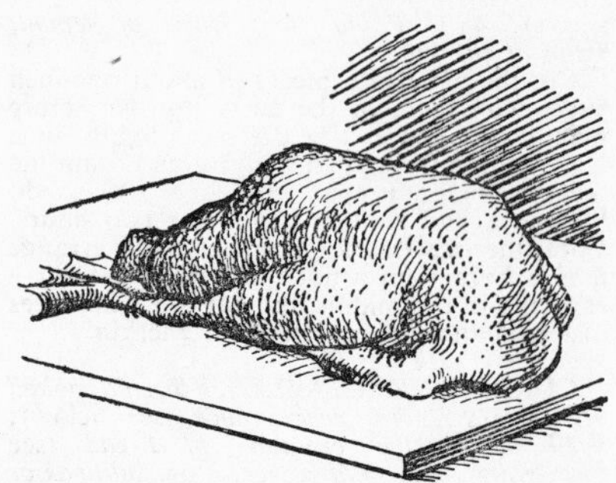

Fig. 20. *Duck during preparation for roasting.*

Sieve the flour, baking powder and salt. Add the chopped suet and mix to a firm dough with cold water. Cut into eight pieces and roll each to a smooth ball with floured fingers. *Either* place the dumplings on top of a stew one hour before it is due to finish cooking, *or* have ready a saucepan of fast-boiling water and drop in the dumplings one at a time. Boil fairly fast for fifteen minutes without lifting the lid. *Note:* if it is desired to cook dumplings in a saucepan in which meat is being boiled, remove the meat for a few minutes so that the dumplings may be put into fast-boiling water for a time, and thus will not toughen the meat with fast cooking. Return the meat to the saucepan when the dumplings are set.

DURHAM CUTLETS. 1 *oz. dripping or margarine;* 1 *oz. flour;* ¼ *pint stock;* ½ *lb. cooked minced meat; salt and pepper;* 2 *teaspoonfuls chopped parsley;* 1 *tablespoonful chopped cooked onion, or* 2 *teaspoonfuls Worcester sauce; egg and coating crumbs* (see COATING); *a few pieces of macaroni.*

Make a sauce with the dripping, flour and stock (see STOCK, HOUSEHOLD) and add it to the cooked minced meat. Add salt, pepper, parsley, and flavouring. Turn the mixture on to a plate, smooth it to a round, and leave to cool. Mark into six or eight pieces, and form into cutlet shapes, using a little flour to prevent sticking. Coat with egg and breadcrumbs and put one inch macaroni in the narrow end of each cutlet to represent the bone. Fry in smoking hot deep fat until brown, and drain on crumpled paper. Arrange the cutlets leaning one against the other on a hot dish, and, if liked, a cutlet frill may be put on each of the upstanding bones. Serve tomato or brown sauce separately.

ÉCLAIRS. *Choux pastry* (see PASTRY, CHOUX); ¾–1 *gill whipped cream or evaporated milk, or mock cream* (see MOCK CREAM); *chocolate or coffee icing* (see ICING, CHOCOLATE and COFFEE).

Make the choux pastry. Put it into a forcing bag fitted with a half-inch plain forcing pipe, and force it in finger lengths of about three inches on to a greased baking tin. Bake in a hot oven set at Mark 6 or 425 deg. F. for thirty-five minutes, reducing the heat after about fifteen minutes. Cook them until quite crisp and a light brown colour. At once slit open down the sides and set on a wire tray to cool. When cold, fill with the prepared cream and ice the tops with a line of thick icing.

EGG CUTLETS. 3 *hard-boiled eggs; salt and pepper;* ¼ *teaspoonful curry powder (optional);* 1 *oz. margarine;* 1 *oz. flour;* 1 *gill milk; egg or substitute and dried crumbs; parsley stalks and sprigs.*

Chop the eggs, and make a thick white sauce (see WHITE SAUCE, FOUNDATION) with the margarine, flour and milk. Add the chopped eggs, salt, pepper and curry powder if used. A raw yolk of egg may be added at this stage if it is available. Stir over slight heat until all is well bound together. Spread in a round on a plate until cold. Mark into six portions and shape each to a cutlet, on a floured board and using two knives. Coat with egg and breadcrumbs, and fry, preferably in deep fat, until golden-coloured. Drain and dish with a short thick piece of parsley stalk stuck into the narrow end of each cutlet. Garnish with sprigs of parsley, fried if deep fat is available. *Note:* tomato sauce may accompany egg cutlets if served hot; they may also be served cold with salad.

EGG SALAD. 4 *hard-boiled; mayonnaise or thick salad dressing* (see MAYONNAISE and SALAD DRESSING); *assorted salad (lettuce, watercress, small cress, etc.);* 8 *anchovy fillets; a few capers (optional).*

Cut the eggs in halves lengthways, or leave them whole. Lay them on a bed of prepared salad (see SALAD, MIXED GREEN) broken small and coat the eggs with the dressing. Garnish with pieces of salad and anchovy fillets: the latter may each be rolled round two or three capers to make little nests if liked.

EGG SAUCE. ½ *pint white sauce* (see WHITE SAUCE, FOUNDATION); 1 *hard-boiled egg.*

Hard-boil the egg and, when cold, chop it coarsely and add to well-seasoned white sauce. If liked, half of the hard-boiled yolk may be pressed through a coarse strainer, and used to garnish the food, after coating it with the sauce.

EGGS, anchovy. 3 *hard-boiled eggs;* 1 *small tablespoonful anchovy paste;* 1 *oz. margarine or butter; cayenne and salt; brown bread and butter; sprigs of watercress.*

Prepare the hard-boiled eggs and, when cold, cut them across the middle and remove the yolks. Mix the yolks, anchovy paste, cayenne and salt, and rub all through a sieve. Cut a small piece off the bottom of each piece of white to make the halves stand firmly, and fill some of the mixture into each, if possible using a bag and forcer. Spread any of the mixture remaining on slices of thin brown bread and butter, and cut into small squares, one for each half-egg. Arrange the eggs firmly on these and garnish with sprigs of watercress.

EGGS, fricassée of. 2–3 *hard-boiled eggs;* ½ *pint béchamel sauce* (see BÉCHAMEL SAUCE); *chopped parsley; paprika pepper.*

Halve the eggs and put them into the heated sauce. Simmer gently for ten to fifteen minutes and remove carefully to a hot dish so that the pieces are not broken. Arrange a border of chopped parsley round the edge and sprinkle paprika pepper in the middle.

EGGS, poached. *Eggs; a slice of buttered toast for each; salt.*

Make the toast, butter it and keep hot. Have a frying-pan two-thirds full with boiling water, and add a little salt. Break the egg into a cup, and slip it gently into the water, slightly tipping the pan to keep the white from spreading. If the egg is not quite covered with water, baste the top, and cook for about two minutes until the white is set. Remove with a fish-slice or perforated spoon and serve on the toast.

EGGS, sardine. 3 *hard-boiled eggs;* 1 *heaped teaspoonful sardine paste or boned mashed sardines;* 1 *oz. margarine or butter; few drops lemon juice or vinegar; cayenne and salt; brown bread and butter; small cress to garnish.*

Make as for anchovy eggs (see above) and garnish with small cress.

EGGS, Scotch. 2 *hard-boiled eggs;* 2 *sausages;* 4 *croûtons fried bread; chopped parsley; beaten egg (or substitute); dried crumbs.*

Hard-boil the eggs and remove the skin from the sausages. Remove egg-shells and enclose each egg in the sausage-meat, shaping neatly to follow the shape of the egg. Coat with egg and breadcrumbs (see COATING), and fry in deep fat which is just beginning to smoke, for eight to ten minutes to cook the sausage-meat thoroughly. Cut each egg across in two, and serve each half upstanding on a croûton of fried bread (see CROÛTONS). Decorate with a ring of parsley at the edge. Serve cold with salad, or hot, with a suitable sauce and mashed potatoes. Scotch eggs left uncut make a good dish for a packed lunch.

EGGS, scrambled. 2 *new-laid eggs;* 1 *tablespoonful milk;* ½ *oz. butter or margarine; salt and pepper;* 1 *slice buttered toast.*

Beat up the eggs, add salt, pepper and milk. Make the toast, trim it neatly, butter it and keep it hot. Melt the butter or margarine in a small saucepan, add the egg mixture and stir over gentle heat with a metal spoon, until the mixture thickens to a creamy pulp. Avoid overcooking, but the mixture should not be soft enough to flow off the toast. Pile on top of the toast, and sprinkle with a little chopped parsley. If dried egg is used, reconstitute it smoothly, and proceed as foregoing. One teaspoonful of chopped parsley or two teaspoonfuls anchovy essence may be added to improve flavour.

EGGS, tomato. *Rounds of buttered toast. To each slice allow* 1 *egg;* 1 *medium-sized tomato; scant* ½ *oz. margarine or butter; salt and pepper.*

Skin the tomatoes. Cut in slices and cook for a few minutes in the margarine or butter. Beat the eggs and add to the tomatoes in the saucepan, with salt and pepper. Stir over heat until creamy and pile upon the toast. Put a sprig of parsley on top.

FAIRY CAKES. ½ *oz. almonds* (*optional*); 2 *oz. margarine;* 2 *oz. caster sugar;* 1 *egg;* 1½ *oz. glacé cherries or sultanas; few drops carmine or cochineal; flavouring essence;* 3 *oz. flour;* ¼ *teaspoonful baking powder;* 1–2 *tablespoonfuls milk.*

Grease about a dozen small fancy cake tins, and put a pinch of chopped blanched almonds at the bottom of each. Make by creaming method (see CAKE MIXTURES, CREAMED), adding the colouring and flavouring after beating in the eggs. Fill the mixture into the prepared tins, and bake in a hot oven, set at Mark 6 or 425 deg. F. for fifteen minutes.

FISH IN BATTER (fried). 1 *filleted fish; coating or fritter batter* (see BATTER FOR COATING and FRITTER BATTER); *lemon and parsley.*

Make the batter. Wash and dry the fish, remove skin and cut into neat pieces. Have ready some deep fat which is just beginning to smoke, dip each piece of fish separately into the batter, and put it carefully into the fat. Turn it from time to time, and skim off any pieces of batter which float away from the fish. The time for cooking will be about ten minutes, when the fish is evenly golden-brown and crisp. Drain well on crumpled paper and pile on a hot dish, on a plain dish paper. Garnish with slices of lemon and fried parsley. A suitable sauce may be handed separately if liked.

FISH CAKES. ½ *lb. cooked fish;* ¼–½ *lb. mashed potato; a nut of margarine; salt and pepper; lemon juice; white sauce or egg to bind; egg* (*or coating substitute*) *and dried crumbs; lemon and parsley to garnish.*

Remove skin and bones from the fish and flake it finely. Add potato, salt, pepper and lemon juice. Melt the margarine in a saucepan, add the mixture and add sufficient egg or left-over sauce to bind all together. Heat and mix well. Spread the mixture in a round on a plate and mark into eight pieces. When cold, shape the pieces into flat, round cakes, of even depth and width. Coat with egg and breadcrumbs and fry until golden-coloured in deep fat. Drain well and serve the cakes leaning one against the other on a dish paper on a hot dish. Garnish with lemon and parsley, and a suitable sauce may be handed separately in a sauceboat.

FISH CUTLETS. ½ *lb. cooked fish;* ½ *oz. margarine;* ½ *oz. flour;* ½ *gill milk or fish liquor; salt and pepper; lemon juice; egg or coating substitute; dried crumbs; a few pieces of macaroni.*

Remove bones and skin from the fish, and flake it. Make a thick white sauce (see WHITE SAUCE, FOUNDATION) with the margarine, flour and liquid. Add the prepared fish, salt, pepper and lemon juice. Spread the mixture in a round on a plate and mark into six to eight pieces. Form these into cutlet shapes on a floured board, using two knives. Coat with egg and breadcrumbs and insert a small piece of macaroni in the pointed end of each. Fry, preferably in deep fat, until golden-brown. Drain on crumpled paper, and garnish, frying the parsley if deep fat is used. A suitable pouring sauce, such as anchovy or parsley may be served in a sauceboat separately.

FISH, fricassée of. 1 *plaice or sole;* 1½ *gills white coating sauce* (see WHITE SAUCE, FOUNDATION); *salt and pepper; lemon and parsley.*

Wash, dry, skin and fillet the fish. Prepare a small quantity of fish stock from the bones. Place the fillets on a board with the skinned side uppermost. Sprinkle a little salt, pepper and lemon juice on each. Roll up the fillets, from head to tail, and place them in the heated sauce; simmer very gently fifteen to twenty minutes. Remove fillets carefully to a hot dish, season the sauce, add a few drops lemon juice, and strain it over the fillets. Garnish with lemon and parsley. *Note:* a fillet from a large fish may be cut in neat pieces and used similarly.

FISH, fried fillets of. *In deep fat:* 1 *plaice or similar fish;* 2 *teaspoonfuls seasoned flour; egg coating substitute; dried crumbs; lemon and parsley to garnish.*

Wash, scale, dry and fillet the fish; again dry the fish and dip in seasoned flour, and coat with egg and breadcrumbs. Press on the crumbs firmly and fry in smoking-hot deep fat for about one minute until golden-coloured. Drain and serve on a dish paper on a hot dish, garnish with lemon and fried parsley. A suitable pouring sauce may be served in a sauceboat separately.

In shallow fat: 1 *steak of cod or similar fish; or small whole flat fish; seasoned flour or egg and breadcrumbs; clarified dripping or lard; sprigs of parsley.*

Have sufficient melted fat in a frying-pan to give half-inch depth. Put in the prepared coated fish and fry until golden-coloured on one side, then turn and cook the second side. Reduce heat and continue cooking until the fish is cooked through. A cod steak will take about twelve to fifteen minutes in all, and a whole small sole or dab about ten to twelve minutes. Remove the fish with a fish-slice, drain, and serve garnished with parsley.

FISH, grilled. 1 *steak of fish, about* 1 *in. thick, or whole small flat fish such as soles or dabs; melted fat;* 1 *teaspoonful maître d'hôtel butter* (see MAÎTRE D'HÔTEL BUTTER); *lemon and parsley to garnish.*

Wash and dry the fish; dredge it very lightly with flour. Place the fish on a heated greased grid, and grill for six to seven minutes. Brush with melted fat, and turn carefully to the other side. Grill for a further ten to twelve minutes, first dredging with flour and brushing with fat when nearly cooked. Grilling should not be so rapid as for meat. Serve on a hot dish, with pieces of maître d'hôtel butter on top and garnished with lemon and parsley.

FISH PIE. ½ *lb. cooked fish;* ¾ *lb. cooked potatoes;* 1 *gill white sauce* (see WHITE SAUCE, FOUNDATION); *milk; lemon juice;* 1 *hard-boiled egg* (*optional*); 1 *heaped teaspoonful chopped parsley; salt and pepper; a nut of margarine.*

Remove bones and skin from the fish and flake it. Mix it with the lemon juice, parsley, white sauce, salt and pepper, and put in the bottom of a greased piedish, arranging slices of hard-boiled egg, if used. Mash the potatoes with a fork, and add the margarine, salt and pepper, and sufficient hot milk to make it smooth but not wet. Cover the fish in the piedish with potato mixture, mounding it slightly in the centre and fluff the surface with a fork. Brush the top with beaten egg or milk. Bake in a hot oven, set at Mark 8 or 465 deg. F. for twenty-five to thirty minutes, until nicely browned.

FISH SCALLOPS. *¼ lb. mashed potatoes; a nut of margarine; 1 small tablespoonful milk; ¼ lb. cooked white fish; ½ pint white coating sauce* (see WHITE SAUCE, FOUNDATION); *salt and pepper; 3 tablespoonfuls fresh breadcrumbs; a little oiled margarine; lemon and parsley to garnish.*

Heat the milk and add margarine and potatoes. Grease four or five large scallop shells and sprinkle them with breadcrumbs, put a little sauce in each and a mound of boned, flaked fish. Coat each mound with sauce, sprinkle with oiled margarine. Put the prepared potato mixture into a forcing bag, fitted with a large rose pipe. Force a line of potato round the edge of each shell, or arrange it using two forks. Place in a very hot oven, set at Mark 9 or 490 deg. F. for a few minutes. Put a half-slice of lemon on each with a tiny piece of parsley.

FISH, steamed. 1 *medium-sized plaice or sole, filleted and skimmed* (see "The A. B. C. of Cookery"); *salt, pepper and lemon juice; 1½–2 gills white, parsley or anchovy sauce* (see under those headings); *garnish.*

Wipe the fillets, and put them on a board with the skinned side uppermost. Sprinkle each with salt, pepper and lemon juice, and roll up, or fold over in half. Put the fillets on a greased plate, cover with greased paper and place on top of a saucepan half filled with boiling water. Put the lid or another plate on top, and steam twenty to twenty-five minutes, until the fish looks opaque and curd-like. Remove the fillets to a hot dish, and add the liquor from the plate to the sauce as part of the liquid measurement. Coat the fish with sauce and garnish with lemon and parsley, or strips of anchovy fillets, or picked shrimps.

To steam a larger piece of fish. Prepare the fish and place it in an enamelled piedish or casserole in the upper part of a steamer. Cover with greased paper and allow half as long again for cooking as would be allowed for boiling, that is, ten minutes to each pound and ten minutes over (about fifteen minutes if under one pound).

FLAN CASE. Roll out rich short pastry (see PASTRY, RICH SHORT) made with four to five ounces flour, etc., to one inch bigger than the flan ring all round. Grease a flan ring of seven inches diameter. Fold the pastry lightly in half to avoid stretching it, and lift it into the ring, then press firmly to the bottom and sides. Roll off any superfluous pastry with a rolling pin, press up the edge and decorate it with a fork. Prick the bottom. Place on it a round of greased paper, large enough to come up the sides, and snipped at the edges to make the paper set well. Put in pieces of bread crust, and bake "blind."

FLAPJACKS. 2 *oz. margarine;* 1 *tablespoonful golden syrup;* 1 *oz. caster sugar;* 4 *oz. rolled oats; pinch of salt.*

Melt margarine and syrup in a saucepan. Add sugar, oats and salt, and mix well together over gentle heat for one minute. Press into a small, shallow, greased tin. Bake in a moderate oven set at Mark 4 or 375 deg. F. Mark deeply into fingers in the tin when cooked. Leave in tin until cold, and cut up.

FLEURONS. These are small shapes of pastry, usually crescents, which have been cut from thinly rolled pastry, either puff, rough puff, flaky, or short. Brush with beaten egg or milk, and bake on a greased tin for a few minutes, until golden-brown. Use as a garnish.

FORCEMEAT BALLS. *Veal stuffing* (see STUFFING, VEAL); *egg or coating substitute; dried crumbs.*

Make the veal stuffing, mixing in some beaten egg to make the stuffing hold together well. When firmly mixed, but not so stiff as to crack and crumble, roll into small balls with the floured fingers. Coat with egg and breadcrumbs, and fry in deep fat until well browned, or have some smoking hot fat in a small deep tin and bake until browned. Drain well.

FOWL, boiled. 1 *boiling fowl;* 1 *carrot, turnip and onion;* 1 *hard-boiled egg; chopped parsley;* 1 *pint coating sauce, either béchamel, white or parsley* (see under these headings).

Draw and truss the bird for boiling (see below). Put breast downwards in boiling salted water, boil for three minutes and skim well. Add vegetables. Simmer gently until tender. Allow an hour for a young bird. Two or even three hours are necessary for an old bird. Remove string and drain well. Coat with the prepared sauce, and garnish with hard-boiled egg, the white cut into strips, and the yolk pressed through a strainer, and chopped parsley.

FOWL, to draw. Have two bowls of water in readiness: one warm for cleansing the fingers, and the other cold to receive the giblets. Place a sheet of kitchen paper on a board. Hold the bird up by the legs and singe it. Cut off the head, leaving three to four inches of neck. Turn the bird over so that the back is uppermost, insert a small sharp-pointed knife at the end of the spine and slit up the neck. Pull away all loose skin and, gathering it up in the left hand, cut off the neck very close to the top of the spine. From this end remove the crop and windpipe, and any fat which may be present. Turn the bird round, and make a short cut between the tail and vent. Place two fingers of each hand inside the bird at each end to loosen the inside, keeping the fingers high under the breastbone to avoid breaking the gall bladder. Withdraw the left hand and hold the bird firmly while taking hold of the gizzard and drawing down all the inside. Cut the gall bladder from the

Fig. 21. Drawing a fowl: (a) ***hold bird up by the legs and singe it;*** (b) ***remove head and neck, followed by crop and windpipe (leave an uncut flap of skin on the breast);*** (c) ***draw the bird, steadying it with the left hand;*** (d) ***cut off the feet. Have a bowl of water handy for the giblets.***

liver, and place liver, gizzard which has been emptied out, heart and kidneys in the bowl of cold water, with the neck. Cleanse these in salted water; the liver should be used for a savoury, and the remainder used for stock for gravy. Wrap all remaining in the paper and burn it. Wipe out the inside of the bird with a damp cloth. Cut round the skin at the hock joint of the leg, and draw out the sinews. Cut off the feet, scald and scrape scaly skin off the remaining piece of leg (see Fig. 21).

FOWL, roast. 1 *tender fowl; dripping or butter for basting; veal forcemeat* (see FORCEMEAT); 4–5 *streaky bacon rashers* (see BACON ROLLS); *thin gravy* (see GRAVY, THIN); *watercress to garnish; bread sauce* (see BREAD SAUCE); *chipped or browned potatoes* (see POTATOES, CHIPPED and BROWNED).

Place the bird on a grid in a meat tin. Bake in a hot oven at first set at Mark 6 or 425 deg. F. An hour or hour-and-a-quarter would be the average time. Baste frequently, and cover the breast of the bird with a piece of greased paper for the first part of the cooking time. When done remove the string and place the bird on a hot dish. Place the bacon rolls in a mound at the neck end of the bird, and garnish at the tail end with the bunched watercress. Pour a little of the gravy round and serve the remainder in a sauceboat, and also the bread sauce. Drain the potatoes well and serve on a dish paper in a hot dish, sprinkled with a little fine salt and chopped parsley. Fig. 22 shows four stages in the carving of a roast fowl.

FOWL, to truss. *For boiling.* Singe the bird, cut the skin round the hock joints and draw out the sinews. Cut off the legs. Place the first two fingers inside the bird, break through the flesh just below the leg joint, loosen the skin around the legs, place the thumb against the "knee" joint. Push the leg upward until it slips inside the bird. Repeat with the other leg. This is called "pocketing" the legs and is done to make the bird of better shape for coating with the sauce (see Fig. 23). Draw the skin smoothly over the bird to give it a plump, even appearance, and truss with needle and string as for roast fowl (see Fig. 24).

For roasting. Fold the flap of skin smoothly over the back at the neck end, and fold the ends of the wings backward and under to secure it. If the bird is to be stuffed, place the stuffing in this end before folding over the flap. Place the bird on its back and press the legs well down to plump up the breast. Pass the tail through the vent. Place the bird with the neck end to the right of the worker.

Thread a trussing needle with string. Pass it through the first wing joint, through the bird, and out again in a similar position on the other side. Insert the needle in the second joint, leaving a stitch of about an inch showing.

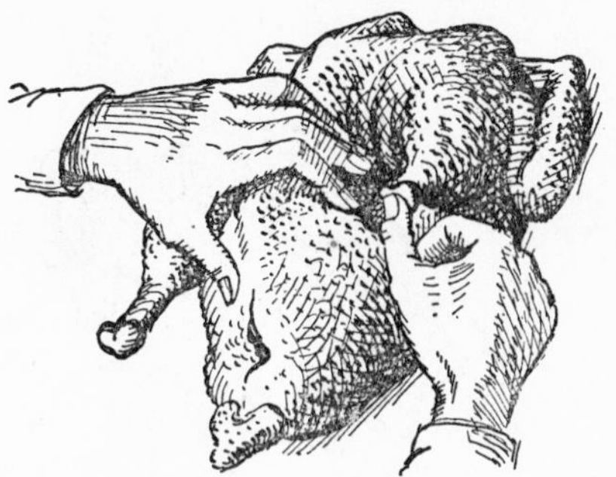

Fig. 23. Pocketing legs of a fowl preparatory to boiling. The legs are cut off halfway up and pressed inside the loosened skin.

Fig. 22. Carving a fowl: (a) *insert the knife between thigh and body and remove the wing and a slice of breast attached;* (b) *press the knife into the leg joint and remove the leg;* (c) *the breast can now be carved;* (d) *remove the wishbone and surrounding meat. With a small chicken, the breast will be served with wings and wishbone. With a larger bird additional portions are obtained.*

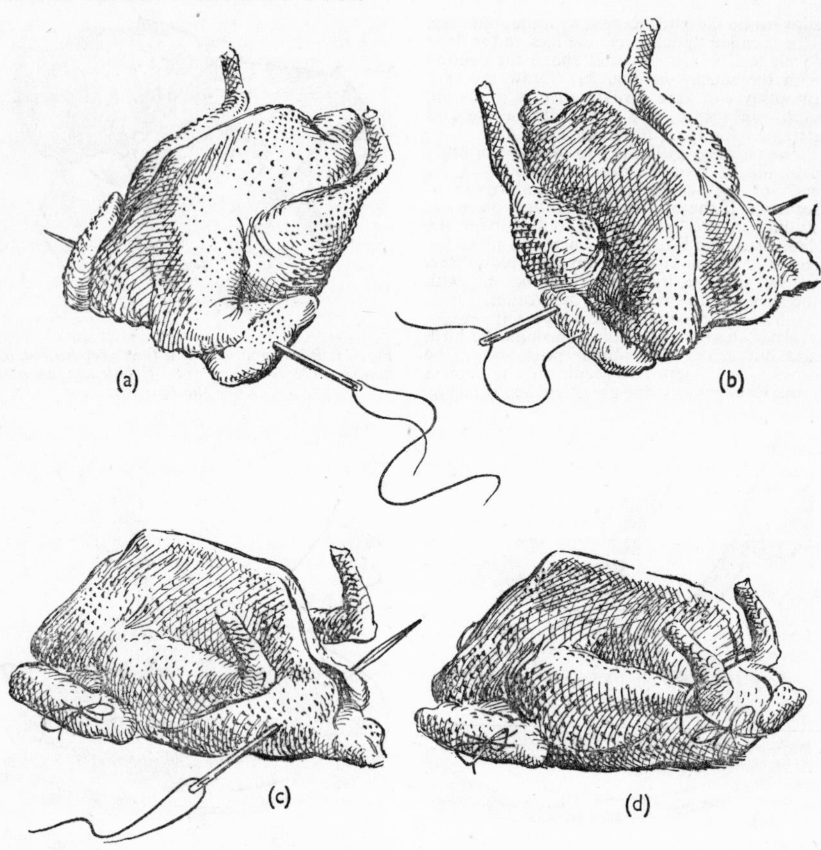

Fig. 24. Trussing a fowl: (a) *pass a trussing needle through the first wing joints;* (b) *return the needle through the second joints, catching in the top of the legs, and tie;* (c) *pass the needle and string through the bird's back beneath the hock joints;* (d) *loop in the legs and tie.*

Catch in the legs, and return to similar joint. Tie the string in a bow, making the bird taut and trim. Re-thread the needle with string and pass it through the back of the bird under the hock joints. Pass the string round twice, and tie in a bow at the side. *Note:* if no trussing needle is available, use two metal skewers, placed in the position followed by the trussing needle, and twist string round (see Fig. 24).

FRITTER BATTER. 2 *oz. flour; pinch of salt;* 1 *dessertspoonful salad oil or yolk of* 1 *egg;* ½ *gill water; white of* 1 *egg.*

Sieve the flour and salt, and make a well in the centre. Put in the oil or yolk, and some of the water, which must be tepid if oil is used. Mix to a smooth paste, adding remainder of water. Beat well. Cover and set aside for half an hour. Just before the batter is required for use, fold in the stiffly whisked white of egg. *Note:* fritter batter is a suitable coating for fruit fritters, fish in batter, kromeskies, etc.

FRUIT, dried. To clean. For a large quantity, place currants or sultanas on a sieve, dredge with flour and rub lightly, so that the soiled flour will fall through the mesh. If no sieve is available, place the fruit on the corner of a teacloth, dredge with flour and rub in the cloth. Pick up the fruit in small handfuls and remove all sticks and stems. There is no need to wash fruit, but, if this method is preferred, it must be well drained afterwards, spread on large dishes or trays, and allowed to dry for a few days in a warm place, and frequently turned over. If allowed to dry rapidly, fruit becomes hard and loses flavour.

Raisins are most quickly stoned if cut open with a small knife first. Put the stones into a small basin of very hot water, as this eases the stickiness of the fingers. Slice them or leave whole as desired. *Candied peel.* Remove all sugar and use for stewing fruit, etc. With a sharp knife, shred along the length of the cap, gather up the shreds in the left hand.

turn them round, and slice finely, in the opposite direction.

FRUIT, dried. Stewed. *For whole fruit, such as prunes or figs, allow 1 brimming pint of water to 1 lb. fruit. For halved fruit, such as apricots, peaches or pears, allow 1½ pints water to 1 lb. fruit. For sliced fruit, such as apple rings, allow 2 pints water to 1 lb. fruit. Allow 2–4 oz. sugar to each 1 lb. of fruit. Flavouring of lemon or orange rind and juice, cloves or cinnamon (optional).*

Wash the fruit thoroughly in warm water. Steep in the measured cold water for at least twelve hours. Stew the fruit in the steeping water, adding the flavouring, over gentle heat and covered with a lid. Alternatively, cook in a casserole in a moderate oven. When almost tender, add the sugar. Serve hot or cold.

FRUIT FLAN. *Baked flan case* (see FLAN CASE); *small tin of fruit or ½–¾ lb. fruit stewed; 1 gill syrup; 1–1½ oz. sugar; 1 teaspoonful arrowroot or cornflour; 1 teaspoonful lemon juice; 1 teaspoonful red, yellow, or green jam, according to colour of fruit; colouring if necessary; cream to decorate (optional).*

Drain the fruit and place it in the case. Dissolve the sugar in the water, mix arrowroot smoothly with a little water, add and boil well, stirring. Add lemon juice, jam, and see that the consistency is that of a thick coating sauce. Strain over the fruit, completely to cover it. Decorate the edge with whipped cream, mock cream, or whisked evaporated milk, if desired. Alternatively, lay baked pastry leaves on top, leaving spaces to show the fruit between them.

FRUIT MOULD. *1 pint well-pulped stewed fruit, sweetened; 1½ oz. cornflour; a little milk to mix; ½ pint custard or custard sauce* (see CUSTARD).

Stew the fruit and mix the cornflour smoothly with the milk. Add the mixed cornflour, stir until boiling and continue for a further ten minutes. Turn the mixture into a mould or basin rinsed with cold water, and leave to set. Prise the mixture from the edges with the finger tips and shake on to a fancy dish. Pour the custard round.

FRUIT PUDDING, boiled. *Suet pastry made with 6–8 oz. flour, etc.* (see PASTRY, SUET); *¾–1 lb. fruit, according to kind; about 2 tablespoonfuls sugar according to acidity of fruit; a little water.*

Grease a pudding basin, and have a pudding cloth and string in readiness. Prepare the fruit according to its kind. Make the suet pastry and cut off a quarter of it for the lid. Roll the larger piece to a round one-and-a-half times larger than the top of the pudding basin, and line the basin with it, pressing firmly. Half-fill the basin with fruit, add sugar, and a little water, then the remainder of the fruit. Damp the edge of the pastry, roll out the remaining piece for the lid. Press firmly into place. Scald and flour the pudding cloth, invert it over the pudding and tie securely with string. Tie the corners of the cloth over the top and boil for two-and-a-half hours. Unmould on to a hot dish. *Note:* if preferred, the pudding may be steamed for three hours or longer. In this case, twist a greased paper over in place of the pudding cloth.

FRUIT SALAD. *1 pint fruits, fresh or tinned; ½ pint syrup from tinned fruits or water; 4 oz. sugar (if water is used); juice ½ lemon or orange; 2 tablespoonfuls sherry or liqueur (optional); whipped cream, mock cream, or whipped evaporated milk.*

Prepare the fruit according to its kind and put into a basin. Sprinkle with the lemon juice and liqueur such as maraschino or kirsche if it is used. Dissolve the sugar completely in the syrup or water, boil up and simmer steadily for ten minutes, skimming as necessary. Pour the boiling syrup over the fruit, stir up, cover and leave until cold. Serve in a glass bowl or in coupe glasses decorated with whipped cream or its substitute, if required.

FRUIT, stewed fresh. *1 lb. fresh fruit; ½ pint water; 3 oz. sugar.*

Put the water and sugar into a stewpan, dissolve the sugar completely and boil up without stirring. Prepare the fruit according to its kind, place it in the boiling syrup and simmer gently until tender but not broken, with a lid on the pan. Remove fruit, and boil the syrup until reduced and syrupy. Pour syrup over the fruit.

FRUIT TART. *Short pastry, made with 4–6 oz. flour, etc.* (see PASTRY, SHORT); *1–1½ lb. fruit, according to kind; 2–4 oz. sugar, according to acidity of fruit; custard or custard sauce* (see CUSTARD).

Prepare the fruit according to its kind; if apples are used, cut the quarters into small chunks and not into thin slices. Put half the fruit into a pint piedish, add the sugar and put the remainder of the fruit on top. Add water to come halfway up the piedish, unless the fruit is very juicy, such as raspberries and red currants, or very young rhubarb, when one tablespoonful will be sufficient. Make the pastry and roll it out an eighth-inch thick, and to the shape of the piedish, but an inch larger all round. Cut a complete strip of pastry from the edge, and place it cut side inside on the damped rim of the piedish. Press the strip of pastry firmly, damp it with water and lift on the cover, being careful not to stretch it. Trim the edges, and flake them with a knife, laying the first finger of the left hand on the edge of the pie to keep it steady. Decorate with small flutings. Bake in a hot oven at first, set at Mark 6 or 425 deg. F. Reduce the heat when the pastry has risen and is brown, cooking slowly until the fruit is tender, about thirty-five minutes in all. Dredge with sugar and hand the custard separately.

FRUIT TRIFLE. *4 oz. sponge cake or stale plain cake; ½ lb. fresh fruit; 1 gill water (average amount); 1½ oz. sugar; ½ pint custard; whipped cream, mock cream, or whipped evaporated milk.*

Stew the fruit with the water and sugar. Small fruits need very little water, if any. Crumble the cake or cut in thin slices. Arrange cake and fruit in alternate layers, beginning and ending with fruit. Leave to become cold and set. Make the custard and leave to become cold. Pour the custard over and when set decorate with the chosen cream.

GALANTINE OF BEEF. 1 *lb. buttock steak;* ½ *lb. sausage meat or bacon;* 6 *oz. fresh breadcrumbs;* 1–1½ *gills stock; salt and pepper;* 1 *level teaspoonful ground allspice;* 2 *eggs;* ½ *teaspoonful meat or yeast extract; mock glaze* (see GLAZE, MOCK); *watercress or small cress to garnish.*

Mince the beef and bacon (or add the sausage meat). Add the breadcrumbs, salt, pepper and spice and mix well. Beat the eggs and add the meat extract dissolved in the stock. Mix all together, form into a roll and tie firmly in a pudding cloth. Boil steadily for two-and-a-half hours. Remove the cloth and tie the galantine up again in a dry, greased pudding cloth. Press between two plates or dishes, weighted on top. When cold remove cloth and brush with glaze, giving three or four coatings. Trim the ends and serve garnished with cress.

GAME, roast. 1 *tender, plump game bird; fat bacon; dripping for basting; flour for dredging; croûte of fried bread. Accompaniments: thin gravy* (see GRAVY, THIN); *watercress; chipped potatoes; bread sauce* (see BREAD SAUCE); *green salad* (see SALAD, MIXED GREEN); *fried crumbs.*

Wipe the bird inside and out with a damp cloth. Cleanse the giblets and simmer them thirty minutes for gravy. Truss the bird as for FOWL, ROAST, but cut off the ends of the wings, securing the wings with the legs to the sides of the body by means of a skewer. A small lump of dripping may be placed inside the bird, and a slice of fat bacon tied over the breast. Cook in a hot oven set at Mark 7 or 440 deg. F., basting every ten to fifteen minutes. Allow time for cooking according to table below. Ten minutes before the bird is ready, remove the bacon and baste well; baste again five minutes later and dredge with flour and return to the oven to froth. Serve the bird on a croûte of fried bread cut large enough to support it, if the bird is a small one. Garnish with watercress and hand the accompaniments separately. *Fried crumbs.* Melt sufficient margarine to supply two tablespoonfuls, and stir in two ounces fresh breadcrumbs. Brown the crumbs slowly, stirring frequently, and giving them constant attention.

GAME, table for cooking. Heat the oven to Mark 7 or 440 deg. F. If the bird is small, keep this temperature throughout, but if large, heat may be reduced after thirty minutes. Cover the breast of the bird with a piece of greased paper, which should be removed ten minutes before it is cooked.

Blackcock	Time for roasting	Forty-five minutes.
Grouse	Time for roasting	Thirty-five to forty minutes.
Partridge	Time for roasting	Thirty-five to fifty minutes, according to size.
Pheasant	Time for roasting	Forty-five to fifty-five minutes.
Teal	Time for roasting	Twenty-five to thirty five minutes.
Wild duck	Time for roasting	Thirty to thirty-five minutes. Should be crisp and brown on the surface, but rather underdone.

GELATINE, rules for using. Powdered gelatine is reliable and easy to use as it requires no preparation. If leaf gelatine is used, cut the sheets in strips with a pair of scissors, and it will dissolve more easily if it is soaked in the measured liquid for fifteen minutes or so. Being a powerful ingredient, gelatine should be weighed or measured accurately, as the resulting food is unpleasant if too stiff, and will not set if too little gelatine is allowed. Melt gelatine in a small saucepan over very gentle heat, stirring all the time, and do not allow it to boil. It is ready for use when all granules or shreds have disappeared, and must be added while still hot to the other ingredients, and last of all.

GINGERBREAD. 12 *oz. flour;* 1 *heaped teaspoonful ground ginger;* 1 *level teaspoonful bicarbonate of soda;* ¼ *lb. sugar;* 2 *oz. chopped candied peel;* ¼ *lb. margarine;* ½ *lb. golden syrup;* 2 *small eggs;* ½ *gill milk.*

Sieve the flour, ground ginger and bicarbonate of soda. Put the sugar, margarine and syrup into a small saucepan and warm gently until all is blended. Add the chopped peel to the dry ingredients and pour in the syrup mixture, then the beaten eggs and milk. Mix well. Pour the mixture into a Yorkshire pudding tin, lined with greased paper. Bake in a moderate oven set at Mark 3 or 350 deg. F. for one to one-and-a-quarter hours. *Note:* a darker gingerbread may be made by using brown treacle, or half syrup and half treacle. Two ounces chopped preserved ginger or sultanas may be added, and also one level teaspoonful mixed spice.

GLAZE, mock. 1 *gill stock, vegetable water, or water;* 1 *heaped teaspoonful powdered gelatine; salt and pepper; few drops gravy browning;* ½ *teaspoonful meat or yeast extract.*

Put the liquid in a small saucepan, add the gelatine and dissolve it completely. Add remaining ingredients and again warm gently until all is well blended. Allow to cool but not to set, and paint it over cold food such as beef galantine or tongue. Three or four coatings may be necessary, allowing each to set before adding the next. If the main bulk of the glaze should set before the coatings are completed, stand it in warm water for a minute or two. *Note:* mock glaze is suitable for cold food only, as heat melts it at once.

GOLDEN PUDDING. 4 *oz. flour;* 1 *teaspoonful baking powder;* 2 *oz. chopped suet;* 2 *oz. stale crumb of bread;* 1 *gill milk and water;* 1–2 *tablespoonfuls marmalade; marmalade or custard sauce* (see MARMALADE SAUCE and CUSTARD SAUCE).

Pass the flour through a sieve with the baking powder, and add the chopped suet. Crumble the bread and soak in the milk and water, then beat smooth, and add to the dry ingredients with the marmalade. If the smaller amount of marmalade is used, a little extra milk and water may be necessary to enable the mixture to be dropped from the mixing spoon, and also two teaspoonfuls of sugar may be added. Put the mixture into a greased pudding basin, twist a greased paper over, and steam for two-and-a-half hours. Turn out on to a hot dish and pour the sauce chosen round the pudding.

GOOSEBERRY FOOL. 1 *lb. green gooseberries;* 4 *oz. sugar;* ¼ *pint water;* 1 *gill custard* (see CUSTARD); 1 *gill evaporated milk or cream.*

Stew the gooseberries with the sugar and water until soft, pass through a sieve and allow to cool. Add the custard to the gooseberry purée, then the evaporated milk or cream; this may be half-whipped before adding. Pour into a glass bowl or serve in coupe glasses. *Note:* other fruits can be used for making fool, and if strawberries or raspberries are used the fruit should be raw when sieved.

GRAVY, thick. 1 *tablespoonful dripping;* ½ *oz. flour;* ½ *pint stock or vegetable water; salt and pepper.*

Remove the meat from the roasting tin and pour off the fat, retaining the sediment and one tablespoonful of the fat. Add the flour to the tin, working it down to one corner. Brown slowly over gentle heat. Add the liquid, stir until boiling and boil well. Add salt and pepper and, if liked, a little meat or yeast extract, and/or one teaspoonful Worcester sauce. Thickened gravy is served with all stuffed meats and also with roast pork and roast veal.

GRAVY, thin. Remove the meat from the tin and keep hot. Strain off the fat, keeping back sediment only. Dredge the tin lightly with flour, and brown it slowly. Add about half a pint stock or vegetable water, and boil up rapidly stirring all the time. Season and skim if necessary to remove grease. Strain a little of the gravy round the joint and the remainder into a sauceboat.

GREEN PEAS. 2 *lb. peas; boiling water;* 3 *teaspoonfuls sugar;* 2–3 *sprigs mint; salt; a nut of butter or margarine.*

Shell the peas, looking them over carefully. Boil sufficient water to cover the peas, and add the sugar and mint. Add the peas and boil gently until tender, time according to age of peas, from ten to twenty minutes. Add salt when the peas are almost cooked. Drain and remove mint, re-heat with a nut of butter or margarine. *Note:* if the peas should be old, a pinch of bicarbonate of soda may be added to the water before the peas are put into it. It is best to avoid this if possible, but if the peas are rather dry it will prevent them from being indigestible.

GRILLED STEAK OR CHOP. *Rump or fillet steak,* 1–1½ *in. thick, or loin or chump chops; maître d'hôtel butter;* 2 *raw potatoes; sprigs of watercress;* 2 *tomatoes.*

Prepare the maître d'hôtel butter as explained under that heading, and cut the potatoes to the required shape for chips or French fried potatoes. Wipe the meat and beat steak lightly with a damp rolling-pin. Brush with oil or oiled dripping on both sides, and leave for half an hour before cooking. Place the meat on the heated and greased bars of the grid, and put it under a red-hot griller. Cook quickly to seal in the juices, turn and again cook quickly to seal the juices on the second side. For time for cooking and further notes on grilling, see "The A.B.C. of Cookery." When the meat appears puffy and no longer spongy, place it on a hot dish, with pieces of the prepared butter on top. Put the fried potatoes at one side and watercress sprigs at the other, and tuck halves of grilled, fried or baked tomatoes in between.

HADDOCK, smoked. Trim off the tail, fins and flaps, and wash the fish thoroughly. Put the fish into an oval frying-pan and cover with milk and water. Place a lid or dish on top. Bring just to boiling point over moderate heat, then leave to cook in its own heat eight to ten minutes. Remove carefully with a fish-slice, and put tiny pieces of butter or margarine over, and sprinkle with pepper. The backbone may be removed, the fish divided into portions and a poached egg put on each if desired. Smoked cod fillet is prepared similarly, except that, being thicker, it will require to be kept at simmering point for a minute or two before heat is turned off.

HADDOCK CROÛTES. 2 *oz. chopped, cooked, smoked haddock;* 2–3 *anchovy fillets or* 1 *gherkin;* ½ *oz. margarine;* 1 *tablespoonful evaporated or top milk; cayenne and salt; chopped parsley or paprika pepper;* 6 *round croûtes of fried bread* (see CROÛTONS).

Heat the fish and chopped anchovy fillets or gherkin in the margarine. Add the milk, cayenne and salt. Heat gently until hot through, and mound neatly on the croûtes of fried bread. Sprinkle with parsley or paprika pepper and serve hot. *Note:* the haddock mixture may be put on a round of buttered toast and served as a breakfast savoury.

HAM, boiled. Soak the ham for twelve to twenty-four hours, wash and scrape off the rust. Boil as for boiled beef (see BEEF, BOILED SALT), adding one teaspoonful vinegar and one teaspoonful brown sugar to each quart of water used to cover the ham. Put the bone downwards in an oval boiler, as the rind is liable to stick to the bottom. For hams up to six pounds in weight, allow twenty minutes to each pound and twenty minutes over. Shorten the time per pound for larger hams, fifteen minutes per pound and fifteen minutes over is sufficient for a fourteen-pound ham. When the ham is cooked, the flesh is ready to separate easily from the bone at the knuckle end. Leave the ham in the liquor until cold, removing the skin at the end of about two hours. When ready, remove the ham from the liquor and drain it, press the outside with pieces of kitchen paper to dry it and press fine breadcrumbs (see RASPINGS) over the surface. If preferred, the ham may be served hot with tomato or parsley sauce.

HARD SAUCE. 1 *oz. butter;* 1½ *oz. caster sugar; flavouring essence or* 2–3 *teaspoonfuls rum or brandy; grated nutmeg.*

Cream the butter thoroughly, add the caster sugar gradually and cream until white. Add the chosen flavouring by degrees, and pile the sauce in a small fancy dish, arranging it neatly and fluffing the top with a fork. Grate nutmeg lightly on top. Set aside in the cool to become quite firm and hard. Serve with any rich steamed or boiled pudding. *Note:* flavoured with brandy, hard sauce is frequently known as brandy butter.

HARE, jugged. 1 *hare;* ¼ *lb. bacon or* 2 *oz. dripping; rind of* ½ *lemon;* 1 *onion;* 1 *large "bouquet garni"* (see BOUQUET GARNI); *veal forcemeat* (see FORCEMEAT BALLS); 2 *oz. flour;* 2 *tablespoonfuls port wine; salt and pepper; red-currant jelly.*

Cut the unwashed hare into joints and roll them in some of the flour which has been seasoned with salt and pepper. Fry the joints with the bacon cut in strips, or in dripping. Put the joints into a casserole with the onion, bouquet garni and lemon rind. Cover with about one quart of household stock, put on a lid, and cook in a cool oven set at Mark 1 or 300 deg. F. for four hours. Parboil the liver for ten minutes (see PARBOILING), mince it and add to the veal forcemeat. Form into small balls and either coat with egg and breadcrumbs or roll them in flour and fry in smoking hot dripping. Dish the hare and keep it hot. Mix the remaining flour smoothly with water, stir into the liquid and boil for five minutes. Add the wine and add more seasoning if necessary. Lastly add the blood of the hare; after this the sauce must not boil. Re-heat the hare and forcemeat balls in the gravy. Pile up neatly in a hot dish and hand red-currant jelly separately.

HASH. *Slices of cold cooked meat;* ½ *pint brown sauce* (see BROWN SAUCE) *to each* ½ *lb. meat;* 3 *oz. macaroni; chopped parsley; croûtons fried bread or toast* (see CROÛTONS).

Make the brown sauce and, when it has cooled somewhat, lay the slices of meat in it. Re-heat in a double saucepan or in a casserole in a cool oven for thirty minutes, being very careful that the sauce does not boil. See that the sauce used is well seasoned, and it may be made piquant by the addition of halved capers or chopped gherkins, Worcester sauce, or tomato ketchup. Dish the hash in a border of cooked macaroni (see MACARONI) sprinkled with chopped parsley, and arrange croûtons of fried bread or toast over the meat and sauce.

HEART, roast, in a saucepan. 1 *sheep's heart;* 1 *tablespoonful veal stuffing* (see STUFFING, VEAL); 2 *oz. dripping;* ½ *pint thickened gravy.*

Cleanse the heart by soaking in salted water for twenty minutes and squeezing out any blood clots. Cut the tubes from the top, but leave the flap for covering down during cooking. Cut the dividing walls in the heart and fill the cavity with the stuffing. Fold over the flap and skewer it down. Melt the dripping in a strong saucepan, and it should be about half an inch in depth. When the fat is smoking hot, put in the heart and brown it on all sides. Lessen the heat considerably and cook for fifty minutes, turning and basting occasionally. Remove to a hot dish, make the gravy and pour a little round, putting the remainder in a sauceboat. A calf's heart will require one to one-and-a-half hours for cooking and a bullock's one-and-a-half to two hours. Either of these may be steamed first for one to one-and-a-half hours and then roasted as sheep's heart.

HERRINGS, preparation of. Remove scales with a knife which is not too sharp, or the flesh may be cut. This may be done under water running from the cold-water tap. Hold the herring in the left hand, begin at the tail and work gently towards the head. Work along one side first, and then the other. Cut off the head, pull out the gills and make a slit about an inch long in the underside of the fish, leaving the roe unbroken. Draw out the inside. Rinse beneath the running tap, and wipe out the inside.

To bone a herring. Use a sharp knife, and make a shallow cut down the front of the fish, beginning at the head end. With the thumb and finger, open the fish and press it flat. Lift up the backbone with the knife and remove as many other loose bones as possible.

HERRINGS, fried. *Allow* 1 *medium-sized herring per person.*

Clean the herrings and dip each into medium oatmeal. Use a little frying fat, a nut of dripping of the size of a walnut being sufficient for two herrings. Fry the herrings on both sides about ten minutes in all, and do not overcook them. Serve at once very hot.

HERRINGS, grilled. Clean and bone the herrings, or they may be left unboned if preferred. For four herrings, melt about an ounce of dripping or margarine, and brush the herrings with it. Grill on each side until cooked, allowing about six minutes in all if the herrings are boned and spread flat, or ten minutes if left whole. Sprinkle with chopped parsley and serve at once.

HERRINGS, soused. 3–4 *fresh herrings; salt and pepper;* 1 *bayleaf;* 6–8 *peppercorns; a blade of mace;* 2–3 *cloves; vinegar.*

Prepare the herrings and bone them (see HERRINGS, PREPARATION OF). Sprinkle each with salt and pepper, and roll up with a piece of roe in each, and the skin outside. Pack the rolls in a casserole or piedish, and add the spices. Cover with vinegar and water in the proportion of three parts of vinegar to one of water. Cover with the lid, or a strong piece of greased paper if the piedish is used. Cook in a very moderate oven set at Mark 3 or 350 deg. F. for one hour. Serve in the dish, either hot or cold.

HORS D'OEUVRE. These consist of a variety of relishes which will stimulate but not satisfy appetite. Serve them daintily, placing them as a rule in a dish divided into compartments, or into separate small dishes arranged on a tray. Hand small pats of butter separately, and a small dinner roll. Suggested variety of six plain hors d'oeuvre would be: potato salad; beetroot salad; thin wafers of liver sausage, garnished with parsley; sardines or anchovy fillets, drained from oil, neatly arranged, which have been sprinkled with French salad dressing (see SALAD DRESSING, FRENCH) and capers; hard-boiled eggs coated with mayonnaise or thick salad dressing (see MAYONNAISE and SALAD DRESSING, BOILED); olives or gherkins.

Oysters are usually served in their shells. Do not open them until at the point of serving them, or much of their aroma will be lost. Hand chilli vinegar or cut lemon, brown bread and butter and cayenne separately.

Olives can be either the French or Spanish variety. The former are considered to have the finer flavour, but Spanish olives are larger.

Fruits such as grape-fruit, melon or pineapple, can be served with sugar, salt and pepper, and ground ginger or powdered cinnamon with melons. One of these fruits only is served as the hors d'oeuvre.

Smoked salmon fillets can be bought by the ounce, or obtained in oil in tins, when they are usually known as lax. Sprinkle with French salad dressing and chopped parsley.

HORSERADISH SAUCE. 1½ *oz. grated horseradish; ½ teaspoonful dry mustard;* 1 *teaspoonful sugar; ¼ teaspoonful salt;* 1 *tablespoonful white vinegar; ½ gill evaporated milk.*

Peel and grate the horseradish. Mix it with the remaining ingredients except for the milk, and lightly stir them into the evaporated milk, or, for a special sauce, slightly whipped cream may be substituted. Serve in a small sauceboat.

HOT-POT. 1 *lb. middle neck of mutton, or* 1 *lb. buttock steak;* 2 *teaspoonfuls seasoned flour* (see SEASONED FLOUR); 2 *onions;* 2–3 *sticks celery;* 1 *parsnip or turnip;* 2–3 *carrots; stock* (see STOCK, HOUSEHOLD); 1 *lb. potatoes, blanched* (see BLANCHING).

Wipe the meat, remove fat and divide into cutlets or cut in neat pieces. Dip in seasoned flour. Arrange meat, and the vegetables cut small, in layers in an earthenware or glass ovenware casserole, or deep piedish. Pour in sufficient stock to come halfway up. Slice the potatoes a quarter-inch thick; the ends may be cut up and put with the other vegetables. Arrange the slices neatly on top and add a few small pieces of the meat fat. Sprinkle with salt and put on the lid, or a strong piece of greased paper. Bake in a moderate oven set at Mark 5 or 400 deg. F. for two to two and a half hours. Remove the lid for the last thirty minutes, so that the potatoes may become crisp and brown lightly. Serve in the dish in which the hot-pot has been cooked. *Note:* in season, lamb or veal may take the place of mutton or beef, and young carrots and peas or runner beans may be used as the vegetable.

ICE CREAM, economical. ¾ *oz. custard powder or cornflour; ½ pint milk;* 1 *teaspoonful flavouring essence; ½ tin evaporated milk;* 1 *oz. caster sugar.*

Mix the custard powder or cornflour with some of the milk, heat the remainder and pour it over. Return to saucepan and stir and boil for four minutes. Add sugar and flavouring stir until cool and add the evaporated milk. When quite cold pour into the ice drawer of the refrigerator.

To prepare the drawer remove the divisions which form the cubes, and scald the drawer; dry it completely inside and out. Set the refrigerator to its coldest degree for an hour before the mixture is put in. Time for freezing varies somewhat according to the size and make of the refrigerator, but about two and a half to three hours is the average. The tray should be removed at the end of the first hour and the mixture beaten and scraped from the edges with a small whisk or fork. Any mixture can be frozen in this way.

ICE CREAM with gelatine. 1 *large tin evaporated milk; ½ large tin sweetened condensed milk; ½ oz. powdered gelatine; ½ gill water;* 1–2 *teaspoonfuls vanilla essence.*

Dissolve the gelatine in the water (see GELATINE). Cool and add to the evaporated milk, then mix in condensed milk and essence. Whisk and pour into the ice drawer of a refrigerator (see previous recipe).

ICING, almond. 1 *lb. ground almonds; ½ lb. sieved icing sugar;* 2 *small eggs; juice ½ lemon; ½ lb. caster sugar;* 1 *tablespoonful brandy or sherry* (*optional*).

Mix the ground almonds and sugars. Add the lemon juice, well beaten eggs and all flavourings. Mix ingredients together and knead thoroughly until smooth.

ICING, butter. 2 *oz. butter or margarine; scant* 4 *oz. icing sugar; colouring and flavouring.*

Cream the butter or margarine very thoroughly and add the finely sieved icing sugar gradually, beating in each small spoonful very well. The icing may be left white and flavoured with vanilla essence; or coloured pink and flavoured with raspberry essence; or coloured green and flavoured with almond or ratafia essence; or coffee essence may be added, which is both colouring and flavouring.

ICING, chocolate butter. *Butter icing* (see above); 2 *oz. plain chocolate; few drops vanilla essence.*

Scrape the chocolate with a knife, put it in a small saucepan with three tablespoonfuls of water. Dissolve over gentle heat, and boil gently while stirring until a smooth batter is obtained. Allow to cool, then beat into the butter icing, adding a few drops of vanilla essence.

ICING, chocolate glacé. 3 *oz. plain chocolate; scant ½ gill water; tiny piece of fresh butter; about* 8 *oz. finely sieved icing sugar; ½ teaspoonful vanilla essence.*

Scrape the chocolate finely with a knife and put it in a small saucepan with the water. Dissolve over very gentle heat, then bring just to boiling point. Beat in the butter, and when the chocolate has cooled somewhat beat in the icing sugar by degrees, then the vanilla essence. Beat well to make the icing glossy. If too thick, add a few drops of tepid water, or if too thin a little more icing sugar, so that the icing is of good coating consistency. Warm the icing slightly, stirring gently to dispel the bubbles caused by beating.

ICING, glacé. 3 *tablespoonfuls warm water; 8–10 oz. icing sugar; few drops flavouring essence; colouring if required.*

Put the water into a small pudding basin and add the finely sieved icing sugar by degrees, mixing very smoothly with a small wooden spoon. Stand the basin on top of a small saucepan, half-filled with very hot, but not boiling, water. Continue stirring until the icing is just warm, and when ready note that it is of the consistency of a coating sauce, and this may be tested over the back of the wooden spoon used for mixing. If the icing should be too thick, add a few drops of water, or if too thin add a little more sieved sugar. Use as required, adding flavouring and colouring to taste.

INFUSION. To infuse is to draw out flavour. Heat water or other liquid to steaming point, and put in the ingredient required. Cover with a lid and leave to stand in a warm place, usually from ten to fifteen minutes. Strain and use the flavoured liquid. This method is used for drawing flavour from lemon rind, bayleaves, stick cinnamon, etc.

INVALID APPLE PIE. 1 *large apple;* 1 *tablespoonful water; lemon juice; caster sugar;* 1 *plain sponge cake;* 1 *egg;* ½–¾ *gill milk;* 1 *teaspoonful sugar.*

Cook the apple with the water and sugar and beat it smooth, or the pulp of a baked apple may be used. Add lemon juice. Put the pulp at the bottom of a small greased fireproof dish, and lay the thinly sliced sponge cake on top. Beat the egg and sugar, add the milk and pour over the whole. Bake gently in a very moderate oven set at Mark 3 or 350 deg. F. for about thirty minutes, until the custard is set. Dredge lightly with sugar and serve in the dish.

INVALID COOKERY. Choose food which is easily digested and assimilated, yet sufficiently nourishing to strengthen. Have all food of the best quality and perfectly fresh, providing variety as far as possible, in food and in method of preparation. Do not prepare any food in the sickroom and do not allow the smell of cooking to penetrate to it.

Serve the food in small quantities and in individual portions when possible, and serve it very daintily. Do not leave food in the sickroom, but have something in readiness to serve if required. Season and flavour the food delicately, as overseasoning aggravates thirst.

Follow the doctor's directions about diet very carefully, and, in infectious illness, burn any remains of food from the sickroom, and disinfect crockery.

Steaming is the most digestible method of cooking, and later in convalescence this may be followed by grilling and stewing. Avoid frying, which is the least digestible method.

IRISH STEW. 1½ *lb. middle neck or knuckle of mutton;* ½ *lb. onions;* ¾–1 *pint water; salt and pepper;* 2 *lb. potatoes;* 1 *heaped teaspoonful chopped parsley.*

Cut the meat into joints or neat pieces. Put them in a saucepan with the cold water and bring to boiling point. Skim well. Add the peeled and sliced onions, add salt and pepper and rather less than half of the potatoes, cut in pieces. Simmer very gently for two to two and a half hours. When half-cooked arrange the remaining potatoes on top, whole unless very large, when they may be halved. Dish with the meat piled in the middle of a hot dish, the potatoes around it, and the liquid and onions poured over the meat. Scatter chopped parsley over the potatoes.

JAM MAKING. General instructions. Use firm, ripe, fresh fruit, avoiding that which is over-ripe. Use good sugar, and this may be either cane or beet sugar, granulated or loaf. Fruit should be allowed to simmer gently before the sugar is added. See that correct proportions of pectin, acid and sugar are used. Sugar should not be added until the fruit is well pulped; it is the fruit that needs thorough cooking and not the sugar. The exception to this rule is that, in the case of whole-fruit jams such as strawberry, all ingredients must be put together and heated gently with constant stirring. After the sugar has been added, boil the jam *briskly* until setting point is reached. Do not skim the jam until it is almost ready, as continuous skimming is wasteful.

Have the jam jars clean and well polished before filling, and also dry and warm. Fill the jars quite full with jam to allow for the slight shrinkage that will occur. To prevent whole fruit from rising in the jars, especially in the case of strawberries, allow the jam to cool in the preserving pan, then stir it up and fill into the jars. Either cover jam down at once, or when the jam is quite cold. In either case, put on the round of waxed tissue immediately, placing the waxed side downwards.

Wipe round the jars with a cloth wrung out from very hot water. Label and store in a cool dry store cupboard, away from light.

General method. Wash or wipe the fruit and pick it over. Put the fruit into a preserving pan with the required amount of water, over moderate heat, and simmer, stirring frequently until a thick pulp is obtained. Add sugar, withdrawing the pan from heat, and dissolve *completely*. Boil up, and boil briskly, stirring very slowly until the jam sets on trial. To test when jam is cooked, cool a little quickly in a saucer. Push the little finger through the centre, and the edges should crinkle, and the two parts should not flow together again. The drop of jam left on the finger should be firm enough to adhere. Pour into warm dry jars, and either cover down at once or when the jam is quite cold (see Fig. 25).

For the amount of water and sugar to allow, and times for cooking, see under individual recipes below. See also PECTIN.

JAM, apricot (fresh). 4 *lb. fresh apricots;* 4 *lb. sugar;* 1 *pint water.*

Wash fruit, cut in halves and remove stones. Crack some of the stones, remove kernels and add about five minutes before the jam

Fig. 25. General method of jam making: (a) *wipe the fruit and pick it over carefully, rejecting unsound or over-ripe fruit;* (b) *put fruit into a preserving pan with water and allow to simmer;* (c) *withdraw the preserving pan from the heat and add the sugar, which may be in granulated or loaf form;* (d) *boil briskly for the time stated in the recipe, stirring slowly, and skimming when boiling is nearly complete;* (e) *test when jam is ready by putting a little on a cool saucer and seeing if the edges crinkle when pushed with the finger;* (f) *use a jug to pour the jam into warm dry jars, cover the jam with waxed paper and place a further cover over the jar and tie down. Label, and store the jam in a cool cupboard, taking care that light is excluded from it.*

is ready. Approximate time for boiling, fifteen to twenty minutes. Follow the general instructions.

JAM, apricot (dried). 1 *lb. dried apricots;* 3 *lb. sugar;* 1 *oz. almonds (optional);* 3 *pints water; juice* 1 *lemon or* 1 *teaspoonful citric or tartaric acid.*

Wash the apricots and soak in three pints of water for twenty-four to forty-eight hours. Simmer the apricots in the same water with lemon juice or acid, for one and a half hours until tender. Withdraw from heat, add sugar and follow the general instructions. Add blanched split almonds when the jam is almost cooked. Approximate time for boiling, fifteen to twenty minutes.

JAM, blackberry and apple. 4 *lb. blackberries;* 1½ *lb. sour apples;* ½ *pint water; sugar.*

Peel, core and cut the apples into small chunks. Stew them until pulped with half of the water. Add the blackberries, the remaining water and cook until a soft pulp is formed. Weigh this and add an equal weight of sugar. Follow general instructions. Approximate time for boiling, twenty to twenty-five minutes. *Note:* if seedless jam is required, cook the blackberries separately with half of the water, and sieve before adding to apple pulp.

JAM, black-currant. 4 *lb. black-currants;* 6 *lb. sugar;* 2 *pints water.*

Remove stems and rinse fruit in cold water. Simmer gently until fruit is completely pulped and the contents of the pan are reduced. Follow general instructions. Approximate time to cook, twenty to twenty-five minutes.

JAM, cherry. 4 *lb. red cherries;* 3 *lb. sugar;* ½ *pint water;* 2 *tablespoonfuls lemon juice, or* 1 *teaspoonful citric or tartaric acid.*

Wash and stone the cherries. Tie the stones in muslin, and simmer with the fruit and water until the fruit is tender, about thirty minutes. Follow general instructions. Remove bag of stones, leave to cool and fill into jam jars. Approximate time for boiling, twenty to twenty-five minutes. *Note:* black cherries are better bottled, as they make a very sweet jam. If morello cherries are used, reduce the amount of acid to half.

JAM, damson. 4 *lb. damsons;* 6 *lb. sugar;* 1 *pint water.*

Remove stalks and wash the fruit. Follow general instructions, removing as many stones as possible as they rise to the surface. Approximate time to cook, fifteen to twenty minutes.

JAM, gooseberry. 3 *lb. green gooseberries;* 4 *lb. sugar;* 1 *pint water.*

Top and tail the gooseberries, wash them and follow general instructions for jam making. Cook slowly at first until the gooseberries begin to crack, then mash well with the spoon and cook until well reduced.

JAM, greengage or plum. 4 *lb. greengages or plums;* 4 *lb. sugar;* ½ *pint water.*

Wash the fruit, halve and stone it. A few kernels from cracked stones may be added towards the end of cooking. Follow general instructions. Approximate time for cooking, fifteen to twenty minutes.

JAM, loganberry or raspberry. 4 *lb. loganberries or raspberries;* 4 *lb. sugar.* Pick over the fruit and wash it. Follow general instructions, but no water is required. Stir the fruit continuously until tender right through, before adding the sugar. Approximate time for boiling, seven to ten minutes.

JAM, marrow. 4 *lb. prepared marrow;* 4 *lb. sugar; rind and juice* 3 *lemons, or* 1 *heaped teaspoonful citric or tartaric acid;* 2–3 *oz. dried root ginger.*

Cut the peeled marrow into cubes, place in a colander over a pan of boiling water and steam until just tender. Add the grated lemon rind and the juice, and arrange with the sugar in layers. Leave to stand until next day. Place in the preserving pan with the bruised ginger tied in muslin, and heat gently until the sugar has completely dissolved. Boil until the marrow is transparent and the syrup thick. Approximate time for cooking, thirty minutes.

JAM, rhubarb. 4 *lb. rhubarb after preparation;* 3 *lb. sugar;* ½ *gill water;* 2 *lemons, or scant* ¾ *pint red-currant or gooseberry juice.*

Cut the rhubarb into one-inch pieces. Put the water in the bottom of the preserving pan to prevent sticking. Add the squeezed lemon juice and rhubarb. Bring to boil and reduce the rhubarb to a thick pulp, frequently stirring to prevent sticking. Add the sugar and follow the general instructions. Fill into jars. If the fruit juice is used, add just before the sugar. Approximate time to cook, twenty minutes.

JAM, strawberry. 4 *lb. strawberries;* 3 *lb. sugar;* ½ *gill water;* 1 *tablespoonful lemon juice, or* 1 *teaspoonful citric or tartaric acid.*

Remove hulls and wash the strawberries quickly to avoid loosing juice. Put the water at the bottom of the preserving pan to prevent sticking, and add acid. Follow general instructions. Stir strawberries lightly to avoid crushing them, but make sure they are cooked right through before adding sugar. Small strawberries make the best jam. Approximate time to cook, twelve to fifteen minutes.

JAM PUDDING. 4 *oz. flour;* 2 *oz. crumb of stale bread;* 1 *gill milk and water;* 2 *oz. chopped suet;* 1 *level teaspoonful bicarbonate of soda;* 2 *teaspoonfuls lemon juice or vinegar;* 2 *tablespoonfuls red jam.*

Crumble the bread and soak it for an hour or more in the milk and water. Pass the flour and bicarbonate of soda through a sieve with a pinch of salt. Add the chopped suet. Beat the soaked bread smooth and add with the jam and lemon juice or vinegar. Put the mixture into a greased pudding basin, twist a greased paper over and steam for two and a half hours. Hot jam may be served with the pudding, or custard or jam sauce poured round (see JAM SAUCE and CUSTARD).

JAM SAUCE. 1 *gill water; scant* 1 *oz. sugar;* 1–2 *tablespoonfuls jam;* 1 *teaspoonful* *powdered arrowroot; juice ½ lemon; colouring if required.*

Simmer the water, sugar and jam together for about five minutes. Strain, return to saucepan and add the arrowroot mixed smoothly with a little water. Stir and boil gently for seven minutes, until the arrowroot becomes clear, and add the lemon juice. *Note:* cornflour can take the place of arrowroot, but does not make a clear sauce as does the well cooked arrowroot.

JELLY, milk. *½ pint milk; scant ½ oz. gelatine; flavouring; colouring (optional).*

Dissolve the gelatine in two tablespoonfuls of water (see GELATINE). Warm the milk slightly, add the sugar, flavouring, colouring if used and the gelatine. Stir gently until the jelly thickens creamily, and pour into coupe glasses.

JELLY, orange. *½ pint water; 3 oz. sugar; rind 3 oranges; ¾ oz. gelatine; ½ pint orange juice; juice 1 lemon; whipped cream or evaporated milk to decorate (optional).*

Scrub the oranges and peel them thinly. Put the water, sugar, orange rind and gelatine into a saucepan, and dissolve the gelatine (see GELATINE). Cover and leave to infuse for twenty minutes. Add the orange and lemon juices and strain. Colour may be improved by adding one or two drops of carmine or cochineal if liked. When cool, pour into a wet mould or into coupe glasses. When set the jelly is ready to turn out of the mould, or to serve in the glasses. Decorate if desired.

JELLY MAKING (for store). Suitable fruits for jelly making are crab apples, currants, gooseberries, loganberries, and quinces. These contain a good amount of pectin and acid and have good flavour. Cooking apples also make good jelly, but need the addition of flavouring, such as ginger, cloves, or lemon rind.

Wash the fruit carefully and remove any that is unsound. Berries need not be hulled, or the stems of currants removed. Large fruit, such as apples, need not be peeled or cored, but should be cut in pieces.

Cook the fruit in water. Small soft fruit needs a small quantity only, black-currants and gooseberries need more, and apples or crab apples should be barely covered with water in the preserving pan. Cook the fruit until soft and broken, when it is ready to strain. Tie an even-threaded teacloth to the legs of a stool or kitchen chair turned upside down on the kitchen table. Scald the cloth with boiling water, then pour on the pulped fruit. Allow to drip, overnight if possible, until all liquid has drained through. Allow three-quarters to one pint sugar to one pint of juice. Dissolve sugar and boil rapidly until set, following the points given in JAM MAKING.

JUNKET. *1 pint milk; 1 large teaspoonful rennet; 1 teaspoonful caster sugar; grated nutmeg.*

Warm the milk with the sugar to blood heat, stirring continuously so that it warms evenly. Pour into a glass bowl, stir in the rennet then leave the junket quite undisturbed to set, at normal kitchen temperature. Grate nutmeg over the surface, and, if available, a little half-whipped cream or evaporated milk may be poured over first.

KEDGEREE. *8 oz. cooked smoked haddock; 4 oz. Patna rice or crushed macaroni; scant ounce butter or margarine; salt and pepper; a little grated nutmeg; 1–2 hard-boiled eggs (optional); chopped parsley.*

Boil the rice or macaroni plainly. Skin, bone and flake the fish. Cut the eggs in pieces if used, and reserve half a yolk for garnish. Melt the butter or margarine, and add the fish, rice, seasoning and eggs. Heat thoroughly and form into a mound on a hot dish. Press the portion of hard-boiled egg yolk through a strainer over the mound, and encircle it with chopped parsley. *Note:* tinned fish, such as salmon, may be used instead of smoked fish. Or, if white fish is used, cook a level teaspoonful of curry powder in the melted fat for a minute before adding remaining ingredients.

KIDNEYS, grilled. *3–4 kidneys; 3–4 back rashers of bacon or bacon rolls* (see BACON ROLLS); *a little melted dripping, bacon fat or margarine; sprigs of watercress.*

Remove all fat and skin the kidneys, wash and dry them. Cut each on the bulging side, and open out, without cutting right through. Place a small skewer through each side of the opened kidney so that it will not close up during the grilling. Brush over with melted fat and grill on each side for about eight minutes in all. Do not overcook, or the kidneys will be tough. Dish with the bacon and garnish with sprigs of watercress.

KIDNEYS, stewed. *4 sheep's kidneys; 1 chopped shallot or 1 teaspoonful chopped onion; pinch mixed herbs; salt and pepper; scant 1 oz. dripping; 1 teaspoonful flour; ¼ pint household stock or vegetable water; bacon rolls (optional).*

Wash, skin and cut the kidneys into halves. Mix together the chopped shallot or onion, salt and pepper, and roll the slices in this. Fry lightly in the hot dripping, remove the slices and add the flour to the dripping. Fry until brown, remove from heat, stir in the stock, and stir until boiling. Put in the kidneys and simmer gently for half an hour. Serve on a hot dish, straining the sauce over. Garnish with rolls of bacon, if desired.

KIPPERS. Baked. Place the washed fish in a baking tin and cover with cold water, and then with another tin or an enamelled plate. Cook in a hot oven set at Mark 7 or 440 deg. F. for about fifteen minutes. Lift from the water with a fish slice, on to a hot dish.

Grilled. Immerse the kippers for one minute in very hot water, then remove and pat them dry. Spread a little dripping over, and grill for four minutes.

Poached. Place kippers in a frying pan and cover with cold water. Bring the water to boiling point, reduce heat and cook for a further two to three minutes. Lift from the water with a fish slice and serve on a hot dish.

KROMESKIES. 4 *oz. cooked veal, rabbit or chicken; 4 rashers streaky bacon; coating or fritter batter* (see FRITTER BATTER); *salt and pepper; grated lemon rind; lemon and parsley; binding sauce:* ½ *oz. margarine;* ½ *oz. flour;* ½ *gill milk; tomato or piquante sauce.*

Make a sauce with the margarine, flour and milk. Add the minced meat and season well, adding a little grated lemon rind. Leave to cool and make into eight cork-shaped rolls. Enclose each roll in a thin slice of bacon. Dip each roll in batter, and put into deep fat which is just beginning to smoke. Fry until crisp and brown, and allowing sufficient time thoroughly to cook the bacon, about ten to twelve minutes. Drain on crumpled paper, and pile in a hot dish, garnished with slices of lemon and fried parsley. Serve the sauce in a sauceboat separately.

LAMB, oven-roast. *Suitable joint for roasting* (see "The A.B.C. of Cookery"); *thin gravy,* ½ *pint for four people* (see GRAVY, THIN); *new potatoes; green peas; mint sauce.*

Follow the general method for oven-roasting meat. Serve it on a hot dish, with a little gravy poured round, and serve the accompaniments separately.

LEEKS, boiled. 6–8 *leeks;* ½ *pint white coating sauce* (see WHITE SAUCE); *slice of toast* (*optional*).

Trim off the roots of the leeks and the upper part of the green leaves, leaving about two inches of green above the solid part of the leek. Remove outer casing. Cut the leeks in two, lengthways, and wash well under running water to remove all mould. Tie in bundles and cook until tender in boiling salted water, about thirty minutes. Lift with a fish slice on to a hot dish to drain, then remove to a hot vegetable dish, with a piece of toast at the bottom if desired. Coat with the sauce.

LEMONADE. *To each large lemon allow:* ½ *pint boiling water;* ½ *pint cold or iced water;* 2 *tablespoonfuls sugar.*

Scrub the lemons and peel thinly. Put the rind with the sugar in a jug. Pour on boiling water, stir well, cover and leave until cold. Add the cold water and lemon juice. Strain into a glass jug and float two or three thin slices of lemon on top.

LEMON CURD. 2 *eggs;* ½ *lb. caster sugar;* 3 *oz. margarine or butter;* 2 *lemons.*

Beat the eggs and put them into a jug with the sugar, margarine and grated rind and juice of the lemons. Stand the jug in a saucepan of hot water and cook until the curd forms a coating on the back of the spoon. Remove jug from saucepan, stir frequently until the curd has cooled. Pour into a jam-jar and tie down as for jam.

LEMON PIE. 1 *baked flan case* (see FLAN CASE); *filling:* 1 *gill water;* 1 *oz. flour; yolks of* 2 *eggs;* 2 *oz. sugar; rind and juice* 1 *large lemon; meringue* (*optional*): *whites of* 2 *eggs;* 3–4 *oz. caster sugar.*

Prepare the flan case. Work together the egg yolks, sugar and flour, using a small wooden spoon. Pour on the boiling water, stirring briskly, return to saucepan and cook until thick. Cool slightly, then add the grated lemon rind and juice. Pour the mixture into the flan case and return to a cool oven to set the top, which should be quite smooth. If the meringue is used, prepare it (see MERINGUE) and heap it on top. Return to the oven to cook the meringue. Serve cold.

LEMON PUDDING. *Short pastry, made with* 3–4 *oz. flour, etc.* (see PASTRY, SHORT); 3 *oz. margarine;* 3 *oz. sugar;* 1 *egg; grated rind and juice* 1 *lemon;* 4 *oz. stale cake crumbs.*

Line the sides of a greased piedish with the pastry and decorate the edge. Cream the margarine, add the sugar and cream again. Beat in the egg by degrees. Fold in the cake crumbs, grated rind and juice of lemon. Pour into the prepared piedish, making the mixture level. Place in a hot oven, set at Mark 6 or 425 deg. F. for fifteen minutes, then reduce heat to Mark 4 until the mixture is firm, and the whole an even golden brown, about forty to forty-five minutes. Serve hot or cold.

LEMON SPONGE. *Whites of* 2 *eggs;* 2 *oz. caster sugar; rind of* 2 *lemons;* ½ *gill lemon juice; scant* ½ *oz. gelatine;* ½ *pint water.*

Dissolve the gelatine in the water, with the thinly peeled lemon rind and sugar. Cover and leave to infuse for ten minutes (see INFUSION). Strain into a basin, and when cooled add the strained lemon juice and whites, and whisk until stiff, fifteen to twenty minutes. Pile in a glass dish or coupe glasses at once. If preferred the mixture may be poured into a rinsed tin or enamelled mould, left to set and unmoulded like a jelly. In this case the sponge should not be so stiffly beaten. Decorate with pieces of glacé cherries and angelica if liked. *Note:* a custard may be made with the two yolks, etc., if desired, and served separately.

LIVER AND BACON, fried. ¼ *lb. streaky bacon;* ½ *lb. liver;* 2–3 *teaspoonfuls seasoned flour;* ½ *pint water or vegetable water.*

Trim the rind and rust from the rashers of bacon, and fry the bacon and rinds. Wash and dry the liver, cut into quarter-inch slices and roll in seasoned flour. Remove the bacon from the frying-pan and keep it hot. Re-heat the fat, adding a little more bacon fat or dripping if required. Fry the liver quickly on each side, then reduce heat and cook through gently, about ten to twelve minutes in all. Remove the liver to the hot dish, and drain off all but one dessertspoonful of fat. Add seasoned flour remaining, made up to two teaspoonfuls, and brown in the fat. Add the liquid, and stir and boil for five minutes. A teaspoonful of ketchup or Worcester sauce may be added, and seasoning. Arrange the liver with the bacon on top, and strain the gravy round.

LIVER, baked stuffed. ¾ *lb. liver;* 3–4 *rashers streaky bacon* (*optional*); *water or vegetable water; stuffing:* 1 *onion;* ¼ *pint fresh breadcrumbs; salt and pepper;* 1 *tablespoonful chopped parsley; pinch mixed herbs.*

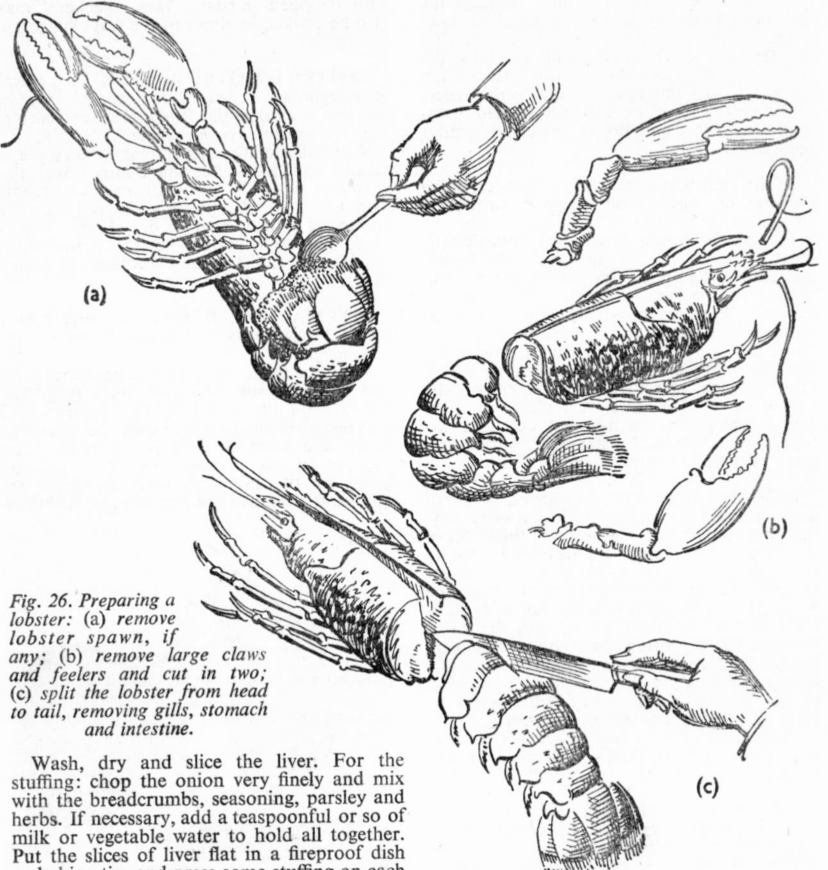

Fig. 26. Preparing a lobster: (a) *remove lobster spawn, if any;* (b) *remove large claws and feelers and cut in two;* (c) *split the lobster from head to tail, removing gills, stomach and intestine.*

Wash, dry and slice the liver. For the stuffing: chop the onion very finely and mix with the breadcrumbs, seasoning, parsley and herbs. If necessary, add a teaspoonful or so of milk or vegetable water to hold all together. Put the slices of liver flat in a fireproof dish or baking tin, and press some stuffing on each slice. Put a small thin piece of bacon on each, or a few shavings of dripping. Pour in liquid to come just to the top of the liver. Cook in a moderate oven set at Mark 4 or 375 deg. F. for forty-five minutes. Dish up the slices of liver, boil the stock, thicken it slightly by dredging in a little flour, add salt and pepper and a teaspoonful ketchup or Worcester sauce if liked. Pour round the liver.

LOBSTER, to prepare. Lobsters are in season all the year round, but are at their best and cheapest from April to October. Buy at a shop having a quick sale so that they are fresh and in good condition. A good lobster is heavy for its size and compact, and when the tail is lifted it springs back again rapidly.

Lobster spawn may be found beneath the tail of a hen lobster, and consists of a collection of tiny greenish-blue eggs. If these are not removed before the lobster is boiled, they become red, or heating gives the same result. Spawn, after heating, may be pounded with a little margarine and sieved, and beaten into a fish sauce or cooked salad dressing to give colour and flavour.

Lobster coral is the red matter, which is immature spawn, found in the body of a hen lobster. This may be removed, dried gently, rubbed through a sieve and used as garnish for any fish dish.

To prepare lobster for serving. Remove the large claws and feelers and cut off the head. *Remove and discard* the soft spongy matter which forms the gills, the sac-like stomach, and the intestine which runs like a vein down the tail of the lobster. This can be noted when the lobster is laid out flat and split from head to tail, which is the next process (see Fig. 26).

LOBSTER, plainly served. 1 *medium-sized lobster; French salad dressing; shredded lettuce; condiments; brown bread and butter.*

Prepare the lobster as described above. Stand the head upright in the middle of a dish, on some shredded lettuce. Arrange the split tail on either side, and the cracked claws pointing outwards at one end. To ensure that the flesh is not bruised while cracking the claws, take each into the hand in turn and tap gently with a small hammer. Bunch the feelers at the other end of the dish. Serve salad dressing, condiments and brown bread and butter separately.

LOBSTER SALAD. 1 *cooked lobster; salad dressing or mayonnaise; lettuce; cucumber; small cress or watercress; hard-boiled egg.*

Prepare the lobster (see above). Set aside the meat from the tips of the claws, the feelers and coral for garnish. Cut the lobster in small pieces, and season with salt and pepper or cayenne. Prepare the salad plants. Arrange a few lettuce leaves in the bottom of a salad bowl. Mix the lobster meat with a little of the dressing, and pieces of salad separately with a little dressing, and arrange in layers on the lettuce leaves. Decorate with pieces of salad and lobster claw, hard-boiled egg and the feelers. *Note:* tinned lobster may be used or a salad prepared from any kind of fish.

MACARONI, to cook. Macaroni, spaghetti and vermicelli are all cooked in the same way, the time varying with the size and thickness of the cereal. Also, any that has been kept in stock for some time will take a little longer to cook. Buy the cereal wrapped in cellophane paper, if possible, as it is better not to wash it. Cook in boiling salted water, with the lid of the pan slightly lifted, as it boils over very easily, and stir with a metal spoon occasionally to prevent sticking. When ready the material should be quite soft, but should keep its shape. Drain well, and use as required.

Average time for cooking: macaroni, twenty-five minutes; spaghetti, fifteen minutes; vermicelli, ten minutes.

MACARONI CHEESE. 3 *oz. macaroni;* ½ *oz. margarine;* ½ *oz. flour;* ¼ *pint milk;* ¼ *pint macaroni water; salt and pepper;* ½ *teaspoonful mixed mustard;* 3 *oz. grated cheese; croûtons of fried bread or toast.*

Cook and drain the macaroni (see above). Make a thin white sauce with the margarine, flour, milk and water in which the macaroni was cooked. Add the macaroni and seasonings to the sauce, then about two-thirds of the cheese. Turn into a greased fireproof or piedish, sprinkle the remaining cheese on top, and brown lightly under a grill. Decorate the edge with croûtons of fried bread or toast (see CROÛTONS).

MACKEREL, baked stuffed. 2 *mackerel;* 1 *tablespoonful veal stuffing* (see STUFFING, VEAL); 1 *oz. margarine.*

Prepare the mackerel as for herrings (see HERRINGS, PREPARATION OF). Split and bone them. Place one of the fish with the skin downwards, on a greased dish or tin, cover with the stuffing, place the other fish on top, skin upwards. Pour the melted margarine over, lay a greased paper on top and bake in a moderate oven set at Mark 5 or 400 deg. F. for thirty minutes. Serve in the dish, sprinkled with chopped parsley. *Note:* mackerel may also be cooked in either of the ways suggested for herrings.

MAÎTRE D'HÔTEL BUTTER. ½ *oz. butter or margarine;* 1 *heaped teaspoonful chopped parsley;* ½ *teaspoonful lemon juice or vinegar; salt; few grains cayenne pepper.*

Work all the ingredients together on a plate, using a rounded knife. Shape into a neat, flat cake and set aside in a cool place to become firm. Cut into small pieces and arrange on the surface of grilled meat or fish. If the food is really hot, as it should be, the butter melts quickly and moistens and flavours the grilled food.

MARMALADE. 6 *Seville oranges* (*about* 2 *lb.*); 2 *sweet oranges;* 1 *lemon;* 6 *pints water;* 6 *lb. sugar.*

Wash the fruit, cut in half, squeeze out juice and pips and slice the peel finely (Fig. 27). Put the fruit into a bowl, add the juice and the pips tied up in muslin, cover with the measured water, and leave for twenty-four hours. Next day put all into a preserving pan, and cook gently for two hours, or until the shreds are quite soft. Remove the bag of pips, withdraw

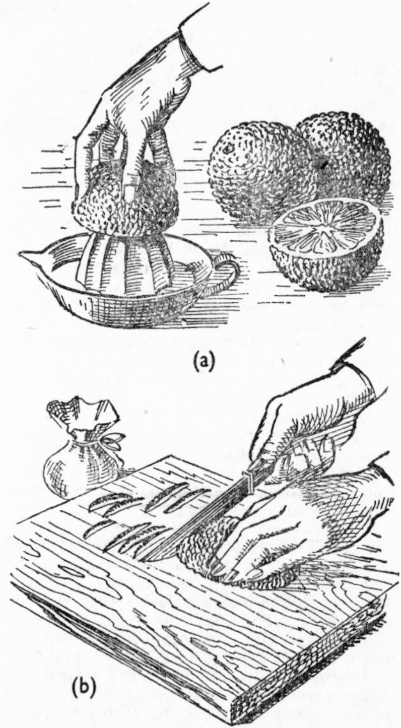

Fig. 27. Marmalade making: (a) *squeezing the juice;* (b) *slicing the peel. The pips are tied up in a muslin bag for use later.*

from heat and add sugar. When the sugar has completely dissolved, boil rapidly until setting point is reached, about twenty to thirty minutes. Allow to cool for ten minutes, then stir well and pour into dry, warm jars. Follow the rules for jam-making throughout, and tie down as for jam.

MARMALADE PUDDING. 4 *oz. flour;* 4 *oz. sugar;* 4 *oz. fresh breadcrumbs;* 4 *oz. suet;* 1 *egg;* 2 *tablespoonfuls marmalade* (5 *oz.*); 1 *level teaspoonful bicarbonate of soda; about* 1 *gill milk; marmalade or sweet white sauce* (see MARMALADE and WHITE SAUCES).

Mix together the flour, sugar, breadcrumbs and finely chopped suet. Beat the egg, add the marmalade, and dissolve the bicarbonate of soda in the milk. Add and mix all well together. Pour into a greased pudding basin and steam for two and a half hours. Unmould and pour the sauce chosen around the pudding.

MARMALADE SAUCE. 1 *gill water; scant oz. sugar;* 1–2 *tablespoonfuls marmalade;* 1 *teaspoonful powdered arrowroot; juice* ½ *lemon.*

Make as for jam sauce, but do not strain.

MAYONNAISE. *Yolk of* 1 *egg; salt and pepper;* ¼ *teaspoonful dry mustard;* 2 *teaspoonfuls vinegar;* ¼ *pint salad oil.*

Work together the yolk of egg and seasonings in a small basin. Add the oil drop by drop from the point of a teaspoon, and, using a small wooden spoon, stir all the time. As the mayonnaise thickens, add a few drops of vinegar and the oil may then be added a trifle faster, but continue to add it from the point of a spoon. While working, wrap a damp cloth round the basin, as this keeps the ingredients cool and helps to steady the basin. When all the oil has been worked in, add the remaining vinegar gradually.

MEAT PATTIES. *Rough puff, flaky, or short pastry, made with* 8 *oz. flour, etc.* (see PASTRY); 4 *oz. raw veal;* 1 *oz. ham or bacon; salt and pepper;* 1 *teaspoonful chopped parsley;* ¼ *teaspoonful grated lemon rind; a little stock or water;* 1 *hard-boiled egg; egg or milk to brush over; sprigs of parsley.*

Prepare the pastry. Cut the veal into very small dice or mince it, also the ham or bacon. Mix in the seasoning, chopped parsley, and a small tablespoonful of stock to moisten. Line six patty tins with the pastry, following the method for mince pies (see MINCE PIES). Put a mound of meat mixture into each, and one or two pieces of hard-boiled egg. Work up the trimmings of pastry, roll out thinly and cut out a ring with two small cutters, to decorate the top of each patty. Make a hole in the centre of each. Brush tops with beaten egg or milk. Bake in a hot oven set at Mark 7 or 440 deg. F. for the first twenty minutes, then lessen the heat and continue cooking for three-quarters of an hour in all. Serve hot or cold. The patties make a good dish for a packed lunch. *Note:* cooked meat may be used, but in this case mix with white sauce or thickened gravy. Bake for thirty minutes. Beef may be substituted for veal, in which case use two teaspoonfuls of finely chopped onion in place of the ham.

MEAT RISSOLES. ½ *oz. dripping or margarine;* ½ *oz. flour;* ¼ *gill stock;* ¼ *lb. cooked minced meat; salt and pepper;* 1 *teaspoonful chopped parsley, or* 1 *teaspoonful Worcester sauce, or* 1 *tablespoonful chopped cooked onion; short pastry, made with* 4 *oz. flour, etc.* (see PASTRY, SHORT); *egg or substitute, and dried crumbs for coating.*

Make the meat mixture as described under DURHAM CUTLETS, but add an extra tablespoonful of stock to make it a trifle softer. Make the pastry and roll it out very thinly. Cut into rounds of about four inches diameter. Put a little of the meat mixture on each, damp the edges, fold in half and seal the edges well. Coat and fry in deep fat, which is just beginning to smoke, for ten to twelve minutes, to cook the pastry, turning the rissoles occasionally. Drain and garnish with fried parsley

MERINGUE TO COVER PUDDINGS. *To each white of egg allow* 1½–2 *oz. caster sugar.*

Whisk the white very stiff and dry, add one teaspoonful of the sugar and whisk for a few seconds. Remove whisk and shower on the remaining sugar, folding it in very lightly. Heap the meringue very quickly on to the pudding, dredge with caster sugar, and put the pudding at once into a cool oven, set at Mark ½ or 275 deg. F. The meringue should become evenly biscuit-coloured and crisp. *Note:* the egg should not be whisked or the meringue made until required for baking.

MILK PUDDING, long method. Suitable for large grains, such as rice, tapioca, sago or crushed macaroni: 2 *oz. cereal;* 1 *oz. sugar;* 1 *pint milk; grated nutmeg; tiny shavings of margarine.*

Wash the grain and put it in a greased piedish. Add sugar, pour over the milk and allow to stand for thirty minutes. Stir well, float margarine and grated nutmeg on the surface. Place in a cool oven set at Mark 2 or 325 deg. F., or put in the bottom of the oven when other cooking is in progress. Cook for two to two and a half hours until the consistency is of soft creamy pulp. *Note:* an egg may be added to the pudding. In this case omit the margarine, and stir the pudding occasionally while cooking to prevent a skin from forming on the surface. When cooked, beat in a whisked egg after cooling the pudding somewhat, and return to the oven for twenty minutes to set the egg.

MILK PUDDING, short method. Suitable for fine grain such as semolina or seed tapioca, or powder such as cornflour, ground rice or arrowroot: 2 *oz. cereal;* 1 *oz. sugar;* 1–2 *eggs; few drops flavouring essence; 1 pint milk.*

If a powdered grain is used, mix it smoothly first with some of the milk. Heat the milk with the sugar, and sprinkle in the cereal or add mixed cereal. Stir until boiling, and stir and simmer for ten minutes. Allow to cool, add the beaten egg and essence. Pour into a greased piedish and bake in a moderate oven, set at

Mark 5 or 400 deg. F., for twenty minutes, until puffed and golden-brown.

MINCED COLD MEAT. 1 *lb. cooked minced meat;* ¾ *pint brown sauce* (see BROWN SAUCE); *salt and pepper;* 4 *oz. macaroni or* ¾ *lb. mashed potatoes; chopped parsley; croûtons of toast* (see CROÛTONS).

Make the brown sauce and allow it to cool. Add the minced, seasoned meat and allow to re-heat thoroughly without boiling. Cook the macaroni, or prepare the mashed potato, and arrange in a border round a hot dish. Pile the mince in the middle, sprinkle with chopped parsley and garnish with the toast. *Note:* baked tomato halves or fried or grilled mushrooms can be used to garnish the dish further.

MINCEMEAT, economical. ¼ *lb. sultanas;* ¼ *lb. currants;* ¼ *lb. dates or raisins;* ¼ *lb. sliced apples;* ¼ *lb. sliced carrots;* 2–3 *oz. sugar;* 3 *oz. chopped suet;* 1 *level teaspoonful mixed spice;* ½ *teaspoonful lemon essence; few drops almond essence.*

Clean the currants and sultanas. Stone and slice dates or stone raisins. Mix these ingredients with the sliced apples and carrots and pass all through a mincing machine. Add remaining ingredients, and mix all very well. Press the mincemeat into dry jam jars and cover down as for jam. *Note:* this mincemeat will be liable to ferment if kept for more than two to three weeks, and must be stored in a cool place.

MINCEMEAT, rich. 1 *lb. apples;* 1 *lb. raisins;* 1 *lb. sultanas;* 1 *lb. currants;* ½ *lb. mixed peel;* 1 *lb. suet; grated rind and juice* 1 *lemon;* ¾ *lb. brown sugar;* 1 *teaspoonful mixed spice;* ½ *nutmeg grated;* ½–1 *gill brandy, rum or whisky;* 2 *oz. ground or shredded almonds.*

Make as for MINCEMEAT, economical. If the mincemeat is securely covered—and glass-lidded preserving jars are best for the purpose—it will store for two to three months.

MINCE PIES. *Flaky, rough puff or short pastry, made with* 8 *oz. flour, etc.* (see PASTRY); *about* ¾ *lb. mincemeat* (see above); 1 *tablespoonful milk or water; caster sugar to dredge.*

Roll out the pastry to a scant quarter-inch thickness and cut into rounds with a cutter of the size of the tops of the patty tins to be used. Gather the trimmings together, and roll them out as thinly as it is possible. Cut out rounds with a cutter of one size larger and line the patty tins with these. Put a teaspoonful of mincemeat in a mound in the centre of each. Damp the edges, and press on the tops, which are the smaller, thicker pieces. Flake the edges, make a small cut in each. Bake in a hot oven, set at Mark 7 or 440 deg. F., for rough puff or flaky pastry, or Mark 6 for short pastry. Bake for twenty-five to thirty minutes, slackening the heat towards the end of cooking. Brush the pies with milk or water, and dredge with sugar. Put the pies back into the oven for a minute or two to dry the glaze.

MINT SAUCE. 3 *heaped tablespoonfuls chopped mint;* 1 *dessertspoonful caster sugar;* 2 *tablespoonfuls boiling water;* 1 *gill vinegar.*

Pick the mint leaves from the stems, wash, dry, shred, then chop very finely with the sugar. Add the boiling water, stir and allow to stand until cold. Stir in the vinegar and serve in a sauceboat.

MIREPOIX. 1 *oz. margarine;* 1 *rasher of streaky bacon;* 2 *large carrots;* 2 *large onions;* 1 *large turnip;* 2–3 *sticks celery;* ½–¾ *pint stock; bouquet garni* (see BOUQUET GARNI).

Melt the margarine and fry the bacon in it to remove fat (bacon rinds only may be used, as an economy). Add the vegetables cut into slices half an inch thick, and cook for ten minutes to absorb the fat. Add sufficient stock to cover the vegetables and the bouquet garni. Boil up. This mirepoix forms the bed of vegetables on which braising is carried out, the vegetables, herbs and stock providing the flavoured steam in which the food to be braised is cooked. See also pages 280-1.

MOCK CREAM. 1 *oz. margarine;* 1 *oz. caster sugar;* ¼ *pint cold stiff custard, made with powder; flavouring essence.*

Cream the margarine thoroughly, add the sugar and cream again. Add a little custard at a time, beating well until all is beaten in. Flavour, and use as required.

MULLIGATAWNY SOUP. 1 *lb. lean mutton or rabbit,* 1 *quart water or* 1 *quart meat stock* (see STOCK, BONE); 2 *heaped teaspoonfuls curry powder;* 1 *oz. dripping;* 1 *onion;* 1 *oz. flour;* 1 *dessertspoonful coconut;* 1 *large apple; lemon juice; salt;* 1 *dessertspoonful chutney;* 2 *oz. rice.*

If meat is used, cut it into small pieces, dip in the curry powder and fry it lightly in the dripping. Remove meat from pan, add chopped onion and fry, then add the flour. Stir in the coconut. Add liquid and salt, stir until boiling and return the meat, with the chutney and chopped apple. Simmer for two hours, skimming when necessary. Strain on a sieve, add lemon juice, pieces of meat and re-heat. Dish the plain boiled rice separately and hand with the soup.

MUSHROOMS, fried. ½ *lb. mushrooms;* 1 *oz. bacon fat, dripping or margarine; salt and pepper; chopped parsley.*

Remove the stems, wash the mushrooms quickly in salted water, and pat dry in a cloth. Peel the outer side of the cap. Melt the fat in a frying pan, and fry the mushrooms on each side until tender, about ten minutes in all. Drain and serve as required. Fried mushrooms can be served with grilled or fried bacon, on buttered toast, as filling for an omelette, etc.

MUSHROOMS, grilled. Prepare mushrooms as for frying (see above). Sprinkle with salt and pepper and brush over with oiled margarine or bacon fat. Place on a heated greased grid, and grill under moderate heat, turning them once, until tender, about eight to ten minutes. Serve with fried or grilled bacon, grilled steak, etc.

MUSTARD SAUCE. ½ *pint white sauce* (see WHITE SAUCE, FOUNDATION); 1 *teaspoonful* *dry mustard, mixed with the flour; ½–1 teaspoonful vinegar.*

Mix the dry mustard with the flour, and make the sauce in the usual way. Add the vinegar last. Serve with boiled beef, or boiled mackerel or herrings.

MUTTON, boiled. *½ leg mutton, knuckle end; 2 carrots; 2 turnips; 2 onions; ¾ pint caper or parsley sauce* (see CAPER and PARSLEY SAUCES); *chopped parsley.*

Wipe, trim and weigh the meat. Place it with the best side downwards in just enough boiling salted water to cover. Bring to boiling point and skim. Boil gently for five minutes. Add the vegetables, whole or cut in large pieces. Simmer for the remaining cooking time. Allow twenty minutes to each pound and twenty minutes over for a joint weighing three pounds or more. Allow one and a half hours for a smaller piece. Lift the meat on to a hot dish, and press with soft paper to dry the top. Coat with the sauce chosen, and garnish with blocks of vegetable sprinkled with chopped parsley. Serve with some broth in a sauceboat, skimmed, seasoned and sprinkled with chopped parsley.

MUTTON, boned stuffed shoulder. *1 small shoulder of mutton; ½ pint thick gravy* (see GRAVY, THICK); *sage-and-onion stuffing* (see STUFFING); *browned potatoes* (see POTATOES, BROWNED).

Make a cut down the length of the knuckle. Loosen the flesh round the bone, working the knife close to the bone. Cut the flesh from the other end, following the line of the bone. Draw out the bone. Put the stuffing into the cavity, and truss it to a neat, plump shape with skewers and string. Follow the general method for roasting meat, allowing the extra time (see "The A.B.C. of Cookery"). Pour a little of the gravy round the meat on a hot dish and serve the remainder in a sauceboat. Serve the browned potatoes in a hot vegetable dish.

MUTTON BROTH. *¼ lb. knuckle or scrag of mutton; 1 tablespoonful pearl barley; carrot, turnip and onion; salt and pepper; 1 teaspoonful chopped parsley; 1 pint cold water.*

Wipe the meat and cut it off the bone, removing all fat; cut the meat into small dice. Put the meat, bone and salt into a saucepan with the water, bring slowly to boiling point, and skim. Add the blanched barley (see BLANCHING). Simmer for two hours, adding the diced vegetables at half-time. Remove the bone, skim, add the chopped parsley, boil up and serve.

MUTTON CUTLETS. *Piece of best end of neck, with five long bones; egg and coating crumbs; about 2 oz. dripping for frying; ½ pint tomato or brown sauce* (see TOMATO and BROWN SAUCES); *cooked vegetables to garnish.*

Cut off the chine bone and divide the meat between the long bones. Trim excess fat off each cutlet, and clear the flesh from about one inch of bone at the end. Coat with egg (or coating substitute) and dried breadcrumbs. Fry briskly at first, on each side, in smoking hot fat, reduce heat and cook for about ten minutes in all. Drain and dish the cutlets, leaning one against the other. Pour the sauce round, and garnish with a small heap of cooked vegetables, such as small brussels sprouts, green peas, etc., at each side.

MUTTON, haricot. *1 lb. best end neck or middle neck; 1½ oz. dripping; 1 oz. flour; 1 onion; 1 carrot; 1 turnip; salt and pepper; ¾ pint household stock or vegetable water; 2 oz. haricot beans.*

Soak the beans overnight, and cook (see BEANS, HARICOT). Divide the meat into cutlets. Cook as for STEWED STEAK. Pile the cooked haricot beans at each end of the dish, and diced vegetables at each side.

MUTTON, oven-roast. *Suitable joint for roasting* (see "The A.B.C. of Cookery"); *thin gravy, ½ pint for four people* (see GRAVY, THIN); *browned potatoes* (see POTATOES, BROWNED); *red-currant jelly or onion sauce.*

Follow the general method for oven-roasting. Serve the joint on a hot dish with a little of the gravy poured round, the remainder in a sauceboat, and the accompaniments separately.

NUT CUTLETS. *4 oz. mixed dried nuts or dried walnuts; 2 oz. fresh breadcrumbs; 1 oz. margarine; 1 oz. flour; 1 gill milk; 1 small cooked onion; 1 teaspoonful chopped parsley; few drops lemon juice; salt and pepper.*

Pass the nuts through a nut mill, or chop them finely. Make a panada with the margarine, flour and milk (see PANADA). Add the nuts to it with the breadcrumbs, chopped onion, parsley and seasoning. Heat and bind well together. Form into cutlet-shaped pieces with egg and dried crumbs and fry in deep fat until golden-brown. Garnish with fried parsley and serve with tomato sauce.

OATCAKES. *7 oz. fine oatmeal; 1 oz. flour; ½ teaspoonful salt; 1 oz. lard or dripping, melted; boiling water.*

Mix the oatmeal, flour and salt. Add the melted fat and just sufficient boiling water to form a stiff dough. Roll out very thinly on a board dusted with fine oatmeal, and cut into triangles. Place on a greased tin, and put into a moderate oven, set at Mark 4 or 375 deg. F., for thirty minutes until crisp.

OMELETTE, cheese. *3 eggs; salt and pepper; 1 tablespoonful milk; 1 oz. cheese; ¾ oz. butter or margarine.*

Add the grated cheese to the egg mixture. Prepare and fry as for French omelette (see below). Sprinkle with grated cheese and serve at once.

OMELETTE, fish. *Puffed omelette, made and cooked as described below; 2 oz. cooked fish; 1 tablespoonful white sauce* (see WHITE SAUCE, FOUNDATION); *salt and pepper; 1 teaspoonful anchovy essence; 1 teaspoonful chopped parsley.*

Remove skin and bones from fish, flake it and add a few flakes to the yolks. Heat the remainder in the sauce and keep it warm while preparing the omelette. When cooked, invert the omelette on to a hot dish, put the fish filling on to it and fold over.

OMELETTE, French. 3 *eggs;* ¾ *oz. butter or margarine;* 1 *tablespoonful water, milk or cream; salt and pepper;* ½ *teaspoonful chopped parsley.*

Have everything in readiness for mixing, frying and dishing, before beginning work. For the above quantities have a thick, smooth frying-pan of six inches diameter. Melt a nut of lard in the pan, and heat it until smoking hot, running the fat over the bottom and sides of the pan, so that the whole is well heated and greased. Pour off the fat. Put in the butter in readiness for frying the omelette. Beat the eggs and add liquid chosen, seasoning and parsley. Skim the butter and, when just smoking hot, add the egg mixture. Stir the top briskly, using a fork held flat and not touching the bottom of the pan. Push the mixture towards the centre; any mixture which is not set will run out at the sides and set quickly, and can be added to the middle of the omelette. Push the omelette to the far side of the pan, folding it into three. Allow the underside to colour for half a minute, then tip it over on to a hot dish. Serve at once. *Note:* if a sweet omelette is required, omit seasoning and parsley, and add one teaspoonful of sugar. A small tablespoonful of jam may be put in, if thought desirable, just before the last fold.

OMELETTE, kidney. *French omelette, prepared and cooked as described above; kidney sauté:* 1 *sheep's kidney;* ½ *oz. margarine; salt and pepper.*

Skin and wash the kidney, remove core and cut the kidney in pieces. Fry in the melted margarine for a few minutes until tender. Prepare the omelette and put in the kidney sauté before making the last fold.

OMELETTE, puffed. 3 *eggs;* 2 *teaspoonfuls caster sugar; few drops vanilla essence; small tablespoonful hot jam;* ½ *oz. margarine.*

Grease a six-inch frying-pan with lard as for French omelette (see above), then brush it out thickly with well skimmed margarine or butter. Cream the yolks of the eggs with the sugar and vanilla essence. Whisk the whites stiffly and fold them in. Pour the mixture into the prepared pan and shake for a minute or two over gentle heat until set at the bottom. Place the pan into a hot oven or under a hot grill until the top is set and golden-brown colour. Turn the omelette on to a piece of sugared paper, place the heated jam in the centre, fold in half and serve at once. *Note:* if a savoury puffed omelette is required, omit sugar and vanilla essence, and use a savoury filling in place of the jam.

ONION SAUCE. ½ *pint white sauce, made with half milk and half onion-water;* 1 *large onion; salt and pepper.*

Blanch the onion (see BLANCHING), cut in quarters, and boil in salted water until tender. Make the white sauce, using some of the water in which the onion was cooked. Add the chopped onion, re-heat and season.

ONIONS, boiled. 1–1½ *lb. even-sized onions;* ½ *pint white coating sauce.*

Skin and blanch the onions (see BLANCHING). Put them into boiling salted water, and boil gently until tender, about thirty minutes, unless they are very large. Drain well and coat with white sauce.

OXTAIL, stewed. 1 *oxtail;* 1 *carrot;* 1 *onion;* 1 *turnip;* 1 *stick of celery;* 1 *oz. dripping;* 1 *oz. flour;* 1 *quart stock* (see STOCK, HOUSEHOLD); *bouquet garni* (see BOUQUET GARNI); *salt and pepper.*

Divide the oxtail into pieces and blanch them (see BLANCHING). Roll the pieces in flour and fry them until golden-brown. Make a brown gravy with the dripping, flour and stock (see GRAVY, THICK). Add the pieces of tail and the vegetables cut in large pieces. Cover closely and simmer until tender, about four hours. Put the meat and vegetables on a hot dish, and pour the gravy over. *Note:* if rich flavour is desired, two tablespoonfuls of port wine, and two teaspoonfuls of red-currant jelly may be added a quarter of an hour before the stew is ready.

Fig. 28. Opening an oyster. Force the point o a knife between the shells. Press the knife in and towards the edge of the shells and twist.

OYSTERS. The season for oysters is from September to the end of April. Oysters should be opened (as shown in Fig. 28) and eaten immediately to prevent deterioration of their flavour. (See HORS D'OEUVRE.)

PANADA. 1 *oz. margarine or dripping;* 1 *oz. flour;* ¼ *pint milk or stock.*

Melt the fat, withdraw from heat and stir in the flour. Return to heat and cook well for a few minutes, but do not brown. Again remove from heat, add the liquid gradually and stir until boiling. Boil until a very thick smooth paste is formed, stirring meanwhile. Use for binding ingredients together, as in Durham cutlets.

PANCAKES. ½ *pint pancake batter* (see BATTER); *lemon juice; about* 1 *oz. lard for frying; caster sugar; fingers of lemon.*

Make the pancake batter and set aside in a cool place for an hour. Stir well and pour into a jug or measure. Melt the lard in a small frying-pan and, when smoking hot, pour it all off into a small basin. At once pour in sufficient batter to cover the bottom of the pan thinly. Shake the pan while cooking and loosen the edges of the pancake with a knife. Fry golden-brown, then turn the pancake by slipping a broad knife under it, and fry the second side. Invert the pancake on to a sugared paper. Dredge lightly with sugar and sprinkle with lemon juice, roll up and keep hot, while frying the remainder of the pancakes in the same way. As soon as the pancake is removed, put in the lard and leave it to heat while flavouring and rolling the next pancake. Dish in a lattice on a paper doily, on a very hot dish, and serve as soon as possible garnished with lemon fingers, made by cutting a lemon lengthways into eight pieces.

PARBOILING. Parboiling means cooking by putting food into boiling water, for the stated length of time, the cooking being completed by another process. This term is often confused with blanching, which is quite another process and carried out for different reasons (see BLANCHING).

PARSLEY SAUCE. *½ pint sauce* (see WHITE SAUCE, FOUNDATION); *2 heaped teaspoonfuls finely chopped parsley.*

Pick the leaves off the main stems and wash the parsley. Squeeze it dry, shred, then chop finely. Add to the sauce when it is completely cooked.

PARSNIPS. *6 medium-sized parsnips; a little margarine and chopped parsley or ½ pint white coating sauce.*

Scrub the parsnips and peel them thinly. Cut in quarters lengthways and, if old, trim off the hard centre. Cook in boiling salted water until tender, about thirty to forty-five minutes according to age and size. Either toss the pieces in a little margarine and chopped parsley, or coat with white sauce. For parsnips au gratin, cook the parsnips as above, add cheese to the sauce, coat and finish as described under CAULIFLOWER AU GRATIN. For baked parsnips, parboil for fifteen minutes, then bake as for POTATOES, BROWNED.

PASTRY CASE. This process is used when it is desired to prepare a cooked pastry case into which to put a filling, either savoury or sweet. Line a sandwich tin or flan ring with short pastry, preferably choosing the rich variety containing some egg, which makes the pastry more binding and so provides a better shaped case. Prick the bottom, and cover with a piece of greased paper with the greased side downwards. Fill the space with small pieces of broken crust, to weight the pastry down and so prevent it from rising. Bake in an oven set at Mark 6 or 425 deg. F. until the pastry is set and brown. Remove crusts and paper and return the case to the oven reduced to Mark 4 to dry the centre. The pastry case is then ready to receive any cooked filling, either hot or cold.

PASTRY, cheese. *4 oz. flour; 2 oz. margarine; 2–2½ oz. finely grated cheese; salt and few grains cayenne; ½ egg yolk; about 1 tablespoonful water.*

Rub the fat into the flour, as for short pastry (see below). Add the cheese and seasoning. Beat the yolk and water together, and mix all to a stiff paste. Use for cheese biscuits, or as a foundation for savouries.

PASTRY, choux. *2 oz. flour; 1 oz. margarine; 1 gill water; pinch salt; few drops vanilla essence; 1 egg and ½ yolk.*

Dry the flour and pass it through a sieve on to a piece of paper. Put the margarine and water into a saucepan and boil up. Draw the saucepan aside and at once slide the flour into it, all at once. Beat until smooth. There should be sufficient heat in the mixture to cook it. Test by pressing a finger on the mixture, none of which should stick to it, and the pastry should have formed a ball. If necessary, cook for a further minute or two, but overcooking will cause the fat to separate and make the pastry heavy. Add the salt and vanilla essence and, when cooled, beat in the half yolk, then the beaten egg by degrees. When the pastry is ready it should be soft but not at all liquid. Use for making éclairs.

PASTRY, flaky. *8 oz. flour; 2½–3 oz. margarine; 2½ oz. lard; pinch of salt; water to mix.*

Sieve the flour and salt. Divide the lard in half and the margarine in half, making four portions of fat. Rub in one portion of margarine as for short pastry, and mix all to a soft and pliable, but not sticky, dough, with cold water. Put the pastry on to a floured board or slab, and knead lightly to a smooth ball. Roll out to a square-cornered oblong strip, and put one portion of lard in small upsticking pieces over the top two-thirds of the strip. Dredge lightly with flour. Fold up the plain piece of pastry, and fold the top piece down on to it. Seal the edges heavily with the rolling-pin, and give the piece of pastry a half-turn, so that the top fold comes to the left hand. Roll again to a strip, and repeat, using the remaining margarine; dredge, fold and turn as before. Repeat using the remaining lard. Set the pastry aside in a cool place for an hour before shaping and baking. Bake flaky pastry in a hot oven set at Mark 7 or 440 deg. F.

PASTRY, hot-water. *4 oz. flour; pinch of salt and of pepper; 1–1½ oz. lard; ½ gill (good measure) milk or milk and water.*

Warm the flour, sieve it into a warm basin with the salt and pepper, and make a well in the centre. Heat the lard with the milk until boiling, pour it into the well, and mix with a wooden spoon. Knead with the hand as soon as the pastry is sufficiently cool. Use the pastry for making raised pies. Bake in a moderate oven, set at Mark 5 or 400 deg. F.

PASTRY, puff. *8 oz. flour; 8 oz. margarine or butter; pinch of salt; 2 teaspoonfuls lemon juice or ¼ teaspoonful cream of tartar; water.*

If the butter is salt, wash it well and squeeze it in the corner of a floured cloth. Otherwise, cream it (or margarine) on a plate to make it pliable. Cut off a piece of the fat used of the size of a walnut and rub it into the sieved flour and salt. Make the remaining fat into a flat oblong cake on a plate and lightly flour the top. Mix the flour with the lemon juice and water to a pliable dough. If cream of tartar is used, sieve it with the flour. Knead the ball of dough lightly to a smooth ball, and roll it out to a square. Invert the cake of fat on to it, lightly flour the top and cover with the remaining pastry. Seal the edges. Roll out to a square-cornered oblong strip, keeping the sides straight. Fold up the lower third and fold the top third down. Seal the edges and turn the pastry half round, so that the fold is to the left. Continue the rolling and folding until the pastry has been rolled out seven times after the fat was placed on the dough. Put the pastry aside to cool for ten to fifteen minutes between each two rollings. Leave between two floured plates for a couple of hours to mellow. Use for patty cases, mince pies, etc.

PASTRY, rich short. *8 oz. flour; 5 oz. margarine or butter; 1 teaspoonful icing or caster sugar (optional); yolk of 1 egg; water.*
Method as for short pastry (see below), adding the sugar, if used, after the fat has been rubbed in. Beat up the yolk with the water for mixing. Use for flans, tartlets, cheesecakes, or for covering fruit tarts to be served cold. Oven temperature as for short pastry.

PASTRY, rough puff. *8 oz. flour; 5–6 oz. margarine; 2 teaspoonfuls lemon juice; pinch of salt; water to mix.*
Sieve the flour and salt. Add the margarine in pieces the size of walnuts, being careful not to break up the pieces in the process of mixing. Mix, without rubbing in the fat, with the lemon juice and water to make a fairly stiff dough. When mixed, press the pastry together, and do not knead it. Roll out into a square-cornered oblong strip, keeping the sides straight. Fold up the lower piece of pastry, leaving a third clear, which fold downwards. Seal the edges together with a rolling-pin. Set the pastry aside in a cool place for ten minutes. Put the pastry with the fold to the left, roll again to an oblong strip. Again repeat folding, sealing and cooling. Repeat rolling, folding, sealing and cooling. The pastry will now have been rolled out three times and folded, and it is now ready to roll out to the shape required. Bake rough puff pastry in a hot oven set at Mark 7 or 440 deg. F. Use for meat pies, mince pies, sausage rolls, cheesecakes, etc.

PASTRY, short. *8 oz. flour; pinch of salt; 2 oz. margarine; 2 oz. lard; water to mix.*
Pass flour and salt through a sieve. Put in the fats, which should be firm, and neither hard nor oily. Cut the fat into the flour with a knife, then rub it in lightly with the finger-tips. Make a well in the middle and add the water gradually, mixing with a rounded knife. Flours vary in the amount of water they will absorb, but for pastry based on eight ounces flour, the amount needed will be about three-quarters of a gill. When about half of the ingredients have been blended, remove the knife and finish mixing with the hand, to make a firm but not hard dough. Put on to a floured board or slab, then mould lightly and quickly to a smooth ball. Bake in a hot oven set at Mark 6 or 425 deg. F.

PASTRY, suet. *8 oz. flour; 3–4 oz. chopped suet; 1 teaspoonful baking powder; large pinch of salt; cold water to mix.*
Sieve the flour, salt and baking powder. Shred and chop the suet, using some of the weighed flour and removing all skin. Add suet to the flour, mix and make a well in the centre. Add water gradually, and mix until the ingredients are bound firmly together. Turn on to a floured board and knead lightly for a few moments to a smooth ball. Suet pastry may be either boiled, steamed or baked, and is used for lining pudding basins for meat or fruit puddings, roly-poly, etc.

PATTIES, chicken or lobster. *8–10 baked patty cases* (see below)*; 4–6 oz. chopped chicken or lobster meat; sprigs of parsley or small cress to garnish; sauce: 1 oz. margarine; 1 oz. flour; 1 gill milk; salt and pepper; few drops lemon juice; 1 tablespoonful evaporated or top milk. For lobster patties, add 1 teaspoonful anchovy essence.*
Make the sauce (see WHITE SAUCE, FOUNDATION). Add the prepared chicken or lobster, fill into the prepared cases, garnish and serve.

PATTY CASES. Prepare puff pastry (see PASTRY, PUFF) and roll it out a scant half-inch thick. Cut into rounds of two and a quarter inches diameter. With a cutter of one-inch diameter cut half-way through each round of pastry, in the middle. Work up the trimmings, roll out a quarter-inch thick and cut a lid for each patty with the one-inch cutter. Leave in a cool place for half an hour. Brush tops with a little beaten egg. Bake in a hot oven, set at Mark 8 or 465 deg. F., for about twenty-five minutes, slackening the heat towards the end of cooking. The lids will not take so long to cook and should be removed as soon as ready. Scoop out the centres from the cases and put them back for a few minutes into a moderate oven to dry. Patty cases can be served hot or cold, and if the former the filling must be heated ready for putting into them.

PEASE PUDDING. *8 oz. dried split peas; 1 oz. margarine or dripping; salt and pepper; 1 oz. flour.*
Soak the peas for twenty-four hours in hot water to which one level teaspoonful bicarbonate of soda has been added. Rinse and tie loosely in muslin. Cook two to three hours until quite soft. Pass through a sieve, add flour, dripping and seasoning. Flour a pudding cloth and pack the mixture closely into it, tying up with string. Boil for forty-five minutes, turn out from the cloth, and serve as an accompaniment to boiled pork, or with a good sauce or gravy.

PECTIN. The reason why fruit will form a jelly-like substance, when boiled with sugar as in jam- or jelly-making, is that it contains a natural gum called pectin. Pectin is present in fruits in varying degree, and is found to be greatest when the fruit is barely ripe. When making jam or jelly the first object is to extract the pectin from the fruit, and the presence of acid helps this. The pectin must be brought into solution before best use can be made of its setting properties, and that is the main reason why the fruit should always be cooked, usually with a little water, before the sugar is added.

Fruits rich in pectin and acid are: cooking apples; black-currants; gooseberries; damsons; plums; red-currants.

Fruits poor in pectin are: cherries; strawberries; marrow; pears. This may be remedied and good setting obtained by (1) adding lemon juice; (2) adding tartaric or citric acid; (3) combining it with fruit which is rich in pectin. See recipes for jam-making.

PICCALILLI. 1½ *lb. prepared marrow;* 1 *small cauliflower;* 6 *oz. runner beans;* ¼ *lb. onions;* 1 *small cucumber;* 1 *quart vinegar;* 3 *oz. sugar (preferably Demerara);* ¾ *oz. mustard;* ¾ *oz. ground ginger; scant* ½ *oz. flour;* ¼ *oz. turmeric; salt.*

Prepare the vegetables and cut into small pieces. Put into a large earthenware basin and sprinkle each layer with salt. Leave to stand for twenty-four hours and drain off all water. Put the mustard, ground ginger, flour and turmeric into a basin and mix smoothly with some of the vinegar. Put the remaining vinegar and sugar into a saucepan, add the vegetables and simmer for twenty minutes. Pour a little of the hot vinegar on to the mixed flour, etc., return all to saucepan stir until boiling and stir and boil for three minutes. Put into jars and cover down as for pickled cabbage (see below).

PICKLED CABBAGE. 1 *firm red cabbage; spiced vinegar* (see VINEGAR, SPICED).

Cut the stump from the cabbage, cut in quarters and remove outside leaves. Cut the cabbage into shreds, across each quarter, and put the shreds into an earthenware basin, sprinkling each layer with salt. Leave to stand for twenty-four hours, drain well and pack the shreds loosely into jars. Cover with spiced vinegar, and seal down closely, being careful that no metal comes in contact with the vinegar. Glass-lidded preserving jars are the best and most convenient to use. Pickled cabbage is ready for use at the end of a week, and becomes soft after two to three months.

PICKLED ONIONS. 4–5 *lb. small silver-skinned onions;* 1 *quart spiced vinegar* (see VINEGAR, SPICED); *brine.*

Soak the onions in brine made from half a pound salt to two quarts of water, for twenty-four to thirty-six hours. Skin the onions, pack into jars and cover well with spiced vinegar. Cover down as for pickled cabbage (see above). Keep for at least three months before using.

PIQUANTE SAUCE. ¾ *oz. dripping;* 1 *small onion; piece of carrot;* 4 *mushrooms;* ¾ *oz. flour;* 1 *tablespoonful vinegar;* ½ *pint stock* (see STOCK, HOUSEHOLD); 2 *teaspoonfuls ketchup;* 1 *blade of mace; small piece of bay leaf; salt and pepper.*

Melt the dripping and fry the sliced vegetables in it until brown. Add the flour and brown it, then add the vinegar and cook to reduce it for three to four minutes. Withdraw from heat, stir in the stock, and stir until boiling. Add the ketchup, mace and bay leaf. Simmer for half an hour, skimming when necessary. Strain, and re-heat.

PORK, oven-roast. *Suitable joint for roasting* (see "The A.B.C. of Cookery"); *gravy* (see GRAVY, THICK); *stuffing* (see STUFFING, SAGE AND ONION); *apple sauce.*

Follow the general method for oven-roasting. Make sure that the joint is well cooked. Serve on a hot dish, with a little of the gravy poured round the joint and the remainder in a sauceboat.

PORK PIE, raised. *Hot-water crust, made with* 4 *oz. flour, etc.* (see PASTRY, HOT-WATER); 4–6 *oz. lean pork or pork sausage-meat;* ½ *teaspoonful salt;* ½ *gill pork stock;* ¼ *teaspoonful pepper;* ¼ *teaspoonful powdered sage or* 2 *teaspoonfuls anchovy essence;* 1 *teaspoonful powdered gelatine; beaten egg to brush over.*

Cut the pork in small pieces, season and add sage or anchovy essence. Make a little strong stock from any bone or gristle obtained with the pork. Fold a piece of foolscap paper into four lengthways, fasten it with a wire paper-clip, and grease the inside. Have a one-pound jam jar in readiness for shaping the pie. Make the hot-water pastry, cut off a quarter for the lid and keep it warm. Roll the pastry until slightly larger than the bottom of the jam jar, flour the jar and flour the centre of the pastry, and place it on the bottom of the upturned jar. Press the pastry over the edge of the jar to the depth of two to three inches. Turn the whole thing over and drop the pastry into the prepared paper "collar." Fill the case, pressing down the meat, and do not add any liquid. Damp the edges. Roll out the piece of pastry for the lid, press in place, trim edges with a pair of scissors and make a hole in the centre. Brush the top with beaten egg, and decorate with small pastry leaves if desired. Bake in a moderate oven set at Mark 5 or 400 deg. F. to set and brown the pie, then reduce the heat and cook the pie through more slowly, fifty to sixty minutes in all. Remove paper collar about fifteen minutes before the pie is ready, and paint the sides with egg. Return to the oven to finish cooking. Add stock, in which gelatine is dissolved, by means of a funnel through the centre hole, and leave until cold.

PORRIDGE. 2 *oz. medium or coarse oatmeal;* 1 *pint water; salt.*

Bring the water to boiling point, add salt, and sprinkle in the oatmeal, stirring all the time to prevent lumps from forming. Boil and stir for the first five minutes until the meal swells. Simmer slowly for forty minutes, or the porridge may be made in a double saucepan, and in this case put the pan over boiling water for an hour. Add a little more boiling water, if necessary, to make the porridge of pouring consistency. If rolled oats are used for making porridge, follow the directions given on the packet. *Note:* if preferred, the meal may be soaked in the water overnight, and will then cook in little over half the time. After the five minutes of initial boiling porridge may be put in the haybox overnight (see "The A.B.C. of Cookery").

POTATOES, baked in skins. Scrub the potatoes, which should be large and even-sized, and prick them well with a fork. Place on a lightly greased baking tin, and bake in a moderate oven until soft when pinched gently, one and a quarter to two hours according to size. Set the oven at Mark 4 or 375 deg. F., or they may be placed on the bottom shelf while other cooking is in progress. Break the potatoes slightly when they are cooked, to allow steam to escape. Serve on a folded table napkin, and hand butter balls separately.

POTATOES, boiled. Scrub and peel the potatoes thinly, or cook them in their skins if preferred. Put them into just sufficient boiling water to cover them, cutting into even-sized pieces if large. Add salt and cook gently until tender when pierced with a fork, about twenty minutes. Drain, using the lid of the saucepan, and put back for a few minutes over slow heat, with the lid lifted, to dry off moisture. For new potatoes, add a sprig or two of mint to the cooking water, and toss them with a nut of butter or margarine when drying them at the end of cooking. Sprinkle them with chopped parsley.

POTATOES, browned. 1 *lb. potatoes;* 2 *oz. dripping; salt; chopped parsley.*

Scrub and peel the potatoes thinly. Cut if necessary and have the pieces of the same size. Blanch briskly and drain. Melt the dripping in a Yorkshire-pudding tin, or cook them in the tin with a joint. Cook in a moderate oven set at Mark 5 or 400 deg. F. if baked in a separate tin, for about fifty minutes, turning and basting them occasionally. If cooked with a joint, put the potatoes in the meat tin an hour before the meat will be done. Drain on crumpled paper and pile in a hot vegetable dish on a plain dish-paper. Sprinkle with fine salt and chopped parsley.

POTATOES, chipped. Choose large potatoes and cut them in half lengthways. Trim off the ends if they are pointed, and slice across thinly down on to a chopping board. If it should happen that small potatoes only are available, take whole slices across. Soak the slices in plenty of cold water, separating to prevent them from matting together. After fifteen to twenty minutes, drain and leave wrapped in a cloth for twenty minutes. Fry the slices, using a frying basket, a few at a time in fat which is just smoking, and remove when the bubbling subsides. Two or three batches may be put together for the second frying in smoking hot fat, as there is less danger of the fat bubbling over, but keep them well separated with a small slice or fork. When evenly brown, lift out the frying basket, drain on crumpled paper, and pile on a plain dish-paper on a hot dish. Sprinkle with a little fine salt and do not cover with a lid.

POTATOES, French fried. Scrub and peel thinly some even-sized potatoes and trim the ends square. Cut in slices of scant quarter-inch thickness lengthways and cut the slices into quarter-inch strips. Soak the strips in cold water for fifteen minutes. Drain and leave wrapped in a cloth for ten minutes, separating the strips. Put the potatoes in a frying basket and then into smoking hot deep fat. Lower the basket gently into the fat, and raise it at once if the fat is bubbling dangerously near the top of the pan. Shake the basket frequently and remove it when bubbling ceases. Re-heat the fat until smoking hot, and brown the potatoes in it. Drain the potatoes on crumpled paper, and pile on a plain dish-paper in a hot dish and sprinkle with fine salt.

PURÉE. A purée consists of food material reduced to a pulp and passed through a sieve, and the process is applied to meat, vegetables, pulse, or fruit, very frequently. The term is also applied to soups which have been passed through a sieve or beaten smooth. As a rule these soups have no garnish, that is, no pieces of material floating in the soup, but are smooth and creamy, and it is with these soups that croûtons of fried bread or toast are served.

QUEEN CAKES. 3 *oz. margarine; grated rind* ½ *lemon or* ¼ *teaspoonful grated nutmeg;* 3 *oz. caster sugar;* 2 *small eggs;* 5 *oz. flour; scant* ½ *teaspoonful baking powder;* 2 *oz. currants.*

Grease about fifteen queen-cake tins. Make the mixture by creaming method (see CAKE MIXTURES, CREAMED). Bake in a hot oven set at Mark 6 or 425 deg. F. for fifteen to twenty minutes.

QUEEN OF PUDDINGS. 2½ *oz. breadcrumbs;* ½ *pint milk; a nut of margarine;* 1 *dessertspoonful sugar; grated rind* 1 *lemon; yolks of* 2 *eggs;* 2 *tablespoonfuls red jam; meringue: whites of* 2 *eggs;* 3 *oz. caster sugar.*

Heat the milk and pour it over the crumbs, margarine, sugar and grated lemon rind. Cover and leave to soak for thirty minutes. Add the yolks of eggs, and pour the mixture into a greased piedish, then cook in a moderate oven set at Mark 5 or 400 deg. F. for fifteen minutes. When set, spread the top with jam, prepare the meringue (see MERINGUE) and heap it on top of the pudding. Put back into a cool oven to become golden-coloured and crisp.

QUEEN PUDDING (economical). 2½ *oz. breadcrumbs;* ½ *pint milk;* 1 *dessertspoonful sugar; a nut of margarine; grated rind* 1 *lemon or flavouring essence;* 1 *egg;* 2 *tablespoonfuls jam.*

Heat the milk and pour it over the crumbs, sugar, margarine and grated lemon rind if used. Cover and leave to soak for thirty minutes. Whisk the egg and beat into the mixture. Add flavouring essence if used. Pour mixture into a greased piedish, and cook in a moderate oven set at Mark 5 or 400 deg. F. for forty-five minutes. When set spread the jam on top and serve hot.

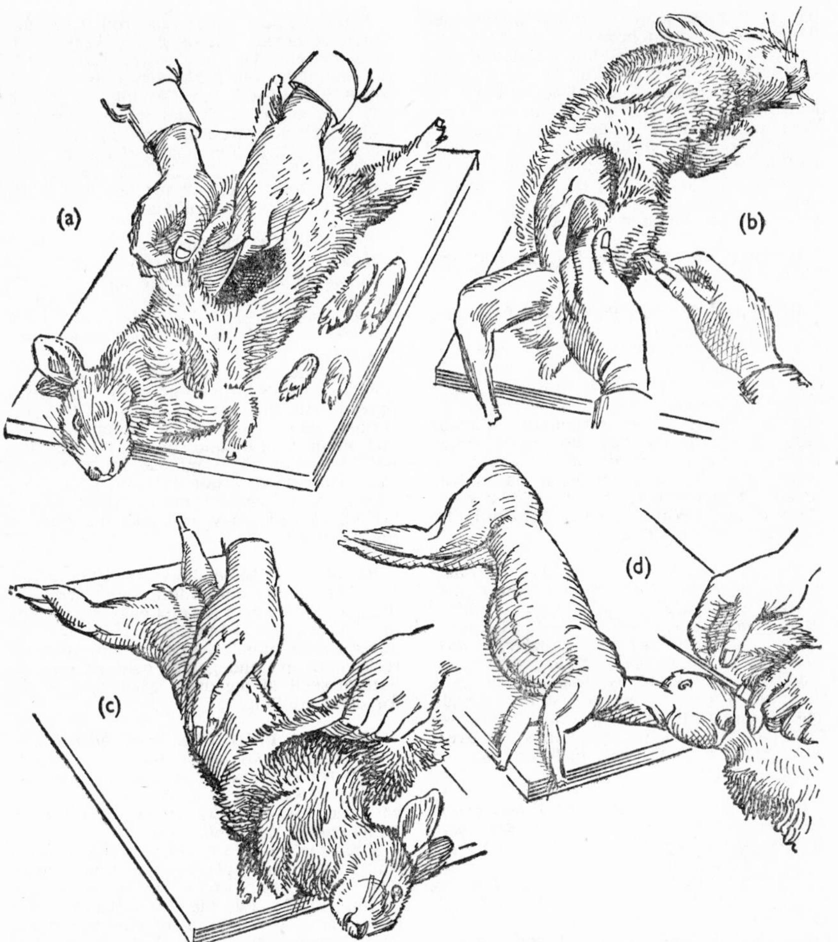

Fig. 29. Skinning a paunched rabbit: (a) *chop off the lower legs and separate the skin from the body;* (b) *bend the joints of the legs and pull them towards the body and out of the skin;* (c) *pull the skin towards the head;* (d) *pull the skin off the forelegs and over the head, cutting off the ears and round the eyes. If a hook is available the rabbit may be hung from it by a slit in one leg, but the process is the same. See also* RABBITS *in "Pets and Livestock."*

RABBIT, baked. 1 *rabbit; slice of fat bacon;* 2–3 *tablespoonfuls veal stuffing* (see STUFFING, VEAL); ½ *pint gravy* (see GRAVY, THICK); *bacon rolls.*

Remove heart, lungs, liver and kidneys. Soak the rabbit in cold salted water overnight. Place the stuffing inside the rabbit, and sew up, using a trussing or packing needle and fine string. Truss the rabbit, using skewers and fine string, with the hind legs drawn forward over the forelegs, and the head fastened upright between the shoulders. If preferred, the head may be cut off, cleansed and used for stock for gravy. Place the fat bacon over the back, or cover with a piece of thickly greased paper. Lay a piece of greased paper over the whole, and bake in a hot oven, set at Mark 6 or 425 deg. F. for an hour and a quarter. Baste frequently, and if liked the liver may be baked with the rabbit for the last thirty minutes. Remove paper, skewers, string and bacon, and place the rabbit on a hot dish, pouring a little of the gravy round. Garnish with bacon rolls and pieces of liver.

RABBIT, casserole of. 1 *rabbit;* ¼–½ *lb. bacon;* 1 *onion;* 1–1¼ *pints water;* 1 *tablespoonful seasoned flour; salt and pepper.*

Prepare the rabbit as for baking and cut into joints. Fry the bacon and cut it into small pieces. Dip the joints of rabbit in seasoned flour and fry them brown in the bacon fat with the sliced onion, adding a little more fat or dripping if necessary. Put the bacon, joints and onion in a casserole and pour the fat off, leaving just sufficient in the pan to absorb the remainder of the seasoned flour. Cook for a minute or two, add the water and stir until boiling. Pour over the rabbit, etc., in the casserole. Cover with the lid, and cook in a moderate oven, set at Mark 4 or 375 deg. F., for two hours. Serve in the casserole.

RABBIT, to skin. See Fig. 29 and also "Pets and Livestock."

RICE, boiled. Select Patna rice, if possible, for boiling plainly, as it is a non-absorbent rice and the grains can be kept separate more easily. Blanch the rice and rinse under the cold-water tap. Sprinkle it into a saucepan containing boiling water and a teaspoonful of white vinegar, or two teaspoonfuls of lemon juice, to whiten the rice. Boil until tender, about ten minutes. Strain off the water, and again rinse the rice. Spread it on a dish, covered with another, and stand in a warm place to dry. Whilst drying, frequently lift the grains lightly with a fork.

ROCK CAKES. ½ *lb. flour;* 3 *oz. currants, sultanas or raisins;* 1 *oz. chopped candied peel;* 1 *level teaspoonful grated nutmeg or mixed spice;* 1 *tablespoonful baking powder;* 1–2 *eggs;* 3–4 *oz. margarine and lard, together; a little milk;* 3–4 *oz. sugar; pinch of salt.*

Make the mixture as described in CAKE MIXTURES, RUBBED-IN. Mix to a stiff dry dough, and arrange in twelve little heaps, using two forks, on a baking tin. Bake in a hot oven, set at Mark 6 or 425 deg. F. for eighteen to twenty minutes.

ROE, cod's. 1 *lb. cod's roe;* 1 *teaspoonful vinegar; salt;* 1 *tablespoonful seasoned flour; dripping for frying or* 4–5 *rashers of bacon.*

Wash the roe, and tie it up firmly in muslin to prevent breaking in cooking. Put an inverted plate or saucer at the bottom of a saucepan. Put in the roe, and pour in sufficient hot water to cover. Add salt and vinegar. Simmer gently for about forty-five minutes, according to thickness. Remove, drain thoroughly and leave to become cold in the muslin. Cut into half-inch slices, coat with seasoned flour, and fry in fat, until golden-brown, turning the pieces occasionally. If the bacon is used, remove rind and rust, and fry the bacon first. Remove and keep warm, add a little more fat and fry the slices of roe. Drain on crumpled paper.

ROES, herring, on toast. Wash the roes well in salted water. Either stew them in milk and water for ten minutes, or fry them in a little margarine until tender. Season with salt, pepper and a few drops of lemon juice, drain and serve on hot buttered toast.

ROLY-POLY, jam. *Suet pastry, made with* 8 *oz. flour, etc.* (see PASTRY, SUET); 2 *tablespoonfuls jam, mincemeat or marmalade.*

Make the suet pastry, and roll it out to a square-cornered, oblong shape, keeping the sides straight. Turn the pastry over, so that the smoother, rolled side comes outside when rolled. Spread with jam, leaving a margin of one inch at the sides and top, which damp with cold water. Roll up firmly, pinching the ends together. Roll in a piece of greased paper cut to fit the length of the roll. Tie up in a pudding cloth, and boil for one and a half hours, or steam for two hours.

ROLY-POLY, savoury. *Suet pastry, made with* 8 *oz. flour, etc.* (see PASTRY, SUET); ½ *lb. raw minced meat or sausage meat;* 1 *tablespoonful finely chopped onion; salt and pepper;* 2 *teaspoonfuls chopped parsley; small tablespoonful water;* ½ *pint thickened brown gravy* (see GRAVY, THICK).

Make the suet pastry and roll it out to oblong shape as for jam roly-poly (see above). Spread with the minced meat as for jam, sprinkle with seasoning and chopped parsley and onion. Roll up and cook as for jam roly-poly, but allow thirty minutes longer in each case. Turn on to a hot dish and pour gravy round. *Note:* cooked meat, mixed with a little thickened gravy, can take the place of the raw mince.

RUSKS. Cut some slices from stale bread. Dip them quickly into a little sweetened milk, drain and place on a greased baking tin. Cook in a hot oven set at Mark 6 or 425 deg. F. for about twenty minutes. Alternatively, cook the rusks until dry and golden coloured, on the bottom shelf of the oven, when it is in use for other cooking.

RUSSIAN FISH PIE. ½ *lb. filleted fish;* 2–3 *tablespoonfuls white sauce* (see WHITE SAUCE, FOUNDATION); 2 *teaspoonfuls chopped parsley; flaky pastry, made with* 8 *oz. flour, etc.* (see PASTRY, FLAKY); *salt and pepper; lemon juice;* 1 *hard-boiled egg.*

Shred the fish into flakes, and mix with the white sauce, salt, pepper and lemon juice. Roll out the pastry to a square of about eight or nine inches. Put the fish mixture in the middle and arrange slices of hard-boiled egg over. Moisten the edges of the pastry and place the corners to the centre in envelope shape. Press firmly, and place a leaf, made from pastry, over each join. Brush the whole with a little beaten egg or milk. Bake in a hot oven, set at Mark 7 or 440 deg. F., for fifteen minutes. Reduce heat and continue cooking for forty-five minutes in all. *Note:* the pie may be made with cooked fish and will then take only thirty to thirty-five minutes to bake.

SALAD DRESSING, boiled. ½ *level teaspoonful pepper;* 1 *teaspoonful salt;* 1 *level teaspoonful dry mustard;* 1 *teaspoonful sugar;* 3 *teaspoonfuls flour; yolk of* 1 *egg;* 1 *oz. margarine, melted;* 1½ *gills milk;* ½ *gill vinegar.*

Mix together the pepper, salt, mustard, flour, yolk, and sugar. Add the milk and margarine mixed, and lastly the vinegar, drop by drop. Cook very slowly until the dressing thickens to a creamy consistency, stirring continuously. Cool and bottle, if not required for immediate use. The dressing will keep for ten days in a cool place.

SALAD DRESSING, French. *½ level teaspoonful salt; ⅛ level teaspoonful pepper; ⅛ level teaspoonful dry mustard; 2 tablespoonfuls salad oil; 1 tablespoonful vinegar.*

Put seasonings into a small basin and mix smoothly with the oil. Beat in the vinegar by degrees with a fork.

SALAD, preparation. Remove coarse and withered parts from all green salad plants. Separate the leaves and wash well. Soak for a short time in very cold water to crisp them. Drain first in a colander, then in a clean teacloth, shaking well.

Mustard and cress. Remove from basket in small bunches and wash under a running cold-water tap to remove all seeds. Trim off ends of stalks and lay bunches aside on a cloth to dry. *Watercress.* Divide into sprigs, removing any threads around the stems. Wash quickly in salted water, then leave in cold water to crisp for a short while. *Spring onions.* Trim off tough green parts and remove skin from outside. *Radishes.* Trim at the root end. If to be served whole, leave half-inch stem at the end of each; or slice them across so that a narrow rim of red shows at the edges. *Beetroot.* Peel and slice thinly, cut into fancy shapes if desired, or cut into dice. Sprinkle with vinegar or French salad dressing (see above). *Tomatoes.* Take each on a fork in turn and dip into boiling water for a minute. The skin can then be stripped off easily. Cut in slices or downwards into segments.

SALAD, mixed green. *1 cabbage lettuce; ½ bunch watercress or ½ basket small cress; 1 skinned tomato or 1 dozen small radishes, or 2-in. beetroot; 2-in. piece of cucumber; 2 tablespoonfuls salad dressing; 1 hard-boiled egg.*

Prepare the salad plants (see above). Line the salad bowl with lettuce leaves, reserving the heart and best pieces of other kinds for decoration. Break up the remainder, or cut small, and mix lightly with the dressing. Pile in the bowl, decorate and serve at once.

SALAD, potato. *¾ lb. cooked potatoes; 2 tablespoonfuls French salad dressing; 1 gill boiled salad dressing; salt and pepper; 2 teaspoonfuls chopped onion; small cress or sprigs of watercress; 1 teaspoonful chopped parsley.*

Cook the potatoes and while hot dice them and mix with the French salad dressing, or oiled margarine mixed with a little seasoning and vinegar may be substituted. When the potatoes are cold, mix them with the onion, salt and pepper, arrange in a mound in the centre of a dish and coat with the boiled salad dressing. Encircle with the cress and sprinkle chopped parsley on top.

SAUSAGE ROLLS. *Flaky or rough puff pastry, made with 4 oz. flour, etc.* (see PASTRY); *2 sausages or about 6 oz. sausage meat; beaten reconstituted dried egg; small cress or sprigs of watercress.*

Make the pastry and set it aside to cool. Skin the sausages, if used, and make six small rolls, using a little flour as necessary. Roll the pastry out to an oblong shape, about twelve by eight inches. Trim the edges, cut lengthways, and cut each strip across twice into three squares. Turn each piece over, put a roll of sausage meat on each and damp the edges. Seal firmly, flake edges with a knife and make three small cuts on top. Brush with egg and bake in a hot oven, set at Mark 7 or 440 deg. F., for fifteen minutes, reduce heat and continue cooking for a further ten to fifteen minutes. Serve hot or cold, garnished with cress.

SCONES. *½ lb. flour; 2 heaped teaspoonfuls baking powder; ¼ level teaspoonful salt; 1 teaspoonful caster sugar; 2 oz. margarine; 1 gill milk (good measure); 1–2 oz sultanas (optional).*

Sieve the flour, baking powder, salt and sugar. Rub in the margarine lightly, add sultanas if used, and mix to a soft, pliable dough with milk. Roll out half an inch thick, prick with floured fork and cut in rounds with a two-inch cutter. Brush with milk and bake at once in a hot oven, set at Mark 8 or 465 deg. F., until set and browned. Split, butter and serve at once, or leave to become cold. *Note:* if sour milk is used, the baking powder may be omitted, and one level teaspoonful bicarbonate of soda and one level teaspoonful cream of tartar used instead.

SEASONED FLOUR. *1 tablespoonful flour; 1 level teaspoonful salt; ¼ level teaspoonful pepper.*

Mix all ingredients thoroughly together.

SHEPHERD'S PIE. *½ lb. cold cooked meat; brown sauce or thickened gravy; salt and pepper; 1 cooked onion; 2–3 teaspoonfuls Worcester sauce; 1 lb. mashed potato; a little beaten egg or shavings of dripping.*

Remove skin and excess fat from meat and mince it. Add salt, pepper, Worcester sauce, chopped onion and sufficient brown sauce or thickened gravy to form a soft pulp. Put the mixture into a greased piedish. Pile the mashed potato on the meat, smooth it with a knife, then flake the surface with a fork. Brush with beaten egg or dot the surface with shavings of dripping. Put into a very hot oven, set at Mark 8 or 465 deg. F., for twenty minutes.

SHORTBREAD. *6 oz. flour and 2 oz. ground rice, or 7 oz. flour and 1 oz. fine semolina; 4–5 oz. butter or margarine; 2½ oz. caster sugar; large pinch of salt.*

Sieve together the flour, salt and ground rice or semolina on to one end of the pastry board. Spread the sugar at the other end and put the butter on top. Work the sugar and margarine together, then draw the remaining ingredients in gradually. Knead lightly until a smooth, firm dough is obtained. Do not add any water unless absolutely necessary. Cut in half and press out each piece to a round, using the finger-tips, and making the rounds quarter-inch thick. Cut across into eight wedge shapes and fit the pieces together again for baking. Cook on a greased baking tin until pale golden-coloured, in a very moderate oven, set at Mark 3 or 350 deg. F., about twenty-five minutes. Divide again into pieces when the shortbread is half cold.

SOUPS, vegetable, general method for. 1 *lb. vegetables; flavouring material, such as onion, bacon rinds, etc.;* ½–1 *oz. margarine or dripping;* 1 *pint stock* (see STOCK, HOUSEHOLD), *water, or half of each;* ½ *oz. cornflour, flour, ground rice or fine semolina to each pint of sieved soup;* 1 *gill milk.*

Prepare vegetables according to their kind, and slice thinly. Toss the prepared vegetables and flavouring material in the melted fat for ten minutes at a temperature below frying point, until the fat is absorbed. Do not allow the vegetables to brown. Add the liquid, boil up and simmer for half to two hours, according to kind of vegetable, until the vegetables are soft enough to sieve or beat smooth. Mix the starchy material used smoothly with the milk, add to the hot soup, stir and simmer for ten minutes. Correct the seasoning and consistency, which should be that of cream.

SOUP, artichoke. 1 *lb. Jerusalem artichokes; scant oz. margarine;* 1 *pint stock or water;* ½ *oz. starchy material;* 1 *gill milk; salt and pepper; croûtons of fried bread or toast.*

Scrub and peel the artichokes thinly, using a teaspoonful of white vinegar or lemon juice in each water to prevent discoloration. Follow the general method (see above). Simmer three-quarters to one hour.

SOUP, celery. 1 *lb. celery, after preparation;* 1 *onion.*

Remainder of ingredients and method as for general method (see above). Simmer one and a half hours.

SOUP, green pea. 1 *lb. green peas;* 1 *small onion;* 2–3 *sprigs parsley;* 2–3 *sprigs mint.*

Shell the peas and wash about half of the pods. Remainder of ingredients and method as for general method (see above), tossing the peas over gentle heat for five minutes in the fat. Add the washed pea-pods, mint and parsley with the liquid. Simmer one hour.

SOUP, lentil, haricot or pea. 1 *gill lentils, haricots or split peas;* 1 *onion;* 1 *carrot;* 1 *turnip;* 2 *sticks celery, or a leek.*

Soak haricots or peas overnight; lentils do not require soaking. Remainder of ingredients and method as for general method (see above). Lentil soup requires simmering for two hours, haricot or pea soup for three hours. Stir occasionally.

SOUP, mixed vegetable. 1 *lb. mixed vegetables; for example,* ¼ *lb. potatoes,* ¼ *lb. carrots,* ¼ *lb. onions or leeks,* ¼ *lb. celery.*

Remainder of ingredients and method as for general method (see above). Simmer one to one and a quarter hours.

SOUP, tomato. 1 *lb. fresh tomatoes or* 1 *pint tin of tomatoes;* 1 *small carrot;* 1 *small onion.*

Ingredients and method as for general method (see above), but substitute water or tomato juice for the milk. Simmer for one hour.

SPINACH. 2 *lb. spinach; salt and pepper;* ½ *oz. margarine; croûtons of fried bread or* 1 *hard-boiled egg.*

Remove the stalks and wash the spinach in several cold waters. Put it into a saucepan, with no added water, cook it in that which clings to the leaves. Put on the lid and cook until tender, stirring occasionally to prevent burning. Drain well, pressing out the water. Either chop the spinach finely or pass it through a sieve. Melt the margarine in the saucepan. Add the spinach, re-heat well and add salt and pepper. Pile up in a hot vegetable dish, and garnish with croûtons or sections of hard-boiled egg.

SPONGE SANDWICH. 3 *eggs;* 3 *oz. caster sugar;* 3 *oz. flour;* 2 *tablespoonfuls warm jam.*

Grease two seven-inch sandwich tins with lard and put a disk of greased paper at the bottom of each. Whisk the eggs, add the sugar and whisk again until the mixture is thick and creamy, and twice its original bulk. Scatter the sieved flour lightly over the surface and, using a large metal spoon, fold it in, passing the spoon round the outer edge of the mixture, then through the centre and folding over. Carry out this process very lightly and merely sufficiently to incorporate the flour, or the air enfolded by whisking will be expelled. Pour the mixture equally into the tins, spread smooth, and bake in a moderate oven, set at Mark 5 or 400 deg. F., until set and golden brown, fifteen to twenty minutes. When cool, spread with jam and dredge with caster sugar.

STEAK AND KIDNEY PIE. ¾ *lb. buttock steak;* 2 *sheep's kidneys;* 1 *tablespoonful seasoned flour;* 1–1½ *gills water; beaten egg to brush over, or milk; rough puff or flaky pastry, made with* 6 *oz. flour, etc.* (see PASTRY).

Wipe the meat, wash and dry the kidney, cut the fat into tiny dice. Cut the meat into thin slices, and the kidney in small pieces. Put a piece of kidney and of fat at the end of each slice of meat, roll up and coat rolls with seasoned flour. Put the rolls in a greased piedish, pour the water over and cover with a thick greased paper. Cook gently in a moderate oven for one to one and a half hours and leave to become cold. Prepare the pastry and set aside to chill. Roll out the pastry rather more than quarter inch thick, and one inch larger all round than the piedish. Cut a strip of three-quarter inch all round the edge of the pastry and press it firmly on to the damped rim of the piedish. Damp the top of this strip and put on the lid of pastry. Trim, flake and decorate the edges. Make a hole in the centre, brush the top with egg or milk and decorate with pastry leaves made from the trimmings. Bake in a hot oven, set at Mark 7 or 440 deg. F., until the pastry has risen and is brown, cover with paper, lessen the heat and leave to finish cooking, for forty-five minutes in all. A little hot seasoned stock may be added through the centre hole.

STEAK AND KIDNEY PUDDING. *Suet pastry made with* 8 *oz. flour, etc.* (see PASTRY,

SUET); 1 *lb. buttock steak;* 2 *sheep's kidneys or* ¼ *lb. ox kidney;* 1 *tablespoonful seasoned flour;* 3–4 *tablespoonfuls water or stock.*

Prepare the meat and kidney as for steak and kidney pie (see above). Prepare the suet pastry, line the basin, fill with the rolls of meat, finish and cook as described under FRUIT PUDDING, BOILED. Boil steadily for four hours. Serve gravy separately.

STEWED STEAK. 1 *lb. buttock steak; carrot, turnip and onion;* 1 *oz. dripping;* 1 *level tablespoonful flour;* ¾ *pint stock or water; salt and parsley.*

Remove excess of fat from meat, and cut in strips about half-inch thick. Fry the meat on all sides in smoking hot fat until browned, then remove it from the pan. Add the sliced onion and fry for a minute or two, then add flour and fry until it is a rich brown colour. Add liquid and salt, stir until boiling. Return the meat and simmer gently two to two and a half hours until tender. Cut tiny dice from the carrot and turnip, add the trimmings to the stew and cook the dice in boiling salted water, cooking the carrot for ten minutes longer than the turnip and about twenty minutes in all. Pile the meat on a hot dish, add pepper to sauce, boil up, skim, and strain over the meat. Drain the vegetable dice and pile at each side of the dish, sprinkled with chopped parsley.

STOCK, bone. 4 *lb. uncooked bones;* 3 *quarts water;* 1½ *teaspoonfuls salt;* ½ *lb. carrots;* ½ *lb. onions;* ¼ *lb. leeks (green part) or* ¼ *lb. onions;* ¼ *lb. turnips;* 2 *oz. celery or* 1 *teaspoonful celery seeds tied in muslin;* 2 *dozen peppercorns.*

Chop the bones, remove fat and marrow, wash well and put into a saucepan with the water and salt. Boil up, skim and boil for one hour. Skim frequently, and it is helpful to pour in half a teacupful cold water and then to boil up again briskly, which collects scum for easy removal. Add vegetables in large pieces, and boil gently for a further two hours. Strain, and next day remove fat. The bones may be added to the stock-pot.

STOCK, household. Fill a large saucepan half or quarter full with water, according to the probable supply of scraps. Add these to the pan, boil up and simmer gently, two to three hours. Strain and discard vegetables. Next day remove fat from surface and cook the stock with fresh scraps, adding more water if the liquid has reduced too much.

Suitable scraps for use: bones, cooked or uncooked; trimmings of meat, cooked or uncooked; water in which meat or vegetables (not greens) have been boiled; giblets; unthickened gravy or broth; bacon rinds or bones; trimmings of carrot, turnip or onion; outer stalks of celery. *Avoid:* anything starchy or floury; anything stale; all fat, which can be melted down and clarified; any green vegetables, or green vegetable water, though this is excellent for quick use for gravy.

STUFFING, sage and onion. ½ *lb. onions;* 2 *teaspoonfuls fresh or dried chopped sage;* 2 *oz. breadcrumbs;* 1 *oz. margarine; salt and pepper.*

Cut the onions in quarters and cook in boiling salted water until soft. Drain well and chop. Add the sage, crumbs, margarine, salt and pepper. Press all together and use for stuffing pork, ducks or geese.

STUFFING, veal. 4 *tablespoonfuls breadcrumbs;* 1 *tablespoonful chopped suet or* 1 *oz. dripping or bacon fat;* 2 *heaped teaspoonfuls chopped parsley; salt and pepper;* ½ *teaspoonful grated lemon rind;* ½ *teaspoonful fresh or dried mixed herbs; a little beaten egg and milk.*

Mix all dry ingredients and bind together with a little beaten egg and milk. Use for stuffing veal, fish, poultry, etc.

SWISS ROLL. 4 *eggs;* 4 *oz. caster sugar;* 4 *oz. flour;* 2 *large tablespoonfuls hot jam.*

Line a Swiss roll tin (twelve by nine inches) with thickly greased paper. Make the sponge mixture as for SPONGE SANDWICH. Bake in a hot oven set at Mark 6 or 425 deg. F., ten to twelve minutes. Turn on to a piece of sugared paper and remove baking paper. Spread at once with hot jam and trim the sides with a sharp knife. Roll up, making the first two twists quite firmly, then lightly to shape. Leave the roll wrapped in the sugared paper until cold. *Note:* if the oven has rather much bottom heat and the sponge cake bakes too firmly underneath, turn the roll on to a tea-cloth wrung out from hot water, instead of a sugared paper. Roll it up in sugared paper to cool. For a chocolate roll, substitute two teaspoonfuls of cocoa for two teaspoonfuls of the flour. Roll up without any filling and when cold unroll, spread with mock cream or butter icing, flavoured with vanilla essence.

TEA CAKES, yeast. ¾ *lb. flour;* 1 *level teaspoonful salt;* ½ *oz. yeast;* 1 *teaspoonful caster sugar;* 1 *oz. margarine;* 1½ *gills milk;* 1 *egg; milk and sugar to glaze.*

Warm the flour and salt and sieve into a warm bowl. Cream the yeast and sugar and add the warm milk in which the margarine has been melted. Add these to the beaten egg, and pour all into a well made in the flour. Mix to a dough, put on to a floured board and knead for a few minutes. Have ready two warm greased five-inch cake tins, and press half the dough in each. Cover, and set the tins in a warm place until the dough has risen to the tops of the tins. Bake in a hot oven, set at Mark 8 or 465 deg. F., for fifteen minutes until well risen and browned. Dissolve a level tablespoonful of sugar in a small tablespoonful of milk and brush the tops, put back into the oven to dry the glaze. Cut through in slices, toast, butter and put together again in the form of a cake. Cut downwards into halves and quarters.

TOAD-IN-THE-HOLE. 4 *sausages;* ½ *oz. dripping;* ½ *pint Yorkshire pudding batter* (see BATTER).

Skin the sausages and form into small rolls, using a little flour for shaping. Put the dripping into a Yorkshire pudding tin and heat until smoking hot. Arrange the rolls in it and pour the batter over. Bake in a hot oven, set at Mark 6 or 425 deg. F., for forty-five minutes. Cut into squares and serve.

TOMATO SAUCE. *½ oz. margarine or bacon fat; ½ onion; small piece carrot; few bacon rinds; ½ lb. fresh tomatoes or ½ pint tinned tomatoes; 1 gill stock or water; 1 teaspoonful cornflour or flour; salt and pepper.*

Melt the margarine or bacon fat and fry the sliced onion and carrot, and bacon rinds, in it for a few minutes, without browning. Add the sliced tomatoes or tomato pulp and cook for a few minutes more. Boil up, add seasoning and simmer twenty-five to thirty minutes, stirring occasionally. Rub through a fine sieve or strainer and return to the rinsed saucepan. Add the cornflour or flour mixed smoothly with a little water, stir and boil gently for five minutes.

TOMATOES, baked stuffed. 4 *large tomatoes; 2 tablespoonfuls veal stuffing* (see STUFFING, VEAL); 1 *teaspoonful finely chopped onion; 2 teaspoonfuls chopped cooked ham or bacon; salt and pepper;* 1 *teaspoonful grated cheese;* 1 *teaspoonful dried crumbs; 4 croûtes of fried bread.*

Wipe the tomatoes and cut a slice from the end opposite the stalk from each. Scoop out some of the pulp, using the handle of a teaspoon. Prepare the stuffing and add the chopped onion and ham. Add sufficient of the tomato pulp to make a soft mixture, season and press the stuffing into the tomato cases, piling it neatly. Sprinkle the tops with cheese and crumbs. Put the tomatoes on a greased tin and cook in a moderate oven, set at Mark 5 for about fifteen minutes, until tender but not broken. Lay the slices at the side to warm through for about five minutes, and put one on each tomato, when baked, to form a lid. Dish each on a croûte of fried bread and garnish with parsley sprigs.

TREACLE PUDDING. 4 *oz. flour;* 2 *oz. chopped suet; ½ level teaspoonful bicarbonate of soda; ½–1 teaspoonful ground ginger; ½–1 egg; ½ gill golden syrup or brown treacle; ½ gill milk; ½ pint treacle or sweet white sauce* (see below).

Sieve all dry ingredients and add the suet. Beat the egg and add the syrup or treacle, and milk. Mix these with the other ingredients. Put into a greased pudding basin, twist a greased paper over and steam for two hours. Turn out on a hot dish and pour the sauce chosen round.

TREACLE SAUCE. 2 *tablespoonfuls brown treacle or golden syrup;* 1 *tablespoonful water;* 1 *teaspoonful lemon juice or ½ teaspoonful lemon essence.*

Heat the treacle and water, add lemon juice or essence and pour around the pudding.

TRIPE AND ONIONS, stewed. 1 *lb. dressed tripe; ¾ pint water; 2 large onions;* 1 *oz. flour; ¼ pint milk; salt and pepper.*

Blanch the tripe (see BLANCHING) and cut it into neat pieces. Peel the onions, leaving them whole. Cover tripe and onions with the water, boil up, skim and simmer for two hours. Remove the onions and chop them. Mix the flour smoothly with the milk, and add to the tripe and liquid in the saucepan, with the chopped onions, salt and pepper. Stir until boiling and simmer for ten minutes. Serve sprinkled with chopped parsley.

Fig. 30. Roasting a turkey in a small oven.

TURKEY, oven-roast. 1 *turkey of about* 16 *lb.;* 6 *tablespoonfuls veal stuffing* (see STUFFING, VEAL); *chestnut stuffing (optional); dripping for basting;* 1 *pint thickened gravy; bread sauce* (see BREAD SAUCE); 1–1½ *lb. sausages.*

Draw and truss the turkey as explained under FOWL, ROAST. If both stuffings are used, put the veal stuffing in the crop and chestnut stuffing in the body of the bird. This may be done overnight. Heat the oven to Mark 6 or 425 deg. F. Smear the breast, legs and wings of the bird with bacon fat, if available, and place it on its side in a large meat tin, on a grid and covered with margarine papers. If the bird is too big for this treatment, hang it from one of the bars of an oven shelf, slid into the top runner of the oven (Fig. 30). Put a baking tin in the bottom, and reverse the position of the bird at about half-time. At the end of the first half-hour baste the bird and turn it to the other side, in a further half-hour turn it to normal position for the remainder of the cooking time and reduce heat to Mark 4. Serve on a hot dish, with fried sausages round, and gravy and bread sauce in sauce-boats. Browned potatoes and brussels sprouts are usually served with a roast turkey.

VANILLA BUNS. 6 *oz. flour;* 2 *teaspoonfuls baking powder;* 1½ *oz. margarine;* 1½ *oz. lard;* 2½ *oz. sugar;* 1 *egg;* 2–3 *tablespoonfuls milk;* 1 *teaspoonful vanilla essence; mock cream or butter icing, or* 1 *tablespoonful red jam.*

Sieve flour and baking powder, with a pinch of salt. Rub in the fats lightly with the finger-tips, and add the sugar. Beat the egg, add milk and vanilla essence. Add these to the dry ingredients, mixing stiffly as in the making of rock cakes. Put the mixture in twelve heaps on a greased baking tin or bun pan. Bake fifteen to twenty minutes in a hot oven, set at Mark 6 or 425 deg. F. Split open when cool and spread with mock cream or butter icing, coloured pink and flavoured with vanilla essence, or with red jam. These cakes are best when used new.

VEAL, fricassée. 1 *lb. fillet of veal;* 1 *onion; small bouquet garni* (see BOUQUET GARNI); *salt and pepper; sauce:* 1 *oz. margarine;* 1 *oz. flour;* 1 *gill liquid from veal;* 1 *gill milk;* 1 *teaspoonful lemon juice; garnish: rolls of bacon; slices of lemon; crescents of fried bread; small parsley sprigs.*

Cut the veal into moderate-sized pieces, put in a saucepan and cover with about half a pint of tepid water. Bring to boiling point, skim, and add bouquet garni, onion, salt and pepper. Simmer one to one and a quarter hours until tender, and strain off the stock. Make a white sauce (see WHITE SAUCE, FOUNDATION), using the margarine, flour, stock, milk, lemon juice and seasoning. Re-heat the meat in this, dish neatly and garnish with the rolls of bacon, lemon slices, parsley and fried bread.

VEAL AND HAM PIE. ¾ *lb. lean pie veal;* ¼ *lb. streaky bacon;* 1 *hard-boiled egg;* 1 *gill water or stock;* 1 *teaspoonful chopped parsley; small teaspoonful salt;* ¼ *teaspoonful pepper; egg or milk to brush over; rough puff or flaky pastry, made with* 8 *oz. flour, etc.* (see PASTRY).

Cut the veal in small pieces, remove rind and rust from the bacon, and blanch it. Cook the egg. Mix the parsley, salt, pepper and shredded bacon with the veal, put into a piedish, with the egg cut in slices or into eight pieces on top. Cover with pastry, as for STEAK AND KIDNEY PIE. Put the pie into a hot oven, set at Mark 7 or 440 deg. F., until the pastry has risen and is brown. Cover with paper to finish cooking, one and a quarter hours in all. If the pie is to be served cold, add half a gill stock with one teaspoonful gelatine dissolved in it, by means of a funnel through the centre hole.

VEGETABLE PIE. *Short pastry, made with* 8 *oz. flour, etc.* (see PASTRY, SHORT); ½ *lb. cooked mixed vegetables, in small pieces;* 2–3 *tablespoonfuls cheese sauce, or thickened gravy;* 1 *tablespoonful chopped parsley; salt and pepper; milk to brush over.*

Make the pastry, cut it in half, and line a greased sandwich tin or flan ring with one piece. Mix together the vegetables, sauce or gravy, parsley and seasoning. Roll out the remaining piece of pastry to fit the top of the tin, fill with the vegetable mixture, damp the edges and put on the lid. Trim and decorate the edge, make three short cuts in the middle, and brush with milk. Bake in a hot oven, set at Mark 6 or 425 deg. F., until the pastry is browned, about twenty-five to thirty minutes. Serve hot, or if allowed to become cold the pie may be used for a picnic lunch.

VINEGAR, spiced (for pickles). 1 *quart white or brown malt vinegar;* ¼ *oz. stick cinnamon;* ¼ *oz. mace;* ¼ *oz. whole allspice; a few peppercorns.*

Tie the spices together loosely in muslin and add to the vinegar. Put on the lid and boil up briskly, turn at once into an earthenware basin, cover with a plate and leave to stand for two hours. Remove the bag of spices and use the vinegar as required. Use the vinegar cold if crisp pickles are needed, such as cabbage or onions, or hot for the softer varieties such as walnuts or plums.

WELSH RAREBIT. 1 *slice buttered toast;* 3 *oz. grated cheese;* 1 *tablespoonful oiled margarine;* 1 *tablespoonful milk;* 1 *level teaspoonful dry mustard; salt and pepper;* 1 *teaspoonful vinegar* (*optional*).

Make and butter the toast. Mix the remaining ingredients together and spread in a thick layer on the toast. Place under a hot grill and cook for a few minutes until pale golden brown. Serve at once.

WHITE SAUCE, foundation. *Coating sauce:* 1 *oz. margarine;* 1 *oz. flour;* ½ *pint liquid. Pouring sauce:* ½ *oz. margarine;* ½ *oz. flour;* ½ *pint liquid.*

Note: the liquid used depends on the use to be made of the sauce. The basic liquid is milk but if the sauce is to be served with fish use half milk and half fish liquor, and the same applies to meat liquor and vegetable water.

Melt the fat in a small saucepan, withdraw from heat and stir in the flour. Return to heat and cook again for a few minutes. This blending of fat and flour is called a roux. Do not allow to brown. Remove from heat and stir in the liquid, about a third at a time, adding the cold milk first, or the sauce may become lumpy. Return to gentle heat, stirring the whole time, and bring to boiling point. Stir and boil four to five minutes, to ensure that the flour is completely cooked. If the sauce is allowed to stand after cooking, a skin forms on top, but this may be minimized by rinsing the inside of the saucepan lid with cold water and putting it on firmly. *Note:* various additions may be made to this foundation, after the sauce is cooked, e.g., chopped parsley, anchovy essence, grated cheese, capers, etc.

WHITE SAUCE, sweet. 2 *teaspoonfuls cornflour* (½ *oz.*); ½ *pint milk;* 2 *teaspoonfuls sugar; flavouring essence or* 2 *strips of lemon rind.*

Mix the cornflour smoothly with some of the milk. If lemon rind is used for flavouring, infuse it in the remaining milk (see INFUSION). Pour the hot milk over the cornflour. Stir and boil for five minutes, adding the sugar. Remove the lemon rind if used, or add the essence.

YORKSHIRE PUDDING. ½ *pint Yorkshire pudding batter* (see BATTER); ½ *oz. dripping.*

Make the dripping smoking hot in a small Yorkshire pudding tin. Pour in the batter and bake in a fairly hot oven, set at Mark 7 or 450 deg. F., for forty minutes. Cut into squares and either arrange them round the oven-roast joint, or pile on a hot dish.

HOW TO SEW

Stitches and processes used in dressmaking, embroidery, repairs and renovations, simply described and illustrated.

ALGERIAN EYE STITCH. An embroidery stitch worked on canvas or on material in which the threads can be counted. It consists of eight single stitches radiating from the centre of a square into the four corners and the centres of the four sides, each stitch being taken over an equal number of threads.

APPLIQUÉ. A decorative form of needlework in which one fabric is "applied" to another, usually with fancy stitchery. The material to be stitched down is cut into the required shape and tacked carefully into place. The edges are then secured with a suitable embroidery stitch, such as a satin, chain, split, herringbone or buttonhole stitch.

A method called *blind appliqué* is frequently used on fine materials that fray easily. For this the raw edges of the pattern shape are turned under and sewn down with invisible slip-stitching.

Another variation of appliqué is *inlay* work, in which the design is cut out of the main material and the contrasting material laid underneath. The pattern shape is marked on the top fabric and the contrasting material tacked in place beneath. The two layers are then stitched together with small running stitches along the outline of the design, the top layer is cut away within the running stitches and the raw edges are securely sewn, usually with narrow satin or chain stitch.

An advanced form of inlay work is used for *counterchange* designs in which the pattern is identical on both background and inlaid material.

In all forms of fabric appliqué work it is most important that the weave of the "applied" material runs in the same direction as that of the background, otherwise the work will pull out of shape.

ARMHOLES. See SLEEVES, TO SET IN.

ARROWHEAD. A triangular formation of close stitches worked in strong embroidery thread to reinforce the tops of pleats, the outer corners of pockets or wherever material is subjected to strain. The arrowhead is worked over an imaginary triangle of approximately ½-in. depth, as shown in Fig. 1.

ASSISI EMBROIDERY. A simple form of embroidery of Italian origin, its characteristic designs of birds and beasts being said to be inspired by the story of St. Francis of Assisi. The embroidery is worked on coarse linen in which the threads can be counted. The design itself is outlined with double running stitch (see HOLBEIN STITCH), and the background is filled in with cross stitch, so that the motif stands out in plain material. Traditionally, not more than two colours should be used for this type of embroidery.

BACK STITCH. A stitch used for hand-sewn seams that need to be very strong. On the right side it gives a line of continuous small stitches, resembling machine stitching. A small amount of material is picked up on the needle, then the needle re-inserted at the beginning of the same stitch and double the length of material picked up. For the second stitch the needle is inserted at the end of the first one and brought out again a stitch length in front of the working thread.

BAR FAGGOTING. See FAGGOT STITCH.

BELTS. Fabric belts need stiffening a little to prevent them folding in wear. Cut a strip of fabric at least 6 in. longer than the waistline measurement and 1 in. wider than the finished belt is to be. Leave one end straight and cut the other into a curve or point, as desired. Take a ½-in. turning along the edges and press well. Over the turned-in edges tack a length of matching petersham ribbon just less in width than the finished belt. Slip stitch or machine the ribbon and fabric together along the outer edges of the belt and press well under a damp cloth. Slip the straight end

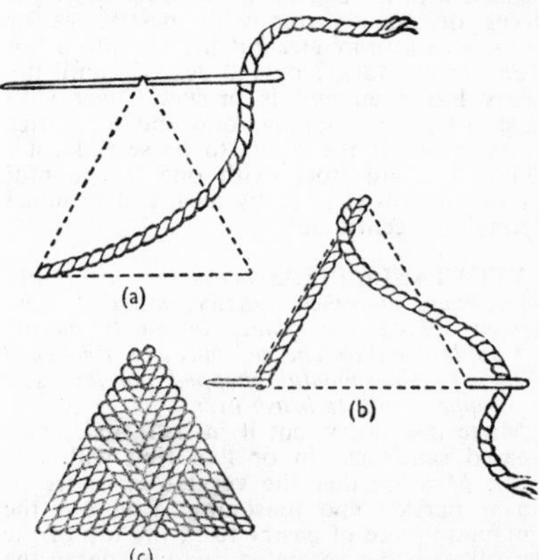

Fig. 1. Arrowhead. (a) *Take thread from lower left-hand corner and pick up small stitch at top of triangle.* (b) *Insert needle at lower right-hand corner and bring out at the left-hand corner inside first stitch. Continue these stitches keeping threads close together and parallel until completed.* (c) *Finished arrowhead.*

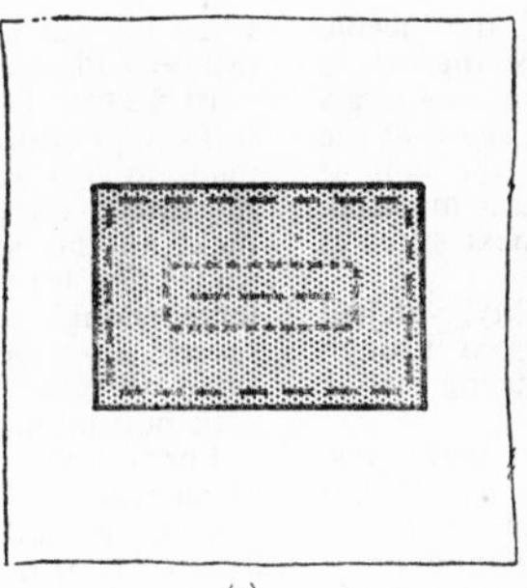
(a)

(b)

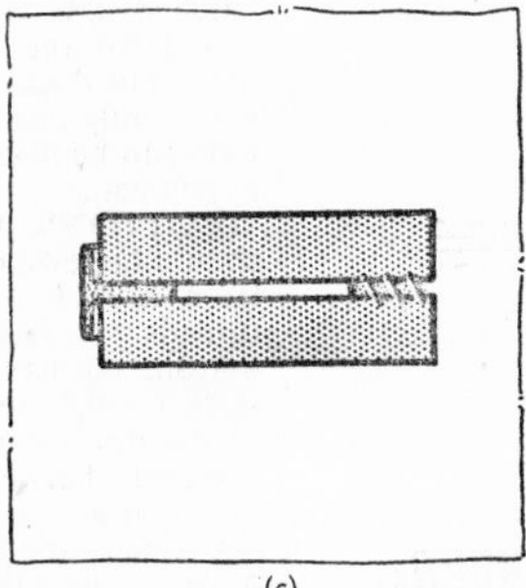
(c)

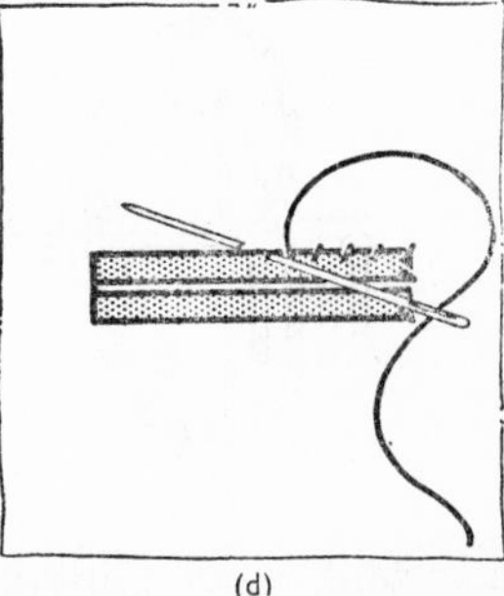
(d)

Fig. 2. Bound buttonhole: (a) *work an oblong of stitching about* ⅛ *in. beyond the centre tacking;* (b) *snip both layers of material through centre and into corners as far as stitching;* (c) *wrong side of work with binding strip pulled through and folded into inverted pleats, the sides of which are caught together;* (d) *right side, slip stitch along edges of binding as nearly invisibly as possible.*

through a buckle, turn under the raw edges and hem securely, then work three or four eyelet holes at the shaped end, for fastening.

An alternative method is to use a strip of stiff muslin or canvas as an interlining. Turn the raw edges of the belt fabric over it and herringbone them down, then line the belt with a second strip of fabric, machining or slip stitching the two layers together round the outer edges.

BIAS BINDING. A narrow strip of material cut diagonally across the warp and weft threads and used to bind the raw edges of another fabric. This bias-cutting allows the material to be stretched where necessary so that curved or circular edges can be bound smoothly. Bias binding can be bought ready-made, or strips may be cut and joined to the required length.

To make an accurate cross-cut, fold the material cornerwise so that the weft threads of the top layer lie at right-angles to the weft threads of the material beneath. Cut along the fold, and continue cutting in strips parallel with the first cut. To join two strips, place one on top of the other at right-angles. Seam them along the straight of the material, then press the seam open and snip off the points that extend beyond the edge of the binding. See also BINDING.

BINDING. A method of neatening a raw edge by enclosing it in a strip of fabric. On a straight edge, the binding can be one woven on the straight, such as ribbon, tape, Prussian binding, etc., but for most purposes bias binding should be used (see BIAS BINDING). To sew on, place the binding strip on the edge of the material, right sides facing, and stitch the two together a short distance from the raw edges. Fold the binding over on to the wrong side of the work, turn in its raw edge and hem down over the previous row of stitches.

BLANKET STITCH. See BUTTONHOLE STITCH.

BLIND APPLIQUÉ. See APPLIQUÉ.

BOUND BUTTONHOLE. A buttonhole in which the raw edges of the cut are bound with material. Mark the width of the button, at the required place, with two pins and run a line of small tacking stitches between them. Tack the binding strip, an oblong about 1½ in. deep and about 1 in. wider than the button, on the right side of the material over this centre line; then proceed as explained in Fig. 2.

BOUND HEM. See HEMS.

BOX PLEAT. See PLEATS.

BRAID, to sew on. Flat braids that have straight edges can be hemmed or machine stitched along both sides, but *ric-rac braid* may be secured with one row of stitching through the centre, or by hemming along its curved edges. *Soutache braid* should be sewn along its centre indentation, with running or back stitches as small as possible so as to be almost invisible. Cord-like braids should be sewn underneath, taking alternate stitches through braid and fabric.

BRODERIE ANGLAISE. Traditional English embroidery worked in white threads on white fabrics, usually linen, lawn, muslin, etc. The designs are dainty and finely detailed with eyelet holes, both round and oval, edged with satin overcast stitch, solid satin stitch fillings, fine stem stitch scrolling and buttonhole-scalloped edges as the most notable characteristics.

BULLION STITCH. A detached stitch, cord-like in appearance, that lies on the surface of the material. It is popularly used for leaves and petals.

Bring the needle through to the front of the material, make a back stitch of the required length and bring the point of the needle through where the thread is. Twist the thread round the needle four or five times and draw the needle through, then insert it again at the other end of the stitch so that the coil of thread lies to the right along the material. Bring the needle out where the next stitch is to begin.

BUTTONHOLES. For durability, stitched buttonholes should always be worked through a double thickness of material, using strong thread or buttonhole twist.

Mark the width of the button with pins, then run two lines of small tacking stitches about $\frac{1}{8}$ in. apart between the pins. Snip the material through between the tacking lines, then work *tailor's buttonhole* stitch over the cut edges as shown in Fig. 3. Begin at the

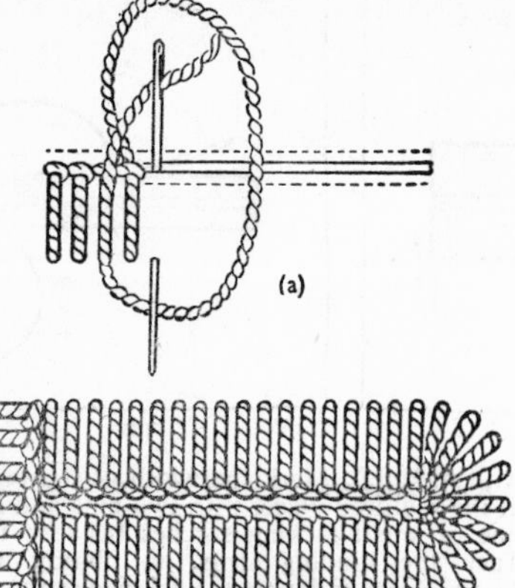

Fig. 3. Buttonholes: (a) *tailor's buttonhole stitch worked over tacked edges of buttonhole slit;* (b) *finished worked buttonhole.*

left-hand end of the buttonhole and work along the lower edge, radiating the stitches out in a semi-circle at the right-hand end and continuing along the top edge. Finish with a bar of stitches at the left-hand end.

See also BOUND BUTTONHOLE.

BUTTONHOLE STITCH. Simple buttonhole stitch has a great many uses, both for neatening edges and as a decorative embroidery stitch. It differs from tailor's buttonhole stitch in the direction of working and is shown in

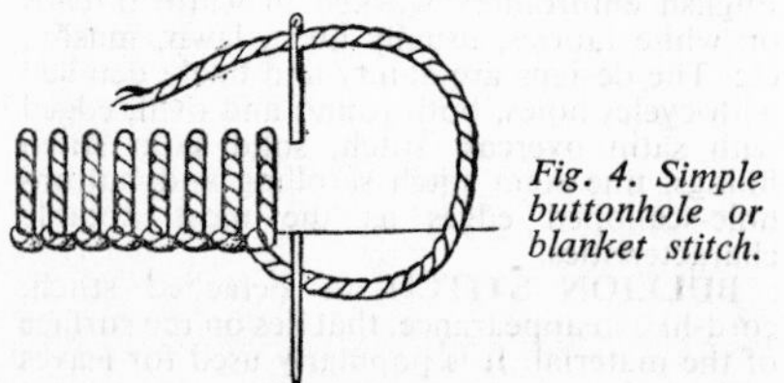

Fig. 4. Simple buttonhole or blanket stitch.

Fig. 4. The depth and closeness of the stitches may vary according to the work in hand, but when the stitches are widely spaced they are usually called *blanket stitches.*

BUTTON LOOPS. Where it is necessary to fasten buttons with loops, the loops can be made in two ways. For worked loops, secure the thread on the edge of the opening; then make another stitch a little farther along the same edge, leaving a loop between the two just large enough to slip over the button. Make several loops between these two points in the same way, then bind all the strands together with buttonhole stitch.

For button loops of material, make a length of narrow rouleau (see ROULEAUX) and stitch one end on the edge of the opening. Leave a loop of the rouleau large enough to slip over the button, then catch it to the material edge again farther along. At each point where it is stitched the rouleau can be either curved round for the next loop or folded back on itself. On thick materials, such as tweeds, and where only one or two loops are wanted, each loop can be made from a separate short length of rouleau.

BUTTONS, to sew on. Two-hole buttons should be sewn on with several threads passing from hole to hole; four-hole buttons with threads running diagonally, or from top to bottom corners. The threads should be left slack enough to allow room for the material of the buttonhole side of the fastening to lie smoothly between the button and the fabric to which it is sewn.

On coats and any garment where the material is very thick, the necessary slackness can be achieved by working the stitches over a matchstick or thin pencil held between button and cloth. When the match or pencil is removed the loose threads can then be bound round to form a shank.

CABLE CHAIN STITCH. A simple embroidery stitch giving the appearance of

Fig. 5. Cable chain stitch. Work from right to left; bring thread to front of material, hold in loop towards left. Put needle inside loop and pick up stitch. Pull loop tight round needle, passing working thread under point. Draw needle through and complete stitch.

cable links. The method of working is explained in Fig. 5.

CANVAS WORK. One of the oldest forms of decorative needlework, the background being of canvas and the embroidery worked over counted threads. The term covers a wide field, for materials may vary from the fine, single-thread canvases and stranded cottons used in delicate petit-point work, to the coarse, double-thread canvases and thick wools used for chair coverings, footstools, carpets and the like. There are many traditional stitches, probably the best known being cross stitch, tent stitch, long stitch, rice stitch and Florentine stitch. Because these stitches are worked over counted threads, the designs used are often formal and geometrical, so that neatness and uniformity are characteristics of the work. See also TAPESTRY WORK.

CHAIN STITCH. One of the simplest and most popular of embroidery stitches, giving a

Fig. 6. Chain stitch. Bring thread to front of work. Insert needle close to where thread has emerged and pick up small stitch. Bring thread from left under point and draw needle through.

chain-like effect on the surface of the material. The working method is shown in Fig. 6.

COLLARS. Although collar shapes and styles vary according to fashion trends, they fall into two classes as regards sewing them on, that is, peterpan and turned-down collars which are stitched to a round neckline, and coat or stepped collars which are stitched to the back of the neck and along the top of turned-back revers.

In the first type the collar should be seamed round its outer edges, turned right side out and pressed. The double inner raw edges are then tacked round the bodice neckline on the outside of the garment with a strip of bias binding on top. The binding is then turned over and hemmed down to cover all the raw edges.

For the stepped collar, used on tailored frocks, blouses and coats, the collar is made up according to the pattern instructions, and one inner edge stitched to the neckline and across the top of the revers on the inside of the garment. The remaining raw edge is then slip stitched down on the outside of the garment.

Collars that must be detached for laundering should have their inner raw edges bound with bias binding.

CORAL STITCH. A fine line stitch, with a surface knot at regular intervals. Fig. 7 gives the working method.

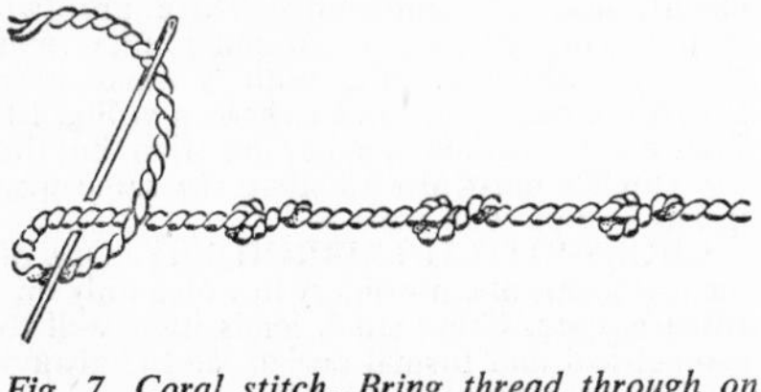

Fig. 7. Coral stitch. Bring thread through on line of stitching and hold to left. Slip needle in above thread, pick up small stitch at an angle to and under thread. Pass thread under point towards right and draw needle through.

CORDED PIPING. Piping cord covered with a bias-cut strip of material and used to emphasize seams, chiefly in furnishings.

The bias-cut strip (see BIAS BINDING) should be at least $\frac{1}{2}$ in. wider than the circumference of the cord. Enclose the cord in the binding and stitch the two layers of material together as close to the cord as possible. Sandwich the covered cord between the two edges to be seamed so that all four raw edges are together, then sew close to the cord.

CORNERS. There are two methods of making a neat, precise corner in a hem, a *squared* corner or a *mitred* corner.

For a squared corner, turn in the raw edges along the top first and then along the side of

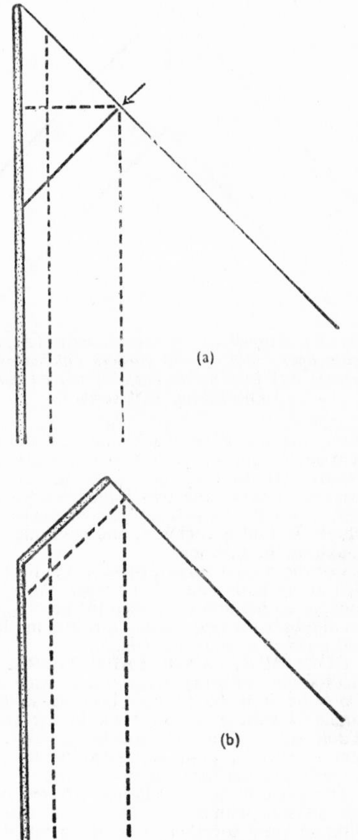

Fig. 8a. Mitred corner (dotted lines show hem creases): (a) *fold corner diagonally and seam between fold and edges from point where hem creases meet (arrowed above) and at right angles to fold;* (b) *leaving narrow turning above seam, snip off corner.*

the corner. Turn over the hem to the required depth, working first up the side and then

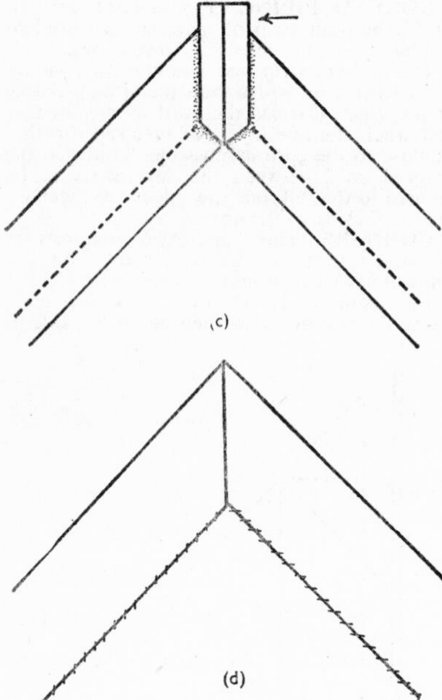

Fig. 8b. Mitred corner (continued): (c) *press seam open, snip off top corners (indicated by arrow) and turn inside out;* (d) *mitred corner finished and hem sewn.*

along the top edge. Tack and sew the top hem down right across to the extreme left edge. From there to the top left of the corner, oversew together the two folded edges, then hem down the right-hand side of the corner where the fold is enclosed, and continue sewing along the side hem.

For the mitred corner, press in the turnings well along both sides of the work as for the squared corner and then open the hems again, leaving only the first narrow turnings in place, and proceed as shown in Fig. 8.

COUCHING AND LAID WORK. A method of covering large areas with embroidery; it is economical because so little thread is wasted on the back of the work. Wool, silk and metal threads can be used very effectively, gold and silver being particularly popular for ecclesiastical work.

The space to be filled is first covered from side to side with long stitches, the threads lying so close together as to leave no background material visible. These threads are then tied down, or couched, with contrasting threads.

Couching stitch itself (see below) can be used in a number of ways, to tie down one or more threads and with the vertical stitches forming brick or diagonal patternings. Other stitches that can be used for couching laid threads include back stitch, chain, split, coral, feather, and surface buttonhole stitches. Laid work should be outlined with raised stitches and should always be worked in a frame.

COUCHING STITCH. A short, vertical stitch used to hold one or more other threads in place. Bring the thread that is to be couched-down through to the front of the work and lay it along the working line. With contrasting thread, make a tiny stitch from beneath the laid thread right over it and at right-angles to it. Insert the needle in the fabric at the top of the thread and bring it out again farther along the line and below the laid thread. See COUCHING AND LAID WORK.

COUNTERCHANGE. See APPLIQUÉ.

CRETAN STITCH. A very popular stitch for leaf veining or filling. Bring the thread through to the front of the material at the top point of the leaf. Pick up a small stitch at the right-hand edge with the needle pointing inwards and draw the needle through over the working thread. Make a similar stitch on the

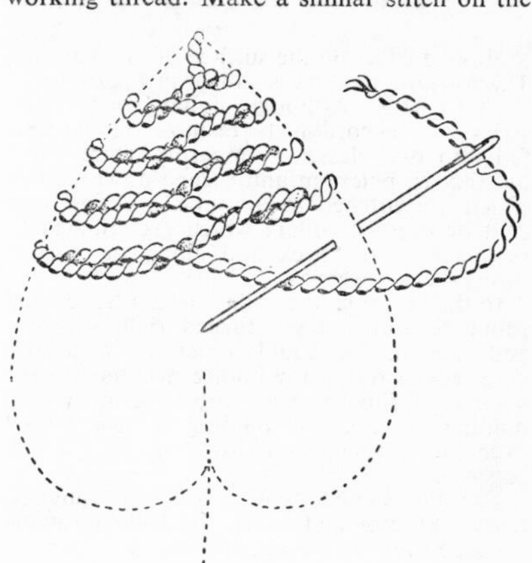

Fig. 9. Cretan stitch.

left-hand edge with the needle pointing inwards and continue working thus from side to side. See Fig. 9.

CREWEL STITCH. See STEM STITCH.

CROSS STITCH. As its name implies, this stitch forms a small cross. It is used in canvas work and in linen embroidery where the threads can be counted, as it relies for its effectiveness on uniformity. There are two methods of working, the double-journey and single-journey methods, both worked over squares of canvas or linen as shown in Fig. 10. They can be worked in either direction, but the top stitches must always slope the same way in any one piece of work.

CROSS-STITCH EMBROIDERY. One of the few forms of embroidery in which only one stitch is used. Cross stitch lends itself well to geometrical and formal design, and is always worked over counted threads.

The background material should be coarse enough for the threads to be counted easily. Where this is not possible, the design can be transferred to canvas and the canvas tacked

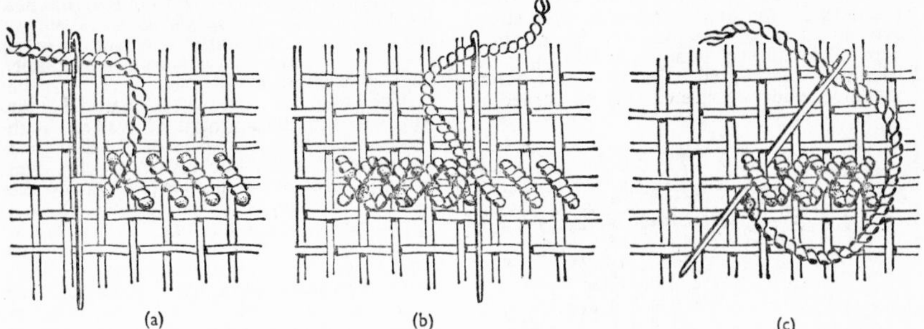

Fig. 10. Cross stitch: (a) *double-journey method, first step;* (b) *double-journey method, second step;* (c) *single-journey method. In* (c) *the first half of the cross is made as for double-journey method; from that point take the needle back to top right of square and bring it out at bottom left, completing each cross before starting to work the next.*

over the finer material. The cross stitch can then be worked over the canvas and the canvas threads drawn out afterwards, leaving the cross-stitch design on the material itself. For this method it is, of course, important that the stitch is worked tightly, otherwise the threads will lie slack on the work after the canvas has been removed. For the method of working the stitches, see CROSS STITCH.

CUFFS. For turned-back cuffs on a plain sleeve, cut a strip of material ½ in. longer than the sleeve edge, and ½ in. deeper than the finished cuff is to be. Join the two short ends of the strip and press the seam. Turn the sleeve on to the wrong side and slip the cuff over it with the right side of the cuff facing the wrong side of the sleeve. Seam the raw edges together, then turn the cuff over, turn in its other edge and hem down on the right side of the sleeve so that all the raw edges are enclosed. Press the lower edge of the cuff and fold back up the sleeve.

Where full sleeves have to be drawn up and set into a cuff, the method of gathering into a band is used (see GATHERS). The cuff is seamed at both ends before being set on to the gathers, and the edges of the sleeve openings are neatened with a facing or bias binding. This type of cuff is usually fastened with a button and buttonhole.

CURVED HEM. To turn up the hem of a flared or circular skirt, first mark, with either a tacking thread or pins, the line where the bottom edge of the hem is to be. Place the garment flat on a table, turn the hem surplus over on to the wrong side and tack the two layers together near the fold.

Because of the circular cutting, the raw edge of the material will have more fullness in it than the garment itself beneath; so distribute this fullness evenly by pinning the top layer to the underneath one at about ½-in. intervals with the pins at right-angles to the outer fold. Turn in the raw edge and sew the hem down, making a tiny pleat between each pin to take in the extra material. See FACED HEM and HEMMING.

CUTTING-OUT. Accuracy is all-important in this, the first step in garment-making, for no amount of care in sewing can make a success of a badly cut garment. See that the material is laid perfectly flat on a smooth surface. Make certain that the pattern is a correct fit, then follow the instructions and diagrams carefully when pinning the pattern on the material, paying particular attention to folds, selvedges and the grain of the fabric. Use sharp scissors and keep strictly to the pattern shape. Do not cut notches or darts, but mark them clearly with tailoring chalk or pins.

CUT WORK. A form of embroidery, mainly floral in design, in which the design itself is outlined and the background cut away. By tradition it is worked on white linen with white threads; but colour can be introduced.

In simple cut work, the design is first outlined with running stitches over which close buttonhole stitches are then worked, the knotted edge of the buttonholing being kept always to the outer edge of the design. When the embroidery is complete the background material is cut away with sharp scissors close to the buttonholed edges. Renaissance and Richelieu embroideries are more ornate forms of cut work, embellished with bars and picots.

DAMASK PATCH. See PATCHING.

DARNED NET. See NET DARNING.

DARNING. A method of repairing thin, worn places and the smaller holes in household linens, garments, woven and knitted fabrics, etc., by weaving in strong new threads. A darning mushroom and fine, large-eyed darning needles are essential.

Where the fabric is merely thin, take threads from some other portion, possibly a seam, and use them to weave in and out of the existing threads in order to reinforce the worn portion. The weaving should extend well beyond the thin part so that any strain is borne by the strong, outer area.

To darn a hole, work on the wrong side of the article and weave in matching threads up and down, roughly in the shape of a diamond, until the hole itself and a small surrounding area are covered. To allow for shrinkage of the darning threads, leave a small loop at each turn. Now work from side to side, weaving threads in and out of the vertical strands until the hole is filled in with close-textured darning. As before, leave small loops of thread at the ends of each row.

Knitted fabrics, such as jerseys, woollen stockings, underwear, etc., can be darned in

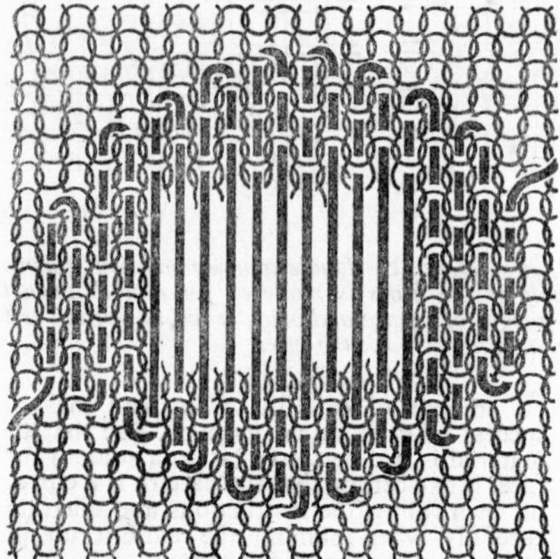

Fig. 11. Darning a hole in stocking stitch with loops picked up by the vertical threads. A second thread is woven across from side to side to complete filling in the hole.

much the same way with the darning threads taken through the mesh of the knitting in the surrounding area (Fig. 11).

The same method of darning, with appropriately finer threads, of course, is used for holes in silk stockings, but even greater care must be taken here to pick up the loop of each stitch at the edge of the hole to prevent laddering. As a further precaution, a thread catching in all the loops can be run round the outside of the hole before the darning is begun.

In addition to filling in holes, darning can be used for repairing cuts and tears in materials.

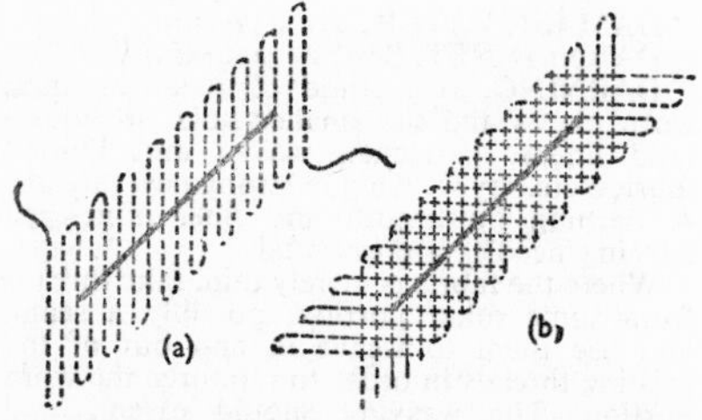

Fig. 12. Cross darning a diagonal cut: (a) *edges of cut caught in with vertical threads;* (b) *the cut cross darned in the opposite direction.*

Tablecloths, for instance, sometimes suffer from diagonal knife-cuts for which a *cross darn* can be used. In this, two parallelograms are darned so that the area immediately surrounding the cut is double-darned (Fig. 12).

DARTS. Triangular intakes of material used for fitting and shaping garments. Their size can vary from the short wide ones, used in sleeve tops, to the long narrow ones for tapering a skirt into the waistline.

Along the raw edge of the material, mark with two pins the amount of material to be taken in at the widest part of the dart. Fold the material, right side inside, so that these two pins meet. With another pin, mark on the fold of the material the point where the dart should taper away to nothing. Tack the double material together in a gently sloping line from the pin on the fold to those at the widest point, then seam along this line. The dart can be either cut down the fold, opened and pressed, or folded to one side of the seam and pressed.

DOUBLE BACK STITCH. See SHADOW STITCH.

DOUBLE RUNNING. See HOLBEIN STITCH.

DRAWN-FABRIC WORK. Embroidery worked on counted threads in which the threads are *not* drawn out but are drawn closely together in groups so as to leave open spaces between.

The best known stitch used for this embroidery is *punch stitch*, and it is worked with a specially thick needle. The design, usually worked in satin stitch, stands out in relief on the background of punch work. See PUNCH STITCH.

DRAWN-THREAD WORK. A form of needlework in which threads are drawn from the material in either one or both directions, and the remaining strands, or the resulting open spaces, grouped or filled with a variety of stitches, to give dainty lace-like insertions.

The work is traditionally white, although colour is often introduced in modern usage. Despite its delicate appearance, it is strong and durable, and is therefore extremely popular for decorating table linen, bed linen, handkerchiefs, and the like. Only evenly woven fabrics such as linens should be used.

The stitch most closely associated with drawn-thread work is hemstitch (for working details, see HEMSTITCH) and, where the threads are drawn out in one direction only, the work is often called "hemstitching."

DRESS SHIELDS, to sew in. Single shields that give protection to the bodice only should be stitched with whipping or buttonholing to the curved underarm seam, so that about two-thirds of the shield lies to the front and one-third to the back of the side seam. The outer curve of the shield should be caught to the side seam with one or two slack stitches to prevent the material from being pulled in wear.

A double shield should be placed over the underarm seam so that one half extends down the inside of the sleeve, the other half protecting the bodice. Like the single shield, it should be placed well to the front of the garment, but should be stitched with slack stitches at each end of its inner curve only and its outer curves caught to the sleeve seam and bodice side seam.

EMBROIDERY FRAMES. Where it is difficult to keep embroidery from puckering when worked in the hand, a frame should be used. The simplest type is the tambour frame, which consists of two hoops of wood, one slightly larger than the other. The embroidery is placed over the smaller hoop and the larger one fitted down over it so that the fabric is held taut between the two.

For larger pieces of work a square frame is best. This consists of two pieces of wood, pierced with holes and fitted with pegs, at the sides of the frame, with wooden rollers top and bottom. Strips of canvas are attached to these wooden rollers, and the embroidery is stitched to these, and the space between the rollers adjusted until the work is held taut. The sides of the embroidery are then laced to the sides of the frame or, if the fabric is delicate, canvas is stitched to the work first and the canvas laced to the frame sides.

EQUIPMENT FOR SEWING. The amount of equipment that a needlewoman requires depends upon the type of needlework she undertakes. A selection of sharp needles, sizes 3 to 10, and darners, sizes 4 to 8, steel pins, a smooth thimble, a bodkin, a mushroom, an inch-tape, a pair of long, sharp scissors for cutting out, and some small, sharp-pointed scissors for snipping cottons, etc., comprise the minimum basic equipment for everyday household sewing and repairs.

Darning wool, silk, sewing cotton and sewing silk will, of course, be chosen specifically for the job in hand. For fine needlework and embroidery, crewel needles, sizes 4 to 8, blunt tapestry needles, a selection of stranded cottons, embroidery silks and wools suitable for the type of embroidery chosen, fine-pointed embroidery scissors, and a frame will be added to the basic equipment.

If dressmaking is to be undertaken, a sewing machine is almost indispensable, while such additional equipment as tailoring chalk, a yardstick, a hem guide and a tracing wheel all contribute to good workmanship.

EYELET HOLES. Small holes, either round or oval in shape, with their edges stitched to prevent fraying. They are used in belt fastenings, and as openings for threading lacings, elastic, etc., while, in embroidery, they are a characteristic feature of white work, particularly broderie anglaise.

To make a small round eyelet hole, work a small circle of tiny running stitches, pierce the fabric inside the stitches with a stiletto and then work close satin or buttonhole stitch over the edges. For oval or larger round eyelet holes, outline the shape with running stitches, then snip the inside fabric vertically and horizontally as far as the outline; turn the cut points back to the wrong side and work satin stitch or buttonhole stitch over the folded edges. Trim away the surplus material at the back.

FACED HEM. A hem in which the fabric that is turned up is added to the main material, either to lengthen a garment or for decorative purposes. The additional strip can be machined to the lower edge of the main material, right sides facing, turned over so that the seam lies along the bottom of the hem, and stitched down as for an ordinary hem (see HEMS).

A curved hem can be faced in the same way,

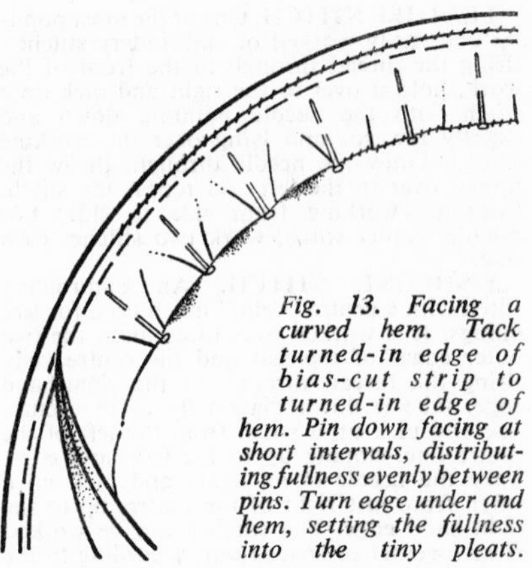

Fig. 13. Facing a curved hem. Tack turned-in edge of bias-cut strip to turned-in edge of hem. Pin down facing at short intervals, distributing fullness evenly between pins. Turn edge under and hem, setting the fullness into the tiny pleats.

but the facing strip must be bias-cut and the inner hem sewn as explained for CURVED HEMS. Fig. 13 shows a facing added to a curved hem.

FAGGOT STITCH. A decorative insertion stitch worked between two edges of material. Turn in the two edges and tack, right sides uppermost, on to a strip of firm paper, leaving about ¼-in. space between them. Join the thread to one edge, then take the needle across to the other edge at an angle and pick up a small piece of material. Draw the needle through with the working thread under it; then take the needle farther on along the opposite edge and repeat, as shown in Fig. 14.

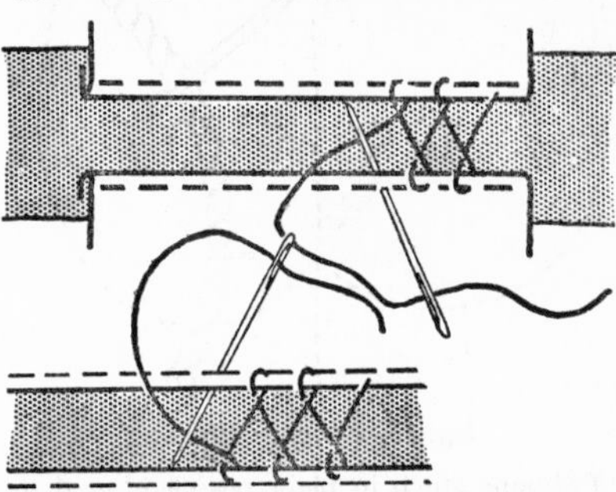

Fig. 14. Faggot stitch is worked over a strip of firm paper, represented by the shaded area in the illustration above. The stitch on both sides is the same but in reverse direction.

Continue working from side to side, keeping the space between the stitches uniform.

Another popular type of faggot stitch is *bar faggoting*. Prepare the work as above, then join the thread to the top edge and pick up a little of the lower edge exactly opposite. Twist the needle two or three times through this single thread and draw it upwards to make a twisted strand between the two edges. Insert the needle at the top edge and bring it out a little farther on, to make the next stitch.

FEATHER STITCH. One of the most popular and easily worked of embroidery stitches. Bring the thread through to the front of the work, hold it over to the right and pick up a stitch with the needle pointing down and slightly inwards and lying over the working thread. Draw the needle through, throw the thread over to the left and repeat the stitch. Continue working from side to side. For double feather stitch, work two stitches each side.

FISHBONE STITCH. An embroidery stitch with a centre "vein," much used for leaf fillings. It is worked over three lines, the two outer edges of the leaf and the centre vein. Bring the thread through at the right-hand edge, take it down diagonally to the centre line and pick up a stitch from the left of the centre line, sloping up to the left-hand edge. Take the needle down again and pick up a stitch from just right of the centre, up to the right-hand edge. The stitches can be worked close together or spaced out, according to the effect desired. Details are shown in Fig. 15.

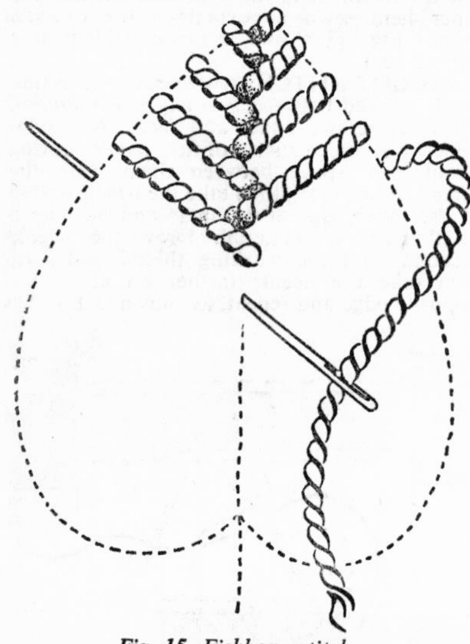

Fig. 15. Fishbone stitch.

Fishbone stitch in plain sewing is used to draw two edges together, the needle being passed between the cut edges from each side alternately.

FLARED HEM. See CURVED HEM.

FLOUNCES. Bias or circular-cut strips of material, stitched at one edge to the main garment. Neaten the outer edge of the flounce with a rolled hem, shell edging or whatever trimming is required. Place the garment and the flounce together, raw edge to raw edge and right sides facing, and tack, easing the flounce on but not gathering it. Machine or hand-sew the two layers together, then whip the raw edges to neaten them. Turn the flounce down and press the seam upwards under the garment itself.

To add additional flounces above the lower one, put in lines of tacking threads and stitch the flounces along these, as along the raw edge, with right sides of the flounce and the garment facing, then turn the flounces down and press the seams.

FLY STITCH. A V-shaped embroidery stitch that can be worked singly or in lines or groups. Bring the thread through to the front of the material and insert the needle at the same level but to the right. Bring the needle out farther down, midway between the two points, with the working thread running under the needle from left to right. Make a tiny vertical stitch to hold the loop of thread down and bring the needle out again wherever the next stitch is to commence.

FOUR-SIDED STITCH. See PUNCH STITCH.

FRENCH BINDING. A practical method of sewing on bias binding when very flimsy material is being used. Fold the bias-cut strip lengthways in half and press it. Sew the double raw edges to the raw edge of the material, on the right side, fold the binding over and hem the fold down on the wrong side of the work.

FRENCH KNOT. A detached embroidery stitch that forms a small knot on the surface of the material. Bring the thread through to the front of the material. Hold it towards the left, then slip the needle under it and twist it two or three times so that loops of thread lie over the needle. Draw the needle through, holding the loops down with the thumb, and insert the needle in the material just to the right of the point where the thread originally came through. Bring the needle out where the next knot is to be.

FRENCH RUN-AND-FELL SEAM. A narrow seam used mainly on lingerie and thin fabrics. Tack the two pieces of the material together, right sides facing, and machine or hand-stitch them a little more than a ¼ in. from the raw edges. Turn over and tack the double raw edge in a narrow turning, then fold over again and hem down over the first line of stitching.

FRENCH SEAM. A neat method of joining two pieces of material so that no raw edges are visible, inside or out.

The two materials to be joined are placed together with right sides outside and are sewn about a ¼ in. below the raw edges, with small running or machine stitching. These edges are then trimmed with sharp scissors until they are neat and level; then the work is turned on to the wrong side and the two layers of material tacked together so as to enclose the raw edges. A second line of stitches is then worked just below the tacking so that no raw edges are visible on the right side.

FRILLS. Strips of material gathered at one edge and stitched on to the main garment as trimming. Before gathering, the frill should be at least one and a half times, but preferably twice, its finished length. Neaten or trim the lower edge of the frill strip as desired.

Take a narrow turning on to the wrong side along the top edge and work a line of small running stitches just below the fold. Draw up the thread to the required length and spread out the gathers evenly. Tack the frill on to

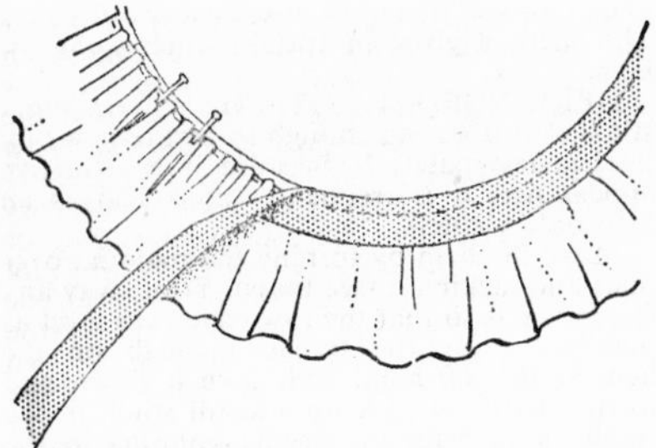

Fig. 16. Attaching a frill to a curved edge. Gather frill to right size, pin on curved edge and stitch with a strip of bias binding. Turn binding over and hem down on other side.

the garment and sew on along the gathering thread. When a long frill is being stitched on, it is advisable to divide both frill and garment into equal sections and to deal with each section separately.

Another method of attaching frills is shown in Fig. 16. Here the frill is sewn to a curved neckline and the raw edges neatened with bias binding.

GATHERS, to set into band. The material to be gathered should be at least one and a half times the width of the finished band. Work a line of small, even running stitches across the material, about a ¼ in. down from the raw edge. Draw this running thread up tightly so that the material is closely gathered; then put a pin vertically in the material at the end of the gathers and twist the gathering thread securely round it.

Beginning at the left and using a fine pin, "stroke" down between each gather so that the material lies in even parallel folds as shown in Fig. 17 (a). Take a narrow turning on to the wrong side along one edge of the band, and pin the band over the gathers at the right-hand end.

Unwind the thread that is round the pin at the left-hand end, and let out the gathers until the gathered piece is the same length as the band; then fasten off the stitching securely. See that the gathers are evenly distributed and tack the band along over the gathering thread. Hem the band down, using rather an upright hemming stitch and picking up one fold of the material with each stitch, as illustrated (b).

On the wrong side of the work, fold the band over, turn its raw edges under and hem it over the gathers again in the same way as the front.

GAUGING. A decorative method of holding gathers in place. Work several parallel rows of small, even running stitches across the material to be gathered, keeping the rows equal distances apart. Leave a length of thread visible at the end of each row without finishing off.

Draw the top thread up to the required width, and wind the thread round a pin; then draw up the other threads similarly until all the gauged section is the same width. Unwind the threads from the pins and fasten them off securely.

GROS POINT. See TENT STITCH.

HEMMING. The method of hand sewing a fold of material over another layer. The folded edge should be tacked in place first (see HEMS).

Beginning at the right-hand end of the work, secure the thread with two small stitches. With the needle pointing upwards and to the left, pick up a small amount of the single fabric and a small amount of the folded edge of the top piece. Draw the needle through and repeat the stitch, keeping all the stitches even in size and sloping at the same angle. They should be just as small and even on the right side of the work.

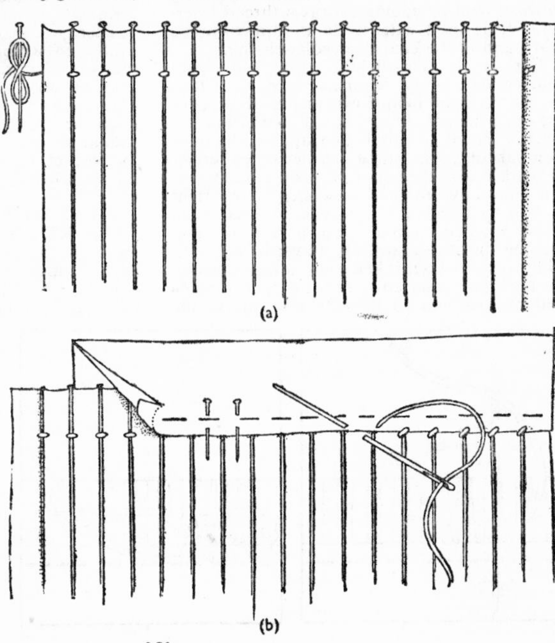

Fig. 17. Gathers: (a) *material drawn up and "stroked" into even folds with the gathering thread twisted round a pin;* (b) *the gathers are eased out to size of band, the edge of which is turned under and tacked in place. The band is then hemmed on with one stitch to each fold.*

HEMS. A method of neatening a raw edge by folding the material on to the wrong side and sewing it down. There are several methods of stitching the hem, the most usual being with hemming stitch (see HEMMING), but the method of preparation is always the same.

Fold the raw edge of the material over in a narrow turning on to the wrong side, pin and then press lightly, afterwards removing the pins. Fold the material over again to the depth the hem is to be, pinning at short intervals and measuring it constantly with an inch-tape, ruler or hem guide to ensure that it is the same width throughout. Tack along the outer edge of the hem and along the pinned fold and press lightly. Beginning at the right-hand end, sew the hem down with hemming stitch.

For hems on garments, the stitches should not show on the right side of the work and slip stitching is more generally used (see SLIP STITCH). If the hem is to be machined, the stitching is done just above the lower fold.

With very thick materials it is sometimes impractical to make the first turning along the raw edge because this gives three layers of material at the sewing line. If the material does not fray very much, the hem can be turned over once to the required depth and well tacked, and the raw edge stitched down with herringboning (see HERRINGBONE STITCH). On a fraying material, the raw edge can be bound first with bias binding or Prussian tape and the binding caught down to the fabric beneath with slip stitching. See also CURVED HEM, FACED HEM, and ROLLED HEM.

HEMSTITCH. A decorative stitch worked over drawn threads and used for fastening down a hem or edging a drawn-thread insertion. It is used extensively in drawn-thread work and in the coarser needleweaving.

For simple hemstitching, draw out about four threads at the required place; then turn in and tack the hem down just to the top of the open threads. Proceed as shown in Fig. 18.

This version of simple hemstitch is the most popular one, but some needlewomen prefer to work it with the hem to the top of the work. An alternative method is worked from right to left by bringing the thread through $\frac{1}{8}$ in. above the hem, taking it down vertically and picking up three strands towards the left. The needle is then taken back to the opening on the right, inserted under the open threads and brought out to the left $\frac{1}{8}$ in. above the hem, ready to make the next downward stitch. This method gives an upright stitch along the hem.

HERRINGBONE STITCH. A criss-cross stitch that is strong enough to secure hems on the heaviest materials. Because of its attractive appearance, it is frequently used also as an embroidery stitch.

Make the hem by turning the material over once and tacking it (see HEMS). Trim away any fraying ends so that the raw edge is as level as possible. Bring the thread through on the hem at the left-hand end, take it down and to the right and pick up a small stitch in the single fabric with the needle pointing to the left. Move the needle up to the right and pick up a stitch in the hem, still with the needle pointing to the left. Continue working up and down, keeping the crosses even. No stitches should be visible on the other side of the work.

HOLBEIN STITCH. An embroidery stitch with the appearance of back stitch, sometimes called *double running*. It consists of two rows of even running stitches worked along the same line but in opposite directions so that the stitches picked up on the first journey are passed over on the second.

HONEYCOMB STITCH. See SMOCKING.

HOOKS AND EYES, to sew on. The hook should be sewn inside the top layer of the placket or opening. Hold it in position with the curve of the hook a little below the outer edge of the material, and then sew it down with close oversewing round the two metal rings and over the bar beneath the hook.

To find the exact position for the eye, rub a little tailor's chalk on the hook and press it down on to the underside of the placket or opening.

There are two types of eyes, loop and bar. Both are sewn on with close oversewing round the two metal rings, but while the bar type is sewn on exactly on the chalk mark, the loop type is sewn so that the outer curve of the loop is on the mark. The hook for this type of eye should be sewn well inside the outer edge of the placket, so that the margin of fabric covers the eye when the fastening is closed.

INLAY WORK. See APPLIQUÉ.

INSERTION, to sew in. Take narrow turnings, on to the wrong side, along the two edges of material between which the insertion is to be sewn. Tack the insertion along these two edges, on the right side of the work; then, with matching thread, sew it down with small oversewing stitches, taking the stitches through the double fabric beneath. Finally, trim away the raw edges of material beyond the line of sewing on the wrong side of the work.

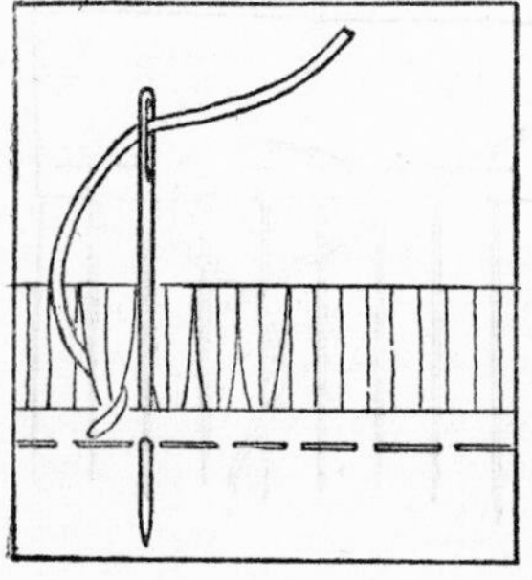

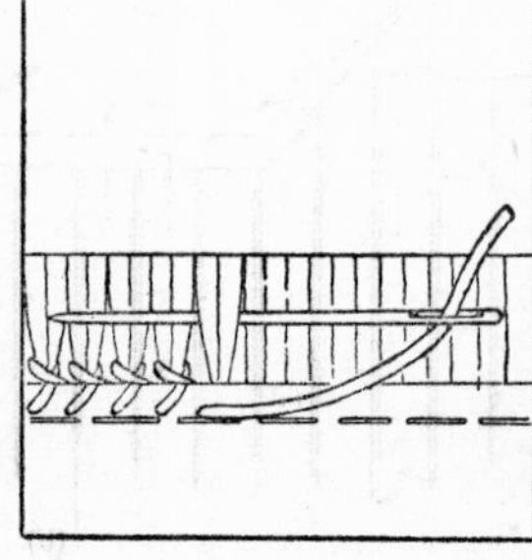

Fig. 18. Hemstitching: bring the thread through on to the tacked hem (dotted line), take needle round three or four threads and pick up a stitch in the hem again.

INVERTED PLEAT. See PLEATS.

JACOBEAN EMBROIDERY. A style of embroidery dating from the seventeenth century, worked in wools on a bleached twill ground. It is sometimes called *crewel work*, and was extensively used for bed- and wall-hangings, and for furnishing draperies of all kinds.

The designs are very distinctive, their characteristics being a leafy well-branched tree, called the Tree of Life, springing from small hillocks, with fruit, flowers and wild life intermingled, the whole design being highly imaginative. The work is colourful, and a wide variety of stitches and laid work is used to achieve interestingly patterned fillings within the outlines of each leaf, flower, etc.

Designs that are typical of Jacobean work are often used in canvas embroideries.

LACE, to sew on. Lace that has one shaped edge looks most effective if appliquéd and the fabric cut away from behind afterwards. Pin the lace carefully into position, then tack with small stitches round the outline, keeping as near to the corded edge of the lace as possible.

Using embroidery silk to match the lace, work round the outline with narrow satin stitch over the cord edge. On the wrong side, cut away the fabric from behind the lace, keeping close to the outline of sewing.

Lace with a straight edge can be sewn on with bar faggot stitch (see FAGGOT STITCH), or oversewn along a turned-in edge (see INSERTION), or whipped on as shown in Fig. 19.

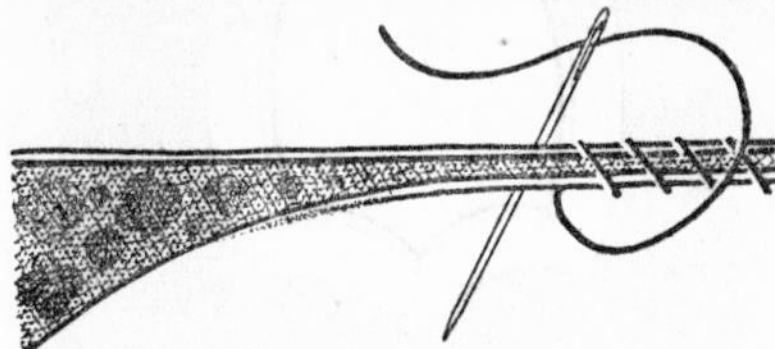

Fig. 19. Whipping lace on to fabric. Roll fabric edge between finger and thumb and stitch over roll and edge of lace. Press lace upwards as soon as the whipping-on is finished.

To gather lace or net edging before sewing it on, draw it up to the required length by the strong thread that runs along its straight edge. The edge of the material should be neatened first with a narrow hem or turning; then the gathered net or lace is placed in front, right sides facing, and the gathered edge whipped to the edge of the material. After sewing, the edging can be turned up and pressed.

LAID WORK. See COUCHING.

LAPPED SEAM. A seam in which one piece of material is folded down over another, with one line of sewing visible on top. It is used mostly in machine-sewn work, to emphasize a seam.

Turn under the edge of the top piece of material and tack the fold on to the lower one, then put in one row of stitching to hold all three layers together. The width between the folded edge and the stitching is varied according to the work in hand. In recent fashions, a good width has often been left so that the lapped seam gives the appearance of a tuck. The turning must, of course, be even wider. On the wrong side, trim the raw edges level, and overcast them for neatness.

LAZY-DAISY STITCH. A detached chain stitch, popularly used in small flower petals. Bring the thread through at the flower centre and hold it down with the left thumb. Put the needle back in again just to the right of the thread, pick up a stitch the length of the petal and draw the needle through over the working thread. Make a tiny stitch to hold the thread down at the top of the petal, and bring the needle out again at the flower centre.

LININGS. The lining for a garment must be cut as carefully as the garment itself. But it is sometimes a help in fitting if the darts in the lining are only tacked and not stitched. The side seams can be stitched and pressed, but the shoulder seams left undone, while all sleeve seams should be sewn, but the sleeves not stitched to the bodice lining.

Slip the lining inside the garment and tack the side seams of both together; then run a line of tacking down the centre of the back to keep the lining in its correct position. Turn in the front edges of the lining and tack, then hem them over the inner edges of the front facing of the garment, working from the shoulder line downwards. Tack the front shoulder edge of the lining to the shoulder seam, and bring the back edge over it, turning it in and hemming it down over the front.

If the lining is to be stitched to the coat at the bottom, turn the raw edge under and tack, then hem it, keeping the lining well above the bottom edge and taking care that it does not drag the garment up. Where the lining is to be loose at the bottom, turn the raw edge to the inside and make a hem.

Tack lining and garment together round the arm-holes. Turn in the lower edge of the sleeve linings and hem them to the garment sleeve well above the lower edge. Tack both together along all the sleeve seams, easing the lining on to prevent it from pulling the sleeve up. Tack and hem the top edge of the sleeve lining over the bodice lining, round the armholes. Remove all tacking and press the edges.

LONG-AND-SHORT STITCH. A variety of satin stitch used extensively for fillings in large shapes. A row of satin stitches is put inside the outline of the shape, with the stitches level on the outer edge, but alternately long and short so that the inner edge is uneven. Succeeding rows of even-length stitches are then worked so that the lower edge is always uneven. This causes the stitches to merge into one another and is of great value where shaded effects have to be achieved.

MENDING. Any necessary mending should be done immediately a garment or article shows signs of wear. Delay means a bigger job when the repair is eventually undertaken. Material that is wearing thin can be strengthened with matching threads woven into it, or reinforced with a piece of similar material herringboned underneath it.

Holes, whether in woven or knitted fabrics, should be patched or darned immediately they appear so that the patch or darn is as small as possible (see PATCHING and DARNING).

Where there are large holes in the fingers or toes of knitted gloves or socks, it is advisable to unravel them and re-knit.

Split gloves can be repaired by working buttonhole stitch along both edges of the split and drawing the loops of the buttonholing together with another thread through the middle. Similarly, holes in gloves can be mended by cutting a patch from an old glove, exactly to size, buttonholing round the outer edge of the patch and the inner edge of the hole and drawing the two buttonholed edges together with another thread.

Torn buttonholes can be repaired by hemming a short piece of tape behind the torn end, darning the material down on to the tape and re-working the end of the buttonhole.

Tape can also be hemmed along the edges of sheets, tablecloths, etc., that show signs of splitting, and the frayed edges darned down on to the tape.

Where the corners of pockets have torn the garment material, the pocket corner should be unpicked and the material beneath neatly patched or darned over a piece of tape. The pocket can then be stitched back into place. Material torn out by buttons can be repaired in the same way, the button removed, the material darned or patched over tape to strengthen it, and the button replaced.

Where the pull on lingerie shoulder-straps has torn lace or the edge of the garment, the strap should be unpicked, the fabric neatly patched or the lace reinforced with net and the strap sewn on again, but a little to the right or left of its original position.

MITREING. See CORNERS.

NECKLINES, to finish. The choice of trimming for a neckline will depend mainly on current fashions and on the type of garment. Collars of contrasting or self-material are always popular, while binding or piping can be used when a small amount of contrasting colour is wanted. Ready-made frilling or pleating can be used to soften a neckline, while, on children's clothes particularly, narrow frills of self-material, set on with bias binding, give a dainty finish. See FRILLS.

A plain neckline that is to be untrimmed must, of course, be neatly finished. Its raw edge can be turned in to the wrong side and covered with bias binding, or the whole neckline can be faced with material cut exactly to shape as shown in Fig. 20.

NEEDLEWEAVING. A simple variation of drawn-thread work in which coarser materials and thicker threads are used. Heavy, evenly-woven linens and furnishing fabrics with thick embroidery silks or wools are most suitable, for its chief use is to introduce borders and insertions of colour into household articles such as curtains, cushions, table mats, etc. The designs are necessarily simple.

The threads need not draw out right across the fabric as in drawn-thread work, but are snipped in the centre of the border space and withdrawn right and left to the ends of the space, where they are then woven into the fabric at the back. The drawn threads are hemstitched and the cut ends of the border space are buttonhole-stitched. When the threads have been drawn across the space, the remaining vertical threads are interwoven with wool or silk and are drawn together in blocks according to the design.

Where the needleweaving is carried out in one colour, the interweaving threads are drawn tight, so that the blocks are separated sufficiently to give a pattern of solids and open spaces. In a coloured design, however, the contrast of colour gives sufficient patterning and the groups of threads are not, therefore, pulled so widely apart.

NET DARNING. Threads woven through the mesh of net to give a lace-like effect. The work covers a wide range, from the dainty patterns woven and embroidered in fine threads on net or tulle to the sturdier types worked in wool or coarse silks on wide-meshed nets. The fine net embroidery and darning has been commercialized, and very little of it is worked by hand these days; but the coarse net darning is still popular for curtains, covers, cushions, etc.

The designs can be worked by counting the spaces or by tacking the net over the drawn

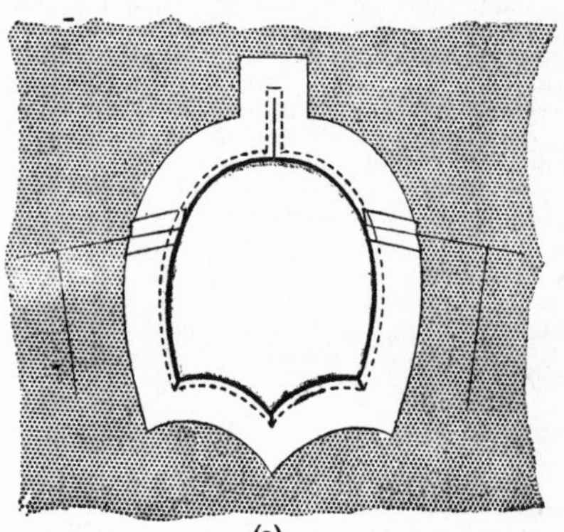

(a)

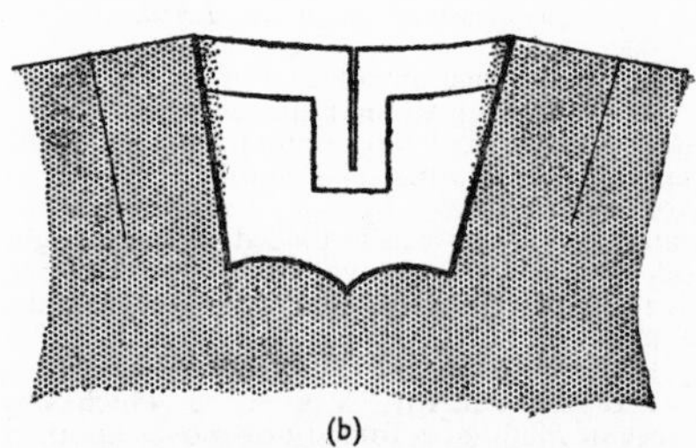

(b)

Fig. 20. Facing a neckline: (a) *facing stitched on with right side of facing to right side of garment and with narrow turnings trimmed neatly; neaten outer edge of facing with whipping or turn in once and machine, and snip into any corners before turning over;* (b) *facing turned to inside of garment, no stitching being visible on right side.*

pattern and working over it. With the use of a blunt needle, the silk or wool is woven in and out in a variety of stitches, filling in the mesh of the net in geometrical patternings.

OUTLINE STITCH. See STEM STITCH.

OVERCASTING. A stitch used for neatening raw edges. It is usually worked from left to right. Take the thread from the front of the material over the raw edge a little to the right, and bring the needle through from the back to the front of the work just below the edge.

OVERSEWING. A stitch used to join two edges of fabric together. Turn in the two edges and tack them together with the right sides outside. Beginning at the right-hand end, take the thread from the front of the work straight over the two edges. Put the needle in at the back and bring it out just to the left of the thread at the front. The stitches must be kept close together and must be even in depth.

PATCHING. A method of repairing a hole in a fabric by stitching another piece of fabric over it. The work should always be done neatly and carefully with the fabric of the patch matching that of the surrounding area so that the repair is as little noticeable as possible. If new material has to be used, it should be well washed first to avoid shrinking afterwards.

There are several methods of patching, the hemmed patch being suitable for most plain-fabric repairs. The patch should be ½ in. larger each way than the area of the worn part and should be cut in a neat square or oblong. Take narrow turnings along each edge on to the right side, and tack the patch on to the wrong side of the article with the weave of the patch matching that of the fabric beneath. Hem the patch down as invisibly as possible. On the right side trim the raw edges of the hole into a square or oblong, snip into the corners and turn the edges under; then hem them to the patch.

For thicker materials, where the turned-in edges would be too bulky, the flannel patch can be used. Tack the patch over the hole on the wrong side of the work and herringbone its raw edges down; then, on the right side, trim the hole into a neat square or oblong and herringbone these raw edges on to the patch.

When patching patterned material, the design on the patch must match in with that of the material surrounding the hole so that the repair will not be obvious. Cut a square or oblong patch, turn its edges on to the wrong side and tack over the hole on the right side of the material, so that the continuity of the patterning is preserved. Hem it down; then, on the wrong side, trim the hole into a neat square or oblong, and finish the raw edges with blanket stitch without sewing them down to the material beneath.

A combination of darning and patching for repairing holes in damask cloths is shown in Fig. 21.

Another type of darned-in patch can be used on loosely-woven materials such as tweeds. The patching material should be two or three inches larger than the hole, and should be tacked on so that the weave matches that of

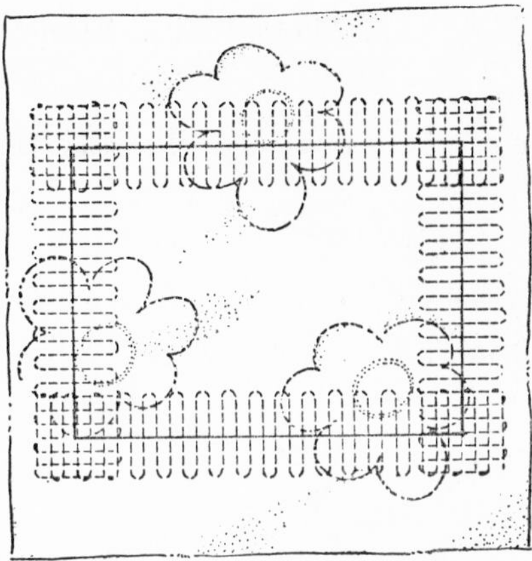

Fig. 21. Damask patch. Cut patch to match pattern round hole and at least 1 in. larger each way. Tack under hole, trimming raw edges of hole away a little at a time. Darn across from patch to cloth along opposite sides, so that the corners are double darned as shown above. Press well when finished.

the surrounding area. The threads in the patch beyond the hole are then unravelled and darned in and out of the surrounding fabric.

PATCHWORK. The art of sewing together small scraps of different materials to make one piece of fabric of pleasing design. It is used mainly for bed covers and cushions. Plain and patterned fabrics can be combined effectively, but in an article that will need to be laundered care should be taken that unwashable fabrics and those with colours that would "run" are not included.

The patchwork can be made up to a specific geometrical design, many of which are traditional, or scraps of irregular shapes and sizes can be used to make crazy patchwork.

Where a design is to be used, small pieces of strong paper are cut to the exact sizes needed for each patch. With these as patterns, the scraps of fabric are cut with a narrow turning allowed on each edge. Each patch is tacked over its paper shape with the raw edges turned on to the wrong side. The folded edges of each are then stitched to the folded edges of its neighbouring patches. When the work is complete, the paper foundations are removed and the article lined. In the case of a bed quilt, it is usually also interlined.

An alternative method and the one generally used for crazy patchwork is to tack odd-shaped pieces on to a foundation fabric, with turned-in edges overlapping raw edges. The joins are then stitched with feather stitching in contrasting thread.

PEKINESE STITCH. A stitch much used in Chinese embroideries. It is worked in rows, and can be used to fill large or small areas. Work a first row of back stitch; then, beginning at the left, take a second thread up under the second stitch and down under the first, up under the third and down under the second, and so on. Contrasting threads may, of course, be used.

PETIT POINT. See TENT STITCH and CANVAS WORK.

PICOT EDGE. An edge with small loops of thread outstanding. Fig. 22 explains two methods of working it on a buttonholed edge.

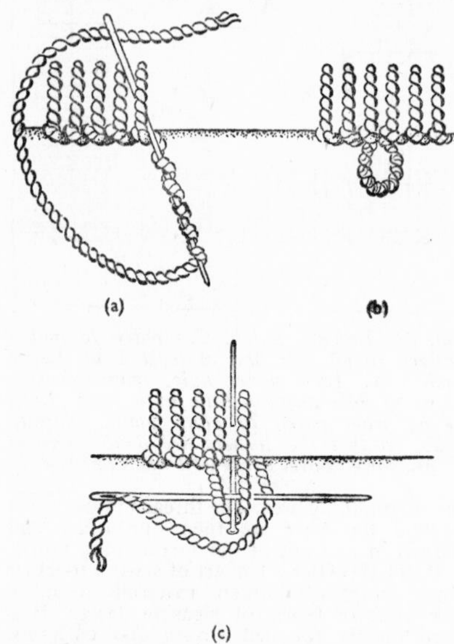

Fig. 22. Buttonhole picots. (a) *and* (b) *show one method. The needle is slipped under the last buttonhole stitch; the thread is twisted round the needle which is drawn through.* (b) *shows the finished picot. Another method* (c) *is to put a pin in the buttonhole edge. Loop thread round pin, pick up next stitch on edge and make a buttonhole stitch over loop of thread round pin.*

The raw edges of fabrics can be neatened with a machine-worked picot edge. This consists of a line of machine hemstitching which is cut through the centre to give a tufted edge to the fabric. It is undertaken by most pleating and button-covering firms.

PIN TUCK. The narrowest of tucks; it is used in groups for shaping or sometimes merely for decoration. Fold the material, with the right side outside, in a perfectly straight line and pin as near the fold as possible. Run a line of sewing not more than $\frac{1}{8}$ in. from the fold for the length the tuck is to be.

Subsequent tucks must be parallel with the first one, as they depend for their effectiveness on precision and regularity. In pressing, they should not be flattened to one side but should stand up to give a ridged effect.

PIPING. A folded strip of bias-cut material inserted in a seam for decoration. Cut the piping material on the cross (see BIAS BINDING). Fold it in half lengthways and press. The folded strip can then either be sandwiched between two layers of material with all four raw edges together and seamed, or be tacked to the right side of one piece, raw edge to raw edge, and the turned-in edge of the other piece sewn down on top of it.

PLACKETS. The openings left at waist, neck and wrist so that a garment can be slipped on easily. They can be fastened with press-studs, hooks and eyes or zip-fasteners.

For press-stud or hook-and-eye fastenings, the front of the placket must overlap the back portion. Stitch a facing, either of self-material or bias binding, inside the front portion of the placket, then widen the underneath part by stitching a double band of material to its inner edge.

In a seam where turnings of an inch or more have been allowed, these turnings can be used instead of facings. Press both turnings towards the front of the garment. Neaten the turning under the top half with a narrow binding along its raw edge, and slip-stitch the binding down to the top layer of material. Neaten the underneath turning by facing it with thin silk on the wrong side of the garment. At the bottom of the placket, snip across the underneath turning so that the seam below can be opened and pressed flat.

If a placket has to be made where there is no seam, sew a continuous strip of bias binding along both raw edges. Hem the binding down on the wrong side, then fold it inside the garment, so that it lies under the front part of the placket but forms an extension to the back half of the placket.

PLEATS. Folds of material pressed and stitched to keep them in place. For each pleat must be allowed three times the amount of material as the finished width of the pleat. Fig. 23 shows how a single pleat is made.

When a group of pleats is wanted, or a skirt is to be pleated all round, the whole of the material should be marked-off first, before any folding and stitching are done, so that the pleats can be accurately spaced. A cardboard guide is useful in ensuring uniformity.

Narrow pleats with their folded edges lying in the same direction are called *knife pleats;* very narrow ones pressed in by machinery are called *accordion pleats.* A *box pleat* is one in which two adjacent pleats lie with their folds in opposite directions; an *inverted pleat* is that in which the two folds are turned in towards one another and meet in the centre. *Sun-ray* pleats are those radiating out on a circular skirt.

POCKETS. Fashion trends influence the styles and sizes of pockets, but in the main there are three types: *patch, slot* and *inset.*

Of these, patch pockets are the easiest to make. Their top edge should be finished first, with a hem, a facing, or even a flap made from a deep hem folded over on to the right side. A narrow turning is taken on to the wrong side along the sides and lower edge, tacked and well pressed. The pocket is then ready to be pinned and tacked in place on the garment, preparatory to machining it round the edges.

Slot pockets are made on the same principle as bound buttonholes. The pocket opening is marked and a wide binding strip stitched

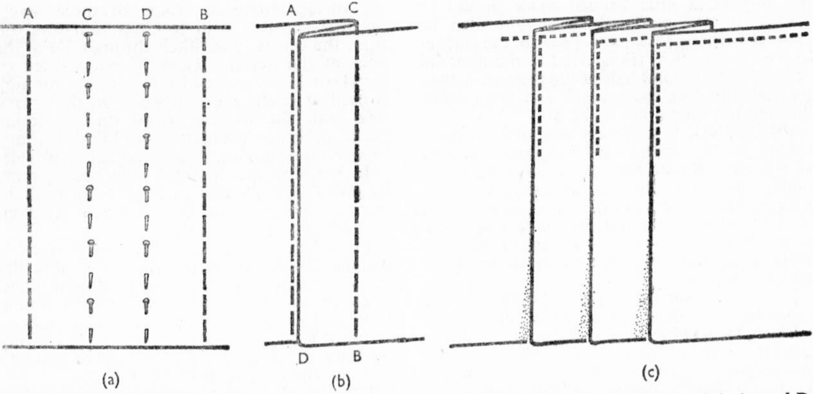

Fig. 23. Pleats. (a) *Mark off amount to be pleated with two lines of tacking (or pins)* A *and* B. *Divide space into three equal parts with lines* C *and* D. (b) *Fold material so that* D *lies on* A *and* B *on* C. *Tack fold* D. (c) *Three finished pleats with edge-stitching at fold and tacks at top to keep layers together. In making a group of pleats, complete marking-off before folding.*

above and below the line. The slit is then made on the line, and the binding is pulled through to the wrong side and stitched so as to leave only narrow bound edges visible on the right side. The pocket lining is then stitched to the bindings on the inside of the garment.

If a flap is wanted, this must be made first. Cut it to shape and turn in its raw edges over a piece of interlining canvas. Herringbone the edges down, then line the flap. Mark where the slot of the pocket is to be and stitch the flap just above it with its right side facing the right side of the garment. Make the slot pocket as previously described, then turn the flap down over the opening and press.

Where a pocket has to be set into a seam, the seam should be left open for the required distance. The two halves of the pocket are stitched to the seam turning on each side on the inside of the garment, then the remaining edges of the pocket are stitched together in a bag shape.

PRESS FASTENERS, to sew on. The stud part of a press fastener should be sewn on first inside the top layer of a placket. It should be secured with close oversewing through each of the four holes provided, the needle being taken through the material when working from one hole to the next.

To mark the position for the lower part of

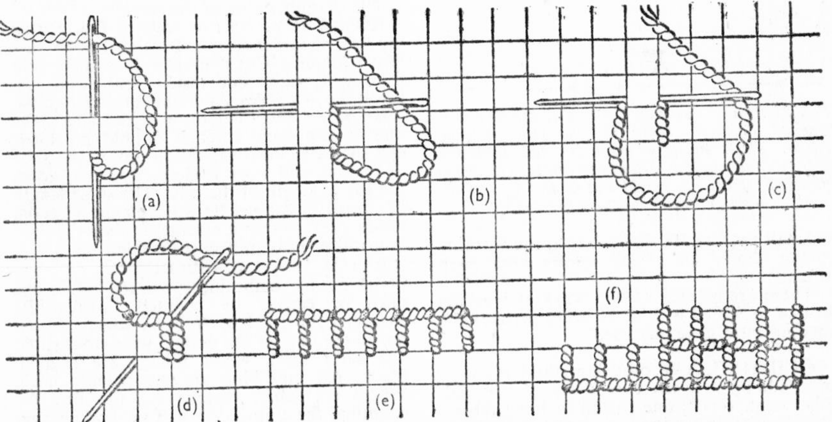

Fig. 24. Punch stitch (squares represent four threads in each direction). (a) *Bring thread out at bottom right of square and pick up stitch four threads away. Draw needle through.* (b) *Pick up stitch on top edge of square.* (c) *Pick up second stitch in same place.* (d) *Put needle in top right-hand corner and bring out at bottom left, ready to begin at* (a) *again.* (e) *One completed row.* (f) *Turn work round and use same movements but on opposite sides of the squares, thus completing squares of the first row. It is essential to pull the thread tight after each stitch.*

the fastener, a little French chalk should be rubbed on the stud, which should then be pressed down on to the lower part of the placket so that the chalk is transferred to the material beneath. The second half of the fastener is then centred over this chalk mark and sewn down through the four holes as before.

PRESSING. It is always advisable to press sewing on the wrong side first, and the heat of the iron should be tested on a scrap of similar material. Rayons, particularly, need a cool iron. A damp cloth, well wrung-out and placed over the material, will take out obstinate creases; but care must be exercised when using it on woollens, as too much moisture will shrink them.

Embroidery should be pressed lightly on the wrong side and always on a well-padded board.

PUNCH STITCH. An embroidery stitch, sometimes called *four-sided stitch*, used for background fillings in drawn fabric work. A special punch needle or the thickest of crewel needles should be used with fine thread. The effect of the stitch is to separate the threads of the fabric and draw them together

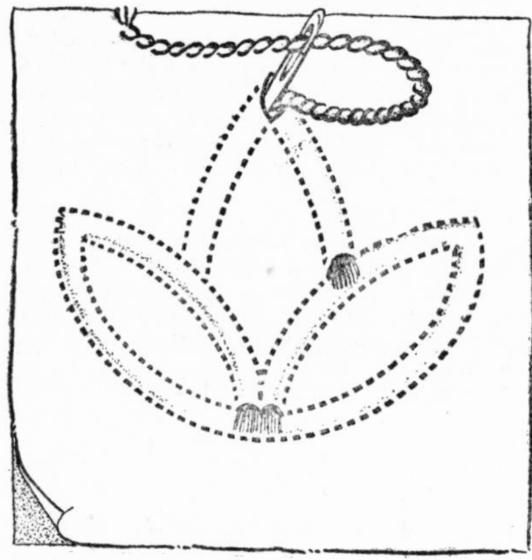

Fig. 25. Italian quilting. Outline of the design is worked through both layers with running stitch. Thick quilting wool is then threaded between the running stitches to produce a design in relief. Bring the needle out at the tops of the points and at corners and re-insert.

in small squares. To achieve this, the working thread should be pulled tightly after each stitch.

There are several known ways of working it, that indicated in Fig. 24 being perhaps the method most generally used.

QUILTING. A decorative method of stitching padding between two layers of material. Silk, satin, velvet, fine cotton or linen fabrics are all suitable for the top surface, while thin lining silk or muslin is most generally used for the backing. The padding between can be of wadding, domett, cotton-wool or soft flannel.

There are various methods of quilting, the most usual being to trace the design lightly on the surface material. Tack all three layers together securely with tackings radiating out from the centre, and stitch through along the lines of the design. Running, back stitch or chain stitch can be used for this, but, if running is used, it is advisable to work on the wrong side with the design drawn on the lining fabric, otherwise the marking will show through between the running stitches on the right side.

In working the stitching, the needle must be taken through and through from back to front so that the stitches and spaces are even on both sides of the work.

In *Italian quilting*, only the design itself is padded to stand up in relief. For this the design, which should be one of double lines, is drawn or traced on to a thin muslin lining. Lining and top surface are then tacked securely together and stitched through along the lines of the design. The method of padding between the lines is shown in Fig. 25.

For the main part, quilting is executed in one colour, the sewing thread matching the surface fabric; but contrasting stitching can be used. As the charm of quilting lies in its highlights and shadows, it should never be pressed flat, but should be only lightly ironed, or its creases removed by steaming.

RENAISSANCE EMBROIDERY. See CUT WORK.

RICHELIEU EMBROIDERY. See CUT WORK.

ROLLED HEM. A very narrow hem suitable for use on thin fabrics only. The raw edge must be trimmed level; then, using thumb and first finger of the left hand, roll the material over towards you in a thin, tight roll. Slip the needle inside the roll and bring it out near the top. Pick up only a thread of the single fabric beneath the roll and, taking the needle along inside the roll again, make the next stitch. The sewing should be scarcely visible on either side of the work.

ROULEAUX. Narrow rolls of fabric used for ties, shoulder-straps, draw-strings or surface trimming. Cut a narrow bias strip, fold it in half, right side inside, and seam just below the raw edges. At the end of the stitching, leave only a short length of thread and make one or two back stitches to hold the loose end securely. Push the needle inside the tube of binding and work it along, eye first, down the whole length of the tube. The short length of thread in the needle will pull the material inside itself, so that it emerges at the other end as a roll with the raw edges inside.

ROUMANIAN EMBROIDERY. A traditional outline embroidery worked on coarse linen or canvas by counted threads. Its characteristic stitch is *Holbein*, which is used for all the lines of the design, with cross stitch and satin stitch where fillings are needed. Black, red and blue are the colours used. Where the fabric threads are too fine for counting, the embroidery can be worked over canvas tacked on to the fabric. The threads of the canvas are then drawn out to leave the stitching on the fabric (see CROSS-STITCH EMBROIDERY and HOLBEIN STITCH).

RUN-AND-FELL SEAM. A firm, strong seam worked with two rows of sewing. With

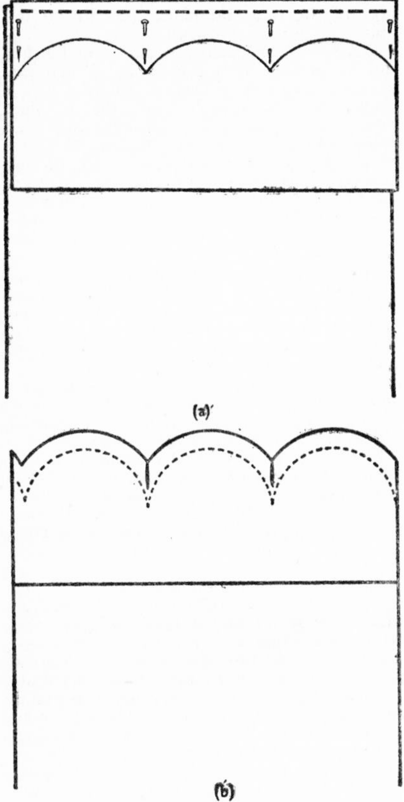

Fig. 26. Scallops. (a) *Tack facing strip to edge to be scalloped, right sides together. Mark scallops on facing, and pin between scallops.* (b) *Sew facing and material together along marking, leaving a small turning. Snip down to the points of the scallops. Turn right side out, tack the scallops into a good shape at the edge and press. This is only one of several methods.*

right sides facing, tack the two pieces of fabric together so that the raw edge of the front one is about ¼ in. below the raw edge of the back one. Sew them together with a line of running, back stitch or machining, just below the front raw edge. Turn the back raw edge down to meet the front raw edge, then fold down again on to the single fabric beneath. Tack near the fold and hem down.

RUNNING. One of the basic stitches of needlework. It consists of picking up and passing over equal amounts of material. The stitches should be small and uniform in size. Running is used whenever a gathering thread is needed, or to join two pieces of material in the first stage of a run-and-fell seam.

SATIN STITCH. Smooth, flat stitches, lying side by side on the surface of the material. Bring the thread through to the front of the material. Insert the needle where the opposite end of the stitch is to be, and bring it out again just to the side of the point where it first emerged. Satin stitch can be worked from left to right or from right to left, the stitches can be horizontal or vertical, or they can slope at an angle. But, in any one group, they must be parallel and lie so close together that no fabric shows between.

SCALLOPS. Where the edge of fabric is cut in a series of small curves, various methods of neatening the raw edge can be used.

In embroidery, buttonhole stitch is the popular method of scalloping. For this the curves are drawn or traced on to the fabric, but the material is not cut. To ensure a satisfactory result, pad the scallop with a running stitch. The buttonhole stitch is then worked along the curved lines, with the knotted edge of the stitch lying to the outer curve. When the stitching is finished, the surplus fabric beyond the buttonhole scalloping is cut away, with sharp scissors, close to the knotted edge.

Scalloped edges can also be bound with bias binding, the binding being stretched along the inner curves and eased on round the outer curves, so that it lies smooth and flat. A method of facing a scalloped edge is shown in Fig. 26.

SCROLL STITCH. A very attractive embroidery stitch, giving a series of small curves. Beginning at the left, take the needle

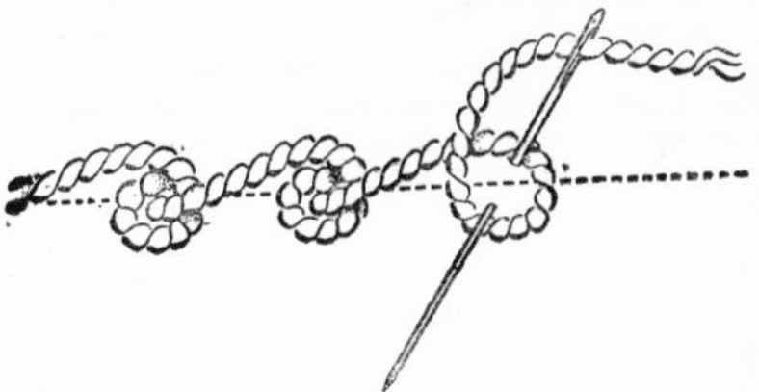

Fig. 27. Scroll stitch.

to the right and, with the thread behind it, pick up a small stitch across the line of work and slanting back towards the left. Pass the working thread under the point from right to left, then draw the needle through over it, as shown in Fig. 27. Hold the loop of thread firmly on the surface of the material until the working thread is drawn right through.

SEAMS. Two edges of material joined together. In the simplest seam, sometimes called a ***flat seam***, the two layers of material are first pinned, then tacked together, edge to edge and with right sides facing. They are then sewn near the tacking line and the turnings are opened and pressed.

The raw edges of the turnings can be bound or can be neatened with whipping or overcasting, or turned under with small running stitches. Alternatively, they can be herringboned down to the fabric beneath. See FRENCH RUN-AND-FELL SEAM, FRENCH SEAM, LAPPED SEAM, RUN-AND-FELL SEAM.

SHADOW STITCH. An embroidery stitch used for fillings where a design has to show through transparent material. It consists of a double row of back stitching on the right side and closely worked herringbone stitch on the wrong side.

Beginning at the right, make a small back stitch on the top line; then take the thread down at the back and bring the needle out a little to the left, on the lower line. Make a

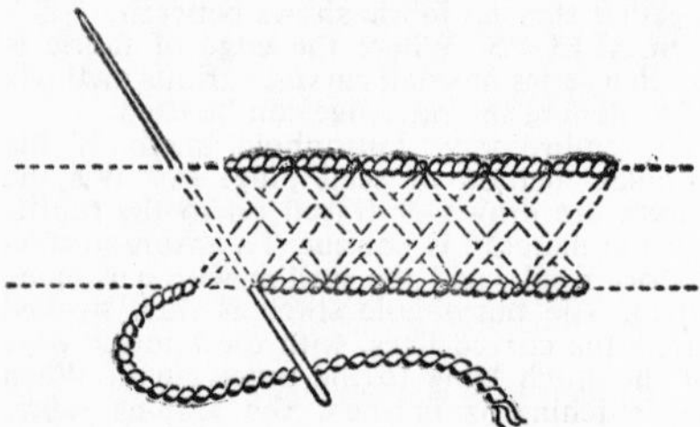

Fig. 28. Shadow stitch or double back stitch used under a transparent material.

small back stitch here, and take the thread up at the back, bringing the needle out on the top line to make another back stitch there, as shown in the illustration. Continue working between top and bottom lines (see Fig. 28).

Delightful soft-toned effects can be obtained by working shadow stitch in bright colours under organdie.

SHELL EDGING. A dainty method of neatening the edges of fine materials. Make a narrow hem on the wrong side of the material, then stitch it with small running stitches and, at about every third or fourth stitch, take the thread over the top of the hem and draw it down tightly to pull the material into tiny scallops. On springy material, a second stitch over the top of the hem may be found necessary to keep the scallops secure. Narrow tucks and bias binding of thin fabrics also lend themselves to shell edging in this way.

SHOULDER PADS. Ready-made shoulder pads are available in various types and sizes, but they can be made at home if preferred.

Cut a circle of canvas, fold it in half and fill with wadding. Cover this padded semicircle with fabric and bind the raw edges along the curved side.

When sewing in a shoulder pad, the curved side should lie under the shoulder seam with rather more than half of it towards the front of the bodice. The straight edge should extend about 1 in. beyond the arm-hole seam inside the sleeve top. The pad should be stitched lightly, but securely, to the seam turnings so that no stitches are visible on the outside of the garment.

SHOULDER STRAPS. To sew ribbon or rouleau shoulder straps to the edge of a garment, turn in about $\frac{1}{4}$ in. of the end of the strap, and pin it to the wrong side of the garment with the raw edge enclosed. Hem the doubled end down along three sides, then turn to the right side and hem the garment to the ribbon on the fourth side.

On a lace-edged garment, the folded end of the ribbon should be stitched on three sides where the lace and fabric join, then the top edge of the lace should be hemmed to the ribbon farther up the strap.

SLEEVES, to finish. The choice of finishes and trimmings for sleeves is, of course, largely a question of current fashions. For a plain sleeve without a cuff, the simplest method of neatening is to turn the raw edge inside and add a narrow facing of fabric which has been cut to shape, or a strip of bias binding. This applies whether the sleeve is short or long, if it is a type that hangs straight. A short sleeve is frequently tightened-in slightly with a small inverted pleat, before the facing is added.

For the main part, a long sleeve is fitted close to the wrist by means of a placket in the seam. To neaten this type, the facing material for the wrist edge is usually cut in one with that of the placket or opening; or, if bias binding is used, one continuous strip is stitched inside the wrist edge, mitred at the corners and continued down the placket edges. On this type of sleeve the placket is frequently fastened with small buttons and button loops.

SLEEVES, to set in. Sleeve seams should be sewn and pressed before the sleeve is inserted in the bodice. If there are darts in the sleeve top, these should be finished too, or gathering threads put in for a gathered sleeve top. Turn the bodice wrong side out and with the side seam towards you.

Slip the sleeve into the arm-hole so that its right side faces the right side of the bodice. Match the seams and notches of sleeve and bodice according to the pattern instructions and pin the two raw edges together, with the pins at right-angles to the edges. Distribute any extra fullness in the sleeve edge so that it is eased on and, if there is a gathering thread in the sleeve top, draw it up to the required size. Tack securely, then seam the two edges together and press with the turnings opened.

SLIP STITCH. A quickly worked version of hemming, used wherever stitching must not be visible. Tack the hem in the usual way, then, beginning at the right, pick up one thread of the material below the hem (or just the top surface if the fabric is thick), then run the needle along inside the fold of the hem and bring it out on the fold a little farther to the left, ready to make the next stitch.

SMOCKING. Embroidery worked on closely gathered material. It serves the dual purpose of being decorative and holding the gathers in place.

The material to be smocked should be about three times the width the finished work is to be. Mark the material with rows of evenly spaced dots (transfers are obtainable for this), then run a gathering thread along each row, picking up just a few threads of the fabric on each dot. Leave the ends of threads loose until all the rows have been worked, then draw them up tight and tie them together in pairs, so that the folds are held at the same tension from top to bottom of the work.

The embroidery is worked over these gathers, the stitches picking up just the tops of the folds. The four basic smocking stitches are shown in Fig. 29. These and variations of them are combined into pleasing geometrical designs. When finished, the gathering threads

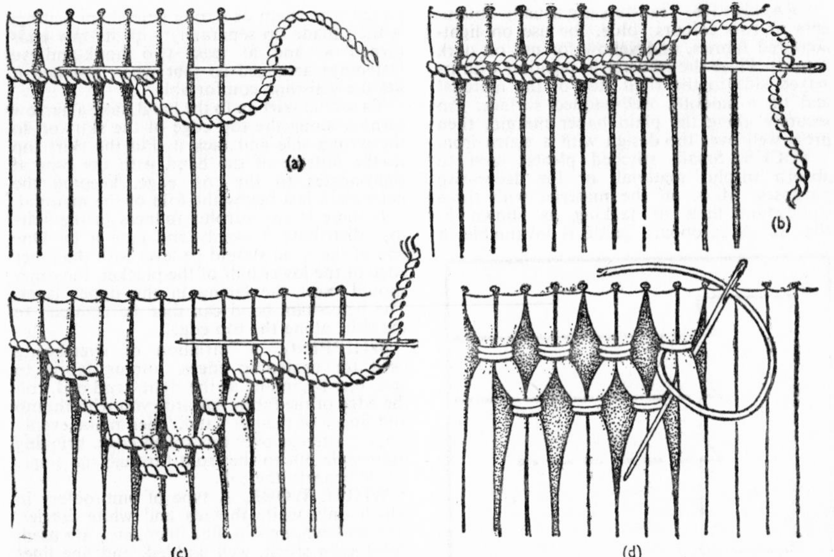

Fig. 29. Smocking stitches. (a) *Outline: take thread across two folds, picking up edge of second fold each time and keeping thread below needle throughout working.* (b) *Cable: this is similar to outline, but with thread alternately above and below needle.* (c) *Wave: take thread across two folds and pick up second fold with thread above needle; make four similar descending stitches; on the fifth stitch work with thread below needle and then work four stitches upwards.* (d) *Honeycomb: make a stitch over two folds; repeat, but bring needle out below to left of second fold. Repeat stitch over second and third folds, then take needle up to left of third fold.*

are removed and the work eased out to the required width.

SOUTACHE BRAID. See BRAID.

STEM STITCH. A narrow embroidery stitch used extensively for stems, or in closely worked rows for fillings. It is known also as *crewel stitch.*

Bring the thread through at the left of the work, take it a little way to the right and pick up a small stitch at a slight angle to the working line, bringing the needle out about halfway along the thread and just to the side of it. The thread can be kept to either side of the needle, but throughout any one piece of work it should be kept to the *same* side.

The larger the angle of the stitch, the wider the finished line will be. By picking up the stitch actually on the line a very narrow result is obtained, sometimes called *outline stitch.*

TACKING. A temporary method of holding material in place while it is sewn with the appropriate stitches. Tacking cotton of contrasting colour and a long, fine needle should be used. The stitch consists of picking up and passing over equal amounts of material. For most purposes, a stitch of ¼ in. to ½ in. in length is sufficient, but smaller stitches can be used on finer materials and longer ones on tweeds or thick woollens.

The first and last stitches should be firm and secure, particularly in garments that have to be tried on at the tacking stage. To remove tacking threads, snip through them at short intervals and draw out each small length carefully so as to avoid dragging the material.

TAILOR TACKING. A simple method of marking the exact position of darts, etc., on more than one layer of material. Use double thread and fasten-on securely, then work small tacking stitches, leaving a loop of the double thread on the surface at each top stitch. Ease the two layers of material apart and snip through the threads between them, so that little tufts remain in each half to mark the sewing line.

TAPESTRY WORK. Fine hand-woven fabrics used in the past for wall hangings, etc., and depicting historical and biblical scenes. The name is also given, erroneously now, to embroidery worked on a canvas background. See CANVAS WORK.

TENT STITCH. One of the simplest of stitches used in canvas work. It consists of a single thread slanting diagonally over the cross of the canvas threads.

Working from right to left, bring the thread through to the front of the canvas. Insert the needle in the line of holes above and one space to the right, and bring it out two holes to the left in the line below, that is, on the level on which it started. It is most important that all the stitches slope at the same angle.

Worked in fine thread on single-thread canvas, it is called *petit-point* work. On double-thread canvas and worked in coarser silks and wools it is known as *gros-point* work.

TRANSFERS. Transfers are usually obtainable in two colours: blue, for use on light-coloured fabrics, and yellow for use on dark colours. Place the transfer in position with its waxed side to the right side of the material and on a smooth, well-padded surface. Pin securely along the plain paper margin, then press well over the design with a warm iron.

TUCKS. Small, stitched pleats, used to absorb surplus material, or for decorative purposes. Mark off the material with three equidistant lines of tacking as shown in Fig. 30. A cardboard guide is invaluable in keeping the lines level. Fold and press the material so that the first line lies over the third and the second lies along the outer fold of the pleats. Tack the top two layers of material together and sew along the tacking line.

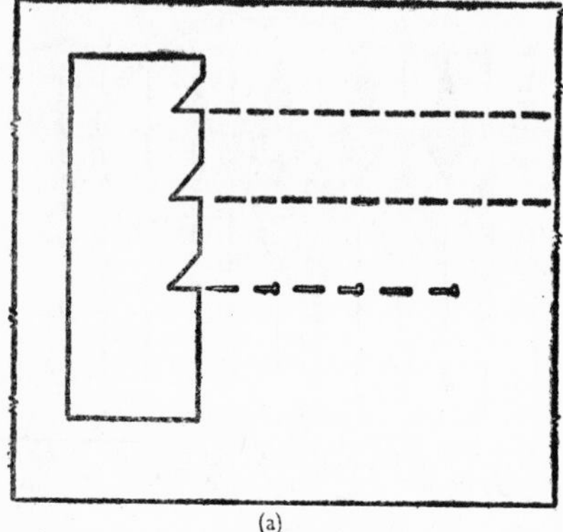

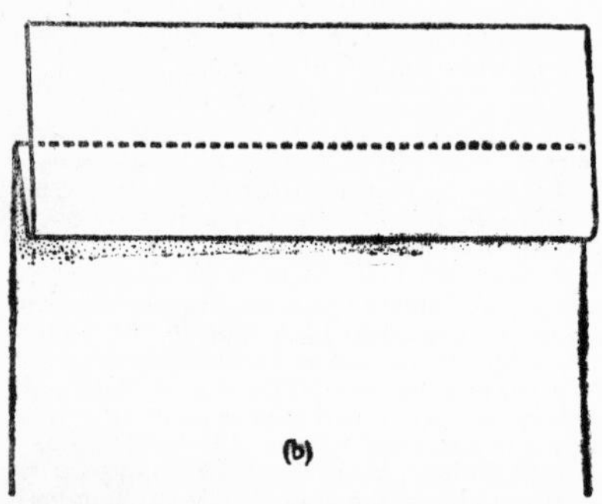

Fig. 30. Tucks. (a) *Mark material in three parallel lines equal distances apart, with pins or tacking. A cardboard guide, as shown here, is useful to keep the lines level.* (b) *Fold material at the centre line to form tuck. Tack and stitch two top layers together and press tuck down flat to produce a smooth surface.*

WAISTBANDS. All necessary darts in the waist of a skirt and the placket in the side seam must be stitched before the waistband is set on. The band, which can be of specially boned petersham or strong petersham belting, is then made up separately with its raw ends turned in and at least two hook-and-eye fastenings arranged so that when fastened it fits the waistline comfortably.

To set the skirt on to the band, take a narrow turning along the top edge of the skirt on to the wrong side and tack it. Pin the skirt top to the outside of the band with the pins at right-angles to the top edge, keeping the petersham just below the fold of the material.

If there is any surplus fullness in the skirt top, distribute it evenly and ease it in. One end of the band should be level with the inner edge of the lower half of the placket, the other should meet the facing in the upper layer. The petersham band can then be hemmed to the skirt along the top edge.

WHIPPING. A variation of oversewing used for neatening edges, joining fabric to lace, etc. Beginning at the right-hand end, roll the edge of the fabric towards you with thumb and finger of the left hand. Then make evenly sloping stitches over this rolled edge, bringing the needle out to the front through the single fabric beneath the roll.

WHITE WORK. A type of embroidery in which only white threads and white fabrics, such as lawn, muslin, fine linen, etc., are used. Solid satin stitch, well padded, and fine lines of narrow satin overcasting stand out in relief on the fabric in pleasing contrast to the lace-like fillings and backgrounds of drawn-thread and drawn-fabric work. Eyelet holes and shadow work are also characteristics of this type of embroidery.

YOKES. If the main part of a bodice is to be gathered, pleated or tucked beneath the yoke, the gathers, pleats or tucks should be completed first. Also, any fastening in the yoke should be made; for instance, a placket faced, buttonholes made, etc.

The yoke can then be joined on, by either a flat or a lapped seam. For the former, tack yoke and bodice together with right sides facing, matching any pattern notches, and machine. Press with both raw edges turned upwards beneath the yoke. A second line of machining is frequently worked near the edge of the yoke to emphasize the seam.

For a lapped seam, turn under and tack the lower edge of the yoke, then pin in position on the bodice with the yoke overlapping the top edge. Tack and machine above the folded yoke edge.

ZIP-FASTENERS. To sew in a zip-fastener. first take a narrow turning along both edges of the opening. Close the fastener and tack the two folded edges along the braid, keeping them well away from the metal centre. The material must on no account be stretched while being sewn. Do not cut off the surplus braid at the end of the fastener, but sew it to the seam turnings.

A zip-fastener can be concealed in a placket by machining the turned-in edge of the underneath part of the placket to the braid on the right of the fastener and slip-stitching the left-hand braid to the facing inside the overlapping part.

HOW TO KNIT

An introduction to the craft of knitting, including stitches, patterns, designing of garments, and alterations.

ABBREVIATIONS. In knitting patterns, abbreviations are commonly used as follows:

k. = knit, which is plain knitting, the right-hand needle being inserted through the front loop of the next stitch on left-hand needle from left to right.

p. = purl, which is the wrong side of stocking stitch, the right-hand needle being inserted through the front loop of the next stitch on the left-hand needle from right to left.

st. = stitch(es).

st.st. = stocking stitch, which is one row plain and one row purl, the plain or knit rows being the right side of the work.

g.st. = garter stitch (knit every row).

w.fd. = wool forward, which is to make a stitch by bringing the wool to the front of the right-hand needle when working a knit row.

w.r.n. = wool round needle, which is to make a stitch by winding the wool round the right-hand needle when working a purl row.

m. = make, which covers w.fd. and w.r.n., unless otherwise stated.

t.b.l. = through the back loops.

rep. = repeat.

tog. = together.

dec. = decrease or decreasing.

inc. = increase or increasing.

beg. = beginning.

patt. = pattern.

sl. = slip, slip stitch off needle.

p.s.s.o. = pass slip stitch over.

The above abbreviations are used in patterns in this section. They appear only in the actual instructions for knitting and not in explanatory or descriptive passages.

ALTERING SIZES. To reduce or enlarge the measurements from a pattern of a hand-knitted garment, simple arithmetic is used. If the garment to be altered is made to fit a 32-in. bust measurement, and is to be enlarged to fit a 34-in. bust measurement, work as follows: Assuming that, with the correct tension, there are 8 stitches to 1 in. in width, the next step is to measure across the back, at the waistline, of the person whom the garment is to fit. If this measurement is 14 in., the number of stitches required at this position will be 14 times 8 (8 stitches equals 1 in.), which is 112 stitches. If the original garment had 96 stitches at the waistline, there will be an extra 16 stitches to add on.

The welt, or first few inches of the knitting, is worked on this amount of stitches. Next, measure across the back at the underarms, if this measurement is 1 in. more than that of the original pattern an extra 8 stitches will be needed at this point. For instance, if the original garment measured 16 in. across the back at underarms there would be 128 stitches, and if it is now to measure 17 in. there will be 136 stitches.

When the arm-hole shaping is reached, measure across the back shoulders and calculate the number of stitches needed for this section, thus finding out how many stitches to decrease in the arm-hole shaping. Having shaped the arm-holes, continue until they are the required depth to the shoulder, then measure the shoulderline from the neck to the arm-hole edge; convert the number of inches into stitches and compare this number with that given in the original directions, adding extra stitches for the shoulder shaping if necessary.

This method of measuring and finding out the number of extra stitches to add to the original number applies to each section of the garment, and, if carried out carefully, will ensure a well-fitting enlargement.

To produce a smaller size than that given in the original pattern, use the same method as above, but, having worked out the difference in terms of stitches, subtract this number from that of the original.

BELL PATTERN. This is a favourite pattern for dressing jackets. There are many variations, and the clever knitter can design her own bell pattern. These can be knitted in rows, one bell above another or in alternate positions and also in clusters. To knit the bell pattern in rows, work as follows:

Cast on a number of st. divisible by 4, plus 4 extra st. *1st row.*—P. 4, * turn work and cast on 8 st., turn work back again and p. the next 4 st.; rep. from * to end. *2nd row.*—K. 4, * p. 8, k. 4; rep. from * to end. *3rd row.*—P. 4, * k. 8, p. 4; rep. from * to end. *4th row.*—K. 4, * p. 8, k. 4; rep. from * to end. *5th row.*—P. 4, * sl. 1, k. 1, p.s.s.o., k. 4, k. 2 tog., p. 4; rep. from * to end. *6th row.*—K. 4, * p. 6, k. 4; rep. from * to end. *7th row.*—P. 4, * sl. 1, k. 1, p.s.s.o., k. 2, k. 2 tog., p. 4; rep. from * to end.

8th row.—K. 4, * p. 4, k. 4; rep. from * to end. *9th row.*—P. 4, * sl. 1, k. 1, p.s.s.o., k. 2 tog., p. 4; rep. from * to end. *10th row.*—K. 4, * p. 2, k. 4; rep. from * to end. *11th row.*—P. 4, * k. 2 tog., p. 4; rep. from * to end. *12th row.*—P. 4, * k. 1, p. 4; rep. from * to end. *13th row.*—P. 4, * k. 2 tog., p. 3; rep. from * to end. *14th row.*—K. *15th row.*—P. *16th row.*—K. These 16 rows form one patt.

To work a smaller bell, cast on fewer stitches for the first row of the bell, and work fewer rows. This pattern should be worked out on graph paper (see GRAPH PAPER).

Note: It is advisable to use No. 7 or 8 size needles, with 3-ply wool for bell pattern. If a smaller size is used the garment will be heavy.

BLACKBERRY STITCH. This pattern produces a "nobbly" effect and is used for jumpers, scarves, gloves and tops of socks. It is worked over a number of stitches divisible by four, plus two extra stitches, as follows:

1st row.—K. 1, p. to the last st., k. 1. *2nd row.*—K. 1, * then k. 1, p. 1 and k. 1 all into the next st., p. 3 tog.; rep. from * to the last st., k. 1. *3rd row.*—As 1st row. *4th row.*—K. 1, * p. 3 tog., then k. 1, p. 1 and k. 1 all into the next st.; rep. from * to the last st., k. 1. These 4 rows form one patt.

BRACKETS. In many knitting patterns, especially when fancy patterns are used, groups of stitches appear between two brackets thus: (w.fd., k. 2 tog., k. 3) 4 times. There may be stitches worked before this group in brackets, but these are ignored and only the stitches between the brackets are worked the number of times stated immediately after the second bracket.

BUTTERFLY PATTERNS. All butterfly patterns are very decorative, and, if an elaborate garment is the choice of the knitter, one of the open butterfly designs would be suitable. Following are directions for a pattern giving the effect of butterflies in flight.

Cast on a number of st. divisible by 11, plus 2 extra st. *1st row.*—K. 5, * k. 2 tog., k. 9; rep. from * to the last 8 st., k. 2 tog., k. 6. *2nd row.*—K. 1, p. 3, * p. 2 tog. (working into the back loops instead of the front loops), w.r.n. twice (to make 2 st.), p. 2 tog., p. 6; rep. from * to the last 8 st., p. 2 tog. t.b.l., w.r.n. twice, p. 2 tog., p. 4.

3rd row.—K. 3, * k. 2 tog., w.fd. twice (to make 2 st.), drop the 2 made st. of previous row, sl. 1, k. 1, p.s.s.o., k. 4; rep. from * to the last 7 st., k. 2 tog., w.fd. twice, drop the 2 made st., sl. 1, k. 1, p.s.s.o., k. 3.

4th row.—K. 1, p. 1, * p. 2 tog. t.b.l., w.r.n. twice, drop the 2 made st., p. 2 tog., p. 2; rep. from * to end. *5th row.*—K. 1, * k. 2 tog., w.fd. twice, drop the 2 made st., sl. 1, k. 1, p.s.s.o.; rep. from * to the last st., k. 1.

6th row.—P. 2, * drop the 2 made st., turn work to the right side and cast on 4 st.; pick up the 4 threads made by the dropped st. and k. them tog., which gives an extra st., sl. this st. on to left-hand needle, then cast on 4 more st., turn work back to the wrong side, p. the next 2 st.; rep. from * to end. *7th row.*—K. *8th row.*—P.

These eight rows form one pattern. The directions may appear to be rather complicated but, when knitting the pattern, it becomes quite easy to follow. For a butterfly pattern worked on to a solid foundation, the following directions knit up into a very pretty design.

Cast on a number of st. divisible by 10, plus 5 extra st. *1st row.*—K. 5, * bring w.fd., sl. the next 5 st., take wool to back of work, k. 5; rep. from * to end. *2nd row.*—P. Rep. these 2 rows twice more. *7th row.*—As 1st row. *8th row.*—P. 5, * p. 2, then pick up the loops formed by bringing the wool to the front of the sl.st., sl. these loops on to left-hand needle and p. them tog. with the next st., p. 7; rep. from * to end.

These eight rows form one pattern. If desirable, the butterflies can be worked in alternate positions, working the next group of butterflies over the five knitted stitches and knitting the slipped stitches of previous pattern. If working alternate groups of butterflies, the first and last five stitches must always be kept in stocking stitch, as these stitches cannot be slipped, and also form the ends of rows.

Another butterfly pattern is worked to give an open effect, and is more simple to knit than the first pattern given. For this pattern, cast on a number of st. divisible by 10, plus 5 extra st. *1st row.*—K. *2nd row.*—P. Rep. these 2 rows twice more. *7th row.*—K. 2, * sl. the next st. off the left-hand needle and let it drop down for 5 rows, then sl. this st., and the five loops made by dropping the st. on to the left-hand needle and k. them all tog., making 1 st. again, k. 9; rep. from * to end, but finishing k. 2, instead of k. 9.

8th row.—As 2nd row. Now rep. the 1st and 2nd rows twice more. *13th row.*—K. 7, * sl. the next st. off left-hand needle, drop it down for 5 rows, sl. this st. and the 5 loops on to left-hand needle and k. them tog., k. 9; rep. from * to end, but finishing k. 7, instead of k. 9. *14th row.*—P. The last 12 rows form one patt. When working the patt. again, always begin with the 3rd row.

BUTTONHOLES. There are two methods for making buttonholes in knitted garments. The first is to make a stitch by bringing the wool forward or winding it round the right-hand needle and then knitting two stitches together. This will produce a small buttonhole and would not be suitable for large buttons.

The second method is to cast off a small number of stitches in the required position and, on the next row, to cast on the same number of stitches over those cast off in the previous row. Always work into the back of the cast-on stitches to procure a firm edge. In some instances, it is advisable to knit into the back of the stitch before the cast-on stitches and of the stitch immediately after the cast-on stitches. When finishing the garment, work in buttonhole stitch all round each buttonhole to prevent stretching. Use a finer ply for this purpose or split the wool used for making the garment.

CABLES. There are many variations of cable patterns; they can be worked with a stocking-stitch basis, with purl stitches between cables, with ribbing or moss stitch between each cable, and, to knit an elaborate garment, a fancy pattern can be worked in between cables. The latter, however, should not be undertaken by inexperienced knitters. To those who have not attempted cable patterns, the directions given below should be easy to follow and should be experimented with before commencing the more complicated forms of cable pattern.

When working cable patterns, a third needle is required. It should be the same size as those used for the main pattern and must be pointed at both ends. Cables can be worked over an even number of stitches from four to as many as twelve. To work a cable pattern with a stocking-stitch background, work as

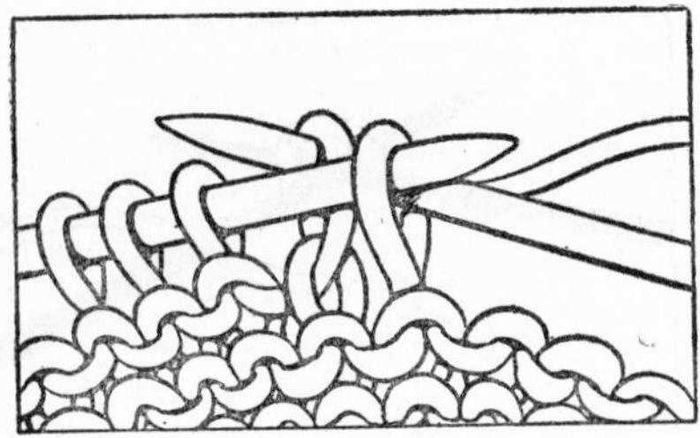

Fig. 1. Casting off. (See page 366.)

follows: This design has two stitches for the cables, with two stitches between each cable.

Cast on a number of st. divisible by 6, plus 2 extra st. *1st row.*—K. *2nd row.*—P. *3rd row.*—K. 2, * sl. the next 2 st. on to the spare needle and leave at the back of the work, k. the next 2 st., then k. the 2 st. from the spare needle, k. 2; rep. from * to end. *4th row.*—P. *5th row.*—K. *6th row.*—P. These 6 rows form one patt.

If preferred, the stitches between each cable can be purled, instead of knitted. When the stitches on the spare needle are left at the back of work, the cables will twist from left to right. To reverse the twist, leave the stitches on the spare needle in front of work.

Plaited Cable. This is worked on a number of st. divisible by 16, plus an extra 4 st., and is worked as follows: *1st row.*—P. 4, * k. 12, p. 4; rep. from * to end. *2nd row.*—K. 4, * p. 12, k. 4; rep. from * to end. Rep. these 2 rows. *5th row.*—K. 4, * sl. the next 3 st. on to the spare needle and leave at back of the work, k. the next 3 st., then k. the 3 st. from the spare needle, sl. the next 3 st. on to the spare needle and leave in front of the work, k. the next 3 st., then k. the 3 st. from the spare needle, p. 4; rep. from * to end. *6th row.*—As 2nd row. These 6 rows form one patt.

Miniature Cable. This is very popular for children's garments, and is very effective when used in between wide cables. A spare needle is not necessary for this pattern as the stitches are twisted, or crossed, with the two working needles. To knit this cable with purl stitches between the twists, work as follows:

Cast on a number of st. divisible by 4, plus 2 extra st. *1st row.*—P. 2, * k. 2, p. 2; rep. from * to end. *2nd row.*—K. 2, * p. 2, k. 2; rep. from * to end. *3rd row.*—P. 2, * k. in to the back of the second st. on the left-hand needle, then k. the first st. and sl. both st. off the needle, p. 2; rep. from * to end. *4th row.*—As 2nd row. These 4 rows form one patt.

The above method twists the stitches from right to left. To reverse the twist, knit into the

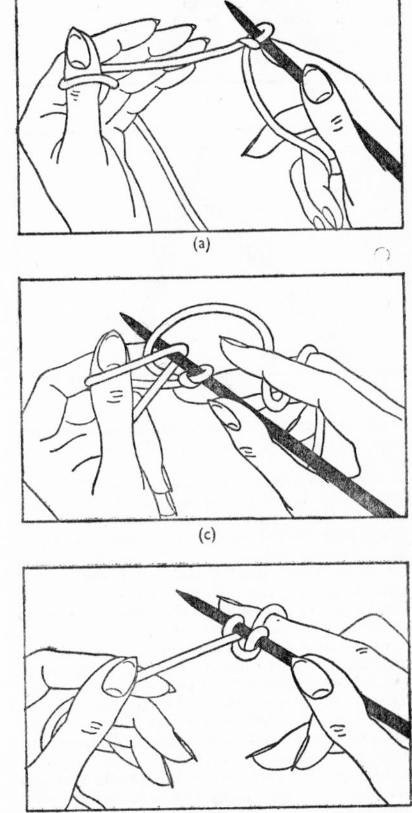

(a)

(b)

(c)

(d)

(e)

Fig. 2. Casting on, using one needle. (See page 366.)

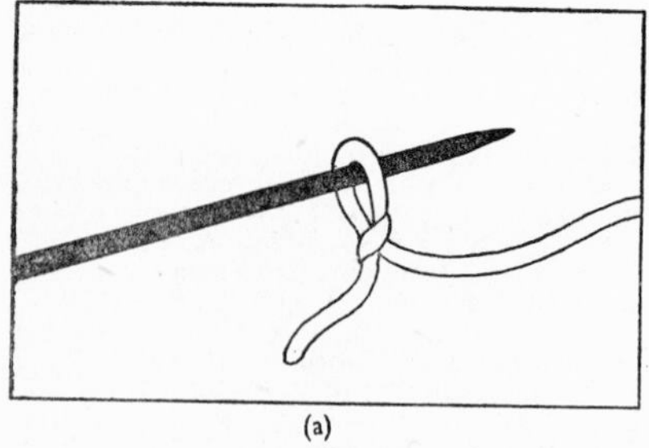
(a)

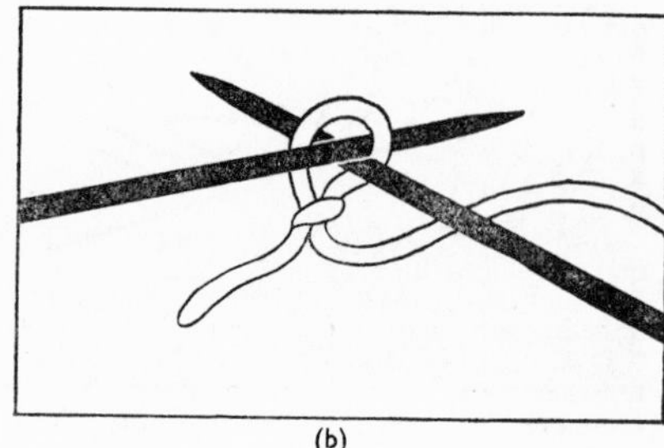
(b)

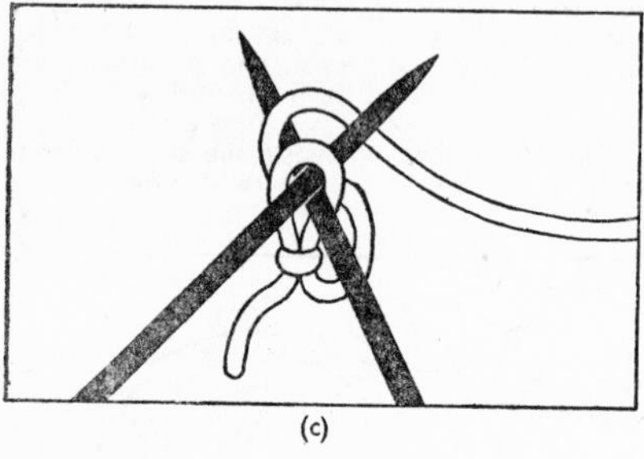
(c)

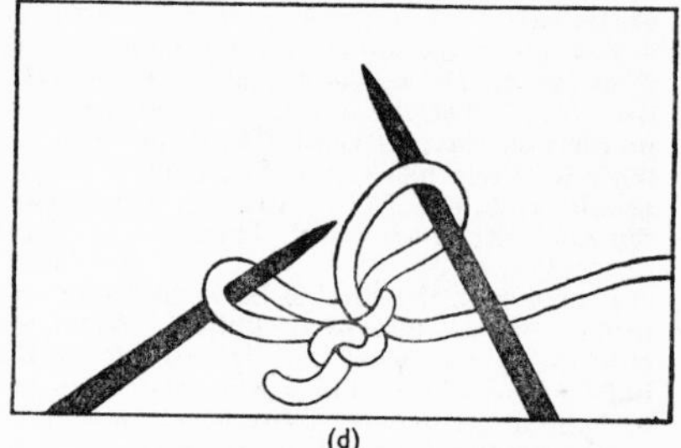
(d)

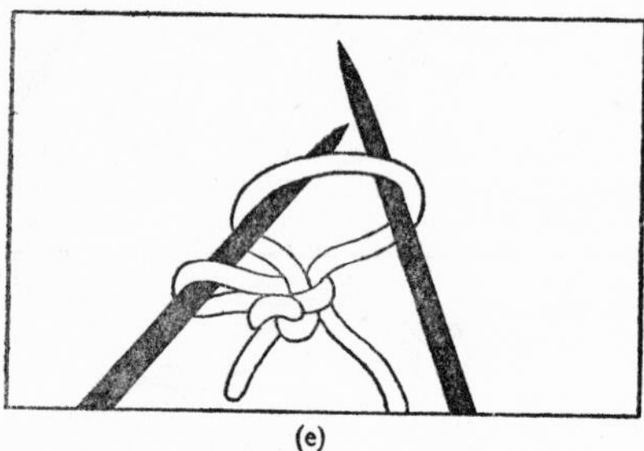
(e)

Fig. 3. Casting on, using two needles.

front of the second stitch on left-hand needle, then knit the first stitch and slip both stitches off the needle.

CASTING OFF. To cast off, work as follows: Knit the first two stitches, then slip the first of these two stitches over the second stitch and off the needle. Knit the next stitch on left-hand needle and slip the first stitch on right-hand needle over the stitch just knitted and off the needle as shown in Fig. 1. Continue in this way until the required number of stitches has been cast off.

CASTING ON. To cast on using the thumb method, work as follows: Leave a long end of wool, then make a loop and slip it on to the right-hand needle. Hold the needle and the wool from the ball in the right hand. In the left hand, hold the long loose end, twist this over and round the thumb of left hand, as shown in Fig. 2(a), insert the needle through the front of this loop (b), and wind wool under and over the needle. Draw the loop through on to right-hand needle (d) and, with the left hand, pull the loose end of wool gently (e) to tighten up the stitch. Continue in this way until the required number of stitches has been cast on.

To cast on with two needles work as follows: Make a loop near the end of the wool, slip this loop on to left-hand needle, as shown at Fig. 3(a), insert the right-hand needle through the front of the loop from left to right (b), pass the wool under and over the right-hand needle (c), and draw the loop through (d) and slip this on to left-hand needle (e). Again insert right-hand needle through last stitch as before, pass the wool under and over this needle, draw the loop through and slip it on to left-hand needle. Continue in this way until the required number of stitches has been cast-on.

Care must be taken when casting on with two needles, as a tight edge can result from this if the loops, or stitches, are tightened up too firmly. With this method, it is necessary to knit into the back of all stitches on the first row to secure a firm edge.

CHEVRON PATTERN. There are several variations of chevron patterns, and they are suitable for pullovers, cardigans and jumpers for men, women and children. The following directions for the pattern are for a small chevron design.

Cast on a number of st. divisible by 12, plus 1 extra st. *1st row.*—* P. 1, k. 3, p. 5, k. 3; rep. from * to the last st., p. 1. *2nd row.*—K. 1, * p. 3, k. 5, p. 3, k. 1; rep. from * to end. *3rd row.*—P. 2, * k. 3, p. 3; rep. from * to end, finishing k. 3, p. 2. *4th row.*—K. 2, * p. 3, k. 3; rep. from * to end, finishing p. 3, k. 2.

5th row.—P. 3, * k. 3, p. 1, k. 3, p. 5; rep. from * to the last 10 st., k. 3, p. 1, k. 3, p. 3.

6th row.—K. 3, * p. 3, k. 1, p. 3, k. 5; rep. from * to the last 10 st., p. 3, k. 1, p. 3, k. 3. *7th row.*—* K. 1, p. 3, k. 5, p. 3; rep. from * to the last st., k. 1. *8th row.*—P. 1, * k. 3, p. 5, k. 3, p. 1; rep. from * to end. *9th row.*—K. 2, * p. 3, k. 3; rep. from * to end, finishing p. 3, k. 2.

10th row.—P. 2, * k. 3, p. 3; rep. from * to end, finishing k. 3, p. 2. *11th row.*—K. 3, * p. 3, k. 1, p. 3, k. 5; rep. from * to end, finishing k. 3, instead of k. 5. *12th row.*—P. 3, * k. 3, p. 1, k. 3, p. 5; rep. from * to end, finishing p. 3, instead of p. 5. These 12 rows form one patt.

DECREASES. The method in which a decrease is worked depends on the pattern or design of the knitting. To decrease a stitch when shaping the side edges of a garment, the usual method is to knit two stitches together on the right side of work (Fig. 4), or to purl two stitches together on the wrong side of work (Fig. 5). In knitting two stitches together, the loops slope from left to right.

To reverse the slope, a decrease is worked in the following way: Sl. 1, k. 1, then pass the slipped stitch over the knitted stitch. The same result is achieved by knitting two stitches together, but inserting the needle into the back loops of the stitch, instead of the front.

To decrease two stitches, there are two popular methods. The first is to knit three stitches together, when the loops will slope from left to right. The second method is as follows: Slip two stitches on to the right-hand needle, knit the next stitch, then pass the two slipped stitches over the knitted stitch and off the needle. These loops will slope from right to left.

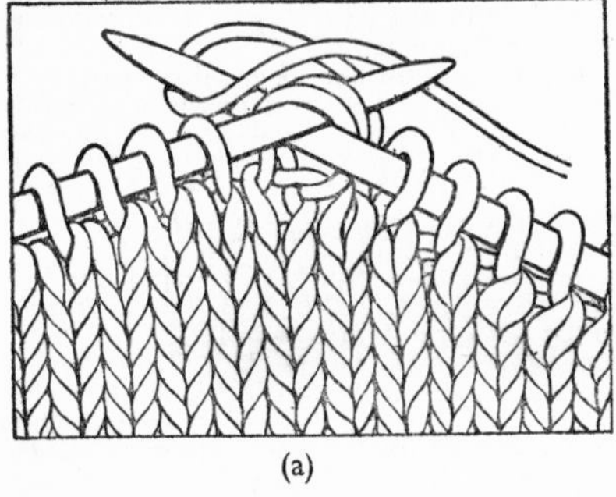

(a)

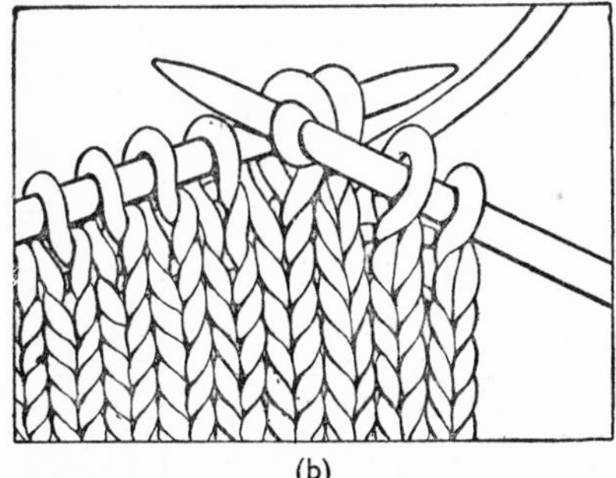

(b)

Fig. 4. Knit two together: (a) *wool round needle and* (b) *wool drawn through stitches.*

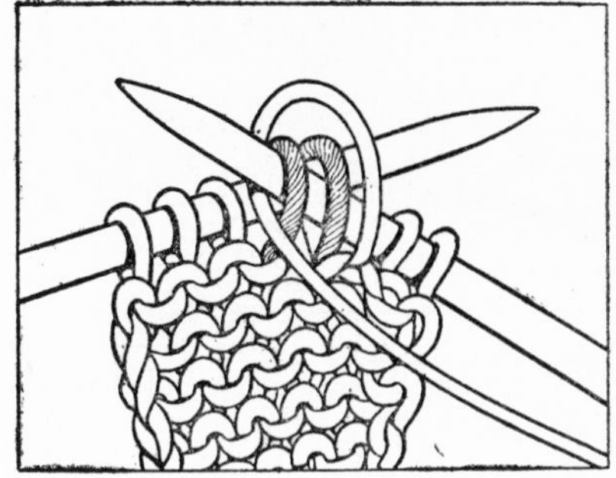

Fig. 5. Purl two together.

When working two decreases as a pair, as when working a pattern, the decreases should slope in opposite directions; therefore, to slope both decreases towards each other work in the following way: *First decrease.*—Sl. 1, k. 1, pass the slipped stitch over the knitted stitch and off the needle. *Second decrease.*—K. 2 st. together. If the decreases should slope away from each other, reverse the process.

When a decrease is worked on a purl, or wrong-side row, by purling two stitches together, it will slope in the same direction on the right side of work as a knit-two-together decrease, that is, from left to right. To work a decrease on the wrong side of work which will slope from right to left, work as follows: P. 1 st., slip it back on to the left-hand needle, then slip the stitch next to it over this purled stitch and off the needle, and then slip the purled stitch back to the right-hand needle.

DESIGNING GARMENTS. This is not complicated and requires no special talents, as it is achieved by simple arithmetic. Beginners should choose a simple style such as a plain button-up cardigan-jumper, preferably worked in stocking stitch. First, take the measurements of the back, which consists of the waist, the width across the back at the underarms, the width across the shoulders, and the depth of shoulderline from the neck to the arm-hole edge.

Now measure the length from the underarm to the waist, then from the underarm to the shoulderline. As an example, presume that the garment is to be designed to fit a 34-in. bust measurement and the knitting is to be stocking stitch; also presume working to a tension of 8 stitches to 1 in. in width and 10 rows to 1 in. in depth.

If the waist measurement across the back is 13 in., multiply 13 by 8 (8 stitches equals 1 in.), which is 104 stitches. This will be the number to cast on, for the waist of the back and the welt, or first 3 in., will be worked on this number of stitches. The next step is to find out the number of stitches needed at the

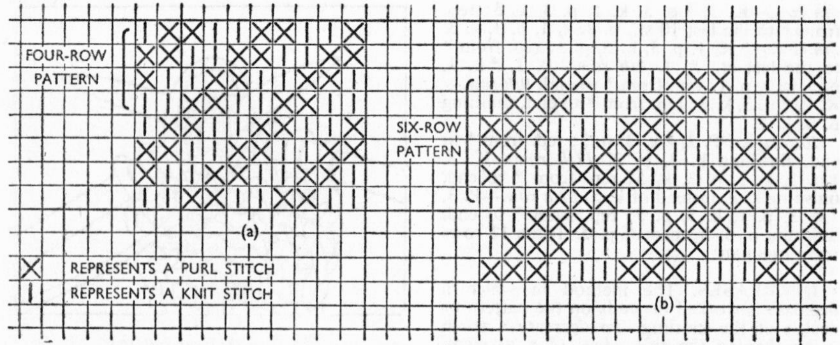

Fig. 6. Four-row (a) *and six-row* (b) *patterns for diagonal ribbing.*

underarm. If the width at this position is 16 in., multiply 16 by 8, which is 128 stitches; thus 24 extra stitches will have to be added to the original number, so 12 increases will be necessary at each side of the back.

If the depth to the underarm measures 12 in., and 3 in. of this comprises the welt, there will be 9 in. in which to work the increases. With a tension producing 10 rows to 1 in. in depth, the number of rows to be worked between the welt and the arm-hole shaping will be 90; therefore, one increase at both ends of every 6th row will bring the number of stitches to 128 and the depth from the cast-on edge to 10 in. The full amount of stitches should be on the needles about 2 in. below the underarm.

Having reached the position for the arm-hole shaping, work out the number of stitches needed for the back shoulder width. If this is 13 in. multiply 13 by 8, bringing the number to 104. Deduct this number from the 128 stitches, which leaves 24. This is the number of stitches to cast off and decrease in the arm-hole shaping.

When this shaping has been completed, continue until the required depth to the shoulderline has been worked. If the shoulder-line measures 4 in. from neck to arm-hole edge, multiply 4 by 8, which is 32. The number of stitches to cast off for each shoulder will be 32, and this shaping is carried out in several rows, the stitches being cast off from the shoulder in sections to give a slope to the shoulder seam.

Work out the stitches needed for each front and, if a ribbed border is to finish the front edges, do not count in the stitches for these with the stitches of the front, as the tension of the ribbing will have more stitches to the inch than that of the stocking stitch; also the ribbed borders cross one over the other if the garment is to be fastened down the front.

Work out the number of stitches required for the sleeves, using the same method as before. Remember that the first and most important part of designing is to work out the tension and make sure that it is measured correctly. If a design is chosen in which there are several sections, such as a yoke on the back and front, it can be very successful, providing that all measurements taken are perfectly accurate.

DIAGONAL-RIB PATTERN. Diagonal-rib patterns can be narrow or wide, according to the garment for which they are intended. For a small garment, the smaller pattern is more suitable. To work this, first cast on a number of st. divisible by 4, plus 2 extra st. *1st row.*—K. 2, * p. 2, k. 2; rep. from * to end. *2nd row.*—K. 1, * p. 2, k. 2; rep. from * to the last st., p. 1. *3rd row.*—P. 2, * k. 2, p. 2; rep. from * to end. *4th row.*—P. 1, * k. 2, p. 2; rep. from * to the last st., k. 1. These 4 rows form one patt. A patt. of this type is shown in Fig. 6(a).

If a three-and-three diagonal-rib pattern is to be worked, cast on a number of st. divisible by 6, plus 3 extra st., and work as follows: *1st row.*—K. 3, * p. 3, k. 3; rep. from * to end. *2nd row.*—K. 1, * p. 3, k. 3; rep. from * to the last 2 st., p. 2. *3rd row.*—K. 1, * p. 3, k. 3; rep. from * to the last 2 st., p. 2.

4th row.—K. 3, * p. 3, k. 3; rep. from * to end. *5th row.*—P. 2, * k. 3, p. 3; rep. from * to the last st., k. 1. *6th row.*—P. 2, * k. 3, p. 3; rep. from * to the last st., k. 1. These 6 rows form one patt., as shown in Fig. 6(b).

DIAMOND PATTERN. Cast on a number of st. divisible by 12, with one extra st. *1st row.*—P. 2, * k. 9, p. 3; rep. from * to the last 11 st., k. 9, p. 2. *2nd row.*—K. 2, * p. 9, k. 3; rep. from * to the last 11 st., p. 9, k. 2. *3rd row.*—* K. 1, p. 2, k. 7, p. 2; rep. from * to the last st., k. 1. *4th row.*—P. 2, * k. 2, p. 5, k. 2, p. 3; rep. from * to the last 11 st., k. 2, p. 5, k. 2, p. 2.

5th row.—K. 3, * p. 2, k. 3, p. 2, k. 5; rep. from * to the last 10 st., p. 2, k. 3, p. 2, k. 3. *6th row.*—P. 4, * k. 2, p. 1, k. 2, p. 7; rep. from * to the last 9 st., k. 2, p. 1, k. 2, p. 4. *7th row.*—K. 5, * p. 3, k. 9; rep. from * to the last 8 st., p. 3, k. 5. *8th row.*—P. 5, * k. 3, p. 9; rep. from * to the last 8 st., k. 3, p. 5. *9th row.*—K. 4, * p. 2, k. 1, p. 2, k. 7; rep. from * to the last 9 st., p. 2, k. 1, p. 2, k. 4.

10th row.—P. 3, * k. 2, p. 3, k. 2, p. 5; rep. from * to the last 10 st., k. 2, p. 3, k. 2, p. 3. *11th row.*—K. 2, * p. 2, k. 5, p. 2, k. 3; rep. from * to the last 11 st., p. 2, k. 5, p. 2, k. 2. *12th row.*—P. 1, * k. 2, p. 7, k. 2, p. 1; rep. from * to end. These 12 rows form one patt.

The *Lacy Diamond Pattern* is very effective for shawls, and should be knitted with 2-ply wool. For jumpers, 3-ply wool can be used, but will make the garment somewhat heavier. The pattern is as follows: Cast on a number of st. divisible by 10, plus an extra 4 st. *1st row.*—K. 2, w.fd. (to m. a st.), sl. 1, k. 1, p.s.s.o., * k. 1, k. 2 tog., w.fd. twice (to m. 2 st.), sl. 1, k. 1, p.s.s.o.; rep. from * to the last 5 st., k. 1, k. 2 tog., w.fd., k. 2. *2nd and alternate rows.*—P.

3rd row.—K. 2, * k. 2 tog., w.fd., k. 6, w.fd., sl. 1, k. 1, p.s.s.o.; rep. from * to the last 2 st., k. 2. *5th row.*—K. 3, * k. 2 tog., w.fd., k. 4, w.fd., sl. 1, k. 1, p.s.s.o., k. 2; rep. from * to end, finishing k. 3 instead of k. 2. *7th row.*—K. 4, * k. 2 tog., w.fd., k. 2, w.fd., sl. 1, k. 1, p.s.s.o., k. 4; rep. from * to end.

9th row.—K. 2, w.fd., sl. 1, k. 1, p.s.s.o., * k. 1, k. 2 tog., w.fd. twice (to m. 2 st.), sl. 1, k. 1, p.s.s.o.; rep. from * to the last 5 st., k. 1, k. 2 tog., w.fd., k. 2. *11th row.*—K. 5, * w.fd., sl. 1, k. 1, p.s.s.o., k. 2 tog., w.fd., k. 6; rep. from * to end, finishing k. 5, instead of k. 6.

13th row.—K. 4, * w.fd., sl. 1, k. 1, p.s.s.o., k. 2, k. 2 tog., w.fd., k. 4; rep. from * to end. *15th row.*—K. 3, * w.fd., sl. 1, k. 1, p.s.s.o., k. 4, k. 2 tog., w.fd., k. 2; rep. from * to the last st., k. 1. *16th row.*—P. These 16 rows form one patt.

DOUBLE KNITTING. This is used for scarves and is tubular. Work as follows: Cast on an uneven number of stitches. *1st row.*—K. 1, * w.fd., sl. the next st. purlwise, wool back, k. 1; rep. from * to end. *2nd row.*—* W.fd., sl. the next st. purlwise, wool back, k. 1; rep. from * to the last st., w.fd., sl. 1. These 2 rows are rep. throughout.

DROPPED STITCHES. If a stitch has been dropped when working stocking stitch, take a crochet hook and, with the right side of work facing you, insert the hook into the dropped stitch, then take up the thread of wool from the row above the stitch with the hook under the thread and draw it through the dropped stitch as shown in Fig. 7. Continue picking up a thread on every row and drawing it through the stitch on the crochet hook until every thread has been picked up.

Care must be taken in picking up dropped stitches, because, should the thread be pulled too far through with the hook, making a large loop, the stitches at each side will be reduced in size and the knitting will appear uneven.

Fig. 7. Picking up a dropped stitch.

EDGINGS. Narrow edgings can be worked widthways or depthways. If an edging is required to trim the neck or sleeve edges of a garment, the stitches on the edge of the garment can be picked up and knitted. The edging is then worked on these stitches.

For a closely woven edging, work as follows: Knit twice into every stitch on the first row to double the number of stitches, then work an inch or required depth in moss stitch. Cast off rather loosely. For a lacy edging, work twice into every stitch on the first row and, if there is an even number of stitches on the needle, work as follows: *1st row.*—K. 1, * w.fd. (to m. a st.), k. 2 tog.; rep. from * to the last st., k. 1. *2nd row.*—K. 2, * w.fd., k. 2 tog.; rep. from * to end. Rep. these 2 rows for 1 in. or required depth. Cast off rather loosely.

To work a strip of narrow edging, cast on 12 st. and k. 1 row, then work in patt. as follows: *1st row.*—K. 2, p. 2, k. 1, p. 5, w.fd. twice (to m. 2 sts), k. 2. *2nd row.*—K. 2, k. 1 and p. 1 into the 2 made st., k. 1, w.fd., k. 3 tog., w.fd., k. 2 tog., w.fd., k. 4. *3rd row.*—K. 2, p. 8, k. 4.

4th row.—K. 5, w.fd., k. 6, w.fd., k. 2 tog., k. 1. *5th row.*—K. 2, p. 9, w.fd. twice, k. 2 tog., w.fd. twice, k. 2. *6th row.*—K. 2, then k. 1 and p. 1 into the 2 made st., k. 1, then k. 1 and p. 1 into the next 2 made st., k. 1, w.fd., k. 1, k. 2 tog., p. 1, k. 2 tog., k. 1, w.fd., k. 2 tog., k. 1.

7th row.—K. 2, p. 3, k. 1, p. 4, k. 7. *8th row.*—Cast off 5, k. 2 more st. (making 3 st. on right-hand needle), w.fd., k. 1, w.fd., k. 2 tog., p. 1, k. 2 tog., w.fd., k. 2 tog., k. 1. These 8 rows form one patt.

Shawls. To work an edging suitable for shawls or, if worked in fine cotton, suitable for the edges of huckaback towels or chair backs; cast on 22 stitches and work as follows, but note that, when commencing a row with wool forward, hold the wool forward and slip the point of the right-hand needle under the wool, so that the wool goes over the needle as the first stitch is knitted.

1st row.—K. *2nd row.*—W.fd. (to m. a st.), k. 2 tog. (w.fd., k. 1) twice, k. 2 tog., w.fd., k. 4, w.fd., k. 2 tog., k. 10. *3rd row.*—P. 8, k. 6, k. 2 tog., w.fd., k. 1, k. 2 tog., w.fd., k. 3, w.fd., k. 2. *4th row.*—W.fd., k. 2 tog., w.fd., k. 5, w.fd., k. 2 tog., k. 1, w.fd., k. 2 tog., k. 5, p. 8.

5th row.—K. 12, k. 2 tog., w.fd., k. 1, k. 2 tog., w.fd., k. 7, w.fd., k. 2. *6th row.*—W.fd., k. 2 tog., w.fd., k. 9, w.fd., k. 2 tog., k. 1, w.fd., k. 2 tog., k. 11. *7th row.*—P. 8, k. 2, k. 2 tog., w.fd., k. 1, k. 2 tog., w.fd., k. 11, w.fd., k. 2. *8th row.*—W.fd., k. 2 tog., w.fd., k. 6, w.fd., k. 2 tog., k. 5 (w.fd., k. 2 tog., k. 1) twice, p. 8.

9th row.—K. 11, w.fd., k. 2 tog., k. 1, w.fd., k. 2 tog., k. 9, k. 2 tog., w.fd., k. 2 tog., k. 1. *10th row.*—W.fd., k. 3 tog., w.fd., k. 2 tog., k. 7, k. 2 tog., w.fd., k. 1, k. 2 tog., w.fd., k. 12. *11th row.*—P. 8, k. 5, w.fd., k. 2 tog., k. 1, w.fd., k. 2 tog., k. 5, k. 2 tog., w.fd., k. 2 tog., k. 1.

12th row.—W.fd., k. 3 tog., w.fd., k. 2 tog., k. 3, k. 2 tog., w.fd., k. 1, k. 2 tog., w.fd., k. 6, p. 8. *13th row.*—K. 15, w.fd., k. 2 tog., k. 1, w.fd., k. 2 tog., k. 1, k. 2 tog., w.fd., k. 2 tog., k. 1. *14th row.*—(W.fd., k. 3 tog.) twice, w.fd., k. 1, k. 2 tog., w.fd., k. 4, w.fd., k. 2 tog., k. 10. The last 12 rows form one patt. When repeating the patt. always begin from the 3rd row.

Bed-jackets. To make a frilled edging suitable for trimming bed-jackets, collars and cuffs and children's garments, cast on a number of stitches divisible by 8, plus 7 extra stitches. Note that this pattern is worked from the edge which is sewn to the garment; therefore, the length required will have to be measured and then the number of stitches to cast on will have to be calculated from the tension of the knitting.

To work the frilled edging, cast on the required number of st. *1st row.*—P. 7, * k. 1, p. 7; rep. from * to end. *2nd row.*—K. 7, p. 1, k. 7; rep. from * to end. *3rd row.*—P. 7, * w.fd. (to m. a st.), k. 1, w.r.n. (to m. a st.), p. 7; rep. from * to end. *4th row.*—K. 7, * p. 3, k. 7; rep. from * to end. *5th row.*—P. 7, * w.fd., k. 3, w.r.n., p. 7; rep. from * to end. *6th row.*—K. 7, * p. 5, k. 7; rep. from * to end.

7th row.—P. 7, * w.fd., k. 5, w.r.n., p. 7; rep. from * to end. *8th row.*—K. 7, * p. 7, k. 7; rep. from * to end. *9th row.*—P. 7, * w.fd., k. 7, w.r.n., p. 7, rep. from * to end. *10th row.*—K. 7, * p. 9, k. 7; rep. from * to end. *11th row.*—P. 7, * w.fd., k. 9, w.r.n., p. 7; rep. from * to end. *12th row.*—K. 7, * p. 11, k. 7; rep. from * to end. *13th row.*—P. 7, * w.fd., k. 11, w.r.n., p. 7; rep. from * to end. *14th row.*—K. 7, * p. 13, k. 7; rep. from * to end.

15th row.—P. 7, * w.fd., k. 13, w.r.n., p. 7; rep. from * to end. *16th row.*—K. 7, * p. 15, k. 7; rep. from * to end. *17th row.*—P. 7, * w.fd., k. 15, w.r.n., p. 7; rep. from * to end. *18th row.*—K. 7, * p. 17, k. 7; rep. from * to end. *19th row.*—P. 7, * w.fd., k. 17, w.r.n., p. 7; rep. from * to end. *20th row.*—K. 7, * p. 19, k. 7; rep. from * to end. Cast off fairly loosely.

The above frilling will measure about 2 in. in depth if worked on No. 10 needles with 3-ply wool. The frilling can be worked to any depth by continuing to use the above method, that is, working two extra stitches between the made stitches on every alternate row.

EYELET PATTERNS. Eyelets are holes in the knitting, and each hole is worked by making a stitch followed by decreasing a stitch, or, for a larger hole, by decreasing a stitch, making two stitches, and again decreasing a stitch. Eyelets are the foundation of all open-lace designs and geometrical shapes, and are most effective when arranged in flower groups. Rows of eyelets are used for a beading through which to thread ribbon or elastic.

To make a row of eyelets work as follows: Cast on a number of st. divisible by 2. *1st row.*—K. 1, * w.fd. (to m. a st.), k. 2 tog.; rep. from * to the last st., k. 1. *2nd row.*—P. This beading is for a stocking-stitch background. Another method for making a beading is to knit one row, make a row of eyelets, then knit the next row, which gives a garter-stitch edge or ridge, above and below the row of holes.

To make larger holes work as follows: Cast on a number of st. divisible by 4 (this is without any extra st. for the edges). *1st row.*—* K. 2 tog., w.fd. twice (to m. 2 st.), sl. 1, k. 1, p.s.s.o.; rep. from * to end. *2nd row.*—* P. 1, then p. the first made st. and k. the second made st., p. 1; rep. from * to end. The knitter can derive great pleasure from designing eyelet patterns on graph paper, using signs for making stitches and for decreasing (see GRAPH PAPER).

FAIR ISLE KNITTING. When working Fair Isle patterns, the wool or wools discarded should be woven in with the knitting on the wrong side of work. When working a right-side row, the discarded wool should be held at the back of the work. Then, to weave it in, bring it in front of the next stitch to be worked and knit this thread with the stitch. Take the discarded wool to the back of the work again, knit the next stitch, or next two, then weave in the unused colour again.

Never carry the discarded wool across too many stitches, as this method tends to tighten up the knitting, making it uneven. Not more than two stitches should be worked without weaving in the wool not in use.

When working a purl row (wrong side of work), the same method for weaving in the wool is used, the discarded wool is held in front of the next stitch to be purled, and the thread is purled together with the stitch. Do not pull the wools too tightly, as this will give an uneven finish to the work and the knitting will not have any elasticity. Beginners should experiment with two colours only, and practise until they achieve a perfectly knitted sample of a Fair Isle design.

FUCHSIA PATTERN. This design gives a raised effect and is suitable for jumpers. The directions are not difficult, although there are many rows to one pattern. The size of the fuchsia can be varied in length and width, according to taste.

Here are the directions for the most popular design. Cast on a number of st. divisible by 8, plus an extra 11 st. *1st row.*—K. 2, * p. 7, k. 1, w.fd. (to m. a st.); rep. from * to last 9 st., p. 7, k. 2. *2nd row.*—K. 9, * p. the made st., p. 1, k. 7; rep. from * to the last 2 st., k. 2. *3rd row.*—K. 2, * p. 7, k. 2, w.fd.; rep. from * to the last 9 st., p. 7, k. 2.

4th row.—K. 9, * p. 3, k. 7; rep. from * to the last 2 st., k. 2. *5th row.*—K. 2, * p. 7, k. 3, w.fd.; rep. from * to the last 9 st., p. 7, k. 2. *6th row.*—K. 9, * p. 4, k. 7; rep. from * to the last 2 st., k. 2. *7th row.*—K. 2, * p. 7, k. 4, w.fd.; rep. from * to the last 9 st., p. 7, k. 2. *8th row.*—K. 9, * p. 5, k. 7; rep. from * to the last 2 st., k. 2.

9th row.—K. 2, * p. 7, k. 5, w.fd.; rep. from * to the last 9 st., p. 7, k. 2. *10th row.*—K. 9, * p. 6, k. 7; rep. from * to the last 2 st., k. 2. *11th row.*—K. 2, * p. 7, k. 6, w.fd.; rep. from * to the last 9 st., p. 7, k. 2. *12th row.*—K. 9, * p. 7, k. 7; rep. from * to the last 2 st., k. 2. *13th row.*—K. 2, * p. 7, k. 5, k. 2 tog.; rep. from * to the last 9 st., p. 7,

k. 2. *14th row.*—K. 9, * p. 2 tog., p. 4, k. 7; rep. from * to the last 2 st., k. 2.

15th row.—K. 2, * p. 7, k. 3, k. 2 tog.; rep. from * to the last 9 st., p. 7, k. 2. *16th row.*—K. 9, * p. 2 tog., p. 2, k. 7; rep. from * to the last 2 st., k. 2. *17th row.*—K. 2, * p. 7, k. 1, k. 2 tog.; rep. from * to the last 9 st., p. 7, k. 2. *18th row.*—K. 9, * p. 2 tog., k. 7; rep. from * to the last 2 st., k. 2.

19th row.—K. 2, p. 3, * k. 1, w.r.n. (to m. a st. before purling), p. 7; rep. from * to the last 6 st., k. 1, w.r.n., p. 3, k. 2. *20th row.*—K. 5, * p. 2, k. 7; rep. from * to the last 7 st., p. 2, k. 5. *21st row.*—K. 2, p. 3, * k. 2, w.r.n., p. 7; rep. from * to the last 7 st., k. 2, w.r.n., p. 3, k. 2. *22nd row.*—K. 5, * p. 3, k. 7; rep. from * to the last 8 st., p. 3, k. 5.

23rd row.—K. 2, p. 3, * k. 3, w.r.n., p. 7; rep. from * to the last 8 st., k. 3, w.r.n., p. 3, k. 2. *24th row.*—K. 5, * p. 4, k. 7; rep. from * to the last 9 st., p. 4, k. 5. *25th row.*—K. 2, p. 3, * k. 4, w.r.n., p. 7; rep. from * to the last 9 st., k. 4, w.r.n., p. 3, k. 2. *26th row.*—K. 5, * p. 5, k. 7; rep. from * to the last 10 st., p. 5, k. 5. *27th row.*—K. 2, p. 3, * k. 5, w.r.n., p. 7; rep. from * to the last 10 st., k. 5, w.r.n., p. 3, k. 2.

28th row.—K. 5, * p. 6, k. 7; rep. from * to the last 11 st., p. 6, k. 5. *29th row.*—K. 2, p. 3, * k. 6, w.r.n., p. 7; rep. from * to the last 11 st., k. 6, w.r.n., p. 3, k. 2. *30th row.*—K. 5, * p. 7, k. 7; rep. from * to the last 12 st., p. 7, k. 5.

31st row.—K. 2, p. 3, * k. 5, k. 2 tog., p. 7; rep. from * to the last 12 st., k. 5, k. 2 tog., p. 3, k. 2. *32nd row.*—K. 5, * p. 2 tog., p. 4, k. 7; rep. from * to the last 11 st., p. 2 tog., p. 4, k. 5. *33rd row.*—K. 2, p. 3, * k. 3, k. 2 tog., p. 7; rep. from * to the last 10 st., k. 3, k. 2 tog., k. 2.

34th row.—K. 5, * p. 2 tog., p. 2, k. 7; rep. from * to the last 9 st., p. 2 tog., p. 2, k. 5. *35th row.*—K. 2, p. 3, * k. 1, k. 2 tog., p. 7; rep. from * to the last 8 st., k. 1, k. 2 tog., p. 3, k. 2. *36th row.*—K. 5, * p. 2 tog., k. 7; rep. from * to the last 7 st., p. 2 tog., k. 5. These 36 rows form one patt.

GARTER STITCH. This is elementary knitting, and all beginners should practise this stitch until an even sample of work is produced. Garter stitch (shown in Fig. 8) is knitting every row; it forms horizontal lines which close up, making the elasticity depthwise. Also it produces fewer stitches to the inch than any other plain pattern, but more rows to the inch.

Fig. 8. Garter stitch.

Garter stitch has a corrugated effect, and can be very attractive if introduced into a stocking-stitch background. The edges of garter stitch never curl up; therefore, it is particularly useful for borders or edging.

GRAFTING. Grafting must be worked over an even number of stitches. This method of joining two sets of stitches together is generally used for toes of socks and stockings.

Divide the stitches equally on to two needles with the wool at one end of a needle. Place these two sets of stitches together with the wrong side of work to the inside. Break off the wool, leaving a long end. Thread this end through a bodkin. * Insert the bodkin into the first stitch on the front needle as for knitting, draw it through and slip the stitch off the needle; insert the bodkin into the next stitch on the front needle, as for purling, draw it through and leave the stitch on the needle; take the wool under the front needle, insert the bodkin into the first stitch on back needle, as for purling, draw it through and slip the stitch off the needle, insert the bodkin into next stitch on the back needle, as for knitting, draw it through and leave the stitch on the needle. Repeat from * until all the stitches have been worked off both needles. Darn in the end of the wool.

GRAPH PAPER. This paper is ruled out in squares, and has either eight or ten squares

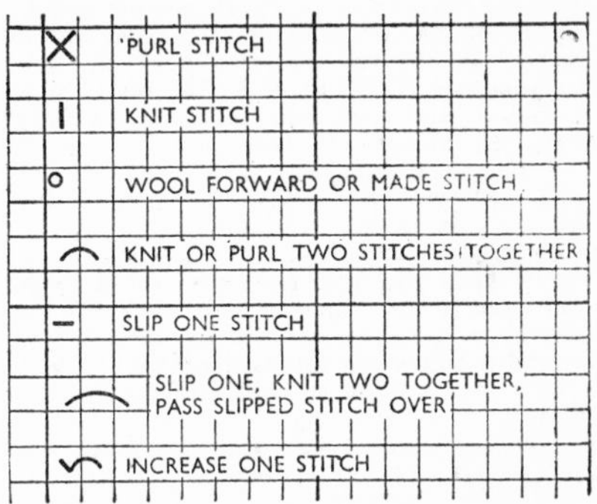

Fig. 9. Signs used in knitting patterns.

to the inch. Patterns are charted on to the paper, various signs being used to represent different stitches (Fig. 9) and each square representing one stitch (see also PATTERNS).

To chart a Fair Isle design on to graph paper is simple and interesting, but it is important to count the stitches and rows of each section in order to ensure that the pattern will repeat (Fig. 10). For example, if a pattern consists of 15 rows, it will not repeat, as the first row of the second pattern or repeat would be on the opposite side of the work to that of the first row of the first pattern; therefore, one complete pattern must consist of an even number of rows. For a Fair Isle chart, coloured

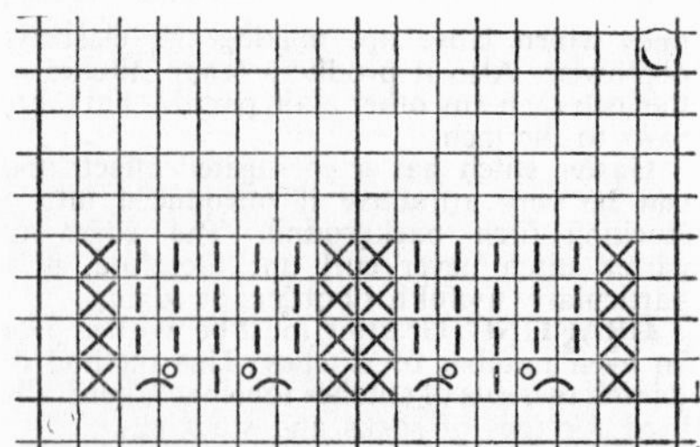

Fig. 10. A four-row pattern showing two repeats and worked over a number of stitches divisible by seven. This is a very simple example.

crayons can be used instead of signs, thus simplifying the working from the chart.

HEELS. The workings for three different heels are given.

Dutch Heel. Half the number of stitches on the needles are used for the heel of a sock or stocking, or one quarter of the total amount are used from each side of the centre back of the sock. The point between the beginning of the first needle and the end of the third needle is, usually, the centre back of the sock.

Let us assume there are 62 st. all round. The first 16 st. on the first needle and the last 15 st. on the third needle will be the heel st. Now begin the heel as follows: Knit the first 16 st. on the first needle, turn and p. these 16 st., then, on to the same needle, p. 15 st. from the third needle, turn. Divide the remaining st. on to two needles and leave for the instep. Work over the 31 heel st. thus: *1st row.*—Sl. 1, k. to end. *2nd row.*—Sl. 1, p. to end. Rep. these two rows 12 times more; then turn the heel as follows: *1st row.*—K. 20, k. 2 tog., turn. *2nd row.*—Sl. 1, p. 10, p. 2 tog., turn. *3rd row.*—Sl. 1, k. 10, k. 2 tog., turn. *4th row.*—P. 10, p. 2 tog., turn.

Continue in this way until all st. are on one needle again (11 st.). K. across these 11 st., then, on to the same needle, pick up and knit 16 st. along the side of the heel. With a second needle work across the instep st. With a third needle pick up and knit 16 st. along the other side of the heel; then, on to the same needle, k. 5 of the heel st. from the first needle.

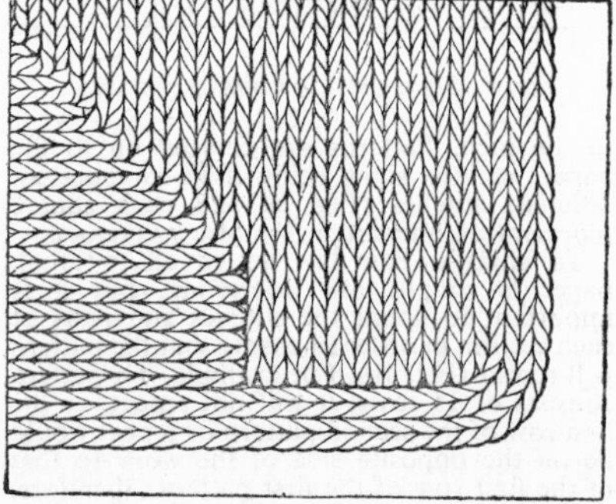

Fig. 11. Dutch heel.

Now dec. for the instep. *1st round, 1st needle.*—K. to the last 3 st., k. 2 tog., k. 1. *2nd needle.*—Work across all st. *3rd needle.*—K. 1, sl. 1, k. 1, p.s.s.o., k. to end. *2nd round.*—Work all st. Rep. these 2 rounds until 62 st. remain. This completes the heel and all shapings, as shown in Fig. 11.

French Heel. Work as given for the Dutch heel until the position for turning the heel is reached, then continue as follows: *1st row.*—K. 19, k. 2 tog., turn. *2nd row.*—P. 8, p. 2 tog., turn. *3rd row.*—K. 9, k. 2 tog., turn. *4th row.*—P. 10, p. 2 tog., turn. Continue in this way, working one extra st. before taking 2 st. tog. and turning, until all the st. are on one needle again. There should be 19 st. K. these st.

Now, on to same needle, pick up and k. 16 st. along the side of the heel. With a second needle, work across the st. of the instep; with a third needle, pick up and k. 16 st. along the other side of heel; then, on to the same needle, k. off 9 of the heel st. Now dec. for the instep as given for the Dutch heel (see Fig. 12).

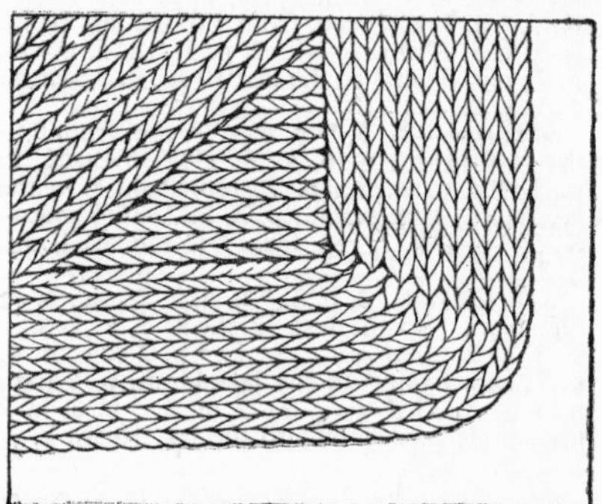

Fig. 12. French heel.

Auto Heel. Divide the st. as given for the Dutch heel; then, having purled the row so that the 31 st. are on one needle for the heel, work as follows: *1st row.*—Sl. 1, k. to the last st., turn. *2nd row.*—Sl. 1, p. to the last st., turn. *3rd row.*—Sl. 1, k. to the last 2 st., turn. *4th row.*—Sl. 1, p. to the last 2 st., turn. *5th row.*—Sl. 1, k. to the last 3 st., turn. *6th row.*—Sl. 1, p. to the last 3 st., turn.

Continue in this way, working one st. less on every row, until 9 st. remain in the centre, then work thus: *1st row.*—K. 9, pick up a loop before the next st. and k. it tog. with the next st., turn. *2nd row.*—P. 10, then pick up a loop before the next st. and p. it tog. with the next st., turn. *3rd row.*—K. 11, pick up a loop before next st. and k. it tog. with the next st., turn. *4th row.*—P. 12, pick up a loop before the next st. and p. it tog. with the next st., turn.

Continue in this way until all st. are on one needle. K. these st., then pick up and k. 3 st. at the side of the heel; with a second needle,

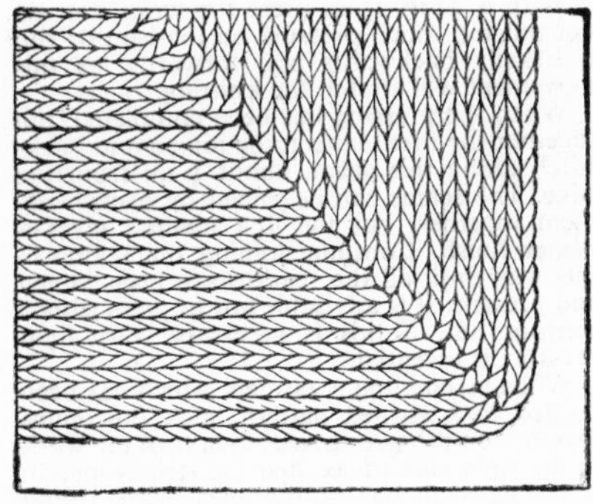

Fig. 13. Auto heel.

work across the instep st.; with a third needle, pick up and k. 3 st. at the other side of the heel, then k. off 15 of the heel st. This completes the heel shaping, as shown in Fig. 13, and from this point the foot is worked on this number of st. until the toe is reached.

HOPSACK PATTERN. Hand-knitted fabric, hardly distinguishable from hopsack material and perfect for tailored suits, is achieved by working a simple two-row pattern. The smaller the knitting needles, the finer the weave; but not a pattern to be chosen by those who like quick results, as this knitting takes many rows to the inch. If hopsack weave is worked on small needles the knitting will not stretch and lose its shape, and can be used as hopsack material.

Directions are as follows: Cast on an uneven number of st. *1st row.*—K. 1, * bring w.fd., sl. the next st., take the wool to the back of the work, k. 1; rep. from * to end. *2nd row.*—P. 2, * take the wool to the back of work, sl. the next st., bring the w.fd., p. 1; rep. from * to end, but finishing p. 2 instead of p. 1, as shown in Fig. 14.

When working this pattern it will be quite easy to increase or decrease without becoming

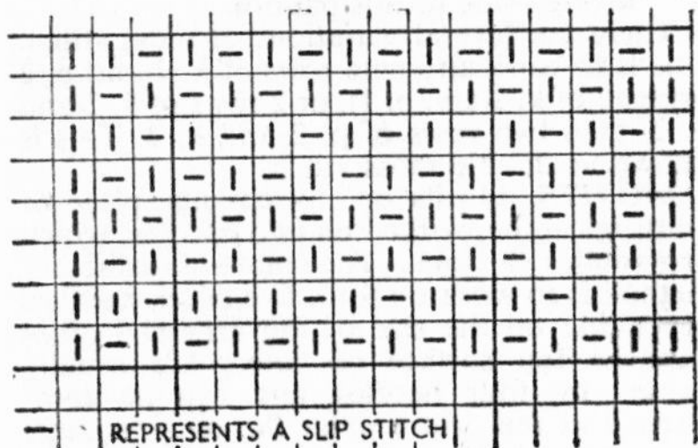

Fig. 14. Hopsack pattern.

confused as to how each row begins, for a slip stitch of the previous row will be a knit or purl stitch on the next row.

INCREASES. There are several methods of increasing, some of which are used to form fancy patterns, and others for adding extra stitches to enlarge the size of the garment. In many patterns, an increase is made by bringing the wool forward before a knit stitch, or by passing the wool round the needle before a purl stitch. This results in a hole, or eyelet. When working a closely woven pattern an increase is made by working into the loop which lies between the stitch just knitted and the next stitch on left-hand needle.

Another method for this type of increasing is to pick up the loop below the next stitch on the left-hand needle and knit it. The usual method for increasing at side edges is to knit into the front, then into the back of the edge stitch. To increase two stitches in a lacy pattern, bring the wool forward twice before a knit stitch, or wind wool twice round needle before a purl stitch.

If four stitches are to be increased from one stitch, work as follows: K. 1, p. 1, k. 1, p. 1, k. 1 all into the next stitch, making 5 stitches altogether, including the original stitch. This method is used when working clusters.

KNITTING ON FOUR NEEDLES. When knitting on four needles begin by casting on the full number of stitches on to one needle. This is more successful than casting on a number of stitches on to each of three needles, which tends to leave gaps between the needles.

Having cast on the full number, divide the stitches on to three needles, the first group on to one needle, the last group on to another needle, leaving the middle section on the original needle, which will be the second needle when working in rounds. With the fourth needle, begin working in rounds, taking care that the stitches are not twisted when joining them into the first round.

LATTICE PATTERN. This is a pattern suitable for knitting in a fine wool or cotton, and is ideal for such garments as gloves, blouses or baby clothes.

Cast on a number of st. divisible by 3. One group of 3 st. to be used for beginning and ending of rows. *1st row* (wrong side of work).—K. 2, * w.fd., k. 3, then sl. the first of these 3 st. to be knitted over the other two st. and sl. it off the needle; rep. from * to the last st., k. 1. *2nd row.*—K. *3rd row.*—K. 1, * k. 3, then sl. the first of these 3 st. over the other two and off the needle, w.fd.; rep. from * to the last 2 st., finishing w.fd., k. 2. *4th row.*—K. These 4 rows form one patt.

LENGTHENING GARMENTS. Hand-knitted garments for children often have to be discarded long before they are worn out, owing to the rapid growth of the wearers. Any garment can be lengthened, providing it has not become too "matted" through constant washing.

If there is a welt at the lower edge of the garment, it is advisable to begin the lengthening above the welt. Having unpicked the seams, take a thread of wool from the side edge and pull it gently. This will give the effect of gathering up the knitting. When the thread has been pulled as far as possible, cut it and smooth out the gathering. The knitting will then fall apart, leaving loops along both edges.

Continue in this way until the same thread has been pulled right across the garment. Slip all the loops on to a knitting needle, join on the wool and continue knitting until the garment is the required length, or until the position for the welt has been reached.

LOOP STITCH. This pattern is very effective for bed-jackets, hoods and scarves. It can be worked over any number of stitches, and produces the best results if 2-ply wool is used. The loop pattern is worked as follows:

1st row.—K. *2nd row.*—K. 1, * insert the needle into the next st., wind the wool round two fingers of the left hand and the right-hand needle, draw the loops through, then k. into the back of the st. and sl. it off the needle; rep. from * to the last st., k. 1. *3rd row.*—K., but counting each group of st. as one st. *4th row.*—K. These 4 rows form one patt.

In the foregoing pattern, the rows of loops overlap, but they can be worked as far apart as required by working more rows between each loop-stitch row.

MAKING UP. Hand-knitted garments can be completely ruined in the making up, and great care should be taken in finishing them. First, darn in all loose ends, then place each section on a thick blanket with the right side of the work to the blanket. Pin down at the outside edges, as shown in Fig. 15, to the measurements given in the directions, then take a damp cloth and place it over the work.

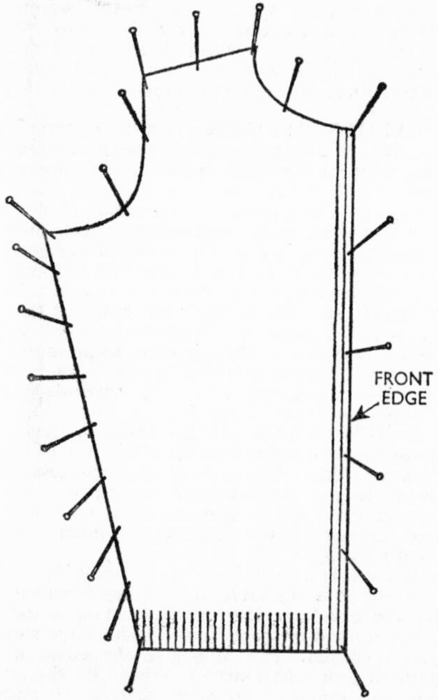

Fig. 15. Left front of a garment pinned down for pressing on the wrong side.

With a warm iron, press the work, but do not put too much pressure on the iron or run it heavily backwards and forwards, as this movement will stretch the knitting.

When the pressing has been completed, pin together the first seams to be joined and back-stitch along this seam, about $\frac{1}{8}$ in. from the edge. The seams can be joined by oversewing them together, but the first method gives a neater finish. Continue joining the seams in this way until all the seams have been joined and pressed. It is advisable not to press ribbed sections but, if this is necessary, very light pressing is essential.

When assembling a garment which has been knitted in a striped pattern, tack the seams together on the wrong side, then turn the work to the right side to see that the stripes match. If the garment has buttonholes, work round these in buttonhole stitch to prevent them from stretching. To keep buttonhole borders firm, back them with ribbon, then cut slits in the ribbon to correspond with the button-holes and sew round the edges of both at the same time. The ribbon prevents the borders from stretching, especially when the garment is being washed.

If a woollen garment is being made up, always join the seams with wool. Never use cotton for this purpose because the seams will split open, the cotton not having the elasticity that the wool has. If the garment has been knitted in a very open, lacy pattern, tape the shoulder seams to prevent stretching.

MOSS STITCH. Moss stitch can be worked over an even or uneven number of stitches. Over an even number of stitches there are two rows to the pattern, but over an uneven number of stitches every row is the same.

To produce moss stitch over an even number of st. work as follows: *1st row.*—* K. 1, p. 1; rep. from * to end. *2nd row.*—* P. 1, k. 1; rep. from * to end. These 2 rows form one patt. For moss stitch worked over an uneven number of stitches work as follows: *Moss-stitch row.*—K. 1, * p. 1, k. 1; rep. from * to end. The effect is alternate rows of a k. st. over a p. st. and vice versa. There is no "wrong" side to this pattern.

There are several variations of moss stitch. One is to work alternate rows of k. 2 and p. 2 (instead of k. 1 and p. 1), or 2 rows of k. 2 and p. 2, then two rows of p. 2 and k. 2. This is known as double moss stitch.

MOTIFS. Motifs or any circular piece of knitting can be worked on two needles, which necessitates a join. The more satisfactory method is to work on four, five or six needles, depending on the size of the article. Doilies and the top surface of berets are usually knitted on four needles, and can be commenced at the centre or at the outside edge. If beginning in the centre, continual increasing is carried out; if beginning at the outside edge continual decreasing is maintained.

The following doily pattern, or circle, is worked on two needles and joined into a circle when finished. With fairly fine cotton and a pair of No. 12 needles, work as follows:

Cast on 9 st. *1st row.*—K. 1, * yarn fd. (to m. a st.), k. 1; rep. from * to end. *2nd and all* *alternate rows.*—P. *3rd row.*—K. 1, * yarn fd., k. 2; rep. from * to end. *5th row.*—K. 1, * yarn fd., k. 3; rep. from * to end. *7th row.*—K. 1, * yarn fd., k. 4; rep. from * to end. *9th row.*—K. 1, * yarn fd., k. 5; rep. from * to end.

11th row.—K. 1, * yarn fd., k. 6; rep. from * to end. *13th row.*—K. 1, * yarn fd., k. 7; rep. from * to end. *15th row.*—K. 1, * yarn fd., k. 8; rep. from * to end. *17th row.*—K. 1, * yarn fd., k. 9; rep. from * to end. *19th row.*—K. 1, * yarn fd., k. 10; rep. from * to end. *21st row.*—K. 1, * yarn fd., k. 11; rep. from * to end.

23rd row.—K. 1, * yarn fd., k. 1, yarn fd., sl. 1, k. 1, p.s.s.o., k. 1, k. 2 tog.; rep. from * to end. *25th row.*—K. 1, * yarn fd., k. 3, yarn fd., sl. 1, k. 2 tog., p.s.s.o.; rep. from * to end. *27th row.*—K. 1, * yarn fd., sl. 1, k. 1, p.s.s.o., k. 1, k. 2 tog., yarn fd., k. 1; rep. from * to end. *29th row.*—K. 2, * yarn fd., k. 3; rep. from * to the last 2 st., yarn fd., k. 2.

31st row.—K. 1, * k. 2, yarn fd., sl. 1, k. 2 tog., p.s.s.o., yarn fd., k. 3; rep. from * to end. *33rd row.*—K. 1, * yarn fd., k. 7, yarn fd., k. 1; rep. from * to end. *35th row.*—K. 2, * yarn fd., k. 7, yarn fd., k. 3; rep. from * to end, but finishing k. 2 instead of k. 3. *37th row.*—K. 1, * k. 2 tog., yarn fd., k. 7, yarn fd., sl. 1, k. 1, p.s.s.o., k. 1; rep. from * to end. *38th row.*—P. *39th row.*—K. *40th row.*—K. *41st row.*—K. *42nd row.*—K.

Now cast off very loosely. Run a thread through the cast-on stitches, draw up tightly and fasten off. Join the seam. Starch the work, and iron it on the wrong side.

To make a doily on four needles work as follows: Cast on 6 st. (2 on each of 3 needles); then, with the 4th needle work in rounds thus: *1st round.*—K. *2nd round.*—* Yarn fd. (to m. a st.), k. 1; rep. from * to end of round. *3rd round.*—K. *4th round.*—* Yarn fd., k. 2; rep. from * to end of round. *5th round.*—K. *6th round.*—* Yarn fd., k. 3; rep. from * to end of round. *7th round.*—K. *8th round.*—* Yarn fd., k. 4; rep. from * to end of round.

9th round.—K. *10th round.*—* Yarn fd., k. 1, yarn fd., k. 2, k. 2 tog.; rep. from * to end of round. *11th round.*—K. *12th round.*—* Yarn fd., k. 3, yarn fd., k. 1, k. 2 tog.; rep. from * to end of round. *13th round.*—K. *14th round.*—* Yarn fd., k. 1, yarn fd., k. 3 tog., yarn fd., k. 1, yarn fd., k. 2 tog.; rep. from * to end of round. *15th round.*—K.

16th round.—* Yarn fd., k. 3, yarn fd., k. 1, but k. into the back loop, instead of the front loop; rep. from * to end of round. *17th round.*—P. *18th round.*—P. *19th round.*—P. *20th round.*—* Yarn fd., sl. 1, k. 1, p.s.s.o.; rep. from * to end of round. *21st round.*—P. *22nd round.*—P. *23rd round.*—P.

24th round.—* K. 1, yarn fd.; rep. from * to end of round. (*Note:* When a repeat ends with yarn forward be careful to keep yarn forward when beginning a needle or round.) *25th round.*—K. *26th round.*—* Sl. 1, k. 1, p.s.s.o., k. 1, k. 2 tog., yarn fd., k. 3, yarn fd.; rep. from * to end of round. *27th round.*—K.

28th round. * Sl. 1, k. 2 tog., p.s.s.o., yarn fd., k. 1, yarn fd.; rep. from * to end of round. *29th round.*—K. *30th round.*—* Yarn fd., k. 1 t.b.l., yarn fd., k. 3; rep. from * to end of round. *31st round.*—K. *32nd round.*—* Yarn fd., k. 3, yarn fd., sl. 1, k. 2 tog., p.s.s.o.; rep. from * to end of round.

33rd round.—K. *34th round.*—* Yarn fd., sl. 1, k. 1, p.s.s.o., k. 1, k. 2 tog., yarn fd., k. 1 t.b.l.; rep. from * to end of round. *35th round.*—K. Now work from the 17th round to the 35th round, then cast off loosely. Starch the doily and iron on the wrong side.

NECK SHAPING. Very often the pattern of a knitted garment exactly suits the requirements, with the exception of the neckline, and many knitters are too timid to attempt an alteration to the design. Following are a few valuable hints on neck shapings.

If a V-neck is desired, work to the position at which the V should start. Count the stitches on the needle, divide these, and on the next row work across one half of the total amount; turn, leaving the remaining stitches on a spare needle. Continue on the first half, but decrease one stitch at the neck edge on the next row and on every following third or fourth row (depending on the number of rows to the inch and the depth of the neckline) until the number of stitches needed for the shoulder remain on the needle.

Having decreased to this number, it may be necessary to continue without further shaping until the shoulderline is reached. If a very deep neckline is required, space the decreasings farther apart, so that the slope continues almost to the shoulder. When the shoulder shaping has been completed on the first side, join the wool to the neck edge of the stitches for the other side and work up this to match the first.

For a round neck fitting fairly high, work until the depth to shoulder is 2½ in. less than required. Count the number of stitches on the needle, deduct the equivalent in stitches to 3 in. from the total amount. Halve the remaining number of stitches; then, on the next row, work as follows:

Work the first half of the remaining number of stitches, then cast off the neck stitches and work to the end of the row. Leave the first set of stitches on a spare needle and continue on the last set, but decrease one stitch at the neck edge on every row until the number of stitches required for the shoulder remains on the needle. Work without further shaping until the shoulderline is reached, then shape the shoulder. Now join the wool to the neck edge of the stitches for the other side and work up this to match the first.

For a square neck, work to the position for the neckline; then deduct the number of stitches required for each shoulder from the total amount. The remaining number of stitches must be cast off in the centre of the work as follows:

Work the stitches for the first side, cast off the neck stitches, then work to the end of the row. Leave the first set of stitches on a spare needle, and continue on the second set until the shoulderline is reached. Shape the shoulder, then join the wool to the neck edge of the stitches for the other side and work up this to match the first.

To knit a garment with a straight neck, continue working the front until the shoulder-line is reached, then shape the shoulders by casting off the equivalent number of stitches to 3½ in. Work about 1 in. on the remaining centre stitches, then cast off loosely. When making up the garment, turn in on the wrong side the 1-in. extension to the level of the shoulderline, and sew down very loosely. If the sewing threads are pulled too tightly, the stitches will break when the neck is stretched in pulling the garment over the head.

NEEDLES. Steel knitting needles are most satisfactory for socks, stockings and gloves, or for any very fine knitting, as they are stronger than needles made from a composition. When knitting a garment it may be necessary to use a pair of needles of a different size from that quoted in the directions from which the garment is to be worked; but this should apply only to a knitter who works to a looser or tighter tension than that given. Do not use larger or smaller needles for any other reason, or the garment will not be satisfactory and the measurements will differ from those of the original.

Successful knitting depends on using the size of knitting needles which produces the tension given in the directions. Large needles produce a loosely woven effect and small needles a closely woven effect.

PATTERNS. Some knitters find fancy patterns very complicated, especially when working from directions giving increasings at the side edges, but without every row being written in detail. On this account, many directions of fancy patterns are rejected as being too difficult to undertake. The following method should greatly assist those who have not the experience or confidence necessary for shaping the work when knitting a complicated design from written directions.

With graph paper ruled in squares of eight to 1 in., patterns can be charted, with various signs used to indicate the different stitches. When charting a pattern, always work over two or three repeats in order to get a clear picture of the pattern. With practice, charting patterns on squared paper becomes quite easy and garments can be knitted directly from the chart, thus making written directions unnecessary (see GRAPH PAPER).

For an example, an eight-row pattern is given, and Fig. 16 shows a chart of three repeats and gives one pattern worked on the original number of stitches, and the second pattern worked with two increases at each side, the first increases being on the first row of the second pattern, and the second increases on the fifth row of the same pattern.

The pattern is worked as follows: Cast on a number of st. divisible by 4, plus 1 extra st. *1st row.*—* K. 2, k. 2 tog., w.fd. (to m. a st.); rep. from * to the last st., k. 1. *2nd row.*—P. 2, * w.r.n., p. 2 tog., p. 2; rep. from * to the last 3 st., w.r.n., p. 2 tog., p. 1. *3rd row.*—* K. 2 tog., w.fd., k. 2; rep. from * to the last st., k. 1. *4th row.*—P.

5th row.—K. 1, * w.fd., sl. 1, k. 1, p.s.s.o., k. 2; rep. from * to end. *6th row.*—P. 1, * p. 2 tog., w.r.n., p. 2; rep. from * to end. *7th row.*—K. 3, * w.fd., sl. 1, k. 1, p.s.s.o., k. 2; rep. from * to the last 2 st., w.fd., sl. 1, k. 1, p.s.s.o. *8th row.*—P. These 8 rows form one patt.

When working from a chart, read the first and alternate rows from right to left, and the second and alternate rows from left to right. As charts always show the right side of the work, the stitches on the wrong side will be reversed when knitting from the chart, thus a sign indicating a knit stitch will become a purl stitch when working a row on the wrong side.

If inexperienced in charting patterns, do not undertake a very complicated design, but begin with a simple pattern, preferably a four-row one, with not more than six stitches to each repeat.

PICOT EYELET DIAMOND PATTERN. This is a very elaborate patt., especially suitable for shawls. Knitted in a 2-ply wool, it

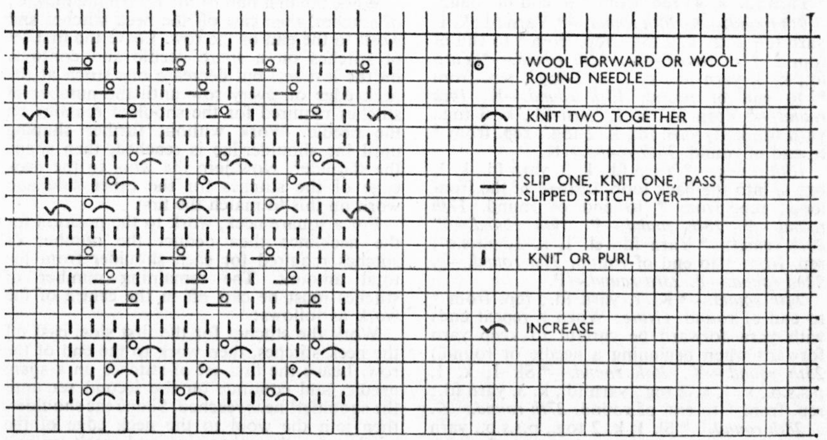

Fig. 16. An eight-row pattern worked on a number of stitches divisible by four, plus one extra stitch.

produces a very gossamery fabric. Cast on a number of st. divisible by 28, plus an extra 12 st., then work as follows:

1st row.—K. *2nd row.*—P. *3rd row.*—K. 2, * (k. 2 tog., w.fd. twice (to make 2 st.), sl. 1, k. 1, p.s.s.o.) 3 times, k. 4, k. 2 tog., w.fd. twice, sl. 1, k. 1, p.s.s.o., k. 4, k. 2 tog., w.fd. twice, sl. 1, k. 1, p.s.s.o.; rep. from * to the last 10 st., (k. 2 tog., w.fd. twice, sl. 1, k. 1, p.s.s.o.) twice, k. 2. *4th row.*—P., but when working the 2 made st., p. the first and k. the second.

5th row.—K. *6th row.*—P *7th row.*—K. 2, w.fd., sl. 1, k. 1, p.s.s.o., * (k. 2 tog., w.fd. twice, sl 1, k. 1, p.s.s.o.) twice, k. 4, (k. 2 tog., w.fd. twice, sl. 1, k. 1, p.s.s.o.) twice, k. 4, k. 2 tog., w.fd. twice, sl. 1, k. 1, p.s.s.o., rep. from * to the last 8 st., k. 2 tog., w.fd. twice, sl. 1, k. 1, p.s.s.o., k. 2 tog., w.fd., k. 2.

8th row.—As 4th row. *9th row.*—As 5th row. *10th row.*—As 6th row. *11th row.*—K. 2, * (k. 2 tog., w.fd. twice, sl. 1, k. 1, p.s.s.o) twice, k. 4, (k. 2 tog., w fd. twice, sl. 1, k 1, p.s.s.o.) 3 times, k. 4, rep. from * to the last 10 st., (k. 2 tog., w.fd. twice, sl. 1, k. 1, p.s.s.o.) twice, k. 2. *12th row.*—As 4th row. *13th row.*—As 5th row *14th row.*—As 6th row.

15th row.—K. 4, * k. 2 tog., w.fd. twice, sl. 1, k. 1, p.s.s.o., k. 4, (k. 2 tog., w.fd. twice, sl. 1, k. 1, p.s.s.o.) 4 times, k. 4; rep. from * to the last 8 st., k. 2 tog., w.fd. twice, sl. 1, k. 1, p.s.s.o., k. 4.

16th row.—As 4th row. *17th row.*—As 5th row. *18th row.*—As 6th row. *19th row.*—K. 2, * k. 8, (k. 2 tog., w.fd. twice, sl. 1, k. 1, p.s.s.o.) 5 times, rep. from * to the last 10 st., k. 10. *20th row.*—As 4th row. *21st row.*—As 5th row. *22nd row.*—As 6th row. *23rd row.*—As 15th row. *24th row.*—As 4th row. *25th row*—As 5th row. *26th row.*—As 6th row. *27th row.*—As 11th row. *28th row.*—As 4th row. *29th row.*—As 5th row. *30th row.*—As 6th row. *31st row.*—As 7th row. *32nd row.*—As 4th row. *33rd row.*—As 5th row. *34th row.*—As 6th row. *35th row.*—As 3rd row. *36th row.*—As 4th row.

37th row.—As 5th row. *38th row.* As 6th row. *39th row.*—K. 2, w.fd., sl. 1, k. 1, p.s.s.o., * (k. 2 tog., w.fd. twice, sl. 1, k. 1, p.s.s.o.) 3 times, k. 8, (k. 2 tog., w.fd. twice, sl. 1, k. 1, p.s.s.o.) twice; rep. from * to the last 8 st., k. 2 tog., w.fd. twice, sl. 1, k. 1, p.s.s.o., k. 2 tog., w.fd., k. 2. *40th row.*—As 4th row. These 40 rows form one complete patt.

PLAITED STITCH. This pattern produces a very solid fabric and is worked on the same principle as cable patterns. The tension has a greater number of stitches to the inch than most patterns, as the continual crossing of groups of stitches tends to tighten up the knitting. Plaited stitch is suitable for pram covers, or for any garment that is required to give great warmth. This pattern can be worked in groups of two, three or four stitches crossing over their equivalent number. An extra double-pointed needle is needed.

To work a medium plaited st. cast on a number of st. divisible by 6, plus 5 extra st., and work as follows: *1st row.*—K. *2nd row.*—P. *3rd row.*—K. 1, * sl. the next 3 st. on to the spare needle and leave in front of work, k. the next 3 st., then k. the 3 st. from the spare needle; rep. from * to the last 4 st., k. 4. *4th row.*—P. *5th row.*—K. *6th row.*—P. *7th row.*—K. 4, * sl. the next 3 st. on to the spare needle and leave at back of work, k. the next 3 st., then k. the 3 st. from the spare needle; rep. from * to the last st., k. 1. *8th row.*—P. These 8 rows form one patt.

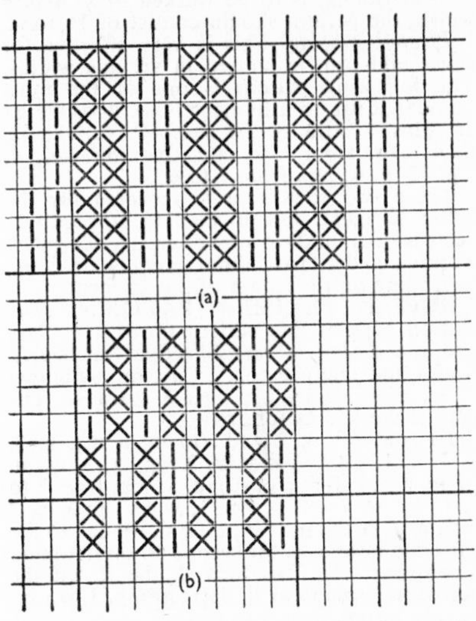

Fig. 17. Ribbing: (a) *knit two, purl two rib;* (b) *an example of broken ribbing.*

RIBBING. Ribbing can be designed in any width, and can be even or uneven. It consists of vertical lines of knit and purl stitches, the purl stitches being almost hidden by the knit stitches, making, therefore, the knitting very elastic. For this reason ribbing is almost always used for welts at waist, neck and sleeve cuffs and for the top of socks or stockings.

When knitting a ribbed patt. always begin and end the rows with the same rib, that is, if the row begins with k. 2, end with k. 2. This means that, for a single rib (k. 1, p. 1), the number of st. to be cast on must be divible by 2, plus one extra st; or for a k. 2, p. 2 rib, the number of st. to be cast on must be divisible by 4, plus 2 extra st., as in Fig. 17. If the ribbing is uneven, such as k. 3, p. 2, the number of st. to be cast on must be divisible by 5, plus 3 extra st.

Single Ribbing. 1st row.—K. 1, * p. 1, k. 1; rep. from * to end. *2nd row.*—P. 1, * k. 1, p. 1; rep. from * to end. For an uneven rib of k. 5, p. 3, work as follows: Cast on a number of st. divisible by 8, plus 5 extra st. *1st row.*—K. 5, * p. 3, k. 5; rep. from * to end. *2nd row.*—P. 5, * k. 3, p. 5; rep. from * to end.

Broken Ribbing. These patterns do not close up, but have a flatter surface and are used for every kind of garment, as they form very attractive patterns. The single broken ribbing is worked as follows: Cast on a number of st. divisible by 2. *1st row.*—* K. 1, p. 1; rep.

from * to end. Rep. this row 3 times more. *5th row.*—* P. 1, k. 1; rep. from * to end. Rep. the last row 3 times more. These 8 rows form one patt., as shown in Fig. 17(b).

The same method applies to all even broken ribbing, but, as the ribbing widens, the number of rows must be increased. For instance, if the broken ribbing is to be worked in k. 4–p. 4 width, the pattern should consist of 16 rows.

Pleated Ribbing. This is very effective for skirts and can be knitted in various widths. The following pattern is one of the most popular. Cast on a number of st. divisible by 16, plus 4 extra st. *1st row.*—P. 4, * k. 12, p. 4; rep. from * to end. *2nd row.*—K. 4, * p. 12, k. 4; rep. from * to end.

These two rows can be repeated for the entire garment, but if shaping is required, decrease 1 st. in the centre of each k.-12 panel, working a dec. row about every 4 or 5 in., depending on the length of the garment.

RUFFLE FEATHER PATTERN. The cast-on edge of this pattern forms a scallop, and the design is very effective for babies' frocks and matinée coats. Cast on a number of st. divisible by 17, plus 3 extra st. The patt. is worked as follows:

1st row.—P. 3, * w.fd. (to m. a st.), k. 3, sl. 1, k. 1, p.s.s.o., k. 4, k. 2 tog., k. 3, w.r.n. (to m. a st. before a p. st.), p. 3; rep. from * to end. *2nd row.*—K. 3, * p. 1, w.r.n., p. 3, p. 2 tog., p. 2, p. the next st., then sl. it back to the left-hand needle, sl. the second st. on left-hand needle over the first, then sl. the st. off the needle (referred to as sl. decrease), p. 3, w.r.n., p. 1, k. 3; rep. from * to end.

3rd row.—P. 3, * k. 2, w.fd., k. 3, sl. 1, k. 1, p.s.s.o., k. 2 tog., k. 3, w.fd., k. 2, p. 3; rep. from * to end. *4th row.*—K. 3, * w.r.n., p. 3, p. 2 tog., p. 4, sl. dec., p. 3, w.fd., k. 3; rep. from * to end.

5th row.—P. 3, * k. 1, w.fd., k. 3, sl. 1, k. 1, p.s.s.o., k. 2, k. 2 tog., k. 3, w.fd., k. 1, p. 3; rep. from * to end. *6th row.*—K. 3, * p. 2, w.r.n., p. 3, p. 2 tog., sl. dec., p. 3, w.r.n., p. 2, k. 3; rep. from * to end. These 6 rows form one patt.

SHADOW PLAITED PATTERN. This pattern consists of small cables with the same number of stitches between each cable. On the first half of one pattern, the cables slope to the right, and, on the second half of one pattern, the cables slope to the left and occupy the position of the intervening stitches of first half.

Cast on a number of st. divisible by 8, plus 2 extra st. The patt. is worked as follows: *1st row.*—K. *2nd row.*—P. *3rd row.*—K. 1, * sl. the next 2 st. on a spare needle, pointed both ends, and leave at the back of work; k. the next 2 st., then k. the 2 st. from the spare needle, k. 4; rep. from * to the last st., k. 1.

4th row.—P. *5th row.*—K. *6th row.*—P. *7th row.*—K. 1, * k. 4, sl. the next 2 st. on to the spare needle and leave in front of the work; k. the next 2 st., then k. the 2 st. from the spare needle; rep. from * to the last st., k. 1. *8th row.*—P. These 8 rows form one patt.

SHORTENING GARMENTS. Some hand-knitted garments are inclined to drop and become too long after having been worn fairly frequently. To shorten a garment without having to re-knit it, first mark the position on the garment at the required length, then separate the knitting as given in the instructions for lengthening (see LENGTHENING GARMENTS). When the work has been separated, slip all the loops on to a knitting needle and cast off.

SPIRAL RIBBING. All spiral ribbing is diagonal, as the stitches continually move from right to left, or from left to right, depending on the directions. When a spiral ribbing is worked on four needles, socks can be knitted without shaping the heels. The knitting is continued without alteration until the position for the toe shaping is reached. When the socks are worn, they should be so arranged on the leg and foot as to appear as vertical ribbing. This ensures a snug fit and is more comfortable to the wearer.

Spiral ribbing worked on two needles is very suitable for jumpers for the fuller figure as it has a slimming effect. The ribs can vary in width, but the wider the ribs, the more rows must be worked before altering the position of the stitches.

To work spiral ribbing on four needles cast on a number of st. divisible by 6 (a minimum of 6 st. on each of three needles). With the fourth needle, work in rounds as follows:

1st round.—* K. 3, p. 3; rep. from * to end. Rep. this round five times more. *7th round.*—K. 2, * p. 3, k. 3; rep. from * to the last 4 st., p. 3, k. 1. Rep. the last round five times more. *13th round.*—K. 1, * p. 3, k. 3; rep. from * to the last 5 st., p. 3, k. 2. Rep. the last round five times more. *19th round.*—* P. 3, k. 3; rep. from * to end. Rep. the last round five times more.

25th round.—P. 2, * k. 3, p. 3; rep. from * to the last 4 st., k. 3, p. 1. Rep. the last round five times more. *31st round.*—P. 1, * k. 3, p. 3; rep. from * to the last 5 st., k. 3, p. 2. Rep. the last round five times more. These 36 rounds form one patt. The knitter will see that the position of the ribbing is altered on every sixth round.

To work spiral ribbing on two needles, cast on a number of st. divisible by 4. *1st row.*—* K. 2, p. 2; rep. from * to end. *2nd row.*—P. 1, * k. 2, p. 2; rep. from * to the last 3 st., k. 2, p. 1. *3rd row.*—* P. 2, k. 2; rep. from * to end. *4th row.*—K. 1, * p. 2, k. 2; rep. from * to the last 3 st., p. 2, k. 1. These 4 rows form one patt.

In the foregoing patt., the ribs slope from left to right, and, to reverse the slope, work as follows: *1st row.*—* K. 2, p. 2; rep. from * to end. *2nd row.*—K. 1, * p. 2, k. 2; rep. from * to the last 3 st., p. 2, k. 1. *3rd row.*—* P. 2, k. 2; rep. from * to end. *4th row.*—P. 1, * k. 2, p. 2; rep. from * to the last 3 st., k. 2, p. 1. These 4 rows form one patt.

If a three and three rib is preferred, it can be worked in the same way, that is, by moving one stitch to the left or right, as the case may be, on every row until six rows have been worked. These 6 rows form one patt.

STOCKING STITCH. This is a smooth fabric on the right side of work, and is worked

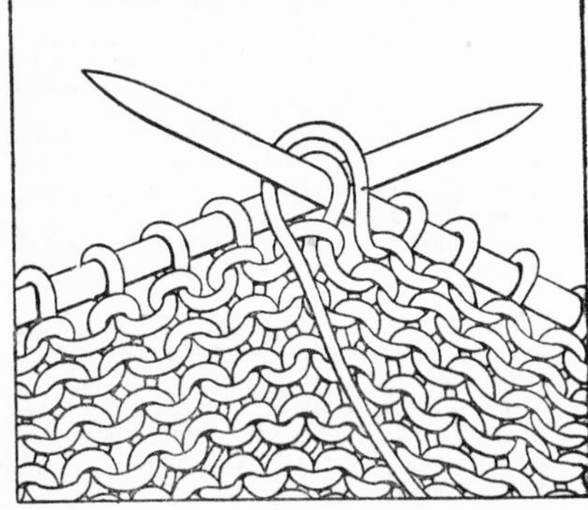

Fig. 18. Examples of stocking stitch: (a) *right or smooth side;* (b) *wrong or purl side.*

by knitting one row plain and one row purl, the plain side being the right side of the knitting (Fig. 18).

TENSION. The foundation of all good knitting is correct tension. Hand-knitted garments should have a tailored appearance, but this will never be achieved if the tension is looser or tighter than that given in the original directions. Unless the work does not require pressing the tension is taken after pressing.

Always work a sample of knitting before beginning to knit a garment, to test the tension. If there are fewer stitches to the inch than the number required, use smaller needles; but, if there are more stitches to the inch, use larger needles. Work the testing sample over a sufficient number of stitches and rows to measure approximately a 4-in. square. This is essential because it is necessary to measure over two or three inches of knitting to ensure that the correct tension is maintained right across and up the work.

An example of how a garment can be a complete failure with regard to measurements, through not working to the correct tension, is easily explained. In the directions the tension may be eight stitches to one inch in width (see Fig. 19) and, should the knitter ignore the tension and work to produce seven stitches to one inch the difference in the width when working over 128 stitches will be just over two inches more than the measurements given in the original. If, on the other hand, the knitter works to a tension of nine stitches to one inch, over 128 stitches, the difference in width will be two inches less than the measurements in the original. The importance of working to the correct tension applies to the depth as well as to the width.

TOE SHAPING. There are two methods for shaping the toes of socks or stockings. One method, when working on four needles, is to work all decreasings at the end of the first needle, the beginning and end of the second needle and at the beginning of the third needle. This is done as follows:

1st round, 1st needle.—K. to the last 3 st., k. 2 tog., k. 1. *2nd needle.*—K. 1, sl. 1, k. 1, p.s.s.o., k. to the last 3 st., k. 2 tog., k. 1. *3rd needle.*—K. 1, sl. 1, k. 1, p.s.s.o., k. to end. *2nd round.*—K. These two rounds are repeated until the toe shaping has been completed, usually leaving about twenty or thirty stitches on the needles. These stitches are then divided into two equal numbers and grafted together (see GRAFTING).

The second method is to decrease about eight times in one round, at equal distances, then working three rounds between each decrease round. The final number of stitches is threaded through a length of wool, drawn up and fastened off.

VEIL STITCH. This is a simple pattern and is most suitable for snoods, lightweight

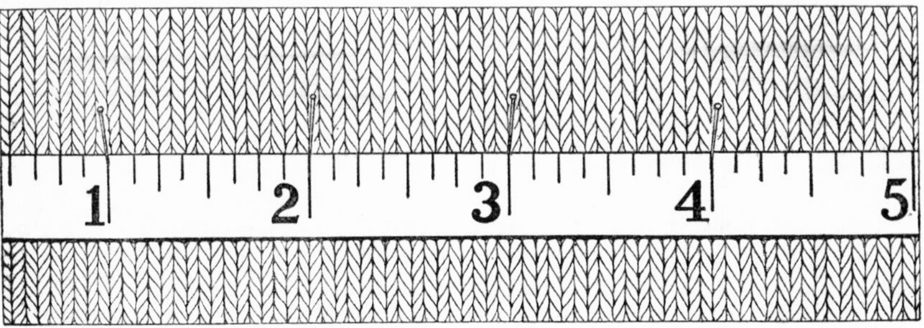

Fig. 19. Measuring the tension. This figure shows eight stitches to the inch.

scarves or veiling, if knitted on large needles. Cast on the required number of stitches, which can be an even or uneven number, and work as follows: *Pattern row.*—* Insert the right-hand needle into the first st. on left-hand needle knitwise, pass the yarn under and over the right-hand needle, then over the left-hand needle, and again under the right-hand needle, draw through a single loop and sl. it off the needle together with the second loop and the st.; rep. from * to end. This row is repeated throughout.

WASHING WOOLLENS. The washing of hand-knitted garments should be undertaken with great care, as careless washing will ruin the wool and the shape. Do not use very hot water or too much soap. Use soap flakes which do not contain soda. Never rub soap on to the woollens, and do not rub the garments but squeeze them and swish them about in the soapy water. Rinse well in two or three lots of water of the same temperature as used for washing.

Squeeze the water out of the garments; never wring them. To dry, place a towel on a flat surface, spread out the garment on the towel and arrange it in shape so that the measurements are the same as before washing. Dry slowly and always away from intense heat. If necessary, press the garment on the wrong side with a warm iron, being careful not to stretch the knitting.

WELTS. All welts should be knitted on fine needles, as they are very elastic and, if worked on coarse needles, will stretch and hang loosely instead of gripping the waist or part of the body at which the welt is to be worn. Do not cast on tightly when beginning a welt as there is always a certain amount of strain on this section of a garment and the cast-on edge will break if the stitches are too tight.

A safeguard against the breaking of a cast-on edge is to use the wool double for the cast-on row, then break off one strand of wool and continue knitting with a single strand. This is advisable for socks, stockings, and especially children's garments. To avoid a loose edge, when casting on with two needles, knit into the back of the cast-on stitches. This is not necessary if the thumb method of casting-on is used.

Welts can be knitted in various ribs, the single rib being the most successful as it has more elasticity than a wider rib.

WINDING WOOL. Do not wind wool into *tight* balls. To avoid doing so, wind the wool over the thumb and first finger of the left hand; then, when the position of the ball needs changing withdraw the thumb and finger and again proceed to wind in the same manner. The result will be a loosely wound ball, thus preventing the wool from stretching.

When winding silk, use a piece of cardboard about 2 in. in width and 6 in. in length, and, when approximately 20 or 25 yd. have been wound over the cardboard, place a piece of soft tissue paper over the wound silk. Continue by winding another 20 or 25 yd., then again place a piece of paper round the wound silk. Repeat the process until all the silk has been wound. This method prevents the silk from slipping off the cardboard, thus avoiding tangles.

WOOL FOR GARMENTS, quantities required. The majority of garments of one type take about the same amount of wool. There are slight variations, depending on the pattern and style, but, for garments of average size, a standard amount covers most patterns —excluding the outsizes, which take more wool.

For a woman, a long-sleeved jumper knitted in 3-ply wool takes from 8 to 10 oz.; a short-sleeved jumper from 5 to 6 oz. of 3-ply wool. In 2-ply wools, a long-sleeved jumper takes from 6 to 7 oz., and a short-sleeved jumper from 4 to 5 oz. 4-ply wool, being thicker and having fewer yards to the ounce than finer wools, is not so economical; but it is more satisfactory if very warm garments are required. A long-sleeved jumper takes from 12 to 14 oz. and a short-sleeved jumper from 8 to 10 oz. of 4-ply wool.

A dress knitted in 3-ply wool takes from 14 to 16 oz. but, for these garments, the style and pattern must be taken into consideration. If a dress is to be knitted on small needles and in a closely woven stitch, more wool will be needed. A knitted suit made in 3-ply wool will take from 18 to 22 oz.

Men's long-sleeved pullovers take from 12 to 14 oz. of 3-ply wool, and a sleeveless pullover from 7 to 8 oz.

A list of baby garments (up to 1 year) and the amount of wool needed for each garment is as follows:

Vest and pilch: 4 oz. of 3-ply or baby wool.
Dress: 3 to 4 oz. of 3-ply or baby wool.
Jersey and knickers: 4 oz. of 3-ply.
Matinée coat: 2 to 3 oz. of 3-ply.
Rompers: 3 oz. of 3-ply.
Pram set (including coat, leggings, gloves and bonnet): 8 or 9 oz. of 3-ply.
Shawl (large size): From 14 to 20 oz. of 3-ply baby wool.

For the toddlers, between the ages of 2 and 4 years, the following list of wool requirements will act as a guide, and will prove useful for the woman who designs knitted garments.

Vest and knickers: 5 oz. of 3-ply.
Rompers: 3 to 4 oz. of 3-ply.
Dress: 4 oz. of 3-ply.
Jersey and knickers: 6 oz. of 3-ply.
Cardigan: 3 to 4 oz. of 3-ply.
Sun suit: 3 to 4 oz. of 3-ply.
Sun suit and bolero: 5 oz. of 3-ply.
Outdoor set (including coat, leggings and bonnet): 10 oz. of 3-ply.

YARNS. Particular care should be taken in the choice of yarns, as it is important to use the most suitable yarn for the pattern, or style, of garment to be knitted. Simple yarns are the best for elaborate or lacy patterns; silk or fancy yarns are heavier and are inclined to drop. With fancy yarns, the beauty of a design is often lost owing to the texture of the yarn. For very lacy patterns, the best yarn to use is a 2-ply. If knitting from written instructions, always use the yarn stated in the directions, as a garment can be quite unsatisfactory if a different yarn is substituted, and the measurements will differ from those given.

EASY ELECTRICAL JOBS

Instructions for repairs, improvements, and maintenance which the handyman can carry out in his own home.

ADAPTORS, USE OF. When a reading lamp, etc., is likely to be used in different parts of the house it is convenient to fit an adaptor to the end of its flex so as to enable it to be fed from either a lampholder or a two-pin socket as required. Such an adaptor is shown in Fig. 1, which also shows other forms of adaptor for sockets. One is easily made up by connecting a lampholder and a two-pin plug by a short piece of flex so that an appliance with a bayonet type of plug can be fed from a two-pin socket. Another type illustrated enables two items to operate at the same time from one 5-amp. socket, while the three-way adaptor shown is plugged into a 15-amp. socket to provide for simultaneous use of a radiator as well as lamp and radio, or for any two of them.

BELLS. Battery-operated. When installing a bell, the first step is to decide whether dry cells or Leclanché (wet) cells are to be used; the former will have to be renewed after about sixteen to eighteen months, while the latter, after a like period, will need recharging only. The number of cells required depends upon the length of wiring; up to 8 yd. of bell wire calls for one cell, up to 14 yd. two cells, and up to 20 yd. three cells, and the actual run that the wires will take from the bell-push to the bell should be carefully planned to keep it as short and as inconspicuous as possible.

Two Leclanché cells are shown in Fig. 2; they are connected in series by a lead from the positive terminal (on the porous pot) of one to the negative (zinc rod) terminal of the other. Separate dry cells to be used as a battery must be similarly connected. The recharging of a Leclanché cell entails renewing the sal-ammoniac solution (4 oz. of sal-ammoniac to 1 pint of warm water) in the glass container; the level of the solution should not be higher than three-quarters of the height of the porous pot. The battery should be as near the bell as possible and yet safely housed on a shelf and in a box to prevent its getting too dusty. The bell should be fixed in a position where it will suffer no accidental knocks.

The construction of a bell for operation from a battery is shown in Fig. 3, and a suitable bell-push in Fig. 4. The twin bell wires should be attached first to the bell-push, one lead on each terminal, and the push then fixed in position. The twin cable is next put in place along its run to the battery. Here *one* wire is cut and its two bare ends (Fig. 5) attached to the two spare (otherwise unconnected) terminals of the battery.

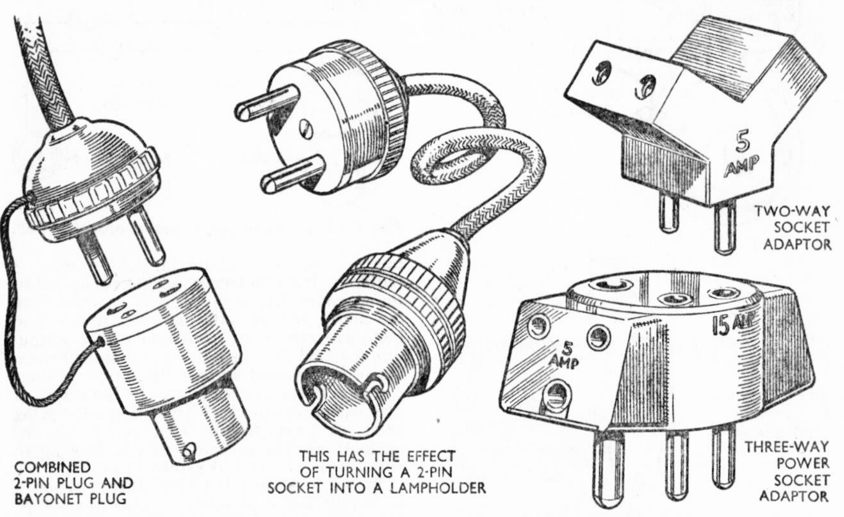

Fig. 1. Various kinds of adaptor which make for convenience in the use of appliances.

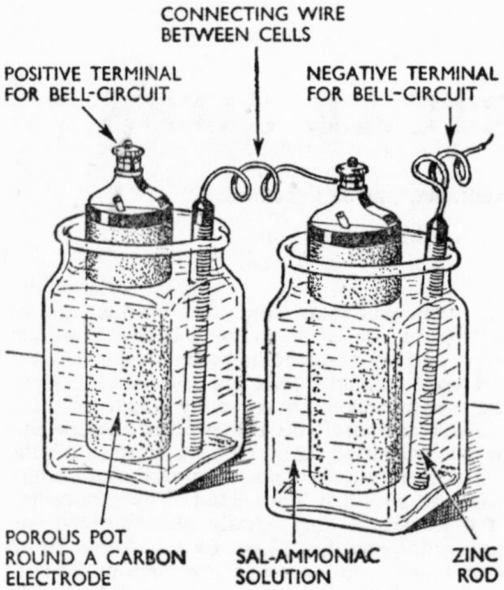

CONNECTING WIRE BETWEEN CELLS
POSITIVE TERMINAL FOR BELL-CIRCUIT
NEGATIVE TERMINAL FOR BELL-CIRCUIT
POROUS POT ROUND A CARBON ELECTRODE
SAL-AMMONIAC SOLUTION
ZINC ROD

Fig. 2. Two Leclanché cells connected in series to form a battery for a bell-circuit.

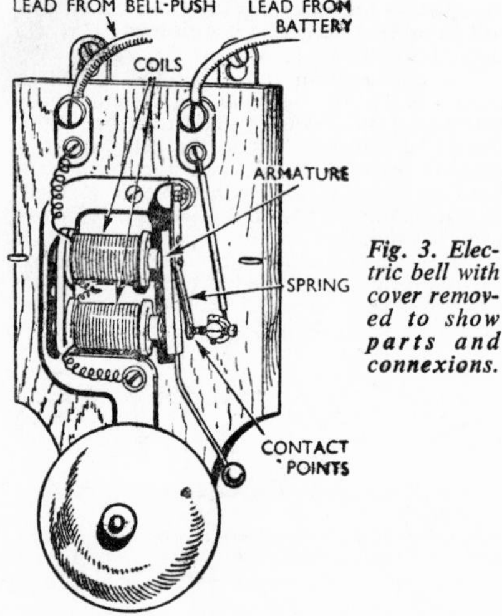

Fig. 3. Electric bell with cover removed to show parts and connexions.

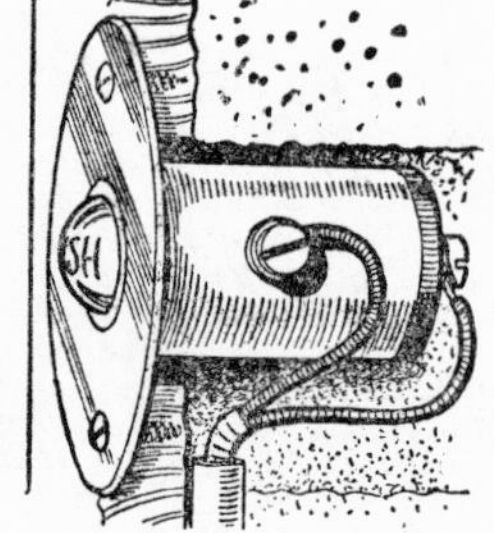

Fig. 4. Barrel type of bell-push suitable for direct insertion in cement or plaster wall.

The leads are finally connected to the bell so that the one from the battery is attached to the bell unit on the side where the striker is, and that coming direct from the bell-push is connected to the other terminal. If the bell does not ring satisfactorily when the push is

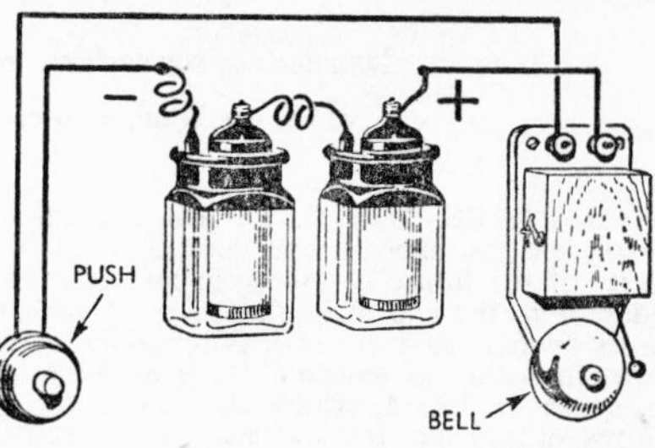

Fig. 5. Complete circuit for battery-operated bell.

depressed, turn the contact screw a little one way or the other until, by trial, correct operation is obtained.

A.C. mains-operated. In this case it is necessary to employ in place of the battery a transformer which will step down the high supply voltage to a mere 3, 5, or 8 volts, according to requirements.

To put the bell transformer in circuit, a feed from the mains is required. This can be taken by means of lead-covered or tough-rubber-covered twin cable from a distribution

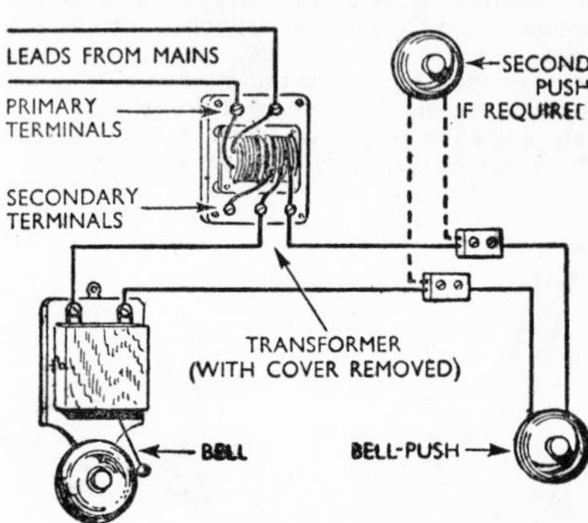

Fig. 6. The circuit for a mains-operated bell.

board as when an additional lighting point is required. The two feed wires are connected to the primary terminals, usually marked with the mains voltage, and the wires to bell and bell-push are taken from two of the output terminals on the other side of the transformer. These are marked so that the output voltage can be selected as necessitated by the length of bell wiring involved; 3 volts normally being sufficient for up to 8 or 9 yd. and 5 volts for up to 15 yd. The complete circuit, showing an additional bell-push, is shown in Fig. 6.

BOWLS AND CHANDELIERS. When a bowl reflector, chandelier or other heavy type of lampshade is to be used, the normal ceiling

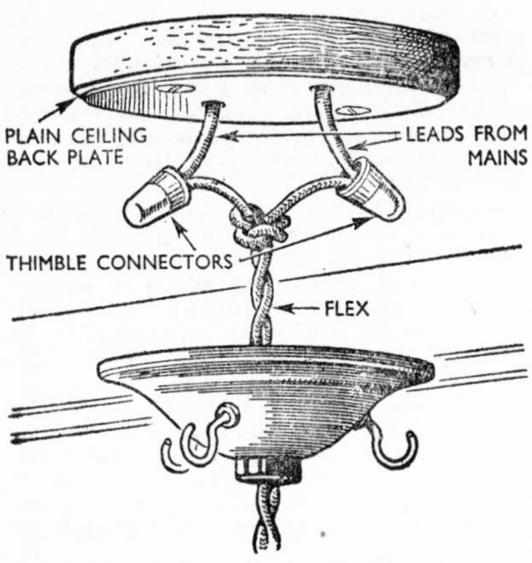

Fig. 7. Joining lamp flex by thimble-connectors.

rose must be replaced by a metal back-plate with one central hook or three or more hooks near its edge from which chains will take the weight. Some back-plates contain a terminal block similar to that of a rose, but others call for the use of special connectors to join the lamp flex to the wires from the mains (Fig. 7).

It is essential that the base be very securely fitted. Long fixing screws should be employed and driven into a joist above the ceiling, or into a cross-member specially inserted between two joists. Laths will not provide a sufficiently strong fixing.

When the base is firmly in position, connect up the flex (of indefinite length as yet) and then screw the back-plate securely to the base. The bowl or other fitting may now be suspended from the hooks provided so that its lowest point is at least 6 ft. 9 in. from the floor. Where a fitting with one central chain is concerned, the flex should be threaded in and out of the links down the chain.

Next attach a lampholder and a 100-watt lamp to the flex, and then switch on at the mains. Hold the lighted lamp over the bowl and lower it until the shadow line cast by the rim of the bowl coincides with the picture rail on the walls nearest to the light (Fig. 8).

Fig. 8. Adjusting a lamp so that the rim of the ***bowl*** *casts its shadow along the picture rail.*

This is the ideal level for the lamp, as not only is the rim's shadow lost, but the maximum reflection will then be obtained. The lamp's position should be noted, and when the current is again switched off at the main, the lampholder should be removed, the flex cut to the correct length, and the lampholder replaced.

DANGERS TO AVOID. An electric current will pass round the circuit of conductors intended for it only provided that it has no opportunity of finding a path to earth on the way. If a bare conductor comes into contact with metal, or touches a damp wall, current will leak away.

More seriously, the human body provides, except in certain circumstances, a suitable path to earth for current from a live conductor. Although contact may be only momentary, the severity of the shock, where domestic supply voltages are concerned, is likely to be considerable and has only too often proved fatal.

And the risk of getting a shock is not reserved exclusively for those who attempt

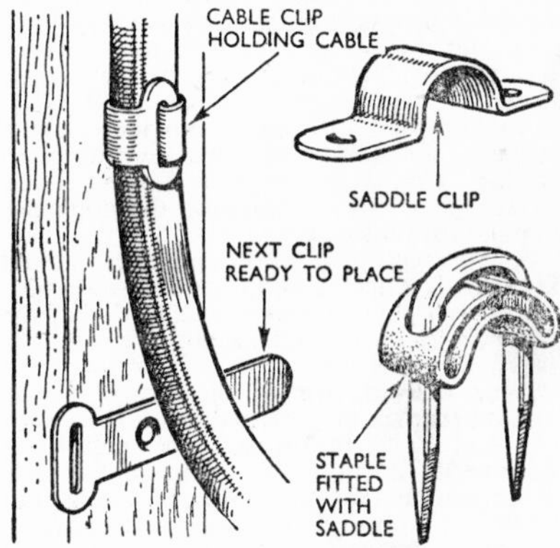

Fig. 9. Three devices for securing cable.

adjustments to components and appliances without first switching off. Anyone operating a switch with a wet or damp hand runs a risk if there is a leak in the switch.

For this reason it is dangerous for a switch to be placed over or near a sink or wash-basin. In a bathroom special care must be taken that switches for light and radiator cannot be operated by anyone while in the bath. A portable electric fire should never be used in a bathroom (it is forbidden by regulation), and the safest control for a bathroom wall radiator is a pull-cord switch in the ceiling.

A similar switch is also the most preferable means of operating the bathroom light; alternatively, a wall switch can be sited just *outside* the door. No socket should be fitted in a bathroom which will make possible the operation of a shaver or hair-drier while the user is in contact with bath or towel rail.

Lights in bathrooms and kitchens, and especially where there are stone, concrete or tiled floors, should be fixed so that the lamp is at least 8 ft. from the floor, and the flex, if any, should be round and with a tough-rubber exterior. The safest type of lampholder for such rooms is that which requires no flex.

Another dangerous practice is the use of a bowl fire or an iron plugged into a pendant lampholder. Both cause undue strain on the lighting flex; the fire is liable to get dragged over if anything catches in the flex, and the movement of the iron while in use is bound to cause trouble in the pendant.

Do not use long runs of flex; they should always be kept as short as possible and never brought through doorways or passed under a carpet. Never attach flex or cables of any kind to walls, etc., with ordinary staples, which may, in time, cut through the insulation; saddle clips or staples which have saddles in them (Fig. 9) should always be employed.

EARTHING OF APPLIANCES. Probably the commonest cause of electrical shocks is the lack of earthing connexions to fittings and appliances with metal exteriors, and in some cases even metal handles.

As mentioned under DANGERS TO AVOID, current will pass through a person's body to earth, but this is true only if there is no path to earth providing less resistance to the passage of current between the conductor and earth. A copper wire, of course, provides such a path and, if suitably connected, constitutes an earth. It takes what current leak there is and thereby gives anyone handling the appliance immunity from shock.

For this reason all power appliances should be earthed. After being in use for some time it may well happen that a lead to one of the terminals in, for example, a radiator (fire) has frayed through movement or vibration, and perhaps one or two of the many strands forming the flex may be making contact with the metal frame. In this case the radiator will continue to function and, therefore, will give no intimation that something is wrong, but the frame, unless earthed, is liable to pass on current to anyone touching it.

Earthing a radiator, iron, electric kettle or vacuum-cleaner involves the use of three-pin plugs and sockets (instead of two-pin types) and a triple flex. The earth socket is connected by a copper wire and earthing clip to the end of the conduit. In the flex, two wires will, of course, be used to carry the current and the third must be connected to the terminal of the third pin designed to fit the earth socket.

At the appliance, the two current-carrying conductors are fitted to their respective terminals, while the third must be attached under the earthing screw where such is provided, or else secured under a nut used in the construction of the appliance or otherwise firmly joined to the frame. At the point where the wire is joined it is essential to remove enamel or rust, if any, to ensure a good contact.

Similarly it is possible to earth a metal lampholder; in this case, a ceiling rose having three terminal plates must be employed, instead of a rose with two, the third terminal being given a connexion to the conduit and taking the third conductor of the triple flex, which also is necessary. Connexion of the other end of third flex conductor is made to the metal casing of the lampholder, which provides several ways of attaching the wire; though this must, of course, be kept well away from the lamp and socket parts.

It will be realized that for the conduit to provide a continuous path to earth, as it ought, the local earth connexions by wire and earthing clips which are necessary at such interruptions of the conduit as Bakelite junction boxes, fuse-boxes, meters and so on, must all be in position and secure. See SWITCHES, TYPES AND FAULTS OF.

ELECTRIC IRONS, FAULTS IN. Failure of an electric iron is much more often due to a fault in the flex or adaptor than to a breakdown of the heating element. The causes are the heat to which the adaptor is subjected and the constant movement of the flex while the iron is in use.

The Bakelite case of the adaptor is made up of two halves which are easily separated for inspection of the wiring connexions by removal of a central screw and nut, or, in other types, two screws. If part of this case has fractured, the adaptor should be promptly discarded.

To replace the heating element of an iron, the handle and top cover are first removed. In modern types these are often removable in one piece, but in older designs two nuts secure the handle and, when these are removed, the handle can be lifted away and then the cover withdrawn; the iron weight is then disclosed; this is clamped down by two more nuts on the same studs used to locate the handle. Upon removal of the clamping nuts the iron weight can be raised, and under it will be found the heating element (Fig. 10), comprising resistance wire contained between two layers of mica sheet or thin asbestos.

When replacing the iron weight over the element, the two clamping nuts must be run down as tight as possible or the life of the element may be considerably shortened.

ELECTRIC KETTLES, REPAIRS TO. If an electric kettle fails to warm up when switched on, and the flex and plug connector are known to be in order, the indications are that the heating element requires renewal.

If the kettle is of the type which has the elements clamped underneath the base, invert the kettle and remove the two or more screws and nuts holding the base.

Removal of the base discloses the heating unit located in a circular recess in the bottom of the kettle. Next undo the central nut and raise the iron plate. Under this will be found the element, which in most designs comprises a resistance wire spiralled round a mica ring placed between two mica insulating disks.

If either of these disks is flaking or crumbling, or if the element wire is fractured, the element must be removed and a new one fitted. The wire receives current through two flexible brass strips attached by nuts to the inner ends of the two contact pins protruding from the side of the kettle.

When fitting the new element, first place it in position and then pass the two brass strips

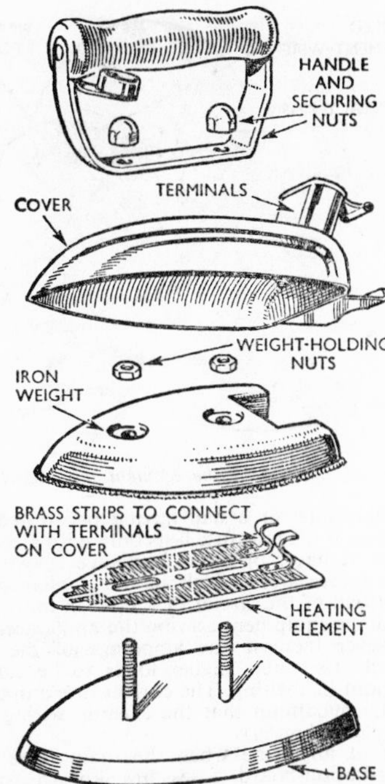

Fig. 10. Parts of an electric iron.

through the slots in the iron plate before doing up the centre nut over both element and plate. The nut should not be tightened unduly, but just sufficient to stop any movement of the parts. When the brass strips have been secured to the contact-pin nuts, the kettle base may be replaced.

Most modern kettles are fitted with immersion elements. This type of element is removed by unscrewing the milled ring on the outside of the kettle body and removing the element through the top of the kettle. The new element is then inserted, taking care to replace the fibre and rubber washers as on the original element to make a water-tight joint. The lip of the element should seat on the kettle bottom.

FLEXIBLE WIRES. A flex that has lost much of its flexibility has undoubtedly perished and should be renewed. If when a flex is passed through the hands it bends weakly at any point, this is probably owing to a break in the wire strands. Should the cotton or silk covering appear frayed at any point other than at the extremities, the flex is best renewed.

Faults near the end of a flex can sometimes be overcome by cutting off a portion. As a temporary measure, a defective portion can be removed from the centre of a flex and the two remaining parts joined by special connectors (see WIRE, JOINTS IN). The practice of merely twisting the ends together and wrapping with insulating tape is never satisfactory for long, and when applied to a pendant flex is highly dangerous.

Best-quality twisted flexible cables should be used for pendants, except in kitchens and bathrooms, where steam is likely to be prevalent; in such places the outer casing must be of tough rubber.

For uses other than lighting, round or oval flexes, that is, two or three cables running parallel in a single outer braiding, should always be used.

Fitting new flex. Commence by threading the flex through first the two wooden wedges retained in the lampholder cap (where this type of holder is in use) and then the cover. Next push back the silk or rubber covering of each cable to expose the rubber beneath. About ¾ in. of the rubber and cotton covering should now be cut or burned away.

The bare ends of the wire should be scraped so that they are clean and bright; the strands of each should be twisted up tightly and secured in the terminals. In the all-Bakelite type of holder there is, between the terminals, a partition which has a hole, or snick, near each end; the cables should be caught one in each of these to remove some of the strain from the terminal connexions.

Cover and socket can now be brought together and secured, and the cap (of a metal holder) screwed home so as to make the wedges grip the flex.

To fit the other end of the flex to a ceiling rose, first pass the rose cover down the flex so that it rests on the top of the lampholder. Next bare ¾ in. at the end of each cable, making sure they are clean and tightly stranded. Pass each through a hole in the dividing bridge of the rose and loop it round the corresponding terminal screw beneath the washer, then do the two screws up tight. Finally pass the rose cover up the flex and screw it into place. The new pendant is now ready for its lamp and shade.

FUSES, RENEWAL OF. A fuse, strictly termed a fusible cut-out, is the "safety valve"

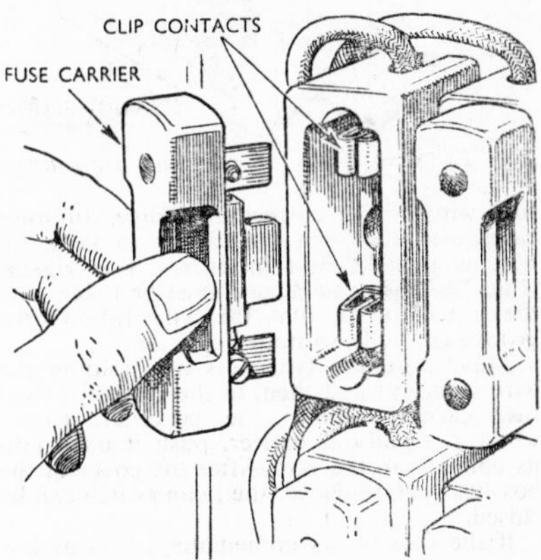

Fig. 11. Pulling out a fuse carrier to examine the condition of the fuse or for replacement.

of an electrical circuit. It contains a piece of special wire that will melt immediately the current passing through it reaches the maximum amperage for which the circuit is intended, so that current can no longer pass. It thus protects lamps and other appliances and, more important still, it prevents excessive current heating the conductors and the consequent damage to their insulation.

The first step in renewing a fuse is to switch off at the main. Where fuses are contained in circular porcelain holders mounted on a large board, it is valuable to have them marked to show which fuse protects which part of the house. This saves unscrewing each fuse cover until the blown one is located.

With the more modern type of fuse-box, however, locating the blown fuse is less trouble because, when the cover of the box has been opened, it will be seen that each individual fuse is secured in a porcelain carrier which is easily pulled out from its clip contacts for inspection (Fig. 11).

Undo the nuts at each end of the carrier and remove what is left of the old fuse wire; then clean the carrier and fit a new length of

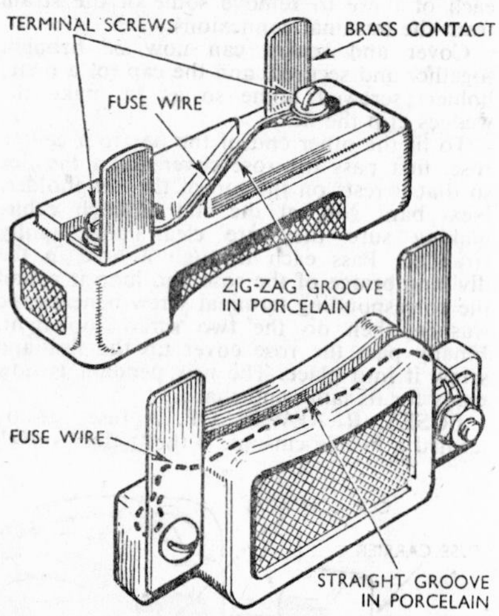

Fig. 12. Two kinds of pull-out fuse carrier.

fuse wire of the correct amperage. In some cases the groove in the carrier to take this wire is straight, but in others it is zig-zag (Fig. 12), and special care must be taken with the latter to see that the wire follows the groove correctly without being taut.

Make sure the two nuts are holding the wire securely; and then, in the case of a fixed fuse carrier, replace the porcelain cover; while if a pull-out carrier, push it back into its contacts in the box. After the cover of the box has been replaced, the main switch can be closed.

If the fuse blows immediately, it is useless to fit another until the fault in the wiring has been tracked down and eliminated. Such a fault may be due to insulation breakdown, a

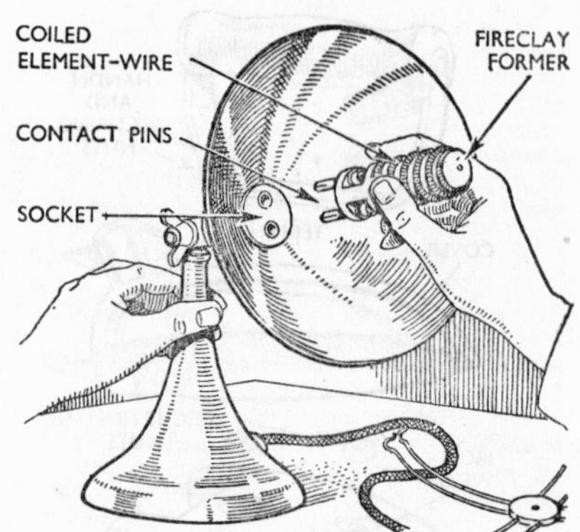

Fig. 13. Removing the element of a bowl fire.

damp cable, or a nail having penetrated the wiring. If the new fuse lasts only until a certain light, radiator or other appliance is switched on, it indicates a fault in the appliance, an overload of the circuit or a fault in the wiring or other equipment serving the appliance.

Never increase the amperage of the fuse merely to enable higher loads to be carried without its melting. The correct fuse amperage is the maximum that the existing wiring will handle *with safety*.

If at any time when the main fuses and distribution-board fuses are known to be intact not a single lamp in the house will light, make certain that the mains switch has not been put off. If it has not, and a check-up shows that your next-door neighbour's supply is normal, it must be concluded that the supply authority's fuse has given out, and they should be notified without delay.

HEATING APPLIANCES, REPAIRS TO.

Every kind of heating unit gives out heat because of the resistance offered to the passage of electric current by a wire (or wires), known as the element. In radiators (fires), boiling rings and bowl fires this element is exposed, and it can be seen that it consists of a long continuous spiral of fine wire. It is mounted on a moulding of fireclay and asbestos; in a large radiator, the wires usually extend straight across from one side to the other to form, with its moulding, one complete fire bar.

In a boiling ring the fireclay moulding is circular and the wire follows a groove, zig-zagging across it, whereas in a bowl fire the fireclay takes the form of a cylinder which has simply to be pushed into a two-pole socket at the centre of the bowl (Fig. 13).

If a radiator or boiling ring fails to warm up when switched on, and it is certain that the fault does not lie in the flex or supply point, it will usually be found that the element wire has broken. This is inevitable after hours and hours of use, but the fracture may be brought about sooner by the presence of dirt and damp on the element. An accidental hard knock will also weaken the element, and failure will often occur when it is switched on subsequently.

When one of the bars of a radiator fails, examine it closely to see where the break has occurred. If it happens to be near the terminal at either end (as is sometimes the case), a repair can be easily effected simply by undoing the terminal, removing the old piece of wire from it and carefully drawing the end of the element out a little so that it can be connected up to the terminal afresh.

Normally, no terminals are visible from the front of the radiator, and the back will have to be taken off, but this is usually merely a matter of removing two of four large securing nuts. An example of the wiring in one form of two-bar fire is shown in Fig. 14.

When the break in the wire has occurred other than near one end of the wire, or if, through a knock, the fireclay moulding is damaged, a complete new firebar should be fitted. Never attempt to make a join in a broken element wire; it is dangerous, will soon fail again, and may lead to arcing and blow a fuse. The faulty firebar is easily withdrawn

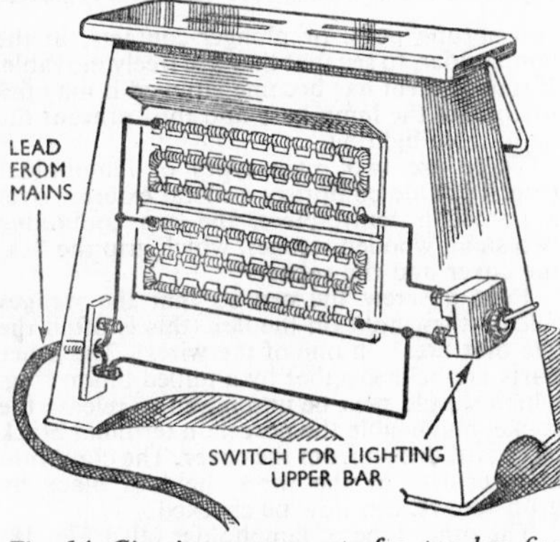

Fig. 14. Circuit arrangement of a two-bar fire.

from the frame after the removal of screws securing it. When purchasing the renewal, the consumption and the voltage of the fire must be stipulated.

It should be remembered that the elements of a fire, when not in use for some little time, should be kept free from dust and damp. And if the heater has a reflector this should be kept brightly polished, because this improves the efficiency of the appliance in radiating heat.

LIGHTS, ADDITIONAL. The simplest method of wiring up a new point and switch is to make use of existing fixtures as circuit connexions. This is particularly useful where the new circuit is to be some distance from the splitter-fuse, or distribution board.

First decide upon the respective sites of the new switch and new ceiling rose and affix their blocks. A length of cable is now taken from one terminal of the new rose to the new switch (Fig. 15).

Having switched off at the mains, a negative must now be run from the other terminal of the new rose to a convenient existing rose,

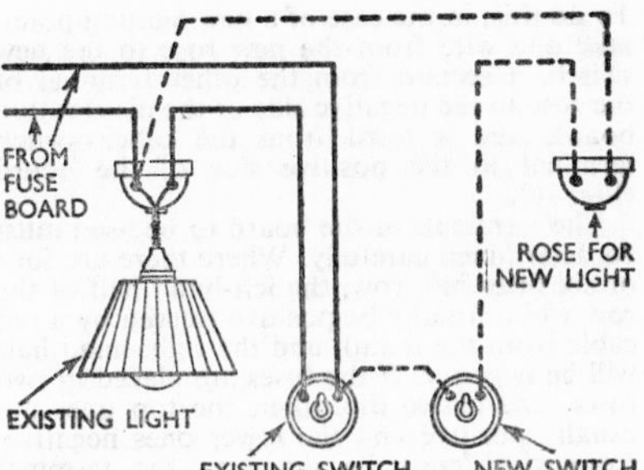

Fig. 15. Making use of an existing rose and switch for wiring a new light-point.

but it must be to what may be called the *negative* terminal ("positive" and "negative" are misnomers in an A.C. installation, but used for convenience) of that rose. If one of its terminals already has more than one wire from it, this is undoubtedly the negative; if not, assume the existing black lead from the rose to be the negative. In any event, should the wrong one be chosen no harm will result. The new light will not function and the lead will then have to be changed over.

The circuit is completed by taking a cable from the second terminal of the new switch to the *positive* side of a convenient existing switch. Here again two leads already entering a terminal indicate the positive side of the switch; failing this, choose that holding a red cable.

For such wiring as this 1/044 or 3/029 (capacity, 5 amp.) vulcanized india-rubber-covered cable may be used, but should be passed through conduit. Otherwise, tough rubber-covered or lead-covered cable will do the job, though the former is best run on the surface of walls and ceilings, not buried.

When lead-covered cable is employed there is the advantage that it can be earthed by suitable connexion from a cleanly scraped portion of the lead to existing conduit or water-pipe. Probably the simplest conductor for the amateur in this kind of work is single lead-covered cable, for its use both obviates the joins necessitated by twin cable and removes the need for additional conduit.

If wiring for an additional 5-amp. socket or a light is required in a part of the house reasonably near the distribution board, the new circuit can be run direct from the board.

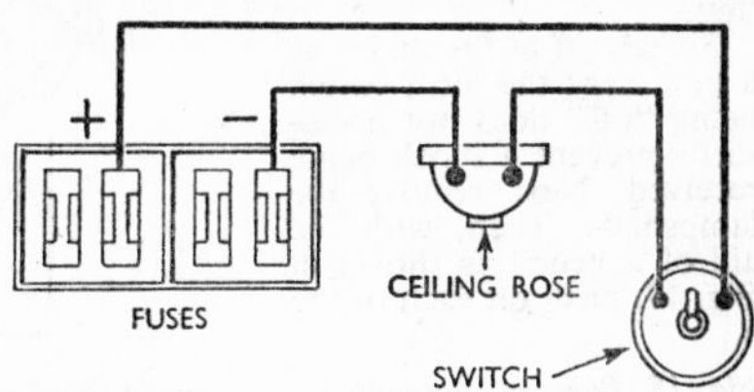

Fig. 16. Circuit for a new light and switch wired direct from a fuse or distribution board.

To do this, in the case of a new lighting point, take one wire from the new rose to the new switch, a second from the other terminal of the rose to the negative side of the distribution board, and a third from the other switch terminal to the positive side of the board (Fig. 16).

The terminals of the board to be used must be determined carefully. Where there are four or six fuses in a row, the left-hand half of the row will normally be positive (served by a red cable from the main), and the right-hand half will be negative. If the fuses are placed in two rows, one above the other, the top ones are usually positive and the lower ones negative. Connexion must be made to the terminal which is contacted by the end of the fuse carrier that is farthest away from the mains connexion in each case, that from the switch to a positive, and that from the rose to a negative.

LIGHTING DEFECTS AND REPAIRS. If a lamp fails to light when expected to do so and nearby lamps are functioning, the first thing to suspect is the lamp. After some hundreds of hours of use the filament in the best of lamps will fracture. Try a sound lamp in its place.

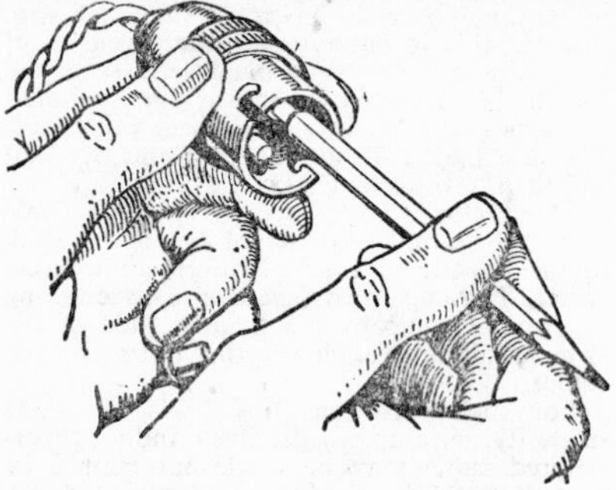

Fig. 17. Testing the contacts of a lampholder.

Failure of a second lamp to light in the holder indicates several possibilities. Of these, a broken flex and a loose connexion are perhaps the most common causes of lighting failure. To deal with either will normally entail the dismantling and/or removal of the lampholder, so this may as well be checked first.

Switch off at the mains as a first step; the local switch being "off" does not necessarily prevent a shock being received. Next remove the lampshade. Then, with the aid of a pencil as shown in Fig. 17, push on each of the two sprung pegs, or plunger-contacts, in the lampholder, to see that they are freely movable. If one of them has become jammed it may fail to contact the lamp base and thus prevent the lamp from lighting.

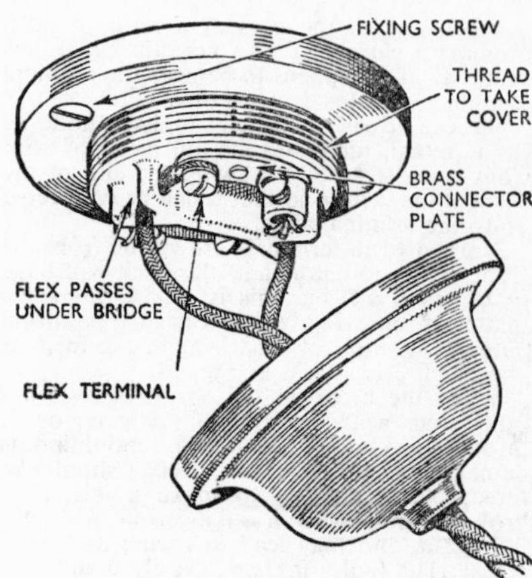

Fig. 19. Bakelite ceiling rose with cover removed.

There are two main types of lampholder (Fig. 18). One comprises a metal exterior over a porcelain centre-piece, the cap containing two small wooden wedges, which grip the flex, the cover and the socket.

First unscrew the cap so that the wedges release their hold on the flex (this is often the site of a break in one of the wires). The other parts are held together by a milled union ring, which should next be unscrewed to release the socket and enable the porcelain terminal block to be withdrawn from the cover. The condition and security of the wires, held in place by grub-screws, can now be checked.

The other type of lampholder (also Fig. 18) is simpler. It is entirely of Bakelite (except for the terminals and a lining to the socket). The

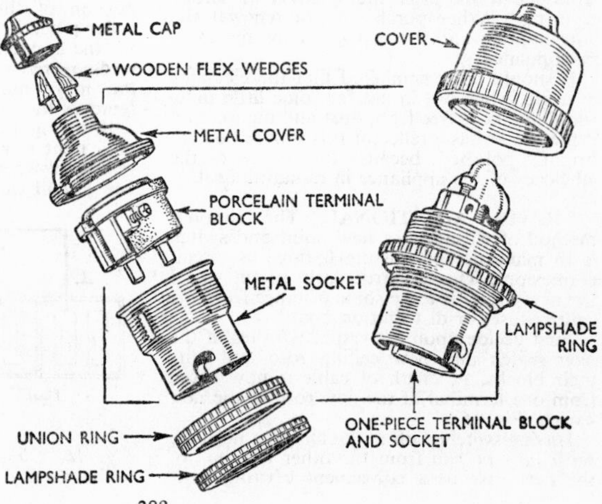

Fig. 18. Parts of lampholders (left) *of metal and porcelain and* (right) *of Bakelite.*

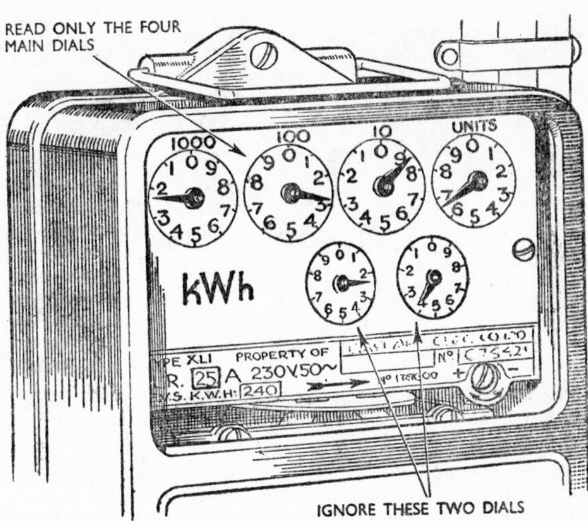

Fig. 20. Electric meter reading 2,286 units.

cover has a milled edge and is easily unscrewed from the one-piece terminal block and socket.

If, by this stage, the cause of failure has not become apparent, attention should be turned to the other end of the flex. In the case of a pendant this will, of course, be in a ceiling rose. It is merely a matter of unscrewing the cover to expose the terminals to which each line of the flex is connected (Fig. 19). On either side of the dividing bridge there is a brass terminal plate; at one end of this is a collar in which, secured by a screw, is a lead from the mains; while at the other end is a slotted pillar-screw with washer for securing the flex. When seeing that connexions are tight, check both screws on the mains as well as the flex terminals.

MEASUREMENT OF ELECTRICITY. The ampere (amp. for short) is the unit used to measure the flow of current in a circuit, as distinct from the volt, which is used for the measurement of supply *pressure*. These two units are related to a third, the watt—a measure of the *energy consumed*—as follows:

Volts × Amperes = Watts
or
Watts ÷ Volts = Amperes

In a 230-volt circuit designed for a 5-amp. flow (and protected, therefore, by a 5-amp. fuse) the maximum load in watts can easily be calculated by 230 × 5 = 1,150. Thus if a bowl fire consuming 650 watts and an iron consuming 450 watts (per hour) are in use simultaneously (total 1,100 watts), the circuit is carrying almost its maximum flow. If now, in addition to the fire and iron, a 60-watt light happens to be switched on, the fuse will ultimately "blow." See FUSES.

A two-bar electric radiator (fire) consumes current at the rate of 2 kilowatts (2,000 watts) with both bars in use. By dividing the voltage —say, 230—into the wattage, it is seen that the amperage required is between 8 and 9; consequently, a 2-kilowatt radiator must on no account be connected to a 5-amp. circuit.

METER READING. The total amount of electrical energy consumed over the complete installation of a house or flat is, of course, registered by a meter fitted near the main switch(es). One type of meter has a window at which five numbers appear, rather like the milometer of a car. The other type, more commonly fitted, has a series of dials on which pointers rotate.

To take a reading from the dial type of meter, ignore small dials marked in red, and study the four larger dials; these are marked in black. Where a pointer is not exactly over a number, take note of the lower of the two numbers between which it lies. Also, it is important actually to *read* the numbers on each dial (and not just go by the appearance of a pointer's position), because the numbers do not progress in the same direction around all the dials. Specimen dials and the correct reading from them are shown in Fig. 20.

PAYMENT FOR ELECTRICITY. The basis upon which payment is made for the supply of current is the "unit of electricity." This unit is the kilowatt-hour, which means that 1,000 watts can be consumed for 1 hour for 1 unit. Knowing the price charged per unit, it is a simple matter to calculate the approximate cost of using lights and other appliances. For the cost of one unit it is possible, for example, to use a 1,000-watt radiator for 1 hour, *or* a 650-watt iron for 1½ hours, *or* a 100-watt lamp for 10 hours, *or* a 25-watt lamp for 40 hours.

Fig. 21. Opening the pins of a 5-amp. plug which fits too loosely in its socket.

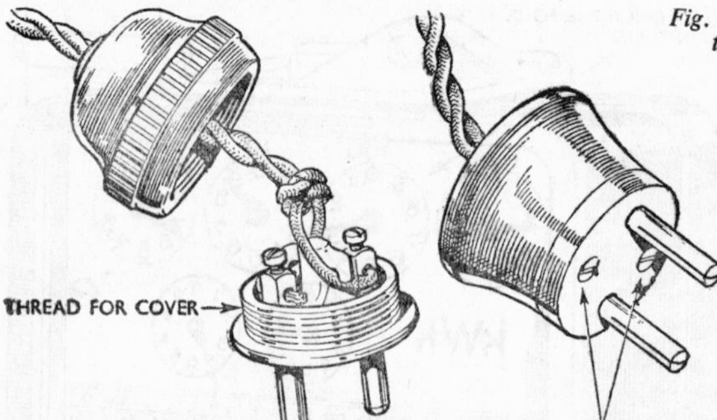

Fig. 22. Two different kinds of two-pin plug in common use.

PLUGS AND SOCKETS. Where the light giving trouble is fed from a plug and socket, as is usually the case with reading lamps, the pins of the plug should be inspected. If they fit too loosely into the socket, they should be spread (Fig. 21) so as to ensure firm contact.

Two-pin 5-amp. plugs are of various patterns; round ones (Fig. 22) often have a milled portion to facilitate unscrewing the cover from the base, which is all that is necessary to gain access to the flex terminals. In other types it is a matter of undoing two screws from the base.

Before attempting to remove the cover of a wall socket, always first switch off at the mains. For lighting purposes, radio, vacuum-cleaner, etc., two-pin sockets of 5-amp. capacity are normal. The cover may be withdrawn after the removal of a screw located between the holes. It may then be checked that the feed-wires are tightly held by the grub-screws.

Power sockets are often designed to accommodate plugs with three pins (one for an earth connexion to the conduit and two for the current). They are usually incorporated in a switch, access to terminals then being gained by removal of the switch cover. In another type of three-pin socket, which has no switch, the earthing pin of the plug, when inserted, opens shutters covering the "live" sockets so that accidental contact is impossible.

Sockets and switches which have become loose on the wall or skirting are dangerous and should be made secure without delay.

SUPPLY—TYPE AND VOLTAGE. There are two kinds of electric current: D.C. (direct current), which flows in one direction only, and A.C. (alternating current), which flows first in one direction and then in the opposite direction. In A.C. supplies for domestic purposes these reversals of current flow take place usually at the rate of fifty in a second.

Whether a D.C. or A.C. supply is received depends entirely upon the nature of the equipment at the generating station. An equally important factor is the pressure, or voltage, at which current is supplied to the house. The supply pressure may be as low as 100 volts D.C., but is usually between 200 and 250 volts, whether D.C. or A.C.

No appliance or component should ever be subjected to a higher voltage than that for which it is designed and marked. When a lamp or radiator is connected to a supply of lower voltage, however, no harm is done, but the resulting light or heat obtained is not the maximum for the appliance. Radio sets, bells, vacuum-cleaners and other motor-operated appliances marked A.C. will not operate on D.C., and vice versa. Only those radio sets and motors termed "universal" are designed to operate on either A.C. or D.C. as required.

SWITCHES, TWO-WAY. On stairways and in rooms which can be entered by more than one door it is often very desirable that the light should be controlled by more than one switch. This is a comparatively simple matter to arrange and depends upon the employment of two-way switches; these have a third terminal (Fig. 23), which is essential for the revised circuit.

Measure off the length of cable required to connect the additional switch to the existing switch position. Lead-covered cable is recommended, and it should be triple cable, as *three* conductors are needed. If, however, triple cable is not available, a twin cable and a single cable can be run over the same route. The cable(s) should be attached in position and the six ends of the conductors prepared.

Having made certain that current is "off" at the mains, remove the present "one-way" switch and wood block. The block will require a third hole drilled in it to coincide with the third terminal of the new two-way switch that is being substituted, and a groove by which the new cable can enter. A block must be similarly prepared for the other new switch.

It will be seen that whereas an ordinary switch takes two feed wires at the top (*A* and *B*, Fig. 23), the new switch has one also at the bottom and to the right (*C* in the diagram). In connecting up, the existing wires from the

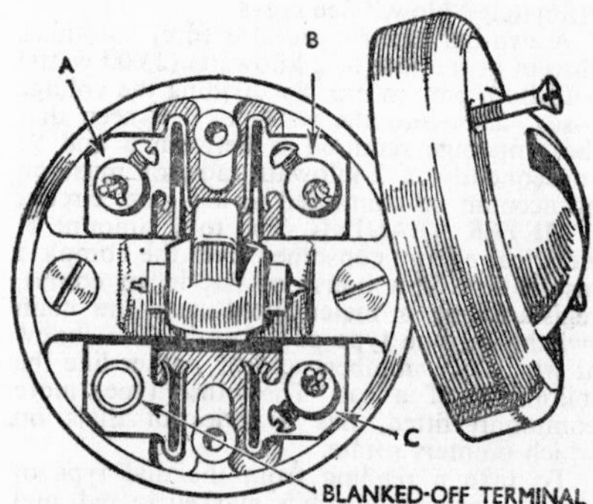

Fig. 23. Two-way switch (the letters refer to wiring instructions given in the text).

mains are placed in terminals *B* and *C*. (If either feed is a double, because of a loop-in for another light, it should go in terminal *B*.)

The new triple cable will have a red lead, a black lead and a white lead. These should now be passed through the block and into the switch so that the red and black leads also enter terminals *A* and *B* respectively, while the white lead is connected to terminal *C* of the switch.

At the additional switch the wiring is very straightforward. Connect the leads of the triple cable in precisely the same arrangement as at the other switch, that is to say, the red to terminal *A*, the black to *B*, and the white to *C*. The completed circuit, now ready for use, is shown in Fig. 24. When the knobs of the switches are either both up or both down, the lamp is out. When either is up and the other down, however, current will pass through the lamp.

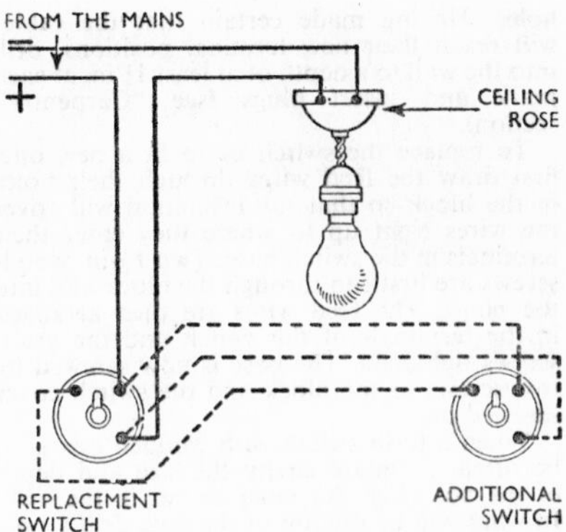

Fig. 24. Complete circuit for controlling a light by two-way switch. New wires required are shown in the diagram as broken lines.

SWITCHES, TYPES AND FAULTS OF. Apart from socket switches, there are three main types of wall switch for domestic purposes: the surface or "raised" switch, the semi-flush switch, and the flush or countersunk switch. The characteristics of all three kinds are evident from Fig. 25.

Switches may be of all-Bakelite construction (except for the current-carrying parts and the spring), or the body, or base, may be of porcelain and the cover and knob of metal. The cover of a round switch is unscrewed for removal, and the ornamental square cover-plate of a flush switch can be removed after unscrewing the milled ring immediately behind the knob.

Before removing the cover of a switch always cut the current off at the mains.

A switch that imparts a shock or a tingling sensation to the fingers when operated is dangerous. Nothing reliable can be done to stop this leak; the switch should be replaced by a new one without delay.

Bad contact in a switch may be the reason for a lamp's failure to light. When the cover is removed, first check that the grub-screws holding the feeds are tight. It will be seen that a pair of brass blades fly up to, and preferably into, two copper slot-contacts. If the blades do not enter their respective slots easily, or if a slot has become too wide for a good contact to be made, the copper can easily be bent until an improvement is effected.

When the knob of a switch tends to drop down again after being pushed up and the contact blades flop loosely instead of jumping with a snap, it can only mean that the mechanism is badly worn and, in some types, that the spring has broken. A switch in this condition should be scrapped.

To remove a switch from the wall, make sure that the current is off at the mains and then unscrew the cover. Next slacken off the two grub-screws securing the feed wires in the terminals. Remove the two wood-screws on either side of the mechanism and the switch will come free.

As a rule, when a switch has become loose on the wall it is because the screws holding the wooden block to the wall have lost their grip. The only way to remedy this state of affairs is to remove the block and any wooden or other plugging for the screws and then fill the holes with cement or stopping. When this filling has set, site the block a little higher or lower than formerly and mark the position of two new

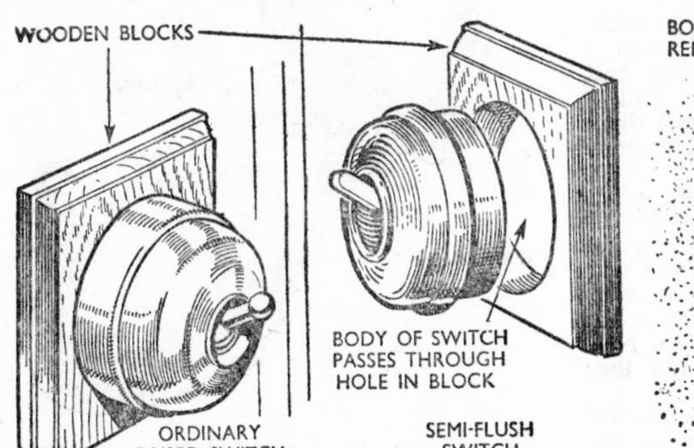

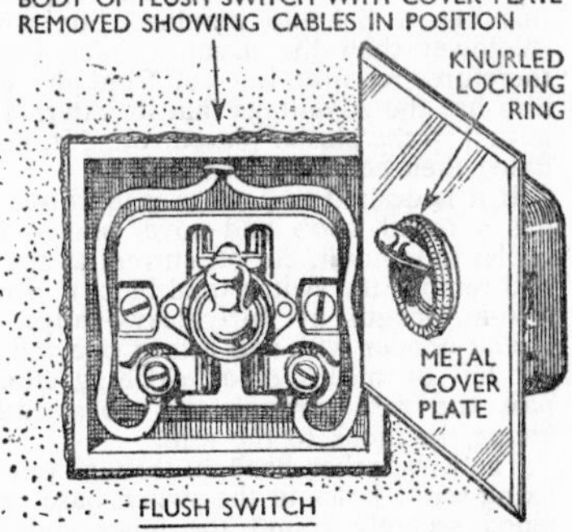

Fig. 25. Three types of switch in common use for domestic lighting.

holes. Having made certain that the cables will reach their new terminal positions, drill into the wall to a depth of at least 1¼ in. at each mark and insert plugs (see "Carpentry" section).

To replace the switch or to fit a new one, first draw the feed wires through their holes in the block so that the insulation will cover the wires right up to where they enter their terminals in the switch base. Two 1½-in. wood-screws are first run through the block and into the plugs. The feed wires are then arranged in the terminals of the switch and the grub-screws tightened. The base is now screwed by two screws to the block and the switch cover screwed on.

When a flush switch with wooden box is to be fitted, a square cavity the size and depth of the box (Fig. 26) must be cut in the wall. In what will be the top of the box, drill a hole large enough to pass the feed cables through. Two 1-in. plugs should be sunk into the back of the cavity to take securing screws into the wall from the switch base through the back of the box.

Sufficient cable should be drawn into the box to pass to each of the switch-base terminals

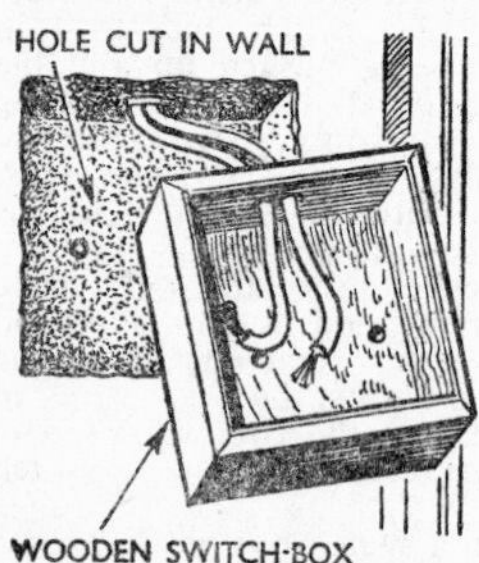

Fig. 26. Preparing to fit a flush switch in a plaster wall.

with a little to spare. When the box is finally in position, the plaster round its edges can be made good with Keene's cement or plaster-of-Paris. The switch base can now be fixed by screws into the plugs prepared at the back, the feed secured by the terminal screws, and the cover-plate attached.

There is another type of flush-fitting switch; this has a Bakelite moulded box which is shallower than the usual wooden box and, therefore, requires less cut from the wall. It also has the advantage that its external shape keys it to the plaster placed round it, no other fixing then being necessary.

If it is desired to earth a wall switch which has a metal knob and cover and is fed by cables in conduit, cut off current at the mains and remove the switch (and block). Now take a 6-in. length of fairly-heavy-gauge single-strand copper wire and attach one end to the conduit by means of an earthing clip. Next pass the wire through the block and then secure the block to the wall.

The wire is then brought through one of the fixing-screw holes in the switch base and fastened securely round the inner end of the thread in the bridge which takes the cover. In

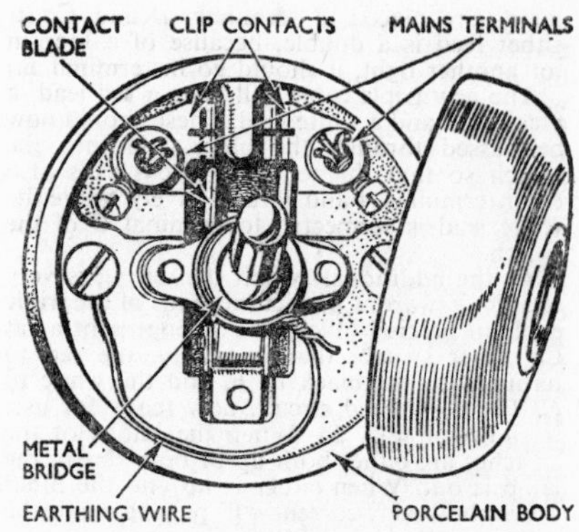

Fig. 27. Method of earthing a metal and porcelain switch by a copper wire from the metal bridge to the conduit behind the switch.

doing this it is important to make the wire, if not insulated, loop first down from the screw hole and then up to the bridge (Fig. 27) so as to keep it well away from all current-carrying parts. The switch base is secured in position in the normal manner and the cover replaced.

When a lamp controlled by a pear switch (Fig. 28) fails to light, the cause is usually to be found on examination of the switch flex. As with all pendants, swinging will eventually cause a fracture of the wires where the flex enters the rose; but the trouble is easily put right, if there are no signs of perishing, by shortening the flex and reconnecting.

A pear switch is made up of two halves, the lower containing terminals and switch mechanism, the upper being merely a cover which unscrews for removal. When attaching flex to the switch it should be noted that some provision is made to relieve strain on the

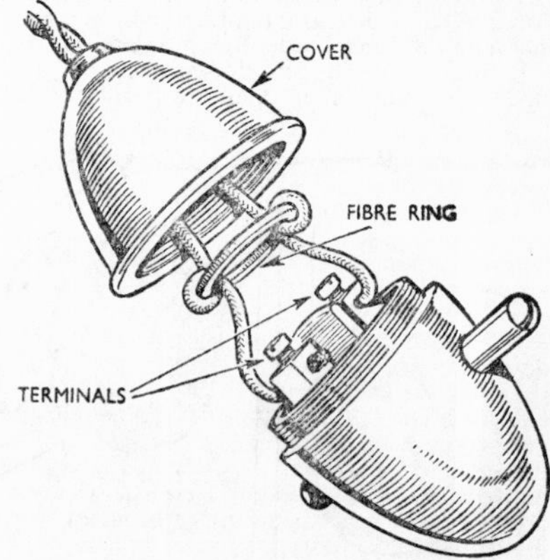

Fig. 28. Pear switch with the cover unscrewed showing the ring round which the flex is twisted in order to take strain off the terminals.

terminal connexions. This, in some designs, takes the form of a dividing bridge between the terminals through or under which the wires should pass. Another pattern has a fibre ring round which each cable should be separately turned before being secured in the terminal (Fig. 28).

VACUUM-CLEANER MOTORS. As with most other electrical appliances, faults are in time liable to occur in the flexes, switches, etc., used in connexion with vacuum-cleaners. But the methods of correcting such faults will be evident from entries on FLEXIBLE WIRES, SWITCHES, etc. Only best-quality round flexes are recommended in connection with vacuum-cleaners, because of the continuous movement and relatively rough treatment to which they are subjected when in use.

Apart from air leaks and defects in the dust bag and hoses, the faults which may occur in the cleaner unit itself are those associated with any kind of electric motor—hence the hints given here apply, at least in broad principle, to other motor-driven appliances, for example, hair-driers.

Suction is produced by a fan (or impeller) turning at high speed. It is turned by being attached to a rotating spindle which passes through the body of the electric motor. Built round the spindle is an arrangement of windings known as the armature. In order to feed current to the moving armature assembly, two carbon-block contacts called brushes are employed, and they are arranged so as to bear lightly upon the segments of a commutator. The commutator is mounted round the end of the armature spindle and is the means of collecting mains current from the brushes and passing it to the armature.

It is obvious, therefore, that wear or dirt causing poor contact between brushes and commutator must result in defective operation of the motor, and a tendency for the motor to run slower than usual, erratically or intermittently, is, as a rule, a sign that trouble of this kind exists.

Where a machine having a separate dust bag is concerned, the removal of a readily detachable cover (Fig. 29) gives access to the parts in question. In the case of a cylinder type of cleaner (Fig. 30), the commutator and brushes are disclosed when the end-piece providing the air-outlet aperture is removed.

The brushes, situated one on each side of the commutator, should slide freely in their holders. Upon unscrewing a cap on the holder it is possible to withdraw the brush by pulling out the spiral spring to which it is attached.

If a brush has cracks in it, or if it has worn down short or is not symmetrically concave in shape at the end, it should be replaced by a new one. The tension of the spring should not be increased by drawing out the coil, as this may lead to unnecessary and excessive pressure between the carbon block and the commutator. Thoroughly wipe all traces of dust from the brushes and from their holders.

The commutator must also be perfectly cleaned. To do this, hold a petrol-moistened piece of clean rag hard against the commutator while it is being rotated (Fig. 30), and

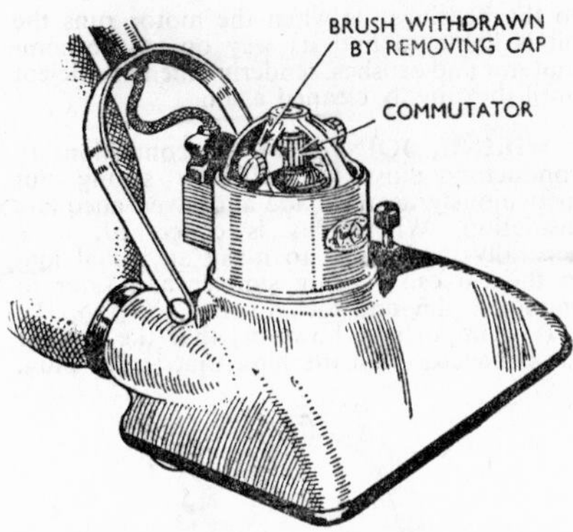

Fig. 29. The cover removed from a separate dust-bag type of vacuum-cleaner for the carbon brushes and commutator to receive attention.

continue the process until the rag no longer comes away marked.

When a vacuum-cleaner fails completely, and the various points already mentioned are known to be in order, it may possibly mean that the armature has burnt-out. If, upon inspection, signs of charring of the insulation are found on the armature, no further confirmation of this unfortunate occurrence need be sought. An armature rarely burns out, however, unless it is subjected to too high a voltage; replacement is usually a matter for the makers of the machine.

If the armature spindle does not turn easily or evenly it may be that the bearings are worn or dry. This is likely to be the case only on old machines, however, since in most designs ball-bearings are fitted and these are packed with high-melting-point grease and sealed.

It is never advisable, except where special provision for it is made, to add lubricating oil

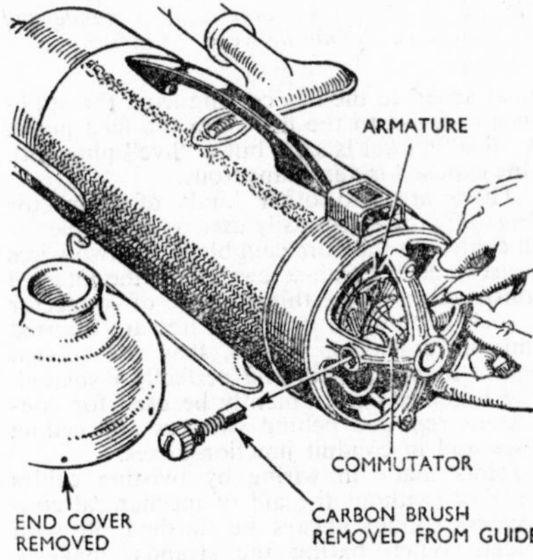

Fig. 30. Cleaning the commutator of a cylinder-type vacuum-cleaner by rotating the commutator against a clean rag moistened with petrol.

to the bearings, as when the motor runs the oil is liable to find its way on to the commutator and brushes, rendering them inefficient until thoroughly cleaned again.

WIRING, JOINTS IN. All connexions in conductors must be not only strong but meticulously neatly made and given adequate insulation. Where flex is concerned, it is generally inadvisable to make an actual join in the cables, it being simpler and safer to employ a plug-and-socket connector (Fig. 31).

It is important, however, that the half of the connector with the pins, that is, the plug,

Fig. 31. A plug and socket make a simple and safe connexion between two flexes.

be attached to the flex coming from the appliance and not to the flex from the feed point. A "live" socket is safe, but a "live" plug with pins exposed is very dangerous.

There are two other kinds of connector (Fig. 32); these are easily used and suitable for all cables. In the porcelain block the two wires are secured by grub-screws, while the internal construction of the thimble type of connector is such that, when the two wires are inserted and the connector turned, they are twisted tightly together, held and perfectly insulated. The latter can conveniently be used for connexions required behind switches and ceiling roses and in conduit junction-boxes.

Joints made in wiring by twisting cables together (without the aid of mechanical connectors) should always be finished off with solder. When baring the strands, make a slanting cut into the insulation to avoid cutting, even slightly, into the copper. To bare $2\frac{1}{2}$ in. of the wire is normally sufficient, but the

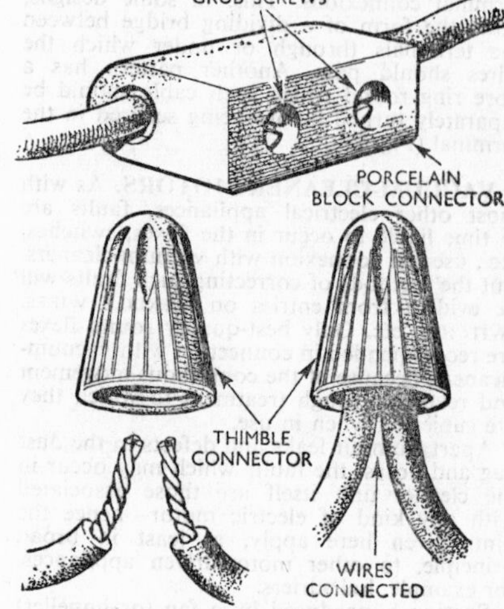

Fig. 32. Two safe and convenient methods of connecting cables.

outer covering or braiding can be taken back an additional $\frac{1}{2}$ in. to advantage.

Single wires should be given at least six turns over each other, and then pulled to test the strength of the joint; cut off or close in the ends with pliers. To join seven-stranded cable, first cut the centre strand away, untwist and straighten the remaining strands, arranging three to each side of the cable (Fig. 33). Then interlace the wires of one cable with the corresponding threes of the other cable, hold those on one side while the strands on the other side are laid round; finish the joint off by taking two pairs of pliers and turning in opposite directions.

In soldering, be careful not to apply more heat to the wire than is essential, as otherwise nearby insulation may be damaged. Wipe away all spare flux when finished.

To insulate the joint, first smear some rubber solution over the join and then tightly wrap with rubber tape, overlapping on to the insulation a little at each end. Two layers of rubber tape should be applied and then a final binding made with adhesive insulation tape.

In making a tee, or branch, joint in seven-stranded cable, the procedure is as described except that the main cable, when bared, is

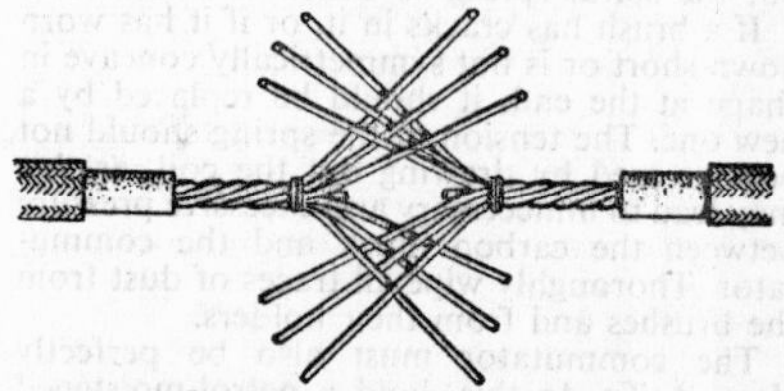

Fig. 33. Preparing a join in seven-stranded cable; the join must be thoroughly insulated.

divided and about 2 in. of the bared branch cable passed through the loop. Three strands of the branch are then laid to one side and four to the other and are turned round the cable in opposite directions.

WIRING OF A HOUSE. The main is brought into the house by the supply authority so that it comes up through the floor at a convenient point by the base of a wall, often in a small cupboard, and immediately enters a sealed fuse-box. Two cables pass from the fuse-box to the meter. Both the fuse-box and the meter are the property of the supply authority, but everything beyond belongs to the owner of the building.

Often houses are wired through separate meters for lighting and power. This is solely because the current consumed for power appliances will be charged at a lower cost per unit than that used for lighting.

But whether separately metered or not, the conductors to and from power points must always be heavier than those used for lighting. This is to enable a greater *flow* of current to pass without the wiring and fittings becoming heated. The wiring to power points for radiators is usually capable of carrying a flow of 15 amp.; similarly, power sockets and switches must be of a type designed to handle 15 amp.

From the meter, two cables pass to a pair of switches, the main switches (Fig. 34), which

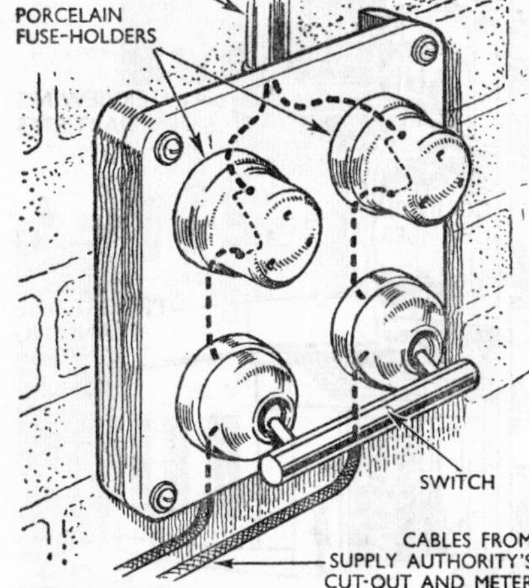

Fig. 34. A domestic main switch comprising two separate switch units connected by a bar.

are often connected by a bar so that they operate together. The cables that leave the switches lead to another fuse-box; in this are the house fuses. In some modern installations, fuse-box and switch are combined in a way which prevents access to the fuses while the switch is closed (as shown in Fig. 35).

Wiring between the fuses and the switches, ceiling roses, sockets, etc., is normally run under the floor and down the cavities or

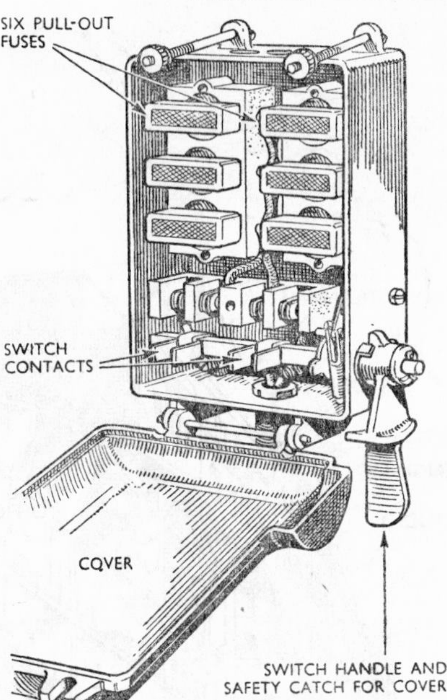

Fig. 35. Combination switch and distribution box for three fused circuits.

channels in the walls. It consists of flexible insulated cables contained throughout in steel tubing known as conduit. Special tough rubber-covered or lead-covered cable is often used, however, where wiring is carried over the surface of walls and ceilings.

There are two methods of employing fuses to protect the various circuits in the house. One is to house four or six fuses in the box by the main switch, each pair then covering different parts of the house (Fig. 35). The other method is to have only one pair of fuses at this point (Fig. 34) and another box, not very far away (but not necessarily in the cupboard containing the meter). In this second box are two or more pairs of fuses for the protection of the various circuits radiating from this point. In such cases, the second set of house fuses are called distribution, or splitter, fuses.

House fuses are finer (capable of passing smaller amperage) than the supply authority's fuse, in order that they shall cut out first. Similarly, where splitter fuses are used, they may each be designed to blow when current flow exceeds 3 amp., while the house fuses will pass up to 10 amp. See FUSES.

Separate wiring and fusing arrangements are required for radiators, immersion heaters, cookers and so on; the cables and fittings for each radiator must be capable of passing up to 15 amp. Where the voltage is 230 or over, however, it is reasonable to fuse individual circuits at 10 amp. if only a 2-kilowatt radiator is to be used. Circuits for immersion heaters and cookers may have to carry up to 30 amp.

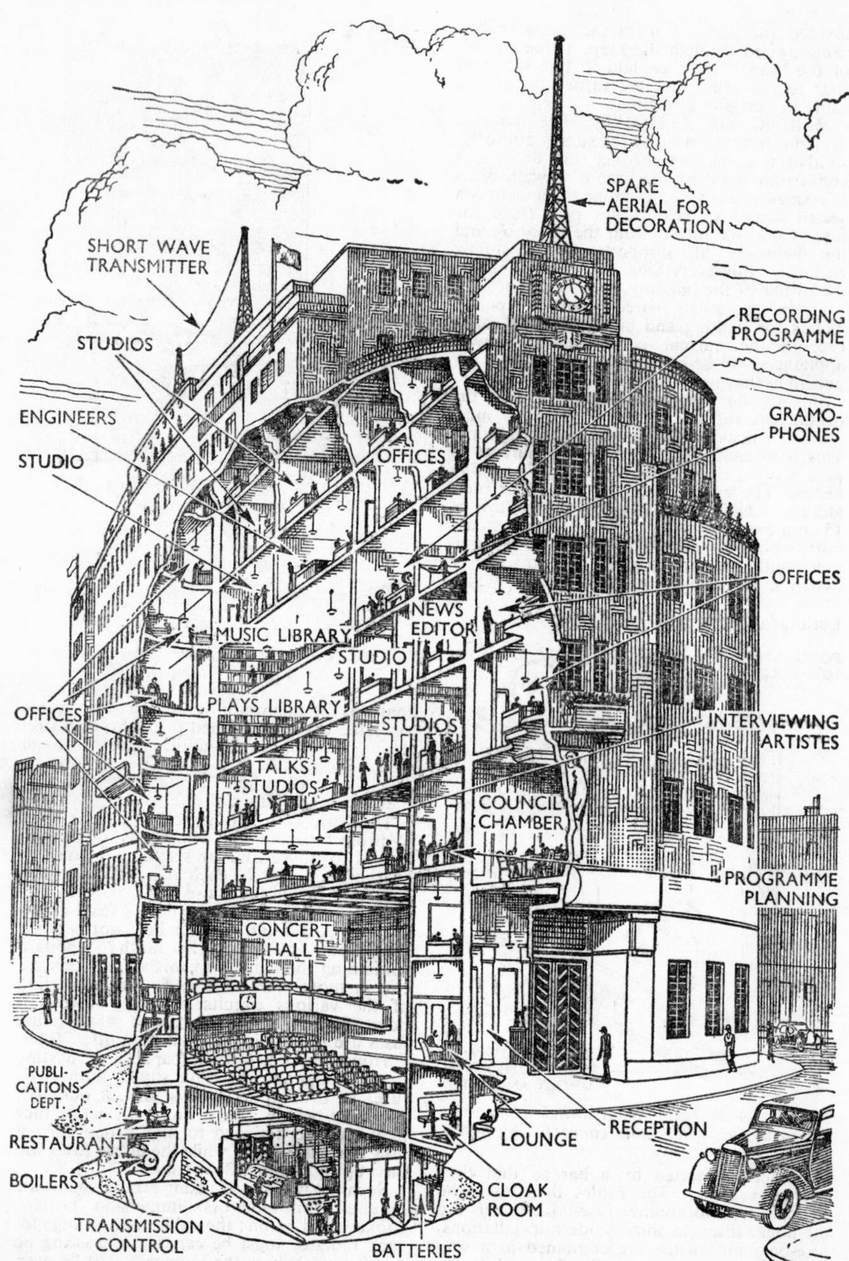

Broadcasting House in London is the centre of broadcasting in Britain. It is the administrative headquarters of the British Broadcasting Corporation and also contains some of its principal studios. The actual transmitters are distributed throughout the United Kingdom and there are studios in several parts of London as well as in a number of the larger provincial cities.

GUIDE TO RADIO AND TELEVISION

A simple introduction to the principles and application of radio, with practical hints and information for the radio and television owner.

This section on radio and television is divided into three parts. The first, entitled "What is Radio?" (pages 397–414), describes in simple language the principles on which the radio transmitter and receiver are based, provides details about different types of valve, and describes extensions of the radio principle to direction-finding, television and radar, and their application to ships and aircraft. The second part (pages 414–30) deals with types of radio receiver in common domestic use, and gives hints as to their choice, installation and faults. Finally (pages 430–2), under the title of "Television in the Home," the section contains some useful general information for present and intending television owners. All the parts are arranged logically so that the whole may be read as a consecutive narrative, but plentiful cross- and side-headings make possible easy reference to particular points.

WHAT IS RADIO?

PRINCIPLES OF THE TRANSMITTER

RADIO WAVES. When a person speaks he creates vibrations in the air which vibrate the ear-drums of those within hearing. A radio transmitter also sends out vibrations, but in this case air is not necessary for their transmission. It is presumed that wireless vibrations take place in a medium known as ether. This is nothing like the ether used as an anaesthetic, but is a hypothetical material that is supposed to exist even in a vacuum and to permeate all matter in the same sort of way as water soaks through a sponge. Not all modern scientists accept the ether theory, but it is a useful means of filling in what would otherwise be somewhat disconcerting blanks in our theory of radio.

These radio vibrations in the ether travel at the same velocity as light waves, 300,000,000 metres (approximately 186,000 miles) a second, and they obey the same kind of laws as light. They can be reflected, focused in beams, and refracted, but, of course, they are invisible.

The length of a wireless wave is measured from the crest of one to the crest of the next; therefore, as the speed with which the waves travel is constant, the shorter the waves the more of them there will be each second. The number of waves a second is called the frequency. A transmission at a frequency of 100 kc/s simply means that during one second a series of 100,000 waves is radiated, for kc/s is an abbreviation for kilocycles per second, and one kilocycle equals one thousand cycles. Cycles is really another word for waves. In the case of very short waves, which is the same as saying waves of very high frequency, the term megacycle (Mc) is employed, this being equal to one million cycles.

As the velocity is constant, either the wavelength or frequency can be worked out if one of them is known, because velocity equals wavelength multiplied by frequency. To discover the frequency of a transmission you merely divide its wavelength in metres into 300,000,000; to discover wavelength you divide the frequency in cycles per second into 300,000,000 and the answer is in metres.

The wireless waves are produced at the transmitter by electrical vibrations in the aerial system; a current of electricity is made to flow backwards and forwards at the required frequency (Fig. 1). If it were a transmission at a wavelength of 300 metres, the current would be flowing backwards and forwards in the aerial system (oscillating) at a frequency of 1,000,000 cycles (1,000 kc or 1 Mc) per second.

PRINCIPLE OF THE RADIO VALVE. Now a current of electricity is a flow of minute particles known as electrons. An electric cell, such as the type which is generally called a dry battery and which is used for electric-bell systems, causes a flow of electricity

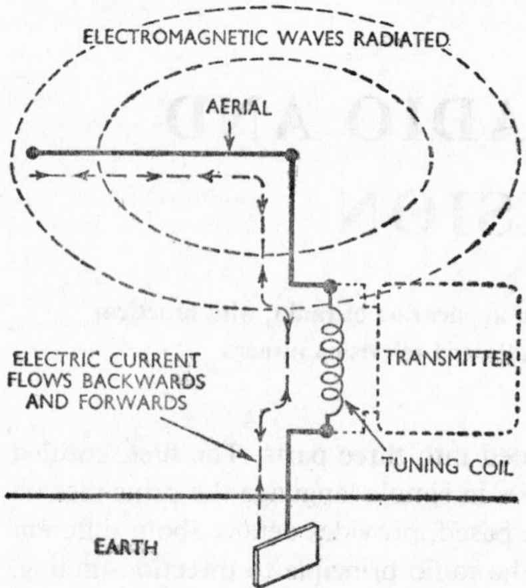

Fig. 1. Principle of production of radio waves.

simply because by chemical action it creates an excess of electrons in that part of it that is connected to the negative terminal as compared with the part joined to the positive terminal. If the two terminals are connected together by a length of wire, the electrons will flow through that wire in an attempt to establish an equilibrium, just as water will flow through a pipe that connects a water tank at a high level to a tank at a lower level.

Remembering this fact, we can now consider another interesting effect. The wire in a lighted electric lamp throws off electrons. If a small plate of metal is enclosed in the same bulb, the electrons will tend to fly to it, as a cold piece of metal will have comparatively fewer free electrons than a piece of wire raised to almost white heat. By means of a second battery connected between this plate and the hot wire (filament), a steady flow of electrons can be maintained from the filament to the plate and through the battery, just as though the path between the filament and plate were

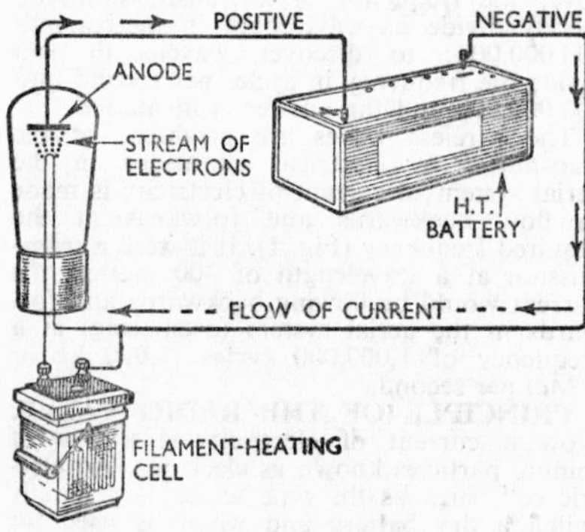

Fig. 2. Principle of the radio valve.

a piece of wire. But there is this difference: current will flow only when the battery is connected so that its negative terminal is joined to the filament and its positive to the plate because the flow of current continues as a result of the out-of-balance condition in the battery, the electron stream within the lamp bulb acting as a bridge.

The electrons from the negative terminal of the battery stream into the filament in an endeavour to get to the plate, and so to the positive terminal of the battery. Electrons stream from the filament to the plate through the vacuum. Electrons stream from the plate to the positive terminal of the battery, and a complete circuit is established (Fig. 2).

An excess of electrons at one point over those at another point constitutes an electrical pressure; there is a difference of pressure between the two points. The lamp with the added piece of metal is a two-electrode valve. And it is clear that it acts as a one-way conductor of electricity.

The term "valve" becomes even more applicable when a third electrode is introduced. This is the grid, and it is situated between the cathode (the correct technical name for the filament) and the anode (plate). The grid

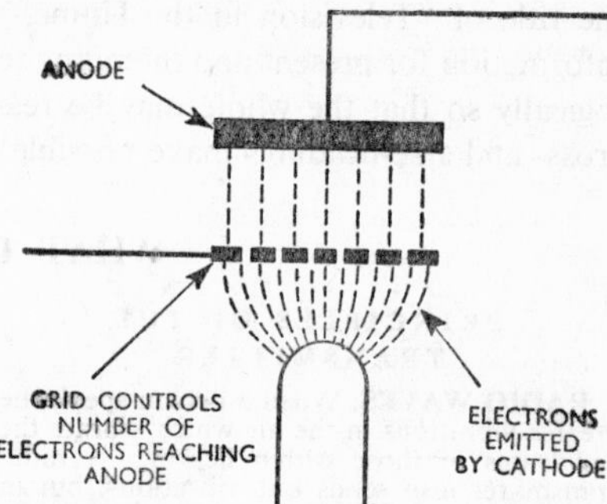

Fig. 3. Purpose of the grid in the radio va.ve.

comprises a spiral or mesh of wire. Normally, the electrons pass through it. But if the grid is given a negative potential, which is the same as saying that electrons from another source are crowded on to it, then the electrons from the cathode are repelled and the stream between the cathode and anode reduced. If the grid is made sufficiently negative, the stream will be entirely interrupted (Fig. 3).

But, and this is the vital thing to note, a small charge of electrical pressure on the grid causes a relatively large change in the anode current. Small variations of electrical pressure on the grid accordingly make comparatively large variations in the anode current. In fact, the three-electrode valve is an amplifier.

Magnetic Fields. When a current of electricity flows through a conductor, such as a length of wire, a magnetic field is set up round the conductor. This magnetic field can be concentrated and strengthened by winding the wire in the form of a coil. If the magnetic force is made to rise and fall by switching the

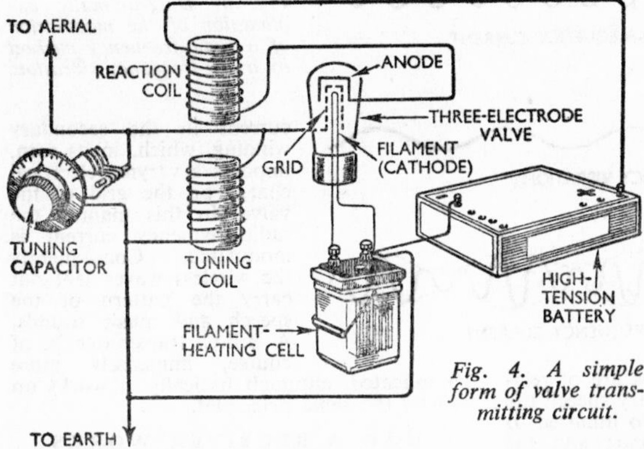

Fig. 4. A simple form of valve transmitting circuit.

current on and off, or change in intensity by varying the current, it will induce electricity into any other conductor it surrounds.

In the simple valve transmitter shown in Fig. 4 we have a coil in the anode circuit through which the anode current passes, and close to it a coil which is in the grid circuit. Any variations in the anode current will produce fluctuations in the intensity of the magnetic force round the anode coil, and induce a fluctuating electro-motive force in the grid circuit. This in turn causes variations in the electrical pressure on the grid. These make the anode current vary to a greater extent; the magnetic force round the coil fluctuates more violently, and the electrical pressure on the grid increases. In short, once the anode current is made to fluctuate in strength, the fluctuation becomes greater and greater until the anode circuit is in a condition of electrical oscillation.

In fact, no artificial stimulus is needed to initiate the regeneration, alternative terms for which are reaction and feedback. This is because, however stable the source of supply of anode current (and you can hardly have a more stable source than a battery), there are bound to be minute fluctuations in it. And these rapidly build up to the maximum strength possible for a given valve and battery.

When an aerial and earth connexion are joined to the circuit, a fluctuating magnetic force is produced around and between the aerial and the earth, and it is this that produces the wireless waves.

INDUCTANCE AND CAPACITANCE. Whatever the speed at which the initiating current fluctuations occur, almost instantaneously the fluctuations settle down to a speed of occurrence, of frequency, to use the proper term, which depends upon the inductance and capacitance of the circuit.

Inductance is a kind of electrical inertia, an opposition to any change in the strength of the current, which is due to the fact that the current has to throw out that field of magnetic force. Increasing the intensity of the magnetic field (by winding a conductor into the form of a coil, for example) increases this electrical inertia or inductance. Increasing the capacitance speeds up the frequency of current fluctuations—but we shall have more to say about these qualities later.

In the meantime we have in Fig. 4 a complete, but not very powerful, wireless transmitter. When the batteries are connected up it will send out a continuous series of wireless waves. And the following is the way the waves can be made to carry speech and music.

CARRYING SPEECH ON RADIO WAVES

HOW THE MICROPHONE WORKS. First of all, some device is necessary to transform the air waves produced by the speech and music into variations in an electrical current. The device which permits this to be done is the microphone. There are various types, one of the most widely used being illustrated in Fig. 5. There is a thin metal diaphragm which vibrates when the sound vibrations strike it. When vibrating it imposes a varying pressure on the carbon granules. Now the electrical resistance of these carbon granules is reduced when they are pressed together; when the pressure is reduced they present a more difficult path for the current to pass through. In other words, the current that can flow through the granules depends upon the pressure with which the granules are pushed together.

So if a battery is connected to the microphone the current that flows will vary in exact accordance with the vibrations of the diaphragm. An electrical pattern of the sound waves has been obtained.

It should be noted that there is a difference between the electrical vibrations representing speech and music and those that cause the wireless waves. Both are certainly variations in the strength of an electrical current, but

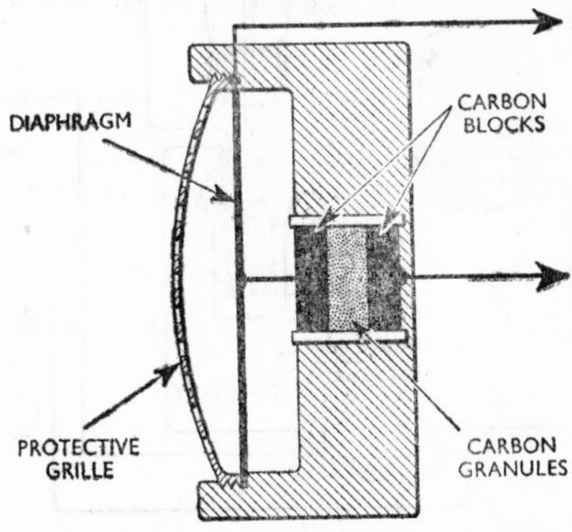

Fig. 5. Sectional diagram of a microphone.

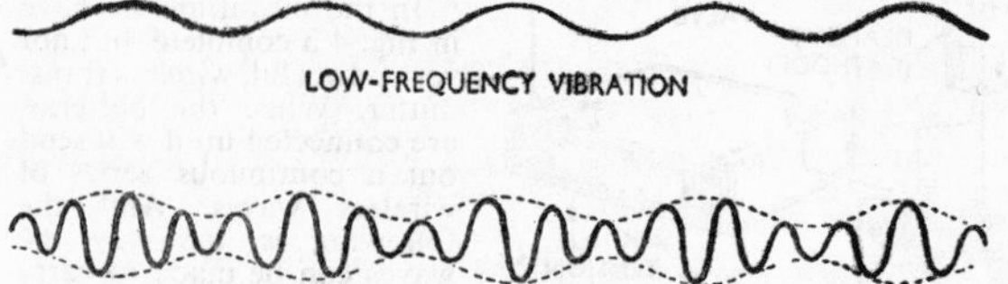

Fig. 6. Diagrammatic explanation of the modulation of a radio-frequency current by a low-frequency vibration.

the speech and music vibrations are of relatively low frequency. For ordinary speech the vibrations range from about two hundred to five thousand cycles per second; and for music from fifty, or even less, to about fifteen thousand cycles per second. These compare with the million or more cycles per second of a radio frequency.

A current of electricity that is varying at a radio frequency can be made to fluctuate in accordance with a low-frequency vibration in much the same kind of way as a singer delivering a steady note of, say, middle C on the piano (256 cycles per second), can raise and lower the strength of that note without altering its pitch (Fig. 6).

MODULATION. Combining the speech and music electrical vibrations with the radio-frequency vibrations is called modulation. It can be done in the case of the simple transmitting circuit shown in Fig. 7 by connecting the microphone circuit to the grid circuit by means of a transformer.

The varying current from the microphone battery sets up a field of magnetic force of varying intensity round the primary winding of the transformer. This induces a varying current in the secondary winding, which, in its turn, imposes a varying electrical charge on the grid of the valve. In this manner the radio-frequency current is modulated. Consequently the wireless waves sent out carry the pattern of the speech and music sounds. A B.B.C. transmitter is, of course, immensely more complicated, although basically it works on exactly the same principles.

HOW A RECEIVER WORKS

TUNING THE AERIAL. When wireless waves ripple past a receiving aerial they act in the same way as a moving magnetic field and induce a current of electricity in it. The largest current is obtained when the aerial is tuned exactly to the frequency of the waves. This is accomplished by adjusting its inductance and capacitance so that it will vibrate electrically at the required frequency.

The greater the inductance and the greater the capacitance, the lower is this natural frequency of the aerial. The tuning circuit shown in Fig. 8 includes a coil of wire to increase the inductance of the aerial, and a variable capacitor which, by enabling the capacitance of the circuit to be controlled, provides a close adjustment of the frequency. That, in brief, is the principle of tuning.

TYPES OF CAPACITOR. There are two kinds of capacitor, the fixed and the variable. The simplest fixed capacitor consists of two plates of metal separated by an insulating material such as air, mica or paper. The capacitance, which is usually measured in microfarads (the fundamental unit, the farad, is too large for practical purposes), depends upon three things: (1) the area of the plates—the greater the area, the greater the capacitance; (2) the distance between the plates—as this is reduced so is the capacitance increased; and (3) the nature of the dielectric (insulating material separating the plates)—with paper the capacitance is greater than with air, and with mica it is greater still.

To increase the effective area of plates without increasing the area of the capacitor when high capacitances are required, sets of plates interleaved are employed. In the variable capacitor the plates take the

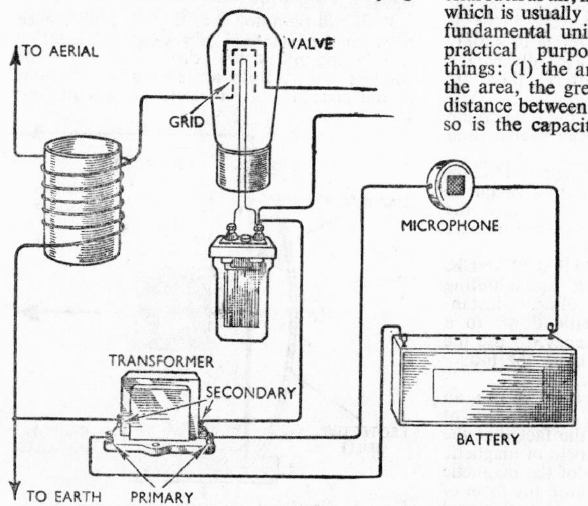

Fig. 7. A transformer used in a simple transmitting circuit in order to modulate a radio-frequency current.

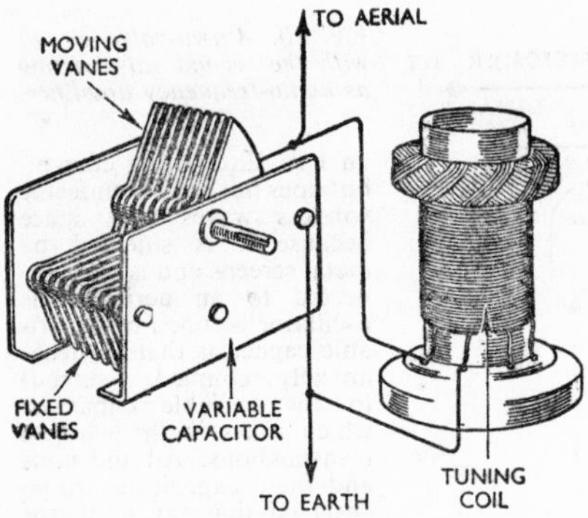

Fig. 8. Basic equipment for tuning an aerial.

form of vanes, the position of one set of which can be varied in relation to the other so that the area of overlap is altered. In this way any capacitance up to the maximum possible with the capacitor can be obtained.

When by such means the aerial circuit is tuned to the transmission of one particular broadcasting station, an electric current is produced which is a miniature counterpart of that which is vibrating in the transmitter aerial. We must define more accurately the nature of this current.

RECTIFYING THE RADIO SIGNAL. The current is an alternating current; that is to say, it flows first in one direction and then in the other. It changes its direction of flow at its stated frequency. If the frequency of the waves is 500 kc/s, which is 500,000 cycles per second, then the current changes its direction 500,000 times a second; and this high- (radio) frequency alternating current varies in strength at the comparatively low frequencies of the speech and music.

A radio-frequency (R.F.) alternating current will not work a loudspeaker; only a current that varies in strength at "speech frequencies" will do that. So one of the main functions of the valve in a receiving set is to change the R.F. signal into an audio-frequency one. This is accomplished by one method with the aid of two components, as shown in Fig. 9a. The grid leak is a high resistance (it is usually about two million ohms in value) that permits a small current to flow from the grid to the cathode. The small unidirectional current is varied in strength by the R.F. signal affecting the quantity of electrons that tends to accumulate on the grid.

The R.F. current has been rectified, or transformed, into a uni-directional current. This process is also sometimes called detection and, at other times, demodulation. The feedback effect, which was explained in connexion with the simple transmitter (Fig. 4), can be applied to make speech and music louder. In this case the feedback or reaction is controlled (Fig. 9b) so as to magnify the sound currents to any extent up to the point where the receiver would burst into oscillation and so become a very low-power transmitter.

Although we now have the right kind of current to operate a loudspeaker, it will not, in normal circumstances, be strong enough to do so unless another valve is used to amplify it.

USING ADDITIONAL VALVES. Fig. 10 shows a two-valve circuit, the first valve acting as a detector and the second as an A.F., or audio-frequency, amplifier. The anode circuit of the first valve is coupled to the grid circuit of the second valve by means of an A.F. transformer. This comprises two windings round an iron core, the core having the effect of concentrating the field of magnetic force and making the transfer of energy from one winding to the other more efficient.

The purpose of the grid-bias battery, the connexions of which can be seen in the diagram, is to give the grid of the amplifying valve a steady electrical charge so that the fluctuating charge, impressed on the grid by the audio-frequency current, produces its correct magnified pattern in the anode current.

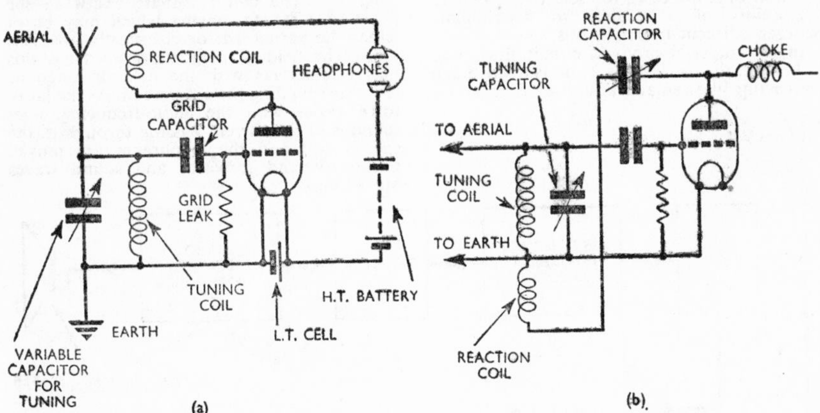

Fig. 9. Circuits showing the principles of (a) *detection and* (b) *controlled feedback or reaction.*

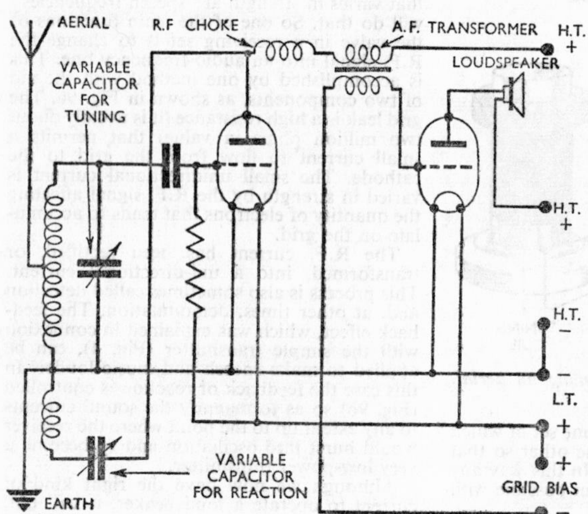

Fig. 10. A two-valve circuit with the second valve acting as audio-frequency amplifier.

A third valve can be added to the circuit in order to amplify the R.F. current before it is detected. This will enable more distant transmitting stations to be heard.

SUPER-HETERODYNE CIRCUIT. The majority of modern radio receivers employ the super-heterodyne principle. The purpose of this is to change any transmission to the one predetermined frequency. This might be, for example, 450 kc/s. Whatever the frequency of the transmitter tuned in, whether it is 750 or 2,000 kc/s, after the R.F. current developed in the aerial has passed through a part of the super-heterodyne receiver it emerges as an R.F. current of 450 kc/s.

The advantage is that it is possible to provide a more efficient amplification of R.F. current if there is only the one frequency to deal with instead of a large number of different ones. Also, it increases the selectivity, that is, the ability of a receiver to discriminate between adjacent transmissions.

In the super-heterodyne circuit illustrated in Fig. 11, the oscillator section is a valve and coils acting like a small transmitter. It generates an R.F. alternating current, but does not send even feeble wireless waves into space because it is shielded by metal screens and is not connected to an aerial. This oscillator is tuned by a variable capacitor that is mechanically coupled (ganged) to the variable capacitor which tunes in the wireless transmissions. All the coils and these capacitors are so designed that the oscillator generates an R.F. alternating current that is always exactly 450 kc/s (or other fixed figure) different from the frequency of the transmission that is tuned in.

The R.F. current from the aerial and the R.F. current from the oscillator are both fed to a mixer valve and in the anode circuit of this mixer appears an R.F. current having a frequency of 450 kc/s. This is called the intermediate-frequency (I.F.) current and it is taken, still modulated with speech and music frequencies, to another valve or valves for amplification.

Then follows the detector which changes the I.F. current into audio-frequency current suitable for the loudspeaker.

MOVING-COIL LOUDSPEAKER. This type of loudspeaker has displaced all others in the good-class modern receiver. It consists of a diaphragm having a conical shape to give it a maximum of stiffness with a minimum of weight; to the apex of this cone is fixed a small coil of wire, known as the speech coil because it is through this that the audio-frequency current from the receiver flows (Fig. 12). The coil is situated between the poles of a strong magnet which may be of either the permanent or electrically operated kind. The field of magnetic force from this magnet interacts with the field of magnetic force surrounding the speech coil. As the latter force varies with the audio-frequency fluctuations in the current passing through it, the speech coil and the diaphragm are moved backwards and forwards and sound waves are set up.

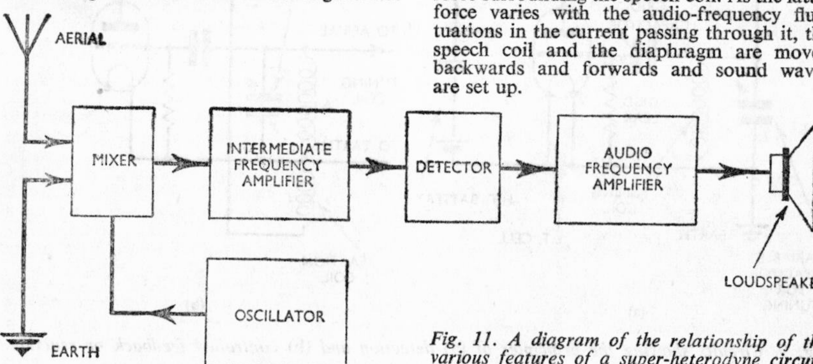

Fig. 11. A diagram of the relationship of the various features of a super-heterodyne circuit.

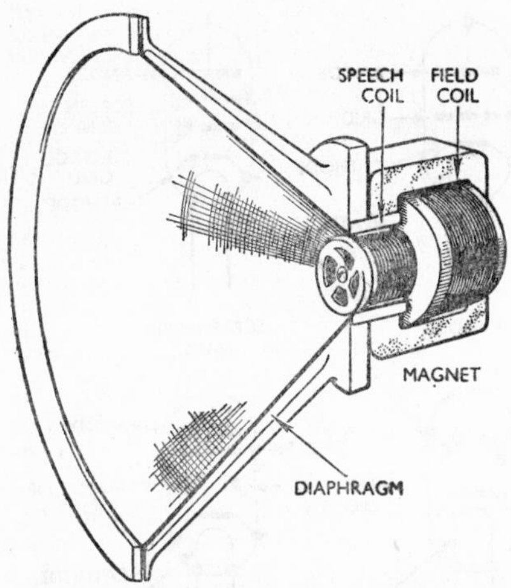

Fig. 12. Section of moving-coil loudspeaker.

It should be noted that it is necessary to match the speech coil to the valve which feeds current to it. The valve may have an impedance (see page 404) of, say, 4,000 ohms. The ohm is the unit of electrical resistance, but in the case of a varying current both the capacitance and the inductance of the component or conductor have to be taken into account. All these contribute to the impedance which limits the flow, and which is also measured in ohms.

The best results are obtained when the loudspeaker has the same impedance as the valve. But to have an impedance of anything like the 4,000 ohms mentioned would mean a speech coil consisting of a very large number of turns of wire. It is not impossible to make a coil of this type, but as it happens there is a simpler method, and that is to use a transformer. The primary winding of this requires to have a high impedance, and the secondary winding an impedance similar to that of the speech coil; this is usually somewhere round about 10 ohms.

This output transformer (sometimes referred to as a matching transformer) is often incorporated in the construction of the loudspeaker. It may have terminals on it, allowing it to be adjusted to suit different valves.

POINTS ABOUT VALVES

TYPES OF VALVE. There are two main classes of valve for receivers, battery- and mains-driven. Battery-operated valves are all designed for direct heating; that is to say, they are heated by current that is supplied by a battery and which passes directly through their cathodes. It is the current flow which causes the heating, and the consequent emission of electrons.

The majority of mains valves are indirectly heated. The supply from the mains, reduced in voltage by a transformer, is passed through a heater which is not in metallic contact with the cathode, but heats it by conduction through the insulating material which separates them. The rise and fall in the current is not communicated to the electron stream of the valve, as the temperature of the cathode does not fluctuate but remains constant. This is because the heat communicated from the heater is unable to rise and fall in time with the alternations in the supply.

The most commonly used types of valve (Fig. 13) are as follows:

Diode. This is a two-electrode valve having only a cathode and an anode. It is usually employed alone only for rectifying alternating current. It cannot be used as an oscillator or amplifier. The diode is frequently combined with other types of valve in the one bulb; hence the double-diode triode, double-diode pentode, etc. Double-diodes (cathode and two anodes) are used for full-wave rectification of alternating current.

Triode. A three-electrode valve. There is a grid situated between the cathode and anode for the purpose of controlling the electron stream, and this enables the valve to amplify or to act as an oscillator.

Screen-grid valve (tetrode). It was found that the grid and anode of a three-electrode valve acted as a small capacitor and tended to introduce an unwanted coupling between the anode and grid circuits when the valve was used as an amplifier of R.F. currents. This capacitance effect is eliminated by the introduction of a second grid situated between the control grid and the anode.

Pentode. Another undesirable effect sometimes encountered is due to the release of electrons from the anode when it is bombarded by electrons from the cathode. This effect is negatived by the use of yet a third grid, which is placed between the screen grid and the anode, and is joined to the cathode inside the valve itself.

Variable-mu valves. Such a valve, normally a screen-grid tetrode or pentode, has a gain which can be controlled by varying the bias on its control grid. See AUTOMATIC GAIN CONTROL in the section on Types of Receiver.

Hexode. This has six electrodes as follows: cathode, control grid, screen grid, second control grid, second screen grid, anode. Some valves are, in effect, combinations of two valves and are primarily designed to combine the functions of oscillator and mixer for super-heterodyne receivers. Such valves include the heptode, triode-pentode, triode-hexode and triode-heptode.

Single-diode tetrode and single-diode pentode. These are combinations of a diode and a tetrode, and of a diode and a pentode respectively. They each combine the electrodes of two different kinds of valve in the one bulb. A double-diode pentode combines two diodes and a pentode. It is a useful valve because it can, at one and the same time, act as a detector and an audio-frequency amplifier and supply the controlling voltage for a system of automatic gain control.

EMISSION OF A VALVE. We have seen that an electron is a particle of electricity and that a flow of electrons constitutes an electrical current. The total electron current that is emitted from the heated cathode of a valve

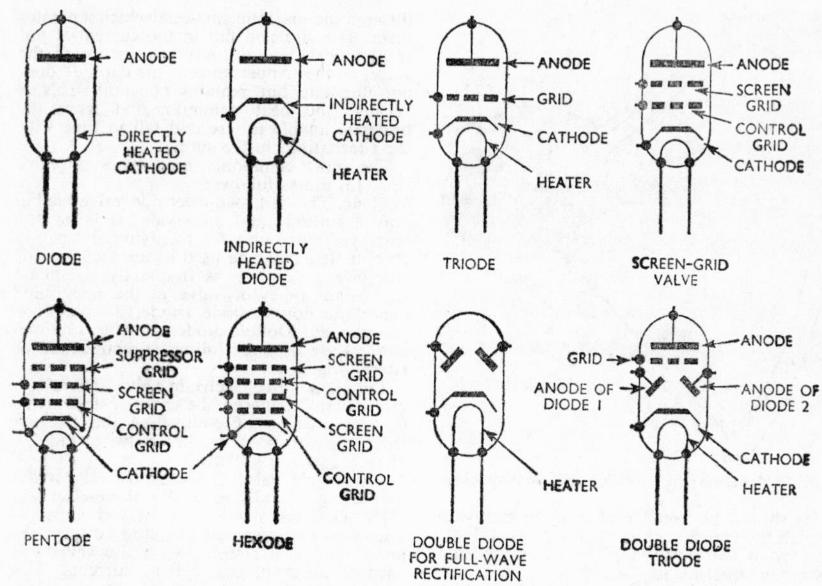

Fig. 13. Diagrams of some of the most commonly used types of radio valve.

is called the emission. It is normally of the order of milliamperes in the case of valves for receivers, a milliampere being one-thousandth of an ampere.

VOLTAGE AMPLIFICATION FACTOR. This is the ratio of the change in anode voltage to the change in grid voltage which produces the same change in the grid current. For example, suppose it is found that a change of 135 to 90 volts in the anode voltage causes a reduction in the anode current of from 12 to 8 milliamperes. To make the same change in anode current without altering the anode voltage of 135, the grid voltage requires to be made 5 volts more negative. The voltage-amplification factor is worked out as follows: Take 90 from 135 to give the change in anode voltage required to reduce the anode current from 12 to 8 milliamperes. 135−90 equals 45. Divide 45 by 5, this being the grid voltage needed to give the same anode current change, and the answer is 9.

The symbol for amplification factor is *mu*; therefore, high mu means high amplification factor. The high-mu valve is made by increasing the space between the grid and anode. The effect is that much greater anode-voltage changes are necessary to produce the various anode-current changes than in a similar valve of normal construction.

The goodness of a valve is given by its mutual conductance; it expresses the relationship between the anode-current changes and the grid-voltage changes which cause them. It is this which gives the best idea of the effectiveness of the valve as an amplifier. If the grid voltage is changed and the change in the anode current is relatively small, the valve does not amplify much; if it is relatively large, the valve amplifies to that greater extent. Mutual conductance is expressed in milliamperes per volt.

IMPEDANCE. Another very important factor is the impedance of the valve, or anode impedance, to be more correct. This is the ratio of anode-voltage change and resultant anode-current change, under conditions of constant grid voltage. It is measured in ohms. To work it out using the figures employed in discussing voltage-amplification factor, a change of 45 volts (135 to 90 volts) in anode voltage resulted, it will be recalled, in a 4-milliampere anode-current change. The milliamperes must be reduced to amperes and this is ·004 ampere.

To make it easier, especially if you know Ohm's Law, the impedance of a valve can be thought of as its resistance. To obtain resistance when the current and voltage are known, divide voltage by current. In the same way to find the impedance of the valve divide the anode-voltage change (in volts) by the anode-current change it produces (in amperes). That in the example is 45 divided by ·004; the answer is 11,250. The valve has an impedance of 11,250 ohms.

It is important to know this, since for the maximum energy to be transferred from the anode circuit of a valve to, say, the speech coil of a loudspeaker, the impedance of the output (anode circuit of the valve) must be matched to the input of the circuit or device to which it is coupled.

The characteristic curves of a valve are graphs which show the relationship between grid voltage and anode current and other factors in the operation of a valve, and from which the various characteristics mentioned above can be calculated.

RADIO DIRECTION-FINDING

DIRECTIONAL CHARACTER OF AERIALS. Generally speaking, the most efficient type of aerial is a wire or wires suspended between two poles or masts. The greater the height of such an aerial, the greater its effectiveness. But for portable radio apparatus a frame aerial is frequently used. This is in principle only a coil of large dimensions and it may be rectangular or circular in shape.

A frame aerial receives best when it is in line with the direction of the source of the radio waves (Fig. 14). It is least effective when it is at right-angles with that direction.

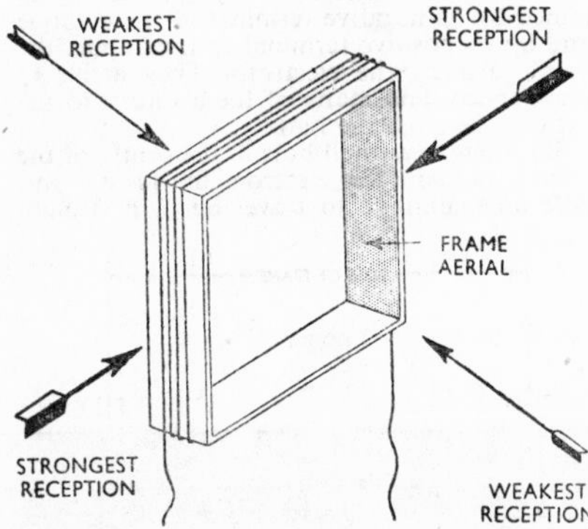

Fig. 14. Reception with a frame aerial.

From this it can be seen that the frame aerial can be used for the specific purpose of determining the line of this direction. As the frame aerial is slowly rotated, the strength of the station, as judged by the volume of the sound from the loudspeaker, will gradually diminish. And at the point where it is weakest the frame aerial will be at right-angles to the direction in which the station lies. This weakest point is taken in preference to the strongest, as it is easier to determine.

SENSING. The information provided by the frame aerial is incomplete, however, for in actual fact all it tells you is that the transmitting station lies in one or other of two directions. It might, for example, be either due north or due south.

In order to discover the absolute direction, a process known as "sensing" must be applied. This necessitates the employment of an open aerial in conjunction with the frame aerial (Fig. 15). They are both connected to the one circuit, and it must be arranged so that the current induced into this circuit by the open aerial is approximately the same as that induced into it by the frame aerial for any one particular transmitting station, and when the frame aerial is in the position for maximum reception. Then it is found that, when the frame lies the one way round, currents from

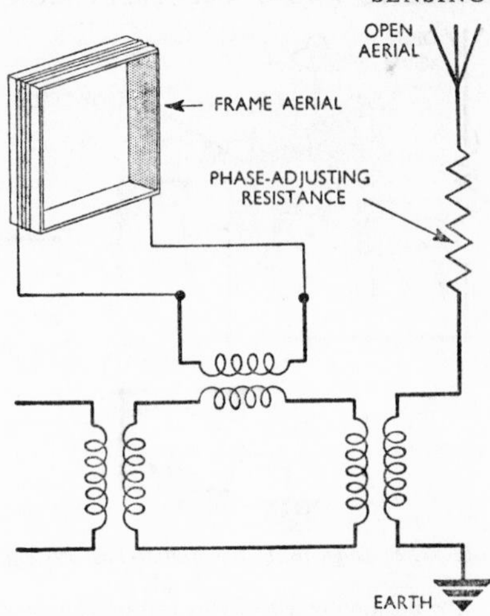

Fig. 15. Aerials required for "sensing."

the two aerials are added together, but when it is turned 180 deg. the currents tend to neutralize each other. So with this arrangement it is possible to discover exactly in what direction the transmitter lies.

In 1907 two scientists named Bellini and Tosi invented a method which overcame the need to rotate the frame, two fixed frame aerials set at 90 deg. to each other being used. These aerials can be fixed at some distant point, such as on the roof of a building, and connected to the rest of the apparatus by means of wires. Each aerial is in fact joined to one of two coils arranged, like the frames, at right-angles to each other (Fig. 16). By

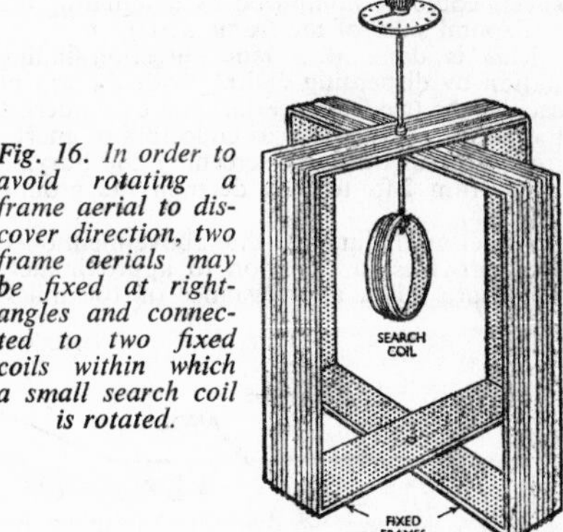

Fig. 16. In order to avoid rotating a frame aerial to discover direction, two frame aerials may be fixed at right-angles and connected to two fixed coils within which a small search coil is rotated.

rotating the "search" coil the line of the transmission can be ascertained. The sensing principle can be applied to the Bellini-Tosi system in order to determine the absolute direction (Fig. 17).

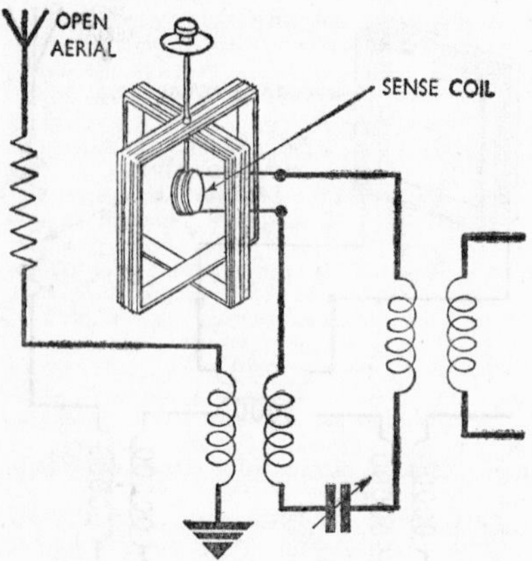

Fig. 17. Sensing, using the Bellini-Tosi system.

The position of a receiving station equipped with a direction-finding radio apparatus can be worked out by taking bearings from two transmitting stations of known location, but sometimes bearings from three stations are taken in order to make the calculation more precise. A ship or aircraft not itself equipped with direction-finding apparatus can obtain its position from two direction-finding stations operating in co-operation with each other.

REDUCING ERROR. There are numerous causes of error in these systems of direction-finding, although most of them are calculable and can be allowed for; but those connected with what are known as night effects are not so predictable. Research has indicated that the night effects are due to the wireless waves being reflected from the conductive layers of the upper atmosphere. And during the First World War Adcock further showed that the effects could be minimized by eliminating the horizontal sides of the frame aerial.

This is done at a land direction-finding station by dispensing entirely with the top of each of the two frame aerials and by rendering the bottoms ineffective as collectors of energy from wireless waves by screening and burying them from 2 ft. to 6 ft. deep in the ground (Fig. 18).

Direction-finding of the above-mentioned kind provides for location to approximately 10 square miles, at a distance of 100 miles. At 500 miles the position may be anywhere within 300 square miles. This is with first-class bearings plotted with the greatest possible accuracy. If the bearings are not first-class, the area of doubt, as it is called, may be 3,000 square miles at 100 miles.

THE CATHODE-RAY TUBE

The cathode-ray tube is a development ot the radio valve and is the key component in several modern developments, such as television and radar.

THE ELECTRON GUN. The main elements of this device are a glass bulb from which as much as possible of the air is extracted, and, inside this bulb, a cathode, an anode and a fluorescent screen (Fig. 19). The cathode is heated in the same way as is the cathode of a valve and, therefore, it emits those tiny particles called electrons. When a battery is joined by its negative terminal to the cathode and by its positive terminal to the anode, the anode attracts the electrons. They arrive at great speed, and many of them return to the cathode through the battery.

But there is a small hole in the centre of the anode, and so a few electrons fly through this hole and continue to travel on in a straight

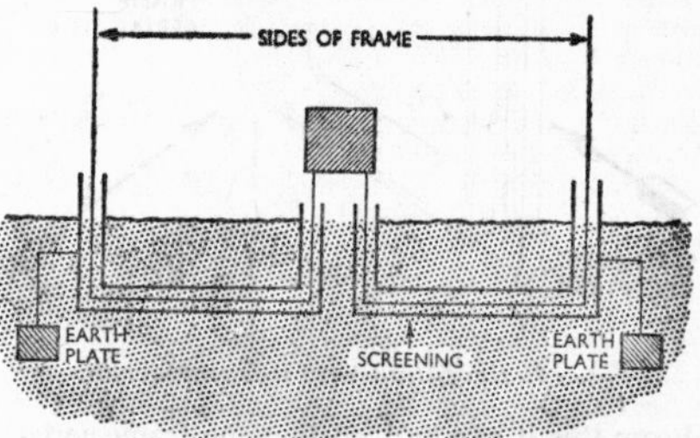

Fig. 18. Screening an aerial to reduce error.

line. They reach the screen, which is merely the inside of the end of the tube covered with some such substance as magnesium tungstate, at a very high velocity. The impact of the electrons on the fluorescent material causes a bright light to be emitted. The point where the electrons strike is seen as a spot of light.

In practice, one or two more anodes may be added to speed the electrons on their way still faster and to focus them into a narrow beam. The whole assembly of the anode is styled the electron gun, for the obvious reason that its purpose is to shoot electrons at the screen. In some modern cathode-ray tubes there is only one anode, and the focusing of the electron stream into a narrow beam is done by a coil wound round an appropriate part of the tube.

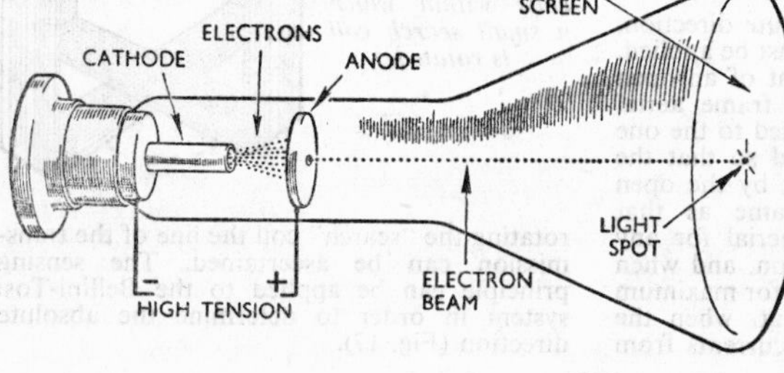

Fig. 19. Principal features of the electron gun.

The brightness of the spot of light on the screen depends upon the rate at which the electrons in the beam strike the screen; if the number of electrons arriving in a given time is decreased, the spot will be less bright. Any brightness up to the maximum, or even a complete cessation of the light, can be obtained by varying the negative voltage on the modulator electrode. This is a small cylinder placed round the cathode (Fig. 20). When it is made

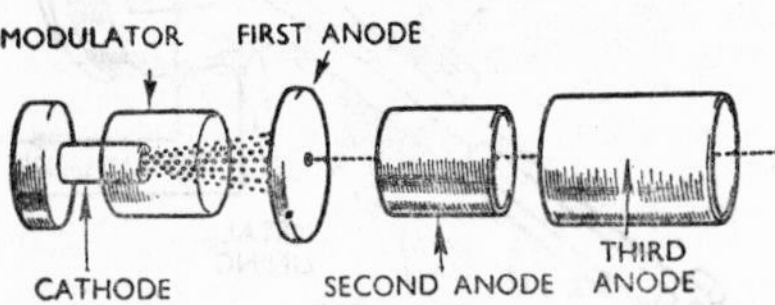

Fig. 20. Position of the modulator electrode.

negative in respect to the cathode it tends to repel the electrons back to the cathode. If it is made sufficiently negative it will act as a complete barrier and prevent any electrons passing through the anodes and reaching the screen.

Now let us see how far we have gone. We have produced a beam of electrons that is sharply focused on to a fluorescent screen and produces a spot of light, the brightness of which can be varied by varying the voltage on the modulator electrode.

DEFLECTING THE BEAM. By placing a pair of plates on either side of the beam and giving one plate a negative charge and the other a positive charge, the electron beam can be deflected, because a positive charge will attract electrons and a negative one repel them (Fig. 21a). By reversing the charges on the plates the beam can be deflected in the opposite direction. Clearly, then, it is possible to move the spot of light on the screen to any point along a straight line merely by adjusting the electrical charges on the two plates.

And the movement is practically instantaneous. The moment the voltage on the plates is changed, the light spot at once moves. If another pair of plates is introduced, these being at right-angles to the first pair, the light spot can be made to appear at any point on the screen by adjusting the voltages on the plates.

The technical name for moving the light spot in the manner described is electrostatic deflection. It can also be done by electromagnetic deflection. Instead of deflector plates, coils are used (Fig. 21b). The electron beam is deflected by the magnetic fields produced by the coils, the intensity of which depends upon the current which is passed through the coils. The direction of deflection is at right-angles to the magnetic field.

HOW TELEVISION WORKS

THE ILLUSION. Television pictures are not transmitted as complete pictures in the same kind of way as a magic lantern sends pictures through the intervening space on to a screen. The pictures are transmitted spot by spot. A picture comes through the ether as a string of radio waves varying in strength in accordance with the amount of light represented by the spots. At the receiver these spots appear on the screen in their correct positions. They actually appear one by one, but so rapidly that the illusion of a complete picture is given.

TIME BASE. To understand how this all happens it is necessary first to inquire how a time base works. This apparatus, used in conjunction with a cathode-ray tube, can make the electron beam in the tube traverse the whole of the screen in a series of lines.

The simplest time base consists of a capacitor and resistor connected to a gas-relay

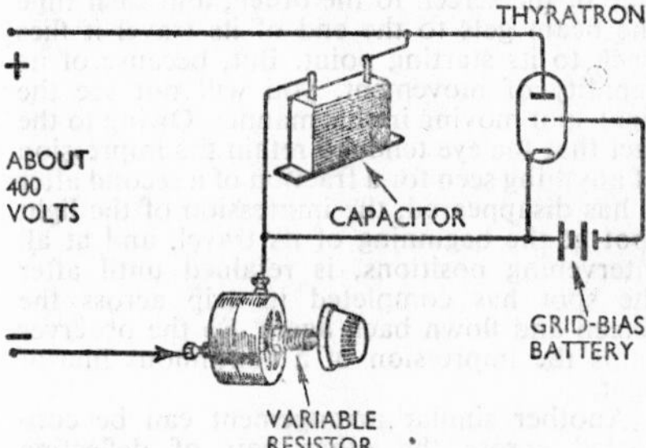

Fig. 22. Principle of time-base circuit.

valve (thyratron). If a high-voltage battery is connected to this capacitor and resistor, the capacitor does not immediately charge up to the full voltage of the battery. It takes a certain amount of time to become charged, depending upon the resistance of the resistor. The charging period can be closely controlled by varying the resistance (Fig. 22).

The thyratron, unlike an ordinary valve, does not start working as a valve with an electron stream passing from its cathode to anode until the voltage on its anode reaches

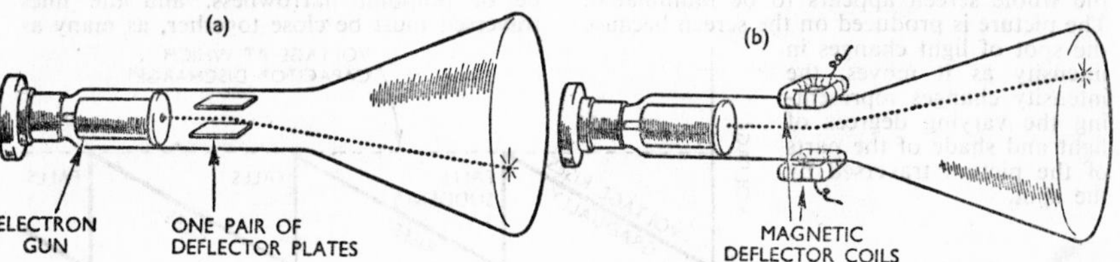

Fig. 21. (a) *How deflector plates affect the electron stream;* (b) *similar effect from magnetic coils.*

a certain value; when it does so there is at once a considerable electron stream and a comparatively high anode current flows.

The thyratron no longer acts as though there were nothing joined across the capacitor, and the capacitor discharges through it. But the capacitor almost completely discharges itself before the consequent falling voltage on the anode reaches the point where the thyratron ceases to function. Then, of course, the capacitor begins to charge again and the whole process is repeated.

If there were a voltmeter connected across the capacitor terminals which could register quickly enough, and the human eye was sufficiently alert to be able to read it, it would be seen that the voltage rises gradually up to a maximum, then falls almost instantaneously back to a minimum, then begins to rise gradually again, and so on (Fig. 23). The word gradually is used in only a relative sense for, in actual fact, the whole operation takes place in a television receiver thousands of times a second!

SCANNING THE SCREEN. This voltage from the capacitor is applied to one pair of deflecting plates in a cathode-ray tube. It deflects the electron beam gradually from one side of the screen to the other; and each time the beam gets to the end of its travel it flies back to its starting point. But, because of its rapidity of movement, you will not see the light spot moving in this manner. Owing to the fact that the eye tends to retain the impression of anything seen for a fraction of a second after it has disappeared, the impression of the light spot at the beginning of its travel, and at all intervening positions, is retained until after the spot has completed its trip across the screen and flown back again. So the observer gains the impression of a continuous line of light.

Another similar arrangement can be connected across the other pair of deflecting plates, and be adjusted so that, while the spot of light is sweeping from one side of the screen to the other it is gradually being pulled downwards, each successive line being just a little lower than its predecessor.

PRODUCING THE PICTURE. In television, this is done at a colossal speed. The point of light explores the whole surface of the screen and returns to its starting point in a matter of a fiftieth of a second. And because of the effect known as persistence of vision by which the eye retains an impression for a brief spell after the object seen has actually gone, the spot of light, when it moves at that speed over the screen, is not seen as a spot, but the whole screen appears to be illuminated. The picture is produced on the screen because the spot of light changes in intensity as it moves, the intensity changes representing the varying degrees of light and shade of the parts of the picture traversed by the spot.

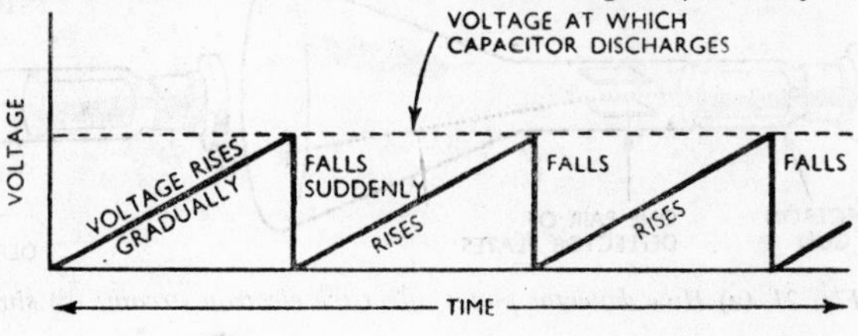

Fig. 23. Diagram showing how a capacitor discharges.

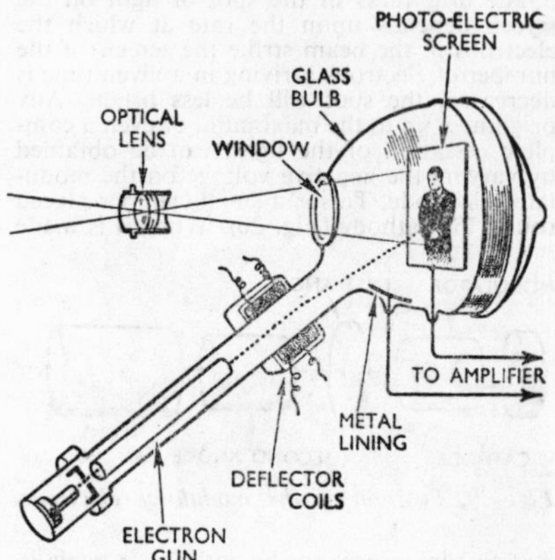

Fig. 24. The principle of the television camera.

TELEVISION CAMERA. If the foregoing is fairly well understood, the principles of the television camera become easy to explain. It is a development of the cathode-ray tube, but, instead of a fluorescent screen, it has a screen composed of thousands of globules of a photo-electric chemical, which is a material that gives off electrons when light is shone upon it. The quantity given off depends upon the intensity of the light (Fig. 24).

Ordinary optical lenses focus the scene to be televised on to this screen. And when it is appreciated that the scene lies over the screen as a pattern of varying degrees of light intensity, it is not difficult to grasp that the photo-electric globules composing the screen each give off electrons in a quantity depending upon the intensity of light at its part of the picture, these electrons building up as a charge of electricity.

The electron beam which sweeps over the picture constitutes a connexion with the outside circuit. And so, to the outside circuit is communicated a current of electricity which varies in strength in accordance with the various electrical charges of the screen globules. The picture has been transformed into a varying electrical current, which can be used to modulate a wireless wave just as can a varying current corresponding with speech or music.

But there is this vital difference. To get a picture of good detail, the electron beam must be of pinpoint narrowness, and the lines traversed must be close together, as many as

Fig. 25. This impression of a television broadcast in progress shows five cameras in use, close-up and long-range cameras on the performer, a superimposing camera for the scenery, and cameras for titles and announcer. The sound system is completely independent and is here using three microphones.

several hundreds for a screen only a few inches high. This means that there will be a tremendous number of light variations during the fraction of a second taken by the beam to scan the whole picture. The consequent current fluctuations will be many times the frequency of speech sounds. The scanning of the picture at the transmitter and the scanning of the received picture are synchronized by special impulses sent out by the transmitter.

There are impulses at the end of each line of the scanning, to make sure that the receiver scan begins correctly at the beginning of each line. And there is a frame scan to ensure that the receiver begins the scanning of the picture at exactly the same moment as does the television camera at the transmitter.

It is easy to understand how an impulse, arriving just as one of the capacitors in the time base is about to discharge will immediately apply the extra stimulus needed to make it do this. Therefore, if that part of the time base is running a trifle slow, it is at once brought into synchronism by the arrival of the synchronizing impulse.

It may be wondered why the synchronizing is not affected by the fluctuations in the current in the receiver which cause the variations in light on the screen. The reason is that the synchronizing impulses are fluctuations that in terms of their affecting the light and shade of the picture, are "blacker" than black.

All the fluctuations necessary for imparting the tones to the picture range from a minimum giving full white to a maximum giving full black; and then from full black comes in the synchronization without in any way being affected by the picture signals or in any way affecting the picture.

A wireless wave cannot satisfactorily be modulated by any frequency that is not several times lower than its own frequency. Therefore, as television currents are of a frequency comparable with the high frequencies of ordinary broadcast waves, then to act as a carrier for them, a radio wave of an extremely high frequency is needed. In practice, wireless waves of a frequency of 40 to 60 million cycles per second, corresponding to wavelengths between about 5 and 7 metres, are found to be satisfactory.

BROADCASTING TELEVISION. An impression of a television transmission in progress is shown in Fig. 25. Two transmissions are necessary for a television programme, one for sound and the other for vision. Therefore, a television receiver is really two receivers in one. But its operation can be and is simplified where there is no choice of programmes. The ultra-short waves of television are limited in their range and do not normally provide good service beyond forty or fifty miles.

RADAR

WHAT RADAR CAN DO. Navigation has been completely revolutionized by the various modern developments of radio. In fact, it is said that when a certain ship arrived just outside Southampton its crew were unable to bring it into port because the radio had broken down and no one aboard knew anything about compasses and other such things!

The story is probably not true, but the virtues it ascribes to radio are not exaggerated. What wonders, for example, can be worked with radar! Even though it is a pitch-black night and foggy into the bargain, by means of radar a ship's officer can quite clearly discern what lies ahead. He can see farther than can a man with a telescope on a bright day. In his cabin, warm and comfortable, he can see on a lighted chart exactly the position of his ship relative to all other objects, from rowing boats to icebergs and coastlines, in an area of many miles around him. His ship can go full steam ahead in perfect safety whatever the weather.

The pilot of an aeroplane can see in the screen of his radar equipment what lies on the ground beneath him, even though it is night and he is above dense banks of clouds. Yet, despite its amazing powers, radar is essentially quite simple. It is a close relation to television, for its key component is the cathode-ray tube and it employs wireless waves of a very high frequency.

But, of course, there have been devices specially developed for radar. For instance, if it were not for radar the cavity magnetron would probably not have been invented. This is a transmitting valve which, though quite small, can develop bursts of enormous power, power exceeding that employed by a broadcasting station. It is called a cavity magnetron because cavities in its internal construction take the place of capacitors and coils, an amazing simplification that is possible only at very high frequencies.

PRINCIPLE OF RADAR. The wireless waves transmitted by a radar installation are focused sharply, just as light is focused sharply by a searchlight. And this focused beam of wireless waves is swept round in a similar manner. When it strikes some such object as an aeroplane, some of the waves are reflected back in the direction from which they came, just as some of the light rays of a searchlight are reflected back when the light falls on the structure of a night fighter (Fig. 26).

The radar waves are transmitted in a series of short bursts, and between these bursts the transmitter goes out of action. The radar receiver has a cathode-ray tube, and on the screen of this a light spot is tracing a single line. Along this line a kink like an inverted V appears to show the reflected waves that are being received (Fig. 27).

Now it can easily be worked out that the light spot takes a certain definite amount of time to travel from one side of the screen to the other. In fact a scale could be drawn under the line showing at intermediate points how long the light spot takes to reach such points. And these will be small fractions of a second.

It is known that radio waves always have exactly the same velocity and that this is approximately 186,000 miles a second. Those kinks, commonly called pips, that appear on the cathode-ray screen can clearly be made

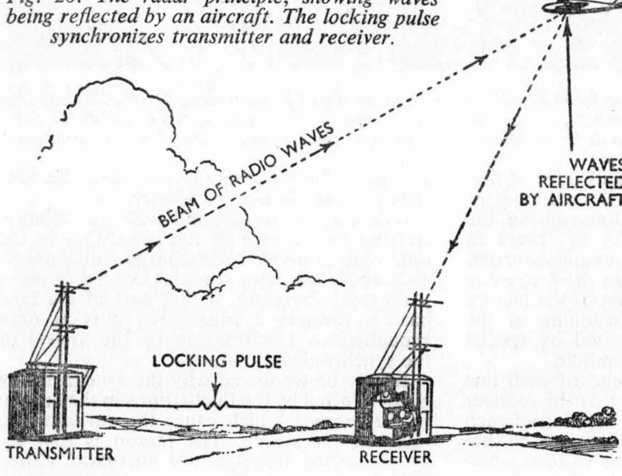

Fig. 26. The radar principle, showing waves being reflected by an aircraft. The locking pulse synchronizes transmitter and receiver.

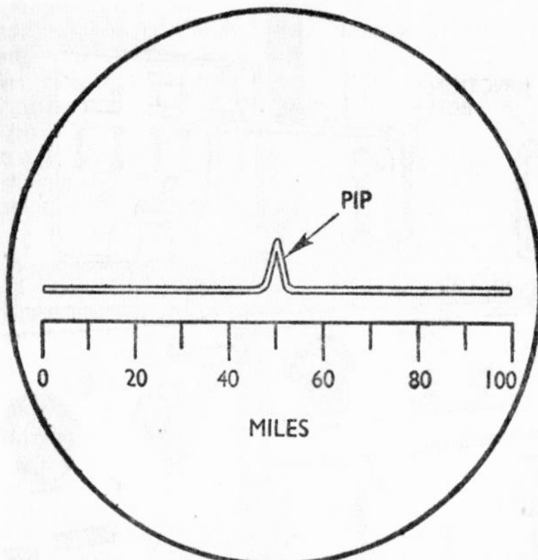

Fig. 27. The reflected radar signal appears as a pip on the cathode-ray tube.

to indicate exactly how long after the transmitter sends each burst its corresponding reflected wave is received by the receiver. If the period is one ten-thousandth of a second, you know the wave has travelled 18·6 miles; the distance to the object that is reflecting the waves and back again is 18·6 miles. That object is obviously 9·3 miles away. The final logical step is that the line on the screen of the cathode-ray tube can be calibrated in distances, so that the observer can, at a glance, see how far away is the object causing the reflection.

The exact direction in which it lies is also known because the controls used in connexion with the directional-aerial system, and by which the operator sweeps the radio beam round in order to search the sky, are calibrated to show at once the direction and elevation of the beam.

The type of radar just described is used for locating aircraft. It has also been used on aircraft, not only for the purpose of enabling the crew to determine, at night, the positions of other aircraft relative to their own position, but also for indicating altitude.

PRODUCING A RADAR PICTURE. A somewhat more complicated system is required to show at once all the objects and ground formation lying within a certain area. The picture seen is not like that which shows on a television screen. It is a pattern of dark and light patches which shows the shapes of smaller objects somewhat crudely. A river is seen by radar in an aeroplane in fairly clear outline; it can be seen twisting and winding on its course. A coastline also is seen clearly enough, but a ship may appear only as a rather shapeless smudge.

In one system of this type of radar that is used on ships, the light spot traces a circle and travels round and round the screen of the cathode-ray tube. The centre of this circle represents the ship on which the apparatus is installed. A directional transmitting aerial is rotated exactly in synchronism with the light spot on the screen of the receiver.

Every time a reflection is received, the light spot is simultaneously increased in intensity and diverted from its normal position to a position which, in its distance from the centre of the screen, is exactly proportional to the distance between the ship and the object causing the reflection (Fig. 28).

Suppose that, at a particular moment, the directional aerial arrangement is sending a burst of transmission due north, and a reflection arrives from another ship lying in that direction. At that same moment the spot on the cathode-ray tube screen will, because it is in synchronism with the aerial, be at a point representing due north. The distance along the line from the centre at which the pip occurs will depend upon the time that the wireless waves have taken to reach the reflecting ship and travel back again to the receiving part of the equipment.

The process is not as rapid a one as television, in so far as the movement of the light spot is concerned. Also, the fluorescent material on the cathode-ray screen has a long afterglow so that a bright spot remains bright for an appreciable time, it may be a second, after the spot has moved on. The process can be speeded up, but there is the mechanical limitation that the speed of scanning an area cannot be faster than the speed at which the aerial system rotates. However, even although the pictures may appear crude to the uninitiated, they can be read with remarkable facility and accuracy by the expert.

RADIO ON SHIPS

Ever since radio played such a great part in the rescue of survivors from the sunken liner *Titanic* in the Atlantic on 15 April, 1912, there has been a steady development of its usefulness on ships. At the outset, sea captains did not welcome the innovation. They saw in

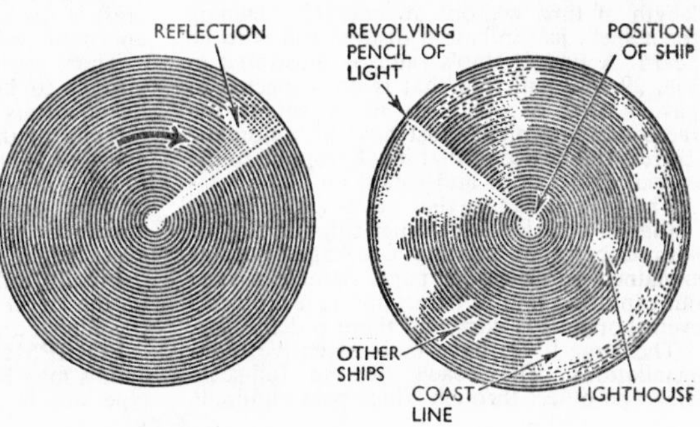

Fig. 28. Radar picture as seen on a ship. The pencil of light brightens where an object is reflected (left) *and as the light revolves it builds up a complete picture, as shown* (right).

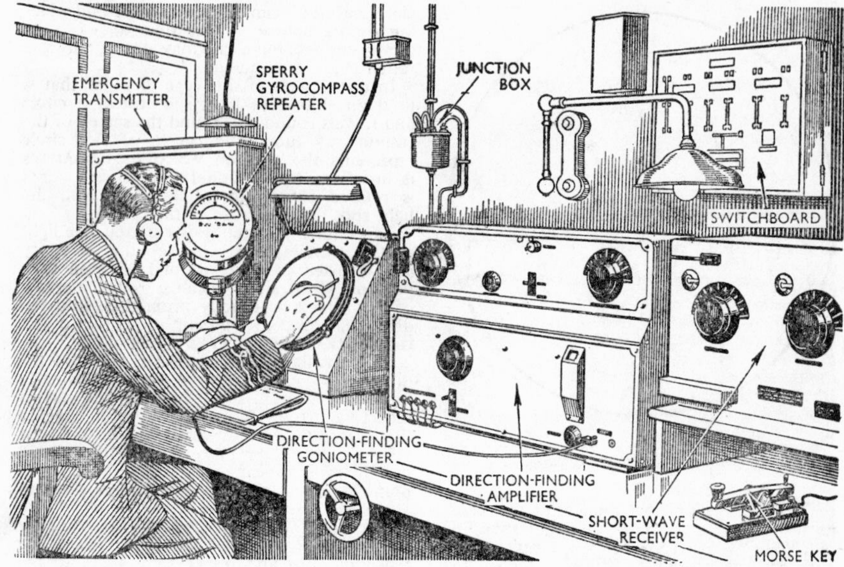

Fig. 29. A typical ship's radio installation with radio direction-finding in progress.

radio a means by which their freedom of action on voyages would be curtailed. By radio the ship would remain in constant communication with ports—and with owners! But it was soon realized by all that radio added a degree of safety in sea travel beyond anyone's greatest hopes, and this swept away all objections to its use.

Any ship, in distress, which was fitted with wireless could at once summon aid from other ships. And many dramatic dashes across the ocean to the rescue of disabled or sinking ships have occurred. No longer does a ship of any size founder alone and unknown in the vastness of the oceans. By the magic of radio it remains in constant touch with the land and other ships. Its progress across the seaways can be followed almost yard by yard.

Every ship above a certain size is compelled by law to carry radio in uninterrupted use through day and night. No ship's radio must be used for transmission beyond a certain length of time without an operator listening for a spell, just in case a distress call is to be heard. A typical ship's radio is illustrated in Fig. 29. A small ship that is not expected to have a staff of operators for attending the radio day and night must have an automatic distress call device so that it will respond to the special distress call and sound an alarm.

The gravest danger that besets a ship at sea is that of collision with other ships in fog, or with icebergs or floating wreckage. But, as explained on an earlier page, radar can send out exploring rays to detect and reveal objects even though it is dark and there is dense fog.

The large liners have most extensive radio installations. They each operate full-scale telegraph offices through which pass hundreds of radio-telegrams every day during the voyage. In addition, news bulletins are received and meteorological information continually passes to and from the ship. Radio-telephone communication is also carried out, and ordinary telephone subscribers on land can be connected to passengers on the liner.

AIRCRAFT RADIO

ITS USES. The most important use for radio in aircraft is for navigation. By means of any one of various methods the navigator of an aircraft can locate his position literally to within yards. So precise is radio as a navigational aid that, were it necessary, an aircraft could fly from London to New York and dip its wings over Broadway with every member of the crew, except the radio operator, blindfolded. Radio is also very useful for enabling the navigator to give information about weather conditions on his journey. Such information, collected from a number of aircraft in the air at widely different places, is of enormous value to the meteorologists.

Then, again, radio permits the captains of aircraft to keep in touch with their various headquarters all the time they are flying. At the end of the journey blind-landing systems are used, which make it possible for the pilot to bring in his plane safely despite the existence of fog. And the radio altitude-determining apparatus gives a visual indication of the exact height on an aircraft.

Finally, radio-telegram services are operated on the larger air-liners for the convenience of travellers during flights.

EQUIPMENT. As many as five or more aerials may be fitted. At one time the trailing type was in general use, but is not now so

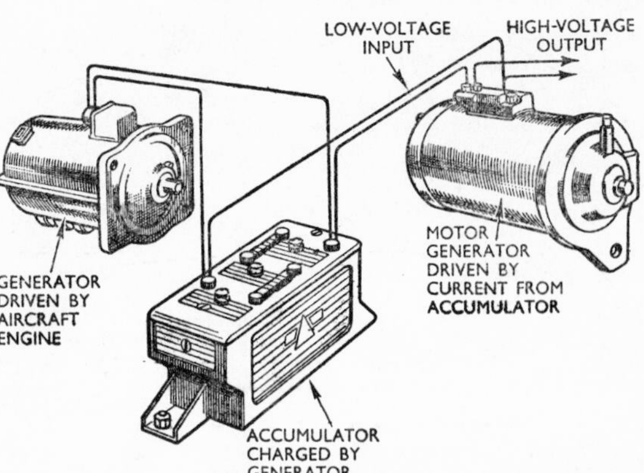

Fig. 30. Apparatus required for the provision of low- and high-voltage current for aircraft radio installation.

widely employed. It consists of a length of wire with a lead bobbin on its end, and this is lowered by means of a winch when the aircraft is in the air, and wound in before landing. More common to-day is the fixed aerial, comprising a wire suspended between two convenient points. Rod-and-frame aerials are also used.

Transmissions are on both medium and short waves. Typical wavebands for the apparatus are 550 to 1,100 metres and 40 to 80 metres. But, in addition, very short wavelengths are employed for the radar and other special equipment, when this is fitted.

The special problem with the design of aircraft radio apparatus is that it must of necessity be as light and compact as possible and sufficiently robust to be unaffected by vibration and considerable temperature changes. The power is usually obtained from a generator coupled to one of the engines in much the same way as a car dynamo is coupled to a car engine. This generator charges an accumulator which, in its turn, supplies current for the radio valves and drives a motor-generator unit the output of which is at a high voltage for the anode circuits (Fig. 30).

In large aircraft there is sometimes a separate, comparatively small petrol engine for the sole purpose of providing power for the radio equipment, thus rendering it independent of the main engines.

AIRPORT RADIO. Radio plays a most important part in the operations at a large airport. From the control tower, messages are sent to and received from aircraft in flight, directing their sequences of landing. The departure of aircraft is also controlled by radio. No aircraft is allowed to take off or land without specific permission from the control officer, conveyed by this invisible link.

The positions of aircraft during their journeys are also carefully plotted; and should an aircraft's own direction-finding apparatus fail, its position can be given to it from the ground. Constant communication is maintained also for the purpose of providing the pilot with the latest weather news. And there is an exchange of weather information between the various ground stations lying on the airway's routes. Frequently, when exceptionally bad weather conditions are reported, aircraft may be diverted so as to avoid the affected areas, and sometimes they may be instructed to land at different aerodromes from those for which they are scheduled.

BLIND APPROACH AND LANDING. The greatest advances in aircraft radio during the past few years have been in connexion with blind-approach and blind-landing systems. Blind approach is the guiding of the aircraft by radio to the aerodrome when it is difficult for the pilot to see the ground beneath him.

The early systems of homing, which is another name for blind approach, involved the use of indicating signals. By listening to a continuous series of morse letters and noting their relative strengths, the pilot could hear whether or not he was on the right course. But it was found that the pilot had difficulty in concentrating on these guiding sounds, as he had, at the same time, to listen to his engines and his captain or co-pilot.

Therefore, a visual method was developed. The general principles are similar. There are two beacon transmitters at the aerodrome (Fig. 31); on the aircraft the transmissions from these beacons affect the pointer of an indicating meter. When the pointer of this meter moves to the right, the pilot knows that he is off course to the left and must steer in the direction indicated by the needle in order to regain his course. When he is flying correctly, the needle remains central and stationary. The apparatus works entirely automatically.

A blind landing demands further information. As well as an outer radio marker-beacon to give an indication to the pilot by means

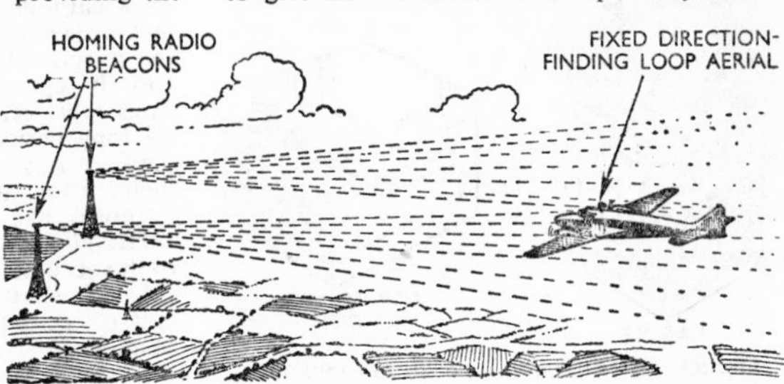

Fig. 31. Two radio homing beacons arranged to provide a blind-approach system.

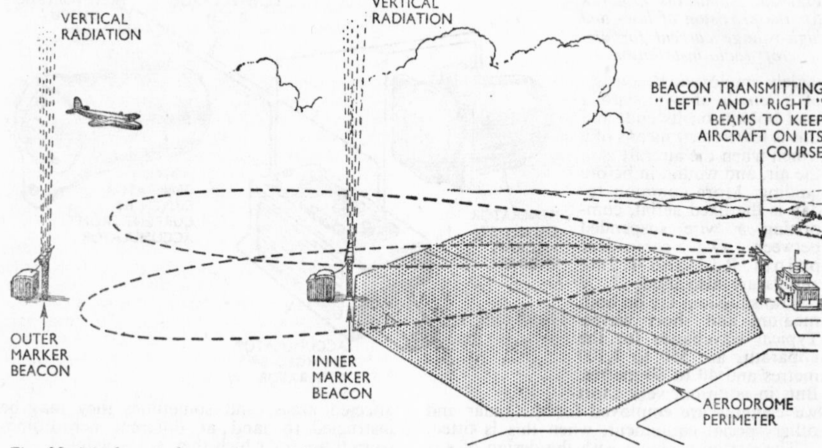

Fig. 32. Markers indicate distance from runway and allow the pilot to adjust height before landing.

of a special signal that he is close to the aerodrome, an inner marker-beacon is required to tell him when he is on or close to its actual boundary. Between these two points he can adjust the height of his aircraft so as to be in the right position to glide down to the ground (Fig. 32). A beacon at the far end of the runway keeps him exactly on the right course. In the very latest blind-landing apparatus all the information is given in visual form by easily seen instruments, but considerable skill is needed to achieve a perfect touch-down in completely blind conditions, such as during a dense fog when visibility is practically nil.

CHOICE, INSTALLATION AND FAULTS OF RECEIVERS

BATTERY SETS

Radio receivers which derive their power from batteries can be used anywhere because they are independent of the power mains.

ACCUMULATORS. Usually an accumulator cell (2 volts) is employed for heating the cathodes of the valves. One of only a comparatively small ampere-hour capacity is required. Twenty ampere-hours is a popular rating. It is advisable to have two such cells so that one can be charged while the other is in use.

Accumulators of the usual type are filled with a solution of sulphuric acid, and this is very corrosive. Therefore, when such cells are not accommodated inside a set they should always be stood on something such as a piece of wood or thick piece of cardboard so that any traces of the acid do not damage the surface of the table or other article of furniture on which the cell is placed. The terminals must be kept clean. If they are allowed to corrode, faulty connexions to them may be caused, or they may even set solid and become unusable.

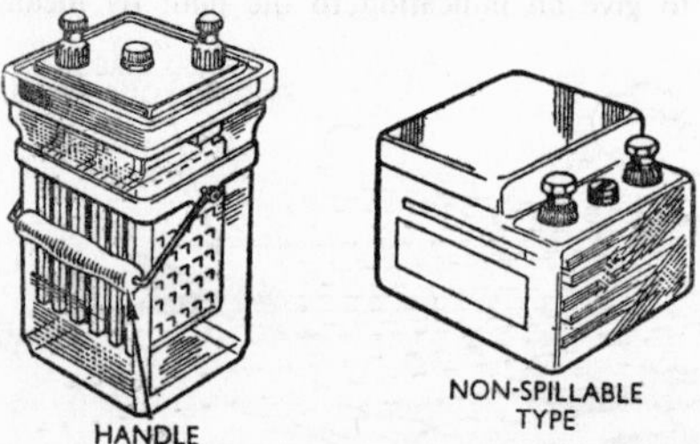

Fig. 33. Two common types of accumulator.

There are two common types of unspillable accumulator. One is packed with glass wool and the other is designed on the principle of the unspillable ink bottle (Fig. 33). Accumulators should never be run until they are entirely exhausted. Regular charging at two- or three-weekly intervals is to be advised, even when they are not being used very much.

DRY CELLS. The "all dry" battery receiver has valves which can be successfully operated on a cathode voltage of 1·5 volts or slightly less. This permits a dry cell to be employed for the purpose but, of course, this needs to be entirely replaced when it is exhausted. In some cases inert cells are used. These can be kept for long periods before going into service, as they are not active until water is poured into them. They then become, to all intents and purposes, like ordinary dry cells.

HIGH-TENSION BATTERY. In addition to the accumulator or the dry cell (often called the L.T. battery) for the cathodes, a dry battery is needed to supply the comparatively small current at high voltage for the anodes and screen grids of the valves (Fig. 34). This

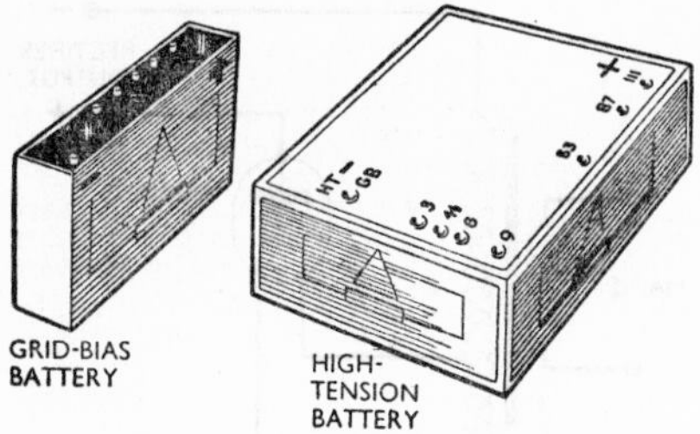

Fig. 34. Types of dry battery.

H.T. (high-tension) battery, which is usually an assembly of dry cells connected in series, cannot be recharged. So when it is exhausted it has no further value and can be thrown away. Its life depends first upon the size of the individual cells. Other things being equal, an H.T. battery of very small cells will not last as long as one having larger cells.

The second factor determining the life of an H.T. battery is the current taken from it by the receiver. Generally, the more valves there are in a set the greater the H.T. current drain. But this is not an invariable rule as some valves take more anode current than others. If kept in a cool place, a dry H.T. battery that is not being used will keep in good condition for several months.

GRID-BIAS BATTERY. A separate grid-bias battery is not always wanted; the set may have automatic grid bias. This is obtained by placing a resistance in series with the H.T. battery at its negative terminal, the component being, of course, built into the set. Tappings taken from this resistance give suitable grid-biasing voltages.

Alternatively, there are H.T. batteries which incorporate some cells for giving grid-bias voltages. This is made possible by the fact that the negative terminal of an H.T. battery is invariably connected to the positive terminal of the grid-bias battery by the wiring of the set. That makes it possible for the two batteries to be combined, although there is the disadvantage that the H.T. part is exhausted long before the grid-bias part. The reason for the long life of the grid-bias battery is that normally it does not have to supply more than a negligible current.

If it is difficult to comprehend why a battery can usefully be employed without any current being taken from it, the following analogy of the water mains may be enlightening.

When a tap is turned on in the normal way, a flow of water comes from it which could be used for, say, driving a small water turbine. The rate of flow (gallons per minute) of the water is analogous to current in electricity which is measured in amperes. The ampere is the unit of rate of flow of electricity and stands for a certain quantity (actually one coulomb) flowing in one second.

Now, the pressure of water from the tap could be applied, by means of a cylinder and piston, to holding a gas tap open against the pressure of a spring that tried to shut the tap. No flow of water would be needed for this; only the pressure by which the water was endeavouring to force its way out.

And so with electricity. A pressure of electricity (voltage) can be extremely useful in, for example, holding the grid of a valve at the particular electrical pressure required for the valve to function in a certain manner. No current flow is required for that.

It is useful for the owner of a battery set to possess a voltmeter having two ranges, one for measuring the comparatively low voltages of L.T. and grid-bias batteries, and the other for measuring the H.T. voltage.

CONNECTING BATTERIES. It is very important that the high-tension or even the grid-bias battery should not be connected across those terminals used for connecting the L.T. battery. In the absence of a fuse, the cathodes of the valves might be destroyed, though many battery sets incorporate fuses to prevent this happening.

A battery set may continue to work, though, perhaps, not quite as satisfactorily, when the L.T. battery is connected the wrong way round. But no results can be obtained if the H.T. battery connexions are reversed. Incorrect grid-bias voltages will not only cause unpleasant distortion, but may also unnecessarily increase the drain of current from the H.T. battery.

MAINS SETS

ADVANTAGES. Wherever power mains are laid on, a mains wireless set should be used. There are few arguments in favour of a battery set in such circumstances. Owing to the necessity for power economy, the average battery set does not possess a performance equal to an equivalent mains set. The mains set is cheaper to run and does not need any maintenance at all equivalent to the changing and charging of batteries.

A mains set derives all its power from the mains and is plugged into them in just the same way as an ordinary domestic appliance, such as a suction cleaner, electric iron, or standard lamp. Components are included within the set to adjust the voltage to those required for the various purposes.

A.C. OR D.C. But it is important to note that not all mains sets will work on any kind of mains. The universal, or A.C./D.C., type is designed to operate on either alternating-current or direct-current mains. But that described as either an A.C. set or a D.C. set will work only on the type of mains indicated.

D.C. (direct current) is current that flows in only the one direction. A.C. (alternating current) is current that continually reverses its direction of flow. The number of times per second that the reversal of direction takes place is called the frequency. The word cycle means the complete succession of changes in the current (or voltage) which occurs for each reversal of direction.

In each cycle the current rises from zero to a maximum and then falls to zero in the one direction, then rises to a maximum in the other direction and again falls to zero. A normal frequency for power mains is 50 cycles per second. The current changes its direction of flow fifty times a second.

The heaters of indirectly heated valves can be supplied by either alternating or direct current. In the case of alternating current, the valves must, in general, be of this type, as otherwise the alternations of the current would be communicated to the various circuits of the set and be loudly heard as a hum from the loudspeaker.

But when the cathode is heated by conduction through an insulating material, as in the case of the indirectly heated valve, the alternations of current, as it rises and falls from zero to maximum in each direction, do not cause a corresponding fluctuation in the heat of the cathode, for heat cannot so nimbly rise and fall in value.

That is why alternating current can be used for the heaters of indirectly heated valves. However, the anodes and screens of the valves must be served with D.C. voltages. Therefore, for these purposes the alternating current must be rectified so that it flows in only the one direction.

ADJUSTING VOLTAGE. But first the current must be adjusted in voltage. The voltage of the mains is usually about 250. In the case of D.C. the low voltage for the cathodes can be obtained by the introduction of a resistance, for whenever current flows through a resistance there is bound to be a voltage drop. With sufficient resistance the voltage can be dropped to any extent desired.

With A.C., any voltage within reason can be obtained without recourse to the wasteful method of introducing resistance. All that is necessary is a component called a transformer. This consists of an iron core on which wire is wound in the form of primary and secondary windings. The mains current flows through the primary winding and causes a field of magnetic force to rise and fall as the alternating current rises and falls in value, first in one direction and then in the other.

This rising and falling magnetic field induces a current of electricity in the secondary winding. The secondary current will have a voltage directly depending upon the number of turns of wire in that winding as compared with the turns of wire in the primary winding. If there are half the number of turns, the voltage induced will be approximately half the voltage in the primary. If there are twice the number, the voltage will be stepped up to about twice that of the primary; hence the terms step-up and step-down transformers.

For the cathodes of the valves there may be a separate secondary winding providing the required step down. Then there will be a larger winding taking off a current of suitable maximum voltage for the anodes and screens. This current is then *rectified* so that it becomes D.C. and its voltage adjusted as required.

RECTIFICATION. By valves. We have shown in an earlier section how the two-electrode valve can rectify. If its cathode and anode are placed in series in a circuit through which alternating current exists, the current will be allowed to flow only in the direction of cathode to anode. (Incidentally, the meaning of the term series should be noted. When a component is placed in series in a circuit all the current flowing in that circuit must flow

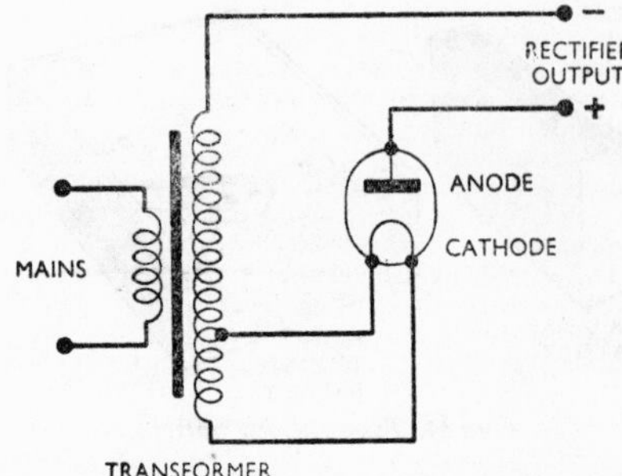

Fig. 35. Circuit providing half-wave rectification.

through the component. When two components are in parallel, they are joined so that they offer alternative paths to the current.)

When one rectifier valve of the single-diode type is used in the manner that has been described, the result is half-wave rectification (Fig. 35). Only one half of each cycle of the alternating current is used, that half which is flowing in the one direction. When the current flows in the reverse direction, the diode presents a barrier against it and it is suppressed (Fig. 36).

Two diodes can be used in conjunction with a centre-tapped transformer in order to give full-wave rectification, whereby the whole of each cycle is used to advantage. This is done, as shown in Fig. 37, by arranging the two diode rectifiers so that one of them always presents a path for the current. When the

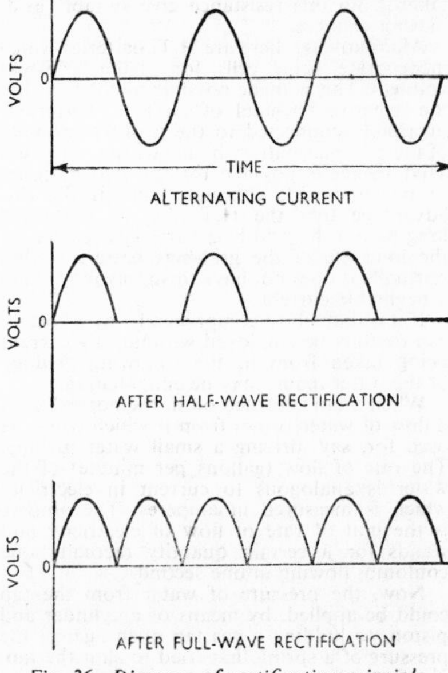

Fig. 36. Diagram of rectification principle.

current flows in one direction, it can flow through number one diode, but not number two. When it reverses its direction of flow it can flow through number two diode, but not through number one. Such are the connexions of the diodes that their anodes feed into a common circuit in only the one direction.

Two diodes can be constructed in the one glass bulb in order to share the one cathode. This results in the double-diode, which has a cathode and two anodes and is used for full-wave rectification (Figs. 38 and 13). A diode and a double-diode designed specifically for

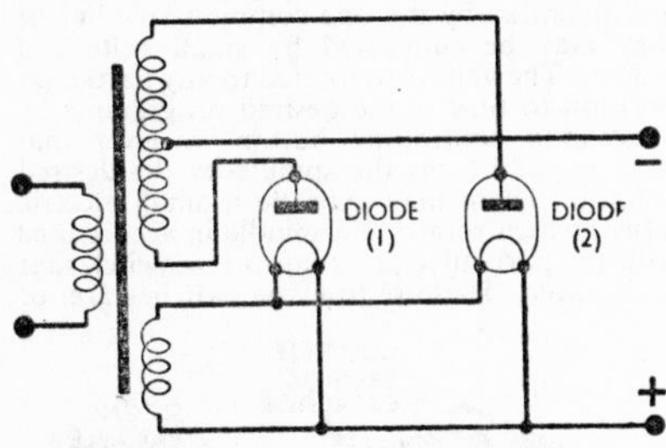

Fig. 37. Full-wave rectification using two diodes.

the rectification of mains current are referred to as a single-wave and double-wave rectifier respectively.

By metal rectifiers. Instead of valves, a device known as a metal rectifier can be employed. The most widely used form of this consists of a copper disk having a layer of oxide on its surface. Rectification occurs because the device has a very much greater resistance to current flowing in the one direction than it has to the current when it flows in the opposite direction.

Metal rectifiers are assembled in banks for higher voltages and greater current-carrying

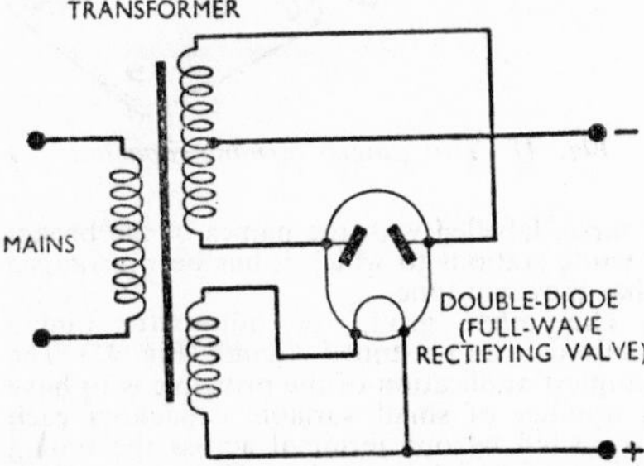

Fig. 38. Two diodes combined as a double-diode.

capacities, and they have the advantage that, so long as they are not overloaded by having a greater voltage applied to them than that for which they are designed, they are practically everlasting.

SMOOTHING. Although after rectification the current is flowing unidirectionally, and although its voltage has been adjusted, it is still not suitable for the anodes and screens of the valves, as it will be fluctuating in strength. The reason for this is that the alternating current is continually rising and falling in strength, first in one direction, then the other, as Fig. 36 shows.

The irregularities in the current flow can be smoothed out by means of capacitors and chokes (Fig. 39). The chokes are coils wound on iron cores to increase their inductances; and it will be remembered that inductance opposes any change in a current.

The smoothing in a good mains set is sufficient to make the mains supply almost as smooth as the current from a battery. Unfortunately, there is a tendency in competitive manufacture to economize at the expense of smoothing. The trade tolerates a certain amount of hum in its cheaper sets. The amount that is tolerated depends upon various considerations, not the least being the conscience of the individual manufacturer. Of course, it is not always poor smoothing that causes a continuous humming noise in a receiver, but it is the most frequent cause.

AUTOMATIC GAIN CONTROL. A refinement that is almost essential in a receiver for broadcasting is automatic gain control. It is sometimes referred to as automatic volume control. Almost invariably there is a great deal of fading after nightfall. The more distant broadcasting stations sometimes fade right away into complete inaudibility and then, a

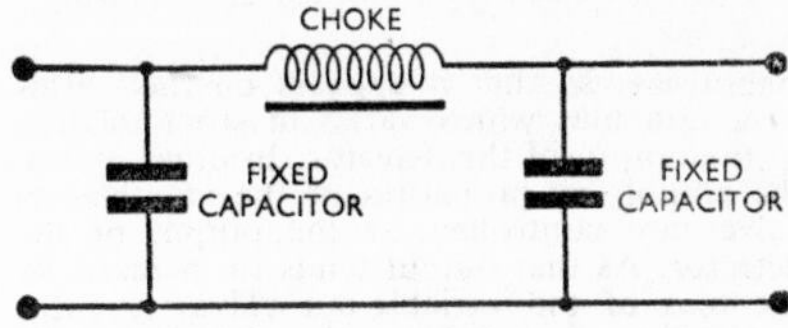

Fig. 39. Circuit for smoothing current flow.

few seconds later, they are heard at the original strength.

Even if there is not this extreme fading, the strength of a station may rise and fall in a disturbing manner. Automatic gain control (A.G.C.) counters this by automatically adjusting the sensitivity of the set as the strength of the received programme changes. When the strength falls, the set immediately makes itself more sensitive; as the strength rises again, so the set makes itself less sensitive. And in this manner it maintains an equal volume of reproduction from the loudspeaker, despite fluctuations in the energy received in the aerial from any station. Once, by means of a manual volume control, the listener has set the level of volume he desires, the set automatically adapts its effectiveness, as occasion demands, to retain this level.

The working of A.G.C. is noticeable when it is dealing with extreme changes. As the set extends its sensitivity, the background noises due to ether disturbances of one kind and another are heard somewhat louder. Sometimes a certain amount of interference from another station may be gathered in by the set at its extremes of sensitivity. The quietest background, the greatest freedom from extraneous noises, will be when the set is receiving a strong wave from a station and it automatically recedes into its least sensitive condition.

Variable-mu valves are used for A.G.C. These are amplifying valves of either the tetrode or pentode type which can be varied in their ability to amplify by varying their grid bias.

A small proportion of the current from the output of the detector valve is fed back to these variable-mu valves (Fig. 40) after suitable

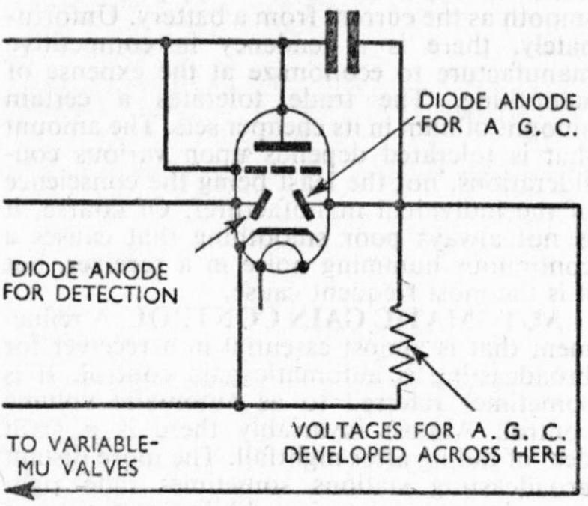

Fig. 40. Circuit for automatic gain control.

smoothing, so that it appears on their grids as a grid bias which varies in strict relation to the output of the detector. In other words, the amplifying properties of the variable-mu valves are controlled by the output of the detector. As that output tends to increase, so the bias of the variable-mu valves is automatically adjusted to reduce their amplification, and vice versa.

This is simple A.G.C. It suffers from the drawback that even weak reception will produce some energy at the detector and a part of this will be fed back to reduce the amplifying effectiveness of the set. In delayed automatic gain control, the principle does not come into operation until the strength of the input to the set reaches a certain point. There is no control when the stations are weak and the set operates at its greatest efficiency. Besides being useful for countering the effects of fading, A.G.C. prevents a set from being overloaded by very strong reception.

TUNING. Not many years ago it was common for a radio receiver to have nearly a dozen dials and knobs that had to be adjusted in order to tune in a programme. Some considerable experience had to be acquired before all these controls could be handled to the best advantage. The development of the super-heterodyne principle permitted considerable simplification of tuning to be obtained. On a modern set there are seldom more than two adjustments for selecting stations. Tuning has still further been simplified on some sets by the provision of switches or press-buttons to select any one of a number of programmes. There is usually a control in addition allowing the listener to do his own tuning.

There are numerous arrangements of this nature, ranging from a dial similar in appearance and operation to the dial of an automatic telephone, to straight rows of lever switches or press-buttons, but they nearly all fall into one or the other of two groups. In the first group are various methods whereby the variable capacitors used for tuning are rotated to predetermined positions by some mechanical means.

All the variable capacitors may be ganged (Fig. 41), that is, they are grouped together and operated by the one common spindle; or they may be connected by small belts and pulleys. The vanes are rotated to any particular position to tune in the desired programme by pressing a controlling button or lever that mechanically turns the spindle by the desired amount. There may even be a small electric motor which rotates the spindle in accordance with the particular press-button or switch that is operated. These buttons or switches are, of

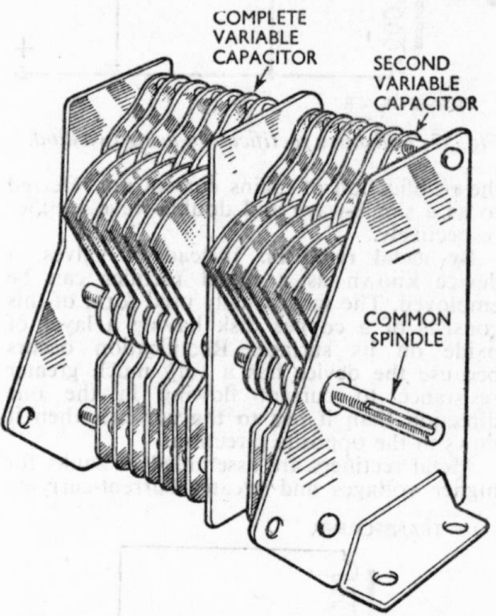

Fig. 41. Two ganged variable capacitors.

course, labelled with the names of the broadcasting stations to which it has been arranged that they will tune.

The other group of automatic tuning methods uses pre-tuned circuits (Fig. 42). The simplest application of the principle is to have a number of small variable capacitors each connected by one terminal across the tuning circuit of a simple receiver. These capacitors are then adjusted so that each will bring the tuning to the point required for a particular station. A number of labelled switches are on the panel of the set and, depending upon which switch is operated, so one or other of the small variable capacitors (pre-set capacitors) is brought into circuit.

It is not quite so simple when the principle is applied to a super-heterodyne receiver. Here

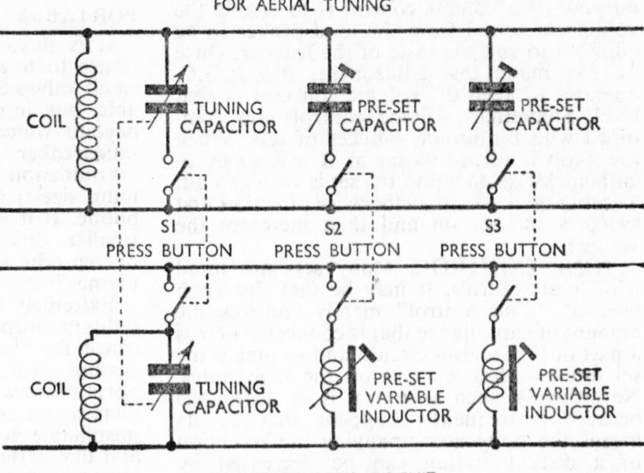

Fig. 42. Three pre-tuned circuits operated by press button.

the oscillator also has to be adjusted precisely as the tuning is altered. The normal pre-set method is to have a series of small variable inductors (tuning coils) which are switched into the oscillator circuit at the same time as the small variable capacitors are connected to the tuning circuit by the operation of one or other of switches or push-buttons.

Any slight discrepancy in automatic tuning can be made good by what is called automatic frequency control, or automatic tuning correction.

It will be appreciated that modern sets are so selective that the slightest maladjustment in tuning is liable to be serious. In automatic frequency control (A.F.C.) there is a discriminator valve to which a proportion of the energy from the oscillator circuit is fed (Fig. 43). If this energy is off-tune, the discriminator valve comes into action in accordance with the degree of error. The control voltage obtained in the discriminator circuit is then passed on to an oscillator control valve. This valve may be connected across the tuned circuit, the frequency of which is governed by the valve reactance, which in turn is altered by the control voltage. Thus, exactly the right amount of correction is applied to bring the set into exact tune. But it is to be noted that A.F.C. cannot apply more than a certain amount of correction. If the error is excessive, the control does not operate.

The A.F.C. also functions when the set is tuned by hand. It does good work here, too, because the average listener has not the skill to obtain very precise tuning. And unless the tuning is precise, there is usually some distortion. With almost any super-heterodyne receiver, high-quality reception is impossible without exact tuning to the station.

A more economical method of ensuring accuracy in tuning is the inclusion of some visual indicator. Some sets have small neon lights on their panels which glow at their brightest when a station is tuned in exactly. Then there is a special form of neon lamp which shows as a small column of light. When the column reaches a maximum length, the set is known to be tuned in accurately.

These neon indicators usually work in conjunction with the variable-mu valves employed for automatic gain control. The grid bias automatically applied to these valves is at its greatest when the signal is at its greatest strength, and the largest amount of controlling voltage is being applied. And it is in consequence of the change in the anode current that the neon lamp is operated.

The most modern and most sensitive form of visual tuning indicator consists of a small cathode-ray tube combined in the one glass bulb with a small triode amplifier. The screen of the miniature cathode-ray tube glows when the set is in operation, and a shadow is cast on this small screen by a control electrode. A variation in the area of the shadow occurs when a station is tuned in and, on one make of set, accuracy of tuning is indicated by the shadow being reduced to a minimum.

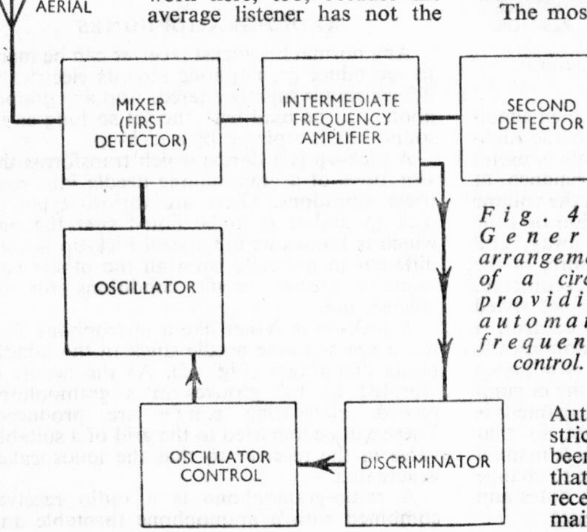

Fig. 43. General arrangement of a circuit providing automatic frequency control.

VOLUME CONTROL.

Automatic gain control is not in the strict sense a volume control. As has been shown, it is a method of ensuring that, despite varying strengths of reception owing to fading, the set maintains a constancy of output. The purpose of a volume control is to enable the volume of sound from the loudspeaker to be adjusted to suit the taste of the listener. Once he has made this adjustment, the A.G.C. operates to keep the volume constant at that level. Sometimes volume controls are combined with the on-off switches of sets. When the knob is turned as far as it will go in an anti-clockwise direction the set is switched off. Turning the knob in a clockwise direction first switches the set on and then increases the volume.

TONE CONTROL. Many sets are fitted with tone controls. It may be that the knob labelled "tone control" merely controls the amount of capacitance that is connected across a part of the receiver circuit, and so makes the set more or less efficient on the high notes. Nevertheless, such a control is of advantage because it frequently happens that by its means the noise accompanying the reception of a distant station can be decreased by reducing the response of the set to high notes. But, of course, this is done only at the sacrifice of high notes in the speech or music being received.

It is to be noted that a tone control of this nature works well with the output circuit of a receiver that tends to give an over-emphasis to high notes. This sometimes happens when a pentode valve is used. The control is then more strictly a tone compensator (Fig. 44).

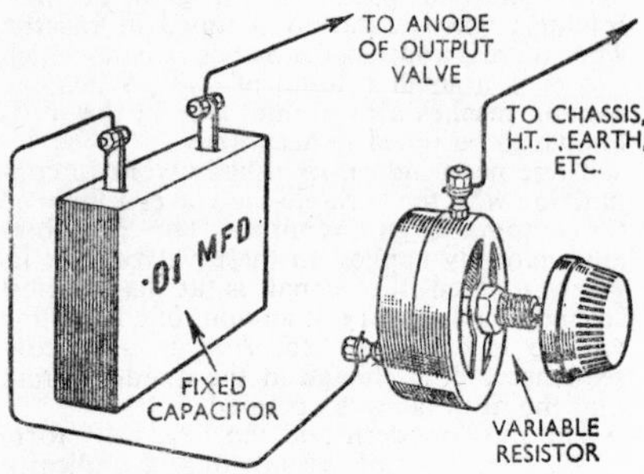

Fig. 44. Tone control or compensator.

There is a type of tone control which simultaneously reduces or increases both the high- and low-note response of a set. This is useful as a means of maintaining a balance at different levels of volume. Reducing the volume often gives the listener the impression that the high and low notes have fallen away, and that the notes lying towards the centre of the range have been correspondingly accentuated.

In a development of this principle, styled acoustically compensated volume control, a compensation of this type is automatically applied. As the volume of sound is adjusted by the listener to suit his mood or the circumstances of his listening, the tone adjustment is automatically made within the set so that the best possible balance is retained. A manual tone control can be used in addition to change the response of the set to only high notes and so diminish some types of interference.

PORTABLE AND TRANSPORTABLE SETS

It is possible to make a portable set no larger than a cigarette case, using the very small valves and batteries that are now available. But, in practice, there is a minimum size beyond which it is impossible to include a loudspeaker capable of giving passable reproduction, especially of music. This minimum size is about that of a portable gramophone. If it is desired that the set should be smaller, this is possible only at the expense of reproduction quality or by using headphones instead of a loudspeaker.

Extremely small sets are manufactured for military purposes, but they have no significance for the domestic reception of broadcasting. Nor, in most cases, have ordinary portable sets. But these latter are useful for picnics and holidays. Some portable sets have unspillable accumulators for the L.T. supply and dry batteries for the H.T. and grid bias. Others embody special valves which are run entirely from dry batteries.

There is a built-in frame aerial and, in some instances, a terminal for the connexion of an ordinary aerial. The sensitivity of such a set, when only its own small frame aerial is in use, will not be very great, but is usually sufficient to provide good reception anywhere in the country of at least two B.B.C. stations.

When a portable set is not likely to be used for a period of some weeks, its batteries should be removed and, if there is an accumulator, this should be kept charged.

A transportable receiver is one that, while not designed like a portable gramophone for carrying about, is sufficiently self-contained to be easily transferred from one room to another in the house. For example, a popular type of transportable receiver for operation from a mains supply is built into a compact case which includes the loudspeaker and frame aerial. It can be plugged into any power point. Usually, terminals are provided for the connexion of an external aerial and an earth in order to increase the range of the set.

RADIO-GRAMOPHONES

Any normal broadcast receiver can be made to reproduce gramophone records electrically if its wiring is slightly altered. And any gramophone can be used with the set so long as its sound-box is replaced by a pick-up.

A pick-up is a device which transforms the vibrations of a gramophone needle into electrical vibrations. There are various types of pick-up and it is to be noted that the one which is known as the crystal pick-up is very different in principle from all the others and requires special circuit conditions for its efficient use.

A pick-up is rather like a microphone that has a gramophone needle stuck in the middle of its diaphragm (Fig. 45). As the needle is vibrated by the grooves in a gramophone record, alternating e.m.f.s are produced. These can be imparted to the grid of a suitable valve in the receiver so that the loudspeaker is actuated.

A radio-gramophone is a radio receiver combined with a gramophone turntable and pick-up. For good results it is essential that there should be a well-fitting lid that can be closed down over the record while it is being played. It is a serious weakness in design if the lid cannot be closed, for there will almost inevitably be a direct transmission of mechanical noises from the pick-up. It acts like a miniature gramophone as its needle and other parts vibrate and, in addition to generating an electrical pattern of the sounds, will mechanically produce sounds that can clearly be heard; they are likely to be harsh and strident sounds which will not blend at all pleasantly with the sounds from the loudspeaker.

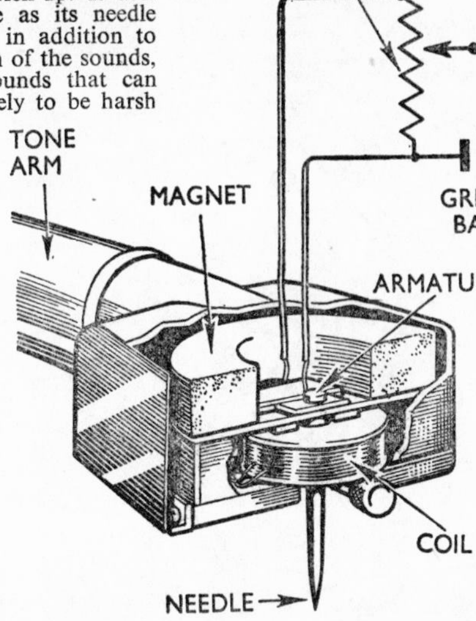

Fig. 45. Section through a radio-gramophone pick-up, showing its principal features and showing diagrammatically its position in the circuit in relation to the amplifier valve.

HOW TO CHOOSE A RECEIVER

SOME GENERAL POINTS. Faced by the very large number of different makes of set, and the various models at various prices in each manufacturer's range, and by numerous specifications of a somewhat technical nature, the prospective purchaser may well wonder how he is to go about the selecting of a good one. The sort of questions he may well ask are, is there any one set which represents much better value for money than any other? Is it possible to buy a wireless pig-in-a-poke? And how is one to steer clear of such a catastrophe?

First of all, it can be accepted as a fact that there is no set now made in Britain by any large firm that has been advertising consistently for some years, that is a bad set. Within the circle of the leading makers of wireless apparatus all the sets produced are good sets. But some are undoubtedly better than others. As a fairly general rule, a set that costs about twenty guineas will be better than most others costing fifteen guineas or less, providing the products of the large concerns are in question. There are still some small firms making wireless sets which are not good value for money. On the other hand, there are small firms making sets that are extraordinarily good value.

In assessing the qualities of a set there are many points to consider and we will discuss these in some detail. It is well worth while to get fully acquainted with them before making a final selection. It is as well, also, to read the makers' specifications of a number of different sets and note how they compare.

There are those who say that the appearance of a receiver is of little importance. On the contrary, it is extremely important, for a radio receiver for the reception of broadcasting has to take its place, and a fairly prominent place, in the home as an article of furniture. Therefore, a pleasing appearance is desirable, and there is no reason why this should be incompatible with a good performance. The radio-gramophone (Fig. 46) is often a prominent item in a room.

Many listeners are attracted by very small sets. Perhaps they are captivated by the wonder that a very small set should be able to function successfully. But it is to be remembered that a small set can have only a small loudspeaker, and good bass reproduction is not possible unless a loudspeaker is of moderately large dimensions Small loudspeakers are referred to as tweeters by radio and talkie engineers, who use them only in conjunction with large loudspeakers to add to the strength of high notes.

It is not so much the size of the magnet and diaphragm that matters as the dimensions of the baffle. Ideally, a loudspeaker diaphragm should be set in the middle of a stout board about 6 ft. square to prevent the sound waves of the low notes from curling round to the back and being neutralized by those which curl round to the front.

The cabinet of a receiver which has a built-in loudspeaker can act as a baffle. It will not be an efficient baffle if it is very small. Nevertheless, the quality from some comparatively small sets is, in the circumstances, extremely good. Fig. 47 shows the lay-out of a typical small set.

The wavebands covered by a set are of importance. Some listeners are satisfied to receive only two of the B.B.C.'s programmes. Others will require the set to be able to bring in the Third Programme clearly, and they do not all do that easily anywhere in the country.

Then there are the short waves. It is necessary for a set to be able to receive these if the very distant programmes, such as those from

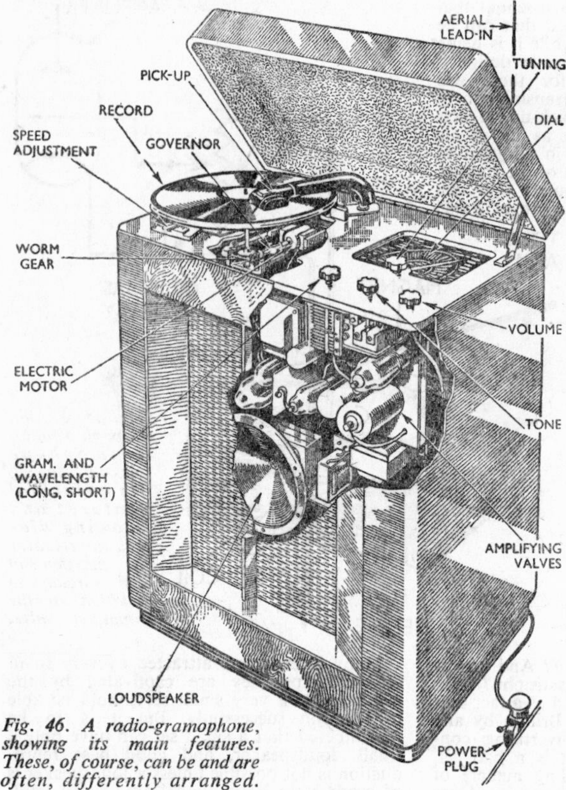

Fig. 46. A radio-gramophone, showing its main features. These, of course, can be and are often, differently arranged.

A set with a large tuning dial on it, giving the names of dozens of different transmitting stations, may appear impressive. It may even be able to give you all those stations when the dial is rotated, or an appropriate control is adjusted. But sometimes there is a certain amount of boasting about such calibrations. All the stations named may certainly be receivable, but only in ideal reception conditions.

Actually, there is not such an advantage in having a set calibrated in station names as at first might be thought, for such a calibration presupposes a permanent state of affairs in regard to the allocation of station wavelengths. Changes do occur now and then which will falsify such calibrations. Therefore, if a set is given a name calibration, then the dial or chart should be easily changeable. Either wavelength or frequency calibration, or both, is usually quite sufficient, because the frequencies or wavelengths of all broadcasting stations are published.

A dial light to illuminate the tuning scale or chart is almost essential and is, in fact, a standard fitting on all modern main sets. Besides enabling the tuning indications to be read easily and quickly, such a light acts as a tell-tale as to whether or not the set is switched on. Some battery sets do not have dial lights, for the reason that even the small amount of current taken by one of these is important when the only source of supply is a small battery.

America, are desired. It should not be accepted that any set that is specified to be an "all-wave" set (the term usually employed to denote that it will receive the short waves as well as the medium and long ones) is as efficient for short-wave reception as it appears to be for that of the medium and long waves.

Many American sets are not capable of receiving long-wave programmes, as long waves are not used in America for broadcasting. Most American all-wave sets are efficient on the short waves.

Although the set which takes a listener's fancy may not be a radio-gramophone, he should ask himself if he may at some time desire to reproduce records electrically on it. If so, he may well enquire if the set has pick-up terminals so that a pick-up can be connected to it. To obtain electrical reproduction from an ordinary gramophone he has then only to replace the tone-arm by a pick-up of a suitable type (see Fig. 48).

If there is a remote possibility that, at some future date, he will require to run one or more additional loudspeakers so that the programmes can be heard in other rooms, he should make sure that the set is equipped with the appropriate socket or terminals.

A receiver should always be heard in domestic surroundings, if it is possible to do so, before it is finally purchased. It is no test at all to listen to one that is standing on a shop counter and blaring right into the listener's face. There should be a thorough demonstration in at least a quiet room, and the following vital technical qualities should be considered.

SELECTIVITY. By the term selectivity is meant the ability of a wireless receiver to discriminate between a desired transmission and all others. But it is to be noted that when two transmitters tend to overlap, there may be a mutual interference which the most selective set in the world could not eliminate.

A transmission of speech or music produces wireless waves which cover a band of frequencies. In the centre is the fundamental frequency, the frequency on which the station is listed as transmitting. At each side (or plus and minus this frequency, to be more technical)

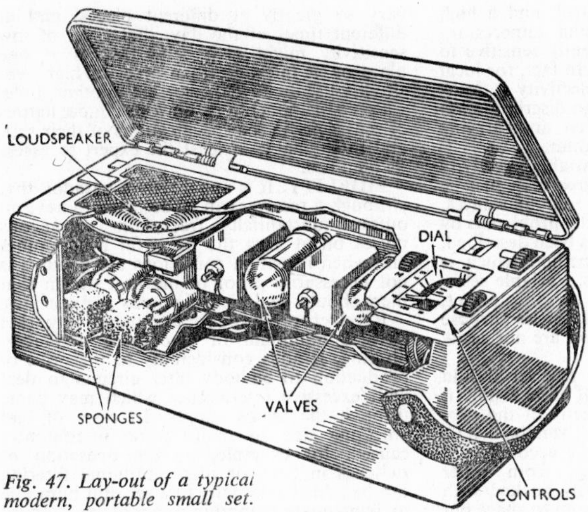

Fig. 47. Lay-out of a typical modern, portable small set.

mission. And when a full orchestra is being broadcast there will be a very large number of additional waves of different frequency. (This example given is rather over-simplified, for a Middle C note on the piano is itself a small family of frequencies with 256 as only the fundamental one.)

It can easily be appreciated that a set must not be too selective or it will discriminate against some of these sidebands of a transmission. Yet a maximum of selectivity is sometimes required to tune in a distant, weak station that is surrounded by other and perhaps more powerful stations.

On the other hand, when a set is tuned in to a nearby broadcasting station its sensitivity can be reduced, and often is reduced automati-

are other wireless waves as much lower and higher than the fundamental as the frequencies of speech and music. For example, a station is said to be transmitting on a frequency of, say, 1,000,000 cycles per second; it is made to carry a Middle C piano note. This has a frequency of 256 cycles per second. Therefore, as well as the 1,000,000-cycles-per-second wave there will be waves of 1,000,256 and 999,744 cycles per second accompanying the trans-

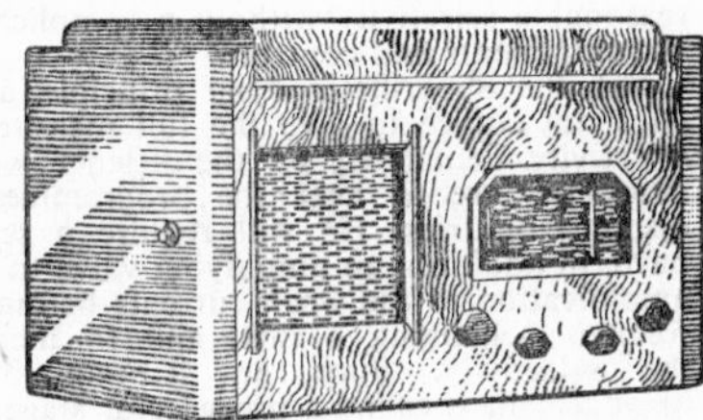

Fig. 48. A table-type radio with sockets for gramophone pick-up and additional loudspeaker.

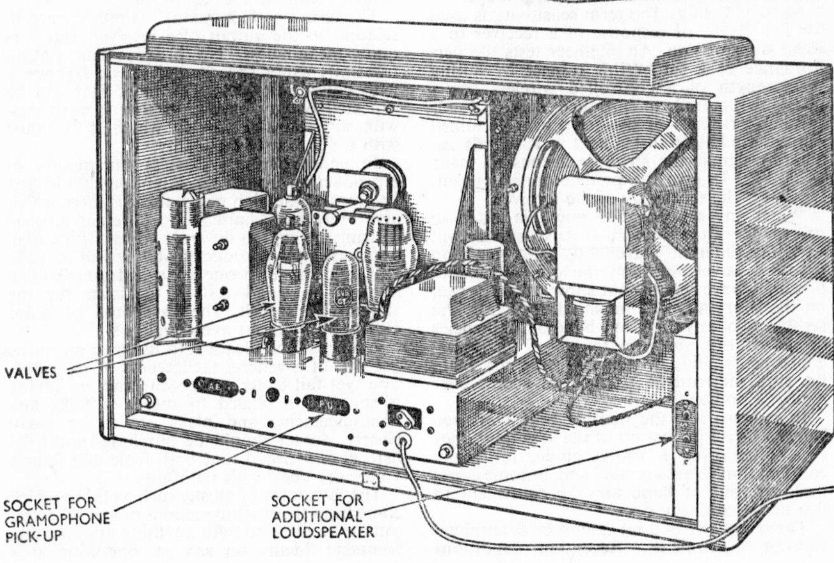

cally by automatic gain control, and a high degree of selectivity is quite unnecessary because the set is not sufficiently sensitive to respond to any other station. In fact, for local station reception a lack of selectivity is desirable so that there is little or no discrimination against those sidebands which are carrying the tone-shades of the programme.

Some sets are fitted with variable selectivity in order that the correct degree of it can be obtained to suit varying circumstances. Another way of dealing with the problem is by means of a tone control, as has been described, and, in general, it is that method which is adopted on most modern sets. Variable selectivity seems, therefore, to be obsolescent, which is probably just as well, as the purpose and operation of such a control are not easily grasped by many listeners.

It is very necessary that a receiver should have reasonable selectivity. If it has not, it may be impossible to hear many of the programmes without interference. Even the B.B.C. programmes may sometimes be accompanied by hissings and whisperings from other stations. The ether is so closely packed with transmitters that there is no room to space out their frequencies very widely. It is because of this that the super-heterodyne principle is universally adopted, as it does permit of reasonable selectivity without a complication of components and controls.

But the super-heterodyne principle alone does not suffice to give the full measure of selectivity demanded by the listener whose ambitions are to hear the programmes of distant countries. He will require a set to have, in addition, an amplifying valve to give amplification to the weak currents before the frequency-changing occurs, and to increase the selectivity. Such an R.F.-amplifying arrangement is called a pre-selector stage.

SENSITIVITY. The term sensitivity is used for the degree of response of a receiver to a weak transmission. An engineer tests the performance of a set in this respect by noting the strength of a controlled wireless transmission required to produce at the loudspeaker terminals of the set a predetermined output. He has an instrument which sends out a radio signal: the stronger he has to make this signal to give the predetermined output, the less is the sensitivity of the receiver.

When any set, however good, is tested in this manner, it is found that its sensitivity will vary on different wavebands, and even on different wavelengths on the one waveband. Some all-wave sets do not show up at all well on the short waves. One should not take the sensitivity of any set at one band of frequencies as necessarily applying to all of its tuning adjustments. But, in this respect, once again the super-heterodyne type of set scores over almost all other types.

In modern sets the number of valves used is not a direct indication of the sensitivity, nor is it often even a rough guide, for many combination valves are used and, in some cases, three or four of these may be equivalent to five or six ordinary ones.

The sensitivity of a set cannot be determined without instruments. Reception conditions vary so greatly at different places, and at different times of the day, that set of low sensitivity might give better results at one place or at one time than a set of high sensitivity used elsewhere or at another time.

Some manufacturers, however, quote figures of sensitivity in the specifications of their sets, and these enable at least the expert to assess its qualities.

FIDELITY. It is apparently a paradox that although a receiver can be designed to have an output substantially free from extraneous noises on at least the powerful programmes and when reception conditions are good, it is not necessarily proof of inexpert design that there should be noticeable hums and crackles.

Receivers produced for a competitive market have a minimum of smoothing and R.F. filtering. It adds considerably to the price of production to embody filter circuits to deal with excessive interference which may come through the mains supply. In cases of bad crackling due to mains-borne interference, caused, for example, by the operation of switches in flats, or lifts, additional filtering can be added externally to a set. But hum due to inadequate smoothing cannot be reduced except by internal modifications and, in a compactly constructed receiver, there may not be room for the additional components.

Therefore, the prospective purchaser of a new wireless receiver should ask himself if hum heard on an inexpensive mains set which he may be considering is more or less than that which he feels he will be able to tolerate. There is this point to remember, that because of its always being present a listener can become accustomed to quite a deal of hum, so that, eventually, it is hardly noticed at all. Generally speaking, it is only with the more expensive mains set that there will be an almost complete absence of hum.

The term "perfect quality" is often heard in relation to the output of a receiver. But it is quite meaningless. No broadcasting station transmits every speech and music frequency with equal efficiency. The most that can be expected of any receiver is that it shall deal with any transmission to which it is tuned with a fair degree of fidelity.

In endeavouring to assess the quality of reproduction from a set, attention should first be given to the high notes, for it is these which give individual character to different musical instruments and to different voices. If the high notes are not reproduced well, it will be difficult to distinguish one wind instrument from another. A good test is to listen for the sibilants in speech. The s's should be heard clearly but without over-emphasis.

A set may be pleasant to listen to on music because of a general mellowness of reproduction, yet fail badly on speech; and, as fidelity is so vital in regard to speech if talks and announcements and plays are to be heard clearly, no set should be purchased until the listener is satisfied that both male and female voices are dealt with faithfully.

The low notes of music, such as those which come from the rhythm sections of an orchestra, cannot be received with anything approaching complete fidelity on any set operating at a general volume level suitable for home listening. The acoustic power represented by the low notes, as compared with the high notes, is such that there is inevitably a rapid falling-off of the low notes at low-volume levels. A certain amount of compensation can be provided by a suitable tone control, but its usefulness is limited.

In any case, in any discussion regarding fidelity of reproduction the point must not be forgotten that the only true reproduction of an orchestra is to create an effect of that orchestra actually being in the room. This would be most uncomfortable for the listener!

The bass should be listened to critically, not so much for a complete rendering as for the existence of spurious booming caused by resonance effects. If these are not listened to critically they might seem pleasing, but there might be a quite serious form of distortion. In general, it is better to have a rather thin bass and good top notes than booming and poor high-note response.

POWER OUTPUT. The power output of a receiver is the amount of power that is available for operating the loudspeaker. It is limited by the valve or valves in the output stage. In other words, it does not matter how many valves there may be in a receiver, it cannot provide an output power greater than that of the final valve.

Others of the valves contribute amplification, but it is only the energy in the final anode circuit that can be communicated to the loudspeaker. The product of the anode current and voltage in this final anode circuit gives the anode dissipation, or power expended. But the figure that matters is the power that is available at the loudspeaker without undue distortion. This is usually about only a quarter of the total power expended.

Therefore, the significant figure in deciding the power output of a set is the total undistorted output. Half a watt is sufficient to work a loudspeaker quite well. But a greater power than that is needed if the low notes are to be heard satisfactorily, and if a fair amount of volume is to be available without distortion occurring.

For a room of average size, an undistorted output power of 3·5 watts is quite adequate for normal reception purposes, but pleasing results are obtainable on a lower power.

POWER SUPPLY. There are special circuits designed to provide an economical use of high-tension current on battery sets. One that is most effective is known as quiescent push-pull; a special valve, which is really two valves in one, is used in the output stage to provide relatively great volume for a minimum drain on the H.T. battery. Another method is known as Class-B amplification. There are also special economizer circuits, for use with ordinary valves, in which the anode current of the last valve is adjusted to suit the power that the output is called upon to give at any particular moment.

The current consumed by the cathodes of the valves is not so important; the difference of a fraction of an ampere is not likely to make it necessary to have the accumulator re-charged more often to any real degree, if it has a reasonable ampere-hour capacity.

But the difference of even milliamperes in the consumption of high-tension current may considerably shorten the life of an H.T. battery, which is a comparatively expensive article to replace. Therefore, in comparing the specifications of a number of battery sets, particular attention should be paid to the total high-tension current consumption.

The total power consumption of a mains set of average size is about that of one medium-sized electric-light bulb. So its cost to run will be no more than a small fraction of a penny per hour, and a difference of ten, or even twenty, watts is hardly worth considering.

It is important that a mains receiver should be suitable for the supply from which it is to be operated.

Most British sets for A.C. operation have adjustments rendering them suitable for mains of any voltage between 200 and 250. A.C. mains sets will not operate on D.C. supplies, and vice versa. But there are universal (A.C./D.C.) sets which will work on either.

INSTALLING A RADIO RECEIVER

EARTH. A great many modern sets will bring in programmes at good volume without the use of either an aerial or an earth. But all sets will work better if they are provided with them. Probably the earth connexion is the more important. It may be valuable not only for assisting stability in the functioning of the receiver, rendering tuning easier and reducing extraneous noises and mains hum, but in a mains set also for providing a measure of safety should anything go wrong with a component concerned with the power supply.

Gas pipes should *not* be used for earth connexions. The best earth is a plate or rod of metal buried two or three feet in the ground (Fig. 49). Connexion to it should be made by means of a thick flexible wire, which need not be insulated anywhere along its length except at the part near the set in case of an accidental contact with some live point. This ought not to be possible.

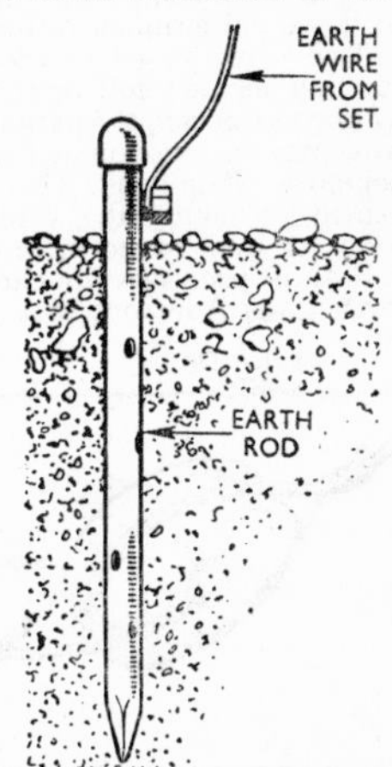

Fig. 49. A good earth.

Quite a good earth is given by a connexion to a main cold-water pipe (Fig. 50). The connexion is best made with a special earthing clip. The surface of the pipe should be scraped clean so as to ensure good contact.

AERIAL. An aerial suspended out of doors is to be recommended, wherever it is possible to fix one, if it is desired to obtain the maximum

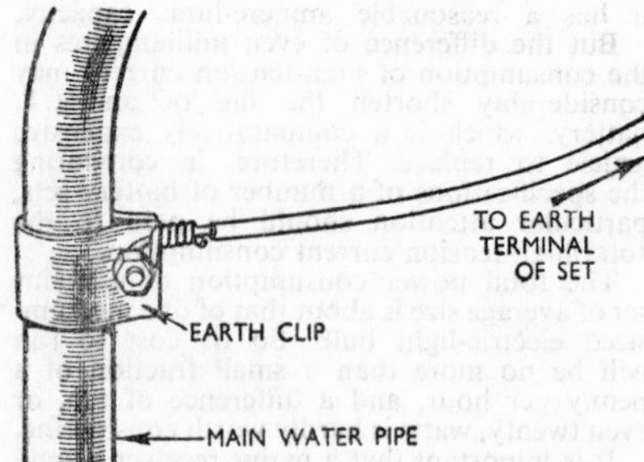

Fig. 50. Earthing to a cold-water pipe.

ranges of reception. The higher it is the better. It must be well insulated by means of insulators at each end (Fig. 51) and a lead-in insulator (Fig. 52) at the point of entry into the house. If it is allowed to come into contact with the branches of trees or walls, not only will there be loss of energy, but also, and especially in wet weather, crackles in the set may be caused.

The actual wire for the aerial need not be of the insulated type, but should be multi-stranded and flexible. It is advisable to have an unbroken length running, if possible, right to the aerial terminal of the set.

Two wires joined together at one end and running across a loft or roof space constitute a quite useful aerial. Alternatively, an insulated wire may be run round two sides of a room behind a picture rail. There is nothing to be gained in taking the wire right round the room, or even round three sides of it.

If it is necessary to carry the aerial and earth leads from one side of a room to the other, they must be kept well apart and not run as a twin cable in the manner of mains wiring. An aerial wire that is to be run along a wall should be insulated; for this rubber-covered wire can be employed.

There is very little danger of lightning dangerously affecting a receiver using an indoor aerial. It is seldom that any harm follows even the use of an out-of-doors aerial, but there have been cases of radio receivers being damaged by violent lightning discharges. However, there are many types of lightning arresters and switches, and it is as well to fix one between the aerial and the earth outside the house.

SITING THE SET. The position of a set in a room is a matter that should be seriously considered. For best listening it needs to be at a little distance from the listeners and placed so that its loudspeaker will be at about ear level, because the high notes come out somewhat directionally like the light from a lantern. It ought also to be in such a position that listeners can look at it without turning their heads right round, for many feel a strong urge to see a radio receiver or loudspeaker and do not listen comfortably if they cannot do so (Fig. 53).

POWER SUPPLY. A mains set ought not to be far away from a power point, as long flexible connexions are tiresome things to have straying round a room. There is an element of danger about them, too, especially if they are run so that they are frequently trodden upon. Flexible connexions from a receiver to a pendant light fitting are to be avoided. If a power point is to be especially fitted for a radio set, it can be of the lowest rating, as there will be comparatively little current. A 5-amp. point will be quite adequate. There need not be a switch and the set can be permanently plugged in; its own on-off switch will suffice.

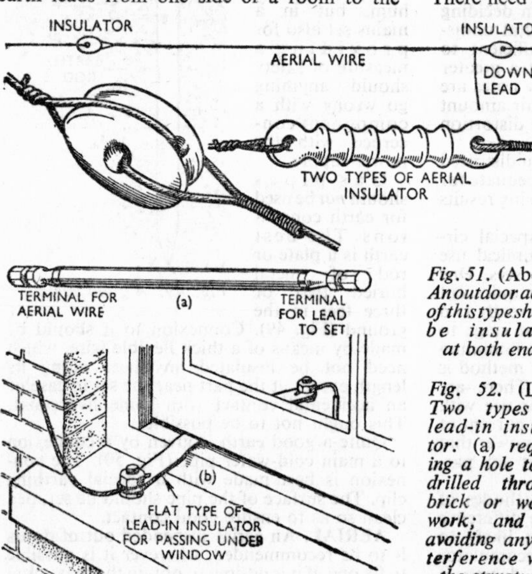

Fig. 51. (Above) *An outdoor aerial of this type should be insulated at both ends.*

Fig. 52. (Left) *Two types of lead-in insulator:* (a) *requiring a hole to be drilled through brick or woodwork; and* (b) *avoiding any interference with the structure.*

It does not matter which way round the plug of an A.C. receiver is inserted in the socket of a power point. But it matters very much in the case of a D.C. receiver, or of a receiver of the A.C./D.C. type connected to D.C. mains. Such sets cannot work at all unless the plug is inserted the right way round.

There is no means by which the ordinary listener can identify the correct way, except by practical test. The plug must be tried first the one way and then the other. As mains valves do not at once work, but require some time to warm up, the plug should be left in position for a full minute before the absence of any results is taken as proof that the plug needs to be reversed. Once the

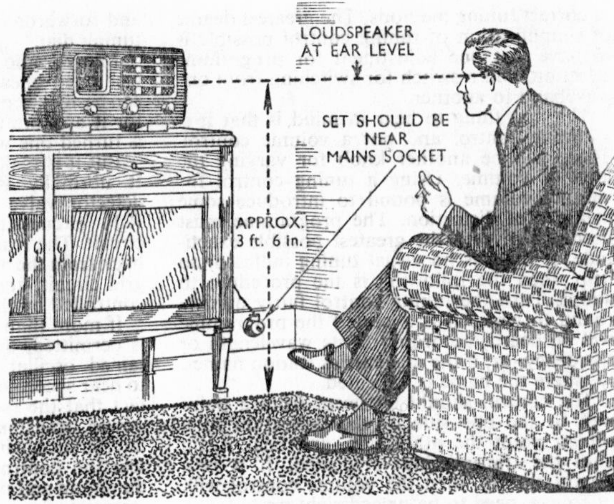

Fig. 53. Siting a set: some worth-while points to note.

correct way has been found, it is a good idea to mark the plug in some manner so that it is not necessary to indulge in the trial-and-error method every time the set is plugged in. It is most improbable that the polarity of the mains will ever be changed.

ADDITIONAL LOUDSPEAKERS. Extra loudspeakers can be fitted to any set, but if terminals or sockets are not provided for them it is necessary to adapt the interior wiring of the receiver. This, however, is a task which should be carried out only by an experienced wireless mechanic.

Loudspeakers have to be matched with the apparatus to which they are connected: this matching is frequently done by means of a special matching transformer, and some loudspeakers, designed to be used separately as

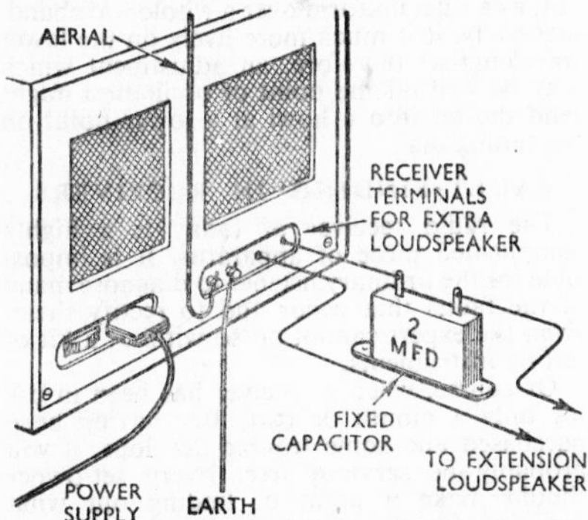

Fig. 54. Wiring for an additional loudspeaker

additional loudspeakers, have adjustable matching transformers permitting them to be suited to almost any receiver. From this it will be seen that it is quite useless to buy any loudspeaker for the purpose. A reputable radio dealer should be consulted.

Ordinary twin-flexible wire, such as is used for light pendants, is quite satisfactory for connecting extra loudspeakers. It can be run round the skirting or picture rail. But when it is to go to an adjoining room, it is always worth while exploring the possibilities of running it beneath the floorboards, rather than out of one room along a passage and through the door of the other room.

Wiring for extra loudspeakers must never go out-of-doors or into damp places unless special lead-covered wire is used. It is to be noted that a proportion of the anode voltage is across the wiring in some instances. If it is known that this is the case, and especially if the wiring is to cover any considerable distance, it will be as well to join a large fixed capacitor in series with that extra loudspeaker terminal which is positive (Fig. 54), so that the wiring is isolated from the anode current and only the low-frequency current passes through the extension wiring.

A switch can be fitted near the extra loudspeaker so that it can be switched on and off when desired (Fig. 55). The switch need be only of the single-pole type and is connected in the following manner: one terminal of the loudspeaker to one terminal of the switch, the other terminal of the switch to one of the extension wires. The other extension wire is joined to the remaining terminal of the loudspeaker. There is normally no economy effected in switching off the extra loudspeaker, because it is not causing any additional drain on the batteries or mains.

TUNING. The owner of a modern radio receiver may not appreciate the necessity for skill in tuning. But it is safe to say that with nine out of ten receivers the expert radio man will make more of it, merely by the way he handles the tuning controls, than will anyone who has not troubled to acquire some knowledge of the theory of tuning and experience

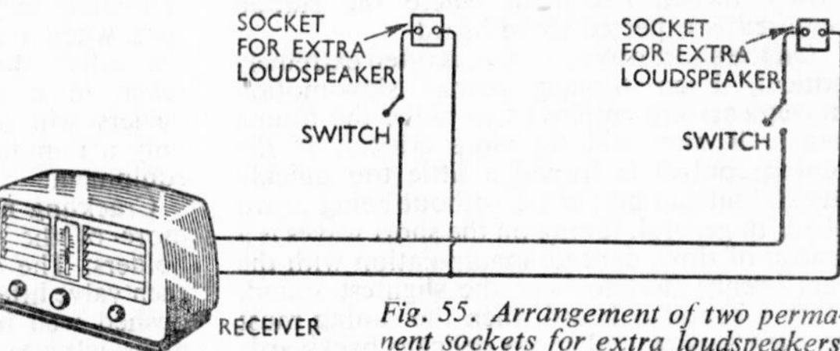

Fig. 55. Arrangement of two permanent sockets for extra loudspeakers.

in correct tuning methods. The greatest degree of simplification of tuning control possible is to have just one adjustment for programme selection, and a switch for switching from one waveband to another.

The first thing to bear in mind is that it is a tuning control and not a volume control. There will be another knob for varying the level of volume. Using a tuning control for varying volume is bound to introduce some measure of distortion. The programme must be tuned in with the greatest possible exactitude. If there is no visual tuning indicator to help, then the following is the procedure to adopt. Turn the tuning control fairly quickly round to where it is expected the programme will be heard, according to its wavelength or frequency, or, if the dial carries station names, to where the name is indicated.

The control should be swept from a point well to the one side of the indication to a similar point the other side, and back again until the transmission is located. If it is a distant station, then the volume control will, of course, need to be turned right up.

Having located the station, the movement of the control should be slowed right down and delicately manipulated, first to the one side and then to the other, making the movement smaller and smaller so that the station is overshot each way to a smaller and smaller extent. In this manner it is possible to find the central point of maximum reception with considerable accuracy. As the final position of the tuning is resolved, the volume level should simultaneously be lowered, for it is impossible to achieve that dead-centre tuning when the loudspeaker is operating loudly.

There are still many sets in use which have a reaction control. If there are also two tuning controls, a great measure of skill is required to tune a programme in quickly and correctly. It is first necessary to learn how the two tuning controls operate. There may be one control for quickly tuning from one part of a waveband to another, the other control merely being a fine adjustment.

Two controls of such a nature are easy to handle, for they do not require to be operated simultaneously. But if each is concerned with its own tuning circuit, then the use of both hands at once will be required. Now, it is almost certain that the tuning on one dial will be more critical than on the other. This is the one on which to concentrate with the one hand, while the other hand continuously turns the other knob or dial slightly backwards and forwards, but always advancing it to keep roughly in step with the other dial as that is slowly turned round to where the station required is expected to be heard.

On the short waves, tuning is often extremely critical. Even though geared slow-motion movements are employed to make the tuning easier, it may still be most critical. If the tuning control is turned a little too quickly the station can be passed without being heard at all. In general, tuning on the short waves is a matter of slow, delicate manipulation with the ears keenly alert to hear the slightest sound. Once a sound is heard, then the tuning must be even slower and more delicate backwards and forwards over that particular part of the tuning dial.

Many radio receivers, mostly rather old-fashioned ones, have a reaction control. This can easily be confused with the volume control, for it appears to increase the volume when it is turned one way or another.

But it is really more of a sensitivity control. It normally works in conjunction with a detector valve in a receiver having a tuned R.F. circuit instead of a super-heterodyne circuit. The reaction arrangement feeds energy back from the anode of the detector valve to its grid circuit, and the degree of feeding back is controlled by the reaction knob.

If more than a certain amount of feed-back is permitted, the receiver will break into sustained oscillation and it will be impossible to hear speech or music. More important is the fact that the receiver is then acting as a low-power transmitter and may cause serious interference with neighbouring listeners. The reaction control should always be turned to minimum and never used unless it is absolutely essential, for any degree of reaction is liable to introduce distortion.

When the reaction control is advanced to bring up the strength of a programme, it should be turned back before tuning the set to another programme. A reaction control is not, as a rule, uniform over a whole waveband. Generally, it is much more lively on the lower wavelengths; therefore, an adjustment which may be well off the point of oscillation might send the set into a howl at a lower point on the tuning dial.

FAULT-FINDING IN RECEIVERS

The radio receiver of today is a highly complicated piece of apparatus. It is impossible for the ordinary listener to diagnose many of the faults that occur and to rectify them. Even the expert cannot do so without a kit of testing instruments.

Of course, when a receiver has been in use for only a month or two after having been purchased and some trouble develops, it will probably be serviced free. Every set-owner should make a point of finding out what servicing facilities are available for his particular model.

VALVE TROUBLES. There are troubles, however, which are extremely easy to put right. Should the receiver have been working for a long time quite satisfactorily and then its sensitivity gradually begins to fall until even the strongest transmissions are hard to tune in at reasonable volume, the valves can be suspected. Radio valves have long lives, but ultimately they are bound to wear out. Therefore, when a set fails in the manner described, the valves should be carefully removed and taken to a local dealer for testing. Most dealers will do so without charge; it takes only a minute or two, using the appropriate equipment.

Crackling noises may be caused by one or more of the valves becoming loose in their holders. The set should be switched off and each valve lifted up and down slightly and then pushed well into position. The lifting movement will clean the contacts between the valve

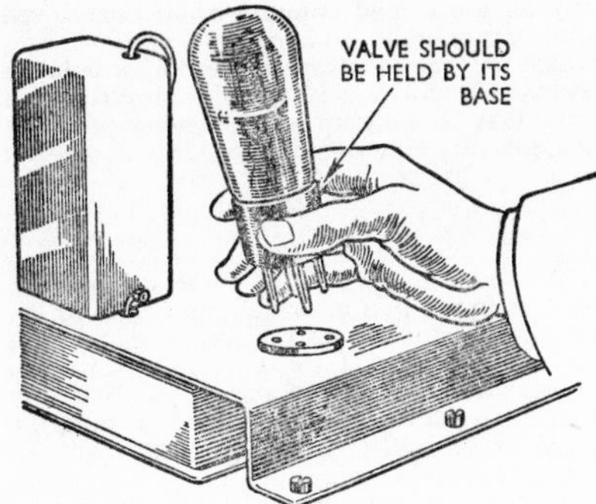

Fig. 56. Correct way of removing a valve.

pins and their sockets (Fig. 56). Should one of the valves appear to fit loosely, take it out and carefully open up the pins slightly with the point of a penknife. The banana type of pin bulges a little in the centre where there are narrow slits, and it is in these slits that the knife should be inserted (Fig. 57). But they must not be opened more than a very little, or the valve may be difficult to replace. Incidentally, it will be noticed that each valve is located either by a special projection in the

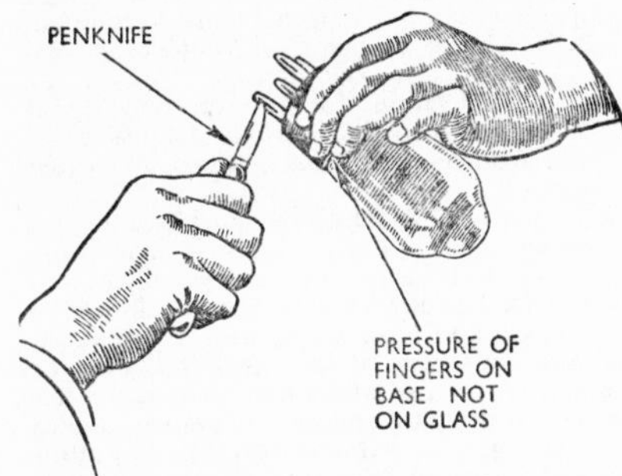

Fig. 57. Widening valve pin to improve contact.

holder or by the pins not being symmetrically arranged; this is to ensure that it cannot be inserted in any other than the correct way. A valve must be pulled out by gripping its base, not by its bulb, otherwise the bulb may be loosened.

Nothing in the interior of either a battery or a mains set should be touched unless the power supply is entirely removed. The batteries must all be completely disconnected, or the mains plug pulled out of its socket. Many valves have been burnt out by listeners removing them or putting them in without taking the precaution of disconnecting all the batteries. Listeners have killed themselves by meddling with the interiors of plugged-in mains sets. The vital things to bear in mind are that a voltage of over four hundred may exist inside a mains set (200 volts can prove fatal), and that faults can, and indeed often do, exist in switches. Safety can be assured only by entirely removing the set from all possible connexions with the mains.

Sometimes loud crackles are due to outside causes. They may be atmospherics when thundery conditions prevail; or there may be some fault in the mains, perhaps there is a sparking in a nearby switch. But if there has previously been no interference, and yet the crackling continues day after day, it is fairly certain that there is something wrong with the receiving apparatus.

It might be a loose contact that can easily be traced. Gentle tugs on the mains leads (or battery leads in the case of a battery set), or the aerial and earth leads to the set, may indicate where the fault lies.

If the set goes absolutely dead, the valves should be inspected to see whether or not they are lighted. If they all appear to be extinguished, then clearly there is an interruption to the power supply, unless, which is not probable, they have all been burnt out. Do not expect to see even a faint glimmer of light from every valve. Some of them may be metal-coated so that nothing can be seen of their interiors.

FUSES. Listeners sometimes forget that the fuse in a circuit serving a point to which a radio receiver is connected may burn out through a fault in some other appliance in the same circuit. There might be, for example, a refrigerator sharing the same fuse. Therefore, it will be as well to test the power point by plugging in a table lamp or vacuum cleaner.

If the fuse has been burnt out, there is, of course, the possibility that some fault in the set has caused it. Replacing the fuse and again plugging in the receiver will soon show whether or not this is the case.

The break in the power supply might be due to a fuse going in the receiver, for many are fitted with these safety devices. But it is not likely to be a mere matter of replacing the fuse, for the fact that it has gone is fair evidence that a serious trouble has developed inside the set which only a trained serviceman can rectify.

FAULTY CONNEXIONS. These are one of the greatest sources of radio failure. Where a wire has to be connected to another wire or to a terminal, or where a pin has to go into

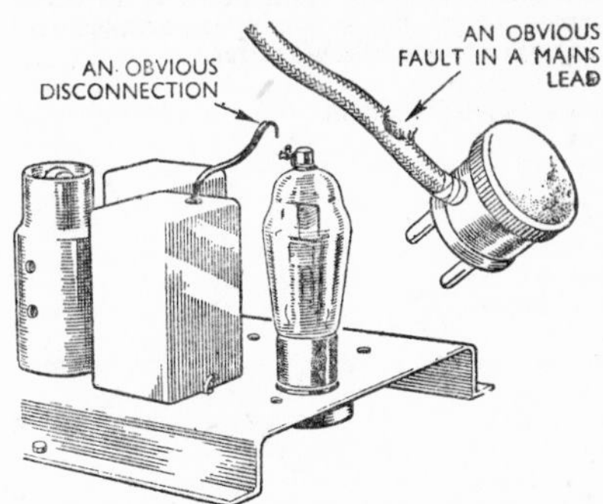

Fig. 58. Some wiring faults to repair.

some socket, it is imperative that there should be a firm pressure between the two surfaces and that those surfaces should be clean. Even the man who has no knowledge of mechanical or electrical matters can at least inspect the connexions of a radio set to see if there are any obviously bad connexions. He may even spot an entirely broken connexion—a wire which has parted company from a terminal to which it ought clearly to be connected, or a wire that is hanging loose instead of being soldered to some point (Fig. 58).

TELEVISION IN THE HOME

An ordinary radio receiver of even the cheapest kind will provide some programmes almost anywhere that it may be installed. Moreover, it will probably work quite well with only a short length of wire slung up in the room for an aerial; perhaps it will give good results with no aerial at all.

Television is more exacting in its conditions for good reception. So much so that it is far from being a matter of buying a receiver and expecting good reception as a matter of course. However, within forty to fifty miles of a television station satisfactory results ought to be forthcoming provided the instrument is properly installed. A special aerial and lead-in are needed.

AERIAL REQUIREMENTS. The aerial is usually of the dipole type, with a reflector and a special matching feeder cable to connect the aerial to the receiver. Usually a receiver is designed for a feeder having certain electrical characteristics. It is necessary to have the aerial arrangement fixed at a good height, and a suitable place is on the roof of a house. Often it is mounted on a chimney stack.

The aerial should point in the direction of the transmitting station, with the reflector (if one is used) behind the aerial (Fig. 59). Its erection is a job for an expert and is not one that the amateur should undertake lightly.

There is, alternatively, the compressed dipole which occupies smaller space and can be fitted up in the roof space of a house quite easily. But it is not as efficient as the other types, and is not to be recommended except in the areas where the television programmes are strongly received.

Incidentally, as television sets are improved it will undoubtedly be found that more and more people will get quite good results by using normal types of aerial of low efficiency. In the meantime, it is safer to work on the principle that a television outfit is no better than its aerial, and to employ the arrangement suggested by the manufacturer.

On the other hand, in some instances it may be found that an installation close to the transmitter receives too strong a signal. But the method of dealing with this is not to reduce the efficiency of the aerial itself. An attenuating device should be fixed between the aerial feeder and the receiver. This results in very good, stable reception.

Severe interference can often be reduced by changing the position of the aerial, or by pointing it in a different direction. The use of a reflector is frequently helpful, and also tends to reduce a curious effect of ghost images that is sometimes troublesome. These are duplicate pictures which are seen on the screen somewhat to the right. If the effect is not very serious, there may be only a blurring of the picture. It is caused by the reception of waves that are reflected from buildings or hills. Obviously, as such reflected waves travel farther than those received direct from the transmitter, they arrive a little later. Fortunately, the receiving aerial, especially if it is equipped with a reflector, is highly directional. That is why it is possible to make it discriminate against the reflected waves by altering its position. In the same way it can often be made to discriminate against interference from electric trains, trams and other sources.

CHOOSING A RECEIVER. There are yet to come many developments in television. The present transmissions are excellent, but the science has already advanced to the extent that bigger and brighter pictures are possible. But the definition, at any rate, is limited by the system of transmission. It is not possible for the B.B.C. to change its system in any material manner without completely putting out of action all television receivers now in use. Therefore, before any drastic change could be made it would obviously be necessary for the B.B.C. to give viewers a fairly long notice that this was to be done. The radio industry would have to have even longer notice. Probably it would never be done at all without the approval of the industry.

Nevertheless, a television outfit is expensive and the prospective purchaser might well ask for some information as to how he might stand in the event of any serious alteration in

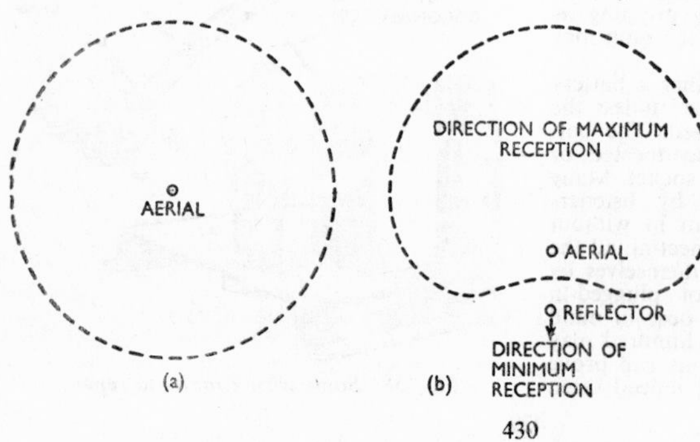

Fig. 59. Television aerials: (a) *without a reflector reception is equally strong from any direction;* (b) *effect of using a reflector.*

Fig. 60. Television faults: "plastic" effect.

the system of transmission likely to affect the instrument's usefulness. Then he ought also to ascertain whether or not good servicing facilities will be available to him.

It is not difficult to choose a television receiver. There are not scores of different makes, as there are with the ordinary sound-receiving apparatus. And there is a fair guide as to the resources behind the maker of a particular model in the proportion of components that that firm has itself manufactured.

Between one good receiver and another there will, however, be differences which the buyer will require to consider. If the controls on one are not quite so accessible or simple as those on another, perhaps the picture is slightly larger, or the instrument may be more compact or of superior appearance. One may have rather more brilliance in its picture, another may approximate nearer to a true black and white.

The technical efficiency of the equipment cannot be judged by any but the expert; to do so, he would require to have it under examination in controlled conditions. But it will probably be helpful to the prospective purchaser if he can recognize some of the symptoms of faults in design and, later, to have knowledge of the troubles that are liable to develop in the best of receivers.

As has been explained previously, a television receiver is really two sets in one, for the sound and vision are transmitted separately on different wavelengths. The sound-receiving part of the apparatus is normal, except that it is designed for the reception of the ultra-short waves. It is useful to have a television outfit that is capable of being used for sound alone on the higher wavelengths. It is then able to receive ordinary broadcasting.

FAULTY RECEPTION. Although the sound and vision come through on different radio channels, some of the parts of the outfit will be shared by both sections of the apparatus. For example, the power may be derived from a common mains unit. The quality of the sound ought to be at least as good as, if not superior to, that provided by normal broadcasting. If it does not appear to be particularly good, then it would seem probable either that there is a fault in the receiver or its installation, or that its design is sub-standard.

Phase distortion. Sometimes a television picture is outlined in duplicate, giving it what is called a "plastic" effect. The outlines of objects appear to be traced round by white lines (Fig. 60), an effect which is more noticeable when the picture is one of sharp contrasts.

The effect is usually due to phase distortion and is caused by unwanted electrical qualities in the receiver. It is not usually a trouble that develops so much as one that is present in a receiver embodying an inherent fault of design and construction. It is to be noted that it is a different trouble from the duplicate pictures that can be caused by reflected waves.

Insufficient frequency response. An ordinary broadcast receiver needs to give a response of only from 50 to 8,000 or so cycles per second for its results to appear very good. But a television amplifier has to respond to a range of from about 40 to 2,000,000 cycles per second in order that a clear picture may be obtained. If the lower frequencies are not dealt with adequately, the picture will show strips of greyness where there ought to be long patches of black. Poor high-note response results in a lack of detail.

Fault in smoothing. The visual equivalent to the hum that interferes with speech and music when there is a fault in the smoothing circuit, or for some other reason, is for the picture to be wavy (Fig. 61). This can be seen

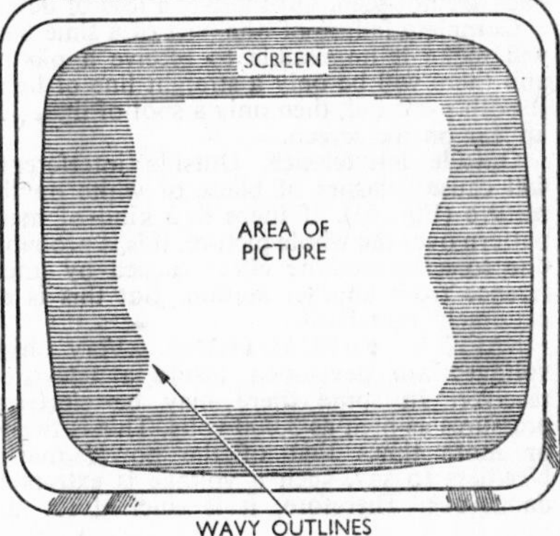

Fig. 61. Television faults: defect in smoothing.

when no picture is being received; the illuminated part of the screen of the cathode-ray tube will have wavy edges instead of being straight and square and there will probably also be black bands running across the screen (Fig. 62).

Faulty deflector setting. If the raster, as this illuminated part of the screen is called, is over to one side, or is nearer to the top or the bottom than it should be, the setting of one or other of the deflectors is faulty.

Time-base faults. White splashes on the picture are sometimes caused by a fault in the time base. Under-modulation gives a very weak picture, and over-modulation produces heavy blacks and poor detail.

One of the most common faults encountered in at least some of the earlier television receivers was incorrect interlacing. If the

Fig. 62. Another sign of imperfect smoothing.

picture is closely inspected it will be seen that the successive scanning does not pair the lines properly. Instead of the second set falling exactly in the spaces left by the first set, they tend to run on the same position.

At any distance, however, the individual lines are not seen, but there is a loss of detail.

Complete failure of one part of a time base will make it impossible to receive a picture and there will be only a straight line of light. If both parts fail, then only a spot of light will appear on the screen.

Outside interference. Outside interference will cause splashes of black or white on the picture (Fig. 63). If there is a kind of mesh pattern over the whole picture, this is probably due to a heterodyne effect caused by interference from another station. But this is an extremely rare fault.

SAFETY PRECAUTIONS. Very high voltages are developed inside a television receiver. In some there may be electrical pressures as high as 3,000 volts. This is twelve or more times that of the power mains. Needless to say, such a voltage is extremely dangerous. Therefore, it is suicidal for the owner to delve into the interior of a television set while it is connected to the mains; though it must be added that in most modern receivers the components and wiring where high voltages occur are well covered with earthed metal shielding and are not easily accessible.

Fig. 63. Television faults: outside interference.

When a television receiver is used normally, it is perfectly safe, and the high voltages are not, and cannot be, communicated to any of the exterior parts of the instrument.

REPLACEMENTS. As with ordinary broadcast receivers, the valves will in due course wear out and need replacement. Also the cathode-ray tube will eventually require to be replaced. But before this stage is reached the receiver should have given many months, if not years, of trouble-free service.

A typical television receiver has eighteen valves. Three are employed for the power supply and four for the time base; the sound-receiver section has four and the vision section seven.

RECEIVER CONTROLS. A number of the controls are at the back because, once set by the engineer installing the receiver, they seldom require further adjustment. These controls regulate the width and height of the picture and its synchronization. On the front are controls for sound volume, picture focus, brilliance and contrast.

Fig. 64. Television faults: wrong setting of Brightness control.

Focusing affects the definition just as focusing affects the definition of a picture taken by a camera.

Contrast is the range of tone covered from black to white (Fig. 64). It is governed by two factors—the strength of the television waves and the amplification of the receiver. Therefore, the contrast control is rather similar to the volume control on a sound receiver.

By adjusting the contrast control correctly, just the right range of "full black" to "full white" with correct intermediate tones is obtained. The increase of brilliance without a proper adjustment of contrast is not a sufficient compensation for poor tone values.

CARE OF CARS AND CYCLES

Instructions for maintenance and repairs which can be carried out by every car and cycle owner

Part 1 deals with motor-cars under the main subdivisions of the engine, transmission system, suspension and tyres, steering and brakes, electrical equipment, and the body, in that order. Parts 2 (pages 451-7) and 3 (pages 457-8) deal with bicycles and motor-cycles respectively, and are subdivided for ready reference.

1. CARE OF THE CAR

THE ENGINE

The operational life of a motor-car engine, between overhauls entailing the replacement or reconditioning of worn parts, can be lengthened by proper maintenance. To be effective, however, this must be systematic.

Regular maintenance following a routine will prove most successful, and will, on the whole, entail less time and trouble than spasmodic attention. It will, at the same time, keep the engine working at its highest possible efficiency and save many a small repair bill.

MAINTENANCE ROUTINE. The following is a suggested plan for the routine maintenance of a petrol engine (Fig. 1):

Daily (or whenever the car is used if less frequently). Check level of engine oil; top up if required. Check level of water in the radiator; top up if required.

Every week. Check level of electrolyte in the battery; top up with distilled water if the plates are not completely covered.

Every month. If the car has an Autovac unit, drain off sediment. Check over all high-tension leads for cracks in the insulation and make sure all terminals are tight. Check gaskets for signs of leakage, particularly the cylinder-head gasket.

Every 1,000 miles. Drain all engine oil from the sump. On engines where an oil filter of the gauze type is accessible this should be removed, washed clean in petrol, allowed to dry off and then replaced. Refill the sump to the correct level with new lubricant of the type and grade recommended by the manufacturers of the engine for the time of year.

Remove the sparking plugs, clean them and inspect the condition of the insulators. Check

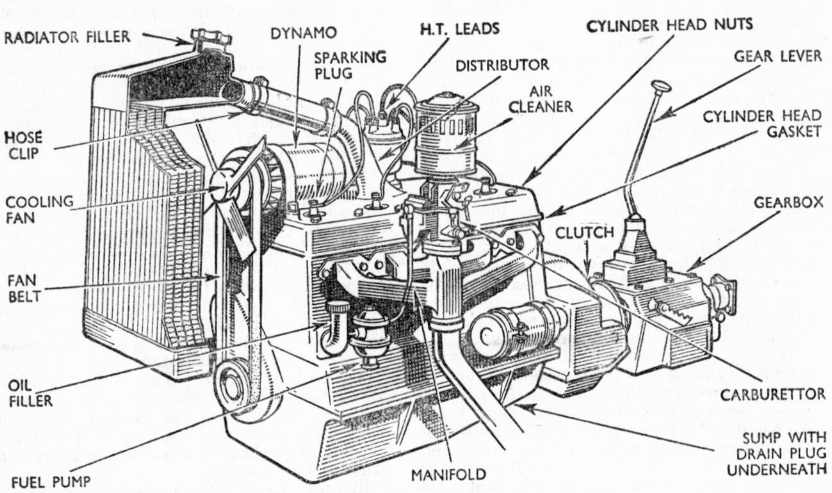

Fig. 1. Four-cylinder engine, showing many of the points requiring particular attention.

the gap between the electrodes and adjust it, if necessary, before replacing each plug. Check over all cylinder-head holding-down nuts for tightness.

Inspect the distributor or magneto contact-breaker points for condition; also check the breaking gap and adjust it if necessary.

If the air-cleaner is of the "concertina" type, this should be freed of the dust it has collected.

Clean out the carburettor, jets and any filters in the fuel system, including that of an Autovac unit if fitted. Lubricate the accelerator and choke-control linkages with thin oil. Make sure that the controls return fully to their stops on the carburettor when not in use.

Every 2,500 miles. Drain off sediment from fuel pump, and take out and clean the gauze screen or filter of the pump.

Check the clearance of all valves with the engine warm, and reset any incorrect clearances to those recommended by the engine manufacturers.

Inject high-melting-point grease into the water-pump lubricator, unless of the greaseless type.

If the distributor or magneto unit has an oiling hole or oil cup fitted, give three or four drops of engine oil. Where provision is made for lubricating the dynamo and fan bearings, give them four to six drops of engine oil. Tighten, if necessary, belts driving the fan, the dynamo and water pump. Make sure that the dynamo is quite secure. Check that the starter motor is secure.

If the air cleaner is of other than the "concertina," or dry, type, clean the gauze or element and re-oil it.

Every six months. Drain, flush out thoroughly and refill the cooling system. If this is done at the end of October and the end of April each year, the flushing-out operation will conveniently coincide with the changes-over to and from the use of anti-freeze solution.

Check over all nuts and bolts which hold the engine in place.

In the notes that follow, many of the jobs so far given but brief mention are more fully described, and several useful hints are included so that time spent on the engine of the car may be employed to the best advantage.

LUBRICATION. To take a reading of the engine-oil level, first withdraw the dipstick and wipe it with a *clean* rag. Insert the dipstick and push it in as far as it will go; then draw it out again and note the level of the oil. While there is no point in adding lubricant to the sump so that the oil-level is above the "full" mark on the dipstick (this is merely wasteful), it is essential never to allow the level to descend beyond the lower limit of the safe-driving range, or below the line marked "Low" or "Danger," or "D" on some dipsticks.

Incidentally, excessive oil consumption—usually signified by blue clouds from the exhaust pipe when the engine is revved-up—means worn cylinder bores and piston rings. An engine which is in good condition will not require much oil added to it during a thousand miles of running, but by the time this mileage figure is reached the best of lubricants will have deteriorated and should be replaced.

To drain the sump. Choose a time when the engine is warm from a run; or else let the engine run for five minutes or so to warm the oil up thoroughly. Then make sure that the car is standing on level ground, and have a suitable receptacle close at hand in which to collect the old oil. Next remove the sump drain plug and allow the oil to drain out until it drips only occasionally. The longer it is left to drain the better. After making sure the plug is right home and will not leak, fill up with fresh oil to the correct level on the dipstick.

On every third occasion of draining the sump it is as well to clean the engine out with a flushing oil. After draining old oil away, replace the sump plug and pour a quart or more of the flush (according to size of engine) into the oil filler. Then run the engine slowly, but a little above tick-over speed, for about four minutes. Switch off and allow all the flushing oil to drain out before filling up with new lubricant. *Never* use paraffin oil as a flushing medium. Oil filters of the cartridge type should be renewed after every ten thousand miles of running.

COOLING SYSTEM. Always use clean water when topping up the radiator, and soft water in preference to hard or chalky water. If more than an occasional topping-up is necessary it will be as well to examine the system for leaks. These may occur at the ends of hoses and can often be stopped by tightening up the hose clip. Make sure the drain taps on the radiator and cylinder block are properly turned off.

If a water pump is fitted, the point at which the drive spindle enters may be a source of leakage, and the glands may need adjusting or renewal. If the radiator itself is leaking, a slow dripping can often be sealed by using a tin of one of the special preparations which, when poured into the system, form a sort of crust over such a leak and stop it up.

If it appears to be leaky in several places, or runs fairly fast from a particular point, the radiator should be sent away for repair and testing by a specialist, particularly if anti-freeze solution is likely to be employed. An anti-freeze mixture is far more searching than water and may show up other weaknesses in the radiator. Furthermore, continual topping-up with water will soon reduce the solution's effectiveness against frost.

When the cooling system contains water only, and the car is likely to stand for several hours in frosty weather, the system should, of course, be drained. But never simply turn the radiator drain tap and walk away; stay to see that the water is *all* drained out. It often happens that when the water has run for a few seconds a particle of rust will reach the tap and block it. This must be moved with a piece of wire if the draining is to be complete.

There may be, in addition to the radiator tap, a cock at the base of the cylinder block. Make sure whether the engine in question has one, for draining the radiator does not necessarily drain the whole system and the freezing of pockets of water in the block can cause serious damage.

In order to rid the radiator and cylinder-block cooling jacket of a good deal of rust and sediment liable to cause blockages it is good practice to flush out the system thoroughly at least twice a year. Whether or not a special preparation is purchased to assist in this cleaning, a length of garden hose should be used, and water from the main allowed to run through the system for about fifteen minutes.

BATTERY. Normally, the only attention required is topping-up the cells with distilled water to maintain the level of the electrolyte at about ¼ in. above the top of the separators. Distilled water for this purpose should be stored in a clean glass or china container and kept covered. If the weather is very cold, top up the battery only while the engine is running, or is about to be run, at a rate sufficient to provide charging from the dynamo. This will ensure prompt mixing of the newly added water with the electrolyte and thus avoid freezing.

Only if there has been a leak from the battery should it be necessary to add acid. To ascertain the state of a battery, a hydrometer (Fig. 2) should be used to measure the

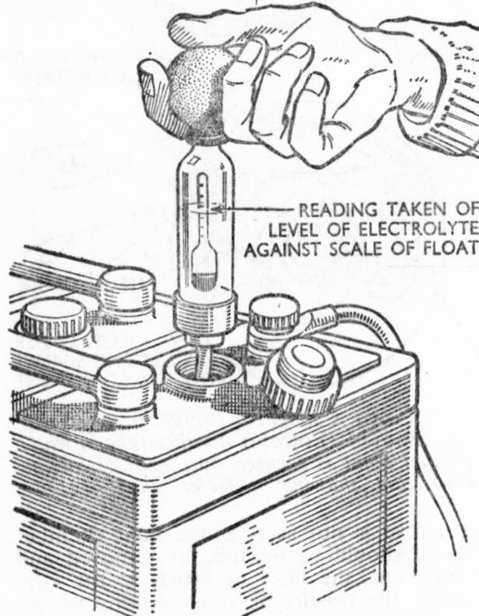

Fig. 2. Measuring the specific gravity of a battery by means of a hydrometer.

specific gravity of the electrolyte in each cell. A fully charged cell will give a reading of between 1·27 and 1·29, and a completely discharged cell one of 1·15. The hydrometer reading will not be reliable, however, if recently added water has not had an opportunity of mixing well with the electrolyte.

The battery should never be allowed to stand in a discharged condition; and if it soon loses its charge without current being taken from it, this is usually due to the plates being faulty, new plates or a complete new battery then being necessary.

Keep the filler plugs and terminals tight and the top of the battery clean. A little ammonia, applied with a rag, will counteract the effect of acid on the outside of the battery case. The battery should always be clamped firmly in its place on the car.

The terminals must be cleaned should any sign of verdigris appear on them; a film of petroleum jelly should be smeared over them to protect them from corrosion.

SPARKING PLUGS. These play a vital part in the petrol engine, and their condition has a marked effect upon the performance of

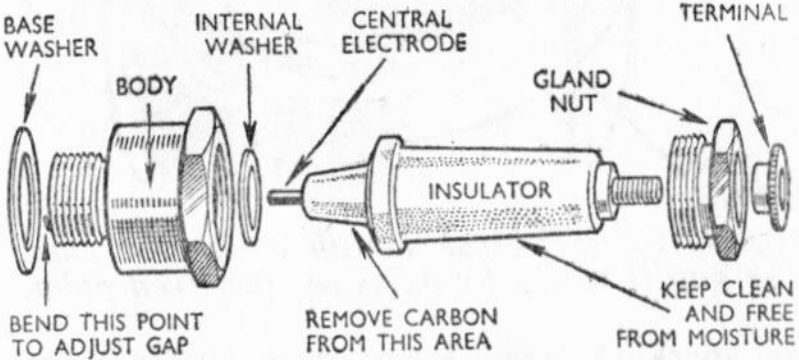

Fig. 3. A sparking plug dismantled for cleaning of the porcelain insulator with a petrol rag.

the car. Such troubles as misfiring and difficult starting can often be brought about by dirty plugs or incorrect spark gaps. Plugs should, therefore, be removed periodically. The points may easily be cleaned (before checking the gap) by brushing with a fine wire brush, care being taken not to scratch the insulation.

Detachable plugs should be taken apart so that the centre is withdrawn from the body (Fig. 3), thus allowing the insulator to be wiped clean with a petrol rag. The non-detachable type of plug does not provide easy access to the insulator, but if the carbon deposit appears to be considerable and cannot be easily removed, the set of plugs can be cleaned and tested in one of the special machines installed at many garages.

The gap between the electrodes should be checked with a feeler gauge and adjusted, if incorrect, by bending the earthed electrode, that is, the point or points on the outside of the plug, nearer to, or farther away from, the centre electrode. The correct gap is that specified by the car or plug manufacturers for the particular engine in which it is to operate. Recommended gaps are mostly between 0·018 in. and 0·030 in., and usually about 0·020 in.

When replacing plugs in the cylinder head, all washers which are no longer compressible should, for preference, be renewed. Check over the sparking-plug leads for cracking of the rubber insulation and for weakening of the wire strands near the terminal spades, and renew leads in which these faults occur.

CONTACT-BREAKER. This is another member of the ignition circuit which pays a good reward for systematic attention. The contact-breaker mechanism is disclosed by the removal of an end-cover in the usual types of magneto, and by removal of a distributor side-plate or, more often, the distributor head in coil ignition systems (Fig. 4).

It is important that the breaker points should have their meeting surfaces smooth and flat so that they connect squarely and make a good all-over contact with each other.

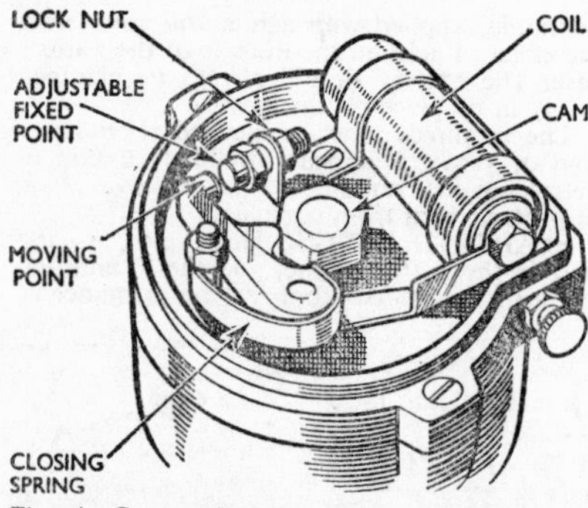

Fig. 4. Contact-breaker with a six-lobe cam. The gap is varied by adjusting the fixed point.

As sparking takes place these surfaces are liable to become pitted and dirty; the points should be removed and cleaned by rubbing with a flat carborundum slip or on an oilstone until no sign of pitting remains; a file should *not* be used. Be careful to clean away dust or oil resulting from this operation before the points are replaced. If the points are badly burnt it is advisable to have the condenser tested.

Attention must now be paid to the gapping of the points. This is specified by the car manufacturers and should be adhered to strictly as it affects, among other things, the timing of the sparks at the plugs. Recommended gaps for coil systems are usually between 0·010 in. and 0·015 in., though some are up to 0·020 in. for magnetos.

The gap is set by turning the engine (slowly with the starting handle) until the cam has forced the movable contact fully open. Now insert a feeler of the thickness of the gap required, loosen the locking device of the fixed contact and move it until the correct gap is obtained (Fig. 5). Tighten up the locking device and then, after bringing another cam lobe round into operation, check the gap again. A thin film of petroleum jelly may be imparted to the cam lobes to reduce wear; but always be careful to see that no grease, oil or moisture gets near the breaker points.

Before turning attention to another part of the engine, it is as well to see that the H.T. pick-up brush is making proper contact with the distributor rotor and that there is no evidence that the rotor is burning away.

CARBURETTOR. As a rule there is little that can actually wear out or get out of adjustment on the modern carburettor. Almost the only thing likely to cause faulty carburation, unless the carburettor is tampered with, is the presence of dirt and water which are apt to accumulate when gallon after gallon of petrol passes through it.

To keep down to a minimum the possibility of blocked jets, and of flooding because the

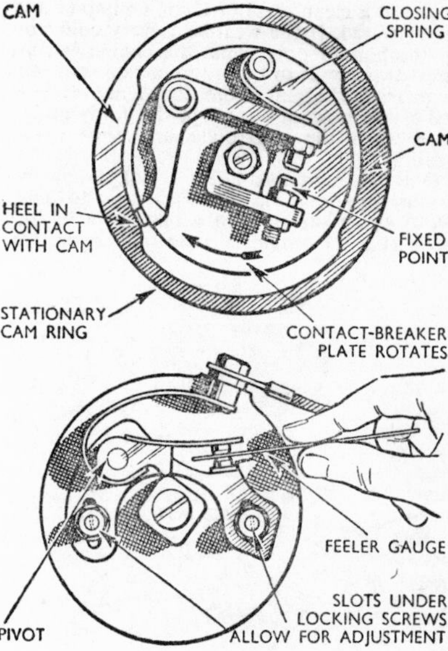

Fig. 5. (Top) *A magneto contact-breaker with cover removed.* (Bottom) *Another type in which the fixed point is secured by means of locking screws and showing a feeler gauge in use.*

inlet valve is not seating, the float chamber (Fig. 6) should be periodically removed and cleaned out, the filter (if fitted) at the inlet cleaned, the needle, or valve, seating wiped, and the float shaken to see whether it has allowed any petrol to leak into it. If so, the leak will be located and contents evaporated by immersion of the float in very hot water.

Jets should be removed occasionally and blown through strongly in each direction with a tyre inflator to make sure of removing any foreign body. Wire, unless very thin and soft, should not be pushed through a jet, as this may damage the bore or tend to make the hole slightly larger, the latter often entirely upsetting

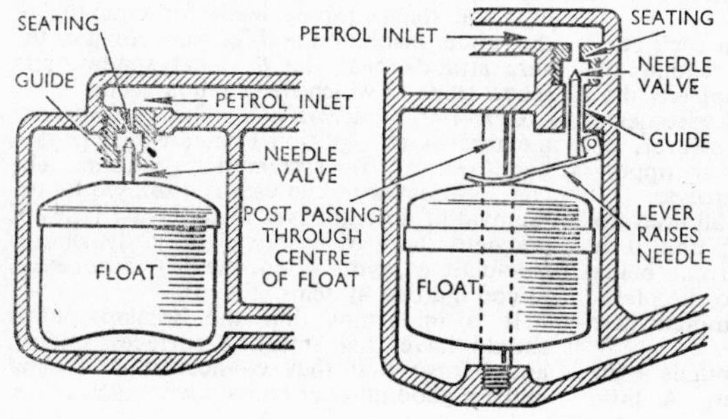

Fig. 6. Two common float-chamber arrangements in carburettors.

the operational balance of the carburettor. All internal passages in the carburettor should be cleaned out and traces of sediment removed from jet wells.

There are so many different types of carburettor, precision-made to give economy, rapid acceleration and/or high speed according to the design of car in question, that no generalizations here would be of value in re-tuning the unit. If flat-spots, too rich a mixture, or too weak a mixture become apparent, and cannot be accounted for by the discovery of such things as a blocked pilot or progressive jet, a choked air cleaner, or an air leak, respectively, it may be felt that an alteration to the jets or other adjustment is desirable. In this event, obtaining advice from a carburettor expert or from the manufacturers is the only course that can be recommended.

Changes in the condition of the engine and also sudden changes in air temperature sometimes affect the slow-running of an engine. Adjustment for this is provided on all carburettors, but getting it right is usually a matter of trial and error.

Generally, the air bleed should first be fully closed and then opened a very little. The petrol jet (often governed by a throttle-stop adjustment) is then opened until slow-running of a kind is achieved, though this may be very "bumpy." By next opening the air bleed very gradually, a setting should be reached when the engine fires fairly evenly. Usually the correct slow-running speed of a small four-cylinder engine is much higher than that of a larger unit. The adjustment should always be made with the engine well warmed up.

AIR CLEANER. This requires periodical attention if it is to perform effectively its function of extracting a high percentage of dust and other abrasive particles from the air drawn into the engine. The frequency with which attention is paid to it depends largely upon the conditions in which the car is used, for obviously the motorist who continually travels along gravelly or chalky lanes collects more dust than does one whose mileage is done almost entirely on main roads.

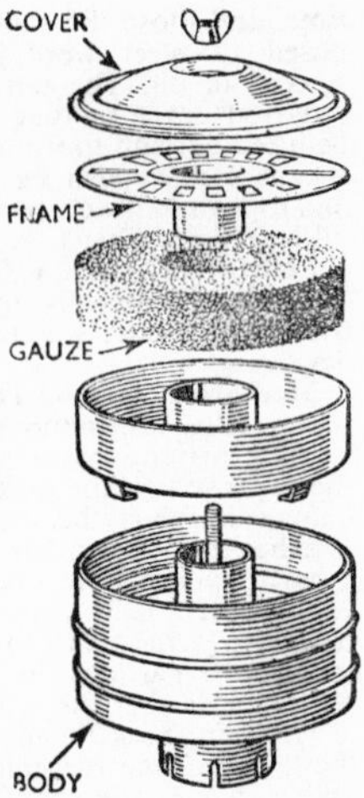

Fig. 7. Parts of a dismantled gauze-type air cleaner.

A "concertina" type of cleaner should be cleared every thousand miles or less, by releasing the lid from its catches and then steadily alternately compressing and expanding the concertina element until no more dirt appears to be expelled from it; no oil must be introduced into this kind of filter. Replace the lid so that it is held by the catches.

The gauze type of filter (Fig. 7) should be effective for at least three thousand miles. By removing the cover-securing nut, the cover and the frame, the gauze may be withdrawn and washed clean in petrol. When dry the gauze should be dipped in clean engine oil and replaced. When reassembling the cleaner, make certain that the solid portion of the frame is towards the *front* of the engine.

Other types of filter include those which require renewal of an insert from time to

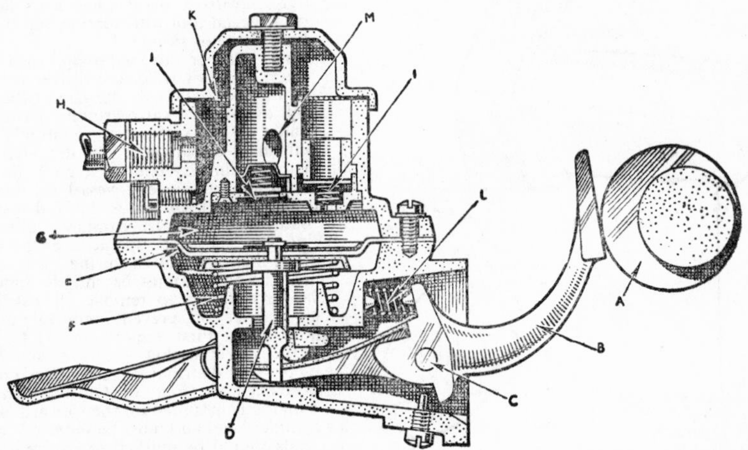

Fig. 8. Mechanically operated fuel pump: A, *cam;* B, *rocker arm;* C, *pivot;* D, *pull rod;* E, *diaphragm;* F, *diaphragm spring;* G, *pump chamber;* H, *petrol inlet;* I, *suction valve;* J, *delivery valve;* K, *filter gauze;* L, *rocker-arm-operating spring;* M, *fuel-delivery opening.*

time, and those the element of which is composed of steel wool, or similar material, soaked in oil. The latter type has an easily removed cover so that the filter element can be lifted out and thoroughly washed in petrol; the base must also be emptied, cleaned out and topped to the correct level with new engine oil before the filter is reassembled.

FUEL-FEED DEVICES fall into three classes: mechanically operated pumps, electrically operated pumps and siphonage devices.

Mechanical pumps. To clean a mechanical pump (Fig. 8), remove the screw or bolt holding the top cover and carefully take off the cover so that the gasket under its rim is not damaged. When the gauze is lifted off, note whether there is another gasket under it; some types of pump have one, others do not, but where fitted it is essential to preserve airtightness. Wipe and blow through the screen to remove particles in the gauze, and then replace it so that the reinforcement is on top.

To drain the sediment chamber, first loosen the union of the fuel-inlet pipe, then unscrew and withdraw the drain plug; this is usually situated below and a little to the left of the inlet, but just above the flange locating the pump diaphragm (Fig. 8).

Electrical pumps. Servicing an electrical pump is similar, but usually the filter takes the form of a cylinder mounted on a hexagon nut and is easily withdrawn from the underside of the pump body (Fig. 9). The electrical components of the pump require no regular attention, and unless unsatisfactory working occurs are best left undisturbed.

When a pump fails to operate satisfactorily it is often due to air leaking in at some point

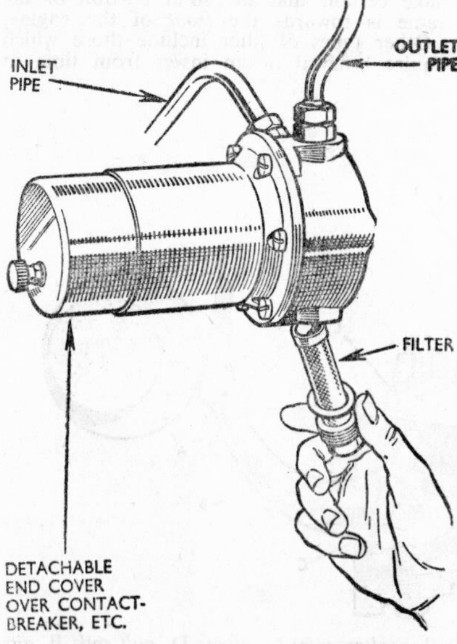

Fig. 9. Removing filter from underside of an electric fuel pump for routine attention.

of the pump or of the pipe from the tank. Always see that all washers and gaskets are sound and in place, and that union nuts are kept right home to ensure airtightness. In electrical pumps faulty operation can sometimes be traced also to a loose terminal or a bad earth connexion from the contact-breaker.

Siphonage devices. To gain access to the filter of an Autovac unit, release the pipe from the petrol inlet elbow at the top of the unit. After undoing the elbow-locking nut, remove the elbow and thus expose the cone filter, which should be wiped and blown through to free it completely from particles of foreign matter. At least every month, and preferably more often, sediment should be drawn off by means of a drain tap or hexagon plug located at the lowest point of the unit's base, it being unnecessary to undo any other connexion for this purpose. Check over all unions regularly to ensure that they are airtight.

DECARBONIZING. When an engine has run about eight thousand miles, and often less, it may show signs of the need for decarbonizing. The indications are general loss of power, less compression in some cylinders than in others, and pinking when the engine is under load or when the accelerator is depressed. These things are due to excessive carbon deposits on the cylinder head and piston crowns and to inefficient operation of the valves.

Decarbonizing an engine, although a longish job and one that needs care and method, is fairly simple and entails nothing which cannot be carried out successfully by anyone who is reasonably handy with tools.

Tools required. Before starting work, make sure that all the tools needed are to hand; they are as follows:

- Spanners to fit engine nuts.
- Socket wrenches to fit cylinder-head nuts and sparking plugs.
- Tappet spanners and feeler gauge.
- Suitable valve-spring compressor.
- Large screwdriver if valve heads are slotted, or a special tool with suction cup if valve heads are not slotted.
- Carbon scraper for removing carbon (a blunt chisel or wide screwdriver will do).
- New manifold and cylinder-head gaskets.
- Small quantity of valve-grinding paste.
- Paraffin oil and some clean, non-fluffy rags.

Preliminary dismantling. The first step is to drain the cooling system. If it contains anti-freeze, collect in a clean vessel so that the coolant can be used again. Next disconnect the battery. If they are available, old rugs, sacking, etc., should be spread over the wings to afford them protection during work on the engine. The bonnet must be entirely removed.

The next step is to remove all auxiliaries which restrict or prevent removal of the cylinder head. First remove the H.T. leads from the sparking-plug terminals and mark them or the distributor to ensure correct replacement later (Fig. 10). On many engines the dynamo is mounted on the forward end of the cylinder head and must be removed; again the leads should be marked to ensure correct re-connexion. The belt drive should be slackened, and the dynamo and carrying bracket removed together.

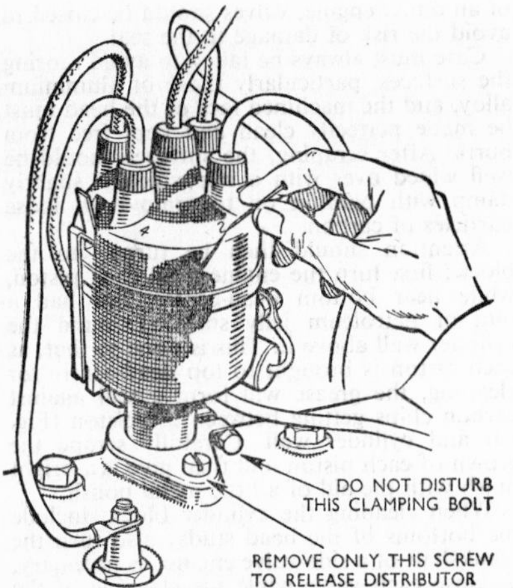

Fig. 10. To ensure correct replacement of plug leads, the cylinder numbers should be scratched on the distributor head before disconnecting.

Then disconnect the throttle and choke controls at the carburettor (on some engines there may be pipes to the distributor and suction windscreen-wiper in addition), also the petrol pipe to the float chamber. And, having taken off the air cleaner, remove the carburettor and induction manifold.

Turning attention once again to the ignition system, disconnect the wires between the induction coil and distributor where, as on many side-valve engines, the distributor drive passes through the cylinder head. It is important not to disturb the clamping bolt at the side when preparing to remove the distributor, otherwise the unit will need to be timed when re-fitted (Fig. 10). All that is necessary is to undo and remove the set-screw securing the plate to the cylinder head, when the distributor unit and drive shaft may be withdrawn.

Finally remove the length of hose connecting the cylinder-head jacket with the top of the radiator—a matter of releasing two hose clips and easing the hose off the pipe ends.

If the engine has overhead valves which are push-rod-operated, it is often necessary to remove the rocker mechanisms before the cylinder head can be lifted off; also some of the nuts holding rocker-shaft posts quite often act as cylinder-head nuts as well. On an engine with valves operated by an overhead camshaft, the chain or gears driving the camshaft will need to be disconnected.

Before this is done, however, turn the crankshaft with the starting handle until the piston of No. 1 cylinder is at the top of its stroke with *both* valves closed and then note whether timing marks on the chain and chain wheel or on the gears are there to assist reassembly to the correct timing (Fig. 11). If no marks exist, make some with a punch or a small file before breaking the drive.

Be careful to see that any oil pipes to the rocker mechanism or camshaft bearings attached to the cylinder head are disconnected and turned out of the way.

Removing cylinder head. If it now appears that there is nothing left to interfere with raising the cylinder head clear of the block, proceed to slacken off the head nuts by commencing at the centre of the head and working outwards evenly in all directions (Fig. 12), giving each nut not more than one turn. Now go back to the first nut and repeat the process.

Fig. 11. Overhead-camshaft gearing with timing marks to ensure correct remating.

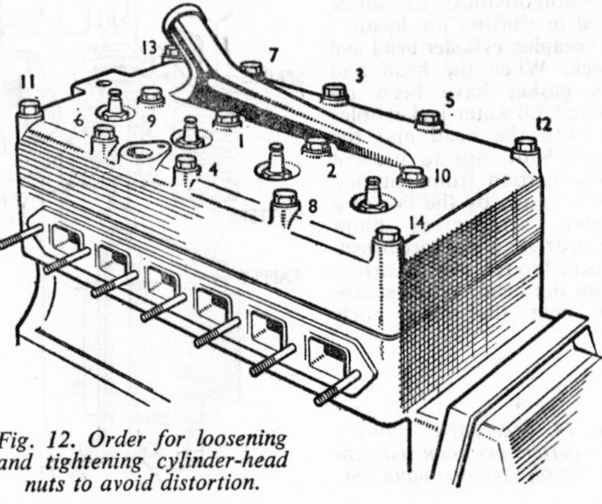

Fig. 12. Order for loosening and tightening cylinder-head nuts to avoid distortion.

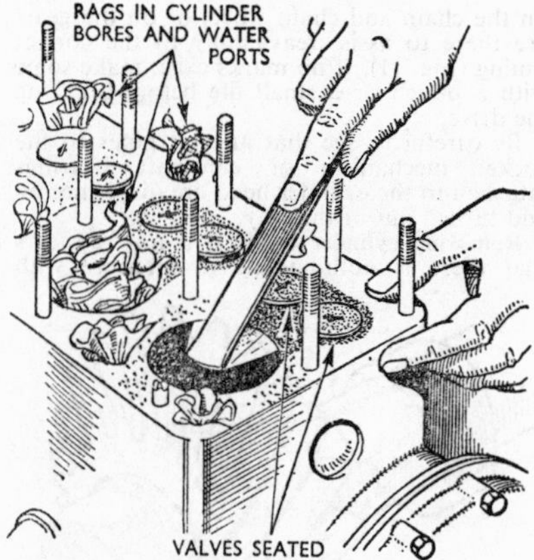

Fig. 13. Scraping carbon from piston crown.

Pressure on the head is thus evenly released (to avoid distortion) until all nuts are loose, after which they may be run off in any order.

The head is now ready for lifting; but if difficulty is experienced in moving it, *do not attempt to prise it up* by inserting a tool at the joint, as this will be almost certain to damage the joint faces. Run penetrating oil into the stud holes, and tap all round the joint with a wooden mallet. Then give the engine a few turns with the starting handle, as the compression should help to break the joint.

When the head has been moved, but before it is lifted finally from the block, it is as well to remove the sparking plugs, not only for cleaning purposes, but to avoid the risk of damage during the scraping of carbon from the cylinder head. Plugs may have been taken out earlier if lifting screws were available for use by screwing into the plug holes, but if all plugs are removed, engine compression obviously cannot be used in shifting the head.

Scraping cylinder head and block. When the head and the gasket have been removed, fill water-jacket holes in both the head and the block with rags to prevent loose carbon from entering them. Now, by the use of a carbon scraper or blunt screwdriver and a wire brush, proceed to remove all carbon from the head. When scraping near the valve ports of an o.h.v. engine, valves should be closed to avoid the risk of damage to the seat.

Care must always be taken to avoid scoring the surfaces, particularly those of aluminium alloy, and the machined face of the head must be made perfectly clean and kept free from burrs. After scraping, the surfaces should be well wiped over with a rag which is slightly damp with paraffin oil to remove all loose particles of carbon.

Attention should then be turned to the block; first turn the engine until each piston, while near bottom dead-centre, has had a film of petroleum jelly smeared round the cylinder wall above it. This is done so that, as each piston is brought to top dead-centre for cleaning, the grease will form a seal against carbon chips getting between the piston (Fig. 13) and cylinder wall. Carefully scrape the crown of each piston and then give it a bright finish with the aid of a little metal polish.

When cleaning the cylinder block, include the bottoms of the head studs; also turn the crankshaft of a side-valve engine, as necessary, to close each valve while the cleaning of the valve head and the area near its seat is in progress. Cylinder bores and pistons should be protected as far as possible from carbon chips and dust by the insertion of rag in the bores. The use of caustic cleansing preparations is not recommended for the removal of carbon from any part of the engine.

Removing and cleaning valves. The valves now require attention. Where they are overhead they are more accessible than those of a side-valve engine. The latter are exposed by the removal of a cover plate; the exhaust manifold must also be removed to permit a thorough cleaning of the ports.

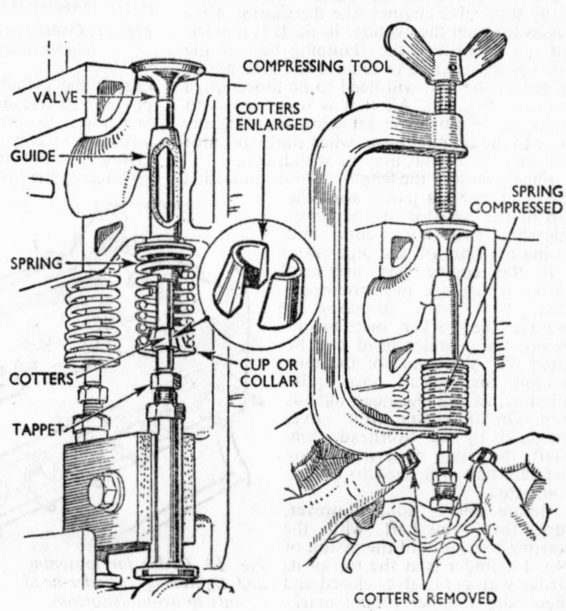

Fig. 14. Side valve, showing how cotters are removed with the aid of spring-compressor.

Before commencing work on the valves, see whether they are numbered. If they are not, it is imperative to place them aside in their correct order when withdrawn, so that their respective positions are maintained on reassembly. Also, plug oil-holes in the valve compartment with rag so that no small parts can fall down them.

Begin with a valve near the centre and see that it is hard down on its seat. Then, with the use of a compressing tool (Fig. 14), compress the valve spring with cup sufficiently to permit the removal of the cotter. This may be a pin through the valve stem, a horseshoe cotter, or one made up of two parts fitting round the stem. Once this is extracted the compressor may be allowed to release the spring pressure and should be removed.

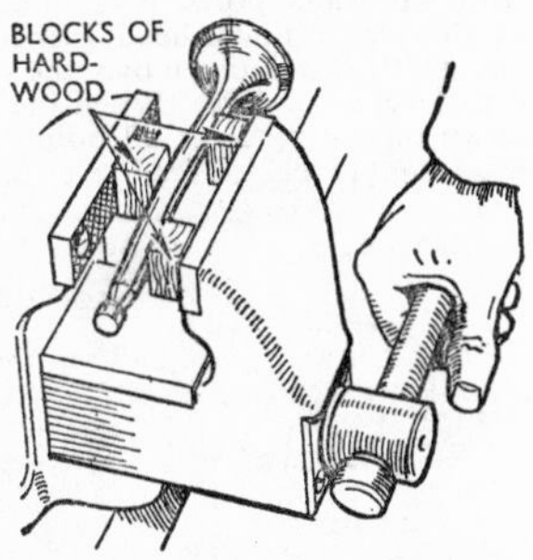

Fig. 15. A bend in a valve stem may be removed by applying slight pressure in a bench vice after blocks of wood have been suitably placed.

The valve can then be withdrawn, by the head, up through the guide, thus releasing the spring and cup. The process must, of course, be repeated on each valve until all are dismantled. Take care to put each set of parts with the valve to which it belongs.

The procedure described does not apply to Ford valves, which have split guides, special instructions and tools for valve removal being issued by the manufacturers.

Every valve and guide should be thoroughly cleaned, carbon being scraped or chipped off, and must then be examined closely. If the valve face is badly ridged or has patches of severe pitting, it will need re-facing in a grinding machine; if in fairly good condition, however, grinding-in the valve on its seat will be sufficient.

Before doing this, look along the valve stem to see whether it is at all bent; alternatively, check with a straight-edge and pass the valve stem up and down its guide. If the indications are that the stem is bent, it is sometimes possible to straighten it by the careful use of a bench vice (Fig. 15), but, as a rule, it is better discarded in favour of a new valve and guide. If the stem seems to be unduly slack in the guide. both should be renewed.

Next chip away carbon from the valve ports and wipe them out with a paraffin-oil rag, at the same time wipe and inspect the valve seats. Where badly burned, ridged or pitted, a new seat or at least a re-facing at the correct angle will be needed.

Grinding-in. Grinding-in a valve on its seat is a finishing process which ensures a gas-tight joint; it is just as necessary with new valves and new seats as with worn ones. To carry out this job, take a little valve-grinding compound and smear it round the face of the valve; insert the valve through its guide, and make sure that the cam and tappet are allowing it to rest fully on the seat with a clearance to spare.

If the valve has a slot in the head, place a screwdriver in the slot and, bearing down slightly on the valve, rotate it smartly to and fro (Fig. 16). If the valve has no slot, a suction tool must be used and worked between the hands (Fig. 17). The valve should be lifted off the seat every few turns to allow proper disposition of the paste; give the valve about half a turn before fresh contact is made with the seat. If a light spring is placed under the head of the valve (Fig. 16), it simplifies this periodic lifting of the valve; a suction tool, however, will usually lift the valve as well as turn it.

When the valve is fully ground-in, the face and seat will be evenly grey and matt in appearance, and entirely without signs of shine or pitting. All the valves should be ground-in similarly on their seats, after which great care must be taken to see that every trace of grinding paste is removed from the engine, particularly from valve seats and ports, while the valves should be washed in paraffin oil and then dried with a cloth.

Reassembling valves. Valves may now be reassembled in the engine. The end valves are invariably the most awkwardly situated and may well be tackled first. Oil each valve stem before inserting it through the guide; then,

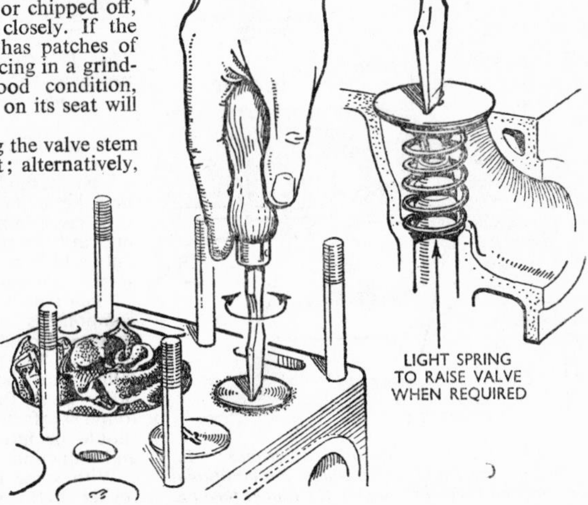

Fig. 16. Grinding-in a side valve with a screwdriver.

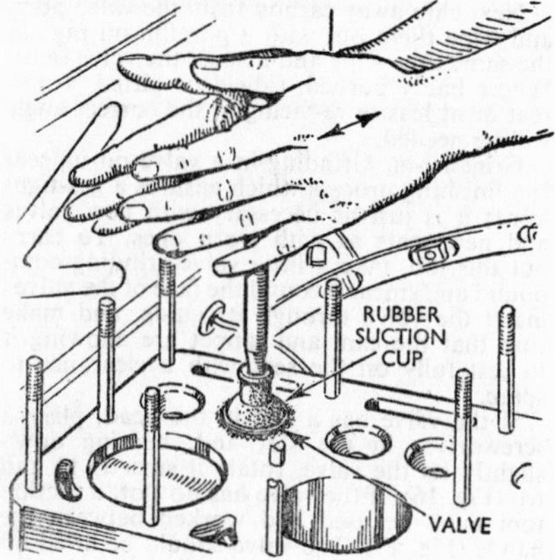

Fig. 17. Grinding-in a side valve by means of a suction tool rotated between the hands.

with the spring and cup in place, use the compressing tool until the cotter is properly in position and the spring can be gradually released. When the valves are back in position, remember to remove all rag plugs from apertures in the valve chest of a side-valve engine.

The grinding-in of the valves will undoubtedly have upset the tappet clearances. A feeler gauge will probably show that these have been reduced to below the figure stipulated by the engine manufacturers, whereas it is better to have clearances a little wider, if anything, on a cold engine, since they are reduced when the valves are hot. On a side-valve engine the clearances should be adjusted at this stage; with an o.h.v. engine this cannot be done until the cylinder head is down.

Bring the piston of the first cylinder nearly to the top of its compression stroke so that both valves are closed and the cams are at their lowest positions. Then, with tappet spanners, undo the locking nut, turn the adjuster to give the correct feeler clearance, and then hold the adjuster still while tightening the locking nut (Fig. 18). The same should be done on the valves of the other cylinders, after which the cover plate of the valve compartment should be replaced. Note that clearance increase for a Ford valve is effected only by the removal of metal from the base of the valve stem.

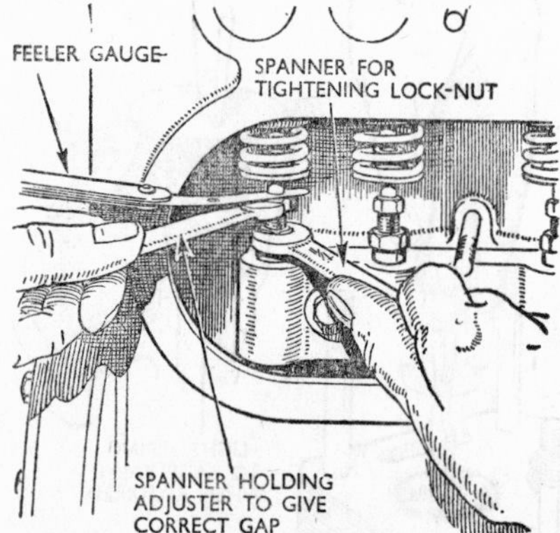

Fig. 18. Adjusting side-valve clearances with tappet spanners and feeler gauge. An additional tool may be necessary to stop the tappet turning.

Replacing cylinder head. The cylinder head may now be put back. First remove all rags and grease from the cylinder bores, and plugs from the water ports. Next smear both sides of the new cylinder-head gasket with grease and gently ease it down over the studs, keeping it as level as possible. When the gasket is flat down on the block at all points, the cylinder head should be lowered over the studs into position. Then run a nut down each stud until it touches the cylinder head.

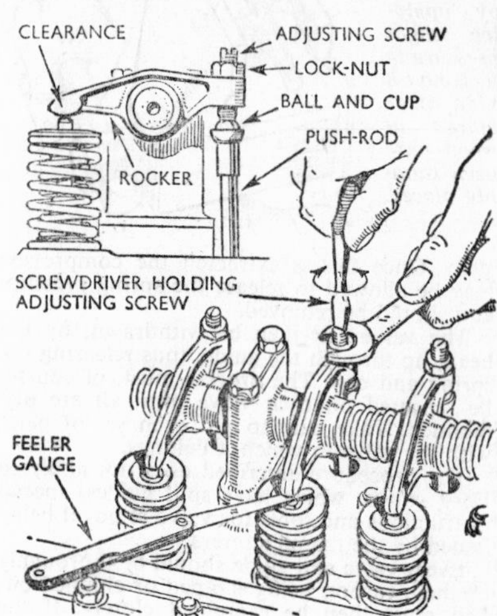

Fig. 19. Clearance of a push-rod-operated overhead valve is governed by an adjusting screw above the rocker-arm ball.

The method of tightening-down the nuts must be similar to that of removing them; that is to say, beginning at the centre and working outwards systematically, turning each nut only a little at a time and going over the head several times until all are tight.

Final reassembly and adjustments. All other components and auxiliaries may now be replaced, commencing with the sparking plugs to avoid the risk of small nuts or washers falling into the cylinders. The reverse of the order given for dismantling will usually be found satisfactory. For preference, new gaskets should be fitted when replacing the exhaust and induction manifolds.

With some o.h.v. engines, as soon as the rocker shaft is secured, and on others, as soon

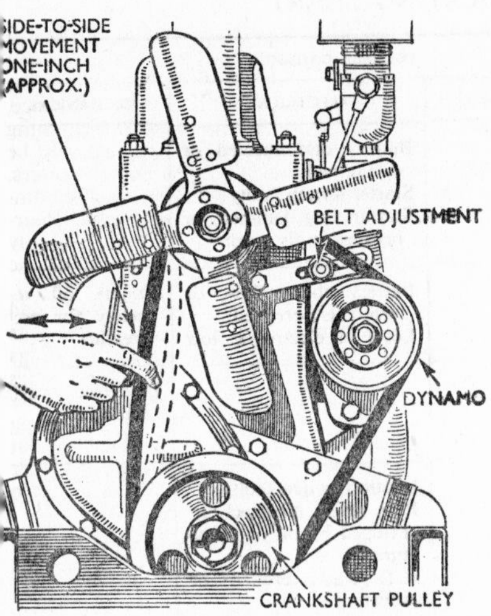

Fig. 20. Testing the tension of a three-cornered belt drive to dynamo and fan pulley.

as the camshaft drive is connected up so that the timing marks are correctly mated, the valve clearances should be re-set (Fig. 19). Make sure, when all auxiliaries are in place, that all carburettor controls and ignition leads have been connected up; the last connexions to be made should be those to the starter motor and the battery terminal.

Do not refill the cooling system yet, but start the engine and allow it to warm up thoroughly. Then go over the cylinder-head nuts and tighten them down again. When the engine is nearly cold, the cooling system should be filled and the engine run for ten minutes, when a further tightening of cylinder-head nuts should be made. This time also check for tightness other engine nuts recently replaced, such as those at the manifolds, exhaust-pipe joint and dynamo.

In connexion with fan and dynamo drives, care should be taken not to make the belt too tight when reassembling, otherwise undue wear on the spindle bearings may result. The correct tension for the belt is normally that which will permit a 1-in. movement of the belt from side to side at a point about halfway between the two pulleys (Fig. 20). The dynamo position is usually adjustable so that the tension can be varied (Figs. 20 and 21).

When the car has done thirty or forty miles after decarbonizing, the valve clearances should be checked and adjusted if necessary with the engine warm.

MAJOR OVERHAULS. There will come a time when the engine, having run a total of 25,000 miles or more, may be in need of a major overhaul. Cylinder bores, pistons and piston rings may have become worn to such an extent that compression is poor and oil consumption high. Sounds of piston slap and of crankshaft and big-end wear may also become apparent. This kind of overhaul is a lengthy job and should normally be undertaken only by the specialist.

TRACING ENGINE FAULTS. Before passing on to details of the maintenance required on other parts of the car, it may be of value to set out, on the accompanying chart (pages 444-5), in a form which allows easy reference, the possible causes of engine failure, so that trouble can be diagnosed and rectified as quickly as possible.

THE TRANSMISSION SYSTEM

The transmission system of the modern car, although comprising the complex mechanisms of the clutch, gear-box and the final-drive axle (Fig. 22), usually requires nothing in the way of maintenance beyond correct and regular lubrication and the occasional adjustment of the clutch pedal to compensate for wear.

CLUTCH. On most cars the clutch is of the dry, single-plate type, and will slip should oil at any time gain access to the friction faces. A type of wet clutch, fitted on some older cars, however, runs in oil but should receive an adequate supply from the engine. Thus, the only part of the clutch that may need lubrication is the release bearing, which may be fitted with a grease nipple or grease cup for attention every thousand miles.

If neither of these is fitted, it is because the bearing is of the greaseless type, no maintenance being required. A fluid flywheel should be checked for fluid level in accordance with the maker's instructions, as topping-up will occasionally be necessary.

To avoid clutch-slip developing as the linings of a friction clutch become worn, steps must be taken to maintain the pedal's range of movement as fully operative. As the clutch friction faces get thinner, the pressure plate will have farther to go before full pressure of the centre plate against the flywheel is achieved. Because of this the pedal will need to travel increasingly farther up when released, though it will be prevented from doing so by a buffer or the floorboards acting on the pedal arm.

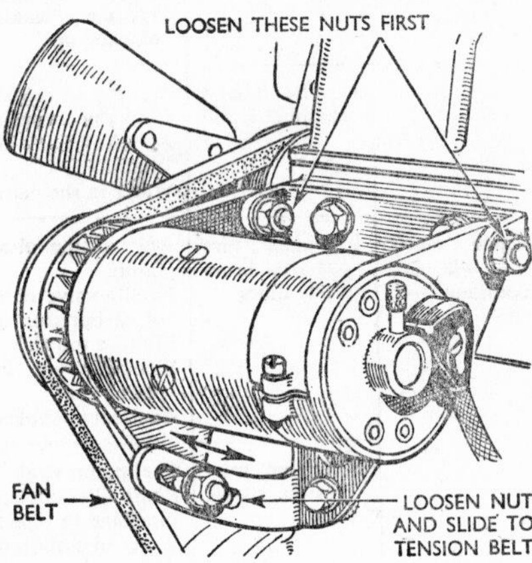

Fig. 21. One way of adjusting dynamo position to obtain correct tension of the fan belt.

ENGINE FAULT-LOCATING CHART

NATURE OF FAILURE	GOVERNING CONDITION	POSSIBLE CAUSES		
		IN FUEL SYSTEM	ELECTRICAL	MECHANICAL
Engine will not start on the starter	If starter will not turn engine		Battery disconnected or discharged Starter switch faulty Starter dog jammed or brushes badly worn	
	If starter turns engine slowly		Battery charge low, or terminals corroded Level of electrolyte low	Engine oil too heavy for cold weather
Engine will not start on handle or starter	When ignition and fuel systems are in order			Incorrect valve timing
	If there is no spark at the plugs		Ignition switch faulty Plug gaps incorrect or bridged by oil or moisture H.T. leads broken or shorting	
	If there is no spark at the distributor		Contact-breaker points dirty or wrongly gapped Contact-breaker arm seized Magneto or distributor damp, or drive sheared Loose L.T. leads H.T. pick-up faulty Rotor damaged Condenser faulty	
	If there is no spark at the coil		Coil burnt out H.T. leads broken or disconnected	
	If float chamber of carburettor is empty	Petrol turned off or tank empty Fuel pump or Autovac faulty or leaking air Pipe-line leaking or blocked up		
	If the float chamber is full	Starting jet blocked Choke not working Air leak at induction manifold Water in the petrol		
Engine starts but will not continue to run	If engine dies out after firing a few times	Any of the above fuel faults Needle valve or dashpot of carburettor sticking Mixture too rich Blocked vent hole to petrol tank Air-cleaner choked	Faulty ignition switch Plug leads loose Distributor clamping-screw loose Plugs wetted by unburnt petrol Plugs dirty or gap at points too wide	Burnt valve Sticking valve Broken valve spring
	If engine misfires or blows back	Fuel pump weak Pump filter choked Blockage in pipe-line Water in carburettor	Plug leads connected in wrong order Ignition timing wrong Contact breaker faulty or points wrongly gapped Plug insulator cracked	Any of the above valve faults Incorrect valve clearances

NATURE OF FAILURE	GOVERNING CONDITION	POSSIBLE CAUSES		
		IN FUEL SYSTEM	ELECTRICAL	MECHANICAL
Engine will not slow-run but runs normally with throttle open	If engine is cold			Oil too heavy when cold
	If engine is warm	Slow-running adjustment wrongly set Slow-running jet blocked Air leak at induction manifold (if a suction windscreen-wiper is fitted, line should be checked for leaky rubber or other connexion) Excessive wear on the throttle spindle	Magneto weak	Sticking valve Worn valve guides Incorrect valve clearances
Engine will not open up		Restricted petrol supply Air leak at the induction manifold Main jet or jets dirty	Retarded ignition Defective plugs Condenser damp or defective Faulty coil	Back pressure in exhaust pipe due to blockage Burnt valves
Engine becomes overheated			Retarded ignition	Pistons and bearings tight if insufficiently run in Fan belt slipping Blockage in cooling system Cooling pump defective Brakes binding

Adjustment of the pedal's travel must, therefore, be made periodically, according to the means provided (Fig. 23), so as to give the pedal pad at least one inch of free travel upwards *after* the clutch is fully engaged. Care must be taken, when adjusting, to see also that the clutch can be completely disengaged before the pedal is depressed to its lowest possible point.

If the pedal arm turns about a cross shaft, the latter is fitted with a grease nipple; this should receive attention approximately every thousand miles.

GEAR-BOX. It is important that high-pressure gear oil be maintained at the correct level in the gear-box. The level should be checked every thousand miles by the use of the dipstick, if provided, or by inspection after removal of a level plug. Every five or six thousand miles the gear-box should be completely drained out, by removal of a drain plug at its base, and then refilled with new oil.

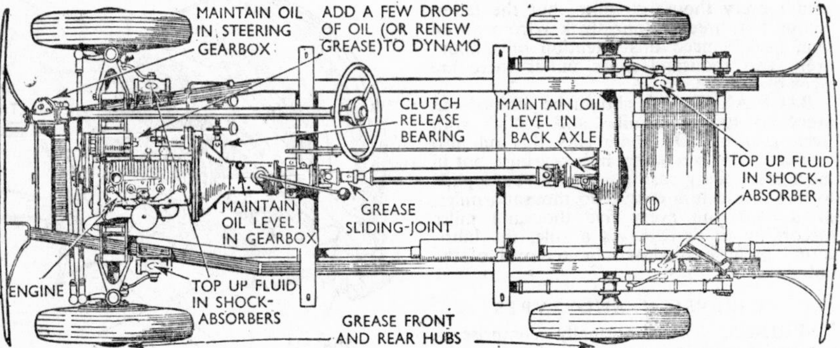

Fig. 22. General view of a car chassis, showing some of the principal items which should be given regular maintenance in the transmission, steering-gear and wheels.

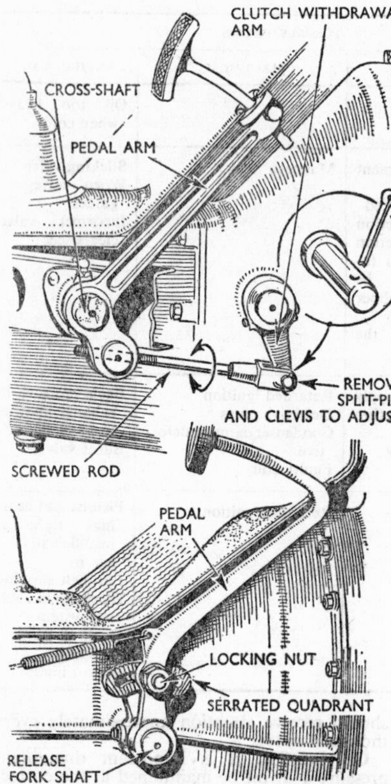

Fig. 23. Two ways in which a clutch pedal may be adjusted to compensate for wear.

UNIVERSAL JOINTS. On most cars, only the joint at the gear-box end of the propeller shaft requires lubrication. Some designs are grease-lubricated, while others require gear oil. The former type should be injected with grease every thousand miles, but the latter, calling for three or four strokes from an oil gun, usually need this attention only about every two thousand miles unless there are signs of leakage.

BACK AXLE. This should be drained out every six thousand miles and refilled with fresh gear oil. On some cars this oil also lubricates the rear-wheel hub bearings, but in most cases the grease gun has to be applied to hub lubricators every two thousand miles, or the oil gun every five thousand miles (according to design). As a rule, the lubrication point is disclosed by removal of the hub disk.

SUSPENSION AND TYRES

SPRINGS. These normally comprise a number of steel leaves per spring and require attention about every two to three months, except when they are specified as dry springs. Most types must be protected from rust which may cause the leaves to bind or break and this is best done by the regular application of penetrating oil.

To lubricate the springs effectively, first remove all dirt, particularly from the indentations between the edges of the leaves. This can usually be done by the combined use of a screwdriver blade and a wire brush. Next jack-up the car, with the jack acting on the chassis frame, sufficiently high for all load to be lifted off the spring. Then the oil should be applied; in the absence of a spray, an oil-can will do, provided that the oil can be got *between* the leaves, which, with no load on them, can sometimes be parted slightly with the aid of a thin wedge. A special tool is made for the purpose.

On some transverse springs a grease nipple is fitted at the U-bolt or anchoring bracket so that the highest point of the spring, normally covered, does not remain dry.

The most usual way of securing a spring to a side member of the chassis frame is by a bolt through the eye at one end of the master leaf, and by a shackle attached to the eye at the other end (Fig. 24). On other springs (particularly transverse), shackles are fitted at both ends of the master leaf (Fig. 25).

Unless the shackles have patent rubber bushes, they are fitted with two grease nipples to which the grease gun should be liberally applied at least every thousand miles. Never allow oil or grease to penetrate shackles of the rubber-bush type.

SHOCK-ABSORBERS. On most modern cars these operate hydraulically, being dependent for their spring-damping effect upon the resistance to displacement of fluid by vanes or pistons. Normally, a car is fitted with four shock-absorber units (two per axle); each unit is secured to the chassis frame and has an arm connected with the axle. On some types a screw, disclosed by removal of the filler plug, provides adjustment of the resistance which the arm offers to up-and-down motion.

Every five thousand miles the shock-absorbers should be topped-up with the special

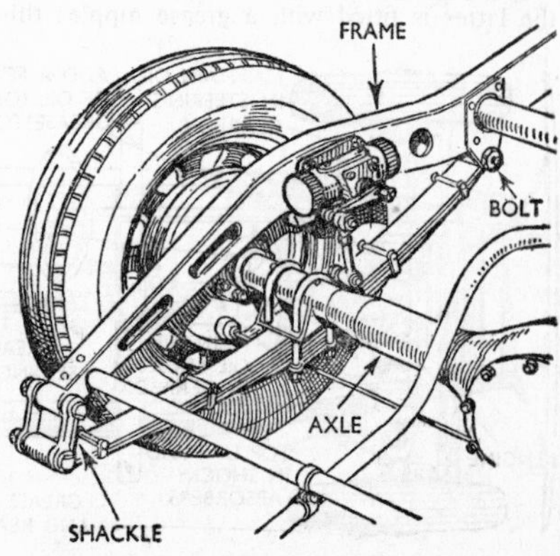

*Fig. 24. Semi-elliptical spring secured by a **bolt** at one end and a shackle at the other.*

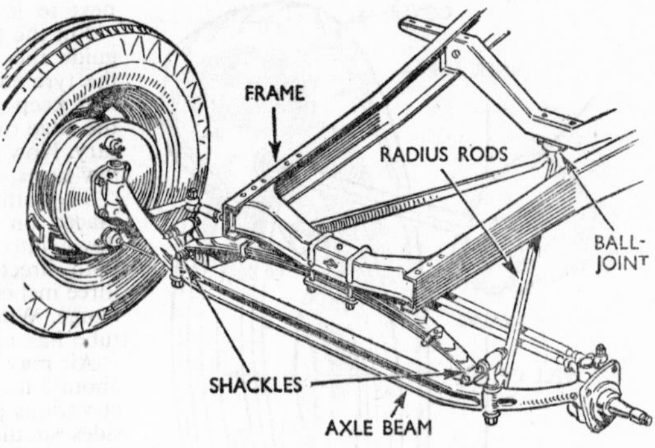

Fig. 25. Transverse spring fitted with a shackle at each end.

fluid recommended by the makers. Use of the correct fluid is essential, as some kinds of unit require a much more viscous medium than others. Before removing a filler plug (Fig. 26), always be careful to brush away dirt from the plug and from the area surrounding it, as grit must not be allowed to get in.

When refilling a dry or nearly dry shock-absorber the arm must be disconnected from the axle link so that it can be continuously worked up and down to remove the air from inside the chambers while the fluid is being added.

WHEELS AND TYRES. Three types of wheel are in use: the wire wheel, with or without spoke-enclosing disks; the one-piece, or solid-disk, wheel; and that which is by far the most popular—the pressed-steel wheel in which the disk is not solid but has holes formed in it in such a way that the wheel has the appearance of possessing very thick, readily cleaned spokes.

Car wheels nowadays are always easily removable. The usual method of securing the wheel to the hub is by a number of nuts on studs near the centre. Another method, sometimes adopted on sports cars, provides for the wheel to be quickly detached after removing one large hub nut.

Slackness in hub bearings of the front wheels can be taken up by first removing the wheel and then unscrewing and taking off an inner hub cap. This reveals the hub-bearing nut, which, after a split pin has been withdrawn, can be turned up until the bearing is tight and then taken back about a third of a turn. The split pin *must* be replaced.

Removing wheel. To remove a wheel which is not of the type held by one large central nut, slacken off with a wheel brace, but do not entirely remove, the various securing nuts round the hub. In some cases these are exposed, but in others an outer hub cap or plate, held by a central screw, will need to be removed first of all.

Next jack the car up so that the wheel in question is well clear of the ground; then remove all the loosened nuts. The wheel can now be withdrawn from the hub bolts. When the wheel is being replaced, it is important that, if there are more than three nuts, they should be done up, *not* in sequence round the hub, but by going from the first nut to one which is opposite or nearly opposite to it, and so on. Each nut should be gone over several times, because, as the wheel settles into position on the hub, it often allows a previously "tight" nut to take another turn or so.

Removing a tyre. Almost all car wheels now have well-base rims, which, if the correct procedure is followed, make the removal of a wired tyre a comparatively effortless matter. The first step, of course, is to remove the wheel from the car, and the second to make sure that the tube is *completely* deflated, by removing the valve dust-cap and depressing the valve needle. Remove the locknut from the valve.

Now lay the wheel on the ground and, by pressing on the side of the tyre (or by tapping

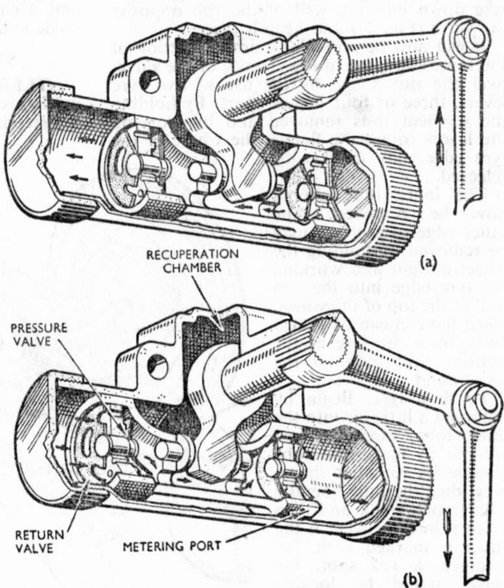

Fig. 26. Two positions of a hydraulic shock-absorber with the arm rising (a) *and descending* (b). *Arrows indicate the direction of movement of oil through the piston. A filler plug would normally be fitted to the top of the recuperation chamber.*

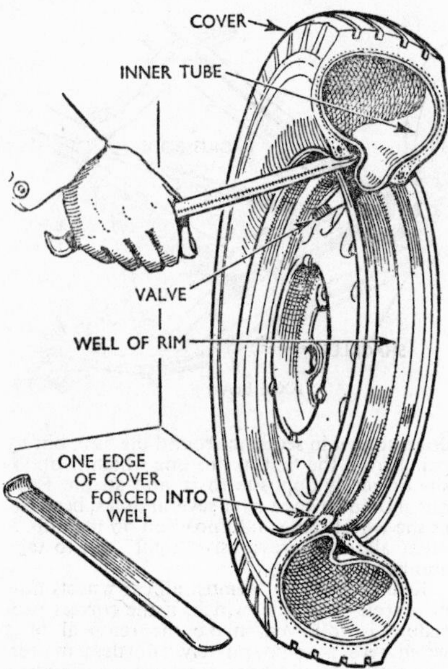

Fig. 27. Removal of a wired tyre from a well-base wheel rim. Note position of valve.

with a mallet), free the edge of the tyre from its contact with the wheel rim all the way round. Then turn the wheel over and similarly free the other edge. Next force one edge of the tyre down into the well of the rim opposite the valve (Fig. 27) and keep it there.

It will now be possible to draw a section of the same edge, but in the vicinity of the valve, over the rim flange by the use of two tyre levers, three or four inches apart. By holding the segment thus removed and by working the levers round the flange, the whole of the tyre edge may quickly be released.

The inner tube should now be removed. The other edge of the tyre may be removed by holding the wheel upright and working the tyre edge into the rim well at the top of the wheel, when the rim can be pulled away from the tyre at the bottom, and then all the way round.

To fit a tyre. Begin by pumping a little air into the inner tube, but only just enough to make the tube assume its rounded shape. Next dust the tube liberally with french chalk and then place it in the cover; if the cover is marked with, for instance, a red **spot,** the valve should be located next to it to preserve perfect wheel balance.

Put the tyre over the rim near the valve and guide the valve through its hole; then push the tyre edge at the valve down into the well and keep it there while working the rest of the edge over the flange, using levers if necessary. Now put the valve locknut back; give it a few turns, but do not run it down tight.

The other edge of the tyre can now be placed on the rim at the valve and worked down into the rim well. From here work in both directions round the rim, forcing two or three inches of the tyre edge at a time over the flange. When this is done, make sure that the tube has not become pinched near the valve.

Air may now be applied up to a pressure of about 3 lb. The wheel should then be bounced at various points round the tyre tread and the sides should be pressed in here and there so that the cover is eased into its correct seating. The moulded line running round the side of the cover near the rim should be used as a guide. When satisfied that the seating is correct, screw the valve locknut up tight and inflate the tyre to the recommended pressure.

It is as well to remember that running the car on under-inflated tyres increases tyre wear considerably—and also petrol consumption. Every three thousand miles the covers should be inspected and all flints, nails, etc., picked out of the treads. Bad cuts should be filled with tyre stopping. If a valve is suspected of leaking, the core should be unscrewed and removed (the slotted head of the dust cap is designed for this purpose) and the seating face wiped and inspected. It may be that grit is interfering with the seat, but if damaged or perished the core should be renewed.

Abnormal wear on front tyres is often caused through incorrect setting of the wheels, and a check should be made of the camber angle and the toe-in (usually $\frac{1}{8}$ in).

STEERING AND BRAKES

STEERING. Maintenance of the steering mechanism (Fig. 28) consists of topping-up the steering box with gear oil when necessary

Fig. 28. Lay-out of a typical steering system, with principal components.

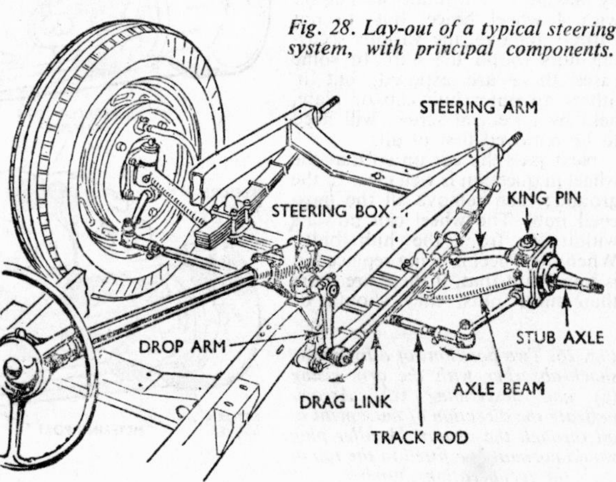

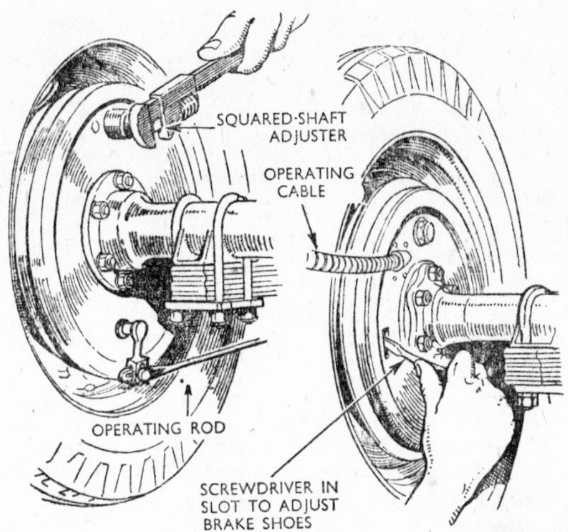

Fig. 29. Examples of two ways in which brake shoes may be adjusted.

(the level should be checked every two thousand miles), and of applying a grease gun to nipples of the drag link, track-rod ends and king pins. In some designs means of adjusting the steering-column races and steering worm for wear are provided; but it is more often wear on the track rod and king pins which brings about slack steering, particularly wheel wobble at low speeds.

The cause of wobble may also be found in a front spring that has weakened badly, become loose or has a broken leaf, because such defects upset the castor angle of the king pins. Wander in the steering may be the result of worn king pins, too much play in wheel bearings or steering box, or even of undue tightness at some point. Excessive or uneven wear on front tyres usually indicates that the wheels are wrongly tracked or that the camber angle is excessive. The steering geometry of a modern car is complicated and, if unsatisfactory, should be checked and adjusted only to maker's specifications.

BRAKES. Apart from being of vital importance to the driver and passengers, the brakes of a car must, in the interests of road users generally, be kept up to a high standard of efficiency.

Mechanically operated brakes, that is, those operated by pull-rods or cables, require regular inspection and lubrication of the operating mechanisms; while in hydraulic systems it is important that the level of fluid be maintained in the reservoir. The shaft on which the brake pedal works must be kept greased, as also must rod linkage points and the actuating arm of each brake. Detachable conduits usually provide for the lubrication of cables.

To compensate for wear of the brake linings it is seldom advisable to alter the effective length of rods or cables, and in many designs adjustment of the brake shoes is provided by a squared shaft (Fig. 29) protruding from the back plate of the brake, or in some cases by a slot in the plate through which a screwdriver will turn a notched adjuster.

The car should be jacked up and the adjuster turned until a drag on the wheel is effected; the adjuster should then be turned back just enough to let the drum turn freely. Hydraulic brakes have two adjusters, one for each shoe. The top of each adjuster is turned away from the centre of the plate to spread the shoes.

It is not always advisable to leave renewal of the linings until adjusters cease to improve braking, because, as the linings become very thin, the rivets come into contact with the drum and score it; grit in the drums will also cause scoring. It is not good policy to fit new linings without having scored drums skimmed so as to present an even braking surface.

Re-lining. Re-lining the brakes is a matter of riveting new linings to the shoes, though on some systems it is preferable to exchange old shoes for new shoe-and-lining assemblies complete. High spots on new linings should be removed with a rasp before the brakes are finally adjusted, and they may be easily detected by chalking a small area inside the drum and rotating it.

Faults. If brakes suddenly become inefficient or unbalanced, the drums should be inspected for the presence of oil. Over-filling of the back axle or a defective seal at the hub or at a shoe expander may be the cause. Washing the drums and linings in petrol and preventing further ingress of oil should restore efficiency, but if the linings are fairly saturated they will have to be renewed.

Binding brakes may be caused by some part of the operating gear becoming dry, clogged

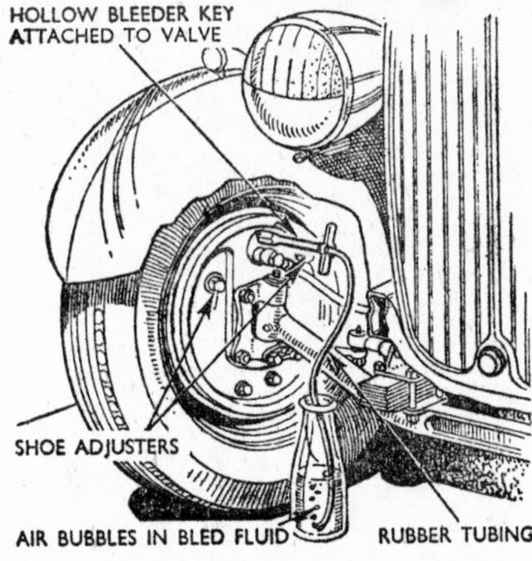

Fig. 30. Drawing off fluid and air from a hydraulic brake system bleeder valve.

with mud or partly seized; cleaning and lubrication are the remedy. If, however, the rods, cables, compensator, etc., are operating freely, and the trouble is confined to one wheel, it is probably caused by a broken pull-off spring in the brake.

Bleeding. Hydraulic brakes require bleeding occasionally to rid the system of air which produces a springy effect upon the brake pedal when depressed.

First make sure that the reservoir is full; next attach a rubber tube to the bleeder valve on the back plate of one of the brakes, placing the other end of the tube at the bottom of a glass jar containing about two inches of brake fluid. Then undo the bleeder valve a half to one turn and depress the brake pedal. Continue to work the pedal up and down until air bubbles cease to appear in the jar (Fig. 30).

Finally do up the bleeder valve and top-up the reservoir before proceeding with the next brake. All the brakes must be similarly bled.

ELECTRICAL EQUIPMENT

DYNAMO. Second in importance only to the battery (which is discussed, as an essential part of the engine, on page 435) is the dynamo. In some types of dynamo no provision is made for periodical lubrication, while some have a grease cup which should be unscrewed, cleaned out and refilled with petroleum jelly every ten thousand miles; others have lubricators to which no more than three or four drops of engine oil should be added every three thousand miles.

If at any time, with the engine running fast, the full charge suitable for the battery is not indicated by the ammeter, the cover band should be removed and the commutator and brushes of the dynamo examined (Fig. 31). Blackness on the commutator, caused by excessive sparking, may indicate insufficient brush pressure, an unevenly worn commutator, protruding mica between copper segments or a breakdown in the armature winding.

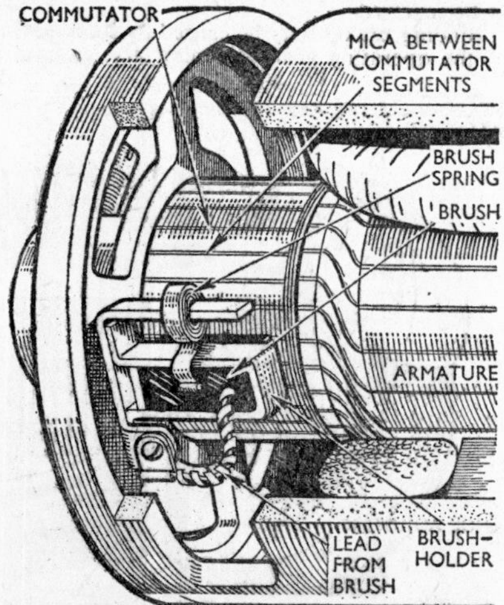

Fig. 31. The commutator end of a dynamo, showing a brush together with spring and holder. An adjustable third brush is sometimes fitted.

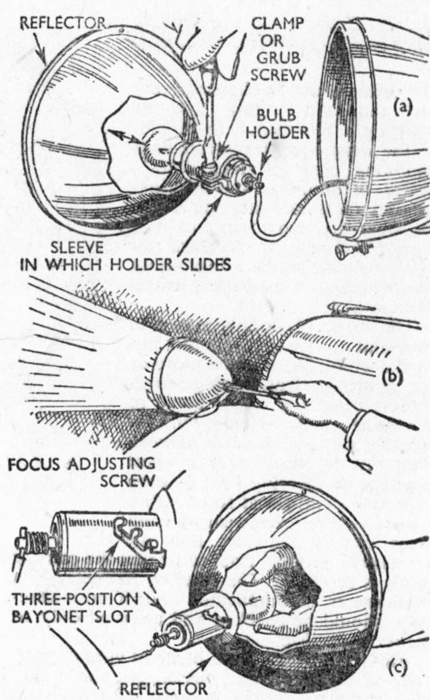

Fig. 32. Three commonly used methods of providing focusing adjustment in headlamps.

Brushes should be washed in petrol if they bear any signs of grease, but renewed if badly worn; the commutator must be cleaned, and can be trued up in a lathe, the insulation having first been cut back about 0·030 in., if necessary.

Should the ammeter indicate excessive discharge when the engine is ticking-over and there is no sign of a short, it may be that the points of the dynamo cut-out have failed to open and that the battery is, therefore, discharging through the dynamo windings. The cut-out, together with fuses, etc., may be accessible from the driving seat, or it may be mounted on the dynamo casing. Remove the cut-out cover and note whether the points are closed. If so, they may be dirty and damp through condensation and after switching-off the engine should be wiped; or the tension of the opening spring may require resetting.

STARTER MOTOR. Usually this requires no periodical lubrication. But like the dynamo, it depends upon the good condition of brushes and commutator for efficient operation. An easily removable band round the motor gives access to the brushes, which should be checked for free movement in their holders and cleaned of carbon dust. It is important that the cable connexions be kept clean and tight and the insulation perfect.

WIRING. The wiring to auxiliaries, such as the horn, windscreen-wiper, trafficators, and to the various lamps should be inspected regularly for tight connexions and to see that insulation is not being chafed by movement. This is particularly important in circuits which do not include a fuse if damage from short-circuiting is to be avoided.

A blown fuse (usually of the cartridge type) should not be replaced by a new one until the cause of the overload has been tracked down. A heavier fuse than that which has blown should never be fitted.

LAMPS. If a lamp fails to light when switched on, and if it is certain that the bulb is in order, check that wiring connexions to the lamp are clean and tight. Single-pole lamps may fail to light if rust or dirt is impairing a good earthing contact with the chassis.

To focus and align headlamps correctly the car should be placed on level ground so that it is facing and about eight yards from a wall. Adjustments should be made, after switching on the headlamps, until the patches of light on the wall are circular and well defined. The centres of these circles should be the same distance apart as are the lamps' centres, the former, however, being three or four inches lower than the latter.

Various means of adjusting focus are employed (Fig. 32): bulb holders are sometimes provided with stepped slots, while others are slidable and locked by a screw behind the reflector or moved by turning a screw at the back of the lamp.

THE BODY

Little need be said about maintaining the body of the car in condition except, perhaps, that the task of cleaning it is made easier if the following points are noted.

On warm, sunny days the car should be washed in the shade. Hot water should never be employed. Use plenty of water, preferably from a hose at a trickle and *not* under pressure, although a strong jet of water is best for knocking dirt from underneath the car, the axles, inside mudguards, etc. Remove dirt from the cellulose finish with a sponge, then wipe with a damp chamois leather. Polish should not be applied frequently.

Metal polish should not be used on chromium-plated parts—the leather, followed by a dry cloth, should be sufficient. Spots of tar can be removed from the body by rubbing them with a cloth dipped in a mixture of two parts of petrol to one of engine oil.

The catches and hinges of doors and bonnet should be regularly given a few drops of oil to ensure free operation and to prevent rust from the penetration of rainwater.

LAYING-UP

When a car is not to be used for a period, the following steps should be taken to prevent deterioration during storage.

Drain used oil from the sump and refill with new oil; then run the engine for one minute, and afterwards drain the cooling system. Next loosen the inlet pipe union at the fuel pump or Autovac and then remove the plug from the base of the petrol tank and drain off all petrol. Also empty the fuel pump and the float chamber of the carburettor. (Petrol, when kept for a long time, forms a gum which will lead to trouble in the fuel system if left in the car.)

Remove the battery from the car and have it fully charged up; thereafter the battery should be kept in a cool, dry place and be recharged every six weeks. Take out the sparking plugs, clean them in petrol and store them in a dry place. Insert bungs of clean rag into the plug holes of the engine, as this will help to reduce condensation of atmospheric moisture in the cylinders. Raise the car on blocks.

Remove the tyres and clean away with petrol any signs of grease on them before storing. The tubes should be extracted, inflated slightly and dusted with french chalk before being stored in a cool place. Finally, clean the car and cover it with a dust sheet.

2. CARE OF THE BICYCLE

The general-purpose roadster type of bicycle is remarkably sturdy for its weight. It will give many thousands of miles of efficient running without more than an occasional adjustment, regular lubrication, cleaning and proper storage.

When a cycle is new it is a good idea to smear a film of petroleum jelly over the parts which provide adjustment of handlebars, brake rods, etc., as this will prevent rain from penetrating and rendering subsequent adjustment at these points difficult.

The height of the saddle should be that which enables the rider to reach the ground with the toes of both feet at once, so that when brought to a stop in traffic he can, by moving slightly to one side, place one foot *flat* on the ground without leaving the saddle.

Having settled the adjustment of the saddle, it is well worth while trying the handlebars at various heights until that which provides the greatest riding comfort is obtained, for this proves a very important factor on long journeys.

LUBRICATION. Use a good-quality cycle oil, and remove all dirt from the vicinity of the lubrication point before applying fresh lubricant so as to avoid grit being unnecessarily introduced into the bearings. Fig. 33 shows the points on a typical bicycle which require regular oiling, though some designs have more lubrication points than others.

The ideal is to insert a little oil *often*, rather than swamp the bearings only when they have become dry. If, say, six to ten drops of oil are administered to each lubricator every two or three hundred miles, this will ensure adequate lubrication without the risk of excess oil draining down to damage tyres, or to reduce the efficiency of brakes through brake-blocks coming into contact with oil on the wheel rims.

In addition to parts which are provided with oil holes, nipples or cups, there are, of course, the brakes and the levers or cables

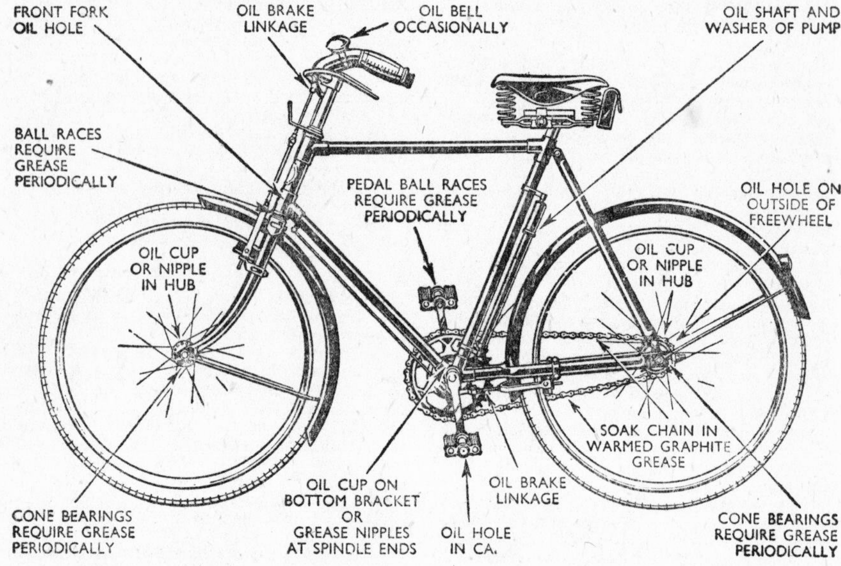

Fig. 33. Principal lubrication points of a bicycle.

operating them. Generally, no more than an occasional drop of oil on each of the linkage points is needed, though in the case of a brake which works on the flat of the rim (not on the edge) failing to release promptly, it will often be found that a smear of grease on the guide (Fig. 34) will greatly improve its operation.

The cables operating calliper or hub brakes should, once a year, be removed at the handle-

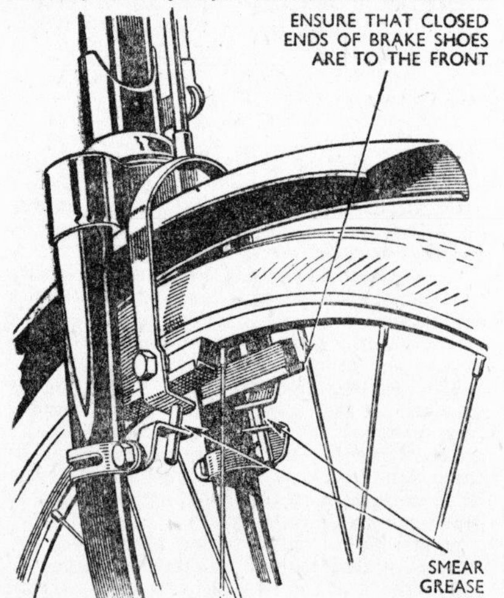

Fig. 34. Brake guide-stems should be greased.

bar end, unclipped from the frame, and straightened out while thin oil is allowed to run through between wire and sleeve from one end to the other.

When oiling hubs, crank-spindle bearings and pedals it is advisable to lay the cycle over first on one side and then on the other to ensure good distribution of lubricant. The free-wheel requires oiling thoroughly and often if it is not to become "sticky." Hold the cycle to one side and spin the wheel as the oil is injected. A little paraffin oil will loosen up a sticky free-wheel, but this must always be followed by the injection of lubricating oil. Be careful never to over-lubricate a hub which incorporates a hub brake, as surplus oil may reach the braking surface and render the brake unreliable.

Lubricating the chain. It is a waste of time and oil to run thin oil along the links of a chain, since very little will stay inside the rollers (where it is needed), and the oil that does penetrate will introduce rust and grit from the outside to form an abrasive paste which will only increase wear in the rollers.

The only satisfactory way of lubricating a chain is first to remove it. This is done by releasing the spring clip and taking out the connecting link. Now go to work on the chain with a good stiff brush until all external dirt has been removed.

The chain should then be loosely coiled and placed in a pan or shallow tin containing thick oil which has been well warmed up. Semi-solid lubricants, some containing graphite, may be obtained especially for chains. Move the chain about in the oil for a few minutes so that the latter will work its way inside the rollers, and thereafter leave the

Fig. 35. Marking the rim of a wheel with chalk when testing it for truth.

chain submerged till the lubricant is cold. Excess lubricant may then be removed from the outside of the chain before replacement on the cycle. This should be done every six months, or every two thousand miles.

WHEELS. To avoid uneven tyre wear and to provide reasonable operation of rim brakes, wheels must be kept dead true. They very often go slightly out of true, however, and if the cycle is inverted and the wheels spun it is usually apparent to the eye. To make certain at which point or points a rim is out of true, it is a good idea to hold a piece of chalk lightly against it at the fork and then spin the wheel (Fig. 35); the rim will then show marks at the points which require adjusting.

The nipples of two spokes which come adjacently on the chalked side (*A* in Fig. 36) to the part of the rim to be corrected should be slackened off two whole turns. Then the spoke (*B*) between them on the rim (coming, of course, from the other side of the hub) is taken up one whole turn. This should correct the rim if only slightly out; but correction may be needed over a larger part of the rim, in which case the same principle is applied to more spokes.

In some cases the whole rim may be pulled over to one side, that is to say, the rim is not centred on the hub. Every one of the spokes coming from one side of the hub should be slackened off two turns therefore, while those from the other side of the hub should each be taken up one turn.

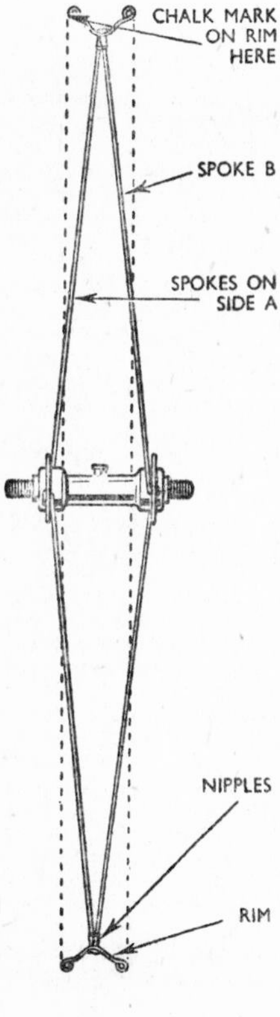

CHALK MARK ON RIM HERE
SPOKE B
SPOKES ON SIDE A
NIPPLES
RIM

Fig. 36. Section through cycle wheel showing adjustment of spokes.

TYRES AND TUBES. The following few points will help to reduce the need for repairs and ensure the efficiency of repairs that have to be made.

Keep the tyres inflated when the cycle is not in use; otherwise, invert the machine so that the rims will not pinch the tubes and the tyre walls will not become cracked.

Tyres should be very hard for riding for the same reasons as above, plus the fact that, when hard, they are less likely to be punctured, provide easier running and suffer less wear on the treads than do under-inflated tyres.

Go round the covers every two hundred miles and remove, with a bradawl or similar tool, all grits, flints, thorns, glass, etc., that can be found. They are all potential punctures and will become positive punctures when continued riding has gradually pushed them through to the inner tube. A tyre which has been cut through to the fabric should have a patch of strong canvas stuck to the inside of the cover. The patch has not only to cover the cut, but must be large enough to give a good sticking area all round it.

Whenever a tyre is flat take the opportunity of seeing that the rim tape adequately covers the heads of all the spokes—another, and often unsuspected, cause of punctures. The tape may have worked to one side, or it may have

[. . .]pierced by spoke heads here and there, in [. . .] case it should be renewed.

[. . .]a tyre goes down rapidly while riding, [. . .]ount and look round the cover for the [. . .] of the puncture immediately as, if the [. . .]ler is a nail, tin-tack or piece of glass and [. . .] removed, even walking the cycle will be [. . .]led by the risk that a new hole or cut [. . .]be made with every turn of the wheel. [. . .]en it is not plainly evident that a flat [. . .]s due to the penetration of a sharp object, [. . .]ys test the valve before removing the tube, [. . .]se the valve rubber has split and requires [. . .]ving. Remember that oil and grease are [. . .]damaging to rubber, and for this reason, [. . .] repairing a puncture in the back tyre, [. . .]ys take off the tube on the side away from [. . .]chain. Care must always be exercised to [. . .]hat the tube, during removal or replace[. . .], does not get caught, for instance, [. . .]een a brake-block and the wheel.

[. . .]ever apply a patch without first cleaning [. . .]area of the tube to which it is to adhere. [. . .]l-paper or glass-paper is supplied for this [. . .]pose in most puncture-repair outfits.

[. . .]ever place a new patch over the edge of an [. . .]one that is leaking, but remove the faulty [. . .]h, clean the tube and affix a new and per[. . .]s larger one. A tube which has a split (as [. . .]nct from a cut) in it requires special pre[. . .]ions to be taken to prevent the split from [. . .]ing longer even after it is covered by a [. . .]ch. Make two short cuts at right-angles to [. . .] split, one at each end (Fig. 37), before [. . .]ering with a patch.

[. . .]efore putting a tube back on to the rim, [. . .] worth while feeling slowly right round the [. . .]de of the cover to make sure that no sharp [. . .]trusion is left; this may not have caused [. . .] trouble which has just received attention, [. . .] will, in time, most certainly result in [. . .]other puncture.

When both tube and cover are in place on [. . .] rim and the valve is replaced, it is as well [. . .]t to inflate the tyre hard straight away, but [. . .]give it only about twelve to fifteen strokes of the pump; then press together the sides of the cover with the fingers progressively around the wheel. This helps to get rid of pinches and twists in the tube.

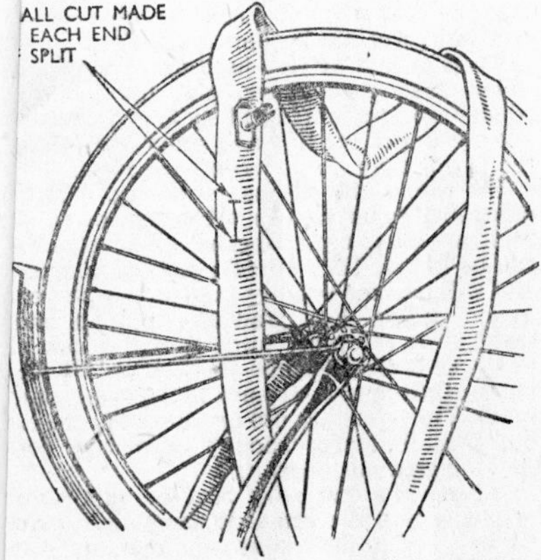

Fig. 37. Small cuts prevent a split in an inne[r] tube from becoming larger after patching.

BRAKES. To compensate for the wearing down of the blocks of a rim brake on the front wheel, it is necessary to take up the linkage at the rod unions below the handlebars, though for the back brake there is a special screwed adjuster located below the rear-wheel fork near the chain wheel (Fig. 38).

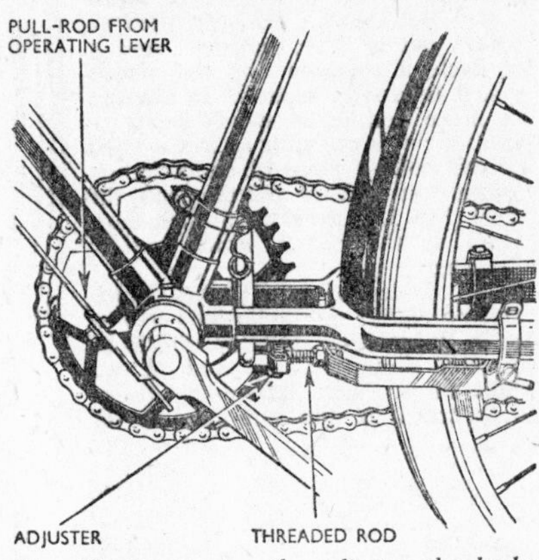

Fig. 38. By turning the adjuster the brake-blocks are drawn nearer the rim.

A block should never be allowed to wear right down so that the walls of the brake-shoe score the wheel rim when the brake is applied hard. New blocks cost only a few pence per pair and are easy to fit, being designed to slide in at the open end of the shoe. Be careful, however, when refitting the shoes, to see that each is replaced so that its closed end is towards the direction of normal wheel rotation, otherwise the blocks will soon be displaced and lost when brought into contact with the rim (Fig. 34).

Calliper brakes are similarly dealt with; shoes can often be adjusted to take up wear in the blocks and to prevent excessive movement of the control lever; an adjustment at the lower end of the cable is usually provided to vary the closing distance of the callipers.

Internal-expanding hub brakes are sometimes provided with a shoe-adjusting wedge as well as a means of varying the operative length of cable. The linings will need renewing from time to time and the most satisfactory way is to buy new shoes and linings complete. When a hub brake becomes suddenly and prematurely inefficient it may be that oil from the hub bearings has got into the brake-drum. To overcome this the drum should be washed out with petrol. It is difficult completely to free the linings of the oil they have absorbed, but soaking them in petrol for an hour or two and allowing them to dry off before reassembling the brake will go a long way towards it. Extra care should, of course, be taken thereafter not to over-lubricate the hub.

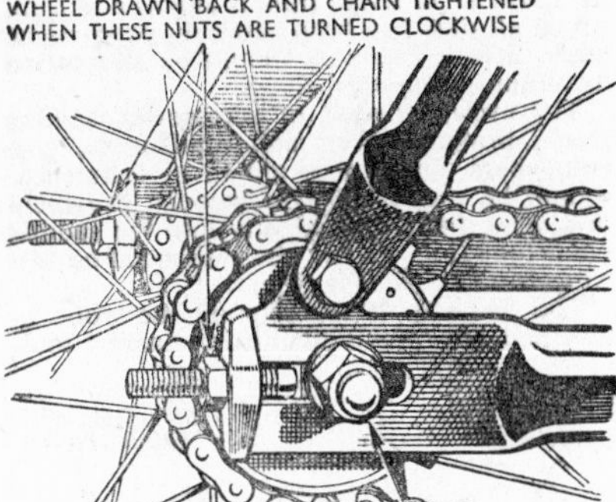

Fig. 39. Parts involved in moving the rear wheel backwards to tighten the chain.

ADJUSTING THE CHAIN. A cycle chain always stretches in time—that is to say, each link of the chain becomes slightly longer than when it was made. A chain that is subjected to severe strain, such as that which it undergoes when the cyclist decides to ride up a steep hill when others would walk, will stretch sooner than one used more considerately. A loose chain will become a nuisance and perhaps a danger, as it will frequently get jerked off the driving sprocket. A chain that is too tight, on the other hand, will exact more effort from the cyclist in turning the wheel.

To adjust the tension of the chain, slacken off the locking nuts on each end of the rear-wheel spindle and then draw the wheel back (or allow it to go farther forward, as required) by means of the small nuts behind the adjusting brackets at the tips of the fork (Fig. 39). The chain is at the correct tension when a slight sag is perceptible in both lines of chain.

A seriously stretched chain should, however, be discarded, because its continued use will wear the teeth of the driving sprocket badly. To ascertain the state of a chain, press the two lines together near the centre (Fig. 40) and see whether any links can be moved away from the opposite side of the hub sprocket; if so, the links are badly stretched and a new chain is desirable.

It is not usually satisfactory to run a new chain over an old sprocket, the teeth of which have a one-sided appearance, but to save the cost of a new free-wheel it is sometimes possible to grind the teeth down shorter and to a more symmetrical shape.

PEDALS. These are exposed to rain and dirt from the road at all times; also to hard knocks against kerbstones and often jabs into gateposts and the like. For these reasons a pedal's life is shorter than would be the case if wear were the only factor. In addition to regular lubrication with oil, a periodical dismantling of the bearings should be made; they should be cleaned and then repacked with grease or petroleum jelly before reassembly.

If the pedal does not spin freely, or if it is inclined to bump during rotation, there can be little doubt that the balls are wearing and *all* must be renewed. Never replace *some* of the old balls with new ones, as this is likely to cause jamming and damage to the ball-race. Ball-bearings are much more easily placed in the cup if this is packed with grease first.

The foregoing remarks concerning the periodical inspection of ball-bearings, their lubrication and renewal, apply equally to other bearings on the cycle, namely the hub bearings (Fig. 41), the crank, or bottom-

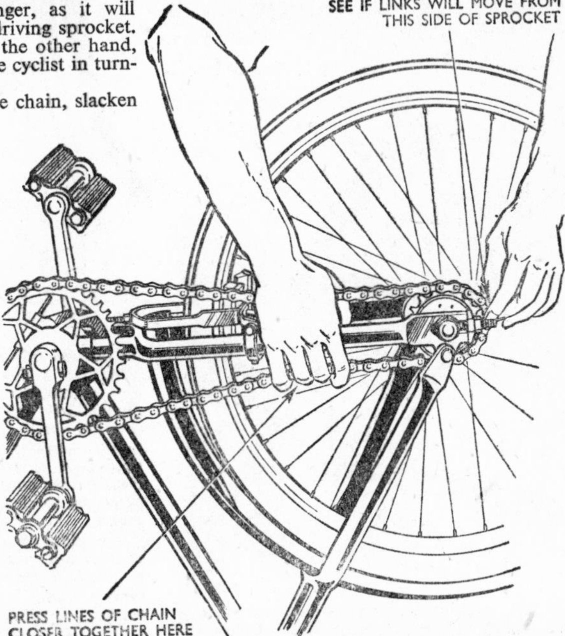

Fig. 40. Finding out the amount of stretch in the links of the chain. This test should be made periodically, for it is a false economy to continue to use a chain which has been stretched excessively.

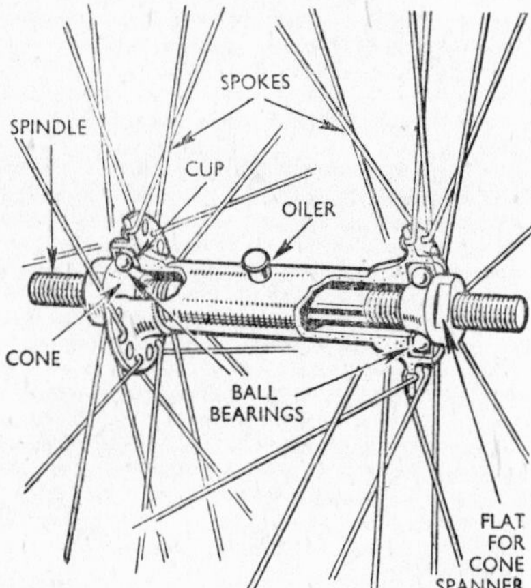

Fig. 41. Construction of the hub and bearings of a front wheel. The cones should be turned clockwise to take up play in the bearings, and unscrewed to remove the ball bearings.

bracket, spindle, the head race and that just above the shoulder of the front forks; the last two must promptly be given attention should the handlebars fail to turn easily at any time. When inserting new balls, always get in the maximum number that the cup will reasonably take.

RENOVATION. Ideal conditions for enamelling are provided by a room which is warm (or at least free from draught) and from which all dust has been carefully swept some hours before. No dust should be allowed to fly about during enamelling.

The cycle, stripped of accessories, saddle, chain, brakes, wheels and mudguards, also handlebars, unless they are to be enamelled, should be supported by a wooden peg (held in a vice) that will fit tightly into the saddle-pillar tube (Fig. 42), or else suspended on two wires from above (Fig. 43).

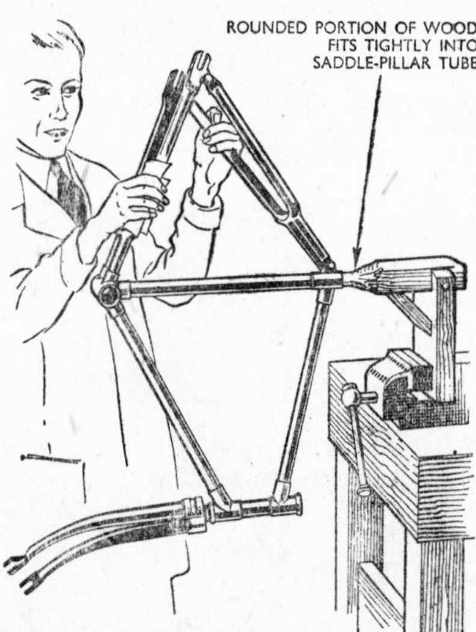

Fig. 42. A cycle frame mounted on a wooden peg and jig held by a vice ready for repainting.

The first step is to clean off the worst of the road dirt. Next, all existing enamel must be burned off, or scraped away with an old knife; it is always unsatisfactory to spread new enamel over old. The parts to be treated, particularly the inside of mudguards, must then be well scoured with emery-cloth or pumice-powder on a felt pad, care being taken to remove all rust. Finally, wipe over all surfaces with a cotton rag wetted with turpentine or petrol to clean away all traces of dust and grease.

Fig. 43. Cycle frame suspended on wires from the roof while enamelling is in progress.

The ideal dressing consists of three coats of enamel and a finish. Each of the first two coats is allowed three days to harden properly before being rubbed down with pumice-powder, washed and dried in readiness for the following coat. The third coat is allowed forty-eight hours and is then only washed before a transparent finish is put on, the whole job, by the time the cycle is reassembled, having occupied about ten days.

To reduce the whole operation to a matter of two or three days at most, patent quick-drying enamels can be used, though these are generally regarded as less durable since they are more easily chipped. However, if a reputable make of quick-drying enamel is to be used the first coat should consist of a matt enamel or flatting. This should dry in four to six hours, and then the glossy enamel can be applied without rubbing down first.

The brushes used for enamelling should be soft, the most suitable size being 1 in. for the bulk of the work; but a ½-in. brush will be valuable for small corners and the spokes.

When the glossy enamel has set, transfers may be used to imprint linings of gold or colours on the frame and mudguards, and the maker's badge on the head, if desired. The protective paper is removed from the transfers and they are given a coat of gold size on their facings. Each is then pressed firmly into place, care being exercised to see that all the transfer is making good contact and that no part is disturbed once it is down. The transfers must be allowed to dry out slowly and completely, after which the backs are thoroughly wetted and, when soaked through, are carefully peeled off.

When all traces of moisture have gone from the new transfer impressions, the final transparent coat of cellulose may be applied thinly with a perfectly clean brush. This will not only protect the transfers, but will impart a splendid finish to the enamel. Do not attempt to reassemble the cycle until certain that the final coat is dry and hard.

3. CARE OF THE MOTOR-CYCLE

As far as operation and maintenance are concerned, a motor-cycle is, of course, something of a cross between a motor-car and a pedal-cycle. For this reason there is little point in dealing in detail here with the care of the wheels, tyres, chains and renovation of the frame, because they are fully covered for cycles in preceding pages. The information and hints given apply equally to motor-cycles in regard to general principles and, to a large extent, in detail.

Similarly the hints given for the maintenance of engine and components in connexion with cars apply, broadly, to motor-cycle engines. The latter, as far as adjustments and decarbonizing are concerned, generally present far simpler tasks, because the units are almost always air-cooled and usually comprise only one or two cylinders. Also the valve gear of a four-stroke engine, being normally exposed, is readily accessible.

PISTON AND RINGS. The motor-cycle engine cylinder is usually secured to the crankcase at its base by studs, and this makes attention to piston, rings, gudgeon-pin, etc., possible without disturbing the big-end.

The cylinder is lifted off the crankcase when all nuts have been removed from the studs through the cylinder-base flange. As the cylinder is raised, care should be taken to prevent the connecting-rod and piston (preferably kept at bottom dead-centre) from falling to one side and being damaged when the piston is clear of the bore.

If the piston shows signs of distortion, it must be removed and renewed; if there is excessive play between gudgeon-pin and piston, or the bosses are wearing oval, either or both will need renewal. The gudgeon-pin should be pushed out of the piston after removal of a circlip at one end of the pin in some designs, or of soft end-pads in others.

Assuming the piston to be satisfactory, its withdrawal from the bore offers the valuable opportunity of removing the rings and cleaning the grooves thoroughly. The rings can often be eased off by the careful use of an old knife blade, but an easier and perhaps safer way is to insert three strips of tin under each ring at the gap and then work them round the piston so as to be equally spaced (Fig. 44). The ring is then sufficiently spread to be withdrawn. Before the new rings are fitted or old ones replaced, the ring grooves should be thoroughly cleaned of carbon (Fig. 45) by means of a suitable scraper or the end of an old ring.

When fitting new rings it is important to see that each is of the correct thickness so as to have no up-and-down play in the groove, but, at the same time, ability to spread and contract unhindered. Emery-cloth should be used

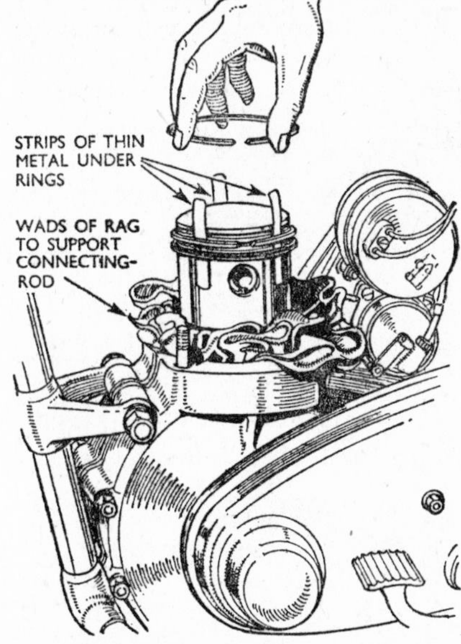

Fig. 44. Method of spreading piston rings so that they can be easily withdrawn.

Fig. 45. The easiest way to clean the grooves of a piston is to roll it along a bench whilst holding an awl or piece of old piston ring in the groove. Care must be taken not to scratch an aluminium alloy piston, easily damaged during the process.

to reduce the thickness of a new ring which is too tight.

Before a new ring is fitted the working gap should be measured. To do this fit the ring into the top of the cylinder bore and guide it into its true position by pushing it down a little way with the piston crown. Then remove the piston, without disturbing the ring, and measure the gap with a feeler gauge.

If the gap is slightly larger than stipulated by the manufacturers, this does not matter; but if smaller, metal must be filed away from one end of the ring until the gap is that recommended, or at least 0·020 in., or damage may be done to the bore when the engine gets hot.

The condition of the gasket between cylinder base and crankcase is very important because, if there is not a perfect joint when the cylinder is replaced, considerable oil leakage will occur; on a two-stroke engine it is even vital, for a fault here will provide also a gas leak.

MAGNETO. Ignition in motor-cycle engines is generally provided by a magneto. In order to ensure efficient operation, the following points must be checked periodically:

(1) The slip-ring must be kept clean. To clean it, first remove the collector-brush assembly at the end of the H.T. cable (it is held in place by a spring clip or two screws), and then hold a petrol-moistened rag against the ring while the armature shaft is rotated several times by the use of the kick-starter (Fig. 46).

(2) Before replacing the carbon brush see that it is free in its holder and wipe it clean. The holder must be renewed if there is any sign of a crack in it.

(3) The small earthing brush, situated behind the contact-breaker plate on some units, should be cleaned.

(4) The contact-breaker points should be reset if necessary so that, when fully open, the gap is between 0·010 in. and 0·014 in. The points should be cleaned and re-faced so as to make good all-over contact with each other when closed. If the points are known to be platinum a suitable small file can be used, but for tungsten points a carborundum slip is necessary.

(5) Make sure that the rocker arm of the contact-breaker is not even slightly tight on its pivot. It is worth removing, first, the spring, and then the rocker arm, occasionally to clean or polish the pivot, and then to give it a touch of petroleum jelly.

Many manufacturers recommend that the magneto be dismantled every ten or twelve thousand miles so that the bearings can be thoroughly cleaned and repacked with high-melting-point grease. To avoid serious damage when dismantling, the earthing brush (if fitted) and the safety-gap screw must be removed before any attempt is made to take off the end plate and withdraw the armature.

CYCLE PARTS. Apart from maintaining chains at the correct tension, and seeing that they are cleaned periodically and thoroughly lubricated in the manner described for push-bike chains, it is as well to check, from time to time, that the sprockets of both primary and rear chains are in perfect alignment.

Wheel-hub bearings should occasionally be tested for backlash and judiciously tightened up if necessary. A plain roller- or ball-bearing hub should have no perceptible play, but a taper-roller bearing must be allowed a little. Hub bearings are not always properly serviced by injecting grease into the hub nipples, and it is generally much more satisfactory to remove them and wash out all grit every six or eight thousand miles. They should then be repacked with high-melting-point grease.

When greasing the steering head and fork spindles, always inject until a reasonable amount of the old grease, which contains grit, has been squeezed out. This should be done regularly as, otherwise, wear or lack of lubrication in these parts will soon have adverse effects upon the steering.

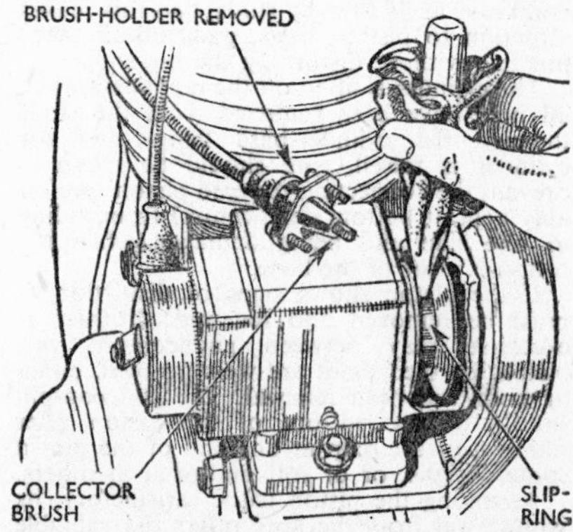

Fig. 46. Part-cut-away view of a motor-cycle magneto, showing how the slip-ring is cleaned with a rag over a screwdriver which is inserted in the hole after removing the brush-holder.

PAINTING AND DECORATING

Essential information for the amateur, alphabetically arranged, on the application of paints, distemper and wallpaper.

ABRASIVES. In the preparation of painted surfaces a variety of materials are used for bringing about a smooth finish.

Glass-paper. This, being glue-bound, can only be used for dry rubbing down.

Waterproof abrasive paper. This material, which can be used either dry or in conjunction with water, came into prominence when the dry rubbing down of lead-painted surfaces was prohibited. It is more expensive than glass-paper, but results may be obtained quickly and effectively, justifying the extra cost (Fig. 1).

Pumice-stone. The lumps of natural pumice are sawn across the grain to provide a flat rubbing surface.

Powdered pumice-stone. The powder, used in conjunction with a felt pad and with water as a lubricant, is employed in the rubbing down of finishes in paint and varnish (Fig. 2).

Prepared rubbing blocks of proprietary brands. Made from abrasive powder, such as pumice, they usually contain a material which acts as a paint solvent during the rubbing down, and may only be employed over old painted surfaces. A wash with weak vinegar is advisable before painting is commenced.

Steel wool. The finer grades of steel wool are useful for rubbing down mouldings, as they fit the shape better than other abrasives.

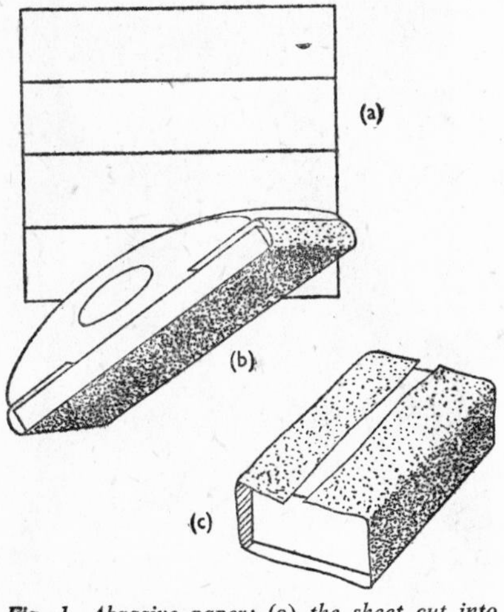

Fig. 1. Abrasive paper: (a) *the sheet cut into strips of suitable size;* (b) *fitted to a rubber;* (c) *folded round a wooden block.*

Steel-wire brushes. These are used for scouring off paint and rust from iron and steel.

Mild abrasives. The finer grades of waterproof paper, cuttle-fish bone, putty powder

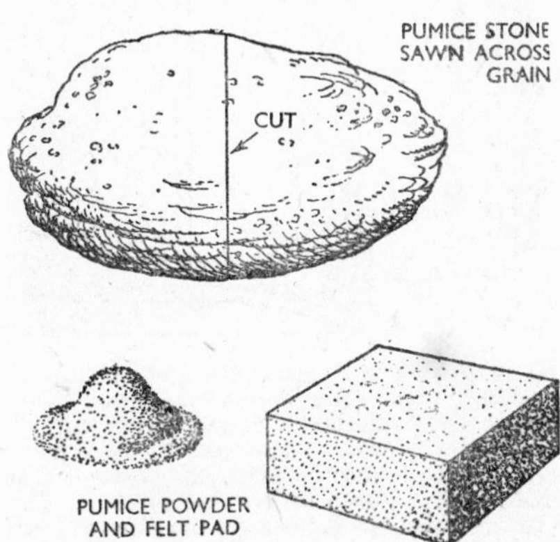

Fig. 2. Pumice-stone can be used in the lump or as powder applied with a felt pad.

and rotten-stone are used on the final coats of varnish to produce a fine finish.

ADHESIVES. See WALLPAPER AND PAPER-HANGING.

ALUMINIUM AND BRONZE PAINTS. The powder is in the form of fine flakes of ground metal which when mixed with a suitable medium and applied to a surface make a complete metal covering of good protective value. These paints are obtainable either ready-mixed in oil-varnish, spirit or cellulose medium; as powder and medium, to mix as required; or the powder may be mixed with japanner's gold size diluted with white spirit. Good grades of aluminium paint or lacquer will retain colour and lustre for a reasonable time, but the bronze paints, which tarnish quickly, should be clear-lacquered.

Clear lacquer can be made from 1½ oz. of white shellac dissolved in 1 pint methylated spirit.

ASBESTOS SHEETS. These are often charged with moisture which in drying out deposits alkaline salts which are fatal to paint. Neutralize by treating the surface with weak acetic acid, or zinc sulphate solution, though results are not always satisfactory. Afterwards wash the sheets to remove surplus acid and leave to dry. An alkali-resisting primer should

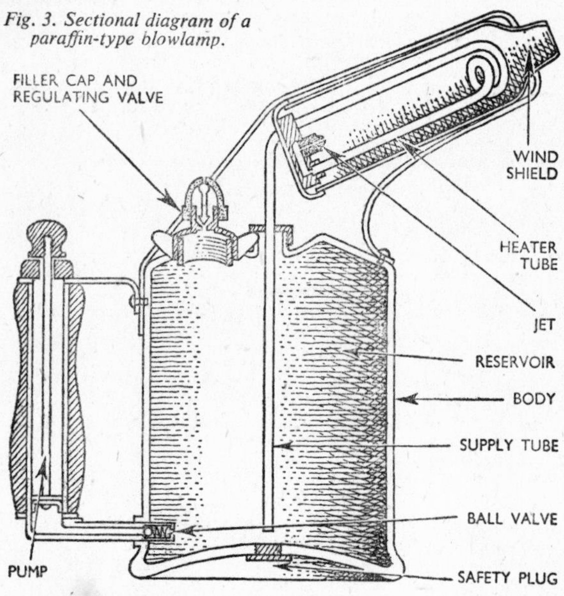

Fig. 3. Sectional diagram of a paraffin-type blowlamp.

be used. Do not use linseed-oil paint for priming; paint containing China wood oil is better and is obtainable already prepared.

BLOWLAMPS. These are of two main types, petrol and paraffin, the latter being fitted with a pump to increase pressure. The general directions for use are the same in both types. The reservoir should be filled to within ½ in. of the top, the cap screwed firmly in place, and the surplus supply of spirit removed to a safe distance. The cup on top of the reservoir should be filled with methylated spirit and lit to warm the condenser or heater tube. Do not open the release valve until the cup is almost empty or a jet of spirit may be ejected instead of the gas which provides the heat (see Fig. 3).

Fig. 4 shows the use of a gas jet as an alternative to a blowlamp.

In using a blowlamp to burn off old paint, burning should be started at the bottom, mouldings being scraped first with a shavehook. Adjacent flat areas should be tackled next with a broad knife. Keep a hot flame with the lamp constantly moving to avoid charring the wood. Drop the debris into a bucket of water. When all the paint is burnt off, rub down the wood with glasspaper, dust down and cover knots with two thin coats of shellac knotting.

BRONZE PAINTS. See ALUMINIUM AND BRONZE PAINTS.

BRUSHES. The initial cost of good brushes is relatively high, but careful use and storage after use make them a more economic outlay than are the cheap varieties.

Bristle and substitutes. The chief component of a good brush is the bristle from the hog or pig. Bristles have a natural bend and spring, not found in other materials from which brushes may be made. In use they become compact, holding paint well and allowing of even spreading. The alternatives to bristles are, chiefly, horsehair and Mexican fibre. These lack compactness, cause splashing, and make it difficult to lay off paint in a satisfactory manner. Many brushes contain one of these adulterants, and although they compare unfavourably with the pure bristle brush, either in life or usability, they make useful tools if the proportion of adulterant is not too large.

Brushes with thin tips and thickness near the handle, caused by the excessive use of short-length bristles, soon wear down and become stumpy.

Test for bristle. If held in a flame, bristle will frizzle, giving off the odour of burning horn or skin. It always splits at the tip, tapers from root to tip, and

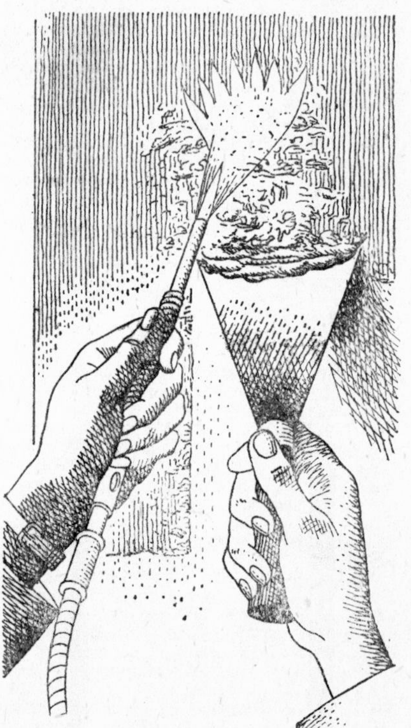

Fig. 4. Using a gas jet to remove paint.

when bent will spring back into its original position. Horsehair is cut into lengths, does not taper and lacks spring. Mexican fibre is of vegetable origin, irregular in section, and when bent is easily cracked and broken. It burns quietly, with a bright flame, leaving little ash or residue. But it is useful for lime-washing and for applying caustic solutions, which destroy animal matter.

The chief source of supply at present is India, from which black bristles of good quality are obtained, but these are less hard-wearing and shorter than grey. They make useful brushes of the flat type, and are often short enough to use without binding, or with a temporary metal binding (Fig. 5), removable as the brushes wear down. They may be regarded as the handy brushes, quickly broken-in and easily washed out after use.

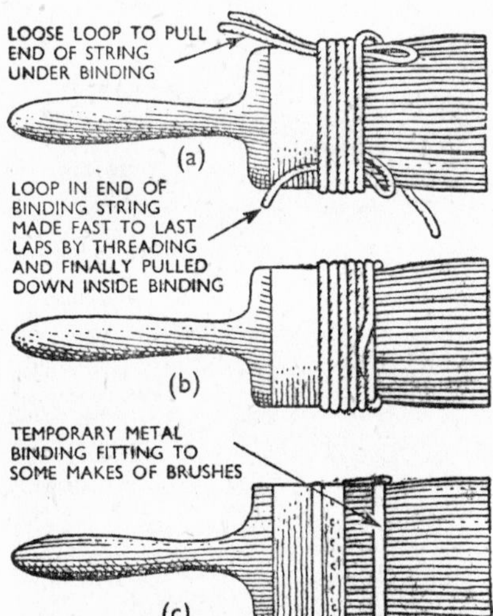

Fig. 5. (a) *and* (b) *Two stages in binding a brush to strengthen the fibres;* (c) *an alternative method which is sometimes employed.*

Care of brushes. A new brush contains dust and loose bristles, which can be removed by twirling and shaking. Some brushes are stamped "soak before use," in order to tighten the binding, and prevent the bristles falling out. Brushes not so marked may usually be put into paint after the preliminary twirling.

After use brushes must never be left standing in the paint; they should be washed out in white spirit, followed by soap and water, and then left to dry. If in constant daily use, they may, after the final washing, be suspended in a can containing water which should just cover the bristles (Fig. 6). Distemper brushes, after use in either distemper or water-paint, must always be washed out in several changes of water and suspended to dry.

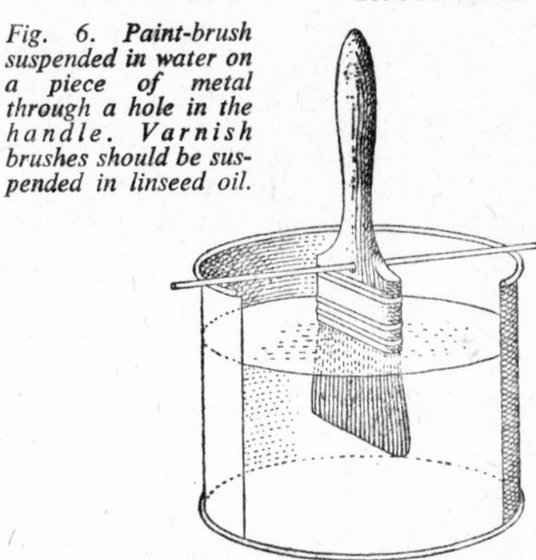

Fig. 6. ***Paint-brush** suspended in water on a piece of metal through a hole in the handle. Varnish brushes should be suspended in linseed oil.*

Types of brushes. The flat black-bristle painting brushes may be obtained in sizes ranging from ¼ in. to 3 in., while wall-painting brushes may be of 4 in. to 5 in. in size.

Distemper brushes are known by the weight of bristle built into them, for example, 6 oz., 7 oz., 8 oz., etc.

A dusting brush, an essential tool of the painter's kit, is used for removing dust particles from a surface before painting.

BRUSHWORK. Good brushwork is the hallmark of craftsmanship.

Holding the brush. When taking up the paint-brush it should be held in the same way that a pen is held in writing (Fig. 7). With the larger wall brush the same grip may be adopted, but with all fingers lying along the shank of the handle and the thumb at the opposite side (Fig. 8). The still larger distemper brush is held in the same way that a stick would be held, with the handle in the palm of the hand, fingers round the shaft, and the thumb down the side of the shaft (Fig. 9). It will be found, in practice, that these two latter grips may be interchanged as the position and purpose changes; for example, when working on a ceiling the latter grip would be employed, while on a wall surface

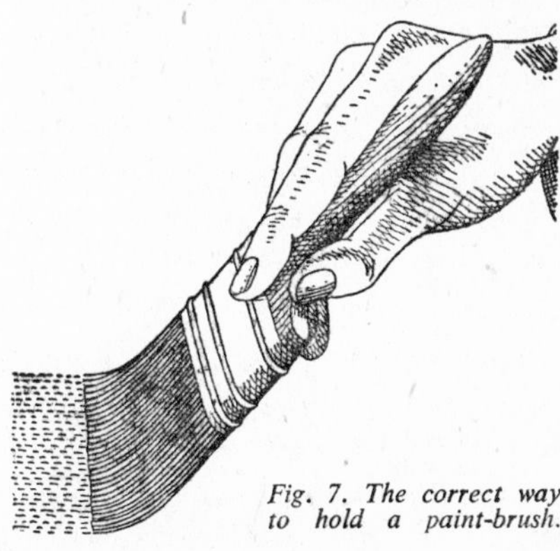

Fig. 7. The correct way to hold a paint-brush.

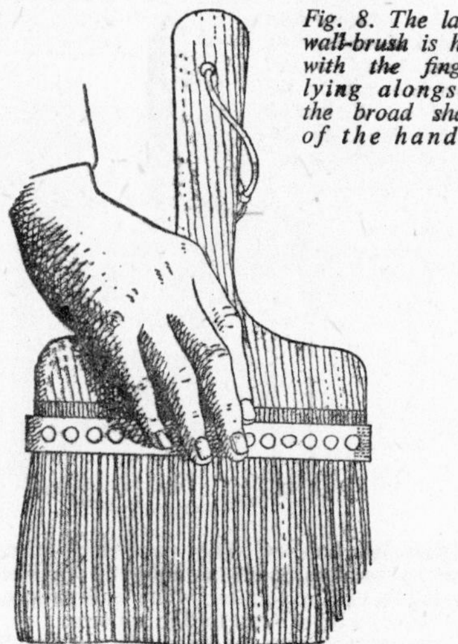

Fig. 8. The large wall-brush is held with the fingers lying alongside the broad shank of the handle.

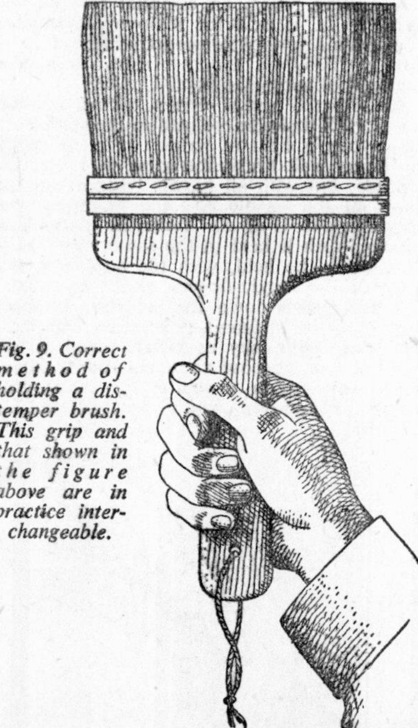

Fig. 9. Correct method of holding a distemper brush. This grip and that shown in the figure above are in practice interchangeable.

the laying-in might be with the first grip, and the laying-off with the second.

Applying paint. Dip the brush about an inch into the paint; slap off excess on the side of the paint-kettle. If the brush requires scraping, twist the can round and scrape the brush on the dirty side. Spread the paint evenly over the whole immediate surface to be covered. Cross-off either diagonally in both directions, or at right-angles to grain of the wood, and finally lay-off with a light touch up and down, or with the grain of the wood. This procedure should be adopted for every coat; careless brushwork in the preliminary coats will show through in the finishing. All brush strokes must "follow through"; do not use short, finicky strokes.

Never allow paint to get into the stock of the brush; never stand the brush in the kettle of paint; and when not in use, lay the brush across the kettle with the tip resting on the side opposite to the handle of the kettle (Fig. 10). When, as is sometimes necessary, the

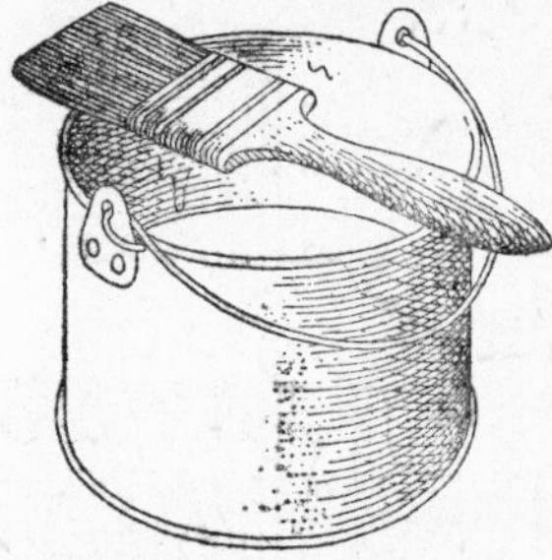

Fig. 10. When resting a brush on a paint-kettle see that the bristles are always on the same side and away from the handle.

brush has to be scraped out, make a practice of doing it at one side of the kettle only; the other side, which should be held towards the clothing, should be kept clean.

CELLULOSE. Composition. Lacquer: nitrocellulose, resin, solvent, diluent, plasticizer; enamel: suitable pigments are added to the lacquer. Cellulose has a very strong and penetrating odour to which many people object. The spirits which cause it, however, evaporate so quickly that once the surface is dry no smell remains. It does not linger as with oil-paint.

Application. The condition of the surface to which it is intended to apply cellulose is important. The solvents used in its composition are similar to those used in paint-removers; therefore, it follows that it cannot be used over new paint, although it may go over old. It is advisable to make a test before carrying out the work. If the cellulose, after application to a small area, causes the paint to become soft and to crinkle, stripping is necessary.

Painted surfaces should be rubbed down to secure a level ground before applying cellulose. If the surface is new, or is one from which the paint has been removed, a special primer and undercoat should be employed to obtain a good finish.

Application by spray is the most satisfactory method: (1) because drying is so quick, and (2) because the first coat is softened as the second is being applied. Special lacquers and enamels are made for application with the brush, but even these call for quick handling to avoid unevenness; despite these disadvantages, there are many small jobs to which this medium is specially suited.

Lacquers made for application with a brush are free-flowing and should be evenly applied, with one or two strokes of the brush, and allowed to flow out. Crossing and laying-off are not possible as in paintwork.

Cellulose does not make so thick a coat as does paint, and careful preparation and rubbing down are required to obtain a good finish.

CELLULOSE FINISHES. Lacquer over hardwoods. This covers application to woods such as oak and mahogany. The wood should be rubbed down with fine sandpaper in the direction of the grain only, or left as it comes from the plane. The filler (see STOPPING AND FILLING) may be obtained ready prepared, and should be applied with a cloth pad without thinning. It should be rubbed into the pores, left for about fifteen minutes, and then rubbed again with a coarse pad, working across the grain, leaving the pores filled and the surface clear (Fig. 11). Two coats of clear cellulose should be applied, time being allowed for the first to set. The coats are much thinner than two coats of varnish and the pores will be found to be slightly recessed.

Fig. 11. Applying the filler across the grain in preparation for a cellulose finish to a smooth wood surface.

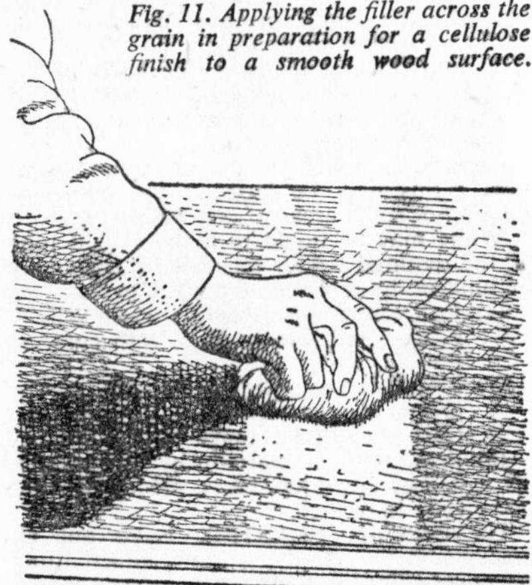

Level up the surface by using a levelling or pull-over solution, supplied by the cellulose manufacturers. A pad of soft cloth or cotton-wool covered with chamois leather is well moistened with the solution and passed over the surface with light, circular movements, finally finishing off in the same direction as the grain.

Flatting and polishing. For a medium finish the work may be left at the stage described above, but for a high-class finish flatting and polishing are essential. Allow at least two hours after the last operation. Use grade 320 or 400 waterproof paper on a rubbing block, and with water as a lubricant rub down the surface to an even dullness. Commence with the mouldings and narrow portions and do large areas last. Allow the work to stand overnight.

For finishing the following materials are required: burnishing paste, paste or liquid polish, soft rag, and clean, soft, dry cloth. Begin with the burnishing paste, applied thinly on soft rag; use the rag with light, circular movements, going over the surface until a semi-gloss is developed. Follow this with the polish, also applied by means of the soft rag, and in the same way, finishing with long, straight strokes.

Pigment or enamel finishes. For new surfaces the following are required: priming, either an oil or synthetic paint; filling, made from either a flat oil-paint thickened with good-quality whiting and slate powder and applied with a filling knife, or several coats of synthetic filler applied with a brush.

When dry the work should be rubbed to a level surface with abrasive and water as described above. Cellulose sealer primer is then applied, allowed to dry, and prepared for the enamel coat by facing down with 320 abrasive paper and water.

Two coats of enamel are applied, and the work is finished by flatting down and burnishing as described for lacquer finishes.

Other finishes. Cellulose bronzes (gold paints) keep their colour well. They do not require further lacquering. To obtain lustre effects, add bronze powder to an enamel which has been reduced in body with clear lacquer.

Small articles, such as toys, may be decorated in distemper and protected with two coats of clear lacquer.

CEMENT AND PLASTER. Painting over. Most cement and plaster surfaces (especially Portland cement) contain alkaline salts which in the presence of moisture become active and destroy oil-paint. The safest way to prepare such surfaces for painting is to leave them for six months to dry out; distemper (which can afterwards be washed off) may be used as a temporary decoration. If the above is not possible, a proprietary primer for cement can be obtained for application before painting. It should always be remembered that structural moisture may work through from the back, and if this happens this measure cannot be effective to any degree.

COLOUR. Colour harmony is the pleasing arrangement of a scheme embracing two or more colours, or tones of a colour. Harmony is dependent on the tone and proportion between the colours used. The following notes apply to interior decoration.

Things to consider. An interior is first of all a background for a purpose and that purpose may not be fulfilled until the interior is peopled. In other words, not only the ceiling, walls, furniture and furnishings, but the people to occupy a room must be considered in the planning of a colour scheme, and with all this will have to be considered the means of illumination, daylight or artificial, which will have a bearing on the amount of light and shade.

Tone and proportion. In the building up of a colour scheme, tone and proportion do not always receive the attention due to them. *Tone* is the varying degrees of light and dark, irrespective of colour value. *Proportion* is the relationship between contrasting tones and/or colours; there is no proportion between equal things or areas. The value given to the above may be best appreciated by taking a scheme built up from white and black, and greys made from the admixture of the first two:

Ceiling and walls. A neutral white (a colour may be so near to white that it is difficult to name, and such terms as blue-white, warm-white, ivory-white arise as different degrees of whiteness).

Curtains. Light grey.

Furniture. Deeper grey, with white and black in small proportions.

Upholstery. Deeper grey, also with white and black added to relieve plain areas.

Carpet. Dark grey.

Woodwork. Medium grey; door, black.

Although this scheme lacks colour in the accepted sense, it has these qualities. White predominates, both in itself, and also in the

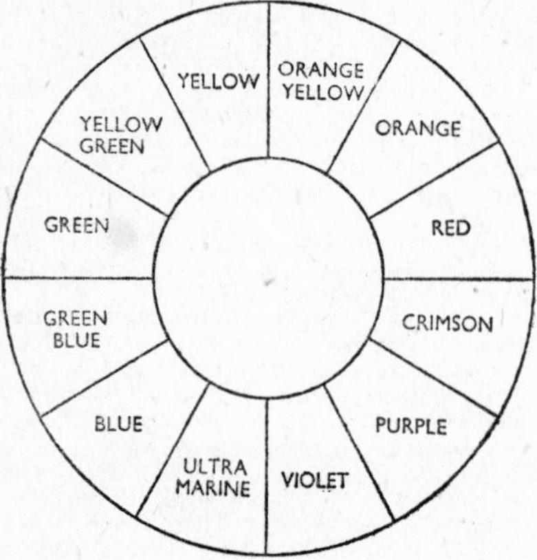

Fig. 12. Colour circle. Allied colours are adjacent; complementary colours are opposite.

mixture of greys, while the darker tones of grey and black in smaller proportions give a contrast of dark to light. In addition, the white and the lighter greys receive other tones by light and shade; the window side of the room is darker in tone than the rest of the room and pieces of furniture may cast shadows, making other tones. The original colours are affected by the play of light and shade, the scheme making a range of tones from the ceiling downwards, with curtains, furniture, etc., making a pattern of form and shape on a foundation of the dark carpet.

Texture. Flat wall surfaces, fabrics, glossy surfaces, all receive light and break up the effect in different ways and degrees. This scheme has endless possibilities: the walls may be in stripes or bands of tones, the curtains may be spotted, and pattern be introduced in other ways, without adding other colours.

Theory of colour. The colour circle (Fig. 12) —adopted by most authorities—is an ordered arrangement of colours (hues). The colours, it will be noted, gradually change in hue and tone; yellow, being the lightest, is followed down one side of the circle by orange, red, etc., and down the other by yellow-green, green, blue, etc., each colour being deeper in tone than its neighbour, with purple, opposite yellow, as the darkest colour. This is the natural order, an order which is generally adopted in colour schemes; when departed from, a discord is produced; for example, a light pink is discordant with deep yellow.

Opposite each colour is its complementary or contrasting colour. By the side of each colour are those which contain some of that colour, so that all have a family likeness. Simple colour schemes may be built up in a number of ways:

(1) Monochromatic, using tones of one colour.
(2) Using related colours and tones of those colours.
(3) Introducing the complementary colour.
  (*a*) As in (2), but adding small areas of the complementary.
  (*b*) As in (2), but adding proportions of the complementary by mixing as well as small areas.

Both (*a*) and (*b*) form the basis of the majority of colour schemes, the addition of the complementary in one way or another making for completeness.

Sometimes a scheme suffers from "prettiness"; this may be lessened by the introduction of small areas of discord colour.

White may be tinted to make a light tone of the required colour scheme. Schemes may be built up by replacing the white by:

(1) Pale yellow, supported by warm yellow, orange, red, brown, etc., with contrast in blue.
(2) Pale green, supported by pale yellow, green, blue-green, grey, etc., with contrast in reddish colours.
(3) Blue-grey, supported by cool-white, deeper grey-blue, blues, etc., with contrast in orange.

CRACKS IN PLASTER. Rake out all cracks with the point of a knife, undercutting the edges (Fig. 13). Soak the crack with water,

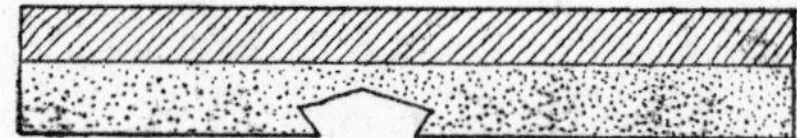

Fig. 13. Section through plaster with the edges of a crack undercut for replastering.

which may be applied by slashing with the distemper brush. Take plaster-of-paris and whiting, in equal proportions, and mix with water to a thick paste. When using distemper, this may be added to the plaster-of-paris in place of the whiting. Plaster-of-paris used alone sets too quickly for amateur use. Press the plaster well into the cracks with a broad knife and level off to the surface. When the plaster is nearly set, go over it with a damp distemper brush. When the plaster is dry it should be rubbed down with glass-paper.

Before repainting, distempering or papering, all cracks should be painted, as new plaster is more absorbent than the old.

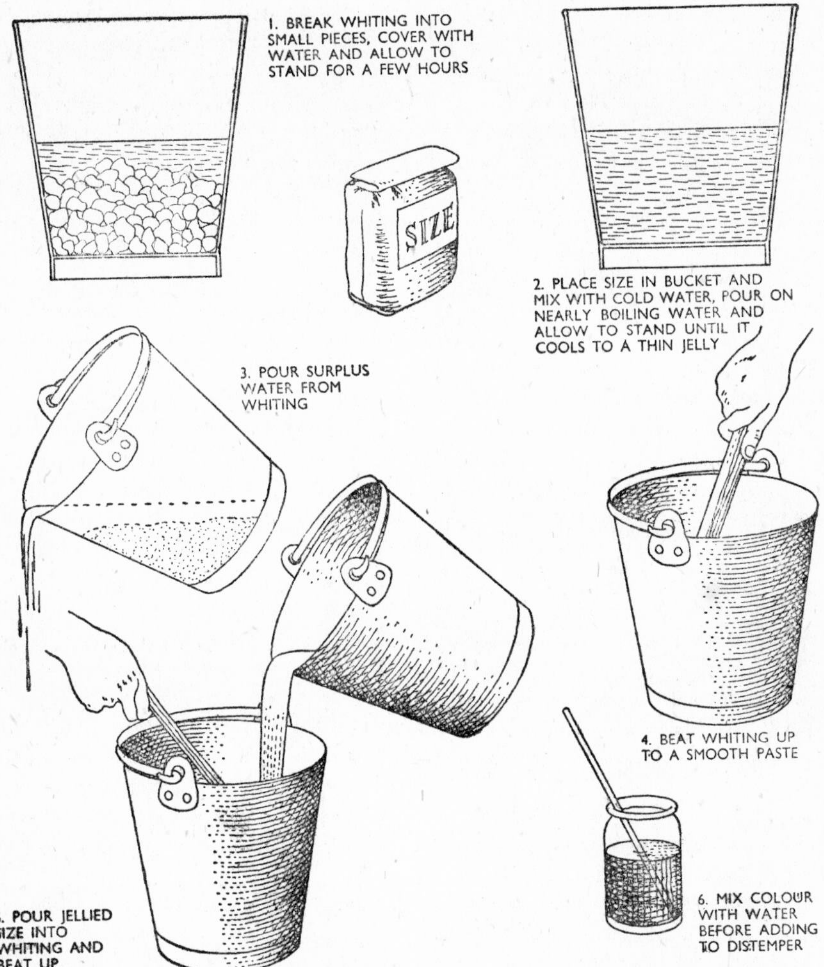

Fig. 14. Six stages in the preparation of distemper. It can, of course, be bought ready-mixed.

Hair cracks. These are very fine cracks which sometimes appear in plaster. They are too fine to be filled with plaster, and paint filler should be used instead.

DISTEMPER. Preparation (Fig. 14). Break 7 lb. of whiting in small pieces, place in a bucket, cover with water and allow to stand for several hours. Concentrated glue-size is used as a binder. Mix ½ lb. of size with water and soak for a few minutes; add ½ gal. of very hot water (not boiling); allow it to stand until cold, when the size should be a thin jelly.

Pour surplus water from the whiting, well beat up and add colours, previously wetted, to obtain the required tint (as distemper is very much lighter when dry than wet, tests should be made by putting samples on a piece of white paper and drying before the fire); add the jellied size, slightly warmed if necessary; mix thoroughly and strain through hessian.

Preparing the surface. If the surface has been previously distempered it must be washed off (Fig. 15). Take a bucket three-parts full of water, and with a distemper brush soak a portion of the surface, scrub with the brush, frequently washing it out in the bucket, taking off the remaining distemper with a large sponge or wet cloth. It is an advantage to fill in any cracks as the washing proceeds.

Application of distemper. To obtain the best results, apply a preparatory coat of clearcole (size to which a little distemper has been added) and allow to dry. As distemper dries

Fig. 15. Washing a wall with a distemper brush.

quickly, close windows and doors to exclude draughts. Commence distempering at the window side and, once begun, carry the work through to keep all edges wet, until a break in the surface occurs. Apply the distemper quickly and evenly, and when finished open the window to hasten the drying.

Colours used in distemper. Zinc-chrome, ochre, raw and burnt sienna, raw and burnt umber, venetian red, indian red, orange-chrome, lime-blue, lime-green, and black; all bought in powder form. It is important that these colours be well wetted with water before being added to distemper.

To make tints, use the following mixtures:

Cream: white and ochre or white and raw sienna.

Straw colour: white, ochre and raw umber.

Stone colour: white, ochre and burnt umber.

Grey-green: white, ochre and black.

Pale yellow: white and zinc-chrome.

Primrose green: white, zinc-chrome and lime-green.

Pink: white and venetian red.

Salmon-pink: white, venetian red and ochre.

Sky-blue: white, lime-blue and touch of black.

Lavender: white, lime-blue and indian red.

DOORS. Sequence of parts in painting. The order in which the various parts should be painted is shown in the illustration of a four-panel door (Fig. 16), and it is important that this order should be maintained for all coats. Where the panels are moulded the moulds should be painted first. The same principles should be applied for more or fewer panels.

ENAMEL. See under CELLULOSE and CELLULOSE FINISHES.

FAULTS IN PAINT AND VARNISH. **Blistering.** Usually due to moisture in or on the surface painted; caused also by spirits, which form gases, being locked under the surface-dry paint, usually when thick coats of paint have been applied.

Cracking. Chiefly caused by addition of too much driers, which results in the paint drying on the surface while remaining soft underneath; when the undercoat finally dries it cracks the surface. There are other causes, such as the application of a hard-drying coat over one that is more elastic.

Flashing, that is, unwanted glossy patches on flat or semi-flat finishes. Caused by allowing edges to dry partially when coating a surface. May occur in distempering, painting or varnishing.

Loss of gloss, smeariness. Caused by uneven suction in undercoats or by a draught striking the partially dry surface of a gloss finish.

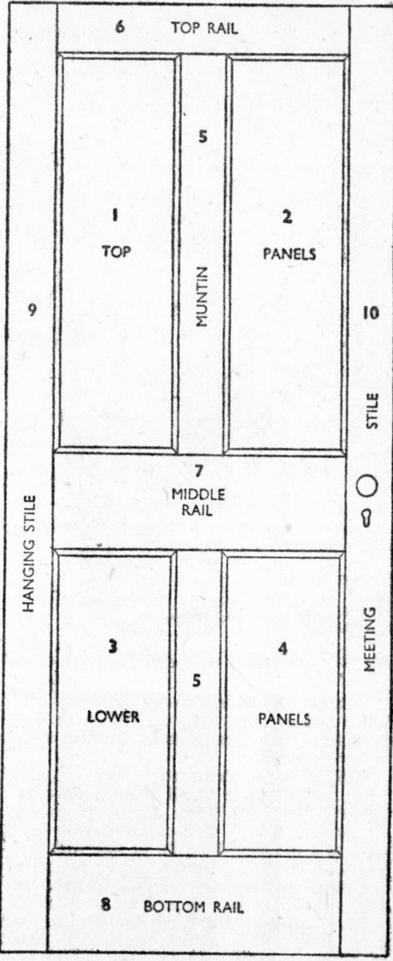

Fig. 16. Sequence for painting the parts of a door. It must be maintained for each coat.

Fig. 17. Using a drag or graining brush to obtain a woody effect on a painted panel.

FILLING: See STOPPING AND FILLING.

GLAZING. See RELIEVING PLAIN SURFACES.

GRAINING. This is the representation of a woody effect in paint. It is obtained by means of a ground coat glazed over with a semi-transparent medium in which the woody effects are worked. The ground colour should be made to dry hard and with a slight gloss, and coloured to represent the lightest tone of the wood.

For oak grounds use a buff shade depending upon whether the finished effect is to be warm or cool, light or dark; for mahogany ground use salmon colour or yellowish red.

Glazes may be purchased ready-made, usually under the name of scumbles. These require thinning only with either oil or turpentine.

Oak Brush-graining. This aims at a broad woody effect and not at a faithful imitation of woods. Apply the graining colour (glaze) as a thin film over the surface; do not apply it so thickly as paint. Drags or tools for brush-graining (which can be purchased) are best for the purpose, but a paperhanger's brush or a coarse, dry paint-brush may be used for putting in the straight grain marks represented in brush-graining (see Fig. 17).

Commence with the panels, bringing the brush from the top to the bottom at each stroke; as each panel is finished, follow on with the mouldings, then the other panels, cross-rails and stiles. Surplus glaze should be wiped off the stiles as each panel is laid on. Otherwise the glaze will partially set and leave dark patches when the stiles are grained.

KNOTTING. Shellac dissolved in alcohol is used for sealing knots in wood before painting.

LACQUER. See ALUMINIUM AND BRONZE PAINTS, CELLULOSE and CELLULOSE FINISHES.

LADDERS. To reach high places it is often necessary to fasten two or more ladders together; failure to adopt the correct method may lead to serious accidents (see Fig. 18).

LEAD. Lead is injurious when taken into the system by breathing in the dust, or by dirty hands conveying particles to the mouth. Trouble may be avoided by rubbing down all lead-painted surfaces with pumice-stone (or waterproof paper) and water, and by keeping the hands clean.

ODOUR OF PAINT may be changed by adding a few drops of oil of spike lavender to

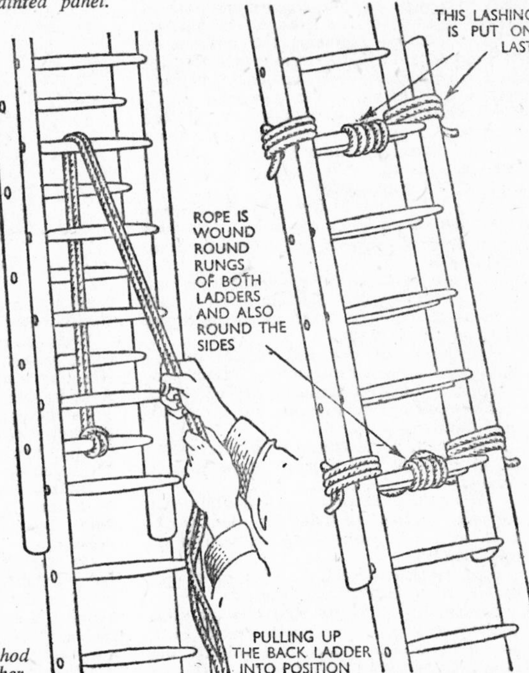

Fig. 18. Correct and safe method of joining two ladders together.

the paint, or lessened by placing buckets of water in the room. Hay may with advantage be added to the water.

OIL-PAINT, COMPOSITION OF. To understand the relative composition of paint which may be employed, and the variations of

Fig. 19. Ingredients from which paint is made.

purpose, a brief résumé is given of its chief components, characteristics and uses.

Ingredients of paint (Fig. 19).

Pigment. The solid portion of the paint (usually obtained ready-ground in oil, making incorporation in the paint easier).

Binder. May be any drying oil, usually refined (raw) linseed oil, varnish, etc.

Drier. A drying agent, incorporated in a paste (patent driers), or liquids (terebene, liquid oil driers, gold size, etc.).

Thinner. Turpentine or white-spirit.

Drying of paint. Oil-paint dries by oxidization of the oil content, turning the oil from a liquid to a solid and binding the particles of pigment together on the surface. The amount of oil, therefore, regulates the amount of driers required. There are certain exceptions to this. Lead pigments enter into chemical combination with the oil, so that in a paint with a base of white lead less driers are required. Red lead itself is a powerful drier, and little or no driers are required. Some pigments, such as blacks, retard the drying action and an addition of driers is necessary.

During the drying of the paint the thinner should evaporate without leaving residue; inferior types of thinner may cause cracking of the paint.

Variations in paint composition. Assuming that the same weight of pigment in oil is used for each type of paint, the following broad variations can be made:

Priming paint. For soft woods or dry semi-porous plaster surfaces, a larger proportion of oil over thinners, say 65 to 35.

Undercoating. 50 per cent oil to 50 per cent thinners.

Flat paint. A minimum of binder, either oil or varnish, and a large proportion of thinners.

Gloss paint (interior). Would contain only sufficient thinners to make the paint workable, with a corresponding increase of oil or boiled oil.

Gloss paint (exterior). An addition of pale varnish to replace some of the oil.

Specimen priming for new deal or pine. White lead in oil, 7 lb.; patent driers, 7 oz., or liquid driers, 4 oz.; raw linseed oil, 11 oz.; turpentine or white-spirit, 7 oz.

PAINTING. On new woodwork, or woodwork from which paint has been stripped. Scrape off any glue, plaster, etc., adhering to the surface, sandpaper rough places, and dust down. Soft woods invariably contain knots, which must be covered to prevent them from staining through to the finished surface. Patent knotting (a quick-drying varnish) is brushed over them, preferably in two thin coats; sappy places should be likewise treated (Fig. 20). Priming paint is applied to even the suction and to provide a key for the

Fig. 20. Applying knotting before painting.

following coats of paint, while it also, being tinted, evens up the tone.

Evenness of paint at this stage, as well as at other stages, will lead to good results and straining is a first principle. Straining may be done by tying a piece of thin muslin, or old silk stocking, over a can and pouring the paint through it (Fig. 21). Brush the paint well into the nail holes and mouldings, and lay-off the surface in the direction of the grain.

On new plaster. Stop up cracks (see CRACKS IN PLASTER), allow to dry, and prime with paint, adjusting the oil content to suit the porosity of the surface.

On previously painted surfaces. Do not remove the paint unless it is badly cracked or loose, as the paint now on will act as a filler, giving a good surface when rubbed down. If the paint must be removed, it may either be burnt off (see BLOWLAMPS), or removed with a paint-remover (see PAINT-REMOVERS).

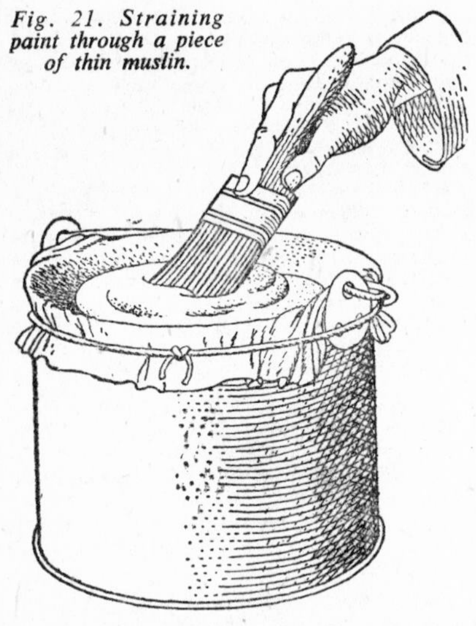
Fig. 21. Straining paint through a piece of thin muslin.

When priming is dry, all nail holes and cracks should be stopped up, the stopping being well pressed in, leaving the surrounding surface clean. If it is desired to make a first-class job, the surface must be filled up, and the filling when quite hard rubbed down to a level surface (see STOPPING AND FILLING).

Sequence of coats in painting. Follow the priming with an oily coat, next with one containing more turpentine, alternating one oily, one flat, the last undercoat depending on the type of finish. If the finish is to be flat, the last undercoat must be oily; if finish is to be glossy, the undercoat must be flat.

When painting woodwork, mouldings should be painted first, taking care that the paint is well worked into the angles of the members. Use a larger brush for the flats, crossing-off the paint and laying-off in the direction of the grain of the wood. In painting the bars of windows, paint downwards in long strokes. Paint should be taken on to the glass so that the joint between putty and glass is well sealed. See also BRUSHWORK.

PAINT MIXING. Take a clean paint-kettle, rub linseed oil round the inside to prevent lumps of paint sticking to the sides, put in the required colours, and with a mixing stick beat up the stiff paste to an even consistency, adding linseed oil gradually and stirring it in as each part is added. Put in driers and mix well and add turpentine to thin. Straining will improve mixing, and remove coarse particles.

Ready-mixed paints. On opening the tin it may be found that the solid portion of the paint is at the bottom in a more or less stiff mass, while the thinners are at the top. Pour off the thinners into a paint-kettle and beat up the thick paint until it becomes more plastic; then put the thinners back gradually, continuing with the beating.

These paints, if made by firms of good repute, are convenient to use, and do the work for which they are made. They are more finely ground, with the ingredients more intimately mixed, than paints made by hand; but the amateur should be warned that there are many inferior kinds on the market.

PAINT-REMOVERS. These are of two main types, caustic and spirit. Caustic potash is dissolved in hot water to make a solution which when applied to a painted surface will penetrate the paint film so that it can be removed with scrapers. There are certain disadvantages to its use. Being a water solution, it raises the grain of the wood, and great care must be exercised in its use to avoid burning of the skin by splashing or other ways of contact. If this method is used the surface of the work must afterwards be washed with weak vinegar to neutralize the alkali. There is some doubt about the effectiveness of this process, and caustic-type removers are best avoided.

Spirit-removers, although more costly, give better results if the directions are followed.

PAPERHANGING. See WALLPAPER AND PAPERHANGING.

PERSONAL KIT. Whatever operation the painter may be engaged on he usually carries in his apron pocket a dust brush, 3-in. broad-knife, 1-in. or 1½-in. chisel knife, putty knife, shave hook and clean rag; and in his bag a palette knife, screwdriver, hammer, pincers, 2-ft. rule, chalk and plumb-line (see Fig. 22).

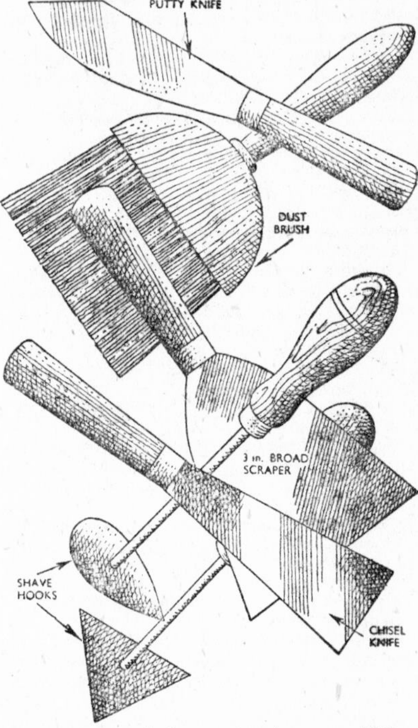

Fig. 22. Tools for a painter's personal kit.

PIGMENTS IN OIL. Kinds in use. The following are of general utility:

White. White lead, zinc white, antimony oxide, and titanium white.

Yellow. Ochres, raw sienna, lead chromes (lemon, middle and orange).

Red. Red lead (for priming paints), venetian red, indian red, red oxide (for ironwork), red lakes such as signal red, post-office red, crimson, etc.

Brown. Raw umber, burnt umber, burnt sienna, vandyke brown.

Green. Brunswick green (pale, middle, deep); also under various names such as privet, holly, etc.

Blue. Prussian blue, Chinese blue, Brunswick blue, and ultramarine blue.

Black. Vegetable black, ivory black.

General characteristics of pigments. *White lead.* This gives greater protection to surfaces than any other pigment, and is therefore specially valuable for outside work. Colour is affected by sulphur-laden air, such as that found in manufacturing towns, but a 25 per cent addition of zinc white will lessen the chances of deterioration.

Zinc white, antimony oxide, titanium white. All these are good interior whites, though their use need not be limited to interiors. The latter two have greater density and all have better colour and smoothness of finish than white lead. A good interior white may be made from 75 per cent zinc white to 25 per cent white lead; this composition makes a paint which tends to correct the faults of either pigment used alone.

Yellow ochre. A useful permanent pigment which makes clean, creamy tints when mixed with white.

Raw sienna, raw umber, burnt umber, burnt sienna. These are semi-transparent and permanent, and used chiefly as glaze colours, but also make good stainers.

Chromes (lemon, middle, orange). More expensive than the ochres, but their bright colour makes them indispensable for bright tints and for use as self-colours.

Venetian red, indian red. These make good tinting colours for pinks, etc., and are also used with other pigments to make a variety of intermediate and deep rich browns and reds.

Red lakes. In a variety of colours, from bright red to crimson and purple. They do not cover well, and being fairly permanent are usually used as finishes for undercoats made from less permanent reds.

Vandyke brown. Very bad drier in oil, usually used as a glaze colour.

Brunswick greens. These are the base of most outside greens, poor qualities being liable to fade badly. They make useful tints with white; but as the colour is destroyed by alkalis, they should not be used directly over new plaster surfaces.

Chromium oxide. More expensive than the above, but more permanent.

Prussian blue. Very strong stainer, and care should be taken not to add too much at once when making pale tints. Being semi-transparent, it makes a good glaze colour.

Ultramarine blue. Although a bright blue in itself, it makes indifferent tints with white. Inclined to be unstable, when mixed with white it is liable to leave blue streaks under the brush. It is not affected by alkalis, and may therefore be used on new plaster.

Blacks. Work well under the brush; mix well with other pigments, but are poor driers.

PLASTER. See CEMENT AND PLASTER and CRACKS IN PLASTER.

RELIEVING PLAIN SURFACES. Methods. There are numerous ways of adding a distinctive note to plain surfaces, such as the walls and ceiling of a room, without an extended knowledge of design. These include glazing, scumbling, blending, shading, spatter finish, stippling (broken colour), stencilling and masking, and texturing.

Glazing, scumbling and blending. *Glazing* is the covering of a non-absorbent surface with a semi-transparent colour to add richness, or in some cases texture, the ground or surface colour showing through the glaze.

Scumbling is the dispersion of glaze colours, or of opaque colours used thinly over a surface, in an irregular manner and with unequal density, giving a clouded effect. Tones of one colour or of different colours may be used.

Blending is the merging, by brushing lightly, or by stippling which will remove brush marks, over any of the effects produced by above methods.

Glazing and scumbling are so nearly akin in operation that the description of one may be applied to the other. Glazes can be medium-oil (linseed oil, liquid oil driers, and turpentine) or medium-water (stale beer, vinegar, or a solution of sugar in water may be used as

Fig. 23. Effect of rag-rolling over wet glaze.

binders for dry colours). Glazes, either oil or water, may be purchased ready-made, usually under the name of scumbles. Colours—for adding to the glaze medium—may be any of the semi-transparent colours, that is, raw and burnt sienna, raw and burnt umber, vandyke brown, Prussian blue, emerald green, crimson lake, and any opaque colour used so thinly that the ground may be seen through.

Glazes may be used to enrich or modify a coloured surface. For example, a front door, painted blue, may be enriched by a glaze of Prussian blue, stippled with a hog-hair stippler to an even texture. The stippling of any painted surface may be varied from fine stippling to

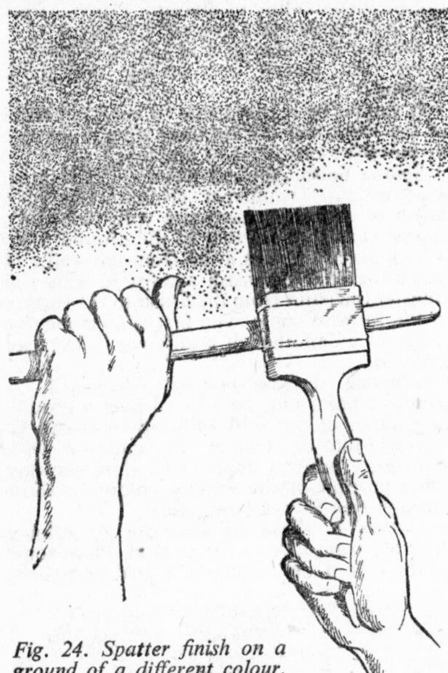

Fig. 24. Spatter finish on a ground of a different colour.

coarser textures by rubber stipplers of varying degrees of width in the size of the rubber or by dabbing with sponges of various and irregular textures (use the sponge damp with water for water glazes, and with white-spirit for oil). Another variation is obtained by rag-rolling. Damp a piece of soft rag with either water or white-spirit, crumple it up to make creases and roll it into a loose cylindrical shape. Then roll it over the surface of the wet glaze in an irregular manner (Fig. 23).

In all these operations the glaze should be laid over the ground in an even film and the operation carried out while the glaze is still wet. When using any particular tool, avoid leaving its definite shape by twisting the hand at different angles when making impressions.

Shading. A wall may be shaded from a light tone or hue at the top to a darker tone or different hue at the bottom, either with glazes or with opaque paints.

Method 1. Paint the surface in bands of colour, varying in either hue or tone; over this

Fig. 25. Stippling in broken colour with a sponge.

Fig. 26. Stippling with a stiff brush. This removes ordinary brush marks and gives a more even texture to the paint surface.

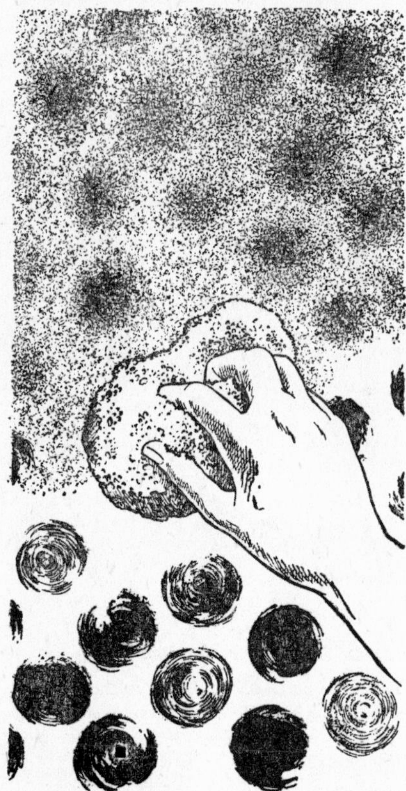

Fig. 27. Stippling by breaking up and blending dabs of colour with a sponge.

apply a glaze and stipple. This is the safest way of getting an effect of gradation, as the glaze may be applied evenly over the whole surface.

Method 2. The wall is painted in one colour. Set out the area with chalk lines to define limit of each tone of glaze, make up glaze in three tones, start by brushing on and stippling the lightest tone; when the division line is reached, begin using the next lightest tone by brushing it along the wet edge of the first used tone. Soften off the tones by stippling out the definite line of division. Proceed from this to the final glaze in a similar way.

Method 3. Make up three tones or hues of paint (not glaze), and follow the above method.

It should be realized that to keep the edges of the work wet during these operations two or more persons must be employed.

Spatter finish. Applied over any flat-painted, distemper, or wallpaper ground. Charge a brush of any convenient size with paint of a colour varying from that of the ground, hold a stick several inches away from the wall and strike the charged brush against it. This will transfer the paint from the brush to the surface in the form of spots. The first spatter may be followed by another of a different colour (see Fig. 24).

Stippling (broken colour). *Method* 1. A coloured paint may be applied over a ground of another colour and while still wet can be worked into a texture by dabbing with sponges, crumpled paper, etc., thus allowing some portion of the ground colour to show through (see Figs. 25 and 26).

Method 2. Make up a colour or colours differing from that of the ground. Place some of the colour on a piece of board or palette,

***Fig. 28.** An example of the kind of pattern obtained by using masks and stencils.*

Fig. 29. A good example of a more complicated design created with masks and stencils.

take a sponge or other texturing tool, dip it in the colour on the palette and dab with the sponge against the surface, transferring the colour in an irregular manner (see Fig. 27).

Stencilling and masking. Stencils are made by cutting holes in a material through which paint may be applied to form a pattern. Masking is done by the use of templates; the pattern is cut on the outer edges of a material and the colour applied to the edges. (See Figs. 28 and 29.)

Preparing a stencil. Take a piece of stout cartridge-paper, give it a coat of linseed oil, and allow it to stand until dry. The design can be traced upon it and cut out. The cutting is done by placing the paper on a sheet of glass and cutting round the design with a sharp knife. Always carry the work through by working continuously away from the starting point, so as not to isolate any portions. If this is not done there is a risk of breaking the stencil when taking out the isolated pieces.

When applying the colour, see that the stencil tool is not overcharged. The best way to avoid overcharging is to place a spot of colour on a palette and work the tool into it; apply the colour by dabbing it away from the edges towards the centre of each cut-out piece, to avoid working the colour under the edges, making them look ragged.

Other methods of texturing. Prepare a ground of one colour and, when this is dry

Fig. 30. The effect obtained by graining with (left) *a rubber or steel comb and* (right) *a coarse brush. This process is worked in a wet coat applied over a dry coat of a different colour.*

and hard, apply over it a coat of another colour or tone; while this coat is still wet, work over it with either rubber or steel combs, coarse brushes (Fig. 30), crumpled rag moistened with turps, or any other tool which suggests itself as likely to give an interesting texture.

SCUMBLING. See RELIEVING PLAIN SURFACES.

STIPPLING. See RELIEVING PLAIN SURFACES.

STOPPING AND FILLING. Stopping is the filling up of nail holes, cracks or deep indentations in a surface. Filling is the application, to either the whole or part of a surface, of a material which when dry can be rubbed down to obtain a level surface; it should be employed whenever a first-class finish is required. Before stopping or filling is done the surface must be painted, otherwise the material will not adhere.

Stopping. Putty (whiting made into a stiff paste with linseed oil) is the commonest form of stopping. While it may be employed for small holes, it is unsuitable for large ones, as it skins over on the surface but remains soft underneath for a long time.

White-lead stopping should always be used for good-class work, as its texture when dry is more in keeping with that of wood or plaster. The stopping is made from white lead, whiting, mixed with gold size, and a little turpentine and beaten up to a stiff paste. Lead stopping must not be held in the hand, but must be placed on a piece of board and taken from it with a putty or stopping knife.

Filling. This can be made (1) from the same materials as the stopping, but with an increase in the proportion of whiting and turpentine, so that it will rub down fairly easily; (2) from water-paint to which has been added 25 per cent of fine dental or modelling plaster; or (3) from distemper stiffened with a little plaster. The first filling, which dries in about three hours, may be applied in several coats with a brush, or both this and the other fillers may be applied in one coat by spreading over the surface with a filling knife in one coat (Fig. 31). The filling knife has a broader and more flexible blade than the broad or stripping knife. The filling, which should be of a consistency to spread easily, is made as level as possible with the knife and allowed to dry hard. The lead filling must be rubbed down wet; the others must be rubbed down dry.

Wet rubbing down. *With pumice-stone.* Prepare the lump of pumice by sawing it across the grain, and, with water as a lubricant, rub the two faces of sawn pumice together to obtain level surfaces. Wet the painted surface and, using water freely, rub down with a gentle circular motion until the surface is smooth and level.

Fig. 31. Filling up a surface with a broad flexible knife.

With waterproof abrasive paper. This paper is more costly than pumice, but is more constant in grain and does the work more consistently. Rubbing blocks of cork or rubber may be purchased of the right size and shape to fit comfortably in the hand (Fig. 32). Cut a piece of the paper to fold round the block and use it in the same way as was advised for the pumice. When rubbing down mouldings, cut pieces of wood to fit the shape of the mould and use strips of the paper over them.

When rubbing down is complete, wash the surface down to remove all sediment and allow the work to dry thoroughly before any further painting is done.

Dry rubbing down. Sandpaper or glass-paper must be cut and used on the block in the same way as in wet rubbing down. Dry rubbing down should be carried out with reserve. Wet rubbing is preferable if possible.

Rubbing down between coats of paint and varnish. This may be done with finer grades of waterproof paper and water, or with a felt pad, pumice powder and water, and the finer abrasives mentioned under ABRASIVES. Sandpaper and steel wool may be used dry, but generally they are not so effective as the wet methods.

TEXTURE. See COLOUR.

TONE. See COLOUR.

WALLPAPER AND PAPERHANGING. English paper is 21 in. wide by $11\frac{1}{2}$ yd. long. To calculate the number of rolls required for the walls of a room, divide the length of the roll by the height of the wall, measure the full lengths a room will need by going

Fig. 32. Wet rubbing down a filled surface with waterproof abrasive paper.

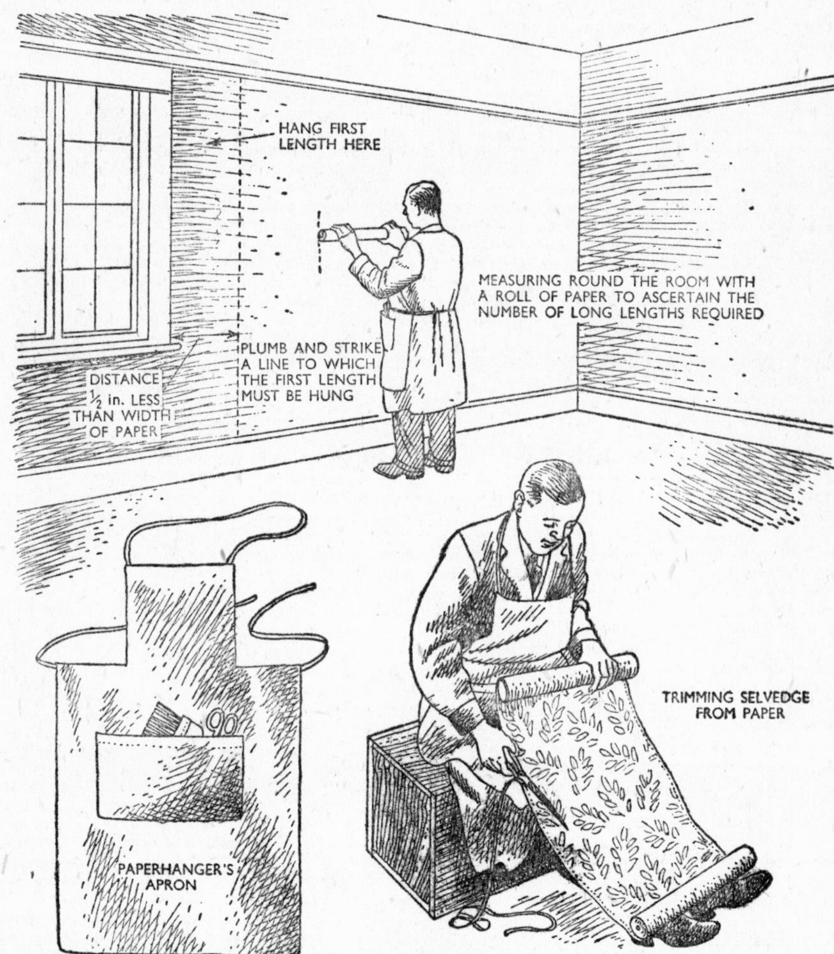

Fig. 33. Trimming wallpaper and measuring the number of lengths required preparatory to hanging.

round the room with a roll of paper, and divide the number of widths by the lengths which may be cut from a roll. Ignore short lengths, as under windows.

Paperhanger's kit. The minimum requirements of a paperhanger's kit are: scissors, 10 in. to 12 in. long, and a short pair for trimming round electric points, etc.; paperhanger's brush; smoothing roller and seam roller; two-fold 2-ft. rule; plumb-bob and chalk line; pasting brush; paperhanger's board; sponge and clean rag.

Preparing paper for hanging. For a "butt" joint both edges must be wholly removed. For a "lap" joint the forward edge and most of the back edge must be removed.

Many retail shops have a machine which will trim both edges at once. Hand trimmers, costing up to 25s. each, will quickly remove the edges, but failing any of these mechanical aids the paperhanger's scissors are generally used (Fig. 33).

Take a low seat, place the roll of paper against the outstretched feet and pull the end of the roll towards the body. As the scissors make a cut with one hand, the other hand rolls up the paper. Some amount of practice is required, but these hints will help.

Don't snip; take a full, firm cut.

Don't jerk the roll with the other hand; pull the roll steadily upwards and see that the paper winds up neatly.

A paperhanger's table is usually 6 ft. long by 22 in. wide. This length is not essential, but the width should approximate to that given to make pasting easy. Paper should be cut to length, leaving 2 in. excess at top and bottom to be cut away later.

A pattern paper may be either side-to-side repeat or with a drop-pattern; the former should be cut through at a point which will leave a full design at the top when hung, the latter must be matched on the board by placing the edge of the second length against the back edge of the first to find the place of match. When a number of lengths have been cut, place them on the table pattern side down and with the top at the left hand of the operative (Fig. 34).

Setting out the wall. Very few corners of rooms will be found to be plumb and it is not possible to hang a paper without having a method of keeping the paper plumb. Hanging is usually commenced by the window, that is, the lengths must be hung from the light.

Make a mark ½ in. less than the width of the paper away from the window. From this mark suspend the plumb-bob, and when it comes to rest make another mark lower down which is in the vertical line made by the plumb-line. Strike a line with chalk between these two points (see Fig. 33).

Making paperhanger's paste. Put the paste powder into a bucket and beat it up into a fine batter with cold water. Pour boiling water on to the paste, stirring with a stick until the paste thickens. Then stand the paste on one side to cool, after covering it with cold water to prevent skinning. Thin or lumpy paste must be avoided; otherwise the paper may come away from the wall, or be uneven.

Pasting the paper. Correct pasting and folding of the paper on the board are essential to a good job. Avoid getting paste on the board or on the front of the paper, and never lift a piece of unfolded paper from the board. The length to be pasted should be pulled forward within an inch of the edge of the board and the top in line with the left-hand end.

Dip the pasting brush (distemper brush) into the paste and brush the paste smoothly over the surface, leaving an inch unpasted at the top; lift the back edge of the length and brush outwards over it, taking great care that none is missed; draw the paper forward to the edge of the board and finish that last (Fig. 36). Fold the paper over from the left and draw another portion of the length on to the board. The length may be short enough to require folding only once at the top and at the bottom, if not, several folds must be made at the top until only 3 ft. remain at the bottom, which should be folded from the right hand. The folding must always be true, that is, with the edges level. This makes hanging easier, prevents paste getting on the front of the paper,

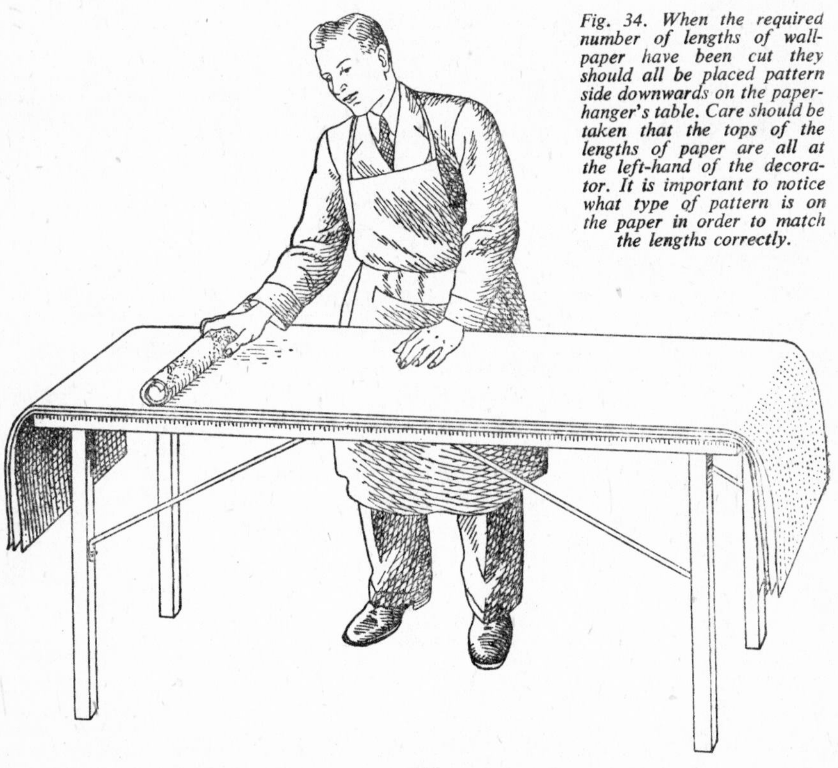

Fig. 34. When the required number of lengths of wallpaper have been cut they should all be placed pattern side downwards on the paperhanger's table. Care should be taken that the tops of the lengths of paper are all at the left-hand of the decorator. It is important to notice what type of pattern is on the paper in order to match the lengths correctly.

Fig. 35. A length of paper hung on the fingers just before being attached to the wall. The top fold has been released, uncovering the wet paste. The bottom section will not be unfolded until the top has been stuck down.

and is very necessary when narrow pieces have to be cut off, as when turning corners.

Hanging the paper. Before taking up the paper the paperhanger must have in his apron pocket two pairs of scissors, one 10 in. to 12 in. in length and a shorter pair for cutting round obstructions; hanging brush; smoothing roller and an edge roller. Near at hand he must have a damp sponge or cloth.

Take the paper on to the left arm with the top nearest to the body. When in position for hanging (usually standing on a pair of steps), take hold of the top right-hand corner of the paper in the fingers of the right hand, slide the left arm from underneath and take hold of the left-hand corner, allowing the top fold or folds to fall gently down. The length should now be swinging freely, the bottom fold still in position acting as a weight and also preventing the paper sticking to the wall at the bottom (Fig. 35). It is essential that this method be closely followed, as otherwise it is

Fig. 36. When pasting wallpaper the paste should always be applied outwards towards the edge. If the brush is pulled inwards paste will inevitably get on the front of the paper and will not only cause a stain but will make it impossible to fold the paper correctly before hanging.

Fig. 37. The paper has been hung to the plumb-line and is being attached to the wall before the decorator takes the roller or brush from his pocket to smooth the paper. A small amount of paper is allowed to overlap the picture rail. This overlap is creased against the underside of the rail, pulled lightly away from the wall and then cut off along the crease.

almost impossible to plumb the paper and avoid creases.

With the paper hung on the fingers, place the right-hand top corner to the wall and with the edge of the hanging paper in line with the struck line on the wall. Place the left-hand corner against the wall and attach the top edge (Fig. 37). If the paper is not quite in position, grasp the bottom fold, easing the paper away from the wall, at the same time sliding the paper into position with the other hand. Brush the paper from the top, downwards and outwards, pressing out all air towards the edges. Never try to smooth a crease out without first lifting the bottom edge away from the wall.

When the top half is in position, pull out the bottom fold, smooth down and press the paper well into the angle where the skirting board meets the wall. Run the scissors along

Fig. 38. Wallpaper has often to be cut to allow for obstructions. First pierce the paper in the centre of the obstruction and make cuts radiating to the edge of the obstruction. Press the paper down well and leave the cutting off of the surplus paper until the whole length is in place. The inset (below) *shows a circular mark made by running the point of the scissors round a switch before trimming with small scissors.*

the angle, pull the paper away from the wall for a short distance, and cut along the crease to remove surplus. With the sponge wipe paste from the skirting and brush the paper back into position; cut off top in the same way. It is sometimes necessary to paper round obstructions such as light switches, gas brackets, bell pushes, etc. How this should be done is explained in Fig. 38.

Hang the next length to match the first, and so on until the space remaining between the last length and corner is too narrow for a full width. Measure the distance remaining and, allowing ½ in. for turning the corner, cut off a strip from the next pasted length. See that this strip when hung is well pressed into the angle of the wall. The remaining strip of the cut length must be plumbed as the corner is turned. At this stage it is advisable to go back on the lengths already hung and run down the seams with the seam roller.

Hanging ceiling paper. Place a plank on two pairs of steps at a comfortable height for working. Paste the length as before, but with a number of rather shorter folds at the left hand. Place a roll of paper under the folds and lift the paper from the table. A line should have been struck along the ceiling so that the first length can be hung along it.

With the roll held in the left hand, pull out the first fold with the right and place the end against the ceiling with the edge against the struck line. With the paper in position, take the brush and smooth the paper down as each further fold is allowed to come away from the holding hand. When the whole length is in place trim off the ends.

VARNISHING. Necessary dusting or sweeping should be done before the work is commenced and time should be allowed for any dust to settle. See that dust is removed from the bottle before opening. Do not shake the varnish up and see that the container into which it is poured is perfectly clean.

It is not advisable to use new brushes for varnishing; the brushes should have been "broken in" on other work and well washed out, first in white-spirit and finally with soap and water. Dip the brush about an inch into the varnish and without letting it touch the bottom of the container.

Apply varnish liberally on small areas at a time; in other words, get the coat as full-bodied as possible without the varnish running (Fig. 39). Outside varnish is elastic, inside varnish is hard-drying; they should be used only for the purpose for which they are made.

WASHABLE DISTEMPER AND WATER-PAINT. Materials sold under these names, although thinned with water, partake of the nature of oil-paint. Their binding solution is an emulsion of oil and water mediums, and when the directions regarding the preparation of the surface and the application of the materials are faithfully followed the surface is washable.

There are no special difficulties with regard to application; in fact, they are easier to apply than glue-bound distemper. They do not dry out solid in one coat, as distemper very often does, but require two good coats. They dry hard and brittle; they having no elasticity, the surface to which they are applied must be thoroughly fast, that is, all loose material must be washed off to prevent scaling and cracking. A good plan is to wash down the old surface, especially if it was glue-bound distempered, with a solution of sugar-soap, wipe clean and allow to dry.

Scaling will often occur when the water-paint has been applied over other water-paints. If there is any doubt, it is advisable to give the surface a coat of thin oil-paint to bind any loose material to the surface. If it is desired to change the colour of a water-paint, it is not advisable to use a very large amount of dry colour. It is better to make changes by adding other colours of water-paint.

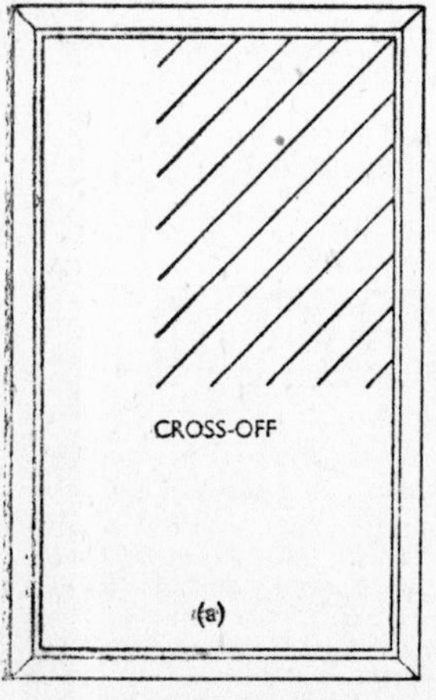

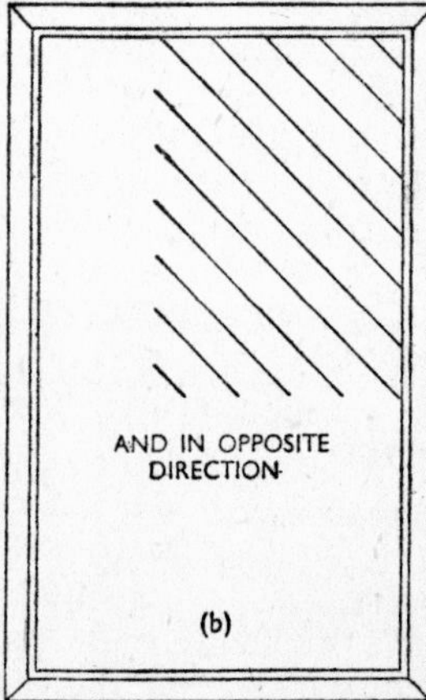

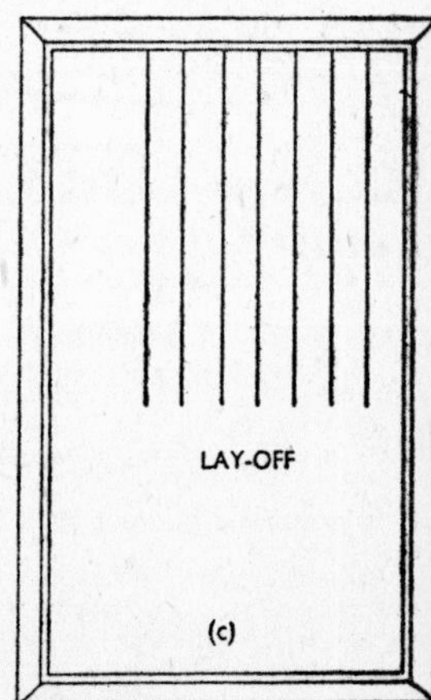

Fig. 39. Varnish should be worked on in three stages as shown in (a), (b) *and* (c). *The brush marks will flow out if a full-bodied coat has been applied, but if the varnish has been over-brushed out it will not flow, the brush marks will remain and a good gloss will not result.*

PLUMBING AND GLAZING

Instructions for the maintenance and repair of water and sanitary systems, and the replacement of windows.

It is important to remember that all works dealing with water supplies and sanitary fixtures have a direct bearing on public health and are governed by regulations and bye-laws. Local authorities have their own interpretations of these and should be consulted before any plumbing alterations or additions are carried out. The following material is arranged under four headings: **(1) Cold-water supplies; (2) Hot-water supplies; (3) Sanitary fixtures;** and **(4) Glazing.**

1. COLD-WATER SUPPLIES

TYPES OF SUPPLY.

Direct supply. In areas of supply where the mains are new and a good pressure can be maintained, it is usual to have all water fittings supplied directly from the main, so that for repairs and alterations it is necessary only to shut off the main control or stop-tap.

The chief advantage of this type of supply is that the accommodation of a weighty storage cistern is avoided; but it has disadvantages, such as fluctuation of pressure, excessive wear of washers, and rushing-water noises.

Storage supply. This type is now becoming more extensively used in order to avoid the disadvantage resulting from having old mains shut off for repair. Some authorities also experience difficulty in keeping up sufficient pressure to supply effectively the higher points of buildings at all periods of the day. Therefore this system, with its accompanying storage cistern, is introduced to give a continuous supply within a building at all times. It not only overcomes the disadvantages of the direct-supply system, but affords a reserve supply which allows the use of boilers, etc., to which a failure of the cold supply may cause serious damage. (See Fig. 1.)

Piping details. In both direct and storage systems the entry of the supply is carried out

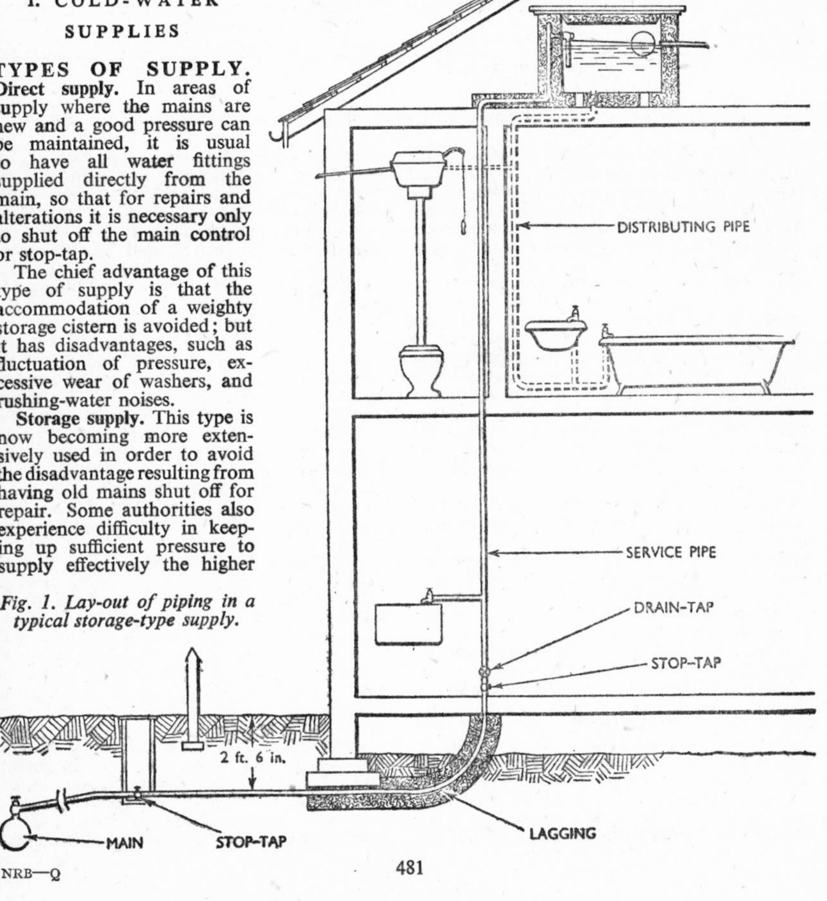

Fig. 1. Lay-out of piping in a typical storage-type supply.

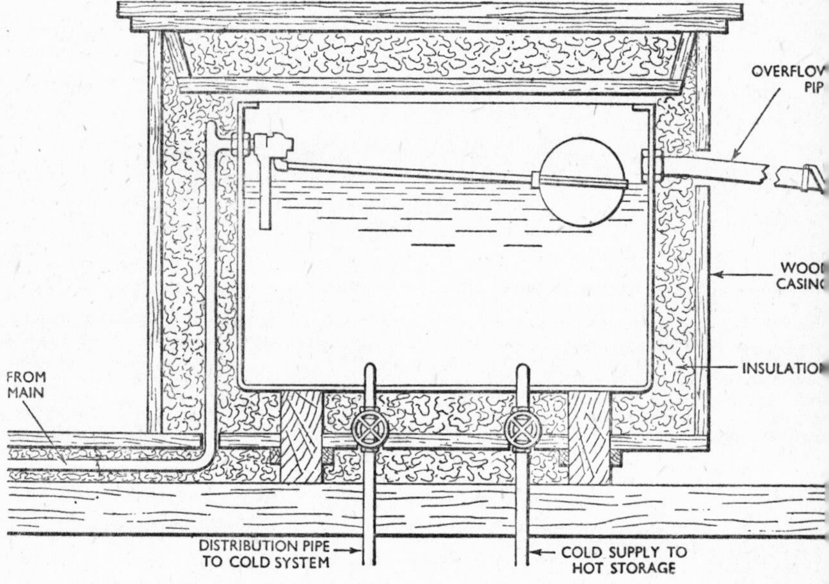

Fig. 2. Storage cistern surrounded by a wood casing filled with an insulating material.

in the same manner. A supply is brought into the premises from the company's main and controlled by a stop-tap fixed close to the consumer's premises. This stop-tap, usually fixed in a chamber and covered with a concrete block and hinged iron cover, is the responsibility of the consumer and, together with any other extensions, must be maintained by him.

The underground piping, if made of lead, should be laid zigzag in a trench to allow for any subsidence and should lie on and be covered by garden loam or sand. Nothing of a sharp or corrosive nature, such as builder's rubbish or stokehold ashes or clinker, should be allowed to come into contact with the pipe. To prevent damage by frost, etc., the pipe should be at least 2 ft. 6 in. beneath the surface until it has the protection of the building (Fig. 1).

Where premises have under-floor cavities, the piping must be insulated and fixed on an inside wall to prevent freezing. An inside stop-tap should be fitted, or a combined stop-tap and drain-tap, if allowed by the supply authorities. Care should be taken that all piping in the building falls to this point, or where this is not practicable falls towards the draw-off taps, so that the system can be completely emptied in case of necessity.

Under the direct-supply system the water is fed from this stop-tap directly to the fittings, but on the storage system it is fed to the ball-valve in the storage cistern (usually fixed in the roof), one or more taps being taken off this rising main to supply drinking-water only.

Storage cistern. This should be fixed in a well-lighted and ventilated space, free from draughts and away from the direct rays of the sun. The cistern should be easy to get at, and the rafters boarded up to and surrounding it.

The materials used in the construction of the cistern depend on the nature of the water stored, but whatever kind is used the same form of insulation can be used. This serves as a guard against extreme temperatures. Thus adequate insulation of cistern and piping prevents freezing during hard weather and helps to keep the water cool in hot weather.

The best method is to construct a casing (wood for preference) round and below the cistern to allow for a 3-in. cavity between casing and cistern (see Fig. 2). This cavity should be *loosely* filled with an insulating material, the best of which is silicate cotton, commonly called slag-wool. This is not only a first-class insulator, but vermin-proof. Alternative materials are cork chippings, shavings, sawdust, etc. A dust-tight removable lid, constructed in a similar manner, should be provided.

All cisterns should be fitted with an overflow large enough to carry the water away as fast as it enters. This pipe should fall to and terminate outside an outer wall, clear of any obstruction, and fixed in such a manner that overflows will quickly be noticed and the fault speedily rectified. A flap or cowl should be fitted to the discharge end of the pipe to prevent cold air being blown over the water or on to the ball-valve.

DISTRIBUTING PIPES. Supplies to sanitary fittings are (under the storage system) taken from the storage cistern by distributing pipes. Each pipe should be controlled by a correctly labelled and marked valve, fixed as near to the storage tank as possible so that any section can be isolated with the least inconvenience.

Insulating pipes. All piping, etc., exposed or subject to extreme temperatures should be insulated against heat loss. This particularly applies to piping in roof spaces.

The best materials to use are those which are poor conductors of heat and are cellular in construction, such as "glass silk," slag-wool, etc. These are especially suitable, as they can be obtained sewn on to canvas and be applied in the manner of bandages. Failing them, substances such as corrugated cardboard, strips of felt or blanket bound on with hessian, make good substitutes if rendered moisture- and vermin-proof.

PIPING SYSTEMS. Choice of materials. Lead, galvanized iron and copper are the most common metals used for piping for conveying water for domestic purposes.

Generally, lead and galvanized iron are safe where water is hard. But for soft water and water of an acid nature copper should be used, as lead and galvanized iron quickly perish and there is a risk of these metals being dissolved and held in solution. Copper will likewise dissolve, but to a minute degree. A green tinge, especially in soapy water, is an indication of this. It is a good plan to run to waste the whole contents of the piping if the water has been standing for some time.

Jointing and repairs. It is sometimes necessary to replace a damaged pipe. This will involve removing the old pipe and connecting in the new pipe by means of some form of jointing.

Threaded joints. Iron pipes are jointed by means of threaded fittings having a standard clockwise (or right-hand) pipe-thread. Copper pipes are jointed in a number of ways. If of strong gauge—11G—the standard pipe-thread is used; if slightly lighter—14 or 15G—a finer thread; while those of the lightest gauges—16 to 19—are joined by means of compression fittings of various types, or by solder capillary fittings (see below).

It is often possible to cut a threaded pipe with a hacksaw. A defective part can therefore be removed and replaced, the new pipe being connected by using a union or connector, care being taken that allowance is made for the join. Before screwing into position, a wisp of hemp should be wound clockwise round the thread, starting at the end of the pipe, the covered thread being then coated with thick paint or proper jointing compound.

With medium-gauge copper piping disconnexion can be carried out in a similar manner or at an appropriate compression or capillary fitting. If a new pipe is not available a burst can be closed by hammering followed by brazing.

Compression fittings. Other than wrenches, few tools are needed for most compression fittings (Fig. 3). To make a joint, cut the ends of the pipes square and remove any burrs with a fine file. Smear a little fine oil on the ends, place fitting in position, and tighten the nuts.

Capillary fittings. These require a blowlamp played on them until the solder is melted, disconnexion of the pipes being carried out at this stage (Fig. 4). If, during this process, there is danger of burning woodwork or paint, a piece of asbestos board should be used as a protection. The board will also help to heat the pipe by reflecting the flame. Should an additional connexion be required, little preparation of the pipe is necessary.

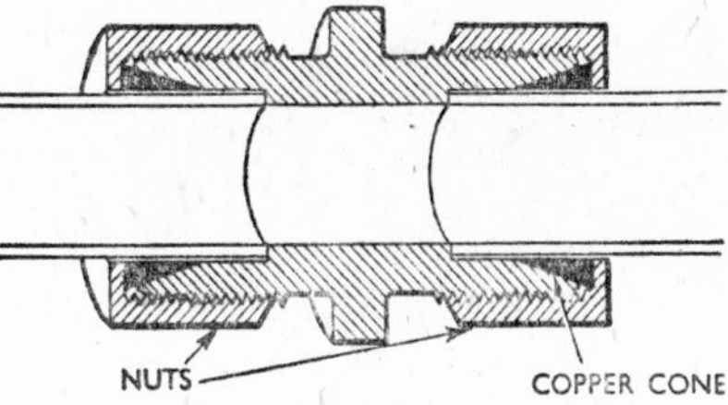

Fig. 3. Pipes joined by a compression fitting.

Capillary fittings require pipe preparation as described for compression fittings. But instead of adding oil, both pipes and the interior of the fitting must be thoroughly cleaned with steel wool (*not* emery cloth), fluxed, and the ends of the pipes assembled on the fitting. Heat should then be applied until the solder shows at the fitting ends. There are many types of capillary fitting; some have sufficient solder contained in them, while others need solder applied either to the ends of the fitting or to a hole in them.

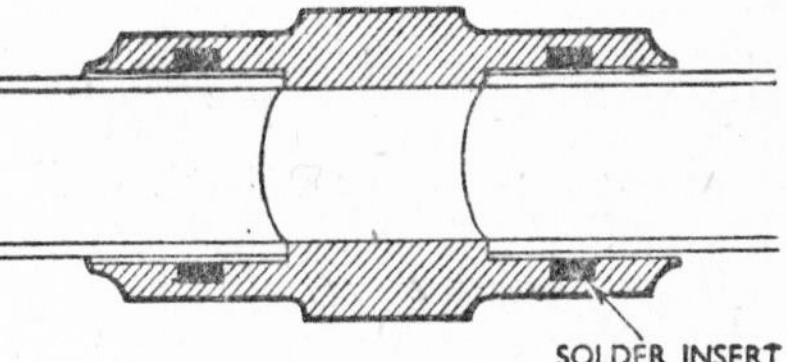

Fig. 4. Pipes joined by a capillary fitting.

Whichever type is used the preparation is the same.

Wiped joints. Lead pipes are jointed by means of wiped joints, which employ coarse or plumber's solder and need considerable skill to execute. The correct way of wiping these may be beyond the scope of the handyman, but the method of preparation is shown in Figs. 5 and 6. An effective, but not so neat, method of connecting or wiping joints for straight piping is illustrated in Fig. 7.

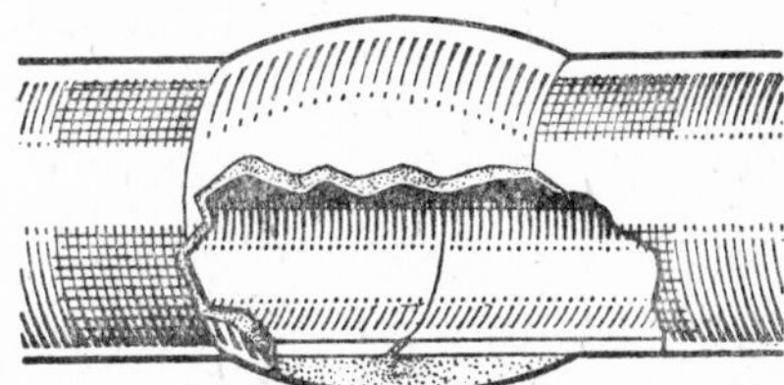
Fig. 5. Cut-away view of a wiped joint

After belling out and rasping down the respective ends these are roughed on the surface by means of carding wire, a wire brush, or sandpaper and chalk is rubbed on to destroy

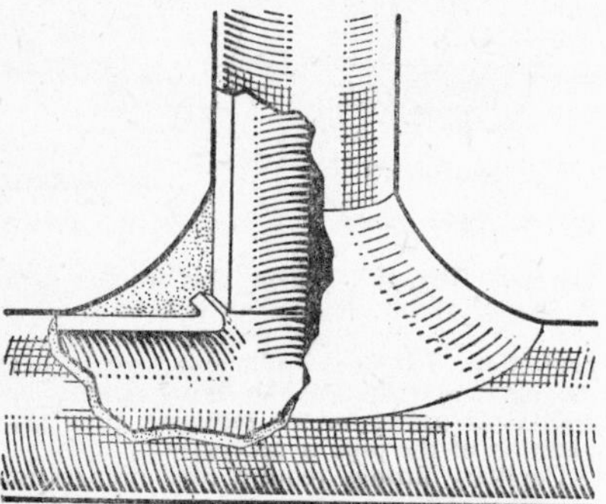

Fig. 6. Details of a wiped angle-joint.

any traces of grease. Plumber's black or smudge, consisting of lamp-black, size and water, is then painted on and allowed to dry. The area of soldering is then thoroughly shaved or cleaned, exposing the bright virgin metal. The parts are then firmly assembled

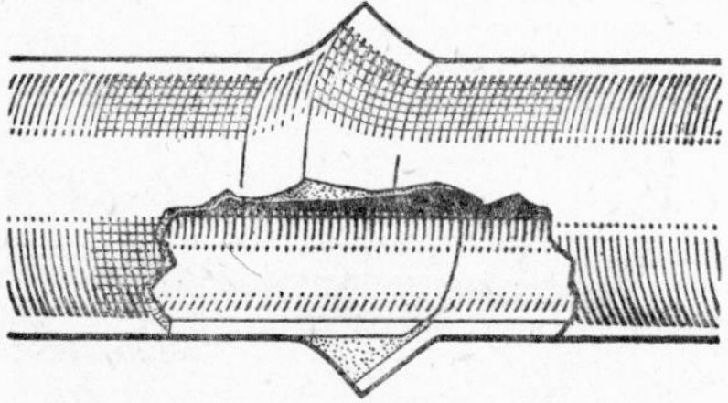

Fig. 7. Alternative method of wiping a joint.

and a little Russian tallow or saltless mutton fat rubbed over them to act as a flux. Heat is then applied, taking care not to melt the lead, the solder being rubbed on until the whole area of the joint is "tinned." A piece of well-greased fustian is used to shape the joint, heat being applied as necessary during the process.

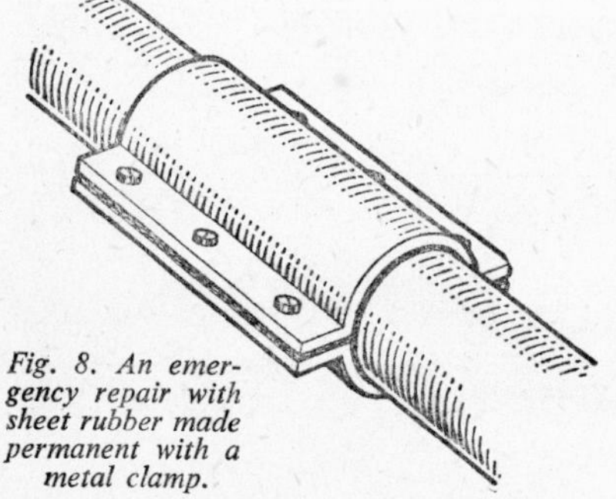

Fig. 8. An emergency repair with sheet rubber made permanent with a metal clamp.

With a small burst or hole, the required heat may be applied by means of a copper bit or soldering iron, fine or tinman's solder being used, after the cleaning and fluxing of the pipe have been done.

For an emergency repair, empty and dry the piping, and close the gap as much as possible by tapping with a light hammer. Place a piece of soft rubber sheet over the crack and bind tightly with adhesive or insulating tape. For a permanent repair, the rubber can be held more tightly in position by means of a metal clamp (Fig. 8).

Repairs to water fittings. Before beginning any repair make sure that the water supply is shut off.

Tap repairs. Save in exceptional cases, all threads of domestic fittings are right-handed. Therefore, in order to tighten, the nut or fitting must be turned clockwise; to loosen or undo, turn the other way.

If force is necessary for loosening or tightening a fitting, especially if fixed into earthenware, counter force must be employed on the body of the fitting, etc., to prevent its turning and breaking the basin. This can usually be achieved by holding the nose and body of the tap firmly with one hand and using the wrench with the other. It is advisable to place a thick cloth in the basin, to soften the blow should the wrench or other tools be dropped.

The modern bib-type tap (Fig. 9) is usually fitted over sinks, etc., but there is no marked difference in the working of other types.

Fitting a new washer. Open tap to the fullest extent. If of the shield type (as illustrated), unscrew the shield or case and expose the square or hexagonal nut of the core. With some types the shield will lift high enough to allow the wrench to be applied. Otherwise the crutch must be removed. Unscrew the core and remove the jumper and washer.

Care should be taken that the fibre ring washer between the core and the body is not damaged or lost; should this happen the washer should be renewed or replaced by a piece of soft well-greased string wound clockwise at the top of the thread.

Remove the nut on the jumper, taking off the old washer, and reassemble using one of correct size and material. Washers for cold water should be of leather and fixed with the flesh or rough side to the seating. Various compositions are often used for washers, but these substitutes, unless carefully fitted, alter in shape and give rise to noises when the taps are turned on and off.

It should be noted that the jumpers of hot-water taps are "fixed," that is, while they can turn in the core, they cannot be removed from it and are lifted automatically as the spindle is turned. This fixing is effected by means of a groove cut into the spindle of the jumper, and a pin is inserted into it, through the thread of the core spindle. The reason for this is that pressure at the hot taps is normally low, and no further reduction in pressure is caused by the water having to lift the weight of the jumper and washer. If pressure is also low in the cold taps, similar jumpers can be used.

With shield-type taps, the flange of the jumper will require holding while the washer

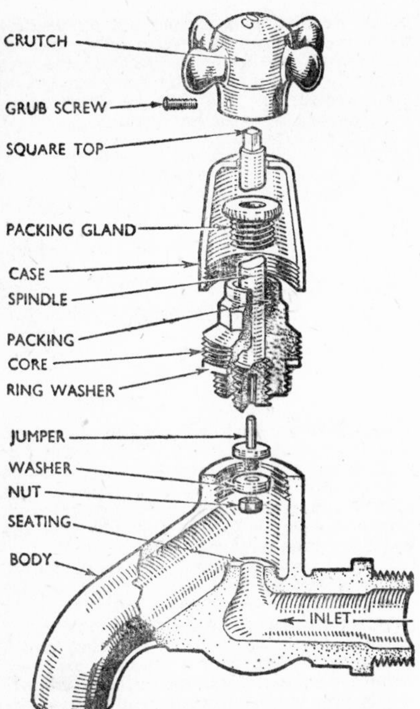

Fig. 9. Components of a bib-type tap.

is removed and the new one fitted. Compressed fibre is the material used for hot-water washers, and on no account should they be cut to fit: the correct size must be used. Leather should never be used for hot-water work or it will soon become hard and brittle and consequently useless.

On reassembly, the spindle should be kept fully extended in the open position, the jumper inserted into the core, which is then screwed into the body of the tap. The core should be turned by means of the hexagonal nut near its base, a wrench being applied only when it is almost screwed home. If difficulty is experienced in this it is probable that the jumper has become dislodged. This should be replaced in the core, or damage to the jumper, washer or seating will result.

If washers wear out frequently, the seating should be inspected. If the seating is pitted, it should be lightly refaced, using a standard seating-tool, or one made for the purpose. For light pitting and in an emergency, a circular piece of emery cloth mounted on a rounded stick with a dead-square end can be rotated on the face.

Leaking packing gland. Leakage often occurs at the packing gland. Unless the tap is much worn, this can often be remedied by tightening the knurled screw of the packing gland until the spindle turns easily, but with no water escaping around it.

Should the nut be already screwed up to its full extent, repacking of the gland will be necessary. Undo the nut completely and take out the old packing. Grease thoroughly some stout soft cotton-string, wind round the spindle and pack tightly into the gland-opening. When packed three-parts full, replace the nut and screw down. Undo the nut again, and on top of the string fit a strip of leather for cold water, or fibre for hot water, completely covering the string packing and fitting tightly to the spindle. Replace the screw and tighten as required.

Ball-valves and cocks. The main causes of trouble are:

(1) Failure of the washer.
(2) Corrosion of the moving parts.
(3) Puncture of the ball-float.

Figs. 10 and 11 show the two most common types, and although the leverage is of a different order their action is much the same. The ball-float, which rises or falls according to the water-level, is attached to one end of the lever-arm. The other end of the lever is so shaped that, as it pivots on a pin passing through the body of the valve, it presses forward a plunger on to the valve seating, so that when the ball-float has reached a desired level the water is shut off.

In case of failure and subsequent overflow the two types shown require the same treatment. The pin, which may be either a screwed

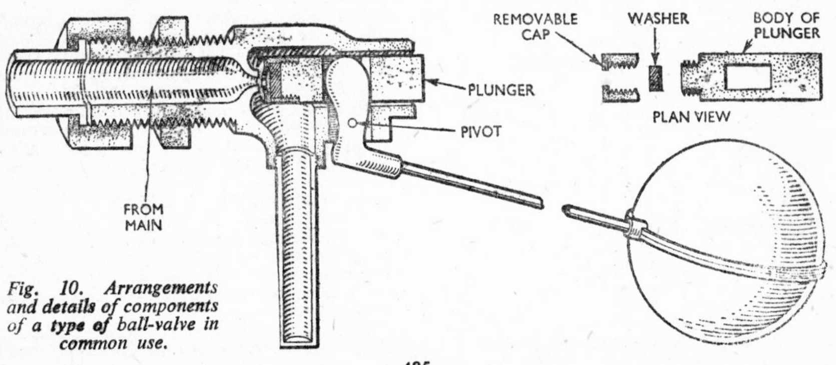

Fig. 10. Arrangements and details of components of a type of ball-valve in common use.

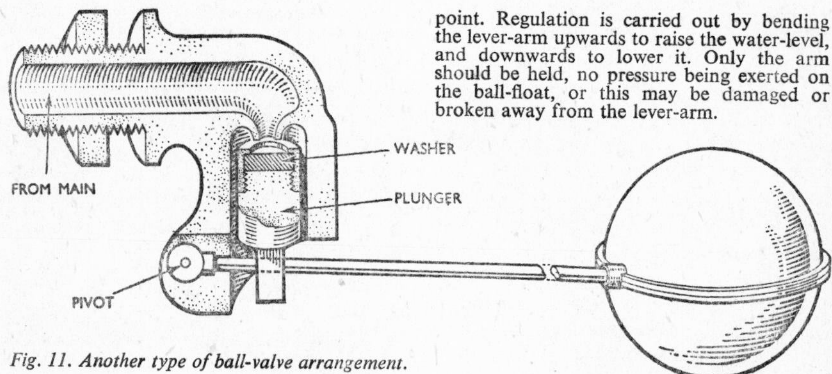

Fig. 11. Another type of ball-valve arrangement.

point. Regulation is carried out by bending the lever-arm upwards to raise the water-level, and downwards to lower it. Only the arm should be held, no pressure being exerted on the ball-float, or this may be damaged or broken away from the lever-arm.

one or a split brass cotter, is removed, freeing both the lever-arm and plunger, which should be withdrawn. The plunger should be cleaned to expose the point where the removable cap joins the body of the plunger. Insert a screw-driver into the slot and, firmly gripping the cap near the join with pliers, unscrew the cap and remove the rubber washer. Insertion rubber is often used, but for long wear a washer cut from good red rubber is recommended.

A new washer of correct size and thickness should now be fitted and reassembly of the plunger carried out. If the washer is fitted correctly, a slight concave should appear on the face, packing of the washer being carried out if necessary to effect this.

All movable parts should be lightly but thoroughly cleaned with a smooth file or emery-paper, exposing the metal. Any sharp edges in the plug or on the lever end should be removed to allow for the smooth working of all parts, but oil or grease should not be applied.

After reassembly, it is often necessary to adjust the ball-valve to the correct water-level. In flushing cisterns this level is indicated by a line and the letters W.L. In most cisterns the water-level is ⅝ in. below the overflow

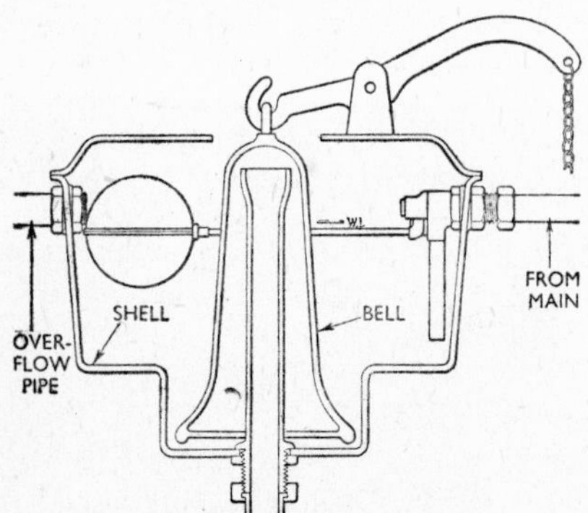

Fig. 12. Bell-type flushing system.

A punctured float will contain water and lose its correct buoyancy. If of plastic or earthenware the float must be renewed, or an attempt made to mend the puncture with suitable adhesive. Should the float be of metal, usually copper, it can be soldered *after* the water has been removed.

If the puncture cannot readily be found, gently warm the float over a flame, or, for greater safety, immerse in hot water, when the escaping warmed air will show in the form of bubbles. Mark the position, and then punch a hole in the top with a bradawl, etc., and remove the water. Clean the surface surrounding the hole and puncture, flux, and then solder first the puncture and then the hole while the float is still warm. The punched hole permits the free escape of water and air and allows for resoldering while the float is still warm.

Flushing cisterns. Of the two types illustrated the bell type (Fig. 12) is perhaps the more common.

Little can be done, if the failure to flush is due to wear (generally of the ball), beyond renewal of the worn parts. A fracture of the shell may be repaired by clamping or bolting a plate over it, using paint and putty as bedding material. If the shell is of earthenware and the fracture not large, thorough drying, followed by adhesive squeezed into the crack and allowed to dry and then painted over, could be resorted to.

Corrosion is another cause of failure, especially in the bell type, which is nearly always made of cast-iron. The cistern should be taken down, lever and bell removed, and all parts cleaned and thoroughly dried. After scrubbing with a wire brush and removing all dust, the iron parts should be painted with a bituminous paint, and allowed to dry before reassembly and before water is admitted. Good warming of the parts with a blowlamp will assist the paint to flow more easily and dry much faster.

The main cause of failure of the type of cistern shown in Fig. 13 is that the loose brass plate becomes wedged or twisted. If this has happened or the slides have become worn the body must be removed for repairs and the shell painted.

Sometimes cisterns fail to flush because the flush pipe contains bits of corroded metal

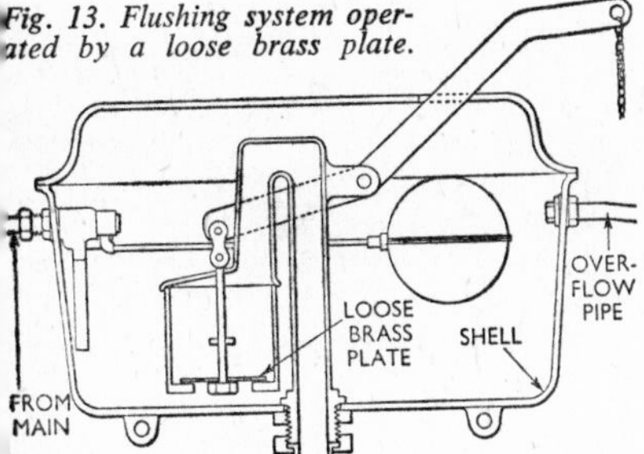

Fig. 13. Flushing system operated by a loose brass plate.

or, if the water is very hard, pieces of lime and shale. These can be removed by a piece of wire by way of the basin; failing this, the flush pipe must be taken down, cleaned out and refixed. The joint between the flush pipe and basin can be made by means of a rubber cone or paint and putty, the latter being retained in position by a metal shield or calico wound round and bound with string.

2. HOT-WATER SUPPLIES

PIPING SYSTEMS. Of the many piping systems in use for the storage and supply of hot water the cylinder system is not only efficient in working and supply, but its safety factor is such that if the cold supply fails, the fire can be kept going for a considerable time. This is because the storage vessel cannot be emptied through the household taps, and therefore the stored water would have to evaporate before damage could result to the boiler, etc.

Fig. 14 shows the piping arrangements and the position of the various fittings. The water is heated in the boiler and circulates via the flow and return pipes to the storage cylinder. The feeds to the taps are taken from the top of the cylinder to the various points required. An open vent or exhaust pipe is also taken from this point and all pipes (circulating pipes in particular) should rise to this point to allow for the free escape of air, etc.

The piping materials used for the conveyance and storage of hot water are usually of hard metals, that is, galvanized iron or copper. Lead, being soft, is liable to sag unless adequately supported; this sagging produces air-locks. The final choice of material will depend on the type of water.

Provided that the installation has been carried out correctly in the first place, little maintenance will be necessary beyond the renewal of worn washers (see under COLD-WATER SUPPLIES), taps, etc. In hard-water districts a gradual furring up by lime scale may occur principally in the boiler and flow and return pipes, with corresponding decrease of flow and increase of noise. The fur may be removed from the boiler by removal of the cleaning covers. In recent years the use of descaling solutions has become practicable, but this is a job for the specialist.

SAFETY-VALVES. A common source of annoyance is leakage at the safety-valve, the two main types of which are the spring and the deadweight (Fig. 15).

Little can be done with the spring type, as failure is often due to weakening of the spring. This can, of course, be replaced, but one of the correct tension would be difficult to obtain, especially as it is constructed of non-corrosive material. The deadweight type is now generally used, as there is little fear of failure.

It often happens that leakage results from an accidental blow on either the valve or the piping holding it. In this case lightly rotate the weighted portion and, while holding the

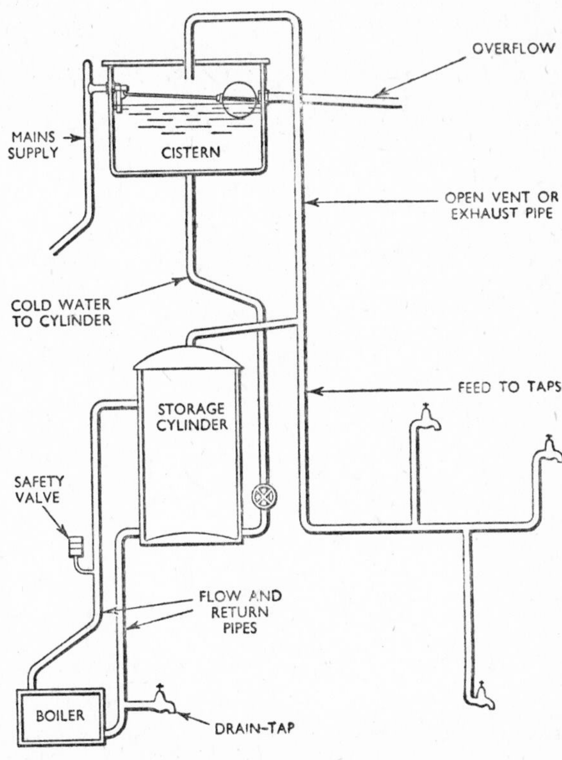

Fig. 14. General arrangement of cylinder-type hot-water system, frequently employed.

Fig. 15. Safety-valves: (a) *a spring type;* (b) *dead-weight type. The latter is in more common use.*

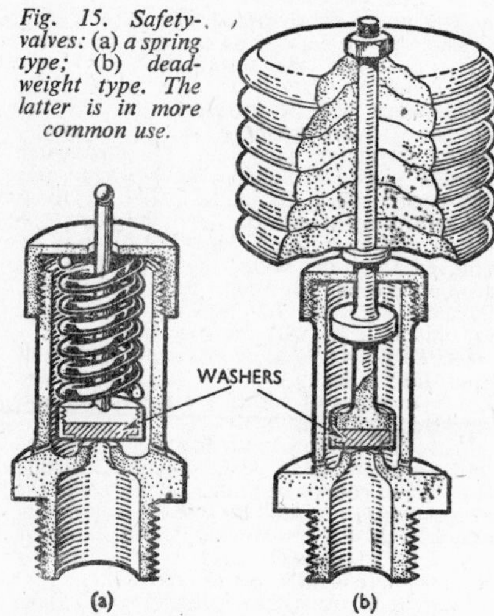

weights and stem steady with one hand, lightly tap the top of the weights downward with a small hammer. This will reset the valve firmly on its seating.

Should leakage persist, rewashering of the valve will be necessary. Shut off the water by means of the stop-valve and drain the system through the drain tap, not forgetting to draw the fire. Dismantle the valve and replace the defective washer with a well-soaked fibre one. Reassemble, and turn on the water, not lighting the fire until water can be drawn off through the hot taps.

GEYSERS. Many water-heaters are erroneously called geysers, a term which should be applied only to those discharging hot water as fast as it is heated. The chief source of danger in the use of geysers is that a large amount of gas is burnt in a comparatively short time. As adequate ventilation must be provided for complete combustion, geysers must never be fixed in confined places. The average bathroom, under normal conditions, lacks sufficient ventilation, and the consequence is that the oxygen content of the air becomes lowered. A person having a bath may be overcome by drowsiness, with perhaps serious results. Again, if the products of combustion are not kept out of the bathroom and discharged into the open air similar conditions will be produced. A greater danger exists if combustion is incomplete, through dirty burners, etc., or from choked or obstructed fume-pipes. Carbon monoxide is produced, very little of which is sufficient to bring about fatal results.

It will be seen, therefore, that it is essential that the following conditions are carried out for the use of this type of geyser:

(1) Correct positioning of the geyser.

(2) Adequate ventilation and correctly arranged flue and baffle.

(3) Regular cleaning of burners and interior flues of the geyser and inspection and cleaning of the main flue or fume-pipe.

Most types work in the same manner. Interlocking taps are arranged in such a way that the water tap must be turned on before it is possible to turn on the gas. A pilot light is arranged so that the lighting of the main burners is automatic. Geysers have very little storage of water in them, therefore note should be taken that water flows from the outlet before the gas is turned on. In most modern types this pre-lighting cannot occur, as the gas is automatically controlled by the water pressure. The valves, etc., controlling this action should not be interfered with unless the maker's instructions are strictly followed.

ELECTRIC HEATERS. The use of electric geysers is generally frowned upon by electricity authorities, on account of high current consumption and loading over a short period, and have been superseded by the storage type of heater. With these heaters the whole of the contents is heated to the required temperature, this being automatically controlled. The water is drawn as required.

Little servicing will be required beyond an occasional rewashering of the cold supply tap or renewal of the heating element. Should the latter become necessary, care should be taken that an identical fitting is obtained and the connexions made in exactly the same manner, with particular attention to cleaning and reconnexion of the earthing terminals.

When disconnecting any electrical fitting, particularly one used in conjunction with water-heating, not only should the switch be in the "off" position, but all fuses controlling that fitting should be withdrawn.

3. SANITARY FIXTURES

CARE OF FITTINGS. Sanitary fittings are made of various materials, but their preservation depends on one common factor: the retention of their high polish if of metal or plastic, and of the glazed surface if constructed of earthenware, etc.

Hard usage and the use of coarse abrasives or scourers will contribute largely to ruining the surface, but quicker deterioration is caused by submitting them to violent changes of temperature. The glaze has a different ratio of expansion from that of the body of the article, and a sudden change of temperature will cause the surface to crack and bring about the familiar crazing and ultimate flaking.

To reduce this risk to a minimum, a small amount of cool water should always cover the base of the fitting, the heated water being gradually added. Should the glaze become stained, use a non-scratching powder or paste.

PIPING AND JOINTING. The common materials used for piping for conveying waste products are cast-iron, copper, lead, or cement asbestos. The jointing of and repairs to lead pipes can be carried out in a similar manner to that used for lead water-pipes.

Minor damage to copper piping may be repaired with solder, but beyond effecting a temporary mend to piping made from other materials with paint and putty and compression bands, the damaged portion must be replaced by new.

The connexions between the fittings and the piping are generally carried out by one of

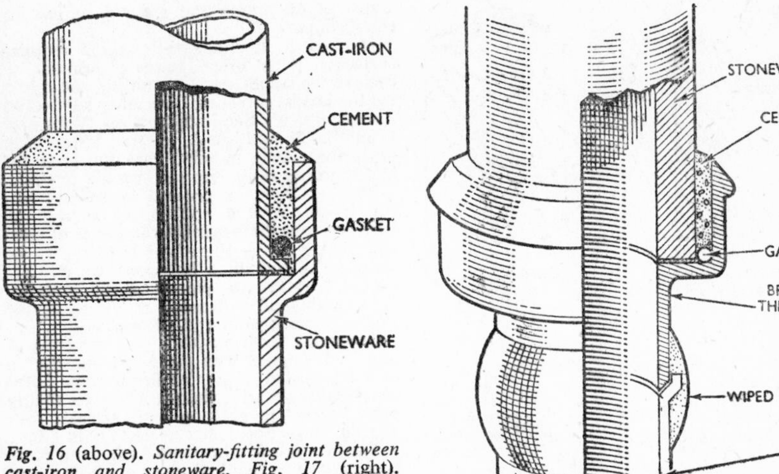

Fig. 16 (above). *Sanitary-fitting joint between cast-iron and stoneware. Fig. 17* (right). *Similar joint between stoneware and lead.*

two methods. The larger outlets, such as those from water-closets, etc. (Figs. 16 and 17), employ a socket-and-spigot method, while those from baths, sinks, and so on, have a compression putty joint (Fig. 18).

The materials used for jointing vary according to conditions, but the following may be taken as a general guide: (1) socket-and-spigot joints, earthenware to earthenware or earthenware to hard metals: Portland cement or one part cement and one part sand; (2) iron to iron or iron to brass, metallic lead, either run molten or caulked in the form of lead wool; (3) waste-pipes and rainwater pipes, red-lead putty; (4) in addition to the foregoing a proprietary cement asbestos jointing material may be used.

If compression can be applied to a joint, such as the outlet to a lavatory basin or sink, paint and red-lead putty are the materials to use. Whenever a putty joint is made, the surfaces should first be coated with paint; with the socket type of joint alternate layers of putty and spun yarn are caulked in, the final layer being putty followed by a coat of paint.

The cement joints should be made in a similar way, omitting the paint, and allowing twelve hours before the joint is put into service.

REMOVAL OF STOPPAGES. In the best practice each sanitary fitting has a U-shaped tube, commonly called a trap (Fig. 18), fixed directly beneath it. Its purpose is to prevent the return of foul gases, but because of its shape it is often the cause of stoppages. Particularly with pipes of small diameter, cleaning screws or plugs are fitted on the traps where the stoppage is liable to occur. These plugs should be unscrewed and the obstruction cleared with a piece of hooked wire.

Should the stoppage be located lower down the pipe, a longer flexible wire or thin cane may be used. If this fails, replace the cleaning plugs, refill the pipe with water, and, by means of a rubber force-cup or a flannel tightly packed, create alternate positive and negative pressures on the waste-pipe.

Another remedy is to fill the waste-pipe from time to time with a strong soda solution, first stopping the outgo with a plug of rag.

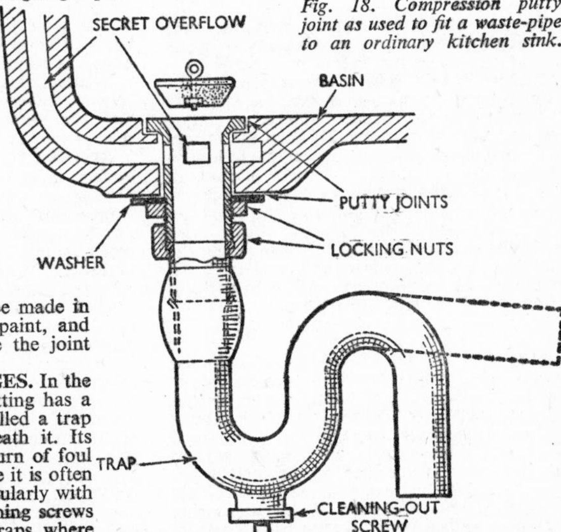

Fig. 18. Compression putty joint as used to fit a waste-pipe to an ordinary kitchen sink.

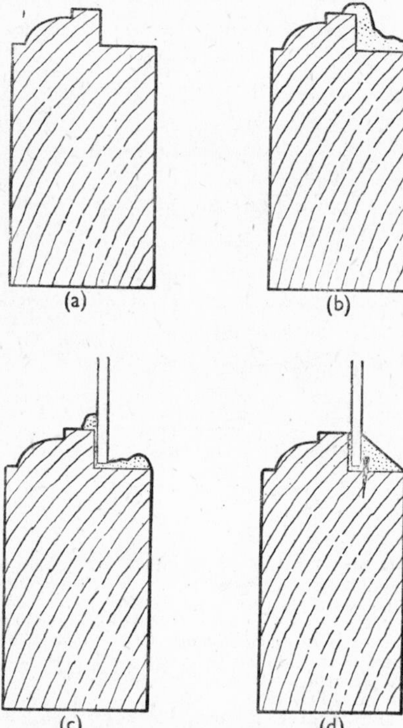

Fig. 19. Glazing a window: sections through (a) *prepared frame;* (b) *frame bedded;* (c) *glaze pressed home;* (d) *finished frame.*

Allow to stand for twenty minutes, then thoroughly flush, thus removing any soapy or greasy coating on the wall of the piping.

TEMPORARY REPAIRS. If sanitary fittings become cracked, they must be replaced, but some delay is often experienced in getting the necessary work done. To keep the fittings in service while awaiting renewal, the following method can be adopted. Obtain a piece of linen or calico sufficient to cover the crack. Paint the material with gold size and smear on some white lead in the form of a plaster. Also paint the fitting with gold size and apply the plastered material, pressing it well over the crack and its surroundings. Allow to dry and cover the whole with white paint.

4. GLAZING

GRADES OF GLASS. Most glass in use to-day for general glazing of houses, etc., is drawn sheet glass. It is obtainable in various grades from "firsts," which is used for cabinet and other fine work, to "fourths," for general work, and "horticultural" for greenhouses and the like, and is specified by its weight per superficial foot, for example, 18 oz. or 22 oz.

REPLACING GLASS. When measuring glass for a replacement, take the exact measurements of the frame and allow $\frac{1}{16}$ in. less for each rebate.

If glass in a sliding-sash frame requires replacing it is often more convenient to remove the sashes, carefully noting and marking the beads, cords, etc. (see entry REPLACING A BROKEN SASH-CORD in the section, "Jobs with Wood"). Should glass in the lower sash be broken, keep in mind that the glass fits into a groove in the top rail and not a rebate.

For replacements proceed as follows (see Fig. 19a-d). With a wood-chisel or hacking-knife, remove the larger broken pieces of glass and the putty (a). If putty is hard it may be softened by running a hot iron over it. Care should be taken to remove *all* old putty. If time permits, all bare wood should be coated with a priming paint and allowed to dry.

Cover the rebates with a $\frac{1}{4}$-in. covering of putty (b), applied with the finger and thumb or a flat-bladed knife, and firmly press home the glass evenly all round (c). The glass should now be held in position with at least four glazing tacks positioned as shown in (d).

The face side is now pointed (d), extra putty being added as required, the knife being held at an angle to prevent cutting into the forward putty. The corners are perhaps the most difficult, and the knife should be used away from them in both directions. The excess putty on the inside of the window must also be cut away. After brushing off surplus putty the frame should be left for twenty-four hours and then a coat of paint applied.

Linseed-oil putty is usually used for glazing wooden frames, and special mastic for iron frames. This can be made by adding red-lead or litharge to linseed-oil putty, using gold size for the resoftening.

If glass is used for roofing of greenhouses, etc., the outside rebates should not be pointed, as the putty will soon fall away. The glass should be bedded in the usual manner and the putty cleaned off flush, all holes or gaps filled at the same time, followed by two or more coats of good lead paint, further coats being added as required.

Figured glass should always face to the rebates, otherwise pointing will be difficult and the weather will embed dirt into the uneven surfaces.

GLASS-CUTTING. To cut glass, a level surface must be provided and covered with newspapers or an old blanket. The cutting instruments are diamond- or wheel-cutters. For handymen the wheel-cutters are perhaps better, single wheel-cutters preferable to the multi-wheel kind, being less bulky and more reliable. Clean the glass thoroughly (on the smooth side, if figured) and, after measuring, place a stout straight-edge half the cutter's width away from the mark on the glass. Holding the cutter upright between first and second finger, draw with a slight pressure smartly towards you along the straight-edge. Place the straight-edge under the glass on the line of the cut and press the piece downward. The glass can also be broken by placing the cut over the edge of the bench and, with hands held apart, pressing downward. Thicker glass may require light taps with a hammer under the cut before hand-pressure is applied.

USES FOR BRICKS AND CONCRETE

Repairs and improvements which the handyman can carry out in his own home.

The handyman builder is advised first to read the general information on this and the following two pages. The items described therein are frequently referred to in the instructions for things to build which form the second part of this chapter.

1. GENERAL INFORMATION

BRICKLAYING. The art of laying bricks demands a far greater degree of skill and experience than is usually appreciated. For the amateur the following details will be found useful as a guide.

The first essential is to be able to pick up the mortar on the trowel, which for bricklaying should have a blade 10 in. to 12 in. long. Place the mortar in the centre of a board, and with a downward movement first to the left with the face of the trowel, and then to the right with the back, form a "vee" about the same size as the trowel. Then twist the wrist slightly to the left, dropping the hand, and the majority of the mortar will rest on the base or the widest part of the trowel. This is then spread evenly with a sweeping motion, at the same time as the trowel is turned from a horizontal to a vertical position, and the point lowered, directing the course of the mortar. This is then spread with an undulating movement of the wrist to form a wavy surface.

Next pick the brick up with the left hand and place it on the wall, back edge first, and press down so as to force forward the excess of mortar, which can be cut off before it stains the face of the work. A line is necessary if a long wall is being built; if only a short wall, then a straight-edge can be placed against the face of the work to ensure that the bricks are in line, and a plumb-bob will ensure that the wall is vertical. Care must be taken that the courses are of equal thickness and also level. The top edge of the bricks should just touch the line. The face joints can be finished as described under POINTING. All bricks should be thoroughly wetted before use.

It is usual when starting to build a wall or small building to lay level bricks at each end or at the corners and then to fix a line to the top edges of these bricks to provide a guide for the other bricks in the course. This can be followed by three or four further courses at the ends or corners. The bricks should be stepped back so that the vertical joints in a course are not directly over or below those in adjacent courses. Ensure that the end or corner bricks are vertical and horizontal. Then, with the aid of the line, bring the main portion of the walls up to the same level, course by course.

CEMENT RENDERING. This consists of covering the surface of a wall with a coat of Portland-cement mortar, which, when applied to the exterior of a building, makes it more resistant to the weather. In lining a pond the rendering will help to keep the water in, or in a cellar or on a wall below the ground it will keep out the damp.

The mortar is mixed in the proportion of 1 part Portland cement to 4 parts of clean sharp sand, and is mixed as described under MORTAR. It is applied to the wall (which has previously had its joints well raked out to provide a key) with a trowel, usually in two coats, the first one being about ½ in. thick and well scratched when the rendering has stiffened to provide a key for the finishing coat, which is usually about ⅛ in. thick. The latter coat is applied before the first coat is completely dry, otherwise it will not adhere properly. The surface is usually finished with a wooden hand float, a flat piece of wood with a handle on the back, which is used in a circular motion to even out any irregularities and to bring the sand to the surface. The result is a closely grained and smooth surface.

CONCRETE. This material is a mixture of Portland cement, which serves as a matrix or binder, and an aggregate consisting of small pieces of broken stone, broken brick, gravel or clinker with enough clean sand added to fill the interstices, the whole being moistened with water. It is easy to make, and is extremely useful for a variety of purposes such as making foundations, walls, floors, blocks for building, paving slabs, tiles or steps.

Suitable mixes of cement concrete for different purposes are as follows: for foundation work: 1 part cement, 3 parts clean sand, 6 parts aggregate; for floors, slabs and walls: 1 part cement, 2 parts sand, 3 parts aggregate. When casting objects in concrete, such as steps, blocks, or ornaments, and a smooth texture is required, use the mix as recommended for walls, the aggregate in this instance.

however, being in the form of ½-in. gravel.

Granolithic concrete is a very hard concrete suitable for the surface of floors, hearths, etc., and is composed of 2 parts cement, 5 parts of fine granite or limestone chippings.

When making concrete, only the best cement should be used; the sand must be clean and free from clay particles. The aggregate, too, must be clean and graded, ranging from ¾ in. downwards for small work.

Mixing concrete. When mixing the materials together a solid platform is essential. Wooden boards laid on the ground will do, or an existing concrete path is admirable. Make a heap of the sand and aggregate, and then put the cement on top a little at a time, turning it over with the spade until the whole is well mixed together and has an even colour, then with the spade make a hole in the top of the heap, pulling the dry mixture outwards. Water is then poured a little at a time into the central hole, and the dry mixture shovelled up from the outside into the water. Continue this until the whole heap is moist but not soaking wet. Turn over concrete until it is thoroughly mixed, when it is ready for use.

The concrete should be wheeled in a barrow to the place where it is wanted and gently tipped out. Then ram and consolidate the concrete with a rammer, also spearing it well to avoid trapping air. Finally bring it to as level a surface as possible. Concrete must not be added to existing dry concrete; the work should be well saturated first.

Coloured concrete. Cement concrete can be coloured by mixing the following materials in the following proportions. *Red:* Portland cement 86 parts, red oxide of iron 14 parts; *yellow:* cement 88 parts, yellow ochre 12 parts; *blue:* cement 86 parts, azure blue 14 parts; *green:* cement 90 parts, oxide of chromium 10 parts; *white:* cement 67 parts, powdered chalk 33 parts. The coloured aggregate is revealed by brushing the concrete, after it has set but before it is too hard, with a liberal amount of clean water. To obtain an ironstone effect, the concrete can be brushed with a solution made by dissolving green vitriol crystals in water.

MORTAR. This is a mixture of cement or lime and sand and is used for making joints between brickwork or other building materials, its main purposes being to cause the bricks to adhere, to distribute the weight through the brickwork, to act as a non-conductor preventing the transmission of heat and sound, and also to prevent water from entering walls. The strength and weather-resisting qualities of the work will depend a great deal upon the quality of the mortar. Bad mortar crumbles easily, allows easy access of water and the consequent deterioration of the work.

A good cement mortar can be made by mixing 4 parts of sand to 1 part of cement with water. In such places as damp-proof courses, or in the setting of coping stones where great strength is needed, 3 parts of sand to 1 part of cement is better. Cement mortar should be prepared immediately before it is required to be used, as it quickly reaches its initial set, and if water is added after this stage its strength will become seriously impaired. Portland cement hardens by the presence of water and should be always used where dampness has to be resisted.

Lime mortar is made by mixing hydrated or slaked lime with sand, in the proportion of 1 part of lime to 3 parts sand. If this mortar is used in walls which have to resist dampness, the joints should be raked out to a depth of ⅜ in. and then pointed with a cement mortar.

The sand should be clean and sharp and free from foreign matter, such as pieces of earth or clay; it should also be well sifted, or the mortar will contain lumps. Always use clean water.

POINTING. The weather, and particularly frost, is one of the chief causes of deterioration of brickwork. The first sign is the mortar beginning to fall out of the joints. It is then necessary to point the affected brickwork.

The whole of the joints in the affected area should be hacked out to a depth of at least ½ in. to obtain an adequate key for the new mortar. If the joints are narrow, great care must be taken not to damage the arrises, or edges, of the brickwork; otherwise the result will appear very ragged. A narrow-bladed chisel should be used, hitting it with a hammer and then well raking afterwards to clear out any loose mortar. If the joints are wider, they can be well raked out with a piece of metal with one end bent at right-angles and sharpened to a point. Do the vertical joints first, and then the horizontal or bed joints. Next, with a stiff brush thoroughly clear away all loose dust and then moisten the whole of the work with clean water.

A board about 10 in. square with a handle on the underside will be found very useful to hold the mortar, a little at a time. The mortar is picked off with a trowel—not the large size used for laying bricks, but one about 4 in. or 5 in. long. Always start at the top right-hand corner and work across and down; this prevents finished work being spoiled, and always do the vertical joints first. Pat the mortar flat on the board and cut it in strips with the trowel, and then with a scraping movement push the mortar strips towards the edge of the board and the mortar will be adhering to the back face of the trowel. This should be done close to the joint, and the mortar is pressed into the joint, at the same time rubbing the trowel on the edge of the brick. Then press the mortar firmly in. Keep the mortar off the face of the work and trim off any surplus with the edge of the trowel.

When a length has been completed, press the trowel on the top edge of the joint and with a sweeping movement run it along the mortar, giving it a polished effect, finishing the work with a bevelled or weather joint.

Two other types of pointing are the flush joint and the recessed joint. In the flush joint the mortar is left smooth and level with the face of the work. This type of finish is useful for inside brickwork which may have to be painted or distempered. The recessed joint is formed by running a round piece of metal along the joint to form a hollow. A more pleasing effect is obtained, but the edges of the bricks are not very well protected.

TILING. Wall tiles are fixed on a cement bed, which is usually ½ in. thick, of cement and sand in the proportion of one part cement to four parts of clean sharp sand. To make certain that the rendering is finished truly vertical, a series of wood battens or screeds, ½ in. thick, are nailed to the wall. These may be either horizontal or vertical and about 4 ft. apart. After the rendering has been applied a straight-edge is used across the face of the screeds to make a plane surface. When the rendering is stiff the screeds are pulled off and the gaps filled up flush with the rest of the rendering.

Before the rendering has set hard the surface must be scratched to form a key. When the rendering is thoroughly hard the tiles are fixed to it by means of a cement mortar mixed in the proportion of 1 part cement to 1 part sand. The tiles should be soaked overnight in water before fixing. The back of each tile should be liberally spread with the mortar and the tile pressed against the wall, the tile being finally tapped with the trowel handle.

Begin fixing at the bottom of the wall and use a straight-edge across the face of the tiles to make sure they are all in line. The mortar should flush up between the joints as the tiles are fixed; any excess mortar must be wiped off before it sets. Mix only a small quantity of mortar at once, to prevent its setting before it can be used. The tiles may be fixed with their vertical joints immediately over each other or they may be bonded as in brickwork.

Tiles may be cut by making a scratch across the glazed side with a glass cutter and then giving the tile a sharp tap on the back with a hammer. The edges can be trimmed with a sharp pair of pincers.

REPAIRING CRACKS IN CEMENT AND CONCRETE. Where exposed to the weather such things as kerbs around gulleys, paths and steps of concrete show signs of deterioration, particularly after heavy frosts. If left unattended these will get worse, as the next time water freezes in the cracks they will become bigger. When making repairs all loose pieces should be removed. The edges should be cleaned of foreign substances such as dust or vegetation and then roughened with a hammer and chisel. The work to be made good should be thoroughly wetted and a mixture of 5 parts of sharp sand to 1 part of cement trowelled into the cracks.

2. THINGS TO BUILD

BASE FOR A GARDEN SHED. The lower part of many a timber shed suffers from being in contact with the damp ground, and a good combined concrete base and floor can be quite cheaply and easily constructed. Begin by digging out a level shallow base about 3 in. deep in the ground, a little larger than the overall size of the shed, and fill this with hard materials such as broken bricks or stone, afterwards filling in any spaces with ashes or gravel.

With the aid of lengths of boarding held by pegs driven into the ground, make a lining or frame around the edge of these bricks, standing 3 in. above them, and make sure that the frame is level in both directions, using a straight-edge and level (Fig. 1a). Obtain a piece of boarding which will fit just inside the sides, for use as a temporary shutter should concreting have to be left before the work is completed.

Mix the concrete in the proportion of 1 part of cement to 1½ parts of sand and 2½ parts of gravel or fine aggregate. This mixture, when wet, is then poured into the frame, starting at one end and adding concrete until the whole frame is filled. In order to make the surface level, a straight board long enough to reach across the frame should be used with a sawing motion from one end of the frame to the other, any surplus concrete that is gathered being scraped off (Fig. 1b).

If the area to be concreted is a large one, a good plan is to do the work in small bays, using an intermediate board which can be taken out when the next batch of concrete is ready. If desired, strips of flat iron twisted at the bottom can be concreted-in upright, and the frame of the shed screwed to these to hold it down. When the concrete has thoroughly set, a course of bricks is laid round in cement mortar with slightly less outside dimensions than the shed and on which the wooden base can rest. A slanting cement fillet is run around the shed between the edge of the concrete and the brick base, so that water dripping from the sides will be more effectively disposed of (Fig. 1c).

This base, besides being high and consequently dry, has the additional advantage of being a suitable foundation for building a brick shed, should one ever be required.

BIRD BATH. A bird bath can form quite an interesting feature in the garden, particularly if formed in the following manner.

Foundation and base. When the position has been chosen, excavate a shallow hole about 30 in. square and 10 in. to 12 in. deep, fill this with 6 in. of hard material well rammed and watered to a depth of 4 in., and end up by laying 3 in. of concrete finished to a smooth and level surface. Next, when this is set, bed over the top paving slabs, crazy-paving stones or bricks and form a path around the bird bath. This can be linked up with the main path if required.

Begin by building a square base two bricks wide each way (Fig. 2) and fill in the central space, making sure with a spirit-level that the bricks are level all ways. Next lay another course of bricks, one and a half bricks wide, and fill in as before, and upon these lay the third brick course, 9 in. each way. These courses must be so arranged that the vertical joints in a course are not in line with similar joints of adjacent courses. This completes the base, and when thoroughly set the work on the shaft may be commenced.

Shaft. Approximately sixty red or buff quarry tiles, 6 in. square and ⅜ in. thick, or other similar regularly shaped tiles, are required for the shaft. The first tile is laid in

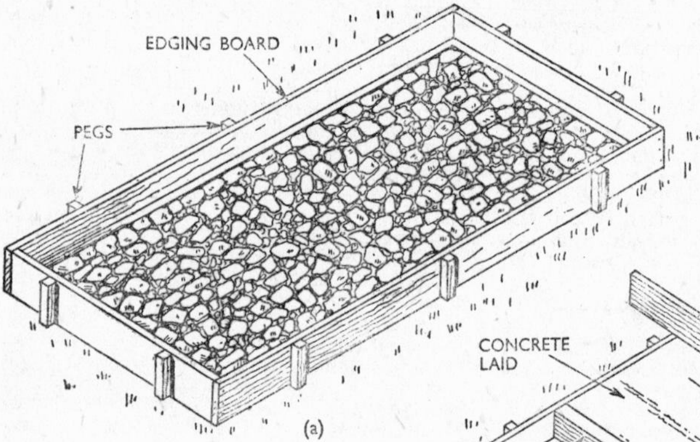

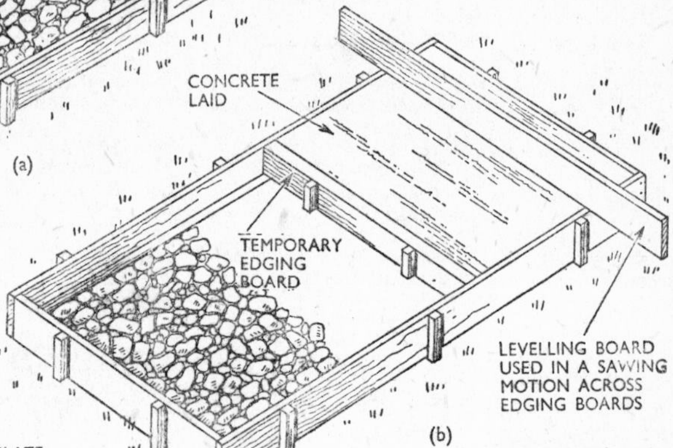

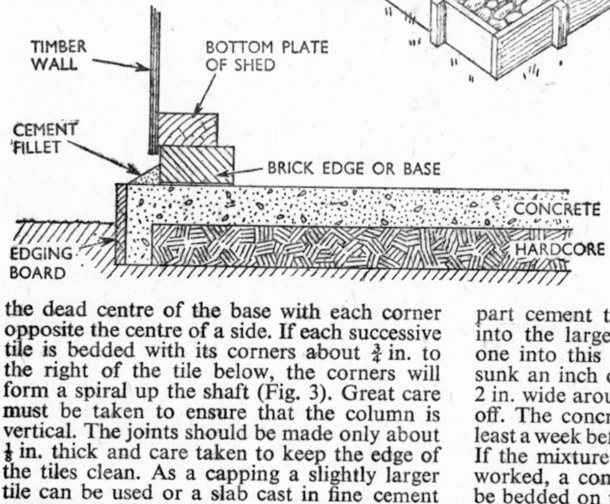

Fig. 1. Concrete base for a garden shed: (a) hardcore rammed home and edging boards pegged down; (b) laying of concrete in progress; (c) section through finished base showing how the woodwork is placed.

the dead centre of the base with each corner opposite the centre of a side. If each successive tile is bedded with its corners about ¾ in. to the right of the tile below, the corners will form a spiral up the shaft (Fig. 3). Great care must be taken to ensure that the column is vertical. The joints should be made only about ⅛ in. thick and care taken to keep the edge of the tiles clean. As a capping a slightly larger tile can be used or a slab cast in fine cement concrete and brought to a smooth finish.

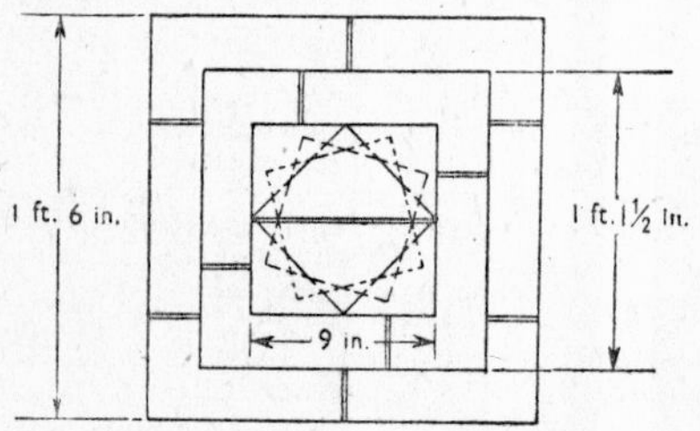

Fig. 2. Plan of base of bird bath.

Bowl and decorations. To form the basin, obtain an enamel wash-bowl of the size required, but a fairly shallow one, and a second bowl which is slightly less in diameter. Mix the concrete very wet in the proportion of 1 part cement to 1½ parts sand and pour this into the larger bowl, then press the smaller one into this and work it about until it has sunk an inch or two. This will leave a margin 2 in. wide around the edge, which is smoothed off. The concrete should be left to set for at least a week before the wash-bowls are removed. If the mixture has been wet enough and well worked, a concrete bowl will result. This can be bedded on the capping with cement mortar and levelled with a spirit-level.

DWARF GARDEN WALL. A garden which is on several levels is considerably improved by the use of dwarf walls (Fig. 4) to hold up flower beds where levels differ, the walls at the same time being ideal places to plant decorative rock plants. This type of wall is laid dry, that is, without any mortar between the layers of stone, and can be safely built to a height of 3 ft. The best-suited stone is usually that found locally, provided that it is in fairly even slabs and not too soft or porous. Stones which are rounded or very irregular should be avoided.

Foundation. When the position and the height of the wall have been decided, dig a

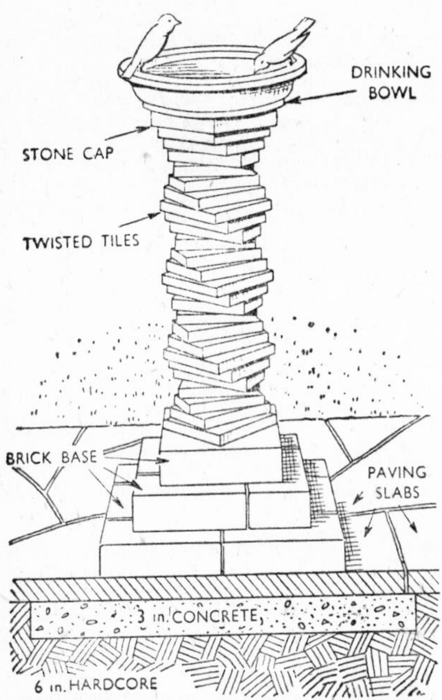

Fig. 3. General view of finished bird bath.

shallow trench along its course for the base, which should be about twice as wide as the top of the wall will be when finished. A good plan is to dig the trench about 12 in. below the surface in order that frost shall not affect the base. Then thoroughly ram in gravel or broken bricks and stones to a depth of 3 or 4 in., thoroughly water to consolidate it, and then lay on top 3 or 4 in. of rough concrete to finish within a few inches of the surface. This concrete can be made by mixing together 1 part cement, 2 parts sand, and 5 parts gravel or broken brick, adding water until the mass is wet but not sloppy. The surface of the concrete should be roughly levelled off and allowed to set. This will take about forty-eight hours, after which time it will be strong enough to stand the wall being built up on top.

Laying the stones. Begin by laying down the largest stones the full width of the trench. As the wall is built, give it a backward slant by setting each course or layer of stones slightly back from the edge of the layer below, so that for about every 12 in. of height the wall sets back 2 in. Also give the stones a slight backward tilt, which will help to make the wall more stable and to collect the rain. It is important that whenever possible the stones are bonded, that is, no two vertical joints are immediately above or below each other. A sprinkling of earth on top of each layer of stones helps to fill the irregularities and give each stone a bed. Should the wall be alongside a lawn, a layer of flat stones about 9 in. wide, or bricks sunk slightly below the surface of the lawn and following the line of the wall, will enable the lawnmower to cut right to the edge, thus avoiding the use of shears.

GARDEN EDGING. Usually some form of boundary between the flower border and path is necessary to keep the soil in its place; and although wooden boards are satisfactory, in time they tend to rot. More permanent

Fig. 4. A dwarf garden wall, laid dry, and with a row of bricks at the base to allow a lawn-mower to be used to the edge of the lawn.

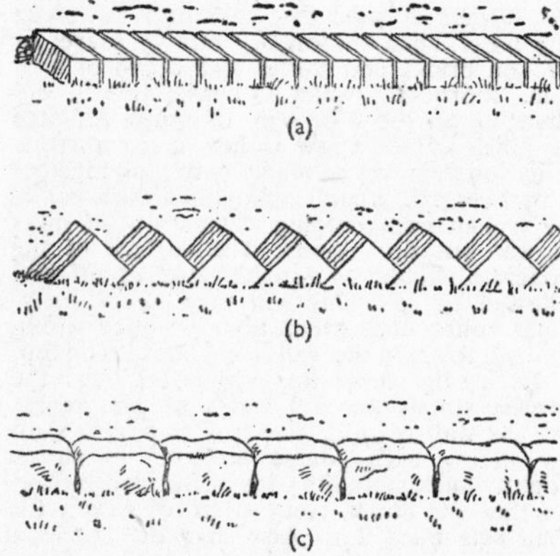

Fig. 5. Garden edging: (a) ***bricks on edge;*** (b) *canted bricks;* (c) ***rough stone edging.***

forms of edging can be quite easily made with bricks, stones or concrete.

Brick edging. The simplest form of brick edging (Fig. 5a) can be formed by digging a trench about 5 in. deep and 5 in. wide along the border, and firmly ramming the bottom. A cord should be stretched between pegs to give the line and height of the edging.

The bricks need not necessarily be all of one colour or texture—the more varied the more interesting the final result will be.

To set the edging bricks, sprinkle a little fine earth in the bottom of the trench and stand each brick upright with its narrow edge to the front, and tap it down gently to give it a good bed, then lay the remainder of the bricks, one by one in this manner, keeping each of them about ½ in. apart until the whole row is complete; the cord will ensure that a straight line is kept, and also that the top edges are in line. The joints should be well filled with fine soil, and the whole well watered to consolidate the edging, refilling with soil and watering as necessary, and at the same time well ramming earth in front and behind the bricks. If this is allowed to weather for a week or two, any bricks which have sunk can easily be lifted and reset.

A more interesting edging can be made by setting the bricks at an angle of about 45 deg. (Fig. 5b), so that each one leans on its neighbour, giving a saw-tooth effect. The top edges need to be kept in line by means of a cord, but no filling is necessary between the joints.

Stone edging. Irregularly shaped stones (Fig. 5c) will also make an interesting edging if sunk in the ground for about one-half of their depth and butted together, providing a picturesque feature if creeping plants overhang the edges. Plain stone slabs, about 10 in. deep and 12 in. long, could also be used. If a permanent edging is required, then 3 in. of concrete should be laid down first to eliminate any chance of sinking.

Concrete edging. Edging slabs can also be made of concrete in the following manner. A mould is built up of wood about 2 ft. 6 in. long, 10 in. deep and 2 in. thick inside size, the top being left open. A mixture of fine cement concrete, with sand as the principal aggregate, is made in the proportion of 4 of sand, 2 of fine gravel (to pass ½-in. mesh), and 1 of cement mixed fairly wet and poured into the mould, well spearing the mixture to release air bubbles. The top edge can be trowelled flat or rounded. With the aid of blocks of wood nailed across the top a crenellated effect could be obtained. the blocks being removed before the mould was emptied. Several similar moulds being used at the same time will speed up production. The slabs should be left in their moulds at least one week before attempting to handle them.

This edging can be set either by digging a trench and ramming the earth round it, or better still by setting it on a 3-in.-thick concrete base about 6 in. wide and then banking up the sides with more concrete.

GARDEN STEPS. Where levels in a garden change, some form of steps is usually required, adding considerably to the appearance of the garden and at the same time having a definite use.

Simple method. The most natural effect is obtained by setting large flagstones on ground which has previously been shaped to receive them, but some means of holding the earth under the steps in place should be provided

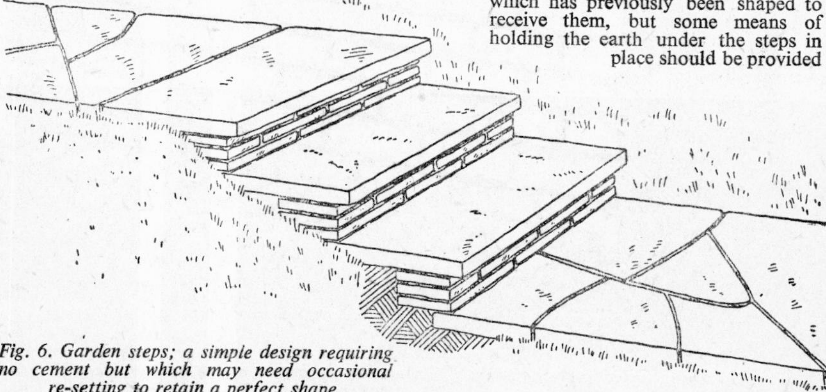

Fig. 6. Garden steps; a simple design requiring no cement but which may need occasional re-setting to retain a perfect shape.

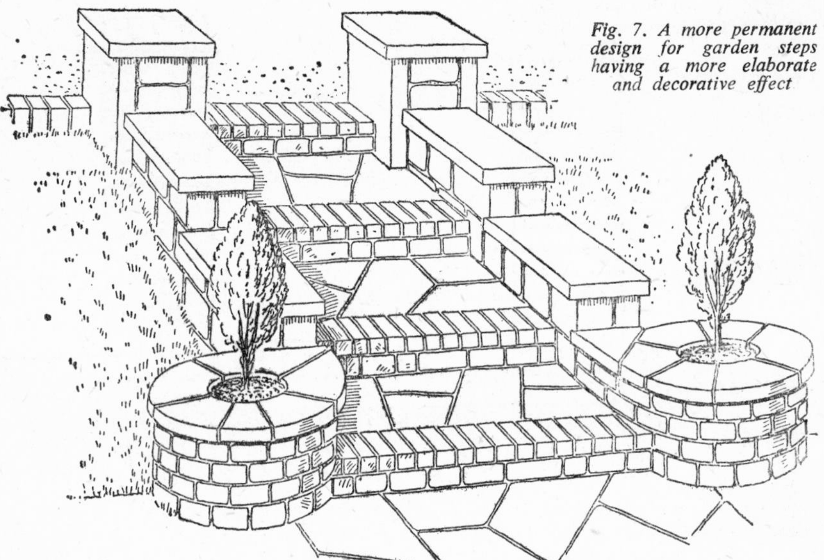

Fig. 7. A more permanent design for garden steps having a more elaborate and decorative effect

by other stones or tiles laid one upon the other under the front edges (Fig. 6). This type of steps might need occasional re-setting.

Begin the steps by laying a course of roofing tiles 3 in. deep along the front edge of the step from bank to bank and then fill in behind with hard material well rammed, or, better still, concrete. Then form the step by bedding on a flagstone or squared stones with their front edges projecting about 1 in. in front of the tiles.

More permanent type. Steps of a more permanent type (Fig. 7) can be constructed quite simply and very effectively with the aid of a little ingenuity in the use of odd bricks, paving slabs and tiles. When the site has been chosen, and the difference in levels taken, the number of steps can be determined by dividing the difference in levels in inches by five, the answer being the number of risers required. These risers should not exceed 5 in. in height, but the treads can be as wide as one pleases.

Begin by marking out the treads on the bank and cutting out the steps roughly in the earth; under the bottom step dig out a trench about 4 in. deep and fill this with concrete. If side walls are required, mark these out in the bank and then spread a layer of concrete 3 in. or 4 in. thick as a base to the walls. When this concrete has set, building the walls can be begun, using either bricks or stones or a mixture of the two. Cement mortar should be used for bedding purposes in the proportion of 3 parts of sand to 1 of cement, and care taken not to spread this over the outside face of the bricks and stones and spoil the general appearance.

These flanking walls can be straight, covered with pieces of stone as copings, curved, or left hollow on top to provide pockets of soil for rock plants. The higher ends of the walls can be finished with brick or stone piers about 18 in. square and capped with tiles and bricks on edge or stone slabs. The lower ends of these walls can be finished normally or added interest provided by building circular tubs in half bricks around oil-drums, thus forming good places for planting shrubs. The bottoms of the drums should be pierced for drainage.

GATE PIERS. To provide a really firm support for a garden gate, brick or stone piers suit admirably, and will last much longer than wooden posts, which are always liable to rot where bedded in the ground. For a single gate, brick piers should be one and a half bricks square; two bricks square is even more substantial.

Foundations. The foundation for each pier (Fig. 8) should be dug to a depth of about 12 in. below the finished ground level, and at least 6 in. wider all round than the size of the pier to be erected. Before any concreting is done, hard material such as stone, broken brick or clinker should be firmly rammed down, filling up the crevices with smaller pieces until a compact mass about 4 in. thick is obtained; water being added at intervals will help in the consolidation. To stiffen the foundations further and to provide a bed for a step, a trench about 6 in. deep and 12 in. wide should be dug between the pier foundations and hard material rammed in this to a depth of 4 in.

Mix concrete in the proportion of 1 part of Portland cement to 3 parts of clean washed sand and 6 parts of gravel. Make sure that these are thoroughly mixed together in the dry state before adding water and mixing to a moist condition. This concrete can then be placed in the trenches and well rammed to consolidate it, working it to as level a surface as possible, at about 2 in. below ground level.

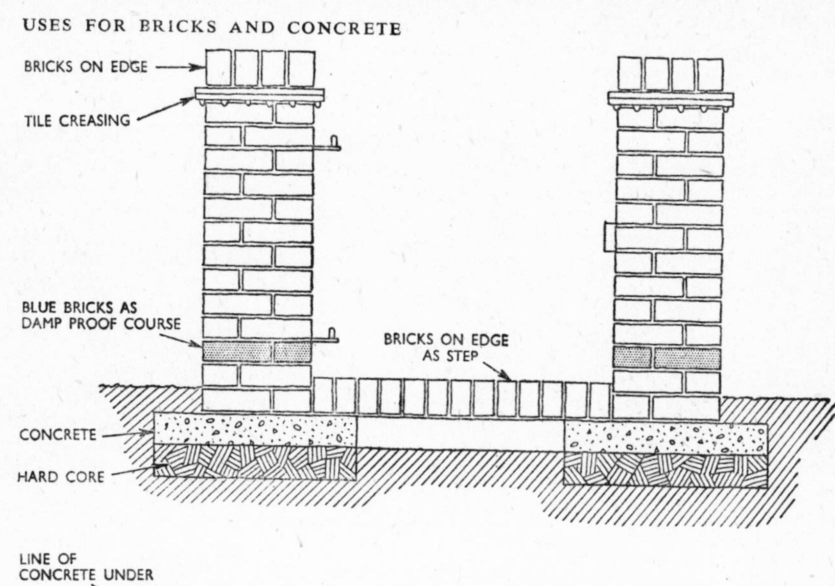

Fig. 8. Elevation and plan for gate piers. The piers can, of course, be made wider if necessary.

Piers. The concrete should be allowed to set for about three days, and then the erection of the piers can be begun. The distance between the inside edges of the piers will be governed by the width of the gate and the projection of the pintles or hooks, which are built into one pier and on which the gate hangs, and the catch, which is built into the other pier.

A quantity of mortar should be mixed to a wet consistency in the proportion of 4 parts of sand to 1 part of cement. As the finished piers will be about 3 ft. high, if they are built one and half bricks square then approximately one hundred bricks will be required. About one dozen blue bricks would be handy to form a damp-proof course at the base of each pier. Well soak all the bricks in water before laying, as otherwise they will suck all the moisture out of the mortar.

Begin by marking on the concrete the position for each pier; a good plan is to prepare a rough drawing showing the main dimensions beforehand. Next put a quantity of mortar on the concrete and form a square with four bricks, so that the end of each brick butts against half the side of its neighbour. The hole left in the middle can be filled with a piece of broken brick, and flushed up with mortar. The next course above is similar, but is twisted round, so that the vertical joints are above the centre of a brick below, and not in line with a joint. This course, if built in blue bricks, will not allow dampness to rise; or, alternatively, two thicknesses of slates bedded in mortar will serve the same purpose. The courses are then built up to the required height, always remembering to break joint as described, and remembering to bed in the pintles and catch at the required height. To keep the brickwork vertical, a plumb-bob or a spirit-level and straight-edge should be used. Either should be applied to all faces at frequent intervals to ensure that each new course is set exactly above the ones below.

As the work proceeds, run a piece of $\frac{3}{8}$-in. rounded iron along the joints, which will give a neat effect. If a wooden fence is to be built on either side of the gateway, wooden plugs built into every fourth course will provide a fixing for nails or spikes.

The top of each pier can be finished off, either with a stone cap projecting 2 in. all round, or by bedding on two courses of roofing tiles, leaving the nibs on the lower course. On top of these finish with a row of bricks on edge, the same size as the courses below. Half bricks will need to be cut with the edge of the trowel.

The step or threshold can be formed either in concrete between two boards as shuttering, or of bricks on edge; here again blue bricks would be more satisfactory, as they are much harder than red.

The foundation work for stone piers is exactly the same, and stones should be fairly regularly shaped. To obtain an even face more mortar would be needed in all joints, but great care should be taken not to smear this over the outer faces; the trowel can be used to improve the appearance of the joints. A stone capping or narrow stones on end can form the top.

The piers should be allowed to set thoroughly before any attempt is made to hang the gate.

Instructions for making a wooden gate are contained in the section entitled "Jobs with Wood."

LILY POOL. Before attempting to construct a lily pool (Fig. 9) a good deal of attention should be given to considering the best site, for it is desirable, although not absolutely necessary, to arrange for an outlet from the bottom of the pool to facilitate draining for odd repairs and preventing the water becoming stagnant. If a stream is nearby it might be possible to direct part of the flow of water through the pool and back to the stream.

The depth of such a pool should be determined partly to suit the type of lilies to be grown (see WATER PLANTS in "Encyclopaedia of Gardening") and should never be less than 15 in. to prevent freezing up solid. The shape of the pool depends upon personal taste or upon other features in the garden, and when the siting, the size, shape and depth have been determined the external dimensions should be staked out with long pegs.

Materials required will be a spade; straight-edge and level; a bricklayer's trowel; cement, sand, shingle and, for a really watertight job, a waterproofing powder to be added to the mixture according to the maker's instructions. When making the excavation, about 6 in. should be added to the internal dimensions of the pond to allow for the floor and sides. Care should be taken not to disturb the surrounding earth, so that it may be used as a mould. If it crumbles, removable wooden shuttering nailed to posts will have to be used if the sides are to be made of concrete.

Floor and sides. When the excavation and formwork are satisfactory and a fairly level bottom obtained, the floor, consisting of 6 in. of concrete, should be laid, the concrete being made in the proportion of 1 part of Portland cement, 2 parts of clean sharp sand, and 4 parts of shingle (to pass a ¾-in. mesh), adding waterproofing powder if desired. Before this concrete has set hard, cut a rough groove, 1 in. deep and 2 in. wide, all round the bottom on the upper face about 6 in. from the outer edge. This is to receive the sides. These can be made up either of concrete poured in between shuttering, or of brickwork or stonework in cement mortar covered afterwards with at least 2 in. of a mixture of 3 parts sand to 1 of cement. It is essential that the sides should slope away from the inside of the pool as they rise, so that any ice forming will ease up them and not crack the sides.

If brick walls are being used for the sides, they will require to be rendered with the cement and sand mixture in several operations until a thickness of at least 2 in. is obtained. Care must be taken to ensure that the mixture fills in the groove in the bottom of the pool during the first coat and when the second is applied, it should also be taken across the bottom. Should either of the rendering coats have to be done in more than one stage it will be necessary to make a 6-in. lap at each joint well away from a corner, and joints made in any subsequent coat must be kept away from any joint underneath.

The top surround of the pool can be finished either with a rockery or with flagstones or crazy-paving, the edges of which could overhang about 1 in.

Outlet pipes and fountain. The outlet pipe, which can be made from a length of 1-in. gas piping, should be laid as the walls are built, and kept about 1½ in. up from the bottom to prevent its being choked by mud; a good cork pushed into the end is easily removable for draining purposes. The other end could discharge into a hole filled with stones, or a ditch.

If complete drainage of the pool is not required, a length of piping fixed just above the

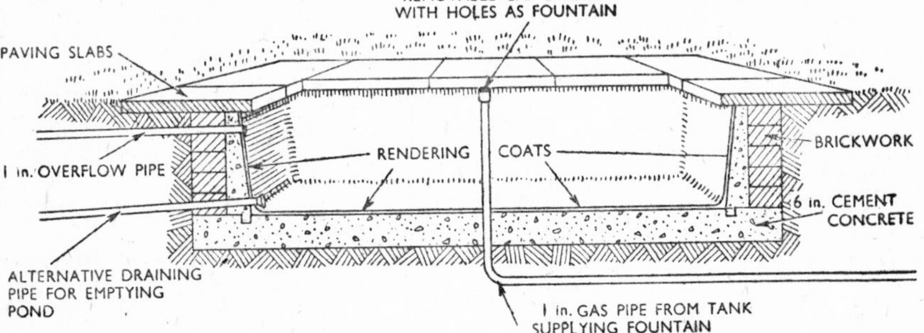

Fig. 9. Brick and concrete lily pool provided with fountain, overflow and drain.

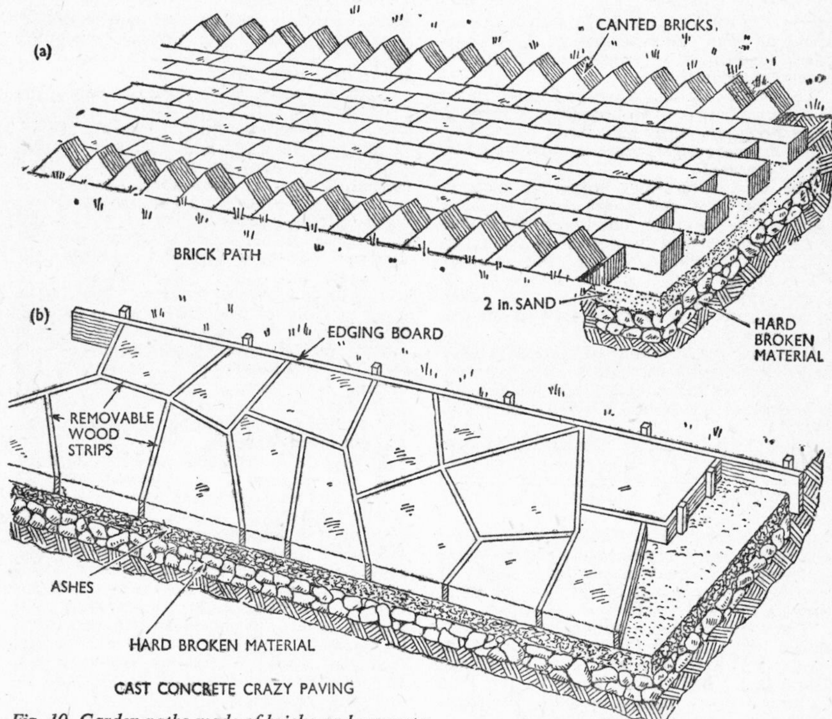

Fig. 10. Garden paths made of bricks and concrete.

required water-level and taken to a ditch or drain will act as an overflow and prevent flooding.

An added attraction can be made by providing a fountain for filling the pool. This can be done by using 1-in. gas piping from a source of water such as a rain-water tank, fitting a stop tap in the piping for controlling the flow. The piping can be buried under the ground and brought up through the centre of the pool, its top finishing just above water-level, with a screw-on cap drilled with small holes to form the spray. The higher the water tank, the better the pressure and consequently the higher the fountain will be. A good safeguard against the piping being blocked by any foreign bodies is to fix a finely perforated grating over the inlet and inside the tank; the removable cap at the fountain will also aid any cleaning operations. (For further information on piping reference should be made to the section, "Plumbing and Glazing.")

PATHS. Of brick. Dig away the top soil to a depth of 6 in. all along the route which the path is to take and then fill in with hard broken materials such as stones, gravel or broken bricks, ramming these well down in the earth and grading it with the coarsest at the bottom and the finest at the top (Fig. 10a). Spread a 2-in. layer of sand over this, well watering it until it is firm.

The bricks can now be laid either in straight rows or in patterns and gently tapping them and trying a straight-edge on them until an even surface is obtained. It will be best to leave the path unused for a few days in order to allow any settlement to take place and be made good. Finally, make a liquid mixture of cement and water and pour this over the surface of the bricks, well brushing it into the cracks with a stiff-bristled brush. The surface should be well brushed over with dry sand and scraped clean before the mortar has set hard. If required, a border can be made on either side of the path by setting up bricks cornerwise (see GARDEN EDGING).

Slabbed and crazy paving. A slabbed path can be similarly made by making the final bed for the slabs in ashes well levelled, rolled and watered. Cement mortar is then applied to the underside of the slabs at each corner and in the middle and each slab is bedded down and levelled. By using odd- or random-shaped pieces of paving slabs, crazy paths can be made in a similar manner.

A more convenient way of making a crazy path is to prepare a solid bed as previously described, finishing with ashes, and then, by use of ½-in.-thick strips of wood, form the shapes of the stones, the strips of wood forming the joints and being levelled to give an even surface (Fig. 10b).

Then pour in a fine cement concrete mix, filling up each mould and levelling off any surplus mixture with a straight-edge, and leave to set. Care must be taken to keep the concrete from setting over the boards, as these are later withdrawn, leaving joints which can be filled in with sand, soil or coloured cement. This method saves a good deal of levelling, as the wet mixture naturally finds its own bed. Care must be taken to bond the stones well, that is, to avoid long continuous joints in several stones by well lapping them.

See also PATHS in "Encyclopaedia of Gardening."

SUNDIAL. Where some special feature or focal point is required in a garden lay-out, a sundial (Fig. 11) is often suitable and can be easily constructed. Assuming that it will stand in the centre of a lawn or green plot, a good plan to ensure that no settlement takes place is to take up the top soil until a firm foundation has been reached and make up again with broken brick or hardcore, finally finishing with 2-3 in. of concrete, brought to a level surface a little below ground level. A centre panel may then be made up with random flagstones laid in cement mortar, or crazy paving; or a paving made of brick in patterns can be effective.

A supply of bricks and a few roofing tiles should be placed handy, after which a sufficient quantity of cement or lime mortar should be prepared, gauging this in the proportions of about 1 part cement to 3 parts of clean sharp sand, or, for lime mortar, 1 part lime to $2\frac{1}{2}$ parts of sand.

Construction of pillar. Lay the first course of bricks by bedding them in mortar, two and a half bricks each way, and filling in any apertures with pieces of brick. The next course of two bricks each way, to form a step, is then laid and similarly filled. Care must be taken to ensure by means of a spirit-level that these courses of brickwork are level.

Next the pillar is built by arranging the bricks alternately, one brick being lengthways and the next brick at right-angles to it; this method is continued in the same way until the tile creasing at the top is reached. This is formed by bedding one course of tiles upon another and lapping them so that no two joints are in line. Next bed on another course of brickwork as before, and after this the next course of bricks is made to oversail, that is, project 1 in. each side. This makes it necessary to insert a closer, a short piece of brick to fill the gaps between the whole bricks.

Lastly, a capping, slightly larger than the top course of brickwork, is formed by a slab of stone or cement. The latter is made in a box of the required size and depth which is filled with a fine concrete mixture in the proportion of $1\frac{1}{2}$ parts of sand to 1 of Portland cement, the surface being trowelled off smooth. This should be left in the box for a week or more until it has set thoroughly hard, after which it is bedded on top of the column after covering this with a thick bed of mortar. Make sure that the slab overhangs equally each side and is perfectly level by placing a spirit-level diagonally from one corner to the other and then the opposite way. If necessary, tap the surface of the slab until it is level.

Fixing the sundial. A good plan is to embed four wooden blocks in the concrete slab to provide a fixing for the sundial, the plate of which should have four holes for screws. Care must be taken to set the position very accurately. The gnomon should point north and south, with the highest part towards the north. A magnetic compass can be used, though an allowance for magnetic deviation from true north should be made. The accuracy of the position can be judged by noting the time given by the shadow of the gnomon, remembering that there will be an hour's difference when summer time is in force.

When satisfied with the position, all that remains is to mark carefully the position of the corners of the plate on the slab, lay a little bed of mortar and screw the metal plate down with wood-screws.

(a)

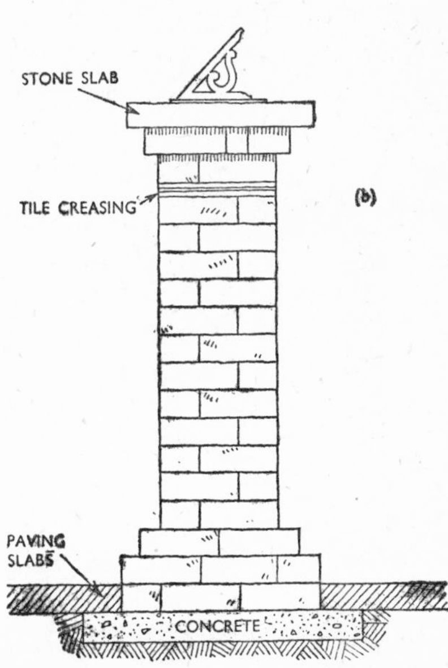

Fig. 11. Sundial: (a) *general view;* (b) *elevation. The paving can be varied to taste.*

JOBS WITH WOOD

Information for the handyman

on carpentry and joinery, upholstery, locks and latches, and staining and polishing.

Under the heading "General Information" the reader will find instructions for such things as making joints and use of tools which have a general application to carpentry and joinery. This information is applied to many of the specific items which are described in the second section, "Things to Make and Repair" (pages 509-25).

GENERAL INFORMATION

FIXINGS. Fixings can be attached to non-metallic substances such as brick, plaster, tiles, concrete, stone, marble and slate, which vary in quality and composition.

Drills and plugs and their use. To make holes in soft stones, cements and tiles, use a rotary drill or tile drill of proprietary make, which will fit in a carpenter's brace and thus make the job much easier.

For very hard stone and brick, a percussion tool is advised. Indeed, this drill suits all

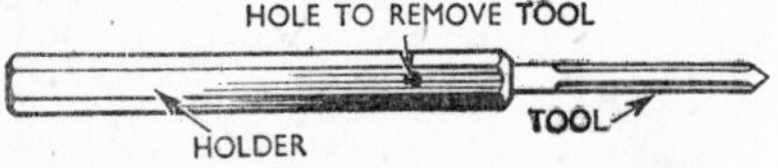

Fig. 1. Percussion drill.

except brittle substances, the hole being chiselled by a steady chipping away of the material with the three cutting edges, which are sharpened to a diamond-shaped point (Fig. 1). In drilling the hole, take care to drill neatly and straight. The rotary drill will do this without trouble, but the percussion tool requires careful handling. Fig. 2 shows the way to use the tool, by holding it lightly in the fingers at right-angles to the wall face, and tapping with a series of light blows.

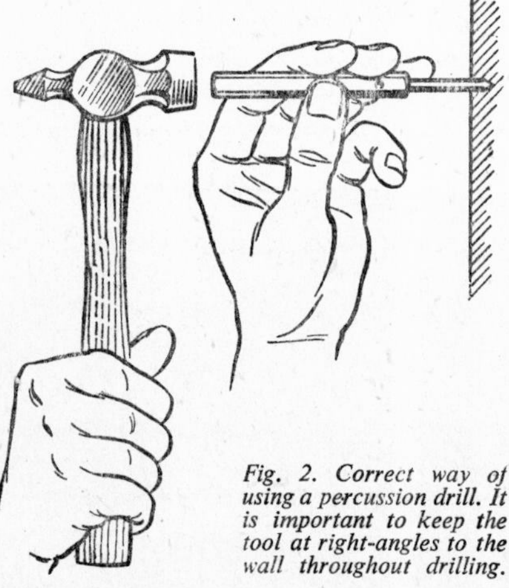

Fig. 2. Correct way of using a percussion drill. It is important to keep the tool at right-angles to the wall throughout drilling.

Various kinds of plug can be bought, such as wood, paper, rubber, lead, asbestos and fibre, but the handyman is advised to use the fibre type.

Drills and plugs are numbered in standard sizes, which numbers tally with the gauge numbers of wood-screws. If you decide on No. 8 wood-screws, the drill or the percussion tool has also the same number; and when the hole has been made insert a No. 8 fibre plug.

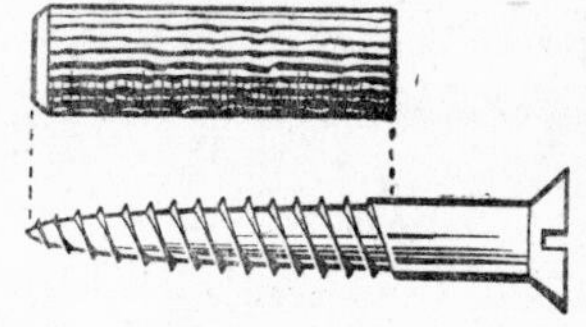

Fig. 3. For best results the plug should be the same length as the threaded part of the screw used.

The length of the plug depends on the length of the screw or the depth of the hole. The procedure, therefore, is to decide which gauge of screw to use, make the hole, determine the length of the screw in proportion to plug (Fig. 3), insert plug, and screw the fitting into place. It is advisable not to have any of the unthreaded part of the screw enter the plug. A little grease on the wood-screw helps to lighten the work.

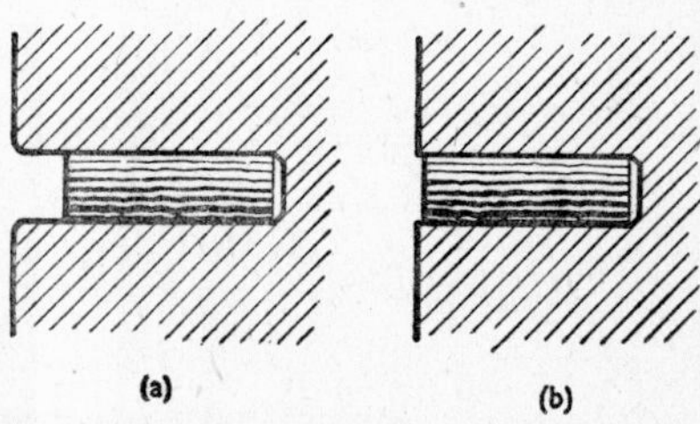

Fig. 4. Plugging (a) *soft brick;* (b) *hard brick*

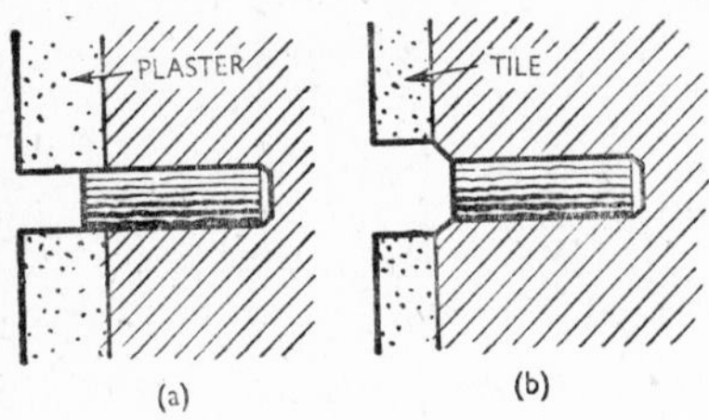

Fig. 5. Plugging through (a) *plaster;* (b) *tile.*

Points to note. Particular substances require special treatment in some respects.

Fixing to brick. If brick is soft, make the hole a little deeper, to allow for the large mouth of the hole (Fig. 4a). With hard brick this is not necessary; the plug can be fixed flush to the surface (Fig. 4b).

Fixing to plaster. As plaster is an unsuitable substance to fix to, drill or punch a hole through the plaster and into the brickwork behind. Insert plug into the brick and screw up as previously described (Fig. 5a).

If the substance is a lath-and-plaster stud partition or wall, lightly tap the surface of the plaster with knuckles or with a hammer until you meet with hard resistance. This is the timber studding, into which the wood-screw can be screwed without holes or plug.

Fixing to tiles. First drill a hole in the tile with a drill twice the size of the screw. Having then made the hole in the material behind with the correct-sized drill, the screw can be screwed into place without touching or leaning upon the tile, so obviating any pressure liable to split the glazed surface (Fig. 5b).

Fixing to concrete, stone, marble. As for brickwork.

Fixing to glass. A hole can be drilled through glass by very slow turns of a twist-drill lubricated with paraffin and turpentine. Care should be taken that the glass is supported behind the hole being drilled, in order to withstand the heavy pressure expended to keep the cutting drill in action.

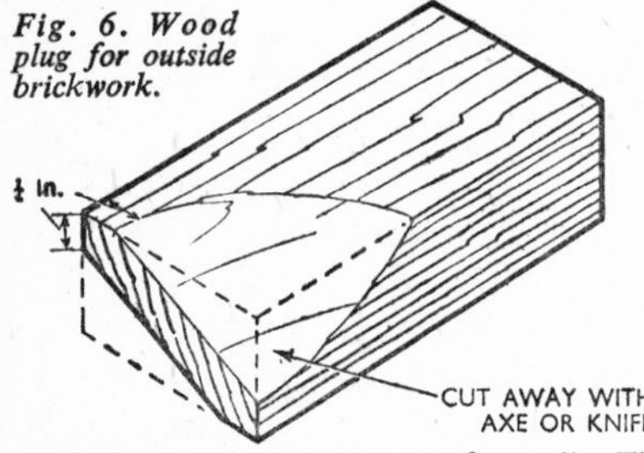

Fig. 6. Wood plug for outside brickwork.

All fixings given above are for walls. The same procedure, however, can be used for ceilings of concrete, floors and the floor surface itself. Here nails will serve instead of screws.

Fixing to exposed brickwork. Fig. 6 shows how to make a wood plug to fit exposed brickwork, if manufactured plugs are not available. With a cold chisel cut out the mortar between the bricks and drive in the home-made plug with a hammer. Cut off flush to the wall, and the plug is ready for the screw or nail to be driven in.

JOINTS. The joints described below are frequently used in carpentry and joinery, and many of them are employed in making the articles described in this section. All the joints mentioned are illustrated in Fig. **7.**

Angle. These are very useful in joinery; Fig. 7a shows three common types.

Cogged. These joints are mostly used for carpentry or framing work (Fig. 7b).

Dovetail. Two sections at right-angles can be joined by means of a dovetail joint (Fig. 7c). The correct splay varies from 1 in 6 to 1 in 8. A happy medium of 1 in 7 can, however, be satisfactorily applied to all dovetail joints. A little templet of corresponding shape will serve as a guide for pencilling the angles of the dovetails on to the work to be cut and will avoid making detailed measurements every time this joint is required (Fig. 7d).

The dovetail halving joint (Fig. 7e) is suitable for holding a framework together without nails or screws.

Housing. This joint is most useful for jointing shelves to standards in open fittings or bookcases without using shelf-bearers. The latter never look nice and take up valuable space (Fig. 7f). The dovetail housing joint (Fig. 7g) does away with having to nail standards to shelves which, when once fitted, remain fixed.

Longitudinal. These vary considerably. Fig. 7h shows a sound type. If this joint is to be subjected to any great strain or weight, the joint can be strengthened by fitting steel plates to both sides, fixed by bolts instead of screws (Fig. 7i). If used horizontally, a square joint is preferable on the top edge.

Mortise and tenon. This is the most common and useful joint employed when a T-shaped joint is required. The size of the material does not matter, but the width of the tenon must not exceed 3 in. in order to minimize the effect of possible shrinkage of the tenon (Fig. 7j).

Mortise and tenon, haunched. Used for an L-shaped joint at the angles of framing, such as cupboard doors, etc. The width of the haunching and tenon should be equal, or half the width of the rail (Fig. 7k).

Notched or halving. Similar in appearance and usefulness to the cogged joint, this joint is mostly used for carpentry or framing work (Fig. 7l).

Widening. Fig. 7m shows three joints used for widening. These joints can be glued together, or a ledge (or cleat) screwed across the joints to hold them together.

STAINING AND POLISHING. This entry is of particular application to furniture and fittings. For other aspects the reader is referred to "Painting and Decorating." First of all, smooth the wood surface of the article to be stained and/or polished with glass-paper. This initial glass-papering puts a final finish where the plane has not left the surface as smooth as could be desired.

Preparation. If deal or any softwood is to be painted, rub the surface diagonally across

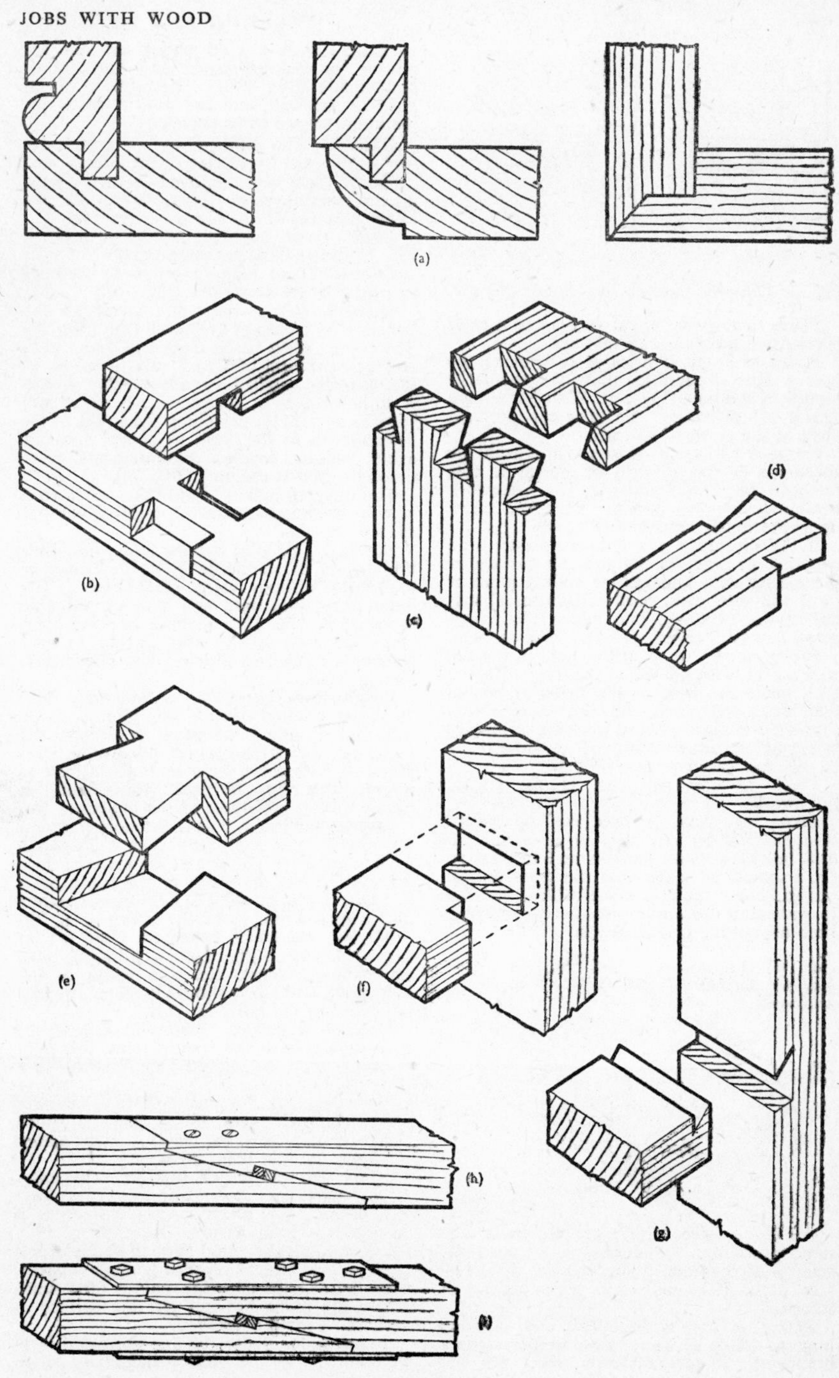
(a)
(b)
(c)
(d)
(e)
(f)
(g)
(h)

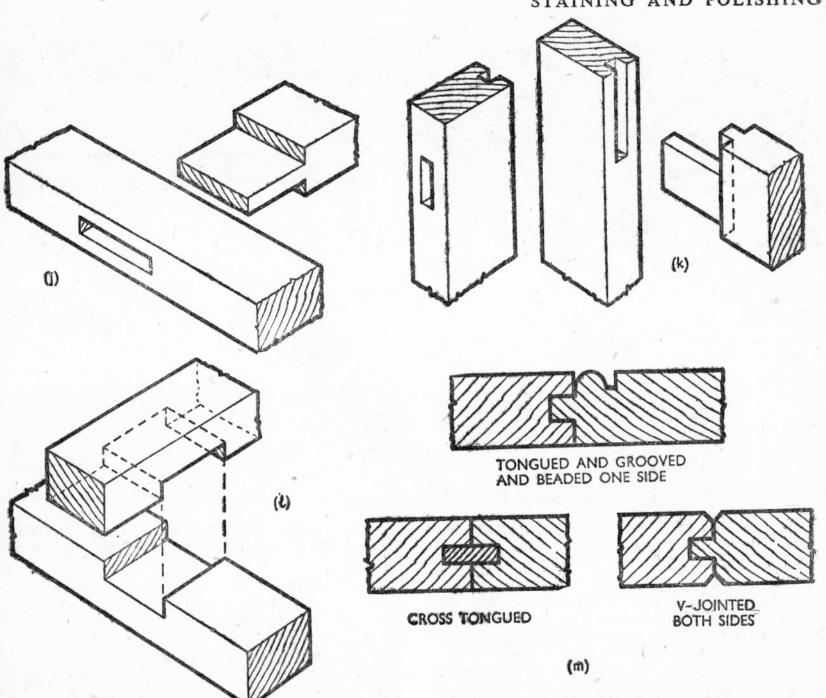

Fig. 7. Opposite and above are shown a number of joints commonly used in woodwork; many of them feature in items described later in this section: (a) *angle joints* (left to right) *tongued and beaded, tongued and ovolo moulded, and lapped mitre;* (b) *cogged joint;* (c) *dovetail;* (d) *templet used in marking out dovetails;* (e) *dovetail halving joint;* (f) *housing joint;* (g) *dovetail housing joint;* (h) *screwed longitudinal joint;* (i) as (h) *strengthened with steel plates and bolts;* (j) *mortise and tenon;* (k) *haunched mortise and tenon;* (l) *notched joint;* (m) *three joints used in widening.*

the grain with "middle 2" glass-paper. If the wood is being prepared for staining and varnishing, apply the finish to the surface with "fine 2" glass-paper, rubbed with the grain.

For hardwoods, such as oak, mahogany, walnut, etc., rub in the direction of the grain with "middle 2" followed by "fine 2." Then rub with a clean cloth dipped in clean hot water, until the whole surface is damp. Allow thoroughly to dry, then rub down with "fine 2" or "0" glass-paper, according to the smoothness required.

Staining. Staining colours new woodwork without obscuring the natural grain. There are three types of stain: water-stain, oil-stain and spirit-stain. This entry deals with water-stain.

Oak. Add cold or warm water to a small quantity of Vandyke brown, allow dye to dissolve, and dilute to the colour required. Before applying, test the solution on a piece of similar wood.

Mahogany. Treat in the same manner as described for oak, using mahogany water-crystals.

Walnut. This looks best if polished in its natural state, without additional colouring.

Softwoods. These can be stained or coloured to look like hardwoods. Vandyke brown will give deal the appearance of oak; Bismarck brown will give deal a mahogany colour.

Do not brush the stain on too thickly. Two thin coats are better than one thick one.

French-polishing. After the wood has been stained to the desired colour it may be given a fine glossy surface, showing natural beauty of the grain, by means of french-polishing. This process is suitable for all hardwoods.

Filling. Fill the wood pores, to prevent absorption. With a wet, clean rag dipped in plaster-of-paris, quickly fill the pores or grain, rubbing in a circular motion, so that all parts are covered uniformly; then with a larger cloth rub off all surplus plaster before it has time to set.

Oiling. When the plaster filling is hard bring the wood back to its finished colour by a moderate application of linseed oil, and rub down the whole surface with old or used "fine 2" or "0" glass-paper. Wipe away all surplus oil, etc.

Polishing. First make a pad, by wrapping cotton-wool soaked in french-polish in a rag about 6 in. square—a pad about half the size

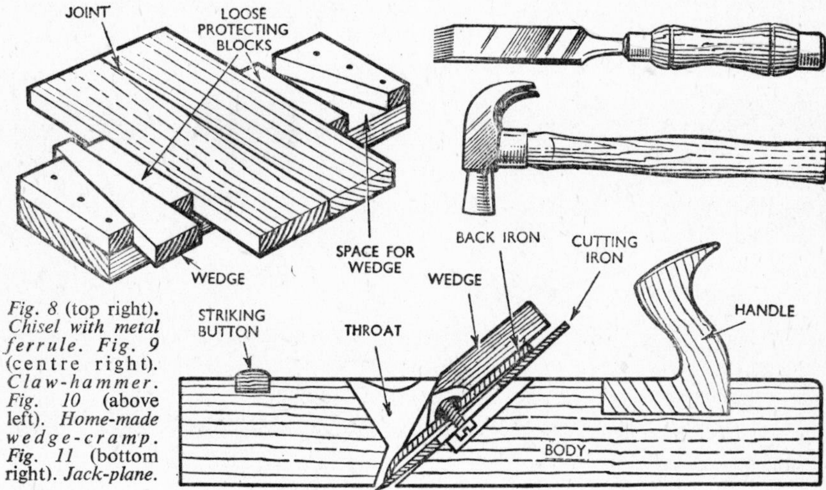

Fig. 8 (top right). *Chisel with metal ferrule. Fig. 9* (centre right). *Claw-hammer. Fig. 10* (above left). *Home-made wedge-cramp. Fig. 11* (bottom right). *Jack-plane.*

of the palm of the hand. In all polishing the rubber must be used so that no place is covered twice, until the whole surface has received a coat of polish. When a second coat is applied, the same sequence should be followed so that the polish has time to stiffen before being rubbed again. Polishing should be carried out in a warm room.

When the first coating has lost its stickiness, resoak the cotton-wool with polish, and apply

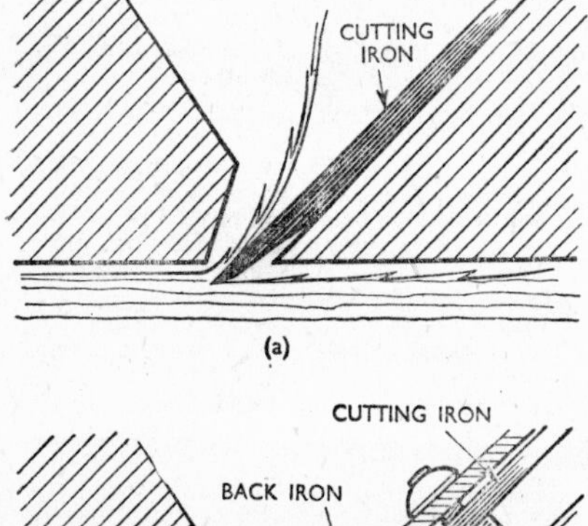

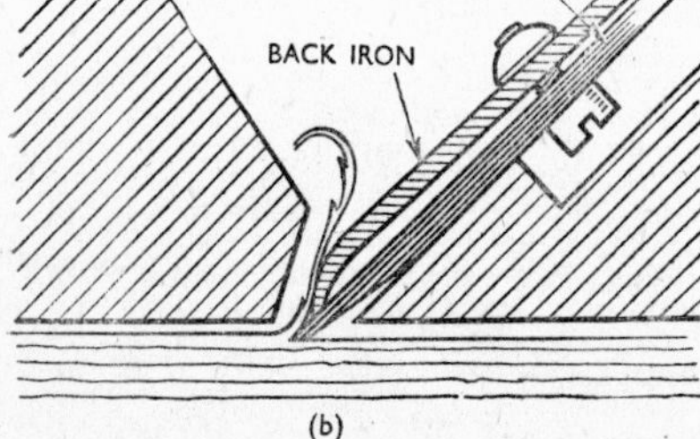

Fig. 12. (a) *Effect of planing with cutting iron only.* (b) *When a back iron is also used the shavings are bent back and a clean cut results.*

the next layer. About sixteen applications will give a good finish; more can be added if desired.

After three or four rubbers of polish have been applied, always working with the grain, the work may become sticky. A drop of linseed oil may be added to the face of the rubber and this will allow the work to proceed until a good body of polish has been put on. Leave the work to harden for a day or two, and then rub down the surface with grade "0" glass-paper.

Repeat the process of applying polish with the rubber, but do not use any oil. After two or three applications thin the polish with methylated spirit and use the rubber nearly dry. This will mean that considerable pressure has to be applied and the rubber must be kept moving slowly across the work to obtain a good polish.

Methylated spirit will remove the polish from the fingers.

Wax-polishing. The handyman is advised against attempting the "spirit finish" in french-polishing. Unless expertly done, the result may be ruinous. An excellent alternative finish may be obtained by beeswax and turpentine.

Melt some beeswax and add a small quantity of turps and linseed oil. Stir the mixture. When cool it should form an easily workable paste. Put on the wax with a flannel (after rubbing down the surface with glass-paper if the wood is stained), and rub in a circular motion. This first coating fills the grain. A second coating will give a bright, even surface, free from tackiness, finger-marks and surplus wax, if the polish is applied "little and often," the secret being the persistent energy that is put into the rubbing.

TOOL OUTFITS. Following are brief descriptions of the principal tools used by the carpenter and joiner. With them the amateur handyman can make all the articles described later in this section and perform many other odd carpentering jobs.

Chisels. Firmer chisels are strongest and best. Those with an iron band at the end prevent the handle from splitting and will stand up to blows from the claw-hammer, thus dispensing with a mallet (Fig. 8).

Claw-hammer, adze-eye. A useful tool, the claw of which is used for extracting nails and may in some cases dispense with pincers (Fig. 9).

Cleat or wedge-cramp. To hold joints together until glue has set. Is easy to make (see SLIDING SASH, REPLACING A) and takes the place of a joiner's iron cramp (Fig. 10).

Jack-plane. English beech is the best wood for this tool (Fig. 11). A generous application of linseed oil to the wood keeps it in constant working order.

The back iron, by bending back the shavings, prevents the cutting iron from tearing or

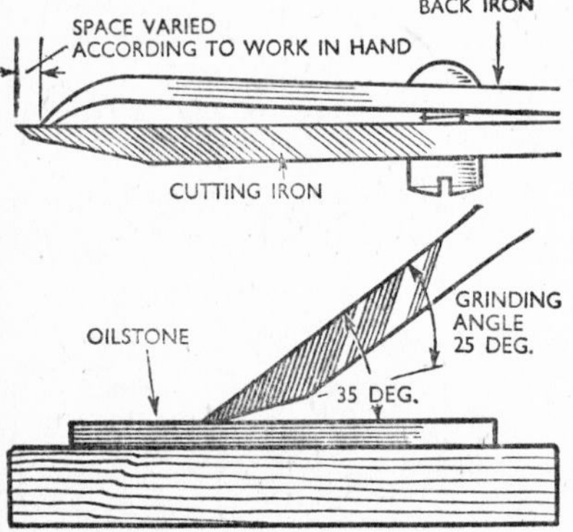

Fig. 13 (upper). *The setting of the back iron is important, and the space should generally be on the small side. Fig. 14* (lower). *This shows the correct sharpening angles for a cutting iron.*

splitting the wood when planing (Fig. 12). The setting of the back iron should be $\frac{1}{16}$ in. to $\frac{1}{8}$ in. from the cutting edge. With a larger space the back iron loses its value (Fig. 13).

The cutting iron should be carefully sharpened on an Indian oilstone, if possible. Fig. 14 shows the angle at which the iron should be held. As this stone is artificial, machine oil can be used with good results. After sharpening, reverse the iron, lay flat on the stone and rub off the surplus metal known as the "burr."

Joiner's dogs. Four are a useful item in a handyman's outfit. Fig. 44 shows one in use.

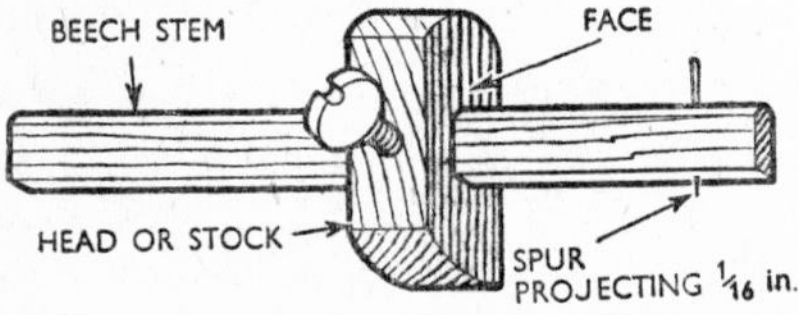

Fig. 15 (above). *Chief parts of a marking gauge. Fig. 16* (right). *How to use this tool.*

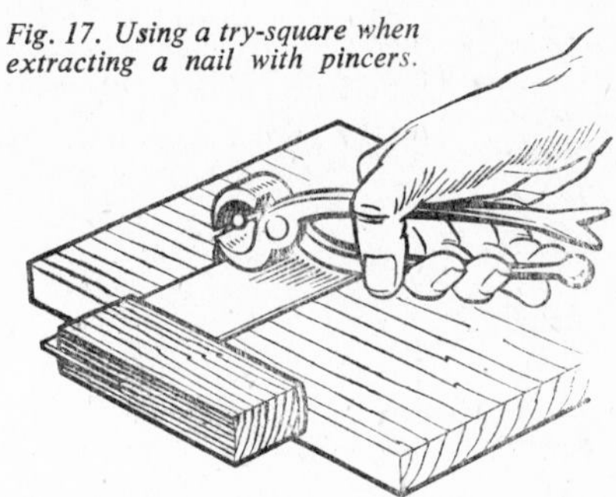

Fig. 17. Using a try-square when extracting a nail with pincers.

Marking gauge. Used, instead of a pencil, for marking accurate lines (Fig. 15). The user should ensure that the spur is slightly inclined, as the gauge is propelled away from the body (Fig. 16).

Pincers. This tool explains itself. A good tip when extracting nails is to put the try-square against the nail. The steel blade then prevents the pincers-head from damaging the surface of the wood (Fig. 17).

Rebate plane. Used mainly to enlarge an existing rebate (a recess cut lengthwise in a piece of wood). Is made of beechwood, and has a cutting iron but no back iron (Fig. 18).

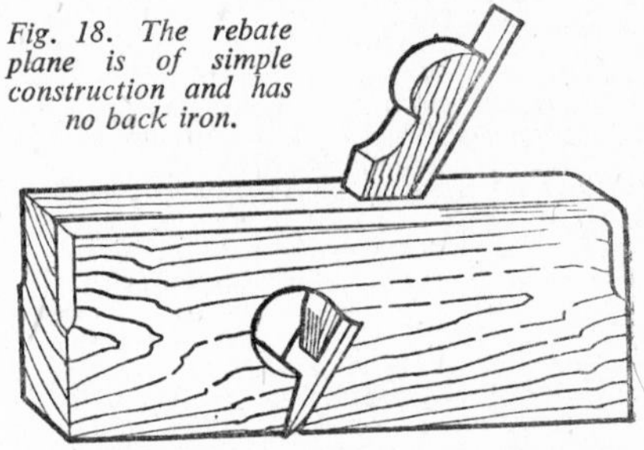

Fig. 18. The rebate plane is of simple construction and has no back iron.

Router. A useful tool for obtaining a level bottom to housings or recesses. It is easy to make one of wood (Fig. 19), but the modern metal router is superior in every way.

Rule. A 2-ft. fourfold boxwood rule, with eighth and sixteenth divisions marked on the edges (Fig. 20).

Saws. Three types of saw are essential to an outfit (Fig. 21). The hand-saw is used for

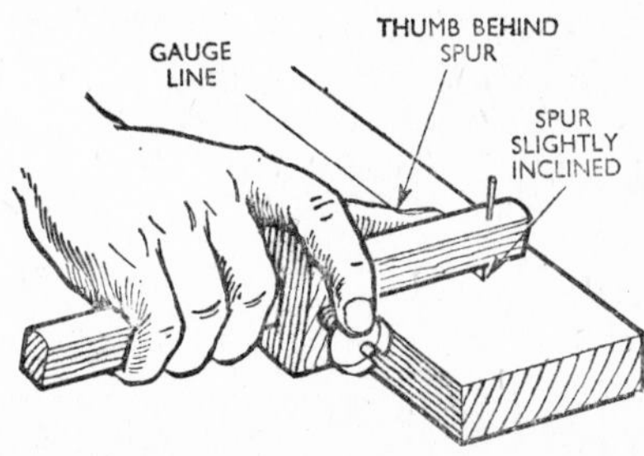

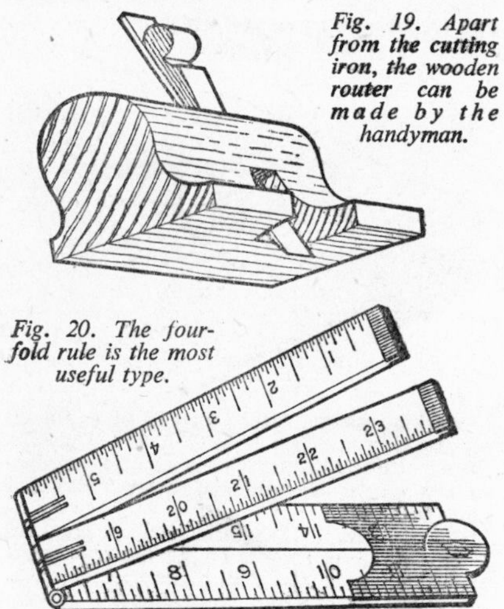

Fig. 19. Apart from the cutting iron, the wooden router can be made by the handyman.

Fig. 20. The four-fold rule is the most useful type.

rougher work and the tenon-saw (designed for cutting the tenons of joints) for finer work. The pad-saw is used for cutting curved work, and the length of projection of the blade can be adjusted to suit the type of work on hand. When saws become blunted, the amateur should not attempt to sharpen them himself. They should be taken to a tool shop.

Sliding-bevel. Used for testing and marking angles other than right-angles (Fig. 22).

Smoothing-plane, steel. This is used for finishing off work or removing last shavings before glass-papering the surface. To ensure easy working, keep the sole slightly oiled. The cutting iron and back iron are similar to those of the jack-plane and sharpening is carried out in the same way (see above), but the setting space between the two irons for hardwoods or across grain should be as small as possible. For softwoods $\frac{1}{16}$ in. is suitable.

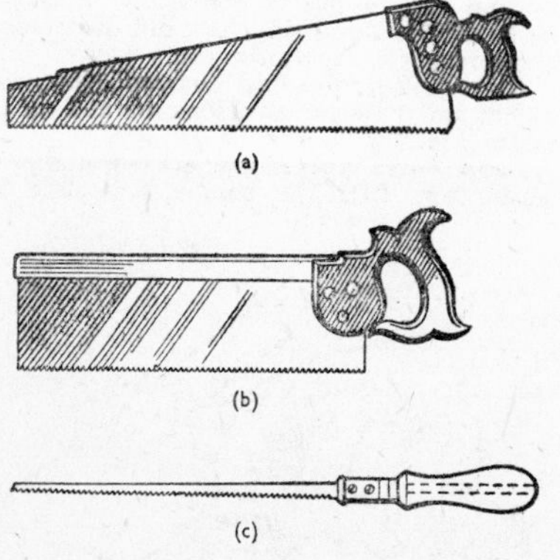

Fig. 21. Three useful types of saw: (a) *hand-saw;* (b) *tenon-saw;* (c) *pad-saw with adjustable blade.*

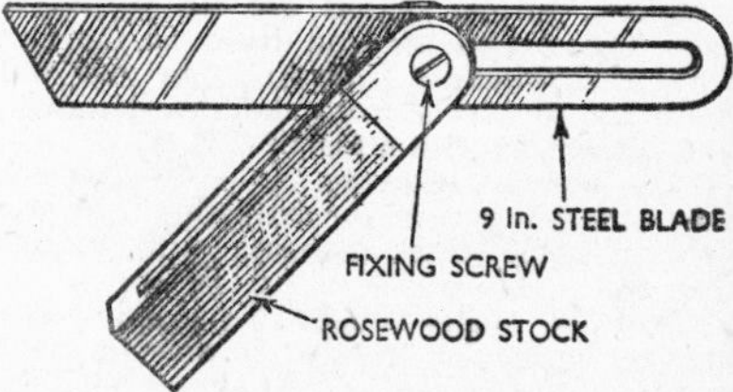

Fig. 22. Sliding-bevel.

Fig. 23. Metal spokeshave.

Spokeshave, iron. Used for trimming or planing curved work. An iron spokeshave is preferable to a wooden one, as it has a finer adjustment (Fig. 23).

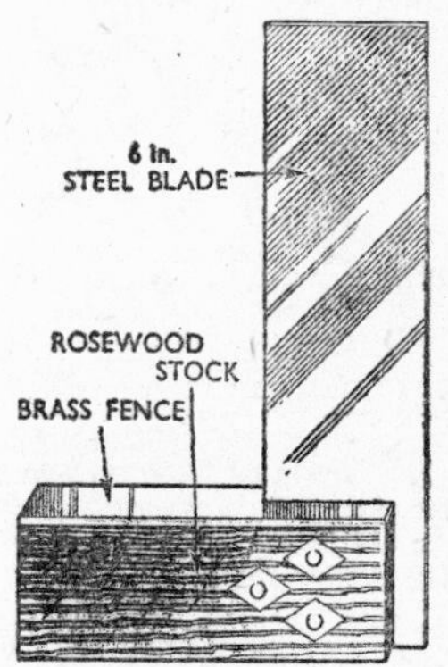

Fig. 24 (left). *The try-square is an essential part of the handyman's equipment. A 6-in. blade is a convenient size.*

Fig. 25 (below). *Testing a try-square. If after reversing the tool against a straight edge the lines are co-incident the square is true.*

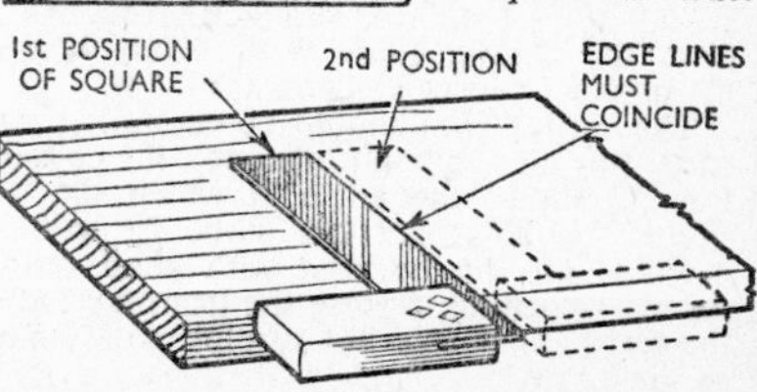

Try-square. For setting out and testing work (Fig. 24). Sizes vary, the 6-in. being most commonly used. This tool must be true and should be frequently tested. It should be noted particularly that the sides of the blade are at right-angles to the brass fence only, so for accurate work do not use the outside of the stock with the blade. A simple method of testing the try-square is shown in Fig. 25. When marking out, always hold the fence firmly against the material.

A half-round wood rasp, twist bits and a brace should complete the outfit.

THINGS TO MAKE AND REPAIR

BOOK-CASE, HOW TO MAKE A. The illustration (Fig. 26) shows an open-fitting type, with fixed shelves, suitable for a recess. 8¾-in. depth will be found suitable for books of average size, 10¾-in. for larger. It is advisable to measure the books before starting the job.

Wood required. This can be bought already machined with smooth, clean surfaces, as follows:

1 top, 4 ft. by depth by ¾ in. thick.
1 bottom, 4 ft. by depth by ¾ in. thick.
2 sides, 2 ft. 11 in. by depth by ¾ in. thick. 1 division, 2 ft. 7 in. by depth by ¾ in. thick.
4 shelves, 2 ft. by depth by ¾ in. thick.

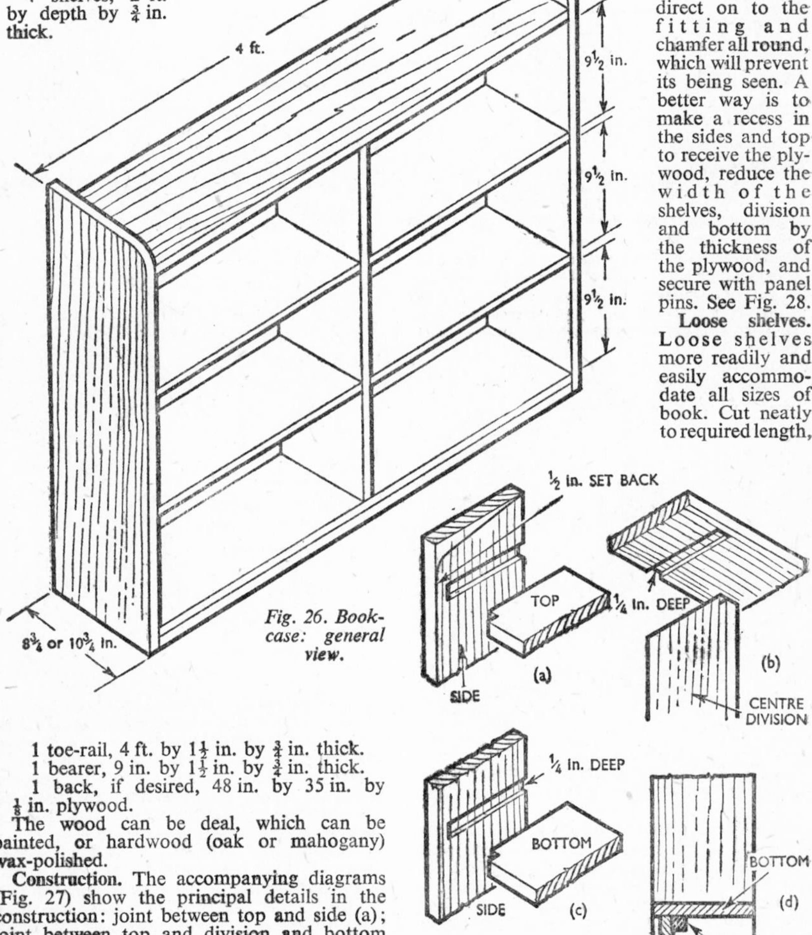

Fig. 26. Book-case: general view.

Fig. 27. Book-case: details of joints.

1 toe-rail, 4 ft. by 1½ in. by ¾ in. thick.
1 bearer, 9 in. by 1½ in. by ¾ in. thick.
1 back, if desired, 48 in. by 35 in. by ⅛ in. plywood.

The wood can be deal, which can be painted, or hardwood (oak or mahogany) wax-polished.

Construction. The accompanying diagrams (Fig. 27) show the principal details in the construction: joint between top and side (a); joint between top and division and bottom and division (b); joint between side and bottom and side and shelf (c); toe-rail, which is fixed in tightly and secured with glue blocks, after fitting has been assembled (d); and bearer, to be fixed in the same way as the toe-rail, but directly beneath the division, under the bottom (e).

Should no back be required, it is advisable to measure the skirting of the wall against which the shelves are to be placed; cut away the back of the sides and centre division to these measurements and reduce the width of the bottom shelf. This will enable the rest of the book-shelves to stand tight against the wall.

The easiest way to fix a back is to nail the plywood direct on to the fitting and chamfer all round, which will prevent its being seen. A better way is to make a recess in the sides and top to receive the plywood, reduce the width of the shelves, division and bottom by the thickness of the plywood, and secure with panel pins. See Fig. 28.

Loose shelves. Loose shelves more readily and easily accommodate all sizes of book. Cut neatly to required length,

Fig. 27 (continued). Book-case: position and fixing of bearer.

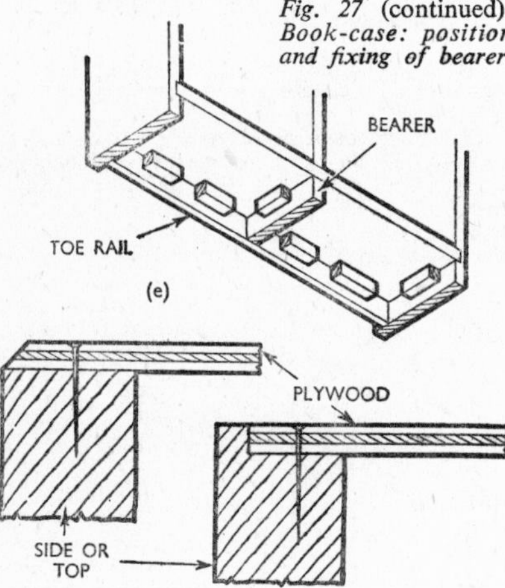

Fig. 28. Book-case: two conventional methods of fitting the back to sides and top.

so that shelves move freely in the fitting. The holes in the division and sides (Fig. 29a) should be made with great care, particularly in respect of their depth. To prevent making the holes too deep, bore through a block of wood, measure on this the depth of hole required, and cut away the wood measured (b).

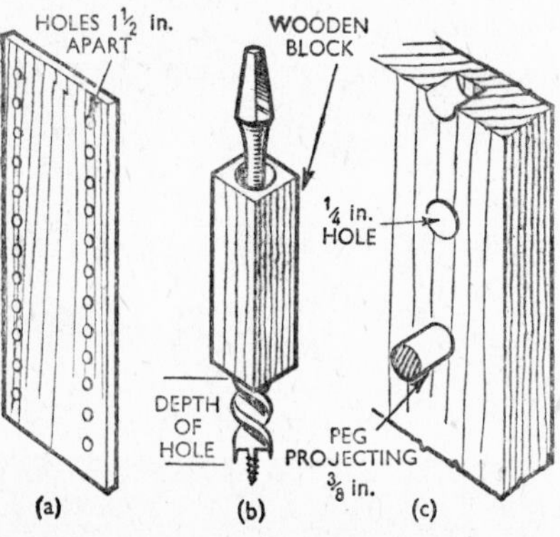

Fig. 29. Book-case: method of fitting loose shelves by means of adjustable wooden pegs.

Drill the holes until the block of wood touches the wood of the sides or division. Four pegs ($\frac{1}{4}$-in. dowelling is suitable) are required for each shelf, and can be inserted where desired (c).

BOOK-REST, HOW TO MAKE A. The illustration (Fig. 30a) shows a small book-rest, the construction of which is well within the scope of the handyman. It can be made of hardwood, such as oak or mahogany, and wax-polished (see STAINING AND POLISHING). The length can be adjusted to suit individual requirements, likewise the design or shape of the ends, but the details of the joints remain the same.

The back and bottom of the book-rest are recessed or housed $\frac{3}{8}$ in. deep into the ends, and made to fit fairly tightly, and except for a little glue no other fastening is necessary (b). The bottom and back are tongued and grooved together, and the joint glued (c). This groove can be quite easily made by cutting with a small saw and then chiselling the surplus piece between the cuts. Cut the tongue by two saw-cuts at right-angles, cleaning up with a chisel. Before assembling, smooth these parts with glass-paper, so that when they are glued together they are ready for polishing.

Fig. 30. Book-rest: (a) general view; (b)—(e) details of joints, with alternatives.

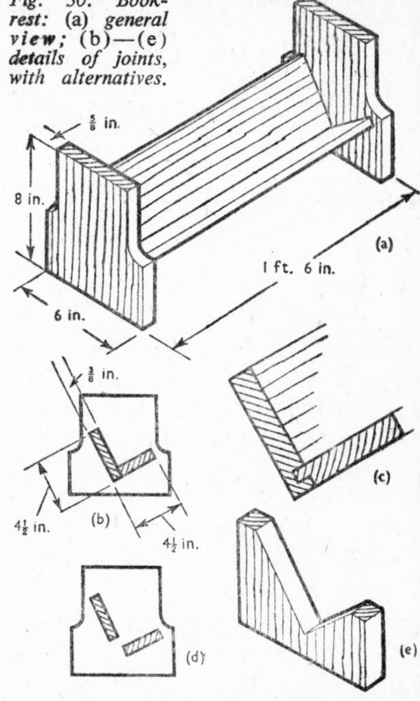

As an alternative make the back and bottom parts square, and recess as shown in (d). This method obviates the dust-trap at the tongued and grooved joint, but the parts require to be of greater thickness if they are to resist bending under the weight of books. To prevent this an extra bearing bracket (e) can be made and the back and bottom parts screwed to it.

CASEMENT SASHES, CONSTRUCTING. Whether the sash (the wooden frame holding the glass) is new or a replacement, the method of construction is the same. Buy from a timber merchant stock sash material, that is, stiles, top-rails, bars (if required), and bottom rail (sections shown in Figs. 31a-c).

Mark in pencil on the stiles the overall size required and a second line denoting the

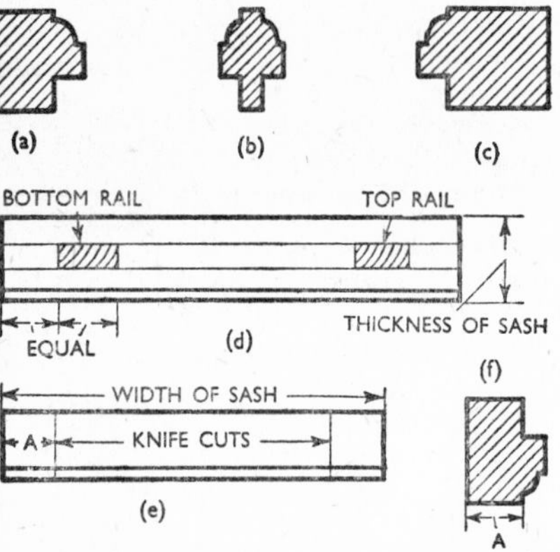

Fig. 31. Constructing casement sashes: (a)—(c) ***sections through top rail and stiles, bars and bottom rail;*** (d) *marking of stiles;* (e) *marking **of rails** before cutting shoulders with fine saw;* A ***equals** the width **of** the rail **as** shown in* (f).

width of the rail. Divide this distance into two equal parts; the portion on the glass side is the mortise and the outer portion the haunching (d). The shoulders on the top and bottom rails and bars are cut with a fine dovetail saw, but before doing this use a knife to sever the fibres on the surface (e).

The joints are fitted as shown in Fig. 32. It is an advantage to use the recessed-rail haunching on sashes as the stiles are so narrow. Assembly is the same as explained for the sliding sash. See SLIDING SASH, REPLACING A.

CASEMENT SASHES, HANGING. In this kind of job pressed-steel butt hinges are generally used, $1\frac{1}{2}$ in., 2 in., or $2\frac{1}{2}$ in. long, according to the weight of the sash (that is, the woodwork into which the glass is fitted). Most hinges have knuckles in odd numbers; also the numbers of screw-holes vary.

Measuring. Measure the distance from flap to knuckle and mark on sash and frame (Fig. 33*A*). The vertical position does not matter; the hinges can be either the same distance, say 4 in., from the top and bottom of the sash, or in line with the edges of the upper and lower rails of the sash.

In the same way, carefully measure thickness and length of hinge and mark on edge of sash and frame (*B*).

Recessing. The measurements being marked on edges and face of both sash and frame, the recesses can now be cut, care being taken not to go too deep. Saw-cut the side, then chisel-cut across the grain and carefully chisel out the surplus wood. To ensure that the ends do not split, place chisel in saw-cut and give a sharp blow with a mallet, to sever the fibres at the back of the recess. Cut each hinge-flap into the sash and frame respectively, keeping the centre line of the knuckle outside the face of the sash.

Fixing. Choose the side of the hinge with the least number of knuckles in the flap and screw to sash. If the recess is cut too deep and the face of the flap is below the wood surface, place a thin wood or cardboard strip underneath. The same process obtains for screwing the corresponding flap to the frame.

DRAINING-BOARD, MAKING A. Of the three best kinds of wood to use, teak will last the longest, with sycamore a good second; the third, white deal, although retaining its whiteness through scrubbing, will not resist the action of water like the other two.

Construction. The length is determined by the distance between sink and wall (Fig. 34), and the width is according to requirements. The surface of the board is cut in

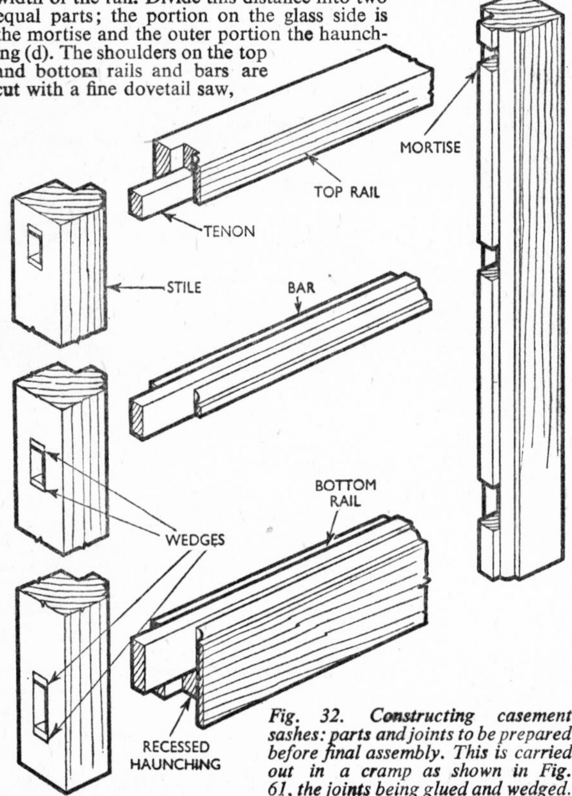

*Fig. 32. **Constructing** casement sashes: parts and joints to be prepared before final assembly. This is carried out in a cramp as shown in Fig. 61, the **joints** being glued and wedged.*

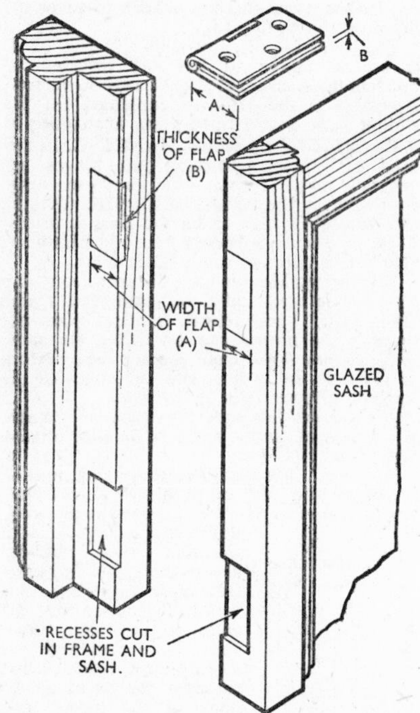

Fig. 33. This diagram shows how the dimensions of the flaps of the hinges should be marked on sash and frame of a casement window.

tapering grooves or flutes, spaced about 2½ in. apart (Fig. 35). A raised fillet is screwed round the edges, to prevent crockery from sliding off (Fig. 36). A small groove is cut on the under edge (Fig. 34) to prevent water seeping back and over the outside edge of the sink.

Fixing in position. If the board is of reasonable length, the only fixings required are a

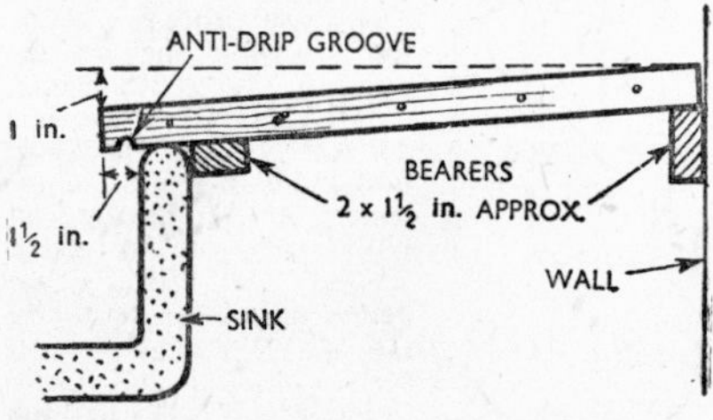

Fig. 34. Side view of draining-board.

bearer or block screwed on the underside to rest against the sink, and a bearer plugged and screwed to the wall (Fig. 34). If, however, the wall is some distance away from the sink, a wall-bracket is needed to support the end of the draining-board. Fig. 36 shows how a

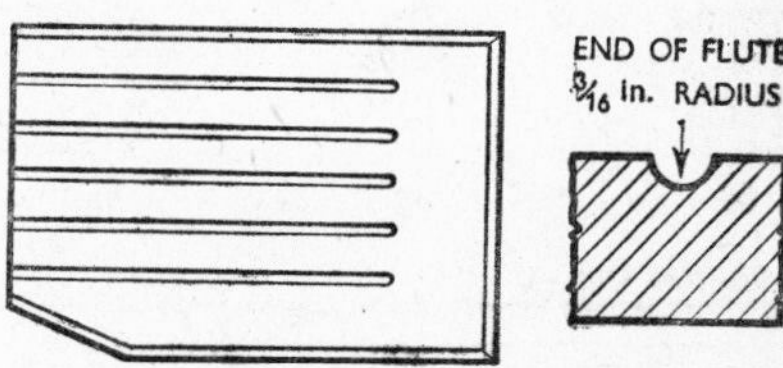

Fig. 35. Draining-board: details of flutes.

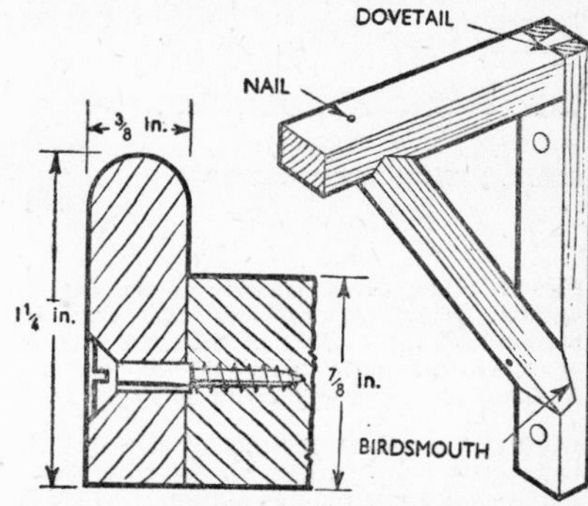

Fig. 36. Raised fillet and supporting bracket.

gallows-bracket can be made for this purpose, of material 2 in. by 1½ in. in section.

DRAWER CONSTRUCTION. Three examples are given, of which two are for a

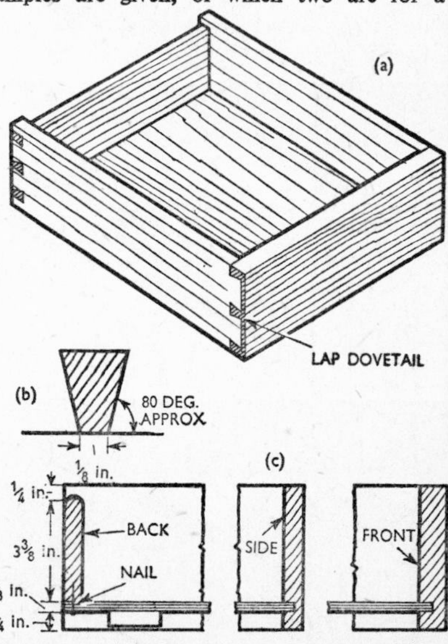

Fig. 37. Construction of dovetailed drawer: (a) *general appearance;* (b) *detail of joint;* (c) *the bottom is grooved into the front and sides but nailed to the back* (*which is very slightly shallower than the sides in this example*).

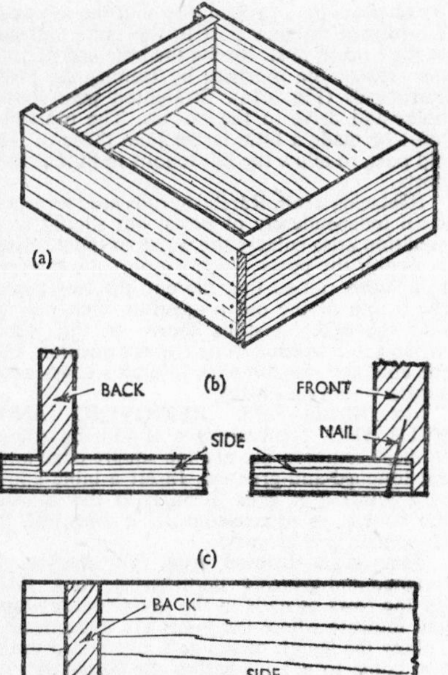

Fig. 38. A simpler type of drawer without dovetails: (a) *general view;* (b) *details of joints at front and back;* (c) *the bottom is grooved into the sides and front and nailed to the back.*

drawer made for a structure that already has an opening to receive it—a kitchen dresser, for instance; and the other example a drawer that can be made for side support only.

Wood required.

1 front, length by 4 in. deep by $\frac{7}{8}$ in. thick ((hardwood is best).

2 sides, length by 4 in. deep by $\frac{1}{2}$ in. thick (deal wood).

1 back, length by $3\frac{3}{8}$ in. deep by $\frac{1}{2}$ in. thick (deal wood).

1 bottom, length by width by $\frac{1}{8}$ in. or $\frac{1}{4}$ in. (thick ply).

Fig. 37 gives details of construction of a drawer to be fitted into an existing structure, with runners already in position for drawer to slide in. This design has dovetailed joints front and back. The bottom is let into grooves in front and sides and nailed to the back. Hardwood blocks are glued under the bottom to the sides.

Fig. 38 is an alternative design which is easier to make as it avoids dovetailing. The front is rebated to take the sides and the back is let into a groove in the sides. The bottom is fitted as in the previous design.

Fig. 39 gives details of construction of a drawer that can be fitted to a tool-shed table, or an extra drawer for the workbench, or any other place where there are sides only for support. A shallow groove is made in each side of the drawer and narrow hardwood runners, designed to run in the grooves, are attached to the supports.

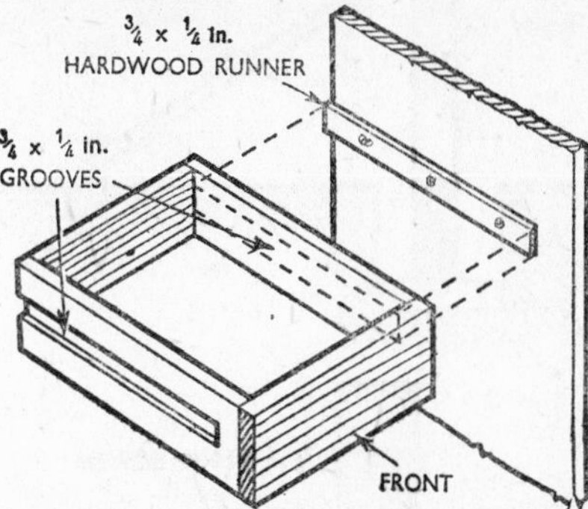

Fig. 39. Drawer made for side support only. Grooves in the sides fit over hardwood runners.

FENCE, CONSTRUCTING A. The type of timber selected will depend on its cost and availability. Of oak, chestnut and deal, oak is the most expensive and deal has the lowest first cost.

Posts. These support the entire structure. To guard against rot at ground level, which may cause the fence to collapse in windy weather, it is important to buy posts impregnated with creosote under pressure, called "pressure-creosoted posts." The average size of posts is 5 in. by 3 in., and they are placed approximately 8 ft. apart. Dig a hole 1 ft. 6 in. to 2 ft. deep. Cover the bottom with concrete. Bed in post, and to keep it upright erect a temporary brace consisting of a piece of wood, one end of which is attached to the top of the post and the other to a peg in the ground some feet away (Fig. 40a). Fill in the hole with concrete, and heap up to 3 in. above ground level. This keeps the post entirely safe from the earth, which can quickly rot it. The surplus earth can be placed round the wet concrete.

Boarding and rails. These can be purchased in the white and creosoted after erection. This will delay rot, and give a uniform colour to the whole fence.

Rails can be bought ready cut to shape and are known as arris rails. These should be on the owner's side of the post. Fig. 40b shows the jointing of two adjacent rails to one post, and sections of alternative styles.

Assembly. Assemble posts and rails before erection, dig the holes, concrete the bottoms, set up fence in required position, complete concreting as described and allow to set. The boarding should be fixed to the rails with galvanized nails as shown in (c). "Featheredge" boarding is the most common type, and the laps can be arranged to suit the spacing of each bay.

FENCE, REPAIRING A. Replacing a post. It is better to replace with a new post than to

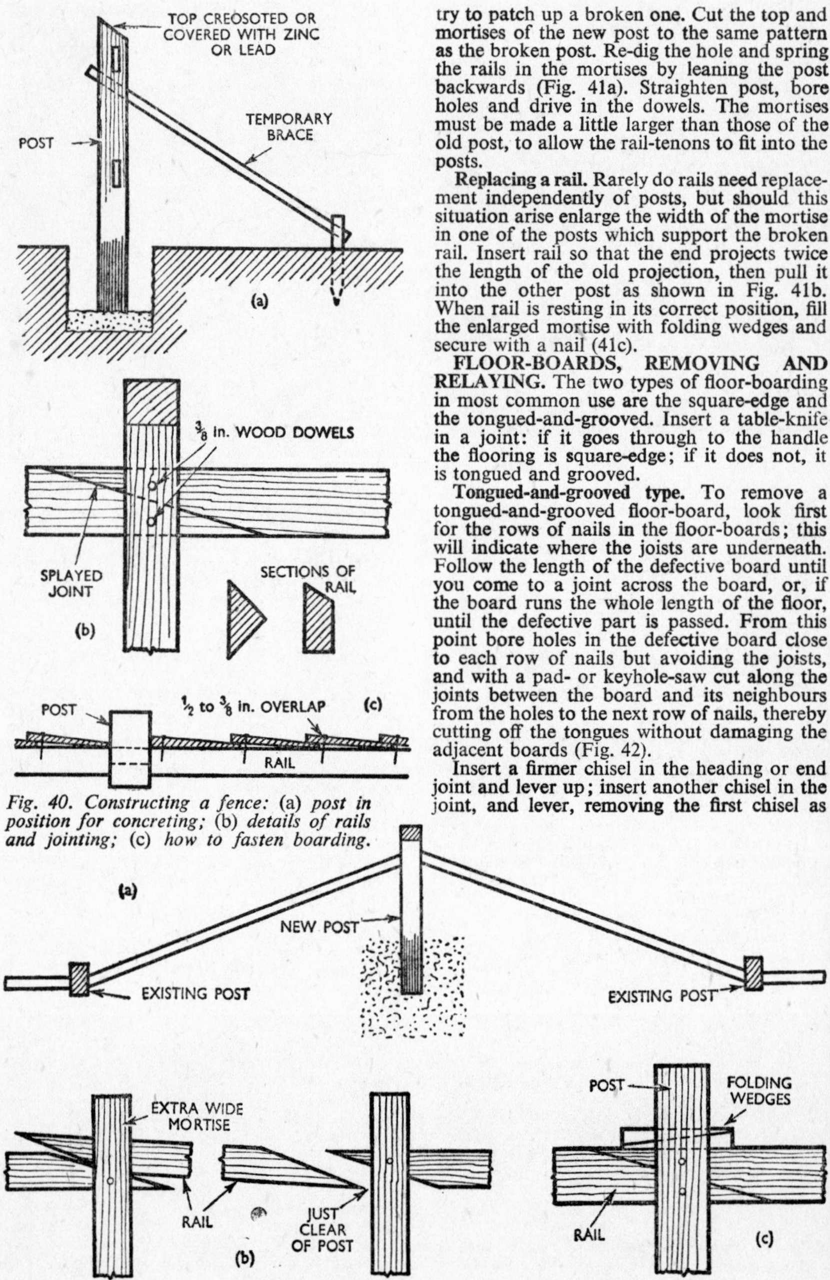

Fig. 40. Constructing a fence: (a) *post in position for concreting;* (b) *details of rails and jointing;* (c) *how to fasten boarding.*

try to patch up a broken one. Cut the top and mortises of the new post to the same pattern as the broken post. Re-dig the hole and spring the rails in the mortises by leaning the post backwards (Fig. 41a). Straighten post, bore holes and drive in the dowels. The mortises must be made a little larger than those of the old post, to allow the rail-tenons to fit into the posts.

Replacing a rail. Rarely do rails need replacement independently of posts, but should this situation arise enlarge the width of the mortise in one of the posts which support the broken rail. Insert rail so that the end projects twice the length of the old projection, then pull it into the other post as shown in Fig. 41b. When rail is resting in its correct position, fill the enlarged mortise with folding wedges and secure with a nail (41c).

FLOOR-BOARDS, REMOVING AND RELAYING. The two types of floor-boarding in most common use are the square-edge and the tongued-and-grooved. Insert a table-knife in a joint: if it goes through to the handle the flooring is square-edge; if it does not, it is tongued and grooved.

Tongued-and-grooved type. To remove a tongued-and-grooved floor-board, look first for the rows of nails in the floor-boards; this will indicate where the joists are underneath. Follow the length of the defective board until you come to a joint across the board, or, if the board runs the whole length of the floor, until the defective part is passed. From this point bore holes in the defective board close to each row of nails but avoiding the joists, and with a pad- or keyhole-saw cut along the joints between the board and its neighbours from the holes to the next row of nails, thereby cutting off the tongues without damaging the adjacent boards (Fig. 42).

Insert a firmer chisel in the heading or end joint and lever up; insert another chisel in the joint, and lever, removing the first chisel as

Fig. 41. Repairing a fence: (a) *replacing a post;* (b) *and* (c) *inserting and fixing a new rail.*

you lever the second. When the board is raised sufficiently to place a bar underneath, remove the chisels and pull up by hand. If only part of a board is defective, cut across to form a new cross-joint as close to the joist as

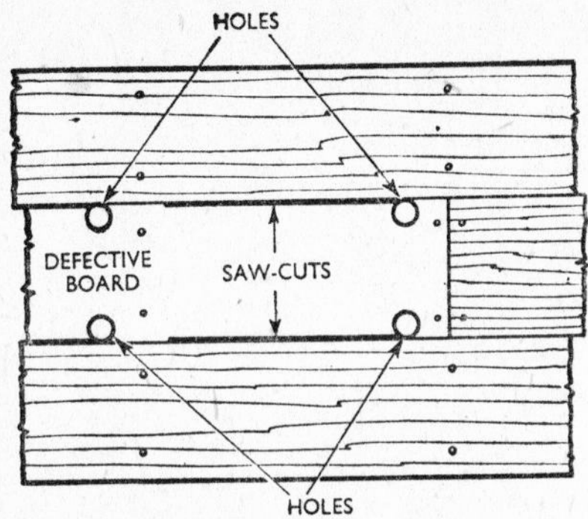

Fig. 42. Removing a part-defective board.

possible (Fig. 43a). Nail a piece of wood 3 in. by 1½ in. on the side of the joist to form a support for the new board. If only one board requires replacement, it must obviously be square-edged, and so must be cut to size and nailed down (b).

Square-edge boarding. The boring of holes and cutting down between the boards is not needed for square-edge boarding. Lever up right away and proceed as described for tongued-and-grooved.

Replacing several boards. Should a large portion of flooring need replacement, once the

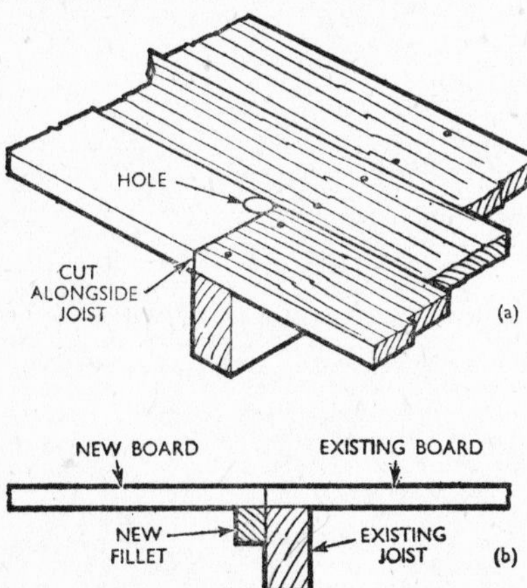

Fig. 43. Replacing a part-defective board.

first board is removed the others can easily be taken up. To overcome the difficulty of tightening the joints when replacing, drive a joiner's dog in the joist, followed by a wedge between the new board and dog (Fig. 44).

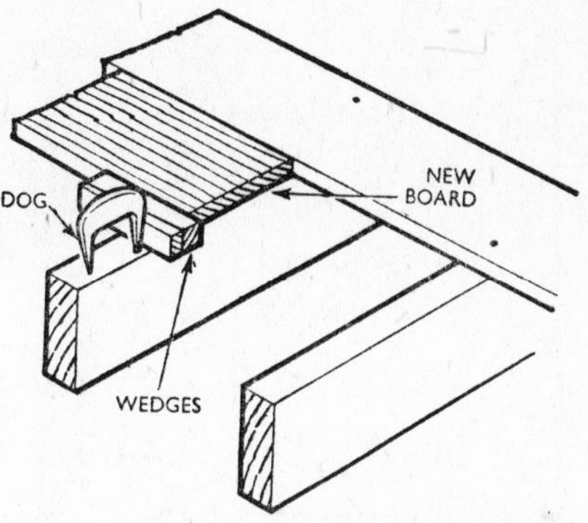

Fig. 44. Tightening joint of a new floor-board.

Secure the board with floor-brads, and remove wedges and dog to the next joist, and so on until the job is completed.

GATE, MAKING AND ERECTING A. The example given is that of a front gate to a house, though the same method of construction would suit other gates. How to build

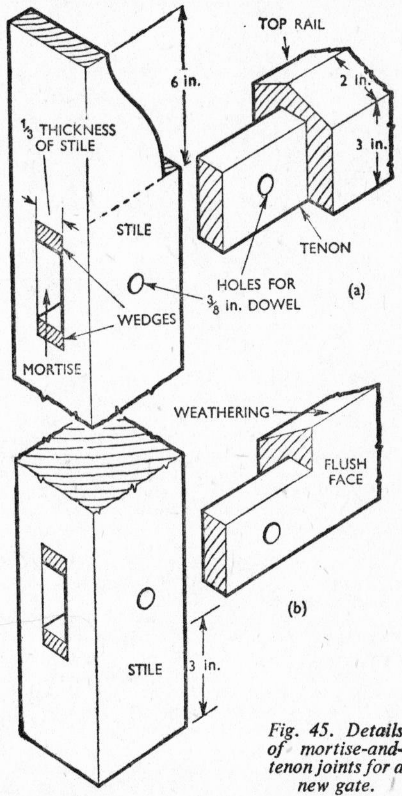

Fig. 45. Details of mortise-and-tenon joints for a new gate.

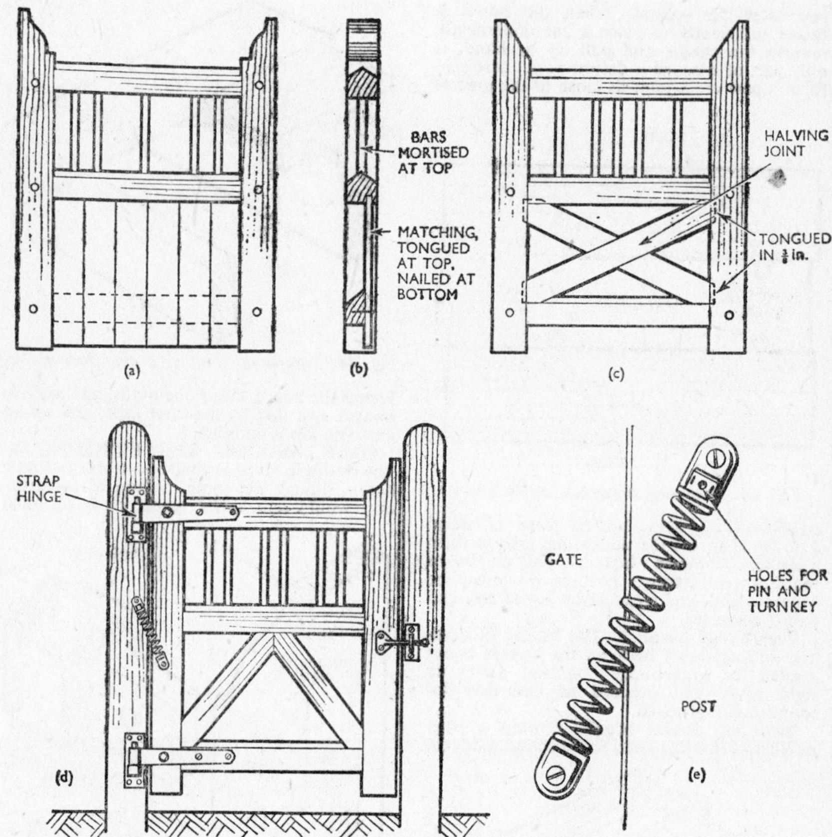

Fig. 46. Making and erecting a gate: (a) and (b) *front and side elevations;* (c) and (d) *alternative treatments for bars, bracing and stiles;* (d) and (e) *show details of hinges, catch and spring.*

brick gateposts is described in the section "Uses for Bricks and Concrete," page 497.

Gate details. The timber can be of varnished oak or painted deal. The mortise-and-tenon joints are wedged and pinned with painted joints instead of glue, as Scotch glues or animal glues do not stand up to outdoor conditions. Waterproof glue is obtainable, and can be used instead of paint. Care must be taken to follow the maker's instructions. Fig. 45 shows the joints between the top rail and stile and the bottom rail and stile. The centre rail joint is similar to the top.

Top rail. Drive in the dowel or pin and cut off flush with the finished surface at both sides, tapering the end of the dowel and dipping it into the paint-pot beforehand. The figure also shows the weathering or sloping top, essential to throw off rainwater (all the rails should be weathered on their top edge). Another point to note is that the top edge of the tenon is cut back square to give the wedge a flat surface on which to fit. The horn can be as long, and cut to any shape, as desired.

Middle rail. As for the top rail.

Bottom rail. This can be as for the top rail or flush, or barefaced. This depends on the construction or design. In this figure one side of the bottom rail is flush with one side of the tenon, called a bareface tenon. Weathering is to one side only.

Fix the bottom rail off ground-level to prevent rotting and cut back top of tenon (as described above) to get a flat wedging surface.

Matching and bracing. Figs 46a and 46b show how the lower half of the gate can be filled in with match-boarding, and a number of bars added to the upper part. As an alternative, and if wood is scarce, bracing can be used (c), in which case the bottom rail will have to be the full thickness (that is, like the top rail).

If the hanging side of the gate is determined beforehand, the shutting or—as it is sometimes called—clapping stile can be 2½ in. or 3 in. wide instead of the 4 in. shown here, thus requiring only one brace or an alternative form shown in (d).

Hinges, latch and spring. The gate can be hung on ordinary butt or tee hinges, but it is advisable to use strap hinges (d). There are various types of latch. If it is decided to fix a spring-catch type, a spring as shown in (e) may not be considered necessary.

To fix a spring to an ordinary latched gate, however, first screw into position. Insert a bradawl in one of the winding holes and turn as with a turnkey, put in spring-pin supplied and place turnkey in next hole, turn, then insert spring-pin as before. If a quick shutting rebound is required, repeat process until sufficient tension is obtained. The spring turns either way. If fixed as shown in (e) the winding will be to leftward.

LOCKS AND LATCHES AND THEIR REPAIR. Rarely do locks and latches fail to work if they are kept oiled. If they do go wrong the trouble is generally with one or more of the springs in the mechanism.

Yale-pattern lock. If the fault lies in the part where the key is inserted, call in a locksmith. It is a job for the expert. Generally, however, it is the back portion (which contains the bolt) that goes wrong. It is the spring which operates this bolt that is likely to be at fault.

Figs. 47a and 47b show the inside of this type of lock, after the screws which hold it to the door have been taken out and the set-screw and the back- or cover-plate removed. First examine the spring. If broken or weak, replace it with a new one. If you raise and remove the loose bar the spring will easily come away, allowing a new one to be inserted. What happens when the spring is working and compressed by a turn of the handle is shown in (b).

Mortise and rim locks. These are similar in principle, but are differently fixed; the mortise is let into the door stile and the rim lock is screwed to the face. Both have two bolts, one of which operates by the turn of the handle, the other by the turn of the key. Both have springs liable to break, so these should be examined at the first sign of trouble.

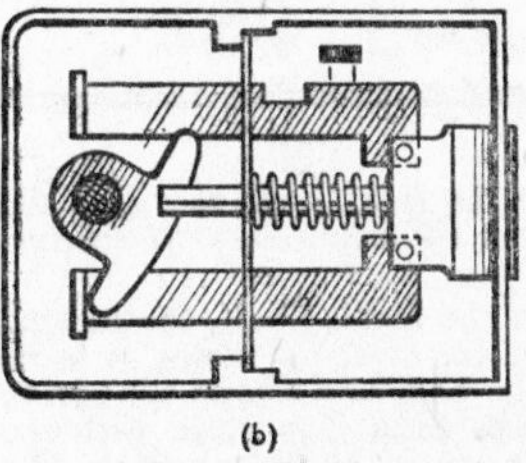

Fig. 47. Back portion of a Yale-pattern lock: (a) *with the bolt closed;* (b) *with the bolt withdrawn.*

To remove the locks one handle should be unscrewed and the shaft removed. The lock should then be unscrewed and can be removed from the door. A screwdriver will be required to lever the mortise lock out. Fig. 48a shows the layout of a mortise lock, together with a sketch of the plate or lever (b) that fits over the rectangular stud ⅛ in. high, above the keyhole. Fig. 49a shows layout of a rim lock, together with sketch of the lever (b) which fits over the lower bolt.

It will be noticed that the locking-bolt and the latch-bolt in these two locks are in reverse positions. But in both cases when the handle is turned (the square in circle, Figs. 48 and 49, is the shaft carrying the handle), the projection on either side levers back the latch-bolt, compressing the springs, and when pressure is released the spring forces the bolt back into position.

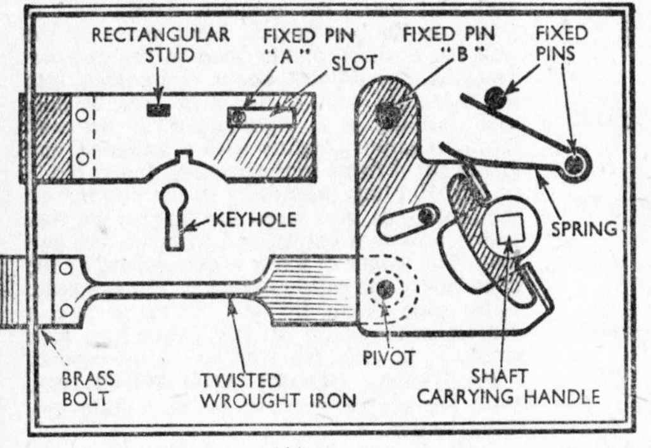

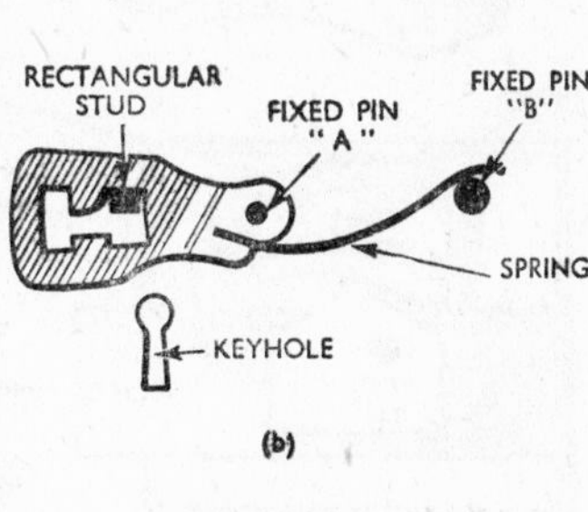

Fig. 48. (a) *Diagram of a mortise lock from which the lever has been removed. The lever is shown at* (b). *When the key is turned the lever is lifted, allowing the bolt to move.*

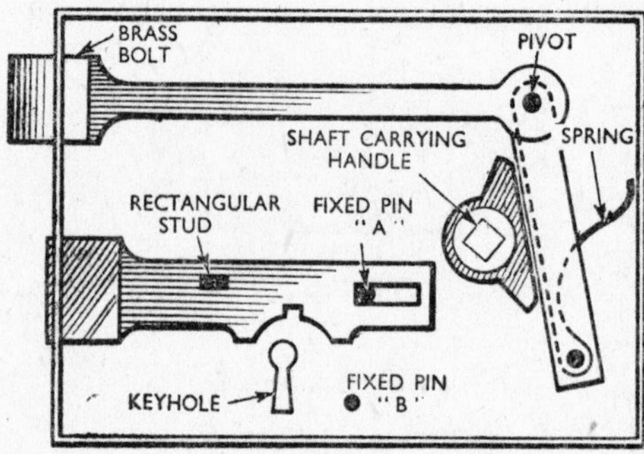

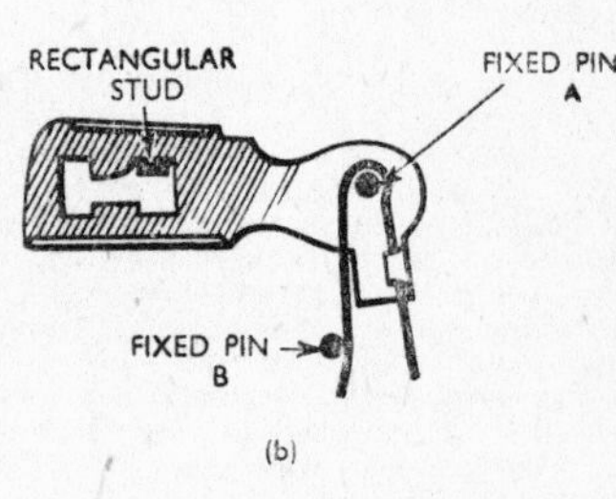

Fig. 49. (a) *The rim lock shown here is similar in principle to the mortise lock shown in Fig. 48, though the arrangement is different. The lever is shown separately at* (b).

In the case of the locking-bolt, the turning of the key raises the lever (or levers, in some locks), moves the bolt, and allows the spring to press the lever back into place with the fixed rectangular pin in the new position. The bolt with the fixed rectangular pin has been drawn along by the key.

Cupboard lock. This reversible lock is suitable for both left- and right-handed cupboards. The springs on the levers are similar to the mortise. The case is about $1\frac{1}{2}$ in. square with a plate on one side about $1\frac{1}{2}$ in. by 3 in. overall. Fig. 50 illustrates (a) the bolt, (b) one of the levers, (c) the whole lock assembled.

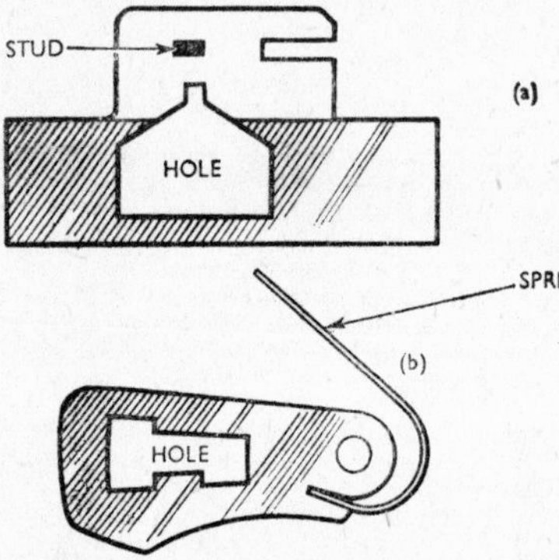

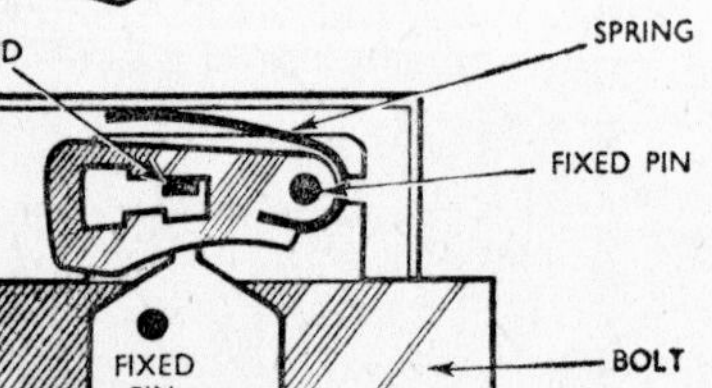

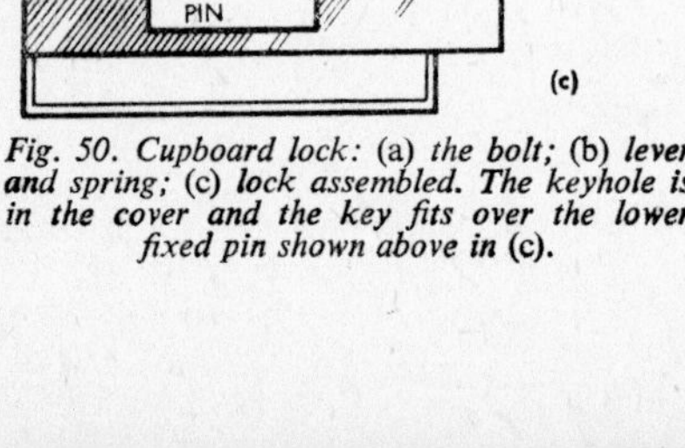

Fig. 50. Cupboard lock: (a) *the bolt;* (b) *lever and spring;* (c) *lock assembled. The keyhole is in the cover and the key fits over the lower fixed pin shown above in* (c).

PLATE-RACK, MAKING A. The example given is for plates and saucers only. A factor in determining the size of the rack is the position of the sink and draining-board. The rack is screwed to the wall above these with wall-plugs and screws.

Construction. Make two gallows-brackets of wood, approximately $1\frac{3}{4}$ in. wide by $\frac{7}{8}$ in. thick, as shown in Fig. 36. The vertical piece should be 12 in. to 14 in. long, the horizontal 12 in. Metal brackets can be bought, but wood ones are preferable for this job.

Make two rails, the length depending on the number of spaces required. Fig. 51 shows the section of the rails with suggested measurements and the fitting of the dowels, in their respective lengths. The rear rail can be parallel with the wall, if desired. Screw the rack to the gallows-brackets, bearing in mind that the plates must not touch the wall. Fig. 51 gives suitable measurements.

Fixing. First plug the wall-holes to receive the rack. To do this, place the rack against the wall and mark the position lightly with a pencil on the plaster-face. Next, mark on the wall the position of the holes in the gallows-brackets. Drive holes, about $1\frac{1}{2}$ in. deep, into the markings with a No. 8 or No. 10 plug tool, holding it at right-angles to the wall face and tapping lightly with a hammer, and giving slight turns in the process. Insert No. 8 or No. 10 plugs (according to the number on the tool used), and screw the rack to the wall with screws that correspond with the tool and plug. The length of screw is determined by the thickness of the gallows-bracket. For example: $1\frac{1}{8}$ in. plus depth in wall, $1\frac{1}{2}$ in., = $2\frac{5}{8}$ in.; nearest stock length is $2\frac{1}{2}$ in.; therefore, four screws $2\frac{1}{2}$ in. long, No. 8 or No. 10, are needed.

RATTLING DOORS AND WINDOWS. Here are simple remedies to stop these irritating noises.

Door. It is the lock or latch that causes the trouble. Measure the strip of space between the door and the frame (that is, the amount of movement or rattle); take off the metal,

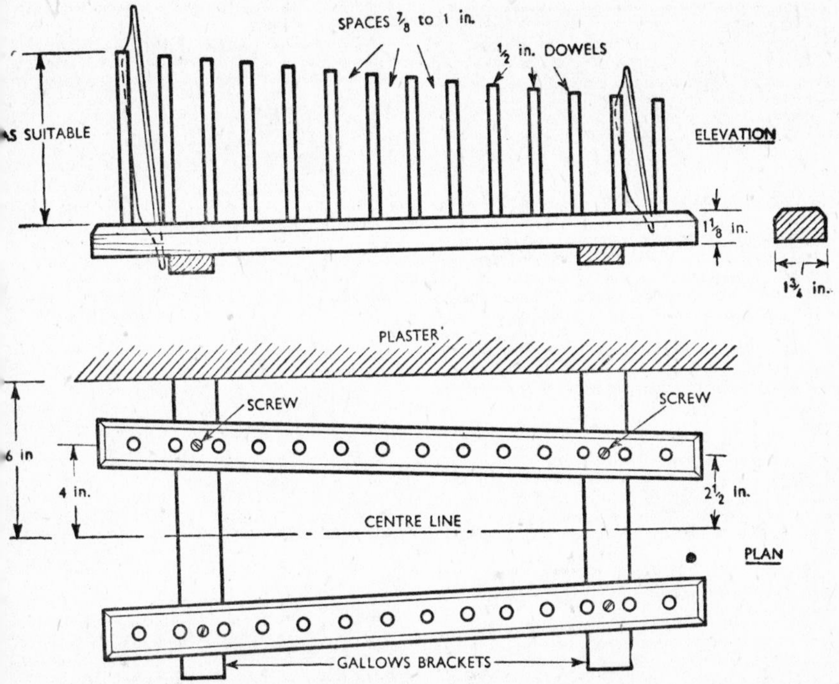

Fig. 51. Side elevation and plan for a plate-rack, and section through one of the rails.

or "striking," plate of the lock from the door-frame. In the recess, cut away the wood on the door-stop edge equivalent to the measurement of the space between door and frame. Plug screw-holes with match-sticks or wood splinters, replace striking-plate and rescrew to door-frame in its new position (Fig. 52).

Casement windows. The two most common types of casement fastener are shown in Fig. 53. To prevent rattle adjust the fastener-plate at (a) by removing the screws, plugging the screw-holes and rescrewing to frame further away from the sash. Clean out the wood to make the mortise the same size as the slot in the metal. To adjust (b) simply slacken the two screws and pack the plate a little farther away from the frame with thin cardboard. Rattling may also be prevented by the adjustment of one of the pins, as shown in Fig. 54

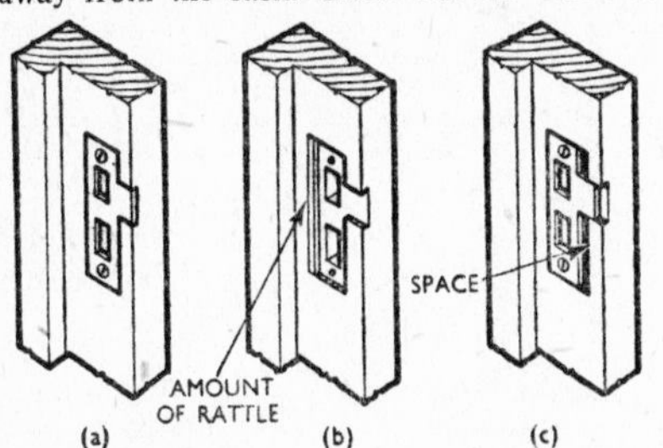

Fig. 52. Rattling door: (a) *before removal of striking plate;* (b) *plate removed and recess enlarged by amount of rattle;* (c) *plate replaced.*

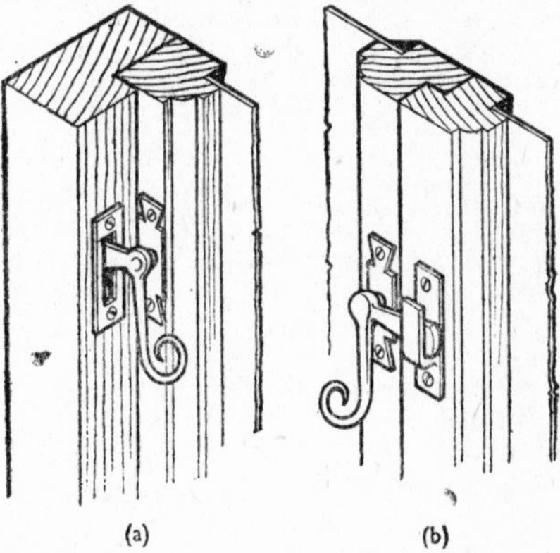

Fig. 53. Rattling casement windows: in (a), *move the slotted plate away from the glass; in* (b), *place cardboard under the right-hand plate.*

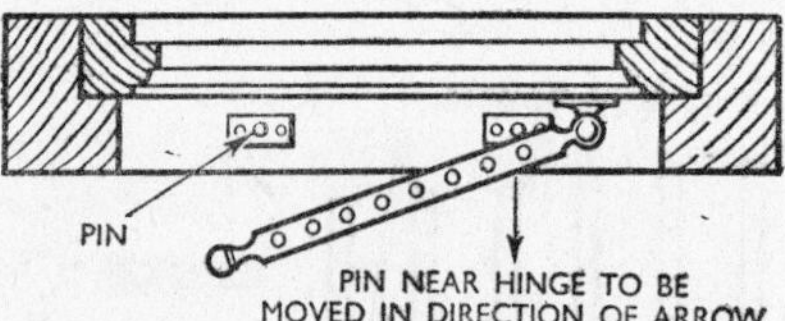

Fig. 54. Method of tightening a casement stay.

Window with double-hanging sashes. For a closed window fix a sash-screw through the meeting rails, by screwing the plate to the outer sash and boring a hole through the inside sash to receive this screw (Fig. 55), or by moving one of the plates of the catch nearer to the other. A tapering wedge, preferably of hardwood, inserted between stile and sash, will hold fast an open window.

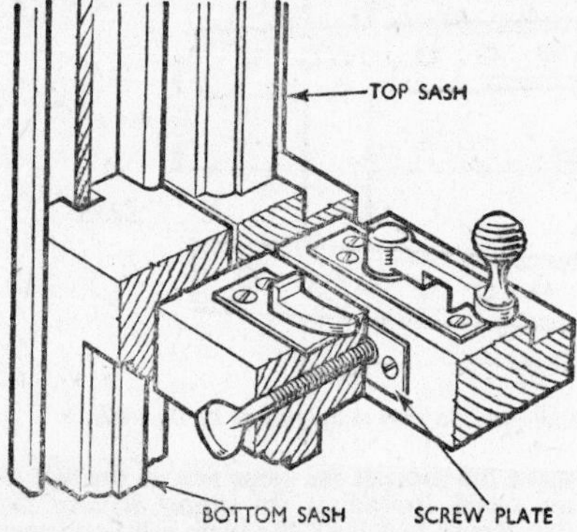

Fig. 55. How to stop a sash window rattling.

SASH-CORDS, REPLACEMENT OF. If only one cord is broken it is nevertheless advisable to renew all four.

To remove sashes from frame. With a chisel or screwdriver remove the two side beads and the top bead of the window frame (Fig. 56), drawing out the nails backwards (that is, drawing the head through the wood) in order to preserve the painted surface. It is now possible to pull out the bottom sash. If both cords are broken it may be lifted down on to the floor, but if worn cords are still attached they must be cut, at the same time holding the cord above the cut and allowing the weight to come down slowly. Remove the parting bead, which is not nailed but usually clotted with dry paint, and take out the top sash.

To remove weights from boxings. To do this, look for a horizontal line about 3 in. above the sill in the painted surface of the stiles. Approximately 14 in. above this mark is another line, and just below it is a screw. Remove this screw, insert a knife or chisel in the top line and lever out the pocket-piece (Fig. 57). Take out the weight from the recess behind. Next to this weight is a piece of wood which seems to hang loose, called a wagtail (Fig. 56). Pull this to one side and withdraw the second weight.

Take out the weights from the other side of the window and remove old cords, making a note of how they are fixed to the sashes, as the new cords will have to be fixed in the same way.

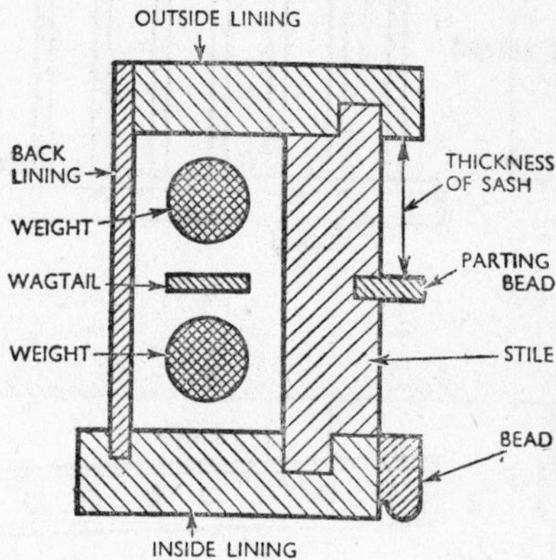

Fig. 56. Section through the boxing of a sash window, with names of component parts.

Fixing new cords. Fasten a piece of twine to one end of the new sash-cord (which should be of the same type as that removed), fix a piece of lead or fishing-line shot to the twine, and thread over the wheels or axle pulleys in the order given in Fig. 58. When the cord

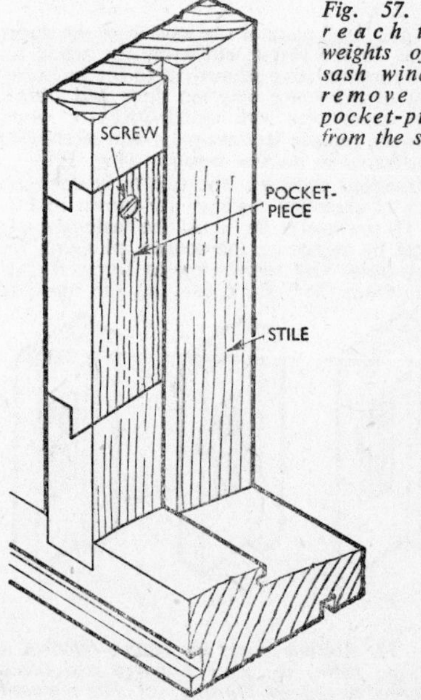

Fig. 57. To reach the weights of a sash window remove the pocket-piece from the stile.

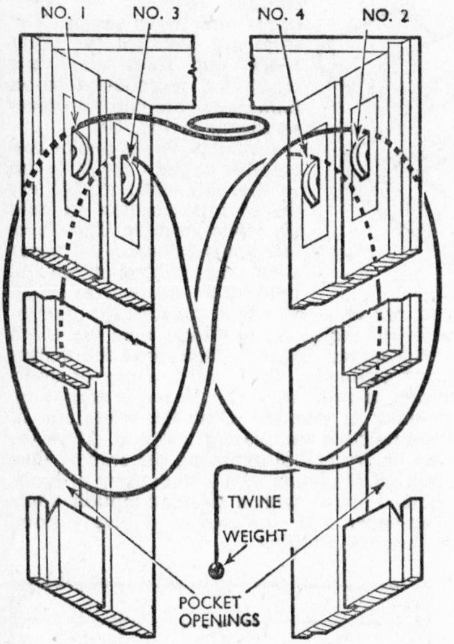

Fig. 58. Sash-cord should be attached to twine and threaded through in the above order.

has been threaded through No. 4 cut off lead and twine, and fasten end of sash-cord to the weight that goes under No. 4. Judge the length of cord required by letting the weight rest on the bottom of the recess; draw cord tight without lifting weight; hold sash against the top of the frame; mark the cord and secure it to the sash by nailing. Do not cut the cord until it has been fixed. This completes cord No. 4, and the new end is now fastened to weight No. 3, and the same procedure adopted. When this is completed the top sash can be left in its proper position.

Begin on the bottom sash by fastening end of cord No. 3 to weight No. 2. This weight will rest on the bottom of the recess, and the length of cord is judged by holding the sash as high as possible in the frame. Mark cord

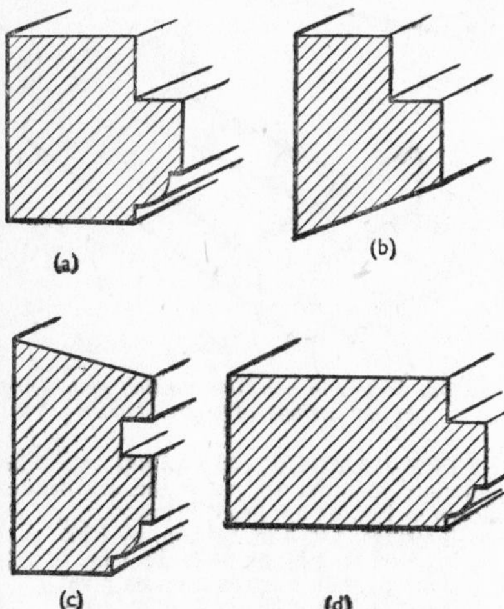

Fig. 59. Sections through the parts of a sliding sash: (a) *stiles and top rail;* (b) *top meeting rail;* (c) *bottom meeting rail;* (d) *bottom rail.*

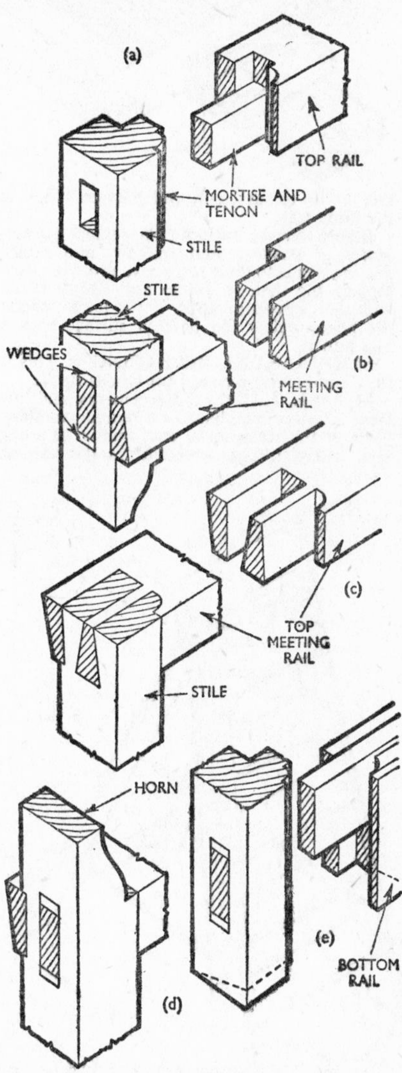

Fig. 60. Joints for sliding sashes: (a) *and* (b) *for the upper sash;* (c), (d) *and* (e) *for the lower sash;* (d) *is an alternative to* (c).

Fig. 61. Cramping a sash while the glue is setting.

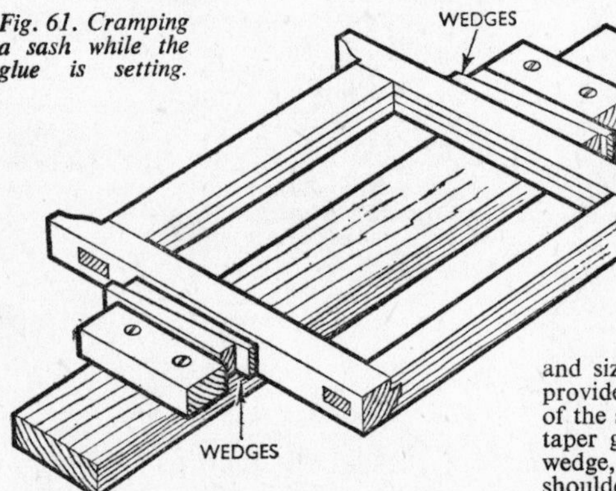

and secure to sash, cut, and start on No. 1 in the same way.

Before refixing bottom sash, replace pocket-pieces in position and rescrew, and return parting beads to their respective grooves. Now replace the sash in frame and secure beads with new screws or nails. If the latter, knock the heads below the painted surface with a nail-punch.

SLIDING SASH, REPLACING A. This is for a double-hung boxed (or cased) frame.

Materials. Take the measurements, and buy from a timber merchant or a builder moulded parts of the stiles, rails, etc., known as stock sash material. Fig. 59 identifies the various sections required for both upper and lower sashes. The stiles are identical for both. Mark out stiles and rails ready for mortise-and-tenon joints, and prepare the joints as shown in Fig. 60.

Assembly. Make one or two cramps, to hold the stiles on to the rails while wedges are driven into position to hold the joints together. The dove-tail joints between the lower stiles and top meeting rail will hold automatically. Any length and size of wood will do to start the cramps, provided the length is greater than the width of the sashes (Fig. 61). Make sure the wedges taper gradually, like a window-peg or door-wedge, and that they grip the tenon as near the shoulder as possible. Glue the joints and fit them together and place in a cramp. Allow the glue to dry before removing the cramp; then clean off the joints with a smoothing or block plane. Finally, with a circular motion apply glass-paper over the joints, to give a good surface for painting.

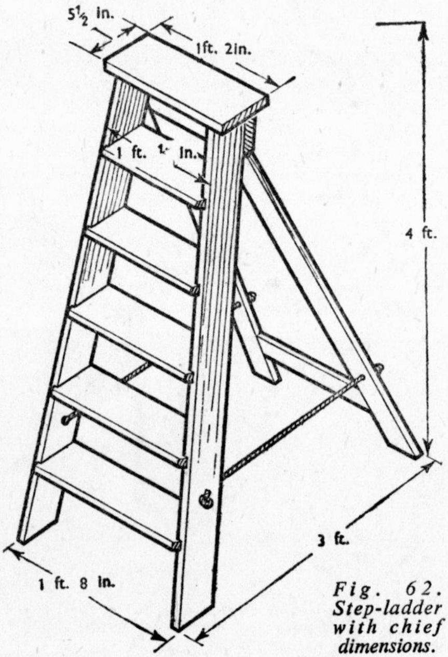

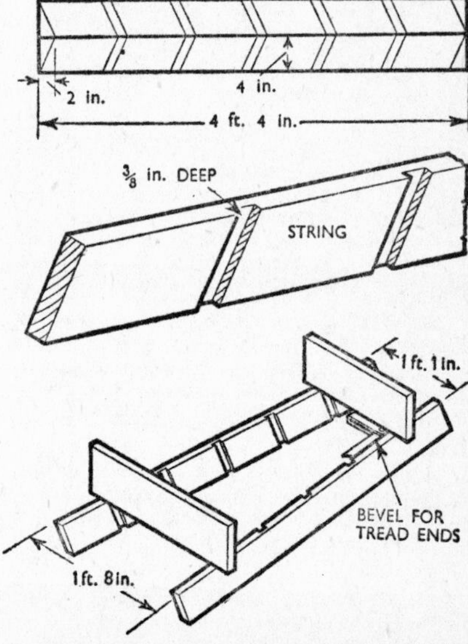

Fig. 63. Stages in marking, cutting and laying out the strings of a step-ladder.

Fig. 62. Step-ladder with chief dimensions.

STEP-LADDER, MAKING A. The materials required to make the step-ladder shown in Fig. 62 are listed below:

2 strings, 4 ft. 4 in. by 4 in. by 1 in.
1 top, 1 ft. 2 in. by 5½ in. by 1 in.
2 treads, 1 ft. 6 in. by 5 in. by ¾ in.
2 treads, 1 ft. 4 in. by 5 in. by ¾ in.
1 tread, 1 ft. 8 in. by 5 in. by ¾ in.
1 back rail, 1 ft. 3 in. by 4 in. by 1 in.
2 stiles, 3 ft. 8 in. by 2½ in by 1 in.

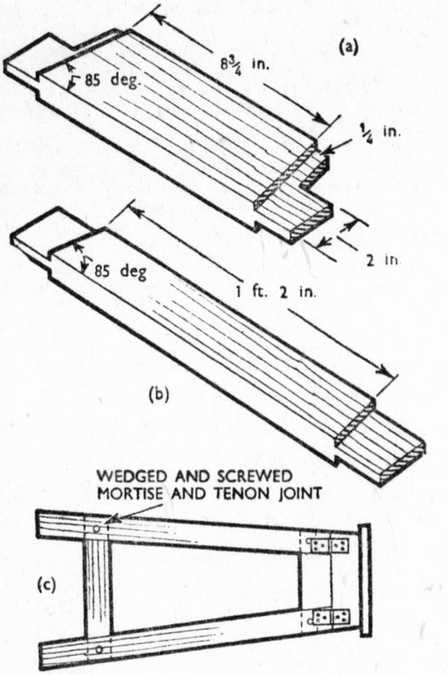

Fig. 64. (a) *and* (b) *top and bottom rails, and* (c) *general assembly of back of step-ladder.*

1 top rail, 1 ft. 3 in. by 6 in. by 1 in.
1 bottom rail, 1 ft. 8 in. by 4 in. by 1 in.
1 pair of 2-in. or 2½-in. back flaps and ¾-in. screws, 2¼-in. oval nails, and sash-cord.

Method of construction. Make the strings first. Mark them out by putting the two together as in Fig. 63; if the first line is marked 2 in. out of square, the rest can be marked with a slide bevel. The depth of the housings for the treads is ⅜ in. and this should be gauged on the edges of the strings. The housings are then made by cutting down the lines with a saw and removing the waste with a chisel.

The two strings are then placed on the floor and spaced to 13 in. at the top and 20 in. at the bottom. The exact length of the top and bottom treads may then be obtained and also the bevel for the ends of the treads.

These two treads may then be cut and fitted, securing them with 2¼-in. nails through the strings. The remaining treads are then marked to length and nailed in the same way.

The top is cut to length, its edges slightly rounded and fixed by nails down into the ends of the strings.

The back rail requires its upper edge bevelling to fit under the top. After this it can be nailed to the strings.

Place the two stiles on the back of the strings and while in this position lay the top and bottom rails (Fig. 64a and b) across them in the correct position. The shoulder-lines may then be marked on the rails and the width of the rails and the angle they make with the stiles are also easily marked. The back frame (Fig. 64c) may now be made. The top rail is jointed with a haunched mortise and tenon. Secure these joints with wedges and a dowel or screw through the framing and tenon.

Fix the back frame by screwing on the hinges. Two lengths of sash-cord, fixed as shown in Fig. 62, will complete the job.

SWING, MAKING AND ERECTING. The children's swing shown in Fig. 66 is a good strong one, made of 4-in.-by-3-in. stock-size timber. The sketch also gives a general idea of materials required and the measurements. It is worth while to plane smooth the surfaces of the timber, and, as the swing is for the garden, it is recommended that the wood

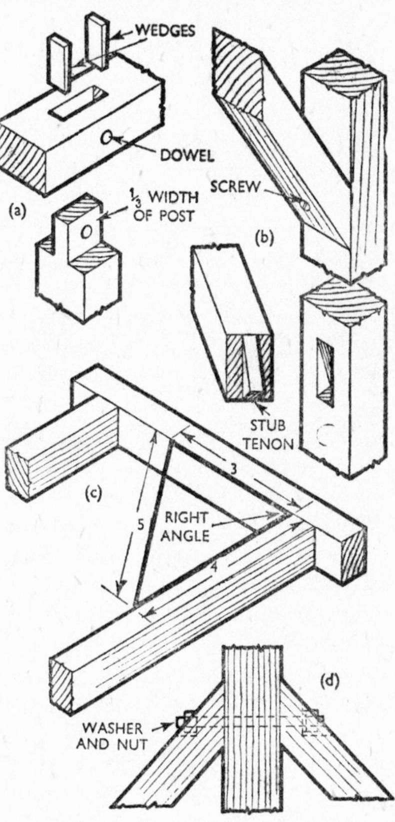

Fig. 65. Details of joints, etc., used in making a garden swing. (a) *Joint between top bar and posts.* (b) *Joint between posts and angle-braces.* (c) *Method of getting the bar and posts at right-angles before cutting the braces. A triangle with the sides in proportion 3:4:5 will contain a right-angle between the shorter sides.* (d) *Bottom bracing of posts, using a ½-in. bolt.*

be purchased already pressure-creosoted. Alternatively, creosote the wood with three or four coats before erecting. The ground-level is the most vulnerable spot.

Construction. *Top part.* Fig. 65a gives details of the joint between head and post. Fig. 65b shows how the angle-braces in the top corners can be screwed or recessed in the head and posts. Fig. 65c shows a method of squaring the head and posts when cutting in the angle-braces.

Bottom part. The posts are tenoned into the sills in the same way as the top. To ensure strong braces at the bottom, bolt parts together with ½-in. diameter bolts, approximately 12 in. long (Fig. 65d). Alternatively, the lower portion of the braces can be stub-tenoned (as in Fig. 65b). One of these two methods should be used: do not just cut off and secure with nails.

The frame can now be assembled and well creosoted. Dig holes 3 ft. deep, place frame in position, and fill by well ramming down the soil as it is replaced in small batches, thoroughly watering each layer to consolidate the disturbed soil as much as possible.

Ropes and seat. Ropes are preferable to chains; they may not last as long, but are more homely and easier to renew. Moreover, chains need special fittings. Fig. 67 shows a No. 2 galvanized-iron eyelet, lashed with fine twine to a good-quality rope of ⅝-in. diameter, and a sketch of a No. 2 black hanger-bolt into which the eyelet fits.

The seat shown is simple and easy to make, in one or several pieces. The edges on all sides should be rounded off and the surfaces plane-smoothed.

For a very small child a ready-made chair-shaped seat can be purchased at most toyshops. Suitable ropes will normally be supplied with the seat.

If desired a wood or tin capping can be fitted along the top of the cross-bar. It will protect the bolts and tenon-ends from the weather, and also improve the appearance of the swing.

UPHOLSTERY, REPAIRS TO. In any repairs to an easy chair or settee a careful note should be made of how the original work was done before any dismantling is undertaken. This is a dusty job and the floor should be covered with a dust-sheet before work is begun.

To renew the upholstery, turn the chair upside down and with a stripping chisel extract the tacks under the seat and remove the canvas cover. Remove the gimp pins (the small nails which hold the covering of the chair to the wooden frame). If the covering is in good condition it can be washed and replaced later, but if a new covering is to be

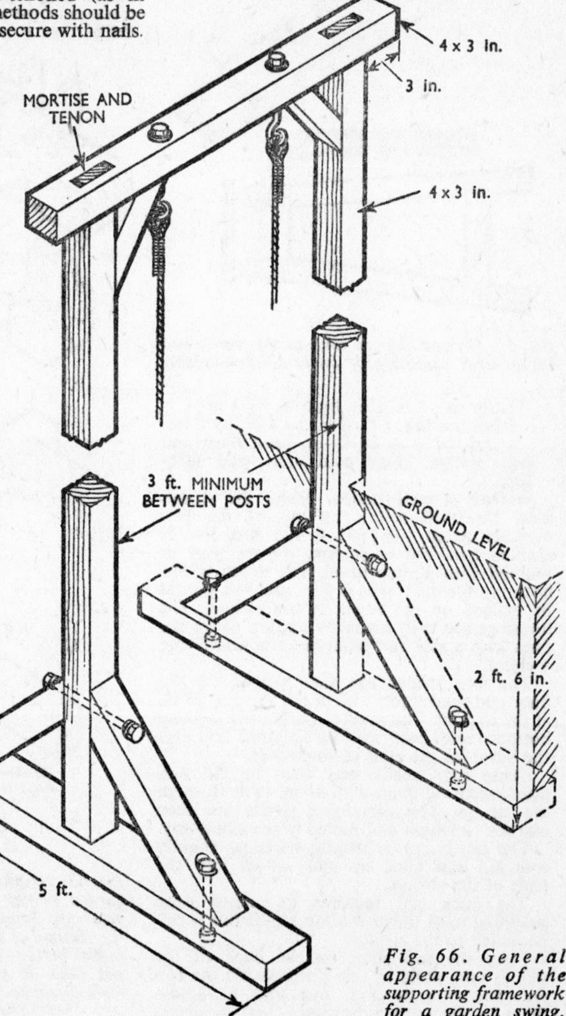

Fig. 66. General appearance of the supporting framework for a garden swing.

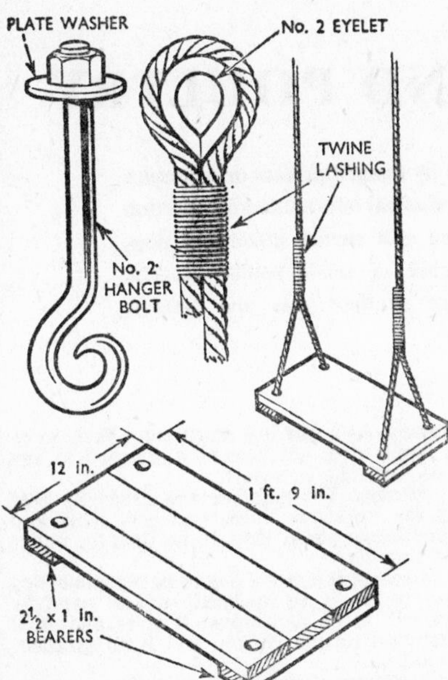

Fig. 67. Details of the seat, ropes and hanger bolts for a garden swing. The rope should be $\frac{5}{8}$ in. diameter and firmly lashed with fine twine. The edges of the seat should be rounded off.

made, use the old one as a pattern and note which way the thread of the material runs.

If there is wadding, hessian, hair, or other stuffing in the seat, cut the stitching in several places and take out the stuffing. Hair can be washed in warm, soapy water (this is most easily done if the hair is put in an old pillow-case or bag). If the stuffing is flock or fibre, dust can be removed by beating.

Make a sketch of the stitching and webbing holding the springs of the seat and remove them. Old, weak, or torn webbing is usually the cause of sagging seats. The best webbing available should be bought for replacements. This should be cut into suitable lengths, slightly longer than the dimension of the chair. Using webbing tacks, nail one end of the strips of webbing to the framing, turn over the surplus and nail again (Fig. 68).

The lower end of each spring rests on a crossing in the webbing and the upper end is bedded in the canvas underneath the seat padding. The larger springs are placed in the centre, the smaller ones round the edge. The springs should be tied up with string to compress them and then stitched in position on the canvas with fine string or upholsterer's twine, using an upholsterer's needle (this is about 9 in. long, curved, and pointed at both ends).

The webbing, which has been attached at one end, must now be drawn taut and nailed at the other end as previously described. To stretch the webbing, a web-stretcher, or a piece of wood and a broom handle, can be used (Fig. 68). The webbing should be interlaced as in the original arrangement. The string compressing the springs can now be cut and the expanded springs guided to the crossings in the webbing to which they should be stitched.

Replace any other stuffing or padding which has been removed and finally the outer coverings and the canvas under the seat.

WOODWORM AND ITS TREATMENT. Furniture can be ruined by this pest. There are several species of beetle which lay their eggs in timber. These eggs develop into larvae or grubs which burrow into the wood, where they live and feed. This tunnelling undermines the structure of the wood, which, if not treated in time, collapses. The three species most common in Great Britain are: death-watch, powder-beetle, and the furniture-beetle. The grubs of the last-named are called woodworms.

The blackish-brown furniture-beetle varies in length from $\frac{1}{10}$ in. to $\frac{1}{8}$ in. It lays its eggs in cracks or bad joints. After hatching, the grub tunnels along the grain at first, and then in all directions. Having done its share of damage, it changes into a chrysalis, and later into a beetle which bores its way out and leaves a hole. The presence of the beetles can be detected by the minute entrances to the tunnels and by the very fine dust they produce. This beetle will attack both hard and soft woods, but prefers the sapwood, especially of birch.

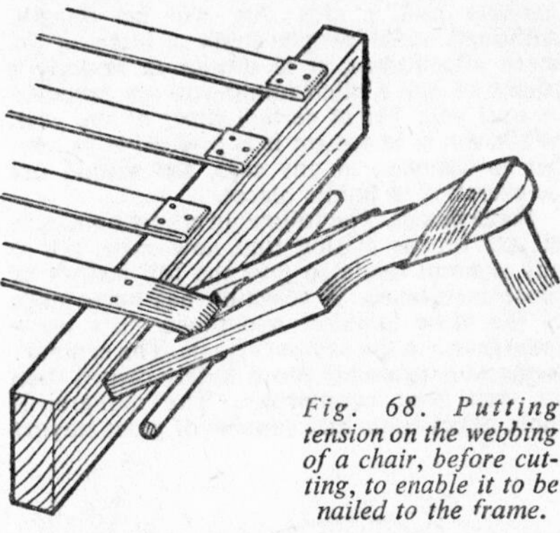

Fig. 68. Putting tension on the webbing of a chair, before cutting, to enable it to be nailed to the frame.

Treatment. Mix a quantity of turpentine and paraffin, in equal parts. Use an oil-can with a forceful thrust, so that when the nozzle is placed against or in each tunnel-mouth the liquid will be strongly injected well into the timber. Cracks and crevices should be similarly treated.

It is important to inject *every* hole, so pencil- or chalk-mark each one after injecting. Repeat the process every two weeks, until no more fresh holes appear.

Proprietary insecticides can also be obtained. Those containing dichlorbenzine are among the more effective.

For garden furniture, application of creosote is a suitable treatment.

DOGS, CATS AND POULTRY

Much suffering can be caused to pets by thoughtlessness or ignorance on the part of owners. The following practical information on selection and treatment, feeding and breeding will enable owners of dogs and cats, and the increasing number of small poultry-keepers, to see to the comfort and welfare of their pets and poultry.

1. DOGS

CHOOSING A DOG. Generally only small dogs should be kept in built-up areas, the larger dogs being limited to people who live in the country. Of the most companionable, the Cairn, West Highland and small mongrels are probably in the forefront. Of the smaller dogs still, the Pekinese and the Yorkshire are perhaps the most noted. All types of terrier need careful handling; whilst not necessarily fighters, they are apt to become so.

In choosing a dog, first decide what breed is required. Application should then be made to reputable kennels, and it is wise to have a veterinary certificate as to the health of the puppy before purchase. If this is done it is unlikely that a sick dog will be bought. Although some people think a bitch is the more affectionate, it is unwise in making a choice to buy a bitch unless you are prepared to part with her at certain times of the year. While she is in season it is preferable to send her to kennels; in any case, she should not be exercised in public places.

Some breeds. The following are by no means all the breeds of dog that now exist, nor is any attempt made to give the full history of those mentioned. A selection has been made of the more popular, and those more likely to be found in the ordinary home. The ordinary mongrel is probably more widely owned than its well bred counterpart. The mongrel is more affectionate and capable of great staying powers. As a rule it is much more likely to be a family dog, not becoming attached to any one particular person.

Bedlington.

Airedale. The Airedale was originally bred in the Yorkshire dales, and first came into prominence about 1850. It was used for water-rat hunting.

Alsatian. It is not a dog to be recommended for town. It is inclined, unless carefully trained, to be dangerous; it gives undivided attention to one person, and is an excellent guard.

Bedlington. Originally bred in Northumberland, the Bedlington is, as a rule, a docile dog and varies in size. The colour ranges from blue to liver, although the blue is most generally known. It is an excellent house-dog and a great companion.

Bull-terrier.

Bulldog. The bulldog, although having every appearance of strength, is prone to chest complaints. It has great courage and is most affectionate and faithful; should it turn nasty, it can be a very dangerous customer.

Bull-terrier. This dog is more popular with owners than the bulldog. It was originally bred as a fighter, and retains many of its earlier characteristics. It varies in colour from white to a dark brindle.

Cairn. The Cairn is a hardy dog adaptable to most climates. Originally bred in Scotland, probably about 1840. They vary in colour from fawn to grey; some have dark muzzles.

Chow. The Chow originally came from China, and was probably crossed with a

Chow.

Tibetan mastiff. As a rule it is somewhat detached, and can turn very nasty, as it is of uncertain temperament.

Dachshund. This dog came from Germany, where they were first bred in the early eighteenth century. It was originally a smooth-haired dog of black or brown coat, but subsequently a long-haired variety was evolved. This breed is long in the body, short in the legs and very tireless. It is very intelligent.

Dalmatian. The Dalmatian was originally a carriage dog. Although it is supposed to come originally from Dalmatia, there is no evidence of this fact. It is distinctive in the fact that it is prominently spotted, and is a most affectionate dog.

Fox Terrier. Not to be confused with its brother, the wire-haired terrier. The fox terrier is smooth and distinctly marked, the ground being white with a black, or sometimes a brown, patch. A very intelligent animal, making a good companion, but needs careful training.

Dachshunds: long- and short-haired varieties.

Dalmatian.

Labrador. The Labrador is a relative of the spaniel, but is a much larger dog, and has little of the present spaniel characteristics beyond its ability to retrieve. It is a very intelligent and faithful dog.

Pekinese. Originally bred in China, they first became known in England after about 1860, although they are known to have existed for at least two thousand years before that. There are two main breeds, the lion and the sleeve, the latter being very much the smaller. They are game dogs and possess extreme intelligence. They usually attach themselves only to one person.

Poodle. Originally bred in France, and usually found in three distinct colours, black,

Clipped and unclipped poodles.

brown and white. The peculiar clipping is merely human fancy, and the poodle looks better with its coat in a natural state. It is a most intelligent dog.

Scottish Terrier. The "Scottie" is probably one of the gamest of all the smaller dogs. Aggressive perhaps, but always a gentleman. In its early days it was a terrier bred in Scotland, and there appear to have been various types. In 1881, however, the Aberdeen arrived,

Aberdeen terrier.

and that may be deemed to have been the beginning of the modern Scottie.

Sealyham. Usually all white and of rather heavy build on short legs. Originally bred in Pembrokeshire.

Spaniel. The spaniel is one of the oldest of English breeds, first mentioned somewhere about 1340. The better known are the cocker and the golden, but there are various other spaniel types. More of a sporting dog, they need considerable exercise.

West Highland. From Scotland, white in colour, and an alert and jolly dog.

Wire-haired Terrier. It is marked similarly to the fox terrier, and has much the same characteristics.

COMPANIONSHIP. If you wish your dog to become really companionable, you should not deprive it at any time of human contacts. A dog's intelligence will rapidly develop if it is talked to in an ordinary voice, and generally treated intelligently. Shouting at a dog rarely does any good, and only makes it more nervous and puzzled. Unless it is absolutely impossible, a dog should live in the house, and should not be left alone for long periods. If for even a short time you have to leave it, see there is some food down so that it does not feel neglected.

TRAINING. All dogs learn quickly and it is not necessary to use a whip; to do so will only ruin the spirit, and more dogs become vicious through this than in any other way. It is, more often that not, the human who is to blame for a vicious animal. Single words of command are best; for instance, on reaching a crossing, use the word "Stop," or "Wait," and when the road is clear say "Over." A puppy will soon learn to be clean in the house

Wire-haired and fox terriers.

if it is shown the mess it has made, strongly spoken to and put outside immediately. Particular care should be taken to take the dog out immediately it asks, otherwise it will not realize that it was wrong and will be puzzled by subsequent punishment.

All puppies are by nature destructive. A puppy should be given, as soon as purchased,

A dog should be trained to obey simple words of command. Before crossing a road it should be made to sit on the kerb on the order "Stop," and not move until it is given the order "Over."

Taking a slipper from a dog and offering it a ball. A dog should be taught as soon as possible to play only with its own property.

an old shoe, a ball and a rubber bone, or any one of these articles. If the puppy takes the owner's shoes or other clothing, it should be admonished immediately, the article taken away and its own particular toy given in exchange. In this way it will assimilate the fact that it is allowed to play only with something that belongs to it.

Probably the most difficult part of a dog's training is to prevent its pulling when on a lead. It is advisable to keep a newspaper, rolled, and threaten or tap its nose each time it pulls. Many people do not wait for their dogs to perform their functions, or to stop for a while at a quite ordinary smell. Once a puppy thinks this will happen it will pull to be ahead in time to do what it wishes.

HARNESS. Every dog, according to the 1906 Dogs Act, must wear a collar or a harness, upon which must be clearly inscribed the name and address of the owner. It is advisable to have both, and when taking the dog out put on the harness and fix the lead to this until open spaces are reached, when it can be allowed to run free. With a collar a dog

It is better to attach a lead to a harness than to a collar. Pulling on the lead is then likely to cause less harm.

takes its full weight on the windpipe, whereas it takes the weight of its pull on its chest when wearing a harness.

EXERCISE. All dogs should be taken for at least one good walk a day. A small dog should be taken for at least two miles, and farther as he becomes bigger. In addition, dogs should be taken out first thing in the morning and last thing at night. They should not be allowed to stray on public highways alone; more accidents are caused this way than by any other. A good way of additional exercise is to have a ball which can be thrown in either a garden or field or even in the house, the dog being taught to retrieve.

CATS. In most cases dogs are not antagonistic to cats, and when it is noticed that they chase these animals the reason is usually traced to the fact that the owner finds it amusing to urge on the dog, using the word "cats." This is not only cruel, but quite unnecessary.

CLEANLINESS. For obvious reasons cleanliness is important, but quite apart from these, dirt will cause the dog irritation and in time will set up various skin diseases. It is therefore essential that a long-haired dog should be brushed and combed each day, and a short-haired dog brushed at least twice a week.

It is not absolutely necessary to bath a dog, but if this course is practised a shampoo powder should be used at least once a week. This should be rubbed well into the coat, allowed to remain for fifteen to twenty minutes and then brushed out. As a variation, insect powder can be used one week in the four.

If the dog is bathed, choose a warm day when possible. It should be dried thoroughly, and, if there is any keenness in the wind, should not be let out for at least two hours; if it is a normal warm day, it should be kept in until its coat is completely dry. It is unwise to use carbolic or other similar rough soaps, as these are too strong for the skin.

Particular care should be taken not to get the soap into the eyes, nor water into the ears, and it is better not to wash the head at all. Behind the ears and the base of the tail, and underneath the legs, must be thoroughly cleansed, as this is where insects may congregate.

SLEEPING ACCOMMODATION. Dogs are very susceptible to cold, and their sleeping quarters should be raised from the floor at least half a foot, or preferably on an old chair; there should be some form of cover which must be changed frequently. If it is impossible

A dog's sleeping basket or box should be raised off the floor clear of draughts.

to have the dog in the house, then a wind- and weather-proof kennel should be placed in the yard, with the entrance facing a wall, to reduce incoming draughts. In the winter much more bedding is required than in summer. If hay or straw is used, it is preferable that this should be changed each day, and certainly every other day. Blankets or something similar should be washed often. Particular care should be taken that no damp bedding is put down, as dogs are prone to rheumatic complaints. In the very cold weather a sack or some similar cover should be placed over the entrance.

CHAINING. It is unwise to keep a dog on a chain continuously. If it is found impracticable to leave the dog free, then a running chain should be used, strongly fastened at each end, of about 30 ft. in length, with a steel link chain fastened to its harness, so that it can obtain plenty of exercise, although not free. If this type of chain is used, its position should be varied so that the dog does not wear away the ground surface. It should not be put near any soft ground that becomes muddy in wet weather, and the ground near should be cleansed each day.

LAW AND DOGS. There are several Acts of Parliament designed for the better treatment and safety of dogs. The main Act is the 1911 Protection of Animals Act, which lays down that no person may cause unnecessary suffering, and if convicted is liable to a fine or imprisonment. Unnecessary suffering can be taken to mean that any dog not taken for treatment when ill, confined to a small space, permanently chained on a short lead or underfed, makes the owner liable to prosecution. General neglect would also come within the scope of this Act.

Under the Roads Act it is obligatory on a motorist who runs over a dog to report the matter to the nearest policeman or police station. Failure to do this can bring, on conviction, a fine of £20. If the dog is injured and no police constable is available, the driver of the vehicle must render such first-aid as he can, and take the dog to a veterinary surgeon or to the owner.

The owner is responsible for his dog and can be held liable for any damage that his dog may do to his neighbour's property. If he fails to keep the dog under control, it is possible that the magistrate will order the animal's destruction. If the owner is convicted that his dog is caught worrying sheep or poultry, that dog will certainly be ordered to be destroyed. An owner can also be made liable if his dog continually barks or creates any other disturbance or nuisance. It is usual for the magistrate first to warn, with a Court order, that the dog must be kept under control, and then, if the owner fails to do so, the animal will be destroyed after a second conviction. (See also page 174.)

Stray dogs. Under the various Acts covering stray dogs no person finding a dog which he believes to be a stray, and which he cannot identify, may keep the animal. He should take it to the nearest police station. He may not

If a dog has to be kept chained, it should be allowed as long a run as possible. One way of increasing the run is to attach the lead to a ring running on a wire fixed to a wall.

hand a stray dog to anyone other than a police constable. A dog so taken in, or seized by the police themselves, must be kept for seven days, and then can be disposed of in accordance with the best advice that the police or a recognized Dogs' Home can obtain.

Owners who lose their dogs should not only notify the police, but should get in touch with their nearest Dogs' Homes, the addresses of which are kept in their police station. There is one exception, which is recognized by the law; any person finding a stray dog and who wishes to give that dog a home, may do so after having reported the finding to the police so that a full description is taken of the dog, obtaining a certificate from the police, and agreeing to keep that dog at the address on the certificate for thirty days. They must also take out a licence. The law is not quite clear on the position of an owner who has lost a dog and has not looked for it, but has discovered the animal in the care of a person who has obtained it after the lapse of the prescribed seven or thirty days; and it seems possible that the original owner can then reclaim the dog should he wish to do so, but is responsible for refunding any expenses that may have occurred in the interim.

LICENCES. Every dog over the age of six months must be licensed. A licence costs 7s. 6d., and is obtained from the Post Office. It is valid for one year.

FEEDING. Regularity in meals is essential. A puppy requires at least five meals a day, which should be gradually reduced to two as he grows older. It is better to give the main meal in the middle of the day and a lighter meal at night. As a general guide, one ounce of food to one pound of weight of animal per day is correct; thus, a dog weighing twelve pounds would require twelve ounces of food, of which eight ounces should be given in the middle of the day, and four ounces at night. In addition, hard biscuits should always be available, as eating these keeps the dog's teeth in good condition. So should fresh water, which should be changed at least twice a day, and in hot and dusty weather no less than four times. Only bones which do not splinter, such as marrow or shin, should be given to dogs.

No meal should be given in a sloppy condition, and it should be particularly noted that dogs, being clean in their habits, do not like their food put on a dirty plate, or with the remains of a previous meal. The smell of the stale food goes through the new and makes the whole meal unappetizing.

Weight of dog (pounds)	*Breed as an index to size*	*Carbohydrate (energizing foods) (ounces)*	*Protein (body-building) (ounces)*	*Fat (ounces)*
10	Cairn	5–6	1	¼
20	Fox terrier	8–10	1½–2	½
25	Large terrier	10	2	½
30	Cocker spaniel	10–12	2–2½	½
60	Airedale	14–18	3½	1
100–120	Alsatians and other large dogs	20–28	5–6	1¼–1½

TABLE 1. *Proportions of different foods required per day by various breeds.*

Dogs prefer, as is only natural, variation in food, and the following are designed largely for this purpose. It is inadvisable to give an animal much raw meat; it tends to make him fierce and is apt also to cause some of the attendant skin diseases.

Balanced diet. For a balanced diet an animal's meal must be proportioned in the types of food (see Table 1). The four specimen diets show that every meal should be made up of a mixture of certain types of food, such as toasted bread, meat or vegetable (see Table 2). These must be mixed in the proper proportions so that the animal's stomach is not overloaded with any one type of food. It is also advisable to give a dose of olive oil or liquid paraffin once a week either in the food, or neat if possible; this helps the digestion, and keeps the coat in good order.

Number one. Toasted stale bread, or oatmeal or whole maize. Mix with 3-4 oz. of any of the following: chopped cabbage, cauliflower, turnip, or other green leaves mashed and boiled for not more than twenty minutes. To this should be added 2 oz. of parsnip, or apple or pear peelings, washed and finely chopped or grated. Moisten the mixture with about half a teacupful of soup or gravy made from stewing bones or scraps from the table.

Number two. Toasted stale bread; oatmeal made into thick porridge or whole maize meal

Energizing foods	*Fatty foods*	*Body-building foods*	*Protective foods*
Dog biscuit, stale bread, baker's scraps, bread crusts, stale ship's biscuit; wheatings, middlings, barley meal, oatmeal; rice meal, flaked maize, whole maize, potato and potato peelings; flaked wheat, rice, pearl barley	Bacon rinds, bacon fats, skimmed fats (from soup, stock, etc.), dripping, margarine, beef and mutton fat, gristle	Soups and stews from meat, bones, fish, scraps, etc.; fish heads and trimmings; game, chicken, rabbit residues; meat and bone; white fish-meal; greaves; horseflesh; carcase residues such as paunches, tripe, guts, spleen, lungs, etc., from sheep and cattle; beans, peas, alfalfa meal, dried green clover leaves	Codliver-oil; other fish liver-oils; milk, whole, skim or dried; whey and whey powder; low-temperature blood and bone meals; raw carrots, parsnips, onions, apples, pears, etc., and most fruit peelings, except banana, orange, lemon and similar fruits; all green vegetable leaves

TABLE 2. *Sources of different types of food.*

Medicine is administered to a dog by pouring it into the mouth behind the canine teeth.

boiled with water for half an hour. Mix this with 2 or 3 oz. of meat scraps from the table, horseflesh or carcase residues from the butcher. These foods mixed together should be moistened with 4-6 oz. of whole or skimmed milk.

Number three. Mix together the following in a dry state: alfalfa meal, 1/10th; dry milk powder, 3/10ths; wheatings, middlings, or similar wheat offal, 5/10ths; dried white fish meal or meat and bone meal, 1/10th. Soak in cold water, enough to form a thick cream, and then simmer for half an hour. Add gravy or soup as in Number one, but no other meat or meat product.

Number four. Mix boiled rice (1 oz. of dry rice to a pint of water; soak and boil for one to two hours) and mashed beans (1 oz. of haricot beans or butter beans or dried peas). To this mixture add a vegetable liquid made by stewing any of the following in a small amount of water fifteen or twenty minutes: green vegetable leaves, dandelions, stinging nettles, carrot, spinach, swede or turnip tops. Add gravy as in Number one.

These meals can be given in any order, and can be varied when wished. They are designed to give alternative diets, a desirable course, and to fit in with available stocks in the shops.

AILMENTS. Generally speaking, it is always desirable to obtain expert veterinary advice whatever the type of illness contracted. There are more than one kind of canker, several types of skin diseases, and internal illness, all of which require expert diagnosis. After contacting a veterinary surgeon and obtaining his advice, the treatment can then be undertaken at home in most cases, following the instructions given. Normally an animal gets well very much more quickly in his home surroundings, and every effort should be made by the owner to keep the dog, however ill, with him.

First-aid. Cuts, provided they are not deep, can of course be treated by the owner. Bathe the wound in a mixture of 1 part of disinfectant to 3 parts of warm water. If the wound is not deep it is better to leave it uncovered, as all dogs have certain disinfectant in their lick, and can very often heal their own wounds by washing them.

Administering medicine. If your dog will not take medicine by himself, that is, through his mouth (an expert only should give any other form), turn back the head, lift the lip, behind the canine tooth, and pour the medicine through the gap between jaws, close the mouth and keep the head held back until the dog has swallowed. If he is difficult, quite a useful aid is to massage the throat. If a pill has to be given it should be crushed and dissolved in a little water or milk, otherwise the dog will try to regurgitate it.

Thorns. If an animal gets a thorn in his pad, stand the whole foot in a solution of disinfectant in hot water, as hot as the dog can bear, and keep it there for at least five minutes. If the pad is then sufficiently soft, squeeze the skin on either side of the thorn until the head appears, then remove with a pair of tweezers.

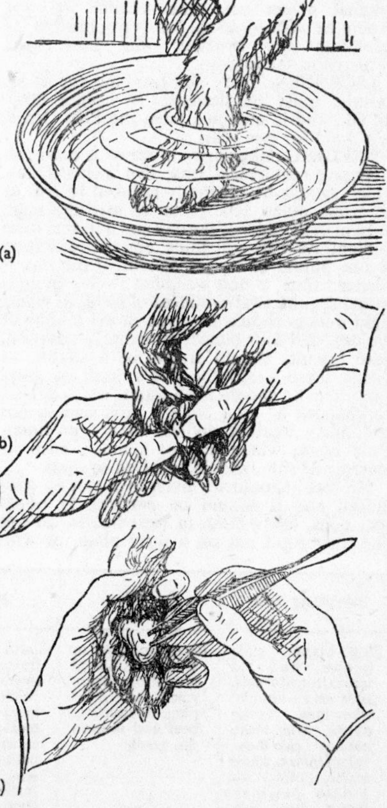

Removing a thorn from a dog's pad: (*a*) *soak the foot in hot water;* (*b*) *squeeze the pad until the head of the thorn emerges;* (*c*) *remove the thorn from the softened pad with tweezers.*

Canker. There are special treatments for canker, but it is advisable before applying these first to discover from an expert whether it is wet or dry canker, and ascertain the correct way to clean the ear. Merely to put a piece of cotton-wool on the end of a matchstick may be dangerous and lead to deafness. Canker can be cured, and once the correct treatment has been found out no further advice is necessary.

Skin diseases. These often result from over-heated blood, caused sometimes by too much meat. As a general rule a piece of rock sulphur kept in the dog's drinking water will help, but once the skin is diseased then it is necessary to obtain advice, and the responsibility should be passed on to a qualified veterinary surgeon.

Worms. Generally speaking, all puppies are infected with worms. There are special worm powders and worm pills which can be given, but it is still better to go to a veterinary surgeon, and get him to administer the dose or give you the correct dosage.

The dog will undoubtedly be distressed for a short while, but once clear and correctly fed there is no need for it to be infected again, as long as it is fed on clean, wholesome and fresh food, and not permitted to pick up anything from dustbins or on the streets.

Diarrhoea. This is usually caused by injudicious feeding, but can also be caused by worms. A good dose of liquid paraffin or other oil should be given to clear the dog, except in the case of worms, when the ordinary worm dosage should be used. Then keep it on a light diet of arrowroot or cornflour, gradually going on to fish and then to normal meals. A dose of bismuth should be given after each meal.

Dew claws. These are the small claws that hang on the inside of the leg and are not used by the dog, and therefore are not kept short by walking. If ignored these claws may gradually grow into the pad and so should be cut fairly frequently to prevent this. Some veterinary surgeons advise that the claws should be removed after birth, but others maintain they should remain. In any case, if they are not removed immediately they should not be removed at all, otherwise the removal will cause considerable pain to the dog.

Foot of a dog showing the dew claw. If these have not been removed at birth, they must be carefully tended to see that they do not grow into the pad.

Distemper. Distemper attacks most dogs, and is one of the commonest complaints, being highly infectious to other dogs. In their interests the affected dog should be isolated. There are many cures suggested, but it is better to obtain the advice of a veterinary surgeon at once. In any case the dog must be kept in an even warm temperature.

Distemper, in its early stages, is often confused with other minor ailments. It usually starts by the dog going off its food, becoming dull and disinterested in its surroundings. His nose becomes hot and dry. After a few days there is a yellowish-green discharge from the nose and eyes, with a rising temperature.

2. CATS

CHOICE AND BREED. It is advisable, particularly in built-up areas, to keep only a neuter; these are less apt to stray, do not produce continual litters of kittens and do not smell as they become older. It is preferable to keep a short-haired cat, particularly in large households, as they do not require the same amount of grooming as the long-haired.

If a female cat is kept, the inevitable litters of kittens must not be drowned, but should be taken to a veterinary surgeon or an Animal Welfare Centre. The cat should not be deprived of all her kittens immediately after their birth.

Breeds. Cats fall into, generally speaking, three categories: the short-haired, the long-haired and those of foreign origin. Most prevalent among those kept by the general public are the ordinary tabby and the black-and-white (or what may be called the mongrel), and these colourings, or markings, appear both in the long- and short-haired animal. The Manx, peculiar to the Isle of Man, although now kept elsewhere in the world, is the only cat born without a tail. The Siamese has many qualities of the dog, and is probably more closely related to the cheetah than the

Tabby cat. This with the common black-and-white variety is the mongrel of domestic cats.

lion. The cat is nocturnal in habit, and is descended from the same stock as the lion.

Blue long-haired. This cat varies from the deepest slate-blue to palest lavender. The eyes are orange in colour, and its coat is very soft on the underside of the body. There is also a short-haired variety of this cat. In a long-haired breed the head is broad, but not so broad on the short-haired.

Cream long-haired. Colouring is cream and the eyes are a golden-yellow. In the white long-haired variety the eyes are pale blue.

Chinchilla long-haired. The fur is in delicate shades of grey, interspersed with some black hairs; the eyes are emerald-green in colour.

Orange and tortoiseshell. The tortoiseshell is the female counterpart of the orange; the coat in itself is a mottled variety of many colours, as the name denotes. The eyes should be orange. The male, which is sometimes popularly called the "marmalade" cat, varies from a very pale to a very deep, almost red, colour. The eyes are usually gold, tinted with green.

Black long-haired. This cat is entirely black, and the eyes are best described as being of the same colour as the yolk of an egg.

Short-haired cats. Most of the long-haired cats mentioned already have their counterparts in the short-haired variety, the markings being exactly the same.

Manx. The ears of the Manx are much more erect than that of the normal cat, and its body

Manx cat.

slopes rather like the wild cat's. It is strange that the Manx does not appear in all colours. There are known to be some black, black-and-white, and even an occasional white. The main feature is that they are born tailless, and they must not be confused with a rarity in the ordinary cat, which is sometimes born with a bob tail. They are, as a rule, very powerful.

Abyssinian. Normally a short-haired cat, it is akin to the wild cat of Britain, except that there are no body markings, though there are rings, faintly indicated, on the tail. The colour is a deep brown with black tickings, and a black line from the nape of the neck to the end of the tail. The ears are tipped with black and the eyes are a deep yellow with a glint of green in them.

Siamese. The Siamese cat, originally bred solely in the Royal Palaces of Siam, is a short-

Siamese cat.

haired cat. Normal colouring is light fawn with the extremities—that is, the tail, paws, face and ears—black. With experimental breeding, whilst not losing the Siamese characteristics, they range in various colours: some even are without any of the characteristic black markings. Their cry is unlike that of the ordinary domestic cat, being somewhat raucous. The eyes are pale blue in colour.

Angora cat. The fur of the Angora is very much softer than that of the long-haired variety, and the combings can be used for the manufacture of woollen articles.

Angora cat.

TRAINING. It is not as easy to train a cat as it is a dog, but they do learn rapidly how to conform with the ordinary needs of a household. They can be kept quite easily in flats and other dwellings which do not possess a garden. In the early stages of kittenhood the cat should be introduced to a box of ashes, sawdust or even newspaper, and made to realize that this is the place for performing its natural function. The ashes or sawdust must be changed frequently each day. It is not necessary to turn a cat out at night; more cats disappear because of this than for any other reason. The last meal should be given last thing at night so that the cat returns for this and remains indoors.

LAW AND CATS. There is no provision for the cat in law as there is for the dog. A cat, for instance, at the moment need not be licensed, does not have to wear a collar and does not come within the provisions of the Roads Acts, but the cat is protected against cruelty and unnecessary suffering by the 1911 Animal Protection Act.

Although the law does not specify that a cat should wear a collar, and the police are not required to seize cats straying on the highways unmarked in this way, those persons who really are fond of their animals will see that their cat is identified, so that a finder may return it to its owner.

It is advisable when choosing a collar for a cat not to have the leather variety; it is safer to use an elastic collar, to which can be attached a small disk with the name and address of the owner. The reason for the use of elastic is that a cat, being prone to climbing, may get its collar caught on a projection or a branch, and perhaps hang, whereas if elastic is used it will stretch and the head will go through. When putting on the collar, it should be possible to insert one or two fingers between the elastic and the neck.

SLEEPING ACCOMMODATION. A cat should be given its own basket, which should be kept raised from the floor, and in the warmest corner of the room. The cat should be provided with bedding which should be frequently changed, and must be kept clean.

If a female cat is kept, she will invariably find her own place in which to have her kittens, but a little human ingenuity may help her to make up her mind. There should be soft material available for the cat when her time arrives. Tissue-paper, soft linen and so on can be left about, and she will take them to make her own nest. Usually a cat prefers a drawer or somewhere where there is a certain amount of darkness, and she should not be interfered with until she brings her kittens out herself.

CARE. The cat, being a very clean animal, washes itself and should never be bathed. In the case of the long-haired cat, it should be brushed and combed at least once a day, particularly in the spring and autumn, when it is changing its coat. The short-haired cat should be brushed at least once a day, and more often at the same periods of the year. The cat when washing itself takes a certain amount of fur into the stomach which can become dangerous if taken in a great quantity. If the owner removes the loose hairs by grooming the animal, this danger will be minimized.

All cats need regular brushing.

It is advisable to give a cat a dose of olive oil or liquid paraffin at least once a week, or, if these are unavailable, the oil from a sardine tin, or some other similar form of oil. This not only helps to keep the coat in good condition and the internal arrangements in working order, but dissolves the hair-ball which forms for the reasons stated above.

FEEDING. It is essential that regular meals should be given to the cat. Milk is not an absolute necessity, many cats preferring water, and in the opinion of many experts it is better to put one part of water to two parts of milk in any case. Kittens should be given three to four meals a day, which should be gradually reduced to two main meals at the age of about six months.

A cat, possibly more than a dog, requires its meals to be reasonably dry. Unlike the dog, it is better to give the main meal at night and the lighter meal in the middle of the day and a useful guide to the quantity of food required is 1 oz. in weight of food to 1 lb. in weight of the animal.

Bones should be removed from the cat's fish.

Particular care should be taken not to give the cat fish-bones, even small ones, as these are apt to stick in the throat and become difficult to remove, nor should a cat have any bone-splinters or the small bones of any poultry or rabbit. A cat should have a certain amount of meat in each week, and should be given as much variety in its meals as is possible. Fish and the flesh of rabbit and poultry can also be given. Unlike the dog, a certain amount of raw meat is beneficial; otherwise, generally speaking, the table on page 531 will be found to provide a useful guide.

It is best to try to make a cat take medicine in its food. If it will not do this and has to be dosed this is best carried out by two people, one to hold the cat and the other to administer the medicine.

AILMENTS. Expert advice should be taken at once if a cat is thought to be unwell. Being a home-loving animal it will naturally recover its health and strength more quickly in its normal surroundings, and once advice has been taken and the correct treatment prescribed it should be taken home and carefully nursed.

First-aid. Should a cat cut itself, or similarly suffer from minor injuries of this nature, the wound should be disinfected with 1 part of a disinfectant to 4 parts of warm water. Unless the wound is particularly deep, or advice has been given to the contrary, it should not be covered, for the cat will lick it and help to heal the cut in this way.

Administering medicine. To administer a dose or a pill to a cat is not quite so easy as to other animals. If it can be induced to take medicine mixed into its food, this is undoubtedly the best course to take. Failing that, its head should be turned back, its mouth opened and the pill put as far back into the throat as possible, or the liquid poured in. The mouth should then be closed and held until the cat has swallowed; an aid to force the swallowing can be effected by massaging the throat. It is better for two people to administer this dosage, one to hold the cat—and the easiest way to do this is to put the animal upon a table, place the hand behind the head and the arm along the length of the cat's back, pressing gently to hold the animal still—the second person giving the dose.

Thorns. The cat, moving as it does through narrow spaces and hedges, has been known to get thorns embedded in the head, quite apart from the pads of the feet. To remove the thorn from the pad is comparatively simple: it should be soaked in hot water until the pad is reasonably soft, and the thorn squeezed out and removed with a pair of tweezers (see DOGS). Unless there is a projection which can be easily gripped with tweezers and pulled out, a thorn in the head is a job for a veterinary surgeon.

Canker. Cats suffer considerably from this trouble. It takes both dry and wet forms. There is a definite treatment, and the proper lotion should be obtained from an expert and the way of administering it carefully learned. It is wrong to put cotton-wool on the end of a matchstick or similar sharp-pointed instrument in an attempt to clean out the cat's ears.

Skin diseases. The cat suffers from many types of disease; they cause considerable irritation, which, if scratched with sharp claws, is apt to result in broken skin and further discomfort. All have their correct ointments and treatments, so expert advice must be obtained.

Cat influenza. The cause of cat influenza is not yet known; it attacks suddenly and takes two forms, the most dangerous of which is the gastric, which can kill a cat within twenty-four hours. The second has in many ways the same symptoms as distemper in dogs, is not so violent, but can also be fatal. It is not necessary to lose a cat from either of these diseases, but very careful nursing is required. The symptoms of the gastric form usually start with a refusal to eat, followed by constant vomiting; the cat becomes dull and listless and in most cases the animal is quiet and remains motionless. Both forms of this disease are highly infectious, and it is advisable not to have another cat on the same premises, certainly for three months, preferably for six. The symptoms of the other form of this disease take the form of a profuse watery discharge from the eyes, and often only one eye discharges. This watery discharge thickens rapidly and finally glues the lids together. The cat becomes very susceptible to light, preferring dark places.

Cystitis. This particular complaint is very common in the male cat, and causes the animal great agony. Taken in its early stages it can be cured, but the cat is prone to have a recurrence. The symptoms are acute discomfort, and inability to pass water; the cat frequently moans with pain.

NEUTERING. To perform this operation is perfectly simple, and in no way affects the growth or mentality of the animal, provided it is done at a reasonably early age. The operation should be performed only by a veterinary surgeon, and in the case of a male should be at the age of about four months, certainly not later than six months, but owners intending to have this done should consult with their veterinarian and fix a date with him.

A female can be similarly neutered (splayed is the correct term). This is an internal operation necessitating an incision in the side, and the cat should stay with the veterinary surgeon until the stitches have been removed. The fur grows quite quickly over the patch. The operation is more dangerous than that of the male, but with modern training the percentage of losses has been reduced to a minimum. It is essential, of course, to keep the wound clear of infection. The operation should be performed at approximately seven months.

3. POULTRY-KEEPING

INCUBATION. In the wild state a fowl lays one or two clutches of eggs in the year. The clutch varies in number, but is usually about twelve or fifteen eggs, which the female bird hatches by brooding them with her own body. The temperature of the eggs during the period of incubation varies from about 97½ deg. F. to approximately 102 deg. F. With natural incubation the mother bird's movements turn the eggs and so prevent the yolks adhering to the membranes adjacent to the shell. The normal period of incubation for the several breeds of poultry is as follows:

Hen egg	21 days
Turkey egg	26 "
Duck egg	30 "
Muscovy duck egg ..	35 "
Goose egg	30 "
Turkey on hen egg ..	24 "
Turkey on duck egg ..	27 "
Hen on duck egg ..	30 "

Incubation by natural means, that is, the **broody** female, probably results in stronger chicks as a result of the survival of the fittest, but this method is obviously unsuited to large-scale undertakings. This need has been met by the introduction of the incubator. In these machines the temperature and humidity are automatically controlled to resemble the natural conditions, and in many incubators automatic turning is a common device. With the small cabinet incubator the operator maintains the temperature at 103 deg. F. and the relative humidity at 48 to 60 per cent—that is, wet bulb reading at 87; with the large machines the temperature reading should be approximately 100 deg. F. and the relative humidity 63 per cent (wet bulb reading 82-85). It is customary to turn the eggs in an incubator two or four times in twenty-four hours.

Candling. A bird may produce fertile or infertile eggs. Obviously the former can be produced only if she has been treaded by the male bird. It is not possible to detect any differences by "candling" the eggs at the time of production. Candling is a process in which the egg is held against a strong light in a darkened room so that the contents may be dimly seen. Originally the apparatus was an illuminated candle shining through a hole in a box or tin; today the "candle" is usually a 60-watt electric bulb in a globular metal container having a circular aperture of about 1½ in. diameter. With this apparatus it is possible to detect a fertile egg about thirty or so hours after being placed in the incubator. The germinating embryo may be detected as a faint red mark on the yolk. In most hatcheries the eggs are tested by the candling light by the seventh day. Those which are infertile, or those fertile eggs which have failed to develop and so do not show the red "spider" of the developing embryo, are removed and are normally quite edible.

SEXING. In theory approximately 50 per cent of all fertile eggs should produce female

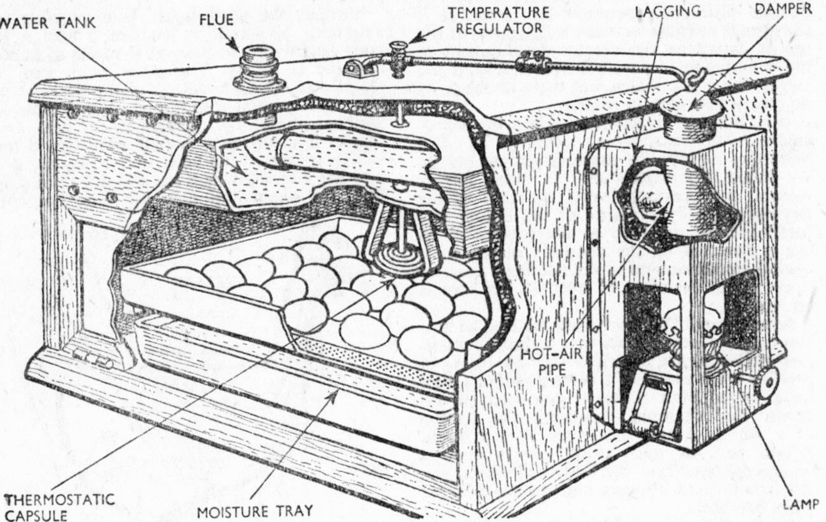

This incubator is provided with automatic temperature regulation. If the temperature gets too high the thermostatic capsule expands and the rod above it is raised, lifting the temperature regulator (adjusted by means of a screw) and with it the damper. Hot air from the lamp is then discharged direct into the atmosphere instead of passing through the hot-air pipe to the flue. When the capsule cools and contracts, hot air once more passes through the incubator, heating the water in the tank, which in turn raises the temperature of the air round the eggs.

Candling and sorting eggs at a big hatchery. Inset: simple apparatus for the small breeder.

chicks and the remainder male chicks. As the latter are of value to the commercial poultry-keeper for flesh or breeding purposes only, it is an obvious advantage to the breeder if the sex of chicks can be determined at hatching time. The appearance of the chicks of pure breeds gives little indication of sex differences. Normally, the secondary sexual characters, such as tail feathers, comb size and shape, and wattle, are not sufficiently developed until six to ten weeks after hatching to allow a definite distinction between the sexes. It is sometimes possible to make a fair guess at the sex of chicks by the greater development of the wing-flights in young female chicks or the larger size of the males, but these methods by no means give certain results.

It is, however, possible to detect the sex of chicks with reasonable certainty by two methods: namely, by manual sexing and by sex-linked characteristics. In the former method the operator everts the vent of the day-old chick by pressure of the thumb and forefinger. In the case of the male bird its sex is detected by the presence of the male genital eminence, and in the hands of a skilled operator an accuracy of over 95 per cent is common.

Sex-linkage. The sex-linked method of sexing follows from the fact that certain plumage characteristics are inherited only by chicks of one sex when males of a certain colour (gold) have mated with different coloured (silver) dams. For example, following the mating of a Rhode Island Red cock with a Light Sussex hen the male chick always appears white-coloured from chickhood onwards, and the female chick appears red or buff-coloured from hatching.

By the use of sex-linked characteristics it is, therefore, possible to detect the sex of chicks at hatching, but, with one exception, the method involves the crossing of two breeds. The exception is that of the auto-sexing breeds, in which the sex-linked factor of barring (found in such breeds as the Barred Rocks), which is the basis of their colouring, allows sex differentiation at hatching.

BREEDING. The actual ability of a bird to produce eggs, or the condition of a bird produced for the table, is the result of two sets of factors, and, generally speaking, these two sets of factors are of equal importance. The bird is produced with certain inherent characteristics. Some of these may be obvious, such as the colour of the plumage, type of comb, and so on. Others may be less easy to distinguish, that is, the bird's ability to lay a large number of eggs, its ability to withstand disease, and so on. These other factors are also less easy to distinguish because they are greatly affected by the second series of conditions, those which may be grouped as external conditions and are in the main those resulting from feeding and management. Thus, a bird may have the ability to lay a large number of eggs, having inherited these abilities, but because she is poorly fed she is unable to give expression to that ability. While, therefore, breeding for any utility factors is of great importance, management and feeding are equally important if the best results are to be obtained.

Poultry scientists have shown that genetic factors control the bird's ability to produce eggs, equally with the determination of the bird's type of comb, shank colouring, plumage and many other characteristics. Unfortunately, these utility factors cannot be as easily distinguished as the latter, and it is only possible to discover whether or not a bird is a good breeder by actual trial, i.e., the results of her progeny.

Spotting the good layer. It is possible to determine by handling whether a bird is in good health and whether at the time of handling she is in lay. The latter point can be established by examination of the beak, vent, legs and general condition. With coloured varieties, the yellow pigment in the beak and shanks is identical with that which gives the yellow colour to the yolk, and obviously if a bird has laid many eggs she will draw not only from the pigmentation in her food but also

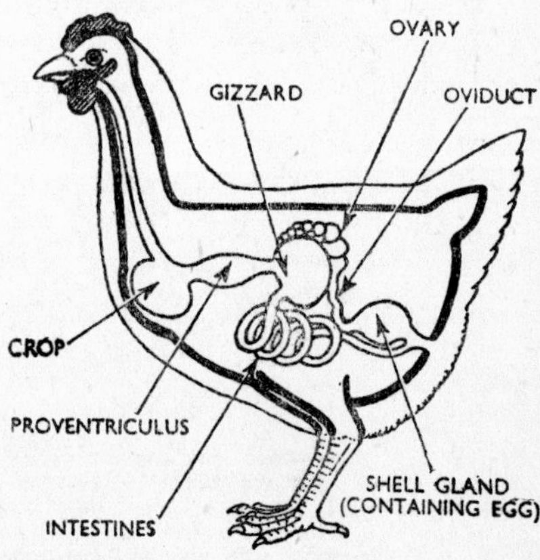

Principal features of a chicken's anatomy.

from that normally in her body. The order in which this pigmentation is lost appears constant and therefore is a good guide as to whether or not the bird is a good layer. This loss is from the vent, then the shanks, and then the beak, and returns in reverse order, vent, shanks, beak; and a close inspection of the bird by a skilled operator will, therefore, indicate whether she has been a good producer during the laying season. A ragged condition of the tail feathers is also indicative of her frequent visits to the nest, whilst the poor doer usually shows a dapper appearance compared with her more hard-working sisters. The flexibility and greater width between the pelvic bones is also a fair indication of a bird in lay.

Progeny testing. Unfortunately, a high-laying bird is no guarantee that her progeny will also be high layers. Quite apart from the fact that the bird itself may not be pure for any of the characteristics exhibited, e.g., although a rose-combed bird she may not be pure for that factor, there is also the additional obstacle that the male to whom she is mated may or may not contribute towards high production in the progeny. A definite check can be made only by an actual test of the progeny. In progeny testing, which is merely an estimation of the breeding worth of a bird by a test of an adequate sample of its progeny, it is important that the sample be adequate. Every chick produced at a mating is indicative of some factor carried by the parents. Some may be excellent egg-producers, but if there are many poor-quality birds it is obvious that one or other of the parents is carrying undesirable factors.

It is possible to carry out a progeny test on a male bird to establish that he at least is a satisfactory breeder. If the majority of all—or a representative sample—of the pullets produced with the several dams show adequate results, then it is reasonable to regard the male as a proven sire. It is more difficult with the dam, because normally she is mated to one sire only and he may have a dominating effect. If, therefore, a test of the female is to be made it is better to mate her to two or more cocks during the breeding season.

Progeny testing requires, however, a good deal of recording and is not suitable for the small breeder. The general method followed by the smaller breeder is individual selection, the mating together of hens with a record of high pullet-production years to sires which appear healthy and in good condition. This method will certainly show an improved production from the progeny, but it is by no means a certain method, and to achieve a further increase in the production figure, once a certain figure is reached, is a task for the high-class specialist pedigree-breeder. This is so because only then can reliable knowledge of the sire's abilities be obtained, and it will be realized that, in any one chick, sire and dam play equal parts.

Table birds. Breeding is not carried out for egg-production alone. With table poultry it is important to produce a bird with a broad, well-fleshed breast, and a bird which will feather rapidly. The last point is important because a slow-feathering bird will have many stubs and pin-feathers (new developing feathering) at the age of thirteen to sixteen weeks, when the bird is normally killed for the table. It has been shown that both broad breast and rapid feathering are factors which are inherited, and thus it is possible to carry out the same breeding principles followed in breeding for egg-production when breeding stock for desirable table characteristics. Progress along these lines with turkeys has advanced to a high degree.

The principles of methods of breeding carried out with fowl are similar to those which must be followed for turkeys, geese and ducks.

FEEDING. The food demands of poultry will vary according to their stage of growth and their status of production. Generally speaking, there is never a normal situation since, apart from the maintenance ration, special feeding-stuffs will be wanted during growth, and in adult life both for egg-production and during the moult, when egg-production is reduced to a minimum. Feeding stuffs are valuable for their contribution of carbohydrates, proteins and vitamins. Generally speaking, carbohydrates provide energy, proteins growth, while vitamins are those important conditioners which assist in the vital processes of life, for example, hatchability of eggs produced. In so far as poultry are concerned, protein is extremely important in egg-production. The following details of the composition of the egg will demonstrate this fact:

Fat	.. ..	10·5 per cent
Protein	.. ..	11·0 ,, ,,
Ash	.. ..	1·0 ,, ,,
Water	.. ..	68·5 ,, ,,
Shell	.. ..	9·0 ,, ,,

The composition of the egg is almost invariable and, therefore, the protein must be drawn either from the diet of the bird or from its own constitution. The latter cannot be a continuous process, and reduction in protein will, therefore, lead to lowered egg-production and finally complete cessation.

It is important to see that laying birds are fully fed. It has been shown that if the supplies of food are reduced by 25 per cent egg production will drop by 50 per cent. The food-consumption of the bird will vary greatly, depending on the type of food and the quality of the ration. The normal adult laying bird will consume about 4 to 5 oz. of good-quality food per day. If the food is eked out with swill, potatoes, etc., the daily quantity may rise as high as 10 oz. The chicken's senses of taste and smell are not strong, and the bird is normally attracted to food by its bright and shining appearance, and thus grain is particularly suitable for poultry. It is important to ensure that grain is not put on a hard unresisting surface. As the bird picks up the food in its beak, if it is placed on a stone or metal surface it results in a shock each time the bird pecks at its food and will reduce the bird's appetite.

Grit. The particular attraction exercised over the bird by bright or shining particles results in a fair amount of grit being picked up. This is important in that the chicken has no teeth, and the crushing of hard substances such as grain is carried out in the gizzard.

The crushing action of the hard and horny walls of this extremely muscular part of the digestive system is assisted by hard stony particles in grinding down grain and other hard substances. Flint or granite grits are ideal, since their edges are not easily worn down by the grinding action, and they are far less soluble than limestone grit, which, in the acid gut of the chicken, soon dissolves and loses its grinding power and leads to excess of calcium in the bird and possibly reduced egg-production.

Poultry have difficulty in dealing with dusty food, since the latter clogs the nostrils. With ducks and geese it will be realized that these birds cannot use their feet for scratching although the bills of both birds are admirably suited for grazing. While chicken can be fed on dry mash, ducks and geese are best suited with wet mash, and with ducks grain is best given in water.

Ration for laying birds. This should be so adapted as to provide a maintenance ration to keep the bird living, and sufficient supplies to promote the production of eggs. Grain foods are mainly carbohydrates and provide energy for the bird. Protein is necessary with adult stock to help in the production of eggs. Proteins may be of vegetable or animal origin, and generally speaking those of animal origin are more valuable to poultry. For the proper production of the egg and for satisfactory shells vitamins A and D are necessary. The fowl on the free range obtains sufficient of these vitamins from sunlight, young herbage and grass, but for birds which are kept on a semi-intensive system it is advisable to have fortified codliver-oil, that is, codliver-oil which has a high vitamin A and D content.

A suitable ration for a laying bird to be fed with grain (50/50) is as follows:

Wheatings	40	per cent
Bran	15	" "
Maize meal	20	" "
Sussex ground oats	10	" "
Fish meal	10	" "
Maize gluten meal	2.5	" "
Grass meal	2.5	" "

In addition about 2 per cent of finely ground calcium carbonate is necessary to provide a mineral supplement, and about ½ per cent of salt. In order to ensure that the bird is getting sufficient vitamins A and D, between 0·5 per cent and 1 per cent of fortified codliver-oil should also be mixed in with the mash. Any form of calcium carbonate is suitable, but preference should be given to oyster-shell, which contains minute traces of manganese. This substance assists in the formation of sound, strong eggshells and also prevents such illnesses as slipped tendon.

The codliver-oil is not essential if the birds are on open range where sunlight can reach them, since the latter synthesizes vitamin D in the bird itself. With intensively reared stock and as a safety measure it is, however, advisable to include the codliver-oil.

The ration can be varied a good deal and individual poultry-keepers may have other materials which can usefully replace some of the materials set out above. Boiled potatoes can be fed—the water should also be used in the make-up of the mash—but it will be found that the birds will consume an increased quantity of mash which includes potatoes. It would also be advisable to increase the protein content if potatoes are to be used, in order to maintain the necessary balance. One of the reasons for feeding animal protein (meat and bone-meal and fish-meal) is that these foods contain phosphorus, which is essential for the metabolism of the bird and the production of eggs. The animal protein can be reduced if phosphorus is fed in the form of a small percentage (1-1½) of steamed bone-flour or a suitable mineral phosphate.

While the diet can be varied a good deal according to the foodstuffs available, it must be borne in mind that for maintenance and egg production the protein content should not fall below 13 per cent, and of this quantity not much less than 5 per cent should be in the form of fish-meal or animal protein, although as stated above a small deficiency can be made up with some form of phosphate. Cereals contain a certain amount of phosphorus, but it is unlikely that the amount fed will supply sufficient of this element. Cereals and root crops are mainly fed to provide carbohydrate or energy food and this energy food is present in the form of starch. Care should be taken that the fibre—woody material—does not exceed a total of 10 per cent in the entire diet, since this is practically useless for nourishing the bird. If the diet contains much fibre, the bird will consume large quantities but still remain undernourished.

Where grain and mash are fed it is better to give the grain in the morning feed and the mash in the evening so that the birds can fill their crops before going to rest. If, however, the mash is bulky because of the inclusion of potatoes, etc., it is best to give a grain feed in the middle of the morning, mash in the morning, and a final mash feed at night.

Ducks can assimilate large quantities of vegetable matter from stream beds, while geese can consume large quantities of grass. In fact, the adult goose needs little except good grazing.

REARING. The newly hatched chick requires no feedingstuffs for the first forty-eight hours of its life. It relies for its sustenance on the reserves of food supplied by the egg-yolk, the remains of which are absorbed into its body before hatching. It is, therefore, important that the diet of the hen or pullet producing the egg should be satisfactory, and the level of that diet has an important bearing on the early health of the chick.

During the early stages of the chick's life it is important that it is neither coddled nor exposed to unnecessarily harsh conditions. Several views exist on this point, but generally speaking chick-brooders of the fold type, which enable the bird to be on grass after the first few days of its life, seem to result in the hardiest type of chick. It is also essential to supply sufficient protein during the growing period to develop satisfactorily. The amount of protein during the early stages of growth should be between 18 and 21 per cent of the complete diet. Excess of protein is unnecessarily expensive and may lead to dietetic troubles. During the later stages of growth the protein in the diet can be reduced as the rate of growth declines, but a fair level is still necessary to ensure the proper development of plumage. At this stage the protein level should not fall below 13 per cent or, better still, 15 per cent. Finally, when the bird comes into lay additional protein above a maintenance ration is still necessary if the bird is to produce a satisfactory number of eggs. In addition to a satisfactory diet, water and grit should always be available to the bird. A saving in both protein diet and expensive foods containing vitamins should be achieved if the bird has access to good-quality well-managed grass. Because of its volume only a small percentage of grass—between 5 and 7 per cent—can be consumed by the bird. If the grass is in poor condition it will be mainly fibre, which is useless as a food and may lead to crop troubles. The strains of grass do not matter so much as its condition, and the swards of poultry pens should be kept short and free from coarse matty tussocks.

Ducks. With ducks, success will attend the rearing if it is carried out on clean grassland, each duck being allowed about 250 sq. ft. They consume a large amount of greenstuff. Because of the nature of their bills the mash should be fed wet, and if running water such as a brook or river is not adjacent to the land on which they are reared, their drinking troughs should be such as to enable them to immerse the whole head. Ducks have a tendency to become fat and maize should, therefore, be given with caution, but it should be remembered that the average well-grown duck will consume about one-third more wet mash than a fowl, which eats about 4-5 oz. daily.

Geese. With geese, green food is again important, and the birds do best on free range where they will graze the pasture better than most animals. They should preferably be within reach of a stream, pond or brook, and again if this is impossible they should be able to immerse their heads in their drinking water.

Turkeys. In the case of turkeys, the young birds are regarded as delicate and should not be allowed to roam amongst uncut tussocky grass. Their diet is similar to that of chicken, but preference should be given to wet mash rather than dry. It should also be realized that turkeys, in common with geese and ducks, do not use their feet for scratching, and grain in their case should, therefore, be placed on the boards of their house. In the later stages of growth the turkey will require up to 8 oz. of grain as its daily ration.

HOUSING AND MANAGEMENT. Apart from geese and breeding ducks, poultry can be managed on an intensive or extensive system or a modification of both methods. In the extensive system full advantage is taken of range conditions, and the operator is saved the task of handling the manure, while the chicken does useful work in harrowing the ground by the scarifying action of its feet. Intensive methods, however, have the advantage of allowing an individual bird to be inspected quickly, so that all passengers can be eliminated, and the method naturally requires much less space.

Extensive systems. The principal extensive systems are those with movable or fixed houses. In the former case the house can be a cabin on wheels or skids, housing fifty to seventy birds, the house being moved over the field by a tractor or horse. It is important to move the house at intervals to ensure that a large bare patch does not develop around the house. In some parts of the country fixed houses of approximately the same size or larger are in popular use. They have the disadvantages already referred to, but their fixed nature allows stouter construction.

A modification of the extensive system is the fold. This ensures that the ground is evenly covered, for the folds should be moved every day, but the moving of the folds is a laborious task. The method is mainly suited for the large-scale farmer carrying a large poultry unit. All these methods ensure that the poultry-keeper is saved the job of spreading the manure on his land and the birds are enabled to graze as much as possible.

Intensive systems. The intensive system is extremely profitable with good-class birds. There is the additional labour of daily cleaning. The average charges of purchasing cages (often referred to as a battery) and the neces

Mobile chicken-house with removable dropping-boards.

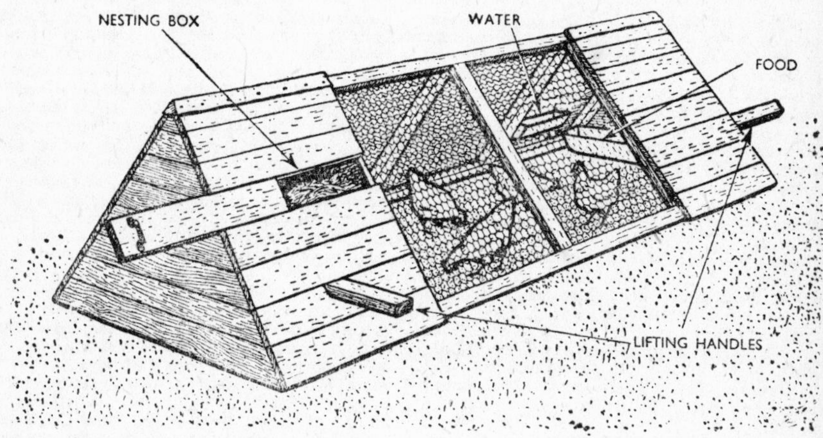

Movable fold suitable for keeping chickens on open grassland. The fold should be moved daily.

sary equipment is approximately double that involved in the extensive systems and it is most necessary to ensure that a complete diet is fed. Under this system there is no possibility of the bird correcting any diet deficiency by grazing and picking up insects. The method is, however, particularly suited to the small farmer and the domestic poultry-keeper who cannot afford much land for his poultry.

HOUSING BY DOMESTIC POULTRY-KEEPERS. The smallholder or dweller in urban areas will not normally be able to follow the methods of managing and housing poultry pursued by the commercial poultry-keeper. If, however, he has a reasonably sized lawn he may be able to follow a fold system. The fold should be made on the same pattern as the large commercial one which is generally about 18 ft. by 6 ft. wide, but, of course, the size will be proportionately reduced for his smaller number of birds. In the fold he should allow approximately 4 sq. ft. per bird. If, therefore, he is housing six birds, a useful size will be 6 ft. long by 4 ft. broad. To get the full value from this particular method, i.e., to enable the birds to obtain protein and vitamin A from the grass and to ensure the grass benefits from the manuring and scratching of the birds, the fold should be moved at least once a day.

Chicken-houses. In many gardens a fold method will not be possible, and in such instances a solid-floor fixed house or some kind of cage is the most suitable. With the former, 4 sq. ft. should be allowed per bird, and so a 6 ft. by 4 ft. house with the roof 4 ft. to 5 ft. high should suffice. It is essential that the house should be well ventilated, airy and light, but not draughty. A good type of house to adopt is one with glass windows which open upwards allowing air and light to come in through the window, which should be covered with small-gauge wire-netting. It is also essential to ensure that the litter is cleaned out and replaced with fresh clean litter at least once a week, and, of course, a supply of green food will be necessary. Open nests filled with frequently changed hay or straw should be provided in a separate section.

Batteries. With the cages, the most successful results are obtained if they are affixed to a wall out of the wind, but where they can receive a good deal of sunshine. The cages should be purchased from a reputable manufacturer or made from stout boxes with wire-netting fronts and false bottoms to ensure the egg rolls away from the bird after having been laid. The cages should have a floor-space of at least 2½ sq. ft. All the precautions necessary with the solid-floor fixed house should be followed in the case of cages, and if the cages are sheltered by an overhanging penthouse roof the birds should be quite comfortable.

In the last two methods the birds cannot forage for themselves, i.e., pick up insects or grits. It is, therefore, essential to ensure that the birds have an adequate ration and a supply of green food and grit together with fresh water.

DISEASE. Poultry come to maturity quickly, live a comparatively short life, and usually fall a prey to disease with remarkable celerity. In view of the value of the bird it is rarely advisable to treat diseased stock. It is more profitable to kill off birds, take the necessary precautions against further outbreaks and purchase new stock. Little information can be given of a practical nature on the diagnosis of poultry diseases by a layman. The symptoms of many poultry diseases appear identical, and those symptoms which can be diagnosed will give no indication whether the bird is also sickening with another entirely different disease.

Some illnesses are due to faults of management and may be quickly cured by the practical poultry-keeper. An example is bumblefoot, due to damage and irritation of the sole of the bird's foot. Crop impaction, due to a highly fibrous diet, can be cured by gently working the contents up through the throat. Our present-day knowledge of the sulpha drugs has given a cure—not a preventative—for coccidiosis.

Inoculation can be used in the cure of blackhead in turkeys and fowl pox in chicken, but these methods are hardly suited for the small poultryman, who is best advised to purchase good stock and keep their living quarters and range as clean as possible.

Poultry are also subject to certain parasites, such as lice and red mite. There are various proprietary cures which involve either the fumigation of the house or the application of powder to the bird. Colds are quickly caused by stuffy or ill-ventilated or draughty houses.

POULTRY ECONOMICS. A well-managed laying bird should produce about 20 dozen eggs per year. There are frequent examples of birds laying 300 and over in the hands of a good poultry-keeper, but the smaller poultryman should make a good profit with a bird laying its 20 dozen per year. The average food-consumption with a good-quality diet will be about 120 lb. per year.

In addition to their value as producers of eggs and poultry-meat, free-ranging birds contribute towards the improvement of pastures. The action of chicken is to harrow the sward besides producing valuable manure, and 100 birds will produce 6 tons of manure per year. The main value of poultry manure lies in its nitrogen and phosphorus content. Usually additions of potash are necessary to make a complete manure, and lime, in which the manure is completely deficient, should always be used on fields where poultry have been raised.

EGGS AND THEIR PRESERVATION. A new-laid egg is produced with a constitution fitted to withstand infection to a marked degree, and will remain in an edible condition for a considerable period.

At the broad end of the egg there is an air space. If the egg is stored with the broad end upwards the air-space prevents the yolk rising to the shell, which it tends to do. The albumen itself has slight prophylactic properties, which the yolk lacks. It is, therefore, important that when packing an egg it should be so done as to reduce the possibility of the yolk reaching the shell. Once this takes place, infection can rapidly reach the yolk and a bad egg results.

There is always the tendency for the water in the albumen to evaporate through the pores of the shell. This can be prevented by storing the egg in a moist, cool room. By so doing the

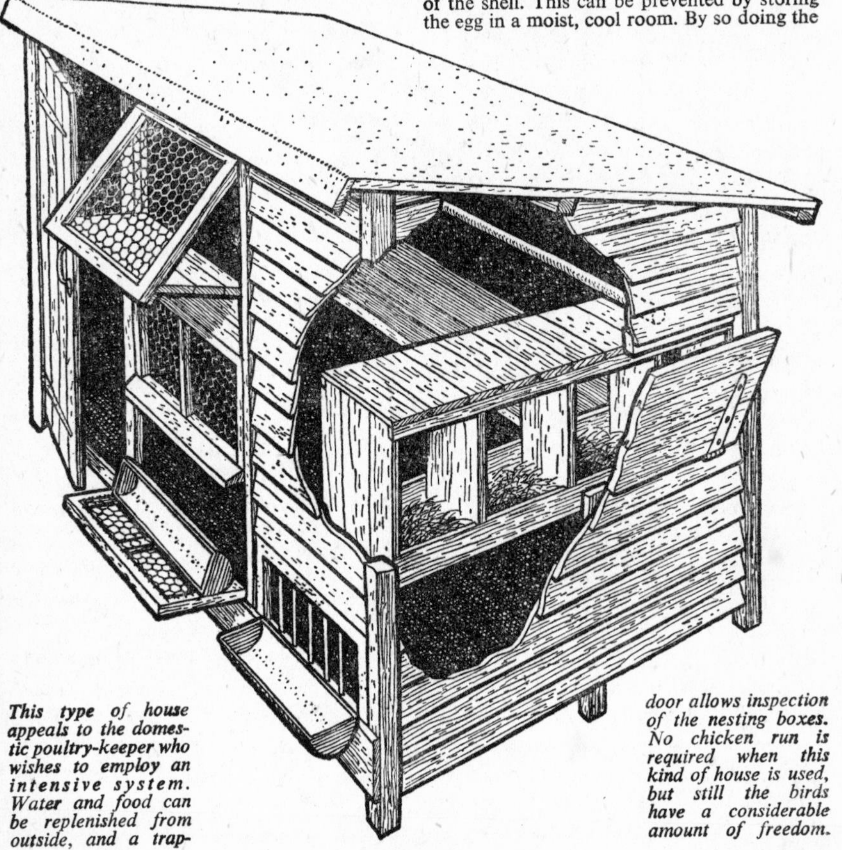

This type of house appeals to the domestic poultry-keeper who wishes to employ an intensive system. Water and food can be replenished from outside, and a trap-door allows inspection of the nesting boxes. No chicken run is required when this kind of house is used, but still the birds have a considerable amount of freedom.

Small battery of six boxes suitable for the domestic poultry-keeper. Each cage has separate troughs for food and water and its own dropping tray. The hen stands on a sloping wire mat down which the eggs roll until they are stopped outside the cage.

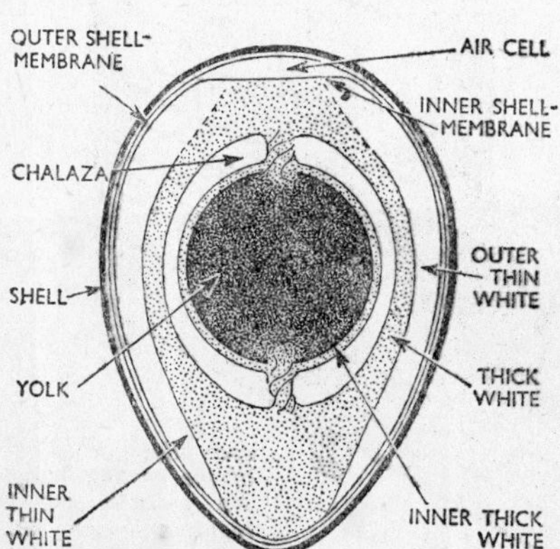

Section through a chicken's egg. This illustration helps to explain some of the problems involved in the preservation of eggs.

rate of evaporation is substantially reduced, the air-space increases but slowly, while, if the egg is stored with the broad end upward, this and the lowered rate of evaporation retain the yolk in a fairly central position, and so deterioration of the contents can be delayed for a period up to, and often exceeding, two months. The rate of evaporation can be still further slowed down by packing the egg in bran or similar material.

More satisfactory systems of egg preservation are the use of water-glass and lime-water. For the housewife the former method is probably the most convenient, and proprietary brands of water-glass can be purchased readily. The principle involved is that the sodium silicate in the water-glass prevents any evaporation at all from the egg. If, therefore, the eggs are immersed in the water-glass when in a fresh condition, and are kept completely immersed with, if possible, the broad ends upwards (although this is not essential), they may be kept stored and will remain in an edible condition for periods up to twelve months.